THE SERAPHIC ORDER

THE SERAPHIC ORDER

A Traditional Franciscan Book of Saints

by

Sr. Aquinas Barth, OSF
Fr. Marion A. Habig, OFM

Republished by:

MEDIATRIX PRESS

MMXX

Nihil Obstat
Geron Fournelle, OFM
Mark Hegener OFM
Censores Librorum

Imprimi Potest
Pius J. Barth OFM
Minister Provincial

Imprimatur
✠Albert Gregory Meyer D.D.
Archbishop of Chicago

ISBN: 978-1-7350601-7-0

Cover art: *The Stigmata of St. Francis*
—Domenico Ghirlandaio, 1485
Santa Trinita, Florence, Italy

Mediatrix Press
607 E. 6th Ave.
Post Falls, ID 83854
www.mediatrixpress.com

TABLE OF CONTENTS

FEBRUARY

MARCH

MAY

JUNE

JULY

AUGUST

SEPTEMBER

NOVEMBER

DECEMBER

INTRODUCTION

T. FRANCIS OF ASSISI is one of the most admired and loved of saints. He is also the father and pattern of a numerous spiritual progeny, of whom very many have likewise attained eminent sanctity.

THE THREE ORDERS

When Francis, as a young man of twenty-five, became a knight of Christ and began to observe the Gospel literally, he had no thought of founding a new religious order. But two years later he was joined by his first followers; and the next year, 1209, just seven hundred and fifty years ago, he founded his First Order, the Order of Friars Minor, an order of priests, clerics, and lay brothers. In place of the first simple rule which he gave his companions in 1209, Francis wrote a longer one of twenty-three chapters in 1221; and in 1223 he revised it and reduced it to the present rule of twelve chapters.

So profound was the impression made on the people of Umbria by the example and preaching of the Poverello, as they called him, that many men and women of every age and rank desired to become his disciples. Because family ties and other duties prevented them from leaving their homes and embracing the religious life, Francis, in 1209 or shortly afterwards, gave these also a simple rule of life, which was replaced in 1221 by a more detailed rule of twelve chapters. Thus he founded another order of men and women who pledged themselves, without vows, to live a life similar to that of the Friars Minor in as far as that was possible while still keeping to their homes and trades and professions. At first they were called the Brothers and Sisters of Penance. Later, not before 1230, they came to be known as the Third Order Secular of St. Francis.

Meanwhile, in 1212, the so-called Second Order of St. Francis, that of the Poor Ladies, was established. This happened when St. Clare of Assisi left her home and placed herself under the guidance of the Little Poor Man, adopting the same life of poverty as that of the Friars Minor and living a cloistered, contemplative life of prayer, penance, and work. Clare was soon joined by others; and Francis gave them a rule similar to that of the Friars Minor. In 1253, shortly before her death, Clare received papal approval for her rule; and after her canonization in 1255 the Poor Ladies were styled Poor Clares.

DIVISION OF THE FIRST ORDER

Early in the sixteenth century, the First Order of St. Francis was divided into three autonomous branches: the Observant Friars Minor, the Conventual Friars Minor, and the Capuchin Friars Minor. Subsequently, within the ranks of the Observants, several stricter groups were formed, especially the Discalced, Reformed, and Recollect Friars Minor. Never entirely independent branches, these latter were united once more by Pope Leo XIII in 1897; and since then, they are called simply the Order of Friars Minor, and popularly, the Franciscans. The Conventuals and the Capuchins have continued as separate orders, although they, like the Franciscans, observe the rule which St. Francis gave his First Order in 1223. Each of the three branches of the First Order, however, has its own general constitutions and its own superior general, called minister general.

THIRD ORDER REGULAR

Since the death of St. Francis in 1226, numerous additional Franciscan religious congregations of priests, brothers, and especially sisters have been founded, many of them in modern times. They adapted the rule of the Third Order Secular to the religious life in the strict sense, and hence all of them together comprise what is called the Third Order Regular of St. Francis. Pope Pius XI gave them a uniform basic rule in 1927. There is one order of priests and brothers which is known as the Third Order Regular properly so called. It was founded in 1447 and uses the initials T.O.R. But all the other Franciscan religious congregations, for instance the Society of the Atonement or Graymoor Friars, the various Franciscan brotherhoods, the numerous Franciscan sisterhoods — all are included in the Third Order Regular.

THE LARGEST ORDER

All of these, together with the Franciscans, the Conventuals, the Capuchins, the Poor Clares, and the Third Order Secular, may rightly be styled Franciscans. In a wide and comprehensive sense, the term Franciscan Order may be applied to all of them; and in this sense, the Franciscan Order is the largest religious family in the Catholic Church at the present time.

The Franciscans, that is the Order of Friars Minor, according to the latest available statistics (June, 1957), have a total membership of 26,351;

the Conventuals number 4,170, and the Capuchins 14,225 — a total of almost 45,000 for the First Order. The Poor Clares have some 13,000 members in 600 convents throughout the world. The many religious congregations of priests, brothers, and sisters, belonging to the Third Order Regular, have an estimated total membership of about 125,000. In the United States alone there are 76 different Franciscan sisterhoods of the Third Order Regular, with more than 30,000 members, which is more than one-fifth of all the religious women in the country. Thus the various religious orders and congregations in the strict sense, which honor St. Francis as their spiritual guide and father, have a grand total membership of more than 180,000. The Third Order Secular of St. Francis has an estimated world membership of 4,000,000.

Mention should be made also of one of the new secular institutes, the Missionaries of the Kingship of Christ, which was founded at Assisi in 1919 and now has about 2,400 members in various countries. Inasmuch as the members of this secular institute are Franciscan Tertiaries, it likewise belongs to the Franciscan family.

Similarly the members of the Archconfraternity of the Cord of St. Francis, called Cordists or Cordbearers, may also be counted among the spiritual children of St. Francis. St. Dominic, founder of the Order of Preachers and friend of St. Francis, is regarded as the first Cordbearer, but it was not till 1585 that Pope Sixtus V established the archconfraternity. It enables those who love and admire St. Francis but for some reason cannot join one of his orders to be enrolled under the banner of St. Francis. Pope Pius XI recommended it especially for children: "Let those who are too young (to join the Third Order) become Cordbearers of St. Francis so that even the children may grow accustomed to the life."

Lastly there are the Franciscanists or "Fourth Order" of St. Francis, scholars who devote themselves to research and to the writing of learned works about St. Francis and the early history of his orders. Of the Franciscanists, among whom there are non-Catholics as well as Catholics, Masseron wrote: "They take no vow of poverty, or of chastity, still less of obedience; indiscipline rules as mistress of their congregation. They promise only to love St. Francis and to work for him." An outstanding Franciscanist was the founder of the Society of St. Vincent de Paul, Frederick Ozanam (1813-1853), who is now a candidate for beatification.

FRANCISCAN SANCTITY

During the seven and a half centuries of its existence, the Franciscan Order, including all its branches, has been blessed by God with a very large number of saints and saintly persons. "Reading your history," declared Pope Pius XII, "one is astounded by the number and variety of the blossoms of holiness, of the fruits of apostolic work, that have budded and matured on the three branches of the thriving and vigorous tree of the Franciscan Order."

In the 1946 Italian revised edition of the Beschin-Palazzolo *Martyrologium Franciscanum*, of which the original Latin appeared eight years earlier, can be found a quite comprehensive list of Franciscan saints, blessed, and saintly persons. It contains a total of 5,604 entries by name or definite number. Not included, therefore, are groups indefinitely designated as "several," "many," or "very many," because the exact number could not be determined.

Among the exhibits at the Vatican Missionary Exposition in 1926, there was a manuscript martyrology, richly illuminated, which listed the names of more than a thousand Franciscan friars who crowned their apostolate among the heathens with the sacrifice of their life-blood but whose cult as martyrs has not yet been approved by the Church.

We cannot arrive at the exact number of Franciscan saints and blessed, that is, those who have been canonized and formally or equivalently declared blessed by the Church. The breviaries and missals of the several branches of the Franciscan Order do not commemorate all the Franciscan saints and blessed; and no complete and satisfactory list has ever been compiled. In various published lists we find different totals, one of the main reasons being the fact that a complete roster of the saints and blessed of the Third Order Secular is lacking.

For this book, we have attempted to prepare a complete and up-to-date list of Franciscan saints and blessed. It will be found at the end of this volume in a chronological as well as alphabetical form; the latter has separate lists for the various branches of the three orders of St. Francis. As far as we could ascertain, the exact number of Franciscan saints and blessed at the present time (January, 1959) is 355. Of this number 113 are canonized saints, and 242 have been formally or equivalently declared blessed.

Not included among the 242 blessed are many allegedly holy persons who have held the popular title of blessed prior to 1534, for instance, "Blessed" John Duns Scotus, "Blessed" Pica, the mother of St. Francis, "Blessed" Blanche, the mother of St. Louis IX of France. A decree of Pope Urban VIII in 1634 permitted that, in popular devotion, the title of "blessed" might be retained in the case of such persons as had from time immemorial held that title among the people; and the term "time immemorial" was set down as a period of at least one hundred years. Such popular "blessed" receive the further sanction of official public worship when their cult is confirmed by formal or equivalent approval through an act of the Holy See. When the Holy See, for instance, confirms the cult of a popular "blessed" by granting a Mass and Office in his honor either locally or generally, we have an example of equivalent beatification. Our total of Franciscan blessed includes only those formally or equivalently beatified by the Holy See.

Although we have included among the Franciscan saints and blessed some Tertiaries, especially modern ones, who founded non-Franciscan religious congregations, for instance, St. John Bosco and St. Frances Xavier Cabrini, we have not included seventeen other founders who are said to have been Franciscan Tertiaries before they founded their own orders or congregations. Neither does our total include four canonized saints who were Cordbearers of St. Francis.

Of the 113 canonized Franciscan saints, 57 belong to the First Order of St. Francis (17 before 1440; 32 Franciscans; 7 Capuchins; 1 Conventual). Five are Poor Clares. One is a member of the Third Order Regular. Fifty are Tertiaries.

Of the 242 blessed, 127 belong to the First Order (38 before 1440; 74 Franciscans; 11 Capuchins; 4 Conventuals). Twenty-two are Poor Clares. Fifteen are members of the Third Order Regular. And 78 are Tertiaries.

Thus the First Order has a total of 184 saints and blessed (55 before 1440; 106 Franciscans; 18 Capuchins; 5 Conventuals). The Second Order has 27; the Third Order Regular, 15; and the Third Order Secular, 129.

The number of Franciscan saints and blessed has been greatly increased in modern times. The number of those canonized and beatified since 1900 is no less than 132.

CAUSES PENDING

Even greater than the present total of Franciscan saints and blessed is the number of causes of canonization and beatification which are now being carried on in Rome, although some of them may be described as temporarily dormant. Of 551 causes which were pending in Rome in 1946, some of them for groups and not merely individuals, no less than 180 belonged to one of the three orders of St. Francis.

The latest list of the Franciscan postulator general, which was published in *Acta Ordinis Fratrum Minorum*, January-February, 1950, shows that at the present writing (1959) and not including any new causes which may have been introduced since 1950, 38 blessed of the Franciscan orders are candidates for canonization, namely 17 Franciscans, 3 Poor

Clares, 7 members of the Third Order Regular, and 11 Tertiaries. The servants of God whose causes of beatification are now pending number 283, namely 206 Franciscans, 25 Poor Clares, 15 members of the Third Order Regular, and 37 Tertiaries. In addition there is one group cause of beatification for Bishop Theotim Verhaeghen and 2,388 other members of the First and Third orders who died as martyrs in China. Not included in these figures are the Franciscan causes which are being promoted by the postulators general of other branches of the Franciscan Order. Some fifty Capuchins are candidates for beatification.

This growing list of Franciscan saints and blessed eloquently testifies to the fruitfulness of the Franciscan ideal and way of life. If we inquire into the reasons for this fruitfulness, the best answer is found in the sources of Franciscan spirituality, as outlined in the encyclical letter *Centenaria solemnia* issued in 1950 by the Most Reverend Father Pacific Perantoni, O.F.M., then minister general of the Order of Friars Minor. They are: (1) the life of St. Francis; (2) the rules of St. Francis; (3) the Franciscan tradition.

The Sources of Sanctity

The first reason why there are so many Franciscan saints lies in their close imitation of St. Francis. They sought to fashion their own lives as much as possible according to his life. As Father Perantoni writes, Francis is "the first incarnation of the Seraphic model in all its native abundance and vigor as conceived by God and by God embodied in the founding father of that new race of people, the family born of Francis. By God's will he became the type and model of all future Seraphic posterity. ... We must regard in him our form of spirituality in its perfection and learn of him the best way to live and practice it."

The second reason why so many of the followers of St. Francis have become saints is their faithful observance of one of the several rules which Francis gave to the orders which he founded. According to the *Revelations of St. Bridget* (book 7, chapter 2), Our Lord Himself said to this Tertiary saint: "The rule of St. Francis, introduced by this saint, was not composed by human genius or wisdom, but by Me, according to My will; every word it contains has been inspired by My Spirit, and as such it has been proposed to its followers and communicated to them."

In his Testament, St. Francis made a similar declaration: "Since the Lord gave me charge over the brethren, no man showed me what I should do; but the Most High Himself revealed to me that I should live after the manner of the holy Gospel." Speaking to his friars about their rule, he grew eloquent in extolling it. "Brethren and most beloved sons," he said on one occasion, "we have been most privileged in accepting this rule. This rule, which has been presented to us, is the book of life, the hope of our salvation, the guarantee of glory, the marrow of the Gospel, the way of the Cross, the state of perfection, the ladder to Heaven, the key of Paradise, the agreement of the eternal covenant."

DECLARATION OF POPES

The popes have likewise bestowed unstinted praise on the rule of St. Francis and have pointed out that it has led many souls to great heights of sanctity. Pope Nicholas III, for instance, in his constitution *Exiit*, referring to the Gospel parable of the sower, compared the order of St. Francis to the fertile soil which brings forth fruit a hundredfold. "This soil," he writes, "is the gentle and docile Order of Friars Minor, founded on poverty and humility and solidly rooted by the noble confessor of Christ, Francis. Growing from that seed, blossoms have developed through the vitality of that rule; and it has brought forth children now scattered over the world, living a life according to the principles of the Gospel. These are the children who, as St. James the Apostle teaches, accepted in all simplicity the Eternal Word, the Son of God, engraved in human nature as in the virgin soil of a garden. These are the keepers of that holy rule, founded upon the evangelical doctrine, strengthened by the example of Christ and confirmed by the words and acts of the Apostles, who were the first founders of the Church militant. This, in the sight of God and the Father, is the pure and spotless religion which came down from the Father of light through His Son, communicated by word and example to the Apostles and at last to St. Francis and his followers, and which was inspired by the Holy Ghost, thus containing the testimony of the three Persons of the Blessed Trinity."

In his declaration *Exivi*, concerning the rule of St. Francis, Pope Clement V declared that the order of St. Francis is a pleasure garden of the Church. "This garden," he says, "is indeed the Order of Friars Minor, surrounded by the walls of religious observance, carefully enclosed within itself, satisfied only with God, and abundantly adorned with new ornamental plants, that is, its children. The beloved Son of God, coming into this garden, finds His pleasure in harvesting there the myrrh of mortification and penance and the spices which spread the sweet aroma of sanctity, so attractive to all. This is the manner of that heavenly life proposed by St. Francis to his children and which he himself by word and example showed them how to practice."

Pope Leo XIII, in his constitution *Felicitate quadam* of October 4, 1897, made the following statement: "The Order of Friars Minor, that numerous and lasting progeny of St. Francis, deserves in the greatest measure our benevolence and solicitude. Their holy founder has bound them by laws and precepts to observe that which at all times will keep them safe. And this has not been in vain. There is hardly any other community of men which has produced so many heroes of great virtue or has given to Christ so many preachers of the Gospel, so many martyrs to the Church, so many saints to heaven. The most profound poverty, so loved by St. Francis, has been emulated to perfection by many of his followers ... also his spotless innocence. These eminent and glorious virtues, in which he excelled, these followers have imitated to perfection."

St. Bonaventure, who is rightly styled the second founder of the Order of Friars Minor, called the 1223 rule of the Friars Minor "a brief summary of perfection." He also declared that "in its entirety this rule has been taken from the source of evangelical purity." No wonder that the great Dominican friar St. Vincent Ferrer believed that "the man who observes this rule is a saint, and when he dies he can be canonized."

These eulogies of the rule of the Order of Friar Minor apply also to a great extent to the rules which St. Francis gave to his Second and Third orders. Of course, they refer not merely to the letter of the Franciscan rule but also to the spirit which underlies them. The many saints who became such by observing one of the rules of St. Francis fully grasped that spirit and unreservedly surrendered themselves to its vivifying force.

"OUR AGE-OLD SPIRITUAL TRADITION"

That leads us to the third reason for the great multitude of Franciscan saints, namely the Franciscan tradition, or as Father Perantoni styles it, "our age-old spiritual tradition." This source of Franciscan spirituality as well as sanctity among the children of St. Francis "gives a practical illustration of the life and the holy rule of our Seraphic Father," and "it is a complete and brilliant documentation of the abundant vitality of that spirit which the Herald of the Great King proclaimed to the world." These are Father Perantoni's words, and he goes on to say that this tradition has taken on a twofold concrete form: "There is first the great host of holy souls such as perhaps other religious orders, however venerable, have not brought forth in like countless numbers. Then there is the great number of masters whose learned spiritual treatises have not only shed luster on the Church of God but have likewise edified souls and inspired them to holiness."

In other words, among the followers of St. Francis there were saints and teachers who were endowed by God with a natural and supernatural kinship with their holy founder. They developed the Franciscan spirituality which had its origin in the simple practical life and the rules of St. Francis; and they gave further, clearer expression to it both by their lives and their writings. Thus they pointed out the characteristic traits of Franciscan spirituality, both in a practical and a theoretical way; and they in turn inspired many other children of St. Francis, by means of the Franciscan way of life, to distinguish themselves by the holiness of their lives.

Concerning the distinctive features of Franciscan spirituality, as contained in the Franciscan tradition, suffice it to say that its essence is doctrinal Christocentrism and practical imitation of Christ, conformity with Christ, prompted by love. Distinctive aspects of Franciscan piety are childlike love of God, our Father, devotion to the Humanity of Christ, His Sacred Heart, the Holy Eucharist, the mysteries of the Nativity and the Passion, His Virgin Mother Mary, and reverence for the Catholic priesthood. Franciscan love of God finds expression also in charity to our fellowmen, understanding them as our brothers, especially in aid to the poor and sick and in apostolic zeal for souls, Christian and pagan. Total poverty detaches the Franciscan soul from creatures, but at the same time it recognizes God in created things and uses the latter to mount to God. Emphasis is placed on the will, and hence on love and action above speculation. The atmosphere in which the Franciscan spirit develops is one of individual freedom of the spirit, absence of coercive and confining methods, love of enterprise, and a sense of realism. On the path of this traditional Franciscan way of life many have attained sainthood.

A Franciscan book of saints, therefore, one which will recount their lives and virtues, can well serve as a practical textbook of Franciscan spirituality. It will undoubtedly help us to learn what the Franciscan spirit is and how to acquire it. Twenty years ago, *The Poverello's Round Table*, by Sister M. Aquinas Barth, O.S.F., containing biographical sketches of Franciscan saints, blessed, and servants of God as well as meditations for every day of the year, was published. For the most part it was a translation of two German works, Seraphischer Tugendspiegel by Father Sylvester Winkes, O.F.M., and Heilige Vorbilder by Father Athanasius Bierbaum, O.F.M. For the past ten years it has been out of print, and many requests have been made for a new edition. It has now finally been revised, corrected, re-arranged, and enlarged; and it is offered to the public as The Franciscan Book of Saints on the occasion of the seven hundred and fiftieth anniversary of the founding of the First and Third orders of St. Francis.

The Franciscan Book of Saints has sketches of all of the 355 saints and formally or equivalently declared blessed, also those who are not in the several Franciscan calendars. Some of the servants of God in the original work had to yield their place to saints and blessed and to some saintly Franciscans of the United States. Thus 40 new lives have been added; a good many of them are sketches of Tertiary saints and blessed.

The entire book was re-arranged to make it agree with the new Franciscan (O.F.M.) calendar. In this calendar there are many days on which the feast of two or three blessed is observed. We have assigned these to different days as close as possible to their feast day; and we have also indicated the days on which the Conventuals, the Capuchins, and the Third Order Regular celebrate feasts of Franciscan saints and blessed. A composite Franciscan calendar will be found at the end of the volume. The necessary information was supplied by the Very Reverend Basil Heiser, O.F.M.Conv., Very Reverend Claude Vogel, O.F.M.Cap., and Very Rev. Adrian J. M. Veigle, T.O.R.; and we gladly take this opportunity of expressing our sincere thanks to them.

In view of the fact that the lessons on the blessed in the new Franciscan breviary, on those days when two or three blessed are commemorated, are reduced to a minimum, the value of this book has been greatly increased. It supplies more information about the lives and virtues of these blessed, and thus enables us to observe their feasts with greater spiritual profit.

Although this is primarily a book of spiritual reading and of meditation, we have tried to make it historically correct as well, at least in as far as that was possible at the present time. Much research sill remains to be done. To our mind, accuracy in the accounts of the saints and blessed is a real contribution to their honor. For those who would like to know more about them, we have added brief references to some of the sketches, and have placed a select bibliography at the end of the book.

The reading of the lives of the saints in many instances has marked the beginning of a conversion or change from sinfulness or indifference or mediocrity to fervor and holiness. By the example of their lives the saints inspire and encourage us to walk in their footsteps; and by their intercession at the throne of God they help us in our temporal and spiritual needs.

The saints are indeed, not only the friends of God, but also our best friends. But we can not call them our friends if we do not know anything about them and do not speak to them. It is necessary that we become acquainted with them, study their lives, seek to imitate their virtues, and take our recourse to them in our troubles and trials. One of the easiest ways to make a good meditation is to consider prayerfully the life and virtues of a saint. That is also the best way of celebrating the saints' feast days and of paying them their deserved honor.

For the children of St. Francis the saints and blessed and saintly persons whose stories are briefly told in this volume are not only friends but spiritual brothers and sisters. That brings them closer, much closer, to all who have been captivated by the Franciscan ideal and are trying to conform their lives to it.

It is especially to the many members of all the branches of the three orders of St. Francis in English-speaking lands that we humbly offer *The Franciscan Book of Saints* as an aid in the lifelong task of becoming better Franciscans. Despite its defects, it can also make us of the mid-twentieth century saints, Franciscan saints.

M.A.H.

JANUARY

JANUARY 1
THE SERVANT OF GOD JOHN DE PADILLA
Martyr, First Order

UST fifty years after the Franciscan Tertiary Christopher Columbus discovered the New World, the Franciscan missionary Father John de Padilla died on the plains of Kansas as the protomartyr of the United States. Born about 1492 in Andalusia, southern Spain, he entered the ranks of the Franciscans there; and in 1526 he departed for New Spain or Mexico to join the pioneer Franciscan missionaries who had come only a few years earlier. For more than a decade he was very successful in making good Christians of the natives, especially in the states of Hidalgo and Jalisco.

In 1540 he and six other Franciscans accompanied Coronado on his famous expedition to New Mexico. The next year he went along to the Quivira Indians in Kansas. When Coronado and his army returned to Mexico in the spring of 1542, Father John, with some companions, including the Portuguese soldier Andres Docampo and two Franciscan Indian Tertiary Brothers from Mexico, went back to the Quiviras in order to preach the Gospel to them. Within a few months he succeeded in converting a large number of these Indians.

In the fall of 1542, despite the objections of some of the Quiviras, Father John decided to carry the Gospel message also to the Kaws, enemies of the Quiviras. A band of Quiviras followed him and killed him on the way.

The historian Mota Padilla gives the following account of his martyrdom: "The friar left Quivira with a small escort, against the will of the Indians of that village, who loved him as their father. But at one day's journey he was met by Indians on the warpath; and knowing their evil intentions, he requested the Portuguese to flee, since the latter was on horseback, and to take with him the oblates (Brothers Luke and Sebastian) and the boys, who, being young, were able to run and save themselves. Being defenseless, they all fled as he desired; and the blessed Father, kneeling down, offered up his life, which he sacrificed for the good of the souls of others.

"He thus realized his most ardent desire—the felicity of martyrdom by the arrows of these barbarians, who afterwards threw his body into a pit and covered it with innumerable rocks. The Portuguese and the Indians, returning to Quivira, gave notice there of what had happened; and the natives felt it deeply on account of the love which they had for their Father. They would have regretted it still more, had they been able to appreciate the extent of their loss.

"The day of his death is not known, although it is regarded as certain that it occurred in the year 1542. Don Pedro de Tobar, in some papers which he wrote and left at the town of Culiacan (Mexico), states that the Indians had gone out to kill this blessed Father in order to obtain his vestments, and that there was a tradition of miraculous signs connected with his death, such as inundations, comets, balls of fire, and the sun becoming darkened."

Docampo and the two lay brothers, after being held as prisoners for ten months, escaped, and amid indescribable hardships trudged some twenty thousand miles through desert country back to northern Mexico. Some nine years later they reached Tampico and reported the glorious story of Father John de Padilla's martyrdom. Brother Luke later won the martyr's crown in Durango, about 1565.

Two other Franciscan brothers, John of the Cross and Louis Descalona, who had remained as missionaries in New Mexico when Coronado left, were likewise put to death by pagan Indians in the latter part of the year 1542. Thus they share with Father John de Padilla the honor of being the protomartyrs of what is now the United States. Bishop J. Henry Tihen of Denver (1917-1931) declared that people had reported to him the granting of favors through the intercession of Father John de Padilla. (Cf. *Heroes of the Cross*, pp. 212-227; *The Martyrs of the United States of America*, pp. 45-47.)

ON LOVING GOD IN OUR NEIGHBOR

1. By loving our neighbor, we can prove to ourselves and to others that we truly love God. There are other signs which indicate that we love God, such as doing God's will in all things, love of prayer, a tender conscience, and the spirit of sacrifice; but the surest proof is the love of our fellowman. "If we love one another," writes St. John, "God abides in us, and His love is perfected in us" (1 Jn. 4,12). A little farther on the Apostle of Love adds: "If anyone says, 'I love God,' and hates his brother, he is a liar. For, how can he who does not love his brother, whom he sees, love God whom he does not see? And this commandment we have from Him,

that he who loves God should love his brother also" (1 Jn. 4,20).

2. To be a proof of the love of God in us, our love of neighbor must be a supernatural, not merely a natural, love. We must love our neighbor because he is a child of God and a member of Christ. All men were created by God out of love, and Christ died for all. Every baptized person, when in grace, is a living member of Christ; and those who still live far from God by reason of sin or unbelief are nevertheless called, if they will only repent, to be "citizens with the saints and members of God's household" (Eph. 2,19). Our Lord assured us: "Amen, I say to you, as long as you did it for one of these, the least of My brethren, you did it to Me" (Mt. 25,40). Hence, the love of God and the love of our fellowman, regardless of race, creed, or color, are inseparably one, forming one divine virtue. Both have their cause in God, tend to God, and rest in God. Both stem from the one great double commandment, of which the second is like the first: "You shall love your neighbor as yourself" (Mt. 22,39). Our love of neighbor must be as sincere and active as the love we have for ourselves. "All things whatsoever you would that men should do to you, even so do you also to them" (Mt. 7,12).

3. Loving our neighbor as ourselves is not a matter of choice, but of obligation. Christ demands such love of neighbor from His followers. We are not deserving of the name of Christians if we do not practice such love. There is also a higher degree of love of neighbor which is not strictly demanded but recommended to us. It consists in loving our fellowman, within the proper limits, more than ourselves. This ideal of Christian charity requires a heroism similar to that practiced by Father John de Padilla. It means forgetting ourselves for the sake of our neighbor's temporal and spiritual welfare, sacrificing ourselves in his service, and even giving up our life for him. "This is My commandment," declared our Saviour, "that you love one another as I have loved you. Greater love than this no one has, that one lay down his life for his friends" (Jn. 15,12-13). He sacrificed His life on the Cross, not only for His friends, but also for His enemies. Our everlasting reward or punishment will depend on whether or not we showed our love of Him in the person of the hungry, the thirsty, the strangers, the needy, the sick, and those in prison (Mt. 25,31-46).

PRAYER OF THE CHURCH

O God, who by the grace of the Holy Spirit didst pour the gifts of charity into the hearts of Thy faithful, grant to Thy servants and handmaids, for whom we entreat Thy mercy, health of mind and body; that they may love

Thee with all their strength and by perfect love do what is pleasing to Thee. Through Christ our Lord. Amen.

CRANGRANGRANGRANGRANGRAN

JANUARY 2
THE SERVANT OF GOD JOHN PARENTI
Confessor, First Order

JOHN was born in a town of northern Italy about the year 1180, and devoted himself to the practice of law. He was judge in the city of Castellana, when, as reported in the chronicles of the order, he saw a herd of swine resisting the herdsman's efforts to drive them into their pen. Their herdsman finally shouted in rage: "Get in there, ye cursed swine, like godless lawyers and judges into hell." Immediately the animals struggled helter-skelter into the sty.

The incident set John thinking on the dangers of his profession, and he decided to withdraw from it. Chancing to hear St. Francis of Assisi preach some time later—it was in the year 1212—he joined the order and led a most exemplary life in it.

At the general chapter in the year 1219, the holy Founder appointed him provincial of Spain. After that the Order of Friars Minor spread so rapidly, and its labors were so bountifully blessed in that country that, upon receiving the information, St. Francis broke out in loud praises of God.

Upon the death of the holy Founder in the year 1226, John was unanimously elected general of the order. He administered the duties of the office with great zeal. He made all his visitation journeys with unshod feet, and placed great importance on the observance of religious discipline.

On the occasion of an uprising in Rome, Pope Gregory IX called John to the city to bring the rebels back to obedience. When they refused to listen to his words John prophesied that the Tiber would overflow. This actually took place soon after, and the terrible devastation caused the insurgents to submit.

In spite of his efforts on behalf of the order, John found that he was not able to restrain certain friars who were causing a relaxation of discipline. So the devout and humble man resigned his office in the year 1233. With the permission of his successor, Brother Elias, he went to the island of Corsica, where he wished to establish convents of the order among the rugged inhabitants.

In the latter years of his life, John applied himself mainly to prayer. He was called by God to his eternal rest in 1250, having been glorified on earth by many miracles.

ON THE OCCASION OF SIN

1. Consider how scrupulous the servant of God John was to avoid the occasion of sin. Made aware of the danger which accompanied his profession, he forsook an honorable and profitable calling, and entered a strict order in order to save his soul. "For what does it profit man," he undoubtedly reflected, "if he gain the whole world, and suffer the loss of his own soul?" (Mt. 16,26).

2. Consider what may have been an occasion of sin for you in the past. Perhaps it is your business, the place where you work, a house to which you often go, a person with whom you associate, society which you frequent. How often has this occasion led you into sin in the past year? Will it be the same in the new year? Change matters at once, today. If you find it difficult, if your heart clings to the occasion, then removing it is all the more necessary, and postponement will be more dangerous, for "he that loves danger shall perish in it" (Eccli. 3,27).

3. How happy saintly John was after he had carried out his heroic resolution! God rewarded him for it with rich blessings, and he used the latter so faithfully that from the very beginning he lived a holy life in the order. He accomplished much good in his official position, and when he was not able to do that any longer, he obtained the grace to be closely united in prayer with God, with whom he is now enjoying his eternal reward. God will also lighten every sacrifice you make out of love for Him. Make a generous start today, and God's grace will be meted out to you in great abundance this year, and the eternal reward will plentifully compensate everything. "It is better for you having one eye to enter into life, than having two eyes to be cast into hell fire" (Mt. 18,9).

PRAYER OF THE CHURCH
(Third Sunday after Pentecost)

O God, the protector of those who hope in Thee, without whom nothing is strong, nothing holy, increase Thy mercy towards us, that, with Thee as ruler and guide, we may pass through the good things of time that we may not lose those of eternity. Through Christ our Lord. Amen.

JANUARY 3
VENERABLE MARY LAWRENCE LONGO
Widow, Second Order

ARY LAWRENCE was born in Catalonia. At the early age of fifteen years she married John Longo, a Sicilian court official. A servant whom she had found it necessary to reprimand, took revenge by giving her mistress poison. The result was that Mary Lawrence became completely paralyzed. Placing all her confidence in our Lady, the health of the sick, she made a pilgrimage to Loreto, where she was miraculously cured. Not long afterwards her husband died.

Henceforth, Mary Lawrence devoted herself entirely to works of godliness. Clothed in the garb of the Tertiaries she nursed the incurable in a hospital which she herself had built. She longed to make a pilgrimage to the Holy Land, but it was pointed out to her that it would be far more pleasing to God if she chose to live in the seclusion of a convent. Following this suggestion, she established a convent according to the rule of St. Clare and, taking with her twelve companions, withdrew to its enclosure. The Capuchin Fathers drew up appropriate constitutions for them. This was in the year 1538.

Mary Lawrence was the first abbess of the new convent and as such was a mirror of cloistral discipline. As she lay dying, some of the sisters spoke of her virtues. But Mother Mary Lawrence said to them: "Do not say such things! What I have done is not due to any merit of mine. God gave me all. He alone should receive praise and thanks for it."

Then, as she took the crucifix in her hand and cried out, "Jesus, Jesus, Jesus," her soul hastened to eternal bliss among the saints. Her death occurred on December 20, 1542. Pope Leo XIII declared her venerable.

MARY, HEALTH OF THE SICK

1. Mary is the health of the sick because it is given her to cure disease. Our Lord gave His disciples the power to lay their hands upon the sick so that they would recover (Mk. 16,18). Would He deny His Mother the same power? If so many sick have been miraculously healed through the intercession of the saints, what should not the Queen of saints be able to effect? If our Lord heard the prayer of the centurion at Capharnaum and of Jairus, how much more would He be attentive to the prayers of His Mother. — Then turn with confidence to Mary. Mary is the health of the sick because she has already cured many sick. St. Bernardin of Siena could

not preach because of a hoarseness that affected his voice. While he was yet a young priest, St. Leonard suffered for many years from infirmity. Mother Mary Lawrence was paralyzed. And Mary helped them all in a miraculous manner. It is not without reason that the Church calls on her, Health of the Sick, pray for us! — Let it encourage you to invoke our Blessed Lady with childlike confidence. Think of the many votive offerings that adorn the image of our Blessed Lady at the various pilgrim shrines. They are so many tongues that seem to say: Mary helped us. Mary will continue to help others. Just have confidence.

2. Mary is the health of the sick because she sees to it that sickness leads to a good end. It is not always good for us to recover from illness. Though we may pray for the restoration of our health, our dear Lord, who knows everything better than we, may yet have to say to us: You know not what you ask (Mt. 20,22). On the other hand, it is certain that the best conclusion of sickness is a blessed death. And our Blessed Mother is certainly interested in that kind of death. It is for that reason she is our Mother. — Pray, therefore, with special devotion: Holy Mary, Mother of God, pray for us sinners now and at the hour of our death.

PRAYER OF THE CHURCH

O God, who didst bestow the gift of salvation on the human race through the virginal fruitfulness of Mary, grant, we beseech Thee, that we may experience her intercession who have been made worthy to receive the Author of life, Jesus Christ our Lord. Amen.

JANUARY 4
BLESSED CHRISTINA OF TUSCANY
Virgin, Third Order

BLESSED CHRISTINA MACABAI or Menabuoi of Valdarno (meaning Valley of the Arno) was a holy Tertiary of the thirteenth century, and may have been born while St. Francis was still living. The town of her birth was Santa Croce, in Tuscany, on the lower Arno, between Florence and Pisa. Her parents were poor; and as a girl, Oringa, as she was then called, was a shepherdess. While tending the flocks, she devoted much time to prayer. So sensitive was her purity, that she trembled and even became ill when she heard an unclean word.

Oringa was a very beautiful girl, and hence there was no lack of suitors who came to ask her hand; but she refused all offers of marriage. Her brothers maltreated her, trying to force her into marriage. Oringa fled to Lucca, and found a position as a servant girl. She began to lead a life of severe penance, going barefoot even in winter, sleeping on the bare ground, and fasting at times for several days in succession without taking any food. By her prayers and example she converted many sinners, and came to be known as "the missionary of Lucca."

With her mistress she made a pilgrimage to Rome, where people began to call her Christina or Christiana because of her holy life. From Rome they went to Assisi; and here a young lawyer was so attracted by her beauty that he wanted to marry her by all means. But Christina had made up her mind to lead a life of virginity and once more took refuge in flight.

There is a tradition that St. Veridiana, the holy Tertiary recluse at Castelfiorentino in the Val d'Elsa, who died in 1242, advised Christina to return to her home town, Santa Croce, and to join the Third Order. Anyhow, that is what Christina did; and many young women followed her example and placed themselves under her direction. Thus she founded a religious community, which, according to some, observed the Rule of St. Augustine. That may well have been the case, because at this time religious sisterhoods of the Third Order Regular were still unknown.

Many years later, in 1310, Christina died a holy death. If the story about St. Veridiana is true, she must have been in her eighties. Many miracles followed her death; and Pope St. Pius V (1566-1572) approved the cult paid to her. At Lucca and at Miniato the feast of Blessed Christina is observed on January 4. The Augustinians also celebrate her feast, but not the Franciscan Order although it is now certain that she was a Franciscan Tertiary. (Cf. Biersack, pp. 24-25; *These Made Peace*, p. 42.)

ON THE VIRTUE OF CLEANLINESS

1. Neatness, cleanliness, orderliness — these are an aid to virtue. In fact, if they are coupled with the right intention, they may be numbered among the virtues. Being neat and clean in regard to one's personal appearance is something entirely different from the pagan cult of the body, which is so prevalent today and has made such devastating inroads into the thoughts and the ways of even such as call themselves Christians. Christina was beautiful without trying to be such, and she did not misuse this gift of God as so many do. She was not vain or conceited; and she did not parade her beauty. She was modest and retiring; and she was intent

above all on beautifying her soul. But she must have been neat and clean in her ways; otherwise she would not have been able to hold the position of a servant girl.

2. Some have the erroneous notion that squalor and filth necessarily go hand in hand with poverty. They often do, but there is no reason why they should. Even the poor can scrub their humble abodes and keep them clean, they can patch their torn clothes and wash them, and they can avoid piling up unnecessary junk or carry it away. Dirt is not the result of poverty but of slovenliness and laziness and carelessness. Having a place for everything, and keeping one's person and belongings clean require work and perseverance. A poor home which is kept spick and span has an aura of virtue.

3. The housewife and mother who is busily engaged in cleaning and washing, who keeps her home attractive and inviting, is fulfilling the duties of her state of life. Mary, the Mother of God, did not regard it beneath her dignity to sweep the house at Nazareth, to make and wash and mend clothes, and to cook meals. But she sanctified the performance of her ordinary daily duties by the love of Jesus. The last chapter of the Book of Proverbs has a description of a valiant woman which provides ample food for thought: "Who shall find a valiant woman? Far and from the uttermost coasts is the price of her. The heart of her husband trusts in her: and he shall have no need of spoils. She will render him good, and not evil, all the days of her life ... She has put out her hand to strong things: and her fingers have taken hold of the spindle ... Strength and beauty are her clothing: and she shall laugh in the latter day ... She has looked well to the paths of her house, and has not eaten her bread idle. Her children rose up, and called her blessed: her husband, and he praised her. Many daughters have gathered together riches: you have surpassed them all. Favor is deceitful, and beauty is vain: the woman who fears the Lord, she shall be praised. Give her of the fruit of her hands: and let her works praise her in the gates" (Prov. 31,10-31).

PRAYER OF THE CHURCH

O God, the protector of all who trust in Thee, without whom nothing is strong, nothing is holy, increase and multiply upon us Thy mercy; that, Thou being our ruler and guide, we may so pass through temporal blessings that we finally lose not those which are eternal. Through Christ our Lord. Amen.

JANUARY 5
THE SERVANT OF GOD ORTOLANA DI OFFREDUCCIO
Widow, Second Order

ORTULANA OR ORTOLANA, the mother of the holy foundress St. Clare, descended from a very noble family, and from her youth was devoted to piety. She took special pleasure in making pilgrimages to holy places, and in company with a pious relative she also made a pilgrimage to the Holy Land. Often she visited the tombs of the holy princes of the apostles at Rome and other shrines in Italy.

At the wish of her parents she entered into marriage with Favarone di Offreduccio, a scion of one of the foremost families among the nobility in Assisi. Her new station in life, however, was no hindrance to her in continuing to lead a truly God-fearing life. When the time of her first confinement arrived, she prayed fervently before a crucifix for a happy delivery. Then she heard a voice which spoke to her: "Fear not, you will give birth to a light that will enlighten the world with its brilliance." Soon afterwards she happily gave birth to a daughter to whom she gave the name of Clare, that is, "the brilliant one." How devoutly she reared her children can be attested by their later sanctity.

When Clare had grown into a young woman, she founded, under the direction of our holy Father St. Francis and in contempt of all earthly pleasures, the Order of Poor Clares in a poor convent near Assisi. Her two sisters, Agnes and Beatrice, followed her into the convent she had founded, and after the death of her husband, Hortulana also entered the same convent, in order to close her life under the guidance of her saintly daughter. There she led so saintly a life that almighty God glorified her by many miracles in life and after her death.

CONCERNING PILGRIMAGES

1. Pious sentiment drew Blessed Hortulana to places of pilgrimage, and as long as domestic duty did not demand her attention, she made extensive pilgrimages. That the practice was very pleasing to God and that she obtained many graces from it can be deduced from her saintly life and holy death. Almighty God Himself prescribed in the Old Testament that the Jews were annually to make a pilgrimage to the Temple in Jerusalem,

and, according to the testimony of the Gospel, Jesus, with Joseph and Mary, made this pilgrimage at the cost of a journey of several days. There can, therefore, be no doubt that pilgrimages are good in themselves and highly pleasing to God. — Have you always regarded them in this light?

2. Consider the benefits that derive from pilgrimages. Many a person never really succeeds in emerging from the noise and maze of his daily cares and labors, and his thoughts about them accompany him even to church. Such people have the finest opportunity, on a pilgrimage of several days, to reflect quietly on the salvation of their soul and on eternity. Furthermore, the prayers said in common throughout the day put the soul in a frame of mind such that it is elevated to God more fervently than otherwise. Then, too, meeting the many devout pilgrims at the shrine, the special devotions and sermons, and particularly the special graces which it pleases God to grant at such places, instil the desire for a good confession, a fruitful holy Communion, and not seldom sincere conversion from a bad life. The difficulties usually associated with a pilgrimage are certainly also a pleasing sacrifice to God in atonement for sins committed in the past. — Have you tried to derive these benefits from pilgrimages you have made?

3. There is also such a thing as an abuse of pilgrimages. If a person neglects the necessary duties of his state in life, or unduly burdens others in the household by going on a pilgrimage; if it is made out of sheer curiosity, inordinate love of amusement, or even in a frivolous disposition and in worldly company; if a person seizes every opportunity for such excursions from dislike of work and idle love of change, then truly they cannot be pleasing to God, nor will they benefit the soul. It is to such people that Thomas a Kempis refers when he says: "Those who travel much abroad, seldom become holy." — Do you have to reproach yourself with such a misuse of pilgrimages? In future, may your pious journeyings proceed from motives of grace, as when Mary went to visit Elizabeth.

PRAYER OF THE CHURCH
(Sixteenth Sunday after Pentecost)

Let Thy grace, O Lord, we beseech Thee, ever go before us and follow us, and make us continually intent upon good works. Through Christ our Lord. Amen.

JANUARY 6
THE SERVANT OF GOD CATHARINE, QUEEN OF ENGLAND
Widow, Third Order

ATHARINE was the daughter of King Ferdinand V of Spain and of his spouse Isabella. Reared in piety and in the fear of the Lord, she was espoused as early as the sixteenth year of her age to Arthur, the eldest son of Henry VII of England. Arthur died within five months of their marriage, and Catharine wanted to return to her native country. But King Henry, who had taken a great fancy to her, urgently besought her to remain in England in order to become the wife of his second son, Henry. Since this was also in accordance with her parents' wishes, Catharine consented, and the papal dispensation for the marriage was requested.

Meanwhile King Henry died, and his son ascended the throne as King Henry VIII. Soon afterwards he celebrated his marriage with Catharine, who was then crowned with great pomp as queen of England. But her heart found as little delight in worldly dignity as that of the pious Queen Esther.

She always arose early in the morning, dressed herself as simply as her rank permitted, and wore the penitential garb of the Third Order of St. Francis which she had joined some time previously. Every morning she attended holy Mass and spent several hours in prayer. Every week she received the holy sacraments, and she fasted so rigorously, that on the vigils of the feasts of our Lady, she partook only of bread and water. Withal, she expended great care on the education of her five children.

But King Henry shared not at all in the devout life of his spouse; rather, he gave himself up to all the gratifications of a luxurious life at court, and even conceived an adulterous affection for a young lady at court, Anne Boleyn by name. This affair was to occasion the greatest sufferings for Catharine. Egged on by godless courtiers, Henry now indulged a dislike for his pious queen. He began to allege that his marriage with Catharine was null and void because the dispensation had not been validly issued. His intention was to marry Anne Boleyn. After a careful investigation of the matter, Pope Clement VII declared the marriage of the king with Catharine valid and insoluble. Now King Henry renounced his allegiance to the Catholic Church and declared himself the head of the Church in England; priests and people who were unwilling to admit his authority were executed or sent into exile.

The pious queen, who in nowise consented to the godless designs of her spouse, was cast off, and Henry married Anne Boleyn. Separated from her children, laughed at by her courtiers, Catharine repaired to a secluded spot, where she sometimes suffered the want of things necessary to sustain her life. Yes, because of the persecution of the priests she did not even have the comfort of the holy sacraments. Though crushed with grief, Catharine, nevertheless, bore it all with the most perfect conformity to the will of God until her blessed death on January 6, 1536.

ON CONSTANCY IN SUFFERING

1. Consider what a difference there was between the day on which Catharine was crowned amid great splendor as the queen of England, and the day on which, cast off by the king and despised by her courtiers, she left the royal palace helpless and destitute. Yet, that sad day was more truly glorious in the sight of heaven than that first day. On the day of her coronation, the world undoubtedly praised Catharine as blessed; yet, how soon did this blessedness come to a sad end! When, however she was going into exile, heaven pronounced her blessed: "Blessed are they that suffer persecution for justice' sake, for theirs is the kingdom of heaven" (Mt. 5,10). This blessedness she still enjoys, and it will never end.

2. Consider how saintly Queen Catharine proved herself through prolonged constancy in suffering. Not only did she bear patiently the first attacks, when the king turned away from her; she remained constant also when the entire fullness of suffering came upon her along with her rejection. For years she persevered and bore the greatest tribulations without complaint or murmuring even unto her death, always resigned to the holy will of God. Thus she obtained the heavenly crown, according to the words of St. Bernard: "The crown is offered to beginners, but it is given to those who persevere." But only such constancy and perseverance can ensure for us the eternal crown. Many people bear their sufferings courageously and resignedly in the beginning; but if the sufferings increase, if they last long, they do not persevere, they despair and murmur against the designs of God. Only "he that shall persevere unto the end, he shall be saved" (Mt. 10,22).

3. Consider by what means saintly Queen Catharine preserved that constancy amid such great suffering. In youth she did not allow herself to be dazzled by good fortune and the glamour that surrounded her, but directed her attention to heavenly things rather than to those of earth. Devout practices and love of mortification confirmed her still more in her life of faith. Even in her suffering she was faithful to her pious practices, and so, with her attention directed more to the future than to the present, she could bear all with joy, while she reflected on the words of the

Apostle: "The sufferings of this time are not worthy to be compared with the glory to come that shall be revealed in us" (Rom. 8,18). — If you wish to arrive at the glory of good Queen Catharine in eternity, then you must tread the same path, and God's mercy will also lead you to your goal.

PRAYER OF THE CHURCH
(Tenth Sunday after Pentecost)

O God, who dost chiefly manifest Thy almighty power in longsuffering and in pity, increase Thy mercy towards us, that, hastening after Thy promises, we may be made partakers of heavenly treasures. Through Christ our Lord. Amen.

JANUARY 7
THE SERVANT OF GOD JANE OF ST. ERASMUS
Widow, Second Order

BORN in the year 1575, Jane descended from a distinguished family in Hainaut. She became a model to Christian women in the secular as well as in the religious state. After a pious youth spent in innocence, she was married, in her twenty-eighth year, to a nobleman of the Netherlands, Erasmus of Scheinghen, whose family, at the time when forceful attempts were being made to introduce the Calvinist heresy in the Netherlands, had nevertheless remained true to the Catholic Faith. Erasmus occupied high rank in the army of the king of Spain, to whom the Netherlands belonged at that time. The marriage was blessed with the birth of a little daughter, whom God almighty called very early to Himself.

Jane had very little comfort in her husband. He loved society and games of chance, and his vanity and ambition often caused him to become involved in bloody quarrels. His good wife endeavored to win his heart. She settled many of his disputes, and once even cast herself between two drawn swords in a duel. She sought strength and consolation in her communion with God, with whom she conversed like a child with its father. She was much devoted to prayer—when she was at prayer she experienced neither hunger nor thirst, neither cold nor heat. Yet, she did not on that account neglect any of her household duties. With all courtesy, she also received the company who were at times invited at the wish of her husband; and added to that, she was a true mother to the poor and the sick. Such virtue caused her husband to be converted to better ways. A true believer at heart, as he had always been, he resolved to make a pilgrimage to the Holy Land; he returned from there a pious Christian.

During his absence, his devoted wife experienced a mighty impulse to enter the convent, and after severely testing her vocation, she believed the call came from heaven. Upon the return of her husband, she asked him for leave to follow the call. But, having since his conversion learned to value his virtuous wife, he did not want to hear of a separation. But Jane continued to plead, and as her vocation was approved by the most experienced directors in the spiritual life, even the archbishop of Cambrai supporting her petition, her husband at length resolved on his part to make the sacrifice to God. He himself accompanied his wife to the convent of Philippeville, where the rule of St. Clare was observed in its primitive rigor.

Although she was already fifty-five years old, Jane cheerfully observed the strictest practices of the novices, went barefoot, and looked upon herself as the lowliest servant in the convent. In gratitude to her husband who permitted her to enter, she called herself by his name, Jane of St. Erasmus. She pledged him the best of all her merits, and also offered, when his death drew near, to suffer his purgatory.

Jane survived for nineteen years, a model for everyone in the convent. She experienced extraordinary graces from God; frequently she was seen in ecstasy and raised above the earth. If she so much as glanced at a picture of our Lord at the Pillar of the Scourging which hung in the choir, she broke out in tears of the tenderest compassion. When it was forbidden her to look at it any more, she never again directed her glance in that direction, because she held obedience in greater esteem than sentiments of devotion.

At the last she was tried by long and painful suffering in all the members of her body. In that condition, a glance at the image of the Crucified was her dearest comfort. Looking at it, she used to say the little prayer: "Jesus of Nazareth, King of the Jews! May this victorious title protect us and preserve us from all evil." She actually had the prayer on her lips, and was raising her hand in order to make the Sign of the Cross as she said it, when our Lord took unto Himself the soul that had been found so faithful. It was in the year 1649.

ON PERSEVERANCE IN PRAYER

1. Consider how faithfully the servant of God Jane observed the admonition of our Divine Saviour: "We ought to pray and not to faint"

(Lk. 18,1). In every situation in life she sought by means of prayer to obtain the necessary help from heaven, and her prayer was not in vain. Through prayer she preserved her innocence in all the dangers of her youth. Through prayer she obtained in the married state the conversion of her husband. Through prayer she rose to the highest perfection in the convent. — Do you in like manner avail yourself of the divine assistance in every situation? Do you always endeavor to obtain it through prayer?

2. Consider how this servant of God persevered in prayer in the various situations of life. Never did she allow her usual devotion to suffer. Her devotion was always so lively that she appeared to notice nothing of what was going on about her. At the same time she fulfilled her household duties with fidelity, since prayer cannot otherwise be pleasing to God. And in difficult situations, as when she felt the call to the religious life, she redoubled her prayers, and pleaded with ever greater confidence until God heard her. — Have you been as persevering in the past, in your daily prayers, in their devout performance, in the faithful fulfilment of your duties, in special exercises of devotion? "He that wavers," and has no confidence, "let not that man think that he shall receive anything of the Lord" (Jas. 1,7).

3. Especially do we need persevering prayer in the time of suffering, whether it be exterior or interior. In her long and painful illnesses, therefore, Jane did not desist from recourse to God in short prayers, and from keeping before her eyes the Passion of Christ. As meritorious as suffering can be, we must remember that without special divine assistance we cannot gain that merit, but may very easily make ourselves displeasing to God. Therefore St. James admonishes us: "Is any of you sad? Let him pray" (5,13). In tribulations and temptations call upon the Lord. — Do you observe this admonition?

PRAYER OF THE CHURCH

Lord Jesus Christ, who in the Garden of Olives hast taught us by word and example to pray in order that we may overcome the dangers of temptation, grant us the grace that we may always be devoted to prayer and may merit to obtain its abundant fruits. Who livest and reignest forever and ever. Amen.

JANUARY 8
THE SERVANT OF GOD ADOLPH OF STRASBOURG
Martyr, First Order

T HE SERVANT OF GOD ADOLPH was custos of the Franciscan province of Strasbourg. During the Thirty-Years' War, while he was on a journey to Wuerttemberg in connection with his priestly duties, a heretic soldier fell upon him and out of hatred for the Catholic Faith and the order whose habit Adolph was wearing, sent a bullet through his left shoulder, another through his neck, then gave him a blow on the head with his sword, and ended by tying the half-dead religious, who was bleeding from three severe wounds, to the tail of his horse.

In this manner he dragged him up hill and down dale into the nearby woods, where Adolph died. This was in the vicinity of the fortress of Asperg in Wuerttemberg, on January 8, 1632.

For three days and nights Adolph's body lay there; yet, neither the birds nor any marauding animals touched it. Then the body was found by some Lutherans, who grew very much incensed at beholding the marks of such wanton cruelty. They buried the remains with great respect. Seven years later the body was exhumed and laid to rest in the church of the Poor Clares at Heilbronn.

The just punishment of heaven, however, was meted out to the murderer of the martyr. Two years after the ruthless deed, in the act of conveying a lot of stolen loot to Strasbourg for safekeeping, he was attacked and stoned by his companion robbers on the very spot of his own crimes. He was so terribly mauled that his face became black and bloated and he expired in dreadful torment.

ON DIVINE RETRIBUTION

1. "Never do to another what you would hate to have done to you by another" (Tob. 4,16). This admonition of the elder Tobias to his son arises from the knowledge that divine retribution frequently permits the same evil to befall us that we have occasioned to others. What happened so strikingly in the case of the murderer of the saintly Adolph, still happens in less serious matters every day. Notice in this, how carefully divine providence watches over us. Think of it when you are tempted to do an injustice to another.

2. Divine retribution is signally carried out not only for actions against

brotherly love, but unkind words and even thoughts are frequently punished in this manner. How often does it happen that a person deals sharply and unkindly with others, or severely censures another for some small fault without being authorized to do so, and then shortly falls into the same fault by the permission of God! Have you not yourself experienced the like? Hence the Apostle admonishes us: "And if a man be overtaken in any fault, you, who are spiritual, instruct such a one in the spirit of meekness, considering yourself lest you also be tempted" (Gal. 6,1).

3. Consider that God's retribution for all sins will be exactly in accordance with the offenses committed. "In what things a man has most sinned," says Thomas a Kempis of the pains of hell (1,24), "in those things shall he be most grievously punished. There the slothful will be pricked with burning goads, the gluttonous tormented with extreme hunger and thirst; there the luxurious and the lovers of pleasure will have burning pitch and fetid sulphur rained upon them; and the envious, like rabid dogs, will howl for grief. There one hour of punishment will be more grievous than a hundred years of the most bitter penance here." — Is it not better and easier, then, to overcome our inordinate desires here on earth, and to do penance for the sins we have committed?

PRAYER OF THE CHURCH
(Saturday in the First Week of Lent)

Graciously hear, we beseech Thee, O Lord, the prayers of Thy people, that we who are justly afflicted for our sins, may for the glory of Thy name be mercifully delivered. Through Christ our Lord. Amen.

JANUARY 9
VENERABLE VICO NECCHI
Confessor, Third Order

THE VIGOR of the Franciscan Order is exhaustless. After seven hundred years it has not yet been spent, rather it seems to have taken on additional life in this present age that is so unpropitious to all that savors of the supernatural. On January 10, 1930, Louis (Ludovico, hence Vico) Necchi, professor of biology at the University of Milan, died. His will prescribed that on his headstone be engraved the simple legend, Vico Necchi, Franciscan Tertiary. These significant words tell the story of so extraordinary life, that all who knew the deceased are putting forth every effort for his beatification.

He was born at Milan on November 19, 1876. While still a young man, he joined the forces of Christ and the Church. The Franciscan spirit became manifest in him in a special way from the day he was invested with the garb of the Third Order. Later on, because of his position as a physician, he frequently moved in circles where everything that savored of Christianity was rejected or even attacked. These people he met with the enthusiasm of a Paul and the kindliness of a Francis, and thus he was instrumental in gaining not a few to enlist under the banner of Christ.

Among his converts was a young radical who later became a Franciscan and the rector of the Catholic University at Milan, Augustine Gemelli. Together they founded the University of the Sacred Heart at Milan. And when Rome called for Catholic Action against socialism, Louis Necchi was found at the head of the ranks. He considered his medical profession a holy apostolate which he employed for the welfare of the souls of his patients as well as of their bodies. He lavished his services without cost on the care of backward children.

The spirit of prayer, humility, and charming cheerfulness was the mainstay of this model Tertiary, even though adversities demanded a heavy sacrifice from him. Professor Doctor Vico Necchi is a brilliant example of active Christianity for everyone, but particularly for the representatives of modern learning and culture.[1] (Cf. *Forum*, 1943, pp. 324-327 and 357-362; 1949, pp. 131- 134, 154.)

ON CATHOLIC ACTION

1. What is Catholic Action? The union of Catholic forces for the maintenance, administration, accomplishment, and defense of Catholic principles in the life of the individual, of the family, and of society. Just as the servant of God Louis Necchi has exemplified it for us. In order to do our share toward the proper promotion of Catholic sentiment and Catholic principle in public life, it is not sufficient that our names be entered in the baptismal record, that we approach the Communion railing, and belong to Catholic societies. Catholic in our dealings with others and

---

[1] Editor's note: Subsequent to this book's publication, the Servant of God was declared venerable on 14 January 1971 following a decree of the *Sacred Congregation for the Causes of the Saints*. The cause for Beatification stalled with the death of the chief postulator in 1975.

The Venerable Vico Necchi

Catholic in conduct — that is Catholic Action. Active Christianity! "The kingdom of God is not in speech but in power" (1 Cor. 4,20). — Does your life conform to these principles?

2. Catholic Action is necessary. It aims to erect a barrier against the tide of religious indifference, lack of charity, and immorality of our day. The clergy can no longer do the work alone. Hence the call for Catholic Action of the laity. Catholic, energetic laymen, to the front! If the laity refuse their assistance, the already overburdened clergy must succumb, and with them Catholicity. But what lay apostles can do has been shown us by the servant of God Louis Necchi. — Will you not follow in his footsteps?

3. Remember the patron of Catholic Action. Holy Church has appointed St. Francis of Assisi to this position. St. Francis, who was not a priest, shows the lay apostles the correct way to approach Catholic Action, namely, by loyalty to the Church, the Pope and the Bishops; by unselfish zeal for Christ and His interests; by personal exemplary conduct. Where the Franciscan spirit reigns, there Catholicity will not fare badly. — Beg our Seraphic Father for the spirit of a Catholic apostle. Offer your services to the clergy.

PRAYER OF THE CHURCH

Defend us, O Lord, we beseech Thee, from all dangers of body and soul, and mercifully grant us peace and salvation through the intercession of St. Francis, so that after overcoming all adversities and errors, Thy Church may serve Thee in liberty and peace. Through Christ our Lord. Amen.

JANUARY 10
BLESSED GREGORY X
Pope, Third Order

THIS holy Tertiary pope of the thirteenth century and friend of St. Bonaventure was a true son of St. Francis, distinguishing himself by his love for the holy places in Palestine and his incessant efforts to establish peace everywhere. Theobald Visconti, as he was called before he became pope, was born at Piacenza in 1210. He was conspicuous from his youth by his virtue as well as his success in studies. He devoted himself especially to the study of canon law, first in Italy, then in Paris and Liège.

In Paris, where he was associated with the intellectual circles surrounding the university for more than two decades, his closest friends were the Franciscans, especially St. Bonaventure. After he was named archdeacon of Liège, Pope Clement IV commissioned him to preach the Crusades. Theobald himself took up the cross, but instead was sent on a peace mission to England.

When his friend, the Tertiary King Louis IX died in 1270, Theobald hastened eastward to comfort the king's son and the other Crusaders and also to satisfy his devotion by visiting the holy places. At this time the Holy See was vacant. It had been such for almost three years, ever since the death of Clement IV in November, 1268. Finally, on September 1, 1271, a committee of six cardinals, to whom the rest had referred the election, chose a new pope. Much to the surprise of everybody, their choice fell on Theobald, who was still in the Holy Land. St. Bonaventure had been summoned from Paris to assist in nominating a candidate; and he had recommended the Archdeacon of Liège, who was then about sixty years old.

Returning to Rome, Theobald was first ordained a priest, then consecrated a bishop; and on March 27, 1272, he was crowned Pope Gregory X. His reign as pope was short, only three years and nine months; but in that short time he accomplished much as a peacemaker. Sometimes he called on the Franciscans to work for peace, for instance, during the trouble between Bologna and Venice.

It was Gregory X who convoked the Fourteenth General Council, the Second of Lyons, which was in session for two months from May to July, 1274, and was attended by five hundred bishops. The previous year he made St. Bonaventure a Cardinal, and told him to accept the red hat "in humility of spirit." He wanted the Seraphic Doctor at his side during the Council. On the way to France, the Pope was joined by St. Bonaventure; and together they reached Lyons six months before the opening of the Council. St. Bonaventure died July 15, two days before the final session.

The more public affairs claimed his attention, so much the more did Gregory X strive for personal holiness and perfection. Abstemious in diet and sparing in speech, he managed to devote much time to prayer and to carry out his many duties in a prayerful spirit and constant union with God. His death occurred at Arezzo on January 10, 1276. Benedict XIV inserted his name in the Roman martyrology; and his feast is kept on January 10.

ON THE SPIRIT OF UNITY

1. The spirit of unity should be a characteristic mark of every Christian,

and particularly of a follower of St. Francis of Assisi, the Man of Peace. To his disciples St. Francis gave this commission: "Go two and two about the several parts of the world, proclaiming peace to people. ... While you are proclaiming peace with your lips, be careful to have it even more fully in your heart. Nobody should be roused to wrath or insult on your account. Everyone should rather be moved to peace, goodwill and mercy as a result of your self-restraint" (*Words of St. Francis*, nos. 209 and 210). The holy Tertiary Pope Gregory X, as a true son of St. Francis, endeavored by every means in his power, both before and after his elevation to the papacy, to promote the spirit of unity among Christian cities and countries and peoples. No one who is not an apostle of peace can rightly call himself a disciple of St. Francis.

2. The Apostle St. Paul pointed out the virtues which are necessary for maintaining the spirit of unity. From his prison in Rome he wrote to the Ephesians: "I, therefore, the prisoner in the Lord, exhort you to walk in a manner worthy of the calling with which you were called, with all humility and meekness, with patience, bearing with one another in love, careful to preserve the unity of the Spirit in the bond of peace" (Eph. 4,1-3). A Christian can promote the spirit of unity in himself and others only if he lives up to his faith and views all happenings in the light of faith. He must practice the virtue of humility and be fully aware that all he has is a gift of God; the virtue of meekness, the fruit of humility, which prevents him from becoming perturbed no matter what may happen; the virtue of patience or long-suffering, which causes him to bear with the faults of others, remembering that he too has faults which are disagreeable to others; the virtue of charity, which keeps him from becoming involved in quarrels and dissensions.

3. St. Paul also indicates the reasons why the spirit of unity should prevail among Christians at all times: "One body and one Spirit, even as you were called in one hope of your calling; one Lord, one faith, one baptism; one God and Father of all, who is above all, and throughout all, and in us all" (Eph. 4,4-6). All Christians are members of the one Mystical Body of Christ, which in turn is the foundation for the Communion of Saints, comprising the Church militant, suffering, and triumphant. All have a share in the merits of Christ, the Head, and of the members, the saints in Heaven and Purgatory and the faithful on earth. There is but one Holy Spirit, the soul of the Church, the principle of life of the "one body"; and all its members are temples of the Holy Spirit. The Holy Spirit is also the pledge of everlasting life, "the one hope" of all. All adore and obey one Lord, the risen and glorified Christ; and by the same baptism and faith they are made members of His Mystical Body. There is but one God, the

Creator and Father of all; and He wishes all His creatures, all His children to live in unity and love. He, the God of Peace, is above all, because He rules all; He is throughout all, because He uses all to attain His wise ends; He is in all by His omnipresence and His grace.

PRAYER OF THE CHURCH

O God, who hast united the divers peoples of the earth in the praise of Thy name; grant that those born again of water in baptism may all be one in mind by faith and one in deed by holiness of life. Through Christ our Lord. Amen.

JANUARY 11
THE SERVANT OF GOD VALENTINE PAQUAY
Confessor, First Order

AT TONGERN in the shadow of the venerable basilica of Our Lady, Cause of Our Joy, this holy father, as he was generally known, was born of a pious Flemish family in 1828, the fifth of ten children. While he was still a good and innocent young man, he was invested with the habit of St. Francis. After his ordination, in 1854, he was sent to Hasselt, the chief city of the Belgian province of Limburg, and there the virtues which he had until then practiced in secret, manifested themselves in great splendor.

He achieved his greatest reputation by unwearied labors in the confessional, and he himself practiced what he preached to others when he said: "We priests can and must sanctify ourselves in the confessional." There, like the holy Curé of Ars, he spent the greater part of his life, hardly finding time to say his Breviary or take his meals. Especially on evenings before Sundays and feastdays great crowds besieged his confessional. What was the secret of this attraction? They ascribed to the Father an extraordinary knowledge of the human heart and the rare gift of setting aright with a few words the unhappy and the discouraged.

His humility and contempt for himself, as well as the love he bore our Blessed Lady, caused him to be particularly loved by all. Moreover, he chose as his own the principle of the medieval mystics, "Love to be unknown and to be accounted as nothing."

When Father Paquay died on January 1, 1905, he was seventy-six years of age. During the two days that his body lay in state, a continuous stream of people passed, to take a last look at the countenance of this beloved priest and to beg his intercession. The unveiling of a monument, which the people erected in the cemetery was another grand demonstration for this poor son of St. Francis. It fittingly represents him with his hand raised in absolution. The many miracles that have occurred at his grave led to the introduction of his cause of beatification.

ON CONFESSION

1. Confession is something holy. Father Valentine became an apostle of confession. Hundreds of thousands of people were taught by him to appreciate confession as it deserves. This institution was given us by the hand of Christ Himself, when He said to the apostles and their successors in the priesthood: "Whose sins you shall forgive, they are forgiven them, and whose sins you shall retain, they are retained" (Jn. 20,23). — Excite in yourself a new appreciation of confession.

2. Confession is something easy. No matter what a person may have done, and even if it were the greatest crime — just a sincere act of contrition, a purpose of amendment, and an honest acknowledgment of it, and everything is removed from the soul. "If we confess our sins, he is faithful and just to forgive us our sins and to cleanse us from all iniquity" (1 Jn. 1,9). God could hardly have made it easier for us. Justly then has the sacrament of penance been called the sacrament of the unbounded mercy of God. — Praise the Lord and extol His mercy, and use it to good advantage.

3. Confession brings great relief. The greatest evil is a guilty conscience. It weighs us down and afflicts us more than many of us care to admit. How gladly we would rid ourselves of it! And now God comes to our assistance in a wonderful manner and has placed a means within our reach by which we can rid ourselves of all blame, and that quite secretly. For, confession restores to us that peace which "the world cannot give" (Jn. 14,27). — Use this sacrament of peace with much profit to yourself.

PRAYER OF THE CHURCH

O God, who dost behold our weakness, watch over our interior and exterior, so that we may be protected in body from all adversities and be preserved in soul from all evil thought. Through Christ our Lord. Amen.

JANUARY 12
THE SERVANT OF GOD MATTHEW ROSSI
Confessor, Third Order

ATTHEW ROSSI, of the renowned family of the Orsini, was a knight of extraordinary piety and virtue. Once St. Francis came to Rome and passed by his palace on the way to the home of Jacoba Settesoli. Matthew begged him to pay him a visit too and to teach him how to go about saving his soul. Francis promised to come soon. But a few days later, when he visited Matthew's home, the latter just happened to be away. The servants, who did not know St. Francis, believed him to be one of the poor whom their pious master had undertaken to support. They directed him to the beggars in the courtyard and there gave him something to eat.

Francis cheerfully took his place among them, and gratefully partook of the food. It was there that Matthew found him upon his return. He promptly sat down next to him and ate at the table of the poor. Later on he often said that he never tasted such delicious food as the time the holy Poor Man of Assisi shared his bread with him.

After Francis had said the prayer of thanksgiving, he conversed with his host so impressively on the vanity of the world that Matthew fell at his feet and humbly begged for admission into the Third Order, to work out his salvation in penance. Gladly the saint acceded to his request, for it was revealed to him that this new novice would contribute much to spread the order by his future holy life. In reality, many noble men and women soon followed his example and became like him ornaments of the Third Order.

Later on when St. Francis again sojourned in Rome, Matthew brought his little son, John Cajetan, to him, to be blessed by him. The saint took the little one lovingly in his arms and began in forceful words to commend his order to him, to the great astonishment of the father. But this astonishment mounted to joyful amazement when the man of God solemnly declared: "This boy will at some future time be a religious not in garb but in sentiment; he will be a mighty ruler and a great protector of our order."

The prophecy was fulfilled. John Cajetan became a priest, cardinal protector of the Franciscan Order, and in the year 1277 he ascended the papal throne as Nicholas III.

After a long life rich in virtue and heavenly merits, Matthew died a blessed death about the year 1271.

CONCERNING THE CALL OF GOD

1. Consider how faithfully the servant of God Matthew followed the example of his great patron saint, the holy evangelist Matthew, in heeding the call of God. Seeing how St. Francis went about in humble apparel, modestly reserved, his countenance reflecting his mortified life, Matthew heard God say interiorly to him: There is the man that shall guide you. And Matthew at once went to St. Francis with an invitation to visit him. He was not offended when the saint did not go with him at once, but waited gladly. And when he found Francis in the courtyard among the poor, he sat down sociably with him at the table of the poor. Now God almighty again called him by the mouth of His servant Francis to despise worldly vanity and to strive after greater perfection; and again Matthew obeyed, became a Tertiary and a leader to many others. Surely he must also be more brilliant than many others in heavenly glory, who so faithfully followed the call of the Lord. — Who would not wish to follow the call of God thus faithfully?
2. Consider the purpose to which the call of God is directed. Mostly it points the way to what is more humble, less glamorous, to a life that men despise, and to abnegation. Human nature is often terrified at these things. But if he who is called to them grasps the opportunity, grace, which is always attached to the call of God, will soon make them easy and sweet, sweeter even than enjoying any natural good. Sometimes the call is to lead us out of the dangers of sin, as God called Abraham to leave his idolatrous country; again it is to greater perfection, as He called the apostles to follow Him completely; but always the call is directed to more faithful service of God. — Judge accordingly what you ought to look upon as the call of God in your case.
3. Consider that the call of God is communicated in various ways. Often God calls by means of His servants, the priests, in sermons and other exhortations; sometimes He speaks to our hearts in pious reading, sometimes in quiet meditation. He calls us also and admonishes us through somebody's dying suddenly, through someone else's falling into sin, or through similar occurrences of whatever kind. We must be concerned to keep our hearts ready to follow His call, so that He will not, after calling in vain, be forced to say to us what He once had to say to the Israelites: "I have spoken to you, and you have not heard; and I have called you, and you have not answered: I will cast you away from before My face" (Jer. 7,13-15). — Oh, may we at all times hear Him and with His grace accomplish what He asks of us!

PRAYER OF THE CHURCH
(Friday in the First Week of Lent)

Be gracious, O Lord, to Thy people, and as Thou makest them devoted to Thee, in mercy cherish them with Thy kind assistance. Through Christ our Lord. Amen.

JANUARY 13
BLESSED ROGER OF TODI
Confessor, First Order

OGER was born at Todi in the Italian province of Umbria, and in 1216 was received into the order by St. Francis himself. Like a good disciple, he directed all his energies toward faithfully imitating the virtues of his holy father and master; likewise he adopted as his models the other saints that have so enriched his native country. Because of his earnest efforts at perfection, the Seraphic Founder greatly esteemed him, and often chose him as his companion when he set out to preach or to direct souls.

After St. Francis had led Blessed Philippa Mareri to greater perfection, and the latter with several young women had repaired to a convent of Poor Clares, the holy Father appointed his disciple Roger to be her future director in the spiritual life. He guided the new congregation with great fidelity and led it to high sanctity. He also assisted Blessed Philippa in her dying moments. At her tomb he delivered a brilliant panegyric, in the course of which he declared that she could be invoked as one of the blessed in heaven. Not many years later this judgment was confirmed by the verdict of the Church.

Within a year after the death of Blessed Philippa, Roger also died, on January 5, 1237. Pope Gregory IX, who knew him personally, and who had called him a saint even during his lifetime, at once sanctioned the celebration of his feast at Todi; Benedict XIV extended his veneration to the entire Franciscan Order. His feast is celebrated on January fourteenth by the Franciscans, on January fifth by the Conventuals, and on January twenty-eighth by the Capuchins.

ON IMITATING THE SAINTS

1. Consider what a great benefit almighty God bestows upon us in holding

up the saints as our models on the way to heaven. Just as He sent out the apostles and their successors to announce the Gospel, so He gave a commission to the saints with the words: "Let your light shine before men that they may see your good works" (Mt. 5,16). It is from their example that we should learn how to carry out the teachings of the Gospel. For this reason Blessed Roger attentively studied the lives of the saints. We ought to be glad to make at least a short daily reading in their lives, and, if possible, to read it aloud to the members of the household. One always finds time to read and to listen to idle news; should zealous Christians not deem it worth while to acquaint themselves with the virtuous example of the saints? — How do matters stand with you and your household in regard to this matter?

2. Consider that it does not suffice to read the Lives of the Saints or to listen to the accounts; the principal thing is to imitate their virtues. That alone will take us to heaven. It is necessary that while reading as well as afterwards, we compare their conduct with ours and make resolutions accordingly; that we improve what has been done badly in the past, and amend whatever has been defective. Do not say, what the saints have done is beyond me, I can never achieve such heights. An artist who wishes to become accomplished, carefully studies the works of the most distinguished masters. He knows that he will never arrive at their perfection, but he aims, as far as he is able, to imitate their works. In this way we, too, should aim to imitate the virtues of the saints according to our ability and our circumstances. From their lives we should also draw encouragement for the practice of virtue, and confidence that He who strengthened them, weak human beings though they were, will also strengthen us. — Would that you always read the Lives of the Saints in this manner.

3. Consider that in the lives of the saints certain particular virtues are seen regularly exemplified, such as humility, charity, piety, and patient resignation to the will of God. We should learn from this fact that whoever wishes to reach heaven must likewise practice these virtues. Say with the devout Tobias: "We are the children of saints" (Tob. 2,18), and endeavor to be not wholly unworthy of the name. — Undoubtedly, this or that particular saint will have a special appeal for us and be specially suited for our imitation. Take such a saint as your special model and call upon him, and you will be mightily strengthened by his intercession.

PRAYER OF THE CHURCH

O God, who didst appoint Blessed Roger as companion to Thy seraphic servant Francis and as his foremost imitator, grant us through the intercession of both these saints so to walk in their footsteps that we may also attain to their reward. Through Christ our Lord. Amen.

CRANDRANDRANDRANDRAN

JANUARY 14
BLESSED ODORIC MATIUSSI OF PORDENONE
Confessor, First Order

DORIC was born of noble parents in the year 1265 at Pordenone in Friuli. He entered the Franciscan Order in the convent at Udine when he was only fifteen years old. He felt himself called by God to be a missionary, and so prepared himself for his vocation by a strict life of penance, intimate union with God in solitude, and earnest application to study.

Ordained a priest, he labored as a zealous and forceful preacher of penance. The people came from great distances to hear his sermons and through him to be reconciled to God in the tribunal of penance. But soon his vast field of labor no longer satisfied his burning zeal. He was desirous of winning souls for God in the distant heathen countries and, if God so wished it, even to shed his blood for Christ. In 1296 he went as a missionary to the Balkan Peninsula, and then to the Mongols in southern Russia.

In the year 1314 he sailed for the Orient. From Constantinople he crossed the Black Sea and landed at Trebizond, whence he travelled and preached in Armenia, Media, and Persia. In all these countries the Franciscans had founded mission centers.

With an Irish confrere, Friar James, he sailed to India and the islands of Ceylon, Sumatra and Java. He then pushed forward to China, and, preaching Christ crucified as he went his way, he finally arrived at the capital, Cambalec, now called Peiping. There he met the great apostle of China, the Franciscan friar John of Montecorvino, who had been appointed archbishop of Cambalec in 1307.

After three years of fruitful labor in Cambalec, Odoric resolved to go to Europe and submit a report of his fifteen years of apostolic labor to the then reigning pontiff John XXII, in the hope of securing fresh recruits for the apostolate. He traveled through China and central Asia, and returned to Italy in the year 1330, sixty-five years old, and emaciated by incessant toil and sufferings of various kinds, so that none of his brethren recognized him.

Reaching Pisa, he fell ill, and, as has been recorded, it was revealed to him that he should go to his native town and repair to the convent at Udine. At Padua he rested several days, and, at the command of his superiors, dictated an account of his apostolic journeys to Brother William. In this account the humble son of St. Francis says nothing of the hardships and dangers that he encountered; but his associates report that he suffered torment from evil spirits and wicked men, from wild animals, from hunger and thirst, and from heat and cold. Once he was seized by cruel heathens and tortured nigh unto death, when our Saviour and the Blessed Virgin appeared, consoling and strengthening him.

Having arrived at Udine after a wearisome journey, Odoric patiently awaited death in the convent where he had once received the holy habit. After making a general confession and receiving the last sacraments he departed this laborious life and entered into eternal rest on January 14, 1331.

Moved by the many miracles that were wrought at the tomb of the great missionary, Pope Benedict XIV, in the year 1775, approved the veneration which had been paid to Blessed Odoric. In the year 1881 the city of Pordenone erected a magnificent memorial to its distinguished son. The feast of Blessed Odoric is observed by the Franciscans and Conventuals on January fourteenth, and by the Capuchins on January twenty-eighth. (Cf. *In Journeyings Often*, pp. 80-108.)

CONCERNING THE MISSIONS AMONG THE INFIDELS

1. Consider how pleasing to God must have been the labor and exertion of Blessed Odoric, as he brought the light of the Faith to so many nations, and led them to the bosom of the Church which alone could bring them salvation. "Without faith it is impossible to please God" (Heb. 11,6) and to be saved. If your heavenly Father had so great a desire for the salvation of souls that He sent His only-begotten Son into the world to enlighten them who sat in darkness and in the shadow of death, how pleasing to Him must be the labors of apostolic men who continue the work of our Divine Saviour! They are doing what Christ Himself commissioned the apostles to do in His parting words to them: "Go and teach all nations, baptizing them in the name of the Father and of the Son and of the Holy Ghost" (Mt. 28,19). O happy calling, to co-operate in God's work of leading souls to heaven! — Would you not like to co-operate in such work?

2. Consider how this co-operation can be put into effect. The Catholic Church has not only sent out missionaries at all times, but she has established an official department for the propagation of the Faith, which

supervises all such activity. For its purposes vast financial assistance is needed, in order to support the missions in the distant heathen countries, and all those whom God has blessed with temporal goods can lend their co-operation. The department of Propaganda accepts, through the bishops and the priests, the gifts and bequests of the faithful toward spreading the Faith, in order to apply them where they are most needed. By affiliation with the Society for the Propagation of the Faith, the Holy Childhood Association, the Franciscan Missionary Union, and similar institutions, one can co-operate in the holy work of the missions by easy regular donations. — Have you utilized such opportunities according to your means?

3. But more necessary than the financial aid, is the special grace of God for the propagation of the Faith, and everybody can help to obtain that grace from God by his prayers and by offering up his hardships. St. Theresa, who entertained an ardent desire for the conversion of the poor heathens, offered up all her prayers and mortifications for the purpose, and she received from God the assurance that she co-operated in the salvation of more infidels than St. Francis Xavier had baptized. So you, too, can co-operate daily in the spreading of the Faith, by your daily prayers and by offering up the difficulties you must suffer daily in your state of life, as is required of the members of the Apostleship of Prayer. Should not every Catholic Christian thus profess his gratitude for the grace of having been born of Catholic parents?

PRAYER OF THE CHURCH

O God, who, in order to lead the nations of the East to the bosom of the Church, didst equip Blessed Odoric with invincible strength of soul, graciously look upon all those who are still blinded by the deceptions of hell, that by his glorious merits they may be delivered from their darkness. Through Christ our Lord. Amen.

JANUARY 15
BLESSED GILES OF LORENZANA
Confessor, First Order

ORN of pious parents at Lorenzana in Italy, Giles received the name of Bernardin in baptism. Even as a youth he received the gift of devotion in so eminent a degree that at prayer his

JANUARY

33

countenance glowed with fervor, and he was often seen raised a foot or more from the floor. This attracted general attention, and people came from the surrounding places in order to see him at prayer.

The devout young man, however, desired nothing more than to serve God in seclusion. In order, therefore, to withdraw from the attention of the world, and also to progress in Christian perfection, he asked for admission as a lay brother at the convent of the Friars Minor. This request was granted. He was given the name Giles after the saintly Brother Giles, one of the first companions of St. Francis.

Burning with love for God, Giles knew no greater joy in the order than to devote himself to the contemplation of heavenly things, and since his superiors were convinced that he was doing great things for the honor of God and the salvation of souls, they permitted him to live in a hermitage close to the convent. Here he lived only for God, to whom he sacrificed his body by severe fasting, and his soul by constant prayer. He overcame the attacks of hell, which he had frequently to endure, without ever yielding for an instant. When he had finished his course, God called him to the eternal union on January 10, 1518.

The convent bells rang by themselves when he died, and a very great concourse of people flocked to venerate him. Many miracles occurred at his grave. Several years after his death his body was found still incorrupt, although he had been buried in a very damp place. The veneration which had been accorded to him since time immemorial was approved by Pope Leo XIII, for the entire Order of Friars Minor. His feast is celebrated on January fourteenth by the Franciscans, and on January twenty-eighth by the Capuchins.

ON DEVOTION AT PRAYER

1. Consider that the devotion with which the entire life of prayer of Blessed Giles was permeated, is also the first and most necessary quality which our prayers must have, since prayer must be a raising of the heart to God. Prayer without devotion is only a prayer of the lips that cannot be pleasing to God, as our Lord Himself says of the prayer of the Pharisees: "This people honors me with their lips, but their heart is far from Me" (Mt. 15,8). — Examine your past prayers, whether they, too, must stand condemned in these words.

2. Consider that devotion at prayer is principally a grace and a gift of God. Of course, we must contribute our part in obtaining and preserving devotion: we must remove the obstacles to it, especially we must guard our senses so that distracting thoughts will not occupy our mind. "The

eyes that are cast down," says St. Bernard, "raise the heart to heaven." But that our hearts may then arrive at God and be occupied with Him, is a gift from heaven, which we must ask of God. Here, too, may be applied the words of our Divine Saviour: "No man can come to Me except the Father, who has sent Me, draw him" (Jn. 6,44). — Do you, too, pray for the grace of devotion? Blessed Giles will be a good intercessor for the purpose.

3. Consider that the degree of your devotion depends upon the degree of your love for God and for your neighbor. If you love God and give evidence of the sincerity of your love by doing good, to the best of your ability, to your neighbor as a child of God, then God will love you as a dear child, and He will draw your heart to Himself with grace; then your heart will be where your treasure is. Prayer will be easy and a sweet bliss. — Examine the degree of your love of God and your neighbor, and if you find yourself wanting in devotion at prayer, then see whether this does not proceed from a want of love.

PRAYER OF THE CHURCH

O God, who didst vouchsafe to Blessed Giles, Thy confessor, the gift of heavenly love, grant us through his merits and intercession that we may love Christ while here on earth, and may reign with Him in heaven. Who liveth and reigneth with Thee forever and ever. Amen.

✲❧✲❧✲❧✲❧✲❧✲❧✲

JANUARY 16
ST. BERARD AND COMPANIONS
First Franciscan Martyrs

HEN our holy Father St. Francis learned by divine revelation that God had called him and the members of his order not only to personal perfection but also for the salvation of the souls of others, he entertained an ardent desire to convert the Mohammedans, whose inroads at that time frequently endangered Christian countries and the Christian Faith. While he himself and a companion traveled to the Orient in order to approach the Sultan, he sent six of the brethren to the Mohammedans in the West: Vitalis, Berard, Peter, Accursius, Adjutus, and Otho. On the journey, Vitalis, the superior, fell sick in Spain, and when his illness refused to mend, he submitted to the will of God and remained behind, while he permitted his brethren under the guidance of Berard to proceed.

At Seville, in southern Spain, which the Mohammedans occupied at that time, they preached fearlessly in the mosque that the teaching of Mohammed was falsehood and deceit, and that salvation could be found only in the Faith of Christ. Burning with rage, the Mohammedan ruler, who had been listening to them, ordered that their heads be cut off at once. But his son, who was with him, appeased the anger of his father, and at his suggestion the friars were permitted to sail across the sea to Morocco.

This was quite in accordance with their wishes, since there among the Saracens they were right in the midst of the Mohammedan people. Coming upon a group of Saracens, Berard, who had a good command of the Arabic language, began at once to preach the Faith of Christ to them. On another day when King Miramolin and his suite appeared on the scene, he again fearlessly preached the doctrine of Christ and called Mohammed an impostor. The king gave orders that Berard and his companions should be expelled from the country; but they escaped from their guards and returned a second and even a third time. Then it happened that on their way through the desert they came upon the royal army, which was nearly perishing because of thirst and could find no water anywhere. Berard prayed, struck his staff upon the ground, and at once a spring bubbled forth, which refreshed and saved the entire army.

More gently disposed because of this miracle, the king ordered the brethren to appear in his presence, and promised them wealth, positions of high honor, and all the conveniences of life if they would remain with him and become Mohammedans. But the champions of the Faith answered: "We despise all these things for the sake of Christ." They proceeded to urge upon the king the necessity of his conversion to their Faith. Stung by disappointment as well as by their audacity, Miramolin then seized his sword and split the head of every one in turn. Thus they obtained the martyr's palm on January 16, 1220. Pope Sixtus IV canonized them in 1481 after many miracles had occurred through their intercession.

ON ZEAL FOR THE FAITH

1. When St. Francis and his religious brethren recognized that they were called to labor for the salvation of souls, they also remembered to bring the tidings of the true Faith to those who had not yet received the grace, because they knew that "without faith it is impossible to please God" (Heb. 11,6). Christ Himself has said: "He who believes and is baptized, he shall be saved; but he who does not believe shall be condemned" (Mk. 16,16). — Do you value your Faith as you should? Do you believe that the

true Faith is the most necessary blessing for you and for all those in whose salvation you are interested?

2. Consider the sacrifices these first Franciscan martyrs made in their zeal for the Faith. They did not shrink from distant journeys, nor from privation and persecution; they did not permit themselves to be deterred by threats nor by promises, not even when they were face to face with certain death for preaching faith in Christ. They despised all temporal things in order to merit the eternal blessings, and they cheerfully offered their blood out of love for the immortal souls for which Christ so lovingly shed His Precious Blood. — What efforts have you put forth to acquire a knowledge of the Faith for yourself and in order to be better able to instruct others in it?

3. Consider the great reward which the holy martyrs are now enjoying and will enjoy throughout eternity. They entered the heavenly kingdom bearing the palm of victory, and were adorned with the crown of martyrdom in the presence of the entire heavenly court. Our holy Father St. Francis, who was still living at that time, rejoiced greatly when he heard of this triumph of his sons. — Should this not also urge you on to zeal for the Faith? To be active for its glory in your own circle of acquaintances, as well as for the spread of the Faith in pagan lands? Cheerfully to labor for this end, to contribute towards it, and to pray for it? In this way you will prove that you are worthy of being a child of St. Francis and a member of the order of these martyrs.

PRAYER OF THE CHURCH

We beseech Thee, O Lord, grant us through the intercession of the holy martyrs, Berard, Peter, Accursius, Adjutus, and Otho, through whose glorious martyrdom Thou didst sanctify the beginning of the Order of Friars Minor, that we may at all times desire those things which are heavenly and may love Christ. Through the same Christ our Lord. Amen.

JANUARY 17
THE SERVANT OF GOD ROBERT, KING OF NAPLES
Confessor, Third Order

ROBERT was the younger brother of Bishop St. Louis of Anjou, and the son of King Charles II of Naples. When his father was taken captive in a war with the king of Aragon, Robert and his brothers, Louis and Raymond, were sent to Spain as hostages for their father, and as such were compelled to remain six years in Barcelona. While there, the princes received an excellent education in piety and learning from three learned Franciscans. Robert fostered in an especial manner a great devotion toward the Blessed Sacrament of the Altar.

Upon the death of his father, Robert ascended the throne of the kingdoms of Naples and of Sicily, since his brother Louis, who was first in line for the honor, had consecrated himself to God in the ranks of the clergy. However, even as a king, Robert persevered in his pious disposition, and publicly manifested his lively faith. With his equally devout wife, Sancha, he manifested a special love for the children of St. Francis, whose Third Order both had joined. At Naples they built a convent for the Franciscan Friars and another for the Poor Clares.

When the affairs of government had been attended to for the time being, the king counted it as his most pleasant relaxation to go to the convent of the Friars Minor and to take part in all the exercises there; not infrequently he even took part in the recitation of the Divine Office at midnight.

In the year 1335 he was anxious to resign the government and enter the Franciscan Order, but insurmountable obstacles placed themselves in his way. He did, however, furnish a chapel in his palace together with living accommodations for twelve Franciscan priests, in whose midst he thereafter spent all the time that could be spared from state affairs. He himself lived among them like a religious.

When Robert became ill and felt his end draw near, he put all the affairs of his kingdom in order and forbade the court officials to mention temporal matters to him again. Thereupon he begged for and received the habit of the Friars Minor, in which, a week later, in the year 1343, he gave up his soul while absorbed in quiet prayer.

In accordance with his wishes he was buried in the religious garb, without any pomp, in the church of the Poor Clares which he and his wife had built.

ON PRACTICAL FAITH

1. Consider that faith, which we must acknowledge as the indispensable foundation of the Christian life, does not of itself lead to salvation, but only when good works are built upon this foundation, and it manifests itself through them as a practical faith. Christ Himself testifies: "Not everyone that says to Me Lord, Lord," — that is, not he who just professes his faith in Me — "shall enter into the kingdom of heaven; but he that does

the will of My Father, who is in heaven, he shall enter into the kingdom of heaven" (Mt. 7,21).

2. How practical was the faith manifested in the life of the servant of God Robert! Although he was king over rich and beautiful countries, he did not give himself up to sensual gratification, and did not seek pleasure in vain pomp. Rather, he attended conscientiously to the affairs of state and then found his pleasure and relaxation in the divine services celebrated by lowly religious. That was indeed practical faith in that fundamental truth of Christianity, that man is not upon this earth for the purpose of enjoying material things, but rather to serve God and find his pleasure in Him. — In what manner have you manifested that your faith in these and other truths is practical? Or has your faith been dead? If so, you have much to fear.

3. In order to keep our faith alive, we should frequently, especially after spiritual reading or at the conclusion of a sermon and similar exercises, compare our life with the truths of the Faith that have been expounded to us. If our conduct is not in conformity with these truths, we must at once begin to amend, otherwise our faith will itself be witness against us at the judgment, and the heathens and infidels will fare far better than we who are well instructed Christians. "Oh, that their life," says Thomas a Kempis (1,3), "had been in keeping with their learning! When the day of judgment comes, it will not be asked of us what fine discourses we have made, but how religiously we have lived."

PRAYER OF THE CHURCH
(Over the People on Thursday of the First Week of Lent)

Grant, we beseech Thee, O Lord, to all Christian peoples to acknowledge (in deeds) what they profess (in faith), and to love the heavenly gift which they frequent. Through Christ our Lord. Amen.

҉ ҉ ҉ ҉ ҉ ҉ ҉ ҉ ҉ ҉ ҉

JANUARY 18
ST. CHARLES OF SEZZE
Confessor, First Order

 HARLES, the son of lowly country folk, was born at Sezze in Italy on October 22, 1613. At the urgent request of his grandmother, the rearing of the child was entrusted to her, and the gentle boy acquired a great love of God and of prayer from the example and teaching of this devout lady. He grasped the truths of religion so readily that his parents entertained the sweet hope that Charles would later become a priest.

But when Charles was old enough to go to school, his studies did not meet with marked success; and so, when his schooling ended, his parents were sensible enough to put him to work in the fields with his brothers. There, in God's free nature, a new light came to the boy. From books he had not learned much, but he understood very well the wonders of God's creation. Everything conspired to raise his thoughts to heavenly things, so that his work was constantly mingled with interior prayer. He began to receive the sacraments more frequently, and evinced real zeal for Christian perfection.

Out of veneration for the Virgin Mother of God, he made a vow of chastity at the age of seventeen, and he preserved it so faithfully that the Beloved of pure souls, "who feeds among the lilies" (Cant. 2,16), seemed to have made His dwelling-place in the heart of Charles. He was seized with a great desire for holiness. He read with delight the lives of the saints and related them to the others while at work. In the Franciscan church which he often visited, he used to study the pictures of the saints with a desire to imitate them.

When he was twenty years old he fell dangerously ill, so that his life was despaired of. Then he made a vow that, if he would recover, he would enter the Franciscan Order. At once his illness took a turn for the better, and, true to his vow, although there were many hardships to overcome, Charles received the habit two years later. After his consecration to God through the vows, he advanced visibly not only in piety but in all the virtues of his state of life, so that even the oldest brothers were edified by him and followed his example. He ardently desired to shed his blood for Christ, and asked that he might be sent as a lay brother to the missions in India; but a new illness frustrated the design.

He was sent to a convent in Rome so that he could fully recover his health. But here God Almighty destined him for another field of labor. He received remarkable enlightenment about things divine and about the truths of religion, so that the most learned theologians were astonished at it and consulted with him on some of the most difficult questions. The cardinals and even Pope Clement IX sought his advice. In compliance with the will of God he also wrote several books about spiritual things.

At the same time the pious brother remained deeply humble. Concerning his remarkable gift of enlightenment he used to say to himself, that our Lord in His wisdom hides such things from the wise but reveals them to the simple, to which class he belonged. He so fervently adored his Lord under the appearances of bread that one day a ray of light like an arrow went out from the Sacred Host and impressed a wound in his left side. This wound was still visible after his death.

Charles died on January 6, 1670. Pope Leo XII pronounced him blessed in 1882, and Pope John XXIII canonized him in the spring of 1959. The Franciscans observe his feast on January eighteenth.

ON THE WAY TO MAKE A MEDITATION

1. Consider how Blessed Charles, who had only a meager understanding of book knowledge, easily grasped the higher knowledge of things divine. From the creature he advanced to the Creator, and from the Creator came the light and the strength necessary for a holy life. Thus he lived in a state of almost constant spiritual meditation, since the latter is nothing more nor less than the raising of our thoughts from material things to those that are eternal, to God, and the consequent coming down to us of heavenly enlightenment, stimulation, and fortitude. Meditation is like the mysterious ladder which the Patriarch Jacob saw "standing upon the earth, and the top of it touching heaven: and the angels also of God ascending and descending by it" (Gen. 28,12). In order to be able to meditate, it is not necessary to have great knowledge; it suffices to have a heart that does not cling to material things, but delights in raising itself to God. That, however, is the first requisite for meditation. — How do you stand in this respect?

2. During meditation some souls are led by God Himself, as was Blessed Charles; such souls need no instruction. But most souls must follow a special order so that their minds will not wander about aimlessly. In order to meditate, we first imagine ourselves quite vividly in the presence of God, and beseech God for His aid. Then we read the points of the meditation, to which end also these considerations may serve, or we call to mind a mystery in the life and suffering of Christ. From the mystery we seek to draw a lesson for ourselves in about the form that we would communicate it to another person, or as we would wish to have observed it at the end of our life. Then we reflect on our own past transgressions against it, sincerely repent of them, make definite resolutions for the future, and pray God to grant us the help of His grace. — Have your meditations perhaps often been poor because you did not observe some such order as this?

3. Consider how a person should conduct himself during meditation in times of aridity and dryness of heart. Sometimes this is a trial from heaven. At such times let the person make stronger efforts to collect his

thoughts, and by means of prayers of supplication call on God and the saints, much as a gardener, when rain does not fall from heaven, himself sprinkles or has others sprinkle. Sometimes aridity is caused through our own fault; because we do not utilize the graces given us, and do not derive fruit from past meditations; or because we allow our hearts to be occupied throughout the day with all kinds of strange and distracting thoughts and disorderly inclinations. Such distraction will disturb our meditation too. A vessel will for a long time smell of what it once contained. In future, therefore, endeavor through the day to keep your thoughts collected while you are occupied with the duties imposed upon you. Keep occupied with the resolutions of your last meditation, and with God, in order to love Him more. The more you love God, the easier it will be for your heart to rise to Him during meditation.

PRAYER OF THE CHURCH

O Lord Jesus Christ, who didst marvelously wound the heart of Blessed Charles with a dart from Thy most Sacred Body, through his intercession look graciously down upon us, and in Thy goodness enkindle in our hearts the fire of Thy love. Who livest and reignest forever and ever. Amen.

JANUARY 19
BLESSED THOMAS OF CORI
Confessor, First Order

LESSED THOMAS was born at Cori near Valletri in the Roman Campagna in the year 1655, and in baptism received the name of Francis Anthony. His parents were poor shepherds, but very pious Christians, who by their virtuous teachings and good example reared their children in the fear of God.

It seemed that little Francis Anthony had in a very special manner inherited the gift of piety from them. His innocent demeanor and fervent devotion so distinguished him among his companions that he was quite generally called "the little saint."

He pursued his higher studies with great diligence and success in a school conducted by a devout canon of his native town. However, the poverty of his parents soon compelled him to discontinue his studies and to return to his father's flocks. But even in the quiet pastures amid the cliffs and the woods, he never desisted from prayer and study.

When both of his parents had died, Thomas sold the flocks which he had inherited from them, presented the proceeds to his two sisters for their dowry, and then asked to be admitted to the convent of the Friars Minor at Cori. He was received in February, 1677, and was sent to the novitiate at Orvieto, where he was invested under the name of Thomas. With redoubled fervor he progressed "from virtue to virtue." At Viterbo and Velletri he studied philosophy and theology with marked success, and finally, when he was twenty-eight years old, he celebrated his first holy Mass amid tears of devotion and joy in the convent at Velletri.

After he had spent some time at Orvieto filling the office of novice master with much zeal and success, he begged his superiors to allow him to retire to the exceptionally strict convent of Civitella near Subiaco, situated in a wild mountainous solitude, in order to sacrifice his life to God in strict penance, ceaseless prayer and work. Later on, when he was appointed superior of this house, he instilled into his brethren such love for religious discipline that Civitella soon became the model convent of the province.

He developed his companions into a band of zealous and courageous men, who traveled as missionaries to India and to China. One of them received the crown of martyrdom. His ardent wish to go with them was never fulfilled. Instead, the provincial superiors assigned him the Roman Campagna and the desert mountain region of Subiaco as his permanent field of labor. Here Thomas labored with the fiery zeal of a Paul for the space of twenty years, so that he was generally called the apostle of Subiaco.

When there was question of gaining souls, no journey was too distant or wearisome. Snow and rain, heat and cold, fatigue and vigils, hunger, thirst, and the painful wounds which the sharp stones made in his bare feet, were borne by him with holy joy. As a reward for all this hardship, he saw great bands of sinners approach in order to be reconciled with God through him, who was at the same time gifted in reading hearts. He was often compelled to spend whole days and even nights without interruption in the holy tribunal of penance.

Here it was also that, as a seventy-four-year-old man, Thomas was attacked by a severe hemorrhage, which brought him to his deathbed. With heavenly patience and amid continuous prayer, he continued to suffer severe pain for several days, until, with the Crucifix in one hand and an image of the Blessed Virgin in the other, he went to his eternal reward while pronouncing the holy names of Jesus and Mary. It was on the day and at the hour he had himself foretold, January 11, 1729.

His body reposes before the high altar in the convent church of Civitella. Pius VI beatified him on August 18, 1786. His feast is observed by the Franciscans on January nineteenth.

SAINTLY YOUTH

1. When our Divine Lord saw the little children gathered about Him, brought there by their mothers, He said: "Suffer the little children to come unto Me, for of such is the kingdom of heaven." And He embraced them and blessed them (Mk. 10,14-16). But how much more lovingly will He look down upon children from the heights of heaven if like our "little saint" they distinguish themselves by piety and virtue! We may be sure that God often spares an entire household because of one innocent child, and that its prayer accomplishes more than that of all the other members. And granting that the child develops in grace and virtue along with its growth in years, how pleasing to God must such a virtuous young man or devout young woman be! The cynical world says: "Youth will be served," and under this plea it would have us condone all the vices of the young. But the holy youths Aloysius and Stanislaus, as well as our Thomas, together with Saints Agnes, Elizabeth, and numerous others, prove by their brilliant virtues that this attitude is false. One should rather say: "Virtue's truth rhymes with youth." Or, are people to dedicate the flower of life to the world and to vice, and then, when the flower has withered away, consecrate the leavings to God? — Would you like to enjoy a happy youth? Then remain close to God. He it is "who gives joy to my youth" (Ps. 42,4).

2. Consider to what extent our temporal and eternal welfare depends upon the practice of virtue during the time of youth. The proverb says: "What you have learnt to do in your youth, you will naturally do when you are old," and the Holy Spirit confirms this with the statement: "A young man according to his way, even when he is old, he will not depart from it" (Prov. 22,6). This can be applied to good habits as well as to evil ones. He who in his youth is not concerned about overcoming lesser faults, will by and by commit greater ones and will easily perish. But if we learn in our youth to deny ourselves, as Blessed Thomas did, to sacrifice our wishes — even good ones — and to bear poverty and want with patience, then we shall have the necessary strength to brave the storms of life, and we shall be prepared to endure cheerfully all labor and sacrifice for the good of our neighbor and the honor of God. With how much greater pleasure can such a person look back upon his youthful years, than he who served only the world and sensual pleasures!

3. Consider the terrible responsibility he draws down upon himself who leads an innocent young man or a virtuous young woman into sin. "It were better for him," our Divine Saviour tells us, "that a millstone should be hanged about his neck and that he should be drowned in the depths of the sea" (Mt. 8,6). This condemnation should not astonish us. Since the seducer robs God of a soul, he often ruins the young person's chances for the rest of his life, and with them not infrequently also the high hopes of an entire family, plunging it into nameless woe. Yet, such serious misfortune can be caused in an apparently innocent manner. A sarcastic remark, teasing someone because of his piety, his modest reserve, his submissiveness, may all lead up to it. Endeavor rather, like Blessed Thomas, to encourage youth in the practice of virtue; that is one of the noblest acts of charity.

PRAYER OF THE CHURCH

O God, who didst adorn Blessed Thomas, who was inflamed with Thy love, with the gift of interior mortification and an extraordinary love of his neighbor, grant us through his intercession and merits, that we may deny ourselves out of love for Thee, and by the constant practice of works of charity deserve to arrive at the eternal reward. Through Christ our Lord. Amen.

JANUARY 20
BLESSED BERNARD OF CORLEONE
Confessor, First Order

 ERNARD was born on the island of Sicily in the year 1605. His father was a shoemaker and taught his son the ways of the trade. But it was difficult for the lively youth to interest himself in this work. Upon the death of his father, he immediately left the shop and, led by love of adventure, he took up fencing. It was not long before he became quite adept at wielding the sword. His unusual corporal vigor qualified him to challenge any comer to a contest.
From then on he spent the greater part of his time in training, and eagerly seized every opportunity to match swords with his hot-tempered countrymen.

Although this manner of life led him far away from God, nevertheless many noble characteristics were perceptible in Bernard. In taking up any quarrel he liked to defend old people and other helpless and defenseless persons against violence. He frequently made devout visits to a crucifix that was highly honored by the people, and provided that a lamp be kept burning before it. Moreover, he cherished great devotion towards St. Francis. God and St. Francis soon led him to realize what a disorderly course he was pursuing.

Bernard had been challenged to a sinful duel, in the course of which he wounded his opponent mortally. In order to escape from his avengers, he sought refuge in flight. In this extremity, as so frequently happens, grace knocked at his heart. Bernard heeded the call. He acknowledged his godless and dangerous conduct for what it was, bewailed it bitterly, and resolved upon a complete change of sentiments.

In order to atone for his sins, he begged for admission among the Capuchins as a lay brother, and on December 13, 1632, he was invested with the holy habit. If in the past Bernard had yielded his bodily members to wayward purposes, he now used them as an atoning sacrifice unto salvation. Seven times a day he scourged himself to the blood. His sleep was limited to three hours on a narrow board, with a block of wood under his head. He fasted for the most part on bread and water. If anything delicious was placed before him, he would carry the food to his mouth so as to whet his appetite, and then lay it down without having tasted it. In spite of this austere life, he still underook the most unpleasant and annoying tasks as being his due.

Almighty God showed how agreeable to Him was the penitential life Bernard was leading; he favored him with extraordinary graces, particularly with ardent devotion at prayer. Bernard cherished special love for our Blessed Lady, and encouraged others to do the same. Often our Lady appeared to him and placed the Divine Child in his arms. Moreover, she gave him knowledge of the day of his death four months in advance. He died at Palermo on January 12, 1667.

Attracted by the fame of his sanctity, there gathered for his burial so many people who raised their voices in praise of the deceased, that it was less a funeral cortege than a triumphal procession. Numerous miracles occurring at his grave promoted the cause of his beatification by Pope Clement XIII in the year 1767. His feast is kept on January nineteenth by the Franciscans as well as the Capuchins.

ON THE NECESSITY OF PENANCE

1. Consider the severe penance that Blessed Bernard practiced after his

conversion. He understood what the holy Fathers say and the Catholic
Church teaches, that for such as have not preserved their baptismal
innocence, there is no other way to salvation but the way of penance.
Perhaps we have sinned more grievously than Bernard did. In that event
it behooves us to practice more rigorous penance, for according to the
measure of our guilt should be the measure of our penance. Or do you
perhaps believe that you have no reason to perform any penance? That
would indeed be a sad delusion, for St. John writes: "If we say that we
have no sin, we deceive ourselves and the truth is not in us" (1 Jn. 1,8).
This is the first requisite of penance, that we sincerely acknowledge our
sinfulness before God and repent of our failures with our whole heart. —
Do you have at least this kind of contrition?

2. Consider the words of our Lord: "Except you do penance, you shall all
likewise perish" (Lk. 13,5). In what way? By sudden death. Our Lord spoke
these words after it had been reported to Him that a number of persons
had died a violent death. There is a limit to God's forbearance. Had
Bernard not heeded the call of grace, might he not have perished in his
sins? Hence, heed the admonition: "Today, if you hear His voice, harden
not your hearts" (Heb. 3,8). — Should you not long ago have followed the
call to penance?

3. Consider that penance requires more than the acknowledgment of our
sins and sorrow for the same. The sinner must also produce the fruits of
penance. The precursor of Christ admonishes us: "Bring forth, therefore,
fruits worthy of penance" (Lk. 3,8). An offense against God requires
satisfaction to be made. If you cannot perform the rigorous penance
Blessed Bernard performed, you can surely impose small sacrifices upon
sensuality and the weakness of the flesh. The time of Lent admonishes us
of these practices. Practice works of charity and piety in the spirit of
penance in order to appease the divine justice, and cheerfully accept in the
spirit of penance every cross and suffering that God allows to come your
way.

PRAYER OF THE CHURCH

O God, who didst permit Blessed Bernard, Thy confessor, to distinguish
himself by heroic charity and admirable penance, grant us, through his
intercession, that we may love Thee with our whole heart and bring forth
fruits worthy of penance. Through Christ our Lord. Amen.

JANUARY 21
BLESSED VINCENT PALLOTTI
Confessor, Third Order

HIS unpretentious man, who out of respect for God omnipresent always went bareheaded, is one of the glories of the Catholic clergy, the pillars of the Church in troublous times, and the successful apostles of the people. He was born in Rome in 1795.

From earliest childhood he evinced tender love for the Blessed Mother of God, and the decree on the heroic nature of his virtues emphasizes the following facts: "He possessed an exceptional love for poverty and penance, and was therefore especially devoted to St. Francis of Assisi. Because various obstacles were in the way of his entering the First Order, he desired at least to belong to the Third Order. It was his constant endeavor to imitate and venerate St. Francis."

Vincent became a Tertiary in the Franciscan church of Aracoeli on November 29, 1816. He distinguished himself not only by his piety but also by his brilliant intellect. In time he received the degrees of doctor of philosophy and of theology. He was overwhelmed with joy when on May 16, 1818, he was ordained to the holy priesthood. Then his apostolate began. With prayer and penance, with his labors in the pulpit and the confessional, with his efforts on behalf of the sick and the endangered, and especially on behalf of young clerics in the Roman seminary, he did a measureless amount of good.

To his apostolic zeal must be ascribed the foundation of the Pious Society of the Missions, also called the Pallottine Fathers. The purpose of the society was to arouse faith and charity among Catholics and to propagate these virtues among heretics and infidels. Vincent placed his organization under the protection of the Immaculate Mother of God and under perfect submission to the Holy See.

God glorified His humble servant by the gift of miracles both during his lifetime and after his death in 1850. He was comparatively young when he was called to eternity, but in that short span he had accumulated a wealth of merits. He was beatified in 1950, and his feast is observed on January twenty-second.

ON ENLIGHTENMENT

1. False enlightenment is destructive. False enlightenment is doing even greater havoc today than in the time of Blessed Vincent. The aim today is

to eliminate religion from public life. The oft-repeated cry is: Take politics away from the Church! But what they really mean is: Take religion out of politics! Yet there is the voice of the Almighty addressing the world: "I am the Lord your God!" (Lev. 19,32). God's religion must not be excluded from any phase of life, not from politics either. To do so is to bring harm on the world and on the nations. — Do you allow yourself to be deceived in this matter?

2. True enlightenment brings blessing in its train. True enlightenment, for which Blessed Vincent toiled, is nothing but the correct knowledge of things and their purposes. But it is only by faith and by grace that we can arrive at this correct knowledge. And Christ is the teacher of the Faith. He has said: "He that follows Me walks not in darkness" (Jn. 8,12). Remain firm, therefore, with heart and mind, in your adherence to Christ and His Church, to pope and bishop.

3. False enlightenment is foolish. The so-called enlightened class of our day despise faith and divine revelation, and hold as right and true only what they can comprehend with their puny intelligence. They act like a person who will heavily curtain the windows of his home so that no ray of sunshine can penetrate, and then lights an oil lamp, in the belief that he can trust only the light of his own lamp. To such a one may be applied the severe judgment: "Professing themselves to be wise, they became fools" (Rom. 1,20). — Be on your guard not to follow these foolish, deluded, and conceited people.

PRAYER OF THE CHURCH

We beseech Thee, O Lord, give ear to our prayer and enlighten the darkness of our minds by the grace of Thy visitation. Through Christ our Lord. Amen.

⊗⊗⊗⊗⊗⊗⊗⊗⊗⊗

JANUARY 22
BLESSED JOHN BAPTIST TRIQUERIE
Martyr, First Order

 LESSED JOHN BAPTIST was born in 1737 at Laval, France. At a very young age he joined the Order of Friars Minor Conventual in the friary at Olonne, where he remained, serving also as superior, until 1778. He was then assigned as chaplain and confessor of the Poor Clares, first at St. Elizabeth in Nantes, then at Montmorillon, and finally at the Monastery in Buron near Chateau-Gonthier, in the diocese of Laval.

Here it was that he fell victim to the French Revolution. He refused to take the oath prescribed by the Civil Constitution of the Clergy (1791). Later he refused to take an atheistic oath, euphemistically called the "oath of liberty-equality." On January 5, 1793, he was imprisoned in a former Poor Clare convent named "Patience." The following is a transcript of the trial record when Blessed John Baptist appeared before the Committee of the Revolution:

Pres.: "Have you taken the oath of 1791?"

Fr. John B.: "No."

Pres.: "The oath of 'Liberty-Equality?' "

Fr. John B.: "No, Citizen. When it was imposed, I was sick in bed."

At this point the public accuser, an apostate priest, interrupted:

"That is no reason! I was sick too, but I had the registry brought to my bedside and I signed the oath with my own hand."

Fr. John B.: "Citizen, I am a son of St. Francis of Assisi. In virtue of my status, I am obliged to be dead to the things of this world, hence am not aware of its laws. My entire purpose in life is to pray for my fatherland, and this I have not failed to do."

The apostate priest: "You are not here to preach us sermons. From the time you were no longer chaplain to the nuns and lacked a livelihood, who supported you?"

Fr. John B.: "Citizen, the charity of the faithful."

Father John Baptist then demanded an explanation of the oath required by him.

Pres.: "The oath which we demand of you is to be faithful to the Republic, not to profess any religion, not even the Catholic, which is your religion surely ..."

Fr. John B.: "Ah, in that case, No! I shall be faithful to Jesus Christ unto my very last breath."

The courageous friar was condemned to death and promptly guillotined in the public square of Laval on January 21, 1794, in the company of thirteen diocesan priests.

Father John Baptist was one of nineteen martyrs of the French Revolution who were beatified by Pope Pius XII on June 19, 1955.

ON STRENGTHENING OUR FAITH

1. Faith, our greatest treasure, is a free gift of God, which can be lost if we

do not properly appreciate it and preserve and strengthen it in a pure and humble heart. To do this we must first of all form a philosophy of life which is in accordance with the truths of the faith, that is, with the Gospel as our divine Saviour preached it and lived it. This is all the more necessary because we are living in an atmosphere which is hostile to the faith or at least cold and indifferent to it. The ideas of the world expounded in books and periodicals are opposed to the principles of faith. "See to it," St. Paul warns us, "that no one deceives you by philosophy and vain deceit ... according to the elements of the world and not according to Christ" (Col. 2,8). The truths of our faith tell us what we are to think of God and our duties toward Him, how we are to judge the world and world events, how we are to view the Church and her means of salvation, how we are to evaluate earthly life and goods. There is nothing extraordinary recorded about Blessed John Baptist before his martyrdom; but he always walked in the light of faith and lived a life of faith, and so he did not hesitate one moment to remain faithful to Jesus Christ until his last breath.

2. To have a strong and firm faith, we must also conform our conduct with the principles of our faith. Nothing weakens faith so much as unchecked passions, sinful habits, and a life that is at variance with what one professes with his lips. Faith without works, according to St. John, is "dead in itself" (2,17) — it is useless. On the other hand, if we live our faith, it is like a divine soil in which we have struck roots, a soil whose energies we draw up into ourselves and make our own, and through which we become transformed into true Christians. We are then able to overcome all temptations and to emerge victorious in our struggle with the pride of life, the concupiscence of the eyes, and the concupiscence of the flesh. And if we should be faced with an alternative like that which was presented to Blessed John Baptist, our faith too will be strong enough to make us loyal to Jesus Christ until our last breath.

3. To walk in the light of faith and to live a life in accordance with our faith, our faith must be fostered above all by prayer and meditation. When he rose from meditation, St. Leonard of Port Maurice used to say: "I return from the land of faith." To meditate means to ponder on the realities of faith, to reflect on the words and example of the Saviour, until the mind is enlightened and the heart enkindled. It means to judge our own life in the light of faith and to transform it according to faith. By prayer we obtain the graces to live our faith. Prayer is the language of faith, the pulse-beat and gauge of faith. A plant will wither unless it is watered. So also our faith will dry up unless prayer brings down upon it the celestial dew of grace. St. Francis and the first friars had such a strong and living

faith because they fostered it by a life of prayer. "They passed their time," wrote St. Bonaventure, "in continual prayer, contemplating instead of books the cross of Christ, by day and by night, after the example of their Father, being instructed continually by his discourses on the cross of Christ" (Leg. 4,7). The apostate priest who was Blessed John Baptist's accuser neglected prayer and thus lost his faith. Blessed John lived a life of prayer and became a martyr of the faith.

PRAYER OF THE CHURCH

Almighty and everlasting God, give unto us an increase of faith, hope, and charity: and, that we may worthily obtain that which Thou dost promise, make us to love that which Thou dost command. Through Christ our Lord. Amen.

JANUARY 23
THE SERVANT OF GOD ZACHARY OF ALEMQUER
Confessor, First Order

T the time St. Francis went to Rome to ask the vicar of Christ to grant him authority and blessing to preach the Gospel to the infidels, a young Roman presented himself to the saint and earnestly begged for admission into the order. St. Francis received him and gave him the name of Friar Zachary.

Zachary distinguished himself in the order by his deep piety and ardent love for God and for his neighbor. So the holy Founder considered him capable and worthy to spread the order in other countries. When he was sufficiently trained in the religious life and had received the holy priesthood, he was sent to Spain with several other brothers. He did not, however, find a favorable opportunity to found a new convent.

So the band of friars continued their journey to Portugal. There they succeeded, although only after overcoming many an obstacle, in founding convents at Coimbra, Lisbon, and also at Alemquer, where Father Zachary resided and died as guardian.

The power of his prayers was remarkable. Once there was no food in the convent. Nevertheless, when mealtime came around, he ordered all the brothers to sit down at table with confidence. Then he knelt down in prayer before a crucifix, and presently there appeared at the door of the convent a charming young man, who brought just as many nice white loaves of bread as there were religious in the convent.

On another occasion a man came to the guardian and told him that he had doubts regarding the Real Presence in the Blessed Sacrament and that he was unable to overcome them. Zachary instructed him, but it was all of no avail. Then he asked the man to attend the Mass which he was to say on the following morning. In answer to the devout prayer of His faithful servant, our Lord deigned to show Himself to the doubting man as the Sacrificial victim, from the time of the Consecration to the Communion, whereupon all his doubts vanished.

Zachary was glorified by God through many other miracles, and the Franciscan Order continued to spread throughout Portugal.

ON THE POWER OF PRAYER

1. Christ our Lord has said: "Ask and it shall be given to you, seek and you shall find, knock and it shall be opened unto you" (Lk. 11,9). And speaking in general, He solemnly declared: "Amen, amen, I say unto you: if you ask the Father anything in My name, He will give it to you" (Jn. 16,23). That was said by the almighty and true God, who is able to keep His word, who is minded to keep it, and who will keep it. Numerous examples from Holy Scripture, as also the examples just related in the life of the servant of God Zachary, show how God kept His word. — Have you not experienced this yourself?

2. But in order to be worthy of the response promised, our prayer must be performed in the proper manner, especially with firm trust and with perseverance. For thus says Christ our Lord: "Whatsoever you ask when you pray, believe and it will come unto you" (Mk. 11,24), and St. James (1,7) says: "He who wavers, let him not think that he shall receive anything from the Lord." That our prayer must be persevering, may be learnt from the expressions with which our Lord exhorts us to it—ask, seek, and knock. How successful persevering, trustful prayer is, we learn from the fine example of the Canaanite woman (Mt. 15).

3. Consider that the answer to our prayer does not always take a form which is in accordance with our wishes. Rather, sometimes it takes a much more perfect form. We, of course, believe that the granting of our desires is the best thing for us; yet, often the all-knowing and all-wise God sees that that is not the case. So He answers our prayer, if it was otherwise a good prayer, in a more perfect way: as by granting us the grace of resignation to His holy will; by strengthening our hearts with patience in the distress and suffering which He permits to continue because they are for our welfare; by giving us the grace to resist the

temptations which He intends should purify and humble our soul. In that way we always receive what Jesus Christ would ask for us, and what we also mean to ask for when we petition the Father in His name.

PRAYER OF THE CHURCH
(Ninth Sunday after Pentecost)

Let the ears of Thy mercy, O Lord, be open to the petition of Thy suppliants; and that Thou mayest grant their desires, make them to ask what is pleasing to Thee. Through Christ our Lord. Amen.

JANUARY 24
THE SERVANT OF GOD JOHN THE GARDENER
Confessor, First Order

JOHN was born of poor parents in Portugal. After their death he went to Spain, and for some time was obliged to beg for his bread from door to door. Then, however, he had the good fortune to find employment as a shepherd. Even at this time when he had hardly the bare necessities, he nevertheless managed to spare a little something that he could give to other poor persons, so that his charity drew forth the greatest admiration. One time he heard a sermon on the love of God, and thereafter he was so strongly stirred by it that again and again he used to cry out: "O Jesus, my love!"

One day he met two Franciscans on a journey and greeted them reverently. They entered into conversation with him, and when they became acquainted with the circumstances in which he lived, as well as with his devout disposition, they invited him to come with them to their convent in Salamanca. John gladly accepted their invitation and was hired at the convent to help the brother gardener. Because of his diligence and piety, he was after a short time received into the order as a lay brother. Because of his steady work in the garden, he received the appellation of Hortulanus, that is, the gardener.

After receiving the holy habit, John advanced so rapidly in all the virtues that he soon shone as a model of sanctity. He slept only a very little; the greatest part of the night he spent in prayer and meditation. He fasted practically always, and the little that he did eat, he managed to make unsavory. At his work, at which he neglected nothing, he nevertheless found time to render acts of charity to the poor and afflicted.

His delight was to honor the Blessed Sacrament, and to adorn the altars with flowers from his garden. If he could serve the priests at holy Mass, he was overjoyed and served with unspeakable devotion.

Almighty God granted him the gift of prophecy, and permitted him to read the secrets of hearts. For this reason he was known far and wide, and distinguished personages, even princes, came to seek his advice. Withal, Brother John remained so humble that he obeyed even the slightest wish of his superiors, and he was so loving toward everybody that he never took offense at anything. His principle was that to forget offenses and to forgive one's enemies is an act of penance which is most pleasing to God. John died in the year 1501, on January eleventh, as he himself had foretold. His last words were: "O Jesus, my love!"

ON CHARITY TOWARDS ONE'S NEIGHBOR

1. Consider how the charity of Brother John laid the foundation for his sanctity. Because he gladly shared with others although he himself was poor, and deprived himself on their account, God rewarded him with very rich graces. God regards not so much the greatness of the gift as the greatness of the love with which it is given. "Man sees those things that appear, but the Lord beholds the heart" (1 Kings 16,7). Learn from this how to practice Christian charity. — Do you stand in need of special graces, then try to obtain them through works of charity.

2. Consider that the neighborly charity which Brother John practiced was closely bound up with his love of God. In fact, charity towards one's neighbor can only then be counted a virtue when it is joined with love of God, so that one loves his neighbor because God wishes it and commands it; for to love one's neighbor and do him good from a natural inclination or sympathy, from motives of self-interest, or even from bad motives, is no virtue; even sinners and the heathens do that (Mt. 5,46). — Examine your own motives and test the value of your charity accordingly.

3. Consider that it is one of the most important and worthy acts of charity towards our neighbor to bear with patience, according to the example of Brother John, the weaknesses and the faults of our neighbor. Thus the Apostle admonishes us: "Bear one another's burdens, and so you shall fulfill the law of Christ" (Gal. 6,2). To conquer and mortify ourselves in that way is far more pleasing to God than the strictest rule of life without patient charity. Hence the wise principle of Brother John: To forget offenses and to forgive one's enemies, is an act of penance most pleasing to God. — Have you practiced this kind of charity? Be sure that without it no other kind will please God.

PRAYER OF THE CHURCH
(Number 29 under "Various Prayers")

O God, who makest all things to be of profit to them that love Thee, give unto our hearts an abiding love for Thee; that our desires arising from Thine inspiration waver not through any temptation. Through Christ our Lord. Amen.

JANUARY 25
THE SERVANT OF GOD JOHN BENTIVENGA
Confessor, Third Order

WE do not find any record to tell us when John lived, though it seems to have been before the year 1562. Several historians of the Franciscan Order record that during the entire time of his long life he lived a very saintly life. He was born on the island of Sicily, and in his youth led a very mortified life. He endeavored to withdraw from public notice, for people considered him a saint. Divinely inspired to do it, he repaired to a mountain near Catanea, where other hermits were leading penitential lives according to the rule of St. Francis. Since John was sufficiently educated, the provincial by whom these hermits were guided in their obedience and spiritual direction, had him ordained a priest, so that he could say holy Mass daily for the hermits on the mountain. After holy Mass he was accustomed to hasten to his hermitage, where he spent several hours in prayer and meditation. He knew so well how to utilize his time that no one ever found him idle.

Many people came to him for advice and consolation, and he was gentle and affable with everyone. He had the special gift of setting fearful souls at ease. And so it happened that a certain priest who suffered much from scruples often came to him. Once the priest resolved to give up the administration of the sacrament of penance, lest he should have to give an account to God of the sins of other people. But John calmly showed him what was right, and pointed out to him in such a convincing way how pleasing to God and how meritorious it is to devote oneself to the care of souls, that the priest, reassured, cheerfully continued his office of confessor.

Meanwhile, John was not indifferent regarding his own welfare, but lived in continuous remembrance of the four last things. He used to say: "Another day, another hour, has passed, which has increased our responsibility and led us closer to death."

At length, at a ripe old age, he fell ill. Though it was apparently a slight illness, he recognized that his end was drawing near and received the last sacraments. All the hermits stood about his poor couch, and one of them said to him: "Father, you are fortunate, for you are going to receive your heavenly reward." But John answered: "Who knows that? Although I have now served God for seventy years, still I am not certain." Yet, trusting in God's mercy, he calmly breathed forth his soul.

ON QUIETING FEARFUL SOULS

1. There are souls that by God's permission, and sometimes by their own fault, are tormented with scruples and fears of all sorts. They regard as sin what is merely temptation, take simple imperfections for grievous offenses, and always think they have not confessed their sins sufficiently. They even despair of the possibility of getting to heaven. Such a condition is much to be pitied, it prevents much good, and often creates very great danger. How fortunate for such a fearful soul if it finds a good guide and counselor, and submits to his judgment in a childlike manner; if it follows that guide like God's representative. The guide then bears the responsibility and not the penitent. Fearful souls are in great danger of being lost if they persist in being self-willed.

2. Consider that all who come in contact with such a fearful soul should have the greatest sympathy for it, for it is suffering from a most painful spiritual malady. By severity or ridicule one may draw down upon oneself a heavy responsibility in the sight of God. It is possible that such uncharitable individuals may some day have the same sufferings to endure. Those, however, who have the direction of such souls, should deal firmly although kindly with them, so that the scrupulous person, guided as he is only by his fears, shall not have his way. — Have you always observed the correct course in such cases?

3. Consider how John applied in his own case the best means to preserve a happy medium between exaggerated fear and careless indifference. He was imbued with the sobering sentiment of the fear of God in consequence of thinking about the last things of man, while he cherished childlike confidence in the divine mercy. — Keep ever before your mind these last things, so that you may not sin; but if you have failed, call upon God with confidence for forgiveness. Then you will preserve peace of soul.

PRAYER OF THE CHURCH
(Over the People on Friday after Passion Sunday)

Grant, we beseech Thee, almighty God, that we who seek the grace of Thy protection may be freed from all evils and serve Thee with an easy mind. Through Christ our Lord. Amen.

JANUARY 26
BLESSED JAMES OF PIEVE
Martyr, Third Order

LESSED JAMES was born in the thirteenth century at Pieve di Cadore, or Castelpieve, a little town in Lombardy. Even before his birth his mother was acquainted with his destiny in a twofold vision. Once she beheld a boy who was carrying a church in his hands; at another time she saw a red lily sprout forth. She concluded then that her child would become a priest and that he would shed his blood innocently. And so it happened.

James began his course of studies in order to devote himself to the religious state. So that he could do a lot of good as a priest, he studied, besides theology, also civil and ecclesiastical law, as was frequently done in those days. While he excelled in his classes, he refrained from taking part in the boisterous revelry of the students, and always treasured the grace of holy purity.

After he had become a priest, the love of God so forcefully attracted him to poverty and humility that he decided to devote his entire life in a humble sphere to the service of the poor and the afflicted. He joined the Third Order of St. Francis, and publicly wore the habit of the Tertiaries. He used his knowledge of law to protect the poor and the oppressed, especially widows and orphans, and he preferred to exercise his spiritual ministry in poor churches, where, too, he was most devout in his duties.

At the gate of his native town there was a hospital that had become ruinous, and with it a deserted church. James acquired both structures and spent the entire fortune he had inherited from his parents in restoring them. Then he moved there and rendered to the poor the corporal and spiritual works of mercy.

One day he found among old papers in the hospital one stating that several pieces of land belonged to it which a prominent man had acquired unjustly. James went to him and asked him kindly to yield the land to the hospital; but when he could accomplish nothing by being kind, he defended the claims of the poor sick in court, and a decision was rendered in their favor.

But his defense of the poor was to exact from him his life. The prominent man invited him, as if by way of reconciliation, to a supper, and had him treacherously murdered by his servants on his way home. This occurred on January 15, 1304.

The body was dragged into a deep gully and thickly covered with brushwood and brambles. But after a few days the peasants saw the brambles sprouting in the middle of winter. On clearing them away, the body of the murdered saintly priest was found. He was solemnly laid to rest in the hospital church, where his body was found incorrupt when the tomb was opened after one hundred and seventy-four years. His cult was approved in 1806, and the Third Order Regular observes his feast on January nineteenth. The Servites also claim Blessed James as a member. He is sometimes called Blessed James the Almsgiver. (Cf. Biersack, p. 70; *These Made Peace*, p. 42.)

ON DEFENDING THE UNJUSTLY OPPRESSED

1. Consider the sad plight of the poor and the weak when in addition to their distressful circumstances they have also to suffer from godless persons in power; when they are robbed of their meager possessions; when their rights are curtailed; or when they are even forced to serve a wicked purpose. There are times when the godless boastfully encourage such misdeeds and when, to use the words of Holy Scripture, they seem to say: "Let us oppress the poor just man, and not spare the widow, nor honor the ancient grey hairs of the aged" (Wisd. 2,10). "Their own malice," says Holy Writ, "blinded them" (Wisd. 2,21). Unfortunately for humanity, such crimes that cry out to heaven for vengeance still occur among so-called Christians. — Have you at any time had a share in them?

2. As sinful and atrocious as such oppression of the helpless is, so meritorious and pleasing to God it is if a person, according to the example of the saintly James, renders assistance to the oppressed. A person like that discharges the office of God Himself, who calls Himself "the father of orphans and the judge of widows" (Ps. 67,6). If you cannot appear in court in their defense, you can nevertheless defend them in the circles in which you move. You can intercede for them, console them, pray for them.

3. After the example of the saintly James, one should, however, always first proceed by the path of kindness in order to obtain justice. Should it, however, become necessary to contend for justice in court, one must still

be ready to enter into friendly exchange, as James accepted the invitation of his opponent. If his way of doing things cost him his life, it also made his crown in heaven doubly brilliant.

PRAYER OF THE CHURCH

Almighty and eternal God, the comfort of the afflicted, and strength of those that labor and are burdened, let the prayers of those who call upon Thee in tribulation be heard by Thee, that all may with joy find the assistance of Thy mercy in their necessities. Through Christ our Lord. Amen.

JANUARY 27
THE SERVANT OF GOD LOUIS OF ARAZILO
Confessor, First Order

OUIS OF ARAZILO lived in the Spanish province of Valencia in a convent where, by lawful dispensation, several mitigations were permitted in the observance of the strict rule of St. Francis.

He longed to transfer to a unit of the order which observed the Franciscan rule in all its rigor. But his delicate health would not permit the fulfillment of this pious desire. When, however, his longing for perfect observance continued to grow, he resolved to carry out his design, trusting in Him who is strong even in the weak. And lo, as soon as he entered the stricter convent, he felt himself gaining such strength that he could join in the observance of all the austerities. Only for the hardships of preaching did he lack the necessary strength. But his holy life was a continuous sermon, and his loving kindness won all hearts to himself.

Chosen guardian of the convent, he administered the office with great solicitude and love. Especially in the care of the sick did he manifest his charity, sacrificing himself for them completely. When a contagious disease broke out in that region, he was untiringly active in visiting the sick, in comforting them, and in preparing them for a Christian death.

But his weakened energies began to decline and he himself was seized by the epidemic. After heroically enduring the greatest pains, he died as a martyr of charity in the year 1583. After his death he appeared to his brethren in the convent radiant with glory.

ON BEING USEFUL IN INFIRMITY

1. It is a common temptation to become impatient in times of delicate health and infirmity, as if we were no good for anything, and instead of being useful to others, were only a burden to them. This is a serious delusion, which robs us of great merit. If our dear Lord permits us to become weak and unfit for work, He is offering us the opportunity to accumulate merits for heaven by patient suffering and resignation to His holy will. And if others should be put to much trouble in caring for us, that can also redound greatly to their spiritual benefit, for it will bring them precious merits.

2. Sometimes, too, there is the delusion (and the resultant dissatisfaction with life) that we are of no earthly use, just because we are not in a condition to do everything. As we see in the life of the servant of God Louis of Arazilo, a good will and confidence in God often change a weak man into a strong one, and make him much more useful than others who are in the best of health. But even apart from that, it is sufficient in the sight of God that we work according to the measure of strength and ability given to us. That servant in the Gospel who had acquired two talents with the two that had been given him, received the same reward as the one who gained five with the five he had received (Mt. 25); but woe to the slothful servant who, though he has been given only one talent, has not used it to gain at least another one with it. — Prove yourself on this point.

3. Consider that personal weakness and suffering should especially incline a person to be sympathetic with other sufferers, as saintly Louis was in such an heroic manner. For that very reason the Son of God took upon Himself the weakness of human nature so that He could "have compassion on our infirmities" (Heb. 4,15). — Examine yourself to determine whether you utilize your own experience with suffering to practice loving sympathy towards others.

PRAYER OF THE CHURCH
(Ember Wednesday in September)

Succor in Thy mercy our weakness, we beseech Thee, O Lord: and in pity renew that poor strength of ours which of its own nature is ever wasting away. Through Christ our Lord. Amen.

JANUARY 28
THE SERVANT OF GOD BROTHER JUNIPER
Confessor, First Order

HE PIOUS lay brother Juniper was received into the order by St. Francis himself in the year 1210. All his efforts were directed towards the practice of humility, which is, of course, the foundation and the surest test of all the Christian virtues. Because he considered himself worthless before God and undeserving of any honor, he wished, in the simplicity of his heart, to be considered worthless and contemptible also in the sight of men. That is why he did many things that the world would consider foolish, but which, in the case of Brother Juniper, proceeded from holy wisdom.

Once, at the command of his superiors, he went to Rome. Many of the inhabitants, who had learnt of his arrival and had knowledge of the sanctity of his life, respectfully came out quite a distance from the town to meet him. When Juniper saw so many people coming, he looked for a way out, and he found one that suited him well. Near the road some children had placed a board over a beam and were amusing themselves in playing seesaw. Brother Juniper drew near and played seesaw with them.

The people were not a little astonished at this behavior; nevertheless they approached, greeted Juniper with great respect, and told him that they had come to accompany him to the convent. Juniper paid no attention to their greeting, bent apparently on nothing but to enjoy himself with the children.

Then some of the people began to rail at him: "What a silly, childish person is this!" And they all withdrew. When they were far enough away, Juniper also proceeded humbly on his way to the convent of the friars in Rome, glad at having escaped their demonstrations of honor.

Such and similar instances induced St. Francis to say: "He is a good Friar Minor who has gained the victory over himself and the world as Brother Juniper has done."

God showed how pleasing to Him was this holy simplicity of Brother Juniper by the miraculous power which He granted him over the proud spirits of darkness. On occasion, when the evil spirit refused to leave a possessed person at the prayers of St. Francis, the latter would say, "I will get Brother Juniper if you do not leave." And forthwith the evil spirit would leave.

The last years of the holy brother were one continual burning desire for the possession of God. After he had spent forty-eight years in the order, God finally heard his prayer and took him to Himself on January 4,

1258, in the convent of Ara Coeli at Rome, where his body is also entombed.

ON SIMPLICITY

1. The virtue of simplicity has become so unfamiliar to us that we have lost even the correct understanding of it. Simplicity is considered folly and stupidity, whereas it is really nothing else than the opposite of pretence and sham. It is the simple, honest intention to appear before men as we acknowledge ourselves to be in the sight of God. It is merely the fulfillment of the principle which our holy Father St. Francis so often uttered: "As much as each one is in the eyes of God, that he is and no more."

2. Consider how far our conduct is removed from this principle, though of course we accept the principle. As friends of the truth and of honesty, we ought to represent ourselves at all times and places just as we are. But, are we not rather much concerned to conceal everything that may reflect discredit on us, and do we not endeavor through dissembling and deceit to impress others with an honorable opinion of ourselves? Is not much of what is considered polite and cultured only pretence, hypocrisy, and fraud? What confusion will overwhelm those who have thus acted when they stand at the final judgment, where everything will be disclosed for what it actually was before God! How we shall then be put to shame by the simplicity of Brother Juniper! — Examine yourself.

3. Consider how happy a soul is that makes no account of the opinion of men. In all simplicity it strives only to fulfill faithfully the duties of its walk of life and leaves everything else to God. Such a soul is ever at peace. The praise of people cannot cause such a person to become puffed up, their blame cannot discourage him, for he knows that praise cannot make us better and blame cannot make us worse than we are in the sight of God. This holy simplicity is true wisdom. It leads to perpetual peace, and on judgment day, it will be acknowledged even by the wise of this world, who will say: "These are they whom we had sometime in derision and for a parable of reproach. We fools esteemed their life madness, and their end without honor. Behold how they are numbered among the children of God, and their lot is among the saints" (Wisd. 5,3).

PRAYER OF THE CHURCH
(Wednesday within the Octave of Pentecost)

May the Comforter, who proceedeth from Thee, O Lord, enlighten our minds; and even as Thy Son hath promised, may He lead us into all truth. Who liveth and reigneth forever and ever. Amen.

✦✦✦✦✦✦✦✦✦✦✦

JANUARY 29
ST. FRANCIS DE SALES
Cordbearer of St. Francis

THE CITY of Geneva in Switzerland is situated at the western end of the forty-five mile long lake of the same name, near the French boundary. In the sixteenth century the Dukedom of Savoy lost this city, as well as the province of Vaud on the north side of the lake and that of Chablais on the south side, to the Calvinists of Switzerland. By giving up his claim to Vaud, the duke of Savoy finally regained Chablais; but the people of the latter province had meanwhile become fanatical Calvinists. The bishop of Geneva resided at Annecy, some twenty miles south of Geneva.

A prominent noble family of Savoy at this time was that of De Sales; and St. Francis de Sales, who was born in 1567 at the Chateau de Sales, near Annecy, became its most illustrious member. His father had the title to the Signory of Nouvelles by inheritance and that of Boisy by marriage. At baptism, St. Francis de Sales received St. Francis of Assisi together with St. Bonaventure as his patron saints; and after he was appointed coadjutor bishop of Geneva, he had himself enrolled in the Archconfraternity of the Cord of St. Francis. He was not a Franciscan Tertiary, but a member of the Third Order of the Minims, founded by St. Francis de Paul. However, he accepted affiliation to the First Order of St. Francis from the Capuchins in 1617; and his spirit undoubtedly has a close kinship with that of the Seraphic Saint. He once told the Capuchins that he belonged to the Franciscan Order by special ties; and in 1609, the holy bishop, girded with the cord, preached a beautiful sermon and took part in the traditional procession of the archconfraternity. The Portiuncula Chapel at Assisi was especially dear to him because of the great spiritual favors he received here. At Evian, on the south shore of Lake Geneva, St. Francis of Assisi appeared to him and said: "You desire martyrdom, just as I once longed for it. But, like me, you will not obtain it. You will have to become an instrument of your own martyrdom."

From early youth, St. Francis de Sales had a great desire to devote himself entirely to the service of God, although his father had other plans for him. With the pious Abbé Déage as his tutor, Francis was a student at the University of Paris from his fourteenth to his twentieth year; and after studying jurisprudence at the University of Padua for four more years, he was awarded the degree of Doctor of Law. In 1593 he finally obtained the consent of his father to enter the sacred ministry; and since he had devoted much time to the study of theology during his student years, he was ordained a priest six months later.

Not long afterwards he volunteered for the difficult and dangerous task of leading the people of the province of Chablais back to the fold of the Church. Several times he miraculously escaped death at the hands of assassins. But he persevered in his heroic and patient efforts, and after four years succeeded in converting a large number of Calvinists. In 1599 he was appointed coadjutor to his bishop; and in 1602 he became bishop of Geneva, a position which he filled in an exemplary manner for twenty years.

St. Francis de Sales has rightly been styled "the Gentleman Saint" because of his wonderful patience and gentleness. He always tempered his unflagging zeal by imperturbable meekness and kindness. He is a model for every priest and bishop. Though a learned man, he insisted on simple catechizing and preaching and himself set the example. The people came in crowds to hear him preach, not only in Savoy, but also in various cities of France. He began his writing career as a missionary to the Calvinists, by preparing leaflets explaining the principle doctrines of the Church as opposed to the errors of Calvinism. His best known works are: Philothea, or Introduction to a Devout Life and Theotimus, a treatise on the love of God.

At Dijon, in 1604, he became acquainted with St. Jane de Chantal, for whom and through whom he founded the nursing and teaching order known as Visitation Nuns. He died at Lyons on December 28, 1622, was beatified in 1661, and canonized in 1665. He was declared a doctor of the Church in 1877; and he has been chosen also as the special patron of Catholic journalists and the Catholic press.

ON BEING A CHRISTIAN GENTLEMAN

1. A Christian gentleman is one who practices the supernatural virtues of kindness, meekness, patience, and charity, in thought, in word, and in deed, at all times and under all circumstances. St. Francis de Sales, who was a model in this respect, describes the Christian gentleman in these words: "The man who possesses Christian meekness is affectionate and tender towards everyone. He is disposed to forgive and excuse the frailties of others. The goodness of his heart appears in a sweet affability that

influences his words and actions, and presents every object to his view in the most charitable and pleasing light. He never allows himself to use a harsh phrase, much less any language that is haughty or rude. There is always a gentle serenity in his expression which distinguishes him from those violent characters who, with looks full of fury, only know how to say no, or who, when they grant, do it with so bad a grace, that they lose all the merit of the favor they confer." The world too has its gentlemen who know how to control themselves and to put on an exterior mask of meekness for the sake of material gain or advancement; but theirs is merely a sham meekness which hides their real thoughts and intentions. They are not Christian gentlemen.

2. The Christian gentleman remains kind and meek even when he is unreasonably harassed and provoked. St. Francis de Sales was often tried in this way when the crowds came to him for help in their various needs, scarcely allowing him a moment to breathe; but he always remained affable, and that encouraged them to come all the more. "God," says he, "makes use of such occasions to try whether our souls are sufficiently strengthened to bear every attack. I have myself been sometimes in this difficulty: but I made a covenant with my heart and with my tongue, in order to confine them within the bounds of duty ... The most powerful remedy against sudden movements of impatience is a sweet and amiable silence. If one speaks at all, however little, self-love will have a share in it, and some word will escape that will sour the heart, and disturb its peace for a long time. When nothing is said, and cheerfulness is preserved, the storm subsides, anger and indiscretion are put to flight, and the only thing left is a joy, pure and lasting."

3. The Christian gentleman is kind and loving also towards sinners. When some criticized St. Francis de Sales for being too indulgent towards sinners, he replied: "If there were anything more excellent than meekness, God would certainly have taught it to us; and yet there is nothing to which He so earnestly exhorts all, as to be meek and humble of heart. Why would you hinder me from obeying the command of my Lord, and following Him in the exercise of that virtue which He so eminently practiced and so highly esteems? Can we really be better advised in these matters than God Himself?" He justified the tender welcome which he extended to returning apostates by observing: "Are they not a part of my flock? Has not our blessed Lord shed His blood for them, and shall I refuse them my tears? These wolves will be changed into lambs: a day will come when, cleansed from their sins, they will be more precious in the sight of God than we are. If Saul had been cast off, we should never have had a St. Paul." Of St. Francis de Sales another saint, St. Vincent de Paul, said:

"Going over his words in my mind, I have been filled with such admiration that I am moved to see in him the man who, of all others, has most faithfully reproduced the love of the Son of God on earth."

PRAYER OF THE CHURCH

O God, by whose gracious will Blessed Francis, Thy confessor and bishop, became all things unto all men for the saving of their souls: mercifully grant, that, being filled with the sweetness of Thy love, we may, through the guidance of his counsels and by the aid of his merits, attain unto the joys of life eternal. Through Christ our Lord. Amen.

JANUARY 30
ST. HYACINTHA MARISCOTTI
Virgin, Third Order

T. HYACINTHA, born in 1585, belonged to a wealthy and prominent family. Her father was Count Antonio of Mariscotti, her mother descended from the princely Roman family of the Orsini.

After her younger sister had been given in marriage, the disappointed Clarice, as Hyacintha was then called, entered the convent of the Tertiaries at Viterbo, but apparently only as a secular Tertiary. She permitted herself to be supplied with all sorts of things by way of eatables and articles of dress which enabled her to enjoy quite an agreeable and comfortable existence. Her rooms were furnished with much worldly apparatus. The spirit of mortification and of penance with which every Tertiary ought to be equipped was in no wise discernible in her.

Then it happened that she was afflicted with a strange illness, and her confessor was obliged to go to her rooms to administer the sacraments to her. When he saw the worldly and frivolous objects in her cell, he sharply reproved the sick sister. Following her confessor's advice, she afterwards went to the common refectory and there, with a rope around her neck, begged forgiveness of her fellow sisters for the scandal she had given them. However, it was only after she had invoked the aid of St. Catharine of Siena, that she dispossessed herself of all frivolous and unnecessary objects and thereupon resolutely entered upon a life of heroic virtue.

She began to lead a very penitential life, in which she persevered unto the end. She went barefoot, wore an old habit that had been discarded by

another sister, and performed the lowliest and most trying tasks. She ate
only inferior food with which she mixed bitter herbs. Her bed consisted
of a few bare boards, on which there was but a single blanket; a stone
served as her pillow. She fostered a special devotion to the sufferings of
Christ; and in memory of them, she subjected herself to special austerities
on Fridays and in Holy Week. She also entertained a filial love for Mary,
the Mother of Mercy, who sometimes appeared to her and comforted her.

Enriched by every virtue and held in great repute by her fellow sisters,
she died in the fifty-fifth year of her age, in the year of our Lord 1640.
Many miracles occurred at her grave for which reason Pope Benedict XIII
placed her in the ranks of the blessed.

In the year 1807 she was canonized by Pope Pius VII. (Cf. *These Made
Peace*, pp. 203-209.)

ON ACCEPTING REPRIMANDS IN THE PROPER SPIRIT

1. How fortunate it was for Hyacintha that her confessor rebuked her so
severely though he knew of her distinguished descent and saw that she
was on her sickbed. It is really a great charity to us if a person points out
our faults to us in a becoming manner. Every man has his faults. But often
we are unaware of them; self-love hides them from us and, unfortunately,
those that call themselves our friends, also try to palliate them and justify
them, so that we can truly say, "Those who praise me, do not love me."
Thus it is also written in Holy Scripture: "Open rebuke is better than
hidden love. Better are the wounds of a friend than the deceitful kisses of
an enemy" (Prov. 27,5). — Have you always counted those as your
benefactors who have reprimanded you, and do you have the courage to
extend this charity to others when it is seasonable?

2. Consider what folly it is to resent a well meant reprimand. What would
have happened to Hyacintha if she had not accepted the reprimand given
her by her confessor? When a person corrects you, he gives you a mark
of his confidence, for evidently he regards you as virtuous enough to
accept it in good part, otherwise it would be foolish to reprimand you. If
you resent it, he will certainly be very careful not to correct you again; but
in the end you will have to hear more severe reproaches when you stand
before the judgment-seat of God. Therefore do not shut the door of your
heart to wholesome admonition, but be grateful to him who administers
it. — Has this been your way in the past? Do you perhaps also have the
courage calmly to accept an unmerited reprimand?

3. Because friends that are true enough to correct us are so rare, we should
be all the more anxious to profit from admonitions that are given in

general. Such admonitions are given in sermons and in spiritual reading. On such occasions one is so readily inclined to refer everything that is faulty to others, or, when a reproof does strike home, to take offense at the author. It is the enemy of the soul who is back of all this and who is endeavoring to prevent our amendment. Do not let yourself be led astray by him, but rather be grateful to God, who so kindly leads us, erring sheep, back to the fold. From now on, strive to apply to yourself all the admonitions you meet with in sermons or in spiritual reading.

PRAYER OF THE CHURCH

O God, who didst transform the holy virgin Hyacintha into a sacrifice of continual mortification and love, grant through her example and intercession that we may bewail our sins and love Thee at all times. Through Christ our Lord. Amen.

JANUARY 31
ST. JOHN BOSCO
Confessor, Third Order

T. JOHN BOSCO, one of the greatest saints of modern times, was born in a Piedmontese village in 1815. When he was two years old, he lost his father, a humble peasant farmer; and he was brought up by his saintly Tertiary mother, Margaret. It was no doubt due to her example and influence that John too joined the Third Order of St. Francis.

Even as a youngster, John recognized that it was his vocation in life to help poor boys; and he began to teach catechism to the boys of his own village and bring them to church. Acrobatic stunts and conjuring tricks were the means he used to get them together.

At sixteen he entered the seminary at Chieri. He was so poor at the time, that the mayor contributed a hat, the parish priest a cloak, one parishioner a cassock, and another a pair of shoes. After he was ordained a deacon he passed on to the seminary in Turin; and there, with the approbation of his superiors, he began to gather together on Sundays poor apprentices and waifs of the city.

Not long after his ordination to the priesthood in June, 1841, he established what he called a Festive Oratory, a kind of Sunday school and recreation center for boys, in Turin. His mother came to be his housekeeper and mother of the Oratory. Two more Oratories in the same city followed. When Father John Bosco's mother died in 1856, the Oratories housed 150 resident boys; and there were four Latin classes and four workshops, one of them a printing press. Ten young priests assisted Father John in his work. Father John was also much in demand as a preacher; and he spent half of his nights in writing popular books in order to provide good reading.

Father John's confessor and spiritual director was the saintly Tertiary priest Joseph Cafasso; and Father John too gained the reputation of being a saint. Miracles, mostly of healing, were attributed to him. By his kindness and sympathy and his marvelous power of reading the thoughts of his boys, he exercised a profound influence upon his charges. He was able to rule them with apparent indulgence and absence of punishment, something which the educationists of the day could not understand.

In 1854 Father John founded the religious order of Salesians, so called in honor of St. Francis de Sales. Its members devote themselves to the education of poor boys. The new society grew rapidly. Father John lived to see thirty-eight houses established in the Old World and twenty-six in the New World. Today it is one of the largest orders of men in the Church.

Father John also founded a sisterhood called Daughters of St. Mary Auxiliatrix; and he organized many outside helpers into the Salesian Co-operators, who are pledged to assist in some way the educational labors of the Salesians. In 1930 they totalled 800,000.

Father John's last great work was the building of Sacred Heart Church in Rome, a task which was entrusted to him by Pope Pius IX after it had seemed to be a hopeless project. The holy priest, who was everywhere acclaimed as a saint and wonderworker, gathered funds for the church in Italy and France; and somehow he succeeded where others had failed. But in doing so he wore himself out, and on January 31, 1888, he was called to his reward. Forty thousand persons came to pay their respects as his body lay in state in the church at Turin; and his funeral resembled a triumphal procession. St. John Bosco was canonized in 1934.

ON THINKING KINDLY OF OTHERS

1. What was the secret of St. John Bosco's wholesome influence on the boys who came under his care? Was it not the spirit of St. Francis of Assisi and of St. Francis de Sales, with which he was deeply imbued? A spirit, which made him think kindly of these boys in the first place, and then caused him to do all he could for their temporal and spiritual welfare? Thinking kindly of others, we will have understanding for them, judge

them charitably, and show them our esteem. To understand another means to put ourselves in his place and to take into consideration everything which has made and makes him what he is: his character and disposition, his background and environment, his interests and strivings, his problems and needs. To understand another means to go beyond the narrowness of human judgment and to acquire something of the depth and breadth of the vision of God, who has the deepest understanding for every human being. It means to become similar to our divine Saviour, in whom the goodness and love of God became visible, and who during His sojourn on earth showed such deep and loving understanding for His Apostles and all who came to Him with their problems or listened to His word. When there is perfect harmony between two persons, we say that they understand each other; when there is disharmony, it is often due to misunderstandings.

2. He who has understanding for others, will also judge them with charity and mercy, even when their faults are evident and undeniable. He will not be inflexible and harsh in his judgment, for he will discover mitigating circumstances and recognize many good qualities. The all-holy God does not cast off and despise the sinner, even when his sins are grievous and inexcusable. His love and grace pursues every human soul in order to bring the good in it to victory and perfection. Thinking kindly of others and judging them charitably makes us like God; it is a sign that we are united with God in love. It is an indication of greatness of soul and spiritual maturity. Like St. Francis de Sales, St. John Bosco was criticized for being too kind and indulgent; but he understood his boys and judged them charitably because of his nobility of soul and his constant union with God.

3. He who thinks kindly of others will also show them esteem; and sincere esteem is a source of great pleasure and encouragement to the recipient. It makes him feel that we believe in the good that is in him, or at least that we believe in his final victory. By showing esteem to another we appeal to his sense of honor, and this is a powerful moral force which the Creator Himself has implanted in all men. On the other hand, a culprit who receives only contempt from his fellowmen often loses the last particle of his self-respect and self-confidence and with it all moral support and incentive. St. John Bosco believed in the good that was in his boys; he encouraged them to keep on trying; he had compassion with them in their difficulties; he was solicitous about their temporal and spiritual progress. Always to think kindly of our fellowman, and to prove it by seeking to understand him, to judge him charitably, and to show him our esteem — that is the Franciscan way of dealing with our neighbor and loving him

sincerely.

PRAYER OF THE CHURCH

O God, who hath raised up in Thy confessor St. John Bosco a father and teacher of youth, and didst will that through him with the help of the Virgin Mary new religious families should flourish in the Church, grant, we beseech Thee, that enkindled by the same fire of charity we may be able to labor in finding souls and serve only Thee. Through Christ our Lord. Amen.

FEBRUARY

FEBRUARY 1
THE SERVANTS OF GOD
JUNIPER VEGA AND HUMILIS MARTINEZ
Martyrs, First Order

IN SPITE of the fact that for more than a century Mexico was a prey to Freemasonry and to laicism, the worst offspring of Freemasonry, it was reserved for this unfortunate country to be the first with which we associate the kingship of Christ in the sense of the new feast of Christ the King. To Mexico may also be attributed the first martyrs to Christ the King. Prominent among these are thirteen secular priests, one Augustinian, one priest of the Society of the Heart of Mary, two Jesuits, three Franciscans, and several Tertiaries.

Today we commemorate Father Juniper de la Vega and his faithful companion, Brother Humilis Martinez. Both received the habit of St. Francis in the same convent in 1901, remained together later on, suffered together for Christ, and were awarded the crown of martyrdom at the same time.

Father Juniper and Brother Humilis were both born in Mexico, the former in 1874, the latter in 1873. Juniper was another Nathaniel, a man in whom there was no guile, with a pronounced tendency towards the interior life. Humilis was impetuous by nature and possessed a tireless impulse for work.

During the persecution under the notorious Calles, both were twice cast into prison for the cause of Jesus Christ. In February, 1928, Brother Humilis wrote to his provincial: "I am in a prison which held a martyr captive before me. One can still see the traces of his blood. I am sending you a bit of ground that is saturated with his blood." On February eighth, Father Juniper was questioned in court. "How many Masses have you read?" an officer demanded. In all simplicity the Father answered: "Figure it out for yourself, for I was ordained to the holy priesthood in 1905." "I did not ask that," the officer replied, "but how many Masses have you read since the prohibition was issued that no Masses be said at all?" The priest asserted in his simple, upright manner: "If I am to tell the truth, as many

Masses as I could." That was a crime punishable with death. Both the father and the brother were again led back to prison and were fully aware of what was awaiting them.

Brother Humilis again wrote to his provincial: "I spent the entire night in humbly asking God to forgive me my sins and in recommending my soul to the ever Blessed Virgin Mary, for it is clear that we must die. You need not, however, reply to this letter, for without doubt I shall not receive the answer any more."

During the night Father Juniper heard the confessions of his fellow prisoners. Early the next morning he cast himself upon the ground and prayed. When Brother Humilis begged him to take a little rest, since he had spent the night without any sleep. Juniper answered: "There is no longer any time to sleep; the hour has arrived to prepare for death." And so it happened.

The executioners soon arrived. Both friars were forced to board a military train. At Ecuandureo Father Juniper was forced to alight and run. A rain of bullets followed him. Meanwhile, the rude soldiery were making sport of Brother Humilis. At Zamora he, too, was forced to alight, and was shot down in his tracks.

The funeral of the two martyrs was like a triumphal march. Father Juniper was solemnly interred at Ecuandureo, Brother Humilis at Zamora. Over the graves of both martyrs the jubilant cry of many thousands of voices could be heard repeating: "Long live Christ the King!"

ON LAICISM

1. What are we to understand by laicism? This pestilence of our modern era consists in the determination no longer to recognize a place for God, religion, and the Church, and to eliminate them from the lives of the people and of the state. Laicism has been most unhappily successful in Mexico and in other countries. The name of God is purposely disregarded at state, political, and business sessions. It has been forgotten that God is "the blessed and only mighty, the King of kings and Lord of lords" (1 Tim. 6,15).

2. How did laicism arise? At first the authority of God was denied, as also that of His Anointed One over the nations, then the right of the Church of Christ to teach and guide the people. After that the religion of Christ was assigned to a place alongside the false creeds, and grossly subjected to civil authority. Finally, every Christian conviction was rejected. And yet, the God-man has solemnly commanded the representatives of the Church: "Going therefore, teach all nations" (Mt. 28,19). — Let us, then, be

the more faithful to Christ and His Church, the more others attack them. 3. What results are bound up with laicism? Pope Pius XI gives the answer in his encyclical of the year 1925: "Dissension has been sown everywhere, the flame of envy and jealousy is kindled among the nations. Human society, which has rebelled against God and Christ, has been shaken, brought to the verge of perdition, and is threatened with unavoidable dissolution." The representatives of laicism are "blind and leaders of the blind" (Mt. 15,14). And matters must come to a still worse turn before they will recognize the real state of things. — Pray for these deluded souls, and, following in the glorious footsteps of the Mexican martyrs, take your stand unflinchingly for the rights of Christ and of His Church.

PRAYER OF THE CHURCH

Almighty and eternal God, who didst make Thy glory known to the whole of Christendom; protect the work of Thy mercy, so that Thy Church, which is spread over the world, may remain firm in its confession of Thy name. Through Christ our Lord. Amen.

FEBRUARY 2
THE SERVANT OF GOD MARY FIDELIS WEISS
Virgin, Third Order

THE SIMPLE greatness of this woman's life is testimony enough that holiness is still with us in the world, even though it may appear that the world has succumbed to Antichrist.

Eleonore, as she was known in the world, was born at Kempten, Germany, in 1882. She inherited her cheerful disposition from her father, her generosity from her mother. She was chosen by Providence to attain to the heights of mysticism. Yet, her exterior life was undisturbed and in no way out of the ordinary. Except for her prudent spiritual director, no one knew of the unusual graces that flooded her soul. Even her fellow sisters knew nothing of the singular way she trod until after her death.

As a child she was a quiet and well-behaved girl. Then, for the space of two years, she was employed in a store in Kempten. For another period of two years she was a model pupil of the school sisters in Lenzfried. Finally, as Mary Fidelis, she entered the convent of Franciscan Sisters in Reutberg, Bavaria.

As a child she was raised to the first degree of mystical prayer, and from then on she passed through all the degrees of this form of prayer until she arrived at the mystical nuptials on Good Friday of 1919. Her first holy Communion on Low Sunday, 1893, made a very deep impression on her. At Lenzfried she took the habit and cord of the Third Order, in order thereafter to scale, with our holy Father St. Francis, the La Verna of union with God.

But since mystical prayer cannot exist without suffering, Sister Mary Fidelis had to empty the chalice of trial down to the dregs. Spiritual sufferings were joined to the corporal ones, and so, on the path of loving and suffering, she became a victim for the sins of her fellowmen. Patiently and staunchly she persevered on the altar of sacrifice until, after a long and painful illness, she went home to God on February 11, 1923, altogether wasted away, as was our holy Father St. Francis, with love for Christ.

Her writings, known in her day only to her spiritual director, are a wonderful summary of mysticism. The miracles that occurred after her death, lead us to believe that this mystical rose in the Franciscan garden will some day adorn our altars. The cause of her beatification is now under way.

TO WORK AND SUFFER FOR OTHERS

1. Mary Fidelis gives us a remarkable example of interior sacrifice for others. Prolonged suffering in atonement for others was in fact the central point in her life as a victim. She endured the terrible sensation of abandonment by God in atonement for the sins of modern unbelief; disgrace, because of the sins of immorality; acute interior torture, for the dying. And all this with the same unchanging joy, patience, and peace. Meanwhile, she even played the organ for the sisters' choir. Much in the same way as St. Paul could say of himself: "But I most gladly will spend and be spent myself for your souls" (2 Cor. 12,15). — What do you do for sinners, what sacrifices do you make for them, what expiation do you render?
2. Every Christian should labor and suffer for his brethren in Christ. Leo XIII once wrote to Cardinal Gibbons: "It is a universal law whereby God in His divine providence has decreed that almost in every case human beings are to be saved through other human beings." How many a soul may have been saved through the prayers and sufferings of Mary Fidelis. — Do you perhaps ask with Cain: "Am I my brother's keeper?" (Gen. 4,19).
3. Perhaps divine providence means that certain persons shall be saved through you, through your prayers, through your Communions, through

your acts of suffering and self-denial. Let this thought take possession of you as it did of Mary Fidelis. It will be well with you if you can finally declare at the judgment, as Christ could declare before His Father: "Those whom Thou gavest me, have I kept, and none of them is lost" (Jn. 17,12). — If in this our day there are so many erring, ignorant, and sinful souls, good Christians must come to their rescue and save them. You must co-operate.

PRAYER OF THE CHURCH
O Lord, we beseech Thee, through the intercession of the ever Blessed Virgin Mary, defend Thy Church from all adversities, and graciously protect her, who has recourse to Thee with her whole soul, from all the snares of the enemy. Through Christ our Lord. Amen.

FEBRUARY 3
BLESSED ELIZABETH AMODEI
Virgin, Third Order

Born in the little Sicilian town of Amelia or Ameria in 1475, Elizabeth manifested an extraordinary zeal for holiness and a remarkable maturity in spiritual matters while still very young. She never lost her baptismal innocence, and before her First Communion she bound herself by the perpetual vow of virginity. It is not surprising, therefore, that she joined the Third Order of St. Francis as a girl, and most faithfully and exactly observed every point of the rule.

While other girls enjoyed their games and amusements, Elizabeth preferred to retire to a quiet spot and spend her time in prayer. Her example had a wholesome effect on her companions, and many of them were inspired to lead a holy life. Elizabeth was never seen to be idle, but always occupied either with work or prayer. However, she carefully avoided making a show of her piety; and she possessed a winning manner which made her everybody's friend.

She died at the early age of twenty-four on February 4, 1498. Though the people mourned her passing deeply, they began at once to honor her as a saint. This cult continued, and Pope Clement VIII approved it in 1603. Blessed Elizabeth is one of several beati of the Third Order whose names are not mentioned in any of the Franciscan calendars. (Cf. Biersack, p. 37.)

EARLY DEATH

1. When a young man or a young woman in the bloom of life dies, people lament their death with loud voices. However, a true Christian looks up to heaven on such occasions. He knows that not a sparrow falls from the roof without the will of our heavenly Father, and that "God created man and gave him the number of his days and time" (Eccli. 17,1-3). He adores Him as the Lord over life and death and recommends to Him his own days upon earth. — How have you conducted yourself on such occasions?

2. Consider why God often calls home some of the most promising persons by an early death. You may think it would have been better if He had called away some that are apparently useless and even a burden to others. Still, such are the counsels of Eternal Wisdom. Could any human being presume to advise God? God's goodness and mercy are manifested when He takes away young people, who are, so to say, ripe for heaven, in order to preserve them from a wicked world and reward them in eternity; whereas, in His compassion, He lets many useless servants and foolish young women continue to live in order that they may reflect on the early death of others and, entering into themselves, save their souls. Moreover, the early death of a companion should remind us that "all flesh is as grass and all the glory thereof as the flower of grass; the grass is withered and the flower thereof is fallen away" (1 Pet. 1,24). — Hence, do not make vain plans, but employ your time well and reflect on eternity.

3. Consider that an early death is not a misfortune and that the thought of it should not be terrifying. Whoever has spent his life well, as did the Blessed Elizabeth, has been "made perfect in a short space (and) fulfilled a long time" (Wisd. 4,13). He may rejoice to receive his reward. If, on the other hand, we have incurred guilt, ought we not to fear that a longer life will only increase our guilt? Were that the case, then surely a long life were nothing to be desired. It has been well said that life is not the greatest of goods, but sin is the greatest of evils. For this reason the Church does not teach us to pray for preservation from an early death, but rather from a bad and unprovided death. Take heed that you may always be prepared. Leave the length of your days in God's hands; pray only that He may grant you the grace of a happy end.

PRAYER OF THE CHURCH
(Seventh Sunday after Pentecost)

O God, whose providence erreth not in its ordinance, we humbly beseech Thee to remove from us all that is harmful and to grant us all that is profitable to us. Through Christ our Lord. Amen.

FEBRUARY 4
ST. JOSEPH OF LEONISSA
Confessor, First Order

N the year 1556, at Leonissa in the Abruzzi in the kingdom of Naples, the devout couple John Desiderius and Frances Paulina were blessed with a son, to whom they gave the name Euphranius at baptism. Under their faithful guidance, the little boy made such progress in piety that at a very tender age he resolved upon certain fastdays, and took the greatest pleasure in practices of piety. Later on, pursuing his studies at Viterbo, he attracted the attention and admiration of everyone by his industry and virtuous life to such a degree that a nobleman in that city offered him his daughter in marriage together with a large dowry. But Euphranius had already made a nobler choice. He left school and entered the Franciscan order among the Capuchins at Leonissa, in the year 1573, under the name of Joseph. Here he found happiness and peace in things which an effeminate age abhors most: mortification and penance.

His dwelling was a poor cell, so small and narrow that he could hardly stand, sit, or lie down in it. His bed was the bare earth, a block of wood was his pillow. He ate by preference food which the others could not or would not eat, such as stale beans and mouldy bread. In spite of the great strain associated with a life of preaching, he persevered in doing such penance even after he had been entrusted with that task. With works of penance he strove to win over those souls to God that he could not move with words.

In the year 1587, his zeal for souls urged him to go to Constantinople. He could not long conceal from the fanatical Turks the good that he was doing, especially among the Christian captives on the galleys. They seized him, pierced his right hand and right foot with sharp hooks, and hung him up on a high gibbet, then kindled a weak fire under him in order to roast him alive slowly, and gradually to suffocate him. He suffered untold tortures for three days. On the fourth day he was miraculously freed by an angel and received the command to return to Italy to preach the Gospel to the poor.

From now on he traveled untiringly through all the villages and country towns of Umbria. He strongly denounced evils of that day, such as frivolous dances and plays. In his associations with the people, however, he resembled a lamb in his meekness and charity. His very bearing won for him the affection of the people, and effected the most remarkable reconciliations between persons who had been living in enmity for years, and between families and communities that had been at variance with each other.

Often while at work or at prayer he would be rapt in ecstasy. He wrought many miracles, and was vouchsafed the gift of prophecy and of reading human hearts. He also foretold the day of his death. It was February 4, 1612, when he entered into the joy of his Lord in the convent at Amatrice. His body was taken to his native town of Leonissa, and reposes there, glorified by many miracles.

Pope Clement XII beatified Joseph, and Pope Benedict XIV canonized him in the year 1745. His feast is observed on February fourth by all three branches of the Friars Minor as well as the Third Order Regular.

ON MORTIFYING THE APPETITE

1. Consider how at a very tender age St. Joseph of Leonissa mortified his appetite by voluntary fasting, and later went so far as to seek his necessary nourishment by preference only in food that was repugnant to the natural taste and might even have injured his health, if the Divine Spirit who urged him to do it had not protected him. Thus he proved himself a true son of St. Francis, of whom St. Bonaventure writes: "When he was well, he seldom ate cooked foods and when he was obliged to eat them, he would mix ashes and water with the food. He did not only abstain from wine, but never even desired to drink water." Our Seraphic Father did this because he had considered the words of the Apostle: "They that are Christ's have crucified their flesh" (Gal. 5,24). — According to their rule, Tertiaries also are required to be temperate in eating and drinking. In this matter, have you proved yourself a true child of St. Francis?

2. Consider how easily and in how many ways we can indulge the appetite: by eating too much, by eating too often, by eating too greedily, by eating too daintily. Many who guard against the first three instances, are caught in the meshes of the last. God has ordained that our food should naturally have a pleasing taste in order that it may be conducive to good health, and it is no fault if we relish our food. But fondness for delicacies serves merely to satisfy an inordinate desire for food and drink; as St. Chrysostom says, some people seem to live in order to eat instead of eating in order to live. — Do you belong to this class?

3. Consider the means to overcome the inordinate desire for eating and drinking. It is related of St. Adelgundis that upon reflecting how difficult it is to satisfy the needs of the body without yielding to sensual pleasure, she asked God to deprive her of all pleasure in eating and drinking. Then St. Peter appeared to her and gave her a piece of bread from heaven. Thereafter no earthly food could again rouse her appetite. If we, too, partake of heavenly food, that is, if in the frequent contemplation of the joys of heaven we gain a foretaste of their sweetness, and if we recall that it was through eating of forbidden fruit that heaven was closed to be reopened only when Christ drank the bitter chalice of His Passion and the nauseous gall, then perhaps earthly food will tempt us less than before. We will be glad daily to offer a sacrifice to God by mortifying our appetite as did St. Joseph of Leonissa, so that we may grow in the relish of pious practices and hereafter be made partakers of heavenly sweetness.

PRAYER OF THE CHURCH

O God, Thou rewarder of faithful servants, who didst make of blessed Joseph an extraordinary laborer in preaching the Gospel, mercifully grant us through his intercession that we may never cease to serve Thee in a pleasing manner here on earth, and may finally receive from Thee the full reward in heaven. Through Christ our Lord. Amen.

FEBRUARY 5
ST. PETER BAPTIST AND COMPANIONS
Martyrs of Japan, First and Third Orders

ABOUT the year 1592 Hideyoshi, the military dictator of Japan, planned to invade and conquer the Philippine Islands, situated near his domain but belonging at the time to the Spanish crown. To negotiate peace, King Philip II of Spain delegated Father Peter Baptist Blasquez, a Franciscan of Manila, as his ambassador to Hideyoshi.

Peter Baptist, who came from an ancient Spanish family of the nobility, was learned, capable, and known for his holy life. He arrived in Japan with three companions at the end of the month of June in 1593. He succeeded in winning the dictator to terms of peace, and even obtained permission to spread Christianity throughout Japan without interference.

So Peter Baptist founded several convents of his order, built churches and hospitals, and in company with his associates converted hundreds of pagans to Christianity. Hideyoshi even offered them a neglected temple in his capital city Miyako, with permission to rebuild it as a church.

The Japanese bonzes were much incensed at the turn of events. They got the dictator to believe that the missionaries had in mind to dethrone him and deliver up the country to the Spaniards. Enraged, Hideyoshi ordered the Franciscan missionaries and their helpers to be imprisoned and put to death as offenders against the crown. Forthwith the soldiers invaded the friars' convents in December, 1596, and imprisoned the inmates. Peter Baptist was among the prisoners, together with his companions, the two priests Martin of the Ascension and Francis Blanco, the cleric Philip of Jesus, who was a native Mexican, the two lay brothers Francis of St. Michael and Gonsalvo Garcia. Included were also seventeen Tertiaries who rendered services to the missionaries as catechists, teachers, sacristans, and infirmarians; likewise three Jesuits.

On January 3, 1597, they were all led out of their cruel prison to the public square at Miyako. Here they were informed that they were to be crucified, and as a mark of dishonor a portion of their left ear was cut off. Then they were driven through the city on hurdles, while the sentence of death was carried on a pole at the head of the procession, and the rabble was given free hand to illtreat and insult them.

On January fourth they were again bound and thrown on hurdles, to be taken to Nagasaki for execution. The sad journey lasted four weeks, which in itself was cruel martyrdom because of the brutality of the bailiffs and the fury of the people in the towns and villages through which the martyrs passed. To this were added cold, hunger, and privations of every sort.

They arrived at Nagasaki on the morning of February fifth. The crosses on which the glorious confessors were to die had been prepared on a hill outside the town. The martyrs were immediately taken there and each one was bound to his cross. With loud voices they thanked God for the grace of being permitted to die like Christ their Lord, and they praised Him with psalms and hymns. As the martyrs hung crucified, executioners ran the body of each one through transversely with two spears, Father Peter Baptist being the last.

Hardly had the martyrs breathed forth their souls when God glorified them with extraordinary signs and marvels. In consequence, Pope Urban VIII beatified them in the year 1627 and permitted the annual celebration of the feast of the Japanese martyrs. On the feast of Pentecost, June 8, 1862, in presence of a great number of bishops assembled from all parts of the world, Pope Pius IX inscribed them in the catalog of the saints as powerful intercessors against the enemies of the holy cross. Their feast is observed on February fifth by the Franciscan orders, except the Conventuals who celebrate it on the eighth. (Cf. *In Journeyings Often,* pp. 246-251, 258.)

ON VENERATING THE HOLY CROSS

1. Consider how the cross became a mark of honor through the death of Christ. Before that time it was the tree of shame for the execution of the basest criminals, so that it was said: "Cursed is everyone that hangs on a tree" (Gal. 3,13). Today it gleams high up on the towers of our churches, it glitters on the crowns of princes; bishops wear it as a sign of their great dignity, and not only do women wear it as an ornament, but even men are proud to wear a cross as a badge of honor. At the last judgment the cross will shine in the heavens and precede the true adorers of the cross to never ending honors of heavenly glory. — Oh, that we may then be among its followers!

2. Consider how Holy Church venerates the cross. She has instituted two feasts in its honor: the feast of the Finding of the Holy Cross, and the feast of the Exaltation of the Holy Cross. She assigns to it the most honorable place on her altars; she dispenses all her means of grace and her blessings with the Sign of the Cross because it is the source of all blessings for us. Thus should we also honor it: we should celebrate the two feasts with special devotion, assign the cross and the crucifix the most honorable place as ornaments of our rooms, erect it in our gardens and along the highways as a guidepost to heaven, and plead for the blessing of God through the Sign of the Cross, making it not only before and after prayer, but also while at work and in all our undertakings. — Have you been honoring the holy cross properly, and have you gladly signed yourself with this means of blessing?

3. Consider that the best and most salutary way to venerate the cross consists in willingly bearing for love of God the suffering, the neglect, the hardships, in short, the cross which falls to our lot in life. Only in this way can we be united with Him who died on the cross out of love for us, for He says: "Whosoever does not carry his cross and come after Me, cannot be My disciple" (Lk. 14,27). Our holy martyrs of Japan counted it a reward for their labors in the missions that God so honored them as to allow them to die on the cross. Does our Lord not, perhaps, reward many of His faithful servants by permitting them to live under the cross? That will be made known on the day of final retribution. Then, just as the cross was changed through Christ from a mark of disgrace to a mark of honor, so

will all the contempt which we have borne out of love for Christ appear as great honor. — Who will then not wish to have carried his cross cheerfully? Happy he who has persevered under the cross until death!

PRAYER OF THE CHURCH

O Lord Jesus Christ, who in imitation of Thy painful death on the cross didst sanctify the first-born of the faith among the people of Japan in the blood of the holy martyrs Peter Baptist and his companions, grant, we beseech Thee, that we who today celebrate their feast, may be spurred on by their example. Who livest and reignest forever and ever. Amen.

FEBRUARY 6
THE SERVANT OF GOD MARY TERESA BONZEL
Virgin, Third Order

A PERSON who was acquainted with her in life writes that Mother Mary Teresa lived a holy life, practiced many heroic acts of virtues, and became a brilliant model for all the members of the congregation which she had founded and which was so richly blessed by God. The writer then expresses the assured hope that the day may not be far distant on which she will be honored and invoked as Blessed.

Mary Teresa saw the light of day in the little town of Olpe, in southern Westphalia, as the eldest daughter of the merchant Bonzel. This was in 1830, on the feast of the Stigmata of our holy Father St. Francis. A singular coincidence, when we remember that she was called to present to the Franciscan family a flourishing new branch and to renew in her person the spirit of the Poor Man of Assisi.

Already at her first holy Communion she espoused herself with our Saviour and prayed again and again: "O Lord, I am Your victim, accept me as Your victim, do not reject me." She entered the Third Order when she was not quite twenty years of age. Her whole being impelled her toward convent life. But a heart ailment and the opposition of her mother interfered with her plans.

Then it was that a devout woman made the unusual statement: "You are called to found a convent of perpetual adoration in your native town." Providence guided her. Already on December 30, 1860, Mother Mary Teresa and eight young women who were similarly minded, received the holy habit in the parish church at Olpe. After many difficulties, the foundation was incorporated in the great family of the saint of Assisi under the name of the Poor Franciscans of Perpetual Adoration.

The members pledged themselves to acquire the spirit of the Poor Man of Assisi, to carry on perpetual adoration before the Blessed Sacrament, to engage in the education of youth and the care of the poor and the sick.

When death summoned the foundress to receive her well earned reward on February 6, 1905, her sisters were active already in both the Old and the New World. The servant of God had no doubt earned this blessing from on high, particularly through her Franciscan spirit, the piety which permeated her whole being, her willing and resigned acceptance of bodily and spiritual afflictions coupled with complete trust in God, and last, but not least, through the charity which she never refused either to her sisters or to the poor, the sick, and poor sinners. "To become all to all" was the motto of her life, and it appears that even now she wishes to become all to all through her intercession at the throne of God.

ON CHARITY TOWARDS OUR NEIGHBOR

1. Charity will always bring us blessings. It was not in vain that the Saviour said: "As long as you did it to the least of My brethren you did it to Me" (Mt. 25,40). From this we can understand that the great and tender charity of the servant of God Mother Mary Teresa laid the foundation for her holiness and merited so many blessings for her community. — Love God in your neighbor, and do good to your neighbor, if you wish to receive special graces from God.

2. The love of God must be joined to the love of our neighbor. Thus it was in the case of Mother Mary Teresa. That is the reason why she united the works of mercy with perpetual adoration of her dear Lord in the tabernacle and with deep-seated piety. To do good from mere natural motives or even from selfish motives is no virtue. "Do not also the heathens and the publicans do this?" (Mt. 5,46-47).

3. It is an essential point of charity that we bear with the weaknesses and faults of our neighbor. "Bear one another's burdens" (Gal. 6,2). That, too, Mother Mary Teresa did most faithfully. Such patience and self-denial are more pleasing to God than a long series of prayers and works of penance. "To forget injuries, and to forgive one's enemies is the most godly act of penance." — Have you always fostered patient and forbearing charity?

PRAYER OF THE CHURCH

Thou dost permit, O Lord, that to those who love Thee, all things tend to their good. Grant us the imperishable sentiments of charity, so that in those things which we feel impelled to do in charity through Thy inspiration, we may not be made to waver because of any adversity. Through Christ our Lord. Amen.

⊗⊗⊗⊗⊗⊗⊗⊗⊗⊗

FEBRUARY 7
BLESSED RIZZIERO OF MUCCIA
Confessor, First Order

N the feast of the Assumption of the Blessed Virgin Mary in the year 1220, St. Francis was preaching in the public square at Bologna before an immense crowd of people. One of those present, who was later archdeacon of Spalato, gives the following account of the event:

"It seemed as though the entire town had congregated in that place. The holy preacher spoke of the angels, of men, and of devils; everything he said was calculated to end the dissension existing in that city. He spoke of those intelligent beings so clearly and purposefully that many learned men in the audience were in admiration. He did not speak in the usual manner of preachers, but in a popular style and with only his purpose in mind. His external appearance was plain and unpretentious, but his words were imbued with such supernatural force that many among the nobility, whose violent and unbridled passions had been the cause of much bloodshed, were reconciled with one another. The veneration of the people was so general that crowds of men and women pressed about him and considered themselves favored if they could but touch the hem of his garment."

So much for the account. Another result of the sermon was the vocation to the Franciscan Order of two young men in the audience, who were later beatified — Rizziero and Peregrin.

Rizziero was born of a noble family in Muccia in central Italy. He studied in the University of Bologna, but was so affected by the sermon of the holy Founder that he renounced all the world offered him in order to become a follower of the Poor Man of Assisi. In spirit, Francis saw the great designs of God regarding the young man and said to him: "You will be a priest and will preach the word of God with great success; you will serve God and your brethren in various offices of the order."

When Rizziero received the holy habit it seemed that also the spirit of his seraphic Father had come upon him. He was inflamed with the love of God and zeal for souls, treasured holy poverty and practiced it to extremes. Together with consummate virtue he manifested singular prudence, and for this reason, after several years of successful preaching he was appointed provincial for the March of Ancona by the holy Founder.

But God did not exempt Rizziero from trials. Although he was an admirable director to others, he found himself entangled in a mesh of temptations that caused him great sorrow and confusion of mind. He prayed, fasted, and practiced severe penance, but all to no avail. He believed that he was rejected by God, that blessed Father Francis knew it, and for that reason did not love him any more and consider him his son. The thought tortured him so terribly that one day he resolved to go to Assisi in order to learn whether it was really true.

Francis, who was lying seriously ill, was informed by God of the sad trial Rizziero was suffering and of his arrival in Assisi. He sent two of the brethren to meet him. They were to receive him in his name and greet him as one of Francis' most beloved sons, and conduct him into his presence. The greeting brought great relief to Rizziero as he hastened to the bedside of the sick saint. Francis rose from his couch, pressed Rizziero to his bosom, assured him again of his great affection for him, and made the Sign of the Cross on his forehead.

At once Rizziero was transported, so to say, from hell up to heaven. Francis said to him: "This temptation, my son, has served very much to increase your merit; but in future you will be delivered from it." Francis kept him close to him until his death soon afterwards.

After the death of St. Francis, Rizziero lived another ten years in undisturbed peace of mind, steadily advancing in virtue. He died in his native town of Muccia, in 1236. Veneration of him began at once, and many sick people, especially those who suffered from fever, were restored to health through his intercession. Pope Gregory XVI approved the celebration of his feast. It is observed by the Franciscans and Conventuals on February seventh, and by the Capuchins on the fourteenth.

ON PEACE OF MIND

1. Reflect on the blessing of peace of mind. Blessed Rizziero enjoyed it from the moment of his entrance into the order and in still greater measure after he had conquered the temptation, even to the close of his

life. The world with all its goods cannot provide us with it, they do not satisfy the heart of man. Rizziero had wealth, but he felt within him the impulse to sacrifice it for the love of God; then he found peace of heart in yielding to the impulse of grace. No creature finds peace and rest except in that for which the Creator has destined it. Man has been made for the service of God. "Our hearts are made for Thee, O God," says St. Augustine, "and they cannot rest until they rest in Thee." — Have you not experienced this yourself? Have you ever found peace of mind in anything but fidelity to God?

2. Consider how you can attain to lasting peace. "My son," says our Lord through Thomas a Kempis (3,23), "I will now teach you the way of peace and of true liberty. Study to do rather the will of another than your own; ever choose to have less rather than more; always seek the lowest place and to be subject to everyone; desire always and pray that the will of God may be entirely fulfilled in you. Behold, such a one enters within the borders of peace and rest." — Endeavor to impress these four lessons deeply on your heart.

3. Consider that affliction and temptation, no matter how violent they may be, can never destroy true peace of mind; they are rather like a disturbing dream from which one awakens with a special feeling of relief. Our peace is destroyed only when we turn away from God in order to follow our inordinate inclinations. Sadly enough, there are many who expect to find peace in that way. They cry out: "Peace, peace, when there is no peace" (Jer. 8,11). Concupiscence is of evil and leads to evil; but self-renunciation and entire submission to the will of God bring peace and blessing from on high. Through Blessed Rizziero's intercession may we be delivered from the fever of concupiscence.

PRAYER OF THE CHURCH

Almighty and merciful God, who didst give Blessed Rizziero, Thy confessor, the gift of healing the sick, grant, we beseech Thee, that through his intercession we may be delivered from all evil and may deserve to obtain the crown of glory. Through Christ our Lord. Amen.

FEBRUARY 8
BLESSED GILES MARY OF ST. JOSEPH
Confessor, First Order

LESSED GILES MARY was born on November 16, 1729, at Taranto in southern Italy. His parents were very poor. They were, however, highly esteemed by all because of their God-fearing conduct. They noted with great joy that their son was blessed with deep piety and a maturity of mind that was far beyond his age.

When Giles attained the proper age, he was sent to a craftsman in town to learn a trade. Here, too, he distinguished himself by his diligence and the progress he made, and was at the same time so modest and sociable towards his fellow apprentices that they adopted several of his pious practices.

Every morning on his way to work he would stop at the church to attend holy Mass, and on returning home in the evening, he again stopped there to perform some special devotion. His love of piety awakened in him the desire to withdraw from the world in order to live only for God. He prayed long and fervently for enlightenment, and then, feeling himself divinely called, he entered the Order of Friars Minor in the year 1754. At his investiture he received the name of Giles Mary of St. Joseph.

Even during the days of his novitiate his future sanctity was discernible; but after he made his vows, it was noticed by all with what holy zeal he strove for the highest perfection. The ordinances of the order were like so many signs on a highway, according to which he regulated his conduct most scrupulously. God was always his only objective. He venerated his two patron saints, Mary and Joseph, with the greatest confidence, so that through their intercession he might, like them, become pleasing to God.

Religious poverty he observed most carefully. When he gathered alms to alleviate the needs of his brethren, he never wanted to accept anything for himself. A poor habit and meager food satisfied him; frequently he partook only of bread and water. In the convent he edified his brethren by his humble submissiveness. He was always ready to perform any task assigned to him, but he preferred those that were lowly and mean. His work finished, he would spend his spare time in church before the altars of our Lady and of St. Joseph pouring out the most ardent prayers by day and by night.

For many years Brother Giles was occupied in gathering alms for the convent in Naples. He was beloved by everyone he met and highly esteemed for his virtues. He had permission from his superiors to share the alms he gathered with such needy persons as he would meet on the way, and he experienced the keenest joy in providing the poor at one time with food, at another with clothing, and then again with household articles. He was the most active person in the entire city in succoring the needy, and many a tear was dried through his ministrations. However, he turned these opportunities to account also by exhorting his clients to lead peaceful, Christian lives. In his prudence and charity he was instrumental in bringing many a hardened sinner back to the right path.

Having spent all his energy in the service of God and the poor members of Christ up to a ripe old age, he died a blessed death on February 7, 1812, clasping a crucifix in his hand and directing his look to images of the Blessed Virgin and of St. Joseph.

So many miracles were performed upon his prayers during his lifetime and through his intercession after death, that as soon as the prescribed fifty years had elapsed the process of beatification was begun, and Pope Leo XIII solemnly enrolled him among the blessed on February 5, 1888. His feast is observed by the Franciscans on February seventh.

ON DEVOTION TO ST. JOSEPH

1. When Giles entered the religious state, he received as his special protector, along with the Blessed Virgin, her chaste spouse St. Joseph. He devoutly honored his patron throughout life, and St. Joseph led his client along the road to sanctity even unto his death. St. Joseph is a special patron of all the children of the Catholic Church, for Pope Pius IX selected him as a special patron of the Catholic Church. The Father of Christendom said to us what Pharaoh once said to the people of Egypt: "*Ite ad Joseph* — Go to Joseph" (Gen. 41,55). Call upon the holy foster-father every morning and ask his assistance with the indulgenced prayer:

> Help us, Joseph, in our earthly strife
> Ever to lead a pure and blameless life.
> (300 days indulg.)

2. Consider that if you wish to be favored with the protection of St. Joseph, your conduct must be as much like his as was that of Blessed Giles. St. Joseph distinguished himself by fidelity in the performance of his duties. With all his power he protected the Blessed Virgin and the Divine Child when He came into this world. He did not shirk the difficult journey to Egypt in order to escape the danger that was threatening Him. He worked day by day to earn a livelihood for his family. At the same time he

led a very humble, retired, and devout life. Mark well, not a single utterance is recorded that St. Joseph ever made. He spoke little, but prayed and labored much. — How do you follow this example?

3. Consider how powerful St. Joseph is to assist those who call upon him. On earth Jesus Christ "was subject to him"; now that he is in heaven, would Jesus refuse him a request? Take recourse to St. Joseph in all your needs of body and soul. He is a special patron for fathers and mothers in the performance of the duties of their state, and for devout persons to obtain for them the grace of devotion at prayer. All Christendom thinks of him as the patron of a happy death. — Let us recommend ourselves to him every day of our life, but especially for the hour of our death, that we may, like Blessed Giles, have the name of Jesus, Mary, and Joseph on our lips.

PRAYER OF THE CHURCH

We beseech Thee, O Lord, that we may find help in the merits of the spouse of Thy most holy Mother, so that what we cannot obtain of ourselves may be given to us through his intercession. Who livest and reignest forever and ever. Amen.

FEBRUARY 9
BLESSED ANTHONY OF STRONCONE
Confessor, First Order

ANTHONY, scion of the ancient and noble family of the Vici, was born in the year 1381 at Stroncone, a small town in the province of Umbria. He was blessed with very devout parents, who provided their son with an excellent education. Both parents were members of the Third Order and great benefactors of the Franciscan convent at Stroncone; the Franciscan Friar John of Stroncone was the youth's uncle.

From his earliest years, Anthony cherished great love for St. Francis, and under the guidance of his devout parents he emulated him in his love of prayer, retirement, and mortification. Soon after his twelfth birthday, Anthony begged the superior of the Franciscan convent in his native town for admission into the order. But the superior thought it fit to defer his reception to a later time, because of the boy's youth and delicate constitution. But Anthony was not to be discouraged. He repeated his pleas until the superior, who had refused him on three different occasions, relented at his tears, and gave him a postulant's garb.

Because the boy possessed great talents, it was the intention of the superiors to educate him for the priesthood. But Anthony's inclinations were toward a hidden life; he humbly begged to be received among the lay brothers.

When his year of probation was completed, he was sent to Fiesole, where he was thoroughly initiated in the spiritual life under the excellent guidance of his uncle John, at that time guardian of the convent there. Later on, Father Thomas of Florence, an eminent director of souls, whom the Church has beatified, was appointed as his second master of perfection. Under his direction Anthony made such progress in virtue that the superiors assigned him, though only a lay brother, as assistant to Blessed Thomas in the education of the novices. He filled this position for three years. Because he himself was a model of all the virtues and was likewise especially inspired by God, he trained a great number of excellent religious in this time.

In the year 1428 he was sent by his superiors to the island of Corsica to assist in the establishment of new convents there. Here, too, he won the hearts of the rugged island folk by his meekness and humility, and he was highly venerated by them. After two years he was sent back to his native country to a quiet convent near Assisi. There he spent the remaining thirty years of his life in prayer, work, vigils, and fasts, a source of edification and admiration to all the brethren. With the greatest humility and reserve he went out daily to gather alms for the convent; he was extremely happy whenever he could serve the priest at holy Mass.

He died on February 7, 1471, in the eightieth year of his life and his sixty-eighth as a religious. A year after his death, St. James of the March had his body removed from the common vault in order to bury it in a separate tomb. The corpse was found incorrupt and exhaling a sweet perfume. "This is a sign from God," exclaimed St. James. But this was only the first of such signs; many others followed by way of remarkable answers to prayer, the restoration of health to the sick, and numerous other graces.

The veneration of Blessed Anthony, which continually increased, was approved for all time by Pope Innocent XI in the year 1687. On August 21, 1809, the body of Anthony was transferred from the convent of St. Damian near Assisi to its native town of Stroncone. It is still incorrupt, and the confidence of the faithful in Anthony's powerful intercession has in no way decreased. His feast is observed by the Franciscans on February seventh, by the Capuchins on the fourteenth.

ON CHRISTIAN EDUCATION

1. Consider how the fruits of a good training manifested themselves in
Blessed Anthony. Trained to virtue by both of his parents who were
Tertiaries, he rose to still greater heights of perfection under the guidance
of his uncle and of Blessed Thomas, and became for many others a teacher
and a leader to sanctity. Withal, he remained a model of humility even in
his old age. —St. Basil says: "Just as a person may fashion whatever kind
of figure his fancy suggests out of soft wax, so are human beings
fashioned by education." True, he who has been reared well may still go
astray, while a person whose education has been deficient may turn out
well, because God leaves every man his free will, and it is according to it
that He will judge him in eternity. But in most instances it is a person's
early rearing that determines his future development. — How great a
responsibility rests on parents and educators!
2. Consider what constitutes a Christian education. It will, of course, take
into consideration the body and the temporal welfare of the child, but it
must above all be concerned with the soul of the child and its eternal
salvation. It must be begun at an early age. In his Confessions, in which
he tells of his return from an evil course, St. Augustine says: "From my
mother's womb I was signed with the Sign of the Cross and strengthened
with the salt of Christian doctrine." We must also frequently recommend
our children to God and their guardian angels, instil in them a tender
devotion to the Mother of God, and encourage them in all that is noble
with our own good example. To many parents, children are merely a kind
of plaything to be used for their own gratification. Hence, many an evil
inclination takes root in their tender souls: vanity, the desire to attract
attention, hypocrisy, nipping sweets, and even graver faults. But our
Divine Saviour pronounces a terrible woe on those parents who scandalize
even one of His little ones, that is, lead them into evil ways. — As regards
the training and education of children, have you always done your duty?
3. Consider that, as a result of original sin, the root of evil is present in
every child. Correction, therefore, and punishment will often be necessary
to keep it from following its evil inclinations and deter it from them.
"Folly is bound up in the heart of a child," says Holy Writ, "and the rod of
correction shall drive it away" (Prov. 22,15). But punishment may not be
inflicted in anger or rancor over the faults the child has committed; it
must be meted out from a holy sense of duty. Remember, too, that all
efforts to root out faults in children will be ineffective unless we call on
God for His assistance. A mother once complained to St. Francis de Sales
that in spite of all the good admonitions she gave her daughter, the latter

did not get any better. The saint answered: "It is well that you often speak to your daughter about God, but it is better to speak more frequently to God about your daughter." — With this purpose implore the help of Blessed Anthony, and rest assured that a child of tears and prayers cannot be lost.

PRAYER OF THE CHURCH

We beseech Thee, O Lord, protect Thy family through the intercession of Blessed Anthony, that it may through his mediation be spared from all adversities, and by the performance of good works be devoted to Thy name. Through Christ our Lord. Amen.

FEBRUARY 10
BLESSED CLARE OF RIMINI
Widow, Third Order

E learn from the life of Blessed Clare what a misfortune it is for a child to lose its mother at an early age. Born at Rimini in Italy about the year 1300, Clare lost her mother when she was but seven years old, and because her father could not devote much time and attention to the training of the vivacious girl, she grew up into maidenhood in a frivolous rather than in a Christian manner. As a young woman she gave herself up so completely to worldly pleasures, that the few religious exercises she still practiced were a mere formality, external functions without any devotion or Christian motive. She married a man who was also a perfect child of the world.

Then, one day, as she attended holy Mass in a Franciscan church, and was gazing about in her usual distracted way, she suddenly felt an inward urge to pray at least one Our Father with devotion. She yielded to this impulse of grace, and lo, in the course of the prayer her soul was so enlightened as to show her the very sad state in which she was living. Clare became alarmed at the consideration of her past life; she shuddered at the thought of the account God could require of her at any moment. Penitently she turned to the God of all mercies with the firm resolve earnestly to change her life.

Henceforth she avoided all worldly festivities, and with the consent of her husband, she entered the Third Order. When he died a short while later, she embraced a very strict life of penance. She wore iron girdles, slept on hard boards, lived on bread and water, and devoted herself entirely to prayer, meditation, and works of charity. She was especially interested in encouraging young women to keep from sinful vanity and frivolous living, and in reconciling persons who were at variance with one another.

Almighty God blessed her efforts with great success; in fact, He granted her the heavenly gifts of prophecy and miracles. Filled with holy longing for heaven, she died on February 10, 1346. Her cult was approved in 1784, but her feast is not observed by any of the Franciscan orders.

ON WORLDLY PLEASURES

1. Consider how vain and deceptive are worldly pleasures, to which so many people, especially in the time of inexperienced youth, allow themselves to be lured. How many young men, how many young women are like Clare! If they are not held back by well meaning parents, they abandon themselves to vanity, to the enjoyment of sensual friendship and worldly pleasure. Yes, there are many who do this in spite of all the warnings of parents and priests! But what do they find? After a short period of intoxication mingled with envy, jealousy, and bitterness, there follow so frequently the long suffering of a ruined life, public contempt, and sometimes poverty and want. Worldly pleasure is poisoned honey which we swallow with delight, but once down, it causes agonizing pain. — Have you always regarded it in this light?

2. Consider that the wicked pleasures of the world, far from bringing us much-sought material good fortune, rather burden the soul with a great weight of sin. For their sake, how many sins are committed against the fourth commandment, against parents and superiors; how many against the fifth commandment, in the harm done to one's own health, as well as by scandal and leading others astray; how innumerable the sins against the sixth commandment; how many against the seventh, through unjust dealings of all sorts! — Examine yourself, in how far you have yielded to worldly delights. Fortunate, however, is he whose eyes have been opened and who does penance, as the saintly Clare did.

3. Consider that the purest and best joys even in this life are the portion of him who serves God faithfully, who preserves a good conscience, and who subdues carnal desires. Only then do people share in the true joys of the children of God to which the Apostle exhorts us: "Rejoice in the Lord always; again I say, rejoice" (Phil. 4,4). Then shall they taste the bliss of innocent pleasure, which is never abated, and which will only be enhanced in the eternal, immeasurable joy of heaven.

PRAYER OF THE CHURCH
(Fourth Sunday after Easter)

O God, who makest the minds of the faithful to be of one will, grant us, Thy people, to love what Thou commandest and to desire what Thou dost promise, that amid the changing things of this world our hearts may be set where true joy is found. Through Christ our Lord. Amen.

FEBRUARY 11
THE SERVANT OF GOD STEPHEN ECKERT
Confessor, First Order

NOTHER child of St. Francis of our own day, Father Stephen Eckert, was born in Dublin, Canada, on April 28, 1869. He received the habit of St. Francis among the Capuchins in Detroit, Michigan, and was ordained to the priesthood in 1896. For several years he labored in New York, and was highly esteemed as a missionary, confessor, and retreat-master.

The glory of the metropolis and the honor accorded him there were not agreeable to his humble disposition. He was attracted to the poor and the outcast. On his request, his superiors appointed him to take charge of the Mission of St. Benedict the Moor, for Negroes, in Milwaukee. There Father Stephen felt completely at home.

His iron constitution, his gift of oratory, his unlimited optimism, and his invincible trust in God he placed at the complete service of the colored people. He was determined, cost what it might, to raise their cultural level and to promote their religious and moral life. With this in mind, he brought his influence to bear on both the Negroes and the white people. To the former he was a father, with the latter he was the spokesman of the despised and oppressed black race. He left no opportunity pass to destroy prejudice and promote understanding and love for the Negro.

On a journey devoted to that purpose, he contracted pneumonia, which caused his death on February 16, 1923. One of the last utterances of this apostle of love was this: "Here I lie and do nothing, and meanwhile thousands of souls are being lost!" The many answers to prayer that have been attributed to his intercession have caused the process of his beatification to be introduced. (Cf. *Forum*, 1947, pp. 366-370.)

ALL TO ALL

1. It is Christ-like to become all to all. All men are one in God: "Have we not all one Father? Has not one God created us?" (Mal. 2,10) All men are one in our Saviour: "Christ died for all" (2 Cor. 5,15). How right it was, then, of Father Stephen to interest himself as much in the colored people as in their white fellowmen! — Let us never guide our actions by the race or nationality, but rather by the souls of men.

2. All such discrimination is unchristian. Our Lord points that out in the parable of the Good Samaritan. The latter did not ask the victim with sectarian narrowness: Do you pray in Jerusalem or on Mount Garizim? He did not insist on the victim's nationality and ask: Are you a Jew or a Samaritan? Neither did he calculate on exploiting the man and ask: What will you give me for my services? Such discrimination should never be made by a true Christian. — Do you have to reproach yourself with unchristian conduct in this matter?

3. When shall we have become all to all? When we have been filled with a spirit of love and of peace. We shall have to sing more than our national anthems, we shall have to sing the hymns to the Holy Ghost. And any modern league of nations shall have to permit itself to be guided by the Holy Ghost, just as did that first league of nations at Jerusalem. Only then will the nations attain to that measure of success which this latter achieved, and become "one heart and one soul" (Acts 4,32). — Do not forget to pray much to the Holy Ghost in these days of ours which are so devoid of peace, that peace, love, and unity may finally reign among the nations.

PRAYER OF THE CHURCH

O God, who didst send the Holy Ghost upon Thy apostles, grant to Thy people the effects of their ardent prayers, so that Thou mayest grant peace to those whom Thou hast favored with the gift of faith. Through Christ our Lord. Amen.

FEBRUARY 12
BLESSED EUSTOCHIUM
Virgin, Second Order

USTOCHIUM was born in the year 1430 at Messina, Sicily, and received in baptism the name Smaragda, which means the emerald. Following the example of her devout mother Mathilda, of the princely family of the Colonna, she shunned intercourse with the world even while still very young. She wore a coarse penitential garb under her outer clothing and strove zealously to cultivate all the virtues, but especially purity of heart, which she resolved to preserve throughout life.

Several times her hand was asked in marriage by young men of distinguished birth, even such who came from princely families, and her relatives, especially her own father, urged her to give her consent. But Smaragda steadfastly declined all the offers of her suitors, and redoubled her fasts, vigils, and prayers, so as not to swerve in her fidelity to her Divine Bridegroom.

Her father died while she was still quite young. Then she entered the convent of the Poor Clares which was located near her home town. At her reception she received the name of Eustochium.

In the convent she lived completely absorbed in God, devoted to prayer, work, and ministering to her sick sisters. Her spare time she devoted to the contemplation of the life and sufferings of Jesus and Mary. She fostered special devotion to our Blessed Lady. Her favorite prayer was the Hail Mary, which she was wont to recite as often as a thousand times on our Lady's feastdays.

One time when the plague ravaged Messina, Sister Eustochium volunteered to take care of her fellow sisters who had been stricken, and regardless of any danger to her own life, she nursed them with tender charity and patience, and prepared them for a happy end.

Eustochium had spent eleven years in the convent when she was seized with a strong impulse to lead a stricter and still more secluded life. She sought permission of Pope Callistus III to found another convent in Messina where, with several other sisters who were of the same mind, she could observe the original rule of St. Clare without any mitigations, under the guidance of the Friars Minor. The permission was granted, and her mother and sisters built a modest convent for her on a height known as Virgin Mount. There Eustochium with several companions and a few relatives entered in the year 1457, when she was but twenty-seven years old.

Like all the works of God, this new foundation was severely persecuted. But Eustochium overcame all hardships with confidence in God, steadfast patience, and the miraculous assistance that was frequently granted by God Himself.

At the age of thirty years, which was the age prescribed by the Church for those who hold the office of abbess, Eustochium was elected to that position. As time went on, a select band of spiritual daughters developed about her, who, guided by her equally loving and enlightened direction, became a delight to God as well as an object of admiration and edification to the people.

After about twenty years spent in working for God and her fellow sisters, while she received much evil from the world, but also much consolation from God, her pure soul took its flight to the eternal mansions. A star was seen to rise aloft from her cell at the moment of her death. Her body, which is still incorrupt, is preserved in the convent church at Messina. Many miracles have occurred through her intercession, and the inhabitants of Messina have frequently experienced the effects of her powerful protection in the time of earthquakes. Pope Pius VI approved the public veneration that has been accorded her. The feast of Blessed Eustochium is observed by the Franciscans on the sixteenth and by the Capuchins on the thirteenth.

ON VIRGINITY

1. Consider how highly Blessed Eustochium valued this virtue, since she declined so many splendid offers of marriage and refused to yield to the urgent representations of her family, in order to preserve her virginity. She recognized by the light of faith how much nobler than mere worldly marriage are the tender nuptials with the heavenly Bridegroom, out of love for whom she preserved her purity. While Christ dwelt on earth, He wished to have only pure souls near Him. His precursor was a virgin, His mother was a virgin, His foster-father was a virgin, the virginal John was His beloved disciple; and when the apostles entered upon their vocation as His followers, they, too, observed perfect purity. How sublime the vocation of those souls whom God calls to the state of virginal purity! They become the intimates of our Lord, and, although still living in the flesh, they lead, so to say, the lives of angels. — Have you always esteemed the state of virginity thus in the light of faith?

2. Consider that virginal purity can be preserved here on earth only at the cost of many a struggle and effort. It is the "lily among thorns." Eustochium understood this even before she entered the convent. That is

why she fasted and practiced severe penances, avoided association with the vain and pleasure-loving world, devoted herself assiduously to prayer and spiritual exercises, and honored the Queen of Virgins and Mother of God with special affection. If you wish to be faithful in preserving purity of heart, you must apply the same means. You must not indulge softness and the pleasures of sense, but rather keep rebellious nature submissive by means of Christian mortification. You must love seclusion, and when it is necessary to mingle with others in the world, you must not try to attract attention to yourself, nor be too free with your attentions toward others. You must fortify yourself by means of prayer and the frequent reception of the sacraments, and cultivate a tender devotion to the Mother of God. — Have you been properly careful to use these means? Is it not on account of neglecting them that you have to suffer so many assaults of temptation?

3. Consider the reward that accrues to the souls that faithfully preserve their purity. If they do it out of love for God, they may justly be called "spouses of Christ" even here on earth. If the Divine Spouse jealously watches over them, He also rewards these faithful brides here below with the sweetest consolations. It will be easy for them to deprive themselves of worldly joys, for they can say with the Psalmist: "Better is one day in thy courts, O Lord, above thousands" (Ps. 83,11). And when her last day arrives, the day of death, which is such a bitter thing to worldlings, then the spouse of Christ will go forth joyfully. It is the day of her nuptials, which shall bind her forever to the Beloved of her heart. — Should you not be glad to live detached from the world in order to partake of such joy?

PRAYER OF THE CHURCH

Almighty and merciful God, who didst glorify the life of Blessed Eustochium hidden entirely in Christ as it was, grant upon her intercession and our imitation of her, that, buried with Christ in this world, we may deserve to rise to eternal life. Through Christ our Lord. Amen.

FEBRUARY 13
BLESSED JOHN OF TRIORA
Martyr, First Order

OHN LANTRUA was born near Triora in Liguria on March 15, 1760, of pious and respectable parents, and passed his boyhood days in great innocence. In his seventeenth year he joined the Order of Friars Minor. He pursued his studies for the priesthood, and after he was ordained he was appointed lector of theology at Corneto. He governed the communities at Corneto and Velletri with the singular prudence with which God blessed him.

Feeling himself called by God to a life of greater sacrifice, and, burning with zeal to go to the Chinese missions, he petitioned this favor, which was granted in 1790. He hastened from Rome to Lisbon, and from there intended to take passage to China. As no opportunity presented itself to sail from Lisbon, he was forced to remain there a whole year. At the end of this time he boarded a ship for Macao, from where he shortly entered the Chinese empire.

For sixteen years he labored with apostolic zeal in the provinces of Shensi and Hunan, which offered an abundant harvest. He was the only priest in this vast region, but he visited each and every Christian community. The difficulties involved could not deter him, neither could the dangers of the journeys restrain him. He restored sacred institutions which had practically fallen into decay, and expelled the shadows of superstition.

He meditated assiduously on the sufferings of our Lord, and the ardent zeal with which he was inflamed, led many idolaters to the true Faith. His zeal for the salvation of souls prompted him to pass whole nights in prayer and in scourging himself. God rewarded this ardor in spreading the Gospel by working great miracles through him. He caused a spring which had run dry to flow again by merely making the Sign of the Cross over it. Another time someone struck him while at prayer, and the offender was instantly killed by a serpent's bite as John had predicted.

John continued the work of spreading the Christian religion, but at last he was apprehended and brought before the magistrates. To the questions that were put to him he answered in a manner worthy of the ancient martyrs. He was bound with chains and forced to make a long journey on foot. He spent seven months in prison, enduring tortures too cruel to describe. With iron chains around his neck, and his hands and feet tied, he was dragged violently to a cross which lay on the ground, that he might tread on it. But this he refused to do. Then the sentence of death was pronounced upon this athlete of Christ.

John was led to the place of execution, where he prostrated himself five times to adore our Lord and to give public testimony of his faith. He begged the executioners not to strip him completely of his garments. This favor having been granted, he directed the guard to give his commands. He was fastened to a cross and strangled at Changsha on February 7, 1816.

His death was followed by great signs and wonders from heaven. The body of the martyr was taken to Rome, where it lies under the altar in the church of Aracoeli. Pope Leo XIII, in the jubilee year 1900, beatified him and seventy-six others who had suffered martyrdom in Annam and China. His cause of canonization is now under way. The Franciscans observe the feast of Blessed John on February thirteenth.

TRUE ZEAL FOR SOULS

1. Not satisfied with providing for the salvation of his own soul by entering a religious order, there to consecrate himself entirely to the service of God, Blessed John was anxious to save the souls of others also, particularly those who were still sitting in the darkness of idolatry and paganism. Hence his ardent desire to go to China, where a vast field of labor awaited the missionary. Is this not a picture of unselfish and loving zeal? The Great Commandment finds a true observer in this saintly son of St. Francis. What thought do we ever give to the souls of those about us who have not been so favored as we in receiving the gift of faith? It is not necessary for each one of us to go out proselytizing. Frequently our non-Catholic friends and acquaintances come to us for information regarding the Catholic Faith, with a sincere intention of learning the truth. Do we show sufficient interest in them and their inquiries when they appeal to us at such times? Have we any zeal for the salvation of their souls? Yet this zeal is an integral part of our love for God.

2. True charity for our neighbor consists in doing all in our power to procure his eternal salvation. The providence of God directs everything to this end. Impelled by His eternal love, God created us; His Son became man, lived on earth poor and unknown, spent three years of His life in toil and in labor, and finally died a disgraceful death on the cross in order to redeem us. For our salvation He instituted the holy sacraments, founded His Church, and commanded His apostles to go forth and teach all men. Moreover, His constant care of us, the many blessings He bestows on us, are all the result of His zeal for our salvation. If God Himself is so concerned for souls, should we not, in grateful tribute, be correspondingly mindful of the souls of those of His children who know Him not? Do we

ever offer them an opportunity of gaining a knowledge of the Faith and the beauties of the Catholic Church? There are various means at our disposal to do this. But does our zeal for souls prompt us to use these means?

3. No fatigue, no hardship, no danger could deter Blessed John from fulfilling his missionary duties. In this he imitated our holy Father, who traversed not only Italy, but also Spain, France, Illyria, Palestine, and Egypt. And to what end? Was it not for the glory of God and the salvation of souls? That was, moreover, his aim in instituting his three orders; not only were his followers to imitate him by preaching, but still more were they, by the holiness of their lives and by fervent prayer, to save souls from the snares of the devil and lead them to Christ. What was the burden of those long prayers St. Francis said and which he sometimes prolonged far into the night? The conversion of sinners and the salvation of souls. If we are incapable of preaching or teaching or giving missions, we can still find many other works of charity in which to employ ourselves. Our weak health may be a hindrance to our undertaking great labors or much active work; but we can edify others by our religious and domestic virtues, and by our prayers labor for the salvation of souls. Let us recall the words of St. Paul: "In doing good, let us not fail; for in due time we shall reap, not failing. Therefore, while we have time let us do good to all men, but especially to those who are of the household of the Faith."

PRAYER OF THE CHURCH

O God, who didst adorn with the crown of eternal glory the sufferings which Blessed John, Thy martyr, endured for the Christian Faith, mercifully grant that by his merits and intercession infidel nations may be freed from the shadows of death and be led to the light of salvation. Through the same Christ our Lord. Amen.

FEBRUARY 14
ST. JANE OF VALOIS
Widow, Third Order

ANE, the daughter of Louis XI, king of France, was born April 23, 1464. Favored with great gifts of mind and heart from her earliest years, she despised the pomp of the court and sought her joy in solitude, prayer, and meditation. This manner of life greatly displeased her proud and morose father as being unworthy of a royal princess, and he always treated her harshly.

Jane, however, bore it patiently and complained of her sufferings only to God. One time the Blessed Virgin Mary appeared to the distressed girl and spoke to her: "Be consoled, my daughter! A time will still come when you will belong to me entirely. A large group of young women consecrated to God will join you in serving me and proclaiming my praise everywhere." At these words a stream of heavenly consolation flooded Jane's soul, and she resolved anew to persevere in the service of God, cost what it might.

Her divinely guided director, Blessed Gabriel Mary or Father Gilbert Nicolas, a Franciscan, encouraged her in her resolution and was her support and director on the way to perfection. From him she also received the habit of the Third Order. From then on she entertained the thought of entering a convent in order to live and die as a bride of the Crucified.

Suddenly her father announced his decision that she should marry Louis, duke of Orléans, and she was to obey without remonstrance. In filial obedience and for love of God Jane made this difficult sacrifice in the year 1486.

Her marriage was not a happy one. Even before the ceremony took place, Duke Louis protested secretly before a notary and witnesses that he yielded to force and was marrying against his will, in order to escape the anger of the king. He always treated Jane as a stranger, and if he ever permitted her to appear before him, he reproached and illtreated her.

When Duke Louis ascended the throne of France in the year 1498 as Louis XII, his first act was to send the queen a bill of divorce. Because of the compulsion employed, the pope declared the marriage null and void. Jane accepted this great humiliation with a heart resigned to God and said: "God has now detached me from the world and has made it possible for me to serve Him better than heretofore."

She now repaired to Bourges, and there the revelation that had been made to her in her youth was to be realized. She united a group of young women to form a religious community which would devote itself to the special veneration of the Blessed Virgin Mary. Her regular confessor, Father Gilbert, drew up the statutes, which treat in ten chapters on imitating the ten virtues of the Blessed Virgin, to wit: the chastity, prudence, humility, faith, obedience, compassion, devotion, poverty, patience and piety of Mary.

In the year 1500 Pope Alexander VI approved this new institute, the members of which were called Sisters of the Annunciation of Mary, or Annunciades. The pope placed them under the obedience of the minister general of the Franciscans, and gave Father Gilbert the name of Gabriel Mary. Jane herself took the veil in the convent of Bourges which she had built, and on Pentecost, 1503, she pronounced her solemn vows.

Having for so long a time been prepared in the school of suffering and humiliation, she soon reached the summit of religious perfection and was ripe for heaven. God called her to Himself on February 4, 1505. Her body was entombed in the church of the Annunciation and many miracles occurred at her tomb.

In the year 1562, the heretical Huguenots stormed the city of Bourges. Also the convent and the church of the Annunciades were plundered and destroyed. They tore Jane's body, which was still incorrupt, out of the vault, and when they pierced it with swords, blood flowed from the wounds. The holy body was then burned. But Pope Benedict XIV sanctioned the public veneration of Jane in the year 1742; and in 1950 she was declared a saint. Her feast is observed by the Franciscans on February fourteenth. (Cf. *Forum*, 1949, pp. 57-59; 1955, pp. 102-106, 123.)

THE HAIL MARY

1. Consider how Holy Church has us announce the praises of Mary at all times and in all places, just as did Blessed Jane and her pious congregation, when we are taught to add the Hail Mary to the Our Father. How greatly it honors the Mother of God, and how much it must please her Divine Son that she is daily greeted thousands of times by all Catholic Christendom with the sublime greeting addressed to her by the Archangel Gabriel, who had come from God, and by her cousin Elizabeth, who was inspired by the Holy Ghost. The children of St. Francis especially should contribute to this veneration; that is why the office of the Third Order prescribes that they should recite the Angelic Salutation twelve times daily. — Do you recite it with proper devotion and reverence, so that it may rejoice the Queen of Heaven and her Divine Son?

2. Consider how wisely Holy Church added to the greeting of the angel the fervent petition: Holy Mary, Mother of God, pray for us sinners, and the rest. As Mother of God, Mary has power through her intercession to obtain for us everything necessary for our salvation, and being also our gracious mother, she is ever ready to intercede for us. And we are in great need of it. For, as poor sinners we are not at all worthy to be heard by God, although we are in need of His assistance every hour, and most of all in the hour of our death in order to be saved for eternity. How good it is, then, that we are directed to call upon the intercession of Mary throughout the twelve hours of the day "now," and what a consolation it

will be in dying if we have often devoutly called upon her for "the hour of our death!"

3. Consider that in order to give due praise to the Mother of God, and to make oneself worthy of her intercession, it is necessary to strive, like Blessed Jane and her spiritual daughters, to imitate the virtues of Mary. Only those are worthy children of so holy a mother, who make an effort to be like her. — Compare your life with the ten virtues of Mary named above. Endeavor earnestly to acquire what you now lack, and ask Blessed Jane, the true imitator of Mary, to intercede for you.

PRAYER OF THE CHURCH
O God, who hast willed that a new congregation of consecrated virgins should be founded by Blessed Jane to imitate the virtues of the Blessed Virgin and Mother of Thy Son; grant us through her intercession and merits that we, too, may imitate those virtues. Through the same Christ our Lord. Amen.

FEBRUARY 15
BLESSED VERIDIANA
Virgin, Third Order

ERIDIANA was born in the year 1182 at Castelfiorentino, near Florence, of the noble family of the Attavanti. Her vocation to a higher life was discernible even in her youth; she loved seclusion, prayer, and works of penance. As she advanced in years, she grew in grace, and her innocence and virtue won for her the love and veneration of everyone with whom she came in contact.

As a young girl, Veridiana was sent to the home of a relative to assist his wife in the administration of the household. Here she displayed good sense that was quite extraordinary for one of her age. She also utilized every opportunity to practice works of charity.

Once in a famine she distributed to the poor a great quantity of beans from the storerooms, not knowing that they had already been sold by her uncle. When the buyer arrived to get them and the bins were found empty, her uncle reproached her bitterly. Veridiana, deeply grieved, prayed all night long, and lo, in the morning the bins of the storeroom were again filled to the brim.

The news of this miracle spread far and wide, and in order to avoid the marks of respect that were being shown her on all sides, she undertook a pilgrimage to Compostela, in Spain, to the grave of St. James the Apostle, and later also to the tombs of the Apostles in Rome.

Upon her return home, Veridiana had an anchorage built hard by the chapel of St. Anthony in Florence. The cell is preserved to this day. It is ten feet long and three and a half feet wide. For furniture there is only a ledge, a foot wide, projecting from the stone wall and serving as a seat. A small window in the cell opens upon the chapel. Through it she could attend holy Mass and receive holy Communion as well as the necessary bodily nourishment.

Veridiana was only twenty-six years old when, with a crucifix in her arms and escorted by her spiritual director and a great number of people, she entered the narrow cell and permitted the door to be immediately walled up. In this voluntary retirement she spent the remaining thirty-four years of her life as an anchoress in prayer and severe penance. In summer her bed was the bare earth; in winter she lay on a board with a block of wood serving as a pillow. Her food consisted of bread and water and herbs. Her only living associates were two large snakes which crept in and out of her cell, with whom she shared her food and her dwelling, in the spirit of penance, for many years.

About the year 1222, when St. Francis was preaching penance in the vicinity of Florence, he also went to visit the poor anchoress, gave her the habit of the Third Order and many beautiful lessons on the proper way to live a contemplative life.

After a very saintly life in which she had been granted the gift of miracles, Veridiana was also privileged with the revelation concerning the hour of her death. She prepared herself with the devout reception of the holy sacraments. While praying the penitential psalms she died on February 1, 1242, being sixty years old. Moved by the many extraordinary miracles that had occurred, Pope Clement VII approved the devotion to her in the year 1533, and later on Pope Innocent XII added his approbation in 1694. Her feast is observed by the Franciscans on February sixteenth, and by the Third Order Regular on the first. (Cf. *These Made Peace*, pp. 12-16; *Forum*, 1948, pp. 41-42.)

ON THE CONTEMPLATIVE LIFE

1. Consider that Blessed Veridiana, after several years spent in a devout active life, was led by divine inspiration to devote herself entirely to a life of contemplation. Perfect contemplation cannot be enjoyed by man until he has entered heaven, where the sole happiness of the blessed consists in beholding God. But the perfect contemplation in heaven gives its name to that form of life here below in which men renounce all aspiration to

material things and, as it were, forget them entirely, in order to spend their lives only in contemplation of the things of heaven. Only souls that have been specially called by God can pursue this kind of life. A previous holy life, as in the case of our anchoress, or severe penance and complete contempt for material comforts, are usually signs of such a vocation. — What high esteem we owe a life so heavenly spent here on earth!

2. Consider the great benefits that accrue to the world from the life of contemplation which is led in so many convents and at times even by private individuals. It is for souls of that kind that almighty God was ready to spare Sodom if even no more than ten of them could be found. Souls of that kind pray for the faithful living in the midst of the turmoil of the world, that the world, the flesh, and the devil may not destroy them, as Moses of old prayed with outstretched arms when Israel was set upon by the Amalekites. "And when Moses lifted up his hands, Israel overcame; but if he left them down a little, Amalec overcame" (Ex. 17,11). What a lack of understanding, then, to say that such a life is useless, or that talent which could have been used to advantage in society is wasted there. Shall we perhaps also call it wasteful to burn the very best oil in the sanctuary lamp?

3. Consider that we are all destined to lead the life of contemplation, inasmuch as it is the only kind of life that is led in heaven. Our first parents lived in most intimate association with God; but sin separated them from Him. They themselves realized that they were no longer worthy to behold Him, and they hid themselves from His sight. Our hearts are, so to say, encrusted with personal sins and evil habits, so that even if we keep ourselves free from mortal sin, we are not capable of permanent intimate association with God. This crust must be removed, and the soul must be cleansed from its scars either here on earth with perfect penance or in the next life in the flames of purgatory. — Let us aim with the help of grace and by means of sincere penance to become worthy of the vision of God soon after death.

PRAYER OF THE CHURCH

O God, who didst unite in Thy servant Veridiana extraordinary fruits of penance with the flower of virginity, grant us, we beseech Thee, that we may through her merits and intercession cleanse our souls with tears of repentance and, thus purified, deserve to be admitted into Thy presence. Through Christ our Lord. Amen.

FEBRUARY 16
BLESSED PHILIPPA MARERI
Virgin, Second Order

PHILIPPA, who belonged to the illustrious family of the Mareri, saw the light of day at the castle of her parents near Rieti in Italy, toward the close of the twelfth century. At a very early age she was the favorite of all who knew her, not only because of her natural gifts, but principally because of her steady advancement in perfection. As a young woman she lived quietly at home, devoted to prayer and the cultivation of her high mental endowments. She took particular pleasure in reading the Holy Scriptures and studying the Latin language, in which she became very proficient.

About this time, St. Francis often visited the valley of Rieti, where he established several convents and sometimes called at the home of the devout Mareri. His forceful admonitions, filled with holy simplicity and unction, and his severe life of penance made a deep impression on Philippa.

It was not long before she resolved to imitate our holy Father, foregoing wealth and consecrating herself entirely to God. She rejected a proposal to marry with the words: "I already have a spouse, the noblest and the greatest, our Lord Jesus Christ." Neither the remonstrances of her parents, nor the ridicule of her brother Thomas, had any effect in changing her mind. She cut off her hair, donned a very coarse garment, and with several companions withdrew to a cave in the rocks of a nearby mountain.

Her austere life of penance and intimate union with God changed the resentment and mockery of her family into admiration. Thomas visited the mountain recess to ask Philippa's forgiveness, and placed at her disposal the church of St. Peter and an adjacent convent once occupied by the Benedictines, over which he was the patron. Full of joy the young community took up its abode there, accepting the place as a gift from heaven. They lived according to the rule of St. Clare under the direction of Blessed Roger of Todi, to whom St. Francis had entrusted the care of their souls.

The new foundation flourished remarkably, and many of the noblest young women joined their ranks. Philippa's excellent example and loving manner were particularly instrumental in bringing about these results. Although she filled the capacity of superior, she was the humblest member of the community. She had no equal in zeal for prayer and mortification, and, like St. Francis and Blessed Roger, she held poverty in the highest esteem. She exhorted her sisters to have no care for the morrow, and more than once in times of need her trust in God was signally rewarded with miraculous assistance.

Philippa had lived and labored and made sacrifices for God for many a year, when it was revealed to her that the time of her dissolution was at hand. She was seized with a fatal illness. Gathering her sisters around her deathbed, she bade them farewell and exhorted them to persevere in their efforts toward perfection, and to remain united in sisterly love. Having received the last sacraments at the hands of Blessed Roger, she addressed to her sisters the words of the Apostle: "The peace of God which surpasses all understanding keep your hearts and minds in Christ Jesus" (Phil. 4,7). Then she expired quietly on February 16, 1236.

Striking miracles occurred on the very day of her burial and many more have occurred since then throughout the years. Shortly after her death Pope Innocent IV approved the veneration paid to her, and Pope Pius VI in 1806 renewed the approbation. To this day very many people journey to the church in which her body, still incorrupt, reposes. The feast of Blessed Philippa is observed by all three branches of the First Order on February sixteenth.

"GODLINESS IS PROFITABLE TO ALL THINGS"

1. Consider how the words of the Apostle, "Godliness is profitable to all things," were verified in Blessed Philippa. In youth she preserved godliness from the dangers which wealth and social position are so apt to bring in their train. Godliness protected her from an unhappy choice of a state of life. It made her happy in her holy vocation in which even her family considered themselves blessed. Finally, it gave her happiness in having so many spiritual daughters gathered about her in the service of the Lord, while it secured her a crown of bliss in eternity, of which the Church herself assures us in her beatification. Hence we see fulfilled in her what the Apostle adds about godliness "having promise of the life that now is and of that which is to come." — If godliness and the fear of the Lord were heeded everywhere by youth, if they were the determining factors in choosing a state of life, everybody would be happier in his state, while the members of the family, though they may have opposed it in the beginning, would thank God that the choice turned out as it did. May you never have the opposite experience!

2. Consider that godliness is as useful in secular life as in the religious state. It takes into consideration, first of all, what is eternal and is

concerned at all times that the soul suffer no harm. That is really the only thing that deserves consideration; for, "what does it profit a man if he gain the whole world and suffer the loss of his own soul?" (Mt. 16,26). What benefit has Dives now of all his wealth? He is suffering the torments of hell. But we may be sure that godliness will avail even in this life to help us receive "what we shall eat and drink and wherewith we shall be clothed" (Mt. 6,31), for "seek first the kingdom of God and His justice and all these things shall be added unto you." Even if godly people ever suffer poverty and want, because God sees that that is profitable to them, they need not be unhappy on that account, though they should suffer as great want as Lazarus; for they know that "the sufferings of this time are not worthy to be compared with the glory to come that shall be revealed in us" (Rom. 8,18). — Have you valued godliness according to its true worth? Consider how piety that proves useless or even hurtful to a good Christian life can by that very fact be recognized as false piety. Through it God is not honored, but "the name of God is blasphemed among the Gentiles" (Rom. 2,24). Praying a great deal, spending a lot of time in church, communicating frequently, going on pilgrimages, and indulging every pious fancy is not necessarily piety. True piety is minded, first of all, to discharge its obligations and attends no services that would interfere with them; for "nothing is pleasing to God," says St. Bernard, "whereby we neglect duty." Genuine piety, furthermore, prefers to do the will of another as far as is possible, rather than its own; it prefers to be governed rather than to govern. It patiently bears with the imperfections of others, and it considers the service it can render the poor and the afflicted as the best service of God. — Is this the kind of piety you possess? May it be given us through the intercession of Blessed Philippa to manifest in ourselves, for the honor and glory of God, the admirable fruits of true godliness.

PRAYER OF THE CHURCH
O God, who dost glorify Thy servant Philippa with great miracles, mercifully grant us that we who devoutly implore her intercession may be granted the wholesome fruits of her prayer. Through Christ our Lord. Amen.

FEBRUARY 17
BLESSED LUKE BELLUDI
Confessor, First Order

HEN St. Anthony in his apostolic zeal was occupied in reforming the inhabitants of Padua, a young man presented himself to him and humbly begged for the habit of the Friars Minor. This was in the year 1220.

Luke Belludi—such was the name of the young aspirant—belonging to one of the noblest families of Padua, had received a brilliant education. Far from imitating the usual conduct of his fellow students at the university, he kept to himself and employed his leisure hours in useful and holy occupations. St. Anthony, who had discovered that Luke had a pure and humble soul, joined with a well-cultivated and talented mind, gladly recommended him to St. Francis, who received him personally into the order.

St. Anthony chose Friar Luke as his companion in the numerous missions which he gave from that time until 1231 at Padua, Rimini, and elsewhere. Luke made wonderful progress in religious perfection under the skillful direction of St. Anthony, whose apostolic labors he continued after the death of the latter.

Padua had at this time fallen into the power of the truculent Ezzelino. Events of the year 1239 filled up the measure of her misfortunes. Many of her nobles were condemned to death, the mayor and his counsellors were banished, and Luke Belludi, the guardian of the Friars Minor, was expelled from the city. Ezzelino gave the government of the city to his nephew Encelino, a man as wicked as he himself. The tyrant, irritated against the unhappy city by reason of her long and heroic resistance, ruled her with an iron grip. This unwarranted conduct was fatal to the university. Padua, formerly so flourishing, rapidly declined; and the beautiful church dedicated to St. Anthony, which had been begun toward the close of the preceding administration, was left unfinished.

Friar Luke, however, had secretly re-entered the city, and remained in careful hiding in the convent of St. Mary. After the night office he and the new guardian frequently spent some time in prayer at St. Anthony's tomb, begging him to come to the assistance of the good city of Padua. One evening as these two holy persons were praying in the chapel dedicated to the saint, a voice suddenly issued from the tomb, assuring them that their prayer was heard, that the city was shortly to be delivered from its tyrannical master. The prediction was verified on June nineteenth.

Because of his great prudence, Luke was elected provincial minister, and as such founded many convents of his order. He was also instrumental in furthering the completion of the basilica of St. Anthony. God granted him the gift of miracles and confirmed his sanctity even in this life.

After he had died in 1287, his body was laid to rest in the same church in which St. Anthony reposes, and was placed in the same marble sarcophagus in which the remains of the great saint were once enclosed.

The veneration accorded to Blessed Luke from the time of his death was continually increased, and Pope Pius XI added his name to the list of the beatified. His feast is observed by the three branches of the First Order on February seventeenth.

ON THE EFFECTS OF THE TRUE LOVE OF GOD

1. The love of God is active in the interests of God. St. Ignatius says that true love of God can be distinguished from false love of God in that it is active; if it does not act, then it is not true love. This love of God produced such powerful effects in Blessed Luke that he sacrificed to God the glory of a great name and the honors and joys which he could lawfully have enjoyed. Such sacrifices are not required of all of us. We should manifest our love of God by keeping His commandments. "If you love Me, keep My commandments" (Jn. 14,15). — Can you lay claim to such love of God?
The love of God causes us to do everything out of love for God. Our Saviour says: "Where your treasure is, there is your heart also" (Mt. 6,21). The fervor of our love must have its source in our heart. Blessed Luke was imbued with but one idea, to be entirely devoted to the service of God and to accomplish his duties from the motive of pure love of God. — Can you say in truth, All for the love of God?
2. To the love of God is attached a great reward. It ennobles the lowliest deeds and makes them meritorious for eternity. It procures for us the remission of our sins, for Christ said of the sinful woman: "Many sins are forgiven her because she has loved much" (Lk. 7,47). Finally, there is reserved "the crown of life which God has promised to them that love Him" (Jas. 1,12). — Strive, therefore, to acquire true love of God and pray earnestly that it may be granted to you.

PRAYER OF THE CHURCH

O God, who hast prepared invisible gifts for them that love Thee, pour forth into our hearts the spirit of Thy love, that we may love Thee in all things and above all things, and may become partakers of Thy promises which surpass all our desires. Through Christ our Lord. Amen.

FEBRUARY 18
BLESSED ANDREW SEGNI
Confessor, First Order

NDREW was born in the thirteenth century at Anagni in the Roman Campagna, of the noble counts of Segni, a most ancient and illustrious family. Many great princes of the Church had already proceeded from this noble family. Among them were the two great popes and protectors of the Franciscan Order, Innocent III and Gregory IX. Alexander IV was Andrew's uncle, Boniface VIII was his nephew.

The road to high honor had opened its portals to him too, but even as a young man he recognized the vanity of the world and renounced it entirely. He left his father's castle and sought another home in the newly founded Franciscan convent of St. Lawrence in the Apennines. There he found a solitary grotto, where, with the permission of the superiors, he made his abode. The cavern was so narrow and low that, because of his tall stature, Andrew was obliged either to kneel or to bend over considerably when he was inside.

In spite of this inconvenience he spent almost his entire life there in the contemplation of heavenly things, practicing great austerities, and struggling almost continually against the evil spirits, over which, with the grace of God, he always emerged the victor. He was diligent also in pursuing the study of the sacred sciences, and was the author of a treatise on the veneration of the Blessed Virgin, which was treasured by his contemporaries, but which has, unfortunately, not survived to our day.

In the year 1295 his uncle, Pope Alexander IV, visited him with the purpose of presenting him with the cardinal's hat. But neither Alexander, nor later Boniface VIII, succeeded in inducing the saint to accept the dignity. This humility made such an impression on Boniface VIII that he expressed the wish to outlive Andrew so that he might have the privilege of canonizing him.

In the last years of his life Andrew was favored with the gift of miracles and of prophecy, and on February 1, 1302, the humble servant of God went forth to receive heavenly honors. His body reposes with the Friars Minor Conventual at St. Lawrence, and he is still signally honored by the people and invoked by them as special protector against the attacks of evil spirits. The uninterrupted veneration accorded Andrew was solemnly approved and confirmed by Pope Innocent XIII, a scion of the same noble family. Blessed Andrew's feast is observed by the Franciscans on February seventeenth, by the Conventuals on the third, and by the Capuchins on the fourteenth.

ON RENOUNCING ONE'S COMFORT

1. Consider how Blessed Andrew sacrificed all the comforts of life he might have enjoyed in the ancestral home of his distinguished family, in order to lead a life of mortification and penance in a poor convent, later repairing to a low and damp cave in which he could not even stand upright. It was their exalted spirit which prompted the saints to renounce the comforts of the body. They understood that the soul soars the higher to its God the more the body is kept in subjection through Christian mortification. They preferred, therefore, to afflict the flesh and cause it discomfort rather than to indulge the natural propensity to ease and comfort. That is what St. Paul teaches us when he says: "For if you live according to the flesh, you shall die; but if by the spirit you mortify the deeds of the flesh, you shall live" (Rom. 8,13). — To what extent have you conformed your conduct to this teaching?

2. Consider how the majority of people are bent on procuring every possible comfort for their bodies. After food and drink, it appears that the main object of all their aim and efforts is their comfort; a fine, comfortable residence, comfortable clothing, a comfortable bed. They consider it so sensible and proper to consult only their comfort that they compliment themselves on not lacking anything by way of comfort for the sake of fashion and vanity. They escape one vice only to succumb to another, and that perhaps a worse one. He who serves the weakness of the flesh often forgets his soul completely; the few devotions he may still be practicing lack vigor, and the worst of it is that he encourages and strengthens in his body an enemy of his soul, laying the latter open to some of the worst temptations. If St. Paul believed that he should discipline his body in order not to be eternally lost, will not a person who is concerned only with pampering the flesh surely glide into the eternal abyss? — Do you perhaps also find yourself on this precipitous path?

3. Consider whence this inclination to effeminacy and love of ease proceeds. On the one hand, it is the result of the general corruption of our nature due to original sin; hence, "the imagination and thought of man's heart are prone to evil from his youth" (Gen. 8,21). On the other hand, it proceeds from the enemy of mankind, the infernal tempter. Those whom

he cannot destroy with vanity, he seeks to pervert by means of sensual pleasure and effeminacy, that after urging them to yield to every bodily delight, he may torment them forever in hell. How many have already been entrapped in his snares! Should we not prefer, like Blessed Andrew, to subject our bodies to occasional inconvenience rather than expose ourselves to such dangers of body and soul?

PRAYER OF THE CHURCH

Protect us, good Lord, in body and soul, through the intercession and merits of Thy blessed confessor Andrew, against all the attacks of the evil spirits, that they may not succeed by their craftiness in making us share in their wickedness, as they aim to make us share in their damnation. Through Christ our Lord. Amen.

FEBRUARY 19
ST. CONRAD OF PIACENZA
Confessor, Third Order

ONRAD was born at Piacenza, Lombardy, in the year 1290, of a very noble family, and while still quite young, he married Euphrosyne, the daughter of a nobleman of Lodi. He had a great fondness for chivalrous sports and was an eager hunter. One time when out hunting, his quarry hid itself in dense underbrush. To force it into the open, Conrad directed his attendants to set fire to the brushwood. The wind, however, drove the flames upon a nearby grain field, where it continued to spread, destroying the entire crop and a large forest besides. The governor of Piacenza at once sent out armed men to apprehend the incendiary.

Filled with consternation at the unfortunate turn of the conflagration, Conrad meanwhile fled into the city along certain lonely roads. The posse, however, came upon a poor peasant who had gathered a bundle of charred fagots and was carrying them into the city. Believing him to be the guilty person, the men seized him. He was tortured on the rack until they wrung from the poor man a statement that he had set fire to the woods out of sheer spite. He was condemned to death.

Not until the unfortunate victim was passing Conrad's house on the way to execution, did Conrad learn why the sentence of death had been imposed on the peasant. Driven by his conscience, Conrad rushed out, saved the man from the hands of the bailiffs, and before all the people acknowledged that he was the guilty person. He went to the governor and explained that the conflagration was the result of a mishap; that he was willing to repair all the damage done. His wife joined him in his good will and sacrificed her dowry to assist in making restitution.

The incident taught Conrad the vanity of the goods of this world, and he resolved to give his attention only to eternal goods. He communicated his sentiments to his wife, and found that she entertained the same ideas. She went to the convent of Poor Clares and received the veil there, while Conrad, who was only twenty-five years old, left his native town and joined a group of hermits of the Third Order.

In a very short time he made such progress in virtue that the fame of his sanctity attracted many of his former friends and acquaintances to his hermitage. But it was Conrad's wish to forsake the world completely; so he slipped away to Rome, and from there went to Sicily, to the Noto valley, near Syracuse, where he hoped he could remain unknown and in utter seclusion. He lived there for thirty-six years, the last of which he spent in a lonely cave on a height since named Mount Conrad.

There Conrad lived an extremely penitential life, sleeping on the bare earth and taking only bread and water with some wild herbs for nourishment. Nevertheless, he was subjected to some of the most terrible assaults of the devil. But by means of prayer and bodily chastisement he put the evil spirit to flight and became so pleasing to God that he was granted the gifts of prophecy and of miracles.

When Conrad perceived that his end was drawing near, he went to Syracuse to make a general confession of his life to the bishop. On the way flocks of birds flew about him and perched on his shoulders as they used to do to St. Francis, and on the way back to his solitude they accompanied him again, to the astonishment of all whom he met. On the very same day he was seized with a fever, which resulted in his death a few days later. He was kneeling before an image of the Crucified when he peacefully passed away on February 19, 1351. In accordance with his wishes he was buried in the church of St. Nicholas at Noto, where his remains still repose in a silver shrine. Many miracles have taken place there. In the year 1515 Pope Leo X permitted his feast to be celebrated at Noto. Urban VIII canonized him in 1625. St. Conrad's feast is observed on February nineteenth by the entire First Order as well as the Third Order Regular.

ON MAKING RESTITUTION

1. Conrad and his wife generously put up their entire fortune to repair the damage caused, without even stopping to think whether they were really bound to make restitution. As a matter of fact the damage was the result of a mischance rather than of any guilt on Conrad's part. But the spirit of God urged him, after overcoming his first fear, to do rather too much than too little, as Zacheus said to our Lord: "If I have wronged any man of anything, I restore him fourfold" (Lk. 19,8). And how did almighty God reward Conrad's magnanimity? The apparent misfortune turned out to be his greatest fortune. Without doubt he would have lived as an ordinary distinguished gentleman, and as such he would have died and appeared before the judgment-seat of God. True, he now led a hard life of severe penance, but at heart he was much happier than before, and he is today numbered among the saints of heaven. Thus are sacrifices, made for conscience' sake, rewarded by God a thousand times.

2. Consider that it is a strict duty to restore what one has unjustly acquired, and to repair the damage one has caused, be it through malice or through guilty carelessness. "If the sinner do penance for his sins," says the Holy Ghost, "and do judgment and justice, and restore the pledge and render what he has robbed, he shall surely live and shall not die" (Ezech. 33,14-15). To regret the wrong done and to confess it, is not sufficient; even if you have prayed much and given plenteous alms on that account, it does not help. "The sin will not be remitted," says St. Augustine, "if that which has been taken is not restored if it can be restored." If you are not in a position to restore, or to restore to the full extent, or if you fear the loss of your good name in consequence, then consult your confessor; he will be able to point out means and ways of fulfilling your obligation and of quieting your conscience. — In serious matters of this nature, have you perhaps set your conscience at rest by means of empty excuses?

3. Consider that in cases where it is entirely impossible to make restitution, a Christian that is interested in his salvation will strive to repair the injustice of which he has been guilty, according to his means and as well as he is able. He can do that, for instance, by prayer, by offering up holy Masses, by penance and other good works, applying the merits to the injured person. In this way he can hope that God will restore what he is physically unable to restore. — In a similar way we must all make restitution to God for whatever we enjoyed against the will of God and His commandments by intemperance, sensuality, and the like, making amends by mortification and renunciation for sins committed by indulging the senses. May the example and intercession of St. Conrad

animate us in such atonement.

PRAYER OF THE CHURCH

Grant, we beseech Thee, O Lord, that as Thou wert pacified by the
penance of Blessed Conrad, so we may imitate his example and blot out
the stains of our sins by crucifying our flesh. Through Christ our Lord.
Amen.

⚜⚜⚜⚜⚜⚜⚜⚜⚜⚜

FEBRUARY 20
BLESSED PETER OF TREJA
Confessor, First Order

 ETER was the son of pious parents at Treja, formerly called
Montecchio, not far from Ancona. He was born about the time
that St. Francis died. Even as a child he was so intent on
perfection that when he was asked on a certain occasion,
"Well, little one, what do you intend to be?" he answered, "I want to be a
saint."

He was no more than a young lad when he decided to escape the
dangers of the world, and sought admission in the recently founded order
of St. Francis. Having stood his probation and made his religious vows, he
went on to higher studies in which he made rapid progress.

As soon as he was ordained a priest, he was appointed to the task of
preaching. He discharged this duty with great zeal, for the honor of God
and the salvation of souls was the only goal he had in mind. He venerated
St. Michael with special confidence as his patron in the struggle against
hell. He had formed an intimate friendship with Blessed Conrad of Offida,
with whom he lived for a time in the convent at Forano. They encouraged
each other in holy zeal, and vied with each other in practicing virtue
rather than in speaking about it.

Peter was often found in ecstasy at prayer and had frequent visions.
St. Michael once appeared to him and asked him what favor he could
obtain for him for all his labor in saving souls. Peter replied humbly: "I ask
only that you obtain for me the remission of my personal sins." He then
received the assurance from heaven that all his sins had been forgiven.

He cherished an ardent devotion for the sufferings of Christ. In his
meditations, he represented them to his mind in so vivid a manner that
they seemed to be enacted before his eyes. His whole body was so affected

at the contemplation that he was often found hovering high in the air before the crucifix.

After a long life of labor and of rigorous mortification, he slept peacefully in the Lord, famed for the miracles he performed both before and after his death. He died on February nineteenth; and his tomb in the Franciscan church at Sirolo near Ancona before the altar of the crucifix became an object of veneration from the beginning. In 1654 his remains were transferred to Treja; and in 1792 Pope Pius VI permitted his feast to be celebrated in the Franciscan Order. It is observed by the Conventuals and Capuchins on February twentieth, and by the Franciscans on the seventeenth.

HOLY FRIENDSHIP

1. How edifying and fruitful of blessing was the holy friendship between Blessed Peter and Blessed Conrad. What is said of the friendship between St. Augustine and Alypius, and between St. Basil and St. Gregory, could readily be said of these two saintly friars: "There appeared to be but one soul in the two bodies." It is as if two flames joined and shone forth in a greater glow. When truly pious souls are joined in intimate friendship, the fire of the love of God and neighbor as well as zeal for virtue are increased. Therefore Holy Writ says of the soul of a faithful friend: "He that has found him has found a treasure; no weight of gold and silver is able to countervail; it is the medicine of life and immortality" (Eccli. 6,14).

2. Consider the path that leads to such friendship. "They that fear the Lord," the Wise Man says again, "shall find a faithful friend; and he that fears God shall likewise have good friendship" (Eccli. 6,16). Genuine and holy friendship can exist only where the fear of the Lord reigns; and if you are God-fearing, you will also prove a true friend. Do not choose your friends only according to their natural good qualities and what you like in them; such friendship will not pass the test and there often results nothing but bitterness. "Of all, therefore, that are dear to you, let Jesus be your special Beloved" (Imit. 2,8). Then you will never trust too securely to human friendship no matter how good it may be, and if you find that you have been deceived, you will not be too disappointed.

3. Consider that if after mature deliberation you have entered upon any friendship, you should also assume certain responsibilities. You owe it to your friends in true charity to encourage them in all that is good and to preserve them from harm. To flatter their faults is really to be a traitor to them. You must stand by your friend in time of need and be willing to make sacrifices for him after the example of our best Friend, Jesus Christ, "who gave His life for His friends" (Jn. 15,13). True friends will also pray

for one another frequently and fervently that their mutual friendship may always become holier and that they may steadily grow in the love of God.

PRAYER OF THE CHURCH

O God, who didst lavish Thy heavenly gifts upon Blessed Peter, Thy confessor, grant, we beseech Thee, that we may rejoice in his protection here on earth and may be partners with him in heavenly glory. Through Christ our Lord. Amen.

FEBRUARY 21
THE SERVANT OF GOD JORDAN MAI
Confessor, First Order

OPE PIUS X once remarked that it is peculiar to the saints of our day that they attain to prominence less through extraordinary deeds than through simple fidelity in their ordinary duties. Such was also the case with this servant of God, all of whose life of virtue and estimation in the eyes of God became known only after his death.

Brother Jordan was born on September 1, 1866, in Westphalia. His parents were poor in earthly possessions, but rich in the fear of God and in thrift. Until he was twenty-nine years old, Henry, as Brother Jordan was known in the world, worked as a simple laborer and a good soldier. In 1895 he became a Franciscan brother and spent the last fifteen years of his life in the Franciscan friary at Dortmund.

In the convent he lived a quiet and retired life, although those who were more closely associated with him, knew him to be a very conscientious, diligent, and humble religious. In his interior life he attained to a high degree of mysticism. After the reception of holy Communion holiness radiated from his eyes. In his humility he copied from our Blessed Lady, and he always regretted that the invocation, "Virgin most humble," was not added to the Litany of Loreto.

His charity towards his neighbor made him particularly agreeable to his fellowmen. No one who ever had any dealings with him, could recall his having in any way, either in word or deed, failed against charity. But he was always on the alert to perform acts of charity for others.

It was one of his greatest delights to serve the priest at holy Mass. Franciscan cheerfulness radiated from his whole being. Only God knows all that he did and suffered and prayed for the conversion of sinners during his lifetime, and still more after his holy death.

On February 20, 1922, he prepared himself for death. "Now I am going to heaven," he said in his simple way to his confessor. The extraordinary answers to prayers directed to him cover such a variety of needs and are so striking that the faithful believe he is really with God, and he has been called "the St. Anthony of Dortmund." The great host of Brother Jordan's clients in the Old and the New World are firmly convinced that the honor of the altars will be granted to him in the near future. His cause of beatification is now under way.

With the approbation of the bishop of Paderborn and in the presence of his representatives, the body of Brother Jordan was exhumed and placed in a new coffin on October 10, 1932. (Cf. *Forum*, 1943, pp. 34-37; 1947, pp. 227-231.)

ON BEING USEFUL IN INFIRMITY

1. Many people are dissatisfied in time of infirmity. They are ill-advised. The Apostle of the Gentiles even says: "I glory in my infirmity" (2 Cor. 11,30). And Brother Jordan, who was exteriorly not attractive, whose talents were hardly average, who was somewhat awkward in his ways, never complained about these deficiencies nor about corporal sufferings. He accepted all with resignation to God, and abided by the principle: "Always be cheerful; God will continue to see you through." — May you also be as happy and as resigned to God's will.

2. Many people consider themselves useless in infirmity. That, too, is foolish. Brother Jordan performed his duties as well as he could; in the eyes of God, that is the main thing. The sense of the words, "Peace to men of good will" (Lk. 2,14), applies in a striking way to Brother Jordan. God looks more to the will than to the deed. And the servant who gained two talents in addition to the two that had been given him, received the same reward as the one who gained five in addition to the five he had (Mt. 25) — Hence, do not lose heart.

3. Infirmity has its advantages. It keeps us little and humble, and preserves us from pride and conceit. It inclines us and prepares us to be indulgent with others. For that very reason our dear Lord took upon Himself the miseries of our human nature so He could "have compassion on our infirmities" (Heb. 4,15). Are you in misery, then pray much for poor sinners, as Brother Jordan did, and you will accomplish more than you imagine. — Rejoice, therefore, in your infirmities.

PRAYER OF THE CHURCH

We beseech Thee, O Lord, through the saving means of Thy mercy, support our infirmities, so that what of its nature tends to sink to earth, may be supported by Thy mercy. Through Christ our Lord. Amen.

***

FEBRUARY 22
ST. MARGARET OF CORTONA
Penitent, Third Order

 HIS Magdalen of the Franciscan Order came into the world in the year 1247 at Laviano near Cortona in the province of Tuscany. When she was seven years old, she lost her pious mother. She was neglected by her careless father, who married again within a short time, and her unsympathetic stepmother dealt harshly with her, so that when Margaret was eighteen years old, she left home to earn her bread among strangers.

She was possessed of rare beauty, and ere long this became a snare for her. For the space of nine years she gave herself up to a life of sin and scandal. Then one day she waited a long time in vain for her accomplice in sin to return home to the place where she lived with him. Presently his dog came to her whining and tugging at her dress. She followed the animal into the heart of a forest, and there she suddenly stood before the blood-stained corpse of the unfortunate man; his enemies had murdered him.

At the appalling sight, Margaret was stunned like one struck by lightning. Filled with terror she asked herself: "Where is his soul now?" Then and there she firmly resolved in future to be even greater in penance than she had been in sin. Like the prodigal son she returned repentant to her native town of Laviano.

In a penitential garb, her hair cut short, a cord around her neck, she knelt at the door of the church and publicly asked all the congregation to forgive the scandal she had given. Many people were edified at this public humiliation, but her stepmother was all the more embittered at it. She, as well as Margaret's father, forbade her to enter the parental home again. This reception severely tempted Margaret to return to the road of vice, but God's grace sustained her.

Led by divine grace, she repaired to Cortona, made a contrite general

St. Margaret of Cortona

confession to a Franciscan there, and submitted to the spiritual direction of her confessor. In a poor little hovel she now lived a secluded life, in penance, tears, and prayer, earning her scanty nourishment by hard manual labor.

Again and again she begged for the habit of the Third Order, that she might be recognized by all the world as a penitent. But not until three years had elapsed and she had been severely tried, was her wish granted. She received the habit in 1277. Now her fervor increased, and it is almost incredible what rigorous penances she practiced from then on. Day and night she wept over her sins, and often sobs so choked her voice that she could not speak. Satan made use of every wile and snare to cause Margaret to relapse, but prayer, mortification, and humiliation successfully put him to flight.

When finally, after uninterrupted struggling, she had triumphed over every earthly inclination, God assured her that her sins were fully pardoned and granted her special proofs of His favor. She was favored with the gift of contemplation and a knowledge of the innermost secrets of hearts. In many an instance, even when people came from great distances, she recalled grievous sins to their mind, while her exhortations and prayers were instrumental in bringing about their conversion. Many souls were released from purgatory upon her prayers. Almighty God wrought many miracles through her even in her lifetime. Health was restored to the sick, a dead boy was raised to life, and at her approach evil spirits shuddered and left those whom they possessed.

Finally, after twenty-three years of rigorous penance, in the fiftieth year of her life, God called the great penitent to the Beatific Vision on February 22, 1297. Her body is preserved in a precious shrine in the Franciscan church at Cortona which bears her name. It is incorrupt even at the present day and frequently emits a pleasant perfume. Several popes have confirmed the public veneration accorded her. Pope Benedict XIII canonized her amid great solemnity in 1728. Her feast is observed by the entire First Order as well as the Third Order Regular on February twenty-second. (Cf. *Forum*, 1947, pp. 35-37; *These Made Peace*, pp. 75-82.)

ON CONTRITION FOR SINS

1. How remarkably the effects of divine grace and mercy manifested themselves in St. Margaret! From all appearances she seemed destined only to become a vessel of divine wrath, and yet she became a brilliant vessel of election. And what brought about the marvelous change? It was her sincere contrition. We must never despair of the conversion of any

sinner; contrition can make a saint of him. You yourself must never despair of your own conversion. No matter how difficult it may be to lay aside certain sinful habits, with the grace of God you will succeed, and He will never deny this grace to a contrite heart. "A contrite and humble heart, O God, Thou wilt not despise" (Ps. 50,19). But sincere contrition is in itself a grace. Do you ever implore the gift from God? Pray especially during the season of Lent for the spirit of penance.

2. Consider what constitutes true contrition. It is sorrow of the soul which detests the sins committed and has the firm resolution not to sin again. Seeing what he has done, considering the punishment he has deserved from a just God, realizing the unworthiness of offending God, who is his greatest benefactor and the greatest and most lovable of all good things, the sinner cries out with a contrite heart: "Oh, how badly I have behaved! Would that I could undo it! Not for all the world will I do it again! Oh, once more, good Jesus, have mercy on me!" If tears follow upon this grief of the soul, they help to increase your remorse and the efficacy of your sorrow; but you can have perfect contrition without tears. On the other hand, no matter how bitterly you were to weep merely on account of disgrace incurred or temporal loss suffered by your sins, it would not suffice for the remission of sins in the sacrament of penance. The thought of having offended God and deserved His punishments must be the cause of your sorrow. Indeed, you should endeavor to awaken perfect contrition, saying for example to your dear heavenly Father: "O my God, so worthy of all my love, greatest and best of all that is good! I grieve from the bottom of my heart that I have offended Thee. Let me rather die than ever offend Thee again." St. Margaret had such contrition; so did St. Mary Magdalen. That is why their many sins were forgiven them, "because they loved much." — Have you endeavored to acquire perfect contrition?

3. Consider that it is a fatal error to believe that, after you have once made an act of contrition for your sins, you may be as unconcerned about them as if nothing had ever happened. "Man knows not," says the Holy Ghost, "whether he be worthy of love or hatred" (Eccli. 9,1). We should again and again make acts of contrition for past sins, and it is good also to confess them again and again subject to the direction of the priest, according to the words of the prophet: "Wash me yet more from my iniquity" (Ps. 50,4). Even if, like St. Margaret, you were assured by divine revelation of the full pardon of your sins, love of God should induce you, as it did her, to keep up in your heart lively sorrow for having offended so good a God. This sorrow should move you to lead a life of penance, and for this reason the holy Fathers tell us that the life of a Christian should be one uninterrupted act of penance. — Can you say this of your life?

PRAYER OF THE CHURCH

O God, who didst bring back Thy servant Margaret from the road of perdition to the way of salvation, grant in the same mercy, that we who once were not ashamed to follow her astray may now be glad to imitate her in penance. Through Christ our Lord. Amen.

FEBRUARY 23

THE SERVANTS OF GOD FREDERICK BACHSTEIN AND COMPANIONS
Martyrs, First Order

EMPEROR RUDOLPH II founded a convent at Prague in the year 1607. It was called St. Mary of the Snow, and committed to the care of the Franciscans, in the hope, as the legal document states, that, true to the tradition of their forebears, they would oppose with zeal and power the rapidly growing spirit of immorality and indifference to God in Bohemia, and would lead the erring back to the right path.

The godly friars began at once by word and deed and by their writings to preach Catholic truth and to refute heresy. In a short time they effected many extraordinary conversions. The Hussites and Calvinists looked with bitter hatred at the flourishing convent and its blessed activities. They waited impatiently for a suitable opportunity to rid themselves forcibly of the entire community of Franciscans.

On February 13, 1611, when the Archduke Matthias and his troops encamped before Prague, a group of conspirators recognized that the long-awaited opportune moment had come. The inmates of the convent of St. Mary of the Snow themselves sensed the evil that was threatening them and prepared themselves for death by prayer and the penitent reception of the holy sacraments. On the morning of February fifteenth an enraged mob, armed with every sort of deadly weapon, stormed into the church and began their work of destruction and of massacre. The marauders pulled down the crucifixes and holy images, robbed the church of its sacred vessels and vestments, and demolished the altars.

The first Franciscan whom they met was Father John Martinez, a Spaniard, who was attempting to save the Blessed Sacrament. With one fell blow they struck off his hand, which fell to the floor together with the ciborium, and the sacred Species were scattered all about the church.

Amid horrible blasphemies the Calvinists trampled on them, and when Father John tried to ward them off, they split his head with a sword. Then the furious mob forced their way into the convent and murdered all who were in it at the time, fourteen in all, including Father John.

They thrust a dagger in the heart of the superior, Father Frederick. Father Simon they struck down with clubs and then stabbed him with daggers and swords. With cudgels they broke every bone in the body of Father Bartholomew of Bergamo, confessor of the Italians. Jerome of Milan, a deacon, was run through with a long sword as he knelt before an image of the Mother of God. The head of Clement, a student in minor orders, was hacked open with a hatchet. Even the aged Brother Christopher was slain with their battle-axes. Jasper of Varese, a subdeacon, and James of Augsburg, in minor orders, as well as the lay brother Didacus, were driven into the tower of the church amid blows from the butt of a gun and jabs from their dirks. From there they were forced on to the roof, where, amid the wild cheers of the mob, they were shot down. They stabbed the novice John of Germany, the lay brother John of Pisa, and the Brothers Emmanuel and Anthony, with swords and halberds till their bodies were hacked and torn to pieces.

The horrible massacre lasted over three hours. On the third day, when the rabble had gradually dispersed, devout Catholics ventured to wrap the precious remains in canvas, and buried them secretly in the transept. Five years later they were exhumed and found wholly incorrupt, their wounds still bleeding and fresh. They were placed in the chapel of St. Michael the Archangel, where they repose to this very day, glorified by many miracles and highly honored by the people. The cause of beatification of these fourteen servants of God has been introduced in Rome.

ON OUR CONDUCT TOWARD PEOPLE OF OTHER FAITHS

1. Consider the inhuman cruelties with which the holy martyrs of Prague were tortured by the heretical Hussites and Calvinists. It happens so often that fanatical heretics entertain a deeper hatred against the Catholic Church and her confessors than do the heathens and the infidels. This is due, principally, to the fact that they have inherited this hatred from the originators of the heresy, who were renegades from the Catholic Church, and, besides, they entertain the lowest ideas of the Catholic Church because she has been misrepresented to them in the grossest way. — What a terrible responsibility the originators of heresy take upon themselves, and how greatly are those people to be pitied who have been born and reared in heresy!

2. Consider how carefully we must guard against being infected with erroneous ideas, especially since we live among people of all faiths and no faith. A mind addicted to faultfinding readily seizes on things it has heard against the faith, or begins to waver in the faith, especially in the case of matters opposed to sensuality or to pride. Yet to depart even from a single teaching of the Catholic Church is to lose the faith and incur the judgment of God. Neither is it of much use to let yourself be involved in a religious argument. Not seldom it only leads to loss of temper and rash assertions, and the other side does not profit by it in any case, for faith is not acquired by disputing about it, but only by childlike submission to the authority of the Catholic Church, "the pillar and ground of truth" (1 Tim. 3,15). St. Peter and the apostles were sent by Christ to teach the nations, and whoever wishes to acquire a knowledge of the true faith, must pay heed to what they taught. So that, if you meet anyone who is really seeking information, introduce him to some priest as a representative of the apostles. But keep aloof from intimate ties with non-Catholics as you would remain away from contagion. — Have you always behaved in such cases as you should have done?

3. Consider, however, that non-Catholics are not to be cut off from our charity, as Christ Himself teaches in the beautiful parable of the Good Samaritan. We must assist them too, should they be in need. In our business and social dealings with them, we should be courteous and friendly, respect them as is proper, and avoid all bitterness toward them. In that way we shall give them the best possible idea of the true Faith. By the fruit they see in us, they will recognize it as a good tree. Finally, following the example of Holy Church, we should pray for non-Catholics, for there are many who are laboring under delusions through no fault of their own.

PRAYER OF THE CHURCH
(Good Friday, for Heretics and Schismatics)

Almighty and eternal God, who savest all and willest none to perish, look on the souls that are seduced by the deceit of the devil, that the hearts of those who err, having laid aside all heretical malice, may repent and return to the unity of Thy truth. Through Christ our Lord. Amen.

FEBRUARY 24
BLESSED MARK MARCONI
Confessor, Third Order

HE son of poor and simple parents, Mark was born about 1480 at Milliarino near Mantua. From early youth he was endowed with a deep sense of piety and gave signs of extraordinary sanctity. At this time there was in Mantua a community of the Poor Hermits of St. Jerome, who had been founded by the Tertiary Blessed Peter of Pisa. In other cities of Italy there were similar communities of hermits; and all of them observed the rule of the Third Order of St. Francis until the year 1568, when they adopted that of St. Augustine. Mark entered the Hermitage of St. Matthew at Mantua when he was still quite young.

From the very beginning of his religious life, Mark won the admiration of the other hermits by the cheerfulness and promptness with which he carried out all the spiritual exercises, those which were ordinary as well as the most difficult. His one desire was to become as perfect an imitator of Christ as possible. He possessed the gift of prophecy and of miracles. The people revered him as a saint, and considered themselves fortunate if they could touch the hem of his garment.

Mark was only thirty when he died on February 24, 1510. His incorrupt body is venerated in the cathedral, and he is called "the Glory of Mantua." The cult of Blessed Mark which continued through the centuries was finally approved by St. Pope Pius X on March 2, 1906. The feast of Blessed Mark is observed on January 25 by the Jeronymites; but his name does not appear in any of the Franciscan calendars, although he may also be counted as one of the "glories" of the Third Order of St. Francis. (Cf. Biersack, pp. 113-114; *These Made Peace*, p. 174; and Heimbucher, vol. 1, p. 595.)

ON LIVING IN THE PRESENCE OF GOD

1. Almighty God said to Abraham: "I am the almighty God; walk before me and be perfect" (Gen. 17,1). Blessed Mark followed this advice in order to arrive at perfection, and his holy life points out what an excellent means it is. By constantly living in the presence of God, he succeeded in avoiding all infidelity in the good use of his time. It will help us to avoid deliberate sin if we keep in mind: Almighty God sees me. For, who would dare to offend a powerful king in his very presence? There is no place on earth nor any secret nook in our heart where God's eye cannot penetrate.
— Have you always thought of this?

2. Consider how living in the presence of God provided Blessed Mark with special light, by which he also learnt to know himself better day by day. Just as, when the sun's beams penetrate a room, we can more plainly see all the particles of dust in the air, which would otherwise be invisible and which we had not realized were there, so will the remembrance of an all-holy God who beholds us, reveal the stains and defects in our hearts of which we should not otherwise have been aware. So, too, when God appears in His glory on the last day, the brilliance will bring all wickedness to light. — Is it not better now to be enlightened by His holy presence, while we can still atone for our sins?

3. Consider that living in God's presence makes us more concerned about the practice of good works. Is there any greater incentive for a servant to do his work well than the fact that his employer is watching him? Will not the thought, then, that God's eye is watching us, be an even greater incentive for us? Often say with Job "Does not He consider my ways, and number all my steps?" (Job 31,4). The remembrance of the presence of God will also support us in suffering and every sort of affliction, as David attests in his tribulations: "I remembered God and was delighted" (Ps. 76,4).

PRAYER OF THE CHURCH
(Twenty-first Sunday after Pentecost)

We beseech Thee, O Lord, of Thy loving kindness, ever guard Thy household, that it may be freed from all adversities by Thy protection and in good deeds may be devoted to Thy name. Through Christ our Lord. Amen.

❦❦❦❦❦❦❦❦❦❦❦

FEBRUARY 25
BLESSED SEBASTIAN OF APARICIO
Confessor, First Order

 EBASTIAN was born of poor peasants in the year 1502, at Gudena in the Spanish province of Galicia. In his youth he attended his father's sheep. When he was twelve years old, he was seized with a pestilential disease. His anxious mother carried him to a little hut far out in the field, so that no one else would be infected by him. While he lay there one day quite helpless and alone, a wolf from the neighboring woods approached by the providence of God, and bit open the plague spot with the result that Sebastian recovered completely.

When he arrived at young manhood, he left home to look for work among strangers in order to support his poor parents and his brothers and sisters. Because he was comely in appearance, wicked women frequently set snares for his purity. In order to escape them, he resolved, at thirty-one years of age, to sail for America which had been discovered recently. On the voyage he had to endure much ridicule from the sailors and his fellow passengers because of his piety and reserve.

Arriving safely at Puebla, Mexico, he at once resumed work in the fields. Also, he made plows and wagons, which were until then unknown to the half-civilized inhabitants, and taught them how to use them. With his team he plowed the fields of as many of the people as possible, never asking any compensation. He also built roads through the forests and mountains to the cities and seaports, making it easier to transport the produce. The main highway that to this day connects the mountain city of Zacatecas with the capital of Mexico is his work.

He undertook, in a carrier of his own, to transport grain and other wares, thus acquiring great wealth. He used the money for worthy purposes, while he himself lived like a poor man. In this way he won the esteem and the love of the natives as well as of the Spaniards. He married twice, each time choosing a poor but devout young woman; and with their consent he lived with them in virginal purity.

When death robbed him of his second wife, he gave all his possessions to the poor and to a convent of Poor Clares which he had established in Mexico City. Then, in the year 1573, when he was already seventy-one years old, he asked for admission among the lay brothers in the Order of St. Francis. It was only after frequent and urgent requests that his petition was finally granted. In the novitiate he would not exempt himself from any of the hardships or works of penance, though he was an old man; he outdid even the most zealous of the young brothers.

After he had made his solemn vows, he was appointed to the task of collecting alms for the convent. He performed this trying task for the remainder of his mortal life to the great edification of the brethren and of the faithful. Despite the many distractions that his work afforded, he was able to keep recollected in God, and his encouragement and example were instrumental in gaining many infidels and sinners for God.

He added certain rigorous penances to his daily labors, and God, who does not let Himself be outdone in generosity, granted him extraordinary graces. Sebastian could read the innermost secrets of hearts and could foretell future events. The wildest animals willingly obeyed him; and frequently, when he was in special need, angels brought him assistance in remarkable ways, at times bringing him food, another time protecting him from falling down a precipice, at other times again directing him on the right road.

In his ninety-eighth year Sebastian died in the convent at Puebla on February 25, 1600. When his body lay in state, the crowds that gathered were so great, and the miracles wrought were so numerous, that he could not be buried for a long time. More than three hundred miracles which he worked in his lifetime were cited at the process of beatification. Pope Pius VI beatified him in 1787; and efforts are being made in Mexico to have his cause of canonization introduced. The Franciscans observe his feast on February twenty-fifth.

ON BEING SOLICITOUS FOR THE GENERAL WELFARE

1. In the life of Blessed Sebastian we see that true piety is not only profitable in many ways, but aims to be useful to all men. As a youth the devout Sebastian went to work among strangers in order to support his parents and brothers and sisters; and as a man, he promoted the interests of his countrymen in temporal as well as in spiritual matters. That is practical Catholicity — to think not only of oneself but also of the welfare of others, first of all of one's family, but then also of the community of which one is a member, the country in which one lives, in fact, of all Christendom and of all men. Thus St. Paul could say of himself: "Not seeking that which is profitable to myself but to many" (1 Cor. 10,33), and: "I became all things to all men" (1 Cor. 9,22). "Nature," says Thomas a Kempis (3,54), "labors for its own interests and considers what gain it may derive from another. But grace considers not what may be advantageous and profitable to self, but rather what may be beneficial to many." — Do the interests of nature or of grace dominate your soul?

2. Consider that many are obliged by their position to promote the general welfare. Office-holders, whether in temporal or spiritual matters, must administer their charge conscientiously, faithfully, and well, since the welfare of many depends on it. The head of any society and all who as members of his staff take part in its government, must do their best to make the society function properly for the common good. Finally, those whose duty it is to vote for an office-holder in the State or in the Church, must conscientiously cast their ballots without regard of persons, so that the result will advance the common good of those to be governed. — Have you perhaps taken an indifferent attitude in such matters, or been unmindful of your duty?

3. Consider that every member of society can and should be solicitous for the common good. This can be done by joining societies organized for purposes of charity and the general welfare, or by gifts and regular contributions to such purposes and institutions. It is far more meritorious to make such gifts according to one's means during one's lifetime than to do it only after one's death by way of legacy. Another way in which we can be solicitous for the general good is to pray for it. Christ our Lord taught us to pray in the "Our Father" not only for ourselves individually but for "us," that is, for all our fellowmen. Say this prayer frequently just for that purpose. Holy Church also urges prayer for the general welfare when she has the priest pray with the people at Sunday Mass for the special needs of Christendom. — May the grace of God grant us the spirit of charity with which Blessed Sebastian was endowed!

PRAYER OF THE CHURCH

O God, who didst permit Blessed Sebastian, Thy confessor, to live in simplicity of heart and to be overwhelmed with heavenly gifts, mercifully grant at his mediation, that we may serve Thee with chaste hearts and obtain the gifts of Thy grace. Through Christ our Lord. Amen.

***

FEBRUARY 26
BLESSED ANGELA OF FOLIGNO
Widow, Third Order

NGELA was born in 1248 of a prominent family in Foligno, three leagues from Assisi. As a young woman, and also as a wife and mother, she lived only for the world and its vain pleasures. But the grace of God intended to make of her a vessel of election for the comfort and salvation of many. A ray of the divine mercy touched her soul and so strongly affected her as to bring about a conversion.

At the command of her confessor she committed to writing the manner of her conversion in eighteen spiritual steps. "Enlightened by grace," she wrote in this account, "I realized my sinfulness; I was seized with a great fear of being damned, and I shed a flood of tears. I went to confession to be relieved of my sins, but through shame I concealed the most grievous ones, but still I went to Communion. Now my conscience tortured me day and night. I called upon St. Francis for help, and, moved by an inner impulse, I went into a church where a Franciscan Father was then preaching.

"I gathered courage to confess all my sins to him, and I did this immediately after the sermon. With zeal and perseverance I performed the penance he imposed, but my heart continued to be full of bitterness and shame. I recognized that the divine mercy had saved me from hell, hence I resolved to do rigorous penance; nothing seemed too difficult for me, because I felt I belonged in hell. I called upon the saints, and especially upon the Blessed Virgin, to intercede with God for me.

"It appeared to me now as if they had compassion on me, and I felt the fire of divine love enkindled within me so that I could pray as I never prayed before. I had also received a special grace to contemplate the cross on which Christ had suffered so much for my sins. Sorrow, love, and the desire to sacrifice everything for Him filled my soul."

About this time God hearkened to the earnest desire of the penitent: her mother died, then her husband, and soon afterwards all her children. These tragic events were very painful to her; but she made the sacrifice with resignation to the will of God. Being freed from these ties, she dispossessed herself of all her temporal goods with the consent of her confessor, so that being poor herself, she might walk in the footsteps of her poor Saviour. She also entered the Third Order of St. Francis, and presently found herself the superior and guide of others who followed in her path. Many women joined her, even to the point of taking the three vows. She encouraged them in works of charity, in nursing the sick, and in going personally from door to door to beg for the needs of the poor.

Meanwhile, Angela became still more immersed in the contemplation of the Passion of Christ, and she chose the Sorrowful Mother and the faithful disciple John as her patrons. The sight of the wounds which her Lord suffered for her sins urged her to the practice of still greater austerities. Once our Lord showed her that His Heart is a safe refuge in all the storms of life. She was soon to be in need of such a refuge.

God permitted her to be afflicted with severe temptations. The most horrible and loathsome representations distressed her soul. The fire of concupiscence raged so furiously that she said: "I would rather have beheld myself surrounded with flames and permitted myself to be continually roasted than to endure such things." Still, she called out to God: "Glory be to Thee, O Lord! Thy cross is my resting place." These painful trials lasted over two years; but then the purified and tried servant of the Lord was filled with great consolations. She obtained a marvelous insight into divine things and was very frequently found in ecstasy. For many years holy Communion was her only food, until at last, completely purified, she entered into the eternal joy of the Supreme Good on January 4, 1309.

Pope Innocent XII approved the continual devotion paid to her at her tomb in Foligno. He beatified her in 1693. The Franciscans celebrate her feast on February 28, but the Conventuals and the Third Order Regular observe it on January fourth. (Cf. *These Made Peace,* pp. 82-88.)

ON THE BENEFIT OF TEMPTATIONS

1. Consider how Blessed Angela had to pass through many painful steps in order to arrive at true conversion. True conversion is not accomplished as easily and as soon as many people believe. One of these steps consisted in enduring temptations. This was one of the most painful stages, but it is in this way that God wishes to try the fidelity of His servants. Moses spoke thus to the chosen people of God: "The Lord your God tries you that it may appear whether you love Him with all your soul, or no" (Deut. 13,3). What pleasure it is when the temptation has been overcome, to know that one has stood the test! — Have you ever partaken of this joy after your temptations?

2. Consider that temptations are also a means by which we may learn to know ourselves and our weaknesses. Thomas a Kempis (1,13) says: "Temptations show us what we are." Sometimes we do not think it possible that we could fall into this or that sin into which a fellowman has fallen. But if severe temptation assails us, we readily join with the Psalmist in declaring: "Unless the Lord had been my helper, my soul had almost dwelt in hell" (Ps. 93,17). Temptation does not make us weak, it merely shows us how weak we are. Such experiences cause us to be kinder in our judgments of others and more cautious in our own conduct. If David became an adulterer and a murderer through a glance at Bethsabee, may we then play with danger like a gnat flying about a glowing flame? "Watch and pray that you enter not into temptation" (Mt. 26,41).

3. Consider that temptations impel us to draw nearer to God and to unite ourselves more closely to Him. As a child runs to its mother when danger threatens, and hides itself in her lap, so a Christian who loves his soul will have recourse to God in time of danger. And just as the tree strikes its roots deeper into the earth when storms whip its crown, so does the Christian attach himself more firmly to God during the storm of temptation. While we acknowledge in the time of temptation that of ourselves we are nothing, we also acknowledge that God is our all: our

only hope, our support, our salvation. This acknowledgment is a great boon. Blessed Angela says: "To know oneself and to know God, that is the perfection of man; without this knowledge, visions and the greatest gifts are of no account."

PRAYER OF THE CHURCH

O God, Thou sweetness of hearts and light of the inhabitants of heaven, who didst refresh Blessed Angela, Thy servant, with a marvelous insight into heavenly things, grant us through her merits and intercession so to know Thee upon earth, that we may be found worthy to rejoice in the vision of Thy glory in heaven. Through Christ our Lord. Amen.

FEBRUARY 27
BLESSED LOUISE ALBERTONI
Widow, Third Order

LOUISE first saw the light of the world at Rome in the year 1474. Her parents belonged to the distinguished families of this city because of their wealth, but still more because of their piety. They bestowed great care upon the training of their daughter, and she responded fully to their efforts, so that she developed into a model for all young women. She had resolved to remain unmarried; but when her parents urged her to be betrothed to an illustrious young man, she believed she recognized the will of God in their desire and agreed to the marriage.

But even in the married state, in which she remained attached to her husband in genuine love, she sought above all things to please God. Her attire was very plain, and even away from home she avoided frivolous pomp and luxury. God blessed their union with three daughters, whom she was careful to rear above all in the love and fear of God.

When she was but thirty-three years old, she lost her husband in death. After her daughters were provided for, Louise thought of nothing but to dedicate herself to the service of God. Publicly she took the habit of the Third Order, practiced the severest penances, and was so irresistibly drawn to the contemplation of the sufferings of our Lord and they were so constantly before her mind, that she continually wept, and it was feared that she would lose her sight.

She bore a special love toward the poor as special members of Christ. She used the abundant income of her fortune entirely for their support. But she strove to conceal her liberality. With this intention she often hid pieces of money in the bread that was given to the poor at her door, and then begged almighty God that He would let it fall to the lot of such as needed it most. Her benevolence knew no bounds. Sometimes she lacked even the necessaries for herself. But then she rejoiced to be like Christ, who, being rich, became poor out of love for men.

God repaid her with extraordinary graces. He granted her the gift of miracles and frequent ecstasy. He also told her beforehand of the day of her death.

When her end drew nigh, she received the last sacraments with great devotion. Then looking at the crucifix with the tenderest pity, she kissed it and said: "Into Thy hands, O Lord, I commend my spirit." Thereupon she breathed forth her soul on the day that had been announced to her, which was January 31, 1533. Her body rests in the church of St. Francis on the Tiber, and her feast is celebrated in Rome with great solemnity. Pope Clement X beatified her in 1671. The Franciscans observe her feast on February twenty-eighth, and the Third Order Regular on January thirty-first. (Cf. *These Made Peace*, pp. 182-187.)

TO LOVE GOD ABOVE ALL THINGS

1. Consider that amid all the things in this world that were dear to her, Blessed Louise loved God above them all. She loved her parents, she loved her spouse, she loved her children, but she loved God more. In fact, she loved them only because and as God wanted it, and never out of love for them would she have done anything displeasing to God. Thus must every Christian love God above all things, because God is the highest good, the most worthy to be loved. — Do you love God in this manner? Have you not, perhaps, preferred the friendship of men to the friendship of God? Have you, perhaps, even loved your convenience, your vanity, your honor more than God?

2. Consider that we should love God with our whole heart, with our whole soul, and with all our mind, that is, all our thoughts, words, and actions should be directed toward God. Even thus did Louise love God above all things, and truly lived only for Him throughout her life. Can you say that of yourself? To what are your first thoughts in the morning directed? Through the day, what do you most frequently think about, and with the greatest pleasure? Oh, what shame if we must say that we are filled with the world and ourselves, and that we love God very little or not at all!

3. Consider how the charity of Blessed Louise towards God showed itself especially in active love towards the members of Christ. Such charity is a fruit of true love of God, and at the same time a means to grow in that love. In order, however, that charity towards our neighbor may produce this fruit, we must see in the poor and in every person to whom we render an act of charity, the person of Christ, who, as a matter of fact, is ready to accept it as if done to Him, since He Himself says: "As long as you did it to one of these My least brethren, you did it to Me" (Mt. 25,40). Accordingly, too, as St. Augustine assures us, He will requite it the way He repaid the food He received in the house of Martha and Mary: while He was being fed corporally, He fed them spiritually, so that Martha and Mary advanced in grace and the love of God.

PRAYER OF THE CHURCH

O God, who, among other exceptional gifts, didst mercifully grant to Blessed Louise a remarkable and truly singular love towards the poor of Christ, grant us, Thy servants, through her intercession and merits, that charity with which we may love Thee above all things with our whole heart. Through Christ our Lord. Amen.

FEBRUARY 28
BLESSED ANTONIA OF FLORENCE
Widow, Second Order

ORN of a noble family at Florence, Italy, in 1401, Antonia entered the married state at a very early age, in compliance with the wish of her parents. When her husband died in 1428, she allowed nothing to induce her to contract a second marriage, but resolved to withdraw from the world and live only for God and the salvation of her soul.

In the following year she entered the convent of Tertiaries which Blessed Angelina had recently founded at Florence. Here she so distinguished herself by virtue and wisdom, that after a few years the superiors called her to Foligno to preside as superior of the convent there.

Although in her humility she found it difficult to accept the advancement, she was happy to carry out the appointment under the guidance of Blessed Angelina, who, as superior general of the several convents she had founded, dwelt at Foligno. Antonia so availed herself of the opportunity to profit by the holy example and the good counsel of the foundress, that she could be held up as a model superior.

In consequence, after a few years, she was sent to establish a convent in Aquila. There, under her maternal direction, a veritable sanctuary of holiness budded forth, the fame of which brought joy to that city and the entire vicinity.

Although the religious community zealously served God according to the rule of the Third Order, it did not satisfy Blessed Antonia in her yearning for personal perfection. She felt strongly drawn to a stricter life, to more perfect poverty, and to more complete renunciation of the world, as practiced in the Order of St. Clare.

At a visitation she communicated her desire to her spiritual director, St. John Capistran. He approved it, and at his suggestion and with the sanction of the Holy Father, a new convent of the Poor Clares was founded at Aquila, which Antonia with twelve consecrated virgins entered in 1447. She was appointed superior and abbess; but, while she occupied the highest place, she always strove to find the last. The lowliest tasks, worn clothes, the most disagreeable occupations she assigned to herself, while she shunned all honor and distinction. In all she did and said there shone forth the most sincere humility.

Just as pronounced was the patience with which she bore the burdens of her position, the weaknesses of all her subjects, the many importunities of her relatives, and finally the sufferings of a lingering illness.

While she was extraordinarily severe with herself, she possessed truly motherly concern for her sisters. They in turn clung to her with filial love, and when after seven years of administration she was relieved of the burden, she was still considered by the sisters as their mother and model.

God distinguished His faithful servant with special graces. Her prayer amounted to perfect contemplation of heavenly things, the ardor of her devotion sometimes causing her to be raised aloft bodily. Once a glowing sphere was seen suspended over her head.

She reached the age of seventy-one years, and died on February 18, 1472, addressing words of comfort and holy exhortation to her sorrowing fellow sisters about her. Numerous miracles occurred at her grave, and her body is a constant miracle, for, up to the present time it is preserved wholly incorrupt and is of an extraordinary freshness which is emphasized by the open eyes. The uninterrupted veneration which began with the day of her death received the sanction of Pope Pius IX. The feast of Blessed Antonia is observed by the Franciscans and the Capuchins on February twenty-eighth.

ON STRIVING FOR PERFECTION

1. Consider the earnest endeavor to reach perfection which filled the heart of Blessed Antonia; it carried her to the heights of holiness. In a more eminent way religious are obliged to strive after perfection, but Christians in every station of life must aim to become better and more perfect. Christ Himself holds up for all the highest pattern of perfection when He says: "Be you therefore perfect as also your heavenly Father is perfect" (Mt. 5,48). He who does not strive to become better will become worse, because a standstill is not possible on the road to Christian living. "He who does not go forward," says St. Bernard, "goes backward." — Are you advancing or going backward?

2. Consider how Blessed Antonia laid the foundation of profound humility for the structure of perfection. We cannot arrive at perfection in any other way. "Do you wish to be great," says St. Augustine, "then begin with the least; do you plan to erect a stately edifice, then think first about the foundation of humility." Humility is also a necessary companion on the road to perfection; the more perfect a person becomes, so much more humble he becomes indeed. Just as in studying the sciences, the farther a person proceeds the more he realizes how far the sphere of learning extends and how little he knows about it, so do we learn more and more how great and sublime virtue is as we advance in perfection; and our humility grows as we realize more and more how far we still are from perfection. — If you wish to know how far you have advanced in perfection, test the measure of your humility.

3. Consider how Blessed Antonia arrived at perfection on the path of patience. It is not necessary to do extraordinary things in order to advance in virtue. One needs only to make use of the circumstances that Providence sends. If in our daily reverses, small as well as great, we always preserve holy patience, we shall find ourselves advancing daily in perfection much as one is pushed forward by the press in a crowded church. The salvation of our soul is wrought through Christian patience, as our Lord says: "In your patience you will possess your souls" (Lk. 21,19), and St. James (1,14) writes: "Patience perfects the work." — May we practice it faithfully in imitation of Blessed Antonia!

PRAYER OF THE CHURCH

O God, who didst marvelously lead Blessed Antonia, Thy servant, through all the paths of life to Thee, grant, we beseech Thee, that through her merits and example we may arrive at our heavenly home. Through Christ our Lord. Amen.

MARCH

MARCH 1
VENERABLE FRANCIS GONZAGA
Confessor, First Order

FRANCIS, a scion of the illustrious house of Gonzaga, was born in the year 1546 at Gazzolo near Mantua, and was given the name Hannibal in holy baptism. Indications of his high calling were in evidence early in life; has companions were accustomed to call him the "little friar," because of his modesty, his piety, and his special attraction for religious. When his elementary studies had been completed, he was sent to the Spanish court to be educated with the son of King Philip II; but here also he lived not for the world but for God and for his studies.

He had listened to a sermon on the vanities of the world delivered by a renowned Franciscan preacher, and this, together with the reading of the history of the order, caused him to resolve to don the Franciscan habit. Despite all obstacles and contrary to the will of the king, Philip II, who had great plans in mind for this talented young man, he entered the convent at Alcalá on May 17, 1562, and received in religion the name of Francis.

When his studies were completed, he was sent back to Italy. There he taught theology in the convent at Mantua; and in the year 1578 he was elected provincial of the province of St. Anthony in the duchy of Mantua. The general chapter which convened in Paris in 1579, elected him minister general of the entire order.

For eight years he administered this responsible office with superior wisdom, great zeal for religious discipline, and such deep humility that he joined his brethren in the performance of the lowliest duties, and was not ashamed to beg from door to door for food for the brethren. Filled with zeal for the welfare of his order, he undertook the visitation of the provinces of Spain, France, the Netherlands, and Germany, always making his journeys on foot.

At the Spanish court he put the vocation of his holy nephew, Aloysius Gonzaga, to the test, because the youth's father had requested it of him. Having recognized his calling to the Society of Jesus as coming from on

142

high, Francis took him along on his return journey to Italy and zealously strove to remove the obstacles that were preventing his admission.

Francis also wrote a famous history of the Seraphic Order which enjoys great distinction even to this day. It is dedicated to Pope Sixtus V, who himself belonged to the Franciscan Order.

Several times Francis was nominated by the popes for the highest ecclesiastical honors; but the humble servant of God was able to induce them to refrain from the nomination. However, in the year 1587, by order of Pope Sixtus V, he was obliged to accept the bishopric of Cefalu in Sicily, and from there he was transferred to the bishopric of Mantua. But even as a prince of the Church he wore the coarse habit of St. Francis under the episcopal robes, and despite the great strain of his labors, he practiced the same rigorous penance as formerly in his convent.

When King Philip II of Spain and Henry IV of France waged a bitter war against each other, Pope Clement VIII sent Francis as his legate to the princes to negotiate terms of peace. His great prudence effected the desired result.

After a successful administration of the diocese of Mantua, which extended over twenty-seven years, Francis died in the odor of sanctity on March 11, 1620, in the seventy-fourth year of his life.

When Pope Paul V learned of his death, he cried out: "He was a great servant of God, a mirror and example to all prelates of Holy Church." Many miracles have occurred at his grave, and the Holy See has introduced the process of his beatification. His body, still garbed in the Franciscan habit beneath the episcopal robes, reposes before the high altar in the cathedral at Mantua, and was found intact as late as the year 1866.

ON CHRISTIAN WISDOM

1. Consider how Christian wisdom shone forth in the life of Venerable Francis. This virtue consists, first of all, in estimating all things according to their true worth. Francis did that. In consequence, he preferred the service of God to the service of an earthly king. For that reason, too, he declined high honors and preferred to serve God in poverty and seclusion rather than in wealth and in an elevated position with its great responsibility. It is wisdom of this type that Christ recommends: "Be wise as serpents" (Mt. 10,16): for serpents protect their heads, the most important organ, above all else, even though their bodies must suffer. And so a wise Christian should above all else concern himself about that which is most important, his soul. In order to protect it from harm and to preserve a good conscience, he readily foregoes material things. The

wisdom of the world and of the flesh, on the other hand, eagerly strives for the false goods of wealth, of honor, and of appetite, even if the eternal goods must thereby be sacrificed. — Have you until now possessed worldly wisdom or Christian wisdom?

2. Consider that Christian wisdom must manifest itself in applying the proper means for the acquisition of the true and eternal goods, according to the circumstances of time, place, and person. Venerable Francis did this so prudently that he met with the happiest results in the government of the order no less than in the episcopate, and in mediating peace between princes. Many a one desires what is good, but his imprudent zeal, his lack of patience and foresight cause him more frequently to be hindered than benefited by it. Hence the Holy Spirit says: "Wisdom orders all things sweetly" (Wisd. 8,1); and in the Book of Proverbs (14,29) we read: "He that is patient is governed with much wisdom; but he that is impatient, exalts his folly." — How do you conduct yourself?

3. Consider how necessary it is to possess Christian wisdom. Theologians class it as the first of the four cardinal virtues, and St. Bernard says: "Prudence is the regulator and guide of the other virtues; take it away and virtue is no more a virtue but a fault." It is not only a necessary qualification for men in official positions or in public life, but also for women in the circle of their homes. Hence the Apostle writes: "The aged women may teach the younger women to be wise," — and how? —"to love their husbands, to love their children, to be discreet, chaste, sober, having care of the house, gentle, obedient to their husbands" (Tit. 2,4-5). Christian wisdom is not a gift of nature, but rather a gift of grace, for which we should, like Solomon, earnestly beseech God.

PRAYER OF THE CHURCH (Sixth Sunday after Epiphany)
Grant, we beseech Thee, almighty God, that being ever occupied with holy thoughts, we may seek, both in words and works, to do what is pleasing in Thy sight. Through Christ our Lord. Amen.

MARCH 2
THE SERVANT OF GOD PHILIPPA OF LORRAINE
Widow, Second Order

HILIPPA, the daughter of Adolph, duke of Gelderland, was born in 1462 and spent the early years of her life in innocence and piety. Later on she married René II, duke of Lorraine and governor of Sicily. God blessed their marriage with three daughters and nine sons, of whom only four outlived their father: Anthony, called the Good, duke of Lorraine; Claude, duke of Guise; John, archbishop of Narbonne and cardinal; and Francis of Lorraine.

Philippa had her children carefully educated. She exercised a wholesome influence also over her husband and urged him to many good works. He built a Franciscan convent at Nancy, and Philippa, special benefactor of the friars, provided the altars and the sacred vestments for their church.

When René died in 1508, the eldest son was still a minor. Philippa was obliged to govern the duchy for eleven years. She proved to be as prudent as she was pious. As soon as her son became of age, she transferred the government to him and, in 1520, entered the convent of the Poor Clares Colettine at Pont à Mousson. Here she submitted to all the austerities of the order with great zeal, and became a mirror of obedience and humility to everyone.

The former princess cheerfully performed the lowliest duties, and steadfastly declined every preferment and position of honor. Through her son the cardinal she managed to obtain a mandate prohibiting the sisters from ever electing her abbess. Every reminder of her noble descent and former rank was unpleasant to her. She said: "I have no other name but Sister Philippa, the poor little earthworm."

The fame of her sanctity attracted many devout and noble women to her to obtain advice and consolation, and she gladly used every opportunity to comfort the sorrowing, strengthen the wavering, advise the doubtful, and encourage the wealthy to be beneficent. But she found her greatest delight in prayer and in the meditation on the Passion of our Lord, especially at the Gethsemane or Calvary grottoes which she had built in the convent garden. Often she was so affected interiorly during these meditations that the sisters would find her unconscious.

Her love of God and neighbor was generously repaid by God Himself. She received the gifts of contemplation, of ecstasy, and of foreseeing future events. Thus, on February 24, 1525, she beheld how her son Francis fought bravely and fell in the bloody battle of Pavia, and urged her sisters to pray for him and the others who had fallen. After several days word was brought which confirmed her vision in detail.

Philippa had spent twenty-seven years in the convent and had borne her last painful illness with admirable patience, when she died peacefully in the Lord in 1547 at the age of eighty-five. She was laid to rest in the chapel of the Immaculate Conception which she had built adjoining the church of the Poor Clares at Pont à Mousson.

ON THE DUTIES OF ONE'S STATE IN LIFE

1. Consider the zeal with which Blessed Philippa performed the duties of her state both as mother and as reigning princess, although they held no natural appeal for her. She would very much have preferred to remain a virgin and devote herself to a quiet and contemplative life. Still "the heart of man disposes his way, but the Lord must direct his steps" (Prov. 16,9). God's way led her to the married state and she became the mother of twelve children. In addition she had to take over the government of her country. Neither may we follow our inclinations, even if they tend toward what is good and pious, if we thereby neglect the duties of our place in life. How could we justify that neglect when God calls us to account for the discharge of the duties He has entrusted to us?

2. Consider how many people neglect the duties of their place in life under pretext of working for the common good. They are much concerned about the administration of matters both temporal and spiritual, they are active in various societies and collect for them, and in the meantime they neglect their household duties. That cannot be pleasing to God, for the Apostle, inspired by the Holy Ghost, writes: "But if any man have not care of his own, and especially for those of his house, he is worse than an infidel" (1 Tim. 5,8). And to the Thessalonians he writes: "Use your endeavor to be quiet and do your own business" (1 Tim. 4,11). Moreover, it is impossible to promote the common good in that way. We all make up one body, of which each one is an individual member, and just as the welfare of the entire body depends on each member functioning properly, so the welfare of human society depends upon each member faithfully performing the duties of his vocation. You may lend yourself to the care of others and the common good only so far as your special duties permit. — Have you acted in this way in the past?

3. Consider that no doubt some people neglect their vocational duties and more readily follow their pious inclinations or concern themselves about others, because they have not the courage and confidence necessary to face the duties of their state. Always to fulfill those duties in a perfect

manner is indeed impossible if we are left to ourselves. But God, who has called us to our state in life, will also help us perform its duties properly. We must do what lies in our power, and then confidently count on His assistance. It is Catholic teaching that if we do our part, God will provide His grace for the accomplishment. — Has a lack of confidence and of prayer been the cause of your negligence?

PRAYER OF THE CHURCH
(Third Secret under "Various Prayers")

Grant unto us Thy servants, O Lord, the pardon of our sins, comfort in life, and continual guidance; that, serving Thee, we may deserve duly to attain to Thy mercy. Through Christ our Lord. Amen.

MARCH 3
THE SERVANT OF GOD LIBERATUS WEISS
Martyr, First Order

ATHER Liberatus Weiss was born on January 4, 1675, at Konnersreuth, Bavaria. He entered the Franciscan Order in 1693 at Graz in Styria, and was ordained to the priesthood on September 14, 1698, at Vienna, Austria. After his ordination he labored in the vineyard of the Lord at Langenleis and Graz in Austria. Full of enthusiasm for missionary work, he was sent to the missions of Abyssinia in Africa in 1704. Appointed superior of the mission, he set out with two Italian Franciscan missionaries, Fathers Samuel and Michael. After unspeakable difficulties they reached Gondar, the capital of Abyssinia, in 1712. With intrepid courage they preached the true faith to the schismatic inhabitants.

When the missionaries began to reap the first fruits of their labor, a persecution broke out against them. They could have saved their lives by adopting the schismatic religion of the country, but they refused to accept this offer of the king, declaring publicly: "If we had a thousand lives to lose, we would rather die a thousand times. You may do to us whatever you wish. We are ready."

They were led out of the city and stoned to death. This was in 1716. The veneration given them by the faithful has been rewarded with miracles and the granting of many favors. Their beatification is pending. Let the faithful have recourse to the servants of God in all their needs.

May God glorify them still more, and grant many graces to all who ask for their intercession.

ON INTREPID COURAGE

1. Is there any vocation that calls for a greater amount of physical and spiritual courage than that of the missionary to foreign lands? These men and women are obliged to leave their kindred and friends to live not only among strangers, but among people who in many instances are only half-civilized or meagerly educated, and frequently very inimical to them. They must adapt themselves to customs that frequently prove a severe test even to the strongest physique. Hardships are for the most part their daily bread, and yet, knowing all this in advance, they undertake the work, mindful that the results they hope to achieve are worth it all. They volunteer to undertake this work in addition to their regular duties as Christians. — What can we say for ourselves and the courage we need to perform our God-given obligations, let alone voluntary works of charity? Do we not wince even when we are called upon to make the little sacrifices of time and convenience, and the like? Are we not rather base cowards compared with these courageous men and women?

2. Besides these personal sacrifices, the missionary is always faced with the possibility of persecution and death. Good Father Liberatus and his companions fearlessly preached the Gospel to the schismatics, and were reaping the first fruits of their labors when persecution reared its head to thwart them. But this did not daunt them. They knew that to adhere to the tenets of the Catholic Faith meant that death awaited them, yet the courage that supported them until then continued to infuse further strength, and so they declared themselves ready to give a thousand lives if they had them to give rather than deny their faith. Undoubtedly they were mindful of the words of the Gospel: "He that shall lose his life for My sake, shall find it" (Mt. 16,25). — We are seldom, if ever, called upon to make a formal profession of our faith, but in certain instances obedience to the Church may require us to show that we are Catholics. On such occasions we must not hesitate. How can we expect to get to heaven if we are ashamed to acknowledge our membership in the army of the Lord of heaven? We ought rather to aim to make ourselves worthy of the reward promised by our Lord when He says: "And I say unto you, whosoever shall confess Me before men, him shall the Son of Man also confess before the angels of God" (Lk. 12,8).

3. To complete God's plan in creation, our Lord Jesus Christ agreed to assume human form and unite it to His divinity. But this union was to be

carried out in a life of glory. Man's sin, however, changed this part of the plan, and instead of glory, suffering was substituted to appease the wrath of God for man's infidelity. Humanly speaking — and we venture to use such terms, since in taking upon Himself our nature, our Lord became human in all things save sin — Jesus made a supreme sacrifice in foregoing this life of glory and assuming a life of suffering. A high degree of courage was needed to do this, yet the God-man did not shrink from it, but set an example which we were to imitate cheerfully and readily when the honor and glory of God required sacrifices of us. Our Abyssinian martyrs belong to this band of courageous souls, on whom our Saviour can look with complacency as most faithful followers; for, as the Wise Man tells us, "As gold in the furnace he has proved them, and as a victim of a holocaust he has received them" (3,6). Let us reanimate our courage, and strive to follow in the footsteps of these holy men by making a more pleasing oblation of the little sacrifices God gives us occasion to make daily for love of Him. Then, too, we can daily preach the Gospel by manifesting in our lives the lessons of the Gospel. We can be martyrs, by courageously battling against the world, the flesh, and the devil. And our reward? "The kingdom of heaven suffers violence, and the violent bear it away" (Mt. 11,12).

PRAYER OF THE CHURCH (For the Beatification)
Eternal Father, I offer Thee all the holy Masses that will be offered today that Thy servants may soon receive the honor of our altars and the public veneration of the faithful. Amen.

⊙⊙⊙⊙⊙⊙⊙⊙⊙⊙⊙⊙⊙

MARCH 4
THE SERVANT OF GOD SYLVESTER OF ASSISI
Confessor, First Order

YLVESTER was one of the first twelve associates who gathered about St. Francis, and he was, moreover, the first priest in the order. Just as the Apostle St. Matthew was called from the tax collector's bench, so was Sylvester called from an avaricious life to one of perfect poverty.

He was a descendant of a noble family in Assisi and possessed an estate near the city, from which, even though he was a priest, he expected to draw considerable gain. It was he who sold a quantity of stones to St. Francis for the restoration of St. Damian's. He had received his price for them. But some time later he saw Francis and Bernard of Quintavalle, who was the first to join the pioneer group of Franciscans, distributing the latter's wealth among the poor of the city. Spurred by avarice, Sylvester approached St. Francis and complained that he had been poorly paid for those stones and that he ought to give him more money. St. Francis, who could not be induced to quarrel over worldly goods, reached down into the bag and gave Sylvester a handful of money with the words: "Here, take as much as you want, although I owe you nothing." Sylvester eagerly took the money and went away.

Suddenly he was touched with remorse. Entering into himself, he reproached himself severely that he, a canon of the cathedral of San Rufino and an older man, should allow himself to be so deluded by avarice, whereas Francis, who was still a young man, was abandoning all his temporal goods for the love of God. He resolved to rectify the wrong he had done and to renounce his avarice. Almighty God, who advances to meet the repentant sinner, led him on to still greater generosity. During the night, in a dream, Sylvester saw St. Francis. A brilliant cross that reached up to heaven and had its cross-beam stretched out to the ends of the earth, proceeded from his mouth. A monstrous dragon that sprawled over the city of Assisi fled at the sight of the cross. This dream was repeated on three successive nights. Sylvester understood from this that the order of St. Francis was destined by its preaching of the cross to drive out the devil everywhere. He began to lead a very penitential life. Soon afterwards he sold all his goods, divided the proceeds among the poor, and humbly asked St. Francis for admission into his order. Francis received the penitent with great joy, and esteemed him highly as the first priest of the order, being especially fond of him because of his earnest efforts in acquiring perfection.

Sylvester became a special lover of solitude and prayer, at which he was so favored that, according to the account in the annals, he spoke with God as Moses once did, as a man does with his friend. Hence, at times, when St. Francis was in doubt about certain matters, he would go to Sylvester to determine what was the will of God in his regard. So it once happened that Francis sent a message to Sylvester when he was trying to decide whether he should serve God by going out to preach or by devoting himself to prayer. "And the Holy Spirit," so St. Bonaventure relates, "revealed to the venerable priest as also to St. Clare, that Francis should go forth to preach the Gospel."

On his missionary journeys through Tuscany, the holy Founder chose Sylvester as his companion. At Arezzo they found furious civil war raging. As one of his early biographers relates, Francis saw a host of jubilant devils hovering over the city, spurring on the inhabitants in their strife. He commanded Sylvester to go and drive out the devils in his name. With simple trust the servant of God went up to the city gate and cried out aloud: "In the name of almighty God and by virtue of the command of His servant Francis, depart from here, all ye evil spirits!" The devils disappeared, and from that moment on the citizens came to terms of peace.

Sylvester lived for fourteen years after the death of St. Francis, constantly advancing in perfection. He died in the odor of sanctity at Assisi in the year 1240, and was buried in the church of St. Francis.

CONCERNING AVARICE

1. Consider what a detestable vice is avarice. It respects no state of life nor any position of honor. Sylvester was a prominent, well-to-do man; he was a priest, Yet avarice drove him to descend to contemptible haggling. But did it not also make a traitor of Judas, an apostle of the Lord? It does not set in at once with serious things; taking advantage of others, and all manner of small injustices are the living germs of this vice. If we allow them to take root in our hearts, this vice will gain strength and make its slaves capable of all sorts of wickedness, so that the Apostle can say in truth: "The desire of money is the root of all evil" (1 Tim. 6,10). — Do you perhaps perceive the germs of covetousness in yourself?

2. Consider that the Holy Ghost (Eph. 5,5) designates covetousness as a "serving of idols," because the avaricious man places worldly goods on a level with, and sometimes even above, his God. His thoughts and ambitions are concentrated solely on material gain; he is little interested in prayer and the divine services; he pretends that his work will not permit him to attend holy Mass during the week, although he could readily arrange for it; even the Sunday is frequently profaned for the sake of work. On the other hand, worldliness and vanity are frequently coupled with avarice, and constantly stir it up to greater intensity. We want to amount to something in the world, we want to have everything grand and fashionable; in order to achieve our purpose, we hanker and inordinately strive after money and temporal goods. "Know," says the Apostle, "that no such man has inheritance in the kingdom of Christ" (Eph. 5,5). — Is it possible that you may forfeit the heavenly inheritance for that same reason?

3. Consider how we can escape from the baneful vice of covetousness. The example of St. Francis, who strove only for heavenly treasures, brought the avaricious Sylvester to his senses. From then on he, too, directed his

attention to higher things, to the eternal, and shortly he was satisfied in temporal goods with the least, and happy to possess only what was necessary. You, too, will profit by turning your attention to the things of eternity, to the imperishable treasures which await us, and by heeding the admonition of the Apostle: "But godliness with contentment is great gain. For we brought nothing into this world and certainly we can carry nothing out. But having food and wherewith to be covered, with these we are content" (1 Tim. 6,6-8).

PRAYER OF THE CHURCH

O God, in whom we live, move, and have our being, grant that, being sufficiently helped in our temporal needs, we may seek with more confidence the things that are eternal. Through Christ our Lord. Amen.

ᏚᏬᏁᏉᏚᏬᏁᏉᏚᏬᏁᏉᏚᏬᏁᏉᏚᏬᏁᏉ

MARCH 5
ST. JOHN JOSEPH OF THE CROSS
Confessor, First Order

THE island of Ischia is the flower among the beautiful islands with which the Gulf of Naples is surrounded. In this earthly paradise a saint was born on the feast of the Assumption of Our Blessed Lady in the year 1654, who sacrificed himself to God in a life of rigorous penance and contempt of all earthly comforts. This was John Joseph of the Cross. Even as a boy he practiced extraordinary virtue and self-denial. At the age of sixteen, he proved to be the first Italian to enter the reform movement of St. Peter of Alcantara, a convent of which had been established in Naples.

In his novitiate he exercised himself in humility and poverty according to the example of our holy Father St. Francis, and strove to nourish the spirit of mortification and prayer in imitation of St. Peter of Alcantara. Ere long he attained to so high a degree of perfection that, even before he was ordained a priest, he was commissioned with the building of a new convent. Wherever there was hard work to perform during the construction, he was the first at hand to do it; he worked now as a hod-carrier, now as a mason. The building itself was arranged according to the strictest poverty.

Like St. Francis, John Joseph preferred not to become a priest, but obedience compelled him to receive holy orders. Because he gave evidence of great theological knowledge and experience in the ways of spiritual life, he was entrusted with the direction of the novices, into whose youthful hearts he was able to inculcate so admirable a religious spirit that several of his novices became distinguished for their sanctity.

Several times Father Joseph was obliged to accept the office of guardian. When the convents in Italy were no longer dependent on the Spanish houses, but were formed into a separate province, he was appointed provincial in spite of all the objections he raised. Just as every good work meets with many obstacles in the beginning, so it happened to the new province. In the spirit of humility Father Joseph had not put himself forward, but it was in this position that his humility had to contend with the severest tests. Nevertheless, he bore all with heroic patience and constancy, and thus drew down blessings and success on the holy work.

When his term of office expired, he lived as a simple subject in the convent at Naples, where he devoted all his time to the care of souls and the practices of piety. His mortifications were exceptionally rigorous, so that no one may venture to imitate him without a special grace from God. He wore several iron crosses, studded with sharp points, on his shoulders, his back, and on his chest. Daily he scourged himself to the blood. He went either entirely barefoot or wore sandals in which small nails stood out. During the last thirty years of his life he abstained from drink of every sort in honor of the thirst of our Lord.

But he was still more intent on interior mortification. In order to keep his soul recollected, he kept a strict guard over all his senses; he strove constantly to deny his own will in order to do only the will of his superiors and thus fulfill the will of God. He emphasized this point also when giving advice to those who came to him for guidance. An optician named Vincent Lainez was a penitent and a great admirer of our saint. He had a little son, five months old, who was very sick and near death. Full of grief Lainez came to Father Joseph and begged him to obtain the recovery of his child by his prayers. "But, Vincent," said Father Joseph, "God calls him to Himself." "No, no!" said the distressed father, "He must leave this child to me. Last year He took my daughter, that is enough; one for Him and the other for me." Reluctantly Father Joseph answered: "You should submit to the will of God; but since you will not, very well! You will suffer the consequences." The child recovered, but it ceased growing; it attained its third year, but gave no signs of intelligence. The unhappy father, whom Father Joseph evaded during this time, could stand it no longer; he went to the cell of the Father, cast himself contritely at his feet and acknowledged his sin. After praying a while, the saint turned to him with sincere compassion and said: "You deprived God of the honor, and the child of the happiness which it should have enjoyed in heaven during all this time in praising God. So God punished you. But now He sees your sorrow, and the punishment is at an end. Return to your home." Arriving there, the father beheld his child in the throes of death. With a sweet smile, the first ever to be seen on his countenance, the boy turned his little head towards his father, and his innocent soul took its flight to heaven.

As an old man, Father Joseph was severely troubled with ulcers on his legs, so that he could hardly make a step without the use of a cane. One day when he was in the cathedral, to venerate the blood of the holy martyr Januarius (which is miraculously liquefied each year when the vial containing the blood is placed near the head of the saint). Father Joseph's cane was lost in the crowd that pressed about him. He was obliged to support himself at the walls until he arrived at the church door. There he paused while he asked the saint to return his cane to him. A distinguished gentleman, who had come to the church in his carriage, asked Father Joseph what had happened. Raising his hand, Father Joseph said: "My hobby-horse has run away, but St. Januarius will bring him back." At this moment the people in church began to cry aloud: "A miracle! A miracle!" Father Joseph's cane was seen passing through the air till it reached his hand. Later on, a cardinal asked the favor of possessing the object of so charming a miracle; he had it encased in a precious shrine.

At the age of eighty, Father Joseph died, like an innocent and beautiful child, his final glance resting on a picture of the Blessed Virgin Mary. It was on March 5, 1734. His grave at Naples is a constant object of great veneration; many miracles still occur there. Pope Pius VI beatified him, and Gregory XVI solemnly canonized him on Trinity Sunday in the year 1839. His feast is observed by the entire First Order as well as the Third Order Regular on March fifth.

ON EXTERIOR AND INTERIOR MORTIFICATION

1. Consider how wise it was of St. John Joseph that from his youth he determined to foster the spirit of mortification and of prayer. He continued in this practice throughout his life. The spirit of prayer is the union of our heart with God in all its undertakings. All temporal affairs, says our holy Father St. Francis, must be subservient to this spirit; without it, it is impossible to please God. The spirit of prayer, however, cannot subsist without mortification. He who grants his body and his sensual desires all that they crave, will find his soul retarded like a flame that is covered with ashes. Therefore the Wise Man says: "The corruptible body is a load upon the soul" (Wisd. 9,15). But the mortification of the body

gives the soul wings, as it were, with which to fly to God. Thus the angel said to Tobias: "Prayer is good with fasting" (Tob. 12,8). — Do you practice this necessary mortification?

2. Consider that there are two kinds of mortification, exterior and interior. Both are necessary, for without exterior mortification the interior cannot hold out, and without interior mortification the exterior is of no value. Exterior mortification sets itself against comfort, effeminacy, the pleasures of the palate, and the like, not only so far as it prevents the body from indulging in what is forbidden and sinful, but even denies it what is permissible, punishing it for former transgressions and so preventing it from committing new sins. Thus St. Paul says: "I chastise my body and keep it in subjection" (1 Cor. 9,27). Corporal mortification, however, must be practiced within bounds; and for the performance of extraordinary mortification, one should always ask the consent of one's confessor. Do you probably neglect mortifications entirely? You could easily practice them in small things, such as in eating and drinking, in dress, in your repose.

3. Consider that interior or spiritual mortification is the more important of the two kinds. This consists in keeping our interior affections in hand: in repressing our impatience, conquering anger, breaking self-will, yielding our own opinion; in curbing our eyes in seeing, our ears in hearing, our tongue in speaking. This type of mortification is far more difficult than the exterior, and yet, in another sense, easier, since everybody can practice it. But everybody must keep on practicing it if he wishes to save his soul and arrive at heaven, for, the Apostle says: "If you live according to the flesh, you shall die; but if by the spirit you mortify the deeds of the flesh, you shall live" (Rom. 8,13).

PRAYER OF THE CHURCH

O God, who didst raise Thy servant St. John Joseph through the rugged way of poverty, humility, and patience to heavenly glory, grant, we beseech Thee, that by mortifying our flesh we may follow the example of the saint and so partake of the eternal joys. Through Christ our Lord. Amen.

MARCH 6
ST. COLETA
Virgin, Second Order

OR centuries the little town of Corbie in France was famous for a Benedictine convent there in which several saints had lived as well as many men renowned for their learning. Usually several hundred religious dwelt there at one time. They were divided into three groups, who took turns in solemnly chanting the Divine Office before the Blessed Sacrament, so that day and night the "perpetual praise of God" resounded there—that was the name applied to this way of imitating the heavenly choirs, as established by devout princes in many a convent of the Middle Ages.

In this little town of Corbie, Coleta was born on January 13, 1381, of exemplary working people. She was a child of grace, an answer to her mother's incessant prayers, for the latter was already sixty years old then and had been childless up to that time.

The little girl took great pleasure in prayer, in compassion for the poor, and in rigorous mortification, making of her soul and of her tender body a sacrifice to God. Up to her fourteenth year she remained unusually small in stature; this was a great grief for her father. Coleta begged God to console her father in the matter, and then she began to grow very rapidly to normal height. On the other hand, she asked God to deprive her of the rare beauty she possessed, which she believed might be the occasion of danger to herself and others; that request, too, was granted, and Coleta developed features of a severe cast which inspired great respect.

When both her parents had died, Coleta, at the age of twenty-two, obtained the permission of the Church authorities to shut herself up in a small abode directly adjoining the church; from a small window in it she could see the Blessed Sacrament. There she expected to spend the remainder of her life as an anchoress. She had embraced the rule of the Third Order of St. Francis, in accordance with which she endeavored to live in perfect poverty, severe mortification, and constant prayer in order to become daily more and more like the Seraphic Father. She received many consolations from heaven, but on the other hand she also experienced severe temptations and even corporal abuse from the spirits of darkness.

Almighty God had destined Coleta for something extraordinary. He excited in her the desire to re-introduce the strict observance of the rule of St. Clare, which many convents of Poor Clares then observed in a modified form. The humble virgin recoiled at the thought, which she tried

Saint Coleta

to persuade herself was an illusion of the proud spirit of darkness. But the inspiration returned again and again, and when she continued to resist it, she was struck dumb and later on blind, until she finally resigned herself to the will of God, like Saul before Damascus. "Lord," she sobbed in her heart, "what wilt Thou have me do? I am ready to do anything Thou desirest of me." At once her speech and her sight were restored. The Lord sent her a special director under whose guidance she was to perform extraordinary things. And so, after spending four years in her retreat, and with the authority and the blessing of the pope, she established one convent of Poor Clares after another, so that the number reached seventeen during her lifetime. After her death similar foundations were established in countries other than France, in which the primitive rule of St. Clare began to flourish anew.

St. Coleta endured untold hardships in fulfilling the task assigned to her, but heaven supported her even in visible ways; numerous miracles, including the raising to life of several dead persons, occurred in answer to her prayers and in confirmation of her work. So, the great foundress remained ever humble, regarding everything as the work of God, who often chooses the lowliest of people as His instruments.

On this foundation of humility she endeavored to foster in her convents the spirit of prayer and simplicity of heart. She placed great value on the recitation of the Divine Office in choir, undoubtedly in remembrance of the practice existing in her native town, and infused this esteem into her fellow sisters. She was also filled with zeal for the salvation of souls, and once in a vision she saw souls falling into hell more swiftly than the snowflakes in a winter's storm.

After laboring for forty years, she was to receive her eternal reward. She died in her convent at Ghent on March 6, 1447. At the moment of her departure from this world she appeared to several sisters in different convents. Pope Urban VIII beatified her, and Pope Pius VII solemnly canonized her in 1807. The entire First Order as well as the Third Order Regular observe her feast on March sixth.

ON CORPORAL BEAUTY

1. The Holy Spirit says: "For many have perished by the beauty of a woman" (Eccli. 9,9). St. Coleta reflected on this truth, and fearing nothing more than to give anyone occasion to sin, she asked God, as did also St. Lidwina, to deprive her of her corporal beauty; God heard her prayer by means of a miracle. How different is the example of the young women who not only prefer to be beautiful to plain-looking, but endeavor in every

possible way to enhance their imaginary beauty and to make themselves more attractive. Such persons lay snares for souls and draw down upon themselves sin and misery. A Christian young woman will not act in that way; whoever does do it, does not deserve the name Christian any more. Moreover, it is not the Christian fashion to make little girls conscious of their beauty; it is in this way that we nourish that evil propensity for personal admiration. — Have you need to reproach yourself on these points?

2. Consider that we should place little stock in personal beauty. "Favour is deceitful, and beauty is vain," says the Wise Man (Prov. 31,30). How little, oftentimes, does interior merit conform with the external beauty, and how soon the latter disappears! Hence Thomas a Kempis (1,7) admonishes us: "Boast not of your stature or beauty of body, which, with a little sickness, is spoiled and disfigured; but glory in God, who gives all things and desires to give Himself above all things." "The woman who fears the Lord, she shall be praised" (Prov. 31,30). — Have you perhaps also paid much attention to corporal perfections?

3. Consider, that if you possess personal beauty, it should urge you to achieve beauty of soul through purity of heart, sincerity, modesty, piety, genuine love of God and neighbor; otherwise your beautiful body will be but the fair peel of a rotten apple. On the other hand, even if you are not now possessed of bodily beauty, you can possess it later if you now beautify your soul; for then even your body will be beautiful in the resurrection and throughout eternity. For "one is the glory of the celestial, and another of the terrestrial" (1 Cor. 15,40). The one is a gift of nature, the other is the result of the virtue which a person has acquired on earth. Impelled by virtuous motives, St. Coleta asked almighty God to deprive her of bodily beauty, and so the beauty of her glorified body will be the greater on the last day.

PRAYER OF THE CHURCH

O Lord Jesus Christ, who didst overwhelm St. Coleta with heavenly gifts, grant, we beseech Thee, that we may zealously imitate her virtues here on earth and deserve to share with her the eternal joys of heaven. Who livest and reignest forever and ever. Amen.

MARCH 7
THE SERVANT OF GOD MARGARET LEKEUX
Virgin, Third Order

ARGARET Lekeux, or Maggie as she was called by the poor of
Liège, was born at Arlon, Belgium, on August 2, 1892. Her
father had become an invalid two years after his marriage;
and her mother gained a livelihood for the family as a school
teacher. The family moved to Liège when Maggie was seventeen. At the
time, she was attending a normal college; and in Liège she continued her
studies for two more years. Her brother and biographer, Father Martial,
then entered the Franciscan Order. Before he left home, Maggie went to
him for advice. She knew that her parents wished her to take a position
as a teacher in a grammar school; but she desired nothing more than to
continue her studies. Father Martial suggested to her a life of self-sacrifice
and renunciation in the world.

Maggie made the sacrifice, and found strength for it in prayer. She
chose as her motto: "I want to live in the world to do good." She was a
school teacher for the rest of her short life, first in a school conducted by
the Daughters of St. Vincent de Paul in a suburb called "the Congo of
Seraing," then in a school of the Sisters of St. Mary not far from her home,
and lastly in one which was in the care of Benedictine Sisters. During
vacations and after school hours she devoted herself with singular zeal,
patience, and charity to the corporal and spiritual works of mercy.
Although frequently misunderstood, she persevered in her self-imposed
task. Accompanied by her helper, Joan, she visited the homes of the poor,
helped the needy and the sick by every means in her power, and brought
about numerous conversions. To the families of the poor and rough
Flemings, who were miners and employees of factories and railroads, she
became an angel of charity.

She lived with her parents in Hesbaye Street, opposite the Franciscan
friary; and one of the fathers who was likewise engaged in apostolic and
social work among the Flemings became her spiritual director. Maggie
joined the Third Order Secular of St. Francis in 1913; and gradually she rid
her soul of all self-love, embraced a life of complete self-renunciation, and
surrendered herself unreservedly to the love of God and her neighbor.

On August 7, 1914, the German army captured the fortress of Liège,
and the First World War was on. Maggie had taken a course in nursing
with the Red Cross a short time before; and she nursed the wounded
soldiers in the improvised hospitals of the Jesuits and Franciscans. But as
soon as a semblance of normal conditions was reestablished, she resumed

her social and apostolic work among the Flemings.

When the war broke out, her three brothers, two of them Franciscans, were called into the midst of the bloody fray. Her aged parents were almost inconsolable. But Maggie repeatedly assured them that their sons would return home safe and sound. She was sure of it, because she had secretly offered her life to God that He might spare her three brothers. God accepted her sacrifice. On Ash Wednesday, March 8, 1916, at the age of twenty-three years and seven months, having predicted her death several months beforehand, she died of a mysterious illness and went to receive the guerdon of her self-sacrifice. Her three brothers passed unscathed through the war, although they were at death's door again and again. The dangers which they encountered were so great and imminent that their escape was truly miraculous.

Maggie's life exemplifies in a striking manner that true greatness and genuine happiness come not from self-seeking and self- indulgence but from self-renunciation and self-sacrifice. Her example demonstrates that in the midst of the world, occupied with many cares and activities, one can lead a life of union with God, unencumbered by the passing things of earth. Her life and work is a practical exemplification of heroic Catholic action. Not a few who have turned to Maggie in their needs, report remarkable favors received through her intercession. (Cf. Lekeux-Habig, *Maggie, the Life-story of Margaret Lekeux*.)

ON THE CHOICE OF A VOCATION

1. Consider how earnestly Margaret strove to know her vocation. Every man is chosen by God, the ruler of the universe, for some particular state of life. God fashioned Margaret both corporally and spiritually for this vocation rather than for another. God also predetermined certain graces for her, the easier to fulfill the duties of her vocation. It is really important that every man enter the state to which God has called him. He who misses this vocation is not only quite miserable in this life, but runs the risk of losing his soul. "Such a man," says St. Alphonse, "is like a dislocated member that finds it very difficult to do its appointed duty." — Have you ever thought of the importance of a vocation, and how unfair it is to force anyone into a certain state of life?

2. From the example of Margaret consider what should be done to know one's vocation. Margaret accepted advice, reflected and prayed. One must above all pray God as did the Prophet: "Make the way known to me wherein I should walk" (Ps. 142,8). Be attentive to the voice of God, especially after holy Communion. Try to discern whither your inclinations

tend. Examine impartially the advantages and disadvantages of the state you have in mind, and the special duties and dangers connected with it. Consider your talents and the means at your disposal to carry out your designs. Finally, consider which vocation will give you the greatest peace in the hour of death. Do not act without having sought the advice of another in so important a matter; above all, consult your confessor. "Do nothing without counsel, and you shall not repent when you have done" (Eccli. 32,24). — Would that youth paid more attention to this counsel.

3. Consider that when, after due consideration, we have made a choice, we should not easily let ourselves be frightened by the first difficulties that present themselves. The servant of God Margaret entered bravely on her chosen vocation; and eventually she was happy in it, labored with much success, and merited a glorious crown in heaven. Every state has its difficulties, and it is in the beginning that we feel them the most. In time, however, we bear them more easily, the grace which God attaches to the state assists us, and later, what in the beginning seemed hardly bearable, frequently becomes sweet to us. Should you have reason to believe that you have thoughtlessly chosen a state of life which God has not intended for you, carry the cross as a penance; it is the one way in which you can save your soul even in such a state.

PRAYER OF THE CHURCH
(Sunday within the Octave of the Epiphany)

Hear, O Lord, we beseech Thee, of Thy heavenly goodness, the prayers of Thy suppliant people, that they may both perceive what they ought to do, and may have strength to fulfill the same. Through Christ our Lord. Amen.

❦❦❦❦❦❦❦❦❦❦

MARCH 8
VENERABLE FIACRE TOBIN AND JOHN B. DOWDALL
Martyrs, First Order

FIACRE TOBIN was born in Kilkenny, Ireland, in 1620 and entered the order among the Capuchins at a very early age. In the persecution to which Catholics were subjected on Cromwell's accession, when other priests sought safety in flight, Father Fiacre remained steadfast at his post, to strengthen Catholics in their faith and especially to assist the sick.

Following the law of expulsion in 1653, Father Fiacre went to France for a while, but soon he returned to his native land and exercised his sacerdotal ministry in secret. Then he was discovered by the officers and led bound to the magistrate at Dublin.

In reply to the question of his identity, he answered without hesitation: "I am a Capuchin priest, and have returned to my native land to shed my blood for the Faith." It was feared that if they would execute him, it would put new strength into the faith of the Catholics. So he was cast into prison.

His bed was made of hard boards, a block of wood was his pillow, half-cooked peas were his food. A month later he was taken aboard ship, in order to be sent anew into exile. But his broken body was no longer able to hold out under the hardships. He died on the voyage on March 6, 1710, a martyr to the cause of the Faith. His cause of beatification, and that of another Irish Capuchin martyr, Father John Baptist Dowdall, who died in the same year, are now under way in Rome.

ON THE EXCELLENCE OF THE SACRAMENTS

1. The value of the sacraments is great. It was for that reason that Venerable Fiacre shunned no danger in order to administer the sacraments to the faithful. The sacraments are the channels through which the salutary graces of Christ flow to us. Happy he who may drink at these channels! Happy he who can make them available to others! — Have you respected the sacraments and their ministers accordingly?

2. By means of the sacraments all the needs of Christian life are provided for. Baptism cleanses us from original sin and makes us children of God. Confirmation gives us strength for all the storms of life. The Holy Eucharist nourishes the soul. Penance raises us up again when we have fallen. Extreme Unction supplies the necessary strength for the journey to eternity. Holy Orders consecrates the servants of God. Matrimony sanctifies human association. And thus provision is made for everything and everybody. — Let us admire the wisdom and charity of our Saviour. We should cooperate with the sacraments. We must cultivate a responsive heart in order to receive the sacraments with greater fruit. After receiving them we must manifest a grateful heart. By means of love of God, purity of soul, and a virtuous life we should endeavor to increase the effects of the sacraments to the fullest measure. We should manifest a growing holy enthusiasm, again and again "to draw waters with joy out of the Saviour's fountains" (Is. 12,3). — Is there nothing with which you have to reproach yourself on this score?

PRAYER OF THE CHURCH

We beseech Thee, O Lord, let Thy sacraments perfect in us all that is contained in them, so that one day we may taste in unconcealed reality the things which we now celebrate in a veiled manner. Who livest and reignest forever and ever. Amen.

MARCH 9
ST. CATHARINE OF BOLOGNA
Virgin, Second Order

THE birth of Catharine was foretold to her devout father by the Blessed Virgin, with the announcement that the child would be a brilliant light throughout the world. On the feast of the Annunciation of our Lady in the year 1413, Catharine was born at Bologna. Her father, John of Vigri, was a relative of the marquis of Este, who resided in Ferrara. It was his wish that little Catharine, who charmed everyone with her beauty and lovableness, be brought to his court, to be educated there with his daughter. Here Catharine learnt the foreign languages and especially Latin, painting, and everything that belongs to the culture of a young woman of high rank. People admired in her the singular wisdom and insight with which she read the profound works of the Fathers of the Church, along with her great modesty and such purity of soul that she was looked upon more as an angelic than as a human being.

The court with all its splendor was not able to fascinate Catharine. The most distinguished suitors were compelled to withdraw without the least hope of obtaining her hand in marriage; she entertained no other desire than to be plighted forever to Jesus Christ, the spouse of her heart. When she was seventeen years old, she obtained the consent of her mother—her father having already died—to join a pious company of young women in Ferrara who led a religious life but had not yet adopted a definite rule. Catharine appeared among them as a mirror of all the virtues, but meanwhile she was also being subjected to very severe temptations of the evil spirit.

Four years later, a royal princess founded a convent for this society according to the rule of St. Clare; and several zealous sisters from Mantua introduced the young women to the Poor Clare rule of life. Catharine was charged with the duties of the bakery; she cheerfully undertook this laborious service, and even when the heat began to affect her eyes, she remained at her post as long as the abbess required it.

One day, just as she had placed the loaves in the oven, the bell called her to the choir for some very special religious service; she made the Sign of the Cross over the loaves and said: "I commend you to our Lord." She was not in a position to return to the bakery until five hours later, and certainly believed that everything had been burned by that time. However, when she removed the loaves from the oven, they were nicer than ever.

After a time she was entrusted with the duties of mistress of novices. Catharine tried, indeed, to be excused, explaining that she was entirely incapable for this task; but she was compelled by obedience to accept it. Her diffidence in herself drew down God's blessing on her efforts to give the novices a good training. She endeavored, above all, to impress on their young hearts that they should desire nothing but the honor of God and the fulfillment of His holy will, and so she recommended that they look upon the holy rule and obedience to their superiors as their guides. Her own experience taught her how to protect them from the snares of the devil. "Sometimes," she said, "he inspires souls with an inordinate zeal for a certain virtue or some special pious exercise, so that they will be motivated in its practice by passion; or again, he permits them to become discouraged so that they will neglect everything because they are wearied and disgusted. It is necessary to overcome the one snare as well as the other." She also taught them to use the golden mean that leads to solid virtue.

For a long time she herself was troubled with the temptation to sleep during the spiritual exercises. Once when she was again heroically struggling against it during holy Mass, God almighty permitted her to hear the angelic choirs singing after the elevation. From then on the temptation was overcome, and she was even able to devote hours to prayer during the night.

Catharine had spent twenty-four years in the convent at Ferrara and had trained many sisters in the way of sanctity when, at the request of the city of Bologna, she was sent with fifteen sisters to establish a similar convent in her native town. She was appointed abbess, and governed her community with wisdom and motherly love. She was particularly solicitous for the sick sisters. In dispensing to them spiritual consolation she said: "My dear sisters, you are now the true brides of the Divine Saviour, who chose pain and sufferings as His portion."

Although she was sickly from the time that she was twenty-two years old, she never complained. When at times it seemed to her that her afflicted body would be justified in complaining, she would say to herself:

"O bundle of corruption, that will soon turn into dust, why should you complain? It appears as if you had not yet learnt to be a true servant of Christ."

She was particularly tactful in preserving peace within herself and peace among the members of her community. Hence she was also loved by all of them.

When she died on March 9, 1463, sounds of sobbing and weeping were heard everywhere in the convent. But even after her death her sisters were to be made joyful through her. Her body, which had been the temple of so chaste and immaculately pure a soul, diffused a sweet odor. It remained incorrupt and retained its quality of flexibility like that of a living body. Thus it can still be seen in Bologna, robed in a costly garment presented by St. Charles Borromeo and seated on a throne, under a crystal shrine. Innumerable miracles reward the faithful for their devotion to her. Pope Clement XI canonized her. The three branches of the First Order and also the Third Order Regular celebrate her feast on March ninth.

ON THE VIRTUE OF CHASTITY

1. On the throne on which the chaste body of St. Catharine of Bologna is honored, one reads the words in which the Holy Ghost pronounces the praise of chastity: "O how beautiful is the chaste generation with glory; for the memory thereof is immortal. It triumphs, crowned for ever, winning the reward of undefiled conflicts" (Wisd. 4,12). Undefiled purity requires a struggle in every state of life, in every period of human life; but such a reward is well worth the struggle. — Have you fought faithfully for this precious treasure?
2. Consider, on the other hand, what an abominable vice impurity is. While chastity makes men similar to angels and sometimes preserves them from corruption after death, impurity degrades them to the level of the beast and sometimes produces corruption even before the soul has left the body. The unchaste person becomes an abomination in the sight of God, in the sight of men, and in his own eyes. Here on earth, impurity deprives a man of all peace of heart and of all the joys of life; and if he is not sincerely converted, he shall in eternity have "his portion in the pool burning with fire and brimstone" (Apoc. 21,8). — Who would not be frightened at beginnings which lead to so terrible an end?
3. Consider the dangers that lead to the defilement of chastity. The softness and sensuality with which we pamper our bodies are the principal ones among the dangers. In the sensual appetite we carry a slumbering serpent in our bosom. If we nourish it with sensuality, it will

not be long ere we feel its poisonous sting. Reading dangerous books, looking at shameless pictures, attending frivolous plays and dances, and associating with dissolute companions aggravate to a still greater degree this evil propensity. No poison is so infectious as that of impurity. Amid so many dangers, Christians may well say with the Apostle: "Unhappy man that I am, who will deliver me from the body of this death?" (Rom. 7,24). But we, too, can gain the victory with the help of God and through the intercession of the Immaculate Virgin Mary, as did all the other chaste souls who are now triumphing in heaven.

PRAYER OF THE CHURCH

Grant, O God, that we, Thy servants, may receive help through the intercession of the holy virgin Catharine, that by the sweet odor of her virtues, we may be joyfully attracted to Thy sanctuary. Through Christ our Lord. Amen.

***

MARCH 10
THE SERVANT OF GOD HUGH OF DIGNE
Confessor, First Order

N the thirteenth century there lived in France a member of the order known as Hugh of Digne, who was widely renowned as a man of great piety, wisdom, and learning. His fame reached the king of France, St. Louis, who was reigning at that time. When the latter returned from a crusade in the Orient in 1254, he ordered Hugh to preach before him and his assembled court. With apostolic frankness the servant of God spoke forcefully against the vices that were prevalent among the courtiers: pride, intrigue, envy, and sensuality.

Neither did he spare the many religious found among the king's retainers. He made it clear to them that by remaining longer at court amid the business and pleasure of court life, they were exposing themselves to the danger of damnation.

Finally, he addressed the king himself, earnestly appealing to him ever to govern with justice and without regard of persons if he wished to keep his dynasty reigning in peace; for, according to the words of Holy Writ, "a kingdom is translated from one people to another because of injustices and wrongs and injuries and diverse deceits" (Eccli. 10,8).

The king, who preferred truth to flattery, was edified and deeply moved at Hugh's words. He besought him to remain about him as his preacher and spiritual adviser. Hugh, however, steadfastly declined the invitation, and on the following day withdrew to a secluded little convent in the mountains. There he wrote many inspired works for the benefit of the order and of pious Christians. His principal work was a thoughtful explanation of the rule of the Friars Minor, which enjoys great prestige even to this day.

God, so to say, placed the seal of approval on the sanctity of Hugh's life by many miracles, some of which are recorded as having occurred in his lifetime. The gift of prophecy was also granted to him. History records the following incident in proof:

Hugh once visited the convent of the Order of the Knights Templars at Marseilles. When they showed him into their magnificent dining hall, he walked up and down a few times and thoughtfully looked at the walls. Then someone asked him what he thought of the hall, and he answered: "This hall will one day be a comfortable stable for horses." Before fifty years had elapsed, Pope Clement V dissolved the Order of the Knights Templars, and Hugh's prophecy was literally fulfilled: the great dining hall became a stable for the king's horses.

Hugh died a blessed death at Marseilles in 1285. The process of his canonization was begun many years ago, but it was interrupted because of political disturbances and never brought to a conclusion.

ON THE RELIGIOUS LIFE

1. Consider what constitutes the essence of the religious life. When St. Dominic was near death, the brothers gathered about and asked him to explain, by way of legacy to them, the essentials of the religious life. The dying founder answered: "The substance of the religious life is to love God with our whole heart, and to love nothing else." Indeed! Perfect love of God is the goal of the religious life, and the three vows of poverty, chastity, and obedience are its fundamental requisites, because it is through them that we defeat the principal enemies to the love of God — the concupiscence of the eyes, the concupiscence of the flesh, and the pride of life, while we lovingly surrender to God the goods of the world, of the body and of the soul. Hence it can truly be said that the perfect religious really loves God with his whole heart, and nothing besides. Each congregation has its special rules and constitutions, in order to direct its various exercises and activities towards this end. Zeal for the perfection of the religious life was a worthy objective of Hugh's labors, and well worth the frank warnings he administered to those religious whom he

believed in danger of losing their hold on it. The holy Council of Trent says that well-regulated religious communities are a blessing and an ornament to the Church of God, and any person who speaks or thinks disparagingly of the religious state can certainly not be a good Catholic. Consider that the Third Order of St. Francis belongs to the religious orders. True, Tertiaries do not live in communities separated from the world and from their families, neither do they take the three vows as is done in convent orders. But instead of the three vows, which the duties of their state in life would not permit secular Tertiaries to fulfill, the Third Order lays down a certain rule of life based on the spirit of the vows, and the members pledge their word, even though not under pain of sin, to this rule after their period of probation. In the spirit of poverty they are forbidden luxury and extravagance; they are to dress simply and eat and drink with moderation. To preserve chastity according to their state, they should keep away from questionable amusements, dances, plays, and other dangers. In the spirit of obedience and submission they should be an example to others in their family circle as well as in their public associations, while they comply with the orders of their superiors and the work of the fraternity. In this way the life of the Tertiaries, with due allowance for their vocational duties, has the same goal in view as the religious state. — As a Tertiary, have you always faithfully observed your rule in the true spirit?

2. Consider that those who because of their circumstances cannot join the Third Order, must nevertheless, if they aspire to eternal bliss, observe a rule of life similar in its essentials to that proposed to Tertiaries. They must, therefore, also keep in mind the principal aim of the religious life, which is Christian perfection and true love of God. Jesus Christ addressed to everybody the words, "Be perfect as also your heavenly Father is perfect" (Mt. 5:48), just as He laid down for everybody the commandment: "You shall love the Lord your God with your whole heart, with your whole soul, and with all your mind" (Mt. 22,37). The purpose and aim of the religious life must therefore, so to say, act as leaven and permeate the life of every Christian, and the regulations contained in the Third Order rule must guide the conduct of every Christian, if he is to survive the dangers of the world and walk in the path of salvation as a true follower of Christ. — Are you walking on that path?

PRAYER OF THE CHURCH
(Tuesday in the Second Week of Lent)

In Thy mercy perfect within us, we beseech Thee, O Lord, the strength acquired by this holy observance, that what we know Thou hast appointed us to do, we may, by Thy assistance, be enabled to fulfill. Through Christ our Lord. Amen.

MARCH 11
BLESSED AGNELLUS OF PISA
Confessor, First Order

IT was the privilege of Blessed Agnellus to have been received into the order by St. Francis himself. He descended from an ancient noble family at Pisa. The government of the Parisian province of the order was entrusted to him. Later on the holy Founder sent him to England with eight companions. Here Agnellus found it possible to establish several convents of his order and to unite them into a province. Due to his zeal and to his virtuous life, many young men, some from the most prominent families in England, took the habit of the Poor Man of Assisi.

In order to provide the young clerics with a thorough education he established a school of theology at Oxford. Meanwhile, however, he infused into them a great desire for perfection and a holy fidelity to the rule of the order, in all of which he led them by his own good example.

His humility was so profound that under no circumstances could he be prevailed upon to receive holy orders. Finally, however, he yielded in obedience to the general chapter. A great part of his time was devoted to meditation. At holy Mass and in choir he was so overcome with interior affections that he was frequently found weeping.

He died the death of the saints in the year 1232, when he was but thirty-eight years old. His grave and the church in which he was buried were destroyed during the persecution of the Catholics in the reign of Henry VIII. Pope Leo XIII solemnly confirmed the uninterrupted veneration that had been accorded to Blessed Agnellus. The Franciscans celebrate his feast on March eleventh, the Conventuals on the twentieth, and the Capuchins on the thirteenth.

ON SENTIMENTS OF HUMILITY

1. Consider the benefits of a humble disposition. While the ambitious are always ill at ease as to whether or not they will be properly esteemed, or whether their dignity will be duly acknowledged, the humble live in

continual peace of soul. They do not wait for approval and do not fear ill success. Their will is directed solely to the honor of God. They expect a reward from Him alone. The principle underlying all their activities is that of their Saviour: "I seek not my own glory" (Jn. 8,50). — Accustom yourself to similar sentiments and you will be spared much anxiety, vexation, and grief.

2. It is not difficult to associate with humble persons. They can bear contradiction; they are not anxious to be everywhere in authority, and to be the first at every gathering. Humble superiors, such as Blessed Agnellus was, are so thoroughly impressed with their own deficiencies that they never expect too much of their inferiors, while humble subjects are cheerfully submissive. Why was Christ affability personified? Because He could say: "I am humble of heart" (Mt. 11,29). — If you are ever at variance with your relatives, with your inferiors, with your superiors, is it perhaps due to the fact that you are not sufficiently humble? Away, then, with "I, me, and mine."

3. Humility makes us worthy to be loved. Blessed Agnellus was welcome everywhere, and everywhere he was successful. While the proud and haughty man does damage everywhere, the example of the humble man exercises a kind of magic power. His presence is appreciated, he is missed when he is absent. Of the humble it may well be said: "He went about doing good" (Acts 10,38). — Would you not prefer to be numbered with the humble rather than with the conceited?

PRAYER OF THE CHURCH

Lord Jesus Christ, who didst release Thy blessed confessor, Agnellus, from the snares of the world and direct him to follow the way of Thy cross, grant that we may so follow His example that we may merit the crown of glory which he has received in heaven. Who livest and reignest world without end. Amen.

⊘⊗⊘⊗⊘⊗⊘⊗⊘⊗⊘⊗

MARCH 12
BLESSED JOHN BAPTIST RIGHI OF FABRIANO
Confessor, First Order

 LESSED John Baptist Righi descended from a noble family in Fabriano, Italy, and already as a child manifested a special love for prayer, together with unusual obedience towards his parents, and a tender compassion for the poor. After he had become a Franciscan, he chose to live in a cave in order to contemplate the sufferings of Christ without being disturbed or seen by others. In regard to food and clothing, he observed the greatest austerity and abnegation, and was, above all, firmly established in humility.

The faithful gathered in great crowds to attend his sermons. He was favored with the special gift of arousing great confidence in the mercy of God, so much so, that many sinners repented of their wickedness and some of the most hardened among them were converted. Even during his lifetime he healed many sick persons by merely making the Sign of the Cross over them.

After a life of rigorous penance, he went to his eternal rest at the ripe old age of seventy years. He died on March 11, 1539. Pope Pius X confirmed the veneration that had been paid to him from the time of his death. His feast is observed by the Franciscans on March eleventh.

ON THE REMEMBRANCE OF THE PASSION OF CHRIST

1. Consider the love and gratitude which impelled Blessed John to meditate on the Passion of Christ. The words of the Apostle were ever before his mind: "Christ suffered for us" (1 Pet. 2,21). For our sins, for our eternal salvation, our dear Lord suffered unspeakable tortures from the day on which He was born in an inhospitable stable until the last drop of blood flowed from the wound in His sacred side on the cross. Hence, it is most ungrateful and unkind to pass over His sufferings in an indifferent manner. — When you say the sorrowful mysteries of the rosary, lay special stress on the little thought that it was "for us."
2. Consider the benefit that accrues from the contemplation of the sufferings of Christ. It provides us with consolation in sorrow and in the sufferings of life; for, although Christ was innocent, He suffered more than you. It affords strength in times when slander and contempt have touched you, for Christ has suffered a greater share of this affliction than you. It affords hope for the remission of sins. For, the Apostle says: "If any man sin, we have an advocate with the Father, Jesus Christ, the just: He is the propitiation for our sins" (1 Jn. 2,1-2). — You will surely be rewarded for the frequent contemplation of the sufferings of our Lord.
3. Consider in what manner we should contemplate the sufferings of Christ. Holy Scripture admonishes us: "Look, and make it according to the pattern that was shown to you on the mount" (Ex. 25,40). In other words, we must keep our thoughts steadfastly directed to Mount Calvary and Mount Olivet. If sufferings come to you, then ask yourself at once: What

has my Saviour suffered? Above all, familiarize yourself with the phases
of the Passion of Christ by making the Way of the Cross, or say the
sorrowful mysteries of the rosary at least once a week. — What have you
done in this regard in the past?

PRAYER OF THE CHURCH
Grant, we beseech Thee, O almighty God, that the example of Blessed
John may serve for the amendment of our life, so that we may not only
celebrate his feastday, but may imitate his virtues. Through Christ our
Lord. Amen.

MARCH 13
BLESSED CHRISTOPHER OF MILAN
Confessor, First Order

BLESSED Christopher came into this world at the beginning of
the fifteenth century. The place of his birth was Milan. His
family were members of a noble house of that city. As a youth
he had distinguished himself by the piety and purity of his
life, but his virtues certainly advanced to a state of singular perfection
after he had donned the garb of St. Francis. The exactness with which this
young man of noble descent practiced Franciscan poverty, was admirable.
After he had been ordained to the priesthood, all his efforts were directed
towards saving immortal souls. The convent of Our Lady of Grace, which
he had established, soon developed into something like a national shrine.
Everybody wanted to hear his inspired sermons and through him to find
the path that led to God. The people came from far and near in order to
recommend themselves to his intercession with God.

Rich in merits, he died in the year 1485. Pope Leo XIII confirmed the
veneration which had been paid to this apostolic man of God since time
immemorial. His feast is observed on March eleventh by the Franciscans
and the Capuchins.

ON THE USE OF THE TONGUE
1. Much good can be effected by the good use of the tongue. "The tongue
of the just is a choice silver; the lips of the just teach many" (Prov. 10,20-
21). Thus it was with Blessed Christopher, who used his tongue to give
good advice and to preach the Word of God, and so to point out the way
to salvation. — Can you say as much about the way you use your tongue

and about the conversations you engage in?

2. Much evil results from a bad use of the tongue. First of all, for the one who speaks evil. "A man full of tongue shall not be established upon the earth" (Ps. 139,12). But then also for those who hear the evil spoken. Not without reason does the Apostle St. James write: "So the tongue also is a little member and boasts great things. Behold how small a fire, what a great wood it kindles! And the tongue is a fire, a world of iniquity" (3,5). How much suffering, contention, discord, and enmity may be traced to evil talk! — Do you belong to those of whom Scripture says: "A man full of tongue is terrible in the city" (Eccli. 9,25)?

3. The correct use of the tongue means keeping the golden mean between speech and silence. "Let your speech be always in grace seasoned with salt, that you may know how to answer every man" (Col. 4,6). Sometimes the honor of God and of the Church or the welfare of inferiors require us to speak and to warn and to admonish. It is advisable to be silent, if one sees in advance that no good will come of it, or that it will only be like oil poured on a fire. — Reflect calmly and in counsel with God whether you should speak or keep silence.

PRAYER OF THE CHURCH

O God, Thou dispenser of peace and friend of charity, grant us, Thy servants, perfect conformity to Thy holy will, so that we may be delivered from all the temptations that assail us. Through Christ our Lord. Amen.

⊱❧⊰❧⊱❧⊰❧⊱❧⊰❧⊱❧⊰

MARCH 14
THE SERVANT OF GOD APOLLONIA OF BOLOGNA
Widow, Third Order

APOLLONIA came from a very noble family in the city of Bologna. Already as a child she was conspicuous for modesty and retirement. While other parents could not do enough to provide their children with beautiful garments and elegant attire, little Apollonia besought her mother not to dress her in that way. Even as a young woman she dressed as simply as her station in life permitted. She preferred being active at home, or entertaining herself with good books, to going abroad.

In accordance with the wishes of her parents she married a good young man of her social rank. Her husband agreed to let her continue living a retired life even in the married state. He gave her free rein in the management of the household, and, as a result, everything in it was well ordered; for, although Apollonia was much devoted to practices of piety, she was no less diligent in the performance of the duties of a provident and prudent housewife. The maxim of St. Frances of Rome can also be applied to her: "A Christian housewife must ever be prepared to leave off her practices of piety if the needs of her house require her presence." She gave no thought to increasing her wealth, which was sufficient for their maintenance, but she was solicitous to obtain God's blessing for her house and to acquire everlasting treasures for eternity through generosity and pious gifts.

When her husband died, she laid aside all marks of her distinguished rank and clothed herself in the ash-gray habit of the Third Order. She used her wealth to found several institutions for the poor and the sick, and to these she repaired each day to administer to the distressed whatever service Christian charity could suggest. Finally, she herself was visited by God with a severe illness. She used this opportunity further to purify her soul and to increase her merits, and bore it with admirable patience until death led her to her eternal reward on March 12, 1500. She was buried in the church of the Friars Minor just outside the gate of the city of Bologna, and was glorified by God with several miracles.

ON CURIOSITY

1. Behold in this servant of God how a young woman in the world, also a married woman, can serve God perfectly amid the varying cares of a large household. It is not the duties of their state that hinder young women and housewives from serving God as Apollonia did; it is rather that very general curiosity which is so much at variance with Apollonia's retirement. This is what leads so many to see that they are kept well-informed about everything that occurs in their locality, to hear everything that others have said, to relate and to have related to them everything that is thought about others or expected of them. That such hearts are not sufficiently tranquil to serve God by the fulfillment of their duties; that, on the contrary, they neglect many a point in these duties; and that even their prayers, if they do say any at all, do not amount to much—that is very obvious. Because curiosity is so destructive, our Lord chided St. Peter when he asked about the destiny of John: "What is it to you? Follow Me" (Jn. 21,22). — How often would our Lord have to address such a reproof to you?

2. Consider that because others interfere in our affairs, we are not, on that

account, justified in examining into and criticizing their affairs. Thomas a Kempis (3,24) puts these words into the mouth of our Lord: "Let the unquiet man be as unquiet as he will. Whatsoever he shall say or do, will come upon himself, because he cannot deceive Me. You need not answer for others, but you shall have to give an account of yourself. Why, therefore, do you meddle with them?" — Would that all curious persons and such who are ever occupied with other people's concerns would take this advice to heart.

3. Consider the peace of heart that is our portion if we do not concern ourselves with the doings of others. "How can he long abide in peace," says Thomas a Kempis again, "who entangles himself in other men's concerns? When you followed your inclination to hear news, what did you derive from it but disquietude of heart? If you will let men alone, they will leave you alone to do as you will. If you do not entangle yourself in matters that do not concern you, it will undoubtedly happen that interior peace will be disturbed seldom and but little." — How happy will he be who will behave in this manner! Pray God that He may help you to acquire these sentiments during the holy season of Lent!

PRAYER OF THE CHURCH
(Monday of the Third Week in Lent)

Pour forth in Thy mercy, O Lord, we beseech Thee, Thy grace into our hearts, that as we abstain from bodily food, so we may also restrain our senses from hurtful excesses. Through Christ our Lord. Amen.

❦❦❦❦❦❦❦❦❦

MARCH 15
THE SERVANT OF GOD PETER OF MALINES
Confessor, First Order

ABOUT the year 1250 there lived in the Franciscan convent at Malines in Brabant, Father Peter, a model of perfection. He fostered special devotion toward the Blessed Sacrament; the holy sacrifice of the Mass he celebrated with the greatest reverence and ardent devotion. Once when he raised the consecrated Host on high at the elevation, children who were kneeling near the altar saw a beautiful little boy in his hands instead of the Host. Filled with astonishment, they drew the attention of their mothers, who were also attending the Mass, to the miracle.

After Father Peter's death, his body was laid to rest before the altar of the Blessed Sacrament; but so many miracles occurred there and the concourse of people became so great that it seriously disturbed the divine services. So, the guardian of the convent commanded the deceased, in virtue of holy obedience, to desist from working further miracles, just as several historians relate that St. Francis commanded Brother Peter of Catani to do. Our saintly Peter rendered prompt obedience even after his death: the miracles at his grave ceased from that time on.

ON THE PRESENCE OF CHRIST IN THE HOLY SACRAMENT OF THE ALTAR

1. Consider how almighty God performed the miracle during the holy Mass said by Father Peter. For him it was to be a reward for his ardent devotion, but for those in attendance, a means of strengthening their faith in the real presence of Christ in the holy Sacrament. Through this lively faith their devotion and their reverence, in which children especially fail at times, was to be increased; for, on the measure of our faith in the most holy Sacrament, depends the measure of our reverence for it. The same miracle once occurred in the royal chapel of King St. Louis. The king had not been in attendance at that Mass; so someone called him to see the miracle. But Louis answered and said: "Let those who do not believe go and see it; thanks be to God, I have no need to do so." — Would it be necessary for you to witness such a miracle in order to revive your faith and your devotion?

2. Consider how our Faith vouches for the real presence of Christ in the holy Sacrament. Christ had promised to give us His sacred flesh and blood under the appearance of bread. When the multitudes of people came to Him a few days after the miraculous multiplication of bread, He said to them: "Labor not for the meat that perishes, but for that which endures unto life everlasting" (Jn. 6,27). Then, when they expressed their desire for this food, He said: "I am the living bread which came down from heaven. If any man eat of this bread, he shall live forever: and the bread which I shall give is My flesh for the life of the world" (Jn. 6,51- 52). — What a blessed promise! Let us not fail to thank God for it.

3. Consider how Christ fulfilled this promise. On the eve of His Passion, when His disciples had gathered in the Upper Room, He said to them: "With desire I have desired to eat this Pasch with you before I suffer" (Lk. 22,15), because He intended to fulfill the great promise immediately afterwards. Then "taking bread, He gave thanks and broke and gave to them saying: 'This is My Body which is given for you.' In like manner also

the chalice, after He had supped, saying: 'This is the chalice of the new testament in My Blood which shall be shed for you. Do this for a commemoration of Me' " (Lk. 22,19-20). Under the separate appearances of bread and wine our Lord gave His sacred Body and His sacred Blood, and ordained that as a remembrance of Him the priest should make the same change at holy Mass, in order to renew the memory of His sacrificial death on the cross. However, under each appearance, even in that of bread alone, the faithful Christian receives the flesh and blood of Christ, for it is the living body of the Lord, which cannot exist without blood; it is the bread that lives and gives life, as the Lord Himself said: "He that eats this bread shall live forever" (Jn. 6,59). — May we ever honor it, and so partake of it that it may lead us to eternal life!

PRAYER OF THE CHURCH
(Feast of Corpus Christi)

O God, who in this wonderful Sacrament hast left us a memorial of Thy Passion: grant, we beseech Thee, so to venerate the sacred mysteries of Thy Body and Blood, that we may ever feel within us the fruit of Thy redemption. Who livest and reignest forever and ever. Amen.

MARCH 16
BLESSED TORELLO OF POPPI
Confessor, Third Order

BORN 1202 in the Tuscan town of Poppi, Torello came from the noble family of Torelli. When he lost his parents at the age of eighteen, he was thinking of devoting himself to the service of God and gave generous alms to the poor. But he had two bad friends and was soon corrupted by their example and influence, so that he became the scandal of the town. One day, when he was about thirty-six years old, he was amusing himself with his associates at the game of bowling. During the game a cock perched on his arm and crowed three times. Torello took this as a warning from heaven, deserted his friends without delay, and went to confession to a priest at the abbey of San Fedele, one of the houses of the Vallombrosan Benedictines.

Torello then went into the nearby Casentino mountains to look for a suitable place for a hermitage. After wandering around in the woods for eight days, he found a cave in a secluded spot called Avellaneto, not far from Poppi. After purchasing the land around this cave and giving what remained of his property to the poor, he built a little hermitage at the cave and cultivated a small vegetable garden to provide himself with food. But he ate very little and fasted for days at a time. He limited his sleep to three hours daily, and slept on a bed of brushwood and thorny twigs. To overcome the persistent temptations of the flesh and the devil, he scourged himself unmercifully and sometimes immersed himself in freezing water. Under his woolen habit he wore a shirt of pigskin from which only some of the bristles had been removed. He kept up this life of penance for about forty-five years; and as Wadding tells us, he became a member of the Third Order of St. Francis in the fourth year of his conversion.

Like St. Francis, he possessed a supernatural power over the wolves, of whom there were many in the Casentino mountains during the thirteenth century. He worked several miracles in behalf of children who were carried off by wolves, and for others who were attacked and bitten by wolves, both before and after his death.

When he was eighty years old, Blessed Torello went back to the abbey of San Fedele to make a general confession of his whole life and to ask that his body be buried at the abbey. Despite the entreaties of the monks that he spend his last days in their care, Torello returned to his hermitage, where another hermit, Peter of Poppi, had joined him. And there he died on March 16, 1282, while kneeling in prayer. He was beatified by Pope Benedict XIV.

At the tomb of Blessed Torello in the abbey church, a man who was an exile from Siena prayed that he might be permitted to return to his native city. He promised to observe the feast of Blessed Torello every year and to have a picture of the holy hermit painted. His prayer was answered, and he engaged the services of an artist. But the latter had never seen Blessed Torello and did not know what to do. Then he had a dream or vision in which he saw Torello, wearing the habit of the Third Order and holding a wolf-cub in his arms. And this is how the painting represents Blessed Torello of Poppi.

The feast of Blessed Torello is not celebrated by the three branches of the First Order of St. Francis; but the Third Order Regular, as well as the Vallombrosan Benedictines, observe it on the day of his death, March sixteenth.

ON AVOIDING CAROUSALS

1. Compare the mortified life of Blessed Torello with the life of many

Christians who are slaves to gluttony and who delight in all sorts of feasting. He was a servant of God, and even if a rigorous life like his is not obligatory for every Christian, it points out, nevertheless, what the sentiments of a true Christian in regard to these matters should be. "And they that are Christ's have crucified their flesh with the vices and concupiscences" (Gal. 5,24). That is why the Third Order rule prescribes that Tertiaries should refrain from all forms of dissipation. Whoever hankers after them is not a follower of God and St. Francis, but rather of Dives, the man who "feasted sumptuously every day" (Lk. 16,19). — To which group do you belong?

2. Perhaps you will say, Christ Himself took part in the wedding feast at Cana. True. He, who became all things to all men, wished to give us an example in the event that we are obliged under circumstances to attend such banquetings. Think of the moderation with which that wedding dinner was prepared, so that the wine soon gave out. Imagine the conversation that went on in the presence of Jesus and Mary. It was like the wedding feast of Tobias, of which it is said: "They made merry, blessing God" (Tob. 7,17). Would that Christian feasting were always conducted in this way. Then, when circumstances arise, every Christian could attend without detriment.

3. Consider how unworthy of a Christian it is to be fond of sumptuous feasting and to be a slave to his appetite. Almighty God has ordained that eating should serve to support our lives, nor does He forbid us to refresh mind and body with better food on feastdays or noteworthy occasions. But he who on such occasions thinks only of glutting sensual pleasure, disgraces a Christian festivity with the feasting of pagans, and, sad to say, that sometimes happens at Christian weddings, baptisms, and even at funerals.

PRAYER OF THE CHURCH
(Thursday in Passion Week)
Grant, we beseech Thee, almighty God, that the dignity of human nature, impaired by intemperance, may be restored by the practice of wholesome self-denial. Through Christ our Lord. Amen.

MARCH 17
THE SERVANT OF GOD PAULA MALATESTA
Widow, Second Order

AULA was the consort of the marquis of Mantua, John Francis Gonzaga. She was a very devout woman. Even during the lifetime of her husband, while she was the ruling marquise, she visited the community hospital three times a week and there ministered to the sick like a Sister of Mercy, dressing their wounds and washing their feet. She also cherished great veneration for the Holy Sacrament of the Altar; with touching devotion she would accompany It in processions, and in the sense of her own nothingness in the presence of the Divine Majesty on such occasions she always went barefoot.

Through her efforts St. Bernardin of Siena came to Mantua in 1420 to preach the Lenten sermons. These discourses produced such blessed results that extraordinary zeal for Christian perfection seized particularly the more distinguished members of society. The pious marquise founded several convents, among which was the monastery of Poor Clares at Mantua, where twenty young women immediately entered. Following the statutes of St. Bernardin, they were trained to perfect observance of the rule of the order.

After the death of the marquis, Paula herself entered this convent as an ordinary sister in the year 1440. She so completely forgot her former station in life that she performed the most difficult and servile tasks like the lowliest sister, and one would have believed that she had been a servant-girl all the days of her life. At the same time she practiced rigorous penances, and was so intimately united with God in prayer that several miracles are recorded as resulting from the power of her intercession.

Rich in merits and honored as a saint because of her virtues, she died in the monastery of the Poor Clares at Mantua in the year 1449. She had definitely stated that her grave was to bear no special inscription and that she was to be buried at the door of the sacristy where she would be trampled under foot, but also where the priests would be made mindful of her as they approached the altar.

ON VISITING THE SICK

1. In the sight of heaven, Paula must certainly have appeared more glorious than all the splendor of the princely household, when she ministered to the sick in the hospital and washed their feet. In the eyes of

the world such service appears lowly and contemptible, but viewed with the eyes of faith, it is so high and sublime that perhaps the pious marquise even considered herself unworthy to perform it, since to her it was nothing less than rendering a service to Christ our Lord Himself. Christ will one day say to those who have acted similarly and with faith: "I was sick and you visited Me. Amen, I say to you, as long as you did it to one of these My least brethren, you did it to Me" (Mt. 25,36-40). — Oh, how precious it is to visit the sick in Christian fashion! Do you ever perform this act of charity?

2. Consider that, aside from the heavenly reward that awaits us, we can derive great benefit here on earth from devoutly visiting the sick. In the sickroom we see what man really is. How weak and miserable he is after he has lain there for months, even if he could boast of his strength in the days of his health! What an object of pity he is if he is obliged to lie there for years, and cannot live and cannot die! Surely then we can forgive the occasional complaints he may make, and endeavor compassionately and sincerely to console him. Try to picture yourself lying there; what will then be your interest in the world and its pleasures? There will be nothing to comfort you then except a good conscience. At a sickbed you also learn to treasure your health, to thank God for it, and never rashly to expose it to danger. — Visit the sick frequently, if your duties permit it; do not only send them things, but take the things there yourself and look on this as paying a visit to our Saviour. In that way visiting the sick may often be better than a visit to the church. Tertiaries are encouraged by their rule to do this (2,13).

3. Consider that you ought to visit the sick in such a manner that it will be beneficial to the sick. Arrange your visit so that it will not be a burden to them; not calling on them too frequently, not unduly prolonging the visit, not speaking too much, not suggesting all sorts of remedies. Endeavor to put cheer into your visits, to console the sick person in a Christian manner, and if necessary to prepare him for a Christian end. Where it is appropriate, pray with him at times, and pray frequently for him and all the sick.

PRAYER OF THE CHURCH (From the Mass for the Sick)
Almighty, everlasting God, the eternal salvation of those who believe, hear us on behalf of Thy servants who are sick, for whom we humbly crave the help of Thy mercy, that, being restored to health, they may render thanks to Thee in Thy Church. Through Christ our Lord. Amen.

MARCH 18
ST. SALVATOR OF HORTA
Confessor, First Order

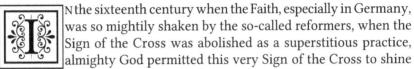N the sixteenth century when the Faith, especially in Germany, was so mightily shaken by the so-called reformers, when the Sign of the Cross was abolished as a superstitious practice, almighty God permitted this very Sign of the Cross to shine with special power and radiance, in order to strengthen the Faith in another country. This was in Spain, and it was through the great miracle worker of the sixteenth century, St. Salvator of Horta.

Salvator was born of poor parents in the year 1520. Orphaned when still quite young, he tended cattle and was later sent as an apprentice to a shoemaker in Barcelona. His devout heart, however, was constantly prompting him to consecrate himself to God; so, when he was twenty years old, he entered the Franciscan Order as a lay brother. He distinguished himself among his brethren by rigorous mortification, profound humility, and extraordinary simplicity. Almighty God, who chooses the lowly to make known the wonders of His power, manifested His power in Salvator at the very beginning of his religious life.

Salvator was sent to assist the brother in the kitchen, and one day, when the cook was ill, Salvator had to undertake the entire round of duties alone. When it was close to the noon hour, the Father Guardian went to the kitchen to see what Brother Salvator had prepared. He found the kitchen locked. After looking for Salvator for a considerable time, he finally found him kneeling before the Blessed Sacrament, deeply absorbed in prayer. Salvator had been there since early morning without being aware of it. The superior reproved him severely, and Salvator acknowledged his guilt amid many tears, begging for a severe penance. How astonished, however, were both men when they arrived at the kitchen and found all the food ready to be served; the angels had substituted for Salvator.

After pronouncing his vows, Salvator was sent to the convent at Tortosa. Although he was assigned in turn to the duties of cook, porter, and quester of alms, he was nevertheless continually recollected and intimately united with God. While gathering alms, he often came upon sick people for whom his prayers were requested. He would make the Sign of the Cross over them, and immediately they were healed. News of this fact soon spread abroad and many sick were brought to the convent. All were restored to health through the Sign of the Cross which Brother Salvator made over them.

The concourse of sick people, however, finally became so great that it disturbed the good order in the convent. So the superiors sent Brother Salvator to the nearby convent of Horta, where he spent the greater part of his religious life; hence his surname "of Horta." Although the transfer was made in perfect secrecy and no one had been informed of it, the sick presented themselves at the convent at Horta already in the first days after his arrival there, and their number increased daily. The deaf, the blind, the dumb, the lame, the epileptic, came; the paralytic, the dropsical, those afflicted with fevers, and sufferers of every type were brought to him on beds, so that Brother Salvator might restore their health. Usually there were as many as two thousand a week, sometimes that many in one day, and once, on the feast of the Annunciation of the Blessed Virgin, as many as six thousand made their appearance.

One time the grand inquisitor, a renowned theologian, whose duty it was to guard the purity of the Faith, came in order to learn whether anything occurred there that savored of superstition. Without giving any indication of his rank, he took his station at a corner of the church where the sick were expecting the healing hand of Brother Salvator. When the good religious arrived, he had the sick make way for him as he passed through their ranks till he reached the grand inquisitor. There he reverently kissed the latter's hand, and begged him to come to the upper church, where he could watch the entire proceedings. Astonished at finding himself recognized, the inquisitor was already assured of the power from on high which held sway there. Nevertheless, he followed the brother. Salvator began, as usual, to admonish the sick to examine their conscience and to receive the sacraments of penance and of the Holy Eucharist worthily. Then he blessed them with the Sign of the Cross while he called upon the Blessed Trinity and imposed on them a few prayers in honor of the Immaculate Conception of the Blessed Virgin Mary, to whose intercession he ascribed all the cures. The sufferers were then all suddenly cured, except, as Salvator had foretold, those who were not sincere in their conversion.

In order to test the humility of the brother and to preserve him in it, his superiors frequently imposed heavy trials, but he always remained an obedient, humble, and contented religious. A prominent gentleman once warned Salvator that he should be on his guard against pride and presumption. The good brother answered: "I always think of myself as a sack full of straw; the sack is indifferent as to whether it lies in a stable or is brought into a magnificent room."

The last two years of his life were spent on the island of Sardinia, and there he died in the convent of Cagliari on March 18, 1567. Innumerable miracles occurred also at his grave. The uninterrupted devotion to the saint was confirmed by Pope Clement XI. He was canonized by Pope Pius XI in 1938. His feast is observed by the Franciscans, Capuchins, and Third Order Regular on March eighteenth, by the Conventuals on April fourth.

ON THE POWER OF THE SIGN OF THE CROSS

1. Consider what great miracles Blessed Salvator wrought by means of the Sign of the Cross. That should not at all astonish us, for, since it is from the cross that all salvation proceeds, especially the saving of souls from hell, why should it not be able to heal the body, too, of its diseases? Yet, only those were cured that in all sincerity first cleansed their souls in the sight of God; "for," said St. Salvator, "God does not confer special favors on His enemies." If we would, first of all, secure the friendship of God, and then with the reverence, the lively faith and firm hope of St. Salvator make the Sign of the Cross, we, too, would surely even today experience its miraculous powers. — How have you acted in the past?

2. Consider that we ought to make the Sign of the Cross to obtain the blessing of God on all our undertakings. With the Sign of the Cross we call the attention of our heavenly Father to the death which His beloved Son suffered for us. Will He refuse to hear us for its sake? Thomas a Kempis says: "In the Cross is salvation, in the Cross is life. In the Cross is strength of mind, in the Cross is joy of spirit, in the Cross is infusion of heavenly sweetness. In the Cross is height of virtue; in the Cross is perfection of sanctity." We do not make the Sign of the Cross often enough. We should make it especially on awakening in the morning, before and after prayer, before and after work, on entering our home as well as the church. Then everything will be placed under the protection of Christ crucified, of whom St. Peter says: "Neither is there salvation in any other" (Acts 4,12). — Have you made diligent use of the Sign of the Cross?

3. Consider that we should protect ourselves from evil with the Sign of the Cross. On the cross, Christ atoned for sin, which is the source of all evil, and vanquished the devil, the enemy of our salvation. That is why the child is so frequently signed with the cross at holy baptism, so that the devil may have no more power over it. If he tempts you, sign yourself with the cross. Bless yourself confidently also in all dangers to which your body or your temporal affairs are exposed. In times of worry and heavy suffering that threaten to depress you, again make the Sign of the Cross. Just as the bitter water which the Israelites found in the desert, became palatable when at God's command they threw the fagots of wood into it,

so does the devout use of the Sign of the Cross make the bitterness of suffering sweet and meritorious.

PRAYER OF THE CHURCH

Grant, we beseech Thee, O almighty God, that we who celebrate the memory of Thy servant Salvator, may, through his intercession, be delivered from all evils here on earth and may one day attain to the eternal joys. Through Christ our Lord. Amen.

MARCH 19
BLESSED HIPPOLYTE GALANTINI
Confessor, Third Order

HE parents of Blessed Hippolyte were simple laborers of Florence. The father was a weaver, whose scanty income was hardly sufficient to provide for the daily sustenance of his family. Their chief riches consisted in their probity and virtue. Their son, Hippolyte, however, was destined to prove a veritable treasure to them. He was remarkable for his obedience and kind-heartedness, which caused him to be beloved by his parents and all with whom he came in contact. He might have been taken for an angel in human form. When he was five years old, he would gather the little children of the neighborhood about him, mount some improvised platform, and repeat to them the sermons which he had heard in church. At the age of nine he was admitted to holy Communion, and from then on gave himself up to the practice of interior prayer. He endeavored to do this also at his work while he assisted his father.

Having attained his twelfth year, he felt strongly inclined to embrace the religious life. But because he was delicate in appearance, little hope was held out to him to gain admission in a convent. Moreover, his father did not feel that he could spare him. Heaven had destined Hippolyte for another calling.

Impelled by an interior prompting and with the approval of his confessor, Hippolyte gathered the children together, taught them Christian doctrine, and prepared them for the reception of the holy sacraments. Later on he also gathered about him young men and young women and such that were not well instructed in their religion, in order to teach them during the evening hours and on Sundays.

This undertaking was not without its hardships and also met with opposition, but faithful to the advice of his devout and experienced confessor, he persevered in it. He lived to see the blessed fruits of his labors. The archbishop of Florence, Alexander of Medici, who later on became Pope Leo XI, interested himself in the undertaking. A chapel was turned over to Hippolyte where he could drill the ignorant in the prayers and fundamental doctrines of religion; also a house in which neglected children were provided with a home. Several young men joined him in his labors of love; many prominent persons contributed to the support of the work and encouraged it in every way.

A confraternity arose out of these beginnings, and Hippolyte placed it under the special protection of his seraphic Father Francis. It was called the "Confraternity of Christian Doctrine of St. Francis," and was approved by Pope Clement VIII in 1602. Its principal objectives were to instruct youth in the truths of Christianity and to keep them away from dangerous amusements; but the members also interested themselves in every type of misery and dereliction as need required. The members of the confraternity engaged in their pious practices, after their daily duties had been performed, in place of recreation. Hippolyte himself never neglected his weaving on that account.

By means of set prayers and spiritual exercises they aimed also to sanctify themselves more and more. The good which the confraternity effected in Florence was so considerable that Hippolyte was requested to establish similar institutions in other cities: Volterra, Pistoia, Lucca, Modena, Parma, and elsewhere. He continued to live as a simple workingman and submitted minutely to the guidance of his spiritual director. But God, who chooses the weak to confound the strong, glorified him by means of heavenly inspirations and the gift of miracles.

The servant of God saw the most bountiful blessings proceed from his labors when God called him to his eternal reward in the year 1620. He was at once honored as a saint, and in 1824, Pope Leo XII approved the celebration of his feast in Florence and several other dioceses in Tuscany. His feast is observed on March twentieth by the Franciscans and the Third Order Regular. (Cf. *Forum*, 1947, pp. 71-73; *These Made Peace*, pp. 191-195.)

ON CONFRATERNITIES

1. Consider what boundless good Blessed Hippolyte, who was only a simple workingman, effected for the salvation of souls. The confraternity which he established proved a source of many blessings even in places where he himself could not labor, and these blessings continued long after

his death. Saints and zealous men have thus done good far and wide over long periods of time by the establishment of pious societies or confraternities. The ardent desire of their hearts to promote the honor of God and to benefit their neighbor was the germ of undertakings which almighty God made so productive of good. "To the just their desires shall be given" (Prov. 10,24). — If you accomplish so little good, is it not, perhaps, because you have so meager a desire for it?

2. Consider the good effects these confraternities produce in their members. The prayers which the various confraternities prescribe are said by the members in intimate union with one another, and the word of God can be applied to them: "If two of you shall consent upon earth concerning anything whatsoever they ask, it shall be done to them by My Father who is in heaven" (Mt. 18,19). How effective, then, must be the well-said prayers of a confraternity! But the various confraternities also encourage the performance of other good works: care for the poor and the sick, a good education for children, the avoidance of dangerous amusements, preparation for a good death, and similar objectives. Consequently, Holy Church has blessed them and granted various indulgences to its members. — Who would not gladly have a part in these blessings by being a member of a confraternity?

3. Consider that the blessings accruing from a confraternity are gained only when we join it in the spirit of the Church. But this spirit of the Church is concerned with the actual purpose of the society, not with its externals. For example, you may not join a confraternity because of the attractive scapular or other insignia that its members wear, but rather to foster veneration for the Mother of God, the spirit of penance, devotion to the Passion of Christ, active charity towards your neighbor, or whatever other purpose the confraternity has proposed as its goal. Hence, you must faithfully observe what is prescribed, and not join too many of them. A well-managed confraternity can change the whole aspect of a parish and renew in it the right spirit.

PRAYER OF THE CHURCH
(Friday in the Fourth Week of Lent)

O God, who renewest the world by wonderful sacraments: grant, we beseech Thee, that Thy Church may profit by Thy eternal institutions and be not deprived of succor in her temporal needs. Through Christ our Lord. Amen.

MARCH 20
BLESSED JOHN OF PARMA
Confessor, First Order

OHN OF PARMA was the seventh general of the Franciscan Order, and labored zealously during his administration to reanimate the spirit of the order. He was a descendant of the ancient noble family of the Buralli, and was born at Parma in the year 1209. He was in high repute for learning and piety, and was professor of philosophy in his native city, when the love of God urged him to forsake the world and devote himself wholly to God in the Order of Friars Minor. At the time he was twenty-five years of age. Already during his year of probation he was imbued with the spirit of our holy Father St. Francis; he loved poverty above all things, not only so far as the renunciation of external goods is concerned, but also in the sacrifice of his will and the esteem tendered him, so that he was a model of humility, abnegation, and self-sacrifice.

After his profession he was sent to Paris to complete his course in theology. After he was ordained to the priesthood, his superiors employed him in the apostolic ministry. Then he was appointed professor of theology, and acquitted himself of this task with remarkable success at Bologna, Naples, and Rome.

Pope Innocent IV convoked a general council in the city of Lyons in the year 1245. As the minister general, Crescentius, was unable to attend the council because of age and infirmity, he deputed Father John to go to the council in his stead. Here John won for himself the admiration of all the prelates of the Church by his wisdom, knowledge, and virtue; and the sovereign pontiff gave him his full confidence.

Two years later, when the pope himself presided at the general chapter of the Franciscan Order for the election of a general, the pope pointed out John as the man best qualified for the office. So, he was elected minister general of the order in 1247. Universal rejoicing reigned among the good religious, especially among the surviving disciples of St. Francis. They trusted that the spirit of poverty and humility would bud forth anew, and they were not disappointed in their hopes.

As general of the order, John visited practically all the convents in the various countries. He always journeyed on foot, clothed in a poor habit, accompanied by only one or two friars. Sometimes it happened that he spent several days in a convent as an unknown guest, and could without trouble observe everything that occurred before he revealed his identity.

Everywhere he set the example of a perfect Friar Minor and made the best possible provision toward promoting religious perfection.

The pope, who called him an angel of peace, sent him as his legate to Constantinople to bring back the schismatic Greeks to Catholic unity. For two years John labored at this task with remarkable wisdom and much success. Upon his return he deemed it best that someone else be appointed to govern the order. This was in the year 1257. Upon the urgent request of his brethren, he named St. Bonaventure as a worthy successor. He it was who completed the work begun by his predecessor.

John now withdrew to a hermitage in Greccio, where he spent a life far more angelic than human. One morning when the server failed to appear for his holy Mass, an angel came instead. John had spent thirty-two years in this solitude when he learned that the Greeks who had been reconciled with the Church, had again relapsed into schism. Although he was then eighty years old, John was eager to undertake the journey to the East in order to restore unity. Pope Nicholas IV gladly assented to the plan. But, arriving at Camerino, John felt that his end was near. He himself exclaimed: "Here is the place of my rest."

He received the last sacraments with great devotion, and departed from this life on the twentieth of March, in the year 1289. Numerous miracles occurred at his grave. Even those who had formerly persecuted and calumniated him came to beg his forgiveness. Pope Pius VI beatified him in 1781. All three branches of the First Order observe his feast on March twentieth.

RENOUNCE AND ENDURE

1. Even worldly-wise heathens recognized with the faint light of reason that the secret of a perfect life is contained in the words: Renounce and endure. Blessed John of Parma found the source of happiness and holiness in these words. — We, too, must renounce, if we wish to be happy and to lead a life that will be pleasing to God. We must renounce the many inclinations that impel us to sensuality, avarice, and the love of honor. By nature man needs little to satisfy his needs; but cupidity is a glutton that will not be satisfied. If we wish to be happy, then, we must deny ourselves whatever the passions crave for. In order to be a servant of Christ, you must even deny yourself necessary things: "Every one of you who does not renounce everything that he possesses, cannot be My disciple" (Lk. 14,33). —What progress have you made in renunciation?
2. Just as we must renounce what our interior and inordinate desires crave for, so must we endure whatever occurs externally to cause us vexation.

Heat and cold, hunger and thirst, fatigue and infirmity befall us in this earthly life ever since the day of original sin, and we must patiently endure them as universal punishment for sin. No man escapes them: "Man, living for a short time, is filled with many miseries" (Job 14,1). In his religious life as well as on his many journeys, Blessed John willingly submitted to innumerable hardships; should we not, then, accept the necessary ones with patience? — How do you bear them?

3. Consider that while we must suffer from the inclemencies of the seasons and the frailties of our nature, there is much more to endure from the people with whom we come in contact. But such things, too, we must suffer with patience. Others must bear with us, why should we not have to bear with their frailties? Particularly we shall have much to endure if we wish to lead others to do what is right. At the same time we should modestly withdraw if we notice that others are more competent at such work. When Blessed John perceived that another was better able than he to conclude happily what he had begun, he withdrew and confined himself to ceaseless prayer that God's blessing might rest upon the labors of his successor. Nor was this blessing wanting. "The patient man is better than the valiant, and he who rules the spirit, than he who takes cities" (Prov. 16,32).

PRAYER OF THE CHURCH

O God, who, in order to promote the honor of Thy name, didst bestow upon Blessed John invincible strength of soul, grant that we may merit the assistance of Thy almighty hand in attaining to the triumph of heavenly glory. Through Christ our Lord. Amen.

☙☙☙☙☙☙☙☙☙☙☙

MARCH 21
BLESSED MARK OF MONTEGALLO
Confessor, First Order

ARK was the scion of a distinguished family of Montegallo in the diocese of Ascoli. He was extraordinarily devout already in his youth, and undertook the study of medicine in order to be able to assist the sick poor. He received his doctor's degree at the University of Bologna. At the urgent wish of his father he entered the married state although he would rather have completely severed himself from the world and the things of the world. Not long afterwards his father and mother died. Again the devout longing for the religious state seized him. When he confided the fact to his wife, she told him she was of the same mind, and so both of them yielded to their pious desire, Mark entering the convent of the Friars Minor, and his wife joining the Poor Clares at Ascoli.

In a very short time Mark displayed all the virtues that are distinctive of a true Friar Minor, so that as soon as he was ordained to the priesthood, his superiors placed him in charge of the community at San Severino. There he set a most extraordinary example in mortification, prayer, and works of charity. One day, while deeply absorbed in prayer, he heard a voice which said: "Brother Mark, go out and preach charity!" That was, indeed, a call from heaven, in compliance with which he now labored unceasingly during the space of forty years as a missionary.

The principal topic of his discourses was the love of God and neighbor, always a most timely one, but notably at that time, for Italy was torn by factions that caused the inhabitants of almost every town to be at variance with one another. Mark's words, animated by true charity, affected them in an unusual way and produced the blessed fruits of peace and harmony. However, he did not only preach charity, he also practiced it and thereby induced others to follow his example. He knew just how to influence wealthy people generously to support the poor, and he was instrumental, wherever he perceived the need for it, in establishing people's banks of the kind called "Mounts of Mercy," in order to protect the people of moderate means from the hands of usurers.

Frequently God blessed his undertakings in a remarkable way. The plague had broken out in Camerino. Every day the terrible epidemic claimed new victims, and the entire citizenry was seized with a mortal fear. Father Mark went out among them like an angel of consolation sent by heaven itself. He rendered aid wherever he could; but as a physician of souls, he gave a sermon in which he told the people that the deadly plague came to them as a punishment for their indifference and their sins. If they would sincerely repent of their sins, God would withdraw the scourge. His admonition touched their hearts, they besought God for mercy, and were sincere in their conversion; soon the disease abated.

Mark was well nigh seventy years old when he conducted the Lenten sermons at Vicenza. About the middle of Lent he was seized with diphtheria, which brought him to death's door within a few days. After he had received the last sacraments, he had someone read to him the history of the sufferings of our Lord. At the words: "He bowed His head and gave up the spirit," Blessed Mark also bowed his head and surrendered his soul into the hands of his Maker on March 19, 1497.

Immemorial devotion to him was sanctioned by Pope Gregory XVI. His feast is observed on March twentieth by the Franciscans and the Capuchins.

ON ACTIVE CHARITY TOWARDS OUR NEIGHBOR

1. Blessed Mark took to heart the admonition of the beloved disciple: "My little children, let us not love in word, nor in tongue, but in deed and in truth" (1 Jn. 3,18). While even his sermons and the reconciliation of enmities which he effected were extraordinary acts of charity, nevertheless, religious though he was, he found means to relieve the needs of the poor and even to provide for an institution that would permanently assist many in their distress. "The accomplishment of deeds" says a holy doctor, "is the best proof of the motives of the heart." — Does your charity for your neighbor manifest itself in this way?

2. Consider that works of charity, if they are to be accounted as virtue, must proceed from unselfish motives. The love of God, who so desires charity, must be the motive; to relieve the need of our fellowmen, must be the purpose. It will not make any difference to us, then, whether the needy person is a relative or a stranger, a friend or an enemy. "If the enemy be hungry, give him to eat; if he thirst, give him water to drink" (Prov. 25,21). The desire to be praised by men may not actuate our acts of benevolence; we should even be, so to say, unaware of our charity and think nothing of it. "But when you give alms, let not your left hand know what your right hand does" (Mt. 6,3). — Were your past acts of charity as disinterested as that?

3. Consider how sweet will be the reward of our charity when it is motivated by the love of God. Even here on earth it is decidedly a joy for any person who is not entirely without sentiment to have been instrumental in aiding another person in his need. The more unknown to others the good work has been, the more one has had to sacrifice personally to accomplish the good deeds, so much the purer will be the joy of heart that we shall experience. Then we shall perceive that the words of Holy Writ, which the world finds so difficult to believe, are actually true: "It is a more blessed thing to give rather than to receive" (Acts 20,35). Hence, he who is wise will bear in mind not only to make bequests after his death for charitable purposes, but will contribute already in this life with the joy of heart which is granted in reward. The complete reward, of course, will be dispensed only in eternity, when on the last day, which otherwise holds so many terrors, God will say to those who have practiced works of charity for His sake: "Come, you blessed of My Father, as long

as you did it to one of these My least brethren, you did it to Me" (Mt. 25,40).

PRAYER OF THE CHURCH

O God, who through Blessed Mark, Thy confessor, didst stir up Thy faithful people to love of God and neighbor, we beseech Thee, that through his merits and intercession we may obtain the grace ever to discharge the duties of charity. Through Christ our Lord. Amen.

MARCH 22
ST. BENVENUTE OF OSIMO
Confessor, First Order

THIS holy prelate was born at Ancona, of the distinguished family of the Scotivoli. He studied theology and law at the University of Bologna. After his return to Ancona and his ordination to the holy priesthood, the bishop made him archdeacon or auxiliary in the administration of the diocese, because of his eminent knowledge and striking virtues. In this capacity he rendered such remarkable service to the Church, that the attention of Pope Urban IV was drawn to him, and the Holy Father believed that he could find no more capable person to whom he could entrust the administration of the diocese of Osimo.

The city of Osimo, which belonged to the Papal States, had formed an alliance with Emperor Frederick II against the pope and the Church. In penalty, it had, for the space of twenty years, been deprived of a bishop. Governing the people gently yet firmly, Benvenute pacified them and succeeded in convincing them of what was for their best interests, so that they repented and returned to the obedience of the pope.

Now that they desired to have a bishop again, the pope chose the former administrator Benvenute, whom he called "a man according to his own heart." Far from allowing himself to be elated over the preferment, Benvenute asked the Holy Father for permission to be invested with the holy habit of St. Francis and to profess the rule before he was consecrated bishop, for he believed that in the practice of poverty, humility, penance, and constant prayer, he would best be able to govern his diocese properly. Touched by this request, the Holy Father gave his consent, and Benvenute wore the habit of the Friars Minor from that day until his death, observing the rule most faithfully.

He continued to govern the diocese of Osimo for thirteen years with so much wisdom, and succeeded in putting such order into affairs, that at the end of his administration the words of the Psalmist could be applied: "Mercy and truth have met each other; justice and peace have kissed" (Ps. 84,11).

When he felt that his end was drawing near, he caused himself to be carried into the cathedral, and there, after the example of his holy Father St. Francis, he begged to be laid upon the bare earth, where, amid the prayers of the priests, he passed away peacefully on the twenty-second of March, 1282. He was buried on the spot where he died, and God at once glorified his tomb with so many miracles that Pope Martin IV canonized him within three years after his death. The First Order observes his feast on March twenty-second, and the Third Order Regular on the twenty-third.

ON THE ADMINISTRATION OF OFFICES

1. Consider, that, in the designs of God, there are various offices in the Church and in the State. God wishes it so, first of all, so that society may be well regulated. Furthermore, so that human beings, duly graded one beneath the other, be preserved from the dangers of pride. In this way, too, God's sovereign authority is exercised in the various positions through mortal men as His representatives. For, rightful authority in all its degrees, great or small, even if it be only the charge of watching over children, is given by God Himself. "There is no power but from God" (Rom. 13,1). — Let us admire the wisdom of God. "(Wisdom) reaches therefore from end to end mightily, and orders all things sweetly" (Wisd. 8,1).

2. Consider that every Christian should strive to fulfill the obligations of his office faithfully; for he acts as God's representative, who will some day require an account of his administration. That thought was constantly before the eyes of Bishop Benvenute; for that reason he humbled himself so profoundly and besought God unceasingly for His assistance. In that way he obtained the necessary strength with all firmness and gentleness to carry his responsible burden through to a successful issue. With humility, fear of the Lord, and trust in God, we, too, shall obtain from God the necessary grace to fulfill the duties of our office with marked fidelity. — If you were asked now to "give an account of your stewardship" (Lk. 16,2), could you hope to be accounted as a faithful steward?

3. Consider how we offend God by the misuse of authority entrusted to us

in any office. When Pilate, priding himself in his power, said to Christ: "Do you not know that I have power to crucify you, and I have power to release you?" (Jn. 19,10), our Lord reminded him that he received this power from God alone, and that he would be guilty of sin if he abused it through weakness, although the sin of those who had delivered Him up was still greater. Nor should anyone use his office for his own profit; because offices are entrusted to people not for their benefit but for the general welfare: to promote what is good, to prevent what is evil, to punish the guilty, to protect the innocent.

PRAYER OF THE CHURCH

O God, who didst grant to Thy holy confessor and bishop Benvenute the grace always to watch over his flock with a shepherd's solicitude, grant, we beseech Thee, that we may be enabled through his mediation to accomplish what Thou hast ordained, and thus happily to attain to the enjoyment of Thy glory. Through Christ our Lord. Amen.

MARCH 23
ST. CATHARINE OF GENOA
Widow, Third Order

ATARINETTA (little Catharine) Fieschi, child of a noble family of Genoa, was born 1447. At thirteen she wanted to enter a convent, but was refused admission because of her youth. When she was sixteen, she was given in marriage to a young nobleman, Julian Adorno by name. For this reason she is sometimes called St. Catharine Fieschi-Adorno. Her husband turned out to be pleasure-loving, quick-tempered, unfaithful. This was a great trial for Catarinetta; and for a while she tried to drown her disappointment in a whirl of pleasure. However, she retained her trust in God and did not give up her religious exercises.

One day in 1473 she visited the convent where her sister was a nun, and there went to confession. That confession was a turning point in her life. In her sadness and desperation she had turned to God; and He now filled her soul with a large measure of grace, making her realize vividly her own sins and inflaming her heart with seraphic love. She began to receive holy Communion every day, and continued to do so for the rest of her life. She entered upon a most intense spiritual life. After reforming herself, she converted her husband, and then lost herself in service to the poor and the sick.

Financial ruin, brought on by the spendthrift life her husband had been living, served as a reason for disposing of their palatial home on the Via Lomellini and to take up their abode in the Pammatone, largest hospital of Genoa. Living henceforth as brother and sister, Catharine and her husband now devoted themselves completely to the works of mercy. In 1490 Catharine was made matron of the women's division of the hospital; and she held this position for twenty-one years until her death.

After her husband's death in 1497, a terrible plague broke out in Genoa and lasted for four years, carrying off four-fifths of the population. Catharine heroically sacrificed herself for the sick, day and night. At the same time she continued her accustomed penances and religious exercises. Frequently she was lost in ecstasy; and even when she was busily engaged in work, her mind was occupied with the things of heaven. She succeeded in a marvelous manner in combining complete "other-worldliness" with the most capable "practicality." She also wrote an excellent treatise on Purgatory and another which is a Dialogue of the soul and the body. The Holy Office declared that these works alone are proof enough of her genuine holiness.

Purgatory, she points out, is not a joyless place, but rather one full of joy in God, which however does not abate one particle of its excruciating suffering. Bidding farewell to her goddaughter, Tomasina Vernazza, Catharine said to her: "Tomasina! Jesus in your heart! Eternity in your mind! The will of God in all your actions! But, above all, love, God's love, entire love!" That, too, had been the program of her own life.

A mystical and mysterious illness, which was really the fire of divine love, consumed the last nine years of her life. One night in August, 1510, she requested that the windows of her room be opened that she might see the starry sky. A large number of candles were lighted, and the dying seraphic lover sang the Veni Creator Spiritus. "Let us go!" she exclaimed. "No more of earth, no more of earth!" She died two weeks later, on September fifteenth, the feast of the Exaltation of the Holy Cross. Pope Clement XII canonized her in 1737.

Although Butler-Thurston's Lives states that she "never became a religious or even a Tertiary," it has now been proved quite convincingly that she was a member of the Third Order Secular of St. Francis. It is certain that her converted husband joined the Third Order at the Del Monte friary of the Observant Franciscans in 1488 and remained a faithful member till his death in 1497. He himself declares in his will that he became a Tertiary at the urging of his pious spouse. Furthermore, the friars were her spiritual directors; and Blessed Bernardin of Feltre put a number of souls under her guidance. Blessed Angelo of Chiavasso helped to found the hospital of which she was superintendent. In her writings Catharine follows St. Bonaventure, especially in the doctrine on Purgatory. Two penitential habits of hers, which are still extant, are like those used by the Franciscans of the time. The Genoese people were wont to call her Catarina Serafina. Her remains are venerated in the Capuchin church at Genoa. Although no date can be assigned for the exact time when she was received into the Third Order, there is every reason for regarding and honoring her as one of the great Tertiary saints. As yet the Franciscans and the Conventuals do not celebrate her feast; but the Capuchins observe it on March twenty-third and the Third Order Regular on the twenty-second, which latter is her feastday in Genoa. (Cf. *Forum*, 1946, p. 192; 1949, pp. 79-80, 92-93; 1951, p. 32. Also Biersack, pp. 19-20.)

ON FREQUENT HOLY COMMUNION

1. No doubt, the effects of holy Communion, which St. Catharine received daily, kept her so intimately united with God wherever she was and however she was occupied. Our Lord has said: "He that eats My flesh and drinks My blood, remains in Me and I in him" (Jn. 6,57). And this intimate union with God was the cause of Catharine's saintly life. She could surely say with the Prophet: "As the hart pants after the fountains of living waters, so my soul pants after Thee, my God" (Ps. 41,2). — Do you appreciate holy Communion to that extent? Do you entertain such a desire for it? Are you willing to make sacrifices for it?

2. Consider that frequent holy Communion is not meant only for perfect souls, but also for those who are sincerely striving to become holy. But to that goal Christ our Lord called every Christian. Because we are weak, we need the bread of the strong; because we fall so readily, we need this means of grace, which, as the holy Council of Trent teaches us, cleanses us from our daily imperfections and preserves us from mortal sin. Thomas a Kempis (4,3) therefore says: "Because I so often fail and commit sin, so quickly grow torpid and faint, it is necessary for me that by frequent prayer and confession, and by the sacred receiving of Thy Body, I may again be renewed, cleansed, and inflamed to do that which is good." — If you so frequently relapse into sin, are so torpid in doing good, find it so difficult to adapt yourself to the vicissitudes of life, is the reason perhaps to be found in your infrequent reception of holy Communion? Hear our Lord saying to you: "Come to Me, I will refresh you."

3. The number of times a person may go to holy Communion depends on

the state of his conscience. Pope Pius X following Pope Leo XIII (May 28, 1902), urged the faithful to receive often, even daily, so long as they are in the state of grace and approach with the right intention of pleasing God and benefiting their soul. The rule of the Third Order prescribes for its members that they must receive at least once a month. The popes explain, however, that such rules in religious institutes must be taken as the mininum. The good fruits which holy Communion produces, especially fidelity to everyday duty and to the Commandments, in turn make us the more worthy to receive often. — Helped by frequent reception of the most Holy Sacrament and by ardent longing for the heavenly food of souls, may you grow more and more worthy of the grace of frequent holy Communion.

PRAYER OF THE CHURCH

Hear us, O God our Saviour, and grant that as we are gladdened by the festival of blessed Catharine, so we may learn from it loving devotion toward Thee. Through Christ our Lord. Amen.

MARCH 24
THE SERVANT OF GOD ADOLPH OF SCHAUMBURG
Confessor, First Order

DOLPH IV, duke of Schaumburg, lord of Holstein, Ditmarsch, and Wagria, had hardly taken possession of the lands he inherited from his father, when the Danish King Waldemar II took up arms to rob him of his paternal inheritance. On July 22, 1227, a hotly contested and bloody battle took place at Bornhovede in Holstein. Sorely pressed, Adolph made a vow that if God gave him the victory, he would forsake the world and don the habit of St. Francis. Immediately the tide of battle turned to his advantage. The Ditmarsch troops, who had allied themselves with the Danes, came over to his side. Shortly four thousand Danes lay slain on the battlefield, while their king was wounded, and only by dint of great effort did he escape from being taken prisoner.

Because his sons had not yet attained to maturity, Adolph could not at once fullfill his vow. Nevertheless he attached himself to the Seraphic Order more intimately from day to day, and built several Franciscan convents at Luebeck, Hamburg, and Kiel.

In the year 1239 his sons were of an age that he could resign the government into their hands, and now he entered the novitiate in the convent at Kiel. In the year 1244, he was ordained to the priesthood and celebrated his first holy Mass in the convent church at Schwerin. After this he labored with blessed success in various convents of his order, particularly at Luebeck, Hamburg, and Oldenburg. Withal he was as modest and retired, as obedient and humble as if he had completely forgotten his noble birth and former rank.

On one occasion when he was returning to the convent with a jug full of milk which he had obtained as an alms for the brethren, he was met by his sons and a retinue of nobles and servants on horseback. The first impulse that came over him was one of shame at carrying a jug of milk; but he reproached himself for it at once, poured the milk over his head so that he was completely doused with it, and said to himself: "So, you are ashamed of the poverty of Christ? Everyone shall now see on your head what you were ashamed to be found carrying in your hand."

A serious illness seized him in the convent at Kiel in the year 1261. When he was assailed by fear a the thought of death and judgment, the Queen of heaven, accompanied by many saints, appeared to him and said: "Why do you tremble, my son? Why do you fear to let your soul leave this prison of its body to enter into eternal freedom and bliss? See, my Divine Son is approaching in order to receive your spirit and to reward you for the many years you have spent in the poverty and austerity of the order. Come, then, O soul, with joy and confidence, for a blessed dwelling awaits you."

Filled with heavenly consolation on hearing these words, Adolph departed blessedly in the Lord. In the Franciscan church at Kiel, which has since been destroyed, a memorial tablet with the following inscription was in evidence for many years:

> "Holstein, mourn not the death of thy ruler.
> With Francis he reigns on heaven's high throne."

ON THE VOWS

1. Consider how agreeable to God must have been the vow which Duke Adolph made, since He at once turned the tide of battle in favor of the prince. Truly, what he promised was something of very great value, of greater worth than any battle he could win. It is clear that the vow was not merely an offering made to God under stress of necessity, but a voluntary sacrifice to Him, whose supreme dominion is more clearly

recognized in the time of need than at any other time. Such voluntary promises to do a good tiling which we are not bound to perform, but to which we bind ourselves with pious intent, must be especially pleasing to God, since, besides the good work that is promised, a person also sacrifices his liberty. If it is in itself highly meritorious that some particular thing be promised to God, such as a voluntary fast, a pilgrimage, some little prayer to be said daily, an alms to be given weekly, then it is all the more agreeable when a man offers himself for a lifetime to the service of God, as Duke Adolph did. Is it surprising, then, that God should reward a vow like that with such extraordinary assistance?

2. Consider that, aside from the special assistance which a vow may bring us in the time of need, a good work is always more meritorious when vowed than if the same work were done without a vow. The vow sanctifies the work even before it is given to God, and the deed becomes the more precious, in the way that a blessed candle is more precious than an unblessed one. Binding ourselves with a vow to do anything for a definite time or for a lifetime, we offer to God the tree itself together with the fruit. Furthermore, vows made with contrite sentiments in the determination to give up a habitual failing prove a strong remedy against relapsing into sin. — But, you say, the vow deprives me of my liberty, and I place a new burden upon myself. True! But should you not rather say with St. Augustine: "O blessed necessity that leads me to do good and preserves me from relapsing into sin"?

3. Consider that a serious obligation attaches to the taking of a vow. "Vow," says the Psalmist (75,12), "and pay to the Lord your God." And the Wise Man admonishes us: "If you have vowed anything to God, defer not to pay it. It is much better not to vow, than after a vow not to perform the things promised" (Ecclus. 5,3-4). There may be reasons for deferring the fulfillment of the vow, as was the case with Duke Adolph — if he had died meanwhile, he would not have been responsible to God for it. But he who can do so and has not been duly dispensed, must fulfill the vow without delay, otherwise he commits not an ordinary sin, but rather a sacrilege, since he withholds from God a gift which he has given to Him. Be cautious not to make a vow rashly, and in matters of consequence, consult your confessor. But if you have made a vow, do not hesitate, but fulfill your promise as soon and as cheerfully as possible, so that you may enjoy the entire fruit of your offering.

PRAYER OF THE CHURCH
(No. 29 under "Various Prayers")

O God, who makest all things to be of profit to them that love Thee, give
unto our hearts an abiding love for Thee; that our desires arising from
Thine inspiration, may not waver through any temptation. Through
Christ our Lord. Amen.

MARCH 25
VENERABLE JANE MARY OF THE CROSS
Virgin, Second Order

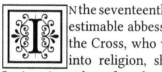N the seventeenth century there lived at Roveredo in Tyrol the
estimable abbess of the Poor Clare monastery, Jane Mary of
the Cross, who was born in 1603. Even before her entrance
into religion, she had surrendered herself to her Divine
Saviour in such perfect charity that He espoused Himself to her with the
bridal ring, as He had done on another occasion to St. Catharine of Siena.
In fasting and mortification, Jane led so austere a life in the convent that
for several years the amount of food she ate week by week was so meager
that it could readily be held in the hollow of one hand. Holy Communion,
which she received daily, seemed to be the only nourishment not only of
her soul but of her body. During her administration the community
flourished in every possible way; she established another house in Borgo
in the diocese of Trent.

Jane was known far and wide for the divine inspirations with which
God favored her, and persons of every state in life came to ask her advice
in serious matters. Even Emperor Leopold I came to the abbess of
Roveredo with his wife, in order to seek counsel in matters of conscience.

When Jane Mary had any spare time, it was spent in profound
meditation, generally on the bitter Passion and Death of Christ. Just how
intimately she was united with her suffering Saviour during these periods,
our Lord wished to indicate in a visible manner by allowing a crown of
thorns to grow out of her head. He caused her also to share with Him the
disgrace heaped upon Him. She was slandered and persecuted, was
subjected to the most embarrassing investigations, and along with all this,
had to endure the most painful maladies. But she bore everything with
heroic patience and the desire to suffer still more.

A few days before her death, our Lord favored her with the stigmata.

The marks were visible after her death, and were still red and bleeding in her hands and feet. The wound in the side was so deep that her heart could be seen through it.

Worn out in body, but aglow in spirit with the desire for God, she died on March 25, 1675, at the age of seventy-two. As her body lay in state, her countenance appeared in the freshness of youth like that of a growing young girl. Shortly after her death the process of her beatification was begun, but as yet it has not been concluded.

ON THE FIVE WOUNDS OF CHRIST

1. Consider how the heartfelt sympathy for the sufferings of our crucified Saviour, with which Venerable Jane was imbued, made her worthy to share with other saints the privilege of bearing in her body the wounds of her Lord. We, too, should be mindful of the excessive torture which our Lord suffered when His hands and feet were pierced with nails and He was fastened to the cross. If we impress this well upon our hearts as we look upon the wounds of Christ, there will doubtless be awakened in us fervent and grateful love for Him, for we must all say to ourselves meanwhile: "He loved me and sacrificed Himself for me" (Gal. 2,10). — Do you think of this when you look upon the wounds of Christ?

2. Consider that the open wounds of Christ should be places of refuge for us in times of temptation and of suffering. God's precious Blood, which broke the powers of hell and secured for us the necessary strength to meet the hardships of life, flowed from these wounds. The marks of these wounds, therefore, are a refuge where we can find protection against all temptations, and strength in all our sufferings. Blessed Jane Mary of Maillé, who also was severely tried, used to say frequently: "The five wounds of Jesus are my comfort in the hour of trial." — Fly to the wounds of Christ, as did Venerable Jane Mary, and you will experience the same blessed results. Where have you sought your consolation in the past?

3. Consider that Christ bore the marks of the holy wounds on His body even after the resurrection, and showed them to the apostle Thomas. When judgment day dawns, He will re-appear and show us these wounds again: "Behold, He comes with the clouds, and every eye shall see Him, and they also that pierced Him" (Apoc. 1,7). Oh, how grievously will they then lament who by their sins have pierced Him and nailed Him to the cross, and have not done penance! On the other hand, what consolations these wounds will be for those who have devoutly honored them on earth, who have wept for their sins, which caused them, and have taken refuge there in all their needs! Then, as a conquering general, Christ will lead

them triumphantly into His kingdom as a reward for their fidelity.

PRAYER OF THE CHURCH
(From the Mass of the Five Wounds of Our Lord)

O God, who through the Passion of Thine only-begotten Son and by the shedding of the blood from His five wounds didst restore our fallen nature, we beseech Thee, grant us who have honored His wounds here on earth, to partake in heaven of the fruit of His precious Blood. Through the same Christ our Lord. Amen.

MARCH 26
BLESSED DIDACUS JOSEPH OF CADIZ
Confessor, First Order

THIS humble Capuchin, who could make no progress at school, this "dunce of Cadiz," was later on admired by the world as the savior of the Faith in Spain, as a second Paul, as the apostle of his century. His lineage dated from the Visigoth kings. After he had taken the habit of St. Francis with the Capuchins in Seville, had been ordained to the priesthood, and had prepared himself by a holy life, he was appointed to the task of preaching.

Everybody marveled at the singular power and unction of his words, which swayed his audiences and left an impression on their lives. But most astonished of all was the venerable Dominican, Antonio Querero, a fellow student of Didacus, who knew how difficult study had been for him. A child, however, solved the problem one day during a sermon, when he shouted aloud in the church: "Mother, mother, see the dove resting on the shoulder of Father Didacus! I could preach like that too if a dove told me all that I should say!"

And there was the secret. Because of his humility and virtue, the Holy Spirit had converted this unlearned man into the most celebrated preacher in Spain. But how Father Didacus prayed before his sermons! How he scourged himself even unto blood, in order to draw down God's mercy upon the people!

Once when his superior chided him because of the austerity of his life, the saint replied: "Ah, Father, my sins and the sins of the people compel me to do it. Those who have been charged with the conversion of sinners must remember that the Lord has imposed upon them the sins of all their clients. By means of our penances we should atone for the sins of our fellowmen and thus preserve ourselves and them from eternal death. It would hardly be too much if we shed the last drop of our blood for their conversion."

In this disposition he journeyed through all Spain and infused new Catholic life wherever he went. In a very pronounced way he preached the praise of the most Holy Trinity and of the Blessed Virgin Mary.

Honors did not escape him. He was appointed extraordinary consultor of the Church, synodal examiner in almost all the Spanish dioceses, honorary canon, and honorary doctor of several universities. He died in 1801, in the fifty-eighth year of his highly blessed life, and was beatified by Pope Leo XIII. His feast is observed on March twenty-sixth by the Franciscans as well as the Capuchins.

ON THE NECESSITY OF PENANCE

1. Consider the rigorous penance of Blessed Didacus. We do not need, nor are we permitted to imitate him in it. But it would be well if we strove to cultivate the spirit which prompted him to undertake it. Not without reason does the holy council of Trent explain: "The whole life of a Christian should be one continuous act of penance." We are sinners, and the first requisite of true penance is the acknowledgment and confession of our sinfulness and hearty sorrow for our offenses. — Do you possess at least this kind of contrition?

2. Consider the admonition of our Lord: "Except you do penance, you shall all likewise perish" (Lk. 13,5), that is to say, by sudden death. Our Lord spoke these words after it had been reported to Him that a number of persons had died a sudden death. But who is there who would care to be surprised in his sins by sudden death? Let us, therefore, heed that other word also: "Today, if you hear His voice, harden not your hearts" (Heb. 3,8). — Should you not long ago have followed the call to penance?

3. Consider penance as atonement for the sins of others. What fruitful penance Blessed Didacus took upon himself in order to atone for the sins of the people. Hence, his sermons produced "fruits worthy of penance" (Lk. 3,8). He who seriously considers how frequently our good God is offended every day, will count it as a sweet obligation to impose small mortifications upon himself by way of atonement. — Have you ever thought of doing that? On Fridays? During Lent? During the Ember weeks?

PRAYER OF THE CHURCH

O God, who didst endow Thy blessed confessor, Didacus, with the science of the saints and didst work wonders through him for the salvation of his people, grant us through his intercession to think those things that are right and just, so that we may arrive safely at the kingdom of Thy glory. Through Christ our Lord. Amen.

MARCH 27

THE SERVANT OF GOD ARCHANGELA TARDERA
Virgin, Third Order

ARCHANGELA was the daughter of the pious physician Peter Tardera of Piazza on the island of Sicily. There the Third Order of St. Francis was held in high esteem. To manifest their regard for it, although they themselves were not yet Tertiaries, Archangela's parents clothed their little daughter at the age of seven in the gray garment which the Tertiaries wore in public.

The little one had ever been a good child, but now she led the life of a true religious. She practiced various rigorous mortifications, was a model of modesty, and by her conduct in church edified all who observed her. After her father died, Archangela, who was then seventeen years old, together with her mother, formally entered the Third Order. Her sister Laura soon followed her example. From now on the women led such devout lives that they were an edification to the entire town; Archangela gave the example.

She evinced such loving solicitude for poor orphans that she was quite generally known as the mother of the orphans. She had, moreover, a certain talent in reconciling married couples who were living in dissension. She had arranged a chapel in her home where the afflicted and the sorrowing could assemble in common prayer with the pious members of the house. This practice joined with the advice which they received from Archangela, invariably produced peace of heart. She drew her strength from her intimate communion with God. Sometimes she was rapt in ecstasy while at prayer; once she was granted the same privilege that was granted to our holy Father St. Francis—our Divine Lord appeared to her as a new-born infant in His crib, and, to her great delight, permitted her to embrace and caress Him.

However, the servant of God was also to be tried in the fire of tribulation, as gold is tried in the furnace. She was seized with severe maladies, one after the other, so that her limbs were as if withered; continuous palpitation of the heart alarmed her, and her whole body was in torture. These sufferings continued without interruption through the space of thirty-six years. But she bore them with great patience and in devout remembrance of the Passion of Christ.

Towards the end of her life our Lord impressed on her body His own five wounds. This grace she endeavored to conceal as much as possible, so that only a few persons knew of it during her lifetime. After her death the marks of the scourging were also detected on her body.

Amid all these tortures she was always heard to speak only of the sweet love of God. Finally the day arrived on which this faithful and tried soul was led into the glory of her Lord. She had foretold the day of her death, and died on it in the year 1608, at the age of sixty.

PATIENCE IN TRIALS

1. The Holy Ghost teaches us by the mouth of the Apostle (Rom. 5,4) that tribulation works patience, and patience trial, and that only trial gives hope of the glory of the sons of God. This we perceive in the lives of almost all the saints, and especially in the life of this servant of God Archangela. She was faithful in the service of God even in her childhood days, and had been granted many special favors by her Lord; but only the patience required for the long years of suffering proved her sterling qualities and made her worthy of the crown. Not the privilege of caressing the Divine Child, but carrying the cross conducted her to eternal bliss. — There are still many who, as Thomas a Kempis (2,11) says, "desire to rejoice with Jesus, but few are willing to endure anything for His sake. Many follow Jesus to the breaking of bread, but few to the drinking of the chalice of His Passion." — Do you belong to the many?

2. Consider why it is through patience in tribulation that man must be tried. As long as the service of God furnishes us with joy and sweetness, virtue cannot be recognized. Many a person serves God only because he derives profit for himself and experiences pleasure from it; but such people do not really love God, rather they love themselves and their pleasure. They fall by the wayside in the time of tribulation; their service of God is only seeming virtue, not true virtue. True virtue serves God because He is the Lord and the highest unchangeable Good, whom we must serve with fidelity at all times. The truly virtuous person acknowledges God's goodness and wisdom also in the afflictions which He sends. He knows that the Lord tries His faithful servants like gold in the furnace: "God has tried them and found them worthy of Himself"

(Wisd. 3,5). — In the time of trial, did He also find you prepared to stand the test?

3. Consider that the virtue that is tried by afflictions also increases our merits. In the parable of the vine our Lord says: "Every branch that bears fruit, he will purge it, that it may bring forth more fruit" (Jn. 15,2). Consider how the husbandman deals with the branch; he cuts and trims it, binds it, and exposes it to the rays of the sun; then only does it produce sweet and precious wine. Did not our heavenly Father thus lead His only-begotten Son to the glorious throne of heaven? Along that same road we must seek to gather precious merits. St. Rose of Lima, who endured great suffering during her lifetime, wept when death approached, because now she could no longer suffer for heaven.

PRAYER OF THE CHURCH
(No. 28 under "Various Prayers")
O God, who by the patience of Thine only-begotten Son hast crushed the pride of the old enemy; give unto us, we beseech Thee, ever to be devoted to what He lovingly endured for us, and thus, after His example, to bear with serene mind the troubles which come upon us. Through Christ our Lord. Amen.

⚜⚜⚜⚜⚜⚜⚜⚜

MARCH 28
ST. JOHN CAPISTRAN
Confessor, First Order

OWARD the end of the fourteenth century the kingdom of Naples was the scene of many wars. Among those who had been drafted to serve in the army was a German knight—others say he came from France—who married a young woman of great piety in Capistrano and then took up his abode there. St. John was born of these parents on June 24, 1385, and was later identified as Capistran, from Capistrano, the place of his birth.

After he had completed his studies in law at the University of Perugia, he became a lawyer in Naples, where he gained so admirable a reputation for his honesty and ability that King Ladislas frequently called him in for advice.

John was not yet thirty years old when the king made him governor of Perugia. Having tasted of the good fortune of this world, he was soon also to experience its instability. He had repaired to a neighboring town, where war had broken out, in order to arrange for a peaceful settlement. He was treacherously seized, loaded with heavy chains, and thrown into prison. No one bothered about releasing him. Then, quite strangely, a Franciscan surrounded with light appeared to him, and invited him to leave this unstable world and enter his order. Capistran replied: "I had never thought about embracing such a life; still, if God so wills it, I will obey."

At a great price he now obtained his freedom and begged for admission at the convent of the Franciscans in Perugia. After a rigorous trial of his humility, he received the holy habit on October 4, 1416. From the very first he was earnestly minded to put off the old man and to put on the new one in justice and holiness. Because of the extraordinary circumstances surrounding his call to the religious life, he was frequently subjected to severe trials; but his virtue and divine calling always shone forth with increased brilliance. Rigorous mortification, perfect obedience, and a fervent devotion to the bitter Passion of Christ distinguished him among his brethren. He was also a devout client of our Blessed Lady, and felt certain that without her assistance it would not be possible for him to obtain the palm of victory.

When he began the study of theology under St. Bernardin of Siena shortly after he had pronounced his vows, it seemed as if he acquired this holy science more through divine inspiration than through human reflection, so that his saintly master once said: "John achieves more in his sleep than others who study day and night." St. James of the March was one of his fellow students. It appears that God caused to be brought together these three great men, who were faithfully to join their forces throughout their lives to promote the perfect observance of the rule in the order, as well as to combat the immorality of that time. Capistran was destined, however, to be the most conspicuous hero in this fight.

While still a deacon, he was sent out to preach in 1420; but not until 1425 did he begin his apostolic ministry. He began in Italy by taking up the struggle against vice. His former position in the world made him acquainted with the enormity of the evil, against which he now rose like another Elias. His burning words, his ardent zeal, and the holiness of his life caused veritable miracles of conversion. People came from every side to hear him; soon no church was large enough to accommodate the crowds. Sometimes 50,000, 80,000, and even more than 100,000 persons would gather about his pulpit in public squares and broad fields to listen to his sermons. His very appearance touched their hearts.

The holy orator could portray the glories of God and His justice, the depravity of vice and the beauty of virtue, the Passion of Christ, the power

St. John Capistran

of the name of Jesus, and the charity of our Blessed Lady so marvelously that the most hardened sinners were converted, while apostates and unbelievers turned to God and the Church. His presence was requested everywhere, and he was received like an angel from heaven. But amid the demonstrations of honor, the servant of God would always say: "Not to us, O Lord, not to us, but to Thy name give glory."

The pope once entrusted him with the mission against a certain heretical sect, and the eminent success of his labor caused him thereafter to be sent by Popes Martin V, Eugene IV, Nicholas V, and Callistus III as apostolic nuncio to northern and southern Italy, to Sicily, and other countries, to preach against the enemies of the Church.

The last five years of his active life were devoted to missionary labors in Germany. Emperor Frederick III begged the Holy Father in 1451 to send the renowned missionary to him to put a check on the scandalous advances of the heretical Hussites. John wended his way through Carinthia and Styria to Vienna. From there his progress led him to Bohemia, Moravia, Silesia, Bavaria, and Thuringia; and then back again to Poland, Transylvania, and Russia. The most astonishing miracles confirmed his words. He cured innumerable sick persons, raised dead people to life again, and with only his mantle spread upon the waters, crossed rivers with several companions. Seeing these prodigies, some of the most obdurate heretics were converted, and hundreds of young people asked for admission into the order.

During this mission against the enemies of the Church at home, great dangers arose abroad, threatening Christendom itself. Mohammed II had captured Constantinople in 1453, and was determined to force all the Christians in the West to submit to Mohammedanism. His first objective at this time was Germany. He had already reached Hungary and was advancing on the fortress of Belgrade. There seemed to be little chance of saving it; the only hope of salvation seemed to lie in the hands of Capistran. He would have to rouse the princes and the people to a crusade against the Turks. Pope Callistus III proclaimed the crusade and appointed Capistran to preach it.

Although he was now seventy years of age, and so reduced by labor and austerity that he seemed to be nothing but skin and bone, the saint rushed, like the flying messenger of Christ that he was, about Germany and Hungary, summoning volunteers for the war against the enemy of the Christian name. With the troops he had assembled, he then hastened to Belgrade to aid the gallant warrior Hunyady.

An army of several thousand Turks was encamped before the fortress, but Capistran did not allow that to frighten him. Filled with confidence in the holy name of Jesus, which was given the soldiers as their standard, and holding aloft the cross with the banner on which was inscribed the holy name, while frequently calling on the holy name with a loud voice, he led the troops against the enemies, who were at least ten times stronger than the Christians. But the power of the Lord of Hosts and the efficacy of the holy name were to be marvelously manifested. More Turks were slain in the attack by the enthusiastic warriors of Christ than the number of the Christian soldiers, and the rest fled in panic. Once more Christian Europe was saved.

This glorious victory on the feast of St. Mary Magdalen in 1456 was destined to be the crown of John's activities. He fell ill soon afterwards, and died in the Franciscan convent of Illok in Hungary on October twenty-third. Glorified by God after his death with numerous miracles, he was canonized by Pope Alexander VIII in 1690. His feast is observed by the three branches of the First Order on March twenty-eighth.

THE LIFE OF A CHRISTIAN IS WARFARE

1. As St. Capistran fought for the Church of Christ, so must every Christian fight for his soul. Christ Himself has said: "I came not to send peace but the sword" (Mt. 10,34). With the sword of Christ, that is, with His doctrine and His means of grace, as well as with His merits and His promises, we must do battle against the world and not let it attract us with its allurements. "Know you not," says St. James (4,4), "that the friendship of this world is the enemy of God?" Hence, keep on your guard against the children of this world. Thank God inasmuch as He keeps you from mingling with this wicked world, even if it be through suffering and affliction. "We are chastised by the Lord, that we be not condemned with this world" (1 Cor. 11,32). — What are your sentiments concerning the world?

2. Consider that even though we may have withdrawn ourselves from the world, we shall still have enemies. "A man's enemies," says Christ, "shall be they of his own household" (Mt. 10,36). At times our own relatives stand in the way of our salvation and perfection with selfish interests. Hence our Lord adds: "He who loves father or mother more than Me, is not worthy of Me" (Mt. 10,37). This may seem a hard saying to some, but it is God's word. In reality, we are our own worst enemy. Self-love, vanity, and sensuality seek to destroy our soul, that they may have their gratification. That is the tinder supplied by original sin; it came from hell and leads to hell. "If you live according to the flesh, you shall die" (Rom. 8,13). Hence, die now to your inordinate desires so that you may not die the eternal death.

3. Consider that the devil, who led our first parents to commit sin, continues to assail the human race. "Our wrestling is not against flesh and blood; but against principalities and powers, against the rulers of the world of this darkness, against the spirits of wickedness in high places" (Eph. 6,12). As invisible as the air that surrounds us, the wicked enemy struggles against us. Sometimes he incites wicked persons against us, sometimes he stirs up the passions in our hearts: revenge, impatience, pride, avarice, impurity. Let us, then, "take the shield of faith," remembering whither sin leads, and "take the helmet of salvation" in the hope of eternal bliss, which the true soldier of Christ looks forward to, and draw "the sword of the spirit, by all prayer and supplication" (Eph. 6,16-18). — With the battle-cry of St. Capistran, "Jesus and Mary!" you, too, can rout the enemy and win the victory.

PRAYER OF THE CHURCH

O God, who didst marvelously exalt Thy Church through the merits and teachings of St. John, and through him didst lead the faithful to triumph over the faithless tyrants by the power of the most holy name of Jesus; grant, we beseech Thee, that through his intercession, we may obtain the victory over our enemies here upon earth, and merit to receive with him the reward in heaven. Through Christ our Lord. Amen.

MARCH 29
THE SERVANT OF GOD LEO HEINRICHS
Martyr, First Order

FATHER Leo Heinrichs was born in the little village of Oestrich in Germany's famed Rhineland, not far from Cologne, on the feast of the Assumption of Our Lady in 1867. He was baptized on the day of his birth and received the name of Joseph. He was well trained in the love and fear of God and was a model of piety, edifying all with whom he came in contact. No one was astonished to learn of his desire to become a priest.

Joseph was just beginning his classical studies when Bismarck launched the Kulturkampf. So the boy was sent to Holland to finish his preliminary studies under the Redemptorist Fathers. But yielding to his desire to follow in the footsteps of the Poverello of Assisi Joseph applied for admission among the Franciscan Fathers. So it happened that at the age of nineteen he was a member of the band of Franciscan exiles who set out for Paterson, New Jersey.

On December 4, 1886, Joseph was received into the Franciscan Order, and on the feast of the Immaculate Conception, 1890, he pronounced his solemn vows. During the formative years of his religious life it was his good fortune to have excellent masters of the spiritual life. He gave himself wholeheartedly to his holy vocation, forming solid habits of piety that remained with him throughout life. His ordination to the priesthood took place on July 26, 1891, in the friary church at Paterson.

The first years of his ministry were devoted chiefly to parish work in New Jersey. In 1907 Father Leo was transferred to Denver, Colorado, to the pastorate of St. Elizabeth's. Little did he or anyone else think that Providence had destined him to spend but five brief months there, that this would be the scene of his death, and that death, martyrdom.

It was on Sunday morning, February 23, 1908. Father Leo had volunteered to offer the six o'clock Mass in place of one of his sick confreres. The altar bell sounded for the Domine, non sum dignus. Quietly and devoutly the communicants approached the holy table. One sinister figure slouched from a pew and joined the others at the altar rail. No sooner was the Sacred Host placed upon his tongue than he spat It forth, at the same time firing a pistol concealed beneath his coat. Father Leo dropped to the floor with a bullet in his heart.

As he fell, he seemed to be concerned only for his Eucharistic Lord. With reverent precision he tried to replace the sacred particles which had fallen from the overturned ciborium. Amid the panic which ensued in church, two priests from the friary reached the scene, and while one picked up the consecrated hosts, the other administered the last rites of the Church. A moment later, on the sanctuary floor, at the foot of Mary's altar, Father Leo breathed his last.

Remarkable coincidence! Just a few days before, in addressing the young ladies' sodality, Father Leo admonished them always to be prepared for the final summons. He then spoke the strangely prophetic words: "Oh, how sweet it is to die at the feet of Mary!" When Father Leo's remains were prepared for burial, the extent of his sanctity became known. Chains of linked steel were found wrapped around his waist and upper arms. To every link was attached a hook, sharpened to a needle's point, adjusted in such fashion that every movement of the priest caused the hooks to pierce his flesh. The deep calluses furrowed in his flesh indicated that these instruments of penance had been worn for many years. None of his associates knew that Father Leo practiced this form of corporal mortification.

Nearly four years after his death, the remains were transferred to a new plot in the cemetery. When the body was exhumed, not the slightest sign of decomposition was in evidence, although the casket had decayed as well as the brown habit in which the body was clothed. The condition of the body was in remarkable contrast to those buried considerably later and was a matter of comment, because it is generally supposed that the best embalming done at the time could not last longer than eighteen months. Through the intercession of Father Leo also a number of cures both in the physical and spiritual order have occurred. (Cf. *Heroes of the Cross*, pp. 88-98.)

"HOW SWEET IT IS TO DIE AT THE FEET OF MARY!"

1. Father Leo had the most filial devotion towards the Immaculate Mother of God. He always considered himself singularly blessed that his birth and baptism occurred on the feast of the Assumption of the Blessed Virgin. The Immaculate Mother surely heard him exclaim, "How sweet it is to die at the feet of Mary!" and she rewarded her son for the tender affection he bore her by granting him the privilege of breathing forth his soul before her altar. — What can we say of our devotion to Mary? Is it such that she might also incline to give us some rare privilege in the hour of our death? Holy Mother Church encourages us to ask the Mother of God to aid us not only now while we are struggling in this vale of tears, but especially when life's course is run. She places on our lips the words: "Holy Mary, pray for us sinners, now and at the hour of our death." How often have our lips repeated these words! But did we always think of what we were saying and did we mean it? Or could the words of the Evangelist be applied to us: "This people honors me with their lips, but their heart is far from me" (Mt. 15,8)? If we find that we are guilty, we cannot expect Mary to intercede for us in that awful moment. But if we have used this prayer to advantage, we are fortunate; for death is the moment of greatest concern in our lives. Satan knows this, and is prepared to put us to a final test. But if Mary is with us in that hour, we have reason to hope that she will then again crush the serpent's head and lead us safely to the eternal shores.

2. St. Francis, too, died at Mary's feet. It was at St. Mary of the Angels that his soul winged its flight to heaven. For him there was no dearer spot on earth than this sanctuary, and many a night he spent there in prayer. He was an affectionate son, and Mary kept him close to her as he passed from time to eternity. We are children of St. Francis, brothers and sisters of Father Leo. Let us imitate them both in their loyalty to the Mother of Mercy while we are in this valley of tears, so that she may not fail us in the end, and "after this our exile may show us the blessed fruit of her

womb."

PRAYER OF THE CHURCH
O God, who didst will that Thy Divine Son should become man upon the
annunciation of the angel; grant us, who humbly beseech Thee, that we
who acknowledge her to be truly the Mother of God, may obtain
assistance from Thee through her intercession. Through the same Christ
our Lord. Amen.

MARCH 30
ST. PETER REGALADO
Confessor, First Order

HE life of this great servant of God appeared to be merely the
unfolding and an ever stronger exemplification of the virtues
which he received in holy baptism. Born in 1390 of wealthy
and devout parents at Valladolid in Spain, he lost his father at
an early age; but he himself became the comfort of his pious mother, who
with joy and gratitude to God recognized in her little son distinct signs of
future holiness. One could notice nothing childish in him. He loved places
of retirement, where he would sit for hours in deepest devotion. Not only
did the saintly child meditate upon the sufferings of Christ, but he wished
also to have a share in them by inflicting pain on his tender body.

When he was ten years old, he importuned his mother to permit him
to consecrate himself entirely to God in the Franciscan Order. The prudent
woman first tried his vocation for a long time; but after three years, when
she could no longer doubt that the call came from God, she gave her
consent despite his youthful age; and thirteen-year-old Peter was also
granted admittance into the convent, a thing frequently done in those
days. Although he was a child, he practiced all the austerities and virtues
of a perfect religious.

Just at that time there was being introduced into Spain a stricter
observance of the rule, and Peter attached himself to it with lively zeal.
From Valladolid he traveled with his teacher and superior, Father Peter of
Villagarcia, to the quite little convent of Aguilar in the diocese of Osma,
where he prepared himself for the priesthood by earnest study and still
more earnest prayer. He had been a priest but a short time when his
teacher, who had set out on a journey to establish new convents of this
reform movement, believed that he could find no one in Aguilar better

fitted for the superiorship than his pupil, Peter Regalado. In this position he proved himself so efficient that, after the death of Father Peter of Villagarcia in the year 1442, he was appointed head of all the convents of the movement in Spain. Whatever he, as superior, taught the brethren, they saw him observe most perfectly in his own life. He kept almost continuous silence; the greater part of the night he devoted to prayer; holy Mass he celebrated with such devotion that often he was not able to refrain from tears. He scourged his body sometimes even until he bled; his bed was the bare floor or a little straw; nine times a year he kept a forty-day fast, mostly on bread and water. Religious poverty he observed most rigorously, for which reason he had to suffer much opposition and even persecution. He accepted that, however, in patience and meekness out of love for God.

His love of neighbor was so great that he often brought the poor and the sick with him into the convent and cared for them with great love. God rewarded his faithful service with most extraordinary graces. At prayer he was so filled with seraphic ardor that he was seen raised above the ground, with flames radiating from his body. On occasion there occurred a prodigy such as was once observed in the life of our holy Father St. Francis: the flames rose above the roof of the convent though not damaging it. The bishop of Osma, who once saw this prodigy himself, cried out: "Truly, that is the abode of God." It seemed that the body of the holy man possessed the agility and ease which our glorified bodies will once have, because he crossed over rivers as though they were solid ground; and often he was found at the same hour at convents far distant from one another, transacting business pertaining to his office.

God almighty announced the praises of His servant through the mouths of babes. On one occasion, Peter said to a babe in the arms of his mother: "May the Lord bless you, my dear child! Oh, what a beautiful and brilliant soul you have!" At this the babe turned to him and said to the amazement of its mother: "But still more beautiful is your soul, which God has adorned with so many graces."

Soon, however, the great mass of the people was to praise him. Peter died in the sixty-sixth year of his life, on March 31, 1456, and immediately the veneration of the people began. His grave was glorified by innumerable miracles. Pope Innocent XI beatified him, and Pope Benedict XIV solemnly enrolled him among the saints. The entire First Order celebrates his feast on March thirtieth, and the Third Order Regular on May thirteenth.

CONCERNING THE PRAISES OF MEN

1. Fault-finding is a great vice. But one must be on one's guard also in regard to the praise of men. Very seldom is their praise infused by God, as was that which the babe spoke concerning St. Peter; most often it is a snap judgment about some striking deed, or it is the promising beginning of a thing which they praise. There is a wise saying which says: "One should not praise the day before evening has come." But still worse is the praise of those flattering and deceitful tongues which praise even the bad in others, only in order to be pleasing to them. "Woe to you," says the Prophet, "that call evil good, and good evil" (Is. 5,20). — Do you, too, have reason to fear this woe?

2. Consider how dangerous the praise of men is for the one in whose favor it is spoken. Encouraging recognition where it is deserved has, of course, its place and time; but just as many sweets are harmful to the body of a child, so does much praise do considerable harm to its soul. And is it not necessary even in later years and in old age to fear such harm? — Censure is bitter at times, nevertheless, it is medicine; but praise which goes down like sweet honey, is apt to be terrible poison: it makes us proud and arrogant. The Holy Ghost says: "As silver is tried in the refining pot, so a man is tried by him that praises" (Prov. 27,21). Genuine virtue remains serene and indifferent over it, whereas sham virtue becomes inflated. — How do you accept the praise of men? Have you perhaps allowed yourself to be confirmed in evil through flattering praise?

3. Consider what should determine us to be indifferent to the praise or blame of men. "You are not more holy for being praised, nor the worse for being blamed," says Thomas a Kempis (2,6), "what you are, that you are; nor can you be said to be greater than God sees you to be. Great tranquility of heart has he who cares neither for praise nor blame." He who walks uprightly before God and aims to act only in accordance with His good pleasure, will, like St. Peter, be made known when the Lord will make manifest the counsels of hearts: "then shall every man have praise from God" (1 Cor. 4,5).

PRAYER OF THE CHURCH

O Lord, who hast graciously admitted Blessed Peter, Thy well-beloved servant, to partake in the delights of Thy glory, we beg Thee to grant to us through his merits and intercession the grace to lead a mortified life after his example, so that one day we may come to eternal happiness. Through Christ our Lord. Amen.

MARCH 31
THE SERVANT OF GOD LOUIS OF CASORIA
Confessor, First Order

OUIS has been called a newly risen St. Francis, especially because of his touching charity and his invincible trust in God. Casoria, near Naples, was the place where he was born in the year 1814. As a traveling cabinetmaker, the eighteen-year-old boy sought admission among the Franciscans. When he had completed his studies for holy orders, he was assigned to the task of teaching philosophy, physics, and mathematics to the young clerics. God, however, had chosen him to be an apostle of charity.

At first Father Louis opened a dispensary for the poor. Then he founded two colleges, for boys and girls who were ransomed in Africa, and were to be educated as missionaries to their countrymen. Besides these, he founded also a college for the children of the nobility, and a half-dozen other institutions, for orphans, the deaf and dumb, the blind, for old people and for travelers.

In order to secure capable helpers, he founded the "Grey Brothers" and the "Grey Sisters" from among the members of the Third Order. Wherever help was needed or any form of distress was to be alleviated, Father Louis was the first at hand to render aid.

To celebrate the seventh centenary of the birth of St. Francis in 1882, he invited five thousand poor persons to dine with him. Louis Pecci, a nephew of Pope Leo XIII, who was a witness to this singular banquet, asked the generous host in astonishment how he had obtained the means to support all his foundations and organizations. "That I am not permitted to know," was the remarkable yet the only correct answer Louis could give.

So it was indeed. He considered himself not the originator of these projects, but rather the tool for carrying out the will of God, in the measure in which God wished it and the manner in which God arranged it. While Louis needed enormous amounts of money, he was generally not in possession of a cent. Then he would say: "On the appointed day Christ will pay."

A piece of property adjoining a church was to be sold at public auction to the highest bidder. Some sect was about to acquire it. Father Louis ordered his agent to buy it. "How high a price can we pay?" asked the agent. Father Louis answered unperturbed: "There is no limit. One soldo is worth as much to me as a million, for I possess neither. But God is very wealthy and you will see, He pays promptly." And God paid!

Finally, after a lingering illness of nine years, this Franciscan friend of mankind went home to his generous Lord. It was on March 30, 1885. His cause has been introduced at Rome.

ON BENEVOLENCE

1. The obligation to do good. "Do not withhold him from doing good, who is able: if you art able, do good yourself also" (Prov. 3,27). The servant of God acted in accordance with this principle, and his whole life was one great act of benevolence. Even though you cannot perform many and great good works, that does not matter. "According to your ability be merciful" (Tob. 4,8). — Use every opportunity to demonstrate practical Christianity.

2. The blessing of benevolence. It effects the remission of sins. Daniel said to King Nabuchodonosor: "Redeem your sins with alms, and your iniquities with works of mercy to the poor" (Dan. 4,24). It secures for us the special blessing of God. "God provides for him that shows favor" (Eccli. 3,34). Moreover, we are sure of the heavenly reward, for our Lord assures us: "You shall be blessed, because they (the poor) have not wherewith to make you recompense: for recompense shall be made to you at the resurrection of the just" (Lk. 14,14). — Hence, it pays to be charitable.

3. The right way to be benevolent. "When you do an almsdeed, sound not a trumpet before you, as the hypocrites do in the synagogues and in the streets, that they may be honored by men" (Mt. 6,2). To do good in a quiet and unpretentious way is the best way to proceed. — Adopt this way.

PRAYER OF THE CHURCH

Keep, O Lord, we pray, Thy family by Thy continued goodness, that, through Thy protection, it may be free from all adversities, and devoted in good works to the glory of Thy name. Through Christ our Lord. Amen.

APRIL

APRIL 1
THE SERVANT OF GOD CAESAR OF SPEYER
Confessor, First Order

AESAR was born in Speyer on the Rhine, and had already been ordained a priest when he entered the Order of Friars Minor. A sermon of Brother Elias that he had once heard made such an impression on him that he joined the order. When he came to Assisi to the holy Father Francis, he felt strongly attracted to him, because he beheld him so full of love for meditation and for holy poverty. Our Seraphic Father, on the other hand, held his new disciple in great esteem, not only because of his extraordinary talent and his ability for the task of preaching, but especially because of his exemplary efforts to observe the rule of the order even in the smallest details. Full of holy joy he once said to him: "Thou art a priest forever according to the order of Melchisedech, and all the promises that Christ has given me will be fulfilled in you and in all those who will observe our holy rule to the letter and with holy readiness."

When the general chapter of the order was held at the Portiuncula in 1221, St. Francis expressed his intention of again sending brethren into Germany, where on two previous occasions the undertaking had proved unsuccessful. The brethren did not understand the German language, and had met with such ill treatment that the mere name of Germany struck terror into their hearts. But the holy Founder, who applied to himself the words of the Lord to His Apostles: "Teach all nations," and who had often been edified by the Germans who had come as pilgrims to the holy places in Italy, encouraged the brethren anew to volunteer for the German missions, which he could now place in charge of the German, Caesar. Ninety of the brethren volunteered, prepared to suffer all for the name of Christ. At the command of St. Francis, Caesar chose twenty-five of this number, twelve priests and thirteen lay brothers, with whom he set out after being fortified with the blessing of their Seraphic Father.

In Trent they were graciously received by the bishop. Amid great hardships they then crossed the Alps. Nevertheless, in October, 1221, they arrived safely at Augsburg. From here Caesar sent his brethren into the various parts of Germany. John of Piano di Carpine and Barnabas the German went to Wuerzburg, Speyer, Worms, and as far down the Rhine as Cologne. Others were sent to Salzburg, others to Saxony, where the first convents of the Saxon province, which still exists, were soon founded at Magdeburg and Halberstadt. In the year 1222, so many convents had been founded, and so many novices from Germany had been received, that Caesar, as first provincial of Germany, held a chapter at Worms for the purpose of organizing the individual convents and the brethren.

After this had been accomplished, he ardently desired to return to Italy to his holy Father Francis. He appointed Thomas de Celano as his vicar, and then set out again across the Alps for Assisi, where he appeared in 1223 at the Pentecost chapter to report about his mission. At his earnest request he was now released from his obligations as provincial, and remained in Italy, where he lived for many years after the death of St. Francis as the head and support of the true observers of the holy rule. He died in the odor of sanctity in 1239.

ON FIDELITY IN LITTLE THINGS

1. "He that is faithful in that which is least, is faithful also in that which is greater" (Lk. 16,10). These words of Jesus Christ we see verified in His servant Caesar. He observed his rule so faithfully even in the smallest points that he merited the special praise of St. Francis. In consequence, when he was commissioned with the great responsibility of the mission to Germany, he proved himself loyal and executed his charge successfully. Fidelity in little things will also be very profitable to us, since the little things occur daily, such as the opportunities to practice patience, charity towards our neighbor — and they provide us with occasions of doing good, the essence of virtue. The little things also enable us to gain merit which, when daily accumulated, becomes great. In this way is it necessary to win the heavenly reward, as the Judge Himself will one day say: "Because you have been faithful over a few things, I will place you over many things" (Mt. 25,21). Have you hitherto valued the little things according to their true merit?

2. Consider how many a person, while committing transgressions and sins, disregards trifles as though they were of little consequence. "Oh, those are but trifles," one says lightly. The Holy Spirit speaks otherwise: "He who contemns small things, shall fall by little and little" (Eccli. 19,1). Is not that a daily experience? If distracting thoughts are not warded off, evil thoughts will soon follow. He who makes light of useless conversations soon indulges in frivolous and uncharitable ones. He who

does not avoid venial sins will soon fall into mortal sins. Temptation becomes stronger, man becomes weaker, and like a building whose many small defects are disregarded, he falls as soon as a violent storm arises. Therefore, if you love your soul, guard yourself against minimizing small faults.

3. Consider that the Holy Ghost does not say: He who commits small transgressions will fall, but: He who contemns them. Therefore, do not lose courage if you still frequently fail in small matters, and perhaps relapse into the same faults despite good resolutions. At any rate, do not desist from chastising yourself for them and practising the good deeds that are opposed to these failings. "Strive manfully," says Thomas a Kempis (1,21); "habit is overcome by habit." Almighty God will look graciously upon your faithful efforts, and His all-powerful grace will assist you.

PRAYER OF THE CHURCH (Third Sunday after Epiphany)
Almighty and eternal God, graciously look upon our weakness and stretch forth the right hand of Thy Majesty for our protection. Through Christ our Lord. Amen.

APRIL 2
BLESSED LEOPOLD OF GAICHE
Confessor, First Order

FATHER LEOPOLD was born in Gaiche, a parish in the diocese of Perugia, in the year 1732. From his earliest years he was known for his great piety, so that no one was surprised when at the age of eighteen years he was invested with the habit of the Friars Minor. After evincing remarkable talent in his studies, he became a priest in 1757, then an instructor of the young clerics in philosophy, and after that in theology. For several years he filled these offices with blessed results and was then appointed a missionary preacher. This seemed to be the very field for which God had chosen him. His knowledge, his apostolic zeal, but most of all his holy manner of life, soon caused him to become widely known. Everywhere people desired to hear Father Leopold, and his missions produced rich fruit for the salvation of souls.

In the year 1768 he was appointed apostolic missionary for the entire Papal States, and through a period of ten years, he traveled from one diocese to another conducting missions that were signally blessed.

He was then elected provincial of his province. Also in this capacity he continued his apostolic work, but in accordance with a long-cherished desire he arranged for a quiet friary on the lonely mountain of Monte Luco, near Spoleto, whither the missionaries could withdraw, that by interior recollection they might promote their personal sanctification and gather new zeal for their work. The location of the friary and its arrangements for convent life could not have served these purposes better. Pope Pius IX pledged himself, as long as he was bishop of Spoleto, to withdraw to this convent every year for a renewal of spirit.

At the conclusion of his term as provincial, Father Leopold became the first guardian of this lonely convent, and except during the time of the missions it remained his place of residence until the year 1809. This was the sad year when Napoleon, at that time emperor of France, seized the Papal States, carried Pope Pius VII a prisoner to France, and suppressed all the convents in Italy. No religious was allowed to be seen in the habit of his order. In consequence, Father Leopold had not only to leave his beloved convent, but also to lay aside his habit. The seventy-seven-year-old man withdrew into a poor hut and offered his services in the care of souls to the pastor. Later he was commanded to take an oath which he considered unlawful; he resolutely refused, for which reason he had to go to prison. During these sad times he was deeply afflicted, not because of his own sufferings, but because of the sufferings of Holy Church. He prayed much, and quietly sanctified himself more and more. He was destined to see the dawn of better times.

In the year 1814 Napoleon was deposed, Pius VII returned to Rome, and Father Leopold, too, could again withdraw to his beloved convent at Monte Luco, where he put forth every effort to restore everything as it had been in the earlier days. Then God called him to his eternal rest on April 2, 1815, in the eighty-third year of his life. Many miracles were wrought at his grave, for which reason the process of his beatification was begun much earlier than usual. A papal decree of 1844 approved his heroic virtues; and on March 3, 1893, Leo XIII issued the decree of beatification. The feast of Blessed Leopold is observed by the Franciscans on April second.

ON LOYALTY TO THE CHURCH

1. Devotion to the Roman Catholic Church has always been a mark of the true children of St. Francis. When the Seraphic Patriarch wished to draw up a definite rule of life for himself and his companions, he said to them: "Let us go to our mother, the holy Roman Church, and communicate to

the pope our intention, since without his approbation nothing seems to me right or lasting in the religious life." The rule of the Third Order says that, at their reception, members must have been tested as to their loyalty to the Roman Church and the Apostolic See. This loyalty must above all be in evidence when the Church is assailed and persecuted. For such times Blessed Leopold is a model for us. He served the Church as a zealous missionary, not only at a time when men held it in high regard; but also when it was persecuted and forsaken by the people, did he endeavor in his humble position to preserve loyalty in the children of the Church. He preferred to go to prison rather than swerve in any way from its teachings. Do you give evidence of like fidelity to Holy Church, not only where it is esteemed, but also where it is despised?

2. Consider how Blessed Leopold, as a truly devoted son, cooperated in the exaltation of the Church during troublous times. The tears he shed in silence, the fasts and chastisements which he offered up for that purpose, the ardent prayers which he sent up to heaven, were not without fruit; he himself lived to see his prayers answered. In every distressful hour of the Church her true children have felt her sufferings as those of a dear mother, and have earnestly prayed that the afflictions might be averted. When Peter, the first head of the Church, was imprisoned, the Acts of the Apostles records: "But prayer was made without ceasing by the Church unto God for him" (12,5). In your daily prayers do you remember the head of the Church?

3. Consider the lot that befalls the disloyal children of the Church. When Napoleon was excommunicated by the pope for confiscating the Papal States, he said mockingly: "Does he perhaps think that his excommunication will cause the weapons to drop out of the hands of my soldiers?" Five years later the weapons fell out of the frozen hands of his soldiers on the icy plains of Russia; he himself fled in haste in a wagon to France, was dethroned there, and led away a captive. Exiled from human society, he died seven years later on the Isle of St. Helena in the Atlantic Ocean. Such has been the lot of all who have opposed their mother, the Church. It is the fulfillment of the curse which the Holy Ghost uttered: "He is cursed of God who angers his mother" (Eccli. 3,18).

PRAYER OF THE CHURCH
We beseech Thee, O Lord, graciously accept the prayers of Thy Church, that after having overcome all opposition and error, she may serve Thee in security and peace. Through Christ our Lord. Amen.

APRIL 3
BLESSED GANDOLPH OF BINASCO
Confessor, First Order

HIS blessed man was born in the little town of Binasco in Lombardy. He renounced the vanities of the world in the flower of his youth in order to become a religious of the Order of St. Francis. This occurred during the lifetime of the holy Founder. He was remarkable for his deep humility, his great love of prayer, and his boundless zeal for the salvation of souls. His reputation for sanctity was widespread in Sicily. His life was one of continual penance and rigorous abstinence. Besides the fasts enjoined by the rule, he fasted three days in the week on bread and water. His only tunic was a hair shirt. He spent whole nights in prayer and was often rapt in ecstasy. Such was his love of humility and his horror of the praise of men that, on learning that his brethren spoke in terms of admiration of his virtue, he determined to withdraw to a solitary place in order to escape the temptation to vanity. Taking with him Brother Paschal, who shared his taste for solitude, he set out for the wild and rugged mountains of Petralia. On their way they stopped at Polizzi. The people, hearing of their arrival, compelled Gandolph to stay and preach the Lenten course in that town. A few days later, Brother Paschal fell ill and lost his speech before he could make his confession. He remained in this sad condition for five days, during which time he frequently made signs to Gandolph with his eyes and hands, as if to implore his help. When he seemed to be at the point of death Gandolph, moved with compassion at his dear brother's affliction, betook himself to prayer, begging God to make known to him what the dying man desired. He had scarcely ended his prayer, when the dying man recovered his speech and said: "I thank God and you, my Father, because through your intercession I have been delivered from hell. Through negligence, I had omitted to confess certain sins, for which the devil was about to lay hold of me, and he would have dragged me down to hell but for your charitable aid." He then made a most contrite confession and died in great peace.

In his sermons Brother Gandolph spoke with such burning zeal as to inspire his hearers with true devotion, while at the same time he taught them the practice of virtue. One Wednesday in Holy Week in the year 1260, while he was preaching in the church at Polizzi, he told his hearers that this would be his last sermon. On his return to the hospital of St. Nicholas, where he lodged, he fell sick and prepared himself for death. On Holy Saturday he told those who were attending him that he would not see the next day dawn. And so it was. At the moment of his death, all the bells in Polizzi rang out of their own accord. His body diffused a marvelously sweet fragrance, which perfumed the whole house and lasted for a fortnight. The clergy and the people of Polizzi assisted at his funeral, and he was buried in the beloved solitude which he had chosen for himself.

Many miracles occurred after his death. When his body had been buried about sixty years, it was decided to remove it to a more honorable resting-place. The exact spot where he had been buried was not known, but God pointed it out to the workmen in a miraculous manner. The body was found whole and incorrupt, and was then exposed to public veneration. God again honored it with many miracles, which made the name of Blessed Gandolph famed throughout Sicily. Pope Leo XIII confirmed the cult which has been paid to him since his death. His feast is observed by all three branches of the First Order on April third.

ON THE PLEASURES OF THE WORLD

1. Consider the vanity of worldly pleasures. St. John says in his epistle (1.2,17): "The world passes away and the concupiscence thereof." A casket and a shroud are all that remains to us of its splendor. Hence there is much truth in the words that there is little happiness behind high windows and beautiful curtains. Worldly pleasures are like poisoned honey which we swallow with relish, to experience afterwards the excruciating pains of worry, envy, spite, and anger. How wisely, therefore, did Blessed Gandolph act when he disengaged himself from these pleasures. — Have you allowed yourself to be deluded by the pleasures of the world? Have you perhaps envied others on their account?

2. Consider the dangers associated with worldly pleasures. "For all that is in the world is the concupiscence of the flesh, the concupiscence of the eyes, and the pride of life" (1 Jn. 2,16). The number of those who suffer no harm in the midst of the pleasures of the world is very small. Again, how wise it was of Blessed Gandolph to renounce the pleasures of the world and so to guard his soul from much harm. — Have worldly pleasures perhaps been an occasion of sin for you in the past?

3. A rich recompense awaits those who renounce worldly pleasures. When St. Peter asked our Lord what he and the other apostles would receive because they had left all things, he was given this promise: "Amen, I say to you, that you who have followed Me, in the regeneration shall sit upon twelve seats (thrones)" (Mt. 19,28). Even here on earth our Lord gives those who have withdrawn from the world the true joys of the children

of God and the peace of a good conscience. — Adhere, therefore, to God, and use the world as though you used it not.

PRAYER OF THE CHURCH

O God, who dost make the hearts of Thy faithful to be of one mind and one will, grant to Thy people to love that which Thou hast commanded and to strive after that which Thou hast promised, so that amid the vicissitudes of this life our hearts may be directed there where true joy is to be found. Through Christ our Lord. Amen.

APRIL 4
ST. BENEDICT, THE MOOR
Confessor, First Order

THE parents of St. Benedict were Negroes from Africa, who had been brought as slaves to San Fratello, a village in Sicily. There they embraced the Christian faith, and lived so exemplary a life in the fulfillment of all their duties that their master granted Benedict, their eldest son, his freedom. From his youth, Benedict was especially God-fearing. He was austere towards his body, not only through constant labor, but also through various types of voluntary mortification. He served his former master for a wage, and when he had saved enough, he bought a pair of oxen, with which he plowed as a day laborer. Because of his black skin and his lowly origin, he was often mocked and despised by his fellow laborers. This he steadfastly endured with meekness and cheerfulness. When he became acquainted with some hermits who followed the rule of St. Francis, their life so attracted him that he sold his small possessions, gave everything to the poor, and also led the life of a hermit in the vicinity of Palermo.

Until he was forty years old he served God in this manner in the practice of every virtue and austerity. Then an order was issued by Pope Pius IV that all hermits following the rule of St. Francis should betake themselves to one of the convents of the order. Immediately Benedict went to the convent of the Friars Minor at Palermo, and there continued to perform his former pious exercises in addition to the heavy work which he gladly took upon himself. After the example of our holy Father St. Francis, he observed the forty days' fast seven times a year, he slept only a few hours on the bare floor, and wore a very coarse habit. Poverty and chastity he loved and guarded most scrupulously.

Because he was a model for all the brethren of the convent, he was appointed their superior, even though he was only a lay brother without any schooling. His holy example, his humble charity and self-abnegation had the effect that not only did no one despise him in his office, but rather was he venerated by all, and the inmates of the convent advanced in all virtue during his administration. At the expiration of his term of office, he went back to his duties in the kitchen with greater joy than he had previously entered upon his duties as superior.

In his sixty-third year he was attacked by a severe illness, which he recognized as his last. With profound devotion he received the last rites of the Church, and departed this life on April 4, 1589, at the hour he had foretold. Several years later his body was found still incorrupt, and emitting a pleasant odor. Veneration for him soon spread from Palermo through Italy, to Spain and Portugal, even to Brazil, Mexico, and Peru. Pope Benedict XIV declared him blessed, and Pius VII solemnly placed him in the ranks of the saints in the year 1807. The First Order as well as the Third Order Regular observe his feastday on April fourth. (Cf. *Forum*, 1944, pp. 11-14, 41-45, 73-76, 104-108; Habig, *Race and Grace*.)

GOD IS NO RESPECTER OF PERSONS

1. Notice that in St. Benedict there is verified anew what Holy Scripture so often declares, that God is no respecter of persons. Benedict was a Negro, the son of a slave, but because he was a true servant of God, the Lord granted him eminent graces, and glorified him through the Church. Should you happen to be lowly in position, unattractive in person, and receive little attention from people, do not let this cast you down. "In every nation (and in every position) he that fears Him, and works justice, is acceptable to Him" (Acts 10,35).

2. Consider that the elevated position of a person has no value in the sight of God: it will only require a stricter account. A Christian, then, when he achieves power and distinction, must on that account fear God all the more. Consequently, St. Paul exhorts masters to have patience with their subjects, when he says, "Their Lord is also your Lord" (Eph. 6,9); and he warns the mighty against the perpetration of every injustice, since "he who does wrong, shall receive for that which he has done wrongfully" (Col. 3,25). — Have you perhaps allowed yourself to be misled into fearing God less because you happened to have a position of authority?

3. Consider that it should be with us even as it is with God; there should be no regard of persons. Truly, we must render respect towards everyone

according to his vocation and position: "Honor to whom honor is due," says the Apostle (Rom. 13,7), and St. Francis prescribes for his followers, "that they should approach everyone decorously as it is becoming." But where there is question of the salvation of souls or the purity of conscience, one may not allow oneself to be influenced by the position of the person or by any power in this world to depart even a finger's breadth from the right path. Neither may we despise a person because of his insignificant rank and unimportant appearance; under a poor garment there often beats a golden heart. As God, "who made the little and the great, also provides equally for all" (Wisd. 6,8), so ought we to render our love to all, since all are our brothers in the sight of the heavenly Father. May almighty God grant us among His benefits also the grace of this universal love!

PRAYER OF THE CHURCH

O God, who didst enrich St. Benedict, Thy confessor, with heavenly gifts, and didst permit him to be distinguished in the Church through miraculous signs and virtues, grant us, we beseech Thee, that through his merits and intercession we may receive Thy benefits. Through Christ our Lord. Amen.

APRIL 5
BLESSED JOHN OF PENNA
Confessor, First Order

TRUE SON of our holy Father St. Francis, John of Penna, who was born about 1193, in the March of Ancona, was called by a heavenly messenger to be a follower of St. Francis. When our Seraphic Founder sent his first disciples into the provinces of Italy to preach penance and to extend the order, Brother Philip came to Penna in order to preach in the church of St. Stephen about 1213. At the same time, the devout young man John saw a youth of extraordinary beauty standing beside him, who invited him to go to St. Stephen's Church to listen attentively to the preacher. He added: "You will make a great journey, but at the end of it heaven itself will be open to you." John went to the church, listened with astonishment to the zealous preacher, and after the sermon he begged for the habit of the order.

He attended the provincial chapter of the order at Recanati, and in the year 1217 St. Francis sent him to France with many others of his brethren. His unchanging sweetness, his invincible patience, and his angelic purity drew all hearts to him. He spent twenty-five years in southern France, where he accomplished untold good for the salvation of souls and the extension of the order. Meanwhile he earnestly desired that his earthly pilgrimage would draw to a close and that he might be permitted to go to God. Seated under a tree, he prayed as did the prophet Elias, "Lord, take away my soul" (3 Kings 19,4). But he received the same answer, "Thou has yet a great way to go."

Then a messenger arrived from the Father Provincial of the order recalling him to Italy. John set out joyfully in the hope that at the end of the journey our Lord would call him to Himself. But he was disappointed; he had to tarry thirty years before his hopes were realized. In 1248, to settle a civil conflict at Penna San Giovanni, he wrote a pact, which is of basic value in the history of Italian law. It was discovered only recently.

Ever perfectly resigned, he accomplished much good by his patience and gentleness as guardian of several convents in Italy. Finally his end drew nigh. One night after Matins, as was his custom, he remained in contemplation until break of day, when an angel appeared to him and announced that his death was near and left to him the choice of suffering one day in purgatory or of expiating his remaining faults through seven days of sufferings here on earth. John chose to suffer seven days here. At once he fell sick with a high fever and pain in all his bodily members; besides, he was afflicted with great interior troubles of mind and temptations to despair. It seemed to him that he had never done anything good, but had burdened himself with great responsibility. The exhortations of his Father Confessor and his references to God's mercy comforted him. On the seventh day our Divine Saviour Himself appeared to him in all His glory, and with a marvelous sweetness put an end to all his sufferings and told him that eternal bliss was his portion. The soul of John then winged its flight to heaven. This occurred on April third between 1270 and 1275. In 1806 Pope Pius VII approved the devotion accorded to him from time immemorial. His feast is observed on April third by the three branches of the First Order.

ON MEEKNESS

1. Reflect on the meekness which Blessed John displayed in the various circumstances of life. Sent to France at a very early age, he not only bore with meekness all the hardships of the journey, but in a country where he was unfamiliar with the language, and where he was certainly exposed to much contempt in his unusual garb, he bore everything with such

meekness that he drew all hearts to himself. Although he earnestly desired to be with God, nevertheless he submitted patiently to the delay, bore the burden of official positions with meekness, and by means of this virtue was able to correct the imperfections of his brethren. His meekness was put to a final test amid the greatest sufferings of body and soul, and he was then admitted to his reward. Truly he could say with our Divine Lord: "Learn of me because I am meek and humble of heart" (Mt. 11,29). — Is there not, perhaps, a lesson in this for you?

2. Consider how we should comply with the lessons taught by Christ and by Blessed John. Do not permit anger and ill will easily to find place in your heart. "The bee," says St. Francis de Sales, "manufactures sweet honey even out of bitter juices, but the spider turns everything into poison." Should ill will rage in your heart, should the flame of anger be kindled, then let it die there; if you open your lips, it will flare up. Whatever can be corrected, will be more easily achieved with meekness than with passionate anger. "A soft tongue shall break hardness" (Prov. 25,15). But if you have been overcome by anger, or if it is a justifiable ill will at the offenses committed against God, then do not let passion sway you, but remember the admonition of the Apostle: "Be angry and sin not; let not the sun go down upon your anger" (Eph. 4,26). — Do you act in this manner?

3. Consider the reward of Christian meekness. Christ our Lord says: "Blessed are the meek, for they shall possess the land" (Mt. 5,4). They possess the land of their own hearts, since the meek person preserves that peace which surpasses all earthly happiness. Through meekness one also wins over the hearts of others, as can be seen in Blessed John. That holy meekness, which is not weakness or indifference towards others but rather is interested in everything with Christian charity, comprehending and bearing all with an even temper — we love it in a child, we treasure it in a young woman or in a young man, we praise it in a woman, we respect it highly in a man. Here on earth it conquers the hearts of men, and in eternity it secures a place near the heart of God.

PRAYER OF THE CHURCH

O God, who, when Blessed John, Thy confessor, faithfully responded to Thy promises, didst admirably guide him on all the paths of life, grant us by the same kindness, that in all the vicissitudes of life we may ever obey Thy precepts and arrive at the heaven of eternal bliss. Through Christ our Lord. Amen.

APRIL 6
BLESSED CRESCENTIA HOESS
Virgin, Third Order

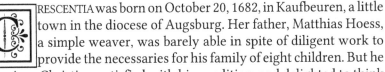RESCENTIA was born on October 20, 1682, in Kaufbeuren, a little town in the diocese of Augsburg. Her father, Matthias Hoess, a simple weaver, was barely able in spite of diligent work to provide the necessaries for his family of eight children. But he was a pious Christian, satisfied with his condition, and delighted to think upon the poor life and the bitter suffering of Jesus Christ. The mother bore a tender love for the sick and poor.

Crescentia received the virtues of her good parents as a precious inheritance. Even as a child she would withdraw from association with her playmates in order to pray in church or in a quiet corner of the house. If a poor person came to the house at mealtime, she often asked permission to give her portion to him. At an early age she was so thoroughly instructed in the truths of religion that her spiritual director permitted her to go to holy Communion at the age of seven. Her answers in catechism class were sometimes filled with such depth of meaning that he said: "My child, you must surely have a higher teacher." It has been recorded that her guardian angel and our Lord Himself, in the guise of a child, frequently conversed with her.

As Crescentia grew older, she not only assisted her mother in all the housework, but also learned weaving from her father in spite of the fact that she was not robust. Her whole deportment, however, showed that she was not destined for this world. In town she was called "the little angel," and she entertained no fonder hope than to be admitted among the consecrated virgins in the convent of the Tertiaries in her native town. But the convent was poor, and the superiors declared that they could not receive her without a dowry. Then the Protestant mayor of the town lent his aid. He had rendered the convent a great service; when the nuns came to offer their expressions of gratitude, he told them that they might now, as a favor to him, accept the daughter of the poor weaver Hoess. "It would surely be a shame," he added, "if such an angel were spoiled by the world."

Now Crescentia was received into the convent, but she was made to feel that she had come without a dowry and was received only through force of necessity. She was compelled to do the lowliest work of a maid; she was regarded as a burden, frowned upon and despised. Her readiness to be obliging and friendly were set down as flattery and hypocrisy; and when visible persecutions came from the devil, she was called a witch. The nuns would gladly have gotten rid of her if they had not been obliged to consider the mayor.

In spite of all these things, Crescentia remained steadfast in her vocation. When the evil enemy said to her, "Go home, there you will not have it so bad as here," she said in answer: "I am ready to suffer still worse things." Often she said that she was only a poor weaver's daughter who was received out of pity, and should consequently not be permitted to make demands. Nevertheless, after four years conditions improved. A new superior soon recognized the eminent virtue of Sister Crescentia; she was appointed portress, and later on novice mistress, in which position she won the love and respect of all the sisters to such a degree, that after the death of the superior she was unanimously elected as the successor.

As superior, Crescentia evinced not only maternal affection for her sisters and holy zeal for their spiritual advancement, but also such prudence in material affairs that the circumstances of the convent became better than they had ever been. Meanwhile, she was entirely devoted to the interior life. God almighty granted her very special enlightenment, so that her advice was constantly sought. Not only did the people come from all parts of Swabia, but princes and princesses as well as bishops and even two cardinals came or wrote to her, to ask for her advice and opinion in most weighty matters. Withal Crescentia, like a true daughter of St. Francis, always remained a model of humility.

In her final sufferings her virtue was to be specially tried. From the very beginning of her convent life, she had been much afflicted with headaches and toothaches. Added to this, she was later attacked with severe pains in the side, so that she could not walk a step. As the years advanced, bodily sufferings increased. She lay so severely ill, that her hands and feet were entirely crippled, and her whole body rolled up like a ball; to this was added severe pain in the back. But remembering the sufferings of Christ, in which she wished to share, she cried out: "O ye bodily members, praise God that He has given you the capacity to suffer." Yes, she drew from her sufferings peace and joy in the Holy Spirit as is indicated by her Hymn in Sufferings, which begins with the following words:

"Thou sweet Hand of God givest joy to my heart,
And grantest that in pain I play the jester's part."

Finally, perfected in the way of sanctity, she went to the joys of her Lord on Easter Sunday, April 9, 1744. Her virtues were pronounced heroic as early as the year 1801. She was beatified by Pope Leo XIII in the Jubilee year of 1900. The Franciscans and the Third Order Regular observe her feast on February sixth. (Cf. *These Made Peace*, pp. 213-215.)

JOY IN SUFFERING

1. Consider what a great grace was granted to Blessed Crescentia, that amid the severe treatment meted out to her in the beginning of her convent life and in the many sufferings that came to her later, she always preserved a cheerful and even temper. The cross was no longer a burden but a joy to her. Often she said, "Lord, not to die, but to suffer," and she attested most sincerely that, if she could ward off all crosses and sufferings by the recitation of a single Ave, she would not pray it on that account. Truly she was a true daughter of St. Francis, for he says: "That is perfect joy to my brethren when they bear joyfully for Christ's sake insult, ill treatment, and wounds." Do you possess this spirit of our holy Father St. Francis?

2. Consider how one arrives at the cheerful endurance of sufferings. In consideration of the reward, even though it be only a transitory one, men will endure great difficulties with pleasure, even with delight. Look at the laborer, the business man, the soldier: they carry their burden cheerfully when a greater recompense beckons them on. But what is a transitory reward when compared with the immeasurable heavenly joy that is destined to be our portion for the sorrows we bear in time? Reflecting upon this, St. Francis cried out: "So great is the good for which I strive, that I deem every pain a joy." — Should heavenly hope not produce similar results also in you?

3. Consider by what means Blessed Crescentia made her joy in suffering more and more perfect. She loved God most intimately, consequently she also loved suffering. She said: "Love that is not desirous of carrying heavy crosses, is not a fire but an icicle." Often she meditated upon our Lord on the cross, and then she rejoiced in as far as she resembled Him. She penetrated into the sentiments of the divine Heart of Jesus, and there her heart was enkindled with the desire for suffering. Her way will also lead us to more perfect joy in sufferings, because Thomas a Kempis says: "If you had once perfectly entered into the interior of Jesus, and tasted a little of His ardent love, then you would care but little for your own convenience or inconvenience, but would rather rejoice at reproach; for the love of Jesus makes a man despise himself" (2,1).

PRAYER OF THE CHURCH
(Over the people on Friday, Fourth week of Lent)

Grant, we beseech Thee, almighty God, that we who, knowing our weakness, trust in Thy strength, may ever rejoice in Thy loving kindness. Through Christ our Lord. Amen.

<hr />

APRIL 7
BLESSED MARY ASSUNTA PALLOTTA
Virgin, Third Order

 N May, 1904, this charming ornament of the Franciscan Missionaries of Mary knelt before Pope Pius X to ask his blessing before setting out on her journey to the Chinese mission. Fifty years later another Pius conferred on her the honors of the altar, when he beatified her on November 7, 1954.

Blessed Mary Assunta hails from Piceno, and was born in 1878. In her youth she was obliged to perform every manner of lowly service in order to help her parents, who were in straitened circumstances. She attracted everybody by her modest reserve, and nobody could have found it in him to speak a coarse word in her presence. Jesus in the tabernacle was the love of her soul.

After she had been invested with the holy habit among the Franciscan Missionaries of Mary, she formed a definite resolution which became the motto of her life: "I will become a saint!" She delighted in taking the last place.

On the journey to the Chinese missions in the spring of 1904, a severe storm arose. She was asked whether she was not afraid. But she calmly replied: "I have nothing to fear. It is all the same to me whether I arrive at my goal or whether I am drowned in the depths of the sea. Just so that the will of God is accomplished."

At the Franciscan mission of Tung-er-kow in Shansi, she was at once appointed to duties in an orphanage. Meanwhile, her union with God was so intimate that no external occupation could disturb it. The task assigned her by Providence, to win the heathens for Christ by her holy and innocent life as well as by her holy death, was shortly to be accomplished.

Within a year after her arrival in this pagan land, Mary Assunta was attacked by typhus and died a victim of love on April 5, 1905, at the early age of twenty-seven years. Pagans as well as Christians hastened to her grave to implore her powerful intercession in the most varied needs. April seventh has been assigned as the feastday of Blessed Mary Assunta, but as yet her name does not appear in the Franciscan calendar.

ON MODEST DEMEANOR

1. A modest demeanor is a means of edification. This is evidenced in the life of Blessed Mary Assunta, who by her modest and reserved conduct fascinated even the rudest characters. She was treading in the footsteps of St. Francis. Taking with him Brother Leo, St. Francis one day went out to preach. The pair walked about the streets of Assisi in silence and with eyes cast down. Presently they returned to the convent without having said a word. Wondering, Brother Leo addressed his saintly Father, saying: "But did we not intend to preach?" St. Francis replied: "We did preach." — Always keep in mind the words of the Apostle: "Let your modesty be known to all men" (Phil. 4,5).

2. Modest reserve is necessary. The senses are the doors and windows of the soul. If we do not keep a guard over them by means of modest reserve, the spirit of the world will enter in by the senses, to destroy the spirit of Christ. And so, by lack of care in guarding them, we readily lose what we have acquired with the grace of God through much effort. "The attire of the body, and the laughter of the teeth, and the gait of the man show what he is" (Eccli. 19,27). — What does your exterior conduct betray? Must you hear and see everything that is going on about you? Do you belong to those who disedify others wherever they go by their lack of self-restraint and reserve? Is it not time for you to be on your guard?

3. Exterior modesty must go hand in hand with a well-ordered interior. If the heart does not put a check on its disorderly inclinations, of what purpose is a modest or reserved exterior? But a well-ordered interior can be developed and preserved by remembering the presence of God and of our guardian angel. Hence the Apostle writes: "Let your modesty be known to all men, the Lord is nigh" (Phil. 4,5). — Often during the day direct your thoughts briefly but fervently to God omnipresent.

PRAYER OF THE CHURCH

We beseech Thee, O Lord, may the offering of our prayer obtain for us the grace of true humility and remove from our hearts the concupiscence of the eyes, of the flesh, and the pride of life, so that we may live soberly, justly, and piously and thus arrive at the eternal reward. Through Christ our Lord. Amen.

APRIL 8
BLESSED JULIAN OF ST. AUGUSTINE
Confessor, First Order

HE FATHER of Blessed Julian was a French nobleman who, in order to escape from the violent pressure exerted on him by the Calvinists to make him apostatize from the Catholic Faith, fled to Spain leaving all his wealth behind. There Julian was born and reared amid unpretentious circumstances, but in a very Christian manner. The boy was devoted to piety, his greatest pleasure being to serve the priests at the altar.

As a young man he accompanied for some time a missionary of the Franciscan Order on his apostolic journeys. The missionary arranged for his admission with the Friars Minor as a lay brother in the convent of Maria of Salzeda. Julian began his convent life with ardent zeal, yes, he practiced such extraordinary acts of mortification that he was considered eccentric; and God almighty permitted, as a means of trial, that he was dismissed from the novitiate. This trial Julian bore with admirable fortitude. He withdrew to a neighboring mountain, where he built a hut in order to live as a hermit. Once a day he came to the gate of the convent from which he had been dismissed, to receive food with the other poor. While waiting for the food to be dispensed, he would instruct the others in the catechism, and when a poor person one day came poorly clad, he took off his own garment and gave it to that person.

On account of such virtues the dismissed novice was again received into the convent, where, after successfully enduring the time of probation, he pronounced his vows. In the zeal that always consumed him, he was impressed with the value of obedience to such a degree that he sometimes said that he would rather die than not obey. He constantly wore iron girdles, and fasted so strenuously that the physicians declared it was a miracle that he could live and work. While on his rounds to gather alms, he edified everyone by his modest and humble demeanor. Full of zeal for God and the salvation of souls, he brought many a sinner back to the right road by his exhortations, and checked much that was wrong among the people, who esteemed him highly. In a special way he denounced frivolous dances. He often exhorted the young people to keep away from such dangerous amusement, and many followed his warning. The fires that had been built in the open for the night dances, he stamped out with his bare feet.

A true son of St. Francis, he loved holy poverty and practiced it so rigorously that he did not even wish to have his own cell. The nights he passed in prayer in the church, or he rested a bit in some corner of the friary. During his fervent prayers he was often favored with visions. In spite of this he always remained so humble that he considered himself the greatest sinner, and accepted all acts of contempt as deserved treatment.

He closed his holy life in the convent of Alcalá on the eighth of April, 1606. At once the people began publicly to venerate him, and Philip III, King of Spain at that time, urged his beatification. The proceedings were, however, often interrupted until the jubilee year of 1825, when Pope Leo XII inscribed him solemnly among the blessed. The Franciscans observe his feast on April eighth.

ON THE DANGERS OF DANCING

Holy and innocent souls recognize more clearly than do ordinary Christians what is dangerous to chastity. If the innocent, pure soul of Blessed Julian proceeded so earnestly against dances, then everything connected with dancing is not so harmless as many Christians believe. He would rather stamp out the flaming fires with his bare feet, than permit innocent souls to be attacked by the flames of evil passions.

Consider what dangers usually accompany dancing. St. Ambrose says: "Dances are the coffin of innocence and the grave of modesty." Love for dress and the desire of women to please, the familiar terms of conversation between the sexes, the fascinating music, the inflaming drinks: all these certainly furnish the greatest dangers for the modesty, propriety, and purity of heart which one values so highly in youth. While the passions are nourished at dancing, piety is diminished. "Love of God and for prayer," says St. Jerome, "decreases in the measure that the love for dancing increases." Consequently, the rule of the Tertiaries warns them (Chap. 2,2) to keep aloof from unbecoming dances as well as plays.

You may say perhaps that St. Elizabeth, the first and foremost Tertiary of Germany, danced. Yes, when a ball took place at the court of the landgrave of Thuringia, whose wife Elizabeth was, she, too, had to attend the ball and could not entirely withdraw from dancing. But when she had taken part in a round dance, she said: "That is sufficient for the world; the others I shall refrain from in honor of Christ." The saintly Queen Adelaide was accustomed after such enjoyments to retire to her room, where for a time she would work at her shroud. Another pious Christian who sometimes had to attend a dance would upon her return home kneel before her crucifix and examine her conscience as to whether she had offended the Crucified while there. If, out of deference, you must attend a dance and you act in like manner, then you may expect to escape danger and to keep your heart clean.

PRAYER OF THE CHURCH

O God, who didst lead Blessed Julian, Thy confessor, on the path of humility and innocence to the full enjoyment of heavenly bliss, grant that we may enter on his footsteps and not follow vanity, but that with a clean heart we may come to Thee. Through Christ our Lord. Amen.

APRIL 9
BLESSED WILLIAM CUFITELLA OF SCICLI
Confessor, Third Order

LESSED William was a nobleman at the court of the king of Sicily. Once while on a hunting trip with the king, he saw the king attacked by a boar and that his life was in danger. William rushed upon the wild animal and saved the king, but was himself severely wounded. The king expressed his gratitude and entreated him to ask a favor, offering him everything that it was in his power to grant. The incident had put William in a serious frame of mind, and he asked the king for permission to leave the court, for he wished to withdraw into solitude in order to devote himself to the care of his soul. After his request had been granted, he went to the hermit St. Conrad of Piacenza, who at that time was living according to the rule of the Third Order near the city of Noto in Sicily. William also entered the Third Order and had himself instructed in all the practices and austerities of a devout hermit's life. He built himself a little hermitage in a forest near the village of Scicli, and there he lived only for God. In a neighboring church he performed the duties of a sacristan. He was always ready to advise and console the afflicted and sorrowing who came to him. In answer to his prayers many a miracle occurred, for which reason he was venerated as a saint in the entire locality.

William lived to the advanced age of ninety-five years. On the morning of his demise, April 4, 1404, he announced his departure to a pious citizen of Scicli. A few hours later the bells of the church rang out without anyone's setting them in motion. The people went to the hermitage and found the lifeless body of the hermit on his knees surrounded by heavenly rays. He was buried in the church at Scicli. In the year 1537 Pope Paul III permitted his feast to be celebrated there with ecclesiastical solemnity. His feast is also observed by the Franciscans on April third, by the Conventuals on the fifth, and by the Third Order Regular on the seventh. (Cf. *These Made Peace*, pp. 129-130.)

CONCERNING THE FAVOR OF MEN

1. Consider how differently from the worldly-minded they who are spiritually enlightened judge concerning the favor of men. A worldly-minded man will use the favor of his king to obtain riches and places of honor; he will endeavor to establish himself ever more firmly in the favor of his prince. Placed in grave danger and enlightened with a heavenly light, Blessed William considered the favor of his king a hindrance in the service of God; he solicited for himself as an only favor that he might be allowed to forsake the court of the king. Also Thomas a Kempis remarks in his third book, chapter 31: "Unless a man be disengaged from all things created, he cannot freely attend to things divine. He shall be little and lie groveling beneath, who esteems anything great but only the one, immense eternal Good." — How do you judge concerning human greatness and human favor?

2. Consider what crooked ways people often adopt in order to gain the favor of rich and powerful persons. Low fawning, words and actions contrary to their own convictions, even against God and their conscience, are frequently the means which are used to curry the favor of men. And what does one possess when it has been obtained? At the most a short, temporal gain. And what must one be ready to put up with later in order to remain in favor? Very often rebuffs and contempt are experienced by him who wishes to derive profit from human favor. At that, in the weightiest matters the influence of men cannot help us at all. That is why the prophet says: "Put not your trust in princes; in the children of men, in whom there is no salvation" (Ps. 145,2-3). —Have you not already found yourself disillusioned in this way?

3. Learn from these considerations that we should exert ourselves so much the more to gain the favor of God, our helper in need. In the spirit of Christian charity be friendly and accommodating to everyone. But if there be a matter in which there is an alternative between the favor of God or of men, then give up the latter, even if they are persons in authority. Trust in God and reflect on the words of Christ: "No one can serve two masters" (Mt. 6,24), and say: I will serve the Lord, my God.

PRAYER OF THE CHURCH
(Saturday in Passion Week)

We beseech Thee, O Lord, may the people who are consecrated to Thee
advance in sentiments of pious devotion: that, instructed by sacred rites,
they may be blessed with the better gifts the more pleasing they are in the
sight of Thy Majesty. Through Christ our Lord. Amen.

⚜⚜⚜⚜⚜⚜⚜⚜⚜⚜

APRIL 10
BLESSED JAMES OLDO
Confessor, Third Order

AT LODI in the territory of Milan, there labored at the end of the
fourteenth century a very zealous preacher of penance, who
at the same time did strict penance in atonement for the
transgressions of earlier years. It was James Oldo, who was
born in 1364. Descended from a distinguished family, and reared
according to the spirit of the world, James, after the death of his father,
gave himself up unreservedly to the enjoyment of the world. Even after
he was married, he and his pleasure-loving wife knew no other purpose
in life but to give themselves up to every amusement. But a friend of his
died, and he accompanied the corpse to the grave. There at the open grave
of his friend divine grace seized his heart. He thought to himself: If your
body were lying here, where would your soul be? — Immediately he
resolved on a radical change in his way of living.

He made a general confession, joined the Third Order of St. Francis,
and began a penitential and devout Christian life. Gladly would he have
led his wife on a similar course, but his own mother detained her amid the
vanities of the world. But later, the mother had a vision in which it
appeared to her that she and her son had been snatched from their
worldly amusements to appear directly before the judgment-seat of God.
She was so strongly affected by the vision that she herself spoke to her
daughter-in-law and urged her to follow the example of her husband. Both
women were likewise received into the Third Order.

The fashionable family mansion, which until then had so often been
the scene of extravagant pleasure, served now as an edification to the
whole city. When his spouse died, James became a priest and then began
to lead a still more rigorous life of penance. On his bare body he wore a

coarse penitential garb, ate neither meat nor drank wine, and observed an almost continual fast. Sometimes he ate only once a week, until he received an order from his bishop to take food at least three times a week. He slept on the bare earth with a stone under his head. Incessantly he preached to the people, admonishing them to do penance. Many turned from their worldly ways to a Christian life, many even left the world to serve God in the religious state. Thus a prominent lady named Mirandola founded a convent of Poor Clares, provided sacred vessels for the church from the sale of her jewels, and herself entered the convent as a Poor Clare.

James obtained from God the gift of prophecy; repeatedly he foretold wars, which always took place as predicted. He also announced the time of his own death, and died in the fullest hope of divine mercy in the year of our Lord 1404. Seven years after his death his body was found still incorrupt. The confirmation of his cult as Blessed, or equivalent beatification, is now being sought.

CONCERNING THE TIME OF MERCY

1. Consider what precious fruit for life and for eternity blessed James reaped from the solemn moment when grace urged him to do penance and to change his life. Truly did he use the time of grace well. In a wider sense, our time of grace is our lifetime here on earth. As long as we live, God offers us His grace toward the forgiveness of our sins and the betterment of our lives. He speaks, as it were, to you when He says: "Behold I stand at the gate and knock" (Apoc. 3,20). If you open the door of your heart to Him, He will enter. He will enlighten and strengthen you, that with His grace you may produce fruit for life eternal. Do not let Him knock in vain; it is still day, when you can work. Maybe it is already evening; soon the night will come when the Lord will not knock any more, and you will not be able to work any more.

2. There are special times of grace, such as Lent, which invite us to do penance; Easter, a time for resurrection to a new and zealous life; the feasts of the great mysteries of Pentecost and Christmas; the feasts of the saints, especially those of the Blessed Virgin Mary. On such days God dispenses especially abundant and wholesome graces. Concerning this the Apostle says: "Behold now is the acceptable time, behold now is the day of salvation" (2 Cor. 6,2). Improve these occasions particularly through the devout reception of the sacraments and other good works for the salvation of your soul. The prophet admonishes us to do so when he says: "Seek the Lord while He may be found; call upon Him while He is near" (Is. 55,6).

3. Consider that special moments of grace come to every human being as they came to Blessed James at the open grave of his friend and to his mother in her vision. On such moments often depends our entire eternity, and in any case, a higher degree of perfection which has its effect on our entire life, and accordingly also on the greater measure of our blessedness hereafter. Because the graces thus offered form so many links in a chain, if you do not grasp the first link, the entire chain is lost. Oh, that we might not lose through our folly what are intended as moments of grace for our salvation.

PRAYER OF THE CHURCH
(Fourth Sunday in Advent)
Stir up Thy might, we beseech Thee, O Lord, and come and succor us with great power; that by the help of Thy grace, the indulgence of Thy mercy may hasten what our sins impede. Thou who livest and reignest forever and ever. Amen.

⁂

APRIL 11
THE SERVANTS OF GOD NICHOLAS OF MONTECORVINO AND COMPANIONS
Martyrs, First and Third Orders

THE holy places in Jerusalem were always precious to our Seraphic Father St. Francis, that ardent lover and faithful imitator of the Crucified. They have ever been dear to his sons. In the year 1342, the guardianship of these places was solemnly entrusted to them by the Apostolic See, and up to the present time they continue to discharge the duty of guardianship faithfully from their convent on Mt. Sion.

In Holy Week of the year 1358, a Hungarian nobleman named Thomas came to Mt. Sion. He had attained to extraordinary rank in the army of the Turkish sultan at Cairo in Egypt, and was the favorite of that prince. To please the prince he had allowed himself to be influenced into abjuring Christianity and becoming a Mohammedan, to the great scandal of the Christians of Cairo. Nevertheless, he still retained in his heart devotion to Christ our Lord, and had come to Jerusalem to venerate the places of His Sacred Passion.

Here grace touched the heart of the apostate. He bitterly bewailed his unfortunate denial of his Divine Saviour, and wished to make amends in every possible way. He went to the Franciscan convent, and there in the presence of several of the brethren, he asked the learned and zealous Father Nicholas of Montecorvino what he should do to make amends for his crime. The priest told him that, since he had openly renounced the Faith and scandalized many Christians, he was obliged openly to profess the Faith again, in order to remove the scandal.

Thomas declared that he was quite ready to sacrifice his life for the Faith, but he feared that if he should acknowledge himself as a Christian before the sultan, the latter would again bring about his downfall. Then Father Nicholas offered, with Father Francis of Naples and the Tertiary Peter of Rome, to accompany Thomas to Cairo to the sultan, there to assist him in his public profession of the Catholic Faith.

All four undertook the journey. In the presence of the sultan, Thomas revoked his apostasy and solemnly professed his belief in Christ. The sultan listened to him calmly, but then upbraided his companions for inducing his favorite to fall away from Mohammedanism. Then Father Nicholas, filled with zeal for Christ, declared that there is no salvation without Him, and that the teachings of Mohammed were but lies and deception. His other two companions supported his declaration. The sultan caused them to be thrown into a foul prison, but Thomas he had separately confined.

After two days the four were again led into his presence, and when they persevered steadfastly in their profession of Christianity, he caused his bailiffs to cut them to pieces. The Christians, who greatly rejoiced over the conversion of Thomas, and were themselves fortified anew in the Faith, came to gather up the relics of the martyrs. They noticed a heavenly light around the remains, and buried them with the greatest respect.

CONCERNING SCANDAL

1. To amend the scandal which the repentant Thomas had given, the three sons of St. Francis volunteered to accompany him to the sultan, and consequently suffered death with him. What a great evil scandal must be! It is, in fact, a terrible crime, because to give scandal does not only mean to cause others vexation and displeasure, but it means to do something by which one gives his neighbor occasion for sin, in other words, to make him wicked, to make him worse than he was. It is, in consequence, the destruction of the work of Christ's redemption; souls that He has redeemed through His death on the cross are led to apostasy through scandalous example. In order to prevent so great an evil, the religious

gladly sacrificed their lives. He who prevents scandal is a coworker of Christ; he who gives scandal is a co-worker of Satan. To which group do you belong?

2. Consider how one may give scandal. Scandal may be given through whatever serves others as a cause or an occasion of sin. Scandal can happen through bad example, the effect of which is so much the worse, the higher the rank of the person is who gives it and the more influence he has on others who readily follow his example. It may also happen through encouragement and persuasion to sin, through indecent speech and other things that inflame concupiscence, through excusing and palliating sin. One also gives scandal through the prevention of good, as did St. Peter when he endeavored to impede our Lord's bitter passion. "Go behind Me," our Lord said to him, "you are a scandal unto Me" (Mt. 16,23). Much scandal is also given through omission, especially by parents and superiors who do not prevent their charges from doing evil. Oh, how full of scandal is the world! Hence the cry of the Lord: "Woe to the world because of scandals" (Mt. 18,7). — Examine yourself, whether you, too, have given scandal or still give it.

3. Consider that scandal and occasion to sin can be taken without any fault on the part of the giver. Thus the Pharisees often acted scandalized at what Christ our Lord said or did, due to their misconstruction of His actions. Christ also told His disciples beforehand: "You will all be scandalized in me" (Mt. 26,31), for they would desert Him when they beheld Him impotently falling into the power of His enemies. Sometimes apparently devout persons are shocked and take scandal at all kinds of indifferent things. That is no sign of perfection. "Much peace have they who love Thy laws and to them there is no stumbling block" (Ps. 118,165).

PRAYER OF THE CHURCH
(Fourteenth Sunday after Pentecost)

Keep, we pray, O Lord, Thy Church with Thy perpetual favor; and since mortal man must surely fall unless Thou uphold him, keep us by Thy help from all hurtful things, and lead us to those that profit us to salvation. Through Christ our Lord. Amen.

APRIL 12
THE SERVANT OF GOD THEODORIC LOET
Martyr, First Order

ATHER Theodoric was guardian of the Franciscan friary of Emmerich on the lower Rhine at the time when the Calvinist heresy from neighboring Holland was constantly gathering about itself new adherents. In accordance with his duty, Father Theodoric warned the faithful, and pointed out the folly and ungodliness of the heresy. In consequence he was hated by the heretics. In the year 1571, upon his return from Rome, whither he had traveled on business associated with his order, he was accused of having negotiated with the pope for the betrayal of his country. In the following year, the heretics, who were themselves traitors, delivered the neighboring town of Zutphen from the rightful domination of the king of Spain into the hands of the Dutch, and a heretic was set up as governor.

The heretics forcibly dragged Father Theodoric before the governor in order to have him condemned as a traitor to his country. Since the good Father could not admit anything of the sort, but frankly professed his Catholic faith, the governor at first had glowing plates applied to the soles of his feet. Then he was divested of his clothing and put to the rack with such force that all his limbs were wrenched from their joints. Burning torches were held to his sides, and seething fat was poured into the wounds. During all this dreadful torture, Father Theodoric raised his eyes and his heart to heaven, and answered not a word to all the raillery and contempt which was heaped upon him. Finally, he was beheaded and quartered; the four parts were placed at the four cardinal points on the gates of the town. This happened on the twentieth of April in the year 1572.

CONCERNING CHRISTIAN HOPE

1. "In silence and in hope shall your strength be" (Is. 30,15). We see these words of the prophet fulfilled in this glorious martyr. We, too, must at times seek our strength in silence and in Christian hope. Against accusations which arise from obdurate malice on the part of those in authority, there is no better answer than the one which our Blessed Saviour gave before Caiphas: "But Jesus held his peace" (Mt. 26,63). Still, while the lips are silent, the heart should raise itself to God with that assured hope which the Machabee brothers uttered before King Antiochus: "You, indeed, O most wicked man, destroy us out of this

present life: but the King of the world will raise us up, who die for His laws, in the resurrection of eternal life." When one of the brothers was ordered to show his tongue so they could tear it out, he said: "These (members) I have from heaven, but for the law of God I now despise them, because I hope to receive them again from Him" (2 Mac. 7,9-11). We, too, will receive something a hundred times better for all that we have sacrificed and offered up here below for God. Should not this hope make every sacrifice easy?

2. Consider that Christian hope must be our strength and consolation in all the affairs of life. Does the knowledge of your sins by which you have so often and so grievously offended God weigh you down, then trust in the Blood of Christ, which has been shed for you. In bitter sorrow and fervent love take your refuge in the Crucified and listen to our Lord, who says: "If your sins be as scarlet, they shall be made as white as snow" (Is. 1,18). If you suffer want in material things, if sickness and tribulation come over you, if you fear that you will not get to heaven, then pour out your heart before our Lord and say confidently with the Psalmist: "My hope is in God. These two things have I heard, that power belongs to God, and mercy to Thee, O Lord" (Ps. 61,8-12).

3. Consider that we must co-operate with the gift of Christian hope. Without cooperation we would be presuming on the divine mercy. He who does not want to leave off from sin cannot expect forgiveness. "God is not mocked" (Gal. 6,7). He who indulges in sloth cannot expect God to give him bread, because the Word of God says: "If any man will not work, neither let him eat" (Thess. 3,10). And he who does not observe the commandments of God and will not resign himself to the will of God, will not get to heaven through prayer. "Not everyone who says to Me Lord, Lord, shall enter into the kingdom of heaven, but he who does the will of My Father, who is in heaven" (Mt. 7,21). A martyr like Father Theodoric, who made the sacrifice of his life to God, can confidently trust in Him. Let us frequently unite ourselves with the sacrifice of Christ in holy Mass; that will put zest into our sacrifice for God and strengthen our hope.

PRAYER OF THE CHURCH
(Secret, Tuesday of Passion Week)

We bring before Thee, O Lord, victims to be immolated, which we pray may bring us temporal consolation; that we may not despair of the eternal promise. Through Christ our Lord. Amen.

APRIL 13
VENERABLE INNOCENT OF BERZO
Confessor, First Order

HIS saintly and wise educator of youth came from Niardo and was a secular priest before his entrance into the Capuchin Order. On April 16, 1874, when he was already thirty years old, he received the habit of St. Francis and soon attracted the attention of all by his extraordinary virtues. He was appointed assistant novice-master, and director of the candidates for the order.

It was a fortunate choice, especially as Father Innocent followed the educational principles of St. Francis. He paid due attention to exterior mortification, especially to bridling the tongue and to religious decorum. Interior mortification, however, he looked upon as the all-important thing, realizing that external discipline without interior compliance is hypocrisy and unwelcome tyranny, which in time degenerates into outright perversity.

With real prudence he often said with St. Francis: "Let everyone pay attention to his own nature. For, while one person can get along with less indulgence, I would not have another, who requires more, try to imitate him; but rather let him take his own nature into account and grant it what it truly needs. Just as we must guard against superfluity of food, so must we beware of too great abstinence. God wants mercy, not sacrifice."

Charity was the soul of his educational methods. He loved his pupils, and they loved him. Teacher and pupils were united in the bond of most intimate understanding.

He died on March 3, 1890. His hallowed remains rest with the Capuchins in Berzo. The process of his beatification was begun under Pope Benedict XV. (Cf. *Forum*, 1954, p. 191.)

ON PRUDENCE

1. What are we to understand by prudence? That virtue which enables us to select and use the proper means to arrive at our eternal goal. Holy Scripture says: "The wisdom of a discreet man is to understand his way" (Prov. 14,8). Father Innocent was guided by this kind of prudence in his efforts at personal perfection as well as in his direction of others. — In all things let yourself be guided by the virtue of prudence.
2. Whither does prudence lead? It helps to discriminate between what is right and wrong, vital and unessential, of first importance or of secondary

consideration. It tells us that exterior things amount to nothing unless the interior are added to them; that all pious practices are worthless if charity does not elevate them; that the commandments of God are above the ordinances of men; that everything is not proper for everybody. These principles guided Father Innocent's methods. — Let them also be your guide.

3. How do we acquire prudence? Above all, from God Himself. He says to us all: "Prudence is mine" (Prov. 8,14). That is why we should plead with God to grant us this inestimable gift, especially if we are charged with the direction of others. "Lean not upon your own prudence" (Prov. 3,5). After that let us turn to the Mother of God, who is not without reason called the Mother of Good Counsel. She will also prudently advise us if we will take refuge with her. — Humble prayer is always better than proud self-reliance.

PRAYER OF THE CHURCH

Almighty and eternal God, by whose grace the faithful serve Thee in a worthy and pleasing manner, we beseech Thee, grant us to follow Thy promises without hindrance. Through Christ our Lord. Amen.

APRIL 14
BLESSED PICA
Mother of our Holy Father St. Francis, Tertiary

HE FRANCISCAN menologium says concerning the servant of God Pica, that she not only gave bodily birth to St. Francis, but by her prayers and the example of her virtues gave him as a brightly shining light to Holy Church.

Pica was descended from a noble French family of the Bourlemonts. In France she was given in marriage to the wealthy Italian merchant, Peter Bernardone of the house of Moriconi, the father of St. Francis.

Concerning the birth of her first child, our Seraphic Founder, an old manuscript, which is preserved in the Vatican, relates the following: When Pica had for several days suffered the severe pains of labor, there appeared an unknown stranger, in pilgrim's garb, and announced to the mother that her child would not come into the world until she had been conveyed to a stable. Tradition relates that the chapel which now bears the title, "To St. Francis, the Little One," was the stable wherein the mother happily gave birth to her first son.

When the child was carried about later, the manuscript continues, again a mysterious stranger came, made the Sign of the Cross on the child's right shoulder, and recommended that the greatest care be tendered the child. Being a truly Christian mother, Pica did that. One can readily assume that it was she who animated the boy who, as St. Bonaventure records, grew up from his earliest youth with a passionate love for the poor.

His father was not so compassionately inclined. When, at the beginning of the extraordinary career to which God called him, Francis had sold his riding horse, and gathered alms to restore a ruined church, his father went out in search of him, laid hold of him, maltreated him, and cast the twenty-five-year-old young man into a dark room in the cellar of his home. His mother, however, who in dealing with her son recognized the workings of God, did not in any way sanction the actions of her husband; soon after, when he was gone for a few days, she set Francis free. Undoubtedly she had on that account to hear reproaches and angry words upon Bernardone's return, but in this son of hers she had the comfort of seeing the signs of holiness stand out in ever bolder relief.

After the death of her husband, Pica committed herself to Francis's spiritual guidance, donned the penitential garb of the Third Order, and lived a secluded life devoted to piety and the practice of good works. Blessed Pica has never been formally beatified.

ON THE HABITS OF CHILDREN

1. How exceedingly important is the rearing of children and the cultivation of habits in children! When an angel announced to the mother of Samson, who had been long without child, that she should receive a son, and she reported that to her husband, the latter bade God almighty to send the angel again, so that the angel might instruct him how to rear that son. When the angel really came, the father of Samson said to him: "When thy word shall come to pass, what wilt thou that the child should do? or from what shall he keep himself?" (Judges 13,12). To accustom children to the things they should do, and constantly to protect them from the things they should not do, is the most difficult duty in the entire process of education. Blessed Pica received such a great reward because she accustomed her son Francis from his earliest youth to those acts of tender mercy which brought such great blessings to his labors.

2. He who must rear children will often experience how difficult it is to accustom them to what is good: cleanliness, orderliness, obedience,

sociableness — especially when their disordered nature rebels against it. How much effort must be expended to break them of bad habits, of lying, pilfering, quarreling, and the like, if their natures are thus inclined. But the longer and more determinedly one applies oneself to the task, so much the easier will it be for the child to overcome itself. Finally, it will do what is good, and it will as easily desist from evil as it formerly did the opposite; habit will become second nature. Such is the power of habit. Have you not already experienced this yourself? It is, therefore, a weak and pernicious love if one does not want to hurt the child, and as a result gives the child over to the influence of its lower nature. The Holy Ghost says: "He who loves his son, corrects him betimes" (Prov. 13,24).

3. Consider what a fortunate thing it is for a man throughout his life if he has been well trained in his youth. "A young man according to his way, even when he is old, he will not depart from it" (Prov. 22,6). If he has accustomed himself to diligence, self-conquest, obedience, compassion, to regular prayer, attendance at church, and the reception of the sacraments, how many dangers will he then escape throughout life, how many merits will he gather for eternity, how grateful will he be to his parents on his deathbed that they trained him to do good! But if they did not train him thus, how will it be with him then? "The things that you have not gathered in your youth, how shall you find them in your old age?" (Eccli. 25,5).

PRAYER OF THE CHURCH (Sixth Sunday after Pentecost)

O God of Hosts, the Giver of all good things, implant in our hearts the love of Thy name; make us to grow in fervor; foster in us that which is good, and in Thy loving kindness, of that which Thou fosterest, be Thyself the safeguard. Through Christ our Lord. Amen.

⊗⊗⊗⊗⊗⊗⊗⊗⊗⊗

APRIL 15
THE SERVANT OF GOD NICHOLAS WIGGERS
Confessor, First Order

IN COLOGNE on the Rhine, where the brothers who had been sent there by Father Caesar of Speyer had established a Franciscan convent, there shone, four hundred years later, a bright light of holiness and zeal for souls in the person of Father Nicholas Wiggers.

He was born in Holland, and as a priest in his native country, he had made the greatest sacrifices when that country fell away from the Faith. When the Calvinistic heresy came into power, and Catholic priests could exercise their ministry only under great danger to freedom and life, Nicholas and a few other priests traveled over the entire country to encourage the Catholics who had remained true. In the cities as well as in the villages, Nicholas assembled them in secret places, strengthened them in their faith, administered the holy sacraments to them, and encouraged them to perseverance.

Although he was well off, he lived in poverty, and like an apostle. Constantly he traveled on foot, and spent no money on himself, but much for the poor Catholics and their religious needs. Often he was pursued by the police, and escaped from their hands sometimes as if by a miracle.

In the year 1602 he journeyed to Rome. On his return he remained for some time in Cologne to recommend his further ministrations to the Three Magi at the shrine of their relics. There, too, he pleaded to know what was God's will with regard to his future, because he sometimes entertained the desire to serve God in the Order of Friars Minor. He then recognized this as his true calling, and pleaded at once for the holy habit at the Franciscan friary "At the Olives." He obtained his wish on the feast of St. Michael, 1603.

Although he was already forty-eight years old, and quite exhausted by much labor, Nicholas was, nevertheless, a model to all the novices in all the exercises and austerities. After he had made his vows, he was appointed to the task of preaching, which responsibility he exercised with great success. Thereafter he was appointed novice master, then guardian at Cologne, and in 1610 he was elected provincial, to the great joy of the entire city. In all circles of society he was accorded the greatest respect and confidence. Not only many citizens, but also the most distinguished men at the University of Cologne joined the Brotherhood of the Blessed Sacrament which he founded.

While he held the office of provincial, to which he was reelected three times after his first term expired, he strove with all earnestness to lead the cloistral life of his holy vocation as perfectly as possible. At the instance of the archbishop, he was ordered by the Holy See to reform other convents also, which duty carried with it not a few difficulties. Grievously accused, he was even removed from Cologne for a whole year. But when he was pronounced guiltless of the charges brought against him, he returned, and the whole city rejoiced.

Nevertheless, Father Nicholas was happier in exile and desolation than amid the honors of the people. He dearly loved interior prayer, to which he sometimes devoted whole nights. He was sometimes in ecstasy, surrounded by a bright light. At such times he often called out as did St. Francis in an earlier day: "My God and my all, who art Thou and who am I?" Many a sick person was miraculously healed through his prayers.

Tried by severe illness, and confirmed in patience, he departed this life in a holy manner on May 25, 1628. His tomb, splendidly hewn out of stone, was embellished with marble by the Catholics of Holland, where his labors and sacrifices were constantly kept in remembrance. Objects that he had used were venerated like the relics of a saint, and several sick persons recovered after contact with these objects.

ON WILLINGNESS TO MAKE SACRIFICES

1. Consider what sacrifices the saintly Father Nicholas made of his wealth and of his person, in order to preserve his Catholic countrymen in Holland in the true Faith and to save their souls. There are circumstances when the ordinary fulfillment of duty does not suffice, where Christian charity requires the extraordinary; then one must be willing to make sacrifices in order to save immortal souls, for which Jesus Christ consummated the sacrifice of the cross. Therefore St. John writes: "In this we have known the charity of God, because He has laid down His life for us; and we ought to lay down our lives for the brethren" (1 Jn. 3,16). — How do matters stand with you in regard to willingness to make sacrifices?
2. Consider how self-sacrificing the servant of God Nicholas proved to be later, in complying with the will of God concerning his own soul. While venerating the Three Kings, he recognized that God wished him in future to serve Him in the religious state. At once he sacrificed his previous field of labor, his native land, his freedom, and through the three vows of religion he gave all to God. Of us also God sometimes asks a sacrifice for the salvation of our soul, perhaps a sacrifice that is very difficult, as was Abraham's willingness to sacrifice his only son. But when God asks it and the salvation of your soul requires it, then you must make it, because "what shall a man give in exchange for his soul" (Mk. 8,37)? Is there anything you must still sacrifice for the good of your soul?
3. Consider the blessing and the success in the ministry which attended the sacrifices made by the servant of God Nicholas. Often our efforts alone are not sufficient to produce success; sacrifices must first be made, just as the seed produces no fruit if it does not fall upon ground and die, "but if it die; it brings forth much fruit" (Jn. 12,25). If here on earth you do not see the fruit of your labor, effort, and sacrifice, nevertheless, in eternity, where Christ reigns in glory because of the sufferings He endured they will merit

for you the incorruptible crown.

PRAYER OF THE CHURCH

Almighty King, equip Thy combatants with persevering strength, so that those who on the way of this mortal life are made joyful over the crown of Thy incarnate Son, may complete their course and obtain the victor's prize of a blessed immortality. Through the same Christ our Lord. Amen.

APRIL 16
ST. BENEDICT JOSEPH LABRE, *Confessor*
ST. MARY BERNADETTE SOUBIROUS, *Virgin Cordbearers of St. Francis*

N ST. BENEDICT Joseph Labre there was realized the full meaning contained in the words of God: "I will destroy the wisdom of the wise, and the prudence of the prudent I will reject" (1 Cor. 1,19). His entrance into the world took place at Amettes, France. He was the first-born of parents who were favored by God with fifteen children.

It appears that the spirit of God, which moved him strangely throughout life, came over him at the age of sixteen; for, from that time forward, he lost all inclination to continue his studies. For that reason, too, his training for the priesthood, which his reverend uncle so earnestly desired, came to naught.

Because of poor health and lack of knowledge he was refused admission also among the Carthusians and the Cistercians. Then it was that he was interiorly instructed to imitate the life of St. Alexis, leave his native town and his parents, live on alms, and visit the great shrines as a pilgrim. From that day on his soul was flooded with great peace.

His food was composed of the leavings that fell from the tables of others. Alms that had been given to him he gave to the poor. The rags of this beggar of the Lord covered a heart that glowed with love of God and neighbor, and the tenderest devotion to the Blessed Sacrament and to the Mother of God. At Assisi he was received into the Confraternity of the Cord of St. Francis. He has been the pride of that pious society ever since. His repulsive exterior caused him more pain than it did others; indeed, his sensitiveness on the subject was his most poignant suffering. He used to say: "Our comfort is not in this world." In Rome he was called the poor man of the Forty Hours' Devotion. On the day of his death, April 16, 1783, he dragged himself to a church in Rome and prayed there for two hours until he collapsed. He was carried into a near-by house, where he died that night most peacefully.

Immediately after his death the people proclaimed him a saint. The guardians of Christian morals, Popes Pius IX and Leo XIII, have proposed the beggar Benedict as an example to a generation steeped in materialism. The former beatified him, the latter proclaimed him a saint of the Church.

Like St. Benedict Joseph Labre, St. Mary Bernadette Soubirous, to whom the Immaculate Mother of God appeared at Lourdes in 1858, was also a member of the Confraternity of the Cord of St. Francis. She was received into this pious society after she had become a religious sister. Both saints are commemorated on April sixteenth by the Franciscans. St. Benedict Joseph is commemorated on this day by the Capuchins and the Third Order Regular, by the Conventuals on the seventeenth. (Cf. for St. Benedict Joseph, *These Made Peace,* pp. 215-222; for St. Mary Bernadette, *Forum,* 1943, pp. 117-119, 128.)

ON THE CONFRATERNITY OF THE CORD

1. How did this confraternity originate? It is well known that St. Francis of Assisi girded himself with a coarse cord in remembrance of the cord with which our dear Lord was girded. St. Dominic, the very close friend of our holy Father St. Francis, requested and obtained from the latter his cord and thereafter wore it steadfastly. This custom was soon imitated by many of the faithful. So it was that the Franciscan Pope Sixtus V established the Archconfraternity of the Cordbearers of St. Francis in the Franciscan basilica at Assisi in 1585. He, and other popes as well, enriched the confraternity with privileges and indulgences. — This confraternity is well deserving of your consideration.

2. What obligations do the members of the confraternity assume? They are supposed to recite daily six Paters, Aves, and Glorias (five in honor of the Five Wounds of Jesus, one for the intention of the Holy Father, to gain the indulgences). Then, too, they should wear the blessed cord. Moreover, on the feasts of St. Francis, St. Clare, St. Anthony, and the Stigmata of St. Francis, they receive the General Absolution, or the so-called indulgenced blessing, and on the feast of the Immaculate Conception, the Papal Benediction. — There are therefore only a few obligations imposed upon the members of the Confraternity of the Cord, but the favors conferred are great.

3. What is the spirit of the Confraternity of the Cordbearers? At their

reception the members are admonished to be mindful of the bonds of our Lord Jesus Christ. The cord should be for them a reminder of the fear of God, of temperance, and of purity. Finally, they should consider themselves as joyfully bound to the commandments of God. Love of Christ and virtue and fidelity to God, that is the spirit of the confraternity which the members should foster in imitation of St. Francis and under his guidance. — Consider whether you should not join this preparatory school of the Third Order.

PRAYER OF THE CHURCH

Thou, O Lord, didst permit St. Benedict Joseph, Thy confessor, to attach himself to Thee alone by zeal in humility and love for poverty; grant us, through his intercession and merits, to despise all that is material and ever to aspire to what is heavenly. Through Christ our Lord. Amen.

APRIL 17
BLESSED MARK OF BOLOGNA
Confessor, First Order

AMONG the beautiful palaces in Bologna which to this day give evidence of the glory enjoyed by this city in the Middle Ages, one of the most beautiful is the palace of the Fantuzzi. Mark of Bologna was born in it in the year 1405, the only son of this wealthy patrician family. When he had completed his studies in philosophy as well as in civil and ecclesiastical law at the university of his native city, and the question of choosing a state of life arose, this generous young man, for whom the glory of this world was too insignificant, went to the door of the poor Franciscan convent and asked to be admitted there. He received the habit on the feast of his holy patron, St. Mark. He was then twenty-six years old. Blessed James Primadizzi was charged to initiate him in the religious life, and St. Bernardin of Siena was his teacher in theology. Under such direction Mark made rapid progress in perfection and within a few years had developed into so perfect a religious that he was appointed guardian of the convent of Fonte Colombo, that venerable abode where our Divine Saviour dictated the holy rule to St. Francis.

Mark was ever zealous for the faithful observance of the holy rule. After he had given proof of his sterling qualities as superior in several other convents, he was elected provincial, and in the year 1452, vicar general of the Observant Friars Minor. Later again he had to discharge the duties of this office for two terms of three years. Untiringly he traveled about the provinces, announcing the word of God to the people; but above all he was solicitous to maintain the faithful observance of the rule of his convents.

When the king of Bosnia, who had lately been converted to the Faith by the Friars Minor, imposed upon his subjects a special tax for the support of the convents, Mark begged him to leave his people full liberty in the matter, so that the benefactors might not lose their merits and the spirit of poverty of his brethren might not suffer injury. On the other hand, this wise director did not wish to impose any precepts over and above those already laid down in the rule. Hence, when a suggestion was made at one of the chapters that perpetual abstinence should be imposed on all the religious, Father Mark would not permit its adoption, saying: "Our perfection consists in the observance of our rule. It can do no good to add thereto anything more perfect, since in such cases the more perfect is enemy to that which is good."

More edifying than his zeal and wisdom in the administration of his office was the humility he displayed when he completed his trienniate. He prostrated himself before his brethren and with tears accused himself of the many faults which he believed he had committed in the administration of his office.

Because of his wisdom and zeal for the interests of the Church, Popes Nicholas V, Callistus III, Pius II, and Paul II held him in high regard. The last named pope wished even to raise him to the cardinalate; Father Mark, however, withdrew from Rome and found a way to evade this honor. It was not without the permission of God that for a time Mark received little consideration in the order; but the holy man bore all without a word of complaint.

Full of zeal for the honor of God and the salvation of souls, he preached everywhere with the fervor of an apostle, In his seventy-fourth year he still preached the Lenten sermons at Piacenza. It was then that he was attacked by a fever that brought him close to death's door. He asked for the guardian of the convent of the Friars Minor, which was located in the suburbs of the city, and said to him: "Father, although I am a great sinner and not worthy to die in your convent, still I beg you to grant me the privilege that I may be taken to it." There, after devoutly receiving the last sacraments, he died the death of the just in Holy Week of the year 1479. Pope Pius IX approved the immemorial devotion paid to Blessed Mark. His feast is celebrated by the Franciscans on April nineteenth and by the Capuchins on the tenth.

ON THE ACKNOWLEDGMENT OF OUR GUILT

1. In his explanation of the Franciscan Rule, Pope Clement V, as the supreme teacher of truth, says that delicate consciences perceive faults where none exist. Thus it was with Blessed Mark. That he made so humble a confession of supposed guilt even before anyone accused him, is a greater proof of his sanctity than many brilliant deeds would have been. According to the words of the Holy Spirit Himself, he belongs to the just: "The just is first accuser of himself" (Prov. 18,17). Can this mark of the just also be found in you? Blessed Mark also accepted the lack of regard that was shown him for a time, as treatment justly due him. — When you acknowledge your unworthiness, do you also willingly accept as your just due the treatment meted out to you?

2. Consider how human beings usually act when they acknowledge their guilt. They immediately recall their confession again with the excuses they make. Our first parents acted that way already in Paradise. Before God, Adam could not deny that he had eaten of the forbidden fruit, but he excused himself because of Eve, and Eve because of the serpent. People do the same thing to this very day; does one not perceive it daily? In fact, the pernicious desire to excuse oneself does such havoc with some people that even in the confessional, after they have accused themselves of their guilt, they immediately recall the admission, so to say, with the excuses they set forth, so that neither God nor His representative can forgive them; for, there is no forgiveness without sorrow, and no sorrow without the acknowledgment of guilt. Hence, David prayed to the Lord after he had sinned: "Incline not my heart to evil words to make excuses in sins" (Ps. 140,4). — Pray often with him in this manner.

3. Consider whence arises this tendency always to excuse one's faults. It is personal pride and the deceit of the infernal enemy. We have not kept free from guilt, but a humble confession would cleanse us from guilt. "If we confess our sins, he is faithful and just to forgive us our sins and to cleanse us from our iniquity" (1 Jn. 1,9). Pride deceives us by representing to us that we are innocent, and the evil spirit makes us shrink from humble confession, lest we cleanse ourselves of our guilt. Remember, however, what St. Gregory says: "I have greater regard for the type of self-restraint that humbly acknowledges a fault that has been committed, than that which has committed no fault at all." St. Augustine beautifully says: "The man and the sinner are two very different things. God made man, and man made a sinner of himself. Expiate (in humble confession) what you have made, so that God may redeem what He has made. The

confession of our evil deeds is the beginning of good deeds."

PRAYER OF THE CHURCH

O God, who didst grant Blessed Mark the grace to spend his life in the preaching of the Gospel and to merit the crown of glory, mercifully grant, that being truly submissive by our faith, we may persevere in the struggle until death and obtain the eternal reward. Through Christ our Lord. Amen.

<hr/>

APRIL 18
BLESSED ANDREW OF HIBERNON
Confessor, First Order

NDREW was the descendant of an old Spanish noble family which had, however, been reduced to poverty through adverse circumstances. He was born in Murcia in the year 1534. In order to relieve the family, an uncle in Valencia undertook the child's rearing.

People marveled at the innocence which Andrew preserved so unsullied throughout his life that it was believed he never lost his baptismal innocence. The depressing conditions in which his parents lived saddened him very much, and on this account, as a young man, he endeavored in various ways to earn money to support them. After he had saved a considerable amount of money, he undertook a journey to Murcia, very happy in anticipation of the unexpected joy which he would afford his parents. But robbers attacked him and stripped him of all he had. At first greatly cast down, he later derived from this incident the grace to discern how little one can depend on material goods. He resolved to labor henceforth for other goods of which thieves could not rob him.

In the city of Albacete, the twenty-two-year-old young man begged at the gate of the Franciscan friary to be admitted as a lay brother, which favor was granted to him. Here he could be seen zealously engaged in gathering imperishable treasures. He observed all the rules of the conventual fife very punctually, performed cheerfully all the tasks assigned to him, and was so given to penitential observances that he excited the admiration of all the brothers. While he dealt very strictly with himself, he was full of love and kindness towards others. He endeavored to lighten the burdens of his companions whenever he could do so, and took pleasure in relieving them of their most burdensome tasks. His free time he devoted to prayer and meditation. Often he was completely absorbed in the mysteries of the bitter sufferings of Christ, or in the mysteries of the feast which was at hand. At such times he neither saw nor heard what was going on about him.

From this intimate union with God he drew the strength steadily to advance in all virtues, as well as lively zeal to save the souls of others. Many a sinner and unbeliever he led back to the right road through his discourses. He also prayed and made many a sacrifice for the poor souls in purgatory. God granted him extraordinary graces. Many sick persons he restored to health; sometimes he multiplied provisions for the assistance of the poor, and he foretold many future events. He also foretold four years in advance that April 18, 1602, would be the day of his death, on which date he really did die a holy death at Gondia in Spain. To his funeral came a large concourse of people; and they were so loud in their praises of the deceased, that the cortege seemed to be accompanying the body of a saint. Since new miracles were constantly occurring at his tomb, Pope Pius VI pronounced him blessed in the year 1791. The feast of Blessed Andrew is observed by the Franciscans on April eighteenth.

ON THE IMPORTANCE OF MEDITATION

1. Consider what profit Blessed Andrew drew from meditation. When he had been robbed of all he possessed, he began to consider; he recognized the vanity of material goods, and henceforth strove earnestly for the eternal. In the religious life, meditation was the daily bread of his soul, from which he derived strength for all the virtues. To us, too, will meditation bring heavenly light according to the words of the prophet: "Come to Him and be enlightened: and your faces shall not be confounded" (Ps. 33,6). In this light we shall recognize our faults and our needs, in order to correct them and to make us humble. We shall also be made aware of our duties and find the means to perform them faithfully. Meditation will also supply the soul with vigor, whereby our will will be strengthened and the love of God will be enkindled. "In my meditation a fire shall flame out" (Ps. 38,4). A devout and learned religious once said that he would sooner give up all his knowledge than lose a quarter-hour of his meditation. Ought we not, then, value meditation and long for it?
2. Consider how in a certain sense meditation is necessary for the religious life. The spiritual life of a Christian is worthless if it consists only of external exercises. Their value is determined by the interior disposition; but these can be developed only in meditation. As bodily nourishment

must be digested by means of body fluids and internal heat in order to be transformed into flesh and blood, and give renewed strength to our body, so must the truths of Faith be digested in meditation and be applied to ourselves in order to form the food of our souls. Without it we should languish and perish. "Unless Thy law had been my meditation, I had then perhaps perished in my abjection" (Ps. 118,92). — Is it perhaps due to a lack of meditation that your soul is so infirm?

3. Consider that every Christian can make the needful meditation. If you are able to arrange for a formal meditation each day, that will be of incalculable benefit to your soul. A saint has said: "Give me a soul that meditates well for a quarter of an hour daily, and I will give it heaven." If you cannot do it daily, you can perhaps do it at least on Sundays. But if you find yourself too helpless to make your own meditation, then listen the more attentively to the sermon, read devout books of meditations, accustom yourself in daily occurrences to reflect on things eternal, and to take counsel with your soul when more weighty problems arise. He who refuses to do that will be lost in the maelstrom of this world; but even the prodigal son came back to his father when he entered into himself.

PRAYER OF THE CHURCH

O God, who didst adorn blessed Andrew, Thy confessor, with the gift of contemplation and a remarkable innocence, grant us through his intercession, that amid the allurements of this world, we may with our whole heart adhere to Thee alone. Through Christ our Lord. Amen.

APRIL 19
BLESSED CONRAD OF ASCOLI
Confessor, First Order

AT ASCOLI in the district of Ancona, Conrad was born of the noble Migliano family in the year 1234. It was marvelous how the small child practiced mortifications and self-denial in all things as saints would do it. It is recorded that even as an infant he took his mother's milk only once on fastdays. It was discovered that even as a boy he possessed the gift of prophecy. Sometimes, for instance, he would go on his knees before a companion named Jerome, and he always tendered him great respect. When he was asked for the reason, he said: "I have seen the keys of heaven in his hands." Jerome later became a pope, known to us as Nicholas IV.

The two companions formed an intimate friendship. They vied with each other in their application to study, but still more in the practice of virtue. As young men, both entered the Franciscan Order at Ascoli; from there they were both sent to the cloister in Assisi to complete their training in the religious life, and then to Perugia to complete their studies, where both received the doctor's degree in theology. Then they went to Rome, where both had to teach theology, besides instructing the people in sermons. Later when Jerome was called to fill the higher offices in the order, they separated, each going his way. Conrad remained in his lowly condition, and did everything possible to turn aside any regard that might lead to promotion. Although he possessed great learning, his sermons were nevertheless so simple and plain that this great learning never came to the fore.

He went about barefoot and in a poor habit, and lived very austerely. Four days in the week he partook of only water, bread and in consequence he was quite devoid of comeliness.

In 1274 his friend was elected as the successor to St. Bonaventure in the position of minister general of the entire order. Then a desire to save souls and also perhaps of escaping the danger of any preferment led Conrad to beg for a mission to Africa to convert the Negroes. The mission was granted him. Through his holy zeal and gentle charity, the splendor of his virtues and the many miracles that God wrought to confirm his labors, he won many thousands of souls for Christ.

Meanwhile Minister General Jerome received from Pope Nicholas III the responsible errand to persuade the king of France, who was warring against Spain, to accept terms of reconciliation. Jerome asked that his fellow religious, Conrad, in whose enlightenment and holiness he had much confidence, might be appointed as his associate on this embassy. So the missionary had to come back from Africa in order to set out for Paris with Father General. They had the greatest success, whereupon Jerome was raised to the cardinalate.

Conrad remained several years in Rome in order to preach; then he was sent to Paris to teach theology at the university there. While he did this with distinction, he also preached to the people and visited the hospitals in order to nurse the sick and render assistance to the dying. He saw in the poor sick our suffering Saviour, in the contemplation of whom he was so deeply rapt that Christ Himself appeared to him every Good Friday in the manner in which Pilate showed Him to the Jews when he said: "Behold the man."

When in the year 1288 Cardinal Jerome of Ascoli was raised to the papal chair, he recalled his friend Conrad to Rome in order to create him cardinal. Just once more Conrad preached to the people of Paris; it was on the subject that only virtue has any true worth and deserves to be valued. Then he set out. On the way he became very ill at his native town of Ascoli. With the devotion of an angel he received the sacraments, had himself placed on the bare floor and passed away blessedly in the Lord on April 19, 1289. Nicholas IV bewailed his death before the cardinals as a great loss to the Church. The inhabitants of Ascoli prepared for him a beautiful monument and venerated him as their heavenly intercessor. Pope Pius VI approved his uninterrupted cult and thus declared him Blessed. The feast of Blessed Conrad is celebrated by the three branches of the First Order on April nineteenth.

ON RIVALRY

1. Consider how Blessed Conrad from early youth vied with his friend Jerome in the laudable and holy rivalry to grow in virtue. Such rivalry the Apostle recommends to all of us when he writes: "Be zealous for that which is good in a good thing" (Gal. 4,18). We ought to strive and vie with one another continually to improve in what is good. Thus should Christians, especially those of the same age, mutually animate one another in holy friendship by word and example to become perfect in humility, in self-abnegation, in charitable brotherly love, in true love of God and in piety. Would that this holy rivalry existed among all Christian young men and young women.
2. There is a second type of rivalry, but it can become dangerous; it is rivalry for knowledge and accomplishments. To compete in diligence and devotion for the acquisition of useful things is good, since dissipation and indolence are faults. In that way Conrad and Jerome vied with each other in application to study. Thus also may one urge on children to competition in study. But it is not right if competition recognizes no criterion but success and the results achieved. The latter are not always the fruit of diligence, but more often of the gifts and talents a person has received from God, and in this regard, every person must be satisfied with his share. Be not "more wise ... than God has divided to everyone the measure" (Rom. 12,3). — Have you perhaps failed in this regard?
3. Consider the type of competition which is the worst, and unfortunately the most common. It is competition for honor and recognition in the world, to secure a more fortunate and brilliant position than one's associates. Such competition is indicative of pride and sensual desires, and it nourishes these failings. That is why Blessed Conrad fled from rivalry

of that sort so earnestly; the higher his friend rose to honor, the more he sought to keep himself humble. He kept the admonition of the Apostle ever in mind: "Not minding high things, but consenting to the humble" (Rom. 12,16). This deep wisdom he drew from his frequent meditation on the Passion of Christ, "who having joy set before Him, endured the cross, despising the shame, and now sits on the right hand throne of God" (Heb. 12,2). —May humility and the cross lead us to a similar goal.

PRAYER OF THE CHURCH

O God, who didst wonderfully distinguish Blessed Conrad with incessant meditation on the Passion of Jesus Christ, Thy Son, grant us through his intercession, that we may carry the mortification of the cross in our hearts and deserve to arrive at eternal life. Through the same Christ our Lord. Amen.

𝕺𝖄𝕭𝕺𝖄𝕭𝕺𝖄𝕭𝕺𝖄𝕭𝕺𝖄𝕭𝕺𝖄𝕭

APRIL 20
BLESSED ANGELO OF CHIAVASSO
Confessor, First Order

NGELO was born of wealthy and very pious parents at Chiavasso in Piedmont in the year 1411. His pious mother beheld in each of her children a new pledge of God's love, for which reason she endeavored above all to cultivate in their tender hearts the love of God through veneration of the sufferings of Christ. Angelo had been much impressed. It was frequently noticed how the little boy arose in the middle of the night, prayed before his crucifix, and kissed it tenderly. Devotion to the Passion of Christ and the ever Blessed Virgin protected him also through his student years, so that amid many dangers he preserved the purity of his heart unsullied.

At Bologna he was raised to the dignity of a Doctor of Theology and of Canon and Civil Law. These extraordinary mental gifts, as well as his outstanding position, induced the Duke of Montferrat to appoint him councillor and senator for the duchy. Quite remote was the possibility that the brilliant career open to the young man would dazzle him; all these things could not even satisfy him.

In his thirty-third year, when his mother died, he resigned all his preferments, went to Genoa, and begged the Friars Minor for admission into the order. Here he strove for perfection with such lively zeal that everyone admired him. Love of God, devotion to the Passion of Christ and to the Mother of God filled his heart. From these budded forth all the cloistral virtues: humility, obedience, chastity, and love of poverty. He burned with an extraordinary zeal for souls. When he was appointed to the task of preaching, he proved tirelessly active for the salvation of souls. In a special way were the poor the object of his care; he strove in every way to assist them, and to improve the material lot of the poorer classes.

But the influential also desired the services of Father Angelo. Duke Charles of Savoy chose him for his confessor, and Pope Sixtus IV commissioned him to preach a campaign against the Turks who had invaded the coasts of Italy. His successor, Innocent VIII, sent him to repress the heresy of the Waldensians. In his order, he was obliged to take over some of the most responsible positions. He was elected provincial of his province at Genoa, and then vicar general of the Observants for four terms.

In order to turn to profit his knowledge and rich experience, he wrote a book about conscience cases for the service of confessors and directors of souls, which was repeatedly reprinted at Venice.

When he was eighty-two years old, he asked to be relieved of his official duties. The request was granted. He then lived in the solitude of the friary at Cuneo, intent only on prayer and preparation for death. In his eighty-fourth year he died the death of a saint. Immediately the public began venerating him, and the devotion was approved by Pope Benedict XIII. His body has remained incorrupt even to this day, and it emits a pleasant odor. The feast of Blessed Angelo is observed by the Franciscans on April nineteenth and by the Capuchins on the twelfth.

ON ZEAL FOR SOULS

1. If, according to the words of St. Dionysius, it is the most godly of all godly acts to labor with God for the salvation of souls, how much must Blessed Angelo's zeal for souls have pleased God! In fact, he who saves a soul causes all heaven to rejoice. He leads a lost son back to his heavenly Father, he replaces a wandering sheep in the shepherd arms of our Blessed Saviour, he consecrates anew to the Holy Spirit a profaned temple, and he prepares a joy for all the angels in heaven, for "there shall be joy in heaven upon one sinner who does penance, more than upon ninety-nine just who need not penance" (Lk. 15,7). What Christian should not long to engage in such a task?

2. Consider also how useful it is for us to be filled with true zeal for souls. It must first of all be directed to the salvation and preservation of our own

soul, since all well ordered love begins with oneself. How could you attempt to convert another if there were still so many flagrant faults in yourself? Would the other not say to you, Physician, cure yourself? But if in true zeal you govern your own soul and then bring back another, you cancel the debt which is still to be atoned for your own sins, for St. James says: "He who causes a sinner to be converted from the error of his way, shall save his soul from death, and shall cover a multitude of sins" (5,20). Consider how you can practice zeal for souls. If you are not able to do this like Blessed Angelo, as superior and confessor, as missionary in the conflict against unbelievers and heretics, you should nevertheless be a missionary in the quiet circle of your home. A good word can often do much good there; the example of your life of retirement will be a check on frivolity. Pray fervently for those that you see are going astray and falling into error. No Christian may say: "What business is that of mine?" That would mean to take one's stand on the side of Christ's opponents, because our Lord has said: "He that is not with Me, is against me: and he that gathers not with Me, scatters" (Lk. 11,23).

PRAYER OF THE CHURCH

O God, who in order to vanquish the enemies of Thy Church, didst endow Blessed Angelo, Thy confessor, with invincible strength of mind, grant that through his intercession and merits, we may overcome the snares of all our enemies, and enjoy eternal peace. Through Christ our Lord. Amen.

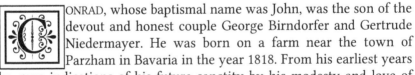

APRIL 21
ST. CONRAD OF PARZHAM
Confessor, First Order

CONRAD, whose baptismal name was John, was the son of the devout and honest couple George Birndorfer and Gertrude Niedermayer. He was born on a farm near the town of Parzham in Bavaria in the year 1818. From his earliest years he gave indications of his future sanctity by his modesty and love of solitude.

The fervor of his devotion was noticeable especially when he prayed in church, the distant location of which was no hindrance to his visiting it frequently even in inclement weather. He was inflamed with great love for the Blessed Virgin, and each day fervently recited the rosary. On

feastdays he frequently made a journey to some remote shrine of the
Mother of God. During such pilgrimages, always made on foot, he was
constantly engaged in prayer, and when he returned in the evening, he
was usually still fasting.

Having spent his youthful years on the farm, closely united to God by
means of interior union with Him, he decided at the age of thirty-one to
bid farewell to the world. After disposing of a very large inheritance, he
received permission to be admitted as a lay brother among the Capuchins.

Immediately after his profession he was sent to the convent of St.
Anne in the city of Altoetting. This place is particularly renowned among
all others in Germany for its shrine of the Mother of Mercy, and hundreds,
even thousands of the faithful come there daily. Because of the great
concourse of people in this city, the duty of the porter at the friary is a
very difficult one. As soon as he arrived, this charge was given to Conrad,
who retained it until his death. Diligent at his work, sparing in words,
bountiful to the poor, eager and ready to receive and help strangers,
Brother Conrad calmly fulfilled the task of porter for more than forty
years, during which time he greatly benefited the inhabitants of the city
as well as strangers in all their needs of body and soul.

Among the virtues he practiced, he loved silence in a special way. His
spare moments during the day were spent in a nook near the door where
it was possible for him to see and adore the Blessed Eucharist. During the
night he would deprive himself of several hours of sleep, to devote the
time to prayer either in the oratory of the brothers or in the church.
Indeed, it was quite generally believed that he never took any rest, but
continually occupied himself in work and exercises of devotion.

On a certain feastday, when he had ministered to a large number of
pilgrims, he felt his strength leaving him. He was obliged to manifest his
weakness to his superior. Obedience sent him to bed. Only three days
later, little children, to whom the news of Conrad's sickness had not been
given lest they be oversaddened, gathered as by instinct around the friary,
reciting the rosary. As Blessed Father Francis had died to the music of the
birds he loved, so his son died with the voices of the children, these lovely
creatures of God, ringing in his ears. On April 21, 1894, the Capuchin
porter heard the sound of the Bell for which he had so patiently waited.
For the last time he ran to the Door. But this time the Door was literally
his Christ.

His heroic virtues and the miracles he performed won for him the
distinction to be ranked among the Blessed by Pope Pius XI in the year
1930. Four years later, the same pope, approving additional miracles
which had been performed, solemnly inscribed his name in the list of

saints. The feast of St. Conrad is celebrated on April twenty-first by the Franciscans, Capuchins, and Third Order Regular; and the Conventuals observe it on the twenty-second. (Cf. *Forum*, 1945, pp. 263-266.)

ON COMBINING THE CONTEMPLATIVE WITH THE ACTIVE LIFE

1. Already as a child, little John gave evidence of his piety, but he was not petted and coddled on that account. There were other pieties to be practiced. He was taught to help in the house or in the fields, and these tasks he undertook cheerfully, thus laying the foundation for his later years. When his parents died, he became the pillar of strength to the bereaved family, and work on the farm could proceed because "Big John" was not merely able but eager to do more than his share in wresting a livelihood from the soil. In spite of his heavy labor, he found ample time for pious practices. We read that he joined no fewer than nine pious associations. Each one seemed to speak to him of some element of Christian piety in which he could afford to make progress. This is a direct challenge to men and women of the present generation who consider it burden enough to belong even to one pious society. — Do you belong to these, or do you possess the material out of which saints are made?

2. As Brother Porter, St. Conrad merely continued to do what he had been taught to do in early life. Though not a contemplative, he must attain to a contemplative's spiritual outlook whilst engaged in the busiest and most exacting services for others ... A thousand times a day, perhaps, he must open the door and hold converse with strangers. Very well, he will see Christ in the busy world of men. He did not shrink away from the crowds. He spoke words of comfort to them and they went away solaced ... At times he is wearied by the importunity of thoughtless people; he will then remember the weariness of his Lord. And so in the midst of his activities, he remained continually recollected in spirit with God. The religious whose life, like Brother Conrad's, is devoted in great part to external duties may take courage from this example of a fellow religious to learn how to use these very duties as stepping-stones to God, the means "whereby he may enter into the inner life of the spirit." Let us thank Jesus that in His infinite love He has chosen us in preference to so many others, to combine the active life with the contemplative.

3. Considered in itself, the contemplative life is better and more perfect than the active. Christ Himself affirms this: Mary has chosen the better part. And St. Bernard, speaking of the active life, expresses himself as follows in his Sermons on the Canticle: God forbid that I should decry this kind of life, but still I would not say that it attains to perfect beauty. But

the mixed life is preferable to the state of those who only lead the contemplative life. This is the opinion of the saints, especially of St. Thomas, who wrote: As it is better to illuminate than merely to shine, so it is more perfect to give to others the fruits of our contemplation than merely to contemplate. And so when St. Francis wondered what was the will of God in this regard, he applied to Brother Sylvester to ask God to make His will known to him. He sent a similar message to St. Clare. Their prayers ended, both informed St. Francis that it was God's wish that he should devote himself to the mixed life of prayer and preaching. Brother Conrad shows us this type of life is possible both within and without the cloister. — Have we reflected sufficiently on this in the past? Have we made the best use of the opportunities at our disposal to arrive at the perfection to which we have been called? If not, let us say in truth what St. Francis said in humility: "Let us begin at last, my brethren, to serve the Lord our God, for hitherto we have done but little."

PRAYER OF THE CHURCH

O God, who hast willed to open to Thy faithful the door of Thy mercy, we humbly beseech Thee, that through the intercession of Blessed Conrad, Thy confessor, Thou mayest bestow on us assistance for both time and eternity. Through Christ our Lord. Amen.

APRIL 22
BLESSED FRANCIS OF FABRIANO
Confessor, First Order

RANCIS was born in the year 1251 in the city of Fabriano. His father was a physician in that city and highly esteemed not only because of his medical ability but still more because of his love for the poor and afflicted and his sincere piety. Daily he recited the Divine Office as the priests do. To the great joy of his parents, Francis gave evidence of the finest talents, an alert understanding, and a meek and devout temperament. As a boy he had a very serious illness which brought him to death's door. Then the pious mother vowed to make a pilgrimage to the grave of St. Francis of Assisi, and at once the illness took a turn for the better.

In Assisi the venerable Brother Angelo, one of the first associates of St. Francis, saw the lovely boy and foretold to the mother that he would later be his companion in the order. In consequence Francis won the love of his parents more and more. The boy's desire for learning and his great progress were especially pleasing to his father. At the age of ten years Francis already understood the Latin language. When he had reached his seventeenth year, he experienced a strong impulse to consecrate himself to God in the Order of St. Francis, and his pious parents gave their consent.

Francis entered the Franciscan convent at Fabriano and there, under the excellent direction of Father Gratian, later minister general of the entire order, he was instructed in all the conventual virtues. In order to gain the Portiuncula indulgence he went to Assisi, and there he heard from the trusted companion of St. Francis, Brother Leo, who was still living, how this popular indulgence had been given and also how the Stigmata had been bestowed. Concerning both these facts Francis later wrote a book, which still serves as evidence.

In theology he acquired eminent knowledge, which he endeavored to use for the benefit of his brethren as also for the conversion of sinners. He eagerly gathered books that could serve the intellectual advancement and the edification of the friars, and when his father made him a rather generous legacy for procuring books, he founded a library for the convent of Fabriano to the great future benefit of the order.

But Francis also faithfully carried out the teaching and the example of the saints as he found them laid down in the books. He lived so strictly that he partook of food only once a day, frequently only bread and water. He slept only a few hours on a hard bed; the remainder of the night was devoted to prayer and meditation. The holy sacrifice of the Mass he celebrated with fervent devotion. Once when he had said the Mass for the departed and at the end said: "Requiescant in pace. May they rest in peace!" many invisible voices answered, "Amen." It is supposed that these were the holy angels or the released souls.

In the new convent at Fabriano, which his fellow citizens built out of veneration for him, the day and the hour of his death were pointed out to him. On his very deathbed he miraculously cured a sick person. Then he departed blessedly in the Lord, with a gentle smile on his lips, on April 22, 1322. His body, which is still incorrupt, rests in the church of the Friars Minor at Fabriano. The celebration of his feast was granted by Pope Pius VI.

ON SPIRITUAL READING

1. Consider the zeal which Blessed Francis unfolded in acquiring good

books, not only learned works for study, but also books of piety which would be of service to him and his brethren as a means of edification. Ages before, the Apostle Paul had admonished his disciple Timothy: "Attend unto reading" (1 Tim. 4,13). What marvelous results has reading often produced! At the direction from heaven to "Take and read," St. Augustine took the open book of Holy Scripture, and what he read, led to his complete conversion. On his sickbed St. Ignatius of Loyola read the Lives of the Saints, and the reading led him to sanctity. The same thing happened to St. John Colombini after he had read the Lives of the Saints for a mere quarter of an hour. — Do you also take pleasure in reading from Holy Scripture and from the Lives of the Saints?

2. Consider how spiritual reading should be made. St. Gregory and St. Augustine say that we should let spiritual reading serve as a mirror in which we search our interior, in order to learn what is good and bad about us, how near or how far away we are from perfection. Hence, we must not make our spiritual reading hastily or superficially, but undertake it with great attention, pausing at times to compare the matter we read with the condition of our interior. Other saints say we should do as the birds do when drinking: after they have partaken of anything, they raise their heads. So should we raise our hearts during the reading, in order to thank God for the truth we have recognized, to acknowledge our imperfections, and to pray for the grace to carry out what we have read. — Have you undertaken spiritual reading in this way in the past?

3. Consider that above all else we should derive profit from our spiritual reading. That is what Blessed Francis did; his saintly life was the fruit of his spiritual reading. Of what profit is it to know of the right path, or to sigh about not being on the right path, if one does not walk on the right path? It is of no profit to the patient to read the prescription to him; he must take the prescribed medicine. And so spiritual reading cannot make one holy, one becomes such only by putting into practice what one has read. Thus Christ our Lord says: "If you know these things, you shall be blessed if you do them" (Jn. 13,17).

PRAYER OF THE CHURCH

Grant, we beseech Thee, almighty God, that as Blessed Francis in heralding Thy Word acted and taught in such manner that he deserved to be great in heaven, so may we at his intercession strive to imitate him, pleasing Thee always in word and work. Through Christ our Lord. Amen.

APRIL 23
BLESSED GILES OF ASSISI
Confessor, First Order

WO companions from Assisi had already joined St. Francis, when Giles, a well-to-do young man of the town, heard about it. He repaired to the poor hermitage hard by Assisi, which the three occupied; and, prostrate upon his knees, he begged St. Francis to accept him into his company. Francis presented him to the other two, saying: "See here a good brother whom almighty God has sent us." This was on April 23, 1209. On the same day, both went to Assisi, where Giles begged in God's name for a bit of cloth to make a habit. Giles divided his entire fortune among the poor. He was plain and simple in mind, of a mild temperament, but also full of power and energy when it served to accomplish anything good.

Recognizing humility as the necessary foundation for perfection, Giles sought humiliation and contempt, but fled from honors. Once when he was passing through the March of Ancona with the holy Founder and at some places special honor was shown to them, he said: "O my Father, I fear we shall lose the true honor if we are honored by men."

Giles entertained a great desire to make a pilgrimage to the Holy Places, and since Francis knew that he did much good everywhere by his holy example, he gladly granted his desire. The pious man betook himself first of all to the grave of the holy Apostle James at Compostela in Spain, then to the Holy Places of the Passion of Christ in Jerusalem. He also visited the sanctuary of the holy Archangel Michael on Mt. Gargano in Italy, and the town of Bari, there to honor St. Nicholas.

His whole appearance preached poverty, humility, and piety. He also utilized every opportunity to encourage penance and love of God. He endeavored to earn his livelihood mainly through manual work; whatever he obtained over and above his immediate needs, he at once gave to the poor; if he lacked necessities, he begged them for God's sake. Once a poor woman who was dressed in the barest necessaries asked Brother Giles for an alms. As he had nothing to offer her, he compassionately took off his capuche and gave it to her.

In the year 1219, at the great chapter of five thousand brothers, St. Francis commissioned Giles to go to Africa with several companions, to preach the gospel to the Mohammedans. But they did not achieve their purpose. As soon as they landed in Africa, the Christians there, who feared a general persecution, led them by force to another ship which brought them back to Italy.

At this time Brother Giles was sent to the quiet convent of Perugia, which remained his abode until his death. He lived practically only for God. Even at his work, thoughts of the last judgment, of eternity, and of the glory of heaven constantly occupied his mind. Once when two distinguished gentlemen asked him to pray for them, he said: "Oh, you do not need my prayers." "Why not?" they asked. Giles answered, "You live among all the comforts of the world and still believe that you will get to heaven; but I, a poor human being, spend my days in labor and penance, and yet I fear I shall be damned." When he reflected on the joys of heaven, he was beside himself with longing. Often when the children in the street called out to him the mere word "Paradise," he was rapt in ecstasy.

Pope Gregory IX had heard of the contemplative gift of Brother Giles, and being just then in the neighborhood of Perugia, he sent for him. When the pope began to speak to Giles about divine and heavenly matters, Giles at once went into an ecstasy. When he came to again, he humbly begged the Holy Father's forgiveness — it was his weakness, he said, that he was immediately beside himself. The pope required that he give him some good advice for the administration of his burdensome duties. Quite confounded, Giles excused himself, saying that he could not advise the head of the Church. But when the pope commanded him in obedience, he said: "Holy Father, you must have two eyes in your soul. The right eye must be kept on heavenly things; the left one, on the things of this earth, which you must regulate."

St. Bonaventure considered himself fortunate to have lived at the time when he could still see and speak with Brother Giles. When he came to Perugia as provincial of the order, Giles said to him one day: "My Father, God has accorded you great kindness, since you are so learned and can, therefore, serve God so perfectly; but we unlearned ones, how shall we correspond to the goodness of God and arrive at heaven?" The learned general of the order answered him: "My brother, in order to get to heaven, it suffices that one love God, and a poor unlearned woman can love God as well as, maybe even better than, a great theologian." Thereupon Giles ran out into the garden that led to the street, and filled with joy, cried aloud: "Come, ye simple and unlearned men, and ye poor women! You can love God as well as, and perhaps even more than, Brother Bonaventure and the greatest theologians."

A religious of great learning, who, however, was much troubled with doubts concerning the virginity of Mary, came to Brother Giles for advice. The holy brother cried out, as he struck the earth with a stick: "Yes, yes! She was a virgin before the birth of Jesus," and immediately a beautiful lily sprouted forth. Giles struck anew and said: "She was a virgin during the birth," and again a lily sprouted forth. Then he beat a third time upon the earth, saying the words: "She was a virgin after the birth," and the third lily sprouted forth.

Finally, pure as a lily, the soul of Brother Giles went to the vision of things divine, which he had so often contemplated. He died on April 22, 1262, on the anniversary of his entrance into the order, to which he had belonged for fifty-three years. His grave in the Franciscan church at Perugia is highly venerated. Pope Pius VI sanctioned the veneration accorded him from time immemorial. The feast of Blessed Giles is observed on April twenty-third by the Franciscans, and on the twenty-second by the Capuchins.

CONCERNING THE GOOD INTENTION

1. What the divinely enlightened brother said to the pope and observed so faithfully himself, we, too, must observe. The right eye of our soul must be directed to things of heaven, while the left eye looks at the things of this earth which we have to deal with, that is, amid all our occupations the higher regard of our soul should be directed towards God, so that we may do everything according to His good pleasure and with a good intention. Yes, the Apostle warns us always to bear about in our hearts the best, the most perfect intention, which desires nothing but the honor of God: "Whether you eat or drink, or whatsoever else you do, do all to the glory of God" (1 Cor. 10,31). If we do everything as God wants it, and because it pleases God, we thereby promote His honor. Have you always been thus minded at your work?

2. Consider how precious in the sight of God our dealings become through our good intention. In order to make our good intention most perfectly, we should unite it with that of the Sacred Heart of Jesus. The first thing in the morning it is well to make the intention which Pope Leo XIII prescribed for the members of the Apostleship of Prayer, offering up all our works, prayers, and sufferings of the day, and everything else we do, for the purpose with which the Son of God, Jesus Christ, offers Himself to the heavenly Father in all the holy Masses of the day. What value our works must thereby acquire in the sight of God! United with the sacrifice of His Divine Son, they appear as a part of the holy Sacrifice itself, and as He once assured St. Gertrude, God hardly knows how to reward such gifts sufficiently. Should that not inspire us never to forget this good intention and to renew it often during the day?

3. Consider how a good and pure intention in our actions preserves us in tranquility of heart and interior peace. What is it, in fact, that makes so

many people restless and tortures them at their work but the thought of what people will say about them, or what success they will have in the eyes of the world. "If God were always the only object of our desires we should not easily be disturbed," says Thomas a Kempis (1,14). Let people think of us what they may, and let us not be fearful about the results which so often are not in our control. Doing what is assigned to us, and directing our whole intention towards God, we shall always preserve interior peace.

PRAYER OF THE CHURCH

O God, who didst deign to raise Thy blessed confessor Giles to the height of extraordinary contemplation, grant through his intercession that in our actions we may always direct our intention to Thee, and through it arrive at the peace which surpasses all understanding. Through Christ our Lord. Amen.

⁂

APRIL 24
ST. FIDELIS OF SIGMARINGEN
Martyr, First Order

BORN at Sigmaringen of a prominent family in the principality of Hohenzollern, in the year of our Lord 1577, St. Fidelis received the name of Mark in baptism. He was fortunately endowed both by nature and by grace, so that while he progressed in learning, he made still greater progress in virtue and piety. When he had completed his studies in philosophy and jurisprudence at the University of Freiburg in Breisgau, the parents of several young noblemen were looking for a tutor who would accompany their sons on a tour through the various countries of Europe. The professors at the university drew their attention to Mark, who qualified for the position by his moral as well as by his mental gifts. Mark accepted the position, as a result of which he spent six years in traveling. To the young men who had been entrusted to him he pointed out, not only everything that was noteworthy from a worldly point of view, but he led them also to the practice of Christian virtue. He himself was to them an exemplary model, since in all the vicissitudes of these six years they never saw him get angry.

Upon his return, Mark followed the profession of a lawyer. He was soon much in demand because of his ability. But when he noticed that many lawyers, corrupted by money, did violence to justice, and that an attempt was being made to lure him also into that course, he gave up the dangerous career.

He had an elder brother among the Capuchins; and he, too, joined them in the year 1612. At his investiture he received the name Fidelis, the faithful one, and in his address, the superior applied to him the words of Holy Writ: "Be thou faithful until death, and I will give thee the crown of life" (Apoc. 2,10). The words were destined to be a prophecy concerning the new candidate in the order. After Fidelis had completed his studies in theology and had received holy orders, he preached the word of God with great zeal. Meanwhile, he was a model in all the conventual practices, and evinced such wisdom that a few years later the superiors appointed him guardian.

In this position he strove earnestly to promote in his subjects religious perfection; he especially insisted on a strict observance of holy poverty, tolerating no violation of it. But he was stricter with himself in this regard than with any of his brethren; towards all the others he cherished truly maternal solicitude and charity. Whenever the salvation of a soul was concerned, no sacrifice was too great. When he was guardian at Feldkirch, a pestilential disease raged among the soldiers there; at once Father Fidelis betook himself to them and tendered them every possible service.

In the year 1622, the Congregation of the Propaganda, which had just been founded by Pope Gregory XV, established a mission for the Grisons in Switzerland, to check the pernicious inroads of the Calvinists and Zwinglians. Father Fidelis was named the head of this mission. For a long time he had been begging God daily at holy Mass to grant him the grace to shed his blood for the Faith; now his prayer was about to be heard. Since Fidelis had the happiest results from the very first months of his mission activity, the rage of the heretics rose to great heights; his death was resolved upon. Fidelis was so convinced of it that on the morning of April twenty-fourth at Sevis he prepared himself for his last moments. Then he mounted the pulpit. During the sermon a band of armed heretics pressed into church. They dragged him down from the pulpit, and inflicted so many blows and cuts on him that he died at their hands.

God almighty glorified His martyr by many miracles, whereupon Pope Benedict XIV solemnly entered his name in the register of saints in 1746. The three branches of the First Order observe the feast of St. Fidelis on April twenty-fourth.

FAITHFUL UNTO DEATH

1. Consider how the holy martyr Fidelis remained true to his Lord and God throughout life. The fidelity which he vowed in baptism, he kept in all the circumstances and manifold dangers to which he was exposed. Not his youthful years at the university, not his many years of travel all over Europe, not the allurement of money in his position as a lawyer, not human respect while he was superior of his convent, not danger to his life during the pestilence, not certain death from fanatical heretics, could make him waver in the fulfillment of his duties, in his fidelity to God. He was faithful unto death, therefore he also obtained the glorious crown of eternal life. — Let us rejoice with him and wish him happiness.

2. We, too, would like to obtain the crown; but that will be the lot of only faithful combatants. "For he is not crowned except he strive lawfully" (2 Tim. 2,5). You promised to do that in baptism as did St. Fidelis; at your first holy Communion you solemnly renewed the promise. How do you keep it? Do you remain faithful to God in all things? In the dangers of youth? Amid unusual circumstances, for instance while traveling? Against the lure of money? Against the fear of displeasing men? In dangers of life? Even when certain death is imminent? Fortunate he who at the end of his life can say with the Apostle: "I have kept the faith" (2 Tim. 4,7). For then there will also be a crown laid up for him.

3. Consider the means that will preserve us faithful unto death. It is firm and lively faith, and strong and fervent love of God. Faith enlightens us to acknowledge that everything else is as nothing compared with God and eternity; love strengthens us to suffer everything rather than displease our Lord and God. May the veneration and the intercession of St. Fidelis obtain for us an increase in both these virtues.

PRAYER OF THE CHURCH

O God, who didst vouchsafe to enkindle in St. Fidelis the seraphic fire of charity, and didst adorn him with the palm of martyrdom and of astounding miracles in the propagation of the true Faith, so strengthen us by Thy grace in faith and in charity that we may merit to be found faithful in Thy service unto death. Through Christ our Lord. Amen.

APRIL 25
VENERABLE FRANCIS XIMENEZ
Bishop, First Order

RANCIS XIMENEZ first saw the light of day in 1436, at Torrelaguna near Toledo in Spain. His father was the nobleman Ximenez de Cisneros, his mother was a della Torre, and at his baptism he received the name of Gonzalez. After a twelve-year course in philosophy, theology, and civil and ecclesiastical law at Alcalá, Salamanca and Rome, he was ordained to the priesthood. Shortly afterwards he was appointed vicar general and chancellor of the diocese of Siguenza in Spain. Only a few years later, he resigned his official positions and entered the newly established Franciscan convent of San Juan de los Reyes, where the religious name of Francis was given to him.

He proved to be a model to his brethren in his holy zeal and his strict observance of the rule. Early in his religious career he was appointed guardian, then minister provincial and visitor of the order. In 1495 Pope Alexander VI made him archbishop of Toledo, in 1504 King Ferdinand the Catholic made him prime minister, and Pope Julius II created him a cardinal in 1507. Despite these high positions he continued to wear the habit of the order, and when he was commanded by the pope to don the splendid garments of his high rank, he still wore the coarse Franciscan garb underneath them.

He always slept on a board and ate only plain food at the princely table he was obliged to have served. He was sparing in words, zealous in prayer, vigils, study, and in reading spiritual books. He considered the honors heaped on him only as a means to do much good. His entire income, which amounted to a considerable sum of money, he used in building churches, hospitals, and schools. Among these edifices were the University of Alcalá, the church of St. Ildephonse, several convents for the Franciscan friars and for sisters of the Third Order. Notwithstanding the great cost, he had the Holy Scriptures printed anew in several languages placed side by side on the single pages.

In 1509 he accompanied the Spanish army on a crusade against the Moors in Africa. With the cry of "St. James and Ximenez!" the victorious Spaniards set the standard of the cross on the battlements of Oran, the conquered capital of the Moors. On the death of King Ferdinand in 1516, Ximenez had still another charge imposed on him, for he was appointed viceroy of Spain.

Worn out with hardship and labor, he died at Roa in the province of

Burgos at the age of eighty-two years, November 8, 1518. His remains rest in the university church of Alcalá, which he had built. His memory is venerated by the Spanish people to this day as that of a saint. King Philip IV on two occasions, in 1650 and in 1655, requested the canonization of Ximenez of the Apostolic See. His cause has been introduced, but is still pending.

ON OPPORTUNITIES TO DO GOOD

1. Consider what great merits for eternity Venerable Francis Ximenez accumulated by using his opportunities to do good in his lifetime. Honorable positions, influential offices, a vast income, which this true son of St. Francis accepted only in virtue of obedience, meant to him only means to do good. In this way he gathered immense treasure for heaven. Many people use honors, official positions, and wealth only for their own benefit; to satisfy their pride, their desire for power, their desire for pleasure. Hardly ever do they think of doing good with the many opportunities afforded them, or of gathering merits for heaven. How will such people fare in eternity? "He who sows sparingly, shall also reap sparingly" (2 Cor. 9,6).

2. Often people think that in their common walk of life they have no opportunity to do good. The truth is, they do not pay sufficient attention to their opportunities. Besides the faithful fulfillment of everyday duties, every vocation offers opportunities for doing good, and circumstances often increase these opportunities considerably. Must you live with rude and ill-humored persons? Is your employment difficult? Are you being calumniated and persecuted? Are you sickly and infirm? How many opportunities are thereby offered you for the practice of patience, meekness, self-denial, and fraternal charity. The example of your virtues may even be instrumental in converting those who annoy you. If we only made use of the opportunities offered us, we could make each day a full day for eternity. — Have you acted thus in the past?

3. Consider what confusion will overwhelm those persons on judgment day who have made so little use of the opportunities afforded them for doing good. Like the foolish virgins, they will look about to see where they can still buy oil — the merits of good works, but it will be too late; they will be shut out from the heavenly wedding feast. Perhaps like the lazy servant, they will complain that they had no grand opportunities; but they will be cast out because they did not use those that were offered them. Therefore, "let us do good whilst we have time" (Gal. 6,10) ... "the night comes when not man can work" (Jn. 9,4).

PRAYER OF THE CHURCH
(Sunday after Christmas)

Almighty, everlasting God, direct our actions according to Thy good pleasure, that in the name of Thy beloved Son we may deserve to abound in good works. Who livest and reignest forever and ever. Amen.

APRIL 26
THE SERVANT OF GOD ANNA OF THE HOLY CROSS
Widow, Second Order

ANNA, the eldest daughter of the duke of Arcos, was born on May 3, 1527, in Andalusia, one of the most prosperous provinces of Spain. The world offered her every comfort that a worldling could wish for. What heaven offered her, her birthday was to indicate; it was the feast of the Finding of the Holy Cross. From her earliest years Anna learned to prefer the gifts of heaven, even when they were crosses, to the allurements of the world. The renowned master of the spiritual life, John of Avila, was her spiritual guide during her youth, and the director of her conscience through life.

She was scarcely sixteen years of age, when, in compliance with the wish of her relatives, she married the noble and pious count of Feria, Peter, marquis of Priego. The married state did not interfere with her former practices of piety, the less so because during the first three years her husband was absent on a campaign with the Emperor Charles V. Upon his return, they supported each other in the true service of God and in the practice of virtue, as truly Christian spouses should do.

Anna had an extraordinary love for the poor. With her own hands she made shirts for the sick and the poor. Often she gave up the jewels she wore for their support.

When a son was born to her and she enclosed him in her arms after holy baptism, God almighty revealed to her that He would soon take the child to Himself again. Although she was shocked at this, the young mother at once submitted her heart to the will of God. After a few days the child died. But this was to be only the beginning of her way of the cross.

A few years later her husband became ill. Anna was constantly with him for his comfort and benefit, scarcely ever leaving his bedside. In the three years during which his sufferings lasted, she did not remove her clothing, in order to be constantly at his service.

The Venerable Louis of Granada assisted the duke at his death. When he breathed forth his soul with the kiss he impressed upon the crucifix, and his confessor then passed the crucifix to the duchess, she also kissed it fervently and said: "From now on, He shall be my only spouse."

The twenty-four-year-old widow thought only of consecrating her life to God. She would gladly have entered the convent of the Poor Clares, but her delicate health did not warrant it. So she remained with her mother-in-law. In order to mortify her own will, she wished to make a vow of obedience to her Father Confessor; but Master Avila did not consider it prudent that a woman should vow obedience to her confessor, and therefore he advised her to vow obedience to her mother-in-law. Anna did that, and ever afterwards she sought her mother-in-law's permission for even the most trifling matters.

After a period of years, during which her desire for conventual life increased, her health also appeared to be wonderfully improved, so that the director of her soul and, finally, also her mother-in-law consented to her entrance into the convent of the Poor Clares at Montilla. Anna was overjoyed.

In the convent she deprecated every distinction and every exception. Just as if she were the servant of the other sisters, she performed the lowliest tasks. She observed poverty so strictly that she did not wish to accept even the smallest gift from her wealthy relatives.

Her devotion to the Blessed Sacrament was animated by the liveliest faith and the most ardent love. Many continuous hours she spent before the tabernacle in the sweetest exchange of sentiments with her hidden Lord, for which reason she was called "the bride of the Blessed Sacrament."

But the cross was also to test her in the convent. Her health again declined, and for thirty years of almost continuous illness, she practiced perfect resignation to the will of God. To this were added vexations from people who were indebted to her, but she never complained. Her brother, the new duke of Arcos, whom she dearly loved, died. Upon receiving the news of his death, she took the crucifix and said: "Lord, as Thou wilt; he belonged more to Thee than to me."

Her prayers effected many wonderful results in ailments, but she never cared to pray for relief from her own sufferings. Finally, the patient sufferer went to her eternal repose on April 26, 1601. Honored like a saint, her cause of beatification is under way.

RESIGNATION TO THE WILL OF GOD

Let the following verses from the German by Luise Brentano serve in place of a meditation:

Lord, *what* Thou wilt, may that be done to me, then it will be well.
May things of earth diminish and decay, my heart will swell; What until now Thy grace has granted me, it was surety,
I place it in Thy hands without delay most willingly.
Lord, *what* Thou wilt!

Lord, *as* Thou wilt, so may it be with me, for I am Thine,
Take all I have, all I possess on earth — be only mine!
'Tis not so hard to give up vanities, there is no smart.
If Thou wilt help, with mercy raise the weight from human heart.
Lord, *as* Thou wilt!

As long as Thou dost will, I will endure what Thou thinkest best,
I will not grieve, nor will I even ask why I'm oppressed;
Full well I know Thou wilt keep me in Thy care, I hold Thee firm,
Thy warding arm doth him more firmly clasp who all doth spurn.
So long Thou wilt!

PRAYER OF THE CHURCH
(Second Sunday after Pentecost)

Grant, O Lord, that we may have a perpetual fear and love of Thy holy name, for Thou never ceasest to direct and govern by Thy grace those whom Thou instructest in the solidity of Thy love. Through Christ our Lord. Amen.

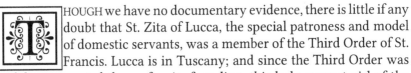

APRIL 27
ST. ZITA OF LUCCA
Virgin, Third Order

THOUGH we have no documentary evidence, there is little if any doubt that St. Zita of Lucca, the special patroness and model of domestic servants, was a member of the Third Order of St. Francis. Lucca is in Tuscany; and since the Third Order was widely propagated there after its founding, this holy servant girl of the thirteenth century would quite naturally join its ranks. She was born at the village of Monte Sagrati in 1218, at the time that St. Francis was entering upon his career as a knight-errant of Christ. Her parents were poor, devout Christians; an older sister afterwards became a nun; and her uncle Graziano was a saintly hermit.

When she was twelve years old, Zita went to Lucca, eight miles from her home, to be a servant girl of the Fatinelli family which carried on a prosperous wool and silk weaving business; and she remained in their employ until she died forty-eight years later. Her daily work became a part of her religious life. She was wont to say: "A servant girl is not pious, if she is not industrious; work-shy piety is sham piety." At the same time she led a very prayerful and penitential life. She rose nightly for prayer; and daily she attended the first Mass in the adjacent church of San Frediano. The good food she received for herself, she gave to the poor, and lived on waste scraps or fasted. She wore only the poorest clothes and never put on shoes, even in winter.

For some years she had much to bear from her fellow servants, who despised her way of life and insulted her repeatedly. Though she performed her work faithfully, her employers too were prejudiced against her for a time and treated her as a common drudge. But in the spirit of the suffering Christ, she bore these trials without complaint and never lost her temper or peace of mind. By her patience she gradually overcame all opposition, and became the friend and adviser of the whole household, including the servants. Her master and mistress, realizing at last what a treasure they possessed in Zita, made her chief housekeeper and the children's nurse. This embarrassed her even more than the slights she had to bear during the earlier years. However, she fulfilled her duties so well that everyone fared so much better as a result.

When Lucca lay under an interdict from 1231 to 1234, Zita used to go on foot into Pisan territory to receive holy Communion. These were dangerous trips at the time; but mysterious strangers befriended Zita on the way, and she was never molested. During the later years of her life, when she was relieved of much of the domestic work, she visited and helped the poor, the sick, and the prisoners to her heart's content.

Absorbed in prayer, her eyes turned heavenward, and her hands crossed on her breast, she died on April 27, 1278, at the age of sixty. At the time, a brilliant star shone above her attic room. After she had been honored as a saint for four centuries, Pope Innocent XII formally approved this cult in 1696. Her feast is celebrated at Lucca on April twenty-seventh; but no place has been assigned to her in the Franciscan calendar. (Cf. Biersack, p. 176; *These Made Peace*, p. 43.)

ON ENDURING CONTEMPT

1. Consider how St. Zita, by the patient endurance of insult, gave proof of great virtue. It is in fact the surest test of true humility, in which a person has a lowly opinion of himself and willingly accepts contempt from others. But where there is true humility, there is also the foundation and the fruitful root of every other virtue. — Do you stand the test of virtue in the endurance of contempt and disdain?

2. Consider that opportunities for enduring lack of regard present themselves daily. Thomas a Kempis enumerates a few when he writes (3,49): "What pleases others shall prosper, what is pleasing to you shall not succeed. What others say shall be hearkened to; what you say shall be reckoned as naught. Others shall ask and shall receive; you shall ask and not obtain. Others shall be great in the esteem of men; about you nothing will be said. To others this or that shall be committed; but you shalt be accounted as of no use. At this, nature will sometimes repine, and it will be a great matter if you bear it with silence." — How do you behave on such occasions?

3. Consider what will help you to bear patiently the contempt of men. It is the thought of our Divine Lord and Saviour, who had foretold through His Prophet: "I am the reproach of men, and the outcast of the people" (Ps. 21,7). Christ experienced misjudgment and lack of consideration from the day of His birth until His passion. He was satiated with disgrace when Herod in derision dressed Him in a white robe and made Him the laughingstock of the populace. The servant is not above the Master; what wonder if it happens to him as it did to the Master. But reflect also on the reward which Christ enjoys in His glory; that will also be your portion, as He promised: "Blessed are you when they shall revile you and persecute you, and speak all that is evil against you, untruly, for My sake. Be glad and rejoice, for your reward is very great in heaven" (Mt. 5,11). — Ask Mary, the Queen of the angels, to obtain for you the strength to endure contempt in a manner pleasing to God.

PRAYER OF THE CHURCH

Hear us, O God, our Saviour, and grant that as we are gladdened by the festival of Blessed Zita, Thy virgin, so we may learn from it loving devotion toward Thee. Through Christ our Lord. Amen.

APRIL 28
BLESSED LUCHESIO (LUCIUS)
Confessor, First Tertiary

UCHESIO, or Lucius, Modestini was a merchant in the little town of Poggibonzi in Tuscany. More than most merchants, he was so entirely and solely concerned with material success that he was quite generally reputed to be an avaricious man. His wife, Buonadonna, was of a similar disposition. Then the grace of God touched the husband. He realized how foolish it is to strive only after worldly goods, of which he could take nothing with him to eternity, meanwhile forgetting about his soul's salvation, as he had, unfortunately, been doing until then. He began to practice works of mercy and to perform his religious obligations with fidelity; he succeeded in winning his wife over to a similar outlook on life.

Since they had no one to care for but themselves, and Luchesio feared that in conducting his business he might relapse into covetousness, he gave up his business entirely. He and his good wife divided everything among the poor and retained for themselves only so much acreage as would suffice for their support. Luchesio tilled this with his own hands.

About this time St. Francis came to Tuscany. After his sermon on penance, hosts of people desired to leave all and enter the convent. But the saint admonished them calmly to persevere in their vocation, for he had in mind soon to give them a special rule according to which they could serve God quite perfectly even in the world.

At Poggibonzi Francis visited Luchesio, with whom he had become acquainted through former business transactions. Francis greatly rejoiced to find this avaricious man so altered, and Luchesio, who had already heard about the blessed activities of Francis, asked for special instructions for himself and his wife, so that they might lead a life in the world that would be pleasing to God.

Francis then explained to them his plans for the establishment of an order for lay people; and Luchesio and Buonadonna asked to be received into it at once. Thus, according to tradition, they became the first members of the Order of Penance, which later came to be called the Third Order. It was so called because St. Francis also founded the First Order for the Friars Minor and the Second Order for the Poor Clares.

If Luchesio and Buonadonna were really the first Tertiaries, they must have become such not long after St. Francis founded his First Order in 1209. The first simple rule of life, which St. Francis gave to the first Tertiaries at that time, was supplanted in 1221 by one which Cardinal

Ugolino prepared in legal wording. And in the same year Pope Honorius III approved this rule verbally. For this reason the year 1221 is often given as the date of the founding of the Third Order of St. Francis.

Later in the thirteenth century, in the year 1289, Pope Nicholas revised the rule of the Third Order and approved it anew. Pope Leo XIII adapted the Third Order rule to modern conditions in 1883. Finally, in 1957, general constitutions were added to the rule, in order to determine in greater detail what is expected of modern Tertiaries and also to render their way of life more uniform and effective in the modern world.

After Luchesio had put on the gray garment of a Tertiary, he rapidly advanced toward perfect holiness. He practiced penitential austerities, often fasted on bread and water, slept on the hard floor, and at his work bore God constantly in his heart. His generosity to the poor knew no bounds, so that one day there was not even a loaf of bread for his own household. When still another poor man came, he asked his wife to look whether there was not something they could find for him. That vexed her and she scolded him severely; his mortifications, she said, had well nigh crazed him, he would keep giving so long that they themselves would have to suffer hunger. Luchesio asked her gently please to look in the pantry, for he trusted in Him who had multiplied a few loaves for the benefit of thousands. She did so, and the marvel of it! The whole pantry was filled with the best kind of bread. From that time on Buonadonna vied with her husband in doing good.

When a plague raged in Poggibonzi and the surrounding places, Luchesio went out with his laden donkey, to bring the necessaries to the sick. When he did not have enough to supply all, he begged for more from others in behalf of the distressed.

Once he carried a sick cripple, whom he had found on the way, to his home on his shoulders. A frivolous young man met him, and asked him mockingly: "What poor devil is that you are carrying there on your back?" Luchesio replied calmly: "I am carrying my Lord Jesus Christ." At once the young man's face became distorted, he cried out fearfully, and was dumb. Contritely he cast himself on his knees before Luchesio, who restored his speech to him by means of the Sign of the Cross.

The time had come when the faithful servant of God was to receive the reward for his good works. When he lay very ill, and there was no hope for his recovery, his wife said to him: "Implore God, who gave us to each other as companions in life, to permit us also to die together." Luchesio prayed as requested, and Buonadonna fell ill with a fever, from which she died even before her husband, after devoutly receiving the holy sacraments. Luchesio passed away with holy longing for God on April 28,

1260. At his grave in the Franciscan church at Poggibonzi many miracles have occurred. His continued veneration as Blessed was approved by Pope Pius VI. The Franciscans, Conventuals, and Third Order Regular observe his feast on April twenty-eighth. (Cf. *These Made Peace*, pp. 2-9; *Forum*, 1945, pp. 99-237; Meyer, *Blessed by a Curse*.)

CONCERNING IMPERISHABLE TREASURES

1. Christ our Lord says in His Gospel: "The kingdom of heaven is like to a merchant seeking good pearls. Who when he had found one pearl of great price, went his way, and sold all that he had, and bought it" (Mt. 13,45-46). Such a merchant was Blessed Luchesio, since, having been enlightened by grace, he found the costly pearl of true godliness. Then he desisted from his covetous chase after perishable goods, gave them up in order to inherit imperishable treasures, which now delight him in his beatitude with God, and will be his eternal joy. May we, too, find this costly pearl!

2. Consider what folly, on the other hand, it is to strive after temporal goods as is done by so many people. They place their body and soul in danger; they have troubles here on earth and hereafter. The body is exposed to fatigue, hardships, privations, and even danger to life; through falsehood and deceit, through disregard of the commandments of God and of the Church, the soul becomes laden with much guilt. And in the end, what does man achieve with the temporal goods he has acquired? "As he came forth naked from his mother's womb, so shall he return, and shall take nothing away with him of his labor" (Eccl. 5,14). Must the same judgment perhaps be passed concerning your endeavors?

3. Consider that not everybody in this world can act as did Blessed Luchesio. Not everyone is free of obligations toward others, who are perhaps entrusted to his temporal care; nor has everyone the grace and the vocation for such extraordinary virtues. If anyone believes himself called by God in that way, he should seek counsel with his spiritual director. But everyone can and should strive, while following his occupation and business, to gather at the same time eternal and imperishable goods. He can do that if he conducts his temporal business as the special vocation assigned to him by God to acquire a livelihood for himself and his family; if through it he endeavors to be of service to his fellowmen; if he tries to promote Christian morality according to the best of his power, himself setting the good example; if, finally, he does not endeavor greedily to hoard what he acquires, but uses it well, gladly sharing it with those in need. "Blessed is the rich man who is found

without blemish; and who has not gone after gold, nor put his trust in money nor in treasures" (Eccli. 31,8).

PRAYER OF THE CHURCH

O God, who in the plentitude of Thy mercy didst call Blessed Luchesio to penance and didst permit him to shine by the merits of piety and liberality, grant us at his intercession, that in imitation of his example, we may produce worthy fruits of penance, and through works of piety and charity merit forgiveness. Through Christ our Lord. Amen.

APRIL 29
VENERABLE PAUL HEATH
Martyr, First Order

HE SON of a Protestant family, Henry Heath was born at Peterborough, Northamptonshire, England, in 1599. Endowed with unusual gifts of the mind, he was sent at eighteen to the University of Cambridge; and four years later he received the degree of bachelor of arts and was placed in charge of the university library. Because of religious misgivings, which became graver as he advanced in his studies, Henry began to investigate the teaching of the Catholic Church. He soon saw how utterly untenable Protestantism was on logical and historical grounds and decided to embrace the old faith. Leaving Cambridge secretly, he went to a Catholic nobleman in London; but, at first, he was taken for a spy. After seeking the aid of the Blessed Virgin, however, he was well received and introduced to a priest, who admitted him into the Church. The young convert then left England and went to the English College at Douai.

Meeting the sons of St. Francis at Douai, he was filled with the desire of joining their ranks, but was discouraged by his confessor. Once more he implored the help of the Blessed Virgin; and in May, 1624, he was clothed with the Franciscan habit and received the name of Friar Paul of St. Magdalene. Four years later he was ordained a priest. Father Paul was highly esteemed for his virtue as well as his learning. He held the important offices of professor of moral and later dogmatic theology, spiritual director of the student clerics, vicar, and then guardian. At the same time he devoted himself to the care of souls, making sinners and heretics the special object of his priestly zeal. Many conversions were brought about through the prayers and labors of Father Paul. Father Peter Marchant, who presided at the chapter of 1637, described Father Paul as "a mirror of meekness, integrity, and sincerity, a beacon light of holiness, a model of religious observance among the brethren, and in the science of theology a shining and glowing star among the luminaries of the Douai University."

From the beginning of his conversion Father Paul distinguished himself by his devotion to Our Lady. Though his father had remained a bitter Protestant, Father Paul begged the Blessed Mother to lead him into the fold of the Church, and a most remarkable conversion followed. The eighty-year-old man crossed the sea to hunt up his son at Douai; and not only did he make his peace with the old faith, but he joined the Franciscans there as a lay brother.

In 1641 the Puritan persecution of the Catholics in England broke out. It was directed particularly against priests. Five Franciscans won the martyr's crown, and Father Paul was the third among these. In December, 1642, he left Douai for Dunkirk. There he had a sailor's suit made out of his habit, and crossed the channel to Dover. On the way to London, he was apprehended. After admitting that he was a priest and making a fearless profession of faith, he was thrown into Newgate prison. There he devoted much time to the spiritual comfort of his fellow prisoners and of the many Catholics who came to visit him. More than five hundred went to confession to him. Several months he spent in prison, and in April he was condemned to be executed at Tyburn. When the final preparations were made for his hanging, Father Paul again and again invoked the names of Jesus and Mary. His last words were: "O Jesus forgive me my sins! Jesus, convert England! Jesus, have mercy on this country! O England, be converted to the Lord thy God!" He died a martyr's death on April 27, 1643. At the moment of his death, the aged lay brother at Douai, who was his father, saw a brilliant light ascending into heaven and told his brethren that his son had just then died for the faith. (Cf. Steck, *Franciscans and the Protestant Revolution*, pp. 272-291; *Forum*, 1943, pp. 194-200.)

ON TRUE SPIRITUAL PROGRESS

1. You are the nearer to God, the lower you become in your own estimation and the farther removed from the world. Be humble, yet trustful. Be patient, yet energetic. Be insistent, yet resigned, always singling out for yourself the last place among God's servants. Whatever good you have the chance to do, take it as something entrusted to you by

God. In such a case, busy yourself hand and foot to achieve the aim, bending your unwilling mind to the task and embracing the cross of Christ with all your heart. And when you have finished the work, do not sit back to indulge vanity and dissipation; but, with due allowance for rest, direct your interior gaze upward and seek out a solitary place to find your way to Jesus. At such times set your mind on contrition and regret for the days of your sojourn. Be ready for hardships, be vigorous in mortifying yourself, be cheerful about prayer. For, such things and all things are to lead you to one destination, to God.

2. The temptation to sin will now and then attack you. Then you must be ready to defend steadfastly the camp of your heart, so that the enemy's power cannot take foot there. Make Christ alone your really intimate friend, for He alone can give you the victory in all cases. When the Devil assails you, Christ supplies the arms against him. He will rouse your sleeping conscience with His secret impulse, so that you may not stray from the right path under the black darkness of temptation. He will show the way for your resolutions, infuse fervor, steady your virtue, and lead your advance to the goal. He understands the wise, and He instructs the ignorant as well — those who have never tasted the rudiments of human wisdom. In Christ's company you will find yourself reaching out to greater progress in a month than you can over long periods of time by cultivating the world's vain companionship. Once you have begun well, do not for anybody's sake desist from your good proposals.

3. If no chance to practice virtue presents itself, still you can go on practicing it interiorly, at one time hanging your head as if you heard Jesus sweetly reproving you, at another bending your back to the rod of mortification as if you felt Jesus lovingly beating you, at still another having recourse to the incentives of virtue, or the aspirations of love, or the sigh of repentance. But let people not see your private austerities, so that you can keep them secretly for God alone. Go your humble way, therefore, as the vilest among sinners, regardless of how far you may have advanced in holiness and virtue. For, the farther you advance, the more you will be assaulted by enemies. Wherefore, so much the more do you need the grace and mercy of God. Never consider yourself safe, never regard yourself as truly perfect, for you do not know how readily you will fall when temptation assails you. Let Jesus, therefore, be all your strength and confidence. Take your stand firmly with Him and do not depart from Him. Pray when you should, so that your prayer may not interfere with your virtuous activity, nor the latter smother but rather promote your life of prayer. In that way seek nothing, either in your prayer or in your activity, but the plain will of God. — These beautiful reflections on true

spiritual progress are culled from the writings of Venerable Paul Heath. If we make them our own, they will lead us onward as they did the saintly martyr. (Cf. Meyer, *Self-Communings of a Martyr.*)

PRAYER OF THE CHURCH
(Tenth Sunday after Pentecost)

O God who dost chiefly manifest Thy almighty power in long-suffering and pity, increase Thy mercy toward us, that, hastening after Thy promises, we may be made partakers of the heavenly treasures. Through Christ our Lord. Amen.

APRIL 30
ST. JOSEPH BENEDICT COTTOLENGO
Confessor, Third Order

IT is the lot of the city of Turin that for almost one hundred years it possessed a line of saintly Tertiary priests who have been raised to the honors of the altar. One of these is St. Joseph Benedict Cottolengo, the man who more than any other man, in the nineteenth century at least, was instrumental in inducing men "to love, bless, and invoke that sweet and ever active providence which rules over the universe and provides for the needs of every man on his way through the toils of life to the rest of the eternal blessedness."

Joseph Benedict was born in the little town of Piedmont called Bra, on the third of May, 1786. His parents were poor in the goods of this world but rich by virtue of noble traits of mind and character. Twelve children were born to this worthy couple. Joseph was the eldest, and was so frail in his infancy that his mother was in constant dread of losing him, but her fervent prayers and faithful care in time brought him health and strength. As soon as he was able to understand, she filled his mind with thoughts of God and of our Lady, and was careful to train him to deeds of charity to the poor.

In preparing His servant for his life work, almighty God provided him with the greatest need of the human soul — that "one in ten thousand" whom St. Francis de Sales recommends Philothea to choose for his confessor. The parish priest of St. Andrew the Apostle, besides being a priest who possessed more than ordinary zeal, eloquence, and piety, had a special love for the poor and the afflicted. He allowed this gentle and pure child to receive his first holy Communion at the then unusual age of nine years.

At school, Joseph was much grieved to find himself always at the foot of his class. Some priests advised him to pray to the great St. Thomas Aquinas, after which he went from the foot to the head of the class. Recognizing the event as a special blessing from God, he was desirous of reciprocating to the best of his ability, and so he frequently declared, "I will strive to become a saint."

In spite of the various obstacles that came in his way when preparing for the holy priesthood, he nevertheless succeeded in passing the various tests of his vocation; and on June 8, 1811, he was ordained a priest in the church of the Immaculate Conception in Turin. He devoted himself with much ardor to all his priestly duties and especially to the poor and the sick; still, his heart was not satisfied, for he felt that God intended him for some special work.

As canon of the collegiate church of Corpus Christi in Turin, he was inspired, by the sight of the misery everywhere apparent and by the reading of the life of St. Vincent de Paul, to take a hand in alleviating human suffering. His first steps were to provide care and shelter for the destitute sick of the parish, by renting some rooms for a hospital and interesting some young women in the work.

In 1832 there was founded at Valdocco what became known as the House of Providence. Pius IX called it the "House of Miracles," and popularly it was styled the University of Charity on account of the diversified work of charity which the saint set afoot there, with no income or outlook but an heroic trust in the merciful providence of God. By the time of his death in 1842 the work, as it may still be seen today, was practically complete, with all its various hospitals, workshops, schools, seminaries, cloistered and non-cloistered convents, asylums for the old, the feebleminded and the insane, the crippled, epileptic, blind, deaf and dumb, and the like. At Cottolengo's beatification in 1917 this "City of Charity" numbered some eight thousand people; and these had resolutely resisted any attempt to settle fixed revenues on the institution, so that it might remain forever what it was at the outset, a monument to divine providence.

While still a young man, Joseph Benedict had been received into the Third Order of St. Francis and had distinguished himself by his spirit of perfect poverty; he assiduously strove also to foster in himself and in others love towards the Blessed Sacrament and the sufferings of Jesus Christ. Along with supreme trust in God's providence, Franciscan good humor adorned the saint, which no opposition, no storms, nor hardships could shake. When the authorities of the city of Turin, giving way to protests from the people, ordered the closing of the original house, the saint smilingly complied and moved the infirmary countryward saying: "Cabbages thrive better for being transplanted." His vast settlement with all its departments he referred to as "Noah's Ark."

He was only in his fifty-sixth year when he was called to his great reward. His last hours were spent in fervent prayer. He died on the evening of April 13, 1842. Many miracles occurred at his tomb, including many cures of bodily ills and maladies of the soul. It is even claimed that some have seen his visible presence. Pope Pius XI enrolled him among the saints of the Catholic Church on March 19, 1934. His feast is celebrated by the Franciscans on April thirtieth, by the Conventuals on the twenty-ninth. (Cf. *Forum*, 1949, pp. 110-112.)

ON TRUST IN DIVINE PROVIDENCE

1. How frequently our Divine Saviour reminded the people of God's watchfulness over them in all the affairs of their life, and how frequently He encouraged them to trust in His provident care. "Behold the birds of the air," He said in the sermon on the Mount, "for they neither sow, nor do they reap, nor gather into barns, and your heavenly Father feeds them. Are not you of much more value than they? And for raiment why are you solicitous? Consider the lilies of the field how they grow; they labor not neither do they spin. But I say to you, that not even Solomon in all his glory was arrayed as one of these. Be not solicitous, therefore, saying: 'What shall we eat, or what shall we drink, or wherewith shall we be clothed?' For after all these things do the heathens seek. For your Father knows that you have need of all these things" (Mt. 7,26-32). — Have we reflected sufficiently on these words of the Divine Teacher and profited thereby?

2. In the account of the Piccola Casa (the Little House of Providence) we read that on the main door is inscribed the ninth verse of Psalm 61: "Trust in Him, all ye congregations of people, pour out your hearts before Him." The faith and trust which St. Joseph Benedict reposed in God seems truly without a parallel even among the saints. Nothing could disturb it. The king of Savoy as well as wealthy people and corporations repeatedly made advances towards endowing his work, but his reply was: "Such a thing is impossible. The Piccola Casa already enjoys the protection of the Blessed Virgin Mary and of God's providence. What other patronage can it require?" — What an example for this present day and age, where our

concerns for tomorrow seem to be even more important than those for today. And this in spite of the fact that our good God reminds us, "And which of you, by taking thought, can add to his stature one cubit?" (Mt. 6,27).

3. Trust in divine providence is a distinctly Franciscan trait bequeathed to us by our holy Father himself. The accounts of the life of the Seraphic Founder give frequent evidence of the trait. One instance will suffice as an example. When St. Francis convened the chapter, since that time known as the "Chapter of Mats," more than five thousand of the brethren assembled from all parts of the world. Encamped on the plain about the Portiuncula, they engaged in prayer and pious exercises. Francis traversed the camp, encouraging them and animating all to fresh fervor, to the love of God, and the observance of the rule. Among other things he said: "I recommend to you above all, nay, I strictly command you, not to be anxious about what concerns your food, clothing, or lodging; for Jesus Christ has bound Himself to provide both you and me with all that is necessary, if on our part we devote ourselves faithfully to His love and service." His worthy companion, St. Dominic, who was present and heard this discourse, considering the difficulty of providing for the wants of this immense family, was tempted to think his friend indiscreet, and mentioned this thought to him. But Francis, confiding entirely in God, answered: "Wait and see how well my children are provided for." As a matter of fact, carts, mules, horses, and men from all Umbria flocked into the plain bringing every sort of food and everything necessary for their service. And all who had come to witness this wondrous sight, considered it an honor to wait upon the humble friars, blessing God for His mercy and love. St. Dominic, amazed at the faith and confidence of Francis, threw himself at his feet, and begged him to forgive the rash judgment he had formed of him. — To what extent have we striven to acquire this truly Franciscan trait? What can we say about our trust in God?

PRAYER OF THE CHURCH

O God, who dost bountifully assist those who place their confidence in Thy fatherly protection, grant us, through the intercession of St. Joseph Benedict, that having served the poor and afflicted, we may deserve the reward Thou hast mercifully promised. Through Christ our Lord. Amen.

MAY

MAY 1
THE SERVANT OF GOD SIMON VAN ACKEREN
Confessor, Third Order

T HE SEVENTH child in a family of twelve children, Lawrence Van Ackeren was born at Humphrey, Nebraska, on February 17, 1918. Even as a boy he stood out by reason of his spirit of prayer and his love of our Lord in the Blessed Sacrament. After completing the grade school, he wanted to go to the Franciscan preparatory seminary at Westmont, Illinois; but he had such a hard time with his studies that he was told to finish high school first. In September, 1936, he was admitted to the preparatory seminary and joined the fourth-year students. But by Christmas he realized that he did not have sufficient talent to pursue the required studies for the priesthood, and he applied for admission as a Franciscan lay brother.

Toward the end of January, 1937, he was sent to St. Joseph Theological Seminary, Teutopolis, Illinois, and was invested as a Tertiary brother about a month later, receiving the name of Brother Simon. His ankle started to bother him about a year after he arrived at Teutopolis, and he began to walk with a slight limp. Soon after, the limb became too painful and he could scarcely walk. He was taken to St. Anthony Hospital in nearby Effingham and received treatments for a month, but his ankle failed to respond. He returned to the seminary on crutches, and was permitted to make his profession as a Tertiary brother on March 4, 1938. The next day he left for St. Louis to consult a specialist. After three weeks he came back, his ankle in a cast. The verdict was tuberculosis of the bone. Soon his general health began to fail. On the last day of April he went to the hospital in Effingham. There the doctors found that he had galloping consumption and gave him only a short time to live.

Brother Simon's condition quickly grew worse, and he was anointed on the sixth day after his arrival at the hospital. The next few days his strength failed rapidly. About ten o'clock on the night of May 10, while the sister on night duty was with him, his innocent soul winged its way to heaven. Though he was only a Tertiary brother for little more than a year, Brother Simon has gained a greater reputation as a saint and intercessor in heaven than any other deceased member of the Franciscan Province of the Sacred Heart. During his illness and suffering no one heard an impatient word escape his lips; and he never ceased praying. His sunny smile never wore off. His greatness consisted in doing the little things well — doing them with extraordinary and always cheerful willingness, fidelity, charity, patience, and piety. "Being made perfect in a short space, he fulfilled a long time" (Wisd. 4,13).

As it was Brother Simon's delight to help others in life, so he has continued to help others in a remarkable manner also after his death. Innumerable favors have been reported and attributed to his intercession. Strangely enough Brother Simon is gaining a growing reputation as a missionaries' broker and a helper in financial difficulties. Constant favors are reported also from sick persons who have gained health or alleviation from ill health through a novena made in his honor. Hardly a week goes by that a note or letter does not mention some favor granted through the intercession of Brother Simon. (Cf. *Heralds of the King*, pp. 727-733; Marquard, *On Crutches to Heaven*; *Forum*, 1943, pp. 98-103, and 1957, pp. 333-335.)

SICKNESS IS USEFUL FOR THE SOUL

1. Consider the great perfection which Brother Simon achieved in the sickness with which he was afflicted. Where does a person have more opportunity for patience, mortification, surrender to God's will, and devotion to the sufferings of Christ? That is why it sometimes happens that almighty God visits His favorites with long-standing or even incurable sickness; because in everything that He does in His wisdom, He has above all our soul and its welfare in mind. "Sickness of the body," says St. Gregory, "is the health of the soul." — Have you also drawn benefit for your soul from sieges of illness?
2. Consider that most people do not make use of sickness for the welfare of their soul, so that Thomas a Kempis (1,23) says, "Few are improved through sickness." How does that happen? The reason is that they look upon sickness as an evil, and think of nothing but to avert this evil. — But have not many persons been saved through illness, yes, even become saints, who would otherwise have been lost? Therefore, "reject not the correction of the Lord, and do not faint when you are chastised by Him. For, whom the Lord loves, He chastises (Prov. 3,11-12).
3. Consider that sickness is also a form of penance. By it God permits us to atone for things which we should otherwise have to atone for in purgatory, only in a more painful manner. Our Divine Lord spoke thus to

the paralytic, who, after enduring much pain on a bed of suffering for a long time, was finally brought to Jesus by four compassionate persons: "Be of good heart, son, your sins are forgiven you" (Mt. 9,2). The penance had been performed, and now He gave the man his health again. If we call this to mind often in times of painful illness, the pain will be less severe and at the same time very useful to us, since our soul will then enter the presence of God so much the sooner in eternity.

PRAYER OF THE CHURCH
(Friday after Palm Sunday)

Pour forth, we beseech Thee, O Lord, Thy grace into our hearts, that we who restrain ourselves from sin in voluntary chastisement may rather suffer in time than be found deserving of eternal punishment. Through Christ our Lord. Amen.

MAY 2
THE SERVANT OF GOD MARIE CELINE
Virgin, Second Order

ISTER MARIE CELINE of the Presentation was, before her entrance into the religious life, Jeanne Germaine Castang. She was born on May 24, 1878, at Nojals, France, the fifth of twelve children. Her parents were poor but deeply religious. They loved their children with true Christian love and tried to rear them in innocence and piety.

An illness with which Germaine was attacked at the age of four left her with severe pains in her limbs, and for some time her left leg was totally paralyzed. She always limped a bit and suffered constantly from it. But her mother taught her even at this tender age to bear it all for the love of Jesus, who also suffered much when He was a child.

Many reverses came to the family during the first decade of Germaine's life, but the hard lessons and trials which she learned during these times equipped her with a courage and heroism unusual in one so young. Due to repeated sieges of illness, she did not receive her first holy Communion until she was fourteen years old. In preparation for this event a kind lady, who had interested herself in her, took her to the House of Nazareth, an institution conducted by sisters. On June 12, 1892, she received the Divine Lover of pure souls for the first time; a happy day, especially after it had been so long delayed. Shortly afterwards she was confirmed, and then came new trials.

Her mother died quite suddenly in the following Christmas season; an older brother of Celine followed their mother to the grave not long afterwards. During this sad period Germaine had summoned all the faith and strength she could command to assist the dying and at the same time to care for her younger brothers and sisters. But she was too delicate to take over the entire care of the house, so it was broken up. Germaine returned to the House of Nazareth.

The desire to become a nun had been engaging her thoughts for a long time, but when she asked for admission among the Poor Clares, for whom she felt a special attraction, she was refused because she was too young and too frail. Applications at other convents met with the same results. Three years later, however, when she was eighteen years old, she was passing the Ave Maria convent of the Poor Clares at Bordeaux, when she decided to make another attempt to gain admission. The Mother Abbess was won by her sweet simplicity and humility, and on June 12, 1896, Germaine was received into the enclosure. At once she set herself with earnestness to acquire the virtues of a good religious. She accepted with sweetness and humility the mortifications and trials sent her by God.

It is related that on one occasion when she was suddenly called away and had to leave her cell without having an opportunity to put things in order, as she was tempted to do contrary to prompt obedience, she found upon her return that everything had been neatly put away. Believing that her novice mistress had tidied the cell for her, she sought her out to thank her. It was found, however, that neither the novice mistress nor anyone else had been in her cell from the time she left it. It was evident that her Guardian Angel had done it as a reward for her prompt obedience.

She was clothed with the holy habit on November 21, 1896, and was given the name Sister Marie Celine of the Presentation. She was a model of charity, humility, unselfishness, and punctuality, and was always cheerful, often being the very life of the recreations in the novitiate.

One evening in the winter following her investiture, she was suffering greatly and told her novice mistress of her illness. As she had been visibly declining, her superiors were not surprised and immediately called a good doctor. She suffered both from physical pain which racked her body and from fear that she would be dismissed, since she was only a novice. Feeble though she was, she still attended the spiritual exercises and the Divine Office, and always wished to be occupied. However, she was obedient and sweetly acquiesced when told to cease working.

As her death seemed but a matter of time, the Mother Abbess obtained the necessary permission for Sister Celine to make her profession on her sickbed. Accordingly, on March twenty-second, after receiving the last sacraments, the dying novice made her perpetual vows, receiving the black veil and the ring of espousal with her Saviour. However, she still had two months of intense suffering to endure before she should meet her Spouse. During the last ten days of her illness she hovered between life and death. The scent of roses was often noticed in her room and in the corridor, though there were no flowers about at that time. This mysterious scent has often been noticed in presence of the remains or other relics of Sister Celine, and cannot be accounted for except as a favor from above.

Before her final moment Celine was tempted by the evil spirit, but courageously resisted his assaults. When she was again calm, she spoke of the beautiful lady who stood near her bed awaiting her, and with acts of love she breathed her pure soul into the hands of her Maker on Sunday, May 30, 1897, at the age of only nineteen years. She has since obtained many favors for those who invoke her intercession.

ON THE TRIALS SENT BY PROVIDENCE

1. Every person who has arrived at the use of reason is tried by God. This trial is not necessary that God may know what each of us is made of. He knows in advance whether we shall stand the test or not. But it is necessary for us that we may acknowledge what we are and be obliged to say at the judgment: "Thou art just, O Lord, and Thy judgment is right" (Ps. 118,37). — How fortunate for us if we shall have stood the test!
2. God tries the faithful souls. "As gold in the furnace He has proved them, and as a victim of holocaust He has received them" (Wisd. 3,6). Hence, it is not surprising that the Servant of God Marie Celine suffered much in her body and no less in mind, from the earliest years of her life up to her blessed death. These trials were a sign of predilection. — Do not falter, do not become discouraged at every affliction that assails you. Remember the words of the Angel to Tobias: "Because you were acceptable to God it was necessary that temptations should prove you" (Tob. 12,13).
3. What means should we use to persevere in trials? We should prepare ourselves in the time of peace and tranquility of soul for this period of suffering, praying for the grace to withstand the assaults of the evil spirit; and we should carry the cross which Providence places upon our shoulders with patience and resignation. Moreover, when the hour of trial arrives, let us encourage ourselves with the hope of the reward promised us in the epistle of St. James: "Blessed is the man who endures temptation: for, when he has been proved, he shall receive the crown of life which God

has promised to them who love Him" (1,12).

PRAYER OF THE CHURCH

O almighty and eternal God! Thou healest whilst Thou dost afflict us, Thou dost preserve us whilst Thou dost pardon; grant us, who humbly beseech Thee, peacefully to enjoy the comfort we desire and ever to experience the grace of Thy love. Through Christ our Lord. Amen.

MAY 3
VENERABLE JANE OF THE CROSS
Virgin, Third Order

N the feast of the Finding of the Cross, May 3, 1481, Jane was born at Hazagna, not far from Toledo, Spain. Even as a child she gave signs of future holiness; for example, she took no food at all on Fridays. Her bodily as well as her spiritual development progressed so rapidly beyond her years, that, on the death of her mother, although she was only ten years old, she managed the household of her father.

Because of her special endowments, she was sought in marriage by a distinguished young man when she was but fourteen years of age. Her father urged her to consent, but Jane definitely declared that she would never get married and wished to serve God in a convent. When her father enlisted the help of relatives, all endeavoring to influence her toward marriage, Jane secretly took flight in men's clothing.

At Cuba, some hours' distance from her native town, Jane again donned her own clothing, which she had brought with her in a bundle, and asked for admission into the convent of the Tertiaries there. She was invested on her fifteenth birthday, and on the same day of the next year she made her profession. She received the surname of the Cross, because of the feast of the Finding of the Holy Cross.

Jane redoubled her zeal in mortification, in prayer, and in all the religious virtues. She had a special devotion to the Blessed Sacrament and a great desire for holy Communion. Gladly would she have received every day, but in accordance with the custom of the time and the wish of her confessor, she contented herself with the general communion days of the sisters. But she was all the more zealous in receiving the Holy Sacrament spiritually. Her ardent desire led her to receive spiritually at almost every hour of the day, and through this practice she felt so wonderfully strengthened that she sometimes cried out: "O my God, if the mere desire for Thy most holy Body has such marvelous effects, what strength must the actual reception afford!"

But she was also to stand in need of this strength. She had to endure much hostility and ill-treatment from her fellow sisters. True, later all of them recognized their injustice, and upon the death of the superior, they unanimously elected Jane in her place. But even in that position, although she greatly promoted the spiritual and temporal welfare of the convent, she met with such vehement opposition, within and without the convent, that she was deposed, until it was recognized that the complaints against her were calumnies and she was reinstated. Jane was also visited with severe physical sufferings; but that seemed to be her one desire, since she always prayed for more suffering.

Christ our Lord rewarded the fidelity of His spouse with extraordinary graces. She saw her guardian angel visibly at her side and constantly received counsel and comfort from him. She was gifted with wonderful insight into the mysteries of our holy religion, and discoursed on them in a manner that astonished the most learned men. Cardinal Ximenez, archbishop of Toledo, often came to the convent and manifested the greatest respect for her.

Our Lord once rewarded her love for the Blessed Sacrament with a marvelous miracle. She was going to church in order to adore the Blessed Sacrament at elevation, which was just about to take place. But the signal for elevation was given while Jane was still in the cloister hall. Promptly she knelt down, and, marvelous to say, the wall of the church seemed to part so that Jane could see the Blessed Sacrament. After the priest replaced the chalice with the Blessed Sacrament on the altar, the gap closed, but a mark of the marvelous opening was left on the wall. King Philip III himself came to the convent later to see this memento of the miracle.

In the fifty-fourth year of her life Jane learned from her guardian angel that she should now enter the celestial vision, and also that she would die in the shadow of the cross. On the feast of the Finding of the Cross, May 3, 1534, she departed after a prolonged ecstasy. God almighty glorified her after death with numerous miracles, which have been examined and approved by the Church; but her cause of beatification has not been completed.

CONCERNING SPIRITUAL COMMUNION

1. Consider that Venerable Jane knew how to use spiritual Communion to

advantage. In following the practice she preserved obedience to her confessor, avoided singularity, and yet fulfilled the ardent desires of her heart for union with her divine Saviour. Spiritually she could communicate more frequently than was possible sacramentally. For this reason God almighty, who accepts the desire for the deed, strengthened her so marvelously. It is good to follow her example. Thomas a Kempis (4,10) says: "If at times a person is lawfully hindered, he should yet always have the good will and the pious intention of communicating, and so he will not be without the fruit of the sacrament." — Do you often communicate spiritually?

2. Consider how one goes about receiving Communion spiritually. The holy Council of Trent says that faith and love dispense the fruit and the effects of the Holy Sacrament to those who long for the heavenly Bread in spiritual Communion. A person must therefore excite in himself a lively faith in the presence of Christ in the Holy Sacrament, be heartily sorry for all his sins out of love for God, and then express to God the loving desire to receive Him in the Holy Sacrament. Thus one communicates spiritually; and one ought never to omit the practice in holy Mass at the Communion of the priest.

3. Consider especially that spiritual Communion is a great help in the real reception of holy Communion. It is the best preparation for it, in as far as it nourishes our desire for the Bread of Heaven, and thus disposes us better for the graces of holy Communion to take effect. And after holy Communion it keeps alive in us the grateful remembrance of holy Communion, so that the strength of the Holy Sacrament continues to produce its effects in us. Thus through spiritual Communion the Holy Eucharist proves to be not only the daily but even the hourly food of our souls.

PRAYER OF THE CHURCH
(From the Mass of the Most Blessed Sacrament)

O God, who in this wonderful sacrament hast left us a memorial of Thy passion, grant us, we beseech Thee, so to venerate the sacred mysteries of Thy Body and Blood, that we may ever perceive in us the fruit of Thy redemption. Who livest and reignest forever and ever. Amen.

MAY 4

THE SERVANTS OF GOD PAULA AND GABRIELA MEZZAVACCHI
Virgins, Second Order

THE MOTHER of these saintly sisters had from her youth entertained the desire to consecrate her life to God in a convent. Constrained by the wishes of her father to give her hand in marriage to the noble John Baptist Mezzavacchi, a professor of law at the University of Bologna, she went to the church as a bride, cast herself on her knees before the altar and said: "O Lord, since I have not been found worthy to serve Thee in the convent, I now already consecrate to Thee all the children that Thou wilt present to me."

God almighty graciously accepted her sacrifice. She gave birth to two sons and two daughters. The first son entered the Benedictine Order and became an abbot. The second became a Franciscan, was provincial at Bologna, and died as guardian of Mount Sion convent in Jerusalem; his brother saw how the holy angels bore his soul to heaven. The two daughters entered the convent of the Poor Clares at Ferrara, in which St. Catharine of Bologna was the novice mistress.

When Catharine went to Bologna in order to establish a new convent, she took with her Paula, the older of the sisters, whom she appointed mistress of novices because of her outstanding virtue. In this capacity Paula directed the novices with zeal, prudence, and great charity. In a special way she devoted herself to her sick, tempted, and worried fellow sisters. To all she was a model of humility, meekness, and mortification. God adorned her with the gift of prophecy and revealed to her the secrets of hearts. She died in the odor of sanctity in 1492.

For a period of nine years after Paula's entrance into the convent, her sister Gabriela continued to be the object of love and tenderness in their paternal home. Yet, she felt interiorly impelled to follow the example of her sister. Generously she overcame the difficulties she encountered, left all, and at Ferrara asked for the poor garb of the daughters of St. Clare. Her progress in perfection corresponded to the heroic beginning she had made, until, rich in merits, she was called to her reward in the year 1493.

ON THE POWER OF A MOTHER'S PRAYER

1. Consider what the pious prayer of a mother can do for her children. Obviously it was the result of the sacrifice and prayers of the mother of

these saintly virgins that her children became such faithful servants of God. The mother of St. Bernard, who consecrated her six sons and one daughter to God immediately after their birth and begged that they might remain faithful in His service, experienced a similar effect of prayer. Three of the children are honored as saints, all died most edifying deaths. If Christ our Lord says: "All things whatsoever you ask the Father in My name, that I will do" (Jn. 14,13), must not then the prayer of a mother for her children's salvation be heard? Christ Himself before His departure directed this prayer to His heavenly Father for all those who are His: "Sanctify them in truth" (Jn. 17,17).

2. Consider that the prayer of a mother has great power even when children have already begun to go their own way. Augustine had delivered himself up to pride and sensuality till his thirty-second year: even St. Ambrose could think of no means to convert him. But when he saw the tears of St. Monica, the mother of Augustine, and heard her pleading prayers, he said: "The child of so many tears and prayers cannot be lost." Augustine served God for forty-four years in great sanctity. Andrew Corsini was also a wayward young man. When he beheld his mother kneeling before an image of the Mother of God and saw how she wept and pleaded, grace touched his heart; he burst into tears, was converted, and became a saint. Does God almighty not give the assurance (Isa. 49,15) that He will be more merciful even than a mother to her own son?

3. Consider that if it is to be effectual, the prayer of a mother for her children must be supported by faithful fulfillment of her duty. From their youth she must rear her children for God and for what is good, must be on the alert to root evil germs out of their hearts, and guard them against the contagion of a bad world; above all she must always give them a good example. — Have you, Christian mother, been wanting in these points? Then you yourself have prepared the cross which you carry because of your children. But, bear it with patience, repent of your faults, do what you can to correct them even now, and beg St. Monica, whose feast the universal Church celebrates today, for her intercession. Then you may expect that God will still grant your prayer and save your children for eternity.

PRAYER OF THE CHURCH
(Feast of St. Monica)

O God, the comforter of the sorrowful and the salvation of those who put their trust in Thee, who, in bringing about the conversion of her son

Augustine didst have merciful regard to the loving tears of Blessed
Monica, grant through their united intercession that we may grieve over
our sins and win grace and pardon from Thee. Through Christ our Lord.
Amen.

꧁꧂꧁꧂꧁꧂꧁꧂꧁꧂꧁꧂

MAY 5
BLESSED AMATUS RONCONI
Confessor, Third Order

LESSED Amatus was a thirteenth-century Tertiary who rose to
great heights of sanctity by serving God as a hermit, as a
pilgrim, and as a nurse. Born at Saldezzo, near Rimini, about
1238, he lost his parents while still very young, and was
brought up by a relative. He was then urged to get married, but he felt
that God called him to a life of prayer and penance. After joining the
Third Order of St. Francis, he fled to a solitary place and began to live as
a hermit. By many he was considered a fool, but God showed how much
He was pleased with the virtuous life of Amatus by marvelous signs. A
mysterious light was seen shining over the hut which served as his
shelter, and heavenly songs were heard to issue from it.

Amatus left his hermitage at times to make pilgrimages on foot to
Santiago de Compostela in Spain and other famous shrines, or to care for
the poor and the sick. He founded the Hospital of St. Mary of Mount
Orciale, near Rimini, and there he spent the last years of his life as a nurse.
In 1304 he died at the age of sixty-six; and ever since then he has been
venerated as a saint. So many miracles were attributed to his intercession
that Pope Pius VI approved his cult as Blessed; and his feast is celebrated
at Rimini on May fifteenth. However, his name has not been placed in the
Franciscan calendar. (Cf. Biersack, p. 3; *These Made Peace*, p. 42.)

ON THE FEAR OF DEATH
1. Whereas the saints eagerly desired death and rejoiced when the hour
came, many people are in terrible fear of death. Why is that? In some
cases it is because such people have sought all their happiness in this
world, eager to taste all its pleasures without a thought of the will of God.
They feel that their comedy is about to end, to be followed by a long
tragedy. The fear that harries them is striking evidence that everything
does not end with death. "O death, how bitter is the remembrance of Thee
to the man who has peace in his possessions!" (Eccli. 41,1). Also mere

attachment to material things without their having enjoyed them may at times fill people with fear at the thought of being separated from them by death. True Christians are mindful of those other treasures which we cannot lose in death and which constitute real comfort in that hour. "The just man has hope in his death" (Prov. 14,32). — Shall this hope be yours?

2. Consider that there is a natural and justifiable fear of death, which even the saints sometimes experienced. Death was not originally intended for man. Had not man sinned, he would at the end of his span of life have passed on to the paradise of heaven in a glorified state without the separation of body and soul. But "by one man sin entered into this world, and by sin death" (Rom. 5,12). When our first parents violated the command of God, the sentence of death was passed on all the human race. The fear of death should rouse in us a fear of sin and all violation of the divine commands. Because we have at times violated these commands fear seizes us in the face of death, for "after this is judgment" (Heb. 9,27). As the fear of death should keep us from committing sin, the fear of judgment should urge us to make a sincere confession of our sins and to do penance. Then the fear will be our salvation. "The fear of the Lord is a foundation of life, to decline from the ruin of death" (Prov. 14,27).

3. Consider that we should not let the thought of death take unreasonable possession of us. St. Augustine says: "Just as we should fear and love God, but must love Him more than we fear Him, so with death, although we fear it, we should still more love it." For, as St. Bernard says so beautifully, death is the gate of life. From this wretched life, where there is scarcely a day without its troubles, and in which we are always liable to sin mortally, death is to lead us forth to an eternal land of bliss, in singing the praises of God. That is why St. Francis in his dying moments pleaded with the Psalmist: "Bring my soul out of prison, that I may praise Thy name" (Ps. 141,8). — When the thought of death worries you, make a prompt and frequent offering of your life to almighty God at holy Mass, in union with the sacrifice of Christ. You may then confidently expect a blessed death.

PRAYER OF THE CHURCH
(Secret, Mass for a Happy Death)
Receive, O Lord, we beseech Thee, the sacrifice which we offer for the good ending of our lives, and grant that by means of it all our sins may be washed away; that we, who by Thine appointment are stricken with Thy scourges in this life, may win eternal rest in the life to come. Through Christ our Lord. Amen.

MAY 6
BLESSED GERARD OF LUNEL
Confessor, Third Order

ERARD (also Gery, Gerius, and Roger) of Lunel, a Tertiary hermit and pilgrim of the thirteenth century, belonged to the same noble family as that of St. Elzéar of Sabran. The son of the Lord of Castelnau, he was born at Lunel, about halfway between Nimes and Montpellier. So precocious was his piety, that he received the habit of the Third Order when he was five years old. In those days it was not uncommon to invest children in the Third Order.

When Gerard was eighteen, he and his brother Effrenaud hid themselves in a cave on the banks of the river Gardon, a tributary of the Rhone, and spent two years there as hermits. They then decided to go on a pilgrimage, because their reputation for holiness was beginning to attract too many visitors. They walked all the way to Rome, and spent two years in the Eternal City, visiting its numerous famous churches and shrines. Intending to go on to Jerusalem, they set out for the port of Ancona; but on the way Gerard collapsed in a lonely cottage at Colombaro, near Montesanto. His brother went to seek help, but when he got back Gerard was dead. His death occurred on May 24, some time between 1270 and 1299.

Many miracles took place at Gerard's tomb, and so it became a favorite place of pilgrimage. Those who were afflicted with headaches or who were subject to epilepsy invoked the intercession of Blessed Gerard with special efficacy. In 1735 a special confraternity, whose members wore a light green habit, was founded in honor of Blessed Gerard; and it became customary to clothe epileptics who were brought to his shrine in this habit. The city of Montesanto has venerated Blessed Gerard as its principal patron from time immemorial. The cult which has been paid to him from the time of his death was approved by Pope Benedict XIV in 1742. At Montesanto and by the Third Order Regular the feast of Blessed Gerard is observed on May twenty-fourth. (Cf. Biersack, p. 60; *These Made Peace*, pp. 125-126.)

ON PREPARATION FOR DEATH

1. The whole life of Blessed Gerard was a preparation for death. We too must keep ourselves ready since we are not sure of another year nor of another day. Will you live as many more years as you have already spent

here on earth? Can you promise yourself to see the end of this year? No man can, but God has said that death will come like a thief in the night, "at an hour you think not; be you then ready" (Lk. 12,40). Are you ready for death? Perhaps you would rather not think about it. It is a snare of the enemy to distract us from the thought of death, so that it may find us unprepared. Woe to you if that should happen! Once you have died unhappily, you are lost for all eternity. That is why the Church teaches us to pray: "From an unprovided death, deliver us, O Lord!"

2. Consider how we should prepare for death. The words of the Prophet apply to each of us: "Put your house in order, for you shall die" (Isa. 38,1). If as you are now you could not appear before God's judgment-seat, go to the judgment-seat of penance, and get everything in order. From now on make every confession as if it were your last one. Also put the house of your eternity in order, by storing up all possible merits of good works. How many a person has concerned himself only with his temporal affairs up to his very last day, paying little or no heed to the voice of the Lord who said to him: "Thou fool! This night do they require your soul of you" (Lk. 12,20). Where are such souls now? — Prepare in time. Every day and hour you are so much nearer to death; have you provided during this time for eternity?

3. Consider that it is part of a good preparation for death to clear away all hindrances to your entering heaven. Such hindrances, however, are the temporal punishment for sins that have been remitted and all inordinate attachments that have not been brought under control. Hence, every good Christian eagerly employs the means of penance and of indulgences to cancel the punishment due to sin, and he aims more and more to bring his unruly inclinations under subjection. It is in this sense that St. Ambrose says: "Die continually as long as you are alive, so that you may always live once you have died." Would that we all followed this advice!

PRAYER OF THE CHURCH
(From the Mass for a Good Death)

Almighty and merciful God, who bestowest on mankind both the remedies of health and the gifts of life everlasting, look mercifully upon us Thy servants, and refresh the souls that Thou hast made, so that at the hour of their going hence, they may be found worthy to be borne to Thee, their Maker, free from all stain of sin, by the hands of the holy angels. Through Christ our Lord. Amen.

MAY 7
BLESSED CRISPIN OF VITERBO
Confessor, First Order

AT VITERBO, Italy, Blessed Crispin was born of lowly tradespeople in 1668. In holy baptism he received the name of Peter. Christian piety was the worthwhile inheritance Peter received from his parents. When he was five years old his mother took him with her one day to the miraculous image of Mary of the Oak near Viterbo. She directed the attention of her little son to the Mother of God and said: "See, that is also your mother. I have made a gift of you to her. Always honor her as a good son would do." Peter did that throughout his life.

When his school days were over, the ambitious boy made the best of a chance to learn a little Latin, and his parents were told that he had the talents to study. But as they had not the means to pay for his education and did not want their son to be half-educated, they sent him to his uncle to learn the shoemaker's trade. At the wish of his parents Peter cheerfully entered the workshop and learned the trade to the complete satisfaction of his uncle.

But meanwhile, child of Mary that he was, he sought to advance more and more in piety and Christian perfection. This endeavor turned his thoughts toward the religious state. Seeing certain Capuchin novices taking an edifying part in a procession, he went to the convent and pleaded so urgently for admission that in spite of his delicate appearance he was accepted. His parents, too, gave their consent, and so he was invested on the feast of St. Magdalen in 1693. He received the name of Crispin, for the holy shoemakers Crispin and Crispinian.

Even as a novice he lived so perfectly that everybody admired him. As his model, especially in humility, self-abnegation, and continual work joined with prayer, he took St. Felix of Cantalice, whose life was still fresh in the memory of many who were living. After making his vows, he was sent as cook to the convent at Tolfa. There he made it his first care to erect in his kitchen a little altar to Mary, at which he offered his beloved Mother all his labors. Mary rewarded her faithful son with special proofs of her favor. Many a sick person was restored to health when he gave them some of the fruit which he had previously placed on his little altar after asking the Mother of God to bless them.

When he was cook at the convent in Albano near Rome, one of the pope's chamberlains, of whose recovery the doctors despaired, was brought to him. Crispin led him to his little Mary altar, and soon the sick person was cured for good. The pope's physician said to Crispin: "Brother, your remedies are more effective than ours." Crispin replied: "You are a skillful physician, all Rome knows that. But, then, the Blessed Virgin can do more than all the physicians in the world."

A distinguished man, who had until recently led a bad life, lay ill and desired that Crispin should come and cure him. The brother went there, but said to him: "Sir, you want the Blessed Virgin to cure you. But, tell me, he who offends the Son, does he not also grieve the Mother? True veneration of the Blessed Virgin consists in not offending her Divine Son in any way." At the mild reproach of the holy brother, the sick man was much ashamed. He burst into penitent tears and promised to amend his life. And he faithfully carried out his promise when Crispin cured him by blessing him with a medal of the Immaculate Conception.

His superiors and brethren were edified at Crispin's perfection. In company with several of the brothers he was once with his Father Provincial, when the latter received word that in one of their convents all the brothers were down with a contagious disease and that help was needed at once. The superior mentioned his predicament. Whom shall he send there? At once Crispin volunteered. Father Provincial expressed his pleasure at the offer, but insisted that he would not send him against his will. Crispin replied: "Will, my Father? What will? When I entered religion, I left my will at home. Here I recognize only your will." When the others called his attention to the danger of death that he would encounter, Crispin said: "That is nothing. I have a marvelous preventive invented by St. Francis — it is the obedience in which I set out." He actually did return in excellent health after all the sick had gotten well under his care.

Wherever Crispin went, he brought pleasure with his holy cheerfulness. Among the sick he banished all discontent and complaint; it was as if an angel had come from heaven. He often held several charges at the same time in the friary, but when work piled up, he used to say: "That is good; Paradise is not for lazybones."

Even at the door of death he preserved this cheerful spirit. When he was near death as a result of weakness and other bodily infirmities, and the physician drew his attention to it, he said joyfully with the Psalmist: "I rejoiced at the things that were said to me: We shall go into the house of the Lord" (Ps. 121,1). With the sweet names of Jesus and Mary on his lips, he breathed forth his soul on May 19, 1750, in the eighty-second year of his life.

His body, which is still incorrupt, is honored in the Capuchin church at Rome. Pope Pius VII beatified him in 1806. His feast is observed on May twenty-first by the Franciscans as well as the Capuchins.

CONCERNING CHRISTIAN CHEERFULNESS

1. What is written of Moses, "He was beloved by God and men" (Eccli. 45,1), could also be said of Blessed Crispin. His Christian cheerfulness contributed not a little to the welcome which was accorded him everywhere. Far from being contrary to holiness and displeasing to God, cheerfulness is as pleasing to God as the sweet smile of an innocent child is to its mother, and it is a sign of true holiness. Most assuredly the saints mourn over their sins and the sins of the world, as St. Francis in his solitude shed hot tears. But at the same time they enjoy in the purity of their hearts and the love of God an interior joy, such as St. Francis showed also exteriorly and wished to see in his children. Thus Crispin proved that he was a true son of St. Francis. Piety which puts on a sour face the moment anybody laughs is not genuine. "Serve the Lord with gladness!" (Ps. 99,2). — Have you done that in the past?

2. Consider the difference between Christian cheerfulness and worldly cheerfulness. Christian cheerfulness proceeds from purity of heart and takes pleasure in the dispensations of divine providence. Therefore, it is just like God's own operations, tempered, modest, not boisterous. It shows itself outwardly too: "A glad heart makes a cheerful countenance" (Prov. 15,13). But it is above all interior. Worldly cheerfulness proceeds from wantonness of flesh or spirit. It is sometimes accompanied by offense of God and a heavily burdened conscience. It is noisy, boisterous, unrestrained, but often changes to bitterness, spite, and unbounded sadness. — Judge for yourself which is worthy of a Christian.

3. Consider that Christian cheerfulness can bear up in the face of all the bitterness of life. It even helps to bear it and to sweeten it. The prophet Nehemias says: "The joy of the Lord is our strength" (2 Esd. 8,10). A cheerful disposition, such as Crispin possessed, easily bears what might weigh a despondent heart to the ground. And if depression besets you, the thought that God, your best friend, has sent the cross, will soon raise your depressed heart. David experienced this: "My soul," he said, "refused to be comforted. I remembered God and was delighted" (Ps. 76,3). The thought of God is the more apt to sweeten the cross for us because, like Crispin, we have Mary, the Cause of our Joy, to think of. Mary is called so because she brought us Jesus Christ, who sweetens all bitterness for us and who gives us an eternal recompense for patiently bearing it. "They that sow in tears, shall reap in joy" (Ps. 125,5).

PRAYER OF THE CHURCH

O God, who didst lead Blessed Crispin, Thy confessor, to the heights of virtue while he served Thee with joy, we beseech Thee, grant that at his intercession and after his example, we may follow in his footsteps here on earth and thereby deserve to partake of the fullness of Thy bliss. Through Christ our Lord. Amen.

MAY 8
BLESSED WALDO
Confessor, Third Order

ALDO, called also Vivaldo or Ubaldo, was a disciple of the saintly Tertiary priest Bartolo. They were natives of the same place, San Gimignano, in northern Italy. When Bartolo was attacked with leprosy and betook himself to the leper hospital near San Gimignano, Waldo offered him his services and for twenty years, until the death of Bartolo, rendered him every possible kindness. In return Waldo received salutary instructions toward progress in Christian perfection from the holy priest, and at his advice joined the Third Order of St. Francis.

After the death of his spiritual father in 1300, Waldo resolved to withdraw altogether from the world and the association of men, in order to converse only with God and live for heaven. He repaired to a large forest several miles distant from his native town. There he found a hollow chestnut tree of great girth, the cavity of which he turned into a cell for himself; he had hardly room enough to kneel in it. There he meant to spend the remainder of his life. Severe penances and the contemplation of heavenly things were his occupation.

Records indicate that Waldo spent about twenty years in this complete solitude. Then one day in May, 1320, the bells of the adjacent village of Monteone began to ring of their own accord, to the amazement of the people. They all ran to the church. There they saw and heard the bells continue in full peal although no human hand was setting them in motion.

Presently a hunter came out of the forest, who told that his hounds had circled around a hollow chestnut tree, barking in excitement. When he went to investigate he found a recluse in the tree dead on his knees. As the hunter finished his tale, the bells ceased ringing.

The inhabitants of Monteone recognized in this incident the holiness of the deceased hermit. In procession they went to the narrow cell of Blessed Waldo, and brought the body to the church, where it was laid to rest beneath the high altar. God glorified the tomb with many miracles. The cell in the tree was converted into a chapel in honor of our Lady, in connection with which a Franciscan convent was later built. Blessed Waldo's feast is observed on May twenty-first by the Franciscans, on December twelfth by the Conventuals, and on May eleventh by the Third Order Regular.

ON LONGING FOR HEAVEN

1. "God is wonderful in his saints" (Ps. 67,36). He leads them in the most varied ways. But all whom He draws to Himself, He detaches in heart from material things and infuses into them holy longing for heavenly things. What a sweet foretaste of heavenly joy Blessed Waldo must have experienced in his deep seclusion. — If you have only a slight longing for heaven, then fear that you will have but a slight share in the childship of God. They that in the hardness of their hearts find their delight only in worldly pursuits and want nothing to do with heavenly things, will incur the judgment which the Lord uttered by the mouth of the prophet: "I swore in My wrath, they shall not enter into My rest" (Ps. 94,11).

2. Consider why it must be very displeasing to God if we have little or no desire for heaven. He has created us for heaven. There in the company of the angels and saints He Himself wishes to be our joy. He sent His only-begotten Son into this world that through His suffering and death He might re-open heaven for us, to whom it had been closed. He lets us live on this earth only to earn heaven, and promises us in return for our earthly hardships a superabundant reward. How grievously, then, it must wound His fatherly heart if we rarely think about heavenly things and do not long for them. Even though we die in God's grace, shall we not have to suffer in purgatory for such indifference, by being made to yearn for heaven in pain?

3. Consider how we should stimulate our desire for heaven. Amid the brief joys of this world and the constant sufferings of this earthly life, look up to heaven and reflect on the glorious City of God, to which God wishes to lead His true servants and to which the best persons we have known have already gone. Remember the words of the Apostle: "Eye has not seen, nor ear heard, neither has it entered into the heart of man, what things God has prepared for them who love Him" (1 Cor. 2,9). Then your heart will be inflamed with holy desire, and you will sigh with Thomas a Kempis (3,48),

"Ah, most happy mansion of the supernal city! A day always joyful, always secure! Oh, that this day would shine forth, and that all these temporal things would come to an end!" Then plead with the same mystic, "Be mindful of me, O my God, and direct me in the right path to Thy kingdom!"

PRAYER OF THE CHURCH
(Secret on the Last Sunday after Pentecost)

Be propitious, O Lord, to our supplications, and accept the offerings and prayers of Thy people; turn all our hearts unto Thee, that, being delivered from earthly appetites, we may pass on to the enjoyment of heaven. Through Christ our Lord. Amen.

MAY 9
BLESSED GODFREY MAURICE JONES
Martyr, First Order

ALWAYS loyal to the Church! That was the watchword of the Franciscans in England during the terrible persecution under King Henry VIII, Edward VI, and Elizabeth. Blessed Godfrey Maurice Jones, who was of their number, came from a good Welsh family which had remained Catholic. He had been in prison at two different times while he was still a secular priest. Then in 1590 he left the prison of Wisbeach Castle, and went abroad; but whether he was banished or made his escape, we do not know.

During his imprisonment, Father Buckley, as Blessed Godfrey is also known in history, had gained a religious vocation. Immediately after he had recovered his liberty, he went to Greenwich and received the habit of St. Francis. He was professed at Pontoise, France, and shortly afterwards went to Rome, where he lived in the convent of Ara Coeli for almost three years. To one who had already borne the cross and practiced the hardships of poverty, the further sacrifice of his worldly goods cost little. But it needed more than ordinary humility to enter the religious life at nearly sixty years of age, to submit to religious superiors, who were probably his inferiors in years, sufferings, and spiritual experience.

When his religious training was completed, he offered himself for the English missions. Before starting, he had an audience with Pope Clement VIII, who, embracing him and giving him his blessing, said: "Go, for I believe that you are a true son of St. Francis, and pray to God for me and His holy Church." He arrived in London in 1593, but remained there only a few months. He then went to the country, where he labored in the vineyard of the Lord for almost three years. Then he was again sent to prison, remaining there about two years.

Not long afterwards, in July, 1598, he was arraigned for going over the seas and being made a priest by authority from Rome, and for returning again to England. He answered: "If this be a crime, I must own myself guilty; for, I am a priest and I came over to England to gain as many souls as I could for Christ." Then he was condemned to be hanged, drawn, and quartered. When he heard the sentence, he fell upon his knees and thanked God for having considered him worthy of martyrdom.

On July twelfth he was drawn on a hurdle to St. Thomas Waterings. Kneeling down at the foot of the gallows he prayed for a short while, and then addressed the crowd which had gathered. When the last moment came, he prayed in a loud voice, "Sweet Jesus, have mercy on my soul." An officer said in derision that he had forgotten our Blessed Lady. Then he added, "Blessed Queen of heaven, be my advocate and pray for me now and ever." Then he repeated the prayer, "Sweet Jesus," and raised his hands as high as he could, which was the sign for a priest who might be in the crowd to give him absolution. Then he asked all the Catholics present to say the Credo and to pray for him.

After the execution his remains were left exposed for several days, as was the custom of the times, but soon devout Catholics secretly removed them. Pope Pius XI added his name to the list of the beatified. His feast is observed on May twenty-second b the Franciscans, and on July twelfth by the Conventuals. (Cf. Steck, *Franciscans and the Protestant Revolution*, 204-212.)

ON PROFESSING THE FAITH

1. We are obliged to profess our faith in words. The Apostle says: "Now faith is the substance of things to be hoped for, the evidence of things that appear not" (Heb. 11,1). But it is not by this inward conviction alone that we comply with our duty. "For with the heart we believe unto justice; but with the mouth confession is made unto salvation" (Rom. 10,10). This is what Blessed Godfrey did. And so ought you to enliven your faith by frequently praying the Credo.

2. We must also profess our faith in our conduct. The words of our Saviour can be applied here: "He who shall be ashamed of Me and of My words, of him the Son of man shall be ashamed when He shall come in His

majesty" (Lk. 9,26). Those who play fast and loose with their faith or who dishonor it in their conduct, certainly act disgracefully, let alone dangerously. — Do you need to reproach yourself on this score?

3. We commit sin if we deny our faith, for we thereby separate ourselves from Christ, from baptism, from the Church, from the Mother of God. What will be the lot of one who denies his faith? "But he who shall deny Me before men, I will also deny him before My Father, who is in heaven" (Mt. 10,33). Blessed Godfrey preferred a cruel death on the gallows rather than swerve even an iota from the Faith. — Are you ready to act likewise?

PRAYER OF THE CHURCH

We beseech Thee, O Lord, strengthen in our hearts the mysteries of the true faith that we may confess Him as true God, who was conceived of the Virgin; and by virtue of His salutary resurrection, may merit to attain to eternal bliss. Through the same Christ our Lord. Amen.

MAY 10
BLESSED JOHN WALL (JOACHIM OF ST. ANNA)
Martyr, First Order

JOHN WALL, in religion Father Joachim of St. Anna, was the fourth son of Anthony Wall of Chingle (Singleton) Hall, Lancashire. He was born in 1620, and when very young, was sent to the English College at Douai. From there he proceeded to Rome, where he was raised to the priesthood in 1648. Several years later he returned to Douai and was clothed in the habit of St. Francis in the convent of St. Bonaventure. He made his solemn profession on January 1, 1652. So great was the estimation in which he was held by his brethren, that within a few months he was elected vicar of the convent, and soon after, master of novices.

In 1656 he joined the English mission, and for twelve years he labored in Worcestershire under the names of Francis Johnson or Webb, winning souls even more by his example than by his words. At Harvington to this day the memory of Blessed Father Johnson is cherished, and stories of his heroic zeal are recounted by the descendants of those who were privileged to know and love the glorious martyr.

Some of the charges raised against Father Wall when he was captured, were that he had said Mass, heard confessions, and received converts into the Church. He was accidentally found, in December, 1678, at the house of a friend, Mr. Finch of Rushock, and carried off by the sheriff's officer. He was committed to Worcester jail, and lay captive for five months, enduring patiently all the loneliness, suffering, and horrors of prison life, which at that time were scarcely less dreadful than death itself.

On April 25, 1679, Father John was brought to court. His condemnation was a foregone conclusion. He was sent back to prison till the king's further pleasure concerning him should be known; and for another four months he languished in captivity. It was during this period that he was offered his life if he would deny his faith, "But I told them," said the martyr, "that I would not buy my life at so dear a rate as to wrong my conscience."

One of Father Wall's brethren in religion, Father William Levison, had the privilege of seeing the martyr for the space of four or five hours on the day before his execution. Father William tells us: "I heard his confession and communicated him, to his great joy and satisfaction. While in prison he carried himself like a true servant of his crucified Master, thirsting after nothing more than the shedding of his blood for the love of his God, which he performed with a courage and cheerfulness becoming a valiant soldier of Christ, to the great edification of all the Catholics, and the admiration of all Protestants."

Father Wall's martyrdom took place on Red Hill, overlooking the city of Worcester, on August 22, 1679. His head was kept in the convent at Douai until the French Revolution broke out and the community fled to England. What became of it, then, is not known. The Catholics of Worcester found consolation in remarking, as a proof of his sanctity, that his grave always appeared green, while the rest of the churchyard was bare. A large crucifix was raised in the little Catholic churchyard at Harvington to the memory of this saintly son of St. Francis, Father Joachim of St. Anna.

Father Joachim of St. Anna was beatified under the name of Blessed John Wall, December 15, 1929, together with a fellow Franciscan, Father Godfrey Maurice Jones, and one hundred and thirty-four companions. The Franciscans observe his feast on May twenty-second. (Cf. Steck, *Franciscans and the Protestant Revolution*, pp. 326-328.)

ON THE VALUE OF THE SOUL

1. The human soul bears the stamp of nobility. God created the universe with one word. "Let it be made," He said, and it was made. But for the creation of man the Holy Trinity holds, as it were, a consultation: "Let us

make man to Our own image and likeness" (Gen. 1,26). And according to His image and likeness God created man. "Remember, O man," St. Bernard cries out, "your dignity!" Your soul is the image of God. Therefore the Holy Ghost warns us: "Keep your soul and give it honor according to its desert" (Eccli. 10,31). Do not let material baubles dim the image of God that is in you, nor let the evil spirit mar it. — Have you preserved this image in yourself?

2. The soul has been bought at a great price. Jesus Christ came down from heaven, led a poor life here on earth for thirty-three years, endured untold pains, and finally shed His precious blood on the cross to redeem the souls of men. The Church reminds us of this when she teaches us to pray in the Litany of the Holy Name of Jesus: "Through Thy labors, through Thy fainting and weariness, through Thy agony and passion, through Thy cross and dereliction, deliver us, O Jesus!" But if Jesus did so much to save the souls of men, what sacrifice can be too great in our effort to save our souls? Ought we not, according to the admonition of the Apostle (Heb. 12,4), strive against sin even unto blood?

3. The value of the soul surpasses that of all created things. Christ said: "What does it profit a man if he gain the whole world and suffer the loss of his own soul?" (Mt. 16,26). The soul outweighs all the things of earth, all treasures, honors, riches. Blessed John strove for a correct appreciation of material things, which are valueless when compared with our immortal souls. — Have you always manifested this correct appreciation and given evidence of it in your actions?

PRAYER OF THE CHURCH

O God, who didst marvelously create human beings, and still more marvelously redeem them, grant us the grace that with the knowledge Thou hast given us, we may resist sinful desires and deserve to attain eternal bliss. Through Christ our Lord. Amen.

MAY 11
BLESSED JAMES OF BITECTO
Confessor, First Order

THE ANNALS of the Franciscan Order contain records of many servants of God who arrived at a high degree of holiness in seclusion and marked simplicity. They are the loveliest blossoms in the Franciscan garden, and attractive examples for simple souls who seek nothing but God alone. Such a model is Blessed James of Bitecto. Born in Illyria, which was later called Dalmatia, he entered the Franciscan convent in his native place as a lay brother.

Soon he distinguished himself in all virtues as a model religious. This prompted the Father Provincial to choose him as his companion when he traveled to Italy for the general chapter of the order. Separated from his native place, his relatives and acquaintances, James felt more closely united to God, for which reason, with the consent of his superiors, he remained in Italy from that time on.

He was sent in turn to different convents, so that his example might animate the brothers to seek perfection. Nothing, however, was further removed from the mind of James than to consider himself an example to others. He was filled with humility and contempt for himself, loved silence, was punctual in obedience, and performed his duties with care. But while his hands were busy at work, his mind was occupied with God.

In the convent at Conversano, where he was cook, he would fall into rapture at the sight of the fire. He thought at such times of the fire of hell, and adored the strict justice of God, while he found himself mightily urged on to acts of penance and to the love of God, who sent His own Son into this world to save us from hell.

The Divine Spirit who filled his soul at such times did not permit his work to suffer on that account. In the convent garden at Cassano there was a grotto with an image of the Mother of God. To it James at times withdrew in the evening, and there he scourged himself until he bled, and remained all night absorbed in devotion to the Mother of Mercy. God almighty favored him with the gifts of miracles and of prophecy.

The closing years of his life he spent in the convent of Bitecto, from which he received his surname. There he died a holy death on April 27, 1490. His grave is held in great veneration. A hundred years later his body was found still incorrupt. Pope Innocent XII approved the uninterrupted devotion paid to him. His feast is observed on May fourteenth by the Franciscans, and on the eleventh by the Capuchins.

PRAY AND WORK

1. *Ora et labora* — pray and work! That was the order of the day in convents even of the earliest Christian times. Would that it were so in every Christian home. Since God created man body and soul, man must also serve God with both his body, by means of work, and his soul, by means of prayer. "Man is born to labor, and the bird to fly" (Job 5,7). To be occupied according to one's vocation, is a duty incumbent on everyone;

indolence brings temporal and eternal misery to the soul. Likewise it is an obligation for us to raise our hearts to God in prayer: "We ought always to pray and not to faint" (Lk. 18,1). Our soul will soon succumb if we do not continually raise it up by means of prayer. Therefore, both prayer and work are necessary. The unbelieving world considers prayer foolishness, while false piety imagines it can make amends for the omission of work by prayer. Blessed James worked diligently and prayed fervently. Do you also work and pray?

2. Consider that just as body and soul are most intimately united with each other in man, so should prayer and work be united with each other. Prayer should permeate your work so that it is done with a good, Christian intention. It should also bring blessing and success to your work, on which account you ought never to begin the day's work without having said a good morning prayer. Everything depends on the blessing of God. Seek it for every new task of the day.

3. Consider that our work should also lead us to prayer. With what devotion was Blessed James inflamed at his work! Everything can lead to pious thoughts, even the thread used in sewing. It can remind you of the thread of life and how soon it can be torn though you be strong and healthy. The steel needle, too, can snap suddenly. Everything created passes, but God remains. Created things are, as it were, footprints of God, that lead us to recognize His power, goodness, wisdom, justice, and mercy. May our association with such things lead us while still on earth to His love and faithful service, so that we may receive the reward of eternal bliss.

PRAYER OF THE CHURCH

We beseech Thee, almighty God, grant us, who are devoutly celebrating the memory of the glorious merits of Blessed James, Thy confessor, that while on earth, we may zealously imitate his virtues, and in heaven acquire with him the crown of glory. Through Christ our Lord. Amen.

MAY 12
ST. IGNATIUS OF LACONI
Confessor, First Order

IGNATIUS, the son of pious peasants at Laconi, Sicily, was born in 1701. As a young man he vowed, during a serious illness, that, if he recovered his health, he would consecrate his life to God in the Capuchin Order. He regained his health, but kept putting off the fulfillment of his vow from day to day. Then, as if to warn him, his life was again threatened when a horse he was riding became shy. Ignatius called upon St. Francis renewing the vow he had previously made, and again received help. This time even his parents raised no objections.

He asked for admission at the convent of Cagliari, but the superiors hesitated at first because of his delicate health. Then Ignatius looked up an influential friend who interceded for him, and he was received. The ardor of his soul made him so strong that he could attend all the exercises of the community and even excel his brethren in perfect observance of the rule.

After being employed in the community for several years at various occupations, he was appointed quester of alms because of his edifying conduct. The citizens of Cagliari soon realized that Brother Ignatius really gave them more than he took away with him. His modest demeanor was a quiet sermon for all who saw him going about. He seldom spoke; but when charity and the salvation of souls required it, he spoke with exceptional kindness. He would also instruct the children and the uneducated, comfort the sick, and urge sinners to be converted and to do penance. Mockery and contempt he accepted calmly, replying only with kind words.

He punctually obeyed his superiors, also when it required the denial of his own will. The good brother was accustomed to pass by the house of a usurer, because he feared that in accepting an alms from him he would share the guilt of this man's injustices. But when the man complained and the superior commanded the brother to accept alms from him, Ignatius always called on the usurer for his donation. Perhaps this is what caused the man's conversion.

The sister of the servant of God had often written to him asking him to pay her a visit, so she could get his advice in certain important matters. Ignatius had no mind to heed her request, but when his superior ordered him to do so, he at once undertook the journey. But he left again as soon as he had given the required advice.

When his brother was sent to prison, it was hoped that, in view of the reputation of Brother Ignatius, the latter could obtain his brother's release. His superior sent him to speak to the governor, but he asked merely that his brother be dealt with according to justice. Not for anything in the world would Brother Ignatius have kept anyone from doing his duty.

Despite his infirmity, Ignatius persevered in his arduous work until he was eighty years old. Even after he became blind, he continued to make his daily rounds for two years. The veneration of the people increased, and many sick persons were miraculously aided by him.

He died on May 11, 1781, and many miracles occurred at his grave. Brother Ignatius was beatified in 1940, and canonized in 1951. The Franciscans as well as the Capuchins observe his feast on May twelfth.

ON RELINQUISHING OUR OWN OPINION

1. Consider how St. Ignatius gave up his own opinion and serenely followed his superior's orders in instances where at first he feared he would be doing wrong. It is the common teaching of theologians that we not only may but must relinquish our opinion when our lawful superiors prescribe the opposite, as long as their command is not openly sinful. But we should not cling too tenaciously to our own opinion even when we deal with other sensible and conscientious people. To persist obstinately in our own ideas is a plain sign of conceit, and it may lead us sadly astray. Thomas a Kempis (3,7) says of it: "If such who are as yet inexperienced will rather follow their own judgment than believe others who have more experience, their end will be perilous, should they refuse to be withdrawn from their own conceits." — Do you perhaps have to fear such an outcome?

2. Consider that especially in regard to our confessors and spiritual directors we must give up our own opinion. The words of the Apostle apply here: "Obey your prelates and be subject to them. For they watch as having to render an account of your souls" (Heb. 13,17). — If you obey your director in a childlike and docile way, he bears the responsibility and not you, and as a conscientious director he will have no fear to give the required account. But insist on sticking to your own course against his advice, and he may now and then let you have your way, but with a sigh he will think of the account he has to render, and that, as the Apostle adds, "is not expedient for you."

3. Consider that, like St. Ignatius, we may not yield to the opinion or accede to the wishes of others if we should thereby fail in duty or cause others to do so. Ignatius did not, therefore, ask the judge to release his

brother just as a favor to himself. Justice and duty supersede human preference, and they must not be violated for the sake of any human being. The words of the Apostle again apply here: "We ought to obey God rather than men" (Acts 5,29). — May God's grace be with us to help us know when we must relinquish our own opinion, and when we may not follow the opinion of others.

PRAYER OF THE CHURCH
(Postcommunion 25 under "Various Prayers")

O God, who enlightenest every man that cometh into this world, shed upon our hearts, we beseech Thee, the brightness of Thy grace, that we may ever think thoughts worthy of Thy majesty and pleasing unto Thee, and ever sincerely love Thee. Through Christ our Lord. Amen.

MAY 13
BLESSED JULIAN OF VALLE
Confessor, First Order

ULIAN belonged to the ancient family of the Cesarelli at Valle in Istria. In the convent of his native town he was invested with the habit of the Poor Man of Assisi, and soon distinguished himself among his brethren for rigid observance of the holy rule and deep spirituality.

As a priest he labored like an angel of peace to reconcile the various political factions in the city and country. He worked with tireless zeal and spared himself in nothing, if he could pacify the hearts of angry partisans and lead them on the road of salvation.

Finally, after he had advanced in years and virtue, he passed on to meet his Lord, in the convent of St. Michael at Valle, the same convent in which he had been invested, about the middle of the fourteenth century. His grave has been glorified by God by many miracles, so that his countrymen have chosen him for their patron. Pope Pius X confirmed the veneration paid to him. His feast is observed on May fourteenth by the Franciscans, on the second by the Conventuals, and on the eleventh by the Capuchins.

ON PEACE

1. Peace is an inestimable blessing. Blessed Julian understood that well. So he directed all his efforts toward the one end of moving warring factions to peace. Not without reason did our Lord give the injunction: "In whatsoever house you enter, first say, Peace be to this house" (Lk. 10,5). That is why we so often see this greeting of peace in the letters and sermons of the Apostles and of our holy Father St. Francis. — May you also be ready always to join the ranks of those who strive to promote peace and charity.

2. We should be careful to maintain peace in the circles in which we move. Holy Writ says: "Joy follows them who take counsels of peace" (Prov. 12,20). Now and then it is better to close an eye to the cold letter of the law in order to preserve peace and charity. The greatest justice often proves to be the greatest injustice, for the simple reason that, in quarreling about what we regard as the greatest justice, the great virtue of love is trampled on. He who wishes to be allied with Christ, the Prince of Peace, must, like Him, be a messenger of peace. — Have you always been that? Or, have you stubbornly adhered to the letter of the law in your alleged rights?

3. We must pray a great deal for peace. The Prophet Isaias said long ago: "Lord, Thou wilt give us peace" (26,12). And the Lord Himself said: "I am the Lord, and there is none else; I make peace" (Isa. 45,6). There is a crying need in these disrupted and troublous times for good people to unite in storming heaven with the prayer, "Lord, give peace in this our day!" — It is time to plead with great fervor at holy Mass: "Lamb of God, give us Thy peace!" — Never omit the prayer of peace before Holy Communion.

PRAYER OF THE CHURCH

O God, from whom are all holy desires, right counsels, and just works, give to Thy servants that peace which the world cannot give, that our hearts being devoted to keeping Thy commandments, and the fear of enemies being removed, the times by Thy protection may be peaceful. Through Christ our Lord. Amen.

MAY 14
BLESSED BENEDICT OF URBINO
Confessor, First Order

ENEDICT was born of the noble family of the Passionei at Urbino, Italy, in 1560. His birthplace was the so-called palace of Urbino, which has since been converted into an orphanage. Indeed, the change happened soon after Benedict's birth; for, ruthless death, which respects a palace as little as it does a hovel, made an orphan of Benedict already in his seventh year.

At the deathbed of his mother, the pious boy recommended himself to the motherly protection of Mary, just as St. Teresa did, and Mary always remained a loving and protecting mother to him throughout his life.

While Benedict was pursuing his studies at the universities of Perugia and Padua, everybody admired his habits of modest reserve and piety. In his studies he sought God alone. Often the pious student prayed: "Grant me, O Lord, that knowledge which will teach me to know Thee. But grant me above all the grace to love Thee; because I desire to know Thee only that I may love Thee."

Scarcely twenty-two years of age, he obtained his degree of Doctor of Laws amid the acclamation of his professors and the rejoicing of his relatives, who believed that he would shed fresh luster on the family name.

On completing his studies, he went to Rome, to begin his career in the household of a cardinal. But high prelacies did not appeal to the heart of Benedict. He retired to his native place, where, after putting his vocation to several tests, he begged for admittance among the Capuchins.

On the first of May, 1584, he received the habit of St. Francis in the novitiate at Fano. With joy and great ease he undertook all the exercises, even the most humiliating. But his weak constitution, which at his admission had caused some misgivings, appeared to necessitate his leaving the convent. His dismissal had already been decided upon when Benedict pleaded so urgently with his heavenly Mother Mary that his health was miraculously improved. At a later date he could even be sent out on missions.

As a missionary priest, Benedict was associated with the great Capuchin apostle, St. Lawrence of Brindisi, in a campaign against the heretics of the sixteenth century in Germany and Bohemia. A few years later he returned to Italy and was also active there as a zealous apostle of the truth against falsehood, vice, and ungodliness. His edifying life of poverty and austere penance gave his words invincible power over the hearts of men. But with all his success he remained so humble that his associates marveled. Even the smallest fault that happened to him in choir or at other exercises, he humbly acknowledged before the community. When anybody objected that that was a practice for novices, he would answer: "Well, I am still a novice in virtue."

Benedict practiced poverty to an extreme degree. He would have nothing but the most necessary furniture in his cell. Whatever books he consulted, he promptly returned to the library. He wrote his sermons on the blank spaces of letters and envelopes. Repeatedly he had often to fill the office of superior, and as such he stressed the observance of holy poverty and fidelity in little things, realizing that perfection is achieved more through little things than through great things. He practiced such severe mortification that his life can be termed one continuous fast. The most uncomfortable cell pleased him most. Often he slept only three hours and passed the remaining time in prayer.

God almighty glorified His servant by many miracles in life and after death. Benedict died in 1625, after serving God forty years in the religious state. With great solemnity Pope Pius IX pronounced him blessed on February 10, 1867. His feast is observed by the Franciscans on May fourteenth, and by the Capuchins on April thirtieth.

TRUTH AND FALSEHOOD

1. Of Blessed Benedict one may say that he devoted his entire life and labor to the truth. He preached the truth, he fought error and falsehood, he admitted the truth, often without being required to do so and although it served to humiliate him. Love for the truth marks a true Christian, a true child of God. God says of Himself: "I am the truth" (Jn. 14,6). But the devil is called "a liar, and the father of lies" (Jn. 8,44). Not for anything in the world will a true Christian consciously tell an untruth. Worldly people, on the other hand, make no account of lying, so that from the word of God it is easy to see whose children they are. — Have you given serious thought to the fact that truthfulness and lying divide human beings into two classes? To which class do you belong?

2. Consider a means of always being faithful to the truth. We notice it in Blessed Benedict. It is childlike veneration of Mary. When lying began, Mary was promised by God as the champion who would crush the head of the serpent. She also protects her children from falling into the snares of "the liar from the beginning." She obtains for us humility, which leads to candor. She instils aversion for even the smallest untruth as a mark of

the poisonous, hissing serpent. "A lie is a foul blot in a man" (Eccli. 20,26).
— Often pray to Mary that she may preserve yon from all falsehood.
3. Consider that no excuse can justify lying, because it is an offense of
God. You may say: It hurts no one if I lie; I merely help myself out of a
difficulty. But are you not at the same time embarrassing yourself deeply
against judgment day when an account of every word will be required of
you? Are you not harming your soul? With each lie you lean more and
more to the side of your worst enemy, until the words are verified, "The
mouth that speaks lies kills the soul" (Wisd. 1,11). You may object, "I tell
an untruth for the benefit of others." Are we permitted to offend God in
order to be of service to men? May one steal in order to give the stolen
goods to the poor? Furthermore, it is at bottom only lack of self-conquest
or some other inordinate tendency that leads to lying. Love God above all
things, die to the world and to yourself like Blessed Benedict, and a lie will
never again stain your lips.

PRAYER OF THE CHURCH
Grant, we beseech Thee, almighty God, that through the mortification of
the cross, which Thy blessed confessor Benedict, in despising the joys of
this world, always bore about in his body, we may renounce worldly
desires and live justly and piously in this world. Through Christ our Lord.
Amen.

๛๛๛๛๛๛๛๛๛๛๛๛๛

MAY 15
ST. MICHAEL GARICOÏTS
Confessor, Third Order

AT IBARRE, in the mountainous region of southwestern France,
not far from Lourdes, there lived at the time of the French
Revolution a poor peasant family named Garicoïts. Their
humble cottage was always open to the proscribed priests
who came from time to time to minister to the faithful in secret. Michael,
the first son of young Arnold Garicoïts and his wife Gratianne, was born
here on April 15, 1797. As a little boy he had to help earn a livelihood by
serving as a shepherd on a neighboring farm. Often he expressed the
desire of becoming a priest; but his parents always told him: "No! We are
too poor."

However, his grandmother went to the parish priest at St. Palais and
told him about Michael. This priest had often found a hiding place in the

Garicoïts home during the Revolution and subsequent years; and he made arrangements so that Michael could study for the priesthood, first at St. Palais and then at Bayonne. The parents would not have to pay anything, and the boy would earn his expenses by working for the priests and in the bishop's kitchen outside of school hours. Later Michael studied philosophy at Aire, and theology at Dax. As a seminarian at Dax, where he was nicknamed "our Aloysius Gonzaga," he also taught a class in the nearby preparatory school. He was ordained a priest at Bayonne in December, 1823.

Michael joined the Third Order Secular of St. Francis; and from the beginning of his priestly career manifested unusual apostolic zeal. His first appointment was that of an assistant to the pastor of Cambo, who was in poor health. In a short time the young priest revived religious fervor and effectively combatted Jansenism by promoting frequent Communion and fostering devotion to the Sacred Heart. He tackled the freethinkers with such earnestness, that one of them declared: "That devil would give his life to save the soul of an enemy."

After two years he was appointed a professor in the major seminary at Bétharram, and after some time rector. Though he filled these offices in an able manner, the bishop suddenly decided to merge the Bétharram seminary with the one at Bayonne; and Father Michael found himself more or less stranded. There was a great need of mission work among the people; and he conceived a plan for training priests to do this kind of work. With a few companions he began to live a community life; and with his bishop's approval he drew up constitutions in 1838.

The number of his associates increased; but then the diocese received a new bishop who did not favor the founding of a new congregation. Father Michael's constitutions were revised; and his community was permitted to work only under the bishop and in the diocese. They were allowed to choose their own superior only in 1852. It was a great trial for Father Michael, but he bore it with patience and left his foundation in God's hands.

Father Michael died of apoplexy on Ascension Day, May 14, 1863. He was beatified in 1923, and canonized in 1947. In 1877, fourteen years after the death of St. Michael, the congregation which he had founded received papal approval according to the original plan. It is called Auxiliary Priests of the Sacred Heart, and follows the rule of St. Augustine. The members of the society take perpetual vows, and devote themselves to teaching and the care of souls. The feast of St. Michael is observed on May fourteenth; but since he is the founder of a non-Franciscan congregation, his name does not appear in the Franciscan calendar.

ON GRATITUDE

1. Gratitude makes us beloved by God and by men. It is a beautiful virtue when we humbly acknowledge that anyone has done us a benefit without any desert of ours, and therefore render him sincere thanks in word and deed. St. Cassian, a school-teacher, was put to death with the iron styluses of his own pupils at the instigation of the pagan governor. Are not the benefits rendered to the souls of others sometimes requited in a similar way? "Ingratitude is the world's reward," has become a proverb. — Has the proverb proved true in your case too?

2. Consider how great is our obligation to be grateful. We owe thanks to God for our life with all the powers of body and soul; we are indebted to Him for every moment of our life, with all the good that falls to our lot. "Every best gift, and every perfect gift, is from above" (Jas. 1,17). We cannot render thanks to God in any better way than by making good use of His gifts and by thanksgiving. The Apostle admonishes us to give thanks with the words: "In all things give thanks; for this is the will of God in Christ Jesus" (1 Thess. 5,18). We owe thanks to many a person, above all to our parents, also to our teachers and the priests, as well as to such who have made sacrifices for us and have done us favors. Hence, the Apostle, speaking of our conduct towards our fellowmen, says emphatically: "Be thankful" (Col. 3,15). — Have you been grateful in the past?

3. Consider whence ingratitude proceeds. In one case it is indifference toward the favor we have received, although it would be painful to dispense with it if we did not have it. Again, it is dissatisfaction at not having received more, and everything that we wanted. Very frequently the cause is self-love and pride, which make us ascribe to our merits the benefits we have received and render us unwilling to give thanks to someone else. Such are the odious sources from which black ingratitude rises. It is like a dark cloud that passes in front of the sun, so that the ingrate sees nothing of his obligation. This dark cloud of ingratitude eventually prevents any further ray of kindness from penetrating to the ungrateful. May your heart be ever bright with gratitude!

PRAYER OF THE CHURCH

(Postcommunion for the Sixth Sunday after Easter)

Grant, we beseech Thee, O Lord, that we, who are nourished with sacred gifts, may ever abide in thanksgiving. Through Christ our Lord. Amen.

MAY 16
ST. YVES OF BRITTANY
Confessor, Third Order

VES, or Ivo, was born of noble parents in Brittany in 1253. The lessons his pious mother instilled in the heart of the boy through Christian training, preserved him amid the grave dangers to which he was exposed during his student years at Paris and Orléans.

To the study of theology Yves joined the study of civil and ecclesiastical law. He applied himself so diligently to his studies that his instructors and fellow students marveled at his knowledge. But he was much more intent on acquiring virtue and piety. Not only did he go to church in the morning to attend holy Mass, but every evening he performed his devotions there. Besides studying his textbooks, he delighted in reading the lives of the saints, and the reading drew him very strongly to imitate them. He drank no wine, and his pastime consisted in visiting the sick in the hospitals.

After he had completed his studies, he was assigned to the diocese of Rennes, and later his bishop appointed him judge of the church court of his native diocese of Treguier. Although Yves in his humility did not desire it or ask for it, the bishop of Treguier also ordained him a priest and entrusted him with a parish.

As judge, the young priest-lawyer always let justice hold sway without regard to persons, and the wisdom of his decisions was remarkable. He did not derive this wisdom only from his learning, but he prayed often and long for enlightenment. Before making grave decisions, he always said a Mass in honor of the Holy Ghost. By preference he helped the poor, the widows, and the orphans to obtain justice, even when the duty of his office did not oblige him to help. As a son of St. Francis, to whose Third Order he had been admitted, he felt particularly attracted to the poor, and interested himself in their needs with such zeal that he was called the attorney of the poor.

The high office with which Yves was entrusted and the honors which were accorded him because of it, were not to his taste. He begged the bishop until he yielded and allowed him to resign his office, for he wished to take personal care of his parish, which until then had been attended by an administrator.

Yves arranged his household and his wardrobe in the simplest fashion. All his time and labor he devoted to his flock, to whom he was a true shepherd and father. He strove to uproot vices of long standing, especially usury and immorality, and by his zeal, charity, holy example, and fervent prayers, he succeeded.

Here, too, the poor were his special friends. His home was an open guest-house for the poor, the blind, the lame, and the helpless of the entire vicinity. During a famine God almighty came to the assistance of his generosity by visible miracles. A flour bin which a domestic had found empty was found filled when Yves himself went with the domestic to examine it. Once he fed two hundred hungry persons with seven loaves of bread; at another time he fed twenty-four persons with a small loaf.

His labors and his strict life sapped all his energy. He was hardly fifty years old when he felt his end nearing. Fortified with the last sacraments, he commended his soul to the hands of his Creator and died with a smile on May 19, 1303. His body was entombed in the cathedral of Treguier. The finest eulogy was tendered him by the poor, who flocked thither in great numbers and raised such lamentations that all present were deeply touched. After many miracles at his grave, Pope Clement VI added his name to the list of saints of the Catholic Church. His feast is observed on May nineteenth by the Third Order Regular.

ON PROTECTING THE HELPLESS

1. How noble it was of St. Yves to use his talents and skill so readily to protect the poor and the helpless. This is the way to use God's gifts according to His good pleasure. Just as the rich man should use his wealth to alleviate the needs of the poor, so should he who has influence and talent, according to God's designs, gladly use these advantages to protect the helpless and the downtrodden. Thus the Prophet warns: "Relieve the oppressed, judge for the fatherless, defend the widow" (Isa. 1,17). Opportunities often present themselves to do this even if one is not a lawyer. — Have you utilized them?

2. Consider how the practice of protecting the poor and helpless preserved St. Yves from pride amid his distinctions while it strengthened him in humility. There is great danger that anyone who holds a prominent position among his fellow citizens may conduct himself arrogantly toward them and despise the lowly. But Christ says to His disciples: "He who is the greater among you, let him become as the least" (Lk. 22,26). The great should serve the lowly. This cannot be done better and with less loss of dignity than by protecting the helpless. In Christian charity St. Yves recognized the defenseless as his brethren. He could say with St. Bernard: "I experience no consolation as long as I behold my brethren without

consolation." — Would that we could all say as much!

3. Consider the reward St. Yves received for his defense of the poor. Their love and gratitude was a sweet consolation to his kind heart already during his lifetime. Their sobs and tears were a grander eulogy at his grave than the most glowing tribute of an enthusiastic speaker. But the greatest reward awaited him in eternity. There the Lord of heaven, who has said, "As long as you did it to one of these My least brethren, you did it to Me" (Mt. 25,40), is still rewarding him. Should that not impel us to imitate him, so that we may merit a like reward?

PRAYER OF THE CHURCH

O God, who didst choose blessed Yves, Thy confessor, as a distinguished minister unto the welfare of souls and the defense of the poor, grant, we beseech Thee, that we may both imitate his charity and be shielded by his intercession. Through Christ our Lord. Amen.

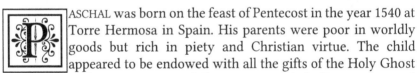

MAY 17
ST. PASCHAL BAYLON
Confessor, First Order

ASCHAL was born on the feast of Pentecost in the year 1540 at Torre Hermosa in Spain. His parents were poor in worldly goods but rich in piety and Christian virtue. The child appeared to be endowed with all the gifts of the Holy Ghost in an eminent degree. He was joyfully attentive and obedient to the good lessons his parents taught him, and he so excelled other children of his age in understanding of the divine truths and zeal for virtue that everybody marveled at it.

As the lowly position of his parents demanded, Paschal, already as a boy, had to tend the cattle of strangers. Although, due to his work, he took no part in the noisy life of the other boys, he was, nevertheless, well liked by them. They had a certain respect for him, they had him settle their quarrels, and they willingly accepted reprimands from him and listened to the Christian instructions he sometimes gave them.

His employer was so pleased with Paschal, who had meanwhile grown to be a strong young man, that one day he declared to him his intention to adopt him and make him his heir. But the young man answered gratefully that he wished to remain poor and was minded to consecrate

St. Paschal Baylon

himself to the service of God in the religious state.

Later, Paschal moved to another province, and at the age of twenty-four begged for admission as a lay brother at the convent of the Friars Minor at Monteforte. His request was granted, and Paschal seemed to run the path of perfection with ease and alacrity. He was so humble that he considered himself the last of all. At the same time he was so charitable that he cheerfully assumed the most burdensome duties for other brothers. He was so strict with his body that even at the most arduous tasks he would permit himself no relaxation in his way of living. He was so devoted to prayer that he spent all his spare time at it.

On the road, while gathering alms, he always had his rosary in his hand and God in his heart. Paschal fostered special devotion to the Blessed Virgin Mary, whom he called his Mother, and to the Blessed Sacrament. His heart glowed with fervor for the Blessed Sacrament, and it proved a constant means to rekindle his zeal.

God showed how pleased He was with his devotion. One day while out-of-doors, Paschal devoutly knelt down to adore the Blessed Sacrament when the bell announced the Consecration. At that moment the Blessed Sacrament was presented to him in a monstrance supported by angels hovering in the air. In the convent church he was frequently found before the tabernacle prostrate or with his arms outstretched or even rapt in ecstasy. At such times his soul was flooded with light from above. At any rate, the simple brother, who had never learnt to read or write, could discourse about the deepest mysteries of religion with marvelous insight to the astonishment of the most learned men.

Because of this heavenly enlightenment the Father Provincial once sent him from Spain on a very important matter to the general of the order, who at the time was staying in France. Paschal made the long and wearisome journey across the Pyrenees barefoot, traveling through regions infested by fanatical heretics, who on several occasions sought the life of the religious brother. But God's angel protected him on the journey to France and back, so that he escaped all danger.

After his return, Paschal remained the same humble brother as before and advanced in every virtue until the day of his happy death. He died at Villareal, on the feast of Pentecost, the feast on which he was born, May 17, 1592. It was during high Mass in the convent church, at the moment of the elevation of the Sacred Host, that Paschal breathed forth his soul.

At the funeral, according to custom, the body of the deceased brother lay on an open stretcher in the church. When the Blessed Sacrament was raised in the Requiem Mass, the dead body raised itself, bowed to the Sacred Host, repeating the act of reverence at the elevation of the Chalice, and then lowered itself again. Numerous other miracles occurred at his grave.

Pope Paul V beatified Paschal and Pope Alexander VIII canonized him in the year 1690. Pope Leo XIII in 1897 made him the patron of all Eucharistic societies and congresses. All three branches of the First Order celebrate his feast on May seventeenth. (Cf. *Forum*, 1943, pp. 148-150.)

ON DEVOTION TO THE BLESSED SACRAMENT

1. Consider that God showed by a miracle of the dead body of St. Paschal how pleasing to Him is devotion to the Blessed Sacrament. How it must offend God when Christians in full health are too indifferent or comfortable to show respect to the Blessed Sacrament. Does not the same Majesty reign in our churches in the Blessed Sacrament before which the angels and archangels, and all the saints and the just offer their homage in heaven? And is it too much for a poor worm of earth to bend his knee in reverence? Where will such Christians seek assurance when the same God appears in glory and majesty to judge the living and the dead? — Will you have no reason to tremble then?

2. Consider the respect Holy Mother Church renders to the most holy Sacrament of the Altar. The God-man really present in the Blessed Sacrament is the motive that explains the magnificence of our churches, the splendor of our feasts, the inspiring music of our choirs, especially as connected with our cathedrals and convent churches, in some of which the chants are heard even at midnight. According to the rubrics, even the poorest village church must keep the sanctuary lamp burning steadily before the Blessed Sacrament day and night. But should the light of the sanctuary lamp alone rise towards Him? Should it not rather remind us that our hearts should glow like it with true inner devotion to the Holy Sacrament? — Have you up till now heeded this lesson of the sanctuary lamp?

3. Consider that devotion to the Blessed Sacrament should not be confined to the walls of the House of God. On the feast of Corpus Christi the Blessed Sacrament is sometimes carried about in solemn procession as in a public triumphal march. On the occasion everybody should do what lies in his power to honor Him whom no words of praise or tokens of honor can ever extol enough. Consider it an honor to take part in such processions. Also on less splendid occasions when the Holy Sacrament is taken to the sick, perhaps in your own home or in that of a neighbor, never omit to manifest your deep devotion. Then our Lord will also come to you in holy Communion so much the more graciously, notably on the

day when He will be brought to you as your Viaticum.

PRAYER OF THE CHURCH
O God, who didst adorn the Blessed Paschal, Thy confessor, with a wonderful love for the mysteries of Thy Body and Blood, mercifully grant that we may draw from the Divine Banquet the same fulness of spirit that he did. Who livest and reignest forever and ever. Amen.

MAY 18
ST. FELIX OF CANTALICE
Confessor, First Order

N the Italian village of Cantalice, in the beautiful valley of Rieti, Felix was born of humble but pious peasants. As a boy he tended cattle, and later he became a farm laborer. Being so much amid God's free nature, his heart was attracted to God, whose gracious ministering to us human beings he had daily before his eyes.

Neither did the hard work make him coarse and worldly-minded, as sometimes happens, but he was gentle and kind towards everyone. When he came home at night all tired out, he still spent much time in his little room engaged in prayer, to which for that matter he applied himself also while at work. It grieved him that he could not attend holy Mass on weekdays. He would indeed gladly have consecrated his whole life to the service of God, but he could see no way of carrying out his desire until one day an accident showed him the way.

Felix had to break to the plow a team of young oxen that were very wild. The oxen shied, and when Felix tried to stop them, they ran him down, dragging the sharp plowshare across his body. Peasants ran to the scene, certain that they would find the man dead, but Felix arose unharmed, with only his jacket rent. But he went straight to his employer and begged to be released from his service. The little he possessed he gave to the poor, and went to the nearest Capuchin convent, where he humbly begged for admission. After careful trial, his request was granted.

Now Felix felt like one newly born, as if heaven itself had opened to him. It was in the year 1543, and Felix was twenty-eight years old. But in his novitiate he was yet to experience the burden and the struggles of this earthly life. The devil attacked him with violent temptations of all kinds. He was also seized with a lingering illness, which made it appear that he was unfit for convent life. But patience, steadfast self-control, prayer, and candor toward his superiors helped him secure admission to the vows, which he took with great delight.

Soon afterwards he was sent to the Capuchin convent at Rome, where, because of his genuine piety and friendly manner, he was appointed to the task of gathering alms, which he did for all the next forty-two years until his death. With his provision sack slung over his shoulder, he went about so humbly and reserved in manner that he edified everybody. When he received an alms, he had so cordial a way of saying Deo Gratias — thanks be to God — that the people called him Brother Deo Gratias. As soon as he got back to the convent and delivered the provisions, he found his way to church. There he first said a prayer for the benefactors, then he poured out his heart in devotion especially before the Blessed Sacrament and at the altar of our Lady. There he also passed many hours of the night, and one time the Mother of God placed the Divine Child in the arms of the overjoyed Felix.

He was most conscientious in observing every detail of his rule and vows. He did not wait for the orders of his superiors; a mere hint from them was enough. Although always in touch with the world, he kept such careful guard over his chastity in every word and look that Pope Paul V said he was a saint in body and soul.

Poverty was his favorite virtue. Because our holy Father St. Francis forbade his friars to accept money in any form, Felix could not be prevailed upon to accept it under any circumstances. How pleasing this spirit was to God was to be proved in a remarkable way. Once on leaving a house, Felix slung his sack over his shoulder, but felt it weigh so heavily that it almost crushed him. He searched the sack and found a coin which someone had secretly slipped into it. He threw it away in disgust, and cheerfully and easily took up his sack again.

Almighty God granted Felix extraordinary graces. Many sick persons he restored to health with the Sign of the Cross. A dead child he gave back alive to its mother. In the most puzzling cases he was able to give helpful advice. Honored by the great and the lowly, he considered himself the most wretched of men, but earned so much the more merits with God.

Finally the day arrived when Felix was to gather the hoard of his merits. He died with a cheerful countenance while catching sight of the Mother of God, who invited him to the joys of Paradise. It was on the feast of Pentecost, May 18, 1587. Pope Urban VIII beatified him, Pope Clement XI inscribed him in the register of the saints in 1709. The entire First Order as well as the Third Order Regular observe his feast on May eighteenth.

ON THE USE OF MONEY

1. For love of poverty in the highest degree and recognizing the dangers to Christian perfection usually connected with money, St. Francis forbade his friars to accept money, as Christ Himself wished His disciples not to carry money about with them (Mt. 10,9). We behold in the life of St. Felix how agreeable to God is the faithful observance of this precept of St. Francis wherever that is possible. But there are instances when no Christian may accept money. That would be the case if anyone were to offer money in order to make you do wrong or be unfaithful to your duty. Solomon complained among the Jews: "All things obey money" (Eccl. 10,19). Must this complaint not be applied to Christians too? To such who accept money for sordid reasons as well as to such who give it, the curse of Peter, the prince of the Apostles, applies: "Let your money perish with you" (Acts 8,20). — Have you perhaps reason to fear this curse?

2. Consider that to acquire the necessities of life, money is something very useful, and as civil life is today, one cannot do without it. But it must be used in the right way. That is why it should not be given freely to such who are apt to abuse it, such as children or shiftless needy people. It is better to give such persons the things they need than the ready money. Neither may we ourselves spend it wastefully or squander it, because God will require an account of the way we spend our money. But it should serve for necessary expenses for ourselves and our charges in accordance with our position in life. The father of a house, for example, must cheerfully provide the necessary money, so that his wife and children are not driven to tell lies and to steal. Money should also be applied, according to one's means, to help relieve the needs of others, as well as to promote good purposes and to further the welfare of the Church and the honor of God. Fortunate is he who uses his money thus. — Have you always used it well?

3. Consider that it is not wrong to lay aside a quantity of money for times of need. A wise proverb reads: "Save in time, and you will have something in the day of need." But be on your guard lest saving should breed love for money, a thing that can readily happen. In that case economy would not save you from distressful experience, but would rather increase the chance, since he who loves money, "sets even his own soul to sale" (Eccli. 10,10). Therefore it is well not to be too saving, but to rely upon God. Should, for example, a particular need arise to help your neighbor, then with the confidence of a child use your savings for him as willingly as for your own need, since Jesus Christ teaches: "Love your neighbor as

yourself" (Mk. 12,31).

PRAYER OF THE CHURCH

Make us, Lord Jesus, walk in the innocence and simplicity of our hearts, since for love of these virtues Thou didst descend from the bosom of Thy Mother into the arms of Blessed Felix, Thy confessor. Who livest and reignest forever and ever. Amen.

MAY 19
ST. THEOPHILUS OF CORTE
Confessor, First Order

T. THEOPHILUS was born at Corte in Corsica in 1676, of a rich and noble family. As a youth he entered the Order of Friars Minor and received the name of Theophilus, which proved to be very appropriate for him. He was a delicate youth and disinclined to the amusements of the young. He loved silence, solitude, and prayer, and by his good example exhorted his companions to exercises of piety, and in general gave evidence of his future sanctity.

When he donned the coarse garb of the Franciscan Order, he appeared already to have acquired an appreciable degree of Christian and religious perfection. The highest hopes were placed in his piety and talent, nor were the results in any way disappointing; by the grace of God, he far surpassed the expectations of his superiors. He pronounced his vows and went to Rome to pursue the study of philosophy, in which he won great distinction. When he entered upon his theological studies at Naples, he was especially ingenious in joining works of piety to his studies, and there was discernible in him a rare blending of virtue and learning.

He had long admired the austere life which obtained in the retreat house at Civitella near Subiaco, and so, after his ordination to the priesthood, he begged his superiors for permission to repair to that convent, in order to join his brethren in their practices of austerity and in prayer. Aglow with zeal for the honor of God, he undertook to establish or restore in the convents of his order the life of austerity which he himself had courageously embraced. Later he was sent to Corsica and to Tuscany, where he founded the retreat houses of Zuani and Fucecchio.

He was pleasant of countenance and possessed a cheerful temperament. Although continually afflicted with various diseases, he was undaunted by hardships, fulfilling the duties entrusted to him while faithfully performing the austerities prescribed by the rule. He was a great lover of poverty, choosing for himself what was poorest, and often begging alms from door to door for the religious entrusted to his care. He distinguished himself in a very pronounced way by obedience, which was remarkable for its promptness. Nothing ever prevented him from immediately carrying out the orders given him, no matter how difficult they might be.

Aflame with love, he fostered special devotion to the sufferings of Christ and the Mother of God. His days and even nights were spent in visiting the sick, assisting the needy, giving advice, and hearing confessions. No obstacle was insurmountable to him when there was question of doing good, no roads were too difficult to traverse, no weather was too inclement, no fatigue or infirmity too exhausting.

At the age of sixty-four he died in the Tuscan retreat house on the seventeenth of June, 1740. God favored him with the gift of prophecy and of many miracles both before and after his death, so that the fame of his sanctity spread far and wide. After the required miracles were duly approved, Pope Leo XIII beatified him; and in 1930, on the feast of SS. Peter and Paul, Pope Pius XI inscribed his name in the catalogue of the saints. His feast is observed on May nineteenth by the entire First Order.

ON THE CONSOLATIONS OF RELIGION

1. The man without religion is a man without consolation. Why are there so many shattered lives today? Why do so many people commit suicide? Because they have divorced themselves from religion, and, with religion lost, they have no hold on life any more. The words of the Apostle about him "who comforts us in our tribulations" (2 Cor. 1,4), are foreign to them. — Let it be a warning to you never to cast from you the anchor of religion. Religion provides abundant consolation in this life. Life brings sufferings in its train. St. Augustine says: "The tribulations of this present life are manifold and oppressive; without the consolation of hope in a future life, we should all perish." It was this thought that filled St. Theophilus with such abundant consolation. God, eternity, eternal bliss were ever before his mind. — Be on your guard, let no one rob you of deep religious trust in God.

2. Religion furnishes us with rich consolation in death. When the man without religion comes to die, he stands before nothingness or before ghastly uncertainty. Religion, however, points to our dying but also resurrected and eternally glorified Redeemer, who addresses His followers

with the words, "Where I am, there also shall my minister be" (Jn. 12,26). — Be grateful for the inestimable treasure of religion and seek to make yourself deserving of it.

PRAYER OF THE CHURCH

O God, who didst grant to Blessed Theophilus, Thy confessor, the grace to imitate the manner of life of our seraphic Father; grant us through his intercession, that, strengthened in Thy love, we may never cease to serve Thee. Through Christ our Lord. Amen.

MAY 20
ST. BERNARDIN OF SIENA
Confessor, First Order

T. ANTONINUS, archbishop of Florence, begins the biography of Bernardin with the words: "The grace of God, our Saviour, has appeared in His servant Bernardin, who shone like a bright star in a dark night, and with the heavenly brilliance of his virtue and doctrine frightened away the darkness."

The great saint descended from the old knightly family of the Albizeschi of Siena, and was born on September 8, 1380, in the town of Massa, a dependency of Siena, where his father was governor. When Bernardin was only seven years old, he had lost both his parents, but he was reared in the fear of God by devout relatives. He evinced a great love for the poor, with whom, as a little boy, he gladly shared his food. He attended divine services with the most edifying devotion, and listened to sermons with such attention that he could repeat them to his companions.

He loved purity above all the virtues. While he attended the secondary school in Siena, he could not hear an unbecoming word without blushing for shame, so that those who had spoken it themselves blushed. When any indecent conversation was going on among his companions, they stopped as soon as they saw him coming. "Be still," they said, "Bernardin is coming."

While the holy youth was otherwise very meek, and was friendly to all, he could nevertheless grow extremely angry if decency was violated. A prominent citizen once purposely told him something indecent in the open market place. Bernardin gave him a resounding slap in the face, and amid the laughter of the bystanders the disgraced citizen had to withdraw.

With his great love for purity, Bernardin united a tender devotion to the Blessed Virgin, whom he used to call his beloved. Out of devotion to her he daily visited an image of Mary just outside the town of Siena; he prayed there especially to learn his vocation. The Mother of Grace, who had protected him in the world, now led him to the sanctuary of the convent. In the quiet little convent of St. Mary of Colombaio, which St. Francis himself had founded, Bernardin received the holy habit on the feast of the Nativity of Mary in the year 1402. On the same feast in the following year, he made his profession, and after he was ordained and appointed to preach, he also gave his first sermon on the feast of Mary's nativity.

Since, however, Bernardin's voice was very weak and hoarse, he seemed ill-fitted for the office of a preacher. Yet, here, too, his beloved Mother helped him. At her intercession his voice suddenly became so powerful and melodious that he became one of the most distinguished missionaries.

Now he journeyed all over Italy in order to announce to the people the virtues and vices, and the reward of the former and the punishment of the latter. In many places such depravity existed that he often found it necessary to preach sermons which he himself called sermons for heathens. The effects, however, were so astounding that Pope Pius II compared him with the Apostle of the Gentiles and called him a second Paul. After he had shaken their hearts with stern truths, he poured into them the soothing oil of the sweet name of Jesus, our Saviour and Redeemer, and preached on Mary, the Mother of Mercy.

His blessed ministry induced many towns to seek him as their bishop. Thus Siena, Ferrara, and Urbino petitioned in turn for this privilege, and the pope offered Bernardin the episcopal dignity. But with unchanging humility, he declined every time. He remained among his religious brethren whom he encouraged in religious perfection.

Rich in merits and virtue he died at Aquila on May 20, 1444. Pope Nicholas V canonized him six years later, whereupon the citizens of Aquila built in his honor a beautiful church with a magnificent marble tomb. The feast of St. Bernardin is observed on May twentieth by all three branches of the First Order.

ON INDECENT CONVERSATION

1. "Blessed are the clean of heart" (Mt. 5,8). This praise was merited by Bernardin in his youth and throughout his life. That is why indecent conversation displeased him so very much. Such talk comes from an

unclean heart and filthy mind, because "out of the fulness of the heart, the mouth speaks." How detestable it is for a Christian to indulge in shameless and double-meaning speech or lewd songs, since all his bodily members have been sanctified in baptism and have, as it were, become the members of Christ, who is our head. Added to this is the fact that a Christian's mouth receives the most holy Body of Christ in holy Communion. Therefore the Apostle says: "Uncleanness, let it not so much as be named among you, or obscenity, or foolish talking, or scurrility" (Eph. 5,4). If such matters do not impress you as abominable, then fear lest your heart be not clean.

2. Consider how harmful indecent conversation is to those who listen. The Holy Ghost warns: "Be not seduced: Evil communications corrupt good manners" (1 Cor. 15,33). The smouldering embers of indecent desire lie in the heart of every man since the time of original sin. He who fears it least is most dangerously exposed to the unclean fire. St. Chrysostom, speaking of conversation and jests that offend against decency, says that nothing so readily destroys chastity as the flame that is enkindled through them. That is why Bernardin dealt so vigorously with the citizen who told him a filthy story. The young man would rather have let himself be struck in the face than be addressed with such speech. — How do you conduct yourself in such instances? In their rule, Tertiaries are especially warned to flee filthy and loose conversation.

3. Consider how there was bound up with this great love for chastity on the part of St. Bernardin, a tender love for Mary. For us, too, devotion to the Blessed Virgin Mary will be a special means of preserving the love of chastity and of being protected against all dangers. To this end honor the Blessed Virgin, the Queen of Virgins, particularly during the month of May. If no other refuge remains for you in time of danger, then say over and over again the holy names of Jesus and Mary. Recommend yourself also to St. Bernardin, that you may remain faithful to God.

PRAYER OF THE CHURCH

O Lord Jesus, who didst grant to St. Bernardin, Thy confessor, a very special love for Thy most holy name, pour forth in us, we beseech Thee, through his merits and intercession, the spirit of Thy love. Who livest and reignest forever and ever. Amen.

MAY 21
BLESSED LADISLAS OF GIELNIOW
Confessor, First Order

LESSED Ladislas was born at Gielniow, a town in the diocese of Gniezno, Poland. The very first fruits of his life he offered to God, who alone had the right to them. In compliance with the wishes of his parents, he pursued his studies at the University of Cracow, and after making great progress in learning and virtue, he recognized the call of God to forsake the world.

In 1464 he entered the convent of Friars Minor at Warsaw, which had been quite recently founded by St. John Capistran. There the young man strove so earnestly for perfection that the highest hopes were placed in him. He observed all the austerities of the order most faithfully, and regarded interior mortification as the goal of all exterior practices of penance. His profound humility and perfect obedience greatly edified all.

As soon as he was ordained to the priesthood, he asked, in his great zeal for souls, for permission to go among the Kalmuks in neighboring Russia, in order to preach the Gospel to this heathen nation. The permission was granted, but Ladislas met with so many obstacles in that country that he was obliged to return without achieving any success. He now labored without tiring at his apostolic work in Poland.

In towns and villages he preached the word of God, and his zeal, coupled with a holy life, produced blessed results everywhere. He had a special way of presenting for the consideration of the faithful the sufferings of Christ and the glories of the Mother of God. Above all he recommended the recitation of the Crown of the Seven Joys of our Blessed Lady.

Because of his outstanding qualifications, Ladislas was five times elected to the office of provincial. During his administration he sent many missionaries to Lithuania and to Russia, where it was now possible to convert many heathens to Christendom, a task which he had once attempted in vain.

Broken with age and the fatigues of an exhausting apostolate, he completed his last term as provincial. The fathers who attended the chapter did not wish to assign him a definite convent for his residence, but left it to him to choose one for himself. But the holy old man said: "My fathers, so you wish that at the end of my life I should live according to my own will and fancy! Never before have I done that, and far be it from me ever to follow my own will. Dispose of me entirely according to your own good pleasure." He was then appointed guardian of the convent at

Warsaw. There he had begun his religious life, there he was also to close it in the very next year.

On Good Friday he preached a sermon on the sufferings of our Lord. All at once his countenance was transfigured. He fell into ecstasy and was raised in the air above the pulpit before the eyes of the astonished multitude. When the ecstasy ended, he was seized with a fever, and about a month later, on May 4, 1505, he went to his reward. Many miracles occurred at his tomb in the church of his order at Warsaw. Pope Benedict XIV sanctioned the veneration paid to him. His feast is celebrated by the Franciscans on May twenty-first, and the Capuchins on the eleventh.

ON DENYING ONE'S OWN WILL

1. Behold how a saint treasures the sacrifice of his own will. Blessed Ladislas was obliged to govern others for many years. In such a capacity self-will is apt to assume additional strength. He was advanced in years, a time when persons are usually more inclined to be self-willed. The fathers of the chapter, whose duty it was to decide where each friar should reside, left it to him to choose a residence according to his own wishes. But the holy man declined the offer. He did not wish to lose the merit which the sacrifice of one's own will brings with it, and he wanted the assurance of obedience that he was where God wished him to be. All religious are obliged by their vows, and subordinates by their duty of obedience, to give up their own will if the authorities decide upon something that is contrary to it. But far from being considered a nuisance, such submission should be regarded as good fortune. "We are happy, because the things that are pleasing to God are made known to us" (Bar. 4,4). — Have you placed the proper store by this happiness?

2. Consider on the other hand the dangers that accompany the pursuit of one's own will. The will of man is a blind power, which must be guided by the light of the understanding and by divine grace. One should not permit children, who do not yet know how to use their understanding properly, to follow their own will. But even in the case of adults, the will too often and too readily follows not the guidance of grace, but rather the passions and inordinate desires, so that it drives people to all kinds of evil. "Self-will," says the holy abbot Anthony, "is a wine so intoxicating that under its influence we no longer recognize the value of virtue and the hatefulness of vice." Therefore the Wise Man admonishes us: "Go not after your lusts, but turn away from your own will" (Eccli. 18,30). Only he who is always prepared to deny his will, will be saved from the danger of being lost through it.

3. Consider that for all men the denial of self-will is the most necessary and salutary means of arriving at Christian perfection. Perfection consists in surrendering our heart to God. In the case of good Christians who forswear wickedness, the evil spirit endeavors to prevent their progress in perfection by luring them on to practice virtue merely because they so will it, not because it is their duty, or because it is pleasing to God. Those, however, who overcome also this last hindrance, who prefer in all things to do God's will and, therefore, accept what is disagreeable to them as readily as what pleases them, have already arrived at great perfection. Hence St. Philip Neri used to say in his brief but significant way, pointing to his forehead:

> "Within a space four fingers wide,
> There holiness doth oft abide."

What folly, and likewise what a scandal, when persons who wish to be especially perfect make themselves conspicuous by their self-will!

PRAYER OF THE CHURCH

O God, who didst will that Blessed Ladislas should distinguish himself before all in the practice of religious perfection, mercifully grant, that imitating his example, we, too, may advance in virtue. Through Christ our Lord. Amen.

⊗⊗⊗⊗⊗⊗⊗⊗⊗⊗⊗⊗

MAY 22
BLESSED JOHN FOREST
Martyr, First Order

HEN King Henry VIII of England, swayed by sinful passion, demanded a divorce from his lawful wife Catharine in order to marry her rival Anne Boleyn, he soon gave signs that he meant to set himself up as the supreme head of the Church in England if the pope did not grant his wishes. At that early stage, a number of Franciscans fearlessly declared the king's designs unlawful and sacrilegious, and thus drew down on them and their order the resentment of the king.

In the year 1533 the open breach between the king and Rome took place. Abetted by willing accomplices, Henry had himself declared supreme head of the Church in England. The country once called the isle of saints and the dowry of the Virgin Mother of God was torn away from Holy Church by the adulterous ruler.

To prevent wholesale apostasy, the Franciscan Friar John Forest wrote a book on the primacy of the Catholic Church and of the pope, in which he demonstrated and refuted the sacrilegious claims of the king. He was one of the most learned theologians in the country. He had been raised to the dignity of a Doctor of Theology by the University of Oxford, was provincial of his order, and had been selected by Queen Catharine as her confessor. Because of his distinguished virtue, he was also greatly esteemed by the people.

In consequence the king was highly incensed when he heard of the book. He had the friar promptly arrested and thrown into prison among criminals of the worst kind. Several days later Friar John was led before the king, who employed threats and promises to make the friar acknowledge him as head of the Church in England. But John replied that for nothing in the world would he swerve a finger's breadth from the truth of the Roman Catholic Faith. Thereupon he was remanded to prison.

Four years Friar John languished there. Often he was maltreated in various ways, and then again flattering attempts were made to make him apostatize. As the steadfast confessor continued to prove invincible, he was sentenced to death for high treason.

On May 22, 1538, the seventy-year-old man was led out of his prison to the place of execution. When he beheld a gibbet built there, and a fire prepared under it, he said: "Neither fire, nor gibbet, nor any other torment shall separate me from Thee, O Lord." Then his body, girded about with iron chains, was hung from the gibbet so that the fire licked the martyr's feet. The fire was purposely kept low, for the intention was to satisfy the cruel pleasure of torturing the victim for a long time. Meanwhile he was derided, and an apostate bishop urged him to yield to the king.

His flesh already aflame, the martyr avowed anew his steadfast loyalty to the Catholic Faith. In order to torture his soul, a wooden image of the Blessed Mother brought from a much-frequented shrine in Wales was placed on the fire. The flame then burst forth with great vigor. The martyr prayed with the Psalmist: "In the shadow of Thy wings will I hope until iniquity pass away" (Ps. 56,2). The gibbet itself now caught fire and together with the saint it fell into the burning heap. Friar John said at last, "Into Thy hands, O Lord, I commend my spirit." Then the torture ended, and his soul winged its flight to heaven.

A decree of Pope Leo XIII of December 9, 1886, approved the veneration accorded to Blessed John Forest and fifty-four other martyrs of England. The Franciscans celebrate the feast of Blessed John Forest on May twenty-second. (Cf. Steck, *Franciscans and the Protestant Revolution*, pp. 138-168.)

SUFFERING PERSECUTION FOR JUSTICE' SAKE

1. If we had witnessed the gruesome torture of Blessed John, who of us would at the time have called him blessed? Would we not rather have pitied him with tears in our eyes? But fifteen centuries before his time Christ called him blessed when He said: "Blessed are they who suffer persecution for justice' sake; for theirs is the kingdom of heaven" (Mt. 5,10). Now the Church assures us that he is among the blessed inhabitants of heaven. On the other hand, who now praises those who tortured him? — If you are being mocked and persecuted because of the Faith you profess, then look up to the holy martyrs. Bear it as they did, and you may expect to share their glory. "Everyone, therefore, who shall confess Me before men, I will also confess him before My Father, who is in heaven" (Mt. 10,32).

2. Consider that the justice for which one must suffer is not only the Faith we profess, but every Christian virtue. If a person suffers annoyance because he is not willing to take part in indecencies, he is blessed. If a man is subjected to derision and persecution because he insists on justice, he is blessed. If you suffer ill-treatment and persecution in your work and service because you have harsh and unchristian superiors, bear it with meekness and patience, for blessed are you. "For this is thankworthy," says St. Peter, "if for conscience toward God a man endure sorrows, suffering wrongfully" (1 Pet. 2,19).

2. Consider that there is such a thing as interior persecution which one must bear for justice' sake. "When you come to the service of God," says the Holy Ghost, "prepare your soul for temptation" (Eccli. 2,1). Those who dedicate themselves to the true service of God and wish to walk the way of perfection, experience this. Dryness of soul, weariness of pious practices, and all sorts of interior struggles, of which they formerly had no notion, come upon them. The enemy, the adversary of all piety, likes to have this happen. At such times take your place under the cross and say with our martyr: "In the shadow of Thy wings, O Lord, will I hope until iniquity pass away." Then will your soul also rise to more intimate union with God. — Offer up to God your interior and exterior sufferings in union with the torture endured by our martyr, for the return to the Catholic Church of those who have been separated from it.

PRAYER OF THE CHURCH

O Lord Jesus Christ, who didst choose Blessed John, Thy martyr, as an invincible defender of the Catholic Faith and of the primacy of the Roman Pontiff, grant, we beseech Thee, that through his intercession all the nations that acknowledge Thee as the true God, may return to the unity of the true faith. Who livest and reignest forever and ever.

MAY 23
BLESSED BARTHOLOMEW PUCCI
Confessor, First Order

OWARDS the end of the thirteenth century, when so many cities in Italy were warring against one another, when on the one hand violence, injustice, and immorality were spread far and wide, there were on the other hand examples of extraordinary piety. One such example was the life of Blessed Bartholomew Pucci. He was a respected gentleman of the city of Montepulciano, who, layman that he was, led a very Christian life. He and his wife were above all anxious to protect the many children God had given them from infection by a wicked world, rearing them in the fear of God.

There came a time when Bartholomew felt a mighty urge to forsake the world in order to serve God in the Order of St. Francis. That was something most unusual and called for careful probation. As a rule, the word of the Apostle applies to such as have already embraced a definite state of life: "Let every man abide in the same calling in which he was called (1 Cor. 7,20).

But He who called Peter from the married state and a fisherman's life to the apostolate, made known His will that Bartholomew should serve Him in future in the religious state. His wife willingly gave her consent and consecrated herself to God by the vow of perpetual chastity, and Bartholomew provided for the future of his children. Then he left his fashionable home and family for Christ's sake, and took the coarse habit of St. Francis in the poor convent of the Friars Minor.

In the practices of religious life he was a most edifying example. Prompted by humility he did not wish to become a priest, but in obedience he prepared himself for the priesthood and the reception of holy orders. Now he trod the way of perfection with still greater zeal. At prayer and meditation his heart burned with the fervent devotion of a seraph. His love for his neighbor was so intimately bound up with his love for God that, like St. Francis, he resolved never to refuse a favor asked of him for the love of Christ.

Almighty God took such pleasure in this love of His generous servant that many a time food was miraculously multiplied on being blessed by Bartholomew, especially one time when famine struck Montepulciano. Often angels were among the poor to whom he doled out bread, and once even the Queen of heaven and her Divine Child. When Bartholomew noticed that he was being honored as a saint because of these miracles, his humility took serious alarm. He would then do things in the street which made people laugh and make fun of him as if he had lost his mind. This derision would then calm him again.

Having gained many merits, he died while embracing the crucifix, in 1330. Pope Leo XIII gave the Church's approval to the constant veneration accorded him. The feast of Blessed Bartholomew is celebrated by the Franciscans on May twenty-third, by the Conventuals on the sixth, and by the Capuchins on the fourteenth.

FOR CHRIST'S SAKE

1. Recognizing it as the call of Jesus Christ that he should follow Jesus on the path of the religious state, Bartholomew found no sacrifice too great to make for Christ's sake. He thought, as Thomas a Kempis (4,9) says, that we ought to sacrifice all for Him who sacrificed all for us. Our dear Lord does not require anything so extraordinary of you as He did of Blessed Bartholomew. But examine, whether He is not asking for something which you have until now denied Him: sacrificing a certain occasion of sin, subduing a certain evil inclination, fulfilling a promise or a duty. Think of Blessed Bartholomew and make the sacrifice now for Christ's sake.

2. Consider how Blessed Bartholomew also practiced Christian charity for Christ's sake. This sentiment made his gifts so valuable in the sight of God that even the angels and the Mother of God accepted them. Would that you accustomed yourself, in all your alms to the poor and all your service to your neighbor, to do it for Christ's sake! What merit you could gain by it all, and how easy would many a thing be which until now has seemed too much for you. For Christ's sake forgive your enemies! For Christ's sake welcome the outcast back! For Christ's sake try to save the soul of the sinner! Some day Christ Himself will thank you for it. "As long as you did it to one of these My least brethren, you did it to Me" (Mt. 25,40).

3. Consider that for Christ's sake we should both plead for everything from our heavenly Father and hope for it with confidence. We are sinners and do not deserve to be heard by God. But for the sake of Christ, His Son, who shed His blood for us, and whose members we became in baptism, He will welcome all our petitions. Christ is the mediator between us and our heavenly Father, and His atoning Blood, as the Apostle says, "speaks better than that of Abel" (Heb. 12,24). Holy Church directs us to plead through Him, since all her prayers are addressed to our heavenly Father through Christ our Lord. Bartholomew breathed forth his soul in the embrace of the crucifix. Through Christ may our last sighs also reach the Father of mercy!

PRAYER OF THE CHURCH

O Lord Jesus Christ, who didst grant to Blessed Bartholomew, Thy confessor, the grace to leave all and follow Thee joyfully, vouchsafe through his intercession and merits that we, too, may for love of Thee despise the things of earth and strive only after heavenly things. Who livest and reignest forever and ever. Amen.

⊗⊗⊗⊗⊗⊗⊗⊗⊗

MAY 24
BLESSED JOHN OF PRADO
Martyr, First Order

 JOHN, the son of prominent parents, was studying philosophy at the famous University of Salamanca, Spain, when, enlightened by the Holy Ghost, he resolved to devote all his energies to the acquisition of the wisdom of Christ. In the light of that wisdom he soon recognized the vanity of the world and received the habit of St. Francis in the province of St. Gabriel. The young novice distinguished himself among the zealous religious by perfection in every virtue.

Burning with love for God and for immortal souls, John soon requested permission to go among the infidels to announce the Gospel to them. But his master in the religious life advised him for the present to offer his burning desires as a sacrifice to God and to prepare himself so much the better for the ministry of saving souls where it would serve his province best. John complied willingly. As soon as he was ordained a priest, he preached with great success. In due time he administered various offices in the order, and was even appointed provincial of the newly erected province of St. Didacus.

But almighty God, who has regard for the desire of pious hearts, so arranged matters that John's long-cherished wish could be fulfilled. Pope Urban VIII, who ascended the Chair of Peter in 1623, sent him with special powers to Morocco, Africa, to comfort the Christians who were being held as captives there by the Mohammedans and who were in great danger of losing their faith.

After endless difficulties, he arrived in Morocco, cleverly arranged for admittance to the prisoners, comforted them, administered the holy sacraments, and fortified them wonderfully by his inspiring exhortations, so that they were ready to suffer everything rather than deny the Christian Faith.

When the Mohammedan king learned of John's activities, he was enraged and had John put in chains and imprisoned. But John kissed the chains with ardent joy and cried out: "Now, O Lord, I am aware of Thy great love for me! How have I merited such a grace?"

Shackled hand and foot, John was then led out to work a treadmill. At the work he was maltreated with blows by a brutal servant. But the holy martyr continued to thank God for the torment and prayed for his tormentors. The king had him brought before him several times in the hope of getting him to apostatize; but always in vain. Still more infuriated, the tyrant had John cruelly scourged, and he himself dealt John a blow on the head with a sword. It is reported that at the moment the martyr's head appeared to be surrounded with heavenly light.

But the obdurate king commanded that a great fire be kindled and that John should be thrown into it. Even amid the flames, however, John continued to preach Christ to the bystanders, until, overwhelmed with stones by the executioners, he sank down into the fire. His soul arose to receive the victor's palm.

The province of St. Didacus, with the consent by the Apostolic See, chose John as the patron of its missions in Morocco; and after many miracles had been wrought at his intercession, Pope Benedict XIII placed John among the number of blessed martyrs. The Franciscans observe the feast of Blessed John on May twenty-fourth.

ON THE NECESSITY OF FAITH

1. "He who comes to God," writes the Apostle, "must believe that He is, and is a reward to those who seek Him" (Heb. 11,6). Faith being so necessary in order to reach God, Blessed John burned with such love of souls that already as a youth he wished ardently to evangelize the

heathens and bring the faith to them. Later the thought of this need made him ready to submit to the greatest hardships in order to keep the captive Christians from apostatizing. It induced him later also to suffer death amid the most cruel torments rather than to deny his faith. — Do you duly appreciate the necessity of faith? Do you know the truths necessary for salvation? Are you ready to suffer death rather than to deny your faith? Consider that faith is also necessary to make our works pleasing to God and meritorious for heaven. Faith is the foundation and root of our justification before God. Just as a building cannot stand without a foundation, and a tree cannot grow and bring forth fruit without roots, so our works cannot find favor before God and produce fruits for eternal life, if they are not done from motives of faith. With that in mind the Apostle says: "Being justified therefore by faith" (Rom. 5,1). — Do you act accordingly at your work, or are you merely motivated by temporal advantage and human considerations?

2. Consider that faith is especially necessary in the time of suffering and affliction. Then faith is the anchor that must hold us if the little ship of our soul is not to be borne away on the waves of dejection and despair. Only in faith could stricken Job exclaim: "The Lord gave, and the Lord has taken away. Blessed be the name of the Lord" (Job. 1,21). Only in faith could Tobias console his family with the words: "We lead indeed a poor life, but we shall have many good things if we fear God" (Tob. 4,23). Only in faith could our Blessed John kiss the chains with which he was shackled and which he saw shining with the glory which Christ has promised for such bonds. — During the last days of May let us very often entreat the Mother of God to obtain steadfast faith for us in times of tribulation, so that we, too, may be worthy of the promises of Christ.

PRAYER OF THE CHURCH

O God, who didst make Blessed John a distinguished preacher of Thy word against the wicked doctrine of the Mohammedans, grant, that as he deserved the palm of martyrdom for spreading the Christian Faith, so we may through his intercession deserve the rewards of our faith. Through Christ our Lord. Amen.

MAY 25
BLESSED JOHN OF CETINA AND PETER OF DUEÑAS
Martyrs, First Order

N a May morning many years ago, the city of Granada was astir early. Men, women, and children, yes, the king himself was awaiting the two Franciscan friars who would presently he dragged to the spot, where they were to die because they had discussed and preached the Faith they loved. The crowd thickened and the tumult increased as the hour approached. Meanwhile, John of Cetina and Peter of Dueñas were thanking God for the coming prize of martyrdom, and giving their last moments to prayer.

In his earlier years John had been in the service of a nobleman of Aragon, living and rejoicing in the midst of every amusement which the world can offer to the young, with neither a thought nor a desire for anything higher and better. We are not told what led to his conversion. We know only that the moment came when he realized that he had been blind to the best of good things, and that the favor of God was the one prize worth possessing. There was no half-hearted surrender. At once and without counting the cost, John severed all ties and retired to a secluded spot, where he could give himself wholly to penance and prayer, and be taught by the Holy Spirit what God would have him do.

It was not long before he was inspired to become a son of St. Francis. He was admitted at the Franciscan convent of Monzon in Aragon, and in due time was professed there. After an interval it was decided that John should devote himself to the work of preaching, and for the necessary study he was sent to Barcelona.

Then the news came of the death of four martyrs in the city of Jerusalem. Their constancy and love awakened a great longing in the heart of John to die in such a manner for Christ's sake. So he went to Rome to obtain permission to go to Jerusalem. The pope gave him permission to preach the Gospel to unbelievers, but bade him go to the Moors in Spain instead of to Jerusalem.

Arriving at Cordova, he asked leave of the Father Provincial to begin his work, but for the time being the superior deferred granting his request. Meanwhile, John applied himself to the normal convent life in a most edifying way.

Finally, the long-sought permission came. John was told that he might leave for the missions and take with him any friar whom he deemed most likely to be helpful. John was inspired to take with him Peter of Dueñas, a mere youth of not twenty years, who, inflamed with the same desire for martyrdom, had abandoned all the splendor of the court and joined the Friars Minor. In the world Peter had been accounted a man who lacked reason and sense. But it was soon discovered that if he possessed no learning, nor even the power of acquiring it, he was in a rare degree gifted with virtue.

This, then, was the companion John singled out from among the many older and more experienced members of the community. Together they went to Granada to fight the powers of darkness. They entered the city, announcing that they had come to have the people open their hearts to Christ, their Saviour, and close them to the teachings of Mohammed. There were some who listened and began to waver in their false religion.

The caliph, however, had the friars summoned to his presence to learn for himself why they had come among his people. Simply, yet fearlessly, they declared it their sole purpose to preach the Faith of Jesus Christ and to point out the errors of Mohammedanism. The king sought to dissuade them from their purpose, but his flattery as well as his threats were all of no avail; the constancy and courage of the martyrs could not be weakened. So it was that on that May morning in 1397 John and Peter were led out to die.

The hand of the king himself severed the head of John from his body with one stroke of the sword. But even a heart like his had some commiseration for Peter. The king paused to give him one more chance at life. But the youth bravely withstood the temptation. Once more the king's hand was raised. The sharp sword did its work, and Peter's body lay bleeding on the ground while his soul mounted up to heaven.

The bodies of the two martyred Franciscans were dragged in their headless condition about the city. Later some Christians gathered their remains and entombed them with great honor in the cathedral of Vich. Because of the many miracles performed by them throughout Spain, devotion to Blessed John and Peter was approved by Pope Clement XII. Their feast is observed on May twenty-fourth by the Franciscans, on the twenty-first by the Conventuals, and on the twenty-second by the Capuchins.

ON THE JOYS OF HEAVEN

1. The joys of heaven exclude all suffering. St. John writes of the inhabitants of heaven: "God shall wipe away all tears from their eyes. And death shall be no more, nor mourning, nor crying, nor sorrow shall be any more" (Apoc. 21,4). For that reason the two martyrs John and Peter eagerly longed for martyrdom. All sorrow is at an end in heaven. — Bear

manfully the sorrows of this life which are, after all, of short duration. 2. The joys of heaven exclude all struggle. We cannot pass through this life without a conflict. "The life of man upon earth is a warfare" (Job 7,1). Always there will be the struggle against evil, always the struggle for what is good, always the struggle with our fellowmen. But those who keep ever before their mind's eye the fact that heaven will bring eternal rest and blessed peace after the strife carry on the struggle with joy. — Do not grow faint on account of the warfare, but fight like a soldier of Christ. The joys of heaven consist principally in the beatific vision. "We shall see Him as He is" (1 Jn. 3,2). What that implies, no human tongue can tell nor portray. To behold God in His eternal beauty and goodness, in His omnipotence and wisdom, in His charity and mercy towards men, and immersed in a sea of bliss which is God, who can comprehend that? — Aspire, therefore, for what is eternal and heavenly, and often say: How loathsome is the world when I contemplate heaven!

PRAYER OF THE CHURCH

May the eternal crown of Thy martyrs gladden us, O Lord, and afford us an increase of virtue and faith; and may we be consoled by their manifold support. Through Christ our Lord. Amen.

MAY 26
ST. MARY ANN OF JESUS DE PAREDES
Virgin, Third Order

FTER the death of Mary Ann, or Mariana, of Paredes, a beautiful lily sprouted forth from her blood, and so she has been styled the Lily of Quito. But in far greater measure did she deserve the name because of the innocence of her life. She preserved it unsullied in the midst of a wicked world, carefully protecting it by the practice of rare austerities.

From her earliest childhood Mary Ann, who was born in 1618, felt altogether drawn to God and to heavenly things. Meanwhile she attached herself to the Immaculate Virgin with unbounded confidence and tender devotion. She received the habit of the Third Order from the Franciscans in her native town of Quito, Ecuador, and in consideration of her great virtue, she was permitted to take the three vows of religion. Then she repaired to her home where she led a life hidden in God and devoted to prayer and penance.

She quitted her home only when she went to attend divine services in church or when charity toward her neighbor required it. On such occasions she won the hearts of all whom she met, even the most depraved among them, by her polite and friendly manner, and succeeded in leading them back to the path of virtue. Incidentally it may be remarked, that almighty God favored His faithful servant with extraordinary mystical gifts in support of her apostolate. By means of the Sign of the Cross or by sprinkling holy water she restored many sick persons to health; she also raised a dead woman to life.

When the plague broke out, she offered her chaste young life as a sacrifice to God in behalf of the stricken citizens. God accepted the sacrifice. She died shortly afterwards, in the twenty-eighth year of her age, in 1645. She was beatified by Pope Pius IX, and canonized in 1950 by Pope Pius XII. The Franciscans and the Third Order Regular celebrate her feast on May twenty-sixth. (Cf. *Forum*, 1945, pp. 3-6.)

ON CONFIDENCE IN MARY

1. Mary wishes to help us. She proved that in the Incarnation of our Saviour. She knew that the mother of the Man of Sorrows would have to become the Mother of Sorrows, yet she acceded for the sake of the children of men, whom she loved most affectionately. That is why she uttered those most saving words: "Behold the handmaid of the Lord, be it done to me according to Thy word" (Lk. 1,38). How commendable it was, then, that Blessed Mary Ann clung with such fervor and fidelity to the Mother of God, the mother of all mankind. — Imitate her in the practice and recommend your chastity to Mary Immaculate.

2. Mary can help us. She can help us because she is the Mother of the eternal Son of God. St. Bonaventure cries out: "Thou canst do all things by Him and through Him." She is the intercessory omnipotence at the throne of God. Blessed Mary Ann experienced her power in an eminent degree. — Foster the most profound and filial confidence in the Blessed Mother of God.

3. Mary will help us especially in the time of danger. That was foretold by the words: "I will put enmities between thee and the woman" (Gen. 3,15). To the evil spirit Mary has become "terrible as an army set in array" (Cant. 6,3). If Satan contrives to destroy souls, Mary is God's appointed champion to save them for eternity. — Pledge yourself to be a good child of this good Mother, and you will insure your salvation.

PRAYER OF THE CHURCH

O God, who didst will that amid the allurements of this world Blessed Mary Ann should blossom forth in virginal purity and continual penance like a lily among thorns, grant, we beseech Thee, that through her merits and intercession we may shun vice and strive ever more and more to attain perfection. Through Christ our Lord. Amen.

MAY 27
BLESSED BENVENUTE OF RECANATI
Confessor, First Order

AT RECANATI in the old province of Piceno, which has given so many saints to the Franciscan Order, Benvenute was born of Christian parents, early in the thirteenth century. Reared in simplicity and piety, he did not care for the world and its pleasures. But the love of God waxed strong in him, and when he had grown to young manhood, he resolved to quit the world.

At the Franciscan convent in his native town he asked for admission as a lay brother, and admission was readily granted to this pious young man. In the convent Benvenute was above all concerned about laying a solid foundation in humility, the foundation of all virtues.

The mystery of the profound condescension of our Lord in the Blessed Sacrament had a marvelous attraction for him. On one occasion when he had to supply the place of the sacristan, he was so absorbed in contemplation in the morning after holy Mass, that he forgot himself and remained kneeling before the Blessed Sacrament, becoming aware of things around him only when it was nearly noon. The good brother was struck with fear. He had not prepared anything for the meal; what would he set before the brethren? But He who had detained him to partake of heavenly bread also provided for the bodily food of his brethren. When Benvenute got to the kitchen, an angel in the appearance of a beautiful young man greeted him with a courteous bow and pointed to the meal he had prepared. Benvenute served it, and all the brethren declared that they had never eaten better food.

But the incident made our Brother Cook all the more devout toward the Blessed Sacrament. He visited our Lord in the tabernacle as often as duty permitted. With the permission of his superiors, he communicated very often and derived such fruit from holy Communion that he seemed to be changed into Christ and to live only for God. Frequently he was filled with rapture and was permitted to embrace our Divine Lord in his arms.

A perfect model of all virtue for his brethren, and rich in grace, he passed to eternal bliss on May 5, 1289. At his grave his intercession was invoked in the most diverse needs, and many miracles constantly increased his veneration. Pope Pius VII permitted the Mass and Office in honor of Blessed Benvenute to be celebrated. His feastday is observed on May twenty-third by the Franciscans, on the fifth by the Conventuals, and on the fourteenth by the Capuchins.

ON VISITING THE MOST HOLY SACRAMENT

1. Consider the abundance of spiritual food Blessed Benvenute found in the Blessed Sacrament. That was the source of his virtues and sanctity. The hours that he could spend there were the sweetest hours of his life. For the benefit of all of us our Lord dwells in the Blessed Sacrament, according to His promise: "Behold I am with you all days, even to the consummation of the world" (Mt. 28,20). And to all the Holy Ghost says: "Taste and see that the Lord is sweet!" (Ps. 33,9). Our Saviour Himself invites us: "Come to Me, all you who labor and are burdened, and I will refresh you" (Mt. 11,28). Should that not induce us to visit Him often in the Blessed Sacrament? The King of heaven lives among us and receives everyone, just as in Bethlehem, where He received the poor shepherds as well as the holy Kings. — Is it not highly proper that we, too, should visit Him to pay Him homage and adore Him? What Christian could be indifferent and remain away?

2. Consider that it is not given to everybody to visit the Blessed Sacrament in the same manner. In the convent where the inmates dwell under the same roof with our dear Lord, they can and must visit Him more frequently than is possible for laymen; and those who live in the world and have the spare time should do it more frequently than those who have household duties to attend to. To go there, or to remain there too long and so neglect one's duty, would not be agreeable to our Saviour. It ought, however, to be the pleasure and the aim of every Christian to attend the public afternoon devotions held on Sundays and holydays. Christ assures us that it is His delight to remain with the children of men (Prov. 8,31), and can it be troublesome to us to go to Him? Whoever has genuine love for Him in his heart, will also greet Him as often as he passes a church, and will send Him a greeting if he sees a church at a distance. — Have you conscientiously visited our Lord in accordance with your circumstances?

Or have you found greater pleasure in Sunday afternoon visits of every other kind but visiting the Blessed Sacrament?

3. Consider the great profit we can derive from visiting the Blessed Sacrament. There the same living Lord dwells who once went about doing good in Palestine. His generosity has not been diminished, and His power is the same as it was then. According to the measure of your confidence you will also receive consolation from Him there. In the Blessed Sacrament our Lord is also our model for the most beautiful virtues. There Blessed Benvenute meditated on His humble seclusion, His poverty under the appearance of bread, His obedience to every priest, His patience at so much profanation, His holy captivity for love of us. Would that we followed his example and learned these virtues, drawing strength from the Blessed Sacrament to imitate them.

PRAYER OF THE CHURCH

O God of mercy, grant that we who celebrate the memory of Blessed Benvenute, may imitate his humble and devout life here on earth, and at his intercession may arrive at the blessed dwelling with Thee in heaven. Through Christ our Lord. Amen.

MAY 28
BLESSED GERARD OF VILLAMAGNA
Confessor, Third Order

BOUT the year 1200, Gerard was born of poor parents at Villamagna, not far from Florence. The parents were tillers of the soil and managed the fields of a wealthy family living in the city of Florence. As Gerard lost both his parents early in life, this family took the boy into their own home and taught him to live a pious and Christian life. The boy pleased his benefactors as much with his natural gifts as with the practice of every virtue.

Gerard had just about reached the age of young manhood, when a son of the family, who belonged to the Knights of Jerusalem, chose him as his companion for his journey to the Holy Land. In an encounter with the unbelievers, both were taken captive, and they were not ransomed before they endured much tribulation.

When his master died soon after, Gerard visited the holy places in Palestine and then returned to his country. There he lived in the cabin of his parents near Villamagna, in order to lead a humble and retired life. But not long afterwards he heeded the request of another Knight of Jerusalem, and joined him on a voyage to Syria. The ship on which they sailed with some twenty other knights, was pursued by pirates with far superior power, but through Gerard's earnest prayer, they were saved as by a miracle.

When Gerard had been in Jerusalem for some time, the superiors of the knight offered him, because of his virtue and piety, the privilege of joining the order as a brother servant, which he gladly did. In his new vocation he rendered the sick and the pilgrims so much charity and was withal so devout at prayer, that he was quite generally called the holy brother. But that wounded the humility of unassuming Gerard, with the result that he obtained the consent of his superiors to return to his native town in Italy.

There Gerard was invested with the habit of the Third Order — it is said that St. Francis himself gave it to him. Then Gerard withdrew to a hermitage near Villamagna. Here he led an extremely austere life, and received the gift of profound contemplation on the divine mysteries. But his charity urged him to devote himself also to the sick and the poor. He himself went from door to door and begged for them. In distributing the alms, he admonished them to lead a truly Christian life.

Gerard also proved his love for souls by visiting week after week three churches situated at a great distance from one another. At the first, he prayed for the holy souls in purgatory. At the second, he pleaded for the remission of his own sins. At the third, he prayed for grace and enlightenment for all believers and unbelievers. St. Leonard of Port Maurice in his day cherished one of these churches, located on Mt. Incontro, so highly that he built a friary there dedicated to holy retirement.

In his hermitage Gerard applied himself so continually to prayer upon his knees, that the latter were covered with thick calluses, as is recorded also of St. James the Apostle.

Rich in merits and regarded by all as a saint, Gerard died in the month of May, 1242, on the day he had previously mentioned to his confessor. Many miracles occurred at his grave, for which reason his hermitage was converted into a church. The veneration steadily accorded him for more than six hundred years was sanctioned by Pope Gregory XVI, in 1833. His feast is observed on May twenty-third by the Franciscans, on the thirteenth by the Conventuals, and on the fourteenth by the Third Order Regular. (Cf. *These Made Peace*, pp. 9-12.)

ON JUSTICE IN THE SIGHT OF GOD

1. One can truly say of Blessed Gerard that he was just before God. He gave to everybody just what was his due: to God his heart in faithful service and uninterrupted prayer, to his benefactors due thanks, to his master loyalty, to his superiors obedience, to the needy sympathy and mercy. Only with himself was he severe. But had Gerard done all this in order to find favor with men, it could not be counted as justice before God, because our Lord says: "Unless your justice abound more than that of the Scribes and Pharisees, you shall not enter into the kingdom of heaven" (Mt. 5,20). These people sought the praise of men. Blessed Gerard, however, fled from it. For that reason he was just before God, as were those simple servants of God whom Holy Scripture calls just — Zachary, Elizabeth, Simeon, St. Joseph, and others. — How do you stand in the matter of justice?

2. Consider that inasmuch as it seeks nothing from men, justice before God draws down the special love of the Most High. Almighty God loves everything He created, but it is said in a very special way: "The Lord loves the just" (Ps. 145,8). And again: "The souls of the just are in the hands of God" (Wisd. 3,1). "Whatsoever shall befall the just man, it shall not make him sad" (Prov. 12,21). Why not? Because he can be sure that God directs everything for the best of a just man. And in fact: "The fruit of the just man is a tree of life" (Prov. 11,30). "The just shall be in everlasting remembrance" (Ps. 111,7). Do we not see all this verified in Blessed Gerard? — How this ought to rouse our efforts to become just in the eyes of God!

3. Consider that of ourselves we cannot find justification before God. We have been conceived in iniquity (Ps. 50,7), and our personal sins make it necessary for us to pray to God daily: "Forgive us our trespasses." Blessed Gerard prayed that way too, and with that purpose he visited a church every week to pray for the forgiveness of his sins. But the saving death of Christ, in which the Just One has suffered for the unjust (1 Pet. 3,18), is our hope. Hence we sing with happy hearts: "We therefore entreat Thee to help Thy servants whom Thou hast redeemed by Thy precious Blood." Strengthened in the holy sacraments by the grace of Christ, and confident of Mary's protection, let us live in the fear of God and in justice before Him, so that one day we may rise with the just.

PRAYER OF THE CHURCH

O God, who through the constant remembrance of the sufferings of Thy

Son didst lead Blessed Gerard, Thy confessor, to the heights of contemplation, and rouse him to penance, grant us, Thy servants that we may follow in his footsteps and obtain the fruits of Thy redemption. Through the same Christ our Lord. Amen.

MAY 29
BLESSED STEPHEN AND RAYMOND OF NARBONNE
Martyrs, First Order

THE pernicious heresy of the Albigenses, named after the city of Albi in southern France, had caused the most frightful havoc. It was directed against all established authority in the Church as well as in the State. Pope Innocent III complained that the heretics were worse than the Turks, and St. Bernard described the sad state of affairs produced by them as follows: "The churches are empty, the people are without priests, the sacraments are not respected; thus the people are dying without the assistance of the Church, without penance and conversion."

The popes, as supreme guardians and fathers of Christendom, had already applied measures of mercy and of severity. St. Dominic and his companions had labored for seven years at the conversion of the heretics and had achieved much success. But the sect, especially in the neighborhood of Toulouse still had many adherents who secretly sought to spread its baneful poison still farther.

To counteract their work Pope Gregory IX sent eleven missionaries from different orders to the scene about the year 1240. Among them were the two Friars Minor Stephen and Raymond. At an earlier date, Stephen had been the abbot of a wealthy Benedictine monastery, but out of love for the poverty of Christ he had resigned his position and become a Friar Minor. Now he and his companion were ready to sacrifice their lives in order to win back to Christ erring and misled souls. With great zeal they put the faithful on their guard against the poison of heresy. They strengthened the wavering, and exhorted the perverted to return to the bosom of Holy Church.

But this roused the hatred of the obdurate Albigenses, and their godless leaders thirsted for the blood of the zealous missionaries. By a ruse, the latter were lured, as if to a parley, to the palace of the count of Toulouse, who favored the sect. Hardly had they passed the gate and entered the outer court, when hired murderers sprang from their hiding places and fell upon the unarmed victims. With devilish fury they inflicted the most gruesome butchery upon them.

No complaint was heard from the lips of the holy men. Together they intoned the Te Deum with cheerful countenance, and continued to sing with jubilant hearts until their souls ascended to heaven, there to join in the eternal song of praise of all the saints.

The martyrdom occurred on the vigil of the Ascension of our Lord in 1242. From the first the faithful rendered the honor paid to martyrs to the treacherously murdered friars, and at Avignon their feast was kept every year with great solemnity. The veneration always paid to these martyrs of the Catholic faith was approved by Pope Pius IX in 1862. All three branches of the First Order observe the feast of these martyrs on May twenty-ninth.

ON OBEDIENCE TO THE POPE

1. In the deplorable state brought about by the heresy of the Albigenses, consider the evil results which result from disobedience to the pope. The pope is the representative of Christ on earth, and the visible head of the Church, through whom Christ wished to dispense His blessings to the world. So, in a certain sense, it can be said of him what was said of Christ, that he is the vine and we are the branches. He who separates himself from him, may be compared to a severed branch, which "shall be cast forth and shall wither; they shall gather him up and cast him into the fire, and he burns" (Jn. 15,6). What a warning against all disobedience to the supreme head of the Church!

2. Consider how fittingly we call the pope the Holy Father, that is, he who is placed over us as a father to lead us to holiness. Our holy Founder St. Francis, who wished to open up the paths of holiness for the various classes of men in his three orders, required therefore, above all, that his followers should render obedience to the pope, and promised such obedience in his own name and in the name of his children. We should, therefore, cheerfully comply with any instructions given by the Holy Father. What he warns us to avoid, we should avoid. What he warns us to do, we should do with pleasure. Should his words require a sacrifice of us, willingly should we make it. The holy martyrs Stephen and Raymond made the sacrifice of their lives in obedience to the pope, who sent them on their mission. The crown of glory is their reward for it.

3. Consider that the pope is our supreme and unerring teacher in matters which pertain to Christian faith and morals. How fortunate for us, amid all the doubt and uncertainty of this material world, to have a certain and

infallible leader in the things which are of the gravest importance, and upon which everything finally depends. Should anyone offer objections on points of faith and morals, no matter what they be, even though we cannot refute them or see through them, we should say with St. Augustine: "Where Rome has spoken, the matter is settled. By this faith I stand, for this faith I lay down my life."

PRAYER OF THE CHURCH
O God, with whose love the holy martyrs Stephen and Raymond were inflamed and succumbed to the swords of the godless in defense of the Faith, grant, we beseech Thee, that through their intercession we may remain steadfast in the Faith, and ever love Thee with our whole heart. Through Christ our Lord. Amen.

𝕺𝕭𝕺𝕭𝕺𝕭𝕺𝕭𝕺𝕭𝕺𝕭𝕺

MAY 30
ST. FERDINAND THE KING
Confessor, Third Order

ING FERDINAND III of León and Castile in Spain, cousin of King St. Louis of France (the mothers of the holy kings were sisters), is one of the great glories of the Third Order. Ferdinand was not yet twenty years old when he attained to the government of the kingdom. He gathered about him a royal council of the most dependable elderly men, in order to have their opinion on all matters of administration. On the advice of his mother, who remained a true guardian spirit to him until her death, he married Beatrice, daughter of the German Emperor Philip of Swabia. She was one of the most devout princesses of that period.

From the beginning of his reign, Ferdinand, although still so young, gave evidence of the finest traits in a monarch: generosity, justice, gentleness. He was always concerned about keeping his subjects free from any unfair burdens. Once when resources were needed to fight the Mohammedans, one of his councillors suggested that a special tax for the purpose be imposed. "God forbid," said the king, "that I should follow your advice. I am more afraid of the curse of a single poor woman who would be oppressed by it, than I am of the whole Mohammedan army."

Throughout his life he had to wage war against the Mohammedans almost continually. They had established themselves in Spain for five centuries, threatening to spread their control and to exterminate

Christianity. Filled with anxiety more for the kingdom of God than for his temporal dominion, Ferdinand armed himself and forced back the enemies of the Christian name farther and farther. His arms had very unusual success. But the king also endeavored to make himself worthy of success. He insisted on discipline and Christian conduct among his soldiers. He himself prayed, fasted, and scourged his body when in the field, that God might favor him. He honored Mary, the Help of Christians, with great confidence, and had her image carried at the head of his troops as their standard. He converted the great mosque in the re-conquered city of Cordova into a beautiful church dedicated to the Mother of God. The archbishop of Toledo accompanied him on all his campaigns, and all ecclesiastical affairs in the re-conquered territory were arranged according to the archbishop's directions.

Ferdinand was arming himself for another campaign when he was attacked with a serious illness. In the spirit of humility and penance he prepared himself for death. He had all the marks of royalty removed from his room, and with a rope tied about his neck he acknowledged himself a poor sinner, receiving the last sacraments with touching devotion. Then he admonished his eldest son to be a father to his younger brothers and sisters, always to treat his stepmother, Ferdinand's second consort, with due honor, and to be a kind ruler to his subjects.

Ferdinand died on May 30, 1252, at Seville, aged fifty-two years. In accordance with his personal wishes, his body was clothed in the habit of the Third Order, and thus appareled, he was laid to rest in the cathedral of Seville, amid the tears of his people. Numerous miracles occurred at his tomb. At his canonization in 1671 his body was found still incorrupt. The three branches of the First Order and the Third Order Regular celebrate the feast of St. Ferdinand on May thirtieth. (Cf. *These Made Peace*, pp. 45-47.)

ON TAKING ADVICE

1. Consider how wisely St. Ferdinand acted as a young king, in gathering trusted men about him as counselors. "Designs are brought to nothing where there is no counsel: but when there are many counselors, they are established" (Prov. 15,22). So many people are quick to give advice, believe even that they can advise the temporal and spiritual authorities including the pope and the president. But they themselves are not ready to take advice, so that often their own temporal affairs are in a bad way, and their souls are still worse off. "I have often heard," says Thomas a Kempis (1,9), "that it is safer to listen to advice and take it, than to give it. Not to accept

the advice of others where reason or good sense requires it, is a sign of pride and self-will." — Do you give advice rather than take it?

2. Mind that one must consider well whom one asks for advice. Tobias said to his son: "Seek counsel always of a wise man" (Tob. 4,19). Ask counsel of conscientious persons and of such who are experienced in the matters at hand, not only such who will speak according to your pleasure or flatter your passions, nor such who know nothing about the matter. One does not seek advice from a religious about running one's business, nor from a layman about entering the religious life. St. Ferdinand asked statesmen for advice in matters of the administration, but an archbishop in church affairs. Do likewise. Always seek advice where knowledge of the matter under consideration goes hand in hand with conscientiousness. "If the blind lead the blind, both fall into the pit" (Mt. 15,14).

3. Consider that a person may not follow all the advice given him, even as St. Ferdinand did not do so. But never to be satisfied with the advice received and always to keep asking others, usually proceeds either from conceit or from sensuality, which want to hear only agreeable advice in order to have an excuse for that which they prompt. Thus says Thomas a Kempis again: "It is true, everybody likes to act according to his own pleasure, and yields more readily to such who agree with him; but if God be with us, we shall at times have to yield our own opinion." In personal affairs our own judgment is often very partial, and our self-love is frequently the enemy against whom we must be mostly on our guard. God's grace and willing obedience to good advice will protect us from that enemy.

PRAYER OF THE CHURCH

O Lord, who didst grant to Blessed Ferdinand, Thy confessor, to fight Thy battles and to conquer the enemies of the Faith, grant that we, helped by his intercession, may be delivered from our enemies, both in body and soul. Through Christ our Lord. Amen.

MAY 31
BLESSED VITALIS OF BASTIA
Confessor, Third Order

HE little village of Bastia, about three miles from Assisi, just off the main road to Perugia, was the birthplace of Blessed Vitalis. His good parents implanted in his heart the seed of the love of God; and, as he began to earn a living by the toil of his hands, the spirit of prayer grew within him. Fearful lest he might offend God and bring harm to his soul while living in human society, he decided to become a hermit.

He sold what little possessions he had, gave the proceeds to the poor, joined the Third Order Secular of St. Francis, and then retired, about 1470, to a remote spot in the hills behind Assisi, where there was a little chapel of Our Lady called Santa Maria di Lendiola. In this solitary place he remained for the rest of his life, spending his time in prayer and meditation and mortifying his body by long watches and severe fasts. His food consisted of vegetables and his drink of water. At times he was sorely tempted to return to the world and enjoy its comforts and pleasures; but by contemplating the things of heaven and invoking the aid of his heavenly Mother Mary, he always emerged victorious and regained serenity of soul.

Vitalis died on the last day of May, 1491, and was buried in his beloved chapel of Our Lady. The people in and around Assisi knew him only as "San Vitale," and numerous miracles were wrought at his tomb. A century later, in 1599, his relics were transferred to the cathedral of San Rufino in Assisi; and the veneration of the holy hermit as "Blessed" was approved. While he has no place in the Franciscan calendar, his feast is observed on May 31 in the diocese of Assisi and by certain congregations of the Third Order Regular. (Cf. Biersack, p. 172; *These Made Peace*, p. 130.)

ON OUR LADY'S INTERCESSION

1. In the life of Blessed Vitalis we see again how remarkably our Lady comes to the assistance of her clients. She is the Mother of Christendom, appointed as such by God Himself when He made her His own Mother. Her maternal heart is concerned about the cares of her devout cl: Holy Church teaches as much when it places upon her lips th' love them who love me; and they that in the morning ear' shall find me" (Prov. 8,17). Christians have so of gracious charity that St. Bernard could say: "O r'

was it known that anyone who fled to thy protection was left unaided." — Should this not encourage us to take refuge with her in all our needs? Consider that Mary's power is as great as her charity. St. Bonaventure, addressing her as the Mother of Christ, says: "Thou canst do all things by Him and in Him." The Son of God was subject to her while He was here on earth. Could He refuse her a request where all power has been given Him? Just as God in His power can do all things that He wills, so can Mary do it by her intercession. At her request Christ worked His first miracle on earth; and at her intercession He is equally willing to send us remarkable help from heaven. The hermit Blessed Vitalis experienced this. Where human aid fails, Mary can assist us. — With what confidence should we call upon her for help!

2. Consider that especially in tribulation of soul and danger of sin Mary can be relied upon to lend her aid. To preserve the purity of his soul was the main reason why Blessed Vitalis fled from the dangers and temptations of a deceitful world to the isolated chapel of Santa Maria di Lendiola, and Mary assisted him in keeping his soul unsullied throughout life. Mary is the woman of whom almighty God spoke to the serpent in the garden of paradise: "I will put enmities between you and the woman" (Gen. 3,15). Just as the devil goes about seeking to ruin souls, so Mary is ever on the alert to put him to flight. She terrifies hell "as an army set in array" (Cant. 6,3). Whoever calls upon her with confidence will be saved. She guides her faithful clients through the dangers of life to her blessed company in heaven.

PRAYER OF THE CHURCH
(Feast of the Holy Name of Mary)

Grant, we beseech Thee, O almighty God, that even as Thy faithful people rejoice in the name of the most holy Virgin Mary, and enjoy her protection, so, by her loving intercession, they may be delivered from all evils here on earth, and be found worthy to attain to eternal joy in heaven. Tʰ ` Christ our Lord. Amen.

JUNE

JUNE 1
ST. ANGELA MERICI
Virgin, Third Order

NGELA Merici was born in the year 1470 at Decenzano, northern Italy, on the banks of Lake Garda. Even as a child she served God very fervently. She so loved modesty and purity of heart that she was quite generally venerated as a little saint in her native town.

When she was in her thirteenth year, she entered the Third Order of St. Francis. Soon afterwards she took the vow of perpetual chastity, renounced all her possessions, and wished to live only on alms. Along with this she practiced great austerities, slept on the bare earth, and fasted almost continuously on bread and water. Sometimes holy Communion was her only food over a period of several days.

When she was twenty-three years old, Angela was praying one day in a secluded place, and there she had a vision of a friend who had died a short while before. Her friend prophesied that Angela would be the foundress of a religious institute which would be devoted to the education of youth, and destined to do an unlimited amount of good for the kingdom of God. That proved to be a great incentive for Angela, not only to lead a life of contemplation, but also to serve her fellowmen in active work.

She gathered about her a group of young women, and together they went out to give religious instruction to little children, to help the poor, and to care for the sick. Often there were great sinners among those to whom she ministered, and in such cases she did not cease instructing, entreating, and encouraging them until they were reconciled with God and began to lead a new life.

Her saintly conduct and the profound knowledge she had, concerning even the most difficult questions of theology, caused her to be greatly respected by high and low and to be regarded as a saint. In order to escape such honor, Angela left her native town of Decenzano in 1516, and went to Brescia, where a wealthy but pious merchant offered her a house. There she lived absorbed in God until the year 1524.

371

St. Angela Merici

At that time Angela was seized with an ardent desire to visit the Holy Land, just as our holy Father St. Francis once was. She visited Jerusalem, Mt. Calvary, and the other holy places with uncommon devotion. She returned by way of Rome, in order to pray at the tombs of the apostles, and thus gain the great jubilee indulgence. Pope Clement VII, who was not unaware of her sanctity, wished to detain her in Rome, and did not permit her to return to Brescia until he understood by divine inspiration that in Brescia lay the field of labor for which God had destined her.

Due to disturbances caused by war, Angela could not undertake her appointed work until 1531. On November 25, 1535, her pious society was founded as the religious congregation of St. Ursula, who was the special patron of their work. The congregation, known also as Ursulines, spread rapidly and is active in many countries, also in America, where its institutions for the Christian education of feminine youth are blessed with much success.

When Angela reached the age of seventy, the day and hour of her death were revealed to her. She received the last sacraments with great fervor, and was then rapt in ecstasy. While pronouncing the holy name of Jesus, she departed this life in the very hour that had been foretold to her. She was laid out in the habit of the Third Order, holding in her hand the pilgrim's staff she had used in the Holy Land. Thus she reposes in a side chapel of the parish church of St. Afra in Brescia. Pope Clement XIII beatified her, and on March 24, 1807, Pope Pius VII canonized her in St. Peter's Church, Rome. The Franciscans and Conventuals celebrate the feast of St. Angela on June first, but the Capuchins on May thirty-first. (Cf. Johnston, *Cameo of Angela*; *These Made Peace*, pp. 187-190.)

ON THE CONVERSION OF SINNERS

1. Consider that St. Angela, whose pure soul would have preferred to devote itself exclusively to the instruction of youth, did not disdain to interest herself for love of God in depraved human beings and great sinners, in order to convert them. As a matter of fact, there can be nothing more pleasing to God than to lead a sinner back to Him. Really, the reason why our heavenly Father sent His only-begotten Son into the world was, that no one should be lost, but that all should have eternal life through Him (Jn. 3,16). The Son of God Himself declares: "I came not to call the just" — they do not need it — "but sinners to penance" (Lk. 5,32). If you can look with indifference on the ruination of sinners and not concern yourself at all with their conversion, then you do not truly love God, and you are not a good Christian, no matter how numerous are your pious

practices.

2. Consider the great personal benefit you derive from interesting yourself in the conversion of sinners. First of all you will then have discharged your duty, especially if you have any responsibility in this matter, because the Prophet, writing of superiors, says: "But if you tell the wicked man that he may be converted from his wicked ways, and he be not converted from his way, he shall die in his iniquity, but you have delivered your soul!" (Ezech. 33,9). But if, by the grace of God, you have succeeded in converting a sinner, then you have acquired invaluable treasures for yourself, for St. James (5,20) writes: "He who causes a sinner to be converted from the error of his way, shall save his soul from death, and shall cover a multitude of sins." —What an incentive, especially for those who themselves have once walked the road of sin!

3. Consider by what means the sinner is converted. Not by corrections, sermons, and reproaches can one hope to achieve this end. If it is tried with bitterness and abusive words, it will serve only to make the sinner more set. A hearty, kind, and gentle word generally does more good than severity. St. Francis de Sales used to say: "One can catch more flies with a drop of honey than with a cask of vinegar." But it is also necessary to pray fervently to God, "who inclines hearts as the divisions of waters" (Prov. 21,1), and to invoke Mary's intercession for the conversion of the soul. Mary is the Refuge of Sinners and the Mother of Mercy. Appeals to her most pure heart have resulted in the most astounding conversions. You will also find grace taking effect in a remarkable way if you aim to appease the divine justice for the sinner by means of works of penance. St. Francis Xavier used to do that. But the most effective appeal to the heart of the sinner is the example of a holy and perfect life, of love, patience, faithful performance of duty, and sincere piety, which we give him. In this way St. Angela converted sinners, St. Monica converted her husband and her son Augustine; and in this same way the sisters in hospitals, like real angels of mercy, still convert numerous souls to God. — May St. Angela help us arrive at the joys of heaven in this way ourselves and be instrumental in helping others get there too.

PRAYER OF THE CHURCH

O God, who through Blessed Angela didst cause a new company of holy virgins to grow up within Thy Church, grant us through her intercession to lead angelic lives, so that, renouncing all earthly joys, we may deserve to enjoy those that are eternal. Through Christ our Lord. Amen.

JUNE 2
BLESSED HERCULAN OF PIAGALE
Confessor, First Order

T THE TIME the Franciscan Order shone with the glory of such saints as Bernardin of Siena and John Capistran, it was adorned also by Blessed Herculan, a celebrated preacher of penance. He was the scion of a wealthy family of Piagale in the neighborhood of Perugia. As a young man he nobly sacrificed all that the world offered him in order to work for God and the salvation of souls under the standard of St. Francis. He received the holy habit in the convent of Sarteano, and there he had the great Albert of Sarteano as his teacher.

When he received holy orders and was appointed to the office of preaching, he proved worthy of so great a master. His sermons soon attracted crowds of people and brought about extraordinary conversions. The most frequent topic of his sermons was the sufferings of Jesus Christ, because he recognized the subject as the most effectual means for the conversion of sinners.

Once on a Good Friday, in the city of Aquila, he so touchingly portrayed the sufferings which the God-man took upon Himself out of love for sinners that the whole congregation broke out in tears. A woman, who was standing near the pulpit and was less affected than the others, said to the enthusiastic preacher: "Father Herculan, there has been weeping enough, do not cause any more tears." "What?" cried the saint. "Never can we weep enough over the sufferings of Jesus Christ. These tears must cleanse our souls. Did our Lord not shed more blood than we can ever shed tears?"

He not only preached about the sufferings of Christ, he also meditated on them day and night, and amid burning tears pleaded the while for mercy for sinners. To this devotion he joined the most severe mortification, fasting sometimes so continuously that holy Communion seemed to be his only nourishment.

While he was preaching in the cathedral of Lucca during the Lent of 1430, the town was besieged by the Florentines. Herculan proved that he was as much concerned for the physical welfare of those to whom he had been sent as he was for their souls. He encouraged the inhabitants to defend their city with courage and perseverance.

When famine broke out, he urged the rich to share their provisions with the poor. By divine inspiration he foretold that a new supply of provisions would arrive at Easter, and soon also assistance against their enemies. And so it happened. At Easter, grain was successfully brought into town, and soon the Milanese came to the assistance of the city, the Florentines withdrawing in haste.

In gratitude to Father Herculan, the city of Lucca offered to establish three convents of his order in its territory. In one of these convents Herculan died after untiring and constant labor, on May 28, 1451. Many miracles glorified his tomb. In 1860 Pope Pius IX sanctioned the veneration paid to him since his death. The Franciscans and the Capuchins celebrate the feast of Blessed Herculan on June second.

THE SUFFERINGS OF CHRIST SHOULD LEAD US TO PENANCE

1. St. Bernard says somewhere in a parable: "As a boy I played in the courtyard of the king's castle. There I saw a beautiful young man going across the yard, laden with a heavy cross, and many people were around him. I was told that he was the son of the king, and that he had volunteered to make reparation for me on the cross though it was I who had been condemned to death. Not another moment could I go on with my game, but I ran weeping to the king's son, ready to follow him even unto death." — Are there not many people living here on God's earth as if they were children at play, since in all things they follow only their good pleasure and comfort? But when we look at the Son of God, who "has loved us and has delivered Himself for us" (Eph. 5,2), then truly our delight in play ought to leave us as we penitently follow our Saviour laden with the cross. Do you also look up to Him in order to put an end to your indifference?

2. Consider that Blessed Herculan described the sufferings of Christ to move the faithful not only to tears of tender compassion but to true contrition for their sins. Thus our Lord Himself spoke on the Sorrowful Way to the women of Jerusalem: "Weep not over Me but weep for yourselves and for your children" (Lk. 23, 28). In memory of Christ's Passion, weep also for your sins and for those of your children, which gave cause to that bitter suffering. Reflect further, that if our innocent Saviour suffered so much for the sins of others, what will guilty man have to suffer in eternity if he has not satisfied divine justice to the best of his power? "Bring forth, therefore, fruits worthy of penance!" (Lk. 3,8).

3. Consider that the sufferings of Christ should in future preserve us from every sin. Of those who relapse and commit sin anew, the Apostle says they are "crucifying again to themselves the Son of God and making Him a mockery" (Heb. 6,6). If you remembered your suffering Saviour, would

you by sins of the flesh scourge anew your bleeding and bruised Jesus? Would you by pride and self-will again crown with thorns His painfully pierced head? Would you again drive nails into His transfixed hands by acts of injustice, and again nail His holy feet to the cross by forbidden parties? Indeed you would not. The lively remembrance of the sufferings of Christ would strengthen you to remain faithful in His service until death.

PRAYER OF THE CHURCH
O God, who by the ministry of Blessed Herculan didst urge the faithful to despise this world, and to be mindful of the sufferings of Thy Divine Son, grant us the grace of despising earthly things and of bearing our cross here below, that one day we may attain to the possession of the eternal blessings. Through Christ our Lord. Amen.

JUNE 3
ST. JOAN OF ARC
Virgin, Third Order

HE DAUGHTER of a peasant farmer, Joan of Arc (Jeanne d'Arc or Darc) was born on January 6, 1412, at Domremy, on the left bank of the Meuse, in Lorraine. At an early age she became a shepherdess. While tending her flock, she sought to live a life of close and constant union with God. She spent much time in prayer and rose to a high degree of contemplation.

Although documentary proof that she was a Tertiary is lacking, there is no doubt whatever that she lived like a Tertiary; and her contemporaries actually called her a Tertiary. Existing evidence establishes "a serious probability in the eyes of the most impartial critics, while others cannot help seeing in it a well grounded motive of certainty" that St. Joan of Arc was a member of the Third Order of St. Francis. "There are plenty of historical questions no better founded" than her membership in the Third Order, and yet they are "commonly accepted" (Cf. Forum, 1932, p. 119).

When Charles VII succeeded to the throne of France in 1422, the so-called Hundred Years War between France and England was still being waged; and the new king was recognized south of the Loire only, while in the north Henry VI of England, who was still an infant, was the acknowledged lord. In 1428 the English began the siege of Orléans. At this

time, Joan of Arc, who was only sixteen years old, was summoned by
heavenly voices to pacify her country which was torn also by civil strife
and to deliver it out of the hands of the English. Leaving her home in
February, 1429, she convinced the doubting Charles VII of the veracity of
her divinely inspired mission in March, entered Orléans at the head of a
small army in April, and by violent sorties relieved the city in May. From
that time on, she was called "the Maid of Orléans" or La Pucelle.

Joan of Arc then drove the English from the Loire, Auxerre, Troyés,
and Chalons, and conducted Charles VII to Reims, where he was crowned
in July, the same year. Since King Charles VII hesitated to continue the
war after a futile siege of Paris, Joan left the court in March, 1430. Two
months later she was taken a prisoner by the Burgundians and sold by
them to the English. Before a carefully packed ecclesiastical court she was
tried for heresy and witchcraft and found guilty. Handed over to the
secular arm, she was burned at the stake on May 31, 1431.

A revision of her mock trial, ordered by Charles VIII in 1456, declared
her innocent. She was beatified in 1909, and canonized in 1920. Two years
later, she was declared Patroness of France. Her feast is celebrated
throughout France on May thirtieth; and the Third Order Regular observes
it on June third.

ON CHRISTIAN FORTITUDE

1. Reflect on the courage of St. Joan of Arc, who, although a weak maiden,
heeded the call of God to deliver her country from the invading enemy,
and before an unjust judge steadfastly, even in the face of death, defended
her mission as coming from God. Truly one can point to her when Holy
Scripture asks: "Who can find a valiant woman?" (Prov. 13,10). If those
who have a special task to perform, a vocation to the religious life, for
instance, would, in the face of difficulties, draw upon the courage of
humility, there would not be so many desertions or apostasies which later
cause such bitter remorse. Rather, we should be able with St. Joan of Arc
to gain many blessings for ourselves and for others, and at the end of our
life we too could address our heavenly Father in the words of our Saviour:
"I have fulfilled the work which Thou hast given me to do" (Jn. 17,4). —
Will the day come when you will be able to say these words?
2. Consider that Christian fortitude must be practiced with every virtue.
That is why it is called one of the cardinal virtues. It is the virtue with
which we must overcome all the difficulties and the opposition which we
encounter in trying to do good. Here in the world, virtue and goodness are
continually meeting with difficulty and opposition. The steadfastness with

which we bear these trials makes up our merits. Heroic Judith urged the Israelites to persevere when she said, "So did our fathers and all who have pleased God, pass through many tribulations, remaining faithful" (Judith 8,23). — Can we not do what they did?

3. Consider how Christian fortitude is acquired. Work faithfully at the task assigned to you. If your conscience is witness to your fidelity, then you can with unbounded confidence expect God to do His part. Without that reliance there is no fortitude. "A troubled conscience always forecasts grievous things" (Wisd. 17,10). He who does his work with an upright heart, and aims only to do God's will, knows that help will always be at hand when needed, and he may say with the Psalmist: "In te Domine speravi — In Thee, O Lord, have I hoped, let me never be put to confusion" (Ps. 70,1).

PRAYER OF THE CHURCH
(Over the People on Tuesday of Passion Week)

Grant us, we beseech Thee, O Lord, perseverance in obedience to Thy will, that in our days the people who serve Thee may increase both in merit and in number. Through Christ our Lord.

✺✺✺✺✺✺✺✺✺✺

JUNE 4
ST. VINCENTA GEROSA AND ST. MARY BARTHOLOMEA CAPITANIO
Virgins, Third Order

 ARY CATHARINE FRANCES GEROSA, the later Mother Vincenta, was born October 29, 1784, in the diocese of Brixen, in the Austrian Tyrol. Her father was a prosperous merchant of leather goods. As a Franciscan Tertiary, she continued to live in the parental home until she was forty-eight. Every morning she attended holy Mass; at noon she visited the Poor Clare chapel; and in the evening she was back for the Angelus. After the death of her parents, she worked as a servant girl in the house of her uncle until she was thirty. The family fortune then passed into her hands, because her brothers and sisters had died; and she opened the doors of her home to the poor, distributing grain, clothes, and money to them, and serving dinner to twelve poor persons three times a week. The sick and girls who had fallen into a life of sin were the special object of her solicitude. When she inherited a small house on Lake Iseo, in Lombardy, in 1823, she transformed it into a hospital and presented it to the French Daughters of Charity. Nine years later, in 1832, she met Mary Bartholomea Capitanio and joined her in founding a new religious sisterhood.

Mary Bartholomea Capitanio was born in 1807 at Lovere on Lake Iseo in the diocese of Brescia, which at the time was in Austrian territory. While her mother was an exemplary Catholic, her father was given to excessive drink; but by self-sacrificing efforts and loving care of him when he was sick, she was able to cure her father of his bad habit. Mary Bartholomea wanted to join the Poor Clare nuns from whom she received her education, but her parents refused to give their permission; and so, with the approval of her father confessor, she took the vow of chastity privately. After attending a normal school, she received a teacher's diploma; and, as a Franciscan Tertiary, she devoted herself to the education of children. Much good was accomplished among her charges by a society which she founded in honor of St. Aloysius Gonzaga, whose ancestral home was not far from Lovere.

Mary Bartholomea was twenty-five, when she and Vincenta Gerosa founded the Sisters of Charity of the Little Child Mary in 1832. Neither of them wanted to be the first superior. Vincenta, who was almost twice as old as Mary Bartholomea, insisted: "I am good for nothing. If God wishes me to become a religious, I desire to comply. But you must be the superior. I know nothing. I have no head. My role is to obey, to wash and care for the sick." And she won her point.

The two of them occupied a humble dwelling in Brescia which housed a hundred orphans; and while Mary Bartholomea continued her work as a teacher, Vincenta devoted herself to hospital work, They placed themselves under the direction of the parish priest, and adopted the rule of the Daughters of St. Vincent de Paul. Others soon joined them. As superior, Mary Bartholomea allowed herself no leisure, although she was a victim of tuberculosis. Her spiritual notes and conferences to her sisters show that she had attained a high degree of holiness. She ceased working only when ordered to do so by her physician. Four months later, on July 26, 1833, she died, only twenty-six years old.

Mother Vincenta now had to take over the duties of a superior, but wished to be called only senior sister. Humility remained an outstanding trait of hers. "I am nothing but a great ignoramus," she said. "We are only poor girls, whom God has asked to do a bit of work. As for me, I spoil everything I touch." But she saw her community grow at a very rapid rate. In ten years it had forty houses in Italy. They were invited to Milan, and began to open houses in the missions of the Milan Foreign Mission

Society. In 1841 Pope Gregory XVI made these sisters independent of the French Daughters of Charity. Six years later Mother Vincenta was called to her reward. In 1943 her sisterhood counted more than seven thousand members in all parts of the world.

Mary Bartholomea was beatified in 1926 and Vincenta in 1933. Both of them were canonized in 1950. St. Mary Bartholomea's feast is observed on July twenty-sixth, and that of St. Vincenta is celebrated on June fourth. (Cf. *Forum*, 1947, pp. 171-173; Biersack, pp. 116 and 170; *These Made Peace*, p. 235.)

CONCERNING ENVY

1. Consider how beautiful were the sentiments of the two saints, St. Mary Bartholomea and St. Vincenta, who vied with one another in avoiding the position of superior of their newly founded community. How odious, on the other hand, is the vice of envy with which so many hearts, even among Christians, are filled. A spiteful person rejoices at public misfortune so long as it does not strike him. On the other hand, he is sad at the good fortune God grants to others, and begrudges it to them. "His eye is evil, because God is good." The envious person may be called a child of the devil. "By the envy of the devil, death came into the world. And they follow him who are of his side" (Wisd. 2,24-25). — If you detect but a trace of it in your heart, tear it out.

2. Consider to what the wicked vice of envy leads. It changed an angel into Satan, the foremost devil. Out of envy Cain slew Abel, Joseph was sold by his brothers, the high-priests brought Christ to the cross. Great envy makes great woe. It still does so daily. But the envious person causes the greatest suffering to himself. The vice gnaws at his heart already here on earth, the way rust corrodes iron and worms burrow in wood; and hereafter, his portion will be the worm that never dies, and the fire that is never extinguished. For St. Chrysostom says: "Even though a person may preserve chastity, though he may fast, sleep on the floor, yes, even work miracles, if his heart is infected with envy, he cannot escape the fire which is prepared for the devil unless he disengages himself of this vice." — Does that fire threaten you, too?

3. Consider the means to overcome this wicked passion. If you sense any stirring of envy in your heart, remember from whom it comes and to what it leads. Consider, too, how odious envy is, since you would have to be ashamed of yourself if others noticed it in your heart. Reject it as you would an indecent temptation. Beware, also, lest you ever stir up envy in the hearts of children or other persons. Thank almighty God for the good

things He has given your neighbor, and pray that He may fortify you as well as your neighbor and all men in the cordial charity proper to children of the same Father.

PRAYER OF THE CHURCH (Seventeenth Sunday after Pentecost)

Grant, we beseech Thee, O Lord, that Thy people may shun all contact with the devil, and with a pure mind follow Thee, the only Good. Through Christ our Lord. Amen.

JUNE 5
BLESSED FELIX OF NICOSIA
Confessor, First Order

 ELIX was born at Nicosia, Sicily, of poor parents. His father was a mender of shoes. But they were good, honest people, who reared their children to be good Christians and useful persons. Their lessons were particularly well received by Felix. His heart was like soft wax, in which the admonitions of his parents were deeply engraved. In a very special way he loathed all lying and indecent speech. Out of veneration for the Passion of Christ, he fasted, even as a boy, on the Fridays of March. In honor of the Blessed Virgin Mary, he prayed the rosary every Saturday.

When the boy was old enough, his father sent him as an apprentice to an able shoemaker. There Felix distinguished himself by great modesty, docility, industry, and patience. When his companions joked about his seriousness and piety, he had a friendly answer for them in such a way that his good master took great pleasure in him.

As he grew older, Felix realized how many dangers there were in the world for virtue. So when his parents died, he applied at the Capuchin convent at the age of twenty for admission. He was refused. But Felix persevered. He prayed, waited, and at opportune times renewed his plea again and again. Finally, after eight years, he obtained the long-desired admission. On October 19, 1743, he was invested at Mistretta.

Now Felix strove to be a true servant of God. His mind was continually set on God alone. He entertained a lowly estimate of himself and welcomed it if others slighted him. Austere as he was, he desired to undertake special works of penance in addition to those practiced in common; however, in obedience he desisted from them.

After his profession Felix was sent to the friary of Nicosia, his native city, to assist the brother who gathered alms. He always showed himself very willing, gladly taking the greater portion of the burden on himself. He kept up that attitude even when he was an older brother. He did not trouble about his relatives and acquaintances in the city. He usually prayed while on his rounds, and in the friary he was happy if he could spend his free time before the Blessed Sacrament. There he was sometimes rapt in ecstasy so that he was seen raised several feet from the ground.

He was always ready for any assignment given to him in obedience. One time his superior said he should go to a certain artist and have a painting made of himself. Felix started out at once. Favored by God as he seemed to be, it was found well to subject him to the most extraordinary trials. But his virtue always proved to be genuine. He foretold future events, cured many sick persons by his prayers and the Sign of the Cross, and was sometimes found to be in more than one place at the same time.

Felix had lived in the order in the greatest perfection for twenty-four years when God called him to eternal bliss. After receiving the last sacraments, he asked his superior to give him his blessing as a father and a priest before he departed this life. His superior tested his virtue even then, and told him not to ask for the blessing until he had been told to depart.

That evening the physician came and felt his pulse, and there was no sign of life any more; but Felix still lived. When the doctor expressed his astonishment, the guardian, deeply moved, said: "Of course, he is waiting for the blessing." Stirred to the heart, the guardian gave him his blessing, and when he had said the words: "Go forth, O Christian soul," in the commendation, he blessed him again. Then Felix called on the holy names of Jesus and Mary, bowed his head and died.

Devotion to him, which Pope Leo XIII publicly approved on February 12, 1888, began immediately after his death. His feast is observed on June second by the Franciscans, and on the first by the Capuchins.

ON THE VALUE OF A BLESSING

1. Consider how highly Blessed Felix esteemed the blessing of his superior. After receiving the last sacraments, he still asked for that blessing before his departure, and God almighty miraculously preserved his life until he received it. To bless means to call down good things on anybody or anything. It is recorded of the early Christian period that Christians used to bless one another by way of greeting by saying: "God bless you!" Thus we also bless ourselves by making the Sign of the Cross, from which all

the blessings of the redeeming death of Christ come to us. We bless ourselves before prayer, before work, on entering and leaving the home, in danger and temptation, in order to be strengthened in doing good and to be preserved from evil. — Do you bless yourself with devotion? Not making a motion with your hand, but raising your heart to God draws down blessing from above.

2. Consider that a father's or a parent's blessing has a special power. God Himself entrusts the care of the children to their parents, and therefore He readily confirms the benediction which parents pronounce over them. "The father's blessing establishes the houses of the children; but the mother's curse roots up the foundation" (Eccli. 3,11). That being so, a pious mother will often and devoutly bless her little children. For that reason, too, grown-up children should be eager for the blessing of both parents. Jacob went to great lengths to get the blessing of his father Isaac. Esau cried out with grief when he had lost it through his own folly. Ruth experienced what good fortune came to her with the blessing of her mother-in-law Noemi. Therefore, "Honor your father that a blessing may come upon you" (Eccli. 3,9-10).

3. Consider that a very particular power is attached to the blessing of a priest. Already in the Old Testament this was made manifest. "Aaron stretched forth his hands to the people and blessed them; and the glory of the Lord appeared to all the multitude" (Lev. 9,22-23). At ordination, the Christian priest's hands are especially blessed with holy oil, while the bishop says: "By this holy anointing and through our blessing, O Lord, consecrate and sanctify these hands, so that everything they bless may be blessed." Hence, all the saints as well as sincere Christians have greatly esteemed the blessing of the priest. You receive his blessing at the close of holy Mass, also when you enter the confessional, when you receive holy Communion and at other times. Receive it always with devotion and with the confidence of Blessed Felix, so that through it the divine blessing may also come upon you and you may one day behold the glory of the Lord.

PRAYER OF THE CHURCH
O God, who dost gladden us with the annual commemoration of Thy blessed confessor Felix, mercifully grant, that we who celebrate his entrance into heavenly glory, may also imitate his actions. Through Christ our Lord. Amen.

JUNE 6
BLESSED JOHN PELINGOTTO
Confessor, Third Order

OHN PELINGOTTO was born of a prominent family at Urbino in the year 1240. At the wish of his father, he became a merchant when he arrived at young manhood. But his efforts in business were directed not so much toward increasing his own profits or the fortune of his family, but rather toward benefiting others.

He did not, however, pursue the occupation very long. With the consent of his father, he turned his back on a career in business, and retired to a solitary place, where he gave himself up solely to God, devoting his strength and his resources to prayer and almsgiving.

He joined the Third Order of St. Francis and became a striking example of virtue to his contemporaries and fellow citizens, distinguishing himself by his exceptional practice of penance, piety, and charity.

Finally, worn out by the austerity of his life, he was attacked with a serious illness. He closed a life replete with merits and good works, with a peaceful and happy death. It was on the first of June, in the year 1304. His body reposes in the church of St. Francis at Urbino.

On November 13, 1918, Pope Benedict XV approved the veneration, which was paid to him since his death and has been increasing with time on account of the many miracles wrought at his intercession. His feast is observed on June second by the Franciscans, on the third by the Conventuals, and on the first by the Third Order Regular. (Cf. Biersack, pp. 145-146; *These Made Peace*, pp. 42-43.)

ON THE OBLIGATIONS OF LABOR AND CAPITAL

1. It is particularly gratifying to read of a merchant who aimed not at acquiring profit for himself and his family, but rather at benefiting those with whom he had business dealings. Greed for money and the gaining of personal advantage at the cost of injury to others, is rampant on every side in the commercial world today. And to what earthly end? Difficulty upon difficulty between labor and capital, and a social order that is constantly in conflict. And to what purpose for eternity? "Better is a dry morsel with joy," says the Wise Man, "than houses full of victims with strife" (Prov. 17,1). — Have you endeavored to be fair in your business dealings, and even generous to your patrons, or have you rather been out for your utmost advantage and thus added your share to the discontent

that exists in the business world?

2. The golden rule is by far the best standard also in the business world. If you are an employer, render to those in your service the kind of consideration that you would wish to receive if you were a laborer. You were perhaps a laborer at one time; what are the complaints you then had against your employers? Do you now deal with those whom you have engaged in your service in the manner in which you used to wish your employer would deal with you? St. Paul admonishes us: "Masters, do to your servants that which is just and equal, knowing that you also have a master in heaven" (Col 4,1).

3. If you are a laborer, you have the obligation to render the kind and amount of service that deserves the pay you are getting. St. Paul again says: "Every man shall receive his own reward according to his own labor" (1 Cor. 3,8). To demand wages that are in excess of the service you are willing to render is an unfairness to those who have engaged your services. Moreover, conditions prevailing at any time must be taken into consideration in the demands you make. The demands must remain within reason. For, the best intentioned employers are at times reduced to straitened circumstances in their effort to meet the unreasonable demands of their employees. — Have you reason to find fault with yourself in this matter? The Gospel maxim applies equally well to you: "Whatsoever you would that men should do to you, do you also to them."

PRAYER OF THE CHURCH

Grant, we beseech Thee, O most merciful Lord, that spurred on by the example of Blessed John, Thy confessor, we may not only celebrate his festival but also imitate his virtues. Through Christ our Lord. Amen.

JUNE 7
THE SERVANT OF GOD JOSEPH PEREZ
Martyr, First Order

OSEPH belongs to the first martyrs of Christ the King in unhappy Mexico. He was born at Coroneo in 1890. When he was seventeen years old, he joined the Franciscans. Civil war drove him to California. There he was ordained to the priesthood at Santa Barbara.

Returning to his native land of Mexico, he served as pastor in the

Franciscan parish at Jerecuaro from 1922 on. There his strong bodily constitution and his skill in riding proved a very useful asset. Even after the outbreak of the persecution under President Calles, Father Joseph, variously disguised, continued his solicitude for his little sheep.

On May 31, 1928, some people took him to Cañada de Tirados, where he celebrated holy Mass. On their return trip, he and his companions fell into the hands of a troop of soldiers. All of his company were forced to dismount. Then their hands were bound behind their backs, and they were despoiled of their shoes. In this manner they had to make the journey to Salvatierra.

In Father Joseph's saddlebag, the soldiers found the priestly vestments used for Mass, and so they knew that there was a priest in the group of prisoners. Father Joseph at once admitted that he was a priest. He looked forward to death with serenity and joy. From Salvatierra the soldiers took their prisoners on to Celaya. A few miles from this place, they led Father Joseph a short distance from the road, cast a rope around his neck, and began dragging him along the ground. Finally, they stabbed him to death with their machetes. This occurred on June 2, 1928.

The body, drenched with blood, was brought in solemn procession to Salvatierra. No indication of decomposition was visible on the body of the confessor. Amid the jubilant cry of "Viva, Cristo Rey! Long live Christ the King!" the corpse was laid to rest.

On Father Joseph's memorial card there were printed among other things the significant words: "May almighty God grant that our prayer, which is supported by the bloody sacrifice of this martyr, may graciously appear in His sight and bring salvation to us and redemption to our country." Many remarkable answers to prayer, attributed to the intercession of Father Joseph, have been reported. (Cf. *Heroes of the Cross*, pp. 118-119.)

ON DEVOTION TO CHRIST THE KING

1. Devotion to Christ the King is the work of Divine Providence. It is an indication of that special guidance promised to Holy Church by Christ: "Behold, I am with you all days even to the consummation of the world" (Mt. 28,20). When the Church was in need of special strength, the veneration of the martyrs was introduced. When she had to wrestle with heresy, the confessors were honored in a special way. When a mystery of the Faith, such as the Blessed Sacrament, the Holy Name of Jesus, the Sacred Heart, was to be proposed for veneration, almighty God sent a Juliana of Liège, a Bernardin of Siena, and a Margaret Mary Alacoque.

Today, when the dominion of Christ is denied everywhere and fails to receive proper recognition, Divine Providence has granted us a new favor in the devotion to Christ the King. — Adore the wisdom of God which "orders all things sweetly" (Wisd. 8,1), and always place your confidence in it.

2. Devotion to Christ the King is a devotion of atonement. The more the godless attack Christ, so much the more must all good Christians unite in homage to Christ the King. The more our modern world cries out, "We will not have this man to reign over us" (Lk. 19,14), so much the more should we insist on the watchword: "Rule thou over us" (Judges 8,22). In that way we should atone for their outrages. — Unite yourself in atoning love with all Christians who are loyal to Christ the King.

3. Devotion to Christ the King is a serious warning. And that, not only for devout persons, but especially for the enemies of Christ and for public officials. The devotion admonishes all to consider that Christ did not lightly avow before Pilate: "I am a king" (Jn. 18,37). Woe to those who permit this admonition to go unheeded! If they have no will to render homage to this King in His mercy, they shall be brought low and punished by the King who will act as their judge. — Behold the heroic martyrs of Mexico, and with your whole soul render homage to glorious King Christ, even if it is necessary to do this at the sacrifice of your life.

PRAYER OF THE CHURCH
Almighty and eternal God, who hast willed to restore all things in Thy beloved Son, the King of the whole world, mercifully grant that all the household of the nations, which are now divided by the wounds of sin, may be brought under His most sweet rule. Through Christ our Lord. Amen.

JUNE 8
BLESSED ISABELLA OF FRANCE
Virgin, Second Order

ISABELLA was the sister of King St. Louis. Her mother, the saintly Queen Blanche, bore this child special affection because, after the death of her husband, Isabella was the only daughter still living.

Isabella was endowed with remarkable gifts, and special attention was paid to educate her in the requirements of her high position. She knew

Latin perfectly and could read the writings of the Fathers of the Church in that language. She was, however, no less capable in accomplishments that are peculiarly feminine. With consummate artistry she embroidered vestments for divine services, and took great pleasure in working for the poor and the sick.

The princess loved and honored her saintly brother Louis, who was her senior by ten years and had then been king for many a year. But her love for God was still greater. One day she was knitting a new-fashioned nightcap. The king asked her to give it to him when finished. "No," she said, "this is the first of its kind and I must make it for my Saviour Jesus Christ." Accordingly, she gave it to a poor sick person, and then made another for the king.

Her life in the royal palace was as retired as that of a nun in her convent. Hardly ever did she speak at mealtime. The choicest food she sent to the sick, and she ate so little even of the ordinary food that it was remarkable how she could live. She fasted three days every week. All the court considered the princess a saint. One of the court ladies, who wrote her life, says: "We beheld in her a mirror of innocence, and at the same time an admirable model of penance, a lily of purity, a fragrant rose of patience and self-renunciation, an endless fountain of goodness and mercy."

Isabella's only desire was to belong entirely to God, and so she took the vow of perpetual virginity. However, Emperor Frederick II sought her consent for marriage with his eldest son Conrad. Her mother, her brother, the king, and even Pope Innocent IV would have liked to see the marriage take place for the good of the State and the Church. But Isabella wrote the Holy Father a letter in which she expressed such high regard for consecrated virginity and so strong a desire to persevere in it, that the pope praised her highly and encouraged her in her noble sentiments.

When her mother died, Isabella wished to withdraw from the court in order to consecrate herself entirely to God in a convent. With the king's assistance she built a convent for the Poor Clares at Longchamps near Paris, and then with several ladies of the court she obtained admission. At the request of the Holy Father, the strict rule of St. Clare was mitigated for this community by St. Bonaventure, who was minister general of the Franciscan Order at that time, and the modified rule was confirmed anew by Pope Urban IV.

At Isabella's request, the convent was named for the Humility of Our Blessed Lady. She lived there nine years and desired nothing more than to be a humble subject although she surpassed everyone in sanctity. At her death in 1270, angels were heard singing. Several miracles occurred also after her death, and so Pope Leo X beatified her. Blessed Isabella's feast is observed by the Franciscans on June eighth, by the Conventuals on March second, and by the Capuchins on February twenty-fifth or twenty-sixth.

ON CONSECRATING ONE'S VIRGINITY TO GOD

1. Blessed Isabella wrote to the pope to say that she considered it greater happiness to be the least among the consecrated virgins than the first queen of the world. And she was right. All the glamour of the world as well as all worldly rank must make way for the dignity and beauty of consecrated virginal souls. "They shall be as the angels of God in heaven" (Mt. 22,30). St. Chrysostom is of the opinion that in a certain sense, chaste souls surpass even the angels, for the angels are not subject to sensual desires because they are not made of flesh and blood, whereas virgins keep sensuality in check by their virtue. Hence he says that virginity is as far above the married state as heaven is above the earth. The Holy Ghost assures us: "No price is worthy of a continent soul" (Eccli. 26,20). — Do Christians regard virginity with this esteem?
2. Consider what happiness consecrated virginity brings to the soul which preserves it intact. If, as the Apostle requires, a virgin is dead to the world though living in it, and if she "thinks on the things of the Lord that she may be holy both in body and in spirit" (1 Cor. 7,34), she will win the special favor of the Bridegroom "who feeds among the lilies." He calls her His beloved, and she, too, can say, "My Beloved to me and I to Him" (Cant. 2,16). This inward consolation outweighs a thousandfold all the sensual pleasures that a person relinquishes. Even death cannot disturb a virgin soul in its pure and holy joy, but rather it conducts the soul to the enjoyment of that peculiar happiness which is shared only by those "who will sing a new canticle that no man can sing, and who follow the Lamb whithersoever He goes" (Apoc. 14,34). — What a great grace to be called by God to the vow of perpetual chastity!
3. Consider the obligations imposed by consecrated virginity. The world and its pleasures must be shut out forever from such a soul, and she must adorn herself with holy virtues in order to be agreeable to the Beloved of her heart. "My sister, my spouse, is a garden enclosed, a fountain sealed up" (Cant. 4,12). Even at the royal court Isabella was "an enclosed garden" by her retired, mortified, and humble life. There the lily of untarnished purity budded forth, there the rose of self-denial and patience bloomed, the holy fountain of loving mercy bubbled forth. Oh, would that we belonged entirely to God as she did!

PRAYER OF THE CHURCH

O God, who didst teach Blessed Isabella, Thy holy virgin, to prefer mortification and humility on the Way of the Cross to royal pleasure and worldly honor, grant us through her merits and intercession to overcome the allurements of this world and to find our joy in embracing Thy cross. Who livest and reignest forever and ever. Amen.

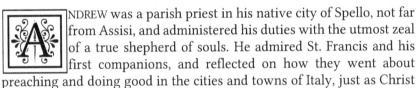

JUNE 9
BLESSED ANDREW OF SPELLO
Confessor, First Order

NDREW was a parish priest in his native city of Spello, not far from Assisi, and administered his duties with the utmost zeal of a true shepherd of souls. He admired St. Francis and his first companions, and reflected on how they went about preaching and doing good in the cities and towns of Italy, just as Christ our Lord and His apostles once traveled about in Judea.

In 1223, when his mother and sister had died, the forty-four-year-old parish priest came to St. Francis and asked to be received among the brethren of his order. The holy founder gladly granted his request, personally invested him with the holy habit, and soon sent him out to preach.

In the year 1226 Andrew was present with other brethren around the deathbed of our Seraphic Father. In giving him his blessing, St. Francis foretold that much fruit would be derived from his preaching of the divine word. The results soon verified the prophecy.

When Andrew was called to Spain to attend the general chapter of the order, a prolonged drought had dried up all the fields of Soria, where the chapter was being held. Andrew told the inhabitants that this was a punishment for their sins, and warned them forcefully to do penance. They were all moved to such deep contrition that they burst into tears. Then he entreated God to ward off the punishment, and behold, at once a plentiful rain fell which restored everything to life. In other places, too, God supported his words with the most unusual miracles; he even restored dead persons to life.

Andrew rejoiced at the blessings which resulted everywhere from his sermons. But at the same time his reputation spread everywhere, and his humility urged him to evade the honors. With the consent of his superiors he retired to the secluded convent of the Carceri, where, engaged in quiet prayer and severe mortification, he led a more heavenly than earthly life. One day the Lord of heaven visited him. In the grotto in which Andrew lived, Christ appeared to him in the form of a beautiful boy. But just then the little bell rang out for Vespers. At the first signal Andrew left the grotto in order to heed the call of obedience. When he returned from Vespers, he found the Divine Child still there, who said to him: "It was well that you heeded the call of obedience; I will be merciful to you."

Not long afterwards Andrew was granted the greatest of all graces here on earth, the grace of a holy death. Rich in virtues and merits, he died on June 3, 1254. Numerous miracles occurred at his grave in the church of the Apostle St. Andrew at Spello. The public veneration accorded him was approved by Popes Clement XII and Benedict XIV. The feast of Blessed Andrew is observed on June ninth by the Franciscans, and on the third by the Conventuals and the Capuchins.

ON TEMPORAL PUNISHMENT FOR SIN

1. Consider that temporal evils are sometimes sent by God as a punishment for sin, as Blessed Andrew pointed out in the case of the prolonged drought in Soria. As a punishment for the sin of our first parents, pain and misery have become the lot of the entire human race. For the Lord said to Adam: "Because you have eaten of the tree, whereof I commanded you that you should not eat, cursed is the earth in your work; with labor and toil shall you eat thereof all the days of your life" (Gen. 3,17). As a punishment for his sins it was announced to David that his son should die, and because he had taken a census out of vanity, he had to suffer the penalty for his pride. In the days of the prophet Elias, no rain fell for three years as a punishment for the sins of the people. Let us recognize from these instances the horror of sin and the severity of the divine justice. If His chastising hand strikes us, we should humbly submit. Have you perhaps murmured at it in the past? That would be a sign of impenitence.

2. Consider that one may not consider all temporal evils a punishment for sin. The Pharisees passed judgment in this rash manner when they said to the man born blind: "You were wholly born in sins" (Jn. 9,24). But our Lord said: "Neither has this man sinned, nor his parents, but that the works of God should be made manifest in him" (Jn. 9,3). Hence we may not look upon every misfortune that assails us as a punishment for sin, and, of course, we should not ask: "How have I deserved this?" Perhaps God just wishes to manifest His works in you, in the patience with which

He strengthens you to endure quietly, and in the glory with which He will reward you in eternity. Still less may we attribute to sins the misfortunes that afflict others. Have you perhaps judged thus rashly?

3. Consider that nothing is so effective in warding off misfortunes that God inflicts because of our sins as sincere penance and earnest prayer. Through these means Ninive, whose destruction had already been decreed, was spared. That is why rain fell for the benefit of those who had heeded the sermon of Blessed Andrew and contritely pleaded with God. Do likewise, for, says Thomas a Kempis (1,24), "now your tears are acceptable, your groans are heard, your sorrow is satisfying and purifies the soul."

PRAYER OF THE CHURCH

O gracious God, who through the merits and intercession of Blessed Andrew didst grant serene weather and rain according to desire and need, pour forth in our souls a shower of graces, that, purified of the filth of sin, we may be found worthy to enjoy Thy blessed vision through all eternity. Through Christ our Lord. Amen.

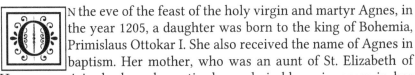

JUNE 10
BLESSED AGNES OF PRAGUE
Virgin, Second Order

N the eve of the feast of the holy virgin and martyr Agnes, in the year 1205, a daughter was born to the king of Bohemia, Primislaus Ottokar I. She also received the name of Agnes in baptism. Her mother, who was an aunt of St. Elizabeth of Hungary, rejoiced when she noticed an admirable seriousness in her infant. At times she saw how the child folded its little hands in the form of a cross, and then, as if absorbed in deep devotion, would lie quite still.

According to the custom of the time, the king's daughter was betrothed at the age of three years to the son of the duke of Silesia, and hence was sent to the Silesian convent at Trebnitz, where St. Hedwig was superior at that time, to be educated there. Her betrothed died after three years, and she was then taken to the convent at Doxan in Bohemia, where the seeds of sanctity which had been seeds sown by St. Hedwig budded forth in marvelous bloom. The child appeared to be destined for the heavenly Spouse rather than for an earthly one; but earthly monarchs renewed their suit for her hand.

Emperor Frederick II desired to secure her as the bride of his son and successor to the throne, Henry, and Agnes, who was now a mature young woman, was sent to the court of the German emperor. But when the union with Henry came to naught as the result of the prayers of the virgin, King Henry III of England sought her hand in marriage, and finally, even Emperor Frederick II himself, whose consort had meanwhile died. All the opposition raised by Agnes, who desired to belong entirely to the Divine Bridegroom, seemed in vain. Then she begged Pope Gregory IX to intervene, and as a result she obtained her freedom. The emperor declared himself satisfied since Agnes chose not a human being but the God of heaven in preference to him.

Now, however, Agnes strove to embrace the religious state in order to achieve her union with the Divine Bridegroom. The fame of Poor Clare convents had reached Bohemia, and Agnes resolved, with the assistance of her brother, who had meanwhile ascended the royal throne, to establish a convent of Poor Clares in the capital city of Prague. Pope Gregory cheerfully gave his consent, and, at his command, St. Clare sent five sisters from the convent of St. Damian in Assisi, to Prague. Agnes and seven other young women of the highest ranks of society entered the new convent together with these sisters.

Within a short time Agnes distinguished herself among them as a model of virtue; in fervor at prayer, in obedience, in religious discipline, in self-denial, and in humility. The command of the pope to accept the position of abbess was a great trial for her humility; however, she obtained permission not to carry the title, but rather to be known as the "senior sister." Holy zeal, similar to that of her holy mother St. Clare, characterized her vigilance regarding the observance of holy poverty; she declined the royal gifts sent to her by her brother, and would not tolerate that any sister possess anything of a personal nature. God blessed her with the gift of miracles; she recalled to life the deceased daughter of her brother.

Enriched with heavenly merits, she departed from this life in the odor of sanctity, to enter into eternal union with her Divine Bridegroom, on March 6, 1282, having served Him for forty years in the religious state. Devotion to her, which has existed since time immemorial, received apostolic sanction from Pope Pius IX, and her feast, which has long been celebrated in Prague on March second, has been extended to the entire Franciscan Order. The Franciscans celebrate the feast of Blessed Agnes on June eighth; the Conventuals and the Capuchins observe it on March second.

SPOUSE OF CHRIST

1. Consider how Blessed Agnes treasured the honor of being chosen by Christ as His spouse. She rejected the crowns of emperors and kings, the emperor himself admitting that he could not take it ill of her to prefer the King of heaven to himself. Indeed, there can be no more honorable union, and every Christian family should consider itself highly honored if one of its members is called to this distinction. One may not, however, choose the vocation arbitrarily and from any human considerations, for here the word of the Apostle is applicable: "Neither does any man take the honor to himself, but he who is called by God as Aaron was" (Heb. 5,4). — Let no one insist on following the vocation without being called to it, and on the other hand, let no one who is called be prevented from following it.

2. Consider that every Christian should, in a certain sense, be a spouse of Christ. By the mouth of the prophet the Lord says to every soul devoted to Him: "And I will betroth you to Me in faith" (Os. 2,20), and concerning heaven, to which every one of us is called, He speaks in terms of the parable of the ten virgins who went out to meet the bridegroom (Mt. 25,1). No matter in what state you are living, or what your associations are with other people, your soul is a spouse of Christ ever since the day of your baptism, and it must persevere until death in fidelity to Him. All the love and attachment we feel for human beings must be idealized and ennobled by our love for Christ, and at no time may human affections make us swerve in our fidelity to Him. — Have you persevered in your loyalty to Him?

3. Consider how easily the glamour, the honors, and the riches of the world delude us and shake our fidelity towards Christ. We are not all so strong as Blessed Agnes was. Hence, we should be on our guard, and not direct our glance to this alluring glamour. Rather, we should pray with the Psalmist: "Turn away my eyes that they may not behold vanity" (Ps. 118,37), and if the devil endeavors to lure us, and if he offers all the riches of this world as a reward for yielding to him, then we should say with Christ: "Begone, Satan, for it is written, the Lord your God shall you adore and Him only shall you serve" (Mt. 4,10).

PRAYER OF THE CHURCH

O God, who didst raise the virgin, Blessed Agnes, to the heights of heaven through her contempt of the pleasures of life at the royal court and her humble following of Thy cross, grant, we beseech Thee, that by her intercession and imitation, we may merit to be partakers of eternal glory. Who livest and reignest forever and ever. Amen.

JUNE 11
BLESSED BAPTISTA VARANI
Virgin, Second Order

APTISTA was the daughter of Duke Julius Caesar of Camerino, Italy. She was born in the capital city of that prince in 1459. In her earliest years she took pleasure in the vanities of the world. Her heart, it is true, remained unstained; but nevertheless she liked to appear in costly garments and beamed with joy when she was adorned with glittering jewels.

But one day she heard a sermon by a Franciscan on the bitter sufferings of Christ. The touching portrayal so wrung the heart of the young princess that she bewailed her previous vanity with many tears and was henceforth a changed person. From then on not a day passed on which she did not meditate on the sufferings of our Lord. Under the spiritual direction of Blessed Peter of Mogliano, a Franciscan, she also practiced various bodily mortifications, and arose every night to pray the rosary in honor of the Mother of God.

Meanwhile her father was contemplating marriage for her, but Baptista desired only to devote herself to God and the contemplation of the divine mysteries in some quiet convent cell. The duke opposed this wish of his beloved daughter for the space of two years. At last, however, he consented that she take the veil in the convent of the Poor Clares at Urbino.

Now Baptista was happier than if she had received a royal crown, and later she often said: "Oh, what sweetness I experienced in the holy convent at Urbino." Some years later, there was an urgent request that the daughters of St. Clare establish themselves in Camerino. The duke built a convent for them, and Baptista was sent there with several other sisters.

But now the servant of God, already firmly established in her vocation, was not to escape the test of suffering. She endured long and painful maladies, to which were added violent interior struggles and also persecution by misguided people. But she thanked God for them all, feeling that she was thereby more intimately united with her suffering Saviour. She prayed for those who persecuted her; and when her father and brother were cruelly murdered, Baptista prayed to God for the murderers: "O Lord, do not hold this sin against them!"

Because of her fidelity in suffering, her crucified Lord constantly drew her more closely to Himself. Christ revealed to her what suffering His own Heart endured, and had her record much of it for the benefit of others.

After she had served her Divine Spouse in the convent for more than forty years, Baptista died blessedly on the thirty-first of May, 1517. Thirty years after her death her body was exhumed, and the tongue which had so often prayed for her enemies, was found incorrupt and fresh, and it is still preserved that way in a special reliquary.

Baptista, who was venerated as a saint immediately after her death, was declared Blessed by Pope Gregory XVI. Her feast is observed on June eighth by the Franciscans, and on the seventh by the Capuchins.

ON DEVOTION TO THE SACRED HEART

1. Consider how our Divine Lord led Blessed Baptista from the contemplation of His bodily sufferings to the consideration of the sufferings of His Sacred Heart. He wished to direct her to honor His Sacred Heart long before He commended this devotion for the universal Church through St. Margaret Mary Alacoque. Baptista did indeed worship the Sacred Heart perfectly. In contemplating the sufferings of our Lord, her heart grew inflamed with love that was at the same time contrite and willing to make sacrifices. That induced her to forsake the vanity and glamour of the palace in order to belong to God alone. Seldom has anyone fulfilled the appeal of our Lord, "Give me your heart" (Prov. 23,26), more perfectly. During this month, which is especially consecrated to the Heart of Jesus, He directs this request also to you. For devotion to the Sacred Heart consists above all, in offering one's own heart to the Heart of Jesus, and in sacrificing whatever is apt to lead our heart away from Him. — What sacrifices of the kind have you to offer Him during this month?

2. Consider how, out of love for our suffering Saviour, Blessed Baptista practiced mortification and cheerfully offered up to God sickness and interior affliction. Because she saw the Heart of Jesus grieving over the sins of men, she found consolation in suffering with Him, and she prepared sweet consolation for the Sacred Heart by offering her sufferings in atonement for sin. Such an atonement is an essential part of true devotion to the Heart of Jesus. Have we no need to render it for our own sins? Offenses committed against God by those who are otherwise numbered among good Christians wound the Heart of Jesus most painfully. He Himself complains: "With these I was wounded in the house

of those who loved Me" (Zach. 13,6). — Have you, too, given occasion for this complaint? How do you offer atonement?

3. Consider how Baptista imitated the Divine Heart in His perfect love. Not only did she sincerely forgive the gravest offenses, but she even pleaded for forgiveness for the murderers of her father, and Christ prayed to His Father for His executioners. Such prayer and forgiveness in imitation of the Heart of Jesus are the most pleasing honor we can render Him. They satisfy in great measure for our own failings against the Sacred Heart. — Frequently look at the pierced Heart of Jesus on the cross and draw from it strength, as did Blessed Baptista, to imitate His sentiments.

PRAYER OF THE CHURCH

O God, who didst inflame Blessed Baptista with the fire of love by the contemplation of the sufferings of Thy only-begotten Son, grant through her intercession that we may always devoutly honor these holy sufferings and deserve to receive the fruits thereof. Through the same Christ our Lord. Amen.

JUNE 12
BLESSED PACIFIC OF CERANO
Confessor, First Order

ACIFIC was born at Cerano in northern Italy in 1424. At an early age he lost both his parents in a plague. As war was raging and every man had more than enough to do to take care of his own family, the poor little orphan boy might have met a cruel fate had not our heavenly Father Himself cared for him. He touched the heart of the Benedictine abbot in the neighboring city of Novara, and the latter interested himself in the boy, seeing to it that he received an excellent education.

Hardly had Pacific arrived at young manhood, when the abbot died. But God's providence had already prepared a new home for him. The young man felt himself attracted to the Order of St. Francis, and was admitted in the convent at Novara. There he devoted himself with great zeal to the study of perfection and the pursuit of knowledge. In both he was blessedly successful.

After he was ordained a priest, he was assigned to the office of preaching. In a truly apostolic spirit he applied himself to this duty with such power that in Novara and its vicinity a noticeable change in public morality set in. Pacific was especially successful in reconciling longstanding enmities and in settling feuds. With great love he also interested himself in the poor and the afflicted. Believing that devotion to Mary is an effective means to obtain results in the care of souls, he introduced a Marian Sodality. In his birthplace he had a special chapel built in honor of the Mother of God, in which the meetings of the sodality were held.

By word and example Pacific was also active in furthering religious order and discipline. For this purpose he also wrote a special rule of life which was named after him the "Pacifica," that is, the way of peace.

Amid such extensive activity he was nevertheless so humble that he was always at the service of everyone, and so cheerful that he made everyone who associated with him happy. Because of his virtue and ability, Pope Sixtus IV chose him as his legate on important business to the Island of Sardinia. This apostolic work was destined to be the last rendered by the servant of God. After successfully accomplishing the papal commission, he died at Sassari in Sardinia on June 4, 1482, being eighty-five years old.

In his last sermon before his departure, given in his chapel of our Lady, he told the inhabitants of Cerano that they would not again see him alive, but that he would like his remains to rest in their midst in the sanctuary of the Blessed Virgin. And thus it happened. His body was buried there.

After Pope Benedict XIV beatified him, a beautiful church in honor of Blessed Pacific was built adjoining the chapel of our Lady. The Franciscans celebrate his feast on June ninth, and the Capuchins on the eighth.

ON THE PATERNAL SOLICITUDE OF GOD

1. Consider how Blessed Pacific in a time of plague and war was a poor orphan boy in a village of northern Italy, forsaken by all the world. Consider, too, how the paternal eye of God watched over him, and how He bears a loving care for each one of us individually. "Is not He your father, who has possessed you, and made you, and created you?" (Deut. 32,6). The Holy Ghost assures us emphatically that our Father is merciful towards all, that He is indulgent and forbearing with sinners, so that they will do penance. "For Thou lovest all things that are, and hatest none of the things which Thou hast made" (Wisd. 11,25). What a consolation for us in the various circumstances of life! What childlike trust in God it ought to evoke in our hearts! — Have you always preserved this trust?

2. Consider more particularly how God almighty provides for our bodily needs. Although He has decreed that in punishment for our sins we should earn our bread in the sweat of our brow, still He does more to help us obtain our bread than we ourselves do. Daily, Christians say with the Psalmist: "Thou givest them food in season" (Ps. 103,27). Yes, even "to the beasts (He gives) their food, and to the young ravens that call upon Him" (Ps. 146,9). "How much more to you?" says Christ Himself. What Christian can still be fretfully anxious that he will not be cared for? Be faithful to God, do your duty honestly, then you, too, will experience what the Prophet said after a lifelong experience: "I have been young, and now I am old: and I have not seen the just forsaken, nor his descendants seek bread" (Ps. 36,25). — Have you not often in the past experienced this gracious solicitude of God in your regard?

3. Consider that God's solicitude for our soul is even greater than that which He has for our body. That is why He sometimes sends physical suffering so that the soul may be preserved and saved. Such chastisements are a sign that He still has faith in our amendment. Therefore David said to the Lord: "Thy rod and Thy staff, they have comforted me" (Ps. 22,4). The Lord casts the proud man down so that he may become humble, but He raises him up again. Even in the act of falling, His paternal hand protects us, not only the children, but adults likewise, "for the Lord puts His hand under him" (Ps. 36,24). With what confidence ought we to abandon ourselves to His solicitude! And if His decrees send us where we know with certainty that death is awaiting us, as happened in the case of Blessed Pacific, we should say with the Apostle: "Whether we live, we live unto the Lord; or whether we die, we die unto the Lord. Therefore whether we live or whether we die, we are the Lord's" (Rom. 14,8).

PRAYER OF THE CHURCH
O God, who didst make Blessed Pacific, Thy confessor, illustrious in word and example, grant, we beseech Thee, that we may follow in his footsteps and thus arrive at our heavenly country. Through Christ our Lord. Amen.

JUNE 13
ST. ANTHONY OF PADUA
Confessor, First Order

NTHONY was born in the year 1195 at Lisbon, the capital of Portugal, where his father was a captain in the royal army. Already at the age of fifteen years the youth had entered the Congregation of Canons Regular of St. Augustine, and was devoting himself with great earnestness to study and to the practice of piety in the monastery at Coimbra, when a significant event, which occurred in the year 1220, changed his entire career.

The relics of St. Berard and companions, the first martyrs of the Franciscan Order, were being brought from Africa to Coimbra. At the sight of them, Anthony was seized with an intense desire to suffer martyrdom as a Franciscan missionary in Africa. In response to his repeated and humble petitions, the permission of his superiors to transfer to the Franciscan Order was reluctantly given. At his departure, one of the canons said to him ironically: "Go then, perhaps you will become a saint in the new order." Anthony replied: "Brother, when you hear that I have become a saint, you will surely praise God for it."

In the quiet little Franciscan convent at Coimbra he received a friendly reception, and in the very same year his earnest wish to be sent to the missions in Africa was fulfilled. But God had decreed otherwise. Anthony scarcely set foot on African soil when he was seized with a grievous illness. Even after recovering from it, he was so weak that, resigning himself to the will of God, he boarded a boat back to Portugal. But a storm drove the ship to the coast of Sicily, and Anthony went to Assisi, where the general chapter of the order was held in May, 1221.

As he still looked weak and sickly, and gave no evidence of his scholarship, no one paid any attention to the stranger until Father Gratian, provincial of Romagna, had compassion on him and sent him to the quiet little convent near Forli. There Anthony remained nine months occupied in the lowliest duties of the kitchen and convent, and to his heart's content he practiced interior as well as exterior mortification.

But the hidden jewel was soon to appear in all its brilliance. Anthony was sent to Forli with some other brethren, to attend the ceremony of ordination. At the convent there the superior wanted somebody to give an address for the occasion. Everybody excused himself, saying that he was not prepared, until Anthony was finally asked to give it. When he, too, excused himself most humbly, his superior ordered him by virtue of the vow of obedience to give the sermon. Anthony began to speak in a very reserved manner; but soon holy animation seized him, and he spoke with such eloquence, learning, and unction that everybody was fairly amazed.

When St. Francis was informed of the event, he gave Anthony the mission to preach all over Italy. At the request of the brethren, Anthony was later commissioned also to teach theology, "but in such a manner," St. Francis distinctly wrote, "that the spirit of prayer be not extinguished either in yourself or in the other brethren."

St. Anthony himself placed greater value on the salvation of souls than on learning. For that reason he never ceased to exercise his office as preacher along with the work of teaching. The concourse of hearers was sometimes so great that no church was large enough to accommodate the audiences and he had to preach in the open air. He wrought veritable miracles of conversion. Deadly enemies were reconciled with each other. Thieves and usurers made restitution of their ill-gotten goods. Calumniators and detractors recanted and apologized. He was so energetic in defending the truths of the Catholic Faith that many heretics re-entered the pale of the Church, so that Pope Gregory IX called him "the ark of the covenant."

Once he was preaching at Rimini on the seacoast. He noticed that a group of heretics turned their backs to him and started to leave. Promptly the preacher turned to the sea and called out to the fishes: "Since the heretics do not wish to listen to me, do you come and listen to me!" And marvelous to say, shoals of fish came swimming and thrust their heads out of the water as if to hear the preacher. At this the heretics fell at Anthony's feet and begged to be instructed in the truth.

The blessings of St. Anthony's preaching were not confined to Italy. St. Francis sent him to France, where for about three years (1225-1227) he labored with blessed results in the convents of his order as well as in the pulpit. In all his labors he never forgot the admonition of his spiritual Father, that the spirit of prayer must not be extinguished. If he spent the day in teaching, and heard the confessions of sinners till late in the evening, then many hours of the night were spent in intimate union with God.

Once a man, at whose home Anthony was spending the night, came upon the saint and found him holding in his arms a child of unspeakable beauty surrounded with heavenly light. It was the Child Jesus.

In 1227, Anthony was elected minister provincial of upper Italy; and then he resumed the work of preaching. Due to his taxing labors and his austere practice of penance, he soon felt his strength so spent that he prepared himself for death. After receiving the last sacraments he kept looking upward with a smile on his countenance. When he was asked what he saw there, he answered: "I see my Lord." Then he breathed forth his soul on June 13, 1231, being only thirty-six years old. Soon the children in the streets of the city of Padua were crying: "The saint is dead, Anthony is dead."

Pope Gregory IX enrolled him among the saints in the very next year. At Padua a magnificent basilica was built in his honor, his holy relics were entombed there in 1263. From the time of his death up to the present day, countless miracles have occurred through St. Anthony's intercession, so that he is known as the Wonder-Worker. In 1946 he was also declared a Doctor of the Church. All three branches of the First Order and the Third Order Regular observe his feast on June thirteenth. (Cf. Habig, Everyman's Saint.)

ON THE VENERATION OF ST. ANTHONY

1. Consider how highly St. Anthony is honored by Holy Church. His feast is celebrated by the whole Catholic Church, and the priests celebrate holy Mass in his honor. In Franciscan churches, not only is this feast observed with great solemnity, but every Tuesday devotions in his honor are conducted before the exposed Blessed Sacrament, at which devotion all the faithful can gain a plenary indulgence. In Padua, where a magnificent basilica has been erected in his honor, he is called the Saint, as if there were no other that can compare with him, as when we style God's Mother the Holy Virgin. Among Catholics there is hardly anyone who does not know the dear saint with the Infant Jesus. — Do you pay him due honor? Do you use the opportunity to gain the indulgence on Tuesday?

2. Consider that, judging by the measure with which God permits St. Anthony to be honored here on earth, his power in heaven must be very great. The experience of the whole Catholic world testifies to the fact. From the day of his death to the present time, he has been invoked in the most diverse needs, and these prayers are answered in a most remarkable manner. — Have you not had the experience yourself? Call upon him with confidence in every necessity, and in case of serious trouble make the devotion of the nine Tuesdays.

3. Consider that in a special way St. Anthony is invoked as the restorer of lost objects. God usually gives the saints a power of intercession in keeping with the way by which they were distinguished in life. Now Anthony once missed a book of the Psalms which he valued very highly because he had written so many comments on the Psalms in it. He prayed earnestly to his dear Jesus to restore the book to him, and behold, soon afterwards a young man who had taken the book came to him, driven by

some indescribable fear, and brought it back to him. Pray to St. Anthony and to the Divine Child with similar fervor, and you will experience his power. But let us not only pray for lost temporal things, but particularly for the more precious gifts of the soul. For example, let us pray for that devotion we used to have and have lost, for our lost patience, our lost zeal for all that is good. May he gladden us by restoring it so that we may one day rejoice with him in eternal bliss.

PRAYER OF THE CHURCH

O God, may the votive commemoration of St. Anthony, Thy confessor and doctor, be a joy to Thy Church, that she may always be fortified with spiritual assistance and deserve to enjoy eternal happiness. Through Christ our Lord. Amen.

JUNE 14
BLESSED LAWRENCE OF VILLAMAGNA
Confessor, First Order

AWRENCE was born May 15, 1476, at Villamagna, a large country estate near Ortona in the Abruzzi, Italy, of parents who were distinguished not only for the nobility of their birth but equally much for the virtue of their lives.

At an early age Lawrence decided to join the Franciscan Order and took the habit in the convent of Our Lady of Grace in the city of Ortona. His father was much displeased at this step and had his son seized and locked up. When presently, however, his father became more composed, Lawrence succeeded in overcoming his objections, and returned in haste to the convent where he was professed in the Order of the Friars Minor.

After his ordination to the priesthood, he preached all over Italy with remarkable success. In this ministry he converted very many people by his words and example. Indeed it was less because of the eloquence of his speech, than by reason of the sanctity and austerity of his life and his devotion to prayer. God favored him with the gift of prophecy. He was greatly venerated by the people, who proclaimed him a saint.

Finally, while he was conducting the Lenten sermons at Ortona, he was stricken in the pulpit. Within a short time he died in the Lord on June 6, 1535. The veneration always tendered Blessed Lawrence was confirmed by Pope Pius XI on February 28, 1923. His feast is observed by the

Franciscans on June ninth.

ON SUDDEN DEATH

1. In the Epistle to the Hebrews St. Paul writes (9,27): "It is appointed unto man once to die and after that the judgment." Death, then, is certain, but the time of death is uncertain. We do not know when we shall die. So often death comes like a thief in the night, when we least expect it. In the Following of Christ we read (1,23): "How many souls have been deceived and snatched unexpectedly from life! Such a one fell by the sword, another was drowned, another falling from on high broke his neck; this man died at table, that other came to his end at play, and so death is the end of all and man's life passes away suddenly like a shadow." For that reason he adds the exhortation: "Be therefore always in readiness and so live that death may not find you unprepared." — If death's summons came to you today, would you be prepared?

2. Consider that it is not a sudden death we should fear, but rather that a sudden death may find us unprepared to appear before our Judge. For thus we pray in the Litany of All Saints: From sudden and unprovided death, deliver us, O Lord. The uncertainty of the day and the hour of our death should impel us to live in such a manner that we may always be prepared to die. "Many die suddenly and unprovidedly," the author of the Imitation again says. The best preparation for death is a holy life, for he adds: "Study, therefore, so to live now that in the hour of death you may be able rather to rejoice than to fear. Do now, beloved, do now what you can; for you know not when you are to die." — Let us daily ask God in prayer for the grace to be conscientious in our work, faithful to His grace, attentive at prayer, regular in frequenting the sacraments, and constant in the performance of those good works and the practice of those virtues which are proper to our state in life, so that if in His designs we are to meet with sudden death, we may be prepared to meet Him in that sacred moment when we depart hence.

3. Consider that a sudden death is not necessarily anything tragic. It may be a blessing and a reward for a life that has been spent in holiness. Cardinal Newman once wrote:

> "Death came unheralded: — but it was well;
>   For so thy Saviour bore
> Kind witness, thou wast meet at once to dwell
>   On His eternal shore;
>   All warnings spared,

For none He gives where hearts are for prompt
    Change prepared."

Our good God spares such souls the agony that usually accompanies death. They do not have to witness the grief of loved ones standing by, they are spared the struggle with the angel of darkness in that final hour, they are not subjected to the pains of sickness nor to the pangs of lengthened agony. Truly such a death may be called a gift from God. — We who are children of a saint who called death by the familiar name of sister, would do well to cultivate a similar attitude towards death. If we lead a holy life by following the path he marked out for us in the rule, we may, like him, joyfully exclaim, "Welcome, Sister Death!" no matter when the summons comes.

PRAYER OF THE CHURCH

O God, who dost gladden us through the merits and intercession of Blessed Lawrence, Thy confessor, grant, we beseech Thee, that we who ask Thy benefits may obtain Thy graces. Through Christ our Lord. Amen.

JUNE 15
BLESSED YOLANDE (JOLENTA) OF POLAND
Widow, Second Order

 OLANDE was the daughter of Bela IV, king of Hungary. Her mother, Mary, was the daughter of the Greek emperor of Constantinople. In the year 1240, when Yolande was scarcely five years old, she arrived at the court of Poland. Her elder sister, Blessed Kinga (Cunigunda), who was married to the duke of Poland, had asked to supervise the child's education. Under such a mistress, Yolande grew not only in age, but also in virtue and grace before God and men.

    When she arrived at young womanhood, Yolande was married to Boleslaus, the duke of Greater Poland. But the young duchess was not enamored of the glory and pleasure of this world. It was a greater pleasure for her to do good in her elevated position. Like a true sovereign, she came to the assistance of the poor and the sick, the widows and the orphans. She and her husband built hospitals, convents, and churches, and she was so great an inspiration to him in everything that was good and pleasing to God, that he received the surname of the Pious.

But Boleslaus was soon to receive the reward of his piety in heaven. After his death and after two of her daughters were married, Yolande and her third daughter left all the glamour and riches of the world and withdrew to the convent of the Poor Clares at Sandec, where, devoted to prayer and mortification, she led a life entirely hidden in Christ. Disturbances resulting from war compelled her after a time to move to the convent at Gniezno, which she herself, assisted by her late consort, had founded.

In spite of the reluctance to which her humility prompted her, she was advanced to the position of abbess. So successfully did she guide her sisters by word and example in the practice of all the religious virtues that the convent flourished like a new garden of God. Even beyond the walls of the cloister she did very much good, so that the fame of the holy abbess spread far and wide.

But, notwithstanding all her fame, she remained entirely devoted to the interior life, as her vocation required. Her favorite devotion was meditation on the sufferings of Christ, during which the Divine Saviour once manifested Himself to her under the appearance of the Crucified. He announced to her that He would soon lead her to glory. Attacked by a serious illness, she asked to receive the last sacraments. Then she admonished her spiritual daughters to persevere in fidelity to the holy rule, and departed blessedly in the Lord in 1298.

After her death Yolande appeared in wondrous glory, together with St. Stanislaus the bishop, to the sick abbess and restored her health. Many other miracles occurred at her grave down to our own time. Pope Leo XII, in 1827, approved the veneration given to her. The feast of Blessed Yolande is observed by the three branches of the First Order on June fifteenth.

ON DESPISING THE WORLD

1. Consider how happy Yolande was already here on earth, when she left the world and all that it held out to her, to serve God as a Poor Clare. Could the enjoyment of all the pleasures and all the goods of this world ever have brought her such happiness? King Solomon tasted worldly pleasure in its fulness, but it did not make him happy. He says: "And, therefore, I was weary of my life, when I saw that all things under the sun are evil, and all vanity and vexation of spirit" (Eccl. 2,17). Did not this duchess make a better choice? Still, what Thomas a Kempis (3,10) says is true: "For it is not granted to all to forsake all things, to renounce the

world, and to assume the monastic life." May you always heed the warning of the Apostle: "And they who use this world as if they used it not" (1 Cor. 7,31), that is, they should not let their hearts become attached to it. — Is your heart attached to this world?

2. Consider how vain and deceitful the goods of this world are. The honors of the world, on which we expend so much energy, cannot make us better, and sometimes they vanish suddenly without any fault of ours. Its riches cause us so much more anxiety the greater they are. Its pleasures are short, and often mixed with much bitterness, as the maxim says:

> "Many a flower grows smooth and fair,
> But bitter the root that it doth bear."

Have you not experienced this yourself? But, as Thomas a Kempis (3,20) says: "The world is censured as deceitful and vain; and yet it is with reluctance abandoned, because the concupiscence of the flesh too much prevails. Some things draw us to love the world; others to despise it." — Examine yourself. What is it that holds you to the world, that keeps you from loving God with your whole heart and serving Him?

3. Consider that our heart should set its goal on something higher if it wishes to despise the world. The heart of man wants to cling to something, yet man was not made for this world and its perishable goods. As Christians we have a higher, a nobler goal, where genuine, imperishable goods await us. That is why the prince of the Apostles says: "Blessed be God, who has regenerated us unto an inheritance incorruptible and undefiled, and that cannot fade, reserved in heaven for you" (1 Pet. 1,4). — Direct the desires of your heart to that inheritance. Then it will soon despise the seeming good things of the world.

PRAYER OF THE CHURCH

Almighty and eternal God, who didst mercifully withdraw Blessed Yolande from honor and riches, and didst graciously inspire her to choose instead the humble cross of Thy Son and the mortification of the flesh, grant, through her intercession and merits, that we may despise temporal things and with upright hearts seek those that are eternal. Through the same Christ our Lord. Amen.

JUNE 16
BLESSED HUMILIANA CERCHI
Widow, Third Order

UMILIANA was a descendant of the ancient noble family of the Cerchi, and was bora in Florence in 1219. From her earliest childhood she was much given to all works of piety, and those who knew her were convinced that she was called for the service of God rather than for the world.

But her father, who had six daughters and twelve sons, and aimed through their alliances to increase the power and reputation of his house, promised Humiliana in marriage to a nobleman when she was but sixteen years old. The humble daughter submitted to the wish of her father and married the nobleman, who proved to be entirely unworthy of her. He was miserly and avaricious, and dealt harshly with his young wife. But she retaliated only with meekness, patience, and charity, seeking consolation with God and in works of charity towards her neighbor.

Her heroic virtues shone forth when her husband fell dangerously ill after five years of married life. She not only nursed him, in a spirit of sacrifice, until his death, but she ceded the entire family fortune to her husband's relatives, with the single condition that they make restitution for all the injustices he had committed.

She then withdrew to her father's house. But when he kept urging her to contract a second marriage, she left the house and family. She now received the habit of the Third Order, becoming the first Tertiary in Florence, and led an unusually austere life in her retirement. She never left her solitude except to visit the churches or to render services of charity to the poor and the sick.

Since her father could not have his way with her so far as his worldly plans were concerned, he strove to deprive her of whatever property rights she still possessed. He succeeded. But, guided by her excellent confessor, Father Michael Alberti, Humiliana was so strengthened in the spirit of our holy Father St. Francis that she rejoiced in being able to fulfill to the letter what our Lord requires when He says: "He who does not renounce all that he possesses, cannot be My disciple" (Lk. 14,33). She only deplored the fact that she could no longer assist the poor. But here, too, she knew how to manage. She was not ashamed to go out begging, and then she distributed the alms among the poor.

In her many tribulations God almighty comforted His servant with extraordinary graces. At prayer she was rapt in ecstasy for hours, sometimes even for days. Once she pleaded, out of heroic charity, to take upon herself the severe pains of a sick person. When that person was relieved and she lay on her couch of suffering amid severe pain, our Divine Lord appeared to her, and with the Sign of the Cross restored her to health again. Her own daughter, who had been reared by her husband's relatives and who had died, she raised to life again. But still more astonishing was the marvelous patience with which she so meekly bore all the reproaches of her relatives no less than the impudence of her own maid.

The ardent longing for God with which her heart was aglow, was soon to be gratified. In her twenty-seventh year she fell seriously ill and felt that her end was near at hand. When her confessor, under whose wise direction she had remained the victor in all her struggles, besought her to be mindful of him after her death, she told him that it would not be necessary for long, because he would soon follow her. And so it happened.

With her confessor at her bedside, Humiliana departed blessedly in the Lord on May 19, 1246. Immediately she was honored by the people as a saint. Pope Innocent XII sanctioned this veneration. The feast of Blessed Humiliana is observed by the Franciscans on June fifteenth, by the Conventuals on May twenty-second, and by the Third Order Regular on May twenty-first. (Cf. *These Made Peace,* pp. 18-21.)

CONCERNING SPIRITUAL DIRECTION

1. Consider how fortunate Blessed Humiliana was to have so dependable a director in the difficult circumstances of her life. Whoever wishes to make progress in the spiritual life, should submit to direction. Thus has God ordained it, so that in everybody the virtue of humility may lay the foundation for the work of sanctification, and ever accompany the work. St. Paul, who as the Apostle of the Gentiles was to be a teacher and leader of thousands, was in his own case sent to another, to Ananias, a disciple of the Lord at Damascus. "And there it shall be told you what you must do" (Acts 9,7). If, then, you were to think you can guide yourself, that would be dangerous presumption.

2. Consider how one should choose a spiritual director. As God singled out a director for St. Paul, so should we above all beg God to let us find the right director. If your ecclesiastical superiors, who are God's representatives, have appointed a director for you, then submit entirely to his guidance. If you are free to
choose among several, then select the one who in knowledge, experience, and virtue is the most suitable for you. If, as may be the case, you have no chance to enjoy advice and guidance, then trust in God and He will

provide, or Himself direct you. Beware of the temptation to change spiritual directors without serious reasons. Thomas a Kempis (1,9) says: "Run hither or thither, you wilt find no rest but in humble subjection. A fancy for places and changing residence has deluded many." — Has it deluded you perhaps too?

3. Consider how you should conduct yourself towards your director. With childlike candor you should reveal to him the state of your soul. You ought never purposely conceal anything from him. He is the physician of your soul, and he can heal and sanctify it only if he knows it perfectly. But then you must, likewise, follow his suggestions faithfully and in a childlike manner. This does not, however, exclude the privilege of asking others for advice. In some instances that may even be obligatory. But you must not place too high an estimate on your own judgment. Rather, as a rule, you should regard the guidance of your director as correct, even though it may not appear so to your own self-love. "The obedient man shall speak of victory" (Prov. 21,28). Then you will also, like Blessed Humiliana, preserve peace of heart in difficult circumstances and make progress in virtue.

PRAYER OF THE CHURCH

Almighty and eternal God, Thou sweetness of hearts and reward of the blessed in heaven, who didst inflame Blessed Humiliana with Thy love and didst fill her with the sweet savor of contemplation, mercifully grant that through her merits and in imitation of her, we may ever follow Thee and deserve to be admitted to the eternal vision of the brightness of Thy Majesty. Through Christ our Lord. Amen.

JUNE 17
BLESSED PAULA GAMBARA-COSTA
Widow, Third Order

LMIGHTY GOD destined this holy woman to be a special pattern for Christian wives and widows in bearing the trials and difficulties of their state. Paula was born in Brescia, in northern Italy, of a very noble family. Even in her youth she showed a special love for solitude and a quiet, devout life. Prayer and spiritual reading were her delight, and she would gladly have exchanged her place in the world for life in a convent. But since her parents promised

her in marriage to the young count Louis Costa, lord of Benasco, Paula
recognized the will of God in this arrangement and complied with the
wishes of her parents.

After the wedding the count conveyed his young wife in great pomp
to the castle at Benasco in the province of Piedmont. He himself was quite
fond of gaiety and amusement, and would have drawn his inexperienced
wife into the whirl of worldly pleasures, for in the beginning she believed
it a duty to yield in everything to the tastes of her husband. But Blessed
Angelo of Chiavasso, whom Paula had chosen as her confessor, kept her
on the path of Christian virtue. He advised her to join the Third Order,
and under his direction she learned more and more to despise the pomp
and pleasure of the world. As far as possible she devoted her services to
the poor, even depriving herself of food in order to bring it to the sick.
One day in winter, meeting a poor woman who was obliged to walk
barefoot over ice and snow, she took off her own shoes and gave them to
her.

The piety of his wife and her devotion to the poor vexed the count,
who had been, meanwhile, pursuing a disorderly and frivolous life. He
reproached Paula severely for her conduct, ridiculed her, and treated her
in a most unworthy manner even in the presence of the servants. The
servants followed the example of their master; they made fun of the
virtues of their mistress, and hurt her feelings on every occasion.

Paula used the saints' way of revenging herself. Ridicule and contempt
she opposed with heroic patience and the meekness of an angel. The
humiliations and persecutions she had to endure, she offered up for the
conversion of her husband, whose disorderly life was her heaviest cross.
She also prayed fervently and performed rigorous penances for the same
intention. Finally her prayer was heard.

The grace of God and Paula's persevering virtue led the count to enter
into himself. He became sincerely repentant, approved entirely of all of
Paula's good works, and even consented to let her wear the habit of the
Tertiaries in public.

After his death Paula lived for God alone. She was constantly occupied
with meditation on the sufferings of Christ. She waited on the poor and
the sick as suffering members of Christ her Lord. She strove to resemble
our Lord in the fasts and the many austerities she practiced.

After a life full of good works and merit, she died in the Lord in the
year 1505. God manifested her sanctity by granting numerous miraculous
answers to prayers at her tomb. Pope Gregory XVI approved the devotion
paid to her without interruption. Her feast is observed on June fifteenth
by the Franciscans, and on January twenty-eighth by the Third Order

Regular. (Cf. *Forum*, 1948, pp. 16, 24; These Made Peace, pp. 181-182.)

DIFFICULTY IN MARRIED LIFE

1. Consider that married life is invariably a cross in one way or another. The Apostle writes: "If you take a wife, you have not sinned; and if a virgin marry, she has not sinned; nevertheless such shall have tribulation of the flesh" (1 Cor. 7,28). Where two persons are so intimately associated, even though it be for their mutual support, it must happen that, taking into account differences of temperament and the changeableness of the human mind, there will be much to overcome, much to endure. Add to this the usual family cares. — On the other hand, to be called to the married state and keep aloof from it merely because of these hardships, might be merely courting a much heavier cross. Married people should rely on the grace of the sacrament of matrimony in accepting the cross of this state of life, and then "bear one another's burdens, so that they may fulfill the law of Christ" (Gal. 6,29). — Have you acted thus?

2. Consider that frequently married people make life hard for themselves, be it through the fault of one of the parties or even of both of them. Most of the sufferings here on earth are caused by human beings themselves. If a husband is remiss in the duties of his state; if he is careless about his work; if, like the husband of Blessed Paula he gives himself up to worldly and sensual pleasures, indulges in drink and in gambling; if he takes no pleasure in being at home with his family, but only gives expression to his ill-humor whenever he is there; surely, that can make life very hard for the wife. Likewise, a man is to be pitied if his wife is lazy and untidy, or wasteful and fond of dress, or garrulous and quarrelsome. "It is better to dwell in a wilderness than with a quarrelsome woman" (Prov. 21,19). If both parties act in that way toward each other, their life may prove to be a very unhappy one and what St. Bernard says is only too likely to come true: "From a hell here on earth they go off to another hell in eternity." In how many unhappy marriages is this the case!

3. Consider that a hard married life has led many people to a high degree of holiness. Blessed Paula is a shining example in point. She shows how one can arrive at holiness under such trying circumstances: by perfect resignation to God, by sincere and profound piety. Sometimes almighty God permits such a cross to afflict them to lead them to true piety. By this means they are taught and strengthened to carry their cross with patience and to requite bitterness with meekness. Thus the cross becomes a ladder to heaven, and on it one's partner in life is also sometimes saved. It was in that way that St. Monica, like Blessed Paula, obtained the conversion of

her husband. The tears which great sorrow causes us to shed during prayer are, as St. Augustine says, like the blood of a heart pierced with pain. Such blood shed in secret cries aloud to heaven and cannot permanently pass unheeded. And when it is heard, how fervently the person will thank God for the cross, at least on his deathbed.

PRAYER OF THE CHURCH

Lord Jesus, who didst perfect Blessed Paula in the path of holiness by imitation of Thee on the way of the cross, grant us through her merits and example so to bear the trials of this life that at the hour of our death we may be consoled by Thy holy cross. Who livest and reignest forever and ever. Amen.

JUNE 18
BLESSED PETER GAMBACORTI OF PISA
Confessor, Third Order

PETER GAMBACORTI was born in 1355. His father was the president of the Republic of Pisa and Lucca. As a youth he led a dissipated life; but, when he was twenty-two, he received the grace of a complete conversion through the example and prayers of his sister Clare who had become a nun. Peter joined the Third Order of St. Francis and retired to a lonely spot on Monte Cessano, near Urbino, in Umbria, and began to do penance there as a hermit.

One day a band of twelve robbers came upon his hut. They were so deeply affected by the hermit's poverty and piety, that they too abandoned their evil ways and joined him in his life of penance. Other disciples increased their number to such an extent that Peter organized them into a Third Order congregation called the Poor Brothers of the Love of Christ; and they moved to the wooded heights of Montebello, overlooking the Adriatic. So severe were the penitential practices of these hermits that they were accused of being in league with the devil. Peter was cited before the court of the Inquisition, but it soon became evident that the charges raised against him were baseless. Because their way of life was so austere, Peter himself made the regulation that only those who were between the ages of eighteen and fifty could be admitted to the brotherhood.

The hermitage on Montebello became the motherhouse of other monasteries of hermits; and in 1421 Pope Martin V gave his approbation to the Third Order congregation. By 1435, when Blessed Peter died, other hermitages of the Poor Brothers had been founded near Venice, Pesaro, Treviso, Fano, Padua, and Urbino; and under Blessed Peter's successor, Bartholomew Malerba of Cesena, convents were established also at Mantua and Vicenza. Blessed Mark Marconi, who died in 1510, belonged to the hermitage at Mantua. In Rome, San Onufrio Convent was opened.

Other congregations of hermits who lived according to the rule of the Third Order of St. Francis were likewise merged with the Poor Brothers founded by Blessed Peter. Among these were the congregations of Angelo of Corsica, of Blessed Nicholas of Forcapalena (who died in 1449), and of Peter of Malerba. Also the Hermits of Monte Segestre.

Long after the death of Blessed Peter, in 1568, the rule of St. Augustine, together with special constitutions, was adopted by the Poor Brothers. A small number still exist today, and they are called the Poor Hermits of St. Jerome of the Congregation of Blessed Peter of Pisa. The cult of Blessed Peter was approved by Pope Innocent XII in 1693; and his feast is observed by the Jeronymites on June 17. Although he was one of the great Tertiary beati, Blessed Peter is not commemorated in the Franciscan calendar. (Cf. Biersack, pp. 148-149; *These Made Peace*, p. 174; Heimbucher, vol. 1, pp. 594-595.)

ON THE NECESSITY AND THE POWER OF GRACE

1. Consider the saying of Holy Scripture: "And where sin abounded, grace did more abound" (Rom. 5,20). These words first of all refer to the time of Christ. When the sins of the world had reached their highest peak, Christ appeared with His infinite measure of grace. But the truth of these words is still continually evident in the lives of individual persons, as in the case of Blessed Peter and his first disciples. When they left their heart a victim to temptation and shut out grace, they fell deeply. But when grace touched them, they opened their heart to it and directed their efforts to return. Grace then proved so super-abundant in them that they gloriously overcame all temptations. How highly we ought to treasure divine grace! "If you knew the gift of God!" (Jn. 4,10).

2. Consider that without the grace of God we can do nothing good. "Without Me," says the eternal Truth, "you can do nothing" (Jn. 15,5). Yes, we are not capable of a good thought without the grace of God, since "it is God," writes the Apostle, "who works in you both to will and to accomplish" (Phil. 2,13). Therefore Thomas a Kempis also says (2,14): "There is no sanctity if Thou, O Lord, withdraw Thy hand. No wisdom avails if Thou cease to govern us. No strength is of any help if Thou cease

to preserve us. No chastity is secure without Thy protection." Therefore pray a great deal that almighty God may grant you His grace, and then be grateful for the grace received, so that it may not again be taken from you. 3. Consider the wonderful power which grace gives us. The same Apostle who acknowledges that man is powerless without the grace of God, says also confidently: "I can do all things in Him who strengthens me" (Phil. 4,13). Truly a Christian would have to give up in despair if in his struggles with the devil, his fallen nature, and the world, he had to stand alone, dependent only on his own power. But an omnipotent God dwells in heaven, who is "rich in grace unto all who call upon Him" (Rom. 10,12). If you ask, who is to lead you happily through all the tribulations and struggles of this life to the eternal goal, then the Apostle answers: "The grace of God by Jesus Christ our Lord" (Rom. 7,25).

PRAYER OF THE CHURCH
(First Sunday after Pentecost)

O God, the strength of those who hope in Thee, favorably give ear to our supplications; and since without Thee mortal infirmity can do nothing, grant the help of Thy grace that, in fulfilling Thy commandments, we may please Thee both in will and action. Through Christ our Lord. Amen.

JUNE 19
THE SERVANT OF GOD MATTHEW TALBOT
Confessor, Third Order

HIS modern penitent and Tertiary is a great miracle of God's grace. He was born in Dublin, the third of twelve children of honest and devout parents, on May 2, 1856. At first he was employed as a messenger boy with a firm of liquor merchants, later he became a laborer.

In spite of good training, however, he took to drinking. He became a drunkard, but the day dawned when grace led him to Damascus. After spending fifteen years as a drink addict, he went one evening to his mother and said: "I am going to take the pledge." On the same day he made a general confession and after that he was a changed person.

Without doubt, Matt Talbot merited this grace of conversion by the way he preserved chastity, never omitted making the Sign of the Cross morning and evening, and was faithful in attending holy Mass on

Sundays. The struggle against a passion that was so deeply rooted in him was not an easy one. He gathered strength, however, from his daily attendance at holy Mass and his visits to the various churches in Dublin on Sundays, as well as from the devotion he had to our Blessed Lady.

At the suggestion of his confessor, he joined the Third Order of St. Francis and entered wholeheartedly into the spirit of the Poor Man of Assisi. His bed consisted of a board, and a block of wood served as his pillow. For hours he would kneel on his bare knees without supporting himself in any way. His nourishment consisted of nothing but bread and tea. In this way he became a model for Christian workmen: conscientious, faithful in small matters, friendly toward everybody. His secret, as he was wont to call his efforts at acquiring virtue, remained his own.

Although his weekly wages in a wholesale lumber yard amounted to hardly five dollars a week, nevertheless he contributed one hundred fifty dollars towards the foreign missions in a single year. But more than this, the holy laborer assisted the sick and sinners by his prayers. Sometimes the results were remarkable.

In 1923 he was laid low by sickness, due to the labor and the penance he performed. Then Matt Talbot became the personification of patience. Once, twice, he was discharged from nursing care, and then he began his penitential life anew. Finally his time came. On Trinity Sunday, 1925, Matt was on his way to church when he fell. Casting one more look toward heaven, he died. When his body was being prepared for burial, a heavy wagon chain was found around his body, another around his arms and feet.

Almighty God has testified by extraordinary signs and wonders that Matt Talbot must be reckoned among the great saints of our day. The process of his beatification has been introduced.

ON THE WAYS OF GOD

1. God's ways are incomprehensible. The Apostle of the Gentiles cries out in astonishment: "Oh, the depth of the riches of the wisdom and of the knowledge of God! How incomprehensible are His judgments!" (Rom. 11,35). Who would ever have surmised that the drunkard Matt Talbot would develop into a saint? And yet that is exactly what happened. Let us learn from his case to leave all things in the hands of God. He knows how to turn all things to the best end, whether we see the issue that way or not. — Try never to be short-sighted in your judgment of God.

2. God's ways lead to a definite goal. God says: "My thoughts are not your thoughts, neither are your ways my ways" (Isa. 55,8). But so much is

certain: Just as we are more definitely sure of reaching our destination if we let the right train take us there, so are we assured of arriving at our goal if we cling to God, even though His ways are concealed from us. He is the best engineer. — Hence, remain closely united to God at all times. 3. God's ways are, above all, directed to the things of eternity. We always imagine that things have to go well with us here on earth. We are always building air castles for ourselves here on earth. Yet, we have not been created for this world, but rather for the happiness of eternity. And this is ever in the mind of God, especially when He sends us suffering and affliction. It is by this means that He wishes to detach us from this earth and to make us ripe for heaven. A true Christian, therefore, will always remember the words: "To them who love God all things work together unto good" (Rom. 8,28). — Resign yourself always to the guidance of God who wills only your welfare.

PRAYER OF THE CHURCH
We beseech Thee, O Lord, that Thou wouldst pour into our hearts the gifts of the Holy Ghost, through whose wisdom we have been created, and by whose providence we shall be guided. Through Christ our Lord. Amen.

<hr />

JUNE 20
THE SERVANT OF GOD JOHN ZUMARRAGA
Confessor, First Order

JOHN was born in the Basque province of Biscay in Spain, and there entered the Franciscan Order. Because of his extraordinary virtue and talent he was frequently appointed to the higher offices in his province. He was guardian of the friary at Abroxo near the capital of Valladolid, when the King of Spain, Emperor Charles V, arrived there to spend Holy Week at the friary, as was his pious custom.

The emperor was greatly edified at the perfect order, the holy zeal, and the austere poverty which prevailed in the convent.

But above all he was delighted with the conversation of Father John, at whose piety, zeal for souls, and enlightened wisdom he could not marvel enough. When, therefore, the question arose in 1528 of appointing a bishop for the recently conquered realm of Mexico, the emperor believed that he could not propose a better person to the pope than Father John.

Only in obedience did John accept this great honor, for there was a heavy burden associated with it. In Mexico it would be his task to set the affairs of the Church in order, promote the propagation of the Faith, and at the same time protect the native Indians against unjust oppression by the emperor's officials, concerning whom many complaints had been sent to the emperor. The latter gave Father John special authority, and urged him to depart for the new country even before he had received episcopal consecration.

John found conditions in Mexico in a very bad state. The highest as well as the lowest officials sought to enrich themselves at the expense of the newly acquired provinces. They treated the natives like slaves, drove them from their property, which they took for themselves, and sent them into the mines to dig gold and silver for them. Many of the Spaniards led scandalous lives and proved to be a hindrance to the conversion of the natives.

With great prudence John began to remonstrate with the officials. But they endeavored to justify themselves on the score that they were the conquerors. They even contended that the Indians were not real human beings and had no claim to be treated as such. Then John informed them of the authority that had been given to him by the emperor, and threatened to punish them if they did not desist from their unjust course. That infuriated them. They sought to take his life, and showed themselves hostile to all priests, especially the Franciscan missionaries.

Since every attempt at kindness was in vain, John publicly pronounced the ban of excommunication on the godless and obdurate officials. A spear was hurled at him as he did so, and only by a miracle did he remain alive. From now on he had to endure no end of annoyance. His letters to the emperor were intercepted, and no mail from Spain was delivered to him, until John got an honest sailor from Biscay to be his secret messenger. Forthwith a new royal governor came, who deposed the recreant officials. John was calumniated and recalled to Spain in 1531; but he easily refuted the charges raised against him. He was highly commended for his courage and firmness, received episcopal consecration, and was sent back to Mexico with new powers as Protector of the Indians.

John returned to Mexico as bishop in 1534, and could now labor for the salvation of souls with less hindrance. His report to the general chapter of the order at Toulouse mentions the following results achieved: More than a million Indians baptized; over five hundred pagan temples deserted; and whereas formerly twenty thousand children were sacrificed to the devil every year by having their living hearts torn out of their bodies and burnt before the idol, now there were just as many children being reared in a Christian way, and they in turn were leading their parents to the Christian religion.

The bishop labored in person and without rest at the conversion of the Indians.

In the last year of his life, John's see of Mexico was raised to an archdiocese, but he never wished to be called archbishop. When he felt his strength leaving him and his end drawing near, he invited all who had not yet received confirmation to present themselves at Pentecost. He had administered the sacrament to fourteen thousand persons in Pentecost week when his strength failed him on Friday. With great edification he received the last sacraments, and died happily on Sunday during the octave of Corpus Christi, June 3, 1548, in the eighty-third year of his life. His last words were: "Into Thy hands, O Lord, I commend my spirit." Several miracles have occurred at his grave in the cathedral at Mexico.

ON CHRISTIAN COURAGE

1. Consider the Christian courage with which Bishop John opposed the despots in defense of the poor Indians. Naturally, he tried first to lead them to justice by milder means, but then he proceeded with severity regardless of danger to his life. The duty of his office was the one thing in his mind, and he feared nothing except to be untrue to his God. A similar duty sometimes falls to the lot not only of spiritual and temporal superiors, but also of husband and wife, of parents, of masters and mistresses, of teachers, and of all whom God has made guardians of what is right and good. Never may they allow themselves to be intimidated through human respect. Rather, the fear of the Lord should impel them to carry out their duty. "Be not afraid of them who kill the body. Fear Him who has power to cast into hell" (Lk. 12,4).
2. Consider that often where there is no official obligation, the love of our neighbor, or the salvation of our soul, or the honor of God may compel us to take the courageous stand of a Christian against evil. If, for instance, you see a woman constantly maltreated by her husband, or children thus treated by unnatural parents, or old parents by their children who are unmindful of their duty, then step in if possible, and speak to the conscience of the erring. Where your own salvation is at stake, fear no one. Think of Susanna, whom the Lord protected. If you hear God's honor blasphemed in irreligious or indecent conversation, then prove that you are a child of God, who cannot remain indifferent when the honor of God is concerned. "He who fears man, shall quickly fall. He who trusts in the Lord, shall be set on high" (Prov. 29,25).
3. Consider what it was that gave Bishop John undaunted courage. Next

to the grace of God it was detachment from material things. He had no desire for riches and honors among men. Where the things of God were concerned, he did not fear death, which at the worst could only bring him eternal life. Hence, he was in a position similar to that of his patron Saint John the Baptist, and could say to those in authority: "It is not lawful" (Mt. 14,4). — Detach your heart from temporal things which perish like grass in the field, and by your courage you will promote the eternal values.

PRAYER OF THE CHURCH
(Postcommunion 34, under "Various Prayers")
Grant unto Thy faithful people, we beseech Thee, O Lord, constancy in the true Faith and in Christian life; that, confirmed in divine charity, they may let no temptation draw them away from its perfect fulfillment. Through Christ our Lord. Amen.

JUNE 21
THE SERVANT OF GOD LEONORE GUSMAN
Virgin, Second Order

EONORE was the daughter of the duke of Medina-Sidonia, one of the wealthiest and most distinguished gentlemen of Spain. When she was eight years old, she had lost both her parents and was placed in the care of an uncle at Seville, who provided for her with a truly paternal love. She requited his affection with childlike attachment and obedience until the time arrived when there was question of a state of life.

When Leonore was eleven years old, at which age Spanish girls were often promised in marriage, her uncle believed he was obliged to provide for his foster-daughter, and arranged for her an excellent opportunity to marry. But Leonore rejected the proposal. When her uncle praised the bridegroom he had chosen for her, and desired that she should at least make his acquaintance, she explained that she had already chosen the heavenly Bridegroom and could not give her attention to anyone else without failing in the fidelity she owed to Him.

A few days later she asked for permission to visit her aunt, who was the abbess of a convent of Poor Clares. Leonore used this opportunity to slip into the enclosure of the convent, and nothing could induce her to leave it again. Her uncle and other relatives were very much embittered at this turn of events. A complaint was even lodged with the king, together with a request that Leonore be forced to return home.

The king decided that Leonore should be taken from the convent of her aunt to another convent of Poor Clares, where she should freely express her wishes before the archbishop and the royal governor. There she declared that in accordance with the desire of her heart she had freely chosen the religious state, adding that she would rather be torn into a thousand pieces than be unfaithful to her vocation. So she was permitted to return to her aunt's convent, where, at the age of twelve, she received the holy habit.

Leonore was a model for all the sisters in complete poverty, deep humility, strict penance, and persevering prayer. After she had practiced perfect obedience as a subject for twenty-eight years, she was elected abbess, which office she administered worthily for the space of forty-one years, until her death. Thirteen months after her death her grave was opened and her body was found entirely incorrupt, for which reason she was buried in a beautiful tomb in the choir of the church.

ON THE FOURTH COMMANDMENT

1. "Honor your father and your mother, that you may live long upon the land" (Exod. 20,12). Thus almighty God spoke solemnly upon Mount Sinai, and thereby made respect and obedience toward parents and their representatives a strict obligation. But did Leonore not fail in this respect when she refused to follow the will of her uncle and foster-father in regard to marriage? No, because this commandment of God requires obedience only in matters that are just and pleasing to God. Children should, indeed, have the advice of their parents, especially when they are about to choose a state of life, and they should seek their parents' blessing for whatever choice they make. But parents may neither force their children into any particular state, nor restrain them from following a chosen vocation. If they do so, their children are in no way bound to obey them. The Boy Jesus in the temple said to His sorrowing Mother: "Did you not know that I must be about My Father's business?" (Lk. 2,49).

2. Consider, however, that in all matters that are legitimate and pleasing to God, obedience to parents is a holy obligation for children. After our duties toward God are set forth in the first three commandments, this commandment is placed at the head of all the duties we have toward men. To whom could we be more indebted than to our parents? And who will be more concerned about what is truly best, than Christian parents are on behalf of their children? Hence Solomon, the Wise Man, after saying, "The fear of the Lord is the beginning of wisdom," immediately adds the

precept, "My son, hear the instruction of your father and forsake not the law of your mother" (Prov. 1,7-8). That holds not only for the years of childhood, but as long as one lives with his parents in the parental home. In that spirit the younger Tobias spoke to his father when the latter sent him on a long journey: "I will do all things, father, which you have commanded me" (Tob. 5,1). What higher praise can come to a young man than if parents say of him what the parents of Tobias said: He is "the light of our eyes, the staff of our old age, the comfort of our life, the hope of our posterity" (Tob. 10,4). — Could your parents say this of you?

3. Consider that in the fourth commandment almighty God adds a promise: "That you may live a long time, and it may be well with you in the land" (Deut. 5,16). General experience definitely confirms the truth that he who honors his parents insures for himself long life and a share in the good things of this world. On the other hand, not infrequently the curse of God rests already in this life upon those who do not honor their father and mother. "The eye that mocks at his father, and that despises his mother, let the ravens pick it out, and the young eagles eat it" (Prov. 30,17). But, if it appears too humiliating to you to obey the orders of your parents, then reflect on the example of Jesus Christ and the little saying found in a children's catechism:

"Obedience is the grandest choice, its act true greatness claims;
Obedient was God's only Son, and He in heaven reigns."

PRAYER OF THE CHURCH
(Number 27 under "Various Prayers")

O God, who withstandest the proud and givest Thy grace to the humble; endue us with that true virtue of humility, the pattern of which Thy only-begotten Son showed in Himself to the faithful; and may we never by our pride, provoke Thee to anger, but rather in lowliness accept from Thy hands the gifts of Thy grace. Through the same Christ our Lord. Amen.

JUNE 22
BLESSED JOACHIMA DE MAS Y DE VEDRUNA
Widow, Third Order

ORN in Barcelona, Spain, in 1783, Joachima was the fifth of the eight children of the aristocratic Vedruna family. When she was twelve she wanted to be a cloistered Carmelite nun; but at sixteen she married a young lawyer, Theodore de Mas, who had been thinking of becoming a Franciscan. Both joined the Third Order Secular of St. Francis. During the seventeen years of her married life, Joachima was a beloved wife and the devoted mother of eight children, the last of whom was born in 1815.

When Napoleon invaded Spain, Theodore served in the Spanish army, after he had moved his family to Vich. When the French troops arrived there, Joachima had to flee with her children; but after the war she returned to that city, the birthplace of her husband. Joachima and Theodore were both members of the Third Order fraternity at the Capuchin church in Vich. She was only thirty-three when Theodore died in 1816 at the age of forty-two.

Though her old desire to enter a religious community was still strong in her, she had duties to perform towards her children; and so, for the first seven years of her widowhood she took care of her children. At the same time, she led an austere life, wearing the Tertiary habit as her ordinary dress, spending much time in prayers, and waiting on the sick in the hospital at Vich.

One day in 1820, as she was passing the Capuchin church, her mount refused to go farther. She went into the church and entered the confessional of Father Stephen of Olot, a noted preacher and director of souls. He told her that she was not to join an existing religious order but to found a new community which would devote itself to teaching in schools and to nursing the sick.

In 1823, two of her children married and one of them took the two remaining girls into their home. Joachima was now free to carry out her plans. Father Stephen assisted her in laying the foundations for a Franciscan sisterhood of the Third Order Regular and drafted the constitutions. The new sisterhood was formally established in 1826 in Joachima's home with six members, but not as a Franciscan community. Bishop Paul Corcuera of Vich, a Carmelite, made it a congregation of the Carmelite Third Order Regular and called it the Carmelite Sisters of Charity. Later St. Anthony Mary Claret revised their rule and constitutions. In 1850 these received the approval of the bishop and in

1880 the approbation of the Holy See.

Though a hospital was opened at Tarrega a few months after its founding in 1826, the new sisterhood had to contend with many difficulties during the first years. During the Carlist Wars, Mother Joachima was put in a prison for five days in 1837; and she, with some of her sisters, was an exile in Perpignan, France, for three years until the fall of 1843. Convents with schools and hospitals were then established all over Catalonia.

Sickness compelled Mother Joachima to resign the superiorship in 1851; and during the last four years of her life, a gradual slow paralysis caused her to die by inches. She was seventy-one when she died in 1854. In 1940, the Carmelite Sisters of Charity had 2,000 members in 150 convents, of which 135 were in Spain and 10 in Spanish America. Mother Joachima, who attained a high degree of prayer, trust in God, and selfless charity, was enrolled in the ranks of the Blessed in 1940; and May 22 was selected as her feastday. (Cf. *Forum*, 1940, p. 454; Attwater, *Butler's Lives of the Saints*, Supplementary Volume, 1949, pp. 76-80.)

ON MEMBERSHIP IN THE FRANCISCAN ORDER

1. Membership in the Franciscan Order should make us grateful. It is a great grace which has been given to us without any merit on our part. It is certainly a privilege to belong to an institute which has given so many saints to the Church and which has accomplished so much for God and souls during the seven and one half centuries of its existence. As members of this order, we should love it, learn more about its history and spirit, promote it in every way we can, and strive to become ever more worthy children of St. Francis. In this way we can show our gratitude for the inspiration, guidance, and help we receive in the order, advantages that we would not have if we were standing alone and shifting for ourselves.

2. Membership in the Franciscan Order should not make us proud but humble. We can not take any credit for the achievements of the many saintly members of the order. We should rather ask ourselves: Do I deserve the name of a child of St. Francis? What have I contributed to the good name of the order? How much has been accomplished by the sainted and saintly followers of Francis who are mentioned in this book, and how little I have done! With St. Francis say: As much as I, as an individual, am in the sight of God, so much I am and no more. The order, at any particular time, is as good as its members are at that time. Superiors especially have the task to see to it that the order, that is, its members, are what they should be. It is not an easy task, and the members of the order

can make it far less difficult by striving earnestly and perseveringly to live faithfully according to the rule and spirit and tradition of the order.

3. Membership in the Franciscan Order should not develop in us a spirit of partisanship. There is something wrong, if it does. Essentially all the religious orders, and that includes the Third Orders, are the same and have the same purpose. All of them were instituted for the purpose of leading souls to perfection and sanctity, and, by united effort, to promote the honor of God and the welfare of souls. We should not be blind to the achievements of other religious orders; and we should gladly lend a helping hand in their good works whenever we can, even if we, or the order, do not get any credit for it. As the rule of the Third Order of St. Francis says, we should promote every good work of piety and charity. The Third Order has often supplied willing workers for the enterprises of other societies, like that of St. Vincent de Paul; and it has been a nursery of religious vocations, not only for the Franciscan orders and congregations, but for others as well. "Be perfectly united in one mind and in one judgment ... Has Christ been divided up? Was Paul crucified for you? ... I have planted, Apollos watered, but God has given the growth ... I have applied these things to myself and Apollos by way of illustration for your sakes, that in our case you may learn not to be puffed up one against the other over a third party, transgressing what is written ... Although you have ten thousand tutors in Christ, yet you have not many fathers. For in Christ Jesus, through the Gospel, did I beget you" (I Cor., chapters 1-4).

PRAYER OF THE CHURCH

O God, who hast united the divers peoples of the earth in the praise of Thy name; grant that those born again of water in baptism may all be one in mind by faith and one in deed by holiness of life. Through Christ our Lord. Amen.

<hr />

JUNE 23
ST. JOSEPH CAFASSO
Confessor, Third Order

 OSEPH was born in 1811 at Castelnuovo of pious parents. The sanctity and apostolic zeal in which he later excelled manifested themselves in him when he was still a child. The usual games of boyhood held no attraction for him. He preferred to occupy himself with God, counting it as a special pleasure if he could attend the holy sacrifice of the Mass and engage in other pious exercises. At the age of six he was already called a saint. As a youth in the public schools and later as a student in Cheri seminary, he continued to be an object of respect because of the innocence of his life, his gravity, humility, observance of rules, and his fervor at prayer. He was frequently referred to as another Aloysius Gonzaga.

Not long after his ordination to the priesthood, Aloysius Guala, an exemplary priest, established a seminary in connection with the church of St. Francis of Assisi at Turin, where young priests were instructed in their sacred calling, and especially fitted to defeat the various errors of Jansenism. Joseph was appointed a teacher at this institution and succeeded the founder after his death.

As head of the seminary, Joseph quickly completed the arduous task which Father Guala had begun but had not been able to finish. He completely rooted out the pernicious doctrines of Jansenism and those of other reformers, reviving the teachings of St. Francis de Sales and of St. Alphonse Liguori, which clearly point out the way to Christian perfection. Joseph continued this mission as long as he was a priest with such constancy and fidelity that the task seemed to have been assigned to him by our heavenly Father Himself.

In his tireless zeal for the divine glory and the salvation of souls, Joseph combined example with words. He did all he could to promote devotion to our Lord in the Blessed Sacrament, toward whom he manifested great love, and never ceased urging the faithful to approach the great banquet daily. Our Blessed Lady had been the object of his devotion ever since his boyhood days, and he now sought to inspire others to love her with filial devotion.

His solicitude extended also to the ministers of the altar, whom he encouraged in zeal and effort to gain souls for Christ. He was a member of the Third Order of St. Francis, and used to recommend this institution as the ideal society, especially for priests who are cut off from worldly associations.

There was no spiritual or temporal need in which he did not interest himself, no kind of calamity for which he did not offer a corresponding means of alleviation, no good work which he did not encourage or support. His heart went out to the orphans, the poor, the sick, and those detained in prison. He shirked no hardship, not even danger to life, in the accomplishment of his undertakings. By his counsel and help he persuaded his dearest pupil, Don Bosco, to found the society of St. Francis de Sales, or the Salesians, whose work for Church and souls has been outstanding.

But the interest Blessed Joseph manifested in the various problems of suffering humanity, was outdone by that which he evinced toward unfortunates who were condemned to death. His sacrifices for them were unlimited. He used every means at his disposal to find an easy approach to their hearts, and the great power of his love overcame their obstinacy. When at last he had restored them to the grace and friendship of God, he accompanied them to their execution, which he regarded not so much as temporal death as the entrance into eternal life.

After doing such great things for God and meriting the veneration of all who knew him, Blessed Joseph humbly begged God to erase his memory altogether after death. Worn with hardships, but enriched with merits at the early age of only forty-nine years, he died the precious death of the just on June 23, 1860, fortified with the sacraments of the Church.

Because of his virtue and the miracles performed through his intercession, Pope Pius XI in the Holy Year of 1925 added his name to the list of the blessed, and in 1947 Pope Pius XII declared him to be a saint. The Franciscans observe the feast of St. Joseph Cafasso on June twenty-third; and the Conventuals observe it on April twenty-ninth. (Cf. Forum, 1947, pp. 167-171.)

"I WAS IN PRISON AND YOU CAME TO ME"

1. Consider how far removed from the minds of most people is the idea of sympathy and compassion for prisoners. The word convict at once suggests the idea of a criminal to them, and as such the prisoner is at once shut out from any share in their charity. Still, records show that sometimes a person detained in prison is innocent of the crime charged to him. He is suffering either from the malice or the ignorance of others. God is the only witness of his innocence, and in the meantime he must content himself with bearing the trial sent him by Providence. His patience is put to a crucial test, not only by the fact that he is suffering unjustly, but also because his family must suffer, first of all, by reason of the stigma attached to the prisoner's name, and secondly, because, being deprived of his physical and moral support, the family have become dependent upon others and have perhaps fallen into bad ways themselves. Up to the present, perhaps no such unfortunate thing has occurred to a member of your family. But is it impossible that it could happen? What sentiments would you entertain towards prisoners if it did, and what attitude would you wish your friends and acquaintances to take? External

evidence has so often proved deceptive that we should be kind in our judgment of those who are sentenced to imprisonment, and remember that God alone can read the heart of man; He alone has the right to inveigh against them. — Pray that God may give patience to those who are in prison, innocent of the crime imputed to them.

2. Consider further, that even those whose guilt has been proved may not be excluded from our charity. Rather, they should be the special objects of our compassion. They are our brothers in Christ, no matter what misdeeds they have committed, no matter what evil ways they have followed. Our Lord evidences His sentiments towards them in clear terms: "I will not the death of the sinner but that he be converted and live" (Ezech. 33,11). In spite of his guilt, our Lord wants this soul back in the fold, just as He wanted the lost sheep there and left the ninety-nine until He found that one. It may not be in our power by personal contact to render charity toward prisoners, yet we can do much by way of bringing these stray members of the flock back to the arms of Christ. We can pray for them, that God may move their hearts to acknowledge their guilt, confess their sins sincerely, and accept in a spirit of penance the punishment meted out to them. — Have you ever prayed for these wayward children of God? If not, do so from now on and remember the words of our Lord in the Gospel: "As long as you did it to one of these My least brethren, you did it to Me" (Mt. 25,40).

3. Reflect on the difficult task that faces chaplains of prisoners. They must win the confidence of these people. They must be able to penetrate a callous exterior and touch the finer sentiments of their hearts, which at times need only the right approach to be revived. They need to break down the wall of prejudice that frequently stands between them and their charges. They need to be gentle, long-suffering, and courageous to meet the many disappointments that await them in a task that at times seems almost futile. They need, finally, to be stout-hearted enough, like Blessed Joseph Cafasso, to perform the extraordinary task of preparing a condemned man for execution, walking with him on the last journey he makes on earth. If the work of priests in general is regarded as fraught with great responsibility, what shall we think of the work of priests charged with the onerous duty of bringing back such wayward souls? Our charity ought to reach out to them, and in that way we may merit a share in the good they achieve.

PRAYER OF THE CHURCH

O God, who didst adorn Blessed Joseph, Thy confessor, with remarkable charity and invincible patience in laboring for the salvation of souls, grant, we beseech Thee, that, urged by his example and assisted by his intercession, we may attain to the joys of eternal life. Through Christ our Lord. Amen.

❦❦❦❦❦❦❦❦❦

JUNE 24
THE SERVANT OF GOD ILLUMINATUS OF RIETI
Confessor, First Order

ILLUMINATUS was the son of wealthy and distinguished parents, but was born blind. Once when St. Francis preached at Rieti, the father of Illuminatus invited him to lodge at his home. Now when St. Francis came into the house, the parents brought the blind boy to him and urgently begged St. Francis to bless him. Filled with compassion, St. Francis made the Sign of the Cross over the child's eyes, and at once the child could see. St. Francis also told the parents in advance that later the boy would join his order. And thus it happened.

When the boy had grown to young manhood and had gained a splendid education, he recognized that all the glamour the world offered him in his eminent position was in reality only passing and dazzling tinsel. He desired better and more lasting treasures, and therefore earnestly begged St. Francis for admission into his order. St. Francis gave him, with the habit, the name of Illuminatus, that is, the enlightened one, not only because he had miraculously received the sight of his bodily eyes, but more so because the grace of God had enlightened his mind to recognize the vanity of the world and devote himself to the service of God.

Illuminatus did indeed evince fine understanding of higher things, and with it lively zeal to advance in perfection. He became one of the most beloved disciples of St. Francis, who chose him as his companion on his journey to Syria. When they arrived at Damietta, they came upon the camp of the Crusaders, who were just then making ready for battle against the unbelievers.

St. Francis said to his companion: "God has revealed to me that if they launch this offensive, great misfortune will befall the Christians. If I tell them this, they will laugh me to scorn, but if I remain silent, my conscience will reprove me. What do you think about it?" Illuminatus answered: "Brother, be not disturbed about the judgment of men; act according to your conscience and fear God more than men." And so

Francis announced to the Christians the revelation that had been granted him and warned them against making the attack. He was scoffed at, but the battle terminated in defeat for the Christian army.

Illuminatus was so trusted by St. Francis that he disclosed to him the miraculous way in which he had received the sacred stigmata, so that Illuminatus could bear witness to the fact after the death of St. Francis. He lived forty years after the death of his spiritual father, and was one of the most reliable witnesses of his admirable life. In 1266 he died on the fifth day of May, regarded by all as a saint, and was laid to rest in the church of St. Francis of Assisi.

ON TRUE ENLIGHTENMENT

1. Consider how the servant of God Illuminatus was granted the gift of true enlightenment. True enlightenment is nothing but true knowledge of things, and he is truly enlightened who has a knowledge of things which corresponds with reality. But there can be no truer knowledge than that which faith and grace bestow upon us, because this knowledge proceeds from the Father of light and the source of all truth. It was this light that made an enlightened man of Illuminatus in his estimation of the glamour of the world. — May it enlighten all of us!

2. Consider, how idle is the false enlightenment of the class of people who like to regard themselves as the enlightened class. They despise faith and divine revelation, and hold as right and true only what they can comprehend with their puny intelligence. They act like a person who heavily curtains the windows of his home so that no ray of sunshine can penetrate, and then lights an oil lamp, declaring that he can trust only the light of his own lamp. "Professing themselves to be wise, they became fools" (Rom. 1,20). — Is not such foolishness to be pitied?

3. Consider how enlightened the advice was which Illuminatus gave St. Francis — to follow the voice of God and his conscience and not heed the judgment of men. The fruit of true enlightenment is ours when we carry out in our lives the truths revealed by God and our faith. The reason why so many people end up with false enlightenment is because they refuse to apply the truths of Christian revelation in their lives. That is why they hate and deny the truth and end up in folly. Christ is our teacher as well as our leader. He says: "He who follows Me, walks not in darkness" (Jn. 8,12). — May His teaching, His example, and His warning grace constantly guide us!

PRAYER OF THE CHURCH (Third Sunday in Advent)
We beseech Thee, O Lord, incline Thine ear to our prayers and enlighten
the darkness of our minds through the grace of Thy visitation. Who livest
and reignest forever and ever. Amen.

JUNE 25
THE SERVANT OF GOD PAUL (PAULUTIUS) TRINCI
Confessor, First Order

LL human institutions are subject to an abatement of their
original glory because of the frailty of human nature. Thus it
is even in religious orders. After a century of existence, the
Franciscan Order also lost some of its first perfection,
especially in the observance of poverty as St. Francis practiced and
prescribed it.

Still, the works of God — be they institutions which God Himself has
founded, like the Holy Church, or be they such that owe their existence
to servants of God, like the Franciscan Order — always give proof of the
presence of the Spirit of God in whom they are rooted, for in the course
of centuries, He causes the original fervor to be revived again and again
and to flourish anew.

In the fourteenth century, the Spirit of God chose a simple lay brother
Paul, who because of his insignificant figure was called Paulutius, as His
instrument in the Franciscan Order. Paul was born in 1309 at Foligno, of
the house of the counts of Trinci, who at that time governed the city of
Foligno. But Paul, who had a generous heart in his small body, resolved
already at the age of fourteen years to renounce the world and its
pleasures, in order to consecrate himself wholly to the service of God in
the Order of St. Francis. Although he had a good education, he wished in
his humility to be only a lay brother.

In 1334, when Father John of Valle began a stricter life according to
the primitive rule, Brother Paul and other zealous brethren at once joined
him. But with the death of Father John, the reform was retarded. In 1368,
when Paul had already entered upon his sixtieth year, he felt an urgent
impulse again to take up the work. Assisted by his brother, Count Ugolino
of Trinci, governor of Foligno, he obtained permission from the general of
the order to repair, with brethren entertaining similar sentiments, to the
secluded convent at Brugliano, there to live in the strictest observance of
the rule of St. Francis.

Some of the brethren did not persevere in that strict poverty, silence, continuous prayer, and practice of penance, and returned again to their convents. But their places were filled by a greater number who now came to Brugliano. Soon there were so many of them that they could establish other convents.

When Pope Gregory XI heard of this reform, he commended it and approved it in 1370. And so it happened that the little convent at Brugliano became the cradle of the form of observance which was propagated in the following century by St. Bernardin of Siena and St. John Capistran, and led the order to new glories. By 1517 it comprised the majority of the order's membership.

Paul gradually established fifteen convents of the reform, over which he was appointed commissary general. His example attracted many of the brethren to the observance, and his fervent prayer drew down upon them the power of divine grace for perseverance in the good work.

When on occasion Paul was detained in Foligno on business pertaining to the order, he would spend hours in an old tower in order to pray undisturbed. Once a flame was seen to burst forth from the top of the tower. The people of the town ran to the place and entered the tower, but they found only Brother Paul deeply absorbed in prayer and aglow with fervor, while flames radiated from his body and flared out beyond the pinnacle of the tower.

Paul died in 1390, in the eighty-first year of his life. Imitating St. Francis in death, he lay on the bare floor, his arms crossed, and a sweet smile playing about his countenance as he pronounced the holy names of Jesus and Mary. His tomb has been glorified by many miracles.

ON FIDELITY TO ONE'S VOCATION

1. Consider the exemplary fidelity of Brother Paul in his vocation. Called by God to the Franciscan Order, the desire of his heart was to answer the call with the utmost fidelity. Every person on earth has his vocation from God and, consequently, also the duties of his vocation. We are all called to Christianity. It is of this call that the Apostle speaks when he admonishes us: "Walk worthy of the vocation in which you are called, with all humility and mildness, with patience, supporting one another in charity" (Eph. 4,1-2). But, in addition, everybody has his particular place in life, and the duties of his station must be the rule of his life. "As God has called everyone, so let him walk" (1 Cor. 7,17). The Apostle adds the special admonition: "Take heed to the ministry which you have received in the Lord, that you fulfill it" (Col. 4,17). God will judge you according to

your vocation. — How would you at this moment fare in that judgment?
2. Consider how Paul descended from the prominent position in which he
was born to a lowly estate. But he brought great honor to this state by his
fidelity, and he is honored for it even to this day by God and men. The
position does not do honor to a man, but a man does honor to his position.
"Were you called, being a bondman? Care not for it" (1 Cor. 7,21). A
servant and a maid, who are faithful to their calling, will have greater
honor for all eternity before God and men than their master and mistress
if the latter have been less faithful in their vocation. Just as at a play, the
actor is applauded not according to the role he plays, but rather according
to the fidelity with which he acts out the role assigned to him, so it will be
with men and their vocation. "We are made a spectacle to the world, and
to angels and to men" (1 Cor. 4,9).
3. Consider by what means Paul preserved perfect fidelity in his calling.
He looked up to the example of his holy Father Francis, so that he in turn
became a model for his brethren, and he prayed fervently and continually
for God's grace to enlighten and strengthen him. You, too, should look up
to those who are most exemplary in your vocation, especially to the saints,
and plead often with God, as did King Solomon: "Give me wisdom that
sits by Thy throne, that she may be with me and may labor with me, that
I may know what is acceptable to Thee" (Wisd. 9,4-10).

PRAYER OF THE CHURCH
(Over the People on Thursday in the Second Week of Lent)

Give ear, O Lord, to Thy servants when they call upon Thee, and grant
them Thy perpetual favor; that whereas they glory in Thee, their Creator
and Ruler, Thou mayest gather and restore to them Thy gifts and mayest
keep alive in them what Thou hast restored. Through Christ our Lord.
Amen.

JUNE 26
BLESSED JUTTA OF THURINGIA
Widow, Third Order

 UTTA, born in Thuringia, was a member of the very noble
family of Sangerhausen with which the dukes of Brunswick
were related. She was espoused to a nobleman of equal rank,
but in the married state she was more intent upon virtue and

the fear of God than upon worldly honor.

In the beginning the piety of Jutta displeased her husband. But later he learnt to value it and was heart and soul with her in her pious endeavors. He made a pilgrimage to the holy places in Jerusalem and died on the way. Jutta received the news of his death with deep sorrow, but also with the most perfect conformity with the will of God, and resolved to spend her widowhood in a manner pleasing to God.

After she had provided for her children, who had all been reared in the fear of God, Jutta, with the consent of her confessor, disposed of the costly clothes and jewels she had until then worn in accordance with her rank, as well as all her expensive furniture. She entered the Third Order of St. Francis, and wore the simple garment of a religious. She devoted herself entirely to the care of the sick, especially the lepers, and to the poor, whom she visited in their hovels and provided with all necessities. The crippled and the blind she led by the hand to her home and took care of their needs.

Many people laughed at the distinguished lady who made herself the servant of the poorest. But she recognized in the poor her Divine Lord, and deemed herself happy and highly honored that she could render them such services. Once when she was at prayer, Christ Himself appeared to her and said to her lovingly: "All My treasures are yours, and yours are Mine." That spurred Jutta on to still greater devotion in serving the poor of Christ.

Another time when she was ill and apparently close to death, our Saviour again appeared to her and gave her the choice of entering into glory at the time, or of suffering still more out of love for Him. Jutta chose suffering. Our Lord gave her strength again to be up and about, but He now destined her for a spiritual work of mercy.

On the eastern boundary of Germany, at the mouth of the Vistula, the Prussians were still living as pagans. St. Adalbert, archbishop of Prague, had indeed attempted to convert them to Christianity, but all in vain; he was martyred in 997. Since 1226 the German Order of Knights labored to bring these stubborn pagans under the yoke of Christ. To offer assistance in the great labor which this undertaking required, God wished someone to pray.

By divine inspiration, Jutta went into this neighborhood about 1260, and built a little hermitage near a large body of water. There she prayed unceasingly for the conversion of the Prussians. The Christian inhabitants of the neighborhood sometimes beheld her raised high in the air in the fervor of her devotion. She had as her confessor the Franciscan Father John Lobedau, who died in the odor of sanctity, and later the bishop of

Kulm.

After Jutta had lived here for four years, her holy life came to a close. With deep contrition she again confessed to the bishop all, even the smallest, faults of her entire life, received the holy sacraments, and surrendered her soul to God with the words, "It is consummated." Her body was brought to the church at Kulm, where without being informed, so many people at once gathered as had not been seen in that city for many years. The church was filled with a wonderful odor.

Since very many miracles were wrought at her grave, a special chapel was built in her honor, in which Jutta has been venerated for centuries as the special patron of Prussia.

ON CHRISTIAN WIDOWHOOD

1. Behold in the servant of God Jutta the model of a Christian widow. After the death of her husband she remained a widow in order to serve God alone. The Apostle writes: "If a woman's husband die, she is at liberty; let her marry whom she will, only in the Lord. But more blessed shall she be, if she so remain" (1 Cor. 7,39-40). Where no weighty reasons urge remarriage, widowhood in Christian continence is very pleasing to God. Hence the holy Gospel praises the eighty-four-year-old Anna, who, after being married for seven years, persevered in widowhood. Thus is holy continence held in esteem in every state of life.

2. Consider how Jutta used the freedom of her widowhood. Above all she faithfully fulfilled her duty towards her children. After she had provided for them, she laid aside all finery and every mark of her distinguished rank, and became the servant of the poor, the guide of the lame and the blind, the mother of the orphans and the neglected. Thus the Apostle describes the exemplary widow as one who has "a reputation for her good works in bringing up children, in practising hospitality, in washing the saints' feet, in helping those in trouble, in carefully pursuing every good work" (1 Tim. 5,10). — May this be the aspiration of every Christian widow.

3. Consider how Jutta was finally called by God to a solitary life of prayer. The widow Anna also "departed not from the temple, by fastings and prayers serving night and day" (Lk. 2,37). Retirement and piety are above all most becoming to a widow. A widow who roams about idly from house to house, is given to gossip and curiosity, likes to speak of things that are not becoming, and lives in pleasure, "is dead while she is living" (1 Tim. 5,6). If a widow is hard pressed and wanting in resources, she has the more reason to remain closely united with God, who delights in being

called the father of the widows and orphans. "But she who is a widow indeed and desolate, let her trust in God, and continue in supplications and prayers night and day" (1 Tim. 5,5). The Sorrowful Mother should be her particular refuge. After St. Joseph died Mary had to stand by while her dearly beloved Son died on the cross. — Can the afflicted widow find better comfort than in this thought?

PRAYER OF THE CHURCH (Collect on Good Friday)
Almighty and eternal God, the comfort of the afflicted and the strength of those who labor; let the prayers of those who call upon Thee in any trouble be heard by Thee, that all may with joy find the effects of Thy mercy in their necessities. Through Christ our Lord. Amen.

JUNE 27
BLESSED GUY OF CORTONA
Confessor, First Order

N the year 1211, when our holy Father St. Francis was preaching in Cortona on his first missionary journey through Italy, a certain young man was so touched by his words that, after the sermon, he entreated St. Francis to dine at his house. The saint accepted the invitation. When the young man learnt further details about the newly founded order, and witnessed the edifying conduct of the founder, he fell at his feet and begged for the habit of the order. The young man was Guy, or Giles, first-born son of a distinguished family in Cortona. He had been reared in piety and virtue, and was quite accomplished in the sciences.

Francis directed him to distribute his wealth among the poor, and gave him the holy habit in the parish church of Cortona in the presence of a great concourse of people. Then Francis chose a spot in a secluded valley near Cortona, where, with the assistance of some devout persons, he built a poor convent. For a few months the saint himself instructed Guy and several other novices there. At his departure he entrusted to Father Sylvester, his companion, the direction of the novices, especially of young Guy, whose eminent holiness he foresaw.

In fasting, prayer, and all the religious exercises, Guy evinced such perfection that he could be held up to the other novices as a model. He would have preferred to spend all his life in the holy seclusion of the convent. But when he was ordained to the priesthood, St. Francis commissioned him to go out and preach, for in accordance with the vocation of the order, he was to sanctify not only himself but others as well.

Filled with zeal for souls, Guy left his seclusion. His words had great influence over the hearts of sinners, his holy life edified everybody, and almighty God confirmed his activities with extraordinary miracles. One time Guy was quite ill with exhaustion, and nothing but water was at hand by way of medicine. Guy made the Sign of the Cross over it, and it became the most choice wine, which restored his health and what was left over later healed the infirmities of others.

After a most blessed and successful career, almighty God announced to Guy, in the sixtieth year of his life, that his death was near at hand. St. Francis, who had long ago entered into heavenly bliss, appeared to him and said: "My son, after three days, at nine o'clock, I shall return and escort your soul to the eternal dwellings." His already decreasing strength then began to ebb rapidly. On the third day he received the last sacraments with great devotion, and when the appointed hour arrived, he called out: "Behold our holy Father Francis! Arise, let us go to meet him!" With these words he jubilantly surrendered his pure soul into the hands of his Maker. It was May 12, 1250.

Upon receiving the news of his death, the people of Cortona came to get the precious remains of their fellow citizen in order to bury them in the parish church. Amid the festive pealing of bells, with palm branches in their hands, and singing spiritual hymns, they transported the holy body in a long procession to the town. There the remains were entombed in the principal church. Many miracles were wrought through his intercession.

After some time enemies invaded the city, the church was pillaged, and the precious coffin containing the body was carried away. But the sacristan hastily wrapped the head in linen cloths and hid it in a well near the church. At the end of three years, when the church was being restored, mysterious light radiated from the well. Upon investigation, the head was found, not even moistened by the water. Amid the jubilation of the entire town it was again placed in the church.

Benedict XIII approved a proper Mass and Office in honor of Blessed Guy for the diocese of Cortona. Pope Innocent XII extended it to the entire Franciscan Order. His feast is observed by the Franciscans on June twenty-seventh, and by the Conventuals and the Capuchins on the sixteenth.

CONCERNING GOOD EXAMPLE

1. Consider that the proverb: "Actions speak louder than words," was verified in Blessed Guy. He was moved by the sermon of St. Francis, but he felt mightily drawn to follow his footsteps when he beheld his edifying life. The power of good example is easily explained. It awakens in the beholders esteem and love for the virtue they behold exemplified before their eyes. Then, too, the example encourages them to practice a virtue which until then appeared too difficult to perform. Finally, one learns from example in what manner the virtue is to be practiced. — Have you profited by the good example of others?

2. Consider that one must avoid as much as possible the bad example given by others, because the saying that example draws, applies also to them. In order not to see the bad example of the world, Blessed Guy would have preferred remaining in seclusion. We who are so weak have even greater need to avoid seeing such example. But when you come upon bad example which you cannot avoid, let it serve as a warning, so that good may result instead of harm. — Have you done this up to the present time, or have you rather used the bad example of others to excuse your own faults? Have you yourself perhaps given bad example to others?

3. Consider how Blessed Guy edified the world by means of his good example. We are obliged to set a good example to others. Our Lord admonishes us to do this in His Sermon on the Mount: "So let your light shine before men, that they may see your good works, and glorify your Father, who is in heaven" (Mt. 5,16). Tertiaries are bound to good example in a special way by their rule (2,8), which prescribes: "They should endeavor to set a good example to others." — Try to do that as did Blessed Guy, without any desire for honor, but purely out of love for God and your neighbor. Then you, too, will partake of the glory of Blessed Guy.

PRAYER OF THE CHURCH

O God, who didst give us Blessed Guy, Thy confessor, as a model of religious perfection and as a zealous preacher of the divine word, we beseech Thee, grant us through his intercession the grace that by good works we may set a good example to our fellowmen. Through Christ our Lord. Amen.

JUNE 28
THE SERVANT OF GOD FRANCIS DE PORRAS
Martyr, First Order

ORN at Villanueva de los Infantes in Spain, Francis de Porras joined the Franciscans as a young man; and on September 12, 1606, he was ordained a priest in the Church of St. Francis in Mexico City. His life as a son of St. Francis was so exemplary that for many years he was entrusted with the task of training the novices of the order. However, he longed to be a missionary to the pagan Indians; and after he had been a priest for about a decade and a half, he was permitted to go to the province of New Mexico which included the northern part of the present Arizona. He was chosen to establish a mission among the Moquis or Hopis in northern Arizona, who had till then stubbornly resisted all attempts to make Christians of them. On August 20, 1629, he arrived at the Moqui pueblo of Awatovi and established the Mission of San Bernardo. His companions were Father Andrew Gutiérrez and Brother Christopher de la Concepción.

After working a great miracle by which sight was given to a boy, about twelve years old, who had been blind from birth, Father Francis enjoyed extraordinary success in converting the Moquis to Christianity. In less than nine months he mastered their difficult language and reduced it to a system. During the four years that he spent among these Indians, Father Francis baptized more than four thousand souls and thoroughly instructed his neophytes in Christian doctrine and life. He also commenced building an imposing church, the foundations of which were uncovered by the Peabody Museum of Harvard University during excavations in 1935-1939. Several other missions were established later among the Moqui Indians, but Awatovi remained the principal one. Even after the Great Pueblo Rebellion of 1680, the people of Awatovi made Christian burials; and they alone, of all the Moquis, were led back into the Fold in 1700, for which reason Awatovi was completely destroyed by the other Moquis. All this indicates that Father Francis firmly established the Christian Faith at Awatovi.

The old pagan medicine men of Awatovi were so angered at the success of Father Francis and the consequent loss of their power, that they tried to kill him openly several times. Not succeeding in this, they secretly poisoned his food. As soon as Father Francis had eaten of this food, he realized what had been done and knew that he had not much longer to live. He hastened to his fellow missionary, Father Andrew Gutiérrez; and on his knees he received the last sacraments from him with great devotion. Father Francis then began to recite Psalm 30: "In Te, Domine, speravi — In Thee, O Lord, have I hoped, let me never be confounded"; and when he came to verse six: "Into Thy hands I commend my spirit," he surrendered his soul to his Creator. The date of his death was June 28, 1633. In 1943 the finding of the remains of a Franciscan missionary in the ruins of Awatovi was reported. They may be those of the holy martyr Father Francis de Porras, or of Father Joseph de Figueroa who died a martyr at Awatovi in 1680. (Cf. *Heroes of the Cross*, pp. 32-33; *The Martyrs of the United States*, p. 61; *Franciscan Awatovi, Peabody Museum*, Report No. 3, 1949, pp. 9-12 and 129-132; *Forum*, 1943, p. 318.)

ON THE PROFESSION OF FAITH

1. Consider that faith consists in inward submission of our hearts to all the truths which God has revealed and the Catholic Church proposes for our belief. But it is not enough to carry the faith in our hearts. Just as man is obliged to serve God with body and soul, so should he profess with his tongue the faith that he acknowledges in his heart. "For with the heart we believe unto justice, but with the mouth confession is made unto salvation" (Rom. 10,10). Moreover, the faith that is in our hearts would grow cold and inactive if we did not frequently express it in words. It is for that reason that we speak of the profession of faith as an "awakening of the faith." — Do you make your act of faith daily?

2. Consider that it is necessary on occasions during our lifetime to profess our faith, and that we may never be ashamed of it. Everybody considers it a disgraceful thing if a son is ashamed of the parents who have reared him perhaps in the sweat of their brow and at the cost of many hardships. Jesus Christ sacrificed His Blood to redeem us from our sins and to make us children of God. How odious, then, would be the ingratitude and how keen the pain offered to our Saviour, if anyone of us were ashamed to acknowledge his membership in the Christian Faith, to venerate the crucifix, to kneel respectfully in church, or to pray before and after meals! Such behavior would certainly deserve punishment. "For he who shall be ashamed of Me and of My words, of him the Son of man shall be ashamed when He shall come in His majesty" (Lk. 9,26). — How will you fare in that day?

3. Consider that the worst sin against faith is the denial of the Faith. He who denies his Christian Faith separates himself from Jesus Christ, from baptism which he received in His name, from the remission of sin which is granted us by His authority, from redemption which He accomplished for our sakes, from the bliss of heaven which He merited for us. "He who

shall deny Me before men, I will also deny him before My Father who is in heaven" (Mt. 10,33). How many there are who deny their faith! All those deny their faith who assent to conversations against the Faith, who say that one religion is as good as another; also those who permit their children to be reared in any other religion. And how many there are who deny their faith by the life they lead! "They profess that they know God, but in their works they deny Him." May the grace of God bring them back, and may it strengthen all Christians to profess their faith in word and in deed.

PRAYER OF THE CHURCH
(Secret in the Mass of the Blessed Virgin during Advent)
Strengthen, O Lord, in our minds, we beseech Thee, the mysteries of the true Faith, that we who confess Him who was conceived of a Virgin to be true God and Man, may by the power of His saving resurrection merit to attain to eternal gladness. Through the same Christ our Lord. Amen.

JUNE 29
BLESSED BENVENUTE OF GUBBIO
Confessor, First Order

IN the Umbrian town of Gubbio, north of Assisi, there lived a knight named Benvenute, who had achieved great martial fame for his valor. When St. Francis came to Gubbio in 1222 in order to preach in that vicinity, Benvenute saw him and listened to him with astonishment. His martial spirit took great pleasure in the saint's perfect mortification and contempt of the world.

The grace of God so touched his heart that, after a few days, Benvenute presented himself to St. Francis in complete knightly attire and entreated him humbly to admit him as a lay brother. Francis always had great esteem for soldiers who distinguished themselves for obedience, self-denial, and fearless courage, for he considered such training a very good preparation for the religious life. Since Benvenute evinced in addition to these good qualities a very profound humility, Francis recognized in him the true soldier of Jesus Christ and gladly received him among his brethren.

Clad in a poor garment and girded with a cord, the stately warrior was now seen heroically overcoming himself. The poorest in clothing, dwelling, and food was his choice. The purity of his heart shone in his countenance and in his entire external appearance. He seemed to have no will whatsoever of his own, so perfect in obedience was he at all times.

St. Francis charged him with the care of the sick in a leper hospital. There he had, in truth, daily and hourly opportunities to practice heroic charity and self-denial. But Benvenute was always seen to wait upon the patients, even the most repulsive among them, with such cheerful devotion and care as if he were serving his Divine Lord. Otherwise very serious and reserved, he was very sociable when he spoke to the sick and the depressed in order to cheer them up.

Benvenute was also favored by God with a high degree of contemplation. Sometimes he spent whole nights in prayer, pleading with God with burning tears for the conversion of sinners. Towards the Blessed Sacrament he entertained an ardent devotion filled with lively faith, and frequently our Divine Lord descended into his arms in the form of a charming child. He also had a very special devotion to Mary, the Blessed Mother of God.

The more completely to purify his soul and increase his merit, God allowed him to be seized with a severe illness, after he had himself tended the sick for many years. As his active charity formerly edified everybody, so his patience and perfect resignation to God's holy will did so now in a greater degree. He died ten years after his entrance into the order, on June 27, 1232, in the city of Corneto.

Astonishing miracles wrought at his grave at once gave evidence of his holiness, and attracted a great concourse of pilgrims, so that only a few years after his death Pope Gregory IX sanctioned his public veneration in Corneto and the surrounding country. Pope Innocent XI extended the devotion to the entire Franciscan Order in the year 1697. The feast of Blessed Benvenute is celebrated by all three branches of the First Order on June twenty-ninth.

ON FULFILLING THE DIVINE WILL

1. Consider how manfully Blessed Benvenute overcame himself and all the human desires of his heart. That made it so easy for him to fulfill God's will in all things, even the most difficult. He entered the order as soon as he recognized that God wished it thus, and he went cheerfully to tend the sick according to the will of God's representative. God also admonishes us in Thomas a Kempis (3,37): "Relinquish yourself and you shall find Me, for greater grace shall be added to you as soon as you have given up yourself." — What has made it till now so difficult for you to do the will of God and that of His representative except that you do not forsake

yourself, but rather cling to your own will?

2. Consider that we must ever be content to let the will of God be done in us, as Benvenute was in his illness. Often we ourselves do not know what is good and wholesome for us. Like unreasonable children, we frequently desire things that would only lead to our destruction. But God, our heavenly Father, preserves us from them and in His good pleasure permits only that to happen to us which is for our good. For that reason Christ our Lord instructs us that before petitioning our heavenly Father for our daily bread, we should pray: "Thy will be done on earth as it is in heaven" (Mt. 6,10). — Do you pray thus each day with all your heart?

3. Consider that the fulfillment of the will of God determines our happiness and perfection here on earth as well as our treasure of merits for eternity. Happy and contented is the man whose will is always accomplished. But that is the case with him who in advance wishes for nothing but what God wills, for God says: "All My will shall be done" (Isa. 46,10). That there is nothing more perfect, however, than such conformity, is manifest in Jesus Christ, the model of perfection, when He says: "My meat" — that is, My life and My joy — "is to do the will of Him who sent Me" (Jn. 4,34). Accordingly our Divine Judge assures us already here on earth that heaven is the reward for those who fulfill God's will: "He who does the will of My Father who is in heaven, he shall enter into the kingdom of heaven" (Mt. 7,21). — May this holy will ever be done in us and by us!

PRAYER OF THE CHURCH

O Lord Jesus Christ, who didst glorify Thy confessor Benvenute with perfect self-abnegation in imitation of Thee, we beseech Thee, grant us the grace always to do Thy will and thus merit to partake of the same glory. Who livest and reignest forever and ever. Amen.

JUNE 30
THE SERVANT OF GOD ORLANDO (ROLAND) OF CHIUSI
Confessor, Third Order

 N one of his missionary journeys through Italy in 1213, St. Francis came into the neighborhood of a castle belonging to a certain count. A great concourse of people was gathering for a festival which the count was giving that day. Since the enemy of our salvation knows how to use such occasions to lead souls astray, the servant of God resolved to go there with his companions to warn the Christian people.

When solemn Mass in the castle chapel was over, Francis ascended an elevated place in front of the chapel and gave an edifying address on the dangers of worldly pleasures. All the guests listened with attention, because the fame of his sanctity had already spread far and wide. In particular, one of the most prominent guests at the castle, Count Orlando (or Roland) Catanii of Chiusi, was very much affected by this address of the saint. He went to Francis and asked for an interview and for advice on leading a life that would be pleasing to God.

Now, while St. Francis was zealous for the salvation of souls, he was also mindful of the requirements of good breeding. He told the count that the present time was not opportune for such an interview, that he should not withdraw himself from the company of his friends to which he had been invited. At a more seasonable time he would be glad to serve him for the advancement of his salvation.

When, shortly afterwards, the saint visited Count Orlando in his gorgeous palace, he spoke to him so warmly about the dangers of a life spent in wealth and every comfort that Orlando resolved to arrange his life entirely according to the principles laid down by St. Francis. He also desired very much to have him and his brethren nearby, and proposed that the saint build a little convent on Mount La Verna, which belonged to him and at the foot of which his palace was situated. He placed the entire mountain at the disposal of St. Francis.

Francis inspected the mount with his brethren, and found the wooded recess with its many caves and ravines very suitable for a quiet life of prayer. He therefore gratefully accepted the offer of the count. Orlando had a convent as well as a church built there at once; later many chapels were added. This place was chosen by God as the scene where the holy wounds were later impressed on St. Francis.

In return, the pious donor, Orlando, desired nothing more than that St. Francis should receive him into the Third Order and become his spiritual director. Under this guidance Count Orlando attained to complete detachment from temporal goods. Thenceforth he practiced works of charity towards his neighbor with great zeal, and distinguished himself in all the virtues of a Christian nobleman. After his happy death he was laid to rest in the convent church on Mount La Verna.

ON THE DANGERS OF RICHES

1. "How hard it is for them who trust in riches, to enter into the kingdom of heaven" (Mk. 10,24). Thus says Christ, the eternal Truth. And because riches keep so many people out of heaven, He says: "Woe to you who are rich, for you have your consolation" (Lk. 6,24). By His example, too, He wished to show us the safest way to heaven. Therefore He chose the carpenter, Joseph, for His foster-father, and shared his laborious life with him. There were then good reasons for it if St. Francis pointed out the dangers of riches to Count Orlando. Under the circumstances, what Christian would still crave to be rich? — Have you perhaps been led by this craving?

2. Consider that the dangers of riches are manifold. Temporal goods so easily enslave the heart and make the owner worldly-minded. To that may be added the anxiety associated with preserving and securing riches as if one were meant to live here on earth forever. Thus it was in the case of the rich man in the Gospel who wondered anxiously what he should do with the fruits of his harvest. "But God said to him: You fool, this night will they require your soul of you" (Lk. 12,20). Then, too, riches are an occasion to lead a life of sensual pleasure, as did Dives: "... and he was buried in hell" (Lk. 16,22). Finally, man readily places all his trust in riches, becomes proud, and forgets the poverty and misery of his soul for which he stands in great need of God's assistance. A rich man is apt to grow domineering toward his fellowmen, despising the lowly, and forgetting the demands of Christian love and mercy. Riches mislead him, and at the end of his life he stands before the eternal Judge with empty hands and a heart laden with guilt. — Is there any reason, indeed, to envy the rich?

3. Consider that a rich man can nevertheless be saved. Christ says: "With men this is impossible, but with God all things are possible" (Mt. 19,26). By the grace of God and Christian sentiments the rich man, too, can enter heaven, yes, store up great treasures for himself there, as God's servant Orlando did. A rich man should not become elated over his temporal goods, he must consider them as a gift of God given into his care in order to do good and earn treasures for eternity. Thus St. Paul writes to his disciple, Bishop Timothy: "Charge the rich of this world not to be high-minded, nor to trust in the uncertainty of riches, but in the living God, to do good, to be rich in good works, to give easily, to communicate to others, to lay up in store for themselves a good foundation against the time to come" (1 Tim. 6,17-19).

PRAYER OF THE CHURCH
(Secret for the Twenty-fourth Sunday after Pentecost)

Be favorable, O Lord, to our supplications, and receiving the prayers and offerings of Thy people, turn the hearts of us all to Thee, that being delivered from the greed of earthly pleasures, we may pass on to heavenly desires. Through Christ our Lord. Amen.

JULY

JULY 1
THE SERVANT OF GOD PHILOMENE JANE GENOVESE
Virgin, Third Order

PHILOMENE Jane belongs to those admirable souls who were strong and courageous despite the weakness of nature, arriving at extraordinary holiness already in their youth, and happily combining penance with innocence of life.

She was born of the Genovese family at Nocera in 1835, and was devoutly educated. The first words and the first greeting uttered by this little angel were "Ave Maria!" The Most High, who chooses to be praised by the mouths of little ones, weaned little Philomene at a very early age from the glamour of the world. She exchanged her beautiful dresses for poor clothes, and she preferred to engage in the lowliest household duties. She used to reprove the maid who was charged with attending to her hair: "You are too particular about such material things. It will be too bad for us if we fail to remember Christ, whose hair was torn from His head!"

She was anxious to enter the religious state, but Providence decreed otherwise. By means of purity and penance, Philomene was to become a spectacle to a dissolute and effeminate world. In order to belong entirely to God, she consecrated herself to Him in the world by the three vows. Then her trials began. Terrible maladies visited her, but Philomene accepted them all with such heavenly patience and joy that the attending physician once said: "You are a saint! Pray for me!"

She lived up to her motto: "Nothing is nearer and dearer to me than to do the will of God." From the day of her admission into the Third Order, she gradually rose to a high degree of perfection. To the various ailments that afflicted her she added scourging and all sorts of mortifications. This heroine of purity, patience, and penance had not yet attained her thirtieth year when she went forth with her lamp well filled to meet her heavenly Bridegroom. She died in the year 1864. The cause of her beatification was introduced in 1919.

ON LUXURY IN DRESS

1. Consider the evil involved in luxury in dress. It was not without good reason that the servant of God Philomene despised it. "Glory not in apparel" (Eccli. 11,4). Whoever pays too much attention to luxury in dress, nourishes vanity and the ambition to please others, is too solicitous for what is exterior, neglects the interior life, and rouses envy and even worse sins in others. — Is there nothing here with which you have to reproach yourself?

2. Consider what should be the style of a Christian's apparel. It should becomingly cover the body, and protect it against the inclemencies of the weather. It may indeed be attractive. The prevalent fashion, however, may not be the sole authority in these matters, but rather a Christian sense of propriety and modesty, and a healthy artistic taste. Everything that savors of sensuality should be avoided, for our Lord Himself says: "They who are clothed in soft garments, are in the houses of kings" (Mt. 11,8). — If our dear Lord examined your apparel, could He approve of it?

3. We must resist the inclination toward luxury in dress. If the inclination arises in you, be mindful of the poor swaddling clothes of our Saviour, and the still poorer loin cloths on the cross. Think of our Blessed Lady, whom you can hardly picture to your mind in luxurious dress. Remember the words of Scripture: "Whose adorning let it not be the outward plaiting of the hair, or the wearing of gold, or the putting on of apparel: but the hidden man of the heart in the incorruptibility of a quiet and meek spirit which is rich in the sight of God" (1 Pet. 3,3-4). — Have you given your main attention to the adornment of your soul?

PRAYER OF THE CHURCH

Be merciful, O Lord, to our humble petitions. Accept the offerings and prayers of Thy people and convert our hearts to Thee, so that freed from sensual desires we may raise them to heavenly ones. Through Christ our Lord. Amen.

JULY 2
THE SERVANT OF GOD BERNARD OF QUINTAVALLE
Confessor, First Order

ERNARD of Quintavalle was the first disciple of St. Francis not only in the order of time but, as St. Bonaventure states, also in the order of sanctity. He was a wealthy man of Assisi, universally esteemed because of his wisdom, experience, and great virtues. When important civic matters had to be decided upon, his advice was usually followed. Desire for greater perfection urged him to remain unmarried.

When Bernard saw young Francis practice the poverty and humility of Christ in such an admirable manner, he felt impelled to follow his way of life. He wished, however, to determine whether it was just sentimentality or sincere love of God that moved Francis, and so he invited him to his home. At their evening repast Bernard conversed with Francis and begged him to remain for the night. A comfortable bed had been prepared for Francis. When everything grew quiet in the house, Bernard observed how Francis arose and, casting himself upon his knees, continued in prayer throughout the night. Sometimes he heard him sigh: "My God and My All!"

At daybreak Bernard told his saintly guest that he had decided to forsake all things of earth and to become his disciple. It was a source of great joy for Francis to receive so distinguished a man as his first companion in the perfect service of God. But he said to Bernard: "Concerning this matter we must determine what is the will of God. Let us go to church, that His will may be made known to us."

Having assisted at holy Mass and spent some time in devout prayer, they asked the priest to open the book of the Gospels for them three different times. At the first opening they read the words: "If you wish to be perfect, go, sell what you have and give to the poor" (Mt. 19,21). The second opening revealed the following: "Take nothing for the way" (Mk. 6,8). The third: "If any man will come after Me, let him deny himself and take up his cross and follow Me" (Mt. 16,24). Then St. Francis said: "This will be the rule of life which we and all those who will join us shall follow."

Bernard went forth and sold all his goods and divided the proceeds among the poor. Then he returned to Francis. He was never happier than when he had a cross to carry or some act of self-abnegation to practice. And many such opportunities presented themselves.

When several other associates had gathered around Francis, he sent

Bernard and a companion to Florence and then to Bologna. Because of their poor garments and the strange life they were observing, they were subjected to much ridicule and persecution in both these cities. This gave Bernard cause for rejoicing. He accepted all with perfect calmness and interior joy for love of Christ. But when Bologna gradually recognized his great virtue, and honors began to be heaped on him from all sides, Bernard asked Francis to take him away, since there was now no more opportunity for gaining merit there.

The holy Founder held Bernard in great esteem, not only because he was an older man, but also because of his great virtue, which made his age still more venerable. St. Francis was accustomed to call him the first-born of the order, and wished all the brethren to respect and honor him as they honored the Founder himself.

When St. Francis went to France and Spain in 1213-1214 to preach to the Mohammedans in Africa, he took Brother Bernard with him. On the way, however, they encountered a poor sick man, and Francis directed Bernard to remain and attend to the man's wants. Bernard did so willingly and cheerfully until Francis called for him again on the return journey.

Before his passing, the holy Founder gave Brother Bernard a special blessing and again charged all the brethren, superiors as well as subjects, to respect him. After the death of St. Francis, Bernard associated little with others. He was indeed sociable, and rated everybody higher than himself, but the spirit of prayer drew him to his beloved solitude, where he kept united with God in holy contemplation and conversed with the holy angels.

He died on July 10, between 1241 and 1246, and was buried in the church of St. Francis next to his spiritual father. Some time later, two of the brethren saw him in the convent of the Portiuncula in heavenly brightness, his eyes beaming like two suns. When the brothers questioned him about that, the glorified Bernard replied that the distinction had been granted to him because he had interpreted everything he saw in the best possible light and had looked upon everybody as better than himself. (Cf. Brown, *The Little Flowers of St. Francis*, pp. 41-57, 325-326.)

ON RESPECT FOR OLD AGE

1. Consider how St. Francis himself respected the servant of God Bernard, who was already advanced in years, and how he desired that the brethren also should honor him. In this St. Francis observed the teaching of Holy Scripture: "Rise up before the hoary head, and honor the person of the aged man" (Lev. 19,32). Old age, which is a gift of God, is in itself a crown

of honor and is frequently the reward of faithful observance of the divine commandments, as is expressly promised by God in the fourth commandment. The troubles which aged people have borne, the merits they have acquired, the experience they have accumulated — all these things make them deserving of reverence, and make their counsels to younger generations valuable. "Despise not the discourse of them who are ancient and wise, but acquaint yourself with their proverbs; for of them you shall learn wisdom and instruction of understanding" (Eccli. 8,9-10). — Have you acted in this manner in the past?

2. Consider that the infirmities of old age should make us compassionate rather than contemptuous. It is well known what punishment the Lord allowed to befall the boys who ridiculed the prophet Eliseus because of his bald head. Moreover, it is well for us, according to the admonition of the Wise Man, to reflect on what we may be like when we have grown old. "Despise not a man in his old age: for we shall also become old" (Eccli. 8,7). If we should perchance be obliged to draw the attention of old people to their faults, we should always do it with the proper respect. Hence, the Apostle writes: "An ancient man rebuke not, but entreat him as a father; old women, as mothers" (1 Tim. 5,12). — Have you always acted thus?

3. Consider that in the divine admonition to respect old age there is included the reminder that old people make themselves worthy of this honor. Holy Scripture says expressly: "For venerable old age is not that of a long time, not counted by the number of years: but the understanding of a man is gray hairs, and a spotless life is old age" (Wisd. 4,8-9). Composure and reflection are seemly to old age, and the glory of old age is humility and holy retirement, as observed in the servant of God Bernard. He who loves to commune with God, then, will be spiritually rejuvenated in Him who never grows old, and prayer will be the sweetest consolation and the keenest joy of his last days.

PRAYER OF THE CHURCH
(Third Secret under "Various Prayers")

Grant unto Thy servants, O Lord, the pardon of their sins, comfort in life, and continual guidance: that serving Thee, they may deserve duly to attain to Thy mercy. Through Christ our Lord. Amen.

JULY 3
THE SERVANT OF GOD ANDREW OF BURGIO
Confessor, First Order

NDREW, the son of wealthy country folk at Burgio on the island of Sicily, was born in 1705. By word and example his parents led their children on to virtue. They soon noticed in their youngest son, Andrew, the beautiful fruits of their training. To modesty, meekness and docility, he also united fervent piety. As a boy Andrew delighted in reading Bible History and other good books found in his home. He was present at all the services that took place in church, and there he edified all by his devotion. At home he prayed a great deal in private, particularly before an image of our Saviour at the pillar of scourging, before which he burned a light each evening.

When he was old enough, he gladly did his share of the work, obeying his parents in the smallest detail, and being friendly with all with whom he had to deal. The careless habits of a near relative who often worked with him caused him much anxiety. Andrew's admonitions brought no results; but by being kind to the offender, humoring him in all permissible things, and praying for him, Andrew finally changed his sentiments so that at length he imitated Andrew's devout life.

When Andrew was twenty-two years old, his father died, and left him the care of the household and of the family. Two years later the mother died also, and then matters took on an unpleasant turn. His elder brother, who had been reared by relatives and was now married, had never previously been concerned about his parental home, but now he claimed possession of the best of all there was. Andrew was given to understand that some smaller items were left to him as a favor. He remonstrated, but in order to keep peace, he yielded. Later, when his brother's wife and then the brother himself died, he sincerely mourned their deaths and took their child into his home and cared for it as if it were his own.

His desire to withdraw from the world and to dedicate himself to God continued to gain strength. He declined some fine proposals of marriage which his relatives commended to him, and took pains to provide for his sisters and for his brother's child. When they were amply provided for, he entered the Capuchin convent in his home town as a lay brother. This occurred in 1735, when he was thirty years of age.

In the convent Andrew led a most austere life. With the permission of his superiors, he partook only of bread and water, scourged his body until he bled and observed the severe regulations of the order with great exactitude. In addition, his superiors considered it necessary, because of his advanced years, to subject him to a rigorous probation. Hence, they frequently found fault with him and humiliated him before the entire community. At such times Andrew acknowledged his unworthiness, asked for a penance, and begged them to have patience with him a little longer, and assured them that he would earnestly endeavor to mend his ways. In this way God increased grace in His humble servant.

At prayer Andrew was completely absorbed in his devotions and was often seen to be raised above the ground. Once when he came upon a cripple lying in the street, Andrew asked him why he did not rise. The unfortunate man answered: "How can I when I have been crippled ever since my birth?" Then Andrew took him by the hand and said: "Rise in the name of Jesus." And he arose and was completely cured.

In his zeal for the salvation of souls, Brother Andrew, at his own request, was sent for seven years to the missions of the Congo in Africa. There his patience in the greatest hardships, his virtues, and his miracles were such that everyone called him a saint. When his term of service expired, the superior of the missions begged him to remain. Andrew promptly yielded to his wishes and remained ten years more, until his superiors recalled him to Sicily.

Worn out in the service of God and of his order, he died at Palermo in 1772, rich in graces. Miracles continued to occur at his grave, for which reason the process of his beatification was introduced in 1835.

ON PATIENT FORBEARANCE

1. Consider how much good Andrew achieved through patient forbearance. Through it he converted a relative, he kept peace with his brother, and prepared his heart for extraordinary graces. Human nature inclines so readily to resist evil with violence, and often we consider it virtue to resist in that way. But Jesus Christ says: "But I say to you, not to resist evil; but if one strike you on your right cheek, turn to him also the other. And if a man will contend with you in judgment and take away your coat, let go your cloak also unto him" (Mt. 5,39-40). Our Lord means that we should be ready to endure injustice and to forego earthly possessions rather than forfeit peace and the things of higher value. Would that we did so, imitating the servant of God Andrew! How much we should then accomplish!

2. Consider also that there is a sinful forbearance. The latter is not the fruit of Christian patience and self-conquest, but rather of sloth and lack of courage, so that we do not resent and punish the faults of others although we know we shall have to give an account to God for them. In this

manner Heli sinned, of whom the Lord said to Samuel: "For I have foretold unto him that I will judge his house forever, for iniquity, because he knew that his sons did wickedly, and did not chastise them" (1 Kings 3,13). — Do not many parents and superiors need to fear the same punishment?

3. Consider how one can acquire Christian forbearance which is so pleasing to God, and be saved from sinful compliance. Imitating the servant of God Andrew, one must foster a deep love for God and for the souls redeemed by the precious Blood of Christ. Love of God will permit us to neglect nothing which will help to bring back to God those who have gone astray from Him. Love for sinners will pour into our hearts the patience and meekness of the Heart of Jesus our Saviour, so that, like Andrew, we will keep ourselves in check, and fulfill the words: "The bruised reed he shall not break, and smoking flax he shall not extinguish, till he send forth judgment unto victory" (Mt. 12,20).

PRAYER OF THE CHURCH

Clothe us, O Lord Jesus, with the virtues and inflame us with the affections of Thy Sacred Heart, so that we may be conformed to Thy image and become partakers of Thy redemption. Who livest and reignest forever and ever. Amen.

JULY 4
BLESSED GREGORY GRASSI AND COMPANIONS
Martyrs, First and Third Orders

ABOUT twenty-five thousand Catholics in China and forty-three European missionaries won the martyr's crown during the so-called Boxer Persecution of 1900. The Boxers were a fanatical sect who hated all foreigners and especially the Catholic Church. With the approval of the empress dowager Tzu Chi, then ruling the Chinese Empire, they went about burning churches and murdering the missionaries and their neophytes.

One of the principal promoters of the Boxer movement was the governor Yu Hsien who resided at Taiyuanfu, Shansi. In this city was also the residence of the Franciscan Bishop Gregory Grassi, vicar apostolic of northern Shansi, and his coadjutor, Bishop Francis Fogolla. Here were also a seminary and an orphanage. The latter was conducted by Franciscan Missionary Sisters of Mary who had arrived only the previous year.

During the night of July 5, Yu Hsien's soldiers appeared at the Franciscan mission and arrested the two bishops, two fathers and a brother, and seven Franciscan Missionaries of Mary. Five Chinese seminarians, and eight Chinese Christians who were employed at the mission were also apprehended. In prison they were joined by one more Chinese Christian who went there voluntarily.

Four days later, July 9, 1900, all of them were taken before the tribunal of Yu Hsien, some of them being slashed with swords on the way. Yu Hsien ordered them to be killed on the spot, and an indescribable scene followed. The soldiers closed in on the prisoners, struck them at random with their swords, wounded them right and left, cut off their arms and legs and heads. Thus died the twenty-six martyrs of Taiyuanfu, of whom all except three belonged to the First Order and the Third Order Regular and Secular of St. Francis. They were beatified on January 3, 1943.

Five of them are Franciscans. Besides Blessed Gregory Grassi, who was sixty-eight years old, and Blessed Francis Fogolla, there were Blessed Elias Facchini, a priest from Italy, Blessed Theodoric Balat, a priest from France, and Blessed Andrew Bauer, a lay brother from Alsace.

The seven Franciscan Missionaries of Mary, the protomartyrs of their congregation and its first members to be beatified, are: Blessed Mother Mary Hermine Grivot from France, the superioress, Blessed Mother Mary of Peace Giuliani from Italy, Blessed Mother Mary Clare Nanetti from Italy, Blessed Sister Mary of Ste. Natalie Kerguin from France, Blessed Sister Mary of St. Just Moreau from France, Blessed Sister Mary Amandine Jeuris from Belgium, and Blessed Sister Mary Adolphine Dierkx from Holland. All of them were between the ages of 25 and 35.

The five Chinese seminarians, all of them Franciscan Tertiaries, are: Blessed John Chiang of Tai-kuo, 22 years old, Blessed John Chiang of Nan-tzu, also 22 years old, Blessed Philip Chiang, 20 years, Blessed Patrick Chun, 17 years, and Blessed John Wan, 16 years.

The six Tertiary laymen who had been employed at the episcopal residence and mission are: Blessed Thomas Shen, 49 years old, servant of Bishop Grassi; Blessed Simon Cheng, 45 years, servant of Bishop Fogolla; Blessed Peter Wu-an-pan, 40 years, servant of Father Facchini; Blessed Francis Chiang-jun, 62 years, janitor of the orphanage; Blessed Matthias Fu-en-tai, 45 years, night watchman of the mission; and Blessed Peter Chiang-pan-niu, 50 years, occasional worker at the mission.

The three laymen who were not Tertiaries are: Blessed James Jen-ku-tun, 46 years old, assistant cook; Blessed James Chiao-chun-sin, 43 years, who voluntarily went to the jail to be of service to the prisoners; and Blessed Peter Wan-o-man, 29 years, cook at the seminary. Thus fourteen of the martyrs were natives of China and twelve were Europeans.

Beatified at the same time as these martyrs and commemorated with them on this day are three other Franciscan martyrs who died as victims of the Boxers in the province of Hunan. All three were missionaries from Italy. They are: Blessed Antonine Fantosati, bishop and vicar apostolic of southern Hunan, who was killed by a mob of Boxers on July 7, 1900, while returning on a boat to his residence at Hengchow; Blessed Joseph Mary Gambaro, priest, who was accompanying the bishop and lost his life at the same time; and Blessed Cesidio Giacomantonio, a young priest, who was severely beaten and then slowly burned to death at Hengchow on July 4, 1900. The feast of all of these martyrs, twenty-nine in number, is observed by the Franciscans on July the fourth. (Cf. *In Journeyings Often*, pp. 288-295; *Forum*, 1943, pp. 44-46 and 295-296; *ibid.*, 1946, pp. 323-326, 350, and 355-358.)

ON MARTYRDOM

1. There are times when martyrdom is a sacred duty. Thus the martyrs regarded it. They testified to the words of our Saviour: "What does it profit a man if he gain the whole world and suffer the loss of his own soul?" (Mt. 16,26). In order to save our soul for eternity, we, too, must be ready to sacrifice blood and life rather than separate ourselves from God and our Faith. "If we suffer, we shall also reign with Him; if we deny Him, He will also deny us" (2 Tim. 2,12). — Have you always taken eternity into account?

2. Martyrdom is a great grace. Many of us shudder when we hear the account of the gruesome tortures inflicted on the martyrs, and we ask in fear, "How could they endure it?" But why should we be afraid? On the one hand, God never asks the impossible of us. On the other, when the decisive moment comes, the same good God raises the soul to such heights of love that it cries out with St. Paul: "Who shall separate us from the love of Christ? Shall tribulation, or distress, or famine, or nakedness, or danger, or persecution, or the sword? But in all these things we overcome because of Him who has loved us" (Rom. 8,35-37). — No one, including yourself, has reason to become fainthearted or to despair.

3. Martyrdom brings a superabundant reward. Christ has assured us: "Greater love than this no man has than that a man lay down his life for his friends" (Jn. 15,13). Therefore, making the sacrifice of our life for our best Friend, Jesus, cancels all our sins and all the guilt of sin and takes us at once to heaven. That is why the martyrs said to their torturers, in the words of the Machabees: "You indeed destroy us out of this present life;

but the King of the world will raise us up to life" (2 Mac. 7,9). — Always keep eternity and the bliss of eternity in mind, and everything will be easy.

PRAYER OF THE CHURCH

O God, who desirest that all men be saved and come to the acknowledgment of truth, grant, we beseech Thee, through the intercession of Thy blessed martyrs Bishops Gregory, Francis, and Antonine, and their companions, that all nations may know Thee, the only true God and Jesus Christ whom Thou hast sent, our Lord. Amen.

JULY 5
THE SERVANT OF GOD JOHN MARTINEZ
Confessor, Third Order

IN the fifteenth century there lived at Viso in the Spanish diocese of Toledo a devout couple, John Martinez and Catharine Lopez, both members of prominent families and blessed with this world's goods. Together they joined the Third Order of St. Francis and from then on they became even more zealous in the performance of works of piety and of mercy.

Because they had no children, they pleaded with God by prayer and almsgiving that He might bless them with offspring whom they could make the heirs of their wealth and good works. But it pleased God to let them remain childless.

Since they were advancing in years, John proposed making God and the poor his heirs and consecrating himself wholly to the service of God. His pious wife consented, and from then on they lived in perfect continence. With the approval of Pope Innocent VIII (1484-1492) they built a convent for Tertiaries, as also a hospital and church in honor of the Immaculate Conception.

After a time, Catharine herself entered this new convent, while John led an unusually holy life of poverty and great austerity. The devout couple were buried side by side in the church they had built.

ON CHRISTIAN MARRIAGE

1. Marriage, by which husband and wife are joined together, was

understood by John and Catharine in the true Christian spirit, as the Apostle designates this holy alliance: "A great sacrament in Christ and in the Church" (Eph. 5,32). Whereas in the Old Testament marriage was chiefly a union intended for the propagation of the human race, in the New Testament Christ elevated it from a purely natural to a supernatural order, raising it to the dignity of a sacrament. "In the Christian Church," says St. Augustine, "the sanctity of the sacrament is of greater value than the fruitfulness of marriage." With good reason does the Apostle call it a great sacrament, since in every Christian family there should be portrayed between man and wife the love of Christ for His bride, the Church. So holy and so chaste should be the love and the union of Christian spouses. — Would that it were always considered in this way.

2. Consider that so holy a union should exist only for sacred purposes. The Apostle acknowledges only honorable marriage among Christians: "Marriage honorable in all" (Heb. 13,4). If God blesses a marriage with children, it becomes the first and holiest duty of both parents to rear them as true children of God. That is a grave responsibility and one which weighs heavily on the mother, but a rich reward awaits her in the end. "The woman shall be saved through child-bearing, if she continue in faith and love and sanctification with sobriety" (1 Tim. 2,15). But husband and wife should also sanctify each other by keeping each other from evil, by urging each other to do good. If married people have no duties towards children, then, like the devout couple, John and Catharine, they should be the more zealous in the joint practice of good works of piety and charity.

3. How closely that will unite them in time and in eternity!

Consider that the grace of wedlock should manifest itself principally when difficulties and crosses strike the family. Because hardship is not spared human beings during their earthly sojourn, almighty God said: "It is not good for man to be alone; let us make him a help" (Gen. 2,18). That is what the wife should ever be. But the Apostle admonishes husbands: "Love your wives as Christ also loved the Church and delivered Himself up for it" (Eph. 5,25). True love between husband and wife will prove itself under the cross, in the sacrifice each makes for the other. It will also preserve peace, should one spouse prepare a cross for the other, for "charity is patient, is kind, is not provoked to anger, thinks no evil" (1 Cor. 13,4-5). — May the grace of the sacrament of matrimony preserve all married people in holy love!

PRAYER OF THE CHURCH (Postcommunion in the Nuptial Mass)
We beseech Thee, almighty God, to accompany the institutions of Thy providence with Thy gracious favor, that Thou mayest keep in lasting

peace those whom Thou dost join in lawful union. Through Christ our
Lord. Amen.

***

JULY 6
THE SERVANT OF GOD SANCIA
Widow, Second Order

IF according to the words of Christ it is difficult for the rich to
enter into the kingdom of heaven, it is all the more admirable
if those who possess riches use them to procure heavenly
treasures. It was thus that the saintly Queen Sancia managed
her possessions.

She was the daughter of the king of Majorca, and the wife of Robert
I, king of Naples and of Sicily. She and her equally devout consort
endeavored to use their wealth only for the honor of God and the welfare
of their subjects. She was much attached to the three orders of St. Francis,
and used to say that this was not astonishing since our holy Father had in
so many ways bound her to himself with his cord. In other words, a great
number of her royal kinsmen were children of St. Francis either as Friars
Minor, or Poor Clares, or Tertiaries.

Sancia built a convent for the Poor Clares in Naples which bore the
title of Corpus Christi, and in which the Blessed Sacrament was honored
in a very special way. Two hundred and fifty cloistered nuns coming from
the most distinguished families among the nobility of the country dwelt
in that monastery and conducted choir services there with great
solemnity. During the octave of Corpus Christi the church was richly
decorated, the altar was a veritable mountain of silver, and according to
Sancia's arrangements, all the clergy of the city participated in the
solemnity.

Her husband also bore the title of king of Jerusalem. This was an
incentive for Sancia to insure worthy veneration of the holy places which
were then in Turkish hands. It cost her and her husband great effort and
large sums of money to obtain from the sultan that the Holy Sepulcher as
well as Mt. Sion in Jerusalem be given into the care of the Friars Minor. In
1342, by a decree of Pope Clement VI, the sons of St. Francis were formally
appointed guardians of the Holy Sepulcher. This commission they are still
carrying out at the present day.

Sancia was also solicitous for her subjects. Immorality was rampant
in Naples at that time and it caused great sorrow to Sancia. She had a

large house of refuge built for public sinners, and so favorably impressed these unfortunates that several hundred became sincerely repentant, the greater number persevering in virtue.

After the saintly death of Sancia's husband, she built another convent of Poor Clares in Naples, named for the Holy Cross. This convent was planned according to the strictest poverty, and the primitive rule of St. Clare was observed faithfully. The queen herself entered there as a plain sister. At her own request the general of the order forbade any distinction to be made in her favor or any reference to be made to her noble extraction. She bore the simple name of Sister Clare, lived in profoundest humility, in great poverty, and in the practice of all the virtues.

She had been a religious only eighteen months when God called her to Himself on July 28, 1345. She died in the odor of sanctity.

ON THE LOVE OF JESUS CHRIST

1. Consider how the love of Jesus Christ was manifested both in the life and in the works of this servant of God. In the Blessed Sacrament she beheld the gracious condescension of our Lord, who wished to dwell among men, not only for a short while here on earth, but to the end of time. "Behold I am with you all days even to the consummation of the world" (Mt. 28,20). It was that thought which urged Sancia to provide a worthy dwelling-place and becoming honor for Him, no cost being too great for her. When a person possesses money, he soon betrays in what direction his love tends. If it leans towards pomp and pride, he will build an elegant house and equip it magnificently. If he loves his body, he will expend much for eating and drinking and all the comforts of the body. If he loves his money, he will cling to it and avoid even the necessary expenses. But if he loves our Lord Jesus Christ, he will take pleasure in spending money for His honor. — For what purpose do you like most to spend your money?

2. Consider that Sancia's love for Jesus Christ was evidenced also in her concern for the holy places. "Greater love than this no man has, than that a man lay down his life for his friends" (Jn. 15,13). That is what our Lord Jesus Christ did for us, and the holy places in which He did so were being dishonored by His enemies. That caused Sancia to shudder, and she made the arrangement according to which the holy places are to this day guarded with great reverence. The same love for Christ induced her to dissuade souls who had been bought with the Blood of Christ from pursuing a life of sin. — Do you experience any sorrow of heart when Jesus Christ and the things that pertain to Him are dishonored? Have you

any zeal for the conversion of even the most despised sinner? You can determine the extent of your love for Christ by your measure of such sentiments.

3. Consider that the love of Jesus Christ finally urged Sancia to leave the world, and in perfect seclusion to serve God in poverty and in a very strict life. Love demands that we strive to become like our Beloved. Christ lived in poverty and mortification, and that is why those souls who love Him feel inclined to adopt a similar life. And because the noise of the world so easily disturbs the love of God, the soul that loves Christ gladly withdraws from all unnecessary contacts with the world. He who has tasted the sweetness of intimate union with Christ in solitude will gladly let the whole world go by without giving it so much as passing attention. It was in this sense that the old hermits said: "O blessed solitude, O solitary blessedness!"

PRAYER OF THE CHURCH
(Fifth Sunday after Pentecost)

O God, who hast prepared for those who love Thee such good things as eye hath not seen, pour into our hearts such tender love for Thee, that, loving Thee in all things and above all things, we may obtain Thy promises which surpass all desires. Through Christ our Lord. Amen.

JULY 7
THE SERVANT OF GOD WALTER LOPEZ
Confessor, Third Order

FROM 1645 to 1648, there were gathered at Muenster in Westphalia, representatives of most of the European powers. They were trying to draw up terms of peace and put an end to the unfortunate Thirty Years' War.

Present in this assembly was the envoy of King Philip IV of Spain. He was Knight of Santiago Count Walter Lopez de Zabata, a man of wide experience, statecraft, and great learning. Among other things, he spoke the Greek language as fluently as his mother tongue. But he was still better versed in Holy Scripture and in the science of salvation. He had been a member of the Third Order of St. Francis for years, and publicly wore the habit of the order, as was frequently the case in those days. He did this without embarrassment even during the negotiations at Muenster, where he found himself in the company of distinguished Protestants and the delegates of Protestant princes. He never drank wine or other alcoholic drinks, and his daily fare was very plain.

Because of his affection for the Franciscan Order, he found quarters in the neighborhood of the Franciscan convent, and often visited the friars. His friendly and affable demeanor won the affection, and his piety, humility, simplicity, and mortification gained the esteem of all with whom he came in contact. His home and hand were always open to help the poor and the oppressed; no one left him without being comforted.

The peace plans were far advanced but not yet concluded, when our Lord put an end to the earthly sojourn of His servant. On May 30, 1648, Walter was suddenly seized with an illness and fell into a coma. The guardian of the nearby Franciscan convent administered to him the sacrament of extreme unction. When his confessor, a Franciscan who had come with him from Spain, pronounced the holy name of Jesus, the dying man regained sufficient consciousness to strike his breast and to raise his eyes to heaven, as if to say that he placed all his hope and his confidence in the mercy of God. He died that same night at twelve o'clock.

While he was being carried to the cemetery, a white dove was seen hovering over the casket. In the plain sight of all, it accompanied the funeral procession up to the place of burial. Then it disappeared.

ON HUMAN RESPECT

1. Consider how courageous was the piety of Count Walter. He did not hesitate to wear the Tertiary garb among the envoys of the European princes. By not being ashamed of something that was near and dear to him, he proved to all the world that he was a true nobleman, a knight of Jesus Christ; and the result was that he won the esteem of everyone. If, without flaunting or making a show of their piety, people generally were to disregard human respect in their practice of religion, they would enjoy more respect than they gain by trying to hide their religious convictions. And then how glorious it will be for them to appear before the Eternal Judge, who has said: "Everyone who shall confess Me before men, I will also confess him before My Father who is in heaven" (Mt. 10,32). — Do you deserve to be recognized by Him there?

2. Consider how foolish and base a thing human respect is. We would like to go to church and attend Mass oftener than we do. We would like to go to the sacraments more frequently, knowing that unless we do, we shall never overcome certain faults. We would like to join some pious organization like the Third Order. But we are afraid people may talk about

us, and so we neglect these things. That is on a level with the silly fear of a child that runs away when it hears a goose cackle. But are there not temporal disadvantages to fear if you profess your Catholic Faith? Nevertheless, you are obliged to profess it when the honor of God, the good of your neighbor, or the salvation of your soul requires it. What did the holy martyrs do? They recalled the words of our Lord, which are likewise addressed to you: "Fear not those who kill the body and are not able to kill the soul; but rather fear Him who can cast both soul and body into hell" (Mt. 20,28). — What is more important to you — respect for men or respect for God?

3. Consider how sinful and harmful human respect is. Not only do we neglect good deeds in our vain fear of talk and ridicule, but it also leads us to take part in what is evil. Uncharitable remarks about our neighbor are made; we know they are unjust, but for fear of our associates we remain silent, or even join in the conversations and agree with the remarks made. Piety is ridiculed and the clergy criticized, and we join in and add our own criticisms. Unbecoming conversation and indecent jokes are heard and we laugh along — that is the extent to which human respect can lead us. For fear of men we remain silent and cower while irreligion makes bolder advances, and immorality grows more shameless. Never could corruption have become so widespread if cowardly human respect had not shrunk from opposing it. What will be the end of such fearful souls? "He who shall be ashamed of Me and of My words in this adulterous and sinful generation," says our Lord, "the Son of Man will also be ashamed of him when He shall come in the glory of His Father with the holy angels" (Mk. 8,38). — Do your part and pray to God for fortitude for yourself and those who are still devoted to the cause of God.

PRAYER OF THE CHURCH
(Postcommunion No. 10 under "Various Prayers")

We beseech Thee, O Lord our God, that Thou wouldst not suffer to be exposed to human dangers those whom Thou givest to rejoice in the participation of these divine mysteries. Through Christ our Lord. Amen.

JULY 8
ST. ELIZABETH, QUEEN OF PORTUGAL
Widow, Third Order

LIZABETH was the daughter of King Peter III of Aragon and of the saintly Constancia. She was born in 1271, and named after the holy landgravine of Thuringia, the sister of her grandmother. An angel of peace seemed to have come to the family with the birth of the child, because great joy over her birth reconciled her father and her grandfather, who had been living at variance with each other. Elizabeth combined great virtue with the most lovable qualities, so that her father sometimes remarked that it appeared this daughter would surpass all the women of the royal court in accomplishments.

Prayer and severe penance were Elizabeth's delight as a young woman; but her austerity had nothing crude or harsh about it. Elizabeth was ever gentle toward others and filled with cordial charity especially towards the poor and the oppressed. Her accomplishments were lauded in all the courts of Europe, and many a prince's son pleaded for her hand.

At a very early age her father betrothed her to Denis, King of Portugal. The first years of her married life were happy ones, her husband loved her, and God blessed the marriage with two sons. While Elizabeth fulfilled her duties as wife and mother, she contrived to find time to devote herself with holy zeal to practices of piety and charity. But ere long she was visited with a severe trial.

Her husband gave himself up to a dissolute life, becoming a scandal to the court and to the country at large, and a great grief to his devout wife. Elizabeth, however, was pained more by the fact that he was offending God than by his unfaithfulness to her. She kept her grief entirely to herself, complaining to no one but to God Himself in persevering prayer. The king never heard her make an unkind remark. Through forbearance and tender love she endeavored to bring him back to the path of duty and virtue. She increased her penitential practices and her works of charity. She visited the hospitals and public asylums, where she nursed the most disgusting patients.

One day she was washing the feet of a sick lady. When she had washed one foot, the patient refused to extend the other because it was badly eaten by a cancerous sore. But the saintly queen urged her to comply. Then she carefully washed the ugly wound, and lovingly pressed her lips upon it. At that very moment the wound disappeared.

The heroic virtue of his wife and the grace of God finally changed the heart of the king. He begged Elizabeth's forgiveness and returned to the path of righteousness. Thereafter she was frequently to play the role of peacemaker. Her husband quarreled seriously with his brother over certain estates. Elizabeth offered her brother-in-law an estate out of her own possessions and thus restored peace between the two brothers.

Later her own son Alphonse became ambitious and rose against his father. All his mother's efforts to effect a change of mind in him were in vain. Alphonse, supported by powerful foes of the king, collected an army and was ready for war against his father and the royal army. Then Elizabeth, mounting her charger, rode between the lines of battle, and spoke so impressively to her son that he cast himself repentantly at the feet of his father, and in the sight of the two armies they were reconciled to each other.

Not long after, King Denis died. Elizabeth then donned the garb of a Tertiary and withdrew to a small house near the convent of the Poor Clares at Coimbra. One other occasion, however, presented itself in which she was to be the peacemaker. Her son was quarreling with the king of Castile, her son-in-law, and war threatened. In spite of her age and the heat of the season, Elizabeth started out on the journey to effect peace between the two kings. Once again she succeeded in averting war and all its evil consequences. But she became ill as a result of the exertions of the journey, which caused her to be seized with a high fever.

After a holy preparation, she entered into eternal peace on July 4, 1336. Numerous miracles occurred at her tomb in the church of the Poor Clares at Coimbra, where the people invoked the intercession of the saintly queen with unlimited confidence. Pope Urban VIII solemnly canonized her in the year 1625. Her feast is observed by the three branches of the First Order of St. Francis on July 8. (Cf. *Forum*, 1949, pp. 142-144; *These Made Peace*, pp. 94-98.)

ON MAKING PEACE

1. Consider what a beautiful and noble work is that of the peacemaker. It was near and dear to the heart of St. Elizabeth. In order to bring peace on earth, Christ came down from heaven, and at His birth the angels sang: "Peace on earth to men of good will!" (Lk. 2,14). Our Lord repeatedly wished His disciples peace; and He praised those who foster peace as being blessed: "Blessed are the peacemakers, for they shall be called the children of God" (Mt. 5,9). Just before His death He pleaded for peace and harmony among the Christians of all times: "Holy Father, keep them in Thy name, whom Thou hast given me: that they may be one as We also

are" (Jn. 17,11). It is also prescribed for Tertiaries (Ch. 2,9) that they should preserve peace, and where it has been disrupted, they should make every effort to restore it. — Have you made efforts in this regard?

2. Consider how detestable it is if people take pleasure in stirring up dissensions and quarrels. Yet, how frequently does this happen, even among those who are considered devout. They carry to one person what another has said about him and then urge him not to tolerate it, often fomenting bitter enmity in that way. If peaceful souls are called children of God, the disturbers of peace surely deserve to be called the children of the devil. If Christ calls the former blessed, no wonder He must curse the latter. "The whisperer and the double-tongued is accursed: for he has troubled many who were at peace" (Eccli. 28,15). — Have you any need to fear this curse?

3. Consider what is required in order to establish peace. Love for the God of peace implies love for the soul of our neighbor; and we must be prepared personally to put up with inconvenience or unpleasantness in order to turn another from his sinful ways. Elizabeth made great temporal sacrifices for this purpose. Of course we must be prudent, patient, and meek, if we hope really to effect a reconciliation. These are the very virtues that made Elizabeth successful in conciliating enemies. We would have greater and more frequent success if we possessed prudence, patience, and meekness, whereas we only increase discord by being violent and angry. "A passionate man stirs up strifes: he who is patient appeases those who are stirred up" (Prov. 15,18).

PRAYER OF THE CHURCH
Most gracious God, who, among other extraordinary graces, didst grant St. Elizabeth the particular grace to allay warlike enmities, grant us through her intercession that we may spend our days on earth in peace and hereafter arrive at joys eternal. Through Christ our Lord. Amen.

⚜⚜⚜⚜⚜⚜

JULY 9
ST. NICHOLAS OF GORCUM AND COMPANIONS
Martyrs, First Order

HERE were especially two dogmas of the Faith that were attacked by the heretics of the sixteenth century: the Real Presence of Jesus Christ in the Eucharist and the Primacy of the Roman Pontiff. The Calvinists in Holland persecuted with relentless fury the confessors of the Catholic Faith. The holy martyrs gave their lives particularly in defense of these two fundamental doctrines.

When the Calvinists, who had set themselves against all ecclesiastical as well as civil authority, took possession of the city of Gorcum, they retained nineteen of the clergy as prisoners, though they had promised to let the inhabitants depart from the town without being molested. There were four secular priests among the prisoners, four priests of other religious orders, and eleven Friars Minor of the convent at Gorcum. The latter were the guardian, Father Nicholas Pieck; his vicar, Father Jerome of Weert; Father Wilhad, an old man of ninety years; Theodoric of Emden; Nicaise Jonson, a learned theologian; Godfrey of Mervelan; Anthony of Weert; Anthony of Hornaer; young Father Francis Rod; and two lay brothers, Peter van Asche and Cornelius of Dorstat.

Cast into a filthy prison, they were cruelly treated during the first night by the drunken soldiers. They seemed to vent their hellish rage principally against the guardian, Father Nicholas. Taking the cord which he wore around his waist and putting it around his neck, they dragged him to the door of the prison and threw the cord across it in order to hang him at once. But as a result of pulling the cord back and forth against its weight, the cord tore, and Father Nicholas fell to the earth unconscious. In order to make sure that he was dead or just for the purpose of outrage, the persecutors took a burning candle and burned off his hair and eyebrows, applying the flame also to his nose and open mouth. With a parting laugh of derision, they then left the motionless body in order to torment the others. They struck the face of the aged Father Wilhad with savage blows, but each time he merely said, "Deo gratias! Thanks be to God!"

After the miscreants had departed, Father Nicholas regained consciousness, for he had only fainted. As soon as he was able to speak again, he encouraged his brethren, declaring that in defense of the Faith he was ready to undergo the same torments again, and even more cruel ones, if it so pleased God, and as often as it pleased God. "For," said he, "the sufferings of this present time are not worthy to be compared with the glory to come that shall be revealed in us."

On the following day several attempts were made to cause the friars, and in particular their superior, to apostatize. The Calvinists opened a discussion with them about the Blessed Sacrament and the primacy of the pope. But the heretics soon found themselves cornered by the clear proofs advanced by the guardian and his brethren. They hoped to be able at least to deceive one of the lay brothers, but he answered very simply that he was in accord with everything that his guardian had said.

Meanwhile, the relatives of Father Nicholas, especially his two brothers, were making every effort to obtain his deliverance. But, like a good shepherd, the guardian declared: "I will not leave prison unless my brethren come with me, and even though there were only one detained, and he the lowliest of them all, I would remain here with him." When his brothers declared that one could renounce the primacy of the pope without denying God, he showed them that he who separates himself from the pope, separates himself from the Church; and that he who renounces the Church, renounces Christ the Lord. And then he spoke with holy zeal: "I would rather endure death for the honor of God than swerve even a hair's breadth from the Catholic Faith."

Eight days later the confessors were taken to Briel, where the Calvinist leader had his headquarters. He had them all hanged there on July 9, 1572. With Christ they shared the disgrace of shameful death, but at the same time also a glorious ascension.

In 1867, at the solemn celebration of the day on which the holy Apostles Peter and Paul suffered martyrdom, Pope Pius IX canonized the martyrs of Gorcum. Their feast is observed by the Franciscans and Conventuals on July ninth, and by the Capuchins on the eleventh.

ON THE PRIMACY OF THE POPE

1. Consider how Christ Himself established the primacy, that is, the supreme authority of the pope of Rome in the Church. He said to St. Peter: "You are Peter, and upon this rock I will build My Church, and the gates of hell shall not prevail against it" (Mt. 16,18). And as the Church was destined to be founded on Peter, so did our Lord actually place him as chief shepherd over His flock with the words: "Feed My lambs," and "feed My sheep" (Jn. 21,16-17). Peter was the bishop of Rome and died as such. The bishop of Rome, that is to say, the pope, is therefore the successor of St. Peter, appointed by Christ as the supreme head of the Church. Whoever does not belong to his communion does not belong to the Church of Christ; he who separates himself from him, separates himself from the flock of Christ. That is why our holy martyrs preferred to suffer death rather than deny their allegiance to the pope of Rome. — Thank God that you belong to this communion, and frequently assure our Lord that you would rather die than renounce the pope.

2. Consider the great benefits that accrue to us from communion with the pope. The supreme power of loosing and binding has been conferred upon him. It was to Peter that our Lord said: "I will give to you the keys of the kingdom of heaven; and whatsoever you shall bind upon earth, it shall be

bound also in heaven; and whatsoever you shall loose on earth, it shall be loosed also in heaven" (Mt. 16,19). Only those priests who are of the same communion as the pope can forgive us our sins. Moreover, it is through the pope that we are confirmed in the true teachings of Christ, for it was to Peter again that Christ said: "I have prayed for you that your faith fail not; and you being once converted, confirm your brethren" (Lk. 22,32). With the pope as the head, the unity of the Church is preserved, whereas those who separate themselves from him have been divided into a thousand sects. — Acknowledge the pope, therefore, as the spiritual father of your soul, heed his word with childlike reverence, and pray earnestly for him who is solicitous for you and for all Christendom.

3. Consider how the power of the pope is attacked by those who have separated themselves from the Church. Not wishing to submit to his authority, they set about denying the validity of that authority. Hence, apostates are for the most part the most insolent enemies of the loyal children of the pope, as can readily be seen from the cruel tortures inflicted on the martyrs of Gorcum. The latter, however, gladly accepted all the torture and derision inflicted on them, even making the sacrifice of their lives to prove their fidelity to the Father of Christendom. Now they are partakers of the joys of eternity and are held in great esteem by the entire Catholic Church. — When occasion presented itself, did you show similar courage and give proof of sincere adherence to the Vicar of Christ, or did you prove weak on such occasions? He who wishes to share the reward of the martyrs must also fight the good fight with them.

PRAYER OF THE CHURCH

O God, who didst adorn the glorious struggle for the Faith which Thy holy martyrs Nicholas and companions endured with the laurel wreath of eternity, mercifully grant us through their merits, that we may do battle as they did on earth and so be made worthy to receive the crown with them in heaven. Through Christ our Lord. Amen.

JULY 10
BLESSED EMMANUEL RUIZ AND COMPANIONS
Martyrs, First Order

ROM the days of St. Stephen all the way down the centuries the Church has had her martyrs, but the nineteenth century is distinguished for the great number, enthusiasm, and heroism of its martyrs for the Faith. The Orient has supplied most of these. China heads the list, but there are also martyrs from Japan, Korea, Cochin-China, Syria, France, Spain, and Peru. The accounts of their martyrdom tempt us to believe that we are reading of a past far removed from our own age; but the fact is that many of them have lived in our own lifetime.

Such modern martyrs are those of Damascus during the frightful massacre by the Druses in 1860. A quarrel between a Maronite and a Druse was the occasion for the opening attack. The Druses were armed, but the Christians allowed themselves to be disarmed by the Turkish authorities under the pretense of preserving order. Within three weeks every Maronite village of the main and southern parts of Lebanon was pillaged or burned, six thousand Maronites were murdered, maimed, or outraged. The massacre broke out in Damascus on July ninth, and in three days the adult males alone numbered three thousand victims.

Among these were eight Friars Minor, who, by the circumstances of their death, are shown to have been martyrs for the Faith. Six were priests, the other two were lay brothers. Emmanuel Ruiz was the superior of the convent, Carmen Volta (Botta) was the procurator, and Engelbert Kolland, the assistant procurator.

Nicanor Miano, Nicholas Mary Alberca, and Peter Soler were studying the Arabian language in preparation for their apostolic labors. The lay brothers were Francis Pinazzo and John James Fernandez.

When the rabble attacked the Christians, these religious and their flocks recommended themselves to God and to our Blessed Lady, and then prepared themselves for death by devoutly receiving the sacraments. At midnight the soldiers entered the convent and in many ways tried the faith of the friars. Promises and threats proved futile, and the tortures to which the Mohammedans resorted to shake the faith of these holy men were hair-raising.

Father Emmanuel Ruiz, realizing that death was inevitable, and fearing lest the Sacred Host in the tabernacle be subjected to profanation by the fanatics after their death, went to the church to consume the Sacred Species. It was not long before he was interrupted, and so, recommending himself to God, he placed his head upon the altar to be cut off with a sword.

Father Carmen Volta was beaten to death with a cudgel; Father Peter Soler's life was cut short with the sword; Father Nicholas Alberca was shot down; Father Engelbert Kolland was killed with an ax. Father Nicanor was also quickly despatched, and the two lay brothers likewise manifested great strength of soul. With their eyes and hands raised to heaven in suppliant prayer, they were hurled from the tower of the church whither they had taken refuge.

The Holy See acknowledged the heroism of their lives when Pope Pius XI enrolled them, as also three Maronite laymen, among the martyrs and conferred on them the title of Blessed in 1926, the seventh centenary year of the death of St. Francis. Their feast is celebrated by the Franciscans on July tenth.

THE GUARDIAN OF THE BLESSED SACRAMENT

1. "Marvelous dignity of the priests!" exclaims St. Augustine. "In their hands, as in the womb of the Blessed Virgin Mary, the Son of God becomes incarnate." And as Mary by virtue of the Incarnation has been appointed by God as the guardian of the humanity of Christ, so the priest by the powers conferred on him at his ordination has been appointed the guardian of the Blessed Sacrament. "Without the priest," says the Curé of Ars, "the death and passion of our Lord would be of no use; the priest has the key of the heavenly treasures; he is God's steward and the administrator of His goods." Let us ask the Holy Spirit, then, to give us knowledge of these truths. It will inspire us with religious veneration for the character of the priest and with lively gratitude towards our Lord who has invested the priest with that character.

2. In this arrangement by which the God-man is entirely subject to the priest during His stay here on earth, we are again given a beautiful example of virtue. If God chooses the priest from among all men as the most suited to direct His sacramental sojourn on this earth, should we not, then, be willing to entrust ourselves to his guidance? Should we not always bear in mind the dignity that attaches to every priest? Has our conduct towards priests always borne the impress of the respect we should tender them?

3. The Blessed Sacrament has been instituted by God for the good of humankind, and the priest, as the guardian of the Blessed Sacrament, has been placed at our service by a kind God to dispense to us the graces of the Sacrament. But it would be the height of rudeness if any of us were on

that account to consider and treat the priest like a hired servant. True, we render the priest material remuneration of a sort in acknowledgment of his services, but this remuneration can never be considered adequate compensation for the benefits he confers on us. Let us remember that it is a privilege for us to be served by the priest, not something that is our due. It would be well for us occasionally to turn our thoughts to the thousands of souls who do not enjoy this saving grace. How welcome would any priest be in their midst! They would know how to appreciate his services. Should we not, then, be doubly grateful for our privilege? In future we will let our words and deeds manifest this gratitude.

PRAYER OF THE CHURCH
(No. 7 under "Various Prayers")

Almighty and everlasting God, who alone workest great marvels, send down upon Thy servants and the flocks entrusted to them, the spirit of Thy saving grace; and that they may please Thee in truth, pour forth upon them the continual dew of Thy blessing. Through Christ our Lord. Amen.

JULY 11
ST. VERONICA GIULIANI
Virgin, Second Order

ERONICA was born of devout parents at Mercatello in Italy. As a child she, too, was of a devout disposition, but inclined to be quite irritable, and, as she herself admits, would stamp her feet at the least provocation.

Her mother died when Veronica was only four years old. In her last moments she assigned each of her five children to one of then five wounds of Christ and bade them take their refuge there whenever they were troubled. Veronica was the youngest. She was assigned to the wound in the side of our Lord, and from that time on her heart became more tempered. Co-operating with the grace of God, her soul gradually went through a refining process by which she became an object of admiration in later years.

When Veronica came of age, her father believed she should marry, and so he desired her to take part in the social activities of the young people. But she had been made aware of another call, and she pleaded so earnestly with her father that, after much resistance, he finally permitted

St. Veronica Giuliani

her to choose her own state in life.

At the age of seventeen, then, the young woman entered the convent of the Capuchin nuns at Citta di Castello in Umbria, where the primitive rule of St. Clare was observed. Imbued with sincere humility she considered herself the lowliest member of the community. At the same time she greatly edified all by her obedience and love of poverty and mortification. Sometimes she was favored with interior conversations and revelations. She resolved that she would reveal all such matters to her superiors and her confessor; she had neglected to do that when she was still in the world, and as a result she had often been misled by the father of lies.

When Veronica had spent seventeen years in various offices in her community, she was entrusted with the guidance of the novices. She endeavored to imbue them with the spirit of simplicity and to lay a firm foundation for humility. She directed them to the truths of the Faith and the rules of the order as their safest guides on the way of perfection, and warned them against reading idly speculative books as well as against everything unusual.

Meanwhile, extraordinary things were beginning to happen to her. On Good Friday she received the stigmata, and later the Crown of Thorns was impressed on her head amid untold sufferings. After a careful examination of these matters, the bishop sent a report to Rome. Then Rome appointed a commission, which was to put her humility to the severest test, in order to determine whether she was an impostor, a person deluded by the devil, or a person favored by God. She was deposed from her office as novice mistress, and deprived of every suffrage in the community. She was even imprisoned in a remote cell, no sisters were permitted to talk to her, and a lay sister who was made her warden was ordered to treat her like a deceiver. Finally, she was even deprived of holy Communion and was permitted to attend holy Mass only on Sundays and holydays near the door of the church.

At the conclusion of these trials, the bishop reported to Rome that she scrupulously obeyed every one of his ordinances, and showed not the least sign of sadness amid all this harsh treatment, but rather an inexpressible peace and joy of spirit.

The test had proved the admirable manifestations to be the work of God. But Veronica did not on that account deem herself a saint, but rather a great sinner, whom God was leading on the way to conversion by means of His holy wounds.

Having filled the office of novice mistress during a space of twenty-two years, Veronica was unanimously elected abbess. Only in obedience could she be prevailed upon to accept the responsibility.

Purified more and more by many sufferings, to which she added many austere mortifications, she went to her eternal reward on July 9, 1727, after spending fifty years in the convent. Because of her heroic virtues and the many miracles that were continually being worked at her tomb, she was canonized by Pope Gregory XVI in 1839. The Franciscans, Conventuals, and Third Order Regular observe her feast on July eleventh, and the Capuchins on the ninth.

ON THE MARKS OF HUMILITY

1. Consider the marks of humility as evident in the life of St. Veronica. She considered herself the lowliest of her sisters. He who is truly humble reflects upon his misery and weakness. He acknowledges that whatever good there is in him has been given to him by God, and that according to the measure of His gifts to him he ought to have achieved much greater perfection. Veronica, therefore, was sincere in believing that she was the least among her fellow sisters, just as St. Francis did, and before his day St. Paul, who said: "Christ Jesus came into this world to save sinners, of whom I am the chief" (1 Tim. 1,15). For the same reason, the humble man never rates his opinion over that of others, his merits above those of others, nor his abilities above other people's abilities. In his humility he considers others as being above him, and cheerfully takes the lowest place. — Are these traits evident in you?
2. Consider how the humility of Veronica was tested by extraordinary humiliations. The evil spirit as well as our evil self-love can conjure up great things before a person, but neither of them can stand the test of humility. To endure humiliations is the way to humility and also an evidence of how much of it we possess. No matter how much they hurt human nature, the soul that wishes to become humble will say with the prophet: "It is good for me that thou hast humbled me" (Ps. 118,71). The more calmly and joyfully a person accepts humiliations, the greater progress has he made in humility. — At what degree of humility have you arrived? Do you at least earnestly desire to acquire this virtue?
3. Consider that humility, which is the root of all other virtues, will also be evident in these virtues. If these virtues flourish and produce good fruit, it is a sure sign that humility is deeply rooted in the soul. There are especially three virtues that manifest the measure of our humility: they are patience, obedience, and mortification. The truly humble person calmly accepts adversities as his due; moreover, he is patient with himself and is not disturbed over his weakness and misery, which he has long

since recognized. He takes pleasure in being guided by obedience and protected against his own frailty. And because he recognizes that he has been guilty in more points than one, he seeks to make satisfaction by penance and mortification. St. Veronica regarded the stigmata as a penance for her sins. We who are sinners can hope to participate in her glory only through the performance of works of penance.

PRAYER OF THE CHURCH

O Lord Jesus Christ, who didst glorify St. Veronica by the marks of Thy suffering, grant us the grace to crucify our flesh and thus become worthy of attaining to the joys of eternity. Who livest and reignest forever and ever. Amen.

JULY 12
THE SERVANT OF GOD ANACLETE GONZALEZ FLORES
Martyr, Third Order

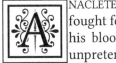NACLETE GONZALEZ was another of the modern martyrs who fought for Christ the King in Mexico, who suffered and shed his blood for Him. He was born in Tepatitlan in 1890, of unpretentious parents. Already as a law student he challenged with Christian courage the godless sallies made by professors of the university in the course of their lectures. Then already he sensed the struggle that was bound to come.

To meet it, he gathered a group of Catholic students about him, and with them he organized the Gironda, a society for the defense of Catholic interests. He himself joined the Third Order of St. Francis, and strove to make himself worthy of the patron of Catholic Action in a way that no one else had yet done.

He was especially concerned to place the press at the service of Catholic interests. He founded a weekly paper called The Word, later another weekly called The Sword, and was a regular contributor to other Catholic publications. Since the government was hostile to the Church, it is not strange to learn that he was frequently thrown into prison. But this staunch Tertiary and lay apostle bore everything with an unruffled mind and continued his apostolate even behind the bars, giving instructions in Christian Doctrine to his fellow prisoners, and praying the rosary with them.

Finally, he fell into the hands of Calles' minions. He was subjected to a gruesome martyrdom. Because he refused to reveal the whereabouts of his archbishop, he was stripped and hung up by his thumbs, then cruelly whipped. When he persevered in his silence, they pierced his feet and his entire body with daggers and knives. The only statement he made was to one of his executioners: "I have labored unselfishly in order to defend the cause of Christ and of His Church. You will kill me: but know that the cause will not die with me. I go, but with the assurance that from heaven I shall behold the triumph of religion in my native country."

Thereupon the soldier pierced the breast of Anaclete with a bayonet. A volley of fourteen bullets put an end to his heroic life. He went forth to meet Christ the King on April 1, 1927, at the same hour at which his Divine Master died. He left a widow and two young sons.

His funeral was a veritable triumphal march. No one shed any tears. Exultant shouts of "Viva Christo Rey! Long life Christ the King!" gave evidence that all were prepared to tread the same path for Christ the King as did the young hero and Tertiary, Anaclete Gonzalez.

ON DEVOTION TO THE KINGSHIP OF CHRIST

1. The kingship of Christ does not conflict with the civil authority of the various governments of the world. Like King Herod, rulers and their partisans sometimes fancy that Christ and His Church wish to contest their authority. No, "He who grants what is eternal, will not take away what is temporal and perishable," as the Church sings on the feast of the Holy Innocents. It is foolish for worldly potentates to persecute the Church, inasmuch as it is through the Church that Christ wishes to dispense to society and to the individual the greatest graces for time and for eternity. In union with the Mexican martyrs, therefore, remain faithful, loyal, and grateful to the Church, notwithstanding the various trends of the time that are hostile to Christ.

2. The kingship of Christ is a saving remedy against forgetting God. Pius XI writes: "Annual celebration of the sacred mysteries is more effective in informing people about the Faith and bringing to them the joys of the spiritual life than the solemn pronouncements of the teaching Church. Documents are often read only by a few learned men; feasts move and teach all the faithful. The former speak but once; the latter every year and forever. The former bring a saving touch to the intellect; the latter influence not only the mind but the heart and man's whole nature." — With a grateful heart, then, celebrate the feast of Christ the King and let it strengthen the faith that is in you.

3. The kingship of Christ is strength for the faithful. What gave the Mexican martyrs such strength that they could sacrifice everything, position, property, parents, family, body, and life? It was the thought: All for Christ the King, to whom is given "all power in heaven and on earth" (Mt. 28,18). Relying upon this regal strength they spoke with the Machabees: "The King of the world will raise us up, who die for the laws, in the resurrection of eternal life" (2 Mac. 7,9). — Hold fast to Christ, the almighty King. Be zealous for Him and His rights according to the example of Anaclete Gonzalez, especially in promoting the Catholic press.

PRAYER OF THE CHURCH

Eternal God, Creator of all things, assist us with Thy all-powerful grace, that we who boast of battling under the banner of Christ the King, may triumph gloriously with Him in the kingdom of heaven. Who livest and reignest forever and ever. Amen.

⚜⚜⚜⚜⚜⚜

JULY 13
ST. FRANCIS SOLANO
Confessor, First Order

 RANCIS SOLANO was born in 1549 at Montilla in the beautiful province of Andalusia, of distinguished and very devout parents. At the special request of his mother, he received the name of Francis in baptism, because she ascribed the fortunate delivery of the child to the intercession of the Seraphic Founder to whom she had recommended herself in her distress.

The boy grew to be a joy to his parents. While he was pursuing his studies with the Fathers of the Society of Jesus, his modesty, gentleness, and piety merited the esteem of his teachers as well as the friendship of his fellow students.

At the age of twenty he entered the Order of Friars Minor. It was necessary to check his zeal rather than to stimulate it, for he knew no bounds in the practice of the strictest penitential exercises. In everything he chose the worst for his own use and spent the greater part of the night in prayer.

After he completed his studies and was ordained to the priesthood, he evinced tireless zeal for souls. The heroic sacrifices he made during an epidemic were especially admirable. He cared for the corporal and spiritual needs of the sick without any fear of infection. He became afflicted with the malady, but was miraculously restored to health. On every hand the name of Father Francis was spoken with the greatest reverence, and he was regarded as a saint. Such veneration offended his humility, and he requested his superiors to send him to the missions in Africa. But another field of mission activity was assigned to him.

Since the discovery of the New World by Columbus, the sons of St. Francis had been active in preaching the Gospel in America. The fearless missionaries advanced farther and farther in their effort to bring the message of salvation to the savage Indians.

In 1589 Father Francis was sent to South America with several members of his order. The provinces of Tucuman (Argentina), Gran Chaco (Bolivia), and Paraguay fell to his lot. He encountered countless hardships; nevertheless he began his mission activities with glowing zeal. He approached the Indians so courteously and kindly that they rejoiced at his very appearance. God almighty assisted him in an extraordinary way. He learned the difficult language of the Indians in a very short time, and he was understood wherever he went, even in those places which he visited for the first time.

God also gave him marvelous power over hearts. Once when he was in the city of La Rioja, a horde of thousands of armed Indians approached in order to slay all Europeans and Christianized Indians. Francis went out to meet them. His words at once disarmed them. All understood what he said although they spoke different languages. They begged him for instructions, and nine thousand were baptized.

Francis would lay his mantle on roaring streams and sail across on it to the opposite shore. He placed his cord around the neck of a mad bull that had everybody in a panic, and led it away as though it were a lamb. Once when a swarm of wild locusts came up and hovered like a black cloud over the fields of the poor Indians, threatening to devastate the entire harvest, he commanded that none of them should alight but that they should depart to the mountains; at once they withdrew. Such miracles and benefits opened to him the hearts of all; they loved and revered him as their common father.

During the holy season of Christmas, he assembled his Indians around the crib, and taught them to sing the most beautiful hymns to the Christ Child, and he himself accompanied them on the violin. He often cheered the sick with song and music. Once he was seen sitting under a tree, playing his beloved violin, and the birds flocked about him and sang along.

After Father Francis had labored twelve years among the Indians, and had won an uncounted number of heathens to Christendom, he was called to the city of Lima in Peru. There Christianity had been established for a longer time, and many Spaniards lived there. But much wantonness and immorality prevailed in this large city. One day, led by divine inspiration, St. Francis passed through the town the way the prophet Jonas once did at Ninive, and proclaimed to the inhabitants the judgments of God if they would not be converted. They were all seized with fear. They called aloud upon God for mercy, and desired the holy sacrament of Penance. The worst sinners publicly declared their determination to reform. The saint thanked God for these fruits of grace, and in devout hymns at her altar gave praise to the Mother of Mercy.

He had labored untiringly for the salvation of souls in South America for twenty years, when God called him to Himself on the feast of his special patron, St. Bonaventure, July 14, 1610. The viceroy and the most distinguished persons of Lima bore the body of the poor Friar Minor to the grave. Almighty God glorified him after death by many miracles, especially in favor of sick children; yes, even dead children were restored to life at his grace. Pope Benedict XIII canonized him amid great solemnity in the year 1726. His feast is observed by the Franciscans and Conventuals on July thirteenth, by the Capuchins on the twenty-first, and by the Third Order Regular on the twenty-fourth. (Cf. Royer, *St. Francis Solanus*; Windeatt, *Song in the South*; Habig, *Saint Francis Solano*; *Forum*, 1949, pp. 291-294.)

CONCERNING SACRED SONG

1. Consider how St. Francis Solano softened the savage spirit of the Indians and made it receptive for Christian teaching by means of spiritual song. Singing exercises a powerful influence on the mind. Not only the words but the very melody has its effect. It affects the heart and inclines the mind, according to the character of the melody, to be worldly and sensual, or Christian and devout. When David, who later composed the psalms for the Israelites to sing, played on his harp for Saul, the evil spirit, who frequently plagued the latter, departed. — Your mind, too, can be attuned to what is Christian and devout by sacred song. What kind of song has hitherto given you the greatest pleasure?

2. Consider that the Church has used vocal music in her services from the earliest time, in order to glorify God on the one hand, and on the other, to edify the faithful. Thus the Apostle admonishes us: "Teaching and admonishing one another in psalms, hymns, and spiritual canticles, singing in grace in your hearts to God" (Col. 3,16). The Israelites also sang

at the command of God, and they were instructed to know their song by heart (Deut. 31,19). The angels sang their song of peace at the birth of Christ, and the blessed will join the choir of heaven in singing God's praise throughout eternity. We should, therefore, have a high regard for the Church's sacred song, encourage it as much as possible, and cheerfully join in the singing ourselves. — Do you do that?

3. Consider the qualities that singing must possess so that it may serve the purpose for which it is intended. It must be devout, since it should be a prayer, exalted prayer. But just as prayer said without devotion does not reach the heart of God, so it is with thoughtless singing, no matter how loud we may shout in the process. Moreover, our singing should be intelligible, so that the words may serve to edify. The Apostle says: "I will sing with the spirit, I will sing always with the understanding" (1 Cor. 14,15). In singing we should also keep in unison with the other voices, otherwise it will not foster devotion but rather disturb it. Whoever cannot sing in harmony should remain silent. Also, whoever believes he has an exceptionally good voice should not try to out-sing the other singers; that may easily result from vanity, and then the devil rather than God is made to rejoice. If, however, like St. Francis, you employ vocal music for the sole purpose of honoring God, of edifying yourself and your neighbor, you will surely obtain grace and mercy for yourself and many others.

PRAYER OF THE CHURCH

O God, who through St. Francis Solano didst lead many of the nations of America to the bosom of Thy holy Church, turn away Thine anger from us through his intercession and merits, and in Thy mercy impart to the nations who still do not know Thee the fruits of Thy holy name. Through Christ our Lord. Amen.

❧❧❧❧❧❧❧❧❧❧

JULY 14
ST. BONAVENTURE
Doctor, Bishop, First Order

Next to God we owe a debt of gratitude to St. Francis for this great Doctor of the Church and minister general of the Franciscan Order.

Bonaventure was born at Bagnorea in the Papal States in 1221, and was given the name John in Baptism. As a child of four years he became seriously ill and was given up by the physicians. Then his mother hastened to St. Francis, who was preaching in the vicinity just then, and begged him to come and heal her child. The saint acceded to her request; he prayed over the child, and immediately it was cured. St. Francis is said then to have uttered the prophetic words: "O buona ventura — O blessed things to come!" For that reason the child was called Bonaventure.

Endowed with most remarkable gifts of nature and grace and reared in the fear of God, Bonaventure entered the Order of St. Francis as a young man. Completing his year of probation with honor, he continued his studies under the great Alexander of Hales. The latter did not know what he should admire most, the talent or the virtues of the young religious. He used to say it appeared that Adam had not sinned in this young man.

During his student years, Bonaventure devoted many an hour to the contemplation of Christ's suffering and he was a zealous client of our Blessed Lady. It is reported that once when Bonaventure abstained from holy Communion for several days from a sense of humility, an angel placed the consecrated Host on his tongue. After his ordination to the priesthood he devoted himself with extraordinary zeal to the salvation of souls.

Because of his extensive and profound knowledge, he was appointed professor of theology at the University of Paris at the early age of twenty-seven. Bonaventure and Thomas Aquinas, of the Order of St. Dominic, at that time shed the greatest luster on that institution. Gerson, the great chancellor, remarked that the University of Paris had perhaps never had a greater teacher than Bonaventure. He grasped theology with his heart as well as with his mind, and it shed its radiance on his conduct as well as his words.

St. Thomas once visited him while he was engaged in writing the life of St. Francis. He found Bonaventure raised in ecstasy above the earth. Reverently he withdrew, saying to his companion: "Let us leave a saint to write about a saint." On another occasion Thomas asked St. Bonaventure from which books he obtained his unparalleled knowledge. Bonaventure pointed to the crucifix as his library.

In 1257, when Blessed John of Parma resigned the office of minister general, Bonaventure was unanimously chosen, at the recommendation of Blessed John, to fill this position. He governed the order for eighteen years, and regulated everything that pertained to convent life and the external activity of the friars with such circumspection and prudence that he has quite generally been considered the second founder of the order.

Both by word and deed he defended the order against great and

learned opponents. Franciscan convents had already been established in
all parts of the world: Bonaventure divided them now into provinces. He
also composed ordinances for the faithful observance of the rule which
formed the basis for all future constitutions of the order. At the same time
he patiently gave audience to the simplest brother and sometimes
performed some of the lowliest duties in the convent. He prescribed that
the Angelus bell be rung daily in all Franciscan churches. This beautiful
custom soon spread throughout the Catholic world.

In spite of all the duties of his important position, the saint still found
time to preach and to write books of great learning and holy unction. He
had steadfastly declined all ecclesiastical distinctions. In 1273, however,
Pope Gregory X obliged him to accept the bishopric of Albano and the
dignity of the cardinalate. The pope himself consecrated him bishop and
then entrusted him with the direction of the Council of Lyons. To the
great satisfaction of the pope and the fathers of the Council, the schismatic
Greeks also attended this assembly. At their arrival Bonaventure delivered
an address, which he opened with the text: "Arise, O Jerusalem, and stand
on high: and look about towards the east, and behold thy children
gathered together from the rising to the setting sun" (Bar. 5,5). Due to his
efforts, the Orientals were reunited to the Church of Rome.

Worn out by the heavy strain, he fell ill after the third session. The
end came very rapidly; the pope himself administered extreme unction.
With his eyes directed toward the crucifix, Bonaventure died during the
night between the fourteenth and fifteenth of July, 1274. Seldom if ever
was there a grander funeral. The pope and all the members of the Council
attended it.

Sixtus IV canonized him in 1482. Sixtus V gave him the title of Doctor
of the Church in 1587. Because of the ardent love which marks his
writings, he is called the Seraphic Doctor. All three branches of the First
Order as well as the Third Order Regular observe his feast on July
fourteenth.

ON THE LOVE OF GOD

1. Let us give our thoughts to what the Seraphic Doctor says on the love
of God. He tells us that it should be the aim of our lives, according to the
words of our Lord: "This is the greatest and the first commandment: You
shall love the Lord your God with your whole heart and with your whole
soul and with your whole mind" (Mt. 22,37-38). Not as though the love of
God were the only virtue and that we need not concern ourselves about
any other, but without the love of God the other virtues are not true

virtues and cannot lead to salvation. Moreover, the other virtues derive their luster and strength from the love of God, as material things do from the sun. — Unless your industry, temperance, charitable activity, and even your piety are enlivened and filled with the love of God, they are worthless. Have you given this sufficient consideration in the past?

2. Consider that the love of God is of such inestimable value because it excludes all sin. "To love God," says the Seraphic Doctor, "means to wish God well. But every sin is something evil, an offense against God. Hence, sin cannot co-exist with the true love of God." The more perfect your love of God is, the more you will abstain from sin. It is, of course, true that the perfect love of God, which implies that all our acts and desires are directed towards God alone, is not possible here upon earth; it will constitute our bliss in eternity. Nevertheless, even here on earth the love of God must exclude everything that is displeasing to God. — If you still fall into many sins, is it due to the fact that you do not love God enough?

3. Consider whence St. Bonaventure derived his ardent love of God. It was from keeping his eyes on the crucifix and meditating on the sufferings of Christ. "The wounds of Jesus," he said, "are arrows that wound the hardest hearts, and flames that kindle the coldest souls." Whoever truly contemplates our suffering Saviour on the cross can hardly yield to sin. The love of Him who loved us to such great lengths must of necessity fill us with zeal to avoid whatever displeases Him and to make our hearts agreeable to Him. May the powerful intercession of the great Doctor of the Church assist us in following his words and example.

PRAYER OF THE CHURCH

O God, who didst give the holy confessor and bishop Bonaventure to the Church as an admirable teacher, mercifully grant that she may merit at all times to have him for her intercessor. Through Christ our Lord. Amen.

༄༅༄༅༄༅༄༅༄༅༄༅༄

JULY 15
BLESSED BERNARD OF BADEN
Confessor, Third Order

hat it is possible to serve God unreservedly in every walk of life, even as a young prince, soldier, and diplomat, is demonstrated by the holy life of the fifteenth-century Tertiary, Margrave Bernard of Baden. Born in 1428, Bernard was the second son of Margrave Jacob I of Baden. Though he spent most of his boyhood at the courts of Charles VII of France and René of Anjou, he grew up to be an exceptionally pious young man. When the king of France made him an offer of marriage with his daughter Princess Magdalen, Bernard refused because he had vowed to live in perpetual chastity.

After the death of his father in 1453, twenty-five year old Bernard left the government of Baden in the hands of his brother and entered the service of Emperor Frederick III as a military officer and ambassador. A Franciscan Father by the name of Friar John, who had received him into the Third Order, henceforth accompanied him as chaplain on all his journeys. So well did Bernard carry out his duties, that the emperor entrusted him with many delicate diplomatic missions, principally in regard to the crusade against the Turks.

Constant contact with worldly affairs, however, did not prevent him from leading the life of a saint. Even at the gay court of Vienna this unusual young diplomat was held in high esteem because of his exemplary and pious life. While others sought relaxation in worldly amusements, he spent hours in prayer. Twice a week at least he received holy Communion. At the time, that was a very unusual practice.

Traveling from Genoa to France in behalf of the crusade, he took sick near Turin, and died in the Franciscan friary at Moncalieri on July 15, 1458, only thirty years old. The people began at once to venerate him as a saint, and miracles took place at his tomb. His body was taken back to Baden and laid to rest in the parish church. In 1481 and again in 1769 the Church approved his cult as Blessed; and the Grand Duchy of Baden honored him as its second patron. At Baden his feast is celebrated on July twenty-fourth; but in the archdiocese of Turin, where he died, it is observed on the fifteenth. He is not commemorated in any of the Franciscan breviaries and missals. (Cf. Biersack, pp. 13-14; *These Made Peace*, p. 174.)

ON AMBITION

1. Consider how the conduct of many, in fact of most people, differs from that of Blessed Bernard. He fled the honors of his high position and endeavored to serve God only by the faithful performance of his duties. Most people, however, seek honors, and there is nothing in the world that gives them greater satisfaction than to be honored by others. The sensible and devout Tertiary Margrave Bernard perceived that worldly honor is a dangerous thing and fled from it. Was he not right? Praise and honor

readily mislead us, we become vain, we strive for still more honor, we perform our good works only to secure the praise of men, and thus we lose all our merit for eternity. We envy others who have received greater honors than we, and we disparage them in order to exalt ourselves. Will God tolerate that? "Let nothing be done by vain-glory; but in humility let each esteem others better than himself" (Phil 2,3). — How have you acted in the past?

2. Consider that, while many Christians do not necessarily lower others in order to exalt themselves, nevertheless they are jealously concerned that due honor is always paid to them. If it is omitted in any way, they are much disturbed and quite unhappy. We should endeavor to preserve our good name: "Take care of a good name" (Eccli. 41,15). But as regards honor, we ought not to be so touchy and overanxious. If our Lord Jesus Christ became "the reproach of men and the outcast of the people" (Ps. 21,7), should we not for love of Him calmly accept it if our honor and our good name are injured through no fault of our own? Reflect that if all our sins were made known to the world, we should be far more despised by others than we are now. — How have you behaved on such occasions?

3. Consider what constitutes the honor after which we should strive. It consists in virtue alone, and principally in the virtue of humility, by which we ascribe to God rather than to ourselves the honor resulting even from the good we do. "He who speaks of himself, seeks his own glory; but he who seeks the glory of Him who sent him, he is true" (Jn. 7,18). He who does not consider himself deserving of honor, as was the case with Blessed Bernard, will be considered deserving of it by others. For, honor is like a shadow; it flees from him who pursues it, but it follows him who flees from it.

PRAYER OF THE CHURCH
(Secret 27 under "Various Prayers")

May this offering, we beseech Thee, O Lord, win for us the grace of true humility, and may it drive from our hearts the concupiscence of the flesh and of the eyes and all worldly ambition; that, living soberly, justly, and piously, we may obtain everlasting rewards. Through Christ our Lord. Amen.

JULY 16
ST. MARY MAGDALEN POSTEL
Virgin, Third Order

JULIE FRANCES CATHARINE POSTEL, the daughter of a rope manufacturer, was born at Barfleur in Normandy on November 28, 1756. After her elementary education, she received further training from the Benedictine nuns at Vologues. There she decided to devote her entire life to the service of God and her neighbor, and privately took the vow of chastity.

Five years after she opened a school for girls in La Bretonne, the French Revolution broke out. During the persecution she played a heroic part in helping the priests who were in hiding or in prison and in strengthening the faith of the loyal Catholics of Barfleur. She was authorized to keep the Blessed Sacrament in her house, and when conditions grew worse to carry the Blessed Sacrament on her person and even to administer Holy Viaticum to the dying in cases of emergency. The Jacobins often suspected her, but she enjoyed the special protection of God and no harm came to her. In the decree of beatification St. Pope Pius X did not hesitate to call her a "maiden-priest."

After the storm had passed, Julie helped to restore the Faith by catechizing young and old, and began to teach school once more at Cherbourg. With the approval of the Vicar Louis Cabart, she and two other women established a religious community there in 1805; and two years later they and another who had joined them pronounced their vows. They called themselves the Poor Daughters of Mercy and observed the rule of the Third Order of St. Francis.

During the first thirty years, the new Franciscan sisterhood encountered many bitter disappointments and trials, but Mother Mary Magdalen, as Julie was now called, persevered courageously in her vocation. The motherhouse of the congregation was transferred in 1832 from Cherbourg to the former Benedictine abbey of St. Sauveur le Vicomte in Courtance; and in 1837 the Vicar General Delamare substituted, in place of the Third Order rule, that of St. John Baptist de la Salle, the founder of the Christian Brothers. Henceforth the members of the community were called Sisters of Mercy of the Christian Schools. During the last few years of her life, Mother Mary Magdalen saw her sisterhood expand and achieve great things. It was at her instigation also that the Vicar General Delamare in 1843 founded the School Brothers of Mercy at Montebourg.

Mother Mary Magdalen was almost ninety years old when she died on July 16, 1846. Her sisterhood continued to grow and spread also to other

countries, especially England and Italy. In 1862 it was established in
Germany when four school teachers adopted the statutes of these sisters;
but in 1920 this foundation became independent, with its motherhouse at
Heiligenstadt. The original French sisterhood received papal approbation
in 1901. Mother Mary Magdalen was canonized in 1925 by Pope Pius XI;
and her feast is observed on July twenty-second. It does not appear in any
of the Franciscan calendars. (Cf. Biersack, pp. 122-123; *These Made Peace*,
p. 235; Heimbucher, vol. 2, pp. 508 and 450.)

MARY, COMFORT OF THE AFFLICTED

1. Consider that the Blessed Mother of God has been appointed as the
consoler of all who suffer, especially those who, like St. Mary Magdalen
Postel, meet unexpected and discouraging difficulties in the work they
have undertaken solely for the honor of God and the good of souls. Holy
Mother Church bids us call on our Lady: "Comforter of the afflicted, pray
for us!" And it is right that she should be so called, because she brought
into this world the God of all comfort, and still more so because she has
been given as a mother to all who suffer. The beloved disciple stood
deeply afflicted beneath the cross of our dying Saviour, and our Lord
pointed to our Lady with the words: "Behold, your Mother!" (Jn. 19,27).
Where does a sorrowful child turn more instinctively than to the heart of
his good mother? — Are you suffering? Go to Mary! Behold your Mother!
2. Consider why Mary is full of pity towards all who suffer. She herself
tasted all sufferings, in fact was satiated with suffering to the utmost. She
can ask of all: "Behold and see whether there is suffering like to mine"
(Lam. 1,12). A mere glance at the Sorrowful Mother brings comfort and
helps us see how small are our sufferings compared with hers. And tender
compassion prompts her to help us in our distress. She could not even
witness the embarrassment of the married couple at the wedding of Cana
without asking her Divine Son to relieve them. Say, therefore, with
confidence: "To thee do we cry, poor banished children of Eve. Turn thine
eyes of mercy towards us in our necessities!" — Have you turned with
confidence to Mary in your sufferings?
3. Consider the power Mary has to help the afflicted. She is now the
Queen of heaven, and has influence through her intercession over the
omnipotence of God. At her wish all our sorrows can be converted to joy.
But because she is also a wise virgin and knows that suffering and crosses
contribute to our salvation, she sometimes leaves them for her best clients
to bear, but then she sends them strength and comfort. That is what St.
Mary Magdalen experienced. That is what thousands of others experience

at the various shrines of our Lady. Beg her that in all the visitations of
God she, too, may visit you and obtain for you God's strengthening grace.

PRAYER OF THE CHURCH

O God, the Sublimity of the humble and the Strength of those who hope
in Thee, who didst make Saint Mary Magdalen Thy virgin wondrous by
virtues, and through her didst enrich Thy Church with a new progeny,
mercifully grant that by her help, and being freed, in imitation of her,
from earthly things, we may always hold on to the things of heaven.
Through Christ our Lord. Amen.

※※※※※※※※※※※

JULY 17
THE SERVANT OF GOD FRANCIS GARCES AND COMPANIONS
Martyrs, First Order

ONTEMPORARY with the twenty-one missions founded by
Father Juniper Serra and his successors along the coast of the
present state of California, there was another chain of
Franciscan missions extending from northern Mexico into
Arizona, which territory was then called Pimería Alta. The latter had been
founded and administered by Jesuit missionaries during the eight decades
from 1687 to 1767, when they were banished. They were then placed in
the care of the Spanish Franciscans of the Apostolic College of Querétaro,
Mexico, who remained until their expulsion in 1827. During those sixty
years, the Franciscans not only constructed entirely new churches in some
of the missions, for instance San Xavier del Bac, near Tucson, but they
also founded several new ones, for instance the two among the Yuma
Indians in the southeastern corner of California.

The first Franciscan missionary at San Xavier del Bac, the
northernmost mission of the Pimería Alta chain, was Father Francis
Garcés, a most enterprising frontier missionary who was consumed by an
unbounded zeal for souls and cheerfully bore the greatest hardships. He
lived on the same food as the Indians and learned to speak the Indian
language perfectly. When he came to San Xavier in 1768 he was thirty
years old; and during the next ten years, with this mission as his
headquarters, he made six expeditions far into the north, going as far as
San Gabriel in California and the Moqui Indians near the Grand Canyon.

He took along no other baggage than his breviary, an extra tunic, and a picture of Our Lady on the rear side of which was another of a condemned soul. The latter he used to instruct the Indians he encountered on the way. He traversed more than five thousand of desert miles, and has been justly styled the Apostle of Arizona.

In 1779 two new missions were founded among the Yuma Indians, La Purísima Concepción on the site of the later Fort Yuma, California, and San Pedro y San Pablo de Bicuñer some miles farther north. Contrary to the prudent advice of the missionaries, the Commandant De Croix, who resided at Arizpe in Mexico, insisted that there must be, not reductions like the other missions, but mixed settlements of Spaniards and Indians in which the Fathers must limit themselves to preaching and the administration of the sacraments. It did not take long for troubles to arise between the Spaniards and the Indians; and in July, 1781, the Indians rebelled and murdered most of the Spaniards including the missionaries. Although it was hatred of the Spaniards which caused the rebellion, those Yumas who killed the missionaries were prompted also by hatred of the Catholic Faith.

At Mission San Pedro y San Pablo, forty-five year old Father John Diaz and his assistant, thirty-seven year old Father Joseph Moreno, were among the first to fall under the deadly clubs of the savages on July 17. The latter was decapitated with an ax. At Mission La Purísima Concepción, forty-three year old Father Francis Garcés and his assistant, thirty-two year old Father John Barraneche had survived the first attack on the same day; but two days later the rebels returned and some of them, contrary to their chief's orders, beat the two missionaries to death with clubs and sticks. All four missionaries had distinguished themselves by the holiness of their life long before their martyrdom.

Some Spanish captives of the Indians, who were rescued later, testified that, for many nights after the massacre and the destruction of the missions, they as well as the Indians saw a procession of people dressed in white at the place where Mission San Pedro y San Pablo had stood. Preceded by a crossbearer and two candle-bearers, they marched around many times, holding burning candles in their hands and singing hymns which no one understood. Then they disappeared. The Indians were so terrified that they finally fled to another place eight leagues down the river.

Five months later a Spanish expedition found the unburied bodies of Fathers Diaz and Moreno on the spot where they had been killed. Their bodies were still incorrupt, but Father Moreno's head was missing. The graves of Father Garcés and Barraneche, who had been buried by an

Indian woman, were found in a plot of ground which was covered by green grass and beautiful flowers, some of them unknown in that region, while all around the soil was parched and bare. Their bodies too were incorrupt. The remains of all four missionaries were taken to Tubutama, Mexico, and in 1794 to the Apostolic College of Querétaro. (Cf. Engelhardt, *The Franciscans in Arizona*, pp. 142-169; Habig, *Heroes of the Cross*, pp. 27-29; *The Martyrs of the United States of America*, pp. 109-110.)

CHRISTIAN MARTYRDOM

1. Martyrdom is part of Christianity. Christ told His disciples in advance: "The hour will come in which whosoever kills you, will think that he is doing a service to God" (Jn. 16,2). And the same hatred that condemned Christ to the martyrdom of the cross, will continue to be the cause of the death of His disciples. It was not so much the sufferings they endured that made martyrs of the early Christians, but rather the confession of their faith, which they sealed with their blood. It was for this same profession and propagation of their Christian faith that the sons of St. Francis were put to death in many of their mission fields. — You may be justly proud of these heroes.

2. Martyrdom reveals Christianity. St. Augustine says of the early Christian martyrs: "They are like bottles of precious ointment, which give forth a more delightful odor after they have been broken." Let us recall the odor of fortitude, patience, love for their enemies, and love for Christ and His Church which they diffused. A religion for whose doctrines so many and such great heroes have testified with their blood must be true! And so the words of Christ can be applied to the martyrs: "You shall be witnesses unto Me" (Acts 1,8). — Are you sufficiently firm in your religion to make you ready to bear witness unto Christ?

3. Martyrdom is recompensed with the reward of Christianity, and principally with that glorious reward to which Christ alluded when He said: "Greater love than this no man has, that a man lay down his life for his friends" (Jn. 15,13). The martyrs sacrificed their blood and their lives for Christ, their best Friend. This love in turn cancels all their sins and the punishment due to them, and immediately makes them partakers of heavenly glory. — In the godless days in which we are living, prepare yourself to make the sacrifice of your life for Christ if necessary.

PRAYER OF THE CHURCH

O God, who dost permit us to celebrate the birthday of Thy martyrs, grant us the grace to be admitted into their company in eternal bliss. Through Christ our Lord. Amen.

⚙⚙⚙⚙⚙⚙⚙

JULY 18
THE SERVANT OF GOD CECILIA JOANELLI-CASTELLI
Housewife, Third Order

ECILIA was born at Gandino in Lombardy. She belonged to the renowned family of the Castelli, who were no less eminent for virtue than for noble birth. One of her sisters was the mother of Blessed Pope Innocent XI, and one of her nieces, the servant of God Cecilia, was christened with her name.

Even as a child, Cecilia evinced a most extraordinary fear of God. If she saw other children doing anything wrong, or if she heard a bad word, she would entreat them: "Do not do that! Do not say that! It is a sin." At that early age, she had such filial devotion to the Mother of God that she edified everybody. Three times every day she knelt down before an image of our Lady at home and said three Ave Marias.

After the child received her first religious instruction, she began to look at everything in the light of faith. She honored Christ our Lord in her father and Mary in her mother; and as she advanced in age and intelligence, she strove so much the more to live like a child of the holy family.

Cecilia had no use for vain attire and the noisy amusements of the world. Before great feasts she would fast for forty hours on bread and water. She took pleasure in reading religious books, and girl companions liked to come and hear her read from them. From her friends, Cecilia once got a number of secular books, the reading of which might easily have changed the course of her life. But just at that time several misfortunes occurred in the family, and she soon realized how little comfort and support could be drawn from books of the kind. So she laid them aside and never picked them up again.

On the other hand, Cecilia set down in writing those virtues which she would henceforth endeavor to practice: deep humility, contempt for the vanities of the world, denial of her own will, loving interest in her neighbor, persevering patience, and union with our suffering Saviour.

It was not surprising that when a new convent for young women was established at Gandino, Cecilia desired very much to enter it. She mentioned her desire to no one, but for the time being prayed much and fervently to know her vocation. Often she pleaded before a crucifix: "Lord, I desire only to do Thy will. Let me recognize Thy holy will!" With this intention in mind, she also practiced severe acts of penance.

Just at this time a young nobleman asked for Cecilia's hand in marriage, and since her parents desired that she give her consent, she believed that she should recognize God's will in the matter. In matrimony she found numerous opportunities to practice the virtues she had resolved to attain. As both her parents-in-law were still living, she decided from the first that she would not give orders but obey.

She was indeed an obedient daughter to her mother-in-law and a great help in the household. She tolerated no indecent conversation among the servants, nor gossip about others. She herself gladly assisted the servants whenever she could make their work easier for them, and continued to do so even after her mother-in-law's death. She also knew how to deal with her husband's older brothers, who lived with them, in order to keep peace with them. Her father-in-law suffered for six months from serious infirmities, but he often remarked that he could easily bear everything, because Cecilia nursed him so tenderly and provided so well for his comfort.

After the death of her father-in-law, Cecilia herself was attacked by a severe illness, which she bore with cheerful resignation. But from now on she was more earnestly minded than ever to withdraw from the world. With the consent of her husband she entered the Third Order of St. Francis; and from then on she made her dress and table as simple as that of a religious. She was, however, so much the more generous to the poor.

She reared her children in the fear of God. Often each day she recommended them to God in prayer, and placed them under the special protection of Mary, particularly her sons when they were obliged to go out into the world. Her daughters were reared in a manner befitting their distinguished rank, but they got no instruction in the vanities of the world; on the contrary, they beheld in their mother a brilliant example of Christian perfection.

As the years passed, Cecilia lived more and more austerely. When her eldest daughter on one occasion asked her to spare herself somewhat, since she was leading a far severer life in the management of her large house than a secluded religious, the mother answered: "I am doing nothing out of the ordinary; I ought to do much more for my God, who did so much for me." Almighty God acceded to her desire for suffering by sending her grievous ailments. Cecilia thanked Him for these, and never wished for relief. Often she prayed like St. Theresa: "O Lord, let me suffer or die."

She died while embracing the crucifix and pronouncing the sweet names of Jesus and Mary, June 20, 1641, in the fifty-eighth year of her life. Pieces of her clothing were preserved like the relics of a saint, and several sick persons were miraculously helped by their use. Emperor Ferdinand III wrote to her husband expressing his condolence, at the same time praising the virtues of the deceased. Her husband himself wrote in a letter: "I can certify on oath that in the thirty years we lived together, she never said an impatient or angry word to me."

ON THE CHRISTIAN HOUSEWIFE

1. Holy Scripture says of a virtuous woman: "Her husband praised her" (Prov. 31,28). If a husband could give the praise which Cecilia received from her husband, she must have been a very virtuous woman, the true model of a Christian housewife. Note whence she obtained the grace and strength to be such a model in her position. It was granted to Cecilia because from the very beginning of her married life she wished for nothing but to do God's will. Not the dictates of sensual nature, not the wish to govern as a mistress, but only the knowledge that God had called her, guided her to enter the married state. She was given as a reward to her good husband: "A good wife is a good portion, she shall be given in the portion of those who fear God to a man for his good deeds" (Eccli. 26,3).

2. In the example of Cecilia, consider the main virtues which a Christian housewife should practice. They are humility, contempt for the world, self-denial, patience. These virtues help her preserve peace in her house and peace in her heart. If a man's strength shows itself in his work, a woman's must appear in patient endurance. It is this strength to which the Wise Man refers when he asks: "Who shall find a valiant woman?" (Prov. 31,10). She is seldom found, because such strength proceeds from genuine piety and true fear of God, as practiced by Cecilia. Too often it is believed that fear of God and piety are necessary only for women who wish to enter a convent, whereas at times they are more necessary for a good housewife. "The woman who fears the Lord, she shall be praised" (Prov. 31,30).

3. In the saintly life of Cecilia, consider what a blessing a truly God-fearing woman is to her house. She is the support of her husband ("the heart of her husband trusts in her," Prov. 31,11), and a comfort to aged parents. She is a model for her daughters, and a guiding spirit for her sons, whom she assists by her constant prayer wherever they may be in the world. She is the guardian of her servants, whom she restrains from evil,

and the augmenter of their comfort, since she herself takes the lead in the work, and her prudent spirit watches over them all. May God in His goodness provide such a housewife for every Christian home!

PRAYER OF THE CHURCH
(First Sunday after Pentecost)

O God, the strength of those who hope in Thee, graciously hear our prayers; and, since human frailty can do nothing without Thee, grant us the help of Thy grace, that in fulfilling Thy commandments we may please Thee both in will and in deed. Through Christ our Lord. Amen.

JULY 19
BLESSED PETER CRESCI
Confessor, Third Order

LIKE St. Francis, Peter Cresci, who was born in or near Foligno some time during the second half of the thirteenth century, was a wealthy merchant's son. But as a youth he was far more of a worldling than the Poverello. Although his parents tried to make a good Christian of him, they were overindulgent; and as a result he became a spendthrift. Because he always had plenty of money in his pockets, he had no trouble in finding bad companions with whom he led a riotous life.

He was thirty years old when he completely changed his manner of life. His parents died at that time, and he was so deeply affected by this loss that the grace of God was able to make him realize the utter vanity of earthly possessions and pleasures. He sold the rich inheritance to which he had fallen heir, and gave all of his money to the poor. Henceforth he gained a livelihood as a laboring man, and even then gave away most of his earnings to the needy. For he subsisted on a very meager fare, and for weeks at a time he ate only dry bread and drank only water. Having no home of his own, he usually took his night's rest on the bare floor of the belfry in the Church of San Feliciano. Often he spent the entire night in prayer and meditation.

Some time after his conversion, Peter joined the Third Order of St. Francis; and frequently he made pilgrimages to Rome and Assisi. The Portiuncula Chapel of Our Lady of the Angels, which St. Francis loved so much, was especially dear to him. Most people were greatly edified that

Peter made amends for the excesses and bad example of his youth in such a drastic manner, but his former bad companions could not forgive him for deserting them and depriving them of the money with which he had so liberally supplied them. They accused him of heresy and managed to have him cited before an ecclesiastical court. However, it soon became evident that he was wholly innocent and his conduct was deserving only of the highest praise. God Himself showed by miracles how pleased He was with Peter's life of heroic sanctity. After Peter's death on July 19, 1323, the people of Foligno began at once to turn to him as an intercessor in heaven. His cult as Blessed was approved by Pope Urban VI in 1385; but his feast is not observed by the Franciscan Order. (Cf. Biersack, p. 147; *These Made Peace*, p. 113, note.)

OUR LIFE IS A PILGRIMAGE

1. Consider that, like Blessed Peter, we are all strangers on this earth and pilgrims to the heavenly Jerusalem. Our departed brothers and sisters, and all the saints of heaven have preceded us on the way and are eagerly awaiting our arrival. What an encouraging thought! This miserable world is not our home, we have no permanent dwelling here; we are merely traveling through it on our way to heaven. Therefore, it is not fitting that we should be so taken up with our sojourn, or make such extensive material plans, or cling so tenaciously to earthly goods, as if we were going to remain here forever. We should rather direct our thoughts and hearts to the things of heaven. — Do you frequently consider the fact that you are but a pilgrim here on earth?

2. Consider that not all men are traveling on the path that real pilgrims should take. There are two roads to eternity: one road leads to eternal life, the other to eternal damnation. The latter is the broad road abounding in pleasure and sinful delight; the former is the narrow road of self-denial and the cross. The narrow road is the pilgrim's true road. On this road Christ went ahead with His cross, and all the saints have followed Him on it. He lovingly extends an invitation also to us: Follow me, take up your cross and deny yourselves! And He adds the comforting assurance: "He who follows Me, walks not in darkness" (Jn. 8,12). — On which road are you traveling?

3. Consider that nothing makes the hardships bound up with this pilgrimage to heaven so easy as a glance at the goal of our journey. The thought of it effectively lightened all earthly hardships for our holy Father St. Francis, and caused him to cry out: "So great is the Good for which I strive, that I regard every pain as naught." If we had no cross to bear in

life, our hearts would cling to earthly things so completely that we would forget the eternal goods and lose them. For that reason God leads all His saints along the way of the cross. Let us contemplate the never-ending reward they have received, and our courage will be revived. Let us beg the dear Lord, who strengthened them, also to assist us. Then we shall not lack the strength to complete our journey happily.

PRAYER OF THE CHURCH
(Third Sunday after Pentecost)

O God, the protector of those who hope in Thee, without whom nothing is strong, nothing holy, increase Thy mercy towards us; that, with Thee as ruler and guide, we may so pass through the good things of time that we may not lose those of eternity. Through Christ our Lord. Amen.

⊗⊗⊗⊗⊗⊗⊗⊗⊗

JULY 20
BLESSED ODDINO BARROTTI
Confessor, Third Order

OMPLETE dedication to the works of charity and mercy is the keynote of the entire priestly life of the fourteenth-century Tertiary, Blessed Oddino Barrotti. Born in 1324 at Fossano in Piedmont, Oddino returned to his native city after his ordination to the priesthood, and for a time served as pastor of the Church of St. John the Baptist.

From the beginning he devoted himself completely to the care of his flock, hardly taking any rest, fasting rigorously at the same time, and giving to the poor almost every penny that he received. The bishop of Turin, to which diocese Father Barrotti belonged, found it necessary to warn him against overdoing it. "Keep at least enough of your income," the bishop counselled him, "so you can have a decent living."

A few years later the young priest was chosen provost of the collegiate church in Fossano; but, in his humility, he resigned this office to become the chaplain of a pious confraternity. It was at this time that he became a member of the Third Order of St. Francis. He then converted his own house into a shelter for the homeless; and he was made director of the Guild of the Cross, an association whose members cared for the sick and for pilgrims. In this capacity he succeeded in having a hospital built at Fossano for the sick, as well as a hospice for pilgrims. Father Barrotti himself made many pilgrimages, especially to the churches of Rome and the shrine of Our Lady of Loreto.

Four years before his death, he yielded to the urgent request of the canons and once more accepted the post of provost or director of the collegiate chapter in Fossano, and with it the duties of a pastor. And when the city was visited by a plague in 1400, the holy pastor cared for the sick with such indefatigable zeal that he too was stricken by the disease and died a martyr of charity at the age of seventy-six.

Though he was honored as a saint after his death, it was not until 1808, four centuries later, that he was declared Blessed. The feast of Blessed Oddino Barrotti is celebrated in the diocese of Mondovi on July twenty-first; but it is not observed by any of the branches of the Franciscan Order. (Cf. Biersack, p. 138; *These Made Peace,* pp. 173-174; *Forum,* 1949, p. 207.)

ON THE THREE DIVINE VIRTUES

1. The three divine virtues of faith, hope, and charity, possessed in a high degree, were the reason why Blessed Oddino became the hero of charity that he was. They must also be the firm foundation of our Christian life. A Christian life must proceed from God and must be directed to Him, and the three virtues are called divine virtues because they proceed from God and tend towards Him. They make it possible for us to arrive at the supernatural goal for which God has destined us, the Beatific Vision. For this purpose our minds must be enlightened with a higher light through faith, our efforts must be directed to higher things through hope, and to an extent we must now already unite ourselves to the greatest Good through charity, in order to derive strength and the higher fife from Him. The Apostle, thinking of this present life in terms of eternal blessedness, says: "Now there remain faith, hope, charity: these three" (1 Cor. 13,13). — Do you esteem these virtues at their true value?
2. Consider that these three divine virtues are implanted in the heart of every man in baptism; that is why they are called infused virtues. At first they are apparently dormant in the child, just as the other faculties are. But they are a supernatural power implanted in the soul, and from them Christian convictions and a Christian life must proceed in maturer years. If anyone from purely natural impulse — and many persons are thus inclined — is merciful or practices justice, preserves his purity, that would be only natural virtue; it is mortal and can never lead to supernatural, everlasting bliss. "Every plant which my heavenly Father has not planted, shall be rooted up" (Mt. 15,13). — From this we can learn how necessary

the divine virtues are.

3. Consider that it is for us to derive the corresponding fruits and merits from these divine virtues. They are implanted in our hearts like a seed. If the seed is choked by mortal sin against any one of these virtues, God will restore it again along with sanctifying grace after the worthy reception of the sacrament of penance. But we must encourage the seed to sprout and grow, we must endeavor to learn from Christian doctrine what we must believe and hope and love, we must frequently make acts of these virtues so that they may be firmly established in us. To encourage us to make these acts more frequently, Mother Church grants an indulgence of 300 days each time any of these acts are made, and a plenary indulgence can be gained once a month by those who make any of these acts daily (*Preces et Pia Opera*, 26). Above all things else, we must endeavor to live in the light of these virtues. Our efforts and desires must be directed to the glorious goal which Christian hope proposes to us, and in order to arrive at it we must accept with love what faith teaches us. Say to God, especially in trying circumstances: I believe in Thee! I hope in Thee! With all my heart, dear Lord, I love Thee!

PRAYER OF THE CHURCH
(Thirteenth Sunday after Pentecost)

Almighty and eternal God, give us an increase of faith, hope, and charity; and that we may be worthy to gain what Thou dost promise, make us to love what Thou commandest. Through Christ our Lord. Amen.

❦❦❦❦❦❦❦❦❦❦❦

JULY 21
BLESSED ANGELINA OF MARSCIANO
Widow, Third Order

NGELINA was born in 1374 in the palace of her father, the duke of Marsciano, near Orvieto in the Papal States. Her devout mother was much pleased to note how the conduct of her child corresponded with the name she bore, little angel. The first words she uttered were the holy names of Jesus and Mary. She delighted in building little altars, which she decorated tastily, and around which she would gather other girls of her age to pray and sing.

Angelina lost her mother when she was but twelve years of age. Her attachment to Jesus Christ then became more intimate and she vowed perpetual chastity. But she had scarcely reached the age of fifteen when her more worldly-minded father told her that he wanted her to marry the duke of Civitella. But Angelina declared that she wished no other than her heavenly Bridegroom, Jesus Christ.

The duke was filled with rage at her opposition. He gave her one week to decide, threatening to dispatch her with his sword if she persevered in her refusal. Angelina increased her prayers and penitential austerities, pleading with her Lord Jesus Christ, with the Blessed Virgin, St. Joseph, and the virgin disciple St. John to help her preserve the virginity she had vowed.

Then an interior voice prompted her to yield to her father's wishes and assured her that God would not forsake her. And God did help. Angelina's husband turned out to be a devout Christian, and, heeding her expostulations as well as her wishes, consented to live with her in perfect continence.

Two years after their marriage her husband died, and the young widow now devoted herself entirely to works of piety and charity. Together with several young women of the vicinity she entered the Third Order of St. Francis, and with them she undertook to care for the sick, the poor, the widows and orphans, and endeavored to win sinners back to the path of righteousness.

Angelina possessed the special gift of awakening in others a love for virginity. Many young women from some of the most distinguished families among the nobility, following her example, left their families and entered various convents. This aroused the ill-will of many people, and Angelina was severely criticized. Some even accused her of being a heretic and a disturber of the peace, saying that she condemned the married state and was disrupting the foremost families of the land. For this reason she was accused before the king of Naples.

The king invited the young duchess to appear before him. Angelina, having received from God the knowledge of the king's intentions, appeared before him and his court carrying burning coals in the folds of her cloak. She exposed the king's secret intention of having her burned as a heretic and disturber of the peace, showed how the coals she had brought had not injured her in any way, and declared herself ready to die upon the coals if it could be proved that she was guilty of the crimes with which she was charged. She attested that she had never condemned the married state, but that she had given due praise to the state of virginity. Struck by the miracle as well as by the words she uttered, the king dismissed Angelina with great respect.

A few days later she raised to life a young man, scion of one of the most prominent families. As a result, she was showered with honors from every quarter of the city. In order to elude them, she went into seclusion in her palace. But several young women of prominent families found their way to her there, and she was again accused before the king, who now banished her and her companions from the kingdom.

The little congregation praised God for the persecution that the world was heaping on it, and then repaired to Assisi. There Angelina was instructed in an ecstasy to go to Foligno, where God would take care of her. In this city she was cordially received by the inhabitants, who evinced great willingness to help build a convent for her and her companions.

There she established a community whose members took solemn vows and lived according to the rule of the Third Order. The Apostolic See sanctioned this sisterhood of the Third Order Regular, and confirmed the election of Angelina as the first superioress although she was then only twenty years old.

Later Angelina founded fifteen other convents of the same type in various towns of Italy, and Pope Martin V appointed her abbess general in the year 1428. This office she administered until her death on July 14, 1435.

When she realized that her death was close at hand, she expressed the wish to make a general confession. She received the last sacraments with great devotion, and assembled her spiritual daughters about her for the last time. She admonished them always to remain faithful in the observance of the rule and gave them her blessing. She was then rapt in ecstasy, during which this faithful bride of Christ was admitted to the eternal joys of Paradise. Pope Leo XII in 1825 confirmed the devotion paid to her from time immemorial. The feast of Blessed Angelina of Marsciano, or of Corbara, as she is sometimes called, is celebrated by the Franciscans and the Third Order Regular on July twenty-first, by the Capuchins on the fifteenth. (Cf. *Forum*, 1941, pp. 168-169.)

THE CROSS LEADS TO SUCCESS

1. The works of God are usually opposed by the world. The apostles experienced that in propagating the Christian Church. Many saints experienced it in their various undertakings. Angelina experienced it too in an exceptional measure. But it did not frighten her. It assured her all the more that her undertaking was the work of God and That He would assist her. — How frequently also in our day do young people experience this opposition when they desire to enter a certain state of life. How often do souls who are urged to undertake a good work for the cause of God

experience the same opposition. Do not allow yourself to become discouraged by such opposition and difficulties. It is a sign that you are undertaking a work that is pleasing to God. Call upon Him in your trial. He has promised to assist you: "I am with him in his trouble; I will deliver him and I will glorify him" (Ps. 90,15).

2. Consider that even in the life of the ordinary Christian, the cross is the only road on which he can arrive at salvation. "By the cross," says Thomas a Kempis, "you shall go into life everlasting. Dispose and order all things according as you will, and you will still find something to suffer, and so you shall always find the cross. If you carry it unwillingly, you make it a burden to yourself, and nevertheless you must bear it. If you fling away one cross, without doubt you will find another, and perhaps a heavier. If you carry the cross willingly, it will carry you, and bring you to your desired end, where there will be an end to suffering." — Who, then, should not be willing to walk the way of the cross courageously?

3. Consider that the souls who are guided by the Holy Spirit must tread the way of the cross throughout life. In the case of Angelina, when persecution from without ceased, she took upon herself the cross of penance and self-abnegation, adopting a very strict rule of life in a convent. Christ says to all: "If any man will come after Me, let him deny himself, and take up his cross daily, and follow Me" (Lk. 9,23). You cannot be admitted to Christ in heaven if you are not willing to renounce your will and carry the daily cross of fidelity to Christian duty. May the virtues and the intercession of Blessed Angelina give us the necessary strength!

PRAYER OF THE CHURCH

O God, who didst adorn Blessed Angelina with the special gifts of humility and charity, and didst increase Thy Church by the founding of a new congregation, mercifully grant that we may follow her virtuous example and may thus arrive at eternal joy. Through Christ our Lord. Amen.

JULY 22
THE SERVANT OF GOD MAGDALEN OF ROTTENBURG
Widow, Third Order

AGDALEN OF ROTTENBURG is one of the servants of God whose fidelity was tried in various stations in life and who was always found to be a model to the members of her sex. She descended from a very noble family, and although the pleasures and good things of life were at her command, she did not give herself up to the enjoyment of them, but rather used them to benefit others through the practice of works of mercy.

She yielded to her parents' wishes and married a young nobleman. She loved him in Christ, and gave proof of her love in the many prayers and holy Masses she offered up for him after his early death. As a widow and a mother, she set herself to the task of giving her daughter and an orphaned relative a good education. When they were both settled in life, almighty God, as a reward for her fidelity, granted her the special grace to spend the remaining years of her life among the spouses of Christ.

By divine dispensation, Magdalen one day paid a visit to the Ridler convent of Tertiaries in Munich, and while there, she experienced a most extraordinary desire to remain there. At her urgent request, she was clothed with the holy habit. She who had spent her days in the world as one of its prominent women, and had been accustomed to give commands and to be respected, now took the greatest pleasure in serving others, in performing the lowliest work, in taking the last place among her sisters in religion.

But God almighty raised her up and drew her to Himself by frequent ecstasies in prayer. It is recorded that once during a procession on the feast of the Ascension she was raised high up in the air as though she were rising to heaven in glory with Christ. In the year 1534 she died a blessed death.

ON GIVING A GOOD EXAMPLE IN EVERY STATE OF LIFE

1. Consider how exemplary the servant of God Magdalen was in every station in life. As a young woman she was not deceived by the vanities of the world, but applied herself to works of charity for the poor and the suffering. As a married woman she loved her husband with the love of Christ and manifested this love even beyond the grave. As a widow she had children to care for, and it was her earnest endeavor to provide for them for time and for eternity. After she withdrew from the world, she

was still in her old age a model for all religious by her humility, her obedience, her sincere piety. — Do you endeavor in your state of life to be worthy of this example?

2. Consider that the servant of God Magdalen became a model to all, by adapting herself to the duties of every new condition of life in which she found herself. It is a grave mistake for people to believe that they would surely be happier and serve God more faithfully in another state of life than the one in which they are at present. The poor man and the unimportant person believe they could lead a more exemplary life if they were better provided for or occupied a more prominent position; married people think they could serve God better if they had not married. The Apostle warns us against such thoughts: "Are you bound to a wife, seek not to be loosed" (1 Cor. 7,27). And the Holy Ghost assures us that "God made the little and the great, and He has equally care of all" (Wis. 6,8). God also gives you the graces proper to your state. If you co-operate with them, you will live a holy and exemplary life.

3. Consider that we ought to look upon every circumstance of life as being part of the plan which God has chosen for us as the road to sanctity. "Good things and evil, life and death, poverty and riches, are from God" (Eccli. 11,14). It is God's will that every person be saved; so of course He must arrange things that all can achieve their goal. Therefore say with Thomas a Kempis (3,15): "Lord, I am Thy servant, ready for all things. I am in Thy hand; turn me hither and thither as Thou choosest. I do not desire to live for myself, but for Thee. Oh! that I could do so in a worthy and becoming manner!"

PRAYER OF THE CHURCH
(Eighteenth Sunday after Pentecost)

Let Thy grace and pity guide our hearts, we beseech Thee, O Lord, for without Thee we are unable to please Thee. Through Christ our Lord. Amen.

JULY 23
ST. LAWRENCE OF BRINDISI
Confessor, First Order

AWRENCE was one of the greatest ornaments of the Capuchin Order, and deserved well of both Church and State at the beginning of the seventeenth century. He was born at Brindisi in the kingdom of Naples in 1559.

From his tenderest years he evinced rare gifts of nature and grace. In remembrance of Jesus in the Temple at twelve years of age, a custom prevails in Italy at Christmas time of permitting boys to preach in public. Lawrence was only six years old when he preached in the cathedral of his native town with such force and point that his audience was deeply affected and many entered upon a more Christian life.

Lawrence entered the Capuchin friary at Verona when he was only sixteen years of age. He distinguished himself from the very beginning as a model of perfection. He was punctual at all the community exercises, perfect in his submission to superiors, and full of respect and charity towards his brethren.

When his novitiate was over, he continued to pursue his studies. He was very successful in the study of philosophy and theology, and acquired so thorough a command of foreign languages that he was able to preach in French, Spanish, German, Greek, and even in Hebrew. He ascribed his success not so much to his talents as to the special help he received from Mary, the Seat of Wisdom, whom he honored with tender devotion.

With such accomplishments Father Lawrence started out on a highly fruitful missionary life. At first he visited the various cities in Italy: Venice, Pavia, Verona, Padua, Naples, where his labors were blessed with remarkable success. He was then called to Rome, where he was entrusted with the conversion of the Jews. His thorough knowledge of the Hebrew language won for him the esteem of the rabbis, and his gentle manner led many an Israelite to baptism.

In 1598 Father Lawrence was sent to Germany with eleven other friars to establish Capuchin convents there and to counteract the heresy of Luther, which was at that time gaining a foothold in Austria.

Emperor Rudolph II entrusted to our saint the task of organizing a crusade against the Turks, who were threatening to invade the whole Christian Occident. Father Lawrence, who loved seclusion, was now obliged to visit the principal cities of Germany to negotiate the cause with the princes, and preach it to the people. Due to his wisdom and holiness, which almighty God permitted him to manifest in astonishing ways, his efforts proved successful.

While he was saying holy Mass in Munich in the chapel of the duke of Bavaria, our Lord appeared after the elevation in the form of a resplendent Child, who lovingly caressed the saint. Frequently he was so affected during the celebration of holy Mass that he shed copious tears. Altar linens thus moistened with his tears were later used on the sick, and they were cured as were the faithful by the kerchiefs of St. Paul.

Father Lawrence was made the chief chaplain of the powerful army of Archduke Matthias, which went to Hungary in 1601 to war against the Turks. Although quite crippled with rheumatism, he mounted his horse and, crucifix in hand, rode at the head of the troops to the battlefield. The first sight of the enemy was most discouraging, for their position was so favorable and their number so superior that the most stout-hearted officers despaired of victory. But in the name of the God of battles Father Lawrence promised victory to the Christians and inspired them all with fiery courage. The enemy was completely routed.

Lawrence now returned to Italy where he hoped he might again serve God in his beloved solitude. But the general chapter of the order elected him vicar general. He was obliged in obedience to accept this heavy burden. In this high office he proved a charitable and vigilant pastor to his brethren. When his term expired, the pope again sent him to Germany, this time on an errand of peace, to reconcile the Archduke Matthias with his brother, the emperor. Again he was successful.

After he returned to Italy, the kingdom of Naples, his native land, was in need of his services. This kingdom which at that time belonged to Philip III of Spain, was governed by a viceroy who cruelly oppressed the people. The only hope lay in presenting the people's grievances to the king through Father Lawrence. The latter sympathized with the people and journeyed to Spain, only to learn that the king was then in Portugal. So on he went to Lisbon, where he pleaded the people's cause and obtained the dismissal of the viceroy.

But this errand of charity cost Lawrence his life. He fell very ill at Lisbon. He knew that his end was drawing near and told his companions so. After devoutly receiving the last sacraments, he fell into ecstasy, during which he went to the sweet embrace of his Lord on the feast of St. Magdalen, July 22, 1619. Pope Pius VI beatified him in 1783, and on December 8, 1881, Pope Leo XIII canonized him. The feast of St. Lawrence is observed by the Franciscans, Capuchins, and the Third Order Regular on July twenty-third, but by the Conventuals on the twenty-fourth. In December, 1958, Pope John XXIII signed a decree declaring St. Lawrence to be a Doctor of the Church.

ON THE GUIDANCE OF THE HOLY SPIRIT

1. Consider that St. Lawrence was not swayed by natural inclinations, but steadily followed the guidance of the Holy Spirit. By nature he inclined towards a life of seclusion, but amid the circumstances of the time, the Holy Spirit and the injunctions of his superiors called him to engage in active life. The blessing that rested on all his undertakings was proof that the Spirit of God was guiding him. — do you permit yourself to be led by the Spirit of God, or do you follow your own inclinations? If you earnestly desire to be guided by the Spirit of God, ask it of Him in prayer. "Your Father from heaven will give the good Spirit to them who ask Him" (Lk. 11,13).

2. Consider that we need the Holy Spirit in everything we undertake. He must counsel us both as to what ought to be done and how we should go about it and how we should plan it in order to achieve our goal. The fact that Lawrence was filled with the Spirit of Counsel enabled him to act so promptly and decisively. We are often so irresolute and fickle and permit every new momentary impression to unsettle us because we so rarely ask the Spirit of Counsel to assist us. All men need the Holy Ghost, and for that reason the Wise Man prayed: "Who shall know Thy thought except Thou give wisdom and send Thy Holy Spirit from above to teach the things that please Thee?" (Wisd. 9,17). — On important occasions say the Veni Creator devoutly.

3. Consider how the Holy Spirit of God guided St. Lawrence in carrying out his undertakings. The Spirit of Strength enabled him to disregard bodily suffering and overcome all hardships. How readily we turn aside from our good purposes because of a few difficulties! "The spirit, indeed, is willing, but the flesh is weak" (Mt. 26,41). We experience this only too often. And yet, "the Spirit helps also our infirmity" (Rom. 8,26). If we are strengthened by Him, we shall also be able to accomplish what the saints accomplished. If weakness and indolence beset you, so that you would like to give up your good resolutions, call upon the Holy Ghost to give you His grace and strengthen your infirmity, to make such sacrifices as St. Lawrence made.

PRAYER OF THE CHURCH

O God, who didst give to St. Lawrence, Thy confessor, the Spirit of Counsel and Strength to enable him to engage in the most difficult undertakings for the honor of Thy name and the salvation of souls, grant, that by the same Spirit, we may perceive what we should do and through his intercession accomplish what we have perceived. Through Christ our Lord. Amen.

JULY 24
BLESSED KINGA (CUNEGUNDA)
Virgin, Second Order

THE ROYAL dynasty of Hungary in the thirteenth century has presented the church with a galaxy of saintly women. Among the most brilliant we find Kinga (or Cunegunda), daughter of King Bela IV, and niece of St. Elizabeth of Hungary. Other aunts of this saint were St. Hedwig and Blessed Agnes of Prague. Blessed Yolande and the Dominican St. Margaret were her sisters. St. Elizabeth of Portugal and Blessed Salomea were her cousins once removed, and she was the aunt of the holy bishop Louis.

Kinga was born in the year 1224, and from her birth seemed destined far more for heaven than for the earth. As an infant she was heard to say distinctly, "Hail, Queen of Heaven, Mother of the King of Angels!" When she was carried to church, she would keep her eyes raised to heaven during the holy sacrifice of the Mass and would bow her little head whenever she heard the holy names of Jesus and Mary. On Wednesdays and Fridays she would take food but once a day.

Kinga was only fifteen years old when at her parents' request she gave her hand in marriage to Boleslaus, duke of Cracow, who later became king of Poland. The angelic virgin, however, spoke to her spouse so convincingly of the excellence of virginity, that he resolved to embrace a life of continence. Later they made a vow of perpetual chastity before the bishop of Cracow, and persevered in it for the forty years of their married life. For this reason history has surnamed Boleslaus the Chaste, while the Church has conferred the title of virgin on Kinga.

At the same time Queen Kinga occupied herself with all the duties of a true mother. She took upon herself the care of her sister Yolande, who was then only four years old, and reared her in true holiness. Faithfully imitating her aunt St. Elizabeth, she evinced a truly maternal solicitude for the poor and the oppressed, and visited the sick in the hospitals, nursing them with the tender care of a sister of mercy.

As the first lady of her country, the constant object of her care was the welfare of her people. At that time Poland was suffering from a scarcity of salt. In answer to the prayers of the queen, valuable salt mines were discovered which not only provided for the wants of the Polish people but permitted considerable quantities of salt to be exported. Desirous of increasing the number of heavenly patrons of her kingdom, she obtained from the Holy See the canonization of St. Stanislaus, bishop of Cracow, and of her aunt St. Hedwig, duchess of Silesia. She and her husband established several convents as sanctuaries of prayer for the welfare of the country.

When King Boleslaus died in 1279, the people of the kingdom strove in vain to make Queen Kinga retain the reins of government. The humble virgin replied that it was her intention to retire from the world and consecrate herself wholly to Jesus Christ. She and her sister Yolande, who had been left a widow some months before, received the habit of St. Clare in the convent at Sandek. When she entered the monastery, which she herself had founded, she said to the abbess and the sisters: "Forget what I once was; I come only to be your servant." It became her greatest pleasure to do the most menial tasks.

Almighty God tested her humility by permitting her to become the object of suspicion. She bore the trial heroically, and was then vindicated by miracles.

Kinga was elected abbess, and in this capacity governed her daughters with great prudence and maternal charity. Her community was suffering from a scarcity of water. She pleaded with God to come to her assistance. Then she went to a neighboring brook and with her staff traced the course that it should henceforth follow. The water flowed obediently to her monastery.

In her last illness she was favored with the most intimate union with her Divine Bridegroom. When she had received the last sacraments and her sorrowing daughters were reciting the prayers for the dying, she suddenly exclaimed: "Make room, do you not see our Father Francis coming to assist me?"

It was on the twenty-fourth of July, 1292, that her virginal soul took its flight to heaven. Fragrant odor filled her cell, and her face became marvelously beautiful. Numberless miracles occurred at her tomb. Devotion to her was approved by Pope Alexander VIII in the year 1690; and with the approval of Pope Clement XI she was chosen in 1715 as the special patron of the Poles and Lithuanians. The Franciscans and Capuchins celebrate her feast on July twenty-fourth, the Conventuals on the twenty-fifth.

HOLY KINSHIP

1. Consider that Holy Writ frequently mentions the kinship of holy persons. Anna, the pious mother of the prophet Samuel, is thus honorably mentioned, the ancestors and descendants of the Patriarch Isaac are spoken of in terms of praise, and we read of the parents of John the Baptist: "They were both just before God, walking in all the commandments and justifications of the Lord without blame" (Lk. 1,6). As St. Ambrose puts it, the glory of the saints lies also in this that they were not necessarily the first to practice virtue, but rather that virtue was at home in their families. And so the kinship of Blessed Kinga reflects credit upon her. But it is even greater honor for her that she perpetuated this glory by her own virtuous conduct. — Will your family have reason to be proud of your virtues?

2. Consider how disgraceful it is if a member of a virtuous family strays and walks the way of evil. Such a person dishonors the whole relationship, and his own shame is the greater in as far as he departs from the virtuous path of his relatives. David's son Absolom, who was beset with the ambition to rule, was a stain on the family name. Dina, the daughter of Jacob, brought disgrace and suffering to her father and brothers. The evil repute of such persons clings to them for all times. — Carefully avoid everything that may bring disgrace on you and your family.

2. Consider that we should be concerned, like Blessed Kinga, to imitate the virtues of our relatives and preserve the honor of our family. She imitated her sainted aunt Elizabeth in caring for the poor and sick. She reared her own sister in sanctity and obtained the honors of the altar for her saintly relative Hedwig. — Do you, too, endeavor to imitate those of your relatives who have distinguished themselves by virtue, thus setting a good example to the younger members of your relationship? If you are a Tertiary and a member of the Franciscan family, you are related to Blessed Kinga and all the saints of the three orders. As Christians, we are, according to the words of the Apostle, "fellow citizens with the saints and the domestics of God" (Eph. 2,19). — Make a sincere effort to live in a manner worthy of such kinship.

PRAYER OF THE CHURCH

O God, who didst bestow on Blessed Kinga the blessings of Thy sweetness and didst preserve her virginity even in the married state, grant, we beseech Thee, that by her intercession we may ever adhere to Thee in a chaste life, and by imitating her arrive safely in Thy presence, Through Christ our Lord. Amen.

JULY 25
BLESSED PETRONILLA OF TROYES
Virgin, Second Order

 ETRONILLA was a descendant of the dukes of Troyes. When she was still quite young, she renounced for the love of God the brilliant prospects which presented themselves to her in the world as a result of her noble descent.

She went to the Poor Clares of Provins, where she led a life of humility and renunciation, and soon became a model to all her sisters in the practice of every virtue. After establishing a new monastery of Poor Clares in the diocese of Beauvais, at a place very appropriately called Mount of Heaven, she was appointed abbess there.

Due to her prudence and maternal solicitude, the new foundation soon developed into an abode of sanctity and heavenly joy. Daughters of some of the noblest families in France came there and begged for the poor habit of holy Mother Clare. Even Queen Joan often tarried at the convent of Mount of Heaven, in order to derive edification from the saintly life and blessed peace prevailing there. She asked as a favor that she be buried there after her death.

After filling the office of abbess for a period of eight years, Petronilla resigned it in order to prepare herself for death as a plain religious. She lived in this state of retirement for eleven years. On May 1, 1355, the Divine Spouse summoned her to the eternal wedding feast. Pope Pius IX sanctioned the veneration paid to her. The Franciscans celebrate the feast of Blessed Petronilla on July twenty-fourth, the Conventuals on May first, and the Capuchins on May thirteenth. (Holweck's Dictionary of the Saints also mentions as a member of the Third Order of St. Francis a Blessed Petronilla or Pironne of Ghent who was a recluse and had the stigmata of the Lord on her body.)

ON RICHES

1. Riches do not make one happy. Where did Petronilla find happiness? Not in the wealth and splendor of her distinguished family, but in the poor convent of the daughters of St. Clare, who were, however, wealthy in the gifts of God. Ask the rich, ask Emperor Napoleon or Emperor Francis Joseph, ask the wealthy captains of industry or the American millionaires,

whether they are happy, and they will agree with the Scripture text: "The eye is not filled with seeing, neither is the ear filled with hearing" (Eccl. 1,8). Care and vexation multiply with the accumulation of wealth. The heart of man can be satisfied only with God, it can find its happiness only in God. Therefore, desist from foolish craving for wealth and earthly possessions.

2. Riches are dangerous. Our Saviour said: "How hardly shall they who have riches enter into the kingdom of God" (Mk. 10,23). Riches in themselves are not necessarily dangerous, but men too readily set their hearts on money and earthly possessions and, as a result, forget about things eternal. Therefore our Saviour added: "Woe to you who are rich, for you have your consolation" (Lk. 6,24). Blessed Petronilla acted very wisely in preferring evangelical poverty to riches. — Do not ever place your trust in riches.

3. Riches can and should be a means to salvation. If anyone with great wealth at his disposal remains humble and looks upon his possessions as a gift of God; if in spite of his wealth he does not forget God and religion; if he gladly shares his wealth with the poor and the needy — then riches will be to him a source of abundant grace and of great happiness besides. St. Paul writes to his disciple Timothy: "Charge the rich of this world not to be high-minded, nor to trust in the uncertainty of riches, but in the living God, to do good, to be rich in good works, to give easily, to communicate to others" (1 Tim. 6,17). — Take these fundamental principles as your guide.

PRAYER OF THE CHURCH

O God, who didst teach Blessed Petronilla to prefer mortification and humility to the pomp and luxury of this world, grant through her intercession that we may overcome the allurements of this present life and find eternal blessedness in embracing Thy cross. Through Christ our Lord. Amen.

JULY 26
BLESSED FELICIA MEDA
Virgin, Second Order

ELICIA was a descendant of the very distinguished and wealthy family of the Meda. She was born at Milan in Lombardy in 1378. She had good parents, who reared the pious and gifted child in the fear of God, and left nothing undone that could be of advantage in her spiritual development. In a very short time she acquired a remarkable command of the Latin language.

She lost both father and mother at a very early age, and thereafter united herself still more intimately with God. When she was twelve years old, she made a vow of perpetual chastity, and then entered the convent of the Poor Clares at St. Ursula in Milan.

The devil endeavored to make convent life miserable for her by subjecting her to severe temptations and frightful apparitions. But Felicia did not permit herself to be overcome. By fervent prayer and the words of the Psalmist: "O God, come to my assistance! O Lord, make haste to help me!" she put the spirits of darkness to flight and persevered steadfastly in her vocation.

When the abbess of the convent died in 1425, the community unanimously chose Felicia for her successor. In this position she did her utmost by word, deed, and example to promote the true religious spirit in her community, so that its good name spread far and wide, even reaching the ears of Pope Eugene IV. It induced the pope and the vicar general of the Observants, St. Bernardin of Siena, to entrust her with the establishment of a new convent of Poor Clares at Pesaro.

Despite her advanced age Felicia and seven companions made the journey from Milan to Pesaro on foot. When the foundress of the convent, the Princess of Montefeltro, offered her the carriage in which she had come out to meet the new community, Felicia humbly declined the offer and entered the town on foot with the rest of her companions.

Felicia spent four years in this new foundation, received a great number of new members, and reared and strengthened them in the spirit of our holy Father St. Francis.

She died in the odor of sanctity in 1444, and many miracles were wrought by God in testimony of the holiness of His servant. Her body was laid to rest in the convent she had founded. Four hundred years later it was transferred to the cathedral of Pesaro. Pope Pius IX solemnly enrolled her among the blessed. The Franciscans observe the feast of Blessed Felicia on July twenty-fourth, the Conventuals on September thirtieth, and the

Capuchins on October fifth.

ON OUR CONDUCT IN TEMPTATIONS

1. Consider that temptations such as Blessed Felicia experienced in the beginning of her religious life are the lot of all who are sincere in their purpose of serving God. The Holy Ghost Himself tells us: "Son, when you come to the service of God stand in justice and in fear, and prepare your soul for temptation" (Eccli. 2,1). And St. Paul writes: "And all who will live godly in Christ Jesus, shall suffer persecution" (2 Cor. 3,12). Sometimes these temptations come from the devil, sometimes from the world, sometimes from our flesh. Only God can help us at such times. Imitating Blessed Felicia, we must call upon God for help with the plea: "O God, come to my assistance; Lord, make haste to help me!" We may also say with childlike confidence: "Our help is in the name of the Lord, who made heaven and earth." God is powerful enough to help us even if the whole world and hell with all its cohorts should rise up against us. Moreover, He will help us, because He has promised to do so and He is faithful. The infernal tempter has been a liar from the beginning, and as a liar we should resist him when he tortures us with all kinds of anxiety. — Because of lack of confidence in God, have you not sometimes allowed temptation to upset you unduly?

2. Consider that along with confidence in God, the knowledge of our unworthiness and weakness must constantly increase if we wish to retain our balance in temptation. Once when the holy hermit Anthony saw the whole world covered with the snares of the devil, he sighed and asked: "Who can safely pass through this?" He received this answer: "Humility alone can do it." Be humble, therefore, in your judgments of others even when they have had the misfortune to fall into sin. Likewise be humble in your judgment concerning yourself; temptations show you just what you can do if God does not support you. But to the humble He will lend His assistance and He will preserve them from harm. — Examine yourself. Is lack of humility perhaps the reason why you are tempted so much?

3. Consider that when our Saviour once cured a demoniac, He said: "This kind can go out by nothing but by prayer and fasting" (Mt. 9,28). In certain temptations it may be necessary to add acts of mortification to our confidence in God and our humble prayer for assistance. At times we may have to bring the rebellious flesh under the subjection of the spirit by fasting and chastisements. And always it is necessary to place a check on the tongue in speaking, on the ears in hearing, on the eyes in seeing, if we do not wish to expose ourselves to numerous temptations. — Watch over your senses, and sometimes think of the souls who are now suffering the

pains of purgatory because of their lack of watchfulness.

PRAYER OF THE CHURCH

O God, who didst put the virgin Blessed Felicia to the test, by permitting her to be assailed by many temptations, and didst strengthen her with the spirit of fortitude, grant, at her prayers and intercession, that we may mercifully be freed from all the snares of the enemy. Through Christ our Lord. Amen.

JULY 27
BLESSED MARY MAGDALEN MARTINENGO
Virgin, Second Order

LESSED Mary Magdalen came from a prominent family of Brescia. Even as a child she took special delight in the austerities of religious life. Despite many difficulties that confronted her, she joined the daughters of St. Clare when she was only seventeen years of age. The young nun soon distinguished herself by her modesty, patience, and cheerful obedience. The hours prescribed for prayer and meditation, as well as the visits to our Lord in the tabernacle, were the most delightful hours of her day.

Her sympathy for our suffering Saviour was so deep that she was often found kneeling like one devoid of life. As novice mistress, and later as abbess, she guided the sisters to great sanctity by her admirable example and loving gentleness.

The fame of her sanctity caused many lay persons to appeal to her for consolation and advice. On such occasions she manifested the special gifts God had given her to encourage disheartened souls, to reconcile such as were at variance with each other, and to bring sinners back to the path of duty. Not seldom she read the innermost thoughts of others and foretold future events.

Exhausted by labor and austerity more than by age, she died on July 27, 1737, in the fiftieth year of her saintly life. Pope Leo XIII beatified her. The feast of Blessed Mary Magdalen is observed by the Franciscans and the Capuchins on July twenty-seventh.

ON THANKSGIVING AFTER HOLY COMMUNION

1. Consider that it is proper to make thanksgiving after Communion, for in holy Communion we have been favored by a distinguished Visitor. The

words which were written by the Evangelist then apply to us: "This day is salvation come to this house" (Lk. 19,9). For this reason Blessed Mary Magdalen found it a trying duty to leave the house of God after holy Communion. – What can you say of your thanksgiving? Let it not be said of you as it was of Judas: "He, therefore, having received the morsel, went out immediately" (Jn. 13,30).

2. At this thanksgiving we should offer ourselves wholly to our Saviour. After every holy Communion we should say: "What shall I render to the Lord for all the things that He has rendered to me?" (Ps. 115,3). Since God has sacrificed Himself entirely for our salvation, we should be willing to make a complete sacrifice of ourselves for His sake. Let us, therefore, consecrate to Him our hands and feet, our eyes and ears, our mind and our whole heart to be spent only in His service. That will please Him and draw down on us great blessings. – Never forget to offer this oblation to your God.

3. Moreover, let us use this time of thanksgiving to offer our petitions to the Lord. St. Theresa says: "The moments after holy Communion are the most precious moments of our life." Let us use them in placing our needs before our dear Lord. Let us above all use them, according to the example of Blessed Mary Magdalen, to pray for the conversion of sinners. – At every holy Communion remember that a great privilege has been accorded you.

PRAYER OF THE CHURCH

O God, who hast given us in the virgin Mary Magdalen an example of innocence and mortification, grant that we may renounce all worldly desires and come to Thee by the way of truth and justice. Through Christ our Lord. Amen.

※ ※ ※ ※ ※ ※ ※

JULY 28
BLESSED ARCHANGEL OF CALATAFIMI
Confessor, First Order

ORN of a noble family at Calatafimi in Sicily, Archangel was from his earliest youth of a serious turn of mind and averse to the pleasures of the world. In order not to become infected by the world, he withdrew to a hermitage in the neighborhood of his native town, where he devoted himself to meditation and prayer. His tender devotion to the Queen of heaven often brought him the grace of her visitations.

The repute of his piety soon spread through the neighboring localities, so that people came to ask his prayers, to seek advice, and to have the sick blessed by him. Since many received wonderful assistance, the crowds kept on increasing. This considerably disturbed Archangel's piety. He feared, too, the dangerous attacks of vanity.

So he decided to withdraw to the city of Alcamo, where he was unknown, and there rendered service to the sick and the poor in the hospital. But here also his virtues made him the object of veneration, and he repaired to a lonely cave in which he lived until the order was issued by the Apostolic See that all hermits should enter some established convent. Archangel then begged for the holy habit in the Franciscan friary at Palermo, where he received it at the hands of Blessed Matthew of Girgenti. Very likely he received holy orders also about this time.

Since his return to Alcamo was urgently desired, and the people offered to remodel the hospital, which was now empty, into a Franciscan friary, he was sent there by his superiors. Under his guidance a model convent of the strictest observance was established. He himself led in zeal for prayer, in the practice of humility, of poverty, and of rigorous mortification. But his zeal for the honor of God and the salvation of souls urged him sometimes to leave his beloved solitude to preach the Gospel and to lead sinners to repentance. God often confirmed his work by miracles.

Weakened by works of penance and old age, he died in the year 1460. Miracles continued to occur at his grave in the Franciscan church at Alcamo; and for this reason Pope Gregory XVI approved his veneration. His feast is observed by the Franciscans and the Capuchins on July thirtieth.

ON RETREATS

1. As the spirit of God drew Blessed Archangel throughout his life to holy solitude, so the same godly spirit draws many laymen who are really in earnest about their salvation to the solitude of some holy house, to reflect exclusively upon the salvation of their souls in the spiritual exercises of a so-called retreat. There, according to the prophet, a man "shall sit solitary and hold his peace, because he has taken upon himself" heavenly things (Lam. 3,28). The Lord will then speak to His own more clearly than amid the noise of the world. "I will lead her into the wilderness, and I will speak to her heart" (Os. 2,14). — Ought we not to esteem such solitude and

long for it?

2. Consider what is meant by the spiritual exercises. A person retires into solitude for three, five, or eight days, where he follows an exact routine of spiritual exercises, especially serious meditations upon the eternal truths as they are set before him in a discourse or a reading. These truths are, above all, the purpose for which man is here on earth; the great evil of sin; and death, judgment, hell. But there are also proposed for meditation the mercy of God, the Incarnation, the life and suffering of Christ, from which we learn the practice of every virtue and are filled with the love of God. Finally, there is proposed the eternal reward if we remain faithful in the service of God unto the end. Is there not a divine wisdom in this arrangement? It has proved itself so fruitful that St. Francis de Sales could say fifty years after St. Ignatius: "The little book of the Exercises has saved more souls than there are letters of the alphabet in it." — Should it not also be able to save your soul?

3. Consider what fruits a retreat should produce in us. The immediate fruit should be a complete and sincerely repentant confession, to cancel all the sins of our past life and make us ready to appear before the judgment-seat of God. But then, too, as we see from the experience of Blessed Archangel, it must make us faithful to the duties of our state of life as well as zealous, according to our vocation and ability, in leading others on the way of salvation. — Have your past retreats produced this fruit?

PRAYER OF THE CHURCH

Most merciful God, who didst grant Blessed Archangel, Thy confessor, in his love for solitude, the special grace to announce the Gospel, grant us, Thy servants, that following his example, we may also arrive at his reward. Through Christ our Lord. Amen.

⊗⊗⊗⊗⊗⊗⊗⊗⊗⊗

JULY 29
BLESSED PETER OF MOGLIANO
Confessor, First Order

ETER was the son of a prominent family at Mogliano in the March of Ancona. He had studied law at the University of Perugia, and had already received his degree of Doctor of Laws, when he heard a sermon by the Franciscan provincial of the March of Ancona. The sermon made such an impression on him that he went to the preacher and asked for the habit of the order.

From the very first he possessed a holy zeal for religious perfection and became a shining light in all the religious virtues. He devoted himself to the study of theology with such ardor that his learning was admired as much as his sanctity. St. James of the March considered him the right sort of man for the missions. He chose him as his companion, and Peter copied his holy master so closely that after the latter's death he was chosen as his successor in directing missions.

It is almost incredible with what zeal and charity Peter labored for the conversion of sinners. Like a two-edged sword his words pierced the hearts of his listeners, and like a soothing balsam they healed the wounds after he had removed the poison of sin in the confessional. Tirelessly he labored in the confessional by day and by night.

He possessed the special gift of putting an end to enmities. Whole towns that were armed against each other he managed to reconcile. Like a true ambassador of the God of Peace, he brought peace and firmly established harmony wherever he went. When God confirmed his words by miracles, they produced even greater results.

Many persons chose him as their guide on the road to perfection. Among these were the duke of Camerino and his daughter Baptista Varani, whom we honor among the blessed of the Franciscan Order. Once when visiting Camerino with several of the brethren, Peter felt that he was near death. Although he had been seized with a violent fever as soon as he got to the convent, he dragged himself to the church to receive Holy Viaticum. The duke soon arrived and presented his two sons to the sick man. Peter admonished them earnestly always to live in fraternal unity, and then gave them his blessing.

But the holy missionary, who had so zealously fought the infernal enemy, had yet to suffer his attacks on his deathbed. The evil one represented to him that all he had preached had been a lie. But Peter asked one of the brethren to read the story of the Passion of our Lord according to St. Matthew. Immediately the devil left him.

While the bells of the convent church were ringing out the Te Deum during the midnight office, Peter slept away peacefully in the Lord. It was on the feast of St. James, July 25, 1490. Pope Clement XIV approved his veneration; and the Franciscans and Capuchins celebrate his feast on the thirtieth of July.

ON PRESERVING PEACE

1. "How beautiful are the feet of those who preach the gospel of peace, of

those who bring glad tidings of good things!" (Rom. 10,15) That could readily be said of Blessed Peter, and it was felt in the hearts of those to whom he restored peace and concord, be it in towns, in families, or in the souls of sinners. Peace and harmony are the sweetest good fortune of men on earth and are, as far as we can experience it here in this vale of tears, a genuine foretaste of the blessedness of eternal peace in heaven. Hence the Wise Man says: "With three things my spirit is pleased, which are approved before God and men: the concord of brethren, and the love of neighbors, and man and wife who agree well together" (Eccli. 25,1-2). — Do you possess this peace?

2. Consider that peace and concord can be preserved only where an effort is made to suppress inordinate inclinations and to practice Christian charity. "From whence are wars and contentions among you?" asks St. James, and he answers: "Where else except from your concupiscences which war in your members" (Jas. 4,1). Because we speak without heeding the laws of justice and of charity; because we act without giving due consideration to the weaknesses of others; because we seek our own comfort rather than the common good, concord is so often injured and bitter anguish of heart is inflicted on all who are concerned. Is it not better and wiser, then, to war against our inordinate inclinations and to preserve peace? The same mouth that can fan a flame by blowing at a spark could also extinguish it with a little spittle. "A mild answer breaks wrath: but a harsh word stirs up fury" (Prov. 15,1). — Have you always done your part to preserve concord?

3. Consider that there are two vices in particular that disturb concord: pride and avarice. "Among the proud there are always contentions" (Prov. 13,10). It can hardly be otherwise, for each one strives to be the first and in that way pride awakens jealousy, anger, hatred and quarrels. Does not your own experience tell you this? And just as the proud man wants all the honor for himself alone, so the avaricious man wants temporal goods. Hence there follow discord and strife between associates in business, between members of a household, between brothers and sisters. In the days of the early Christians the hard words, mine and thine, were not known among the "multitude of believers who had but one heart and one soul" (Acts 4,32). — Should we not be willing to sacrifice a little of honor and of material goods in order to procure this blessed peace?

PRAYER OF THE CHURCH

O God, the Lover of charity and Author of peace, who didst permit Thy confessor Blessed Peter to excel in zeal for the preservation of peace, we beseech Thee to grant us through his intercession and merits that we may taste the joys of eternal peace. Through Christ our Lord. Amen.

❧❧❧❧❧❧❧❧❧❧

JULY 30
BLESSED SIMON OF LYPNICA
Confessor, First Order

IN the summer of 1453 when St. John Capistran visited Cracow, the capital of Poland, at the invitation of the Polish King Casimir, his sermons produced veritable miracles of conversion. Many of the young people, too, among them many students from the University of Cracow, resolved to renounce the world and begged the holy preacher for the habit of the Franciscan Order. One of these was Simon of the little town of Lypnica not far from Cracow. He had just taken his bachelor's degree in the humanities, and what is of greater consequence, by means of childlike veneration of the Blessed Virgin he had preserved his purity of heart unsullied.

Although he had lived an innocent life, he now lived a life of great penance in the order, observed long fasts, scourged his body, and always wore a penitential girdle. On the feasts of our Blessed Lady he added a second one, in order to win her special favor.

After he had been ordained a priest and had been entrusted with the office of preacher in the convent church of Cracow, his words bore the impress of such zeal and eloquence that he brought back countless sinners from the paths of iniquity; and he then guided them on the path of Christian conduct with loving gentleness. Many of his auditors were moved to aspire to higher perfection.

Simon entertained an ardent desire to shed his blood for the Faith, and he hoped to be sent to Palestine to labor among the Saracens. This hope, however, was not fulfilled. He did have to suffer many hardships, but after devoutly visiting the holy places, he returned safely to Cracow. There another type of martyrdom was destined to procure for him the eternal crown.

In the beginning he resumed his task of preaching with renewed zeal. He was obliged also to accept various positions in the order, including that of provincial. He was ever active for the welfare of his brethren and of all men, and allowed himself only the most necessary repose. He used to say that he hoped to enjoy a real rest when God would grant him eternal rest. His motto was: "Pray, work, and hope."

About the year 1482, an epidemic broke out in Cracow and raged with terrible fury. Filled with love for his neighbor and the spirit of holy zeal for the salvation of souls, Father Simon devoted himself entirely to the service of the sick. It was not long before he, too, was attacked by the dread disease. Filled with gratitude to God for this privilege and with Christian hope in a merciful judgment, he died a martyr of charity on July 18, 1482. Numerous miracles occurred at his grave, whereupon the Holy See approved his veneration. The Franciscans and the Capuchins observe his feast on July thirtieth.

ON LISTENING TO SERMONS

1. Blessed Simon, a learned student, heard a sermon by St. John Capistran and resolved to leave the world and consecrate himself entirely to the service of God. It often happens that when university students and educated people hear a sermon, they are intent only on noting whether the sermon has been well prepared and is being delivered eloquently. At times even the uneducated are more concerned about how the preacher speaks than what he is saying. How foolish! It is just as if a person who is so worn out that he can hardly stand on his feet, were to take a loaf of bread that has been offered to him, and test it according to its qualities and price rather than eat it to restore his dwindling strength. "We fools!" St. Augustine cries out. "The uneducated assert themselves and wrest the kingdom of God to themselves, and we with all our learning will sink into the abyss!" — Do you perhaps belong to these fools?

2. Consider that Blessed Simon not only applied to himself what he heard in the sermon, but actually put into practice in his daily life what he recognized in the sermon as pleasing to God. Moreover, he in turn used his talents in his own preaching career, and was tireless in laboring for the honor of God and the eternal salvation of souls. We, too, must not be satisfied with merely listening to a sermon. That would not make us holy, even if we heard all the sermons delivered in the neighborhood. It is the care and perseverance we have in carrying out the instructions that counts. "For not the hearers of the law are just before God, but the doers of the law shall be justified" (Rom. 2,13). — What fruits do you derive from the sermons and conferences you have heard?

3. Consider that without the assistance of the Holy Ghost we cannot derive fruit from the sermons we hear. The word of God is not like a lecture on some temporal subject. It is the divine seed that must penetrate into the depths of our hearts. For this we need the special grace of God. "Neither he who plants is anything, nor he who waters: but God Who

gives the increase" (1 Cor. 3,7). — Before a sermon or conference ask for the grace of enlightenment and after it ask for strength.

PRAYER OF THE CHURCH

Almighty and eternal God, who didst endow Blessed Simon, Thy confessor, with special grace to announce the Gospel, mercifully grant that nourished by his teachings we may perform the works that are pleasing to Thee and may arrive safely on the way of righteousness at our celestial home. Through Christ our Lord. Amen.

⊙⊙⊙⊙⊙⊙⊙⊙⊙⊙⊙

JULY 31
ST. THOMAS MORE
Martyr, Third Order

T. THOMAS belongs to that class of Tertiaries who have grasped the true spirit of their Seraphic Father. It is a spirit of deep-seated piety and of contempt for the world, as well as of unswerving fidelity to Holy Church practiced in an exceptional degree and sealed with one's blood.

His father was a knight. Thomas was born in London in 1480. Having been a very devout youth, he became a lawyer. His services were constantly in demand, but nevertheless he always found time to attend holy Mass daily and to perform other pious practices.

As the father of a family, he was concerned that his children should be reared in the fear of God. He became famous for his book entitled Utopia. By means of this "Kingdom of Nowhere" he scourged in fine satire the evils that were eating their way into the Church and the State.

Through Henry VIII he became attached to the royal court and was finally appointed Lord High Chancellor. The time had now arrived in which this Tertiary was to manifest how sincerely he had grasped the spirit of the Saint of Assisi. As was to be expected, even as a statesman Thomas More continued to make his accustomed religious exercises. He set aside every Friday as a day of introspection. His charity was without limit.

He experienced special delight in serving the priest at holy Mass, and he received holy Communion daily. He was told, by way of reproach, that it was unbecoming for a layman with so much work to do and so many distractions to communicate daily. But he replied: "You are advancing the very reasons for the need of frequent holy Communion. If I am distracted, holy Communion helps me to become recollected. If opportunities are offered me each day to offend my God, I arm myself anew each day for the combat by the reception of the Eucharist. If I am in special need of light and prudence in order to discharge my burdensome duties, I draw nigh to my Saviour and seek counsel and light from Him."

But it was not long before his doom was sealed. Blinded by unholy passions, King Henry divorced his lawful wife and married Anne Boleyn, a lady in waiting at the court. When Rome justly condemned this adulterous act, the king severed his connections with Rome and set himself up as the head of the Church in England. Whoever disapproved of his conduct was doomed to die.

The first person who opposed the king was his loyal chancellor, Thomas More. He was cast into prison. There he wrote a pamphlet entitled Death Endured for the Faith Need Cause No Fear. When his wife endeavored to persuade him to give up his opposition and prolong his life, he asked her just how long she believed he would still live. She answered, "At least twenty years." "Indeed!" said Thomas More. "Had you said a few thousand years, that might make a difference. But surely even he would be a poor merchant who would run the risk of losing an eternity for the sake of a thousand years." He was beheaded on July 6, 1535.

Pope Leo XIII beatified this great Tertiary, and Pope Pius XI canonized him on May 19, 1935. His feast is not in the calendar of the First Order of St. Francis, but the Third Order Regular observes it on July thirtieth. (Cf. *Forum*, 1948, pp. 77-80; 104-107.)

ON LOYALTY TO CHRIST

1. Remain loyal to Christ by the way you live. Christ, however, "began to do" (Acts 1,1), and then He went out to teach. Thomas More, His faithful servant, acted in like manner. His whole conduct showed that he belonged to Christ. He often remarked: "There are many people who purchase hell at so great an effort that one-half of it would be sufficient to win heaven." — Manifest to the world by a good Catholic life that you belong to Christ.
2. Be loyal to Christ by your love for the Blessed Sacrament. Faith taught Thomas to behold in the Sacred Host Him who said: "This is My Body!" It was, therefore, his greatest delight and duty to attend the holy Sacrifice daily, to serve the priests of Christ, and to receive Christ in holy Communion. — Can this also be said of you?
3. Be loyal to Christ by your loyalty to the Church. She is the living Christ and loved by Him even unto death (Eph. 5,25). St. Thomas refused to

St. Thomas More

swerve a finger's breadth in his loyalty to his Church even though his fidelity brought him prison and death. — Beg St. Thomas for like fidelity, and you will share with him a like reward.

PRAYER OF THE CHURCH

Almighty and eternal God, grant us, we beseech Thee, that we who celebrate the festival of Thy holy martyr Thomas, may through his intercession, be firmly established in our love for Thee. Through Christ our Lord. Amen.

AUGUST

AUGUST 1
THE SERVANT OF GOD JOHN OF PIANO DI CARPINE
Confessor, First Order

ORN at Piano di Carpine, now called La Magione, a town which lies between Lake Trasimene and Perugia, John became one of the early disciples of the Poverello. He was about the same age as St. Francis.

In the year 1221 St. Francis instructed Caesar of Speyer to choose some of the brethren as associates to accompany him on the mission to Germany. Among the first of these, Caesar chose John of Piano di Carpine, whose zeal for the missions and knowledge of various languages made him particularly qualified for this work. He was sent on ahead with a companion to Trent, Wuerzburg, Worms, Speyer, and Cologne. His words and especially his conduct won all hearts and thus prepared a kind reception for his confreres.

When the appointments for the provinces and the various offices were made, John was sent as custos to Saxony, where he laid the foundations of the Saxon province. Later he was elected provincial of Germany, and as such provided for the expansion of the order in Austria, Bohemia, Alsace, Lorraine, and as far as Denmark and Norway.

After the canonization of St. Francis in the year 1228, it was he who immediately and with great solemnity introduced devotion to the saint in Germany. Spain also testifies to his solicitude in imitating the holiness of his spiritual Father. He was sent there in 1230 as provincial and successor of the servant of God John Parenti, and although his predecessor had also been a very holy man, the annals of the order state that the people marveled at the extraordinary holiness of this second John. In 1233 he returned to Germany and served as provincial of Saxony until 1239.

The fame of his outstanding virtues and abilities induced Pope Innocent IV to send him in 1245 as his envoy to the Great Khan of the Mongols, in order to check the wild hordes from invading the eastern European nations. No efforts were too great for John when they were expended in the interests of God or of his neighbor, and so he cheerfully carried out the onerous mission imposed upon him by the Vicar of Christ. He was the first to travel from Europe across Asia to the Far East, and he brought back valuable information about the countries and peoples he visited. The pope was so relieved at John's return in 1247, and at the success of his journey, that he said to him: "Blessed be you by God and by me His Vicar on earth, for in you the words of Holy Writ are fulfilled: As the cold of snow in the time of harvest, so is a faithful messenger to him who sent him, for he refreshes his soul" (Prov. 25,13); and he appointed him archbishop of Antivari in Dalmatia. But the time was not far away when he was to receive the reward of a true servant of God. It was in the year 1252, about five years after his return from Tatary, that he died at the age of about seventy years. (Cf. *In Journeyings Often*, pp. 8-35.)

ON INDULGENCES

1. Since tomorrow is the day for gaining the great Portiuncula indulgence, we shall prepare for it by considering indulgences in general. Consider the great labors and hardships which John of Piano di Carpine endured in his very active life. His reward in heaven corresponds to the merit of his labors. But besides the heavenly recompense granted to him in accordance with the holy intentions with which his works were performed, his merits also prove valuable as reparation or satisfaction for the guilt of sin. Due to the saintly lives they led, this servant of God and thousands of other saintly persons certainly did not need this satisfaction for themselves; so these merits flowed into the treasury of the Church, where are stored up the atonement made by Christ as the head, and the saints as members of the Church. — What a blessing to be among the children of the church, where there is such a treasury for the benefit of those who need it.

2. Consider that besides the guilt and the eternal punishment which follow in the wake of sin, there is also a temporal punishment. This punishment remains to be atoned, even after the worthy reception of the sacrament of Penance, either by works of penance here on earth or by the pains of purgatory. "There," says Thomas a Kempis (1,24), "one hour of punishment will be more grievous than a hundred years of the most bitter penance. Hence," he adds, "it is truly better to purge away our sins and vices here on earth than to keep them for purgation hereafter." But since we are frequently incapable of making due reparation for the sins we have committed even when we are seriously disposed to do penance, Holy Church offers us for slighter works of piety, the chance to draw from her treasury whatever is needed to atone for the temporal punishment due to sin. That is what we understand by indulgences. We can gain indulgences,

for instance, by the devout recital of the rosary, by making the Way of the Cross, and by short prayers and devout exercises. Who will not gladly avail himself of such practices? Who will not employ them to aid the holy souls in purgatory, since most of the indulgences are applicable to them? — In the past, have you valued indulgences as you should?

3. Consider that for the actual gaining of an indulgence the guilt and the eternal punishment of sin must first have been removed. You should, therefore, first make an act of contrition, and if you have a mortal sin on your soul, you should first go to confession. Moreover, a penitential disposition is necessary to gain an indulgence, for indulgences are not to promote indifference and sloth. But the more contrite you are, the better you are prepared personally to make satisfaction, and the more devoutly you perform the works of devotion to which the indulgences are attached, so much the more abundantly you will share in them as a reparation for the punishment due to sin.

PRAYER OF THE CHURCH

In Thy clemency, O Lord, show unto us Thine unspeakable mercy, that Thou mayest both loose us of all our sins and deliver us from the punishments which we deserve for them. Through Christ our Lord. Amen.

AUGUST 2
THE FEAST OF PORTIUNCULA

AT the foot of the mountain on which Assisi is situated, hermits from Palestine had built an oratory in the first centuries of the Christian era. This oratory together with a small plot of land was given to St. Benedict in the sixth century. The name Portiuncula, that is, little portion, is supposed to have been derived from the transfer of this small piece of property. The little church was called St. Mary of the Angels, and the inhabitants of Assisi went there frequently to pray.

When St. Francis forsook the world, it was his first pious act to restore this sanctuary of the Queen of heaven, which had become somewhat dilapidated. Many extraordinary favors were granted to him in this little church. The Queen of heaven designated this place as the cradle of his order. Here, likewise, she implored for him the great indulgence by which the Portiuncula chapel became famous throughout Christendom.

A special impulse led St. Francis on a certain night to go to the chapel. There he saw our Lord and His holy Mother surrounded by a great host of angels. Filled with astonishment and reverence, the saint prostrated himself upon the ground and adored the Divine Majesty. Then he heard the voice of our Lord urging him with ineffable tenderness to ask some special favor. Nothing was so near to the heart of Francis as the salvation of souls, and so, after a few moments of reflection, he asked for the grace of a full pardon for all who, being contrite and having confessed their sins, would visit this little sanctuary. Mary cast herself upon her knees before her Divine Son, and repeated the petition of her faithful servant.

Thereupon our Lord said to Francis: "It is a great favor that you request, nevertheless it shall be granted to you. Go to my Vicar on earth, to whom I have given the power to bind and to loose, and ask him in My name to grant this indulgence."

Forthwith Francis presented himself to Pope Honorius III, who, after having assured himself of the truth of the vision, granted his request, but with the restriction that the indulgence could be gained on one day of the year. The second of August was designated as the day, that being the anniversary of the little church's dedication. At the command of the pope and in the presence of seven bishops, St. Francis preached the extraordinary indulgence at the Portiuncula before a great concourse of people. From that time the Portiuncula was annually the goal of innumerable pilgrims. Subsequently the indulgence was extended to every day of the year.

A large basilica was built over the little chapel, and so the little sanctuary of the Portiuncula has been preserved in its original condition. By virtue of their apostolic power the popes have extended this indulgence to all Franciscan churches, and under special conditions even to some other churches. They have also granted that the indulgence can be gained not only once, but as often as anyone, who has been to confession and to holy Communion, visits the appointed church on Portiuncula day and prays six Our Fathers, Hail Marys, and Glorys for the intention of the Holy Father. Besides, the indulgence can be applied to the holy souls in purgatory.

ON THE PORTIUNCULA INDULGENCE

1. It cannot be denied that this indulgence is one of the most precious favors that comes to us from the treasury of the divine mercy. Not only the Vicar of Christ but Christ Himself granted it at the intercession of the Blessed Virgin, the Mother of Mercy. It is recorded that when the pope

first granted his approval St. Francis departed without having obtained a written document as a testimonial. When his attention was drawn to the fact, St. Francis remarked: "God Himself will testify to this indulgence." Was that not actually verified by the great confidence of all Christians? One may well say of this indulgence what was said of the gracious condescension of our Lord in the Incarnation: "Through the heart of the mercy of our God, the Orient from on High has visited us unto the remission of sins" (Lk. 1,78). — Who would not use this day of grace well?

2. Consider how extraordinary are the graces of the Portiuncula indulgence. If we have contritely confessed our sins and gone to holy Communion, we can gain this indulgence as often as we visit the designated church and pray six Our Fathers, Hail Marys, and Glorys for the intention of the pope. If we have gained the indulgence and leave the church, we can re-enter and gain it again. In the event that we have really gained the plenary indulgence so that there remains no further punishment to be remitted, we can help the holy souls each succeeding time if we apply the indulgence to them. — How many souls may be waiting for this day, to be aided by your charity and mercy. Shall their trust in you be in vain?

3. Consider that the effects of the Portiuncula indulgence depend on the disposition of him who sets out to gain it. It was the spirit of penance and of trust in God that made St. Francis worthy of obtaining this indulgence. His entire life was one continuous act of penance, and when this great grace was granted to him, our Lord and His Blessed Mother, and a great number of angels appeared to him; this increased his confidence still more. With a similar disposition of mind and heart you will assuredly share the benefit of the indulgence. Awaken in yourself the true spirit of penance and of great confidence, so that our Lord may also say to you: "Go, and as you have believed, so be it done to you" (Mt. 8,13).

PRAYER OF THE CHURCH

O God, who dost permit us annually to celebrate anew the dedication day of Thy temple, and dost grant that we may attend the sacred mysteries in good health, hear the prayers of Thy people and grant that everyone who enters this church to ask graces for himself, may rejoice in the complete answer to his prayers. Through Christ our Lord. Amen.

AUGUST 3
THE SERVANT OF GOD MAGDALEN DAHMEN
Virgin, Third Order

HIS FOUNDRESS and mother of the Franciscan Sisters of Penance and of Christian Charity of Nonnenwerth must be regarded as a veritable miracle of Divine Providence. She was not a person of distinction, nor of great learning. But she always said, "God will provide!" and so she became a decided favorite of our heavenly Father.

She was born in 1787 at Laek in Dutch Limburg and received the name of Catharine in baptism. At a very early age her pure heart felt a strong attraction towards God. In 1817 she received the habit of the Third Order of St. Francis and spent several happy years with a group of young women who entertained sentiments similar to hers. In the spirit of St. Francis they devoted themselves to intimate union with God and to works of charity. In 1825 Providence led her to Heythuizen, where she laundered the altar linens for the parish church and opened a school for children. There she lived with three other Tertiaries in religious harmony and in self-sacrificing labors.

After much opposition, which she accepted with resignation and trust in God, the motherhouse of her congregation was established in 1835. On February eleventh of the following year the first reception took place. Catharine received the religious name of Magdalen. This new branch of the Franciscan tree grew with unusual rapidity.

Just as soon as the congregation was established, Mother Magdalen resigned the government into the hands of another sister. No one was happier now than she. From this day forward the chapel and her little Franciscan cell were the kingdom in which she spent a life of intimate union with God. "It is difficult to say," writes a sister, "which was the predominant virtue of her life."

She experienced great joy when the purchase of Nonnenwerth, the isle of our Lady, was completed. This has been the mother-house and novitiate of the congregation since 1890.

On August 7, 1858, Mother Magdalen's last hour arrived. "Yes, I shall pray for all of you!" These were the last words of the humble and solicitous mother. The sisters did not lament nor weep, for all were filled with the blessed conviction that their departed mother was going to watch over her undertaking from heaven. Her trust would not be confounded. God would provide! Steps have been taken to obtain her beatification. (Cf. *Forum*, 1942, pp. 89-90.)

ON THE RELIGIOUS SPIRIT

1. Penance is a requisite of the religious spirit. It was not without reason that Mother Magdalen added to the name of her institute the words "of Penance." She was wise moreover in accepting the discipline of the Third Order with such perfect submission. The very term "order," whether one lives in the world or in a convent, supposes the systematic practice of penance, penance for our sins and penance for the sins of the world. By their practices of penance, religious should be like lightning rods to divert the divine vengeance. — Do not slight the spirit of penance.

2. The religious spirit requires amendment of one's life. Mother Magdalen did not have much to correct in her life, and that is why she advanced from virtue to virtue. Religious life implies striving after that which is better, after that which is more perfect. True religious keep laboring at their own perfection and say daily: "I said: Now have I begun." — Recall the motto, "Resting is rusting."

3. The religious spirit requires fidelity. Mother Magdalen was faithful until her holy death. To begin is one thing, to continue is a greater thing, but to persevere unto the end is the most important thing of all. Hence the admonition: "Be faithful until death, and I will give you the crown of life" (Apoc. 2,10). A life of holy loyalty lasts but a second when compared with eternity. — Remain constant in your fidelity. Almighty God deserves it, and your soul will profit by it abundantly.

PRAYER OF THE CHURCH

Hear our prayer, O Lord, and grant us, Thy faithful servants, to persevere in constancy and in unsullied purity, that, being strengthened by Thy divine love, we may never be separated from Thee by any temptation. Through Christ our Lord. Amen.

𑁍𑁍𑁍𑁍𑁍𑁍𑁍𑁍𑁍𑁍

AUGUST 4
THE SERVANT OF GOD FREDERICK JANSSOONE
Confessor, First Order

 REDERICK JANSSOONE was born of Flemish parents at Ghyvelde, in the diocese of Cambrai, France, the ninth and youngest child of the family. As a boy he loved to frequent the parish church and was often discovered in quiet comers of the farm without book or beads, but with his hands and eyes raised to heaven.

At ten years he lost his father by death. He entered college later, but further misfortunes struck the family, and it fell to his lot to be the breadwinner. His pious mother, however, perceived the call to the priesthood in her son, and offered herself a victim to obtain the religious vocation of her four surviving children. Her oblation was accepted.

On June 26, 1864, Frederick received the Franciscan habit at Amiens. He was especially favored in having as his novice master Father Leo de Clary, whose ambition was to make saints of his novices. He was ordained to the priesthood in 1870.

The Franco-Prussian war was on, and immediately after ordination Father Frederick was made military chaplain at a local hospital. Following the war he was made submaster of novices, then superior of the Bordeaux convent and editor of the Franciscan Review.

Like so many other sons of St. Francis, Father Frederick inherited special affection for the Holy Land. He had frequently expressed his desire for the foreign missions, especially in the Holy Land, but it was not until 1876 that his superiors permitted him to go. Without revisiting his family, he set out for Marseilles after a fervent visit to Notre Dame de la Garde, a sanctuary overlooking the magnificent harbor where ten years previously his eldest brother had set sail for India in quest of souls.

In the Holy Land, Frederick was assigned to the church of the Holy Sepulcher which has been entrusted to the Friars Minor ever since 1342. In the midst of a series of retreats in Egypt, he was brought to death's door by a fever, but God, who had still other work for His faithful servant to do, restored his health.

In less than two years Father Frederick was unanimously elected vicar custodian of the holy places, which office he filled during two terms of six years each. During this period he was constantly busy with such activities as giving retreats and missions and conducting pilgrimages. He was ever the same ardent preacher, the man of intense interior life, the guide whose special interest was the individual soul of the pilgrim.

Difficulties arose. Revolutions were sweeping across the world during the second half of the nineteenth century. Alms to the Holy Land were so meager that it became impossible to meet the most necessary expenses. Palestine itself suffered a disastrous drought followed by a winter of unexplained cold. So Father Frederick offered himself for the thankless task of alms collector abroad.

Efforts to obtain help in Paris proved futile, and the French government was at that time expelling the religious. But a providential meeting with a priest from Quebec resulted in an order from his superiors to leave for Canada to establish a Holy Land commissariat and to act as special visitor of Third Order fraternities there.

Father Frederick was graciously received in Canada. He set out at once to make the canonical visitation of the fraternities. Busy as he was, he compiled a manual for the Third Order and contributed articles to magazines. But again he was struck down by severe illness, and again God intervened. During his convalescence he was recalled to Jerusalem, where he filled out his second term as vicar custodian in the same heroic spirit with which he had labored in Canada.

While the purpose of his first visit in 1881 had been to establish a commissariat of the Holy Land in Canada, it was not until his return there in 1888 that the project could be carried out. To the bishop of Trois Rivières goes the credit of establishing the commissariat and thereby automatically effecting the return of the Franciscans to the land they had been the first to evangelize, in 1615. Father Frederick remained commissary until his death, winning the title of Apostle of the Holy Land.

For many years Father Frederick had been suffering from cancer of the stomach. Although ignorant of the true nature of his pain, he at times suffered veritable martyrdom. Once the attack had passed off, he would set to work again as if in perfect health. Pure love of God and of neighbor alone could inspire such constant abnegation. It was on his return from a three days' pilgrimage, during which he had given himself heart and soul to his people, that his worn-out body finally broke down in June, 1916.

There followed fifty days of acute suffering and gentle patience. Further anguish was reserved for this humble soul in the form of fear of judgment. He who had so chastened his will and body out of love of God, now fought the last combat with the evil one. But several days before the end, the blessed peace of Jesus Christ flooded his soul.

In the afternoon of the feast of St. Dominic, August 4, 1916, with a number of his brother Franciscans praying at his bedside, the dying Father Frederick rallied all his remaining strength to say: "Amen. Come, Lord Jesus, come!" After a few moments of rapt contemplation, his eyes fixed on his crucifix, his dearly loved rosary in his stiffening fingers, this noble apostle gave up his soul.

He lies entombed in the convent chapel at Trois Rivières. Any day people may be seen kneeling there to beg the prayers of the compassionate Father who, while on earth, never turned a deaf ear to suffering or request. Miracles ascribed to his prayers soon led to the introduction of his cause in Rome. His writings have been approved, and the way is open for more immediate steps toward his beatification. (Cf.

Forum, 1947, pp. 201-205; R. Legaré, *An Apostle of Two Worlds*, translated by R. Brown.)

ON ZEAL FOR THE HOLY PLACES IN JERUSALEM

1. We read in the psalms: "The zeal of Thy house has eaten me up" (Ps. 68,10). How aptly this text applies to "good Father Frederick," who consecrated his life and all his energy to the interests of the Holy Land by preserving the Catholic claims there as well as arousing the interest of the faithful to provide for the upkeep of the places sanctified by our Lord's life and death. — What is our knowledge of the needs of the Holy Land? Have we endeavored to understand the great mission of preserving the holy shrines and keeping alive the Faith in those places? What is our zeal for the house of the Lord?

2. Every country prides itself on preserving the scenes, the homes, and belongings of its heroes. It delights in pointing them out to visitors. But can any of the world's great men measure up with the greatest of men, the God-man, who is not the hero of one particular race or nation, but who came to redeem all nations? How fitting that concentrated efforts be made to restore and preserve the places hallowed by His life and death! How deserving of admiration and praise are the sacrifices made by the sons of St. Francis to wrest these places from the hands of the infidel who would otherwise desecrate them, and to inspire the faithful with renewed reverence for them!

3. The history of the Crusades is the story of the faith of great men who gladly gave fortune and life itself to the aid of the Holy Land. If the day of the sword has passed and an era of more peaceful effort has been ushered in, that does not make the work of this mission less important than in the days of Godfrey of Bouillon, Richard the Lion-hearted, and their fellow crusaders. The shrines must still be cared for, pilgrims harbored, the poor and the orphans provided for. We can become crusaders and aid in the welfare and service of the sacred places. We can pray for those who have undertaken this noble work, that they may continue in the path of their predecessors who endured hardship and even death to keep the shrines in the possession of the Catholic Church. We can aid materially by joining the Crusade of the Holy Land, at least by contributing liberally to the Good Friday collection, which has been established for the maintenance of the holy places. — If we have had little interest in this great project in the past, let the acquaintance we have made with "good Father Frederick" rouse our zeal for the future.

PRAYER OF THE CHURCH
(From the Mass of the Holy Cross)

O God, who by the precious Blood of Thine only-begotten Son wast pleased to hallow the standard of the Cross whereby we are quickened, grant, we beseech Thee, that they who rejoice in honoring that same holy cross, may likewise everywhere rejoice in Thy protection. Through Christ our Lord. Amen.

AUGUST 5
BLESSED ALBERT OF SARZIANO
Confessor, First Order

LBERT, of the illustrious family of Bertini, was born in Tuscany in 1384. At the age of fifteen he was entrusted to the Franciscan Fathers that he might pursue his studies with them. Among his professors was the celebrated Bartholomew of Pisa, who died in 1401 at the age of one hundred ten years.

Favored by God with extraordinary talent, Albert soon distinguished himself among his fellow students. Withal, he remained so humble and devout that at the age of twenty he asked his professors for the habit of the order.

After his ordination he was permitted to continue his studies, and soon became so proficient that he ranked among the most eminent scholars of Italy, especially in the knowledge of Latin and Greek. He was equally well educated in theology and was particularly interested in the science of the saints, in virtue and perfection.

In 1414 he met St. Bernardin of Siena, and became a wholehearted supporter of the latter's promotion of strict observance of the rule. His first and greatest care now was to make himself pleasing to God. With the consent of his superiors, and despite his great learning and zeal for souls, he continued to live in holy seclusion for seven years more, devoting his time to prayer, to practices of penance and to religious study. During an entire year he accompanied St. Bernardin on his missionary journeys, and only then did he take up the task of preaching.

The times were turbulent when Albert entered upon his apostolic labors. The Turks were rapidly advancing toward the West; Italy was in constant dread of their arrival. Moreover, the Greeks who had fallen away from the Church of Rome, were the cause of much worry to the Apostolic

See. Within the bosom of the Church, antipopes, who always found adherents, rose against the lawful representative of Christ. Also, there was the continual strife between the Guelphs and the Ghibellines, between the pope and the imperial factions, especially in northern Italy, so that city was armed against city, and frequently one group of citizens rose up against another group. In so disturbed a period, rebellion and barbarity, godlessness and indecency overrode all bounds.

Albert perceived that it would be necessary to undertake his work armed, so to say, with fire and sword. In forceful terms he denounced the vices of the times, and most eloquently did he portray the punishments of divine justice. It was as though the trumpets of the last judgment had sounded. Crowds gathered from all sides to hear him, and no church was large enough to accommodate the concourse of people, which at times reached the number of fifty or sixty thousand. Conversions were numerous, and not infrequently of a very remarkable nature. Factions were reconciled with each other; those who had been enemies of the Church returned to her; sinners desisted from their evil ways. Wherever good will was in evidence, Albert manifested tender sympathy with the weaknesses of men.

In Venice a man came to him and told him about his evil life, saying that he would gladly be converted, but it seemed impossible to get rid of his vices. The missionary encouraged him and imposed upon him the simple injunction to assist daily at holy Mass and to give an alms. A few days later, the poor sinner returned, made a contrite confession and began to lead a Christian life.

When Pope Eugene IV learned of the influence which Albert exercised over the hearts of men, he sent him as his envoy to Greece, and later to Egypt, Armenia, Ethiopia, and India, in all of which places he accomplished much good for the Church and for the salvation of souls. Sometimes God confirmed his works by miracles.

After successfully filling many offices in the order, Albert died on the feast of the Assumption of Our Lady, August 15, 1450. St. John Capistran saw his soul take its flight to heaven. Although the title of Blessed has been conferred on him in popular devotion, this cult has not yet been confirmed by the Holy See.

LEARN FIRST, THEN TEACH

1. Consider how modest and humble it was on the part of Blessed Albert to spend so long a time in study before he began to teach. With his extraordinary talents and persevering diligence he had already acquired

great learning when St. Bernardin received him among the Friars Minor. But he asked for another seven years' leave to reflect upon what he had learned and to interpret in virtuous practice the knowledge he had gained. Even then he preferred to spend another year listening to the sermons of his master before he himself became a teacher. His unusual success can readily be ascribed to this preparation. He kept the example of the Divine Teacher in mind, who, though He was wisdom itself, was found "sitting in the midst of the doctors, hearing them and asking them questions" (Lk. 2,46). He kept his eyes fixed on Him who remained in Nazareth until his thirtieth year before He assumed the office of Master and Teacher. — How do we follow this example?

2. Consider how rarely this example which Christ and His servant Albert give us is followed in our day. We want to teach before we have learned anything; we want to govern and command before we have learned to obey the commands of others; we want to judge and discuss things concerning which we know little or perhaps nothing at all; we want to be masters before we have stood the test of students. Hence it comes that there are such frequent sad results. "Learn before you speak" (Eccli. 18,19), says the Wise Man. He admonishes youth in a special way: "My son, from your youth receive instruction, and even to gray hairs you shall find wisdom" (Eccli. 6,18). — Would that this injunction were observed.

3. Consider that, while it is proper that youth above all accept instruction, still there is much that we all can learn throughout life. It is an error prompted by pride, if one regards it a disgrace to accept direction in age. St. Augustine says that, while it is more becoming for age to teach than to be taught, on the other hand, it is more honorable to learn even in old age than to remain ignorant in things which we should know. Thus Job said to his friends: "If I have been ignorant in anything, instruct me" (Job 6,24). Be not ashamed, therefore, at any time to learn whatever is good. Gladly sit with Mary at the feet of our Saviour, from whom proceeds everything good that we receive as Christians.

PRAYER OF THE CHURCH
(Sixth Sunday after Pentecost)

O God of Hosts, to whom belongeth all that is perfect, implant in our hearts the love of Thy name, and grant us an increase of religion, that Thou mayest foster within us what is good, and by the zeal of Thy loving kindness guard what Thou hast fostered. Through Christ our Lord. Amen.

AUGUST 6
VENERABLE ANTHONY MARGIL
Confessor, First Order

ORN at Valencia in Spain on August 18, 1657, Anthony early in life manifested an extraordinary interest in the things of God. He loved to spend his time in prayer and visits to our Lord in the Blessed Sacrament. After he had become a Franciscan and a priest, his whole soul was aflame with the desire to lead others to God. He was among the first who volunteered when missionaries were recruited for the establishment of the first of the so-called apostolic colleges, that of Querétaro in Mexico; and he arrived there on August 13, 1683.

In the New World he became one of its greatest missionaries. He is sometimes called "the Apostle of Texas," but he was much more than that. He should be styled the Apostle of New Spain, including Mexico, Central America, and Texas. He was in fact a second St. Anthony of Padua and another St. Francis Solano, so successful were his sermons, so astounding the miracles he performed.

During the forty-three years of his missionary career in New Spain, Father Anthony Margil traveled repeatedly through its vast territory, preaching parish missions everywhere among the Spanish and Indian Christians, and devoting himself to missionary work among the pagan natives in Mexico, Guatemala, Costa Rica, and Texas.

Besides being one of the first members of the Apostolic College of Santa Cruz at Querétaro and inaugurating this college's preaching of parish missions in that city in September, 1683, he served as its guardian or superior from 1687 to 1700. He also founded the Apostolic College of Christ Crucified in the city of Guatemala on June 13, 1701, and served as its guardian from 1701 to 1704. And he founded the College of Our Lady of Guadalupe at Zacatecas, Mexico, on January 12, 1707, and served as its guardian from 1722 to 1725.

In 1716 he led the missionaries of the Zacatecas College into eastern Texas; and though he was too sick to be present at the founding of the Guadalupe Mission there (so sick in fact that he received the last sacraments — which had happened also on a previous occasion), he personally founded the Texas missions of Dolores and San Miguel.

When the French, during a war with Spain, invaded eastern Texas in 1719, Father Anthony went to the famous Mission San Antonio, the later Alamo, which had been founded the year before (May 1, 1718). The following year (1720) he founded the no less famous Mission San José near the present city of San Antonio. In 1721 he returned to eastern Texas and restored the missions there.

Recalled to Mexico, he died a holy death in the great Convento de San Francisco in Mexico City on August 6, 1726. Not long afterwards steps were taken toward his beatification. When the French armies entered Rome in 1797, the documents concerning the cause of Father Anthony Margil were lost; but afterwards they were miraculously found again.

In 1836 he was declared "Venerable," but his cause has not made any further progress since then. The reason for this probably lay in the persecutions to which the Church in Mexico was subjected during the nineteenth and twentieth centuries. However, the cause of Father Anthony is still pending in Rome, and greater interest in it on the part of the Catholics of the United States would no doubt hasten the day when he would be raised to the honors of the altar. The body of Venerable Anthony Margil was transferred in 1861 to the Cathedral of Mexico City; and it now rests in the Chapel of the Immaculate Conception. (Cf. Leutenegger, *Apostle of America, Fray Antonio Margil.*)

ZEAL FOR THE HEATHEN MISSIONS

1. Zeal for the pagan missions is in accordance with the will of God. The last command given by Jesus was: "Going, therefore, teach all nations, baptizing them in the name of the Father, and of the Son, and of the Holy Ghost" (Mt. 28,19). This it was that filled Venerable Anthony with enthusiasm and made him strong and cheerful to leave home and native land, and to make the greatest sacrifices in the mission field. All this in order to bring souls to Jesus. – Where is your zeal? Where are your sacrifices?

2. Zeal for the missions is every Christian's business. Some years ago a Catholic gathering stressed the theme: "The work of the missions is not left to the wish of each individual, but it is the duty of the Catholic Christian." What can the missionaries do in the foreign fields, how can they build churches, schools, orphanages, and foundling homes, if the faithful at home do not supply them with the means to carry on their work? – Have you been mindful of your obligation to co-operate in the work of conversion?

3. Zeal for the missions must proceed from gratitude and from compassion. We should co-operate in gratitude for the unmerited grace of the true Faith and from compassion for the pitiful lot of the heathens who as yet know nothing of our Saviour, of the Mother of God, of the

sacraments, of heaven. Trust in the reward promised by Him who said: "Whosoever shall give one of these little ones a cup of cold water to drink, amen, I say to you, he shall not lose his reward" (Mt. 10,42). — Pray, therefore, and make sacrifices for the conversion of the heathens. Be a promoter of mission societies, of mission periodicals, and generously make the necessary sacrifices for Christ and the salvation of the heathens.

PRAYER OF THE CHURCH

O God, our Protector, look upon the face of Thine Anointed One, who has offered Himself as a ransom for all, and grant that from the rising to the setting of the sun Thy name may be glorified by all nations and that in all places a clean oblation be offered to Him. Through the same Christ our Lord. Amen.

AUGUST 7
BLESSED AGATHANGEL AND CASSIAN
Martyrs, First Order

GATHANGEL was born in Vendome in 1589, and Cassian in Nantes in 1607. Both received the habit of the Franciscan Order among the Capuchins and were sent to the African missions shortly after they had completed their studies. They met in Cairo. There they learned of the persecution of the Christians in Abyssinia. Filled with a desire to labor and suffer for Christ among their separated brethren, they went to that country.

They had scarcely begun their work when they were seized and put in chains. They languished in prison for the space of a month, and then during another twenty-five days they were dragged to Gondar amid unheard-of treatment and during the extreme heat of a July sun. The king intended to force them to renounce their faith.

Father Cassian replied with firm determination: "We wish to live and die as children of the Catholic, apostolic, and Roman Church, outside of which there is no salvation. We do not wish to purchase our lives with the price of infamous apostasy. We do not wish to enjoy honors and riches, which you offer us at the price of our immortal souls."

Both confessors were then sentenced to be hanged. When the executioners were looking about for ropes, the two confessors, inflamed with a desire for martyrdom, called out: "If you need ropes, use our cords." So it was done. A few moments later the holy missionaries had won the crown of martyrdom. This happened on August 7, 1638. Pope Pius X beatified them with great solemnity. Their feast is observed by the Franciscans and Capuchins on August seventh.

THE ONLY CHURCH IN WHICH THERE IS SALVATION

1. Because it has been founded by Christ as the institution of salvation, the Catholic Church is the only one in which we can be saved. Christ always speaks of only one Church: "On this rock, I will build My Church," "he who will not hear the Church ...", "there will be but one flock and one shepherd ..." The Church would forfeit its own rights were it to recognize any other churches. The martyrs eloquently proclaimed this truth to the world by laying down their lives for the Faith and in defense of the only saving Church. — We too must have the spirit of the martyrs; we must be ready to act as they did.

2. The Catholic Church, as the body of Christ, is the only saving Church. It is the mystical body of Christ, the incarnate Second Person of the Blessed Trinity. Is it possible to think of more than one body belonging to this Head? That is plainly impossible. Besides, it is the task of the Church to lead souls to God. There is only one such goal, and there cannot be various ways which are opposed to one another, as in the non-Catholic churches. The Catholic Church, therefore, says with Christ: "I am the way" (Jn. 14,6). — Be faithful to this way.

3. The Catholic Church is the only saving Church for all men. Of her it can be said: "Neither is there salvation in any other" (Acts 4,12). That is: He who attains to salvation is saved through the Church, either as a member of the Church or as belonging to the soul of the Church. Non-Catholics and heathens will be saved through the Church, if they live according to the dictates of their conscience and co-operate with the necessary graces which God gives them and thus belong to the soul of the Church. — Rejoice that you are a member of the Church, and pray for those who are not within the fold.

PRAYER OF THE CHURCH

O God, who didst inflame Blessed Agathangel and Cassian with Thy love and grant them to shed their blood for Thee, graciously grant that at their intercession we may in this life so struggle against the enemy of our salvation that we may merit to be crowned by Thee in heaven. Through Christ our Lord. Amen.

AUGUST 8
VENERABLE MARY OF AGREDA
Virgin, Second Order

ARY was born at Agreda in Spain in 1602, of noble parents, whose virtues surpassed the nobility of their birth. Very early the child showed special signs of grace. At the age of six she had attained a high degree of prayer, which was noticeable in her devotion to the Blessed Virgin Mary and to the sufferings of our Lord. Her confessor recognized the great graces with which she was favored, and permitted her at a tender age to receive holy Communion and to practice extraordinary works of penance. Painful illness which afflicted her, she bore with the greatest patience, strengthened by the remembrance of Christ's sufferings.

In her seventeenth year Mary entered the convent of Poor Clares of the Immaculate Conception at Agreda. As a novice she excelled in the exercises of convent life. She made her profession on the feast of the Purification in 1620 as Sister Mary of Jesus.

After she had consecrated herself to God through the holy vows, the young religious strove for perfection with holy earnestness and cheerful surrender to God. At the same time her unassuming humility and kindness of heart made her so beloved by her fellow sisters, that at the age of twenty-five she was elected abbess. The pope confirmed her election to office; and she was obliged to accept it repeatedly for thirty-eight years until her death. Only once, at her most earnest request, was she released for a period of three years.

As the superior, Mary was always the first among her associates to engage in lowly work. She swept the halls, nursed the sick, washed their linens, and appeared to have a special preference for the most menial services. Her way of life was so austere that one wonders how she could do her work. She not only abstained from meat, but never partook of eggs, milk, or cheese; she slept on a board for only two or three hours; the remaining time of the night she spent in exercises of devotion. Every night, laden with a heavy cross, she made the Way of the Cross. Even as the superior she strove to practice obedience, following the suggestions of her higher superiors, and in spiritual matters submitting wholly to the guidance of her confessor. For a time she had a confessor who dealt harshly with her and never granted her any request she made; but Mary obeyed him cheerfully, and often said later: "He acted well; I always thought that he was right, and because of obedience I felt great peace of soul."

She governed her subjects with as much wisdom as love. She was
endowed with great wisdom, so that persons of the highest rank, also
prelates and bishops, and even the king of Spain, asked her for advice.
When she spoke of God, all who heard her were inflamed with the love of
God. She received special revelations concerning the life of the Virgin
Mother of God, which she recorded in a book called The Mystical City of
God.

Mention should be made of Mary of Agreda's work among the Indians
of Texas and New Mexico. Her ardent desire, prayers, and sacrifices for
their conversion were apparently rewarded with the gift of bilocation.
Between 1621 and 1631, when Mary of Agreda was between nineteen and
twenty-nine years of age, she made some five hundred visits to the Texas
Indians, coming, as it seemed to them, from the hills on their horizon and
returning that way after her instructions were over. When these Indians
presented themselves to the Franciscan missionaries in New Mexico and
asked that fathers be sent among them, it was learned that a Lady in Blue
had often come among them, instructed them, and ordered them to seek
out missionaries to baptize them.

Upon investigation it was learnt that this Lady in Blue was Mary of
Agreda, who, when she was put under obedience to tell what had
happened, said she had no explanation. She could not say how she got
there, only that when she was praying for the welfare of the Indians, she
just found herself among them and began to instruct them. Presently she
found herself home again. This happened many times.

Mary died on Pentecost morning, May 24, 1667, at nine o'clock, at the
time the Holy Ghost had descended upon the Apostles and when the
"Veni, Creator Spiritus, Come, Holy Ghost Creator!" was being recited in
the canonical hours. She passed away, saying the words: "Veni! — Veni!
— Veni!" At her grave many miracles were wrought; and her cause of
beatification is now being carried on in Rome. (Cf. Forum, 1955, pp. 259-
265, 272.)

CONCERNING THE OPERATIONS OF THE HOLY GHOST

1. From earliest youth and until the hour of death, Venerable Mary was
guided by the Holy Ghost, so that one can truly say "the Holy Ghost was
in her" (Lk. 2,25). Her life demonstrates His marvelous operations.
Enlightened by the Holy Ghost, she recognized her own nothingness.
Hence her perfect humility with which she regarded the most degrading
tasks as the most fitting for her. Hence her submissive obedience, which

caused her to give up her own opinion and considered her confessor right even when he decided matters entirely against her wishes. — Do you yield to these operations of the Holy Ghost, or are you like the children of the world, full of pride and self-will? If so, your heart is not enlightened by the "Spirit of Truth whom the world cannot receive" (Jn. 14,17).

2. Consider how the fire of the Holy Spirit also warmed the heart of Venerable Mary. Hence came her devotion at prayer, her love of God and of her fellow sisters. Hence the warmth of divine love through which others were enkindled by her. "The charity of God is poured forth in our hearts by the Holy Ghost" (Rom. 5,5). Are the operations of the Holy Ghost evident also in your piety and true love of neighbor? The first Christians, upon whom the Holy Ghost descended on the feast of Pentecost, were of "one heart and one soul" (Acts 4,32).

3. Consider the great strength the Holy Ghost imparted to Venerable Mary. Even as a child she bore with great patience the most painful illnesses. For many years she administered the office of a religious superior in an exemplary manner, and she could advise others, even people in high station, by virtue of the strength with which she was endowed. The sacrament of confirmation, in which we receive the Holy Spirit, strengthens our soul for the duties of a Christian life, and protects us in the dangers and distress of our earthly sojourn. Pray fervently that He may fill you with new strength.

PRAYER OF THE CHURCH
(Holy Feast of Pentecost)

O God, who hast taught the hearts of the faithful by the light of the Holy Spirit, grant us by this same Spirit to relish what is right, and evermore to rejoice in His consolations. Through Christ our Lord. Amen.

AUGUST 9
ST. JOHN MARY VIANNEY
Confessor, Third Order

ELDOM has a priestly life been so holy, so self-sacrificing, so fruitful of good for the salvation of souls as the life of the Curé of Ars in France, St. John Mary Vianney, who died August 4, 1859. It is a distinct honor for the Third Order of St. Francis that he was one of its members.

He was born in Dardilly, not far from Lyons, of simple and devout parents. Very early his pure heart experienced a burning desire to consecrate himself to God in the priestly vocation, and to win very many souls for our dear Lord. His talents were very meager; but his diligence and piety helped him to overcome all obstacles, so that he was ordained in 1815.

Three years later his bishop sent him as curate to Ars, a little village in the diocese of Lyon. This parish was at the time in a very pitiable condition. The fear of God and the practice of virtue were rare things there. Attendance at divine services and the reception of the sacraments were quite generally neglected, and the young folks were mindful of nothing but amusement, a dance taking place practically every Sunday.

It was, therefore, with a heavy heart and yet with great confidence in God that the curate entered upon his duties. He realized that God's help was his first great need. Throughout the entire day he knelt before the Blessed Sacrament and prayed for his erring sheep.

This zeal at prayer was soon noticed, and the grace he had asked for continued its work. The people were astonished at the devotion John Mary displayed while celebrating holy Mass. His very mortified life made a deep impression upon them. His love for the poor and the sick, his mild words to everyone soon won for him all hearts.

He invited them to pray, in the morning to attend holy Mass, in the evening to recite the rosary. He also introduced a Eucharistic confraternity. He strove to eliminate the dangers to which the people were exposing themselves by their weekly dances. When a certain person, who was earning his livelihood by means of these dances, said to him, "But a person must live," the priest replied, "True, but one must also die." He conducted the divine services with all possible solemnity, and this proved an attraction for the people. By means of frequent instructions, especially in catechism, he taught his parishioners about virtue and vice, and portrayed in vivid terms the reward God has reserved for the good and the punishment that will be inflicted on the wicked.

He was tireless in administering the sacrament of penance, always showing not only great zeal but also practicing meekness and charity in an extraordinary degree. In a few years the parish was completely transformed. The few dissenting voices were entirely ignored, and their worldly attractions were not heeded. The fame of the blessed success and the holy life of the priest of Ars spread rapidly. Strangers came in ever-increasing numbers in order to have their consciences set aright and to obtain advice and consolation in every type of need.

From the year 1828 the concourse of people took on the semblance of organized pilgrimages; the number of strangers was estimated to be at least 20,000 annually. Numerous conversions of a most remarkable nature occurred, and many sick persons were miraculously restored to health. These cures the humble pastor ascribed to the intercession of St. Philomena, who was venerated in his church.

The demands made upon the servant of God were, naturally, very great. He spent from sixteen to eighteen hours a day in the confessional. Besides, he conducted a catechetical instruction in the church each day, and led the rosary every evening. Along with these superhuman exertions he also practiced rigorous mortification, fasted almost constantly, and slept on a board. In this way he spent himself in the fullest sense of the word as a good shepherd, and labored for the salvation of souls until he was seventy-four years old.

Completely worn out, he collapsed on the last of May, 1859, and died peacefully in the Lord without any agony on August fourth. Pope Pius X beatified him and Pope Pius XI canonized him and made him the patron of all priests who have the care of souls. His feast is observed by the three branches of the First Order on August ninth.

CONCERNING PASTORAL DUTY

1. The saintly pastor of souls Vianney bore the marks of the true shepherd, according to the words of our Lord: "The good shepherd gives his life for his sheep" (Jn. 10,11). He beheld the sheep entrusted to his care in the claws of the infernal wolf, given over to sensuality and dissoluteness. A hireling would have fled from such a situation. Vianney, however, set himself the task of saving them. He prayed, he admonished, he sacrificed himself for their sake, and he succeeded in saving them and innumerable other sheep of Christ's fold. God has appointed all those as shepherds of souls who have been entrusted with Christian guardianship over others, not only as actual pastors, but also as parents and teachers. — If you belong to these classes, do you also deserve the name of a good shepherd, or do you abandon the sheep to the wolves? If that is the case, woe to you!
2. Consider by what means St. John Mary accomplished so much. By his good example he led his flock forward, and he guided the erring back by his meekness and charity. He kept the picture of the Good Shepherd constantly before his eyes, and thus "began to do and to teach" (Acts 1,1), and pursued the lost sheep until he was able to place it joyfully upon his shoulders and bring it back. The Good Shepherd severely reproved the Pharisees for placing upon the people heavy burdens which they themselves avoided, and he pronounced His judgment on these rude

shepherds: "Because you thrusted with sides and shoulders, and struck all the weak cattle with your horns, I will judge" (Ezech. 34,21). — According to what standard have you performed your pastoral duty?

3. Consider that a pastor's work can only then produce results and blessings when those who are being tended follow their shepherd. When the sheep of St. John Mary's flock perceived the charity and the good intentions of their shepherd, they followed him willingly and no longer gave ear to stranger and seducer. It is thus that the Divine Shepherd describes the good sheep. "And the sheep follow him because they know his voice; but a stranger they follow not but fly from him" (Jn. 10,4-5). Moreover, they should pray for their shepherd, according to the advice of the Apostle: "Remember your prelates" (Heb. 13,7), that God may give them light and strength to lead their flocks to their goal. — Pray with this intention for the supreme shepherd on earth as well as for all other shepherds.

PRAYER OF THE CHURCH
(For the Pope)

O God, the Shepherd and Ruler of all the faithful, graciously regard Thy servant whom Thou has been pleased to appoint pastor over Thy Church; grant, we beseech Thee, that he may profit his subjects both by word and example, and together with the flock entrusted to his care, attain to eternal life. Through Christ our Lord. Amen.

⁂⁂⁂⁂⁂⁂⁂⁂

AUGUST 10
BLESSED AMADEUS MENEZ
Confessor, First Order

HEN noble sentiments are joined to nobility of birth, virtue shines forth the more brightly. That was the case with the servant of God Amadeus. He was a descendant of one of the noblest Portuguese families, one that was related to the royal household. Blessed Beatrice, the founder of the Poor Clares of the Immaculate Conception, was his sister.

Filled with a holy zeal for Christ, the young knight Amadeus marched against the Mohammedans, who were at that time still occupying the southern part of Spain and Portugal. He was seriously wounded during a battle; and because his arm became paralyzed, he was forced to withdraw from the bloody conflict carried on against the enemies of Christ.

He now joined the ranks of the spiritual army of St. Francis, the Third Order, to do battle against the enemies of Christ in his own heart, against thirst for honor, covetousness, and sensuality. In his retirement from the world he arrived at a high degree of perfection in humility, mortification, and purity of heart. He cherished a special devotion to our Blessed Lady; and after a short time felt impelled like his great fellow countryman St. Anthony of Padua, to go to Italy to join the Franciscan Order.

He followed this impulse generously, left all, and joined the Conventuals at Assisi as a lay brother. He was a model to all the brethren in the performance of the lowliest services. After several years had elapsed, he was sent, at the urgent request of the duke of Milan, to a deserted convent in Lombardy, where, in company with a few devout brothers, he observed the rule of St. Francis in its primitive strictness. It was not long before several other convents adopted the same mode of life, and thus joined the ranks of the Observants.

His religious superiors urged Amadeus to be ordained to the holy priesthood, but his humility made him shrink from so lofty a dignity. Nevertheless the command of his superiors and of Pope Sixtus IV compelled him to receive holy orders. In 1471 the pope called him to Rome as his confessor and counselor, for he recognized that Amadeus was being favored with special light from the Holy Ghost. The church of St. Peter in Montorio in Rome was entrusted to his care, and later he built a Franciscan convent adjoining it.

In 1487, while visiting and encouraging his brethren in Milan, he died a holy death on August tenth. God testified to his sanctity by many miracles; and the title of Blessed was conferred on him in popular devotion. The confirmation of this cult by the Holy See is now being sought in Rome.

ON THE GREAT DIGNITY OF THE PRIESTHOOD

1. Consider how Blessed Amadeus, a scion of one of the noblest families and a person well tried in every virtue, became alarmed when he was asked to accept the dignity of the priesthood. St. Gregory says that the priesthood is so elevated a mystery that it causes one to tremble in reverence. This the saints understood more clearly than ordinary men. It is related of St. Francis that he once saw in a vision the purity of soul with which a priest should be adorned; and so this seraph in the flesh always refused to accept the dignity of the priesthood. And it was only the command of his superiors that could induce Blessed Amadeus to yield.

The Apostle says of the priesthood: "Neither does any man take the honor to himself, but he who is called by God, as Aaron was" (Heb. 5,4).

2. Consider what constitutes the high dignity of the priesthood. It is the celebration of the holy sacrifice of the Mass, in which the priest sacrifices the Son of God. For this reason Thomas a Kempis says (4,5): "Great is the mystery and great the dignity of priests, to whom has been given that which has not been granted to the angels. For, priests alone, rightly ordained in the Church, have the power of celebrating and consecrating the Body of Christ." Because of this function, St. Catharine of Siena was willing to kiss the footprints of the priests, and our holy Father St. Francis says: "I will love and revere even the poorest priests in this world, because they consecrate and consume the Body and Blood of Christ and distribute It to others." The Holy Ghost Himself admonishes us: "Fear the Lord and reverence his priests" (Eccli. 7,31). — Do you do this?

3. Consider, moreover, what a blessing the priesthood is for Christians. The priest has been placed as a mediator between God and man. In the name of Christ, who has given priests the power — "Whatsoever you shall loose upon earth, shall be loosed also in heaven" (Mt. 18,18), he reconciles to God the souls who have been caught in the bonds of sin. And as the servant of the Church and the spiritual father of the faithful, the priest presents the petitions of the Christian people before the throne of the Most High. Because he has been placed between God and men, the priest has been cut off from the life ordinarily pursued by men, and has been obliged by ecclesiastical precept to lead a more moderate, frugal, and perfect life. Thus he becomes more worthy to appear before God as the representative of others. — Thank God that He has appointed the priests of His Church for your benefit, and diligently unite yourself to their holy prayers and exercises.

PRAYER OF THE CHURCH
(Saturday in Passion Week)

We beseech Thee, O Lord, that the people who are consecrated to Thee may advance in sentiments of pious devotion; that, instructed by the sacred rites, they may abound in excellent gifts as they become more pleasing in the sight of Thy majesty. Through Christ our Lord. Amen.

AUGUST 11
THE SERVANT OF GOD JOHN BERNAL AND COMPANIONS
Martyrs, First Order

LTHOUGH Franciscan missionaries from Mexico had labored and died in the Spanish province of New Mexico (which included northern Arizona) since the year 1539, it was not until the peaceful conquest and occupation of this territory by Oñate in 1598 that they came in large groups and began to see their efforts crowned with success. By 1630 there were 25 churches and mission centers for 90 Indian pueblos, and some 60,000 Christian Indians were under the spiritual care of 50 priests.

But the pagan medicine men and sorcerers, who saw themselves deprived more and more of the control which they had exercised over the people, were fostering a spirit of revolt which became manifest at times and fifty years later developed into fanatic hatred of the Spaniards and of the Catholic Faith. The result was the Great Pueblo Revolt of 1680, during which 21 Franciscan missionaries and 380 other Spaniards were slain and the others were temporarily driven out of New Mexico.

The leader of the revolution was an Indian sorcerer by the name of Po-pe, who declared that he was directed by three infernal spirits. At his instigation, the medicine men or sorcerers and the chiefs of the northern pueblos held many revolutionary meetings and drew up plans for a general revolt. According to these plans, an uprising was to take place in all the pueblos, except those of the Piros, on the same day. As many as possible of the missionaries and also of the other Spaniards were to be massacred, the churches to be burned, their sacred contents to be profaned and destroyed; and the natives were to return to their ancient pagan religion and customs. Those pueblos which refused to join the plot were to be forced to take part by the threat of extinction.

These plans were carried out on August 10 and 11, 1680, in all the pueblos as far south as Isleta (which did not take part in the revolt) and as far west as the Moqui pueblos in Arizona. Dr. Hackett, who examined the original reports, wrote: "The churches, where not burned, had been stripped of their sacred vessels, robbed of their ornaments, and in every way as completely and foully desecrated as Indian sacrilege and indecency could suggest, while the sacred vestments had been made use of by the Indians as trophies in the dance and festivities celebrating their success."

The 21 missionaries, therefore, who were killed by the insurgents, may rightly be called martyrs of the Faith. Besides Father John Bernal, the custos or superior of all the missions, eighteen other priests and two lay brothers won the martyr's crown in or near the pueblos of New Mexico and Arizona on August 10 and 11. Their names at least deserve to be mentioned. Besides Father Bernal, they were Fathers Joseph de Espeleta, Joseph de Figueroa, John of Jesus, Francis Anthony de Lorenzana, Luke Maldonado, Joseph de Montesdoca, Anthony de Mora, Louis de Morales, John Baptist Pio, Matthias Rendon, Augustine of St. Mary, John de Talaban, Emmanuel Tinoco, Thomas de Torres, Joseph de Trujillo, John Del Val, Ferdinand de Velasco, Dominic de Vera, and Brothers Anthony Sanchez de Pro and John de la Pedrosa. (Cf. *Heroes of the Cross*, pp. 35-44; *The Martyrs of the United States of America*, pp. 62-70.)

ON GRATITUDE FOR THE CATHOLIC FAITH

1. Consider how grateful we should be for the gift of the Catholic Faith. If you had been reared in heresy or paganism, and had then come to a knowledge of the truth of Christian doctrine, would you have had the courage to be converted? But God has permitted you to be born of Catholic parents and to be placed, so to say, right in the bosom of the true Church of Christ. How much the more grateful should you be! — Have you ever thought of that?

2. Consider how fortunate we are to be children of the Catholic Church. When Christ said, "He who believes and is baptized shall be saved" (Mk. 16,16), He could, of course, have meant that only of the true Faith as He Himself preached it and commanded His apostles, with Peter at the head, to teach it. If those who profess other Christian beliefs are saved, it can only be because their error is not of their own fault and because they live in the belief that they belong to the true Church of Christ. But how many of the graces which we have in the Catholic Church are denied them: the remission of their sins in the sacrament of penance, our Lord in holy Communion, strength against the storms of life in confirmation, the final cleansing and strength on the journey to eternity by means of extreme unction. And finally, all the blessings that accrue to us through the communion of saints in the Church. How many graces are yours as a child of the Church! "If you had known the gift of God!" (Jn. 4,10) How grateful you should be!

3. Consider in what manner we should manifest our gratitude for the gift of faith. We should frequently tell God how grateful we are. Out of gratitude we should be careful to preserve this grace by guarding ourselves and our kin from every danger that threatens our faith. We should contribute according to our means that the Faith may be better known and spread throughout the world. But above all we should live in

a manner worthy of our Faith so that we may be worthy members of this Church of which Christ is the cornerstone. For that reason St. Peter admonishes the faithful: "Laying away all malice, and all guile, and dissimulation, and envies, and all detractions, be you as living stones built up, a spiritual house, a holy priesthood, to offer up spiritual sacrifices, acceptable to God by Jesus Christ" (Pet. 2,15).

PRAYER OF THE CHURCH
(On the feast of the Holy Family)

Almighty and eternal God, who in the confession of the true Faith hast given Thy servants to acknowledge the glory of the eternal Trinity, and in the power of Thy majesty to adore the Unity: grant, we beseech Thee, that by steadfastness in this same Faith we may evermore be defended from all adversity. Through Christ our Lord. Amen.

AUGUST 12
ST. CLARE OF ASSISI
Virgin, Second Order

AT the beginning of the thirteenth century, when luxury and sensuality held sway, St. Francis of Assisi made his appearance, giving to men the example of a poor and penitential life. But God wished also to give the vain and pleasure-loving women of that period an example of contempt of the world's vanities. For this mission He chose Clare, the daughter of a prominent and noble family of Assisi, born on January 20, 1194. Her father was Favarone di Offreduccio, count of Sassorosso; her mother, the servant of God Ortolana, who died in the odor of sanctity.

Before the child's birth it was revealed to the mother that her offspring would be a brilliant light in the world. This light the mother detected in her daughter from her earliest years. Besides being favored with personal beauty, Clare possessed a charming personality and rare qualities of mind. She was a favorite in the family, and hardly had she attained to young womanhood, when several suitors sought her in marriage.

But her virtues surpassed the gifts with which nature endowed her. She interested herself in the poor and frequently denied herself things so as to be able to give more to the poor members of Christ. She loved prayer, and it was her sweetest delight to surrender her heart to sentiments of ardent devotion before Jesus Christ in the Blessed Sacrament. Beneath her beautiful garments she wore a sharp penitential belt in order to honor the sufferings of Christ and to preserve herself a chaste virgin for His sake.

She was eighteen years old when she heard St. Francis preach in the cathedral of Assisi during the Lent of 1212. His words on contempt of the world and on penance, and particularly the holy example he set, so earnestly affected Clare, that she conferred with him and soon recognized that God was calling her to lead a life similar to his in the seclusion of a convent. She did not hesitate to carry out God's plans. Realizing that her family, intent only on a brilliant future for her in the world, would oppose her vocation in every way, she had to leave home in secret.

On Palm Sunday she went to church, dressed in her richest garments, to attend divine services. That night, attended by an elderly relative, she went to the little chapel of St. Mary of the Angels, where St. Francis and his brethren came to meet her with lighted candles in their hands. Before the altar she removed her beautiful head-dress, then St. Francis cut off her hair and covered her head with a veil of common linen. In place of rich garments, she received a coarse penitential garb and was girded with a white cord. This was the way in which the mother and founder of the Poor Clares was invested on March 18, 1212. For the time being, St. Francis placed her in a convent of Benedictine sisters.

When Clare had successfully overcome the great opposition of her family, who had intended to force her to return home, her sister Agnes joined her in her sacrifice. St. Francis arranged a little convent for them near the church of St. Damian. There the number of consecrated virgins soon increased. They served God in great poverty, strict penance, and complete seclusion from the world according to a rule which St. Francis gave them as his Second Order. Clare was obliged in obedience to accept the office of abbess in 1215 and to continue in it for thirty-eight years until her death. But her love for humility found compensation in the performance of the lowliest services toward her sisters. In spite of her great physical sufferings, she set her sisters a striking example of zeal in penance and prayer.

In the year 1240 an army of Saracens who were in the service of Emperor Frederick II drew near Assisi. They rushed upon the little convent of St. Damian that lay outside the city and had already scaled the walls of the monastery. In mortal fear the sisters had recourse to their mother, who was ill in bed.

The saint, carrying the pyx containing the Most Blessed Sacrament, had herself carried to a convent window. There she pleaded fervently with

St. Clare of Assisi

the Lord of heaven in the words of the Psalmist (Ps. 73,19): "Deliver not up to beasts the souls, that confess to thee, and shield thy servants whom thou hast redeemed with thy precious blood." A mysterious voice coming from the Host said: "I shall always watch over you." Immediately panic seized the besiegers. A ray of brilliant light which emanated from the Blessed Sacrament had dazzled them. They fell down from the walls and fled from the place. The convent was saved and the town of Assisi was spared.

After suffering from a serious illness for thirty years, Clare felt that her end was drawing nigh. After she had received the last sacraments, she and one of her sisters beheld the Queen of Virgins coming with a large escort to meet her, the spouse of Jesus Christ. On August 11, 1253, she entered into the joys of eternity, and on the following day her body was buried. Pope Alexander IV canonized her already in the year 1255. She was chosen as the universal patroness of television in 1958. The feast of St. Clare is celebrated on August twelfth by all the branches of the Franciscan Order. (Cf. *Forum*, 1953, pp. 259-261, and 1958, pp. 25, 35-36; Brown, *The Little Flowers of St. Francis*, p. 326.)

THE GREATEST GLORY

1. "Oh, how beautiful is the chaste generation with glory!" (Wisd. 4,1). This praise of heaven St. Clare and her great company of sisters have merited for themselves. Corporal beauty, personal charm, and costly clothes in which the children of the world take so much pleasure, this wise virgin considered as naught. She understood the meaning of the Psalmist's words: "All the glory of the king's daughter is within" (Ps. 44,14). Untainted purity of soul, humility, voluntary poverty, penance, ardent love of God, these were the virtues in which she sought her glory, and in them she found imperishable beauty. Where are now the beautifully dressed women of Assisi of that period? Their memory has vanished. But Clare, like St. Francis, shines in heaven and on earth. Both have made their town famous throughout the world. — Do you want true and lasting glory? It is to be found only in virtue. Where have you sought it in the past?

2. Consider that, like a wise virgin, St. Clare did not make a display of her virtues before the world, but strove to hide them in the strictest seclusion. If the violet, which gives forth such a sweet scent in its seclusion, is planted in an open garden, its beauteous color fades and the sweetness of its scent diminishes. The same thing happens with our virtues and good works. That is why St. Gregory, commenting on the Gospel parable of the

ten virgins, says: "The good that we do must be carefully concealed, so that we do not look for favor and honor among men, otherwise that which externally appears as virtue would be inwardly deprived of its merit." Christians who are interested in their salvation, and especially Christian women and girls, even though they do not live in a convent, are included in the words of the Apostle: "For you are dead, and your life is hid with Christ in God" (Col. 3,3). — Can this be said of you?

3. Consider what happiness St. Clare found even here on earth in her life of seclusion. This did not consist in material comfort, nor even in continual spiritual consolation, but in sacrifices made for God, by which she became ever more intimately united with the Source of all happiness. She once said to a young girl: "Our alliance is arrived at by self-denial and the renunciation of earthly things, by the crucifixion of the body and the sacrifice of the will, but the joys attached to it are eternal, the bond is indissoluble, it begins in the world, death puts the final seal to it." On the morning of the day on which she died she received the holy Viaticum; in the afternoon, Pope Innocent IV paid her a visit and gave her the general absolution. But Clare felt happier at having received the Lord of heaven in holy Communion than at having been honored by a visit from the pope. — May we, too, become indifferent to all earthly glory so that we may be permitted to enjoy the eternal!

PRAYER OF THE CHURCH

We beseech Thee, O Lord, grant us Thy servants who devoutly celebrate the feast day of the holy virgin Clare, to be made partakers of the joys of heaven and co-heirs of Thy only-begotten Son. Who livest and reignest forever and ever. Amen.

AUGUST 13
BLESSED JOHN OF LA VERNA
Confessor, First Order

JOHN was born at Fermo in Italy in 1259, and gave indications of extraordinary piety even during his childhood. At the age of seven, it was noticed how he sought out secluded places to pray to our crucified Lord. Desirous of sharing His sufferings, John practiced rigorous penances. He scourged his tender and innocent body, wore a sharp iron girdle, and fasted three times a week. When he was ten years old, he was placed under the direction of the Canons Regular in Fermo; and at the advice of his confessor, he joined the Franciscan Order at the age of thirteen.

It was not long before he distinguished himself among his brethren as a model religious. Because of his unusual spirit of penance and devotion, he was permitted to go in 1290 to the secluded convent on Mount La Verna. John lived here for about forty years, up to his death; and for this reason, he has been given the surname of La Verna.

John was as eager in performing the strictest sort of mortification as the children of the world are bent on amusement. His cell was a cave on the windy side of the mountain which was exposed to every inclemency of the weather. He slept on the bare earth, and used a stone for a pillow. He fasted uninterruptedly and scourged his body mercilessly. However, he did not place his trust in these penitential acts, but rather in the merits of the sufferings of Christ. But he did wish by his penances to make himself conformable to our suffering Saviour, according to the words of the Apostle. Like his holy Father Francis, he spent whole nights in meditating on our crucified Saviour. On one occasion our holy Father appeared to him and offered him his wounds to kiss. John did so and received the sweetest consolation.

For three months John was favored with the companionship of his guardian angel who appeared to him in human form and conversed with him on the sufferings of Christ and the joys of heaven. John also had great sympathy for the souls in purgatory, especially after he became a priest. On All Souls' Day, while elevating the Sacred Host during holy Mass, he prayed very fervently for their release; then of a sudden he saw a great cone of light consisting of innumerable glowing sparks ascend to heaven.

His holy life and heavenly inspirations attracted many devout souls to his cell on the cliff of La Verna. Even the German Emperor Henry VII stopped with his suite on his way to Rome and was so edified by his conversation with John that he took La Verna under his special protection.

By divine inspiration John left his beloved solitude during the last few years of his life, in order to preach penance in the more important towns of Italy. He was thus instrumental in the conversion of many sinners. His approaching death was revealed to him while he was in Cortona, and he hastened back to La Verna. A few days later he surrendered his soul to God on August 9, 1322. Many miracles occurred at his grave, and in 1880 Pope Leo XIII approved the veneration which had been paid to him from time immemorial. The feast of Blessed John is observed by the Franciscans and Capuchins on August thirteenth, and by the Conventuals on the eleventh.

ON CONFIDENCE IN JESUS CRUCIFIED

1. Amid all the tribulations which the Apostle St. Paul bore for Christ's sake, and after the great revelations that had been granted to him, he did not place his glory nor his trust in these things; he wanted to know only Jesus crucified, "who is made unto us, justice, sanctification, and redemption" (1 Cor. 1,30). In accordance with this apostolic teaching, Blessed John, too, placed no trust in his innocence, in his penitential practices, in the special graces which were given to him, but only in Christ crucified, to whom his thoughts were constantly directed. In like manner, let us not place any confidence in our human acts: "Cursed be the man who trusts in man" (Jer. 17,5). Such a person remains under the curse that weighs down all men because of Adam's sin. Christ took this curse upon Himself, and blotted it out by His death on the cross. "Christ has redeemed us from the curse of the law, being made a curse for us" (Gal. 3,13). Let us, therefore, look up to the cross with confidence and say with Holy Church, "Hail O Cross, our only hope!"

2. Consider that we can place implicit trust in our crucified Lord only if we are willing to share His sufferings. Blessed John did this with a holy eagerness, and St. Paul tells us: "I fill up in my flesh those things that are wanting in the sufferings of Christ" (Col. 1,24). Was not Christ's passion perfect, then? Is it not infinitely valuable? Certainly. But that we may share in its fruits, we must also be prepared to share its pains. — What can you say of your willingness in this matter?

3. Consider that the true Christian, who is willing to follow Christ on the way of the cross, may place unlimited confidence in his crucified Lord. "For in that wherein He Himself has suffered and been tempted, He is able to succor those also who are tempted" (Heb. 2,18). Just before his death, Blessed John encouraged his brethren to have such unlimited confidence saying to them: "Do you wish to have a good conscience, then desire to know nothing else but Jesus Christ, for He is the way. Do you wish to possess wisdom, then desire to know only Jesus Christ, for He is the truth. Do you wish to enter into eternal glory, then desire to know only Jesus Christ, for He is the life."

PRAYER OF THE CHURCH

O God, who didst clothe Blessed John, Thy confessor, with the virtue of penance and other spiritual gifts, grant us through his intercession and by his merits so to conduct ourselves in this life that we may deserve to receive the eternal reward. Through Christ our Lord. Amen.

AUGUST 14
BLESSED VINCENT OF AQUILA
Confessor, First Order

IN 1444 the body of St. Bernardin of Siena was laid to rest in the Franciscan convent at Aquila. In this convent the spirit of perfect observance of the rule was preserved. The perfume of the virtues which was exhaled from the convent attracted Vincent to it. He had been reared by devout parents in the fear of God, and in the convent he distinguished himself even among the more perfect brethren by his efforts at acquiring true sanctity.

After he had pronounced his solemn vows, he endeavored to observe them as perfectly as possible, in order to offer himself to God as an agreeable oblation. To subdue sensuality he ate only bread and herbs, and drank water; but when his superiors directed him to eat the usual food provided for the brethren, he readily complied.

He loved solitude to such an extent that he not only withdrew from association with the world, but even lived retired within the convent itself. At his daily work he united himself to God in prayer. He would spend entire nights in the contemplation of heavenly things and was sometimes raised above the earth in ecstasy. The results of this hidden life manifested themselves in dovelike simplicity, in invincible patience at work amid hardships and various forms of injustice which he experienced, in obedience, which extended even to fulfilling the suggestions of his superiors, and in stainless purity. His love of God enkindled in him great zeal for souls; he became the wise director of many devout souls in their efforts to achieve Christian perfection.

When he departed from this life in the convent of St. Julian near Aquila in 1504, he was celebrated by reason of his miracles and his gift of prophecy. One of his devout clients saw his soul, surrounded by choirs of angels, wing its flight straight to heaven. Pope Pius VI sanctioned the veneration of Blessed Vincent; and his feast is observed by the Franciscans and Capuchins on August thirteenth.

ON A LIFE OF RETIREMENT

1. Consider how the pious inclination fostered in his youth and later strengthened in the convent, attracted Vincent to a life of retirement. The spirit of God is constantly drawing souls away from the world to devote themselves to a hidden and retired life. In this same spirit Christ Himself lived a hidden life at Nazareth for thirty years, and even during the three years of His public ministry. He frequently repaired to some secluded spot. "Manifest yourself to the world" (Jn. 7,4), was a suggestion prompted by flesh and blood. — What suggestion have you followed in the past?

Consider the wealth of grace and virtue which are the fruit of a life of retirement. It was in solitude that Blessed Vincent attained to so high a degree of sanctity, that in it he lived more like an angel than a human being. The good seed, sown in the soul in sermons and in devout reading, germinates in solitude. We purify our hearts, are strengthened in virtue, and arrive at intimate union with God, from whom we receive all blessings. All these things, however, are endangered by association with the world. Thomas a Kempis, repeating the words of a heathen philosopher, says (1,20): "As often as I have been among men, I have returned less a man." Then he adds: "This we too often experience when we talk long. It is easier to keep silence altogether than not to fall into excess in speaking. It is easier to keep retired at home than to be enough upon one's guard abroad." — Should this not be a warning to you?

Consider how the love and practice of solitude and of a hidden life provide the necessary strength to keep us from committing faults when we do have to associate with others. Thomas a Kempis again says: "No man can safely appear in public but he who loves seclusion. No man can safely speak but he who loves silence." Blessed Vincent loved to speak to God, and so it happened that his conversations led his listeners to God. And because he kept himself recollected in God even when he had to leave his solitude, he lived a life of holy simplicity, seeking nothing but the honor of God and His good pleasure. May he aid us by his intercession to follow his example.

PRAYER OF THE CHURCH

O God, who didst clothe Blessed Vincent, Thy confessor, with every virtue, but especially with evangelical simplicity and remarkable strictness of life, grant that we may join the ranks of his followers, and rejoice in the blessing of having found favor in Thy sight. Through Christ our Lord. Amen.

<hr />

AUGUST 15
BLESSED NOVELLON OF FAENZA
Confessor, Third Order

N the great family of saints the shoemaker stands next to the king's son, and the penitent who has atoned for the errors of his earlier life may associate with the innocent man who has never lost the grace of God.

Born of devout parents at Faenza, Italy, Novellon learned the trade of a shoemaker, but his bad conduct caused great grief, especially to his good mother. He married when he was quite young, and it was hoped that now at least he would change his ways; but he continued in the same bad habits, inflicting still greater pain on his family. His mother, however, prayed and sighed without ceasing that the good Lord, who consoled the widow of Naim by raising her son to life, would also raise her son from a spiritual death to a new life.

The prayers and tears of the mother did not remain unanswered. Because "affliction leads to understanding" (Is. 28,19), almighty God caused Novellon to become seriously ill. The nearness of death opened his eyes; he reflected on his past years, grace touched his heart, and with bitter tears of true contrition he vowed that if he recovered he would lead a penitential life. He also resolved to make a pilgrimage to the tombs of the holy Apostles Peter and Paul at Rome, and to the tomb of St. James at Compostela.

A few days later Novellon recovered his health as if by a miracle. He was then only twenty-four years old, but he remained faithful to his promise even up to an advanced age.

From that time on, prayer and work were his daily occupation. Mindful of the words, "Alms purge away sins" (Tob. 12,9), he retained only so much of his wages as was necessary for his support, and the remainder he divided among the poor and the sick. In the beginning his wife, who was somewhat anxious over their temporalities, was much vexed at this liberality, but when she saw the great blessings that attended her husband's charity, she gave full consent.

Novellon severely chastised his body for the sins of his past life and amid great hardships undertook the pilgrimage he had promised to make.

He made several trips to Compostela.

After giving the most edifying example of penance and every other virtue for a space of fifty-six years, he died peacefully in the Lord in 1280. God glorified him in life and in death by miracles. With the approval of the pope his native town celebrates his feast, and shoemakers have chosen him for their special patron. The Franciscans observe the feast of Blessed Novellon on August thirteenth, and the Third Order Regular on July twenty-seventh. (Cf. *Forum*, 1947, pp. 231-232; *These Made Peace*, pp. 27-29.)

ON THE THOUGHTS OF DEATH

1. The nearness of death which Novellon felt, together with the grace of God, worked a marvelous conversion in him. Death actually came many years later, but it was a blessing for him that he had looked death in the face when he was yet a young man. At present you do not feel that death is approaching, perhaps you are enjoying the power and fullness of life. Yet, it may be that the pall will cover you before the snowflakes cover the earth. "You know not the day nor the hour" (Mt. 25,13). — Often reflect on this truth and ask yourself whether your conduct at present would in no way disturb you if you were now to meet death.

2. Consider that the thought of death not only caused Novellon to turn from the path of sin, but also to renounce temporal goods, and to do much good. The thought ought to produce the same effects in you. Arrange your temporal affairs and make your will, if you have an estate, so that if death comes upon you suddenly, you will not be the cause of dissension. Do not think of heaping up further treasures, but set your mind on doing good and heaping up heavenly treasures that you can take with you to eternity. "Their works follow them" (Apoc. 14,13). — Have you given serious thought to these matters in the past? If not, let me address to you the words, "Memento mori! Remember that you must die!"

3. Consider a third benefit which the thought of death produced in Blessed Novellon. Having indulged in sensual pleasures, he now led a very mortified life; in the past he had gone after wicked amusements, now he found his pleasure in pilgrimages, in going to church, and in visiting the poor sick. Should the thought of death not work a similar change in us? Why pamper the body when we reflect that we are only preparing more food for the worms? With the thought of death in mind, who would not rather undertake a pious errand than pursue sensual pleasures? "It is better to go to the house of mourning than to the house of feasting; for in that we are put in mind of the end of all, and the living one thinks what

is to come" (Eccl. 7,3). — Often, especially at night when you are about to take your rest, think on death which no one can escape, so that when it comes, you can go into eternal rest.

PRAYER OF THE CHURCH (For a Happy Death)

Almighty and merciful God, who bestowest on mankind both the remedies of health and the gifts of life everlasting: look mercifully upon us Thy servants, and refresh the souls which Thou hast made, so that at the hour of their going forth, they may be found worthy to be borne to Thee, their Maker, free from all stain of sin, by the hands of the holy angels. Through Christ our Lord. Amen.

ᢆᢙᠪᢙᠪᢙᠪᢙᠪᢙᠪᢙᠪᢙ

AUGUST 16
ST. CLARE OF MONTEFALCO
Virgin, Third Order

LIKE so many other towns in Umbria, Montefalco is a small city set on a hill. It overlooks the valley of Spoleto, and some distance to the north Assisi is visible. Here Clare Damiani was born about 1268; and as a little girl of six she was placed in the convent of St. Illuminata, where her sister Jane was superior. From the beginning little Clare observed the rule of the Third Order of St. Francis and added severe penances, keeping strict silence, taking only bread and water, and sleeping on the ground. About eight years later, Clare and the other sisters moved to a new convent, that of Santa Croce, which had been built for them on a nearby hill. During these years all of them followed the rule of the Third Order; but in 1290 the bishop of Spoleto substituted the rule of St. Augustine.

After the death of her sister in 1298, Clare, who distinguished herself by her spirit of prayer and penance and was then about thirty years old, was chosen superior. Not only did she carry out her duties as a religious and a superior in an exemplary manner, but she exerted an extraordinary influence also on the outside world. She confuted heretics, converted sinners, reconciled families which were at odds with one another, made peace between neighboring warring towns, drove out devils, foretold future events, healed the sick, and raised the dead. During the latter part of her life, she also received the gifts of ecstasy and supernatural knowledge.

It is related that our Lord, carrying His Cross, appeared to her and said: "I have been searching for a long time, daughter, to find a firm and solid place on which to plant My Cross, and I have not found one more suitable than your heart. You must receive it and allow it to take root." Clare herself once told a sister in her convent: "If you seek the Cross of Christ, take my heart. There you will find the suffering Lord." There is good evidence that when her heart was opened after her death, the Cross and other instruments of the Passion were found within, formed solidly in some fibrous tissue. For this reason she is also called St. Clare of the Cross.

Commending her sisters to her Franciscan brother, Father Francis Damiani, Clare died at the age of forty on August 17, 1308, and was buried in the chapel of Santa Croce Convent. Later a church was built next to it and dedicated to her. Here her body, which has been preserved incorrupt in a most unusual manner, can still be seen; in fact, it seems to be that of a living person who is asleep. It is also claimed that the miracle of liquefaction and ebullition of her blood has taken place. The cult which had been paid to her as Blessed from the time of her death was approved in 1624; and in 1881 Pope Leo XIII canonized her. The archdiocese of Spoleto, of which St. Clare of Montefalco is a secondary patron, celebrates her feast on August eighteenth. The Conventuals and the Third Order Regular observe her feast on the same day, and the Capuchins on the seventeenth. The Augustinians not only celebrate her feast on November third, but another of "The Impression of the Instruments of Christ's Passion on St. Clare" on October thirtieth. (Cf. Biersack, pp. 26-27; *These Made Peace*, pp. 109-113.)

ON THE SIGNS OF ELECTION

1. Consider what a consolation it must have been for St. Clare to have the Cross of Christ imprinted on her heart. Who of us would not rejoice at such a sign? Our Faith teaches us that no man, unless it has been divinely revealed to him, is certain of his salvation. But there are general signs from which we may confidently draw hope. If God at times revealed to certain souls that their salvation was assured, they were such who had long before borne these general signs of predestination which the Apostle designates when he says: "For whom He foreknew, He also predestined to be made conformable to the image of his Son" (Rom. 8,29). True imitation of Christ, which consists in denying oneself and carrying the cross sent us, is the first and surest sign of predestination. — Is this sign discernible in you?

2. Consider that other signs of predestination are sentiments of penance and mortification. Even sinners are not cut off from salvation, for "Christ Jesus came into the world to save sinners" (1 Tim. 1,15). But they can get there only on the road of penance. If a sinner has been sincerely converted and lives in the spirit of penance, that is, renounces the desires of the flesh and the dangerous pleasures of the world, he may hope to persevere on the road to justice, and thus his salvation is assured. Of course, he cannot then indulge in the spirit of the majority of men; but this detachment will be a new sign of his election, for, "broad is the way that leads to destruction, and many there are who go in by this way; but narrow is the gate and straight is the way that leads to life, and few there are that find it" (Mt. 7,14). — On which of the roads are you journeying?

3. Consider that the practice of good works is a third sign of predestination. For, although our salvation depends solely on the mercy of God, still in God's will no man is lost except through his own fault, and likewise no one is saved who has not merited it so far as he was able. Hence St. Peter admonishes us: "Labor the more that by good works you may make sure your calling and election" (1 Pet. 1,10). These good works are above all the works of mercy and piety, and in a special way also love for prayer and childlike veneration of the Blessed Virgin Mary. — Rejoice if you can detect these signs in yourself, and pray to God, who wills that all men should be saved, that His holy will may be fulfilled in you and your fellowmen.

PRAYER OF THE CHURCH

O God, who alone knowest the number of the elect to be admitted to the happiness of heaven, grant, we beseech Thee, that by the intercession of St. Clare of the Cross, the names of all who have been commended to our prayers, as well as of all the faithful, may be written in the book of blessed predestination. Through Christ our Lord. Amen.

⊛⊛⊛⊛⊛⊛⊛⊛

AUGUST 17
ST. ROCH OF MONTPELLIER
Confessor, Third Order

ROCH was the only son of a wealthy nobleman in France, who seems to have been governor of the town of Montpellier. In answer to the persevering prayers of the parents, this child was granted to them. His future career was indicated by a birthmark in the form of a red cross that was deeply marked on his breast.

The parents raised their boy in a devout manner. Proof was given when, at the age of twenty, he lost both parents. He did not use the immense fortune he inherited for his personal benefit, but he sold all the personal property and distributed the proceeds among the poor while he transferred the ownership of the real estate to his uncle. This done, he joined the Third Order of St. Francis, put on a pilgrim's garb, and journeyed to Rome to visit the tombs of the Apostles.

When he arrived at Acquapendente in northern Italy about the year 1315, he found that an epidemic had broken out there and was making fearful ravages. Roch did not hasten on, as many another person, fearful of his life, would have done, but according to the example of Christ and the admonition of the beloved disciple (1 Jn. 3,16), he offered his life in the service of his brethren in Christ. He went to the hospital of St. John, which was filled with the plague-stricken, and offered his services to the brothers there. He also went to individual homes and sought out the sick, serving them without rest by day and by night. God rewarded his heroic charity by causing many to be cured at the mere Sign of the Cross which Roch made over them. When the plague abated, Roch proceeded on his journey to Rome.

But there, too, an epidemic had broken out. Besides visiting the holy places, Roch again devoted himself to the care of the sick, many of whom were miraculously cured by him. He performed the same services in many other towns of Italy until he arrived in Piacenza and was himself stricken with the dread disease. In the very hospital where he had cured so many sick, he was now looked upon as an intruder, who as an outsider had no right to claim a place there. In order not to be a burden to others, he arose, left the house, and with the support of a staff dragged himself wearily to a neighborhood woods. There he came upon a dilapidated hut with a bit of straw, where he lay down, thanking God for a quiet lodging.

God also provided for his nourishment. As He once took care of Elias, sending him bread by means of a raven, so He now sent bread to Roch by means of a dog from a neighboring country house. The sick man gradually recovered. When he had regained sufficient strength, he was divinely inspired to return to his native town.

There furious warfare was raging. The soldiers whom he encountered thought he was a spy. He was led before the governor of Montpellier, his own uncle, who, however, did not recognize his nephew in the emaciated prisoner, and had the supposed spy cast into prison. Roch did not say a word in his defense; he wished, like Christ, to accept in silence whatever heaven had ordained for him. Because of the disturbances of the war, he was almost completely forgotten, and languished in prison for five years. Then death put an end to his trials on August 16, 1327.

When he felt that his end was drawing near, he asked that a priest might come and administer the last sacraments. The priest, on entering the prison, beheld it supernaturally lighted up and the poor captive surrounded with special radiance. As death claimed its victim, a tablet appeared on the wall on which an angelic hand wrote in golden letters the name of Roch, and the prediction that all who would invoke his intercession would be delivered from the plague.

Informed of all that took place, Roch's uncle came to the prison and, shortly after, also the governor's mother, that is, Roch's grandmother. She identified the dead man as her grandson by the birthmark of the red cross on his breast. They gave him a magnificent funeral and had a church built in his honor, in which his body was entombed. His veneration was approved by several popes and soon spread throughout Europe. He was canonized by Pope Urban VIII. The feast of St. Roch is observed by the Franciscans, Conventuals, and Third Order Regular on August seventeenth, and by the Capuchins on the twenty-sixth. (Cf. *These Made Peace*, pp. 134-137.)

ST. ROCH, PATRON AGAINST CONTAGIOUS DISEASES

1. The prediction that St. Roch would be a special patron against contagious diseases, has been so remarkably verified that he is invoked by all Christian peoples in such sad times. In 1414, when a general council was held in Constance, an epidemic broke out. A great procession was inaugurated in honor of St. Roch to invoke his intercession, and immediately the epidemic was checked. We read in the annals of the Franciscan Order, that many convents were preserved from contagious disease due to the devotion they tendered the saint, and for this reason prayers are offered daily in the convents of the order to obtain his protection. — Could you not say a prayer each day in honor of St. Roch, so that he will protect you and your house from contagious disease?
2. It was not granted to St. Roch to be preserved from the dread disease, but his patience and resignation to God's will greatly increased his heavenly merits. It may please God also to permit such an evil to befall us and our associates, for many a person to whom it might not otherwise be granted, is thus led back to God, has a good death, and attains eternal blessedness. Our good Lord afflicts the body with sickness in order to save the soul. — When sickness attacks a community, pray fervently to St. Roch

that through his intercession the souls of men may be benefited by it.

3. Consider that certain diseases of the soul are communicable and spread like contagion. They are much worse than the plagues which attack the body. Such diseases are the various vices: impurity, intemperance, inordinate love of pleasure. Roch fled the dangerous occasions of these vices with so much zeal that he relinquished his wealth and prominent position that, in the guise of a poor pilgrim and servant of the sick, he might preserve his soul from sin. — Think frequently of the example he has given, and invoke his intercession for yourself and yours against contagion of the body and of the soul.

PRAYER OF THE CHURCH

O God, who didst grant to St. Roch the promise, which an angel recorded on a tablet, not to permit anyone who sought his intercession to be afflicted with a contagious disease; grant, we beseech Thee, that we, who celebrate his memory, may be preserved from every contagion of soul and body. Through Christ our Lord. Amen.

AUGUST 18
BLESSED BEATRICE DA SILVA
Virgin, Second Order

EATRICE was born of Portuguese parents at Ceuta on Moroccan soil, and manifested a special attachment to our Immaculate Mother very early in life. At the court of the king of Castile she was persecuted and cast into prison by a jealous queen, but by the visible intervention of the Immaculate Queen of heaven she was released and justified with great honor. Then she left the court and went to Toledo. On the journey thither St. Francis and St. Anthony appeared to her and announced that she would be the founder of a new order.

At Toledo she repaired to a convent of Cistercian nuns and remained there for almost forty years. She did not don the religious garb; nevertheless she was a model of religious perfection. Gradually the resolution took shape to establish a new order that would honor the Immaculate Mother of God. With twelve companions who entertained sentiments similar to hers, she withdrew to a separate house. Beatrice wrote the rule and asked Pope Innocent VIII to approve it. This occurred in the year 1489.

A few years earlier, the Blessed Virgin had showed her in a vision that she should wear a habit consisting of a white tunic and scapular with a light-blue mantle. This was the origin of the Order of the Immaculate Conception, also known as the Conceptionist Poor Clares.

The whole life of the foundress was conformed to her religious rule. The rule itself can be summed up briefly in three short mottos: to be silent and submissive in all things that happen to us by God's ordinance or are required of us by holy obedience; to become small in the eyes of God, of the world, and of ourself, and to prefer a life of obscurity; to love everyone with a holy love, and become all to all by prayer, sacrifice, and labor.

At the age of sixty-five, Mother Beatrice departed from this life in 1490, a year after the founding of her order. Pope Pius XI enrolled her among the beatified. The Conceptionists were incorporated into the Franciscan Order and soon spread through Europe and America. Thanks to the efforts of a Franciscan bishop, Amandus Bahlmann of Santarém, a branch of this order, under the name of Missionaries of the Immaculate Conception, is doing remarkable work especially in the missions of Brazil. Their motherhouse is at Paterson, New Jersey. The feast of Blessed Beatrice is observed by the Franciscans on August eighteenth.

ON THE VANITIES OF THE WORLD

1. Consider the danger to which the vanities of the world expose us. Honors and riches arouse the lower passions and tempt us to pride and forgetfulness of God. Blessed Beatrice was well advised when she rid herself of all vanities and chose a life of renunciation. The words of Holy Scripture can be applied to many who have indulged in worldly vanities: "As much as she has glorified herself, and lived in delicacies, so much torment and sorrow give to her" (Apoc. 18,7). — Do not let yourself be ensnared.

2. The vanities of the world are transient. It is written: "Favor is deceitful and beauty is vain" (Prov. 31,30). What will be the end of all worldly vanities? "Of earth they were made and into earth they returned together" (Eccl. 3,20). Therefore, the Wise Man says: "Why is earth and ashes proud?" (Eccli. 10,9). Blessed Beatrice acted wisely when she bade farewell to all vanities. — Frequently recall the words the Church uses on Ash Wednesday: "Remember, O man, that you are dust and unto dust you shall return."

3. Consider that to devote oneself to the infinite Good is the best thing we can do. Blessed Beatrice did that. All for God, that was her maxim. She

found in it interior peace and satisfaction during her sojourn on earth, and in the next world the possession of the highest Good in eternal bliss. Thomas a Kempis is correct when he says (1,1): "All is vanity but love God and serve Him alone." The Franciscan pope, Clement XIV, wrote at the time of his elevation to the cardinalate: "I count this dignity as an accumulation of letters of the alphabet for an epitaph that is of no use to him who lies beneath it."

PRAYER OF THE CHURCH

Hear us, O God, source of all our blessings, that we who rejoice in celebrating the feast of Thy virgin Blessed Beatrice may be ennobled in sentiments and encouraged to loving submission. Through Christ our Lord. Amen.

AUGUST 19
ST. LOUIS OF TOULOUSE
Confessor, First Order

HE SON of Charles II of Naples and Sicily, Louis was born in 1274 and named after his uncle, the holy king of France. It was the great concern of his mother, the niece of St. Elizabeth, to rear her many children as true servants of the King of Kings. The devout queen observed in her son Louis particularly blessed results of this maternal solicitude. He loved prayer, was reserved and gentle, and his whole conduct radiated angelic purity. Even as a child he practiced mortification. On a certain occasion, after he had retired, his mother found him sleeping on a rug on the floor of his room instead of in his comfortable bed.

Sweets and delicious foods he carried to the poor sick with his mother's permission. It is related that once he was leaving the dining-room with a roasted pullet under his mantle and so met his father. The king wished to see what he was carrying. Timidly the boy laid back his mantle, and lo, it was a beautiful bouquet of flowers.

When he was fourteen years old Louis was taken to Barcelona with two of his brothers, as a hostage for the release of his father, who had been taken a prisoner of war. Gladly did Louis accept this misfortune to obtain his father's freedom; but at the same time, the disposition with which he accepted it was astonishing in a boy of his age. "Misfortune," he said, "is more useful to the friends of God than good fortune, for on such occasions they can prove their loyalty to their Lord."

Under the guidance of several excellent Franciscan friars who were appointed teachers to the young princes, Louis made remarkable progress in virtue as well as in secular knowledge. In public debates he manifested his mastery of the various branches of knowledge, both sacred and profane. Theology was his favorite subject. So devoid was he of ambition that he planned to renounce his claims to the throne in order to devote himself entirely to the service of God.

About this time he became seriously ill. He made a vow that if he recovered, he would join the Order of Friars Minor. The sickness immediately took a turn for the better, but the superiors of the order hesitated to receive the young prince without the consent of the king, his father. Louis was thus obliged to defer his pious design.

At the end of six years his captivity ended. On returning home, after much pleading he finally obtained the permission of his father to settle his claims on his brother Robert, and to become a priest. Not very long after his ordination, and although he was only twenty-one years old, he was selected by Pope Boniface VIII for the bishopric of Toulouse. "Whatever is lacking to the young priest in age and experience," said the pope, "his extraordinary knowledge, his maturity of mind, and his holiness of life will amply supply."

Louis had to yield to the pope's wishes, but he requested that he might first be admitted into the Order of Friars Minor. That request was granted. The royal prince was overjoyed to be permitted, for a time at least, to perform the humblest exercises in the garb of a son of St. Francis; in Rome he went from door to door gathering alms.

The pope himself officiated at the ceremony of episcopal consecration, and shortly afterwards Louis left to assume the government of his diocese. His noble birth and above all the fame of his sanctity caused him to be received at Toulouse like a messenger from heaven. The entire city went out to meet him, and everybody was enchanted with the modesty, sweetness, and angelic virtue which radiated from his face and bearing. A sinner who for many years had lived a wicked life, cried out at sight of him: "Truly, this man is a saint!" and then turned away from his sinful habits and led a better life. A woman who doubted the sanctity of the young man went to church one morning to attend the Mass which the bishop was celebrating. Then she, too, cried out: "Ah, yes, our bishop is a saint!"

Bishop Louis led the poor and rigorous life of a Friar Minor and devoted himself with all solicitude to the welfare of his diocese. The poor were his best friends, and he fed twenty-five of them daily at his own table. His ministry, however, was destined to be short-lived. He died in the twenty-fourth year of his life, having been bishop no longer than a year and a half.

He received the last sacraments on the feast of the Assumption of Our Lady; and on the nineteenth of August, 1297, while pronouncing the holy name of Mary, he yielded his soul to God. Because of the many miracles that were wrought at his tomb, he was canonized as early as 1317, during the lifetime of his mother. The feast of St. Louis of Toulouse is celebrated by all three branches of the First Order as well as the Third Order Regular on August nineteenth.

A PATRON FOR YOUTHFUL STUDENTS

1. What better example than that of St. Louis could be held up to youthful students. He distinguished himself from his youth by modesty and docility, and throughout his life he preserved his purity unsullied. He appreciated and loved his teachers, and applied himself diligently to his studies, in which he was very successful. He directed all his efforts to the honor of God and the salvation of his fellowmen, and preserved a cheerful disposition even in adversity. That is the type of student every Christian youth should desire to be. The saint, who gave them so brilliant an example on earth, will also be a powerful patron and intercessor for them in heaven.

2. Consider how important the good behavior of youthful students is to human society. They will be the future teachers and governors, the directors and leaders of society. Their predominant sentiments will be the dominating policies of the majority of the people. For that reason much depends on how youthful students grow up. They are encompassed by many dangers, and how many of them lose their innocence and their faith to the detriment of the many over whom they later exercise influence. Those who are associated with students and can offer them guidance have the obligation to direct them toward virtue and to point out to them such saintly examples as St. Louis of Toulouse. But, it is likewise the duty of every Christian frequently to recommend youthful students to so powerful a patron as St. Louis.

3. Consider how the example and the protection of St. Louis can help youthful students especially in two grave dangers that threaten them: sensuality and ambition. How frequently the one vice wrecks the body and the other gnaws at the young soul! The mortification which Louis practiced from his earliest years and the childlike devotion he fostered to

our Blessed Lady made him secure in temperance and purity. His love for the poor and his lively faith kept him so far away from ambition that he chose the lesser station of a Friar Minor to that of the royal throne. That is why he is now wearing the imperishable crown of heavenly glory. In behalf of students let us frequently invoke him in the words of Holy Church in the office for his feast: "Vernal rose of charity, lily of purity, shining star, vessel of sanctity, pray to the Lord for us!"

PRAYER OF THE CHURCH

O God, who didst teach Thy holy confessor and bishop Louis to prefer the heavenly kingdom to one of earth, and didst marvelously clothe him with stainless purity and extraordinary love for the poor, grant that by imitating his virtues here on earth we may deserve to be crowned by Thee in heaven. Through Christ our Lord. Amen.

AUGUST 20
BLESSED PAULA MONTALDI
Virgin, Second Order

IN the diocese of Mantua near the little town of Volta lies the castle of the Montaldi in which Paula, a member of this noble and devout family, was born. From infancy she was remarkable for rare modesty, angelic innocence, and strong attraction to piety, and was frequently called the little saint.

When she grew into young womanhood and had made her debut in society, she was seized with such loathing for its vain amusements that she left home and repaired to the convent of St. Lucy at Mantua. The rule of St. Clare, as mitigated by Pope Urban IV, was observed in this convent.

Paula was invested with the holy habit in 1458, when she was but fifteen years of age. In spite of her youth she entered upon religious life with unusual seriousness. Desirous of making a sacrifice of her body to God, she added to the prescribed practices of the community many fasts and penitential exercises and observed long vigils. For the short rest she allowed herself, she used the floor for her bed and a stone for her pillow. She kept a careful check on her senses and on the affections of her heart.

She not only avoided idle words, but prevented useless and distracting thoughts from gaining entrance into her heart, for which reason she was almost constantly in intimate union with God. And the God of Love sometimes favored her with raptures and ecstasies. Meanwhile, she looked upon herself as the last and least among the sisters, even after she had spent many years in the convent.

Her sisters duly appreciated her merits and chose her three times for their abbess. With her humble charity and enlightened wisdom this mistress of the spiritual life led many of her fellow sisters to a high degree of perfection. Attracted by the fame of her sanctity, lay people also came to seek advice and consolation, and to obtain the help of God through her prayers.

After she had withstood severe attacks from hell, and her patience had been tried by long and wearisome illness, she passed to the vision of God in 1514. Her tomb in the church of the convent at Mantua became the object of universal veneration. But when, at the close of the eighteenth century, Emperor Joseph II of Austria suppressed even this old and venerable convent, the city of Volta gladly brought the body of their fellow citizen into their church and erected a magnificent tomb for it before our Lady's altar. Pope Pius IX approved the veneration of Blessed Paula in 1866. The Franciscans and Capuchins observe her feast on August eighteenth.

ON DISTRACTIONS AT PRAYER

1. Consider with what recollection and devotion Blessed Paula said her prayers, since her heart was almost constantly united to God. How different it is with us! Though we begin our prayers with heartfelt devotion, we soon find ourselves preoccupied with distracting and foreign thoughts, so that in the sight of God we must seem like idiotic children who begin to speak sensibly to their father but ere long begin to wander and utter only silly talk. We have one consolation, however, since, according to the teaching of the saints and theologians, distractions at prayer are not sinful if we do not wilfully entertain them, but calmly turn our thoughts to God as soon as we become aware of them. Our Lord has compassion on our weakness. "As a father has compassion on his children, so has the Lord compassion on those who fear Him" (Ps. 102,13).
2. Consider that distractions are sinful if we are the cause of them by gazing about or by similar actions, or if, when we become aware of the distractions, we do not check them, but, setting aside all respect, wilfully dwell on them. Then our prayer is not only useless but deserves to be punished by God, who is being dishonored by it. How can we expect God to pay attention to our prayer when we ourselves fail to be attentive to it? He can only say of such Christians: "This people honors Me with their

lips, but their heart is far from Me" (Mt. 15,8). In a certain church St.
Bernard once saw an angel standing beside each Christian engaged in
prayer, and recording the prayers said. Some angels wrote with gold ink,
others with silver ink, others again with ordinary ink, and still others
were not writing at all. — With what kind of ink is your guardian angel
recording your prayer?

3. Let us consider the cause of our distractions and how we can overcome
them. Many of them are the result of human frailty; we must bear these
with patience, and no matter how often they return, we must humbly turn
our thoughts to God again. Many other distractions come from the evil
spirit. That is why the Church provides that each hour of the Divine
Office begin with the prayer: O God, come to my assistance, O Lord, make
haste to help me (Ps. 69,2). In these same words or in similar ones beg God
at the beginning of your prayers for help against disturbing suggestions
of the evil spirit. But the majority of our distractions are the result of the
freedom we give our senses and because our hearts are filled with
curiosity and idle desires. The only remedy for this source is Christian
self-denial, exterior and interior, which Blessed Paula practiced so
conscientiously. You, too, should practice this mortification, so that it may
lead you to intimate union with God in prayer here on earth, and to
eternal union with Him in heavenly bliss hereafter.

PRAYER OF THE CHURCH

O God, who didst give us the virgin Blessed Paula as a model of purity and
penance by reason of her constant meditation on the sufferings of Thy
crucified Son, grant us, by her intercession, the grace to crucify our flesh
and to breathe forth our soul in the embrace of the cross of our Lord.
Through Christ our Lord. Amen.

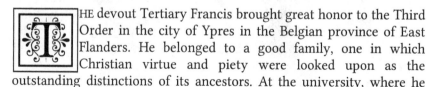

AUGUST 21
THE SERVANT OF GOD FRANCIS OF YPRES
Confessor, Third Order

HE devout Tertiary Francis brought great honor to the Third
Order in the city of Ypres in the Belgian province of East
Flanders. He belonged to a good family, one in which
Christian virtue and piety were looked upon as the
outstanding distinctions of its ancestors. At the university, where he

studied law, he preserved the spirit of piety and never failed to manifest it when an occasion presented itself.

Shortly after completing his studies, he yielded to the wishes of his parents and married. But in order to unite himself more intimately with God, he entered the Third Order of St. Francis, and wore the Tertiary garb publicly at the meetings. He was also very regular in attending the meetings, and if business matters prevented him from being present, he always sent in his excuse.

He made his home the model of a truly Christian household. Because of his love for law and order, everything was well arranged. There was a time appointed for everything, and each member knew just what he was required to do. A point was made of everybody's faithfully discharging his duties, the master and the mistress themselves giving the best example. Love of God was the motive of their dutifulness, and true love of neighbor was the bond that united the members of the household in holy association.

In his profession as a lawyer, Francis soon gained so remarkable a reputation that he was appointed first assessor of the king's council.

When he was thirty years old he fell a victim to a wasting disease, and for a space of eight years he often suffered excruciating pains, but with the most astounding patience. He did not even care to have anyone sympathize with him, but would say on such occasions: "I am grateful to God that He is giving me the time and the opportunity to prepare myself for a happy death, which will, I trust, bring me to eternal life."

Almighty God took His faithful servant home to heaven in the year 1689.

ON ORDER IN A CHRISTIAN HOUSEHOLD

1. Consider the model arrangement established by the servant of God Francis in his household. It is a duty incumbent on the father as head of the family to enforce good order. As householder of the universe God almighty "has ordered all things in measure, and number, and weight" (Wisd. 11,21). So the father of the house, and the mother as his helper, should order their household that from the beginning to the end of the day everything is done at its proper time, and each member of the household is assigned his peculiar work according to his age and ability. There is order among the choirs of the angels in heaven, and in convents good order promotes peace and progress. It will do the same in every Christian household, for, as St. Augustine says: "Peace is the repose of order." — Is there good order in your household?

2. Consider the sad state of a household in which there is no order. One person gets up early and another late; one rises with a prayer on his lips, the other with a curse; some do nothing, others must do everything; nothing is found in its place, and everything goes to ruin because it is not kept in shape by order and cleanliness. Dissatisfaction and dissension reign among the members of such a household because no one wants to take over the disagreeable work, yet each one blames the other for the wreck and ruin of things. A household like that conveys an idea of hell, of which Job says: "It is a land of misery and darkness, where the shadow of death, and no order but everlasting horror dwells" (Job 10,22).

3. Consider the extent to which good order helps the salvation of souls. It teaches self-conquest. Superiors must practice it, because they are bound by their own laws, and subjects must practice it in obedience. If a child has accustomed itself to order and obedience from its earliest years, it will find it easy to obey the commands of lawful authority throughout life. Order preserved in our exterior life will lead to orderliness in our interior as well, for exterior things have a great influence on the interior. Cleanliness and purity have more than one thing in common. Finally, daily prayers said in common, and forming an integral part of every Christian household, will direct the hearts of the members of the family to heaven, whither every Christian father and mother should direct their family, thereby earning a place for themselves in the eternal abode.

PRAYER OF THE CHURCH
(Tuesday in the Second Week in Lent)

Perfect within us, we beseech Thee, O Lord, in Thy mercy, the strength acquired by orderly conduct, that what we know Thou hast appointed us to do we may by Thy assistance be enabled to fulfill. Through Christ our Lord. Amen.

❧❧❧❧❧❧❧❧❧❧

AUGUST 22
THE SERVANT OF GOD FRANCIS QUIÑONES
Cardinal and Confessor, First Order

 RANCIS was the first child of a wealthy Spanish count and heir to a rich family estate. He was endowed with rare mental gifts. When he was scarcely sixteen years of age, he attended the University of Salamanca. At the time, Father John of

Puebla, who was also a count by birth, was introducing a stricter form of life in the Franciscan Order. It was the subject of much conversation among the university folk.

Urged by a sincere desire for perfection, Francis went to the convent of St. Mary of the Angels and asked to be admitted there. Father John himself joyfully received the innocent young man and gave him the name of Francis of the Angels at his investiture. This wealthy heir of a Spanish estate was henceforth seen clothed in a poor habit, cheerfully performing the most menial work, and serving those who in the world had been his father's subjects. As soon as he made his profession, he went out to gather alms and personally carried to the convent the provisions collected.

After his ordination to the priesthood he devoted himself to the salvation of souls with the greatest zeal. His self-sacrificing spirit manifested itself in a special way when an epidemic broke out. Father Francis labored tirelessly in administering corporal and spiritual aid to the afflicted. He even carried the dead bodies, from which others feared contamination, on his shoulders, to their graves.

He ardently longed to go to America to preach the Gospel to the Indians. But God planned another field of labor for him. Because of his extraordinary talents and outstanding virtues, he was chosen for the higher positions in the order at a very early age. After being chosen the head of his province several times, he was elected minister general of the entire order in 1523, when he was only thirty-eight years old.

At this time Emperor Charles V requested the minister general for missionaries to the Indians in Mexico. Father Francis acceded to this request and sent twelve men, the celebrated Twelve Apostles, to undertake the work. When they left Spain, Francis wept because he could not accompany them.

Meanwhile, he administered his office with unusual apostolic zeal. He made all his journeys on foot, and lived in the greatest poverty. He did everything in his power to escape honors that others were so ready to tender him. Where he was not known personally, he would not allow his companions to disclose his identity or use his title in speaking to him. He could not bear it if honor was accorded him because of his noble descent.

Pope Clement VII often called on Father Francis in negotiating with the emperor, who entertained great affection for Father Francis. But when such business matters and the extensive journeys he had to make in the interests of the Church prevented him from giving the necessary attention to the order, he resigned his office of minister general with the approbation of the pope. He sent a last circular letter to the brethren in which he urged them to remain faithful, to persevere in their holy calling, and to look for no other reward than the one promised for eternity, according to the words of our holy Father St. Francis: "Great things have we promised, greater are promised to us."

In 1528 the pope selected him for the cardinalate; but even as a prince of the Church, Francis preserved the simplicity and poverty of a Friar Minor. In the church of the Holy Cross in Rome, to which he was assigned as cardinal, he had his tomb erected with the inscription: "Francis Quinoñes, Cardinal of the Roman Catholic Church, mindful of death and corruption, had this grave prepared for himself during his lifetime."

After accomplishing much good for the Church and his order, and adorning himself with remarkable virtue and great merit, he died an edifying death in September of the year 1540.

ON HUMILITY AMID DISTINCTIONS

1. Consider how edifying must have been the humble disposition of the servant of God Francis. He was never proud of his noble birth, of his high offices, nor of the distinctions that were showered on him by the highest dignitaries in the world. St. Gregory teaches that we should never accept honors and distinctions except when they can help us be of service to others, while for ourselves we regard them as burdensome. That is what Holy Scripture tells us in a few words of the disposition of Queen Esther. She spoke to the Lord with reference to her crown: "Thou knowest my necessity, that I abominate the sign of my pride and glory, which is upon my head in the days of my public appearance" (Esth. 14,16). — When honors are accorded you, do you find them burdensome?

2. Consider how difficult it is to preserve humility amid honors and distinctions. Honor is so sweet a poison that it requires great virtue not to indulge in it and lose humility. It is much easier to endure humiliation with patience, and to think in lowly fashion of oneself when one is in a humble position, than it is to preserve humility amid honors. Saul remained humble while he was a shepherd, so that he could say to Samuel, who anointed him king: "Am I not a son of the least tribe of Israel, and my kindred the last among the families of the tribe?" (1 Kings 9,21). But after he had been made a king, he became so proud that he refused to obey God and was rejected by Him. — When we reflect on such examples, should we not rather fear honor and distinctions?

3. Consider, however, that it is possible to remain humble even amid the honors that are bestowed upon us. We can do so if we refer all honor to God from whom alone worthy actions receive their value. In the Apocalypse St. John thus saw the elders placing their crowns before the

throne to the Most High while they said: "Thou art worthy, O Lord our God, to receive glory and honor and power; because Thou hast created all things" (Apoc. 4,11). As regards ourselves, we should ever keep in mind our baseness, as did the servant of God Francis when as a cardinal he had his tomb prepared, "mindful of death and corruption." — If honors are bestowed on you, or you are appointed to a position of prominence, then "Remember, O man, that you are dust, and into dust you shall return" (Gen. 3,19).

PRAYER OF THE CHURCH
(No. 27 Under "Various Prayers")

O God, who withstandest the proud and givest Thy grace to the humble, endow us with that true virtue of humility, the pattern of which Thine only-begotten Son did show in Himself to the faithful. Nor let us ever by our pride provoke Thee to anger; but rather in our lowliness, may we accept from Thy hands the gifts of Thy grace. Through Christ our Lord. Amen.

AUGUST 23
BLESSED QUEEN BLANCHE
Widow, Third Order

UR DIVINE LORD says: "By their fruits you shall know them" (Mt. 7,16), and in these words He bestows great praise on Queen Blanche, for St. Louis IX of France was her son, and his holiness was in great measure the result of her maternal rearing.

Blanche, the daughter of the king of Castile, Spain, lived in happy wedlock with Louis VIII, King of France, for twenty-six years. She enjoyed the confidence of her husband so perfectly that when he died he entrusted her with the guardianship of their twelve-year-old son Louis and, until his maturity, with the government of the country. There were among the great ones in the land such who were envious of the widow and foreigner, and would have liked to take over the government. But Blanche administered the high and burdensome office with such impartial justice and great wisdom that the envious were silenced and her executive ability was highly commended by all.

As a mother she evinced genuine Christian sentiments. It is in the love for her children that a Christian mother must generally stand the test. Will she allow them to do things that are displeasing to God? Will she love them more than God? "He who loves son or daughter more than Me, is not worthy of Me" (Mt. 10,37). Blanche proved that she was a true Christian mother, for she often said to her son: "Rather would I see you dead at my feet than stained with a mortal sin."

She was not satisfied, however, with helping her son to avoid mortal sin, she was anxious also to preserve him from venial sin. Mother and son therefore had themselves enrolled in the Third Order of St. Francis. In living up to the rule she encouraged him to practice every virtue and to strive after Christian perfection.

The saintly son had such confidence in his mother that, having personally governed the country for several years, he again placed her in charge, while he went to the Holy Land with his army. He did not return until he received the news of her death in 1253. Blanche died surrounded by devout sisters of the Cistercian Order, whose convent at Maubisson she had built. Clothed in the habit of the Third Order, she was buried in their church. The title of Blessed which was conferred on her in popular devotion may still be used, but it has not yet been officially confirmed by the Holy See. (Cf. *Forum,* 1949, pp. 238-240, 252.)

ON VENIAL SIN

1. Next to mortal sin, venial sin is the greatest evil in the world. Though it is not a separation from God, it is at least an offense against God. Though it does not rob the soul entirely of the grace of God, it lessens the divine good pleasure and causes God's special favors to be withdrawn. Though it will not cast us into hell, it will condemn the soul stained with it to the painful tortures of purgatory. We should, therefore, for no consideration on earth ever willfully commit a venial sin. Blessed Blanche recognized how carefully we ought to shun venial sin, and she impressed this fact so deeply on the mind of her son St. Louis that at the end of his life he declared himself far happier to have endured without murmuring all the sufferings and afflictions that befell him during his crusades, than if all the kingdoms of the world had been made subject to his scepter. — Have you taken venial sin so seriously during your past life?
2. Consider that venial sin easily leads to mortal sin if we think lightly of it. "He who contemns small things, shall fall by little and little" (Eccli. 19,1). Just as a storm will cause a house to collapse if it has sprung its joints, so will the storm of temptation cause a soul to collapse if it has been weakened by venial sin. If you are aware of such weakness in

yourself, if you notice that the temptation to impatience, enmity, and impurity is sometimes very hard to overcome, then examine yourself to determine whether your soul has not perhaps been weakened by venial sins. Be careful to avoid them in future. "He who is faithful in that which is least, is faithful also in that which is greater" (Lk. 16,10).

3. Consider that without a special grace of God, as was granted to the Blessed Virgin, it is impossible for us while on earth to avoid every venial sin. "If we say we have no sin, we deceive ourselves, and the truth is not in us" (1 Jn. 1,8). Human weakness and carelessness lead us daily into many a sin. That is why we pray: Forgive us our trespasses (Mt. 6,12), and why we should also say with the prophet: "From my secret sins cleanse me, O Lord!" (Ps. 18,13). But sins that are fully recognized as such beforehand and of which our conscience makes us aware, and be they ever so small, must not be committed by a Christian who loves his soul. Heed the warning of Tobias: "All the days of your life have God in your mind, and take heed you never consent to sin" (Tob. 4,6).

PRAYER OF THE CHURCH

Grant unto us, eternal Saviour, that as we, by Thy grace, receive forgiveness of our sins, so we may henceforth avoid all sin. Through Christ our Lord. Amen.

AUGUST 24
THE SERVANT OF GOD MARGARET OF LUXEMBOURG
Virgin, Third Order

MARGARET was born in Wuerttemberg at the end of the sixteenth century, and was a member of the Lutheran Church. One day two Franciscans came to the palace in which she lived. That evening they spoke of the evil that was resulting everywhere from the heresy of the so-called Reformation, and of the power which the Catholic Church alone has to save the souls of men. Their conversation made a deep impression on Margaret; she recognized that she was not on the road that leads to Christ.

After a time, she became ill, and then and there resolved that she would return to the Catholic Church, through which alone she could be saved. As soon as she recovered, she left her palace and repaired to Antwerp. There she lived in the home of a devout lady, while she was being instructed in the Catholic Faith.

Margaret's love and esteem for the Faith constantly increased. She also fostered a fervent devotion to our Blessed Lady. She was anxious to travel to Loreto, to make her profession of faith in the house of the Mother of God. But when she reached Maria Einsiedeln in Switzerland, she found that she could not continue her journey because of warlike disturbances. She made her profession of faith at this shrine of our Lady before the abbot of the Benedictines, and then, with inexpressible joy, received holy Communion.

Not long afterwards she joined the Third Order of St. Francis in Luxembourg. There she moved into a little house next to the Franciscan church, where she led a life of great austerity and sincere piety for the space of twenty-eight years. She was favored by God with special graces. At holy Mass she was sometimes wrapt in ecstasy, and she foretold the day of her death.

After devoutly receiving the last sacraments she died blessedly in the Lord in the year 1651. She was laid to rest with great solemnity, in the presence of the governor, next to the high altar in the Franciscan church.

THE ONLY SAVING CHURCH

1. Consider how earnestly the servant of God Margaret strove to become a member of the true Church of Christ when she recognized that she was living in error. She acted correctly. For our salvation depends upon renouncing recognized error. Jesus Christ came into this world to save us. He established the Church which He founded on Peter, the prince of the Apostles, as the only institution for leading men to salvation, so that all who are faithful to it are saved. "He who believes and is baptized, shall be saved" (Mk. 16,16). But Christ instituted only one Church and turns away from those who refuse to be members of it. "He who will not hear the Church, let him be to thee as a heathen and a publican" (Mt. 18,17). The Roman Catholic Church, then, with the pope at its head as the successor of St. Peter, is the only prescribed way that leads to salvation, that is to say, it is the only saving Church.

2. Are all those then who profess another belief condemned by the Catholic Church? If they acknowledge that the Catholic Church has the true Faith of Christ and yet will not accept it, then they will be condemned. Christ Himself pronounced this judgment: "He who will not believe, will perish" (Mk. 16,16). But he who lives in good faith and professes a belief which he erroneously considers to be the religion of God can be saved. In the eyes of God he really belongs to the true Church of

Christ, the Catholic Church, in which he is incorporated by holy baptism or by his good will. If he observes the commandments of God and lives in grace or if he regains grace by perfect contrition, he will not be lost. We should pity his error, but we may not condemn him. Not one will be condemned by God except through his own fault.

3. Consider the duties that are incumbent on us who are children of the only saving Church. We should thank God often and fervently for this great grace. We may not ascribe it to any merits on our part, but must acknowledge with the Apostle: "By the grace of God, I am what I am" (1 Cor. 15,10). We must, moreover, be on our guard, never in any way to separate ourselves from the true fold of Christ. Out of love for souls we must also pray for our erring brethren that they may arrive at the knowledge of the true Faith and participation in its treasure of grace. The heart of the Good Shepherd desires this, for He has said: "Other sheep I have, who are not of this fold; them also I must bring, and they shall hear My voice, and there shall be one fold and one Shepherd" (Jn. 10,16).

PRAYER OF THE CHURCH
(For the Removal of Schism)

O God, who settest straight what has gone astray and gatherest together what is scattered, and keepest what Thou hast gathered together, we beseech Thee in Thy mercy to pour down on Christian peoples the grace of union with Thee, that, putting aside disunion and attaching themselves to the true shepherd of Thy Church, they may be able to render Thee due service. Through Christ our Lord. Amen.

⊗⊗⊗⊗⊗⊗⊗⊗⊗⊗⊗⊗

AUGUST 25
ST. LOUIS, KING OF FRANCE
Confessor and Patron of the Third Order

ING ST. LOUIS was born in the castle at Poissy near Paris on April 25, 1215. His devout mother, Blanche, was determined that he should be educated not only for the earthly kingdom he was to govern, but still more for the kingdom of heaven. She accustomed him to look upon all things in the light of faith, and thus laid the foundation for that humility in good fortune and endurance in misfortune which characterized the holy king.

Louis was crowned king when he was only twelve years old. His mother, however, was entrusted with the actual government of the kingdom during his minority. Meanwhile, Louis was being educated in all the duties of a Christian prince. Among his instructors there were several Franciscan friars, and later on the young king himself joined the Third Order of St. Francis.

Louis had governed his kingdom for several years in his own name, when he vowed, in the course of a serious illness, that if he would recover, he would make a crusade to the Holy Land, to wrest the holy places from the hands of the infidels. Upon regaining his health he at once carried out his vow. He took the fortress of Damietta from the Saracens, but was taken captive after his army had been weakened by an epidemic.

After he had borne the sufferings of a prisoner of the infidels for several months with holy serenity, the terms for his release were submitted to him; but there was attached to these terms an oath, that if he did not fulfill them, he would deny Christ and the Christian religion. Hie holy king replied: "Such blasphemous words shall never cross my lips." They threatened him with death. "Very well," said he, "you may kill my body, but you will never kill my soul." Filled with admiration at his steadfast courage, they finally released him without the objectionable condition. After securing many other terms favorable to the Christians, he was obliged to return to France, since his mother had died in the meantime.

In the government of his kingdom, Louis proved how profitable piety is in every respect. He promoted the welfare of the country and of his people in a remarkable manner. His life as a Christian and as a Christian father was so exemplary that he has been found worthy to be chosen as the patron and model of Tertiaries. The most important principle of his life was the observance of the laws of God under all circumstances. His biographer assures us that he never lost his baptismal innocence by mortal sin. He himself set such store by the grace of baptism that, in confidential letters, he took pleasure in signing himself "Louis of Poissy," because it was in the parish church there that he had been baptized.

Louis never tolerated cursing or sinful conversation either among the servants or among the courtiers; and never was he heard to utter an unkind or impatient word. He wished to avoid all unnecessary pomp and luxury at court, so that more help could be rendered to the poor, of whom he personally fed and served several hundred. His wardrobe was as simple as it could fittingly be, and at all times he wore the insignia of the Third Order under his outer garments. On special occasions he publicly wore the habit of the Tertiaries.

In order to curb sensuality he not only observed all the fasts of the

Church with unusual severity, but denied himself certain food for which he had a special craving. He was a most solicitous father to the eleven children with which God blessed his marriage. He himself prayed with them daily, examined them in the lessons they had learned, guided them in the performance of the works of Christian charity, and in his will bequeathed to them the most beautiful instructions.

He fostered special devotion to the sufferings of Christ; and it was a great consolation for him when he gained possession of the Crown of Thorns, for the preservation of which he had the magnificent Holy Chapel built in Paris. When serious complaints concerning the oppression of the Christians in the Holy Land reached his ears, he undertook a second crusade in 1270, but on the way he died of the plague, contracted while visiting his sick soldiers.

Amid exclamations of holy joy because he was going into the house of the Lord, he surrendered his soul to God on August twenty-fifth. St. Louis was canonized by Pope Boniface VIII in 1297. His feast is kept by all the branches of the Franciscan orders on August twenty-fifth. (Cf. *These Made Peace*, pp. 52-65.)

MORTAL SIN IS THE GREATEST EVIL

"Death rather than a mortal sin!" St. Louis frequently said these words when he recalled what his mother had told him. He was right, because mortal sin is worse than death. It is the greatest evil in the world because it means the loss of the greatest good, which is God Himself. He who commits a mortal sin, that is, violates one of God's commandments in an important matter with full knowledge and free consent, even if it be only in thought, hears God threaten him with His displeasure, and still he says: "I will not obey." He separates himself from God, falls from grace, and is changed from an object of the love of God, into an object of hatred: "The Highest hates sinners" (Eccli. 12,7). — Can we think of a greater evil than this?

Consider how King St. Louis actually carried out the great principle of his life in his conduct. He preferred to remain a prisoner of the Saracens, which included the loss of his kingdom and even his own life, rather than to take a blasphemous oath. No material loss can compare with the loss of God, whereas every temporal suffering is quite bearable if we remain in the grace of God; in fact, it becomes sweet if we bear it because we do not want to offend God. But to offend God in order to escape material suffering means to cast oneself into the greatest suffering. "Your apostasy shall rebuke you, and you shall know and see that it is an evil and bitter thing for you to have left the Lord, your God" (Jer. 2,19). — Therefore, say frequently: "Death rather than a mortal sin!"

Consider that St. Louis could not have been happy in the possession of his kingdom if he had been obliged to reclaim it by a blasphemous oath. Can a Christian enjoy temporal goods and honors if he must admit that his claim to them was bought at the price of mortal sin? Can he really accept them while he is confronted with the outlook that the next moment can cast him into eternal hell fire? No more than Damocles could enjoy the grand banquet when he saw over his head a drawn sword suspended by a hair. Surely it is better to die with St. Louis in a strange country among the plague-stricken, and to make the sacrifice of one's life in the practice of charity.

PRAYER OF THE CHURCH

O God, who didst transport St. Louis, Thy confessor, from an earthly kingdom into the bliss of the kingdom of heaven, we beseech Thee, grant us through his merits and intercession to be made associates of the King of Kings, Thy Son, Jesus Christ. Who livest and reignest forever and ever. Amen.

AUGUST 26
BLESSED TIMOTHY OF MONTECCHIO
Confessor, First Order

IMOTHY was born at Montecchio in the diocese of Aquila, Italy. From his earliest years he showed a decided tendency for spiritual things. To escape from the dangers of the world and to consecrate himself wholly to God, he entered the Order of Friars Minor at a very early age. Strict observance of the Franciscan rule was at that time being stressed with renewed fervor, and Timothy distinguished himself among his brethren by the extraordinary exactitude with which he applied himself to it. His outstanding virtues were humility, mortification, and patience, and he was favored by God with a high degree of the spirt of prayer.

After he had been ordained to the priesthood, he celebrated holy Mass with such reverence that one would have believed an angel was at the altar. It is recorded that almighty God favored him with special revelations during the sacrifice of the Mass. On one occasion he was offering holy

Mass to obtain for a novice the grace of perseverance in his vocation; at the elevation of the Sacred Host he received the assurance that his prayer had been heard. Another time, when he was offering the holy Sacrifice for a prominent person who was very ill, it was revealed to him that a longer life would be granted the person if she would give up the vanity of dress to which she was much inclined.

When Father Timothy attained his sixtieth year and had meanwhile given many proofs of holiness, he departed from this life in 1504 in the convent of the Friars Minor at Ocra. He was buried with special honors in the convent church there. Pope Pius IX approved the observance of his feast, which is kept by the Franciscans on August twenty-sixth, and by the Capuchins on September sixth.

ON DEVOTION AT HOLY MASS

1. Consider how important it is that we attend holy Mass with devotion. First of all, it is the wish of Holy Mother Church. In your catechism lesson on the precepts of the Church, you learned that on all Sundays and holydays of obligation we are obliged to assist at the holy sacrifice of the Mass with due attention, reverence, and devotion. But even setting aside the precept, the fuller blessing of the holy Sacrifice depends on the devotion with which we assist at it. How various were the effects of the sacrifice of the Cross on those who stood around as witnesses! The penitent thief received the promise of heaven; his obdurate companion died in despair next to the altar of the Cross. The sincere heathen centurion received the grace to believe in Christ; the Jewish chief priests, who were filled with hatred and envy, mocked Him. Many of the people who had come to the place of execution out of curiosity and in a spirit of indifference, left the place in the same spirit; but many others, who gave careful thought to all that happened there, returned home penitent and striking their breasts. So will the results be at the renewal of the sacrifice of the Cross, at holy Mass, according to the dispositions with which we attend it. — What may you expect from your attendance at Holy Mass?
2. Consider what constitutes devotion at holy Mass. We must direct the attention of our mind and heart to the holy action taking place there. It will be well for us to unite ourselves in a special way with the priest at the three principal parts of the Mass, the Offertory, the Consecration, and the Communion, offering the Sacrifice to our heavenly Father as an offering of praise of thanksgiving, of propitiation, and of petition, reverently adoring Him present on the altar at the Consecration, and receiving Him at least spiritually at Communion. Moreover, we should never omit to

offer ourselves to God, at each holy Mass, as Thomas a Kempis (4,8) suggests: "As I willingly offered Myself to God the Father for your sins with My hands stretched out upon the cross, and My Body naked, so that nothing remained in Me which was not completely turned into a sacrifice to appease the divine wrath; even so ought you willingly offer yourself to Me daily in the Mass, as intimately as you can, with all energies and affections, for a pure and holy oblation." — Would that you attended every holy Mass in that way!

3. Consider the great blessings that are granted to us when we devoutly attend the holy sacrifice of the Mass. We may not, indeed, be favored, like Blessed Timothy, with revelations concerning our fate or that of others — those are communications which God makes for special reasons, and in rare cases only — but we shall receive more salutary communications, namely, enlightenment, inspiration, and interior strength to offer our lives to God in the faithful fulfillment of our duties, and to strive more and more to practice virtue in imitation of the saints, so that we may one day join them in eternal bliss.

PRAYER OF THE CHURCH

O God, who dost gladden us by the annual celebration of the feast of Blessed Timothy, Thy confessor, graciously grant that we who celebrate his memory may also imitate his deeds. Through Christ our Lord. Amen.

***

AUGUST 27
BLESSED BERNARD OF OFFIDA
Confessor, First Order

ERNARD was the son of simple peasant folk. The family lived in the neighborhood of the little Italian town of Offida and were highly esteemed for their honesty and piety. There were seven children in the family, but Bernard proved to be a special joy to his mother, who often held him up as a model to the other children. The little lad, however, so loved his brothers and sisters that, if anyone of them had committed a fault, he would go and ask forgiveness for him and offer to take the punishment.

As he advanced in age his vocation to a higher life manifested itself quite distinctly. Everything attracted him to God. When he tended the cattle, he often took out a holy picture, which he constantly carried with him, posted it in some quiet spot, and then knelt down to pray before it. He would then command his flock not to stray from the pasture, and they obeyed his command. On Sundays Bernard would sometimes remain in church until evening without any food whatsoever. Although he was very useful to his father, still, the latter perceived that he was not destined for the world. He therefore suggested to his son to make choice of a convent that he would like to enter.

Bernard joyfully repaired to the convent of the Capuchins, where he was admitted as a lay brother. He lived in various convents of the order, but always in so simple and unobtrusive a way that nothing special is recorded of him before he was sixty years old. At this age he was sent to his native town, where he was charged with gathering the alms for the brethren, and at a later time, with the duties of porter. It was not long before it was observed that the simple brother was a real saint.

He always went on his way as though he were walking in the actual presence of God. Even for the smallest alms that was offered to him he never failed to express a heartfelt thank you. He never accepted anything for himself personally, and took care never to receive anything that was superfluous. For the temporal alms he received, he returned spiritual alms of far greater value. He was so often instrumental in conciliating persons who were at variance with each other that he was called "the angel of peace."

Once a man intended to tell him what he was suffering because of discord between his mother and his wife. But before he began, Bernard said to him: "Listen, your mother is a cross for your wife, and your mother and your wife together are a cross for you; bear it patiently!" These few words produced perfect peace in the soul of the man and gave him strength to carry his cross.

Sometimes Bernard was divinely enlightened to know the sad state of certain great sinners; he would then disclose to them the great danger to which their souls were exposed and in almost every case they were sincerely converted. Two bishops testified that Brother Bernard had done more good in their dioceses than prominent preachers and missionaries. But Bernard always held priests in high esteem. He would say to the faithful: "When you see priests, you should kiss the ground on which they walk, for it is they who administer the sacraments to us and thereby raise us to the state of grace; the salvation of our souls is in great measure dependent upon them."

He frequently recommended devotion to the Blessed Virgin by means of the holy rosary. "Believe me," he would say, "by means of the rosary Mary is in a special way the dispenser of graces."

When Brother Bernard was eighty years old, he was relieved of all duties. Still he continued to be active for the poor and his dear sick people. But he was no less solicitous to observe poverty. He could not bear to see anything go to waste. He would say: "Let us remember that whatever we do not need, Christ's poor do need."

He died when he was ninety years old, in the year 1694. His reputation for sanctity was confirmed by miracles; and Pope Pius VI beatified him. His feast is celebrated by the Franciscans on August twenty-sixth, and by the Capuchins on September sixth.

ON CHRISTIAN THRIFT

1. Consider that thrift as practiced by Blessed Bernard is truly a Christian virtue. This virtue of Christian thrift does not aim so much at using only a little and saving much, but rather, at providing that nothing superfluous is used and that nothing is wasted that can still be used. In this way Christian thrift protects us from wastefulness and intemperance, and places the true value on the gifts God has given us for our bodily support. Jesus Christ Himself gave us an example of this kind of thrift. Although He miraculously multiplied the few loaves so that thousands were fed, He nevertheless said to His disciples: "Gather up the fragments that remain, lest they be lost" (Jn. 6,12). — Are you as careful that nothing goes to waste?

2. Consider that it is not thrift but rather niggardliness and greed that prompts us to use things sparingly so that we may be able to keep on heaping up and storing away goods. Under the guise of thrift such a person fears to provide what is necessary for himself and those entrusted to him; he hesitates to eat enough at meals. The Holy Ghost says of such people, "There is none worse than he who envies himself. He who is evil to himself, to whom will he be good?" (Eccli. 14,5-6). The virtue of thrift avoids only superfluous expenses, and seeks to make provision that the necessary things of life may be at hand in the time of need. That is the way Joseph stored away supplies in Egypt during the seven years of plenty, so that when the lean years arrived, the necessities of life would be on hand. "Remember poverty in the time of abundance, and the necessities of poverty in the days of riches" (Eccli. 18,25).

3. Consider that the noblest sort of thrift is that which is mindful of others in their need, and avoids all superfluous expenses in order to support Christ's poor. That is the way Blessed Bernard practiced thrift and that is the way exemplary Christians also practice it. A woman criticized her maid for throwing away a burning match because it could have been used

to light another light, but almost in the same breath she gave an alms to a poor cripple who came to her door begging. A farmer reproved his hired man for leaving the horses' harness out in the rain overnight, but he was just then hitching up to bring a wagon load of wood to some poor people who had been made homeless by fire. Such thrift joined to charity will serve us in good stead in the great time of need which will befall each and every one of us — that is, when the last day of our life arrives and we appear before the judgment seat of God.

PRAYER OF THE CHURCH

O God, who didst mercifully grant to Blessed Bernard the disposition carefully to provide for the wants of the poor and the needy, grant that we may follow his example and thereby deserve to be saved on the last day. Through Christ our Lord. Amen.

AUGUST 28
ST. JUNIPER SERRA
Confessor, First Order

ORN at Petra on the Spanish island of Mallorca on November 24, 1713, Juniper Serra entered the Franciscan Order at the age of sixteen and was ordained a priest in 1738. He received the doctorate in theology even before his ordination. For eleven years he taught philosophy in the Lullian University at Palma.

He won great fame as a pulpit orator. As a teacher he was equally successful. The pathway to fame and honor was clearly open to him, but he willingly turned his back on all this, and longed to be a missionary to the Indians of the New World. His superiors yielded to his request and allowed him to join a band of missionaries who were getting ready to go to Mexico. It was on New Year's Day, 1750, that he entered the portals of the College of San Fernando in Mexico City.

From 1750 to 1758, in the wild and isolated Sierra Gorda near Querétaro, Mexico, he taught the fierce Indian worshippers of the sun the way of civilization together with the truth and the life of the Faith. For the next ten years he criss-crossed Mexico for Christ, preaching missions in rowdy seaports, crude mining camps, and cultured cities, recalling innumerable sinners to repentance.

At the age of fifty-six, after a year in the peninsula of Lower California where he founded one new mission, Father Serra began his greatest work, founding the first nine missions along the coast of the state of California. There he confirmed nearly 6,000 Indian converts. "As long as life lasts," he said on one occasion, "I will do all I can to propagate our holy Faith." Combining a deep spirituality and joy in the service of God with a down-to-earth practicality, he laid the foundations of California's present-day agriculture and stock-raising. The state's great coastal cities grew out of the missions he established. His zeal and vision caused him to urge the explorations by sea to Alaska, and overland to New Mexico. In thirty-five years as a missionary, he walked ten thousand miles despite an ulcerated leg. His was a life-long martyrdom of labor, loneliness, and sacrifice.

To become a canonized saint, the candidate must have practiced the three divine virtues and the four cardinal virtues in an heroic degree. Father Serra's faith is seen in his apostolic life; his hope in his spirit of piety; and his charity in both. His prudence is discernible especially in the wise measures he adopted on behalf of the Indians. These Indians often made his labors difficult because of their superstitious ideas. For instance, just as he raised his hands to pour the water over the first child offered for baptism, the fearful parents snatched away their babe and fled. The faithful discharge of his duties despite disappointments, opposition, and bodily sufferings gave evidence of his fortitude. He strenuously defended the Indians and the rights of the Church throughout his hard mission life. His temperance manifested itself in his life of mortification. Already on his journey to America he manifested unusual heroism. The voyage lasted more than ninety days, during which the travelers suffered from want of water. He took the scarcity of water as a training for the future, and naively remarked when he was asked whether he was not suffering from thirst: "Not especially, since I have found the secret of not feeling thirsty, which is, to eat little and talk less, so as not to waste the saliva." Another proof of his heroic virtue is found in his refusal to avail himself of the transportation provided from Vera Cruz to Mexico City. He and a companion started on that tramp of a hundred leagues, relying solely upon Providence and the goodness of the people whom they would meet.

Father Serra died at Mission San Carlos, also called Carmel, on August 28, 1784, and was buried in the mission church. In 1934 preparations began to present him as a candidate for sainthood, and the legal proceedings held in California were forwarded in 1950 to Rome, where his cause of beatification is now pending.[2] (Cf. *King, Mission to Paradise.*)

ON THE EFFECTS OF PENANCE

1. The genuine spirit of penance leads us to sanctity. This we perceive in all holy penitents. It was this spirit of penance also that played such an important role in the sanctification of Father Juniper Serra. All the penances he performed led him to greater perfection. Because he was motivated by sincere intentions, he excelled not only in the spirit of penance but also in "love, joy, peace, patience, mildness, meekness, fidelity, temperance, chastity" (Gal. 5,22). — Do these virtues appear in your conduct as evidence of the genuine spirit of penance you possess?
2. The true spirit of penance rejoices in tribulations. Father Juniper had much to contend with in his dealings with the Indians as well as with the Spanish governors in California. But he had bargained for hardships, had even prepared himself in advance so that he might accept those hardships in the true spirit; so he was not heard to complain when they actually came his way. By cheerfully accepting the involuntary ones, he gave proof that the voluntary ones were not prompted by self-deception. — Do you belong to the class of Christians who stubbornly follow their own inclinations, but who are found wanting in the time of sorrow and tribulations?
3. The sincere spirit of penance effects much good for others. Christ is "the propitiation for our sins" (1 Jn. 4,10). He who unites himself with Christ in a true spirit of penance can achieve much good in the work of the conversion of sinners. Father Serra's great purpose in life was the conversion of the Indians, among whom he chose to live and labor, whose sad lot had inspired him already during his novitiate to offer himself for this arduous task. The history of California testifies to the success he achieved. — You can share in this missionary activity if you offer your slight acts of mortification and of penance for the conversion of sinners.

PRAYER OF THE CHURCH

O God, who despisest no one, no matter how grievously he may have sinned, but art moved to mercy by penance; graciously look upon the

---

[2] Editor's note: Subsequent to the original publication of this work, Junipero Sera was beatified by Pope John Paul II on 25 September 1988, and canonized by Pope Francis on 23 September 2015.

prayers of our lowliness and enlighten our hearts so that we may observe Thy commandments. Through Christ our Lord. Amen.

AUGUST 29
BLESSED GABRIEL MARY
Confessor, First Order

 THIS blessed man belongs to the most outstanding clients of our Lady in the Franciscan Order. He was a native of France. As a result of a sermon on the Immaculate Conception, which had been delivered by a member of the Franciscan Order, he himself became a Franciscan. Due to his great learning and virtues, he was frequently entrusted with the highest offices in the order.

His fame, however, rests on his founding of the Order of the Annunciation, which venerates St. Jane of Valois as its mother. The Blessed Mother of God commissioned him to undertake its establishment. He became the protector and counselor of the order, composed its rules and constitutions, secured many members for it, and was instrumental in establishing ten convents. Later he was given the title of general of the entire order of the Virgin Mary.

Pope Leo X was so impressed by his devotion to our Lady that he changed his name from Father Gilbert Nicolas to Father Gabriel Mary of the Annunciation, or of Ave Maria. Father Gabriel Mary always closed his letters with the words, "Your servant in Mary." The theme of his sermons was always some verse from the Magnificat or from the Hail Mary. He bound himself by vow never to say or do anything which might not be pleasing to his beloved heavenly Queen.

While he was guardian in Paris, a professor of theology ventured to attack the mystery of the Immaculate Conception of the Blessed Virgin Mary in his presence. Father Gabriel was seized with holy anger. He defended this prerogative of Our Lady with such eloquence that the professor declared himself vanquished.

Father Gabriel Mary died on August 27, 1532, following an academic event in which he had proposed ten questions concerning the prerogatives of Mary and had given his explanation of them. He closed by saying: "Today I shall see the glorious Mother of God." Then he began to recite the Vespers of the Blessed Virgin. When he reached the last verse of the Magnificat, he quietly passed away. Pope Innocent granted a plenary indulgence to those who would visit the convent church in Bourges "on the feast of St. Gilbert." A petition has been sent to the Holy See to permit his veneration in the entire Franciscan Order, and the cause of his formal beatification is now pending in Rome. (Cf. *Forum*, 1955, pp. 71-75, 102-106, 123.)

LESSONS TO BE GLEANED FROM THE IMMACULATE CONCEPTION

1. The Immaculate Virgin is an object lesson of serious truths. The Immaculate Conception teaches us that we are tainted, whereas Mary alone is stainless. Hence, we are inclined to evil and must be cautious regarding ourselves and indulgent towards others. Another lesson to be learned is that sin is no trifle; that God chose a poor woman for His Mother, but not one who was stained by sin. — Let these truths take deep root in your heart.

2. The Immaculate Conception teaches us comforting truths. She points out to us the power of God's grace, which made Mary "the beautiful one." This grace of God will always be sufficient; we should, therefore, despair of no one's salvation. Another comforting truth is this, that purity brings joy, for the Immaculate Virgin is also the Virgin most joyful, and it is she who chanted the Magnificat. — Keep these comforting truths always in mind.

3. The Immaculate Virgin teaches us also encouraging truths. Because she is the immaculate one, she is also nearest to the throne of God. She wants us to understand that God is nigh to those who are pure and that they may ask any grace from Him. Besides this she is herself the guardian of the pure, and we never place our trust in her in vain. — Entrust your purity to the Immaculate Virgin and trust in her protection.

PRAYER OF THE CHURCH

Almighty and eternal God, who didst prepare a worthy dwelling place for the Holy Spirit in the heart of the Blessed Virgin Mary, graciously grant, that we who devoutly honor this most pure heart, may live according to the desires of Thine own heart. Through Christ our Lord. Amen.

AUGUST 30
BLESSED DAVANZATO OF POGGIBONZI
Confessor, Third Order

AVANZATO was a young student preparing for the priesthood when Blessed Luchesio was received in the Third Order at Poggibonzi. It was not long afterwards that Davanzato, who associated much with the devout Luchesio, also received the holy habit, in which he shone for many years as a special glory of the order.

Shortly after his ordination the little parish at Casciano in the diocese of Florence was entrusted to his care, and there he ministered to souls for seventy years, until his death. There he labored with remarkable success, more by his prayers than by his words, and above all by the example of a holy life. In the words of our Lord Jesus Christ, he could say of the souls entrusted to him: "For them do I sanctify myself" (Jn. 17,19).

Davanzato lived in a small house near his church, and never left it except when his priestly duties required it. Like the holy hermits, he loved to be alone with God. His life was very strict. Often he sent the meager meal, which a devout young man prepared for him, to a sick person, or he gave it to some poor person at the door, while he contented himself with bread and water. All the provisions in the house were for the use of those who were suffering want. Sometimes it happened that a few more needy persons presented themselves to him after he had disposed of everything. Nevertheless he would send them to the cupboard, confident that they would find something there, and they would, indeed, find a fresh supply. When his attendant expressed his astonishment, the holy pastor would say: "Why are you astonished? Our Lord Himself said, 'Give and it shall be given to you' " (Lk. 6, 28).

On a certain feastday, several priests came to Casciano for the celebration, and the pastor wished to entertain them hospitably. His servant told him that there was no wine in the cellar. The pastor told him to go to a nearby spring with a jar and fill it with fresh water; and when he poured it into the glasses afterwards it was exquisite wine.

Davanzato taught his young attendant Latin, so they could recite the Divine Office together. This spiritual exercise he always performed in church kneeling before the altar. Sometimes both he and his servant could hear heavenly melodies during this time, as if the angels themselves were joining in. Toward the close of his life this was perceived in an increased measure.

The holy pastor died in his ninety-fifth year, surrounded by his weeping parishioners. In order to protect his body from the great throngs that pressed around, it was placed in a vault. When the vault was opened on the next day, a beautiful lily had grown from the mouth of the deceased. Many miracles continued to occur, for which reason the day of his death is kept as a feastday and the title of Blessed is conferred on him in popular devotion, but this cult has not yet been officially confirmed by the Holy See. (Cf. *These Made Peace,* pp. 16-18.)

ON HOSPITALITY

1. Although Blessed Davanzato loved seclusion and led a most mortified life, nevertheless he was hospitable to others. This disposition of the noble priest was so pleasing to almighty God that He wrought a miracle to assist him in his hospitality. Christian hospitality is really a work of charity towards our neighbor, because we aim to honor our guest and make him joyful. God Himself practices this hospitality daily by offering us, who are in reality His guests on earth, so many favors that contribute toward our convenience in life. He who practices Christian hospitality towards his fellowmen imitates this charity of God. Christ rebuked Simon the Pharisee (Lk. 7,14), for having failed in his attention toward his guest. — How do you act in this regard?
2. Consider that hospitality does not mean often inviting guests and indulging in gay festivity. That would be yielding to sensuality. Dives did that, and the rule of the Third Order (Ch. 2,2) very decidedly warns Tertiaries against it. Christian hospitality consists rather in kindness and generosity extended towards guests in accordance with Christian charity or custom; it takes greater pleasure in rendering service than in being served. According to the example of Blessed Davanzato and the teaching of our Saviour, it prefers to invite persons who cannot return the invitation. "When you make a dinner or a supper, call not your friends, nor your brethren, nor your kinsmen, nor your neighbors, lest perhaps they invite you again, and a recompense be made to you. But when you make a feast, call the poor, the maimed, the lame, and the blind" (Lk. 14,12-13). Our Saviour does not mean that we should never invite our friends, but that it should not be done with the intention of being invited in return; and that in practicing this virtue we do not forget the poor, since that is the noblest form of hospitality. — Have you been mindful of the poor on such occasions? Lazarus would have been satisfied with the crumbs that fell from the table of Dives, "but no one did give him" (Lk. 16,21).
3. Consider the reward that has been promised to Christian hospitality.

After urging us to invite the poor, our Lord adds the words: "And you shall be blessed, because they have not wherewith to make you recompense, for recompense shall be made to you at the resurrection of the just" (Lk. 14,14). One of those present, when he thought of this recompense, called out: "Blessed is he who shall eat bread in the kingdom of God!" There the Lord will reward all the hospitality that has been rendered from truly Christian motives; He "shall make them drink of the torrent of His pleasure" (Ps. 35,9).

PRAYER OF THE CHURCH
(Postcommunion No. 29 under "Various Prayers")

May the grace of the Holy Ghost, we beseech Thee, O Lord, enlighten our hearts, and refresh them abundantly with the sweetness of perfect charity. Through Christ our Lord. Amen.

AUGUST 31
THE SERVANT OF GOD MARTIN OF VALENCIA
Confessor, First Order

ATHER MARTIN of Valencia came not from the large Spanish city of that name, but from a little village in the diocese of Leon. There he was born in 1470. Martin manifested a decided attachment for St. Francis and his order from his youth. He begged for the habit of the Franciscans shortly after he had entered upon his studies. In the novitiate he read the book of Father Bartholomew of Pisa on the similarity between the life of St. Francis and that of our Lord. This stimulated in him a desire to conform his life with that of Christ in imitation of St. Francis. He longed especially to devote himself to the salvation of souls. As soon as he was ordained a priest, he applied himself with unusual zeal to this work and had most blessed results.

On one of his journeys he was overpowered by robbers, who beat him nearly to death; but he prayed for his torturers. He was also subjected to many interior trials. A spirit of dryness and many kinds of temptations tortured him for years, and neither prayer nor rigorous mortification afforded him any relief. But they helped him bear the trial by which almighty God was preparing him to do great things for Him. On one occasion Father Martin read in Psalm 58: "Visit all the nations, O Lord, the God of Hosts!" and then found this passage twice: "They shall return at evening" (Ps. 58,7-15). He was then given the comforting assurance that in the evening of his life, very many nations would return to God through him. He did not have to wait long for its fulfillment.

In the year 1524 Emperor Charles V of Spain petitioned the superiors of the Franciscans for missionaries for the recently conquered province of New Spain or Mexico. Twelve apostolic men were chosen for the mission, ten priests and two lay brothers. Father Martin, who was then almost fifty-five years old, was placed in charge. They arrived safely in Mexico and then, according to the instructions given them, they devoted themselves to the conversion of the Indians. Their work was crowned with amazing success. The terrible human sacrifices ceased, numerous idols were demolished, their temples destroyed. In their places, Christian churches were built, wayside crosses were erected, Christian schools and convents were founded.

Father Martin, who was the guiding spirit of this great work, received the name of Apostle of the Indians. In the year 1531 he could report to his superiors in the order: "Each one of the twelve of us who were sent here, has baptized no less than a hundred thousand Indians. They were docile to our instructions, they receive the sacraments with great devotion, and send their children to our schools. These children give promise to our highest hopes, are very intelligent, and love and venerate the Mother of God." What the Church was losing during those very years through Martin Luther in Germany, Father Martin of Valencia was regaining for her in the New World.

Exhausted by hardships and the rigorous mortification he constantly practiced, he died on one of his journeys in the year 1534, in the arms of an associate. God glorified him by many miracles.

ON GOD'S SOLICITUDE FOR HIS CHURCH

1. See how God watches over His Church. When one apostle falls away, another one is called into the fold. If thousands apostatize in one country, hundreds of thousands join the Church in another country. It is immaterial to God where they come from, for He is the Lord of the world and all the ends of the earth shall adore Him. "From the rising of the sun even to the going down, My name is great among the Gentiles, and in every place there is offered to My name a clean oblation" (Mal. 1,11). Admire and adore the loving providence of God, who is constantly dispensing graces to the human race through His Church, and to whom the most distant nations are as close as those that have belonged to the Church for many centuries.

Consider how an entire race, and even whole nations, can lose the blessings and the graces of Christ's Church if they do not remain loyal amid the temptations and persecutions of any period. Large countries in Asia and Africa once flourished under the blessing of the Christian Church and Christian civilization. They apostatized, and the result was that they were plunged into barbarism, while Christianity and good morals flourished in Europe. "Justice exalts a nation, but sin makes nations miserable" (Prov. 14,34). Have we not reason to fear that if godlessness and contempt for the Christian Church continue to increase in our midst, God almighty will gradually move the light farther away, deprive us of the blessings of the Church, and give it to a new world? Let us endeavor wherever and in whatever manner we can to uphold the fear of God and a life governed by the principles of the Church, and let us often pray that God's wrath may not leave the nations of the West to their own wickedness.

Consider that God deals with nations as well as with individuals according to their correspondence with the grace He gives them. If you are not faithful in using the graces God gives you, if you do not profit by the efforts made by zealous priests, God will transfer these graces to someone else, and will give him the crown that was destined to be yours in eternity. "One shall be taken, and one shall be left" (Mt. 24,40). — Be diligent then in using the graces which our Lord places at your disposal, remain faithful in His service, and "hold fast that which you have, that no man may take your crown" (Apoc. 3,11).

PRAYER OF THE CHURCH
(Fourteenth Sunday after Pentecost)

Keep Thy Church, we beseech Thee, O Lord, in perpetual mercy, and because without Thee the weakness of man is wont to fall, save him by Thine aid from all things hurtful, and guide him to all things profitable unto salvation. Through Christ our Lord. Amen.

SEPTEMBER

SEPTEMBER 1
BLESSED JOHN OF PERUGIA AND PETER OF SASSOFERRATO
Martyrs, First Order

HE two Friars Minor, John of Perugia, a priest, and Peter of Sassoferrato, a lay brother, were sent to Spain with a large number of other friars by St. Francis himself. There they were assigned to the kingdom of Aragon, where they built a small convent in the little town of Teruel, and reaped much fruit by their holy lives, their prayers, and their sermons on penance.

Their longing for the conversion of the infidels and the hope of obtaining the palm of martyrdom urged Friars John and Peter to go to the larger city of Valencia, which was governed at that time by the Moorish king Azotus. The friars began to preach in public that Jesus Christ is the true Son of God and that only through Him can we be saved. Azotus was a bitter enemy of the Christians. Hearing of the activities of the friars, he had them seized and cast into prison. He used every possible means to force them to apostatize. But when promises and threats alike failed to shake their constancy, he condemned them to be beheaded. The friars thanked the king, praying fervently to God to enlighten their persecutor and in His mercy to grant him the grace of conversion to the true Faith. Then they were beheaded. This occurred in the year 1231.

A few years later James I, the Catholic king of Aragon, made war on Valencia. His army defeated the army of Azotus, who by this ill fortune and by the grace which the holy martyrs had won for him from God, recognized Mohammed as a false prophet, and Christ as the Saviour of the world. King James rejoiced exceedingly when Azotus asked to be baptized. After his baptism Azotus offered the Friars Minor his former palace for a convent. "When I was still an infidel," he told them, "I caused your brethren to be executed at Teruel. I sincerely regret this crime and desire to make reparation for it. Accept my palace, in which the blood of many holy martyrs has been shed, and convert it into a convent." The palace was remodeled into a convent and, next to it, a church was erected in

605

honor of the two martyrs. Pope Clement XI approved the public
veneration which was paid to them. The feast of Blessed John and Peter
is observed by the Franciscans and Conventuals on September first, and
by the Capuchins on the third.

ON PRAYING FOR ONE'S ENEMIES

1. Consider the marvelous results of prayer said for one's enemies. When
Christ was rejected by His nation and nailed to a cross, He prayed for His
enemies, and the world became Christian. When St. Stephen, whom the
Jews stoned and over whose death Saul gloried, prayed for his enemies,
Saul was converted into Paul, the great Apostle of the Gentiles. The
blessed martyrs John and Peter prayed for the Moorish king who had
them beheaded, and ere long this king became a Christian and changed his
palace into a convent for the Friars Minor. "This is the Lord's doing; and
it is wonderful in our eyes" (Ps. 117,23). Judging from the miracles
wrought by our heavenly Father, we learn how agreeable to Him is such
prayer for our enemies. — Should we not pray in like manner?
2. Consider that Christ imposes it on us as a duty to pray for our enemies.
"Pray for them who persecute and calumniate you" (Mt. 5,44). "Bless them
who curse you, and pray for them who calumniate you" (Lk. 6,28).
Universal charity requires that we wish everyone well and that we pray
for all in common, as our Lord Himself teaches us in the Our Father. And
we are not permitted to exclude anyone from our prayers, not even our
bitterest enemy. No matter how aggrieved we are over the evil done us,
or how much we are irritated by continual malice, we may not exclude
our enemy from our prayers; indeed, his very blindness may be all the
more reason to say extra prayers for him. That is what Blessed John and
Peter did, and the early Christians acted in like manner. "We are reviled,
and we bless, we are persecuted, and we suffer it" (1 Cor. 4,12). — Do you
follow these examples?
3. Consider that we ourselves derive great benefit from prayer offered up
for our enemy. God rewards such prayer. When St. Elizabeth was one day
praying for someone who had offended her, our Lord said to her: "Because
of this prayer, all your sins will be forgiven." Moreover, as a result of your
prayer, your enemy will acknowledge his injustice much sooner than if
you retaliate. The sermons of Blessed John and Peter did not effect the
conversion of King Azotus, but their prayers made him a Christian and a
friend of the friars. Finally, such prayer will best help you to subdue the
bitterness you experience. It will procure for you strength and patience
amid all the adversities of life, so that, like Blessed John and Peter, you

may obtain the crown.

PRAYER OF THE CHURCH

We beseech Thee, O almighty God, grant strength to our weakness, that as we rejoice in the glorious triumph of Thy holy martyrs John and Peter, we may also without tiring imitate their constancy. Through Christ our Lord. Amen.

SEPTEMBER 2
BLESSED JOHN FRANCIS BURTE, APOLLINARIS MOREL, AND SEVERIN GIRAULT
Martyrs, First and Third Orders

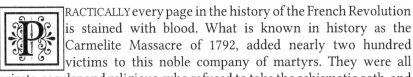 RACTICALLY every page in the history of the French Revolution is stained with blood. What is known in history as the Carmelite Massacre of 1792, added nearly two hundred victims to this noble company of martyrs. They were all priests, secular and religious, who refused to take the schismatic oath, and had been imprisoned in the church attached to the Carmelite monastery in Paris. Among these priests were a Conventual, a Capuchin, and a member of the Third Order Regular.

John Francis Burte was born in the town of Rambervillers in Lorraine. At the age of sixteen he joined the Franciscans at Nancy and there he also pronounced his solemn vows. In due time he was ordained a priest and for some time taught theology to the younger members of the order. He was at one time also superior of his convent.

After Pope Clement XIV, formerly a Conventual friar, had ordered the merging of the province of the Franciscans, to which John Francis belonged, with the Conventuals, Father John Francis was placed in charge of the large convent in Paris and encouraged his brethren to practice strict observance of the rule. His zeal for souls was outstanding, and he zealously guarded the rights of the Church in this troubled period of history.

When the French Revolution broke out, he was reported for permitting his priests to exercise their functions after they refused to take the infamous oath required by the government, and which was a virtual denial of their Faith. He was arrested and held captive with other priests in the convent of the Carmelites. His constancy in refusing to take the sacrilegious oath won for him a cruel martyrdom on September 2, 1792.

Apollinaris of Posat, who was John James Morel before his entrance into religion, was born near Fribourg in Switzerland in 1739, and received his education from the Jesuits. In 1762 he joined the Capuchins in Zug and before long became a prominent preacher, a much-sought confessor, and an eminent instructor of the young clerics of the order. He impressed on their minds the truth that piety and learning are the two eyes of a priest; and humility was a dominating virtue in his life.

In 1788 he was to be sent to the East as a missionary, and so he paused at Paris to study Oriental languages in preparation for his new appointment. But the French Revolution broke out while he was there, and because he steadfastly refused to take the oath of allegiance, he, too, was imprisoned in the Carmelite convent and suffered a cruel martyrdom on September 2, 1792.

The priest of the Third Order Regular was Blessed Severin, formerly George Girault, whose undaunted courage merited the grace to be numbered among these martyrs of Christ. He was born at Rouen in Normandy, and early in life joined the Third Order Regular of St. Francis. Because of his eminent mental gifts he was chosen a superior of his order. In the exercise of his priestly duties he displayed marked zeal for souls, and as chaplain of the convent of St. Elizabeth in Paris he was a prudent director in the ways of religious perfection.

He was also summoned to take the civil oath, and upon his refusal to do this he was seized and confined in the Carmelite convent where so many other confessors of Christ were being detained. On September second, while he was saying his Office in the convent garden, the raving assassins made him the first victim of their cruel slaughter.

These three members of the Franciscan Order, together with one hundred and eighty-two other servants of God who suffered martyrdom at this time, were solemnly beatified by Pope Pius XI, and the Franciscan Order was granted permission to celebrate their feast annually with an Office and special Mass. The Franciscans observe the feast of all three of the martyrs on September second, the Conventuals that of Blessed John Francis on the same day, the Capuchins that of Blessed Apollinaris on the same day, and the Third Order Regular that of Blessed Severin on the third.

ON THE FRANCISCAN SPIRIT

1. The Franciscan spirit is a spirit of piety. For this reason St. Francis says in his rule that "those who are not learned, should not strive to become

learned." Francis was not opposed to learning; he did, however, want to impress it on his brethren that they should guard against false learning, and subordinate learning and study to virtue and piety. The martyrs we are considering today were learned men, yet it was virtue and piety that taught them true wisdom. They were imbued with the true Franciscan spirit. — Go and do likewise!

2. The Franciscan spirit is also a spirit of learning. Hence St. Francis wrote to St. Anthony of Padua: "I am pleased that you are teaching the brethren sacred theology." And when he was asked whether learned men should be received into the order, he replied: "That is very pleasing to me." True knowledge proceeds from the Eternal Wisdom and also leads back to it. — Strive to acquire true learning.

3. The Franciscan spirit is a combination of piety and learning. That is why St. Francis wrote to St. Anthony saying: "The spirit of piety and of prayer should not be extinguished" by study. The most learned men of the order have ever combined learning and piety. Blessed John Francis and his companions did that and taught their brethren to do likewise. — If your vocation requires it, do your part in acquiring knowledge, but let your piety be the main object of your solicitude.

PRAYER OF THE CHURCH

We beseech Thee, O Lord, enable us with filial piety always to love Thy Church, in the defense of whose rights Thy blessed martyrs John Francis, Apollinaris, and Severin suffered a cruel death. Through Christ our Lord. Amen.

※※※※※※※※※※※※※

SEPTEMBER 3
ST. PIUS X
Confessor, Third Order

IT is the way of almighty God to bring honor to those who are mean in their own eyes. That has been demonstrated in the life of Joseph Sarto, later Pope Pius X. He was born in 1835 in the little Venetian village of Riese, where his parents, who were unimportant but devout people, reared a family of ten children during a period of great need.

The clergy of the parish interested themselves in Joseph, the well-behaved leader of the Mass servers, and assisted him in securing an education. In the year 1858, when he was twenty-four years old, he received holy orders. For nine years he was chaplain in Tombolo. His superior wrote of him: "I am convinced that some day he will wear the mitre, and then — who knows?" Chaplain Sarto took the great Franciscan St. Leonard of Port Maurice as his model in life and in the pulpit. At four in the morning he was already kneeling before the tabernacle.

For nine years he was pastor in Salzano. It was during this period that he joined the Third Order of St. Francis and established two fraternities of Tertiaries. Henceforth he strove in his words and in his writings, especially by Franciscan simplicity and frugal standards of life, to emulate the ideals of the seraphic saint.

For another space of nine years he was vicar general, canon, and regent of the seminary of the diocese of Treviso. "He will not die in Treviso," was significantly said of him at that time.

He was bishop of Mantua for nine years. This made no change in his habits of life; he would not tolerate any festive receptions. He devoted himself with unflinching zeal to the ever important apostolate of the press, the pulpit of modern times. At the same time, the poor were his favorites.

As patriarch of Venice he wore the purple of the cardinalate for another period of nine years, always remaining a faithful son of the poor St. Francis.

The death of Pope Leo XIII in 1903 brought him to Rome for the papal election. Who would be the new pope? Cardinal Sarto answered: "Leo XIII, who enlightened the world by his wisdom, will be succeeded by a pope who will impress the world by the saintliness of his life." Without suspecting it, he gave a description of himself.

After he had been elected pope he announced his program to be: To renew all things in Christ. He did much for religious revival, especially by promoting early and daily Communion, by enacting measures for the sanctification of the clergy, by encouraging the Third Order, and last, but not least, by his own holy life.

A great heart broke when the catastrophe of the World War befell us. "I wish to suffer," he said in his illness, "I wish to die for the soldiers on the battlefield." On August 20, 1914, Pius X died peacefully at the age of seventy-nine. His will was genuinely Franciscan: "I was born poor, I have lived poor, and I wish to die poor."

Many miracles occurred at his tomb, and the process of his beatification was introduced in 1923, and he was beatified in 1951 and canonized in 1954. The feast of St. Pius X is observed by the three branches of the First Order of St. Francis on September third. (Cf. *Forum*, 1952, pp. 67-70.)

THE CATHOLIC PRESS

1. We must support the Catholic press. It was not without reason that St. Pius X again and again, no matter what position he was holding, exerted his influence in behalf of the Catholic press. The Catholic press deserves this support when we reflect on the battles it has waged for the Catholic cause in religious persecution, in the struggles concerning the schools, and on numerous other occasions. — You should be grateful, and manifest your gratitude in a practical way.

2. Without the Catholic press we shall perish. That is why St. Pius X showed such zeal for it. "With the tongues of a thousand Goliaths the evil press utters calumnies against everything that is sacred to us; with the tongues of a thousand Davids, therefore, the good press must defend our sanctuary," said Cardinal Faulhaber. But it can do so only if we stand firmly and solidly behind the Catholic press. A rural mail carrier once remarked: "Our pastor would wring his hands if he knew how many filthy newspapers and other printed material we are constantly obliged to deliver to the homes of the people!" — How do matters stand with you in this regard?

3. We must show our enthusiasm for the Catholic press. Pius X said: "In vain will you build churches and convents, yes, all your Catholic projects will be useless, if you neglect to take advantage of the weapon of the Catholic press." — Do not be indifferent in this ever important matter! Promote and participate in the apostolate of the press!

PRAYER OF THE CHURCH

O God, who dost point out to the erring the light of truth so that they may return to the paths of justice, grant to all who profess the Catholic Faith, that they may despise whatever is contrary to this cause, and aspire to that which is agreeable to it. Through Christ our Lord. Amen.

SEPTEMBER 4
ST. ROSE OF VITERBO
Virgin, Third Order

LMIGHTY God did marvelous things in the soul of St. Rose. It appears that her parents gave her that name by divine inspiration, for it was symbolic of her entire career. As long as she lived, she bloomed like a sweet-scented rose in the garden of the Church, and in full bloom was she transplanted to Paradise. Before she was able to speak, Rose attempted to pronounce the sweet names of Jesus and Mary; and as soon as she had learned to walk, she asked to be taken to church and to other retired and quiet places to pray. When religious discourses were given, she would listen with the greatest attention.

When Rose was only three years old, God showed how pleased He was with her in a most wonderful way. One of her maternal aunts died. The family were standing around the bier weeping aloud. Deeply moved by the sorrow of her relatives, little Rose went to the coffin, raised her eyes to heaven, and prayed silently. Then she placed her little hand on the body of her deceased aunt and called her by name. The dead woman immediately opened her eyes and reached out to embrace her little niece, who had raised her to life again.

The child entertained a great compassion for the poor; she always tried to save some of her food to give it to the poor. One day when she left the house with some bread in her apron, she met her father, who asked her in curt fashion what she was carrying off now. The affrighted child opened her apron and fragrant roses were found in it.

When she was seven years old, Rose retired to a little cell in her father's house. There she spent almost all her time in contemplation and in practicing rigorous penance. She prayed much for the conversion of sinners. Meanwhile our dear Lord was preparing her for an extraordinary mission.

Rose was not yet ten years old when the Blessed Mother of God instructed her to join the Third Order of St. Francis. Shortly after, our Lord appeared to her on the Cross, wearing the crown of thorns on His head and bleeding profusely from all His wounds. Rose, aghast at the sight, called out: "O my Lord, who has reduced Thee to this state?" Our Lord replied: "My love, my deep love for men has done this." "But," asked Rose, "who has so pierced and torn Thee?" "The sins of men have done it," was our Lord's answer. "Sin, sin!" cried the saint, and she scourged herself to make atonement for the sins of the world.

By divine inspiration, Rose then took a cross in her hand and went up and down the streets and public squares of her city telling the people of the terrible tortures our Lord suffered and of the heinousness of sin. Every now and then she would emerge from her solitude to entreat the people to do penance.

The town of Viterbo, which belonged to the Papal States, had revolted against the authority of the pope. Disregard for religion and moral degradation were the order of the day. But the sermons of this little missionary had marvelous results. The people came in crowds to hear her. The stone on which she stood was seen to rise in the air, and she was sustained there by a miracle while burning words issued from her lips. The greater part of the citizenry had already resolved to do penance and to return to the legitimate papal allegiance when Rose and her parents were expelled by the civil authorities.

The result was that she now had a wider field of activity. At Soriano and later at Vitorchiano, her preaching had the same blessed results. In the latter place, a sorceress had done much harm among the inhabitants. Fearing that after her departure this woman would undo the good effected there, Rose was desirous of her conversion. Her initial efforts failed. Then our saint had an immense pile of wood prepared in the public square; fire was set to it, and Rose stepped into the fire and mounted to the top of the pile. She remained untouched for three hours in the midst of the flames, singing the praises of God. The sorceress now cast herself at Rose's feet and was sincerely converted.

Meanwhile the rightful authority of the pope had been re-established in Viterbo, and Rose could return. She was now fifteen years old and anxious to enter the convent of the Poor Clares. As she had no dowry, she could not be admitted. "Well," said Rose, "you will not receive me while I am alive, but you will receive me after I am dead." She and several companions repaired to a secluded dwelling, where they intended to live as a community. The ecclesiastical authorities, however, did not approve of the plan, and Rose returned home. She died two years later, filled with the joyous desire of being united with her God.

Two and a half years after her death she appeared three times to Pope Alexander IV, who was in Viterbo at the time, told him to have her body removed to the convent of the Poor Clares. When this was done, her body was found incorrupt; and it has remained in that condition to this day. Miracles are constantly occurring at her tomb. Pope Callistus III canonized her in 1457.

ON THE OPERATIONS OF GOD IN MEN

1. Consider the marvelous operations of God in St. Rose. Entire cities that had fallen away from God and the Church and about whose conversion the greatest missionaries might have doubted, were won to a change of heart by means of a child, and a girl at that. It has often pleased God to reveal His might and wisdom by means of lowly and unimportant creatures. Thus at Milan in a trying period, when it seemed impossible to come to a decision regarding the choice of a bishop, an infant pointed out St. Ambrose as the chosen bishop; and his life story shows that none could have governed the Church at Milan in a more excellent manner. "But the foolish things of the world has God chosen, that He may confound the wise; and the weak things of the world has God chosen, that He may confound the strong. That no flesh shall glory in his sight. But that he who glories, may glory in the Lord" (1 Cor. 1,27; 29; 31). — Have you ever given thought to the fact that it is God who works through human beings?

2. Consider that the operations of grace which God manifests so extraordinarily in children are also effective, generally speaking, in adults. At such time God uses the natural powers and abilities of men in order to effect good. It is not man, however, who produces the good results, but God Himself. The Prophet speaks thus to the Lord: "For Thou hast wrought all our works for us" (Is. 26,12). "God gives the increase" (1 Cor. 3,7). Whatever good, therefore, is done by men, we must recognize as the work of God and thank Him for it. In like manner, we may not ascribe to ourselves the good that we do, nor think well of ourselves on that account, but we must rather give thanks to God who has done this good through us. — Have you done this in the past?

3. Consider that in spite of the fact that God uses men to accomplish His works here on earth, He still leaves them free in their acts. If man resists, He gives him over to his own will. But he who submits himself as a useful instrument for anything God wants of him is "as the clay in the hands of the potter, who will fashion it according to his ordering" (Eccli. 33,13). He will be an instrument of much blessing. Thus it was with St. Rose. When God called her to solitude, she withdrew to her little cell; when He sent her out, she went into the streets and the market places; when He commissioned her to teach others, she undertook the work; and when, despite the fact that He had formerly permitted her to work miracles, He opposed her pious design, she willingly withdrew. — How often have we opposed the operation of God's grace, and instead of doing His holy will, used all our efforts to gain our own ends! Such a course is more apt to bring us the curse of God than His blessing, and guilt instead of merit.

May the intercession of St. Rose obtain pardon for us and her example convert us into more useful tools in the hands of God.

PRAYER OF THE CHURCH

O God, who didst deign to admit St. Rose to the company of Thy holy virgins, grant, we beseech Thee, that at her intercession and by her merits we may be cleansed from all guilt and may be admitted to the eternal presence of Thy majesty. Through Christ our Lord. Amen.

SEPTEMBER 5
BLESSED THOMAS OF TOLENTINO AND COMPANIONS
Martyrs, First Order

ORN in the March of Ancona about 1260, Thomas became a Friar Minor in early youth and soon distinguished himself by his strict observance of the Franciscan rule, especially its precepts concerning the practice of poverty, and by his zeal for the salvation of souls. In 1289 he went with several other friars as a missionary to Lesser Armenia; and two years later King Haython II of that country sent him as his envoy to the supreme pontiff and the kings of France and England to obtain their assistance against the Saracens.

With the exception of a few years during which he made a second journey back to Europe, Father Thomas then continued his missionary work in Armenia and Persia. Thus he conducted a disputation with schismatic Armenians at Sis in 1305. He was in Persia when two letters, written in 1305 and 1306 by Father John of Montecorvino, the pioneer missionary in the capital of China, arrived; and since Father John asked his confreres to communicate the contents of his letters to the Holy See, Father Thomas once more traveled back to Europe, arriving in Rome some time in 1307.

Before a public consistory of the pope and cardinals he made an eloquent address, recounting the marvelous success of Father John's work in China and pleading for effective measures which would develop the promising mission in the Far East. As a result Father John was appointed archbishop of Khanbaliq (Peking); and seven Franciscan bishops, with many other friars, were sent to his aid, although only three bishops and some of the friars survived the long journey of two years to China.

Father Thomas seems to have resumed his missionary work in Persia and remained there until 1320, when he too, together with three other friars, set out for the missions in China. But they got only as far as Thana, near Bombay, in India. There they won the martyr's crown at the hands of the Mohammedans. Father Thomas of Tolentino and James of Padua and also Brother Demetrius of Tiflis were beheaded on April 8, 1321; and Father Peter of Siena was put to death on April 11. Brother Demetrius was a Georgian or Armenian; and, being well versed in Oriental languages, he had served as interpreter for his confreres.

Some two years later Blessed Odoric of Pordenone passed through India; and after he had gathered all known facts about the martyrs, he took along their remains to the Zaitun mission in southeastern China. But the skull of Father Thomas he carried to Khanbaliq; and when he returned to Europe in 1328-1330, he brought this precious relic to the Franciscan church in the city of Tolentino, Italy. Later it was transferred to the cathedral.

In popular devotion the title of Blessed has been bestowed on all four of the martyrs ever since the fourteenth century; but only the cult of Blessed Thomas of Tolentino has been definitely approved by the Holy See, first in 1809 and again in 1894. The feast of the latter is observed by the Franciscans on September fifth, and by the Conventuals and Capuchins on April ninth. Since 1914 his feast is also celebrated in the archdiocese of Goa, India. (Cf. *Forum*, 1945, pp. 291-297; *In Journeyings Often*, pp. 109-121.)

CONCERNING THE REWARD OF THE SAINTS

1. In the life of the holy martyr Blessed Thomas, consider what the reward and the lot of the saints is here on earth. Thomas endured untold labors and difficulties in the distant lands of the heathens, for which he did not even receive ecclesiastical distinction, but in accordance with his lifelong desire, he suffered bloody martyrdom in a new and unknown country. That is what the saints wish for themselves. When Christ our Lord asked St. John of the Cross what reward he desired for so many labors in the service of God, John answered: "Lord, to suffer and to be despised for Thee." The saints realized that this life is the time of sowing, and that nothing produces such rich fruit as when one has suffered something for Christ's sake. Do you delight in such sowing?
2. Consider the reward of the saints in eternity. "Thou hast crowned him with glory and honor" (Ps. 8,6), says Holy Church of the martyrs; "Thou hast set on his head a crown of precious stones" (Ps. 20,4). The glory given to them here on earth after their death is, so to say, a reflection of their

heavenly glory. In the missions of Armenia and Persia Blessed Thomas bore the burden by which he polished the precious stones of his heavenly crown; now its splendor shines from India to the West, his native land. He who desires true glory must not seek the kind which is enjoyed already in this life.

3. Consider how different are our desires from the desires of the saints. They pray for sufferings and contempt, and thank God when they endure them. We fear nothing so much as to have to endure contempt and suffering. When it falls to our lot, our only prayer is that God remove it from us. Of these two opposing views, one must be wrong. The view of the saints has stood the true test, since they have received eternal joys for their short sufferings; in place of earthly contempt they are now enjoying honor and glory in heaven and on earth. We are in error when we wish to avert as an evil every occasion of suffering and contempt. Do you, at least, beg of God that He may give you what is salutary for you?

PRAYER OF THE CHURCH
(Ninth Sunday after Pentecost)

Let Thy merciful ears, O Lord, be open to the prayers of Thy suppliants; and in order that Thou mayest surely grant what they ask to those who seek, make them ask only for those things which are well pleasing to Thee. Through Christ our Lord. Amen.

SEPTEMBER 6
BLESSED LIBERATUS OF LAURO
Confessor, First Order

IBERATUS of Lauro was a count belonging to the noble family of the counts of Brunforte in the March of Ancona. The glory of the world held no attraction for him, and so he left the castle of his forebears and repaired to the solitary little convent of Soffiano where he was invested with the Franciscan habit and consecrated himself entirely to the service of God.

With the consent of his superiors, he led a wholly contemplative life after he was ordained a priest. He was very strict with his body, but his soul was so intimately united with God in heavenly sweetness during prayer and meditation that he often spent whole days and nights in contemplation without even thinking of food and drink or experiencing sleepiness. He became a living model to his brethren, and they were greatly edified by his conduct.

He rarely spoke; but when he was obliged to answer questions put to him, it seemed as though an angel spoke and not a man.

God favored this contemplative soul with very special graces; during his meditations he was sometimes rapt in ecstasy and streams of light radiated from his countenance while his heart experienced a foretaste of the joys of heaven.

Worn out by the ardor of his love and by the austerities he practiced rather than by age, he saw his end approaching. In his last moments he spoke to the brethren, who had assembled around his deathbed, on the joys of heaven which he hoped he would shortly possess. He died about the year 1260.

The place where his body rests was named San Liberato in his honor, and it has been the scene of many miracles. Pope Pius IX approved his veneration in 1868. His feast is observed by the three branches of the First Order on September sixth.

ON THE JOYS OF HEAVEN

1. One can readily perceive how Blessed Liberatus could experience holy joy and ardent longing in his dying moments when he beheld heaven open before him. What a blessed exchange we shall one day make when we pass from a life of faithful service of God in this vale of tears to the eternal mansions beyond! "And God shall wipe away all tears from their eyes; and death shall be no more, nor mourning, nor crying, nor sorrow shall be any more, for the former things are passed away" (Apoc. 21,41). There will be no sickness in heaven, no want, no affliction; neither will there be persecution, or jealousy, or oppression; it is the kingdom of perfect charity, where each one will rejoice at the good fortune of others, and all will be of one heart and mind like true brothers and sisters. There we shall see Mary, the Queen of heaven, in all her wondrous beauty. We shall draw near to her as to our mother, and she will receive us as her dear children. In heaven there will be no diminution of happiness, no night, but always the clear bright day that receives its brilliance from the Lamb of God, from the glorified radiant Body of Christ. In that day we shall say in all truth with St. Peter on Tabor: "Lord, it is good for us to be here" (Mt. 17,4).

2. Consider that there is something higher that will constitute our true and fundamental joy with God in heaven. "We shall see Him as he is" (1 Jn. 3,2). What is not granted to any man here upon earth even during the

sublimest ecstasy will be the portion of all those who enter there: the blessed vision of God. The glorified eye will cling to the highest and most excellent Good with inexpressible joy. We shall behold in God the explanation of all those events in life that appeared puzzling to us. We shall then admire the infinite goodness, wisdom, justice, and mercy of God. Each one of us will then also review his own life and recognize in it the operations of God's grace: the special love with which God favored us in preference to so many others; the long-suffering with which God endured all our ingratitude; the justice with which He punished us; the wisdom with which He guided us through trials to more righteous ways; the mercy with which He repeatedly received us, not casting us off even after we relapsed into sin, but helping us to be faithful unto the end. Boundless gratitude, praise, and glory will then proceed from the hearts of all the blessed and cause them to join the choir of heavenly spirits in saying: "Holy, holy, holy, Lord God Almighty" (Apoc. 4,8).

3. Consider that we shall not all receive the same reward in heaven. Our Saviour says, "In my Father's house there are many mansions" (Jn. 14,2). The happiness of the individual inhabitants of heaven will depend upon the sacrifices they made for God during life, on the sufferings they endured for Him, on the good works they performed, on the loyalty and the charity with which they served God. Whatever material pleasures you give up out of love for God will be repaid with far nobler joys in eternal bliss. Your sufferings according to their number and measure will be the source of so many more and greater joys, the most insignificant will receive a great reward, and our love for God will be recompensed with God's own love for us. What a consolation in our sufferings here below! Who would not be glad to bear all trials and despise whatever is material in order to serve God with perfect charity!

PRAYER OF THE CHURCH

O Lord Jesus Christ, who didst inspire Blessed Liberatus to withdraw from the vanities of the world and to take up his cross and follow Thee, mercifully grant that imitating his example we may despise the perishable things of life and serve Thee with pure hearts. Who livest and reignest forever and ever. Amen.

SEPTEMBER 7
BLESSED GENTLE OF MATELICA
Martyr, First Order

LESSED GENTLE was born at Matelica, a little town in the March of Ancona, of the noble and ancient Finaguerra family. As a young man he entered the Franciscan Order. After he completed his studies and was ordained a priest, he went to Mt. La Verna, where he experienced the sweetness of intimate union with God in prayer and devout contemplation. He also preached the word of God in the neighboring towns and brought about many conversions. His own brethren were so edified by his holy example that he was twice chosen as guardian of the convent.

In time, his love for Christ and for the souls of men impelled him, like our holy Father St. Francis, to preach the Gospel to the infidels. With the consent of his superiors he went first to Egypt. In spite of all his efforts, however, Gentle could not learn the languages of this country. Discouraged by the lack of success, the humble friar had already decided to return to Europe when he was met by a charming young man who encouraged him to preach the Gospel of Christ to these people. Gentle obeyed and found that he was well able to discourse in their languages.

He then went to Persia and preached in the Persian language. The unbelieving Mohammedans flocked to him in great numbers and listened attentively to his words. Frequently it happened that when he was preaching to the people, flocks of birds would fly towards him as if inviting the people to come to his sermons. More than ten thousand infidels were baptized by him. God favored him, moreover, with the gift of prophecy. The Venetian envoy to Persia, Marco Cornaro, fell seriously ill. Gentle foretold that he would recover from the illness, that he would have many vicissitudes and trials to endure after that, but in the end he would be elected Doge of the Venetian republic. Everything happened as Gentle had predicted.

The remarkable success which this apostolic man achieved through his sermons embittered the obdurate followers of Mohammed. They attacked him in the city of Toring, and clubbed him to death on September 5, 1340. The body of the martyr was taken to Venice. During this solemn procession that wound its way through the streets of the city one of the spectators grumbled that such honors were tendered to a person of whose sanctity nothing was known. Amid terrible shrieks, the mouth of the blasphemer was immediately torn wide open so that it extended from ear to ear. But he was healed again as he knelt repentant at the tomb of the holy martyr.

Pope Pius VI confirmed the veneration of Blessed Gentle and his feast is observed by the three branches of the First Order on September fifth. (Cf. *Forum,* 1945, pp. 229-231; *In Journeyings Often,* pp. 172-177.)

CHASTISED BLASPHEMY

1. "God is not mocked" (Gal. 6,7). These words of the Apostle apply also to the insults and blasphemies uttered against God's saints. For the honor we render the saints reverts to God, according to the words of Holy Writ: "Praise the Lord in His saints" (Ps. 150,1). So the blasphemies which are spoken against the saints, also are an insult to God; and God will not let such things go unpunished, as we see in the example of the man who spoke deprecatingly of Blessed Gentle's sanctity. — Have you ever taken pleasure in poking fun and mockery at the veneration accorded the saints? Beware of ever doing so.

2. Consider that we likewise displease God if we make fun of the piety of our confreres. Unfortunately, it is quite a common thing among the people of the world to scoff at and to deride the holy simplicity of God-fearing people and the devout practices of religious persons. Holy Job says: "The just man is laughed to scorn" (Job 12,4). His own friends and even his wife laughed at Job. But the Lord said to Job's friends: "My wrath is enkindled against you because you have not spoken the thing that is right before Me" (Job 42,7). When the great day of wrath comes, the Lord will speak in that manner to all those who have derided devout persons. The just will in that day stand opposite those who ridiculed them, and the latter will be forced to say within themselves, repenting and groaning for anguish of spirit: "These are they whom we had sometime in derision and for a parable of reproach. We fools esteemed their life madness. Behold how they are numbered among the children of God" (Wisd. 5,3-5). —Will we not in that day wish to have imitated their piety rather than to have mocked them?

3. Consider how those persons should act who are ridiculed by others. Above all, see that you do not give occasion for ridicule. Avoid conspicuous singularities, and beware of that false piety which engages in all kinds of pious practices but possesses little virtue and neglects duty. But if you are ridiculed through no fault of your own, then manifest your virtue by patient endurance of the derision. Accept it, as David did when Semei mocked him, as a dispensation of Providence whereby God wishes to establish you firmly in virtue and to cleanse you of the many sins you have committed. Look up also to your Saviour, who has said by His

Prophet: "I am become a reproach to them; they saw Me and they shook their heads" (Ps. 108,25). — Follow His example and pray for those deluded souls; and perhaps you will thus obtain their conversion. On your part praise God that He is giving you an opportunity to increase your merits.

PRAYER OF THE CHURCH

O God, who didst grant to Blessed Gentle the gift of tongues for the purpose of converting the infidels, grant us, we beseech Thee, that Thy praises be ever in our mouths. Through our Lord. Amen.

<hr />

SEPTEMBER 8
BLESSED RAYMOND LULL
Martyr, Third Order

AYMOND belonged to the noble Lull family and was born at Palma on the island of Mallorca in 1236. At a very early age he became a page at the royal court; and before he was thirty years old, he had been advanced to the position of marshal and high steward to King James of Mallorca.

For several years he followed the lead of other courtiers, serving the world and vanity. But God in His mercy soon led him along a better path. On the feast of St. Francis he heard a bishop portray in vivid terms the contempt of the world and the love of Christ with which the Poverello was imbued. For some time past Raymond had perceived in himself the desire for nobler things than human honors. So he recognized in the bishop's sermon the call of God to forsake all things and to win for Christ the infidels on the northern coast of Africa.

Without hesitation Raymond followed the call. He resigned his offices, left the royal court, and founded a college in which missionaries, particularly those who belonged to the Order of Friars Minor, should receive the necessary training in the languages of northern Africa. He himself joined the Third Order of St. Francis, and for nine years retired to the solitude of Mt. Randa in order to prepare himself by prayer and study. God favored him with much heavenly inspiration and granted him extraordinary knowledge so that, in spite of his numerous undertakings, he was able to write admirable things about the most difficult questions in philosophy and theology.

Raymond then made long journeys to Rome, Avignon, Montpellier,

Paris, and Vienne, in order to interest the Holy Father and the various potentates in the work of conversion and the founding of seminaries for missionaries.

In 1314, at the age of seventy-nine he himself undertook a missionary expedition to Africa. It was destined to be his last journey. While preaching the Faith of Christ in the public square at Bougie, a group of fanatical Mussulmans seized him and stoned him. He was bleeding from countless wounds and left for dead in the market place. Genoese merchants took him aboard their ship in order to give him burial in his own country. During the voyage Raymond regained consciousness for a time, but when the ship arrived near Mallorca, he breathed his last.

A very great concourse of people gathered for his burial in the Franciscan church at Palma in Mallorca where he had joined the Third Order. Soon miracles were reported as occurring at the grave of the glorious martyr. Pope Leo X beatified him, and Mallorca chose him as its special patron. His feast is observed by the Franciscans on September fifth, by the Conventuals on July fourth, and by the Third Order Regular on July third. (Cf. *Forum*, 1942, pp. 243-246; 1947, pp. 198-200, *These Made Peace*, pp. 65-73.)

ON THE GREAT VALUE OF CHRISTIAN FAITH

1. As soon as the eyes of Blessed Raymond were opened by the word of God and interior grace, he perceived that all material things are nothing when compared with the inestimable treasures of the Christian Faith. For nine years he retired into solitude in order to make a thorough study of the Faith by reading religious books, by meditation and prayer, and he spent his great fortune and even life itself, in order to bring this precious blessing to others. St. Augustine held the Faith in like regard when he said: "No amount of wealth, no treasure, no honor, no worldly advantage is greater than the Christian Faith." Faith alone teaches us the true value of things; for worldly knowledge is subject to error. Whatever the Christian Faith teaches is infallible truth, for "he believes in the Son of God, who has the testimony of God in himself" (1 Jn. 5,10). This testimony alone indicates the true value of all that is material and eternal. He who judges these things in any other way is eternally deceived. — Have you valued your Faith accordingly and revered it as a teacher?

2. Consider that the Christian Faith is also the greatest consolation in all our earthly sorrows. Here on earth it often happens, and God's wisdom often arranges it thus, that an honest and God-fearing Christian is visited with great troubles and difficulties and misfortunes, while unbelievers and

the godless seem to fare well and everything they undertake seems to succeed. But if you are deeply imbued with the Christian Faith you will recognize in all the sorrow that comes your way the seeds of a rich harvest which awaits you in eternity. Filled with interior consolation, you will then say with the Apostle: "I know whom I have believed, and I am certain that He is able to keep that which I have committed unto Him, against that day" (2 Tim. 1,12). If calumny and persecution come upon you, and it appears that the whole world has conspired against you, but you adhere firmly to the principles of the Christian Faith, you may say confidently: "This is the victory which overcomes the world, our faith" (1 Jn, 5,4). — Thank God for the gift of the Christian Faith. Have you used it well in the time of sorrow?

3. If the Christian Faith is so inestimable a blessing, how concerned should we be to preserve it without stain and to strengthen it! Our Faith is weakened and often lost through association with unbelievers, through the reading of literature that is hostile to the Faith, through conceit and adverse criticism of the truths of our Faith. Be on your guard, therefore, to avoid these snares, and pray often and fervently that God may preserve the Faith in you and permit you to be more and more imbued with it.

PRAYER OF THE CHURCH

O God, who didst adorn Blessed Raymond, Thy martyr, with zeal for the salvation of souls and the spread of the Gospel, grant us, Thy servants, that through his intercession and mediation we may faithfully preserve unto death the faith which we have received in Thy grace. Through Christ our Lord. Amen.

SEPTEMBER 9
BLESSED SERAPHINA SFORZA
Widow, Second Order

ERAPHINA, who belonged to the family of the counts of Urbino, became an orphan at an early age. Her maternal uncle, Prince Colonna, undertook to raise the child. During her stay in Rome, the girl's noble disposition unfolded itself like a flower. God and virtue had the strongest attraction for her, and the vanity of the world had no value in her sight.

Scarcely had she arrived at young womanhood when, at the wish of her relatives, she was betrothed to the widowed Prince Alexander Sforza, governor of Pesaro. A difficult task awaited the young wife, but she proved equal to it. The prince had two children by his first marriage, a son and a daughter. Seraphina embraced them with as much affection as if they had been her own children, and they in turn loved and esteemed their stepmother as their own mother. She also completely won the affection of her husband.

After a few years the prince was obliged to take up arms to assist his brother, the duke of Milan. He believed that he could entrust the government to no one better than to his young wife, for he marveled at her wisdom and skill in the management of the household.

The prince's absence extended over a period of six years. Seraphina carried out her task so perfectly that everyone admired her wise foresight and impartiality. She was loved and honored by all for her brilliant virtues and extraordinary generosity. She sought and obtained God's blessing on her undertakings by abundant almsgiving.

When her husband returned, it was to be expected that she would receive due credit for her success. But God sometimes permits His servants to be treated in a very different way. A woeful change had taken place in the prince. He had abandoned himself to a dissolute life; and he had become so reckless as to bring a paramour into his home and reduce Seraphina to the condition of a servant. But she held her peace, suffered, and prayed. The very presence of his lawful wife, however, was an unbearable reproach to the profligate; he aimed to take her life. When his attempts failed, he forcibly ejected her from the palace, ordering her to hide herself in the monastery of the Poor Clares; and that is where Seraphina went.

Although happy to serve God in the midst of the spouses of Christ, Seraphina nevertheless continued to wear secular garb so as to make it easier for the prince to return to his duties. She prayed unceasingly for his conversion. The prince tried to force her to take the religious habit; but only when she was assured that it was God's will, did she receive the habit and take the vows. She was a perfect religious, faithful even in the most trifling ordinances.

Her perfect sacrifice brought about her husband's conversion. At last he realized what he had done. He came to the convent, and on his knees begged his holy wife for forgiveness. For nine years he lived on, striving to the best of his ability to make amends for his sins and for the scandal he had given. Seraphina lived eighteen years more in the convent, and promoted its temporal and spiritual welfare, especially during the last three years when she was abbess.

On the feast of the Nativity of the Blessed Virgin, September 8, 1478, she went to receive her heavenly crown. Pope Benedict XIV approved the perpetual veneration paid to her. Her body rests in the cathedral of Pesaro. The feast of Blessed Seraphina is celebrated by the Franciscans and the Capuchins on September ninth.

A HOLY WOMAN

1. Behold in Blessed Seraphina the model of a saintly housewife. She loves her children though she is not their natural mother, for God entrusts them to her maternal care through the bonds of matrimony. Every Christian mother should cherish such supernatural love for her children, and not only the natural attachment which she has for them. This latter is too often detrimental to the welfare of the child's soul. Every mother must remember that her children belong to God more than they do to her, as the mother of the Machabees said to her sons: "It was not I that gave breath, nor soul, nor life, but the Creator of the world" (2 Mac. 7,22-23). God will require the souls of the children from their parents. — Have you raised your children for God?

2. Consider how Seraphina expended her energy and abilities attending to the cares of the household. She did so with so much success that she gained the complete confidence of her husband. The care of the house is the particular duty of the wife. Nature provides her with qualities that fit her for this work and God assists her in a special way by His grace. The peace and wellbeing of a home depend in great measure on her devotion and prudent foresight in the management of the household. "A wise woman builds her house" (Prov. 14,1). A truly Christian woman will leave nothing undone to keep the fair name of Christianity from being criticized on her account. — Have you perhaps given occasion for such criticism?

3. It was genuine sanctity that supported Seraphina in her afflictions. To suffer and to endure is the proof of virtue. Generally, it is the long beam of the cross of home life that becomes the mother's portion, whether this is due to the fact that original sin proceeded from Eve, or that God has so ordained it because He has granted women more endurance in suffering. So often we note in the lives of the saints that God leads those women whom He has chosen for a high degree of sanctity along the road of the cross. But woman also has easier access to the divine graces. She is led to God by her natural inclination to piety; and the knowledge of her weakness urges her to pray fervently, while the honor of her sex, Mary, the Mother of Sorrows, and Mother of Grace, is her powerful intercessor. Thus she obtains the supernatural power that works miracles in family

circles. Thus did Seraphina convert her husband, who had strayed far from the path of righteousness; thus she became a model wife and mother as well as an exemplary religious; thus she herself finally attained to the crown of eternal glory.

PRAYER OF THE CHURCH

O God, who didst vouchsafe to give us Blessed Seraphina as an extraordinary example of patience, grant, we earnestly beseech Thee, that we may not only profit by her example, but also be preserved from all adversities through her protection. Through Christ our Lord. Amen.

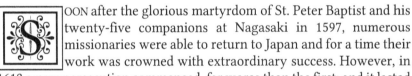

SEPTEMBER 10
BLESSED APOLLINARIS FRANCO AND COMPANIONS
Martyrs, First and Third Orders

SOON after the glorious martyrdom of St. Peter Baptist and his twenty-five companions at Nagasaki in 1597, numerous missionaries were able to return to Japan and for a time their work was crowned with extraordinary success. However, in 1613 a new persecution commenced, far worse than the first; and it lasted until 1638, when Japan adopted a policy of complete isolation.

During this persecution some missionaries were able to hide themselves in the mountains and to continue their work in secret, at least for a time; and some new ones even managed to enter the country. Many of them, together with a large number of their converts, won the martyr's crown.

No less than three hundred and fifty children of St. Francis were put to death for the Faith; and of this number forty-five, who are known as Blessed Apollinaris and his companions, were declared blessed by Pope Pius IX on July 27, 1867. On the same occasion, one hundred and sixty other Japanese martyrs who died between 1617 and 1632 were beatified.

Of the forty-five Franciscan martyrs, seventeen belonged to the First Order, one was a member of the Third Order Regular, and twenty-seven were Tertiaries. Those of the First Order included twelve Franciscan missionaries from Europe and five Japanese Franciscans. Of these one was a bishop-elect, nine were priests, one a cleric, and six brothers. Father Apollinaris Franco was their superior. All the other martyrs were natives of Japan and Korea; and hence their total number was thirty-three.

Though it is not possible to study the life of each of these forty-five blessed martyrs on a separate day, we should at least become acquainted with them and learn their names and the day of their martyrdom.

The first of the twelve European Franciscans to become a martyr was Blessed Peter of the Assumption, who died May 22, 1617. He was followed the next year, on August 16, by Blessed John of St. Martha. Three died on September 10, 1622, namely, Blessed Richard of St. Anne, Blessed Peter of Avila, and Blessed Vincent of St. Joseph, the latter a brother. Two days later, the superior, Blessed Apollinaris Franco won the martyr's crown. Blessed Francis Galvez died on December 4, 1623; and the next year, on August 25, Blessed Louis Sotelo, bishop-elect of eastern Japan.

Two died on August 17, 1627, namely Blessed Francis of St. Mary and Blessed Bartholomew Laurel, the latter being a brother from Mexico. The following year, on September 8, Blessed Anthony of St. Bonaventure joined their ranks. The last was another brother, Blessed Gabriel of St. Magdalen, who died on September 3, 1632.

Among the five Japanese Franciscans was a cleric, Blessed Francis of St. Bonaventure, and a brother, Blessed Paul of St. Clare, both of whom made their novitiate and their profession in prison and died on September 12, 1622. Blessed Louis Sasada, who was admitted into the order in Mexico and ordained a priest in Manila, laid down his life for the Faith on August 25, 1624. The other two were brothers who made their profession in prison, Blessed Anthony of St. Francis, who died on August 17, 1627, and Blessed Dominic of St. Francis, on September 8, 1628.

The martyr who was a member of the Third Order Regular of St. Francis was the Japanese priest Blessed Jerome Torres of the Cross, who was put to death on September 3, 1632.

The first of the twenty-seven Japanese and Korean Tertiary martyrs were eighty-year-old Blessed Lucy Freites and the catechist Blessed Leo of Satsuma, whose death occurred on September 10, 1622. Blessed Louis Baba, the companion and servant of Bishop-elect Louis Sotelo, died on August 25, 1624.

Eight Tertiaries became martyrs on August 17, 1627. Among them was Blessed Gaspar Vaz, a Korean, and his wife, Blessed Mary Vaz. Likewise Blessed Thomas O Jinemon, also a Korean. Another was Blessed Francis Kuhioye, who was baptized in prison. The others were Blessed Louis Matsuo Soemon, Blessed Luke Kiemon, Blessed Martin Gomez, and Blessed Michael Kizaemon.

In the same year, on September 7, died Blessed Tsuji, a Jesuit priest who is counted among the Franciscan martyrs because he was also a Tertiary or at least a Cordbearer of St. Francis. With him died the

Tertiaries Blessed Aloysius Maki, and his son Blessed John Maki.

Thirteen died on September 8, 1628. Among them were one mother and three fathers with one of more of their sons. The mother was Blessed Louise Chikugo of Nagasaki, and her martyr son was Blessed John Romano. Blessed Louis Nihachi, a catechist, was the father of the two child martyrs, Blessed Dominic Nihachi, two years old, and Blessed Francis Nihachi, five years old. Another father, Blessed John Tomachi, a sailor, laid down his life for the Faith together with four sons, Blessed Paul Tomachi, seven years old, Blessed Thomas Tomachi, ten years old, Blessed Michael Tomachi, thirteen years old, and Blessed Dominic Tomachi, sixteen years old. The third father and his son were both sailors, Blessed Michael Yamada and Blessed Lawrence Yamada. The last in this group of martyrs was Blessed Matthew Alvarez, who was the pilot of a ship which was built in Japan for the Franciscan missionaries and was to be used by them to bring new missionaries to the country from the Philippines. The sailors mentioned all belonged to the crew of this ship.

Among the Tertiary martyrs, Blessed Lucy Freites distinguished herself in a special manner by her heroism. Holding aloft a crucifix, she led the martyrs who died with her to the place of execution, encouraging them by her words and intoning Christian hymns in which the others joined her. Even while standing in the fire, by which she was burned to death, she prayed for her country and admonished the pagans who stood about to embrace the Christian Faith. "Can the Christian religion be false," she cried, "when it gives old women and delicate children so much courage and strength? Your gods are false and deceptive, but our God is real and true to His promises; He will receive us into His kingdom and grant us eternal bliss." Then her body sank into the fire, but her soul winged its flight to heaven. The feast of Blessed Apollinaris and his forty-four companions is celebrated by the Franciscans and the Third Order Regular on September tenth. (Cf. In *Journeyings Often*, pp. 251-254, and 259-260.)

ON THE TRIUMPH OF THE CHRISTIAN FAITH

1. Consider what a triumph for our Faith is the glorious death of so many holy martyrs. These heroic souls sacrificed the honors and wealth that were theirs, and let nothing disturb them, neither mother love, nor the weakness of their sex, nor yet the tortures of death by fire. Their death is proof that the Faith for which they died comes from God; for, only God, the Creator and Ruler of men, can give such supernatural strength to weak mortals. The testimony which they gave for the Faith should

mightily strengthen us in our faith, so that we may cry out with the Psalmist: "Thy testimonies are become exceedingly credible" (Ps. 92,5).

2. Consider that it will be revealed before the whole world on the day of judgment how the Faith triumphed in the death of the holy martyrs. They fell, but in dying, they conquered. By the fact that the enemies of the Faith did not succeed in vanquishing them, the world acknowledged the truth of the Faith and became Christian. And so the blood of the martyrs became the seed from which new Christians came forth. The Church of Jesus Christ, which proceeded from the pierced side of the Crucified, assumed new life through the blood of the martyrs and spread throughout the world. That, too, will be revealed before the whole world on the day of the general judgment, and the martyrs will celebrate their triumph when the eternal Judge will say to them: "You are they who have continued with Me in my temptations, and I appoint to you as My Father has appointed to me, a kingdom" (Lk. 22,28). — What a blessed reward is given to the true soldiers of Christ!

3. Consider that we must all share, each in his own way, in the struggle and the perseverance of the holy martyrs, if we wish to have part in their triumph some day. Holy Scripture says: "The life of man upon earth is a warfare" (Job 7,1). The many hardships in life, the self-denial required for the faithful observance of the laws of God and of His Church, the temptations that assail us from within and without: that is the struggle which we as soldiers of Christ must endure. A glance at the holy martyrs, the remembrance of their cheerful disposition, the desire to be admitted to their company, will also strengthen us, and help us to say with the Apostle: "Neither life, nor death, nor principalities, nor powers, nor things present, nor things to come shall be able to separate us from the love of God, which is in Christ Jesus, our Lord" (Rom. 8,38-39).

PRAYER OF THE CHURCH

We beseech Thee, O almighty God, that we may be encouraged by the example of the blessed martyrs Apollinaris and companions, rather to suffer every evil in this world than suffer harm to our souls. Through Christ our Lord. Amen.

SEPTEMBER 11
BLESSED BONAVENTURE OF BARCELONA
Confessor, First Order

SPANIARD by birth, Bonaventure received his surname from his extensive activities in the diocese of Barcelona. While he was a shepherd, he spent all his spare time in prayer and in venerating the Blessed Mother of God. In accordance with his father's wish he married, but he lived with his wife in virginal purity. She died an early death, and then Bonaventure joined the Franciscans as a lay brother. He was sent to Barcelona, and there he attracted attention by his holy life.

Finally, Providence led him to Italy, where he strove to promote the strict observance of the rule. In the little convent of St. Damian at Assisi he heard a voice saying to him: "Go to Rome, and there fill my house with joy!" This he did, and founded the convent of St. Bonaventure on the Palatine, where the rule of St. Francis was observed in its pristine spirit. Similar foundations soon followed, and simple Brother Bonaventure was commissioned to write the constitutions for them. At the pope's command, he assumed the office of superior.

The fame of his supernatural wisdom soon spread beyond the walls of the little convent on the Palatine. Many came to seek consolation and advice in difficult problems; among them were high officials and learned persons, even the pope himself.

When he was sixty-four years old, Bonaventure was attacked by a fever, which resulted in his death. He died a saintly death in 1684, and was beatified by Pope Pius X. The tomb of Blessed Bonaventure is at an altar on the Gospel side of the little church of St. Bonaventure in Rome. In the same church at the high altar is the tomb of St. Leonard of Port Maurice. The feast of Blessed Bonaventure is observed by the Franciscans on September tenth.

CONCERNING THE OBSERVANCE OF THE RULE

1. A religious order is a city of God. "A wall and a bulwark shall be set in it" (Is. 26,1). What the fortifications are for boundaries and countries, the rule and constitutions are for a religious order. "The devil is always lying in wait for us, and, like an enemy, enters through the breach as soon as the ramparts of discipline are broken down," says St. Gregory. As commanders defend the fortifications committed to their charge, so must you defend your fortress and outer wall; that is, you must observe exactly

the rule and statutes of your order. — Are you grateful to God for having prescribed for you a certain program and pattern of life? How do you value your rule, the observance of which has peopled heaven with so many saints?

2. The rules of religious when approved by the Church are, as it were, rays of the divine law itself. Our Lord said to His servant St. Bridget regarding the rule of St. Francis: "This rule which Francis adopted was not dictated and composed by his human intellect and prudence, but by Me, according to My will. Every word written in it was inspired by My Spirit." How strictly ought the rule to be observed since God Himself dictated it, since you promised by a vow to keep it, since it is for you a channel of divine grace, since your perfection depends on the observance of it, and finally, since, if you keep it, it will be the means of your salvation, whereas, if you neglect it, it will cause your condemnation. — Do you give thought to your rule as being the law of God and the expression of His will, according to which you have promised to live? Do you hold even the least of its ordinances with great reverence?

3. By the charity of St. Francis the privileges of religious life in this great order were extended to those who were not in a position to bid farewell to the world and to spend their days in the solitude of the cloister. This he did by means of the Third Order Secular. Tertiaries also have a rule that was given them by St. Francis, the observance of which enables them even in the midst of the distractions of the world to participate in the advantages of the cloister and to attain to perfection. In order to make it possible for all Christians to become members of this holy institution, Pope Leo XIII adapted it to the conditions and requirements of our times, and enriched it with new indulgences and privileges. — If you are a member of the Third Order, ask yourself whether you have a true appreciation of the privilege that is yours, whether you are faithful to the simple rules proposed for your observance. If so, rest assured you will share in the blessings and privileges that have been promised you by St. Francis himself.

PRAYER OF THE CHURCH
(From the Ceremonial of the Third Order)

Grant us, we beseech Thee, O Lord, the help of Thy grace, that with Thy aid we may accomplish what we know Thou hast appointed us to perform. Who livest and reignest world without end. Amen.

SEPTEMBER 12
BLESSED PEREGRIN OF FALERONE
Confessor, First Order

EREGRIN of Falerone in the Papal States was a colleague of Blessed Rizziero of Muccia (February 7), and like him the scion of a noble family. When, after a sermon preached by St. Francis at Bologna, both these young men asked him for the religious habit, St. Francis said to Peregrin: "You, my son, will serve God in the humble vocation of a lay brother, and you should apply yourself to practice humility in a special way."

For the young nobleman who, until now, had studied philosophy and jurisprudence with great success, it was a great trial that the vocation of a lay brother should be assigned to him.

But Peregrin gave proof that he possessed true nobility of soul, and that he valued the lowest place in Christ's service higher than all the honors of the world. Joyfully he received the habit as a lay brother and strove, above all, to lay a firm foundation in humility. On this secure foundation he then built up all the other virtues in a high degree. One of the first disciples of St. Francis did not hesitate to assert that Brother Peregrin was one of the most perfect religious in the whole world.

Moved by his great love for the sufferings of Christ, Peregrin begged permission to make a pilgrimage to the Holy Land, and his request was granted. There, with touching piety, he venerated the holy places. At the sites of Christ's suffering and on the road on which our Lord carried His Cross he shed abundant tears of compassion and of love. Even the infidel Saracens could not suppress their emotion at the sight of him.

After his return to Italy, he led a still more humble life in the seclusion of his vocation. When he met his distinguished relatives, which happened rarely, he spoke only of such things as could strengthen them in the service of God. Almighty God imparted to him the gift of miracles even in this life; and after his death he has continued to work many miracles at his grave in San Severino until our own day.

Several bishops petitioned Pope Pius VII for the Church's approval of the veneration paid to him from time immemorial. This was granted in the year 1821. It is said that persons call upon him with special confidence and blessed results when suffering from toothache. His feast is observed on September sixth by the Franciscans and Capuchins, and on the seventh by the Conventuals.

ON THE DEVOTION OF THE WAY OF THE CROSS

1. He who has received a great benefit and knows how to value it at its true worth joyfully remembers the favor, speaks of it, and aims in every possible way to manifest his gratitude. God's Son, our Lord and Saviour Jesus Christ, conferred on us the greatest benefit when He carried the Cross to Calvary in order to redeem us by His death from the torment of hell. The grateful remembrance of this grace urged Blessed Peregrin to make a pilgrimage to Jerusalem and to visit with great devotion the places made holy by the passion and death of the Saviour. — Should grateful love not urge us to make the Way of the Cross frequently and with great devotion?

2. Consider the many hardships it cost Blessed Peregrin to make the long and perilous journey to Jerusalem. It is so easy for us to make the Way of the Cross, and such rich indulgences are offered for merely passing from one to the other of the fourteen stations. Even when we are ill or are otherwise hindered from visiting the Stations, we can perform the devotion if we hold a Crucifix blessed with the Stations indulgence and say an Our Father, Hail Mary, and Glory for each station, closing with five Paters, Aves, and Glorias in honor of the Five Wounds of Christ, and one more for the intention of the pope. — Why not make diligent use of this easy yet bountiful means of grace? At the same time let us offer up to God the difficulties and the sufferings of our life in gratitude for His love for us, and in lieu of the great sacrifices required, formerly at least, to make a pilgrimage to the Holy Land.

3. Consider how beneficial for our entire life is the devout performance of the holy Way of the Cross. He who reflects on the bitter pains which Christ took upon Himself because of our sins, and sees Him carrying the Cross for us until He is exhausted even unto death, will shirk no effort in faithfully fulfilling the duties of a good Christian. St. Leonard of Port Maurice, who erected more than six hundred Ways of the Cross, testified that in parishes where this devotion was diligently observed, the morals of the people were on a much higher plane than in other places. Blessed Peregrin returned from Jerusalem better fortified to serve almighty God in humility. — May the disgrace suffered by Christ on His sorrowful way strengthen us also, especially in the practice of humility.

PRAYER OF THE CHURCH

Almighty and merciful God, who didst set before us in Blessed Peregrin, Thy confessor, a remarkable model of humility, grant, we beseech Thee, that following in his footsteps here on earth, we may arrive at the eternal reward in heaven, which has been promised to the humble. Through Christ our Lord. Amen.

SEPTEMBER 13
BLESSED SANCTES OF MONTEFABRO
Confessor, First Order

ANCTES first saw the light of day at Montefabro, a little town not far from Urbino, Italy. Since his parents were among the most prominent citizens of that place, they sent their son to Urbino to pursue higher studies as soon as he had grown to young manhood. There, as at home, he lived an innocent life and applied himself so diligently to his studies that the highest hopes were entertained concerning him.

When he was twenty years old, an incident occurred that changed the entire course of his life. An enemy pursued him with drawn sword. Sanctes fled. Reaching home, he found that his pursuer was still following him. He then grasped a weapon that was within reach and dangerously wounded his pursuer with a slash on the thigh which proved fatal a few days later. Although the young man had acted in self-defense, he was nevertheless inconsolable over the outcome, and his conscience grievously tormented him.

In order to appease this trouble of conscience, he resolved to leave the world and lead a life of great austerity in the Franciscan Order. He chose to enter as a lay brother, and distinguished himself among his associates by humility and penance.

The most disagreeable and lowly tasks were the most dear to him. After a time his superiors appointed him novice-master of the lay brothers, and Sanctes filled this office with remarkable success. However, he soon begged so humbly to be relieved of it, that his request was granted. He preferred to be subject to others rather than to rule over them.

In spite of the severity with which he treated his body, he still believed that he had not yet atoned enough for the fatal wound he had inflicted on his enemy, and begged almighty God to allow him to make adequate reparation for it. His prayer was heard. A very painful ulcer formed on his thigh exactly where he had wounded his assailant. He suffered the same pains that the man did, and patiently endured them with resignation until the end of his life.

But God also granted him great consolation and special graces. One day he was busy in the kitchen when the bell rang for elevation at holy Mass. He knelt down to adore the Blessed Sacrament, when suddenly the walls opened and he was able to see the Sacred Host on the altar.

Like his holy Father St. Francis, Sanctes had an extraordinary power over animals. Once he had taken a mule with him to the forest to get some wood. While he was gathering the wood, the mule wandered into a ravine to graze. When the brother returned and looked for the animal, he found that it had been killed by a wolf which was still feasting on him. The holy brother reproached the wolf for having torn the convent's beast of burden to pieces and told him that henceforth he must perform that animal's duties. The wolf followed the brother like a lamb and thereafter allowed himself to be used as a beast of burden.

Other miracles are also reported of Brother Sanctes which caused his name to be revered even in distant places. He was not concerned, however, with the honors rendered him by men. He endeavored only to serve his God and looked for no other reward but that which heaven would grant him. He had not long to wait for this reward. He was in his forty-fourth year when he died in the convent of St. Mary of Scotaneto on the vigil of our Lady's Assumption, August 14, 1390. Pope Clement XIV approved the veneration given to him since his death. The feast of Blessed Sanctes is observed by the Franciscans on September sixth, by the Conventuals on August thirteenth, and by the Capuchins on August fourteenth.

A TENDER CONSCIENCE

1. Consider what a tender conscience Blessed Sanctes had. It was in self-defense that he had wounded his assailant. But who can say with certainty that at such a time excitement and anger play no part at all in our actions. That is what troubled the tender conscience of Sanctes and for that he wanted to satisfy divine justice. God rewarded him by giving him the grace to lead a holy life, with many additional and extraordinary graces, and a great treasure in heaven. Would that you, too, had so tender a conscience. You would then endeavor to satisfy divine justice for the many transgressions of which you have been guilty. Offer up at least the daily sufferings you encounter and which you find hard to endure. "For this is thankworthy, if for conscience towards God, a man endures sorrows" (1 Pet. 2,19).

2. Consider that the tender conscientiousness of the saints was not scrupulosity, which sees sin where there is no sin. We should rather say

that they had a clearer insight than ordinary persons into what is displeasing to the sanctity of God and how even the slightest offenses are deserving of punishment. Hence they drove from their hearts every thought that might be displeasing to the all-holy God. In their words and actions they avoided every wilful transgression of His commandments, and strove to make amends as much as possible for every fault they committed. When St. Paschal was still a farm-hand, he made good, out of his own wages, all damages which his cattle had caused, no matter how small it was; and after his conversion, St. Ignatius made a long detour on one of his journeys in order to repair a theft he had committed as a boy. They were mindful of him who "will bring all things that are done unto judgment for every error" (Eccl. 12,14). When the hour of death approaches, will you not wish to have had a more delicate conscience?

3. Consider how we are to preserve a delicate conscience. The conscience of a child is tender; it trembles at a lie and blushes if it has done anything unbecoming. Whoever continues to follow this clear voice of God, will preserve a delicate conscience even in advanced age as did Blessed Sanctes. But he who has for any length of time neglected to listen to the voice of conscience and has thereby deadened it, must, after praying fervently to the Holy Ghost, make a serious examination of conscience, and must pass judgment on himself as God will sooner or later do. Then he must cleanse his conscience by making a good confession and studying anew the obligations imposed on him by the commandments of God. In this way the interior voice will again become tender and even make him aware of his smaller transgressions. It is the enemy of our salvation that aims to make us careless and light-hearted in matters of conscience, so that he may cause us to despair in the hour of death. Then a conscience that has been constantly ignored cannot be silenced.— Do you wish to subject your soul to so horrible a torture?

PRAYER OF THE CHURCH

O almighty God, Author of our salvation, who didst in Thy admirable providence draw Blessed Sanctes, Thy confessor, out of the dangers of this world and didst lead him on the way of Thy faithful followers, grant us, we beseech Thee, that at his intercession and through his merits, we may serve Thee with holy zeal and may be freed from all the snares of our enemies. Through Christ our Lord. Amen.

SEPTEMBER 14
BLESSED LOUISE OF SAVOY
Widow, Second Order

N the feast of the Holy Innocents in the year 1461, a daughter was born to Blessed Amadeus, duke of Savoy. She was to become more distinguished in the world for her innocence and sanctity than for the nobility of her birth. This daughter was Blessed Louise.

From childhood she showed a marked love for prayer and retirement. On the vigils of the feasts of our Lady she fasted on bread and water. In compliance with the wish of her mother, a sister of King Louis XI of France, Louise wore costly garments and jewelry as was becoming her princely rank; but underneath them she wore a garment of haircloth, and she always looked upon her external finery as a reminder to adorn her soul with virtues.

Louise possessed such innocent simplicity that pride and vanity were wholly foreign to her. Still with the simplicity of a dove she also combined great prudence in evading the dangers of a life at court, to which she was exposed.

She had already decided to consecrate herself to God in the state of virginity, when her uncle and guardian, the king of France, desired her to marry the prince of Chalon. Louise believed that God was thus manifesting His will in her regard; and so she gave her hand to the virtuous young prince.

He was pleased to note how her example and authority checked the excessive luxury and the frivolous customs prevailing at court. Not only did she reform the habits of the ladies of the court, but even the men were won over to a Christian life. If anyone of them was caught cursing or using unbecoming language, she required him to do penance by giving an alms for the poor. She and her husband attended the dances and plays that were given, but never took part in them themselves. They went there only to prevent anything disorderly. She is reported to have said what St. Francis de Sales said at a later date: "Dances and plays are like mushrooms, of which the best are not worth much." When she was but twenty-seven years old, Louise lost her devoted husband. She declined all offers of a second marriage, even those coming from the most honorable suitors. She wished now to live in retirement and very simply, and to devote herself to works of penance, piety, and Christian charity. She used her great wealth in carrying out an extensive program of charity.

There were no children to claim her maternal care; and since she desired to live in close union with God, she entered the convent of Poor Clares at Orbe after overcoming great obstacles. Here the princess was a model to all in humility, poverty, and self-abnegation. She observed all the precepts of the rule and of obedience most conscientiously, and was always very grateful for any reprimands she received. She fostered a tender devotion to the sufferings of Christ and to our Blessed Lady, from whom she sometimes received very special favors.

A serious illness seized Louise when she was forty-two years old. After she had received the last sacraments with great devotion, her death agony began, but she was still able to pronounce the words from the Office of Our Lady:

> O Fount of Mercy, Mother mine,
> Through whom God sends us grace divine,
> Free me from sin, and lend thy aid
> When death's dark hour makes me afraid.

Then she surrendered her pure soul into the hands of her Creator on July 24, 1503. God glorified her by many miracles, and so Pope Gregory XVI confirmed her veneration in 1839. The feast of Blessed Louise is observed by the Franciscans on September ninth, by the Conventuals on July twenty-eighth, and by the Capuchins on August eleventh.

ON FAITHFUL FULFILLMENT OF THE DUTIES OF OUR STATE

1. In every station in life, as daughter, wife, widow, and religious, Blessed Louise distinguished herself as a model of virtue. That is why she merits such great praise. In the sight of God the true worth of a man depends on the fidelity he manifests in fulfilling the duties of his state of life, and God's judgment will also be in accordance with that standard. It is related of a confessor of Emperor Charles V that, after the latter had confessed his personal sins, the confessor said to him: "That was the confession of Charles; now let the emperor confess." The Eternal Judge will surely require an accounting of you also in accordance with your vocation; and when He says, "Give an account of your stewardship" (Lk. 16,3), it will, without doubt, mean an account of your vocation, your work, the office you held while here on earth. May you then stand the test as Blessed Louise did. — Examine yourself now in these matters.

2. Consider that each station in life has its peculiar dangers, and that many a vocation involves greater hardships than the one you have embraced. Innocence and simplicity alone are not always sufficient, but we must add

to these virtues prudence, foresight, and constancy. But no matter how great the hardships, a Christian may never despair. Where human strength seems insufficient, God will come to the assistance of him who does what he is able to do. "He is faithful who has called you, who also will do it" (1 Thess. 5,24). In His wisdom God lets storms come upon us in order to test our fidelity, but He never tries us beyond measure. He "will not suffer you to be tempted above that which you are able, but will make also with temptation issue, that you may be able to bear it" (1 Cor. 10,13). — Was perhaps lack of trust in God the reason why you have become weak and unfaithful in the past?

3. Consider the means that must be employed in every state of life for the faithful fulfillment of our duties. To know our duties well and to have the necessary strength to fulfill them, we must apply the religious means at our disposal: daily prayer, listening to the Word of God, and the frequent reception of the sacraments. To overcome our own personal indolence and the opposition of fallen nature, we must deny ourselves, according to the words of our Lord: "If any man will come after Me, let him deny himself and take up his cross daily" (Lk. 9,23). Finally, it is necessary that we keep before our eyes the first and greatest commandment: To love God above all things and our neighbor as ourselves. This will help you to be faithful to your duty in every station in life, like Blessed Louise, so that you, too, may one day hear the words of the Lord: "Because you have been faithful over a few things, I will place you over many things; enter you into the joy of your Lord" (Mt. 25,23).

PRAYER OF THE CHURCH

O God, who didst raise up in Blessed Louise a remarkable model of virtue in every position of life, grant us, that in every state to which Thou dost call us, we may follow her example and may deserve to attain to Thee. Through Christ our Lord. Amen.

***

SEPTEMBER 15
BLESSED MICHELINA OF PESARO
Widow, Third Order

THE town of Pesaro is situated on the shores of the Adriatic in Italy, not far from the famous shrine of Loreto. There, in 1300, a daughter was born to the wealthy and noble Metelli family, who received the name Michelina in baptism. The child was endowed with superior natural gifts, and in accordance with the tradition of the family she was brought up in the fear of the Lord.

When she was twelve years old, she was married to a nobleman of the powerful family of Malatesta. Although Michelina was good and pious, it is said that her heart was divided between creatures and the Creator, as is often the case. Her husband and a son, with whom the marriage was blessed, occupied her heart more than was becoming to a Christian woman.

The Lord severed one of these ties by taking her husband to Himself when Michelina was only twenty years old. This was a severe trial for the young wife, but she did not yet recognize the higher designs of God. Her maternal affections were now still more centered on her son.

About this time a pious Tertiary from Syria came to Pesaro, and edified the entire town by her fervor at prayer and the holiness of her life. Michelina also conceived a great veneration for this pious lady and invited her to take up her abode in her palace, promising to provide for all her needs so that she could serve God alone. The stranger gratefully accepted this hospitality, and almighty God rewarded Michelina by permitting her to learn to love God above all things, and all other things only in God.

Once on the feast of Pentecost she conversed with her Tertiary guest on the need of surrendering one's heart to God. The latter spoke of it in glowing terms and declared it was necessary. "That may be true," said Michelina, "but I cannot aspire to such perfection. My son, the tenderest object of my affections, occupies my heart too much, and my earthly possessions do not leave me free enough to offer my heart completely to God." "Let us then," replied the Tertiary, "pray together that God may disengage your heart from those things which are an obstacle to your salvation and perfection." The grace of the Holy Spirit was not wanting, and Michelina answered: "Yes, let us. I, too, desire to serve God better than I have till now."

The next morning both attended holy Mass and prayed fervently for this intention. At the close of Mass Michelina interiorly heard the voice of our Lord: "I will set you free. I will take your son to Myself, and you shall henceforth belong to Me alone." When they arrived at home they found the child sick; and soon God took him from this world, in which he would have been in great danger because of the inordinate tenderness of his mother. The two women saw how the holy angels carried his soul to heaven.

The mother was now like one transformed. Her heart was no longer attached to temporal goods. She distributed them lavishly among the poor in spite of the remonstrances of her relatives. After a while she entered the Third Order of St. Francis, and adopted the afflicted and the indigent as her new family. She became a mother to the orphans, the support of poor widows, the nurse of the sick, the comfort of the sorrowful; her house was the refuge of all unfortunate persons. She also practiced severe acts of penance in order to atone for her former life.

Towards the end of her life she made a pilgrimage to the holy places, where she venerated the mysteries of Christ's suffering so fervently that all present saw her in an ecstasy on Mount Calvary. Upon her return to her native country, she redoubled her prayers, practices of penance, and works of charity, until our Lord called her to Himself on June 19, 1356.

Her tomb in the Franciscan church was made glorious by numerous miracles. The Apostolic See approved her public veneration in 1737, whereupon the town of Pesaro chose her as its special patron. The feast of Blessed Michelina is observed by the Franciscans on September ninth, by the Conventuals on June nineteenth, and by the Third Order Regular on June twentieth. (Cf. *These Made Peace,* pp. 137-142.)

ON COMPLETE SURRENDER TO GOD

1. Consider how dangerous it was for Blessed Michelina that her heart was divided between the Creator and His creatures. Almighty God, whose actions are always marked with mercy and who has only our welfare in mind, had to deprive her of what was dearest to her here on earth, her husband and her son, in order to rescue her from this danger. God wants the whole heart, not only of religious, but also of every Christian, since the words, "You shall love the Lord your God with your whole heart" (Mk. 12,30), apply to everyone. At the same time the Lord gives the warning, "You shall not have strange gods before Me" (Ex. 20,2). But how many Christians there are, even among those who consider themselves pious, who carry about in their hearts, next to God, an inordinate attachment to some creature to such an extent that, like Blessed Michelina, they must admit it keeps them from belonging entirely to God! The words of the Prophet may be applied to them: "Their heart is divided," and perhaps also the added judgment: "Now they shall perish" (Os. 10,2).
2. Consider why a divided heart is so easily led to perdition. Following its natural propensity, the heart of man is more inclined toward creatures than toward God, its Creator. If one has already offered half of it to creatures, they easily cause it to forget God and to offend Him on their account, for example when a favorite child is allowed to have something which according to God's will should not be granted, or when a wife acts against her conscience to please a beloved husband. But if, as in the case

of Michelina, God in His mercy tears the object of their earthly affections from such divided hearts, how few of them follow the example of Michelina! Rather, they become bitter toward God and do not want to serve Him at all. They perish because their hearts were divided. — Have you too perhaps been guilty in this respect?

3. Consider how one can and must be prepared for the loss of earthly things. Often reflect that all the blessings that you possess, and that are dear and precious to your heart, have been given to you by God. "What have you that you have not received?" (1 Cor. 4,7). Thank God for it, and in gratitude love Him all the more on that account. But always remember that it is His property, which He has lent you in His goodness, and which He can reclaim whenever it pleases Him. Often acknowledge this before God and let Him govern as He wishes; yes, beg Him even to take it from you according to His will, should it become harmful to you. Then your heart will ever belong to God, whole and undivided. You will serve God in His creatures, in the poor and neglected, as Michelina did after her conversion, and you will grow in His love.

PRAYER OF THE CHURCH

O God, who in a remarkable way didst detach Blessed Michelina from earthly affections and didst lead her to love Thee, we beseech Thee, grant to us that, freed from harmful attachment, we may, through her merits and in imitation of her, accomplish with free hearts what is pleasing to Thee. Through Christ our Lord. Amen.

SEPTEMBER 16
BLESSED THOMAS OF FOLIGNO
Confessor, Third Order

THOMAS was a Tertiary hermit in the diocese of Nocera, Italy. He lived for twenty-four years with Blessed Peter of Gualdo, another holy hermit of the Third Order of St. Francis; and when this hermit died in his arms, he began to lead a still more rigorous life. He chose a very narrow cell for himself, the door of which was walled up. There was a small window in it through which devout persons brought him food on Sundays and Thursdays. The remaining days of the week he ate nothing at all.

He lived in close union with God. The devil, quite naturally, annoyed him with severe temptations, but Thomas manfully overcame them all. It was the earnest wish of Blessed Thomas to spend the remaining days of his life in his cell and to die in it, but God had other plans in mind for him. Some one registered a complaint with the bishop that Thomas was an odd character and had no regard for the precepts of the Church or for obedience to the spiritual authorities. The bishop, therefore, sent for him. At once the servant of God left his enclosure and went to his spiritual superior.

When the bishop recounted the complaints that had been lodged with him, Thomas cast himself upon his knees but said nothing. Not until the bishop urged him to speak, did he state that he had the permission of the pastor of the place, who also administered the sacraments to him. The pastor was summoned, confirmed the statements of the servant of God, and highly praised the sanctity of Thomas. The bishop then dismissed him with his good wishes and his blessing.

But when Thomas again came to the entrance of his enclosure, an angel appeared to him — it is believed that it was really our Lord in the form of an angel — and charged him to go to Umbria, the March of Ancona, and Tuscany. The people there had rebelled against the authority of the pope and no longer observed the precepts of the Church. Thomas was to preach to them, and exhort them to practice obedience to spiritual authority such as he had just practiced so admirably.

At first Thomas hesitated, feeling that he was unfit for this task; but he began timidly to exhort the people, and our Lord Himself placed the words upon his tongue. Many persons ridiculed and mocked him; but he gradually took courage, and warned them of the judgments to come, urging them to do penance. A reform soon set in among the people; they heeded his admonitions. God confirmed his words by miracles, and many thousands returned to the allegiance they owed the Church.

Thomas then returned to his hermitage at Foligno, and died there on September 15, 1377. His feast is annually celebrated in the church of St. Augustine at Foligno, where his body has been laid to rest. Although the title of Blessed is given to him in popular devotion, this cult has not been officially approved by the Holy See. (Cf. *These Made Peace*, pp. 127-128.)

ON OBEDIENCE TO SPIRITUAL AUTHORITY

1. Consider the importance of obedience to spiritual superiors, as Blessed Thomas so zealously preached it and so punctually observed it in his own life. When our spiritual superiors give a command, it is as if God Himself gave that command. Christ says of spiritual superiors: "As the Father has

sent Me, I also send you" (Jn. 20,21), and: "He who hears you, hears Me; and he who despises you, despises Me" (Lk. 10,16). He who is obedient to spiritual superiors follows the path that leads to God; he who lets himself be turned from this path permits himself to be deceived by the devil, as our first parents did in Paradise. That is why persons who have done extraordinary things in life have always been tried in their devotional practices by the test of obedience toward their spiritual superiors; and that test determined by what spirit they were being led. — Would your practices stand the same test?

2. Consider why it is necessary in Christian life to be guided by obedience. As a result of original sin, the mind and heart of man are inclined towards evil, inordinate inclinations assert themselves, and a person readily becomes their slave, unless a higher guide directs him and frees him from his slavery. To shield us from that danger and show us the way to the freedom of the children of God, holy Mother Church makes use of the saving force of her authority, which after all makes us truly free. — Who shall say it is a disgrace to subject oneself to such restraint?

3. Consider that the Church has precepts that affect all Catholics, for instance those which bind us to observe the holydays of obligation, to attend holy Mass with devotion on Sundays and holydays, to observe the days of fast and abstinence, and at least once a year to go to confession and receive holy Communion. Again there are special precepts laid down for certain vocations, such as the religious state. Moreover, amid unusual circumstances and dangers she may prescribe special regulations. Over and above this, the Church places a shepherd in charge of each parish, whose duty it is to protect his flock from spiritual harm. — Resolve always to obey your spiritual superior, so that you may not exclude yourself from the flock of Christ, for our Lord says: "If he will not hear the Church, let him be to you as the heathen and publican" (Mt. 18,17).

PRAYER OF THE CHURCH

O God, who hast united the several nations of the Gentiles in the confession of Thy name, give us both the will and the power to obey what Thou commandest; that thy people, called to eternity, may have one faith in their minds, and show one devotion in their actions. Through Christ our Lord. Amen.

SEPTEMBER 17

FEAST OF THE STIGMATA OF OUR HOLY FATHER ST. FRANCIS

RANCIS imitated Christ so perfectly that towards the end of his life our Lord wished to point him out to the world as the faithful imitator of the Crucified, by imprinting His five wounds upon his body.

Two years before his death, when, according to his custom, Francis had repaired to Mt. La Verna to spend the forty days preceding the feast of St. Michael the Archangel in prayer and fasting, this wonderful event took place. St. Bonaventure gives the following account of it:

"Francis was raised to God in the ardor of his seraphic love, wholly transformed by sweet compassion into Him, who, of His exceeding charity, was pleased to be crucified for us. On the morning of the feast of the Exaltation of the Holy Cross, as he was praying in a secret and solitary place on the mountain, Francis beheld a seraph with six wings all afire, descending to him from the heights of heaven. As the seraph flew with great swiftness towards the man of God, there appeared amid the wings the form of one crucified, with his hands and feet stretched out and fixed to the cross. Two wings rose above the head, two were stretched forth in flight, and two veiled the whole body.

"Francis wondered greatly at the appearance of so novel and marvelous a vision. But knowing that the weakness of suffering could in nowise be reconciled with the immortality of the seraphic spirit, he understood the vision as a revelation of the Lord and that it was being presented to his eyes by Divine Providence so that the friend of Christ might be transformed into Christ crucified, not through martyrdom of the flesh, but through a spiritual holocaust.

"The vision, disappearing, left behind it a marvelous fire in the heart of Francis, and a no less wonderful token impressed on his flesh. For there began immediately to appear in his hands and in his feet something like nails as he had just seen them in the vision of the Crucified. The heads of the nails in the hands and feet were round and black, and the points were somewhat long and bent, as if they had been turned back. On the right side, as if it had been pierced by a lance, was the mark of a red wound, from which blood often flowed and stained his tunic."

Thus far the account of St. Bonaventure. Although St. Francis strove in every way to conceal the marvelous marks which until then no man had seen, he was not able to keep them a complete secret from his brethren. After his death they were carefully examined, and they were attested by an ecclesiastical decree. To commemorate the impression of

St. Francis Receives the Stigmata.

the five wounds, Pope Benedict XI instituted a special feast which is celebrated on September seventeenth, not only by all the branches of the Franciscan Order, but also in the Roman missal and breviary.

ON LOOKING UP TO THE CROSS

1. With the example of our holy Father St. Francis in mind, consider what effect a glance at the cross should have on us. It led Francis from the service of the world to the service of God and to penance. A look at the crucifix should remove from our hearts all delight in the world and fill us with sorrow for the sins we have committed in the service of the world and of our evil passions. For what other reason was Christ nailed to the cross, and his whole body bruised? The Prophet tells us: "He was wounded for our iniquities, He was bruised for our sins" (Is. 53,5). Meditation on the sufferings of our Saviour caused St. Francis to shed so many tears that his eyes became inflamed. – Do you also kneel before the crucifix and bewail the sins through which you nailed your Saviour to the Cross?

2. Consider that a look at the cross is also a consolation for the sinner. Our crucified Lord assured St. Francis of the complete remission of his sins. The Prophet also tells us: "By His bruises we are healed" (Is. 53,5). Moses gave us a picture of our Saviour on the Cross when he raised a brazen serpent on high in the desert, so that those who had been bitten by the poisonous serpent in punishment for their murmuring might be healed by looking up to this sign of our redemption. On the crucifix you behold our Saviour Himself. "Behold the Lamb of God; behold Him who takes away the sins of the world" (Jn. 1,29). – Look up to Him with sincere contrition and lively confidence; He will also take away your sins.

3. Consider how the contemplation of the Crucified finally pierced St. Francis through and through with the fire of love, so that our Lord made him even externally like Himself. A look at the crucifix should also awaken ardent charity in us. St. Augustine points this out to us when he says: "Behold the head that is bent to kiss you, the heart that is opened to receive you, the arms stretched out to embrace you." Do not look at the image of your crucified Saviour in the cold and indifferent way that one looks at a work of art, to marvel at the painful expression there represented. Let it speak to your heart and let your heart speak to it. Serve Him faithfully so that you may one day be united with Him in eternity.

PRAYER OF THE CHURCH

O Lord Jesus Christ, who when the world was growing cold, didst renew the sacred wounds of Thy sufferings in the body of our holy Father St. Francis in order to inflame our hearts with the fire of Thy divine love, mercifully grant that by his merits and intercession we may cheerfully carry our cross and bring forth worthy fruits of penance. Who livest and reignest forever and ever. Amen.

SEPTEMBER 18
ST. JOSEPH OF COPERTINO
Confessor, First Order

T. AUGUSTINE says: "Do you wish to become great, then begin by being small." God often deals in that way with His saints. He often permits the most glorious saints to begin in the deepest lowliness. St. Joseph of Copertino in the old kingdom of Naples is an example in point. His father was a humble carpenter, who had contracted very heavy debts and was in very straitened circumstances at the time Joseph was born. His mother was very strict with him. He used to say in later life that he made his novitiate while still a child. Nevertheless Joseph performed additional penances and appeared to have been given a body merely for the purpose of mortifying it. Even as a child he lived in close union with God, so that he dwelt in heaven rather than on earth.

In time he was sent to learn a trade, but it was soon noticed that this was not his vocation. He was eventually invested with the Franciscan habit among the Capuchins, but was soon dismissed because of his awkwardness. The result was that his own relatives turned him out as a useless creature and a disgrace to his family. Finally, the Conventuals took pity on the young man who so humbly pleaded for admission and employed him to take care of the convent mule. In this lowly service his virtues, especially his humility, obedience, and piety, shone forth with such brilliance that his superiors received him among the clerics, and within three years he was ordained a priest.

Joseph's natural knowledge was of small account, for his efforts to learn by study were never successful. But it was soon perceived that he possessed much infused knowledge, so that even great theologians marveled at it. His life was one of uninterrupted union with God.

Everything in nature lifted him up to heaven and to the supernatural. Not only his spirit but also his body was so frequently raised above the earth in holy rapture and remained in that position for so long a time, that his biographer declares he spent more than half of his religious life above the earth. Sometimes he flew to the objects of his devotion in swiftest flight.

On an elevation near the convent three crosses had been erected. Repeatedly when he looked at them, he would rise in the air with a cry and fly to the cross in the center, embracing it and remaining in that position until the end of the ecstasy. On another occasion, when he visited the Basilica of St. Francis, he saw a painting of the Mother of God high up in the vault of the church; at once his body rose into the air, and he kissed the image with tender devotion. At holy Mass he was usually lifted in the air and remained there swaying over the altar for hours at a time. For that reason, he usually said Mass in the convent chapel rather than in the church.

What impression these ecstasies made on witnesses may be deduced from the story of Duke John Frederick of Brunswick. In 1649 he once attended the Mass offered up by Father Joseph. He was so impressed by the ecstasy that he was convinced of the truth of the Catholic Faith and two years later made his profession of faith before Father Joseph himself.

Because these visions were so extraordinary, Father Joseph's virtue was also tested. God Himself permitted Joseph to be severely tempted by the devil. Added to this, he suffered for years from dryness of heart, so that he felt completely forsaken by God. But all these trials could not embitter his heart; he placed it within the wound of our Saviour's side and preserved peace of mind. He had no other wish but to do the will of God.

After he had stood the test of many storms, he was again rewarded with heavenly consolation. Desiring to be with Christ, he died in the convent at Osimo on September 18, 1663. Numerous miracles occurred at his grave, and Pope Clement XIII canonized him in 1753. Because of his miraculous flights through the air, he is now honored as a patron of those who travel by air. The feast of St. Joseph is celebrated by the three branches of the First Order on September eighteenth. (Cf. *Forum*, 1942, p. 389.)

ON THE WOUND IN THE SIDE OF CHRIST

1. Just as the heart of St. Francis was filled with ardent love for his crucified Lord, so his son St. Joseph was attracted to the cross. He soared to it in marvelous flight as though his body possessed the lightness of glorified bodies, and there he rested at the open wound in the side of his

Lord, at the Sacred Heart Itself. Christ said: "If I be lifted up from the earth, I will draw all things to Myself" (Jn. 12,32). How is it that we are not more attracted to Him, at least in the depths of our heart? We lack the proper interior sentiments. "By two wings," says Thomas a Kempis (2,4), "is man lifted up above earthly things, namely by simplicity and purity. Simplicity must be in the intention, purity in the affection." — Examine yourself. In what are you wanting?

Consider with what sentiments we should be inspired by the wound in the side of Christ. We should have the sentiments of Christ's own Heart. "Let this mind be in you which was also in Christ Jesus" (Phil. 2,5). From this Sacred Heart we should above all learn meekness and humility, that marvelous compassion to which our Lord alluded when He said: "Whosoever shall speak a word against the Son of Man, it shall be forgiven him" (Mt. 12,32), and which He exercised when He hung upon the cross praying for His executioners and blasphemers. In this Sacred Heart St. Joseph placed all his trials and crosses before they could touch his own heart. Act likewise, place your trials and temptations there, so that the meekness of Christ may encompass you.

Consider with what spirit we should be imbued after contemplating the wound in the side of Christ. We should be filled with zeal for the cause of Christ and the desire to promote the honor and glory of God and to gain souls for Him. It was this zeal that burned in the heart of our saint; to this end he directed all his prayers and works of penance. How much zeal have we for the cause of God, for the salvation of our own soul and the souls of our fellowmen? How lukewarm, how indifferent we are in these matters! Go frequently to the wound in the side of Christ, and beg Him to draw you to Himself, so that the zeal of His Sacred Heart may be kindled in you.

PRAYER OF THE CHURCH

O God, who didst ordain that all men be attracted to Thy only-begotten Son, who was raised above the earth, mercifully grant that, by the merits and intercession of Thy seraphic confessor Joseph, we may be raised above earthly desires and deserve to be admitted into his company. Who livest and reignest forever and ever. Amen.

SEPTEMBER 19
THE SERVANT OF GOD PETER DE CORPA AND COMPANIONS
Martyrs, First Order

N 1597, the same year in which St. Peter Baptist and his companions were crucified on Nagasaki Hill in Japan, five Franciscan missionaries in what is now the American state of Georgia won the martyr's crown when they were killed by apostate and pagan Indians.

In colonial times, Spanish Florida comprised the entire southeastern portion of the United States. The first Franciscan missionaries in this territory, if one excepts those who were with the Narvaez and De Soto expeditions, arrived in 1573; and for almost two centuries the sons of St. Francis continued their heroic work in this vast Indian mission field. During the first two decades progress was rather slow; but by 1595 they had founded missions, not only in the vicinity of St. Augustine, but also in Guale, the present Georgia. The latter were situated on the so-called Golden Isles and the nearby mainland.

Father Peter de Corpa was at the mission of Tolomato, on the mainland opposite Sapelo Island. At the mission of Tupique, also on the mainland, just north of Tolomato, there was Father Blase de Rodriguez. The mission on St. Catharine's Island, opposite Tupique, was in charge of Father Michael de Añon, the commissary or superior, and Brother Anthony de Badajoz. The southernmost mission, that on St. Simon Island, was in the care of Father Francis de Verascola.

Many of the Guale Indians had been converted to Christianity, and the missions were in a flourishing condition. However, at Tolomato, the Indian chieftain, Juanillo by name, who had been baptized, was reprimanded and finally deposed by Father Peter because he continued to violate the laws of Christian marriage. Juanillo then became an apostate, gathered a force of pagan Indians, and sought to wipe out Christianity and restore paganism by killing the missionaries and destroying the missions.

During the night the rebel Indians concealed themselves in the church at Tolomato; and on the morning of September 13, 1597, as Father Peter opened the door of the church, two chiefs fell upon him and beat him to death with clubs. Afterwards they cut off the martyr's head and placed it on top of a pole.

Then they went to Tupique, and told Father Blase that he too must die at their hands. But he persuaded them to allow him to offer up the holy Sacrifice of the Mass first. Some time later he made a touching address, saying to them: "My children, for me it is not a difficult thing to die, for death of the body will come even though you be not the instrument of my death ... What hurts me is your loss, and that the devil has been able to make you commit so great an offense against your God and Creator." They held him as a prisoner for two days; and on September 16 one of the rebel chiefs dealt him a mortal blow with a hatchet as he knelt in the mission church.

Proceeding to St. Catharine's Island, the rebels killed the two missionaries there on die next day, September 17. Father Michael, who was in the church at the time, saw how they struck down Brother Anthony in the yard with a large wooden knife which was edged with flint, and knew that he too would die. One blow with a tomahawk put an end to the Father Commissary's life.

On one of the following days Father Francis was returning to his mission on St. Simon Island from St. Augustine whither he had gone to fetch supplies. As he drew up to the water's edge in his boat, the murderers seized him by the shoulders and slew him with their tomahawks, cutting up his body beyond recognition.

The Juanillo Revolt seemed to have succeeded, but in 1605 the Guale missions were re-established and began to flourish once more. The blood of martyrs once more became the seed of Christians.

In 1950 a pro-postulator was appointed for the cause of these five martyrs, and a commission gathered all the historical documents concerning their death. These were sent to Rome and are now in the hands of the Franciscan postulator general. (Cf. *Heroes of the Cross*, pp. 58-63; *The Martyrs of the United States of America*, pp. 56-57, 123.)

ON THE LAWS OF CHRISTIAN MARRIAGE

1. The laws of God concerning marriage are clear, and with regard to them there can be no compromise. Christ, who raised the natural contract of marriage to the rank of a sacrament, declared: "What God has joined together, let no man put asunder" (Mt. 19,6). "Everyone who puts away his wife and marries another commits adultery; and he who marries a woman who has been put away from her husband commits adultery" (Lk. 16,18). "Anyone who so much as looks with lust at a woman has already committed adultery with her in his heart" (Mt. 5,28). No matter what the cost, the Church will not and can not make any mitigating concession in regard to these laws. St. John the Baptist said to Herod: "It is not lawful for you to have your brother's wife" (Mk. 6,18). He was cast into prison, and afterwards his head was brought to Herodias on a dish. Father John de

Corpa said to Chief Juanillo: "It is not lawful for you to have other wives besides the one to whom you are legitimately married." His head too was cut off and placed on a pole. Would that all Christians had the steadfastness and courage of such martyrs! Alas, many of them are so influenced by the spirit of the modern world that they grow weak, entertain false notions regarding the indissolubility and unity of marriage, and in the time of temptation fall and are estranged from God.

The Church has the right and the power to make additional laws and regulations concerning matrimony, for instance those which determine the impediments invalidating marriage. Some of these laws are merely a further expression and explanation of the divine and natural law; others safeguard the sanctity and security of marriage. It belongs to the Church to ordain all that concerns sacred things, especially the sacraments, and to establish the laws which regulate their administration; and matrimony is a religious contract and a sacrament. "He who hears you," said our Lord, "hears Me; and he who despises you, despises Me; and he who despises Me, despises Him who sent Me" (Lk. 10,16).

2. How many young people forget what they have learned in school about the Church's laws concerning marriage, recklessly disobey those laws, and then live in bad marriages! Apostolic-minded Catholics will do all they can to prevent such marriages, or to have them validated if that is possible, or at least to pray for such unfortunate persons who have placed themselves outside the pale of the Church by their marriages. They can, for instance, invoke the intercession of the martyrs, Peter de Corpa and companions, in behalf of those who can not receive the sacraments because they are married outside the Church.

3. The Church abhors and forbids mixed marriages, and only reluctantly grants dispensations for such marriages to avoid greater evils. In such marriages there is no true union between husband and wife in regard to their principal duties on earth. The Catholic party exposes himself to the danger of gradually becoming careless and indifferent in the practice of his religion, and even of losing his faith altogether. Father and mother can not work in harmony at the task of imparting a religious training to their children; and often the children, especially after leaving school, forget the religious instruction they have received, neglect their religious duties, and themselves enter mixed marriages. Good Catholic parents will do all they can to make their children realize from early youth how undesirable mixed marriages are, and to strengthen in them the firm resolution never to enter such marriages. Asking the intercession of the martyrs, Peter de Corpa and companions, will help parents to steer their children away from mixed marriages and to guide and assist them in the observance of all the

laws of God and the Church concerning matrimony. Such private devotion to these holy martyrs may also speed the introduction of their cause of beatification; and once beatified, or even canonized, they could become the special patrons for the solution of difficult marriage cases and marriage problems in the modern world.

PRAYER OF THE CHURCH
(From the Nuptial Blessing during holy Mass)

Be favorable, O Lord, unto our prayers, and graciously protect Thine ordinance, whereby Thou hast provided for the propagation of mankind: that what is joined together by Thine authority may be preserved by Thy help. Through Christ our Lord. Amen.

SEPTEMBER 20
BLESSED CHARLES OF BLOIS
Confessor, Third Order

CHARLES, Duke of Brittany in the fourteenth century, was a brave soldier who was forced to wage a life-long war and lost his life on the battlefield. He was also an exemplary Tertiary of St. Francis who wore a hair shirt and daily assisted at holy Mass and recited the divine office. And about six hundred years after his birth he was enrolled among the blessed by the Holy See.

Born about 1316, Charles was the son of Louis de Chatallon, Count of Blois, and Margaret, sister of King Philip VI of France. Even as a boy he was known for his virtue as well as his bravery. When he was twenty-five, in 1341, he married Joan of Brittany and thus became Duke of Brittany. However, his uncle, John de Montfort, refused to recognize Charles' rightful claim to the dukedom. Charles did all he possibly could to settle the matter peaceably, but his efforts were in vain. A bloody war of four years ensued, during which Charles succeeded at first in repelling the attacks made upon him.

The duke was a model Christian soldier. He required his soldiers to attend holy Mass daily. When they objected, he replied: "We can afford to lose castles, but we can not let a day go by without attending holy Mass." He made careful provision for those who were wounded in battle; and to help his fallen soldiers, he founded religious houses where Masses were celebrated and prayers were offered up for the repose of their souls.

After four years of fighting, de Montfort obtained help from England and defeated Charles in a decisive battle. Charles was taken prisoner and held by the English in the Tower of London for nine years. There he lived like a holy recluse, devoting much time to prayer and never showing any signs of impatience, so that even his jailers were edified.

Finally Charles was released and returned to Brittany; but his implacable uncle renewed his attacks on him, until in the battle at Auray, on September 29, 1364, Charles was killed, fighting bravely. On that day, he had prepared himself for battle by receiving the sacraments with such devotion as if he knew that he would not survive.

Soon after his death, miracles were reported at his grave, and the people began to venerate him as a saint. This cult was kept up through the centuries; and on December 14, 1904, the Holy See gave its official approval and thus declared him blessed. However, his feast is not observed in any of the Franciscan calendars. (Cf. Biersack, p. 23.)

ON ZEAL FOR THE SOULS IN PURGATORY

1. Consider the pious zeal displayed by Blessed Charles for the souls of his fallen soldiers. His kind heart saw them suffering the pain of which the Apostle speaks when he says of the departed Christian whose works are found wanting: "But he himself shall be saved, yet so as by fire" (1 Cor. 3,15). Our good works and principally the holy sacrifice of the Mass can release the holy souls from this cleansing fire. Would it not indicate shocking heartlessness not to concern oneself in the least about them? Like Blessed Charles who had religious houses built, you can practice corporal and spiritual works of mercy at one and the same time if you give alms to worthy causes with the intention that they may benefit the holy souls. It "purges away sins and helps us to find mercy and life everlasting" (Tob. 12,9). — How much zeal for the holy souls have you shown in the past?

2. Consider how this zeal for the holy souls must please almighty God. These souls are the beloved children of God. As they long for God, so God longs for them. But His sanctity and justice have tied His hands so that He cannot release them until they have paid the last farthing. How much it must please Him, then, if we pay off this debt! Our Lord said to St. Gertrude: "God accepts every soul you release, as if you had released Him personally from captivity, and in His own good time He will repay you for the benefits you have rendered Him." — Should that not arouse and increase our zeal for the holy souls?

3. Consider what benefit this zeal affords us personally. We cause God

Himself to look with favor on us. The souls that have been released through us will, in their gratitude, not cease to pray for us at the throne of God until they see us in heaven, and we ourselves will walk more securely if we often remember the sufferings of the holy souls. We will endeavor to remain faithful to God, not only in things that are important, but we will avoid infidelity even in lesser things, since it must be expiated in so painful a manner. So let us often offer up the holy sacrifice of Mass, and pray that God may grant mercy to the holy souls. Let us also induce others to observe this practice. Then we shall also obtain mercy for ourselves.

PRAYER OF THE CHURCH
(Number 12 under "Various Prayers for the Departed")

We beseech Thee, O Lord, to grant everlasting mercy to the souls of Thy servants and handmaids that the faith and hope which they put in Thee may avail them forevermore. Through Christ our Lord. Amen.

***

SEPTEMBER 21
BLESSED JULIAN OF GERMANY
Confessor, First Order

E do not know in what place in Germany Blessed Julian was born. He himself wanted to forget his home and country so that, unknown and undisturbed, he could serve God more perfectly in Italy. He entered the Franciscan Order in Aquila at the time St. Bernardin of Siena died there. Julian lived a very strict life as a friar and a priest. In the forty years he spent in religious life, he never partook of meat or wine; his only sustenance was bread with herbs, and water was his drink.

Although he possessed great intelligence, he was so humble that he never permitted it to be noticed. He shuddered at holding an office to which honors were attached; still, he was obliged to accept the office of provincial in the province of St. Bernardin when he was sixty years old. Because he administered this office in so praiseworthy a manner, his confreres were going to re-elect him; but his tears, prayers, and remonstrances finally prevailed upon them to elect someone else for the position.

Father Julian never wearied of activity in the confessional. By means of solid knowledge, zeal for souls, and piety, he achieved remarkable success as a spiritual director. The remainder of his time he spent in prayer and contemplation, during which he was favored by God with extraordinary graces.

He died in the odor of sanctity on September 30, 1486, in the seventy-sixth year of his life. A magnificent tomb was prepared for him in the church of St. Bernardin in Aquila, where several miracles were wrought. The title of Blessed has been conferred on him in popular devotion.

ON THE BENEFITS OF THE SACRAMENT OF PENANCE

1. Consider the zeal of Blessed Julian in administering the sacrament of penance. He knew the great benefits of this sacrament, of which St. Anthony of Padua said: "In sermons the seed is sown, in the confessional the fruit is gathered in." The fruit consists above all in the reconciliation of the penitent sinner with God. The confessional is like the miraculous pool at Jerusalem, into which an angel descended at specified times, and the first patient to enter the waters was healed "of whatsoever infirmity he lay under" (Jn. 5,4). The priest is this angel of God in the confessional, who has the power to heal the sinner of the disease of his soul, and not only the first sinner that makes his appearance, but everyone who comes properly prepared. — What should keep sinners from hastening to avail themselves of this spiritual bath?

2. Consider that to receive the sacrament of penance with profit, it is above all necessary that we be sincerely sorry for our sins. Of course, we must also seriously examine our conscience after we have called upon the Holy Ghost for help, we must honestly confess all our mortal sins, and we are obliged to say the penance imposed upon us. But the most important and necessary requirement is sincere, supernatural contrition for our sins, to which must be joined a firm purpose not to sin again. Just as there can be no valid baptism without water, so there can be no valid confession without contrition. The more perfect our contrition is, the greater will be the benefit we derive from the sacrament of penance. Therefore, make an act of contrition immediately after you have made your examination of conscience and then repeat it briefly but sincerely while the priest is giving you absolution.

3. Consider that we can derive profit from the sacrament of penance even if we have no mortal sin to confess. For this holy sacrament also remits venial sins, increases sanctifying grace in the soul, strengthens the soul against a relapse into sin, and always remits temporal punishment due to our sins. But since this always takes place through absolution, it is

necessary to confess at least one specific sin; where there is no sin, there can be no absolution. Should it happen that since your last confession you have no actual sin to confess, then accuse yourself of one that you committed in your past life and which you again regret, in the spirit of the Psalmist: "Wash me yet more from my iniquity, and cleanse me from my sin" (Ps. 50,4). Then the holy sacrament will always increase your peace of heart.

PRAYER OF THE CHURCH
(From the Mass for the Forgiveness of Sins)

Give ear, we beseech Thee, O Lord, to the prayers of Thy suppliant people, and punish us not for our sins, which we confess before Thee, but in Thy mercy grant us both pardon and peace. Through Christ our Lord. Amen.

SEPTEMBER 22
BLESSED LUCY OF CALTAGIRONE
Virgin, Third Order

UCY was born of devout and distinguished parents at Caltagirone, in Sicily. Heaven watched over her in a special way from her earliest years. When she was six years old, she went to the country with her mother one day, and there climbed a fig tree to pick figs. As frequently happens in the southern part of Europe, a storm arose very suddenly. Lightning struck the tree and split it asunder. The child lay on the ground as if dead. But an old man suddenly stood beside her, picked her up, and led her, as if nothing had happened, to the house to which her mother had run for safety. At the door Lucy asked her rescuer who he was. He replied: "I am St. Nicholas, whom your parents honor in a special way; as a reward, I have taken you under my special protection."

Thenceforth Lucy was devoted to works of piety. It was her greatest pleasure to attend divine services and to be of assistance to the poor.

She had just about attained the age of young womanhood when a Tertiary from Salerno came to Caltagirone to visit some relatives. She was an object of edification to everybody. Lucy became a companion of this Tertiary and then joined the Third Order herself. When the young woman returned to her native town, Lucy went with her. The young woman received Lucy into her own home as her spiritual daughter, and as a result of her guidance, Lucy made daily progress in perfection. She led a life of recollection and practiced rigorous penance. At the same time she was sympathetic and kind to the poor and the sick.

At the death of her friend, who had been like a mother to her, Lucy entered the convent of the Tertiaries of St. Mary Magdalen in Salerno. Even as a novice she was a model of humility and obedience. Her heart was occupied with the contemplation of the sufferings of Christ, and she endeavored to share His sufferings by crucifying her own flesh. She was favored by God with special graces, and ere long the fame of her sanctity spread far and wide. People came to her from the surrounding towns to ask her prayers or to seek advice. No one in distress ever left her without being consoled, and at her recommendation many sinners were converted and pious souls were encouraged to strive for still greater perfection.

After a long and painful illness Lucy entered the joys of heaven on September twenty-sixth. It is not quite certain in what year she died, but it was about the year 1400. The numerous miracles that occurred at her grave were ample testimony of her sanctity. A great number of silver eyes have been left at her tomb, because many who suffered from diseases of the eyes, and even blind persons were cured through her intercession. Pope Leo X confirmed the uninterrupted veneration with which she has been honored. Her feast is celebrated on September twenty-sixth by the Franciscans, the Conventuals, and the Third Order Regular. (Cf. *Forum*, 1949, pp. 270-272.)

ON THE PROTECTION OF THE SAINTS

1. Consider the great protection which Lucy enjoyed in her youth from St. Nicholas. This saint is a special patron of children because he was so holy a child himself and because he conferred so many favors on children and young people during his lifetime. In order to make known the special love of this saint for children, it is a custom in many places to celebrate his feastday by presenting gifts to children. It would be well if we not only related pious stories about St. Nicholas to the children, but also pointed out the love which he extended to children while he was still on earth, and which impels him in heaven to watch over them, as many instances illustrate. — Often recommend your little ones to the protection of St. Nicholas.

2. Consider how Blessed Lucy was guided through life, away from home, by the protection of her patron, and was led to perfection by this saintly friend. From their own experience the saints in heaven know the dangers that beset us here on earth. While they were in this vale of tears, they took

great pleasure in protecting their fellowmen from these dangers and leading them on the right road. Would this pleasure now be denied them in heaven? We are united to them by the communion of saints as members of one body, the Church. They have come closer to the Head, who is Christ, and can, therefore, be of greater assistance to us now during our pilgrimage on earth. Recommend yourself to them with filial confidence: the patron whose name you bear, the patron of the parish to which you belong, and any other to whom you maybe especially devoted. 3. Consider how Blessed Lucy was a special friend to mortal men after she had joined the saints in heaven. The precious gift of sight was granted to many persons at her intercession. Among these were the abbess of her own convent, who had become almost totally blind, a young woman who had not had the use of her eyes for fourteen months, a blind servant of the bishop of Salerno, and many others. God grants to certain of His saints special power against certain evils, as we perceive in so many instances. Should we not be grateful for such patrons and confidently call upon the saints, without of course neglecting natural remedies? They can doubtless aid us more effectively than the most skilled physicians.

PRAYER OF THE CHURCH
(Feast of All Saints)

Almighty and eternal God, by whose favor we pay honor to the merits of all Thy saints; inasmuch as so many are pleading for us, we beseech Thee, to confer upon us the fulness of Thy mercy for which we long. Through Christ our Lord. Amen.

SEPTEMBER 23
THE SERVANT OF GOD MARY EMMANUELA
Widow, Second Order

MARY EMMANUELA was a Spanish princess, a descendant of the famous dukes of Medina-Sidonia. Her noble rank, the wealth of her family, and her exceptional beauty caused her to give herself up entirely to the world and its vanities. The fact that she remained childless in the married state, only made her seek consolation in dissipating diversions and sinful gratifications.

But the mercy of God caused a fortunate misfortune to tear her away from the abyss to which she was hastening. With another duchess she was crossing a bridge, when the beams suddenly gave way and the bridge fell into the river. Her companion was hurled into the water and drowned; but Emmanuela remained suspended by her clothes from a beam that still stood in place. In this dangerous predicament she made a vow that if she were saved, she would change her life and build a Franciscan convent. She was saved and brought to shore unharmed.

At once she began the erection of the Franciscan convent and church at Seville, and when her husband died, she entered the monastery of the Poor Clares in that city. There she was an object of edification to all the sisters on account of her zeal for penance, her humility, and her unceasing prayer for the divine mercy. Her desire to make satisfaction for her sins urged her, towards the close of her life, to transfer to a Poor Clare community of stricter observance. There she died in the year 1543. When her grave was opened forty years later, her body was found incorrupt.

ON THE BLESSINGS OF MISFORTUNE

1. Consider that the mishap which Emmanuela had on the bridge might seem the worst sort of misfortune if viewed from a human viewpoint; in reality, however, it was the greatest good fortune, the means to preserve her from eternal damnation. It often happens that temporal misfortune contributes to a person's eternal welfare. The loss of temporal goods, sickness and misery, also slander and contempt even from our friends, help us to recognize the nothingness of everything earthly. It helps us to enter into ourselves and to turn our hearts and our efforts to the one supreme and true Good. Sacred history is filled with examples of the sort. Was it not a great misfortune for the prodigal son that he was completely forsaken and indigent? He then entered into himself and returned to his father. — How much of such blessed misfortune there is in the world! Consult your own experience.

2. Consider that it can likewise be said that there is much unfortunate good fortune in the world. What everyone praises as great good fortune is often very real misfortune. The servant of God Emmanuela descended from a very renowned family, was very rich and very attractive. Who would not have considered her very fortunate on that account? And yet, this temporal good fortune was for her an occasion to reach such a pitiable state of soul, that later on she could never bewail it sufficiently. O deceptive fortune of the children of men! How often it is a snare which our enemy lays to destroy us in time and in eternity! Ought a Christian really ever desire such good fortune?

3. Consider that, accordingly, we should look upon the toward and the

untoward in an entirely different light than that with which worldly people look upon diem. We can serve God as well in sorrow and in poverty and be truly happy as in wealth and prosperity; that is plain from the life of Job. Today everyone of us would rather change places with poor Lazarus than with wealthy Dives. We do not know what is most conducive to our true good fortune. Hence, we should let God rule over us, be grateful to Him for the pleasant things of life and be resigned in unpleasant circumstances, ever striving for one thing only — to belong to God. "To those who love God, all things work together unto good" (Rom. 8,28).

PRAYER OF THE CHURCH
(Third Prayer on Ember Saturday in Lent)

Give ear to our prayers, we beseech Thee, O Lord, that through Thy grace, we may both deserve to be humble in prosperity and safe in adversity. Through Christ our Lord. Amen.

ⁿⁿⁿⁿⁿⁿⁿⁿⁿ

SEPTEMBER 24
ST. PACIFIC OF SAN SEVERINO
Confessor, First Order

PACIFIC was born of a distinguished family in the Italian city of San Severino. As a child he evinced unusual seriousness, great piety, and love of mortification.

Early in his youthful life this spirit of mortification was put to the test. He was quite young when he became an orphan, and was taken to the home of his uncle, who brought him up very strictly. Two servants in his uncle's home could not bear the sight of the boy and caused him many unpleasant experiences. If anything went wrong in the house, even if they were to blame for it, they accused the boy; and his uncle would then punish him severely for it. Pacific accepted the punishment in the spirit of mortification, bore it with remarkable patience, and so advanced in virtue.

Our Lord saw to it that his virtue was made manifest. One day a servant knocked the spigot of a wine barrel loose and all the wine ran out into the cellar. She blamed Pacific for it. His uncle took the boy down into the cellar with him to show him what he had done and to give him the punishment he deserved. The boy went along calmly. When they reached the cellar, they found the floor quite dry and the barrel full of wine. The maid was called, and when she saw the miracle, she admitted her fault and praised the holiness of the innocent boy.

When he was seventeen years old, Pacific entered the Order of Friars Minor. After the year of probation, he made his vows, and from that time took great pains to observe them perfectly. He was ordained to the priesthood when he was twenty-five years old. He was first assigned to the surrounding villages of the Apennines, where he found the greatest delight in preaching the Gospel to the poor and the uneducated. No road was too rough, no mountain too steep for him. He looked up the poor shepherds in their out-of-the-way huts in order to instruct and guide them on the road that leads to God. But he was not long to enjoy this apostolic work. After a few years, he became ill and never completely recovered his health, so that he was obliged to serve God patiently with an infirm body for more than thirty years.

Pacific was completely satisfied with God's designs in his regard. "God wills it," he said in a cheerful way, "and so may His will be done." The painful suffering he had to endure, and the many acts of mortification he performed in addition, he joined to his unceasing prayers and offered them up for the salvation of souls and the conversion of sinners. Even in his sickness he was so modest that he would never allow anyone else to dress the ugly sores on his legs, but always took care of them himself.

When he was able to say holy Mass, he did it with the utmost fervor and devotion. In his later years he was often favored with ecstasies after the elevation at holy Mass. His countenance shone with a radiance like that of the sun. The sick were miraculously cured by him, and he foretold many future events.

When death finally summoned him and he had received holy Communion for the last time with admirable devotion, he once more expressed his gratitude to God for all His benefits, and then, with his hands crossed upon his breast, surrendered his soul to his Creator. The day was September 24, 1721.

Many miracles occurred at his grave, and two dead persons were restored to life after his holy relics were applied to them. Pope Gregory XVI canonized him in 1839. His feast is observed by the three branches of the First Order and also by the Third Order Regular on September twenty-fourth.

Vera Effigie del Ven: Servo di Dio P. Pacifico
da S. Severino Sac.~ Minore Osser. Riformato mor-
to nel Convento di S.~ Maria delle Grazie di detta
Città in età d'anni 68. è Mesi 6. l'anno 1721. li
24. Settembre

ON CONFORMITY WITH THE DIVINE WILL

1. Consider how St. Pacific arrived at a high degree of sanctity despite the
fact that he was quite unfit for work. His conformity with the will of God
did it. Already as a child he accustomed himself to accept everything as
coming from the hands of God. And so, when his apostolic career was cut
short so early in life, he did not find it hard to say: "God wills it, may His
holy will be done." The Holy Ghost says: "They who are faithful in love
shall rest in Him" (Wisd. 3,9). This perfect peace, in which we rest content
with all things as happening to us by God's holy will, is a proof that we
are devoted to God in faithful love. That is what true piety and perfection
consist in, not in great undertakings. — Do you strive to acquire this
genuine conformity with the divine will?

2. Consider that man's real accomplishments here on earth depend on his
conformity with the will of God. God has need of no man. The Psalmist
says: "Thou art my God, for Thou hast no need of my goods" (Ps. 15,2).
But almighty God wishes to use human beings as His tools here on earth.
People that are entirely conformed with God's holy will are His most
useful tools. Is it not possible, then, that Pacific accomplished more in his
sufferings than many a missionary in years of toil? You complain, perhaps
that because of your infirmity you are not able to do much work. Be
resigned to God's holy will, do what you can, and pray for your
fellowmen; then God almighty will recompense you abundantly. In a
speeding train, the rusty couplings that bind the coaches together are as
important as the puffing locomotive. — Perhaps God has chosen you to act
the part of such couplings in life.

Consider how happy we can be in trial and suffering if we are resigned to
God's holy will. Faith teaches us that God has only our welfare at heart.
He who is entirely resigned to God's holy will is therefore steering
straight toward the goal of his own happiness. With this in mind, he bears
the sufferings of time as a means to reach his blessed goal, so that even if
nature sighs, he preserves interior peace and joy. "To them who love God
all things work together unto good" (Rom. 8,28). It was from this
knowledge that St. Pacific drew his invincible patience; and that is why he
loved to be alone, because in that way he could more readily attain to true
union with God and make a complete oblation of himself. If we imitate the
resignation of St. Pacific, at the end of our life we shall, like him, render
fervent thanks to God for all His benefits to us.

PRAYER OF THE CHURCH

O God, the Dispenser of all good, who didst clothe St. Pacific, Thy confessor, with the virtue of great patience and of love for seclusion, grant, at his intercession, that we may walk the same way and obtain the same reward. Through Christ our Lord. Amen.

SEPTEMBER 25
BLESSED FRANCIS MARY OF CAMPOROSSO
Confessor, First Order

IN the cemetery in Genoa a statue of Blessed Francis Mary may be seen which bears the following inscription: "Francis of Camporosso was born on December 27, 1804, and died on September 17, 1866. This poor man in Christ was more blessed in giving than in receiving. With bread and advice and consolation, he was ever prepared to minister to the sufferings and needs of all who came to him. His austere and holy life he crowned with the sacrifice he made of himself at the beginning of the epidemic of 1866. The sorrow and gratitude of the people prompted them to immortalize his image in this marble statue."

It needed but a few words to say all that one could wish to have said of this apostle of the people. As a shepherd in the little village of Camporosso near San Remo he was obliged to contribute to the support of his family. Later he joined the Capuchins in Genoa. There he clothed his ideals and intentions in the words: "I came to the convent to be its beast of burden."

The opportunity was presented to him to carry out his intentions when he was made infirmarian, and especially when he was appointed to collect alms. He called at the palaces of the nobles, but oftener at the huts of the poor in order to distribute to them the alms he had just begged. He ventured to go into the ill-famed quarters of the seaport, where he would pick up the stones thrown at him and kiss them. By and by he held all these people fascinated. Soon it was reported of him from all sides that he was working miracles, cures, and conversions of a most unusual kind. People of rank as well as the lowliest souls came to him to seek advice.

His love for our Blessed Lady was most touching. He spent entire nights on his knees before the Blessed Sacrament. When an epidemic broke out in 1866, he was seized with the desire to make his last and most magnanimous sacrifice. He knelt before the altar of the Immaculate Virgin, and through her hands offered himself to God as a victim of expiation. On September seventeenth, he departed this life as a victim. The epidemic ceased that very day. He was beatified by Pope Pius XI. The Franciscans celebrate his feast on September twenty-fifth, and the Capuchins on the sixteenth.

ON SELF-SACRIFICE

1. Blessed Francis Mary offered everything he possessed. He was well aware of our Lord's words: "Everyone of you who does not renounce all that he possesses, cannot be my disciple" (Lk. 14,33). As a child he worked for his parents; in the order, he became a servant to the other members; as the apostle of the people he worked for the poor and the sick. — Does your life agree with the Christian principle, "It is more blessed to give than to receive"?

2. Blessed Francis Mary also sacrificed his life. He lived up to the admonition of the Apostle: "In this we have known the charity of God, because he has laid down His life for us: and we ought to lay down our lives for the brethren" (1 Jn. 3,16). Francis Mary did this literally when he sacrificed his life for the people during the epidemic. — Pray God to give you a share of this heroic courage, of this heroic love.

3. Blessed Francis Mary received an inestimable reward for his sacrifice. Posterity is extolling him. The Church has raised him to the dignity of the altars. Almighty God has fulfilled in him the promise: "And you shall have treasure in heaven" (Mt. 19,21). Whatever we do for God will not go unrewarded. God will not let Himself be outdone in generosity. — Rouse yourself to a similar spirit of sacrifice.

PRAYER OF THE CHURCH

O God, who didst cause Thy humble servant Francis Mary to distinguish himself in an extraordinary way by works of charity, grant that by his merits and intercession Thy love may ever be increased in our hearts. Through Christ our Lord. Amen.

SEPTEMBER 26
BLESSED DELPHINA OF GLANDEVES
Virgin, Third Order

LESSED DELPHINA was the only daughter of the wealthy Count William of Glandeves in southern France. She lost both parents when she was seven years old, but the little orphan was received into a convent school where an aunt of hers was abbess. There she received an excellent education in the fear of the Lord and in everything pertaining to her eminent rank.

Delphina had already consecrated herself to God by the vow of virginity, when King Charles II chose her as Elzear's bride. Filled with consternation, Delphina had recourse to the Blessed Virgin, to whose motherly care she had entrusted herself. Our Lady appeared to her and calmed her fears. Delphina then consented to the marriage, which took place with great solemnity in the presence of the king and of the archbishop of Aix. The holy innocence of his spouse filled Elzear with such love of holy purity that he made a vow to act only as the protector of her virginity, and he was faithful to this pledge all his life. They lived together like two angels, the one ever encouraging the other in more ardent love of God.

Delphina devoted herself to the care of her household. The servants, whom she had to retain because of her high rank, she instructed in piety and the fear of God. She took great personal interest in them all, loving them as if they were her children. They in turn loved and honored her as their mother, young as she was.

Elzear died on an errand to Paris in the interests of the king. Delphina wept bitterly when she heard the news. Nevertheless she prayed: "My God, may Thy most holy will be done!" Urged by the spirit of God toward still greater perfection, she presently renounced all temporal goods and added to her vow of chastity the vow of holy poverty.

The fame of Delphina's holy life induced Queen Eleonore of Sicily to appoint her mistress of the royal household. Delphina so transformed the easy morals of the court that the palace seemed changed into a sanctuary. She lived many years yet, edifying the nobility by the brilliant example of her virtue. She died a saintly death in 1358 at the age of seventy-four. Her tomb is next to that of her husband in the city of Apt in southern France. Numerous miracles increased the veneration paid to her and Pope Urban V solemnly approved this veneration. Her feast is observed by the Franciscans on September twenty-sixth; and the Third Order Regular celebrates the feast of "Blessed Delphina and companions, Virgins" on

December first. (Cf. *Forum*, 1949, pp. 174-176; *These Made Peace*, pp. 98-106.)

ON THE DUTIES OF HOUSEHOLDERS

1. Blessed Delphina is a model to all Christian householders. Like her, they must be interested in the corporal welfare of their domestics and servants. They are obliged to give them proper wages in due time for honest labor rendered, for "the hire of the laborers which by fraud has been kept back, cries into the ears of the Lord of Sabaoth" (Jas. 5,4). Householders must give their domestics wholesome and nourishing food in sufficient quantity. If an employer is so niggardly with wages and food that servants feel justified in helping themselves to what is necessary, it is neither a credit nor a benefit to an employer. Let them rather heed the words of the Apostle: "Do to your servants that which is just and equal" (Col. 4,1). — Do you have to reproach yourself in any way in this matter?

2. Consider, that providing for the corporal necessities of their employees is not the only obligation of a householder. Domestic animals require only care for their bodies. But servants and domestics have souls, and for them employers have greater responsibilities. First of all, they may never keep their servants from performing their religious duties. They must even see to it that their employees perform their religious duties, that they attend holy Mass and receive the sacraments. They must protect them against occasions of sin, against evil companions, and against the vices to which they may become addicted. If a servant is no longer faithful to his God, he cannot expect to be faithful to his employer. Delphina was deeply concerned about the spiritual welfare of her servants and even succeeded in changing those at court into fervent Christians. — What have you done for the spiritual welfare of those whom you employ?

3. Consider the means Delphina used to achieve such success with her household. She gave her subjects the best example by her own conduct and loved them as if they were her children. If a good example were constantly given, if masters had the heart of a father for their servants, and mistresses had the heart of a mother, there would certainly be more filial respect and obedience among servants and employees. "Know you not," asks the Apostle, "that the Lord of both them and you is in heaven?" (Eph. 6,9). In the eyes of God master and servant are brothers; then let masters have a heart for their servants. Without manifesting weakness of character or unbecoming familiarity, be kind in correcting them, do not overburden them with work, and take an interest in them in their needs and in sickness. The centurion in the Gospel, who came to our Lord

pleading for his sick servant, is honored all over the world. — What a comfort to you if your servants, like Delphina's, love you as a father, as a mother!

PRAYER OF THE CHURCH

O God, who in addition to other virtues didst adorn Blessed Delphina, Thy servant, with virginal purity in the married state, mercifully grant that we who devoutly celebrate her festival here on earth, may arrive safely in her blessed company. Through Christ our Lord. Amen.

SEPTEMBER 27
ST. ELZEAR OF SABRAN
Confessor, Third Order

T. ELZEAR was born in 1285 and belonged to a very noble family. His father was the head of the house of Sabran in southern France and count of Ariano in the kingdom of Naples. His mother was a woman of great piety, who, because of her charity to the poor, was known as the good countess. Elzear was her first child. After his baptism she took him in her arms and asked God to take him out of this world if He foresaw that the child would ever stain his soul by sin. With his mother's milk he seems to have imbibed the spirit of piety, for from his babyhood he was always gentle, docile, and modest, without a trace of mawkishness in his piety. He was friendly towards everyone, and was particularly devoted to the poor. When he was only thirteen years old, he undertook severe bodily mortifications in order to keep the flesh in subjection to the spirit.

Conforming to the wish of the king of Naples, who was also the lord of southern France, he married, while still quite young, the Countess Delphina of the Glandeves family. On their wedding day both spouses vowed perpetual virginity, and persevered in living like brother and sister until death.

At the death of his father, Elzear, who was then only twenty-three years old, inherited his father's titles. He considered it his sacred duty to provide for the temporal, and above all, for the spiritual, welfare of his people. He was particularly solicitous that the laws of God and of the Church were observed in his dominions. The poor were the special object of his solicitude. Every day twelve of them dined at the same table with

him and the countess. There was remarkable calmness and self-possession
in his demeanor. Personal injuries did not affect him. If anyone repeated
to him anything uncomplimentary that had been said about him, he did
not even ask who it was that said it, but merely replied: "Worse things
were said about Christ."

Going to Italy in his capacity as count of Ariano, he found that his
Italian subjects were not at all disposed to accept French domination. That
lasted for several years. It was suggested to him that he deal severely with
the offenders, but he would not consent. In four years he had won over
the people by his gentleness and charity, and all looked up to him as to a
father.

Upon his return to France his subjects there prepared a great feast for
him. Delphina was especially happy, and the devout couple now joined
the Third Order of St. Francis in order to be still more intimately united
to God. Elzear redoubled his acts of piety. He prayed the divine office
every day as the priests do, scourged his body severely, and nursed the
sick with as much charity and reverence as if he were actually performing
these services to Christ Himself.

God granted him the gift of miracles, and he cured several lepers. By
his prayers he also restored health to the son of the count of Grimoard,
who was the saint's godchild. On this occasion Elzear told the father that
this child would one day be elevated to one of the greatest dignities in the
Church. The child later became Pope Urban V.

Although engaged in many works of piety, Elzear never neglected his
temporal duties. He was obliged to spend several years at the court of the
saintly King Robert of Naples, where he gave proof of his courage and
talent as army chief and minister of state.

Sent to the court of Paris on matters of state, he was seized with a
serious illness. With the same serenity which he had preserved
throughout life, he prepared himself for death, made a general confession
of his whole life, received the last sacraments with angelic devotion, and
departed from this life in his fortieth year, on September 27, 1323. Because
of the numerous miracles that occurred at his tomb and the urgent request
of the kings of France and Naples, Pope Urban V, his godchild, with great
joy canonized him in the year 1369. The feast of St. Elzear is celebrated by
the three branches of the First Order as well as the Third Order Regular
on September twenty-seventh. (Cf. *These Made Peace*, 98-106.)

ON HOLY SERENITY

1. "A holy man continues in wisdom as the sun; but a fool is changed as

the moon" (Eccli. 27,12). With these words the Holy Spirit Himself has foretold the sanctity of such men as Elzear, who in his holy serenity retained such perfect calm throughout his life. Perfect mastery of self must precede this state of perfection, and only he who is firmly established in God can attain it. The saints were not free from the storms and disturbances of life. As a rule, they had more difficulties to encounter than ordinary men. But just as God, the eternal Wisdom, always remains perfectly serene, so did they, like the sun, retain this holy serenity in the light of true wisdom, whereas the fool seems to change from one mood to another as does the moon. — To which group do you belong?

2. Consider how happy this holy serenity makes men even here on earth. The sufferings of this life do not arise from external things as much as they do from the impressions that these things make on our interior being. He who is convinced that everything that befalls him tends to his best interests will always preserve interior peace. "Whatsoever shall befall the just man, it shall not make him sad" (Prov. 12,21). Moreover, he will not be elated at the praise of men, nor crushed by their criticism; for he knows that the one does not make him any better, nor the other any worse than he really is. Peace of conscience and of soul provide him with lasting joy. "A secure mind is like a continual feast" (Prov. 15,15). — Would you not like to enjoy such a feast for yourself?

3. Consider what is necessary to acquire this peace of mind. The first means lies in directing our hearts to God in the belief that He is directing everything to our own welfare, and with the prayer that He may grant us the grace to preserve interior peace. St. Elzear teaches us a second means in the answer he gave to his wife when she once asked him how he could retain his peace of mind amid affronts: "At such times I recall the insults that my crucified Saviour suffered for me; I do not say a word until I am perfectly calm." A third means is continual exterior as well as interior mortification. St. Elzear practiced such mortification, and thus he was able to preserve his chastity unsullied in the married state. If we practice such mortification of the senses and of the heart, we shall also enjoy peace of mind here below and eternal peace hereafter.

PRAYER OF THE CHURCH

O God, who didst adorn St. Elzear, Thy confessor, with the virtue of virginity in the married state along with other virtues, mercifully grant that we who celebrate his saintly memory here on earth may attain to happy association with him in heaven. Through Christ our Lord. Amen.

SEPTEMBER 28
BLESSED JOHN OF DUKLA
Confessor, First Order

OHN was born at Dukla in Poland, and was raised by his pious parents in the fear of God. Filled with desire for greater perfection, he entered the Order of St. Francis at an early age. He made such progress that his associates beheld in the young religious a model of perfection. His humility and heartfelt charity toward everyone caused him to be generally loved. Frequently he was obliged to undertake the office of superior, and he administered the custody of Lwow with high praise.

When St. John Capistran came to Poland in 1453, and established convents of stricter observance of the rule of St. Francis, Father John of Dukla attached himself to the reformed group. Although he was now forty years old and had been a superior for a long time, he again became a model of obedience, and led the novices in the faithful observance of all the statutes of the order.

Daily he read the rule, and out of love for holy poverty he wished to have no other book. It grieved him deeply to witness even the slightest violation of the rule. He himself submitted promptly and cheerfully to all the directions of his superiors. He practiced severe mortification, kept vigils in prayer through many hours of the night, was continually active as a director of souls, and practiced great devotion to the Blessed Virgin Mary. He had the special gift of reconciling people who were at variance with each other. He also labored with great zeal to bring the schismatic Ruthenians and Armenians back to unity with the Catholic Church.

When he was nearly seventy years old, he was afflicted by God with blindness. But John bore this affliction with great patience, and did not slacken his activities until his blessed death in the year 1484. His tomb in the Franciscan church at Lwow has been glorified by many miracles. Several of the kings of Poland interested themselves in his canonization; and at the request of the people, Pope Clement XII permitted him to be numbered among the principal patrons of the Poles and Lithuanians. The feast of Blessed John is observed by the Franciscans on September twenty-eighth, and by the Conventuals and Capuchins on October first.

ON THE QUALITIES OF OBEDIENCE

1. Blessed John recognized the great value of obedience. He rejoiced that in the prime of life he could transfer from the position of giving commands to that of obeying them, and he did obey with great perfection. In fact, obeying is easier and much safer than commanding; and when it is done perfectly it is also more honorable and meritorious before God. Christ "became obedient unto death, even unto the death of the Cross, for which cause God also has exalted Him" (Phil. 2,8-9). Through the disobedience of Adam evil came into the world; through Christ's perfect obedience salvation has again come to us. — What do you share? The disobedience of the one, or the obedience of the Other?

2. Consider the qualities our obedience should have. Following the example of Blessed John, we should obey cheerfully and promptly. Reluctant and unwilling obedience, rendered only from necessity and outwardly, can be pleasing neither to God nor to man. "That is no virtue," says St. Bernard, "but rather a cloak for one's interior wickedness." Lest our evil inclination get the better of us, we should immediately, without any hesitation, carry out a given order. If you hesitate, the grace of God which was offered you to carry out the lawful command will be withdrawn. If you execute the order promptly and cheerfully, you will be particularly pleasing to God. "God loves a cheerful giver" (2 Cor. 9,7). Has your obedience always been cheerful?

3. Consider that the proper obedience must also be humble and must rest on Christian motives, one should endeavor humbly to carry out the will of the superior without judging whether the command be prudent and profitable. For him who practices perfect obedience it is sufficient that nothing forbidden be involved, but every other consideration is left to the one commanding. The Christian spirit, however, requires that we look up to God in our obedience, and submit to men for His sake. Thus writes the Apostle: "Obey in all things, not serving to the eye as pleasing men, but in simplicity of heart, fearing God" (Col, 3,22). — Then will patience not easily be wanting in our obedience.

PRAYER OF THE CHURCH

O God, who didst adorn Blessed John, Thy confessor, with the gifts of exceptional humility and patience, graciously grant that we may imitate his example and share in his reward. Through Christ our Lord. Amen.

SEPTEMBER 29
BLESSED BERNARDIN OF FELTRE
Confessor, First Order

LESSED BERNARDIN was born at Feltre, Venice, and was the son of an ancient and noble family. In baptism he received the name of Martin. His father was repeatedly appointed ambassador for Venice. The boy gave evidence of rare mental gifts, and at the age of twelve he could speak Latin fluently. At fifteen, on the occasion of a treaty, he read in the public square a lengthy poem he had composed, extolling peace. The composition earned him the universal applause of his fellow citizens. In addition the young man possessed unusual piety and angelic innocence.

In accordance with the wish of his father, he entered the University of Padua to study law. The sudden death of two of his professors, together with the sermons of St. James of the March during the Lent of 1456 induced him to enter the Franciscan Order. St. James who had a short time before attended the canonization of St. Bernardin of Siena, gave him the name of Bernardin, and predicted that, like his patron saint, he would be a true soldier of Christ against the powers of hell.

After a lengthy preparation in thorough study and still more in the virtues required by the apostolate, Bernardin was appointed to the office of missionary at the age of thirty. He approached the task with fear rather than with confidence in himself, and only in virtue of holy obedience. But shortly the extraordinary results of his preaching began to manifest themselves. With severity he inveighed against the vices of the period, sensuality, pride, and avarice. He was no respecter of persons, but he knew just how to word his reproofs so as to infuse into the hearts of his hearers hatred for their own vices and the desire to get rid of them. For twenty-five years he preached in almost all the larger towns of Italy as well as in many villages. At the end of his missions a large bonfire was usually built, in which bad books, indecent pictures, dice and gambling boards, as well as the false hair of women together with other vain and foolish ornaments of theirs were brought together and consigned to the flames.

Following the instructions of St. Francis, Bernardin set himself the special task of composing enmities and removing factions. His success induced Pope Innocent VIII to entrust him with a mission to Umbria to settle various disputes.

The poor were the special object of his solicitude. They were being imposed upon by usurers, who bled them in a merciless way. In order to wrest them from the hands of these men, Bernardin promoted a kind of loan bank called Mounts of Piety. Earlier Franciscan missionaries had introduced them, but Bernardin gave them a new set of rules and gradually popularized them throughout Italy, for which reason he is often considered their founder. Wealthy citizens were prevailed on to contribute sufficient money, from which the less prosperous could obtain sums as needed, against a reasonable guarantee and moderate interest. The plan furnished the wealthy class with a favorable opportunity to practice mercy without too great a sacrifice. At the same time it was more of a work of Christianity than of business. Countless persons in the lesser walks of life were saved by the plan, and the wealthy became the object of their gratitude. This beneficent institution continued to function after Bernardin's death, and in 1515 the general council of the Lateran approved and recommended it.

Rich in merit and virtue, which God frequently attested by miracles, Father Bernardin entered into eternal rest in the convent at Pavia on September 28, 1494. At once the people came to venerate him, and many miracles were wrought. Pope Innocent X beatified him and the cities of Pavia and Feltre chose him as their patron. The feast of Blessed Bernardin is observed by the Franciscans and Capuchins on September twenty-eight.

A beautiful prayer written by Blessed Bernardin is known to every Catholic today — the Anima Christi, "Soul of Christ, sanctify me." It was a favorite prayer of St. Ignatius Loyola, but it is not generally known that it is of Franciscan origin. Pope Pius IX granted an indulgence of three hundred days for each recital of this prayer, and an indulgence of seven years if it is said after holy Communion. If it is said daily for a month, a plenary indulgence can be gained under the usual conditions.

ON DISINTERESTED CHARITY

1. Consider how noble and untainted was the charity of Blessed Bernardin. The temporal need and oppression of the people pressed so heavily upon him that it was for him like a personal problem. In the needy he beheld his true brothers. In his zeal, he resolved to help them. He did not dread the hatred of the usurers nor the disappointment of refusal on the part of those who could have aided the good work. He was not overanxious to learn whether the poor themselves would appreciate his efforts. He thought only of the need of his neighbor and applied to himself the words of the parable of the good Samaritan: "Take care of him" (Lk. 10,35). Have those same words not been spoken to us as well? Our Lord

says to us all: "Love your neighbor as yourself" (Mt. 19,19). — Do you do that?

2. Consider how different is the charity so generally practiced in the world. Many are busy aiding the poor and the needy, but they do it to win the praises of men. Others await the grateful response of the poor, and if this is wanting, they cease their benefactions. Others again speculate on temporal gain. And there are Christians who are as heartless as any usurer, taking advantage of people who are already losing in business, and scheming to acquire the last of their stock and ruin them entirely. The Apostle Paul said already in his day: "All seek the things that are their own" (Phil. 2,21). Are we not obliged to repeat this complaint in our day? Examine your own charity.

3. Consider how well Blessed Bernardin planned his undertaking for the benefit of the poor. He united wealthy persons in an association to lend money to the needy. He obligated the borrowers to furnish security and to pay a moderate amount of interest, so that the undertaking could be supported and not encourage indolence. His work of charity put Christian people of prominence in touch with people in lower walks of life, who at that are so often shiftless, so that the advice, instruction, and encouragement of the former might better the condition of the latter. In this day of ours when so many people are banded in organizations with less noble purposes, should it not be possible to make true charity the object of an organization? The need of many people would be relieved by it, and the bond of charity would bring the members closer to God.

PRAYER OF THE CHURCH

O God, who didst deign to inflame Blessed Bernardin with apostolic zeal, so that he could draw the faithful out of the pool of vice, mercifully grant, we beseech Thee, that through his intercession we may be delivered from all sin and danger, and directed to our heavenly home. Through Christ our Lord. Amen.

SEPTEMBER 30
BLESSED FRANCIS OF CALDEROLA
Confessor, First Order

RANCIS was born at Calderola in the diocese of Camerino. Faithful to the call of God to become a Franciscan, he joined the Friars Minor of the province of the March. The great St. James of the March and other holy men lived in the order at that time and were brilliant models for the younger brethren. Francis strove earnestly to follow in the footsteps of these saintly men.

After his ordination to the priesthood, he was consumed with an insatiable zeal for the salvation of souls, and was occupied for days at a time with preaching and hearing confessions. Then at night he would join in singing the praises of God and spent many an hour in private prayer for strength and blessing on his apostolate.

Although Blessed Francis was a very learned man, he always addressed the people in language that was simple and not above their comprehension. He took great delight in relating anecdotes from the lives of the saints and in encouraging his listeners to follow their example. Wherever the blessed man went, he soon gained the confidence of the people, and as a result he was able to reconcile many enemies and to settle long-standing feuds.

He was also a very devoted servant of the Mother of God, the Queen of Peace. With his own hands he carved a statue of our Blessed Lady, which he presented to a confraternity he had founded. Because of the many miracles that were worked through its means, it became renowned as a miraculous image. On his return from exile in France in 1814, Pope Pius VII himself placed a golden crown on the head of this statue in the church of St. Nicholas at Tolentino.

After Father Francis had reconciled many sinners to God through the intercession of the Mother of Mercy, and had exhausted himself by his great labors, he slept the sleep of the just in the convent at Colfano in 1507. The veneration that had been accorded him because of many miracles was approved by Pope Gregory XVI. The feast of Blessed Francis is observed by the Franciscans on September twenty-eighth, and by the Capuchins on the thirteenth.

ON MIRACULOUS IMAGES

1. The statue which Blessed Francis of Calderola gave to a confraternity as far back as three hundred years ago is now venerated as a miraculous

image. Such an image is not a miraculous image because of any inherent power that it possesses, like the holy sacraments; nor can it procure blessings for us, as, for instance, the intercession of our Blessed Lady can. We call such statues or pictures miraculous images, and the places where they are preserved miraculous shrines, because it pleases God to grant special graces, such as the cure of disease or preservation from other grave ills, to those who pray at these shrines and before the favored images. They are called miraculous images not because they work miracles, but because God works miracles at such places at His pleasure. In some instances the miracles have been so numerous and so extraordinary that the images have been crowned by the pope in thanksgiving for God's bounty to men, as was the case with the statue of Blessed Francis. — Who shall venture to speak of it as unreasonable if we have special confidence when we pray before such images?

2. Consider that such confidence must be directed towards God alone. It is He "who alone does wonderful things" (Ps. 71,18). When and where He will do them, is reserved to His secret judgment. St. Augustine says: "God is everywhere, and we can pray to Him in all places; but He works His miracles only where it pleases Him to do so." In the Old Testament God Himself caused a brazen serpent to be set up by Moses as a miraculous image against the bite of the serpent. "When they who were bitten looked upon it, they were healed" (Num. 21,9). In the Christian era some of these venerated pictures and shrines have been transported to their present locations in a miraculous manner, for example, the Holy House of Loreto and the famous picture of Our Lady of Good Counsel at Genazzano. Would it not be stupid on our part and a sort of obstinacy, not to pray in our special needs at such shrines if we have the opportunity to visit them?

3. Consider that when we cannot visit such places in person, it is quite in order to expect the graces which are granted at the actual shrine in answer to prayer before a reproduction of the miraculous image. Whoever would like to attend holy Mass, but is prevented from doing so, can obtain many graces by reciting the prayers at home and assisting at the holy Sacrifice in spirit. In like manner may he hope to be answered who kneels in spirit before a miraculous image and begs God to grant his petitions. That is why we find reproductions of Our Lady of Perpetual Help, Our Lady of Good Counsel, and others, in so many churches. It is likewise good to pray before such images in our homes. Pray there for help in your special needs; pray above all for the grace to remain faithful to God under all circumstances, and never to turn from Him when crosses and temptations befall you.

PRAYER OF THE CHURCH

O God, who didst give to Thy Church a worthy servant in Blessed Francis, Thy confessor, and didst clothe him with the extraordinary grace to settle quarrels, grant us through his merits and intercession, that being strengthened in Thy love, we may never be separated from Thee by any temptation. Through Christ our Lord. Amen.

OCTOBER

OCTOBER 1
BLESSED FRANCIS CICHI OF PESARO
Confessor, Third Order

RANCIS was the son of a wealthy and devout family at Pesaro in Italy. After the death of his parents, while he was still a youth, he became the master of a considerable estate. This might have been a dangerous occasion for many a young man to give himself over to a life of pleasure; but his earlier Christian training taught him how much bitterness is frequently associated with such a course.

Francis chose rather to follow the advice of Christ to the young man in the Gospel, so that he might attain to Christian perfection. He divided the greater part of his inheritance among the poor; the remaining part he used to build three hermitages and at each of these a chapel in honor of our Blessed Lady. A hospice for poor travelers and pilgrims was added to one of these hermitages. Then he was invested with the habit of the Third Order of St. Francis and lived a holy life as a hermit, devoting himself to prayer and the works of charity.

The tempter did not fail to offer inducements to make Francis return to the world. When he did not succeed with his plans, he endeavored to take Francis' life. One night while the holy man was at prayer, the devil rolled a heavy rock down from the mountainside toward his hermitage. The rock would surely have buried the hermit under the ruins, but it was held suspended on the side of the mountain, and no harm came to the praying hermit.

His devout life did not remain a secret. Soon disciples came to him, and Francis did not have the heart to send them away. He trained them in his devout exercises, and went out humbly to the neighboring town to beg the necessities of life for them. Because he had won the esteem of everyone, he often obtained more than they really needed.

One day when he was returning with the provisions he had collected, two men met him and insulted him by calling him a hypocrite and an idler, who abused the simplicity of the faithful and grew rich at their expense. God immediately chastised the offenders, the one became paralyzed and the other was struck dumb. Francis actually reserved for himself and his brethren only so much of the alms he received as was needed by them; the rest he distributed among the poor.

Once he was asked by some friends to have dinner with them. The savor of an excellent roast whetted his appetite, and he was given a few slices to take home with him. But he kept the meat until it was putrid and emitted a very bad odor. Then he took it, held it up to his nose, and said: "Now, Francis, eat and be satisfied!"

God glorified His servant by many miracles and the gift of prophecy. The veneration which the people paid to him was so great that it was considered a privilege even to touch his habit.

After living the life of a hermit for more than fifty years, he died peacefully in the Lord in the year 1350. The entire town of Pesaro was present when his body was placed in a tomb in the cathedral, where it is still an object of veneration at the present day. Pope Pius IX approved the celebration of his feast, which is observed by the Franciscans on October first, by the Conventuals on August fifth, and by the Third Order Regular on August eleventh. (Cf. *Forum*, 1948, pp. 239-240; *These Made Peace*, pp. 117-120.)

ON DETACHING ONESELF FROM MATERIAL THINGS

1. Ever since our first parents ate of the forbidden fruit, there has arisen in the heart of man an inordinate desire for material things, which manifests itself in avarice, sensuality, and love of honor. Material things are constantly enticing the human heart, and it is only by struggling against this tendency that we can hope to arrive at our goal. "The lust thereof shall be under you and you shall have dominion over it" (Gen. 4,7). How perfectly Blessed Francis controlled his appetites. Grace invited him to heroic detachment, and cheerfully he followed the call; and thus he became a saint. The rich young man of the Gospel whom Christ invited to such detachment did not heed the invitation: "he went away sad, for he had great possessions" (Mt. 19,22), and it is considered doubtful whether he saved his soul.

2. Consider that even the ordinary Christian must detach himself from material things. He may use them only as a means of fulfilling his duties as a Christian, without letting his heart cling to them, without seeking his happiness in them. Hence the Apostle admonishes us that "they who use this world, be as if they used it not" (1 Cor. 7,31). Examine yourself to determine whether your heart is free from inordinate affection for material things. How do you behave if God deprives you of material

possessions? Do you perhaps envy others who have been favored with a greater amount of worldly goods? If so, your heart is still too much attached to them.

3. Consider that as long as the heart of a Christian is still unduly attached to material things, he cannot rise to the interior life and to true prayer. Just as a fluffy feather cannot rise upwards as long as mud clings to it, so the heart of man is not free to raise itself to God as long as it does not detach itself from material things. Thomas a Kempis (1,22) says: "The interior man is greatly weighed down by the necessities of the body in this life, for which reason the prophet devoutly prays: 'From my necessities deliver me, O Lord!' " (Ps. 24,17) The more a man reflects on the things of heaven, as did Blessed Francis, the more he will despise the things of earth. St. Ignatius declared: "How I loathe the earth once I have looked up to heaven!" Frequently direct your thoughts upward, so that you may disengage your heart from the trifling things of earth.

PRAYER OF THE CHURCH

O God, who didst disengage Blessed Francis from all attachment to the things of earth and didst lead him to love those that are heavenly, grant that, strengthened by Thy grace, we, too, may despise the world and may love Thee alone with our whole heart. Through Christ our Lord. Amen.

OCTOBER 2
BLESSED NICHOLAS OF FORCA PALENA
Confessor, Third Order

NICHOLAS spent the days of his youth in the practice of prayer and penance. After he had entered the Third Order and had become a priest, he labored for a time in his native city in a most exemplary way. Then he finally yielded to the strong attraction he felt for a life of solitude, and with several companions who were similarly minded he repaired to a hermitage, first in Rome, then in Naples, and then again in Rome.

When Pope Eugene IV heard of his sanctity, he entrusted to him the direction of several convents in Florence. But in time, Nicholas again returned to Rome, where he founded a convent and a church on the Janiculum in honor of St. Onuphrius. Almighty God attested to the holiness of His faithful servant by signs and wonders.

When Nicholas was one hundred years old, he was called to his eternal reward. The year of his death was 1440. Pope Clement IV approved the veneration paid to him. His feast is observed on October first by the Franciscans and the Third Order Regular. (Cf. *These Made Peace*, pp. 128-129.)

OUR GOAL IN LIFE

1. Our goal is in eternity. Nicholas had this truth ever before his mind. That is why he left the world, so that in quiet seclusion he could prepare for a glorious resurrection from the grave and a blessed eternity. He knew that "the world passes away and the concupiscence thereof. But he who does the will of God abides forever" (1 Jn. 2,17). There were some who shook their heads at the life he led, but he had actually chosen the better part. — Let us frequently think of our goal in life.
2. There is a twofold eternity. It will be either an eternity of blissful joy or an eternity of pain and torment. We decide our own eternity. "What things a man shall sow, those also shall he reap" (Gal. 6,8). Every man is the author of his own fortune or misfortune. It was, therefore, holy wisdom on the part of Blessed Nicholas to direct his entire attention to achieving a blessed eternity. — Is that the case with you?
3. We may arrive at eternity quite suddenly, even this very day. "You know not the day nor the hour" (Mt. 25,13). It would be a terrible thing for us to find ourselves suddenly at the end of our earthly life without being prepared for it. In that case the words of Holy Scripture could be applied to us: "They spend their day in wealth, and in a moment they go down to hell" (Jn. 21,13). — Prepare yourself in time.

PRAYER OF THE CHURCH

O Lord, who dost point out to the wayward the light of Thy truth, so that they may return to the path of justice, give to all confessors of Thy name the grace to despise whatever is displeasing to this name, and to strive after those things which are agreeable to it. Through Christ our Lord. Amen.

OCTOBER 3
THE SERVANT OF GOD MARY MAGDALEN BENTIVOGLIO
Virgin, Second Order

COUNTESS ANNETTA BENTIVOGLIO was born in Rome in 1834. Her father was a general in the papal army, and later governor of Rome. The child early displayed a vivacious spirit, but her religious turn of mind was no less in evidence. She was educated at the convent of the Sacred Heart, where she at times annoyed the good sisters to distraction by her escapades.

After the death of her parents, Annetta's two younger sisters joined the Poor Clares. Four months later she herself carried out the desire she had secretly entertained, and received the habit of St. Clare on October 4, 1864, as Sister Mary Magdalen.

Sister Mary Magdalen found it difficult to adapt herself to her new life. But the iron will she inherited, together with the grace of God and the prudent guidance of the saintly Franciscan Father General Bernardin dal Vago, helped her grow in the love and practice of penance. Out of devotion to the Sacred Heart and the sufferings of Christ she longed to do as much penance as possible for those who forget or neglect their Lord.

The year 1870 stands out as a period of suffering and trial for many religious communities in Europe. In his paternal concern for this section of his flock, Pope Pius IX thought of America as a haven for the Poor Clares of Italy, who could at the same time benefit that country by their devout prayers. So, on August 12, 1875, Mother Magdalen and Sister Constance Bentivoglio set out from their convent of San Lorenzo. After receiving the Holy Father's blessing, visiting the tombs of St. Francis and St. Clare at Assisi, and finally renewing their vows and receiving the blessing of Father Bernardin, they set sail for America, landing in New York on October twelfth.

Their first plans had to be abandoned upon their arrival, and they were forced to await new instructions from Rome. The suspense taxed their endurance to the limit. Meanwhile they were moving about, seeking hospitality from this community and that. Feeling that they were a burden, they finally rented a small room. When their means ran out, they found themselves on the streets of New York without food or home.

On their knees they begged Cardinal McCoskey to give them a place in his diocese, but he did not feel able to do it. Archbishop Purcell of Cincinnati likewise refused their request. Archbishop Wood of Philadelphia received them; but after three weeks, they were obliged to move again.

This is but a small part of the hardships and sufferings they had to endure before they finally settled in Omaha, Nebraska, through the charity of John Creighton. Obstacles again presented themselves, but in July, 1882, the strict enclosure was set up and they were finally established in the United States. Even then calumny nearly wrecked the foundation at Omaha.

By 1905 two additional convents had been founded by Mother Magdalen, and she resided in the one at Evansville, Indiana. She was seventy-one years old, and though her mind remained clear, her body was wasting away. On the feast of our Lady's Assumption she felt she was going to die. But death came August eighteenth. She begged to be lifted out of bed so that, like holy Father St. Francis, she might die upon the floor. The sisters finally acceded to her wish, and there Mother Bentivoglio's earthly sojourn came to an end.

The cause of Mother Magdalen Bentivoglio is before the Roman tribunal, and it is hoped that before long America may call her Blessed. (Cf. *Heralds of the King*, pp. 426-430.)

ON THE DISPOSITIONS OF PROVIDENCE

1. What a great misfortune it seemed to be when Mother Bentivoglio was forced to wander from convent to convent and finally even roam the streets of a strange country for want of the home she expected to find there! What a misfortune when the various attempts at founding an establishment seemed to be thwarted by God Himself! But she accepted her lot with resignation as a disposition of Providence, and with childlike confidence waited until God should send her instructions through lawful authority as to what she was to do. — Do you accept all misfortunes with as much faith as this valiant woman did?

2. It was part of the designs of God that, after overcoming the many physical obstacles in the way of her establishment, Mother Bentivoglio should be attacked with calumnies and deposed from office. Her genuine sanctity became manifest at this time and blessed results followed her final vindication. God still uses the wickedness of men in order that good may result, for those who must endure it and for many others besides. Thus Scripture teaches us, especially in the case of Joseph, who was sold into Egypt by his brothers: "Not by your counsel was I sent hither; for God sent me before you into Egypt for your preservation" (Gen. 45,8,5). — Adore the wise designs of God and amid disagreeable and trying events be convinced that God permits these things for your welfare.

3. Consider that the servant of God Mary Magdalen prepared herself for

this resignation to Divine Providence by early cultivating the habit of meditation on the sufferings of Christ. Early in life she resolved to do as much penance as possible in memory of her suffering Lord, and when the time of trial came, she did not shrink from the cross. God often permits bitter experiences to enter the lives of His faithful servants so as to make them similar to His beloved Son. But He always provides that such experiences tend to their welfare and that of others. — When adversity comes upon you, do not look with envy at the good fortune of the children of this world, which is often deceitful, but reflect with devout faith on the life and sufferings of our Saviour and His saints, and you will always preserve interior peace.

PRAYER OF THE CHURCH (Seventh Sunday after Pentecost)

O God, whose providence erreth not in its ordinances, we humbly beseech Thee to remove from us all that is harmful and to grant us all that is profitable to us. Through Christ our Lord. Amen.

OCTOBER 4
OUR HOLY FATHER ST. FRANCIS
Confessor and Founder of the Three Orders

RANCIS was the son of Peter Bernardone, a wealthy merchant of Assisi. Peter intended that his first-born should follow him in his career. But Francis was in no way avaricious as was his father. Rather, he was very generous, and in gay good humor readily disposed of anything at his command.

Our Lord, whose delight it is to show mercy to the merciful, intended to tear Francis away from the danger of worldly pleasures and draw him to Himself. He permitted Francis to become seriously ill. As Francis lay in the solitude of the sick chamber, exhausted in body, his soul was being prepared by God for higher things. He felt a great longing for perfection, and heroic self-conquest was needed as a foundation for that edifice.

When Francis recovered his health, he was one day crossing the plain of Assisi on horseback, when he met a leper. The unexpected sight filled him with horror, and he was minded to turn back. But he remembered his resolution, dismounted, and hastened to kiss the hand of the leper and then pressed an alms into it. As he remounted and turned to salute the leper once more, there was no one to be seen anywhere on the plain.

Seemingly, Christ had appeared to him in the form of a leper.

Francis so loved the poor that he frequently associated with them. Complying with a divine command, he also begged stones to repare three ruined churches. His father was enraged at this strange conduct, and had his son brought before the bishop of Assisi. There Francis returned to his father not only the money he had but also the clothes he wore, saying: "Now I can truly say, Our Father, who art in heaven." The bishop gave him an old gardener's cloak, on the back of which Francis drew a cross with a piece of white chalk. He now begged our Lord to make known to him His will regarding the futur.e

Soon after, Francis was at holy Mass in the Portiuncula. Hearing the Gospel in which our Lord commissions His apostles to carry about with them neither gold, nor silver, nor two coats, nor shoes, the heart of Francis was filled with joy, for he recognized in it the will of God regarding his own life. In a coarse penitential garb, girded with a cord, without shoes, he entered upon a life of complete poverty and began to preach penance. This occurred in the year 1208. Francis was then about twenty-six years old.

Several companions soon joined him. When they were eleven in number, he went with them to Rome, where Pope Innocent III gave his approval to the new order. They lived in the severest poverty and in brotherly harmony, preaching penance to the people both by their example and by their words. The holy founder called them Friars Minor, so that they might always regard the virtue of humility as the foundation of perfection. He himself was so humble that, when the people proclaimed him a saint, he called himself the greatest sinner. "For," said he, "if God had given the greatest criminal the graces He has given me, he would have used them to better advantage than I have done."

The order grew rapidly. In 1219, at the renowned Chapter of the Mats, more than five thousand brethren were gathered together. As Christ sent His Apostles to preach the Gospel to all nations, so Francis sent out his brethren. He himself courageously faced the Sultan of Egypt and announced to him that salvation could be found only in Christ.

In order to open the way of perfection for all who wished to imitate his life, Francis established a Second Order headed by St. Clare, and a Third order for people of both sexes living in the world. His love for souls inspired him to labor for all his fellowmen.

Still, his desire to be more intimately united with God caused him to retire again and again to a solitary place to fast and pray. He was

St. Francis Contemplating Death

consumed with ever-increasing love for the highest and greatest Good. "In the beauty of things," says St. Bonaventure, "he saw the Author of all beauty, and followed in the footsteps of his Beloved, who has imprinted His image on all created things." Drunk with love, he could call upon creatures to extol the Creator with him, and the birds joined him in singing the praises of God.

It was above all the passion and death of Christ on the Cross that filled his heart with love of his Saviour, and he strove to become as similar to the object of his love as possible. Two years before his death, on Mount La Verna, the crucified Saviour appeared to Francis in the form of a seraph and impressed on his body the marks of the five sacred wounds.

Francis knew in advance the day of his death. Painful suffering preceded it, but Francis thanked God for it and declared himself ready to suffer a hundred times more if God so willed.

Prepared by all the consolations of Holy Church, and lying on the bare ground in imitation of his Saviour's death on the cross, Francis passed to his heavenly home on October 3, 1226.

ON FOLLOWING IN THE FOOTSTEPS OF OUR HOLY FATHER ST. FRANCIS

1. Our holy Father St. Francis can say to us all: "Be followers of me, as I also am of Christ" (1 Cor. 4,16). He felt a strong attachment for the poor, because he saw in them the poor Christ. And because he always beheld Christ in poverty from the Crib to the Cross, he longed for the greatest poverty; he wanted to be deprived of everything material, that he might find God and call Him his own. He would cry out in holy rapture through entire nights: "My God and my all!" — "Whatsoever is not God," says Thomas a Kempis (3,31), "is nothing and ought to be accounted nothing. For a long time shall he be little, and lie groveling beneath, who esteems anything great but only the one, immense, eternal Good. Forsake all, and you shall find all; relinquish desire, and you shall find rest." — Would that all the children of St. Francis were imbued with this spirit.

2. Consider that we must above all forsake ourselves in order to attain intimate union with God. "The one thing that is supremely necessary for a man," says Thomas a Kempis again (2,11), "is that having left all things else, he leave also himself and retain nothing of self-love." "If you would know perfectly," he has our Lord say to us (3,42), "how to annihilate yourself and empty yourself of all created love, then would I come to you with great grace." That was the source of the rich stream of grace that flowed into St. Francis. Free of all self-love, he sacrificed himself for

others, and in humility he called himself and his brethren Friars Minor, looking upon himself in all sincerity as the greatest of sinners. Do you strive as earnestly as your holy Father did, to forsake yourself?

3. Consider how the poor and humble heart of our holy Father raised itself to God by means of the things of earth. He saw in created things whatever they possessed of goodness, usefulness, and beauty. But his heart did not cling to these things; rather, his thoughts mounted to the Author of all that is good, useful, and beautiful. Created things became for him the rungs of a ladder on which he climbed to the uncreated Source of all good. Burning with love, he then called upon all created things to join him in thanking and praising the Creator; thanking Him also for all suffering through which God accomplished His Holy will in him. With the praise of God on his lips, he went into eternity in order to continue it at the throne of God amid the choirs of the seraphim. — May our holy Father intercede for us there today, that we may be enabled to follow in his footsteps.

PRAYER OF THE CHURCH

O God, who didst enrich Thy Church through the merits of our holy Father St. Francis with the establishment of a new congregation, grant us the grace to imitate him in despising the things of this world and to merit in eternity to share the heavenly gifts. Through Christ our Lord. Amen.

⚜️⚜️⚜️⚜️⚜️

OCTOBER 5
ST. FRANCES OF ROME
Widow, Third Order

 ORN in 1384, Frances belonged to a noble Roman family; and at the age of twelve she married another Roman noble, Lorenzo Ponziani by name. She would have preferred to become a nun, but obeyed her father and became an exemplary wife and the mother of three children. Soon after her marriage she fell seriously ill. Her husband called in a man who dabbled in magic, but Frances drove him out of the house in no uncertain terms. St. Alexis then appeared to her and cured her. From that time she began to be conscious of the presence and assistance of her guardian angel. He would give her a little nudge when she fell into any fault.

The Ponziani palace was in the Trastevere section of Rome, and just around the corner was the little church of San Francesco a Ripa. This church had been given in 1212 to St. Francis by the Roman lady Giacoma di Settesoli, who in 1226 was present at the death of the Poverello. By 1414 at least, the adjoining friary was one of thirty-four belonging to the Observant reform movement in the First Order of St. Francis, which was begun in 1368 by Brother Paul or Paoluccio of Trinci and in the following century was promoted by such saints as St. Bernardin and St. John Capistran. It was at San Francesco a Ripa that Frances Ponziani was received into the Third Order of St. Francis; and one of the fathers there, Father Bartholomew Bondi, became her spiritual director.

Living at the Ponziani palace with Frances was Vanozza, the wife of her oldest brother. She too had entertained thoughts of entering a convent before her marriage; and she joined Frances in her works of piety and charity. Together they spent hours of prayer in a disused attic or an old summer cottage in the garden. At seventeen Frances gave birth to her first son, John Baptist; and shortly afterwards her mother-in-law died. Frances was then placed in charge of the household; and she carried out her duties, not only efficiently, but also in a genuinely Christian manner. During a famine she gave away corn and wine to the poor so lavishly that her husband began to object; but when he found an empty granary miraculously filled with forty measures of wheat and an empty cask filled with wine, he allowed his wife full freedom.

Rome was invaded in 1410; and during the civil war which followed, a series of calamities befell the Ponziani family. Lorenzo, who fought with the papal troops, was wounded; and after Frances had nursed him to health, he went back to the war. John Baptist, the oldest son, was taken as a hostage, and did not return until peace was restored. A plague followed in the wake of the war, and Frances' second son and a daughter died of the disease. The peasants from the wasted Ponziani farm came to Frances, begging for food. Frances heroically devoted herself to the care of the sick, the starving, and the dying, and organized a group of Roman ladies to assist her in this work. For a time she too was stricken by the plague, but after she was suddenly cured she at once resumed her works of charity.

After his death, Frances' second son appeared to her and brought her an archangel to take the place of her guardian angel.

The archangel's light was visible to her so that she could read by it. When she committed a slight fault, the archangel would hide himself, and his light would not shine again until she had made an act of contrition.

Shortly after his return, John Baptist married a flighty young lady, who took a strong dislike to Frances. But in the midst of one of her tempers, she was afflicted with a strange illness; and after Frances' hand calmed and cured her, she became a changed person. Frances placed the household in her care, and devoted herself henceforth entirely to works of charity in the city. In 1425, she and a half dozen other Roman ladies, her companions, were clothed as oblates of St. Benedict. This apparently did not cancel her membership in the Third Order; for, at this time she and Vanozza made a pilgrimage to Assisi, walking the one hundred miles from Rome to the city of St. Francis. Near Assisi St. Francis himself appeared to them, and provided the hungry and thirsty pilgrims with fresh, juicy pears by striking a wild pear tree with his stick.

In 1433, after Lorenzo's death, Frances and her companions founded a religious community of Oblates. There they worked and prayed for the Holy Father and the peace of Rome; for the city was once more in turmoil. Returning to this convent after a visit to her sick son, Frances suddenly became ill and was taken back to the Ponziani palace. There she died after seven days, on March 9, 1440. Pope Paul V canonized her in 1608. Her tomb is beneath the high altar in the crypt of the Roman church which is now called Santa Francesca Romana in her honor. She is honored as the principal patron of all Benedictine oblates, but she is also one of the greatest saints who wore the habit of the Third Order of St. Francis. (Biersack, p. 46-47; *These Made Peace,* pp. 168-173.)

ON VALUING ETERNAL POSSESSIONS

1. Consider how well St. Frances acted when she used her ample wealth, not to provide a life of luxury for herself, but in doing good to others and thereby accumulating heavenly treasures. Even in this life she enjoyed many nobler pleasures, and now the heavenly treasures which she acquired constitute her bliss in eternity. Our Lord exhorts us also to direct our attention more to these imperishable possessions than to perishable ones. "Lay not up to yourselves treasures on earth where the rust and moth consume, and where thieves break through and steal. But lay up to yourselves treasures in heaven, where neither the rust nor moth consumes, and where thieves do not break through nor steal" (Mt. 6,19). Which kind of treasures have you been intent on acquiring?

2. Consider that the possession of temporal goods can not make us happy. Of course, people who do not possess them consider the possessors very fortunate. "They have called the people happy who have these things" (Ps. 143,15). But he who possesses them and enjoys them is ill at ease. Solomon reveled in temporal goods, in a life of luxury, nevertheless he said: "And therefore I was weary of my life when I saw that all things under the sun are evil, and all vanity and vexation of spirit" (Eccles. 2,17).

It is quite different with heavenly treasures. Once we possess them, they set our hearts at rest. "I shall be satisfied when Thy glory shall appear" (Ps. 16,15). Even the expectation of them gives the true servant of God such a delightful foretaste, that amid temporal wants he is happy and content. Hence Tobias could say to his family: "We lead indeed a poor life, but we shall have many good things if we fear God and depart from all sin, and do that which is good" (Tob. 4,23). — Should you not aim to acquire such happiness?

3. Consider that most people do not put the proper value on heavenly possessions. Day and night they are busy planning how to acquire temporal possessions, and perhaps weeks go by without one thought about heavenly treasures. They hasten to obtain temporal possessions and expend all their strength in acquiring them, but they put forth no effort to obtain the treasures of heaven. They will even relinquish their rights to heaven because of some momentary pleasure. Is it not to be feared that our Lord's words to the wicked will apply to them: "I have sworn in My wrath: they shall not enter into My rest" (Heb. 3,11). But there is still time. Implore God's mercy.

PRAYER OF THE CHURCH

O Lord, who didst honor Thy servant Frances with the friendly companionship of an angel, among other gifts, grant, we beseech Thee, that by the aid of her intercession we may deserve to be admitted to the company of the angels. Through Christ our Lord. Amen.

OCTOBER 6
ST. MARY FRANCES OF THE FIVE WOUNDS
Virgin, Third Order

ANNA MARIA ROSA, as Mary Frances was christened, was born in Naples in 1715 of a family that belonged to the middle class of society. Her mother, a devout and gentle woman, who had much to contend with from her hot-tempered husband, was quite worried before the birth of this child. But St. John Joseph of the Cross, who lived in Naples at that time, calmed her and recommended special care of the child, as it was destined to attain to great holiness.

She was scarcely four years old when she began to spend hours in prayer, and sometimes arose at night for this purpose. Such was her desire to know the truths of the Catholic Faith, that an angel appeared to her and instructed her regularly. She had not yet attained her seventh year when she desired to receive holy Communion. Her pastor marveled at her knowledge of the Faith, as well as her ardent desire for the Bread of Angels, and felt that he could not deny her the privilege. In fact, it was not long before he permitted her to receive daily.

Meanwhile, although physically of a very delicate constitution, the little saint was making herself useful to her parents by assisting them in their work. Her father, a weaver of gold lace, was anxious to have his children help as early as possible. He found that Mary Frances was not only the most willing but also the most skilled in the work.

Mary Frances was sixteen years old when a rich young man asked her father for her hand. Rejoicing at the favorable prospect, her father at once gave his consent.

But when he told Frances about it, he was amazed to hear her, who had never contradicted him, declare her firm intention of espousing only her heavenly Bridegroom, and asking his permission to become a Tertiary. He became so enraged that he seized a rope and whipped the delicate girl unmercifully, until her mother intervened. He then locked her in a room, where she received only bread and water, and no one was permitted to speak to her.

Mary Frances considered herself fortunate to be able to offer her divine Bridegroom this early proof of her fidelity; she regarded the trial as a pre-nuptial celebration. The earnest representations of a priest made her father, who after all was a believing Christian, realize that he had done wrong; and he consented that his daughter take the Tertiary habit and serve God as a consecrated virgin at home, as was customary in those days.

Filled with holy joy, Mary Frances now received the habit and with it the surname "of the Five Wounds." This name was prophetic of her subsequent life. At home she had much to endure. Her father never got over it that he lost a wealthy son-in-law. When God favored her with unusual graces — she was sometimes granted ecstasies at prayer and suffered our Lord's agony with Him — her own brothers and sisters insulted her as an impostor. Even her confessor felt obliged to deal harshly with her. For a long time she could find consolation nowhere but in the wounds of Christ.

Her confessor perceived at last that it was God who was doing these things in Mary Frances. Since her mother had died meanwhile, he saw to it that she found a home with a fellow Tertiary. There one day, as she herself lay ill, she learned that her father was near death; and she asked almighty God to let her suffer her father's death agony and his purgatory. Both requests were granted her.

Although she suffered continuously, our Lord also gave Mary Frances great graces and consolations. She received the marks of the wounds of Christ and was granted the gift of prophecy and of miracles. When Pius VI was crowned pope in 1775, she beheld him in a vision wearing a crown of thorns. Pope Pius closed his life twenty-four years later as a prisoner of the French Revolution at Valence.

Mary Frances also prophesied the tragic events of the French Revolution; and God heard her prayer, asking that she be taken from this world before they would happen. She died on October 6, 1791, kissing the feet of her crucifix. God glorified her by many miracles. She was beatified by Pope Gregory XVI, and canonized by Pope Pius IX in 1867. Her feast is celebrated on October sixth by the three branches of the First Order as well as the Third Order Regular. (Cf. *Forum*, 1949, pp. 303-304, 318-319; *These Made Peace*, pp. 222-225.)

ON CHRISTIAN DOCTRINE

1. What made Mary Frances so resolute that she never failed in courage amid her many trials, but rather advanced in holiness? The lessons of the catechism did that for her. She entertained such a longing to know them that almighty God had her guardian angel instruct her in them before she received any human instruction. Without a knowledge of Christian doctrine, as it is impressed on the heart in thorough catechetical instruction, man is not safe in the storms of life. Piety itself is built on sand without that knowledge; if the waters of tribulation surround it, it collapses. But the soul that is well instructed in the truths of our Faith is like the house in the Gospel: "And the rain fell, and the floods came, and the winds blew, and they beat upon that house, and it fell not, for it was founded on a rock" (Mt. 7,25). — Have you properly appreciated the lessons of the catechism?

2. Consider how the lessons of the catechism should be taught to children. Before they ever learn to read or go to school, the parents and other members of the household, like visible guardian angels, should teach the children their prayers and the more important lessons of faith, so that the instructions will not be something strange to them later. The first school and the first church of the little ones should be the parental home. And when the children begin to attend instructions in school, the parents should encourage their interest by asking them questions and hearing them recite their lessons. Above all they should not neglect to send the

children regularly to the instructions. Those lessons are the most necessary and the most important of their lives. The Holy Ghost speaks of their importance when He says: "From your youth receive instructions, and even to gray hairs you shall find wisdom" (Eccli. 6,18). — How can parents be guilty of keeping their children ignorant for life of the most important matters?

3. Consider that even in later life we should not neglect the lessons of the catechism. We learn them in youth, but we must use them throughout life. That is why we should frequently review these lessons and reflect on them. Take up your catechism occasionally and re-read it. Its lessons mean much more to us as we grow older than they did when we were children. If public catechism instructions or study clubs are conducted in your parish, or if a series of sermons on these lessons is given in your church, do not fail to attend, for they offer valuable lessons for young and old. If one received money for attending them, no doubt, there would be many present who now prefer the comfort of their homes. But Holy Scripture says: "Receive my instructions and not money; choose knowledge rather than gold" (Prov. 8,10). Christian doctrine is worth more than all the gold on earth. It teaches us that man is made for heaven and not for the earth; and if we live in accordance with that principle, we shall enter the kingdom of heaven when we have to leave the things of earth.

PRAYER OF THE CHURCH
O Lord Jesus, who, together with many other graces, didst give St. Mary Frances the grace of perfect contempt of the world, grant that through her merits and intercession we, too, may despise material things and aspire to those which are heavenly. Who livest and reignest forever and ever. Amen.

෨෨෨෨෨෨෨෨෨෨

OCTOBER 7
VENERABLE GEORGE OF AUGSBURG
Confessor, First Order

EORGE was born in 1696 in the diocese of Augsburg, and was the son of respectable peasants. He learned the baker's trade, and as a journeyman baker he crossed the Alps and went to Rome, the capital of Christendom.

The reason why George went to Rome was his interest in things eternal rather than temporal. Guided by divine grace, he resolved while there to leave the world in order to serve God alone in the Capuchin Order. He received the holy habit on November 4, 1724, in the twenty-eighth year of his life.

Even in the novitiate he was admired for his virtue, and so, after his profession, along with other duties he was assigned to the very difficult task of nursing a sick friar whose coarse ways, aggravated by illness, had taken on so repellent a character that no one could take care of him. George tended the sick man until the latter's death with so much love, humility, and patience that all were astonished. God rewarded him for it by continually drawing him closer to Himself; and George received the grace of prayer in a very high degree.

Brother George was now assigned to gather alms for the convent. While on his rounds, he was always recollected and united with God. Whoever saw him was edified. He had such a kindly way about him that he not only attracted the children, but everybody, high and low, appreciated the chance to speak to him. Those who asked him for religious instruction, or for advice and consolation, were never disappointed. One of his special friends was the Cardinal of York, the last male descendant of the Stuarts.

But George found his greatest delight in associating with the poor and the needy. Many sick persons were restored to health by his prayers, so that the gift of miracles was quite generally attributed to him. His life was so rigorous, it seemed a miracle that his weak body was able to endure the hardships that were his.

After a holy life of thirty-eight years in the order, he died peacefully in the Lord in the convent at Frascati near Rome on October 7, 1762. People prayed at his tomb, which was beneath the sanctuary lamp. Because of the many answers to these prayers his beatification was introduced, and Pope Pius IX conferred on him the title of Venerable in 1852. His cause of beatification is still pending.

ON PATIENCE AMID HARSH TREATMENT

1. The virtue of patience meets its severest test amid circumstances like those in which Venerable George had to practice it. To practice patience in sickness which God sends is not so difficult. Bearing the insults and persecution of wicked men is comparatively easy. And we can close an eye to the shortcomings of others. But it is another matter to preserve patience when serving a sick person who is always complaining, or in daily employment where one finds only annoyance and harsh words, or in waiting on aged parents who are cross or ill-humored. Still, where the

words of Christ have fallen on good ground, they produce "fruit in patience." Every Christian should strive to acquire a virtue so necessary. The prince of the apostles thus admonishes servants: "Be subject to your masters, not only to the good and gentle, but also to the froward" (1 Pet. 2,18). Even the Wise Man said long ago: "Honor your father in work, and word, and all patience" (Eccli. 3,9). — Have you stood this test of virtue in the past?

2. Consider that we should not judge too harshly those who provide us with occasions for patience. St. Gertrude once had a superior who was otherwise an exemplary person but was inclined to be cross and harsh. When she asked our Lord to take this fault from her superior, He said: "Why should I rid her of a fault which offers both of you an opportunity to practice virtue? She is given the opportunity to humble herself, you, to practice patience." Such is the wisdom of God! He permits certain imperfections, of which those who possess them try hard to rid themselves but do not succeed, so that they may become more humble, and others more patient. According to the divine dispensation, the weaknesses of one person thus serve to make perfect the virtues of another. — Profit by these opportunities to achieve your own perfection.

3. Consider the reward that is given to patience which has stood the test. The practice of this virtue is in itself a sweet reward, since it saves us from rancor and preserves our peace of heart. Moreover, God grants the patient man, as He did to Venerable George, special graces to remain faithful in the various events of life. "And patience works trial" (Rom. 5,4). But as tried children of God we receive an eternal share in the glorious reward of His only-begotten Son, "who despised the shame, and now sits on the right hand of the throne of God" (Heb. 12,2). We should direct our thought to Him when our patience is being tried. That is why the Apostle adds: "Think diligently of Him who endured such opposition from sinners against Himself; that you be not wearied, fainting in your minds" (Heb. 12,3).

PRAYER OF THE CHURCH
(Monday in Holy Week)

Grant, we beseech Thee, almighty God, that we who fail through our weakness under so many adversities, may take heart again through the pleading of the Passion of Thy only-begotten Son. Who livest and reignest forever and ever. Amen.

OCTOBER 8
ST. BRIDGET OF SWEDEN
Widow, Third Order

T. BRIDGET was born about the year 1302 in Sweden, and belonged to an illustrious as well as pious family. Shortly after her birth Bridget lost her saintly mother. Her father then undertook to raise her with the aid of an aunt. As a very young girl she manifested a decided inclination for things spiritual. At the age of ten God favored her with a vision of the Crucified. The thought of the unspeakable torments which our Lord endured on Calvary affected her so deeply that she shed copious tears, and from that moment the sacred Passion was the subject of her meditation.

She wished to consecrate her virginity to her Lord, but obedient to the wish of her father she married Prince Ulf, a young man of solid virtue and in every way deserving of her. Both joined the Third Order in order to strengthen themselves in the works of piety and the practice of penance. God blessed their marriage with eight children, and Bridget made it her sacred duty to raise them in the fear of God. Among her charities there stands out especially her service of the poor and the infirm; she waited on them with great care, sometimes even washing their feet and kissing them.

During the return journey from Compostela, where they visited the grave of the Apostle St. James, Ulf fell seriously ill at Arras. St. Denis then appeared to Bridget at night and assured her that her husband would recover. He also foretold events which would take place in their lives. Ulf soon afterwards entered the Cistercian monastery of Alvastra, where he died in the odor of sanctity in 1344.

Bridget now divided her estate among her children and the poor, clothed herself in a coarse garment with a cord for a girdle, and began to lead a very austere life. She built a convent for nuns at Vadstena and gave them the rule of St. Augustine, thus founding the Order of Our Saviour. She spent two more years partly at Vadstena and partly at Alvastra, where her husband had died. Then, at God's command, she went to Rome, where she practiced the virtues in a high degree. She labored much for the return of the papacy to Rome, and was charged by God to deliver several messages to Popes Innocent VI, Urban V, and Gregory XI.

In 1371 she made a visit to the Holy Land, in compliance with a command from our Lord. There He bestowed on her extraordinary graces and imparted to her a knowledge of His sacred mysteries. Upon her return to Italy she was stricken with a grievous illness, which afflicted her for an entire year. Having foretold the day of her death, she passed into the joys of eternity on July 23, 1373, at the age of seventy-one years. She was laid to rest in the Poor Clare convent of St. Lawrence in Panisperna. The following year her body was removed to the convent at Vadstena in Sweden.

Many miracles were wrought at her intercession, and Pope Boniface IX canonized her. The three branches of the First Order celebrate the feast of St. Bridget on October eighth. (Cf. *Forum,* 1947, pp. 297-298; 316; *These Made Peace,* pp. 142-152.)

ON THE FREQUENT REMEMBRANCE OF CHRIST'S SUFFERINGS

1. Love and compassion urged St. Bridget to meditate continually on the sufferings of Christ. Similar sentiments should urge us to do likewise. If you were in straitened circumstances because of a great debt, and were suddenly assisted by a wealthy gentleman who not only stood surety for you but even paid your entire debt, you would never forget that man. Well, your soul was condemned to eternal damnation because of the debt you contracted by your sins. Then the Son of God not only stood surety for you with our heavenly Father, but by His bitter suffering and death on the Cross He paid off your entire debt. Imitate St. Bridget and keep the remembrance of this grace ever before your mind. "Forget not the kindness of your surety, for he has given his life for you" (Eccli. 29,20).
2. Consider how useful it is to think of the sufferings of Christ. There is no better consolation amid the sufferings of life. Are you being ridiculed and persecuted, have you been laid low by painful illness, is your soul worried and sorrowful, then look at your suffering Saviour. Contemplate Him from the time He suffers the agony in the garden until He draws His last breath on the cross. What you are suffering, He endured in far greater measure, and — what is most consoling — His suffering has obtained for you the necessary strength to bear your sufferings patiently and with merit. His death has effected our redemption, so that in time of direst need, when our soul is oppressed because of the sins we have committed, we may look up with confidence to our suffering Saviour. "If any man sin, we have an advocate with the Father, Jesus Christ the just; and He is the propitiation for our sins" (1 Jn. 2,1-2). — Have you always had recourse to your suffering Saviour?
Consider the manner in which we should recall our Saviour's sufferings. St. Bridget's humility, poverty, and austerity prepared her for the grace by which our Lord, so to say, planted His cross in the very center of her

heart. The proud, those who consider themselves better than the rest of men, those who are inclined to pamper their bodies, those who always prefer the company of men, form no part of the group that stands on Calvary. They may grasp the meaning of Christ's Cross and sufferings, but the remembrance of it does not abide with them nor does it produce salutary fruit. Imitate the virtues of St. Bridget, and the sufferings of Christ will also bring consolation to your soul and a foretaste of the joys of eternity.

PRAYER OF THE CHURCH

O Lord, our God, who through Thine only-begotten Son didst reveal heavenly secrets to Blessed Bridget, grant that, through her loving intercession, we Thy servants may rejoice and be happy in the revelation of Thine eternal glory. Through Christ our Lord. Amen.

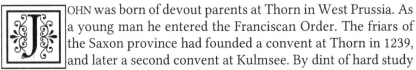

OCTOBER 9
BLESSED JOHN LOBEDAU
Confessor, First Order

OHN was born of devout parents at Thorn in West Prussia. As a young man he entered the Franciscan Order. The friars of the Saxon province had founded a convent at Thorn in 1239, and later a second convent at Kulmsee. By dint of hard study John became quite a scholar, and labored with marked success as a renowned preacher in places where Christianity had recently gained a foothold.

John was no less renowned because of the holiness of his life. At home in the convent, he spent most of his time alone in his cell, absorbed in meditation and holy contemplation. The mystery of the incarnation of the Son of God held a special attraction for him. Over and over he reflected on the boundless love and condescension that induced the infinite God, the Creator and Lord of the universe, to assume human nature for the sake of mankind, to be born, and to be carried about in the arms of the Virgin Mother as a small, helpless child. The Blessed Virgin frequently appeared to him with her Divine Child, and conversed with him on the mysteries of our redemption.

It happened one day, while Father John was living in the convent at Kulmsee, that on passing his cell, certain of his brethren heard someone speaking. Their astonishment at recognizing the voice as that of a woman knew no bounds. The worst suspicions thrust themselves on the minds of his brethren, who had supposed their brother to be a saint. To add to their consternation, they presently heard also the voice of a child crying. Justly shocked, they rapped at the door, but Father John gave no sign that they might enter. But when they threw open the door, they found their holy brother alone, absorbed in prayer and weeping pitifully.

The Father Guardian then commanded John in obedience to tell what had taken place. John admitted that the Blessed Virgin and the Divine Child had been with him, and that the latter had wept to think that the Catholic religion, which had been so recently introduced in those parts, was again to be exterminated and the various places of worship were to be destroyed.

Filled with remorse at their evil suspicions, the awestruck brethren left the cell of Father John and went their ways.

The holy man spent the last years of his life in almost continuous prayer. He died at Kulmsee on October 9, 1264. Many miracles occurred at his grave. So generally was he venerated that his feast came to be observed as the patronal feast of the country until the latter fell away and embraced Lutheranism. But in more recent times, at the request of the bishops of Kulm, the Apostolic See gave renewed approval to the veneration of Blessed John. This, however, seems to have been merely permission to resume the popular veneration of Blessed John which was interrupted for a long time by the Protestant Reformation, and does not appear to have been an equivalent beatification. There is no feast of Blessed John in any of the Franciscan calendars.

ON THE SUSPICION OF EVIL

1. What took place at the cell of Blessed John, reminds us how slow we must be to suspect evil of anyone. There is of course such a thing as a justifiable suspicion, such as parents and superiors must sometimes entertain. And we are obliged to be watchful in the case of those for whose temporal and eternal welfare we have just ground to fear. But there is in many men a tendency to suspect evil in others without sufficient reason, and to pass judgment without first having investigated the matter. If we succumb to that tendency, without doubt we shall only too often find cause for regret, as did the brethren of Blessed John. Such hasty suspicion is a breach of justice, which requires that we never impute evil to anyone without sufficient proof. It is also against charity, for, when we truly love people, we will always interpret their actions in the best light.

"Charity thinks no evil" (1 Cor. 13,5). — Do you possess such charity?

2. Consider whence arises this tendency to suspect evil in others. It is frequently a sign that the suspicious person is inclined to the vice which he so readily imputes to another; we judge others by ourselves. But the real source is found in our inordinate inclinations, ill-will, envy, jealousy, and the like. They easily incite us to suspicion and rash judgment. Persons having these faults no longer believe in solid piety, genuine fidelity, or sincere goodwill. The Pharisees were an example in point inasmuch as they were so ready to interpret everything in our Lord's life in an evil light. Our Lord beholds the hearts of men, and still He dwelt among us. To many of us He could address the words that He once spoke to the Scribes: "Why do you think evil in your hearts?" (Mt. 9,4). —Do those words apply to you?

3. Consider the tragic results which often follow upon evil suspicion. In how many instances has suspicion destroyed harmony between husband and wife for all time! How often have innocent servants been deprived of their good name and their means of livelihood on account of suspicions! How frequently have the best of friends become the bitterest enemies for the same reason! Be careful, therefore, never to incite another person to evil suspicion of anyone; and if you experience it in your own heart, crush it as you would a spark from hell, and pray God to grant you a spark of His charity.

PRAYER OF THE CHURCH

O God, to whom all hearts are open and all wills are known so that nothing remains hidden, cleanse our thoughts and our hearts by the infusion of the Holy Spirit, so that we may deserve to love Thee perfectly and to praise Thee worthily. Through Christ our Lord. Amen.

❦❦❦❦❦❦❦❦❦❦❦

OCTOBER 10
ST. DANIEL AND COMPANIONS
Martyrs, First Order

AFTER the Franciscan Order had been blessed in the glorious death of its first martyrs, St. Berard and his four companions, holy rivalry was aroused among the children of St. Francis to offer their blood in preaching the Faith of Christ.

In 1227, Daniel, provincial of Calabria, a man of eminent sanctity, and six companions, Angelus, Samuel, Donulus, Leo, Hugolinus, and Nicholas, with the blessing of the minister general, went to Africa to preach the Gospel of Christ to the Mohammedans. Landing at Ceuta, they resolved to preach in that large city. Before entering the city proper, they learned from Christian merchants that a strict order prohibited entrance to all Christians. They realized that their undertaking was fraught with the greatest danger, and they prepared themselves accordingly.

On Saturday, October second, they made their confession, received holy Communion, and then spent the remainder of the day in prayer. In the evening, as our Lord did on the eve of His sufferings, they washed one another's feet. On Sunday morning they entered the city and began to preach to the crowds in the streets and public places, boldly declaring that salvation was to be found only in the name of Jesus. The city was in an uproar. The courageous preachers were thrown into prison. There they wrote to the Christian merchants in the suburbs:

"Blessed be God, the Father of mercies, who comforts us in all our tribulations! Our Lord has commanded us: 'Go and preach the Gospel to all creatures.' He has said: 'The servant is not greater than the Master; if men persecute you, remember that they first persecuted Me.' Struck by these words, we poor and unworthy servants of Jesus Christ have abandoned our home, and have come to preach in this country for the glory of God and the salvation of souls, and the confusion of obstinate infidels. ... And although we may have much to suffer, we are greatly comforted in the Lord, hoping He will be pleased to accept the sacrifice of our lives. To Him only be honor and glory forevermore."

A week later the prisoners were led before the governor, and an attempt was made to induce them to renounce their faith, first by promises, then by threats. All remained firm in their profession of Christ and were condemned to be beheaded.

The six companions now knelt down before Daniel, their superior, thanked him for providing them with the opportunity of winning a martyr's crown, and asked for a final blessing. Father Daniel, amid tears of holy joy, embraced each one, blessed them, and said: "Let us rejoice in the Lord, my faithful companions, for this is a festival day for us! The holy angels are already coming to conduct our souls to the eternal mansions, and this day the white-robed martyrs will receive us into their holy company. Heaven is open above our heads, we shall soon be in possession of eternal happiness."

And so their heads rolled from the block, but their souls took their flight to heaven. Their remains were later taken to Spain, where many miracles occurred at their intercession. Pope Leo X canonized them in

1516. Their feast is observed on October tenth by the three branches of the First Order as well as the Third Order Regular.

ON VENERATING THE HOLY MARTYRS

1. In our veneration of the saints, the holy martyrs deserve special attention. We venerate in them, to an extent, the blood of Christ, since the blood they shed is like a continuation of the blood which Christ shed for us on Mt. Calvary. They sealed with their blood the truths for which Christ was crucified. By sacrificing their lives they also gave proof of their perfect fidelity and supreme charity towards Christ, thus giving all Christians an encouraging example. The willing self-oblation of the holy martyrs should impel us to venerate these heroes of the Faith and should fill us with a great love for our holy religion.

2. Consider the special way in which holy Church draws our attention to the veneration of the holy martyrs. On their feastdays the priest approaches the altar clothed in red vestments. The color reminds us of the blood the martyrs shed. In offering their blood and their lives for their holy Faith, they made the greatest sacrifice man can make. We should praise and bless them for it in the name of holy Church, whose glorious heroes they are. The red of the vestments also signifies the fire of love which God kindled in the hearts of the martyrs. That is also the purpose of the red color on the feast of Pentecost. The Holy Ghost descended upon the apostles in the form of fiery tongues and strengthened them remarkably. It is this fire of love that gives martyrdom its value. "If I should deliver my body to be burnt and have not charity, it profits me nothing" (1 Cor. 13,3). Hence, on the feasts of the holy martyrs, we should praise and thank God, who gave this fire of love to so many thousands of His saints, who became witnesses of their Faith by shedding their blood.

3. Consider that the martyrs gave proof of their fidelity even before they shed their blood. Faithful to the call of the apostolate, they went out to face danger after due preparation. They accepted reproach and pain patiently, even cheerfully, for the sake of Christ; promises could not lure them, nor threats frighten them to abandon Him. We must imitate the martyrs in their fidelity even if we are not called upon to shed our blood for Christ. Only in that way may we hope to please them by our veneration. The glorious crown which they have won, should encourage us to remain faithful in our allegiance to Christ. Their powerful intercession will help us.

PRAYER OF THE CHURCH

As we rejoice, O Lord, at the crown which our brethren, Thy martyrs, have won, may it produce in us an increase of virtue, and at their intercession may it also be our comfort. Through Christ our Lord. Amen.

OCTOBER 11
THE SERVANT OF GOD VICTRICIUS WEISS
Confessor, First Order

ATHER VICTRICIUS gives us his own biography in a prayer which he wrote:

"I consecrate myself to the Sacred Heart of Jesus. With my hidden Jesus I wish to remain unknown, misrepresented, and despised. I want to be crucified in body and soul with my crucified Saviour, in order to atone in some way for the insults rendered Him in the most holy Sacrament of the altar. I want to rejoice with my glorified Jesus because He cannot now suffer any more. But I may suffer. I want to offer up all my sufferings for the intentions of His Sacred Heart."

Father Victricius was born in 1842 in the little town of Eggenfelden in northern Bavaria, the son of a deeply religious surgeon. He made his classical studies in Munich; and he studied theology in Freising. During these years he felt a great attraction for the interior life. After his ordination to the priesthood in 1866, he labored as a chaplain in Schwabing and was then appointed prefect and professor of homiletics in the seminary at Freising. In 1871 he received his doctorate in theology.

Although he was very genial and sociable in his dealings with others, he devoted himself resolutely to meditation, self-conquest, and a life of sacrifice. In 1875 he joined the Capuchin Order; and his brethren chose him five times as the head of the Bavarian province. He achieved remarkable results by his exemplary life, the spirit of recollection, and fraternal charity.

From the year 1908, he dwelt in the convent of Vilsbiburg. There he had to suffer much. Deafness, sleeplessness, ulcers, spiritual dryness and desolation, difficulties arising from association with others provided a severe trial for him. But all this only caused him to grow all the more in virtue.

On October 8, 1924, his holy life of atonement came to a close. He was generally regarded as a saint; and the process of his beatification is now being carried on in Rome. (Cf. *Forum*, 1953, p. 318.)

ON THE MERITS OF ATONEMENT

1. The idea of atonement is as old as mankind. It is innate in man. Civil and ecclesiastical authority no less than private individuals in their relations with one another justly require that some form of penalty make up for offenses committed. The penalty, however, may be canceled if the misdeed is atoned for. It was therefore laudable on the part of Father Victricius that he offered himself to God as a victim of atonement for the sins of mankind. For if atonement is in order among men, the supreme majesty of almighty God is a thousand times more deserving of it. — Try to realize the propriety of the idea of atonement.

2. Atonement has been required by God Himself, especially in the laws requiring propitiatory offerings and in the great feast of the Atonement. Both institutions were to prefigure the supreme expiation of the God-man on Golgotha, of which St. John speaks as "the propitiation of our sins" (1 Jn. 4,10). How pleasing to God, therefore, Father Victricius must have been when he offered himself in union with Christ to the Most High in atonement for the misdeeds of mankind! — Should his heroic example not inspire us to make frequent acts of atonement?

3. The idea of atonement must be revived in our day. Our times are like those of which the Prophet of Patmos writes: "Woe to the earth and to the sea, because the devil has come down unto you having great wrath" (Apoc. 12,12). Diabolical crimes that cry to heaven for vengeance are being committed on every hand. God is forcefully thrust out of Society. So it behooves all good people to emulate the spirit of Father Victricius, seeking by prayer, penance, and renunciation to disarm the just wrath of God. — Unite with those Christians who are offering themselves as victims of atonement by practicing at least small acts of mortification and renunciation.

PRAYER OF THE CHURCH
O God, who by sin art offended, but by penance pacified: graciously look upon the humble prayers of Thy people, and ward off the scourges of Thy wrath which we have deserved for our sins. Through Christ our Lord. Amen.

OCTOBER 12
ST. SERAPHIN OF MONTEGRANARO
Confessor, First Order

ERAPHIN'S parents were poor in earthly goods and obscure in the sight of men. But the spirit of prayer which his mother instilled in the boy, was an inheritance of priceless value. The loving lessons of his mother caused Seraphin to make the firm resolve to remain innocent and become a saint.

He fostered tender devotion to the Blessed Mother and occasionally visited her shrine at Loreto, not far from his home. Once, on his way to the shrine, he found the River Potenza so high that no boatman ventured across. In his eagerness to get to the shrine, Seraphin stepped on the water, and it became like solid ground beneath him; he crossed the river on his way to the shrine and back without so much as wetting the soles of his feet.

On the death of his parents, Seraphin was subjected to a severe trial. His brother, a bricklayer and a man of a violent temper, took him into his employ; but no matter what the boy did, he received nothing but harsh words and blows in return. Seraphin bore the cruel treatment with great patience and recognized in it the way to holiness.

Desiring to consecrate himself to the service of God, he entered a Capuchin convent when he was only sixteen years old. The high degree of perfection he had already attained was soon noticed and admired. His brethren were edified at his humility, charity, mortification, and self-sacrifice. Punctual in performing all the duties assigned to him, he still found time to be of service to the other brothers.

He devoted the night to prayer. In the evening he would visit the Blessed Sacrament and remain there for hours absorbed in prayer and contemplation. Then he would take a short rest, after which he would get up once more to attend the midnight office. God seemed to preserve his bodily strength in a marvelous way.

During a famine he ate but a fourth of his own meager meal, in order to have so much more to give to the poor. As porter of the convent, charged with providing for the poor, he once exceeded the bounds of obedience. For, as he had nothing more to give and there were still some poor waiting for help, he went into the garden and gathered a supply of the vegetables growing there. When his superior took him to task for it, the good brother assured him that the community would in no way suffer on his account, and the next morning a new growth of vegetables appeared in the garden.

The miraculous power with which God rewarded the charity of His servant continued to manifest itself. Countless sick were restored to health when he made the Sign of the Cross over them.

Seraphin endeavored, nevertheless, to withdraw as much as possible from contact with the world. While engaged in the quiet work about the convent, his heart was busy contemplating the sufferings of Christ. Consumed with the love of Him who shed His blood for love of us, he yearned to go to the infidels in order to shed his blood for Christ. Since this request was not granted, he made it a habit to pray:

> Holy Mother, pierce me through,
> In my heart each wound renew
> Of my Saviour Crucified.

Inflamed with the love of God, Seraphin departed from this life on October 12, 1604, in his sixty-fourth year. Many miracles occurred at his grave, and Pope Clement XIII canonized him. The three branches of the First Order as well as the Third Order Regular celebrate the feast of St. Seraphin on October twelfth.

ON VENERATING THE PRECIOUS BLOOD

1. The precious Blood which Jesus Christ shed for us inflamed the heart of Seraphin with glowing love for his Lord. When Jesus shed tears at the grave of Lazarus, the bystanders said: "Behold how he loved him!" (Jn. 11,36). But when He shed His precious Blood for us, he proved His love for us more than He could do by tears. One drop of His precious Blood would have sufficed to redeem us, but "what would have satisfied justice," says St. Chrysostom, "did not satisfy His love." He shed all His Blood, even to the last drop. He "has loved us and washed us from our sins in His own blood" (Apoc. 1,5). — When your soul is refreshed with the precious Blood in holy Communion, say, as St. Seraphin frequently said: "My Beloved to me and I to Him" (Cant. 2,16).

2. To promote devotion to the precious Blood, a confraternity of the precious Blood was established in the nineteenth century. Much good has been achieved by it and many members have been enrolled. The only conditions are, to have one's name entered on the membership list and to say daily seven Glorys in honor of the seven times our Saviour shed His Blood: (1) at the Circumcision, (2) at the Agony, (3) at the Scourging, (4) at the Crowning with thorns, (5) on the Way of the Cross, (6) at the Crucifixion, (7) from the open Side. Pope Pius IX, in recommending the

confraternity, reminded the faithful that by way of a figure the blood of the lamb was used in Egypt to mark the houses of the Israelites, so that they would be spared from the wrath of God. He added: "Will not they who devoutly venerate the Blood of our Saviour, more assuredly escape the wrath and experience the mercies of God?" — Let us, then, devoutly venerate the precious Blood.

3. Consider that sincere veneration of the Blood of Christ should hearten us to abstain carefully from every sin and to bear the sufferings of this life in a manner pleasing to God. Our souls have been cleansed by the Blood of Christ, first in baptism, and then in the sacrament of penance. "The blood of Jesus Christ," says St. John, "cleanses us from all sin" (1 Jn. 1,17). And he adds, "My little children, these things I write to you that you may not sin." For, would that not be like treading on the Blood of Christ? We should rather manifest our gratitude and return love for love by patiently bearing the sufferings sent to us and by steadfastly overcoming every temptation to sin. May St. Seraphin's intercession obtain for us a share of his heroic love of God.

PRAYER OF THE CHURCH

O God, who didst inflame the heart of St. Seraphin with the fire of Thy love, grant, we beseech Thee, that at his intercession we may walk in his footsteps and be inflamed with the same fire of love. Through Christ our Lord. Amen.

⁂

OCTOBER 13
BLESSED ROBERT MALATESTA
Confessor, Third Order

 HIS devout Tertiary was a powerful prince in Italy. He died at a very early age, but in such consummate perfection that in the eyes of God he had lived a long life in the service of his Lord. He was the son of the prince of Rimini, Pandolph Malatesta, and was born in 1411.

At a very tender age he denied himself dainty things, and took only the less appetizing portion of the food given him, so that the better part might be given to the sick poor. He also practiced all kinds of mortification with regard to clothing and rest at night. He was so devoted to prayer, that even in sleep he was often found with his hands crossed on his breast and his lips moving as if in prayer. When his uncle asked him on several occasions what he wished to be, the little fellow said: "I wish to be a poor man like Jesus."

His uncle was much pleased with Robert, and so when Robert's parents died, he adopted him as his heir. Although he would have preferred to give himself entirely to God's service, Robert was obliged to accede to his uncle's wishes and married the Princess Margaret of Este. His young wife, however, was also a devout person and they lived together in a very holy union. A year after their marriage, Robert's uncle died, and he became the independent prince of the domains of Rimini, Cesano, and Fano. He governed with justice and charity. He was a father to the poor, and often visited the sick in the hospitals, sometimes even waited on them personally.

It was about this time that he was interiorly instructed by St. Francis, to whom he was tenderly devoted, to take the habit of the Third Order and consecrate himself in a special way to the service of God. On the feast of St. Francis, he was clothed in the holy habit, and from then on practiced the rule of the Third Order very strictly. He prayed the divine office of the priests every day, observed fasts besides those prescribed, and received the holy sacraments often and with the greatest devotion.

Although externally living up to his rank, he always wore the Third Order scapular and cord; and his heart remained humble and detached from the world. Once when he was engaged in prayer, our holy Father St. Francis appeared to him and showed him his five wounds. Robert at once experienced the full pain of the wounds, and for a long time he remained kneeling with his arms outstretched in the form of a cross.

After a very painful illness, yet happy in anticipation of the joys of heaven, he died in 1432 when he was but twenty-one years old. According to his express wishes, he was buried very simply and in the garb of the Tertiaries. God glorified his tomb by miracles. The title of Blessed has been conferred on him in popular devotion. (Cf. *These Made Peace,* pp. 157-161.)

ON WEARING THE SCAPULAR

1. Consider how Blessed Robert was instructed by our holy Father St. Francis, whom he dearly loved, to wear the scapular of the Third Order, thus acknowledging himself as a son of St. Francis. The scapular of the Third Order, as well as the scapular of our Blessed Lady, is a badge or uniform by which we profess to whom we belong and in whose service we are engaged. By the scapular of our Lady we profess ourselves children

of Mary, by the Third Order scapular we profess ourselves sons or daughters of St. Francis. The saints recognize us by these signs as their clients, and consequently protect and watch over us. Be faithful in wearing the scapular — without it you cannot have a share in the indulgences granted. But it should also remind you to live so that you may do honor to this holy garment. — Are you faithful in wearing it? Do you ever reflect on the kind of life you should lead in order to wear it worthily?

2. The word scapular means a shoulder garment. Some religious wear a large scapular over their shoulders, so as to protect their religious habit while at work, and, therefore, the scapular may also be called a working garb. This should remind the persons who wear it, that lazy piety is in disagreement with the scapular. As the cord should remind the Tertiaries to refrain from sensual pleasure, so the scapular should remind them to engage in good works, in faithful compliance with the prescriptions of the rule as well as in fulfilling the duties incumbent on a good Christian, and the obligations of his state of life. Here the words of the Apostle can be applied: "Labor as a good soldier of Christ Jesus" (2 Tim. 2,3). — Think of this every morning when you look at and kiss your scapular.

Consider that the scapular is a garment of humility and penance. St. Francis named his order one of penance. The Blessed Robert practiced penance even in his princely life at court; he ate only common food, fasted often, and sometimes slept on a bare board. Are there not many acts of penance that you could perform? Could you not in the spirit of penance accept the difficulties of your state of life, and the sufferings God permits to befall you? God grant that your scapular may give you that strength. You will then be able to take comfort in the thought of death before it approaches. You will be able to say with the Prophet: "I will greatly rejoice in the Lord, for He has clothed me with the garments of salvation and with the robe of justice" (Is. 61,10).

PRAYER OF THE CHURCH (Palm Sunday)

Almighty and eternal God, who didst cause our Saviour to assume our flesh and to suffer death upon the cross that all mankind might imitate the example of His humility, mercifully grant, that, treasuring the lessons of His patience, we may deserve to have fellowship in His resurrection. Through Christ our Lord. Amen.

OCTOBER 14
THE SERVANT OF GOD ANNA APOLLONIA STADLER
Virgin, Third Order

N MUNICH, the capital of Bavaria, there was a convent of Tertiaries which was called the Ridler convent after its founder. It was also called The Stairs, because of a replica of the stairs on which the bleeding Christ ascended to the judgment hall of Pilate had been built there. But the convent itself was also a holy staircase, since holy zeal for perfection reigned there and many souls ascended from there to heaven.

In the second half of the seventeenth century this zeal for perfection was due in great measure to the efforts of the servant of God Anna Apollonia Stadler, who for a long time filled the office of novice mistress and later of superior of the convent.

A contemporary of the servant of God who has written about the saintly personages of the Franciscan Order says of her, that, for nine years as a novice mistress, and nine more years as a superior of the convent, all her undertakings seemed to have been associated with the holy angels. It is quite certain that the holy angels rejoiced in this true spouse of Christ, since in all her occupations, recollected as she was in God, she was always so cheerful and so pleasant of countenance that she seemed already on earth to be united with the angels in praising God.

Almighty God made known how pleasing to Him was the cheerful spirit of His faithful servant. Once when she approached the Table of the Lord, the Son of God stepped out of the consecrated Host in the form of a lovely infant and Apollonia was permitted to embrace Him with joyful love.

From the praise of God on earth she passed to the eternal praise of Him among the angelic choirs. It so happened that while the *Te Deum* was being chanted in choir, she was suddenly seized with an illness that resulted in her death a few days later. After her death her countenance was even more resplendent than in life.

ON VENERATING THE HOLY ANGELS

1. What a holy life and blessed death was that of the servant of God Apollonia! At work and at prayer she united herself in spirit with the holy angels who sing the praises of the Divine Majesty, and she passed out of this life in the midst of earthly song to take up the heavenly strains. In like manner ought we to unite ourselves in spirit with the hosts of holy angels

who surround the throne of God and thus serve and praise Him. The prophet Daniel who beheld the choirs of angels, wrote: "Thousands of thousands ministered to Him, and ten thousand times a hundred thousand stood before Him" (Dan. 7,10). If, in company with the angels, you do God's will in your work, you will accomplish perfectly what you pray for daily: "Thy will be done on earth as it is in heaven." That is, moreover, an admirable way of honoring the angels and a means of being admitted to their company later.

2. Consider that the holy angels are our helpers in special dangers of body and soul. Two angels saved Lot and his family from the destruction of Sodom. An angel comforted Hagar in the wilderness. An angel protected the young men in the fiery furnace. An angel strengthened our Lord in His agony. And the Apostle writes: "Are they not all ministering spirits sent to minister for them who shall receive the inheritance of salvation?" (Heb. 1,14). What confidence this thought should give us! Invoke their aid frequently, but especially in danger and need. "All ye holy angels and archangels, pray for us!"

3. Consider the great mercy of God in appointing an angel to act as guardian for each and every one of us human beings. St. Jerome says: "So great is the dignity of souls, that everyone has been given an angel for his protection." — Have you not, at times, been aware of the presence of your angel either by some interior light or an urgent warning? Have you perhaps given him cause to hide from you? Honor him, follow his guidance, so that at the end of your life you may be permitted to join him in eternal bliss.

PRAYER OF THE CHURCH (Mass of the Holy Angels)

O God, who in Thine unspeakable providence dost graciously send Thy holy angels to keep watch over us: grant us, Thy suppliants, that we may always be shielded by their protection and ever rejoice in their fellowship. Through Christ our Lord. Amen.

OCTOBER 15
THE SERVANT OF GOD WALTER OF TREVISO
Confessor, Third Order

ALTER was born of noble parents in the vicinity of Spoleto and was very carefully reared by his pious mother. Blessed with rare gifts of mind and heart, he grew up into a likeable young man, equally well versed in the science of the saints and in secular knowledge. His most ardent desire was to become a priest.

The bishop of Treviso, to whom the piety and the zeal of Walter were no secret, joyfully conferred holy orders on him and shortly afterwards chose him as his assistant in the administration of the episcopal office. In this capacity Walter labored with great zeal for the salvation of the faithful, and his efforts were rewarded with the conversion of many hardened and unrepentant sinners.

When the bishop died, Walter was chosen as his successor, but in his humility, he hesitated for a long time to accept the dignity. Finally, the archbishop commanded him to accept it in virtue of holy obedience. Walter hesitated no longer, for he recognized the voice of God in the words of his superior.

Even after his elevation to the episcopate, Walter continued to observe with the greatest fidelity the rule of the Third Order, of which he had been a member for many years. He always led a very plain, humble, and mortified life. The only recreation he allowed himself he sought in the quiet seclusion of a nearby Franciscan convent. There he endeavored to strengthen himself by prayer and religious exercises, and to prepare himself for a happy death.

He died a holy death in 1242. The people venerated him as a saint during his lifetime, and even more so after his death,

ON PREFERMENTS

1. Consider how the saints fled from positions of honor, just as the servant of God Walter did. When, however, they were obliged to accept them, they labored at their post with great success. The true servants of God always act in this manner. They fly from honorable positions because in their humility they regard themselves unworthy of honor while they fear the responsibility associated with such offices. When they must accept them, however, they endeavor very conscientiously to fulfill their duties, and so the blessing of God, which is always given to the humble, is with them. — Have you always thought of honorable positions in this light?

2. Consider that whoever follows the promptings of nature desires preferment. For, it is in accord with human nature to covet distinction over other men and to wish to govern others. Before the coming of the Holy Ghost, even Christ's disciples quarreled among themselves as to who among them should be their leader after our Lord's departure. Everybody engaged in worldly pursuits seeks honors, and everybody believes himself capable of discharging the duties of a superior. But, since God resists the proud, His help is withdrawn from the ambitious once they secure a position of honor. And so it often happens that they reap disgrace in their preferments, while duty unfulfilled increases their deficit for eternity. — Have you exposed yourself to such danger at any time?

3. Consider that while some people are not anxious to have honorable positions for themselves, they are quite set on obtaining them for their children. Like the mother of the sons of Zebedee, they would like to see their sons in places of honor and their daughters educated for social position far above their own. Were our Lord to speak to such parents, He would likewise say to them: "You know not what you desire." Such parents believe that they are promoting the happiness of their children. But how often does such vanity plunge the children and even the parents into the greatest misfortune! — Pray God that He may never permit you to be deceived by such foolish ambition.

PRAYER OF THE CHURCH (No. 27 under "Various Prayers")

O God, who withstandest the proud and givest Thy grace to the humble, endow us with that true virtue of humility, the pattern of which Thine only-begotten Son showed in Himself to the faithful; nor may we ever by our pride provoke Thee to anger, but rather, in our lowliness, accept from Thy hands the gifts of Thy grace. Through the same Christ our Lord. Amen.

᠅᠅᠅᠅᠅᠅᠅᠅᠅᠅᠅᠅

OCTOBER 16
THE SERVANT OF GOD JAMES OF THE ROSARY
Confessor, First Order

BOUT 1422 a young man entered the Franciscan Order in the province which St. Francis himself founded and which bears his name. His name was James; and he became a priest of eminent sanctity and a fervent client of our Blessed Mother.

His sermons and conversations abounded with praises of Mary.

He took a special delight in reciting in her honor the rosary of the Seven Joys of Our Lady, generally called the Franciscan Crown; and he used to exhort the faithful to venerate Mary by saying this rosary which is so pleasing to her. That is why he came to be called Father James of the Rosary. In fact, the origin of this rosary is ascribed to him; and St. John Capistran extols him for it.

He often experienced the power of this beautiful prayer. Once the convent of Borgo San Sepolcro, which lay in the domains of the city of Florence, was marked for destruction to keep the advancing armies of Naples from using it as a vantage point. James, who lived there, influenced the Florentine commanding officer to wait a little longer before proceeding to destroy it, and then went to pray his rosary that the convent might be spared. It was then revealed to him that the enemy would not appear but would be forced to retreat. So it happened and no harm came to the friary.

James spent the last years of his life in this convent in perfect peace, until God called him to eternal rest at the age of seventy years.

ON THE FRANCISCAN CROWN

1. The Blessed Virgin herself pointed out that the Franciscan Crown, like the usual Dominican rosary, is a devotion pleasing to her. The annals of the order state that a young man — it is generally believed that it was James of the Rosary — who entered the order had been a fervent client of our Blessed Lady and had decked her statue daily with a wreath of flowers. Since he was not permitted to continue this practice in the novitiate, he thought of leaving the order. But first he knelt before the statue of our Lady to say a prayer. There the Blessed Virgin appeared to him and said: "Remain here, and do not grieve because you can no longer weave a wreath of flowers for me. I will teach you how you can daily weave a crown of roses that will not wither, and will be more pleasing to me and more meritorious for yourself." And she taught him the rosary of seven decades. — From this incident we can learn not to be selfishly attached to pious practices, and that prayer is of greater value than perishable decorations.

2. Consider the fragrant roses that make up the Franciscan Crown. This rosary consists of seventy-two Hail Marys; and originally these were said in honor of the seventy-two years which Our Lady spent on earth according to the more probable opinion and tradition. As such it was certainly in existence during the first half of the fifteenth century, for St.

Bernardin and St. John Capistran both promoted it. It was not till the seventeenth century apparently that the children of St. Francis began to recite the seven decades of the crown also in honor of the seven joys of Our Lady. The seven joys are as follows: The Annunciation, the Visitation, the Nativity, the Adoration of the Magi, the Finding of Jesus in the Temple, the Resurrection of our Lord, and the Assumption and Coronation of our Lady. At each decade it is well to reflect on the sweet joy our Lady experienced on the occasions indicated. Said in this way, the rosary will be very pleasing to Mary, and you will learn to love it more and more.

3. Consider how effectual this rosary has proved to be. The servant of God James experienced its good effects even in his lifetime; and throughout the history of the Franciscan Order blessed results have been so often achieved in various necessities, that at the request of the superiors of the order the popes have attached rich indulgences to its recitation. It is urgently recommended that all members of the order recite it at least every Saturday. — Make that a rule for yourself. You may then rest assured that you will participate in the joys of our Lady in heaven.

PRAYER OF THE CHURCH
(Vespers of the Little Office of Our Lady)

Grant, we beseech Thee, O Lord, that we Thy servants may ever enjoy health of body and soul, and through the glorious intercession of the Blessed Virgin Mary be saved from present evil and have a share in the joys of eternity. Through Christ our Lord. Amen.

OCTOBER 17
THE SERVANT OF GOD BAPTISTA OF PIACENZA
Virgin, Third Order

IKE her patron saint, St. John the Baptist, Baptista seems to have received the special graces of innocence and love for retirement. For, these were her characteristic marks from childhood. As much as possible she shunned association with the world and sought only to please God in everything she did.

When she attained the proper age, she entered the convent of St. Mary Magdalen at Piacenza, whose members observed the rule of the Third Order of St. Francis while living in the strictest enclosure. Under the guidance of an excellent superior, Baptista was conspicuous among her fellow sisters for the holiness of her life. She loved poverty and practiced it most faithfully. In the spirit of humility she performed the lowliest duties in the house with special delight, and out of love for her companions she undertook to perform the most disagreeable tasks.

She made every effort to keep her heart closely united with God, and always said her prayers with the greatest devotion. Her preparation for holy Communion was made with the greatest care. On the eve before receiving, she would direct all her thoughts and actions to this event, as if, like her holy patron, she was preparing the way for Christ. On the day she received she was filled with joy from the first moment after awaking, and each Communion day was like a great feastday.

The Food of the Soul, for which she always prepared herself with so much care, enabled her to persevere in her efforts to attain to perfection; and when death summoned her in the year 1515, she left the world in the odor of sanctity. Her virginal body was entombed in the sacristy of the convent church. It remained incorrupt for a long time and diffused a delightful fragrance.

ON PREPARATION FOR HOLY COMMUNION

1. Consider how devoutly the servant of God Baptista prepared for holy Communion. Her whole life was really one continual preparation because of her love of seclusion. On the day preceding her reception of the Holy Sacrament, she made special efforts to prepare her soul for this great privilege, and when the day of actual reception arrived, her heart was filled with boundless joy. Thus holy Communion served to lead her to great sanctity. If the Lord of heaven is to find a worthy dwelling-place in our hearts, we may not love the world, and those who receive frequently should endeavor to lead a more retired life. As we remove from our homes whatever displeases a guest whom we are expecting and substitute things that give him pleasure, so before holy Communion we should remove from our hearts whatever is displeasing to our heavenly Guest. "For a house is prepared not for man but for God" (1 Par. 29,1). When you awaken on the morning of your Communion day and don your better garments for the morning's event, adorn your heart with festive sentiments for the great blessing that will be yours. — Is the privilege less great because you enjoy it more frequently?

2. Consider the acts of virtue we should elicit in our hearts before receiving holy Communion. There are three in particular: lively faith, deep humility, and fervent desire. We should make an act of faith in the

presence of the true Body and Blood of Christ in the Sacrament of the altar under the appearance of bread, believing this as vividly as if we were attending the Last Supper and Christ Himself were administering the Sacrament. We shall then humble ourselves deeply, strike our breasts and say with the devout centurion, "Lord, I am not worthy that Thou shouldst enter under my roof" (Mt. 8,8). And, like Zaccheus, we must have a great desire for Him, for we do not merely wish to see Him, but to receive Him into our hearts. He will shower graces on us according to the measure of our desire for Him. "He has filled the hungry with good things" (Lk. 1,53).

3. Consider that you must not let scrupulous worries disturb you during the final moments before holy Communion. If at this time, after you have made your preparation, you are beset with disturbing thoughts and fears which you cannot throw off, go nevertheless confidently to the Table of the Lord and receive Him humbly, and you will experience what Thomas a Kempis speaks of when he says (4,4): "Thou, O Lord, impartest unto Thy beloved much consolation against their various tribulations and Thou liftest them up, so that they who were anxious and without sensible affection before Communion, after receiving find themselves changed for the better. And thus Thou art pleased to deal with Thine elect, that they may more truly acknowledge and plainly experience how great is their weakness when left to themselves, and how much of bounty and grace they receive from Thee."

PRAYER OF THE CHURCH
(Over the People, Tuesday in Holy Week)

May Thy mercy, O God, cleanse us from all deceits of our old nature, and enable us to be formed anew unto holiness. Through Christ our Lord. Amen.

❧❧❧❧❧❧❧❧❧❧

OCTOBER 18
THE SERVANT OF GOD ANNA TELLIER
Widow, Third Order

NNA TELLIER was born of noble and wealthy parents at Pont Andemar in northern France. For many years her father held an important post at the royal court. His wife died at an early age; and after that he never saw his daughter without shedding tears, so overcome was he at the thought of the child's loss.

To provide her with a proper education, he placed Anna in a neighboring convent of Benedictine sisters, where the little girl grew up in the fear of the Lord. Although cordial and affable with the other girls of the institution, she showed a certain seriousness of character that was absent in them. She took special delight in hearing the lives of the saints read by one of the sisters. She kept the lessons learned from these lives ever before her mind, and at times she would remind her companions of them.

If it had been left to her, Anna would have remained with the sisters and have become a religious. But when she had attained to young womanhood, an aunt, who lived alone in the world, desired to have her as a companion; and as her father wished it, she yielded to the aunt's request.

Not long afterwards, she again carried out the wishes of relatives and married a devout young nobleman. But when he died a few years later without leaving any children, Anna resolved to devote all her spare time to the service of God. To forestall further offers of marriage, she made a vow never again to marry. Then she entered the Third Order of St. Francis, and devoted her time to prayer, works of mercy, and charity. She soon distinguished herself so much among the Tertiaries of the town that in two years she was chosen their prefect.

Now Anna felt obliged to lead a still more exemplary life. She dressed so simply that no one would have guessed that she belonged to the nobility. Her relatives reproved her severely. But she had a pleasant way of appeasing them; and they themselves declared that if you wanted her to be particularly good to you, you needed only to offend her.

She retained but one maid and kept the simplest kind of household. During the day her bed was beautifully made up, but at night she used nothing but a straw tick. In churches where the Blessed Sacrament was exposed for adoration, she assisted at the devotions in a most edifying manner. When the Blessed Sacrament was carried to the sick, she would go along, and gradually others joined her in this pious practice. She was a thoughtful mother to the poor and the sick. She visited them, nursed them, and used practically all her wealth to help them. It was her special pleasure to take poor ignorant children home with her, to instruct them, conferring on many of them benefits for time and eternity.

Anna Tellier died at forty-five, on October 18, 1676, deeply mourned by all the poor, sadly missed by the members of the Third Order, and honored as a saint by all the townspeople.

ON INSTRUCTING YOUTH

1. The servant of God Anna gladly used the knowledge she had acquired in youth to instruct poorly educated children, for she perceived on her rounds of mercy what a misfortune it is not to have received the proper education in one's youth. Learning, of course, will not get us to heaven, and many parents undoubtedly provide their children with an expensive education from motives of vanity rather than to make useful citizens of them. But far greater is the number of those who provide little or no education for their children in truly essential matters. Such parents bear the blame for the temporal and eternal misery of their children. Ignorance leaves many people helpless in life; and, as St. Joseph Calasanza says, vicious lives result from lack of Christian training. — Do you have to accuse yourself of neglect in the matter?

2. Consider how meritorious it is to be concerned about the education of youth. St. Joseph Calasanza, a cord bearer of St. Francis, resigned his position as vicar general of a diocese, in order to give instructions to underprivileged children. Although provision is made nowadays so that all children can receive an education, it is still possible to support and promote Christian education. Parents have the obligation to see to it that their children actually attend the classes, and that they do the homework assigned to them. Others can share the merit of educators by taking an interest in the things the children are taught, by encouraging them to be diligent, by giving extra help to the backward, and by teaching the children useful things for which there is no time in school. To teach a child any useful act, is to do him a greater service than to give him bread to eat or clothing to wear.

3. Consider that the most valuable instruction that can be given to a child is instruction in the Christian religion. St. Chrysostom says: "Those who are concerned about providing their children with secular knowledge, while neglecting to instil in them the fear of God, will be the first to reap the fruits of their folly by raising forward and vicious children." It is said of Tobias, who had so much joy in his son: "From his infancy he taught him to fear God and to abstain from all sin" (Tob. 1,10). How pleasing it is to Jesus, to lead to Him the children He so loved! For that purpose St. Theresa always cheerfully interrupted her prayers to be of service to children, saying: "The greatest service we can render Jesus, is to leave Him out of love for the children." In so doing, we do not really leave Jesus at all. Rather we render Him a service, as He Himself says: "He who shall receive one such little child in my name, receives Me" (Mt. 18,5). — Help the children with their catechism lessons, relate and read them stories

from the lives of the saints, and above all pray with them.

PRAYER OF THE CHURCH (Saturday in Passion Week)

We beseech Thee, O Lord, let Thy people who are consecrated to Thee, advance in the spirit of pious devotion, that, instructed by the sacred rites, they may abound in the higher gifts the more pleasing they become in the sight of Thy divine majesty. Through Christ our Lord. Amen.

OCTOBER 19
ST. PETER OF ALCANTARA
Confessor, First Order

ETER was born at Alcantara in Spain in 1499. Already as a child he manifested a remarkable gift of prayer, so that at times, when he became absorbed in prayer, the servants were unable to get any response from him.

At the University of Salamanca Peter resolved to join the Franciscan Order. The tempter left nothing undone to depict the comfortable life he could lead in the world and still have time for the practices of piety. But humble prayer overcame the seductions of the evil one. Peter set out for the quiet convent of Monjarez. On the way our Lord gave him a signal assurance of his vocation. Peter came to a stream which, because of heavy rains, had overflowed its banks considerably. Seeing no means at hand with which to cross, he knelt down and asked God for help. Suddenly, without knowing how, he found himself on the other side.

Once received into the order, he gave himself up completely to union with God. He kept so strict a guard over his senses, that a year later he could not say whether the church in which he prayed each day had a vaulted roof or a flat one. His body seemed to have been given him only to inflict pain on it. The mortifications he practiced upon divine impulse were amazing. For more than twenty years he wore an iron belt studded with sharp points which pierced his flesh, and for more than forty years he daily scourged himself till he bled. At first he was much troubled with sleepiness, but he so mortified himself that in time he got along with one and a half hours of sleep in a day; and this rest he took while sitting on the floor.

God showed His approval of these mortifications by sustaining Peter's strength in a remarkable way. He never tired of going from place to place to give missions, and his success was so astounding that St. Francis Borgia once wrote to him: "Your remarkable success is a special comfort to me." His various activities, however, in no way diminished his spirit of prayer. He lived and toiled in this spirit, and endeavored to impart it to others.

The sufferings of Christ were the special object of his devotion. As Christ sacrificed Himself for us, Peter found nothing too difficult in His service; and as Christ atoned so severely for our sins, Peter practiced the most rigorous penance. The custom of erecting a cross at the close of a mission had its origin with St. Peter of Alcantara. Wherever feasible, he had the cross erected on an elevation, so that it could be seen all over the parish. On one occasion he was so literally carried away with devotion that he sped through the air to such a cross, where with arms outstretched he prayed a long time, while rays brighter than sunlight proceeded from his person.

He wrote a little treatise on prayer and meditation which is celebrated the world over. Pope Gregory XV declared that it was written under the inspiration of the Holy Ghost. The great mistress of prayer, St. Theresa, who lived at that time, wished to have the saint for her spiritual director; and he aided her in reforming the order of Carmel.

He was a very humble man, and fled from honors. Emperor Charles V wanted him for his confessor, but Peter begged him not to press his request since he could easily secure more learned and eminent men. In the order itself he was obliged to accept the position of provincial, and due to his efforts his province rose to a flourishing state of religious discipline. Provincial though he was, he did not hesitate on occasion to perform the lowliest duties in the house.

He was humble and charitable in his judgments. A nobleman was once decrying the various evils which were rampant. The saint said: "Truly, matters in the world are in a bad state; but if you and I begin in earnest to reform ourselves, a really good beginning will have been made."

On October 18, 1562, he died peacefully in the Lord. St. Theresa saw his soul take its flight to heaven. Later he appeared to this saint and said: "O happy penance that has merited for me such wondrous glory!" Many miracles, including the raising of six dead persons to life, occurred in answer to prayers addressed to him. Pope Clement IX enrolled him among the saints. The feast of St. Peter is observed by the three branches of the First Order on October nineteenth.

ON THE REWARD OF PENANCE

1. St. Peter practiced rigorous penance all his life, and what a marvelous

reward it merited for him! He used to say: "I have made a contract with my body; it has promised to accept harsh treatment from me on earth, and I have promised that it shall receive eternal rest in heaven." The reward of penance can be ours if we wish it. And we have more reason to practice penance, since we have not lived from our youth as did St. Peter, but have committed many sins. It is not necessary to imitate him in his unusual penances — without the consent of our confessor it would not even be right to do so — but we can renounce sensuality and atone for our sins by a penitential life. Then our present tribulation will obtain for us "above measure exceedingly an eternal weight of glory" (2 Cor. 4,17).

2. Consider that none of us can say we have no need of penance; only a lukewarm soul could make such a statement. Even if we were stainless from birth, we should still be obliged to mortify ourselves. Blessed Brother Giles was once asked why St. John the Baptist lived so penitential a life. Brother Giles asked by way of reply: "Why do we salt fresh fish? Is it not for the purpose that it may not decay?" Though you may be quite unspoiled and blameless, yet you should apply the salt of Christian mortification and penance, that you may persevere and appear faultless before the judgment-seat of God.

3. Consider that the spirit of penance and mortification also nourishes the spirit of prayer and devotion. He who serves the appetites of the flesh and grants them all they desire, cannot raise his heart to God in prayer. "The sensual man perceives not these things that are of the spirit of God" (1 Cor. 2,14). To be able to pray, you must bridle your senses — eyes, ears, tongue — and withdraw from the world. "When you are about to pray, enter into your chamber and shut the door" (Mt. 5,6). If you shut the door of your heart in the spirit of penance, you will easily raise it to God and enjoy His consolations. Pray to St. Peter of Alcantara for this purpose. St. Theresa says that God revealed to her, that whatever would be requested in the name of St. Peter would be granted.

PRAYER OF THE CHURCH

O God, who didst bestow on St. Peter, Thy confessor, the gifts of marvelous penance and lofty contemplation, grant, we beseech Thee, that with his merits pleading for us, we may so mortify the flesh as to embrace more readily the things of heaven. Through Christ our Lord. Amen.

OCTOBER 20
THE SERVANT OF GOD ALEXANDER OF HALES
Confessor, First Order

LEXANDER was a native of England. He does not, however, take his name from his native place, but from the convent of Hales, where he received his education. About the year 1220 he taught theology in the renowned University of Paris and distinguished himself there by his piety as much as by his learning.

Devotion to our Lady prompted him to make a vow that he would accede to any request made of him in her name. And so the annals of the Franciscan Order relate that a good brother from one of the new convents in Paris called at his home one day while on a begging tour, and asked the celebrated professor in the name of the Blessed Virgin to join his poor order. Alexander was at first much perturbed, but perceiving in this invitation a call from heaven, he carried out the brother's request.

During the year of probation he was once severely tempted to lay aside the coarse garment. The following night he saw in a dream our holy Father St. Francis laden with a very heavy cross which he was endeavoring to carry up a steep hill. Filled with compassion, Alexander advanced to assist him, but he heard our holy Father say: "Begone, miserable man! If you cannot carry the light cross of wool, how can you presume to carry this heavy cross of wood?" On awakening, the novice found that the temptation to leave was no longer bothering him. He persevered in the observance of the rule to the end of his life.

As a Friar Minor, Alexander continued to teach at the university, laying the foundation for Scholasticism, a system of knowledge which marvelously explains the truths of the Faith and defends them against objections even to our own day. For this, Alexander was honored with such titles as the Irrefutable Doctor, the Master of Doctors, and the Fountain of Life. It was from him that his famous pupils St. Bonaventure and St. Thomas Aquinas drew their wisdom. Someone once asked St. Thomas what course in theology he would recommend. St. Thomas replied: "There is just one theologian whom you need to master." Being asked who that theologian was, he named Alexander of Hales.

Though he had become famous and enjoyed honors which he justly deserved, Alexander always remained a humble Friar Minor. He always considered himself the lowly son of the Handmaid of the Lord, the Blessed Virgin, who had directed him into the order. He died while invoking her name on October 20, 1245.

ON LOVE FOR OUR LADY

1. How fervent must have been the love of this learned man for our Blessed Lady, since he vowed never to refuse a request that might be made of him in the name of Mary. And what admirable proof he gave of this love, when he left the world and entered the poor order of the Friars Minor. It appears that our Lady considered him particularly worthy of the order because of his love for her. As we are told by St. Bonaventure, our holy Father St. Francis cherished an indescribable love for Mary and desired that his children should do likewise. The convent of St. Mary of the Angels became the cradle of the order, and St. Francis expressly chose Our Lady as the special mother and patron of the order. And so the children of St. Francis not only honor the Blessed Virgin as the Mother of God, but they love her as their own mother, given to them in a more special way than to ordinary Christians. St. Stanislaus, on being asked whether he loved Mary, answered: "Why should I not love her? She is my mother, isn't she?" — Do you love her tenderly as a good child should?

2. Consider that true devotion to Mary must show itself in deed, first and above all in a God-fearing life. Mary says to us what she once said to the servants at the wedding feast of Cana: "Whatsoever He shall say to you, do ye" (Jn. 2,5). But our love for Mary will manifest itself also in the veneration we pay to her: greeting her morning, noon, and night by saying the Angelus, having a picture or statue of her in our rooms, wearing the medal or the scapular of the Blessed Virgin, saying the rosary, keeping her feasts with special devotion and filial joy. He who sincerely venerates our Lady will also strive to promote devotion to her in others. — Have you been sincerely devoted to our Lady in the past?

3. Consider how fortunate they are who truly love our Lady. They will be loved in turn by her, and they are, so to say, certain of their own salvation. Listen to what the Church itself says of the Mother of God in the canonical hours: "I love them that love me: and they who in the morning early watch for me, shall find me." And again: "He who shall find me, shall find life and shall have salvation from the Lord." St. Alphonsus is right when he says that it is a sign of predestination if we love Mary, and then makes this statement: "A true child of Mary will never be lost."

PRAYER OF THE CHURCH
(At Prime)

O God, who didst choose the immaculate body of blessed Mary for Thy dwelling, grant, we beseech Thee, that we who are shielded under her protection, may by Thy grace join with gladness in her commemoration. Who livest and reignest forever and ever. Amen.

OCTOBER 21
BLESSED JAMES OF STREPAR
Bishop and Confessor, First Order

JAMES was born in the fourteenth century of the noble Polish family of Strepar and was educated in a Christian manner by his pious parents. To escape the dangers of the world, he entered the poor order of St. Francis when he was a young man. Very soon he became distinguished among his brethren for eminent virtue, rare attainments, and zeal for the salvation of souls.

The neighboring realm of Russia presented at that time a wide field for the exercise of his zeal. Partly it was still inhabited by heathens; and where the Catholic Church had flourished for centuries, Greek schismatics had long been endeavoring to win the people from the Mother Church at Rome. With the consent of his superiors James went to Russia to preach the Gospel and to save the faithful from going astray. About 1360, he had a share in the organization of a special group of Franciscan missionaries, called Societas Peregrinantium or Travelers for Christ, who did excellent work in Russia, Wallachia, and Podolia, and in 1401 extended their activities also to the Tatars near the Caspian Sea and other parts of Asia.

Father James' missionary efforts were so successful, and his apostolic virtues were so pronounced, that on the death of the archbishop of Halicz, the pope named him his successor at the request of the king of Poland in 1392. Only because he was compelled, did James accept the dignity. But even as a bishop he wore the Franciscan habit and as far as possible continued his missionary labors.

To preserve the Catholics of the old and the newly acquired districts in Christian truth, he built many new churches and convents. His large income was used only for this purpose and for the support of the poor.

To secure God's blessing on the territory entrusted to his spiritual care, he considered nothing more helpful than veneration of the Mother of God. Next to God he placed his confidence in her. Instead of the family coat-of-arms, he had the image of Mary engraved on his seal; everything he prescribed for his diocese was to have the seal of Mary. He had her image also on his pastoral ring. Every evening devotions were held in her honor in the cathedral or wherever he chanced to be; and he always attended the services. He urged the people to attend these devotions, as well as special devotions of adoration of the Blessed Sacrament, for which he issued special regulations and granted indulgences.

James was also mindful of the temporal welfare of his flock. In order to check the frequent inroads of the Tatars, who were laying the country waste, he proposed such excellent measures to the Polish parliament that he was quite generally called the protector of the kingdom.

After a laborious and blessed episcopate of nineteen years, God called him to receive his heavenly reward in the year 1410. Clothed in the habit of the order and wearing the marks of his episcopal dignity, he was entombed in the Franciscan church at Lwow, to which the archbishopric had been transferred from Halicz. When his grave was opened after two hundred years his body and clothing were found entirely incorrupt. Later the remains were removed to the cathedral.

The continual veneration paid to him was formally approved by Pope Pius VI. The feast of Blessed James is observed on October twenty-first by the three branches of the First Order.

ON THE VENERATION OF MARY
1. The months of May and October are especially set aside by the Church for the veneration of the Blessed Virgin Mary. We should not, however, limit our veneration to these two months. Like Blessed James, we should venerate her throughout the year and all our life. She was the mother of the primitive Christian Church; the apostles and the first Christians at Jerusalem were gathered about her when the Holy Ghost descended. She was the bond which encircled the first Christian community with motherly love, when "the multitude of believers had but one heart and one soul" (Acts 4,32). Blessed James expected veneration of Mary to bring harmony to his diocese as well as the fruits of the Holy Ghost. May those fruits also enter our hearts, our homes, our congregations, and the whole Catholic Church. — Is Mary truly honored in your home?
2. Consider how God Himself honored Mary. He sent one of the most eminent heavenly spirits, the archangel Gabriel, to her who at God's behest said to her: "Hail, full of grace, the Lord is with you, blessed are you among women ... The Holy Ghost shall come upon you; and the Holy One who shall be born of you shall be called the Son of God" (Lk. 1,28-35). The Holy Trinity thus entered into a most intimate union with her, since God the Father was with her, the Holy Ghost overshadowed her, and the Son of God was to be born of her. Could he who would not honor her still be called a child of God? Filled with the Holy Ghost, she herself proclaims: "From henceforth all generations shall call me blessed" (Lk. 1,48). Great

favors will surely be granted to him who venerates her whom the Blessed Trinity has honored. O Mary, Daughter of the heavenly Father, Mother of the Divine Son, and Spouse of the Holy Ghost, pray for us!

3. Consider that Blessed James rightly expected the veneration of Mary to bring special blessings particularly to his sacred ministry. With Mary's blessing the apostles set out to preach the Gospel, and she continually raised her hands to heaven both for those who preached the Faith and for those who accepted the Faith from them. Catholic life flourishes where Mary is honored, and it flourishes the more abundantly the more she is honored. Her maternal protection and powerful intercession will obtain blessings for the shepherd so that he may guide his sheep in a truly apostolic spirit, and for the flock so that it may lead a Christian life and arrive at the blessed goal.

PRAYER OF THE CHURCH

O God, who didst wonderfully renew the apostolic spirit in Thy blessed bishop and confessor James, we beseech Thee, grant us through his intercession that we may ever adhere to Thee in faith and in true service. Through Christ our Lord. Amen.

OCTOBER 22
BLESSED MATTHEW OF GIRGENTI
Bishop and Confessor, First Order

ATTHEW, born at Girgenti on the island of Sicily, entered the Franciscan Order when he was still quite young. When he had completed his studies and had been ordained a priest, the desire to enter upon a more perfect observance of the Franciscan rule led him to transfer to the Observant reform which was being promoted by St. Bernardin of Siena.

St. Bernardin soon perceived the outstanding qualities of the young religious and took him with him as a companion on the missions that he was then giving throughout Italy. By his ardent zeal Matthew was instrumental in the conversion of numerous sinners, and in rekindling the flame of piety where it had long since grown cold. In imitation of his master Bernardin, he did all in his power to promote devotion to the holy name of Jesus.

Believing that religious perfection is particularly meritorious before God, Matthew strove earnestly to promulgate the perfect observance of the rule of St. Francis. He went to Spain, where he was successful in introducing the observance in many convents. Then he went to his own country of Sicily, where, with the approval of the Holy See, he established several convents and labored with much success among the people. In honor of the name of Jesus and that of His Blessed Mother, Matthew gave every convent he founded the title of St. Mary of Jesus.

About this time the bishop of Girgenti died, and clergy and laity joined in the request to have Matthew as their chief pastor. He resisted at first, but Pope Eugene IV commanded him to accept the appointment. He then discharged his office so well that his diocese was soon in a flourishing condition. He took vigorous action against prevalent vices and disorders. As a result powerful enemies denounced him to the pope. The gold was to be tried in the fire. Matthew was called to Rome by Pope Eugene IV, to answer the charges brought against him. But the inquiry resulted in such a clear justification of the bishop that the pope declared him innocent and sent him back with honor to his diocese.

However, not long after, Matthew, worn out by his labors, voluntarily resigned his office in order to return to a Franciscan convent and prepare himself for death.

For several years Matthew then suffered from severe maladies and, thus purified, he entered the eternal bliss of heaven. He died in the convent at Palermo in 1451. His body was taken to the Church on an open stretcher. When the procession arrived before the high altar, to the amazement and terror of all present, the deceased prelate raised himself on the litter, adored the Blessed Sacrament with folded hands, and then lay back again.

Numerous miracles occurred at his grave, and the people honored him as a saint from the time of his demise. Pope Clement XIII confirmed the veneration paid to him, and later Pope Pius VII renewed this confirmation. The feast of Blessed Matthew is celebrated by the Franciscans on October twenty-first, by the Conventuals on January seventh, and by the Capuchins on February third.

ALL FOR JESUS

1. Consider that Blessed Matthew not only preached devotion to the holy name of Jesus, but in the very active life that he led, he always did everything for Jesus. He frequently recalled how our Divine Saviour came down from heaven, spending thirty years in a poor, hard life, and sparing Himself no labor in the course of His preaching, yes, exposed Himself to the most violent persecution in order to announce His holy doctrine, and

finally submitted to bitter suffering and the most painful, disgraceful death in order to redeem us. For that reason nothing seemed too difficult for Matthew in order to win souls for Jesus and to promote His interests. — Was it not for you, too, that Jesus made a complete oblation of Himself? Are you also filled with zeal and do you make sacrifices to further the interests of your holy religion and the salvation of souls? Do you at least sincerely endeavor to make your own soul pleasing to Jesus?

2. Consider that in conducting his missions for love of Jesus, Blessed Matthew labored above all to root out vices. That must also be our main objective: to prevent offenses against God, above all in ourselves, but also in others in as far as we can. If we wish to be followers of Jesus we must never for the sake of a creature do or permit others to do anything displeasing to God. Yes, "we ought rather," says the Venerable Thomas a Kempis (2,8), "choose to have the whole world against us than offend Jesus"; and you may never, he continues, "desire to be singularly praised or beloved; for this belongs to God alone, who has none like unto Himself; neither desire that anyone's heart should be much taken up with you. But let Jesus be in you and in every good man." — What is there, perhaps, in your heart that is displeasing to Jesus?

3. Consider that, imitating Blessed Matthew's love of Jesus, we should not be satisfied with merely preventing evil. We must also do all in our power to promote whatever is good by endeavoring to spur others, but especially ourselves, to greater perfection. Above all, we should strive to detach our heart more and more from all inordinate affection to creatures and to ourselves, so that in all our good works our purpose and intention may be directed to God alone. "If you seek in others your comfort," says Thomas a Kempis again (2,7), "you will more often meet with loss; if you seek yourself you will bring yourself to your own ruin; but if in all things you seek Jesus, truly you shall find Jesus," — here on earth for your consolation, and hereafter as your eternal joy in heavenly bliss. — Often examine the sincerity of your intention.

PRAYER OF THE CHURCH

We beseech Thee, O almighty God, grant us at the intercession of blessed bishop Matthew, Thy confessor, that as he was inflamed with love for the most holy name of Thy Son, so we also being imbued with this love, may strive to despise what is earthly and to love what is heavenly. Through Christ our Lord. Amen.

OCTOBER 23
BLESSED JOSEPHINE LEROUX
Martyr, Second Order

OSEPHINE entered the convent of the Poor Clares at Valenciennes when she was twenty-two years old. In 1770 she made her vows. Then the French Revolution broke out, and the religious were rudely driven from their convents. Josephine at first returned to her family. But when Valenciennes was captured by the Austrians, Josephine could not resist the impulse to return to the enclosure. However, the convent of the Poor Clares at Valenciennes had not yet been rebuilt, and she took refuge in the convent of the Ursulines, where her own sister lived.

But the victorious revolutionary army retook the city, and Josephine was placed under arrest as having been disloyal to her country. Without being in any way perturbed, she confronted the band of soldiers who came to arrest her and said: "It was hardly necessary to make so much ado for the purpose of taking a weak woman captive!" Then, having served her captors with refreshments, she followed them to prison.

Because she had resumed the life of a religious contrary to the laws, Josephine was condemned to death. With holy serenity and perfect resignation to God's holy will she accepted the death sentence and prepared for it by receiving the Bread of Heaven for her journey to the Divine Bridegroom. With a cheerful countenance she went out to the place of execution, singing sacred hymns along the way. She declared herself truly fortunate at being deemed worthy to give her life for the Catholic Faith. "Could anyone fear to leave this place of exile," she said, "when he reflects on the beauty of Paradise?"

At the scaffold she gratefully kissed the hand of the executioner, and in a clear voice forgave everybody. Then she placed her head on the block. Her sister, Mary Scholastic, and four other companions died a martyr's death with her. This occurred on October 23, 1794. Pope Benedict XV enrolled her among the blessed. The feast of Blessed Josephine is celebrated by the Franciscans on October twenty-third.

ON THE TEST OF LOVE

1. The test of love is sacrifice. Christ met the test in the sacrifice of the Cross, and He demands of those who love Him that they prove their love by the test of the cross. Blessed Josephine knew this and desired to show

her loyalty to her Lord. So, after being forced to leave her convent by the civil authorities, she returned to the enclosure of a convent despite the risk it involved. She was arrested and willingly made the sacrifice of her life for the love of Christ. — Are we as ready and as courageous in showing our love for Christ?

2. We can and must make sacrifices in this life. There are thousands of opportunities offered for making small sacrifices for which we need no permission. Let us make them with love and generosity, for it is love that gives value to sacrifice. Each time we deprive ourselves of anything for Jesus' sake, we are thinking of Him and loving Him. — Does He not deserve that much from us?

3. One of the noblest acts of sacrifice is the conquest of self-love. Our Lord builds His sanctuary on the ruins of self-love. "He must increase, but I must decrease" (Jn. 3,30). But to decrease is not enough in this matter. Self must disappear, so that we can say: "I live, now not I, but Christ lives in me" (Gal. 2,20). The secret of sanctity consists in loving much, but this love presupposes interior and daily warfare. Let us be generous, let us be valiant, so that, like Blessed Josephine, we may in the end also be victorious by passing the test of love.

PRAYER OF THE CHURCH

Pour into our hearts. Lord Jesus, fear and love for Thee, so that through the merits and example of the holy virgin Josephine, we may rather choose death than ever consent to offend Thee. Who livest and reignest forever and ever. Amen.

OCTOBER 24
BLESSED BALTHASSAR OF CHIAVARI
Confessor, First Order

THIS saintly man was a descendant of an ancient noble family. He spent his years on earth in unsullied purity. As a Franciscan he was professor of theology and then provincial of the order. He distinguished himself in all the virtues of a good religious, practiced the greatest personal severities, fasted much, and considered it a real pleasure to be accounted the last among his brethren. After he had completed his term of office, he withdrew to the convent at Binasco. There he devoted himself entirely to the contemplation of heavenly things and to the salvation of immortal souls. He labored untiringly in the pulpit and in the confessional.

God sent him very painful diseases. One day, however, he was favored with a visit of the Blessed Mother of God, who greatly strengthened and consoled him. When he was seventy-three years old, he was summoned by Brother Death to enter into eternal rest. He died in the year 1490. His persevering fidelity to the rule and his indefatigable zeal for souls merited for him eternal happiness. Pope Pius XI approved the veneration paid to Blessed Balthassar from the time of death. His feast is observed by the Franciscans on October twenty-fifth.

LABORING FOR SOULS

1. We can labor for souls by our words. Blessed Balthassar did so both in the pulpit and in the confessional. He followed the admonition of the Apostle of the Gentiles: "Preach the word, be instant in season, out of season; reprove, entreat, rebuke in all patience and doctrine" (2 Tim. 4,2). A kind word will always find a place to rest. We should encourage and warn others, not in a meddling manner but rather with loving consideration and tact. — How much good you could promote, how much evil you could prevent, if you had the courage to say the right word at the right time!

2. We can labor for souls by our good example. While Balthassar was a superior in the order, he set a good example to his subjects. Words stir people, but example carries them away, says a Latin proverb. Hence, St. Paul says to Timothy: "Be an example to the faithful in word, in conversation" (1 Tim. 4,12). Can you say to all your fellowmen: Do as I do? If you can, then your words will also have a force that cannot be resisted. — Live so that everybody can take your conduct as his rule of life.

3. We can labor for souls by our charity. The charity with which Blessed Balthassar served everybody virtually forced his fellowmen to follow in his footsteps. Remember, therefore, the words of the Apostle: "Above all things have charity" (Col. 3,14). Diffuse the sweet odor of charity about you, now with a kind word, another time with a good deed, and aim to become an apostle of the Religion of Charity by your kindness. Severity repels, charity attracts. — Have you always thought in that way, always acted accordingly?

PRAYER OF THE CHURCH

O almighty God, who didst appoint Thy blessed confessor Balthassar to serve Thee worthily both in the pulpit and in the confessional, mercifully hear our prayers, and grant us through his merits and intercession, the grace to labor incessantly for the salvation of souls and produce worthy acts of virtue. Through Christ our Lord. Amen.

<hr/>

OCTOBER 25
BLESSED CHRISTOPHER OF ROMAGNOLA
Confessor, First Order

HRISTOPHER had been a priest for many years when the grace of God impelled him to ask our holy Father St. Francis for the habit. In 1219 he was sent to Guienne, in southern France, to establish the order in those parts. He was a man full of holy simplicity and sincere love for the poor and the unfortunate. He took great pleasure in caring for the many persons who were afflicted with leprosy in those days and were outcasts of society.

He was very severe with himself. He wore an iron shirt for a long time, and always a belt having sharp points. He ate but once a day even in his advanced age. He built a small cell for himself of branches and sticks, and covered it with straw. But in spite of these rigorous penances he was always cheerful of countenance and pleasant in his dealings with others.

Realizing the value of time, he never wasted a moment, always busily occupied in prayer, meditation, manual labor, care of the garden, or other work that benefited his brethren. His kindness and affability attracted many sinners, whom he succeeded in converting. God frequently favored him with extraordinary inspirations, and so it was revealed to him that St. Francis was about to die. He hastened from France to Italy and arrived at the Portiuncula shortly before the death of St. Francis. He had the consolation of receiving his last blessing.

When Christopher arrived at the age of nearly one hundred years, his earthly sojourn came to an end. While earnestly exhorting the brethren gathered about his deathbed, he surrendered his soul to God in the year 1272. In death he looked more like a person who had fallen asleep than like a dead person. An unusual concourse of people assembled for his burial which took place in Cahors, France. Many miracles occurred after his death; and his cult as Blessed was approved in 1905. His feast is observed by the Franciscans on October twenty-fifth, by the Conventuals on November third, and by the Capuchins on October thirty-first.

ON BEING SOCIABLE

1. The sociableness by which Blessed Christopher gained the hearts of so many sinners, was a virtue he had learned from St. Francis. Father Christopher had seen how St. Francis dealt with his fellowmen, especially with poor sinners. As in all things else, so in this matter St. Francis kept before his mind the example of our Lord Jesus Christ, who always received sinners with kindness. St. Paul says of Him: "The goodness and kindness of God our Saviour has appeared" (Tit. 3,4). How mistaken it is to believe that piety requires a sour demeanor, and that we must deal harshly with sinners. How many more sinners would be converted, how many more souls would we gain for a holy life, if we approached them with affability. – Have you been wanting in this regard?

2. Consider that sociability is and should be nothing else than the expression of sincere fraternal charity. Mere external polish is unworthy of a Christian. "Let love be without dissimulation" (Rom. 12,9). But the Apostle often recommends that genuine charity which is bound to manifest itself externally: "Love one another with the charity of brotherhood" (Rom. 12,10). "Let all bitterness and anger be put away from you; be kind to one another" (Eph. 4,31). Such goodness of heart will manifest itself also in self-sacrifice for our neighbor: "Walk in love, as Christ also has loved us and has delivered Himself for us" (Eph. 5,2). The early Christians were so devoted to practices of charity that the heathens said of them: "See, how they love one another!" What respect the Christian religion would receive from unbelievers today if similar charity were manifest in the lives of believing Christians! – Are you perhaps at fault that this is not the case?

3. Consider how much depends on not giving in to changing moods and the whims of the moment, but always meeting your fellowmen sociably and kindly. You will then be loved, and others will approach you the same way. "Whatsoever you would that men do to you, do you also to them" (Mt. 7,12). If you do this out of love for God, as a Christian should do it, God will consider this as charity done to Himself and He will reward you for it: here on earth, with the consolations of His grace, and hereafter, when you stand before His judgment-seat, with clemency and mercy.

PRAYER OF THE CHURCH
(Postcommunion No. 29 under "Various Prayers")

May the grace of the Holy Ghost, we beseech Thee, O Lord, enlighten our hearts and refresh them abundantly with the sweetness of perfect charity.

Through Christ our Lord. Amen.

OCTOBER 26
BLESSED BONAVENTURE OF POTENZA
Confessor, First Order

ONAVENTURE was born of poor but virtuous parents in Potenza in the kingdom of Naples. A pious priest gave the boy instructions in Latin. At the age of fifteen, Bonaventure received the Franciscan habit among the Conventuals. After his profession, he resumed his studies with great ardor, but his zeal for perfection was not less ardent.

His superiors sent him to Amalfi, where he lived eight years under the guidance of an eminent director of souls. This spiritual director trained his pupil above all in humility, self-abnegation, and obedience, and Bonaventure achieved a high degree of perfection in these virtues.

One day Bonaventure told his master that the key to the sacristy was lost. "Well," said his master with a smile, "then you will have to look for it in the well; get a rod and fish it out." Promptly Bonaventure went to the well and with rod and line fished for the key. It was not long before he actually drew it out. God rewarded him in a miraculous manner for his blind obedience.

As a priest he labored with remarkable success. His words, conduct, prayer, and mortification combined to produce blessed results. His simple sermons made a deep impression on all hearts. At times a single word of his was enough to move the most hardened sinner to contrition.

At various times he was appointed guardian of a convent, but his humble pleas were always successful in changing the mind of his superiors. Obedience at length compelled him to accept the position of novice-master. In this office he sought to inculcate in his pupils above all the practice of humility and obedience.

An epidemic broke out among the townsfolk, and Bonaventure at once sacrificed himself. Fearless of contracting the disease, he hastened from end to end of the town, rendering every possible service to the stricken, even the lowliest, and administering the sacraments to them. He cured many miraculously; he multiplied their insufficient provisions by his blessing; and he foretold future events.

After Bonaventure had been a shining model of virtue among his brethren for forty-five years, he felt that his last hour was at hand. While the community gathered about his bed during the administration of the last sacraments, the dying man in touching words begged pardon of his superior and the community for his many faults and infractions of the rule, as he called them.

Deeply moved, the superior handed him the crucifix, and amid abundant tears the servant of God kissed the feet of the Saviour, and then died peacefully on October 26, 1711. Pope Pius VI beatified him in 1775. The feast of Blessed Bonaventure is observed by the Franciscans and the Conventuals on October twenty-sixth.

ON SPIRITUAL PRIDE

1. Consider in Blessed Bonaventure the example of a saint who began with humility, advanced by humility, and reached the pinnacle of sanctity by humility. So much is sanctity bound up with humility. It rests on humility as its foundation, only by means of this virtue can it increase, and humility alone makes it possible to persevere in sanctity unto a blessed end. Learn from this how destructive spiritual pride must be. Anybody who is leading a religious life or striving after Christian perfection, and proudly considers himself better than others or presumes to think he amounts to anything in the sight of God, has a worm gnawing interiorly at all the good and pious practices he performs. He actually amounts to nothing before God, and if he persists in being proud he will eventually be lost. When spiritual pride laid hold of the angels, they were cast into hell and became devils. Then the devil seduced our first parents by making them believe they would be like God. — Does he perhaps use the same ruse to tempt you?

2. Consider how pride, like a smooth serpent, creeps in unobserved. It is part of our fallen nature. "Nature," says Thomas a Kempis (3,54), "labors for its own interests; it willingly receives honor and respect, but is afraid of shame and contempt." Hence it happens that we take pleasure in thinking of our good works and advantages, always speaking about ourselves, and in setting ourselves up as models for others. "Not he who commends himself, is approved, but he whom God commends" (2 Cor. 10,18). Recall the parable of the proud Pharisee and the humble publican, which our Lord addressed to those who trusted in their justice while they despised the rest of men. "This man went down into his house justified, rather than the other" (Lk. 18,14). — Which of the two do you resemble?

3. Consider how we should struggle against pride and self-sufficiency. We must often plead with God as did the Wise Man: "O Lord, Father and God of my life, leave me not to their devices. Give me not haughtiness of my

eyes, and turn away from me all coveting" (Eccli. 23,4-5). Then, too, for our humiliation, we should reflect on our faults and our sins. Just as the proud peacock, on spreading its brilliant feathers, immediately drops his wings when he sees his ugly feet, so will a look at our failures soon chase away pride. Finally, imitate Blessed Bonaventure by exercising yourself in acts of obedience and humility. Think of Mary, who called herself a handmaid of the Lord at a time when an angel announced God's greatest prerogatives of grace to her. Say to God: "O Lord, I am Thy servant and the son of Thy handmaid" (Ps. 115,7).

PRAYER OF THE CHURCH

O God, who didst propose Blessed Bonaventure, Thy confessor, to us as an admirable example of obedience, grant, we beseech Thee, that like him we may deny our will and adhere to Thy commandments. Through Christ our Lord. Amen.

❦❦❦❦❦❦❦❦❦❦

OCTOBER 27
BLESSED CONTARDO FERRINI
Confessor, Third Order

THE CITY OF MILAN has abounded in men of learning and virtue. Our present age has revealed a new star there, which is destined to show an amazed modern generation that profound learning and humble faith can well go hand in hand.

Contardo Ferrini was born of a distinguished family on April 4, 1859. When he was still a student in high school and college, he encouraged his companions to lead good lives and exercised a kind of lay apostolate among them. After winning his doctorate in law, he obtained a government scholarship to study abroad. He went to Berlin, where he studied Roman-Byzantine law, a field in which he achieved international fame. In the capital of the German empire prejudices against Catholics did not keep Professor Ferrini from publicly professing his faith. On returning to Italy, he taught in various higher institutions of learning and eventually at the University of Pavia.

It must be stressed here that Ferrini's life was practically an unbroken elevation of his soul to God. His keen intellectual ways penetrated to the Last Principle of all things. "Our life," said he, "must reach out towards the Infinite, and from that source we must draw whatever we can expect of merit and dignity."

Every day he approached the Holy Table. He made a short meditation daily, and also read from Thomas a Kempis. His favorite books were those of the Bible. The better to savor the spirit of their contents, he read them in the original languages, of which he had a perfect command. Like another Joseph of Egypt, he preserved his purity unsullied amid the dangers of big city life. He practiced many and varied mortifications to arm himself against harm.

In 1886 he joined the Third Order of St. Francis, and for the rest of his life he faithfully observed its rule. He also enrolled himself in the St. Vincent de Paul Society. In his speeches and writings as well as in his conduct, he made it a point to show that faith and science are not only not opposed to each other, but that faith is rather a shield to protect us from error and guide us to true heights.

In 1900 Contardo Ferrini was afflicted with a heart lesion in consequence of excessive labor. In the autumn of 1902, feeling the need of rest, he repaired to his country house at Suna. There, however, he was stricken with typhus. Due to his weakened condition, he was unable to resist the malignant fever, and died on October 17, 1902, at the age of forty-three.

The high esteem in which the deceased was held, now became evident. Letters of condolence from the professors of the university praised him as a saint. The people of Suna promptly expressed a desire to see him numbered among the saints. The demand for his beatification grew more insistent with time, and there was universal rejoicing when in 1909 Pope St. Pius X appointed Cardinal Ferrari to begin the process. Pope Pius XI conferred on him the title of Venerable in 1931; and Pope Pius XII beatified him in 1947. The feast of Blessed Contardo is celebrated by the Franciscans on October twenty-seventh. (Cf. *Forum,* 1947, pp. 131-135; 1952, pp. 295-298.)

ON THE HOLY SCRIPTURES

1. Holy Writ is not the only source of faith. It is incomplete for one thing, for St. John says: "There are also many other things which Jesus did" (Jn. 21,25). Then, too, the prophecies about the kingdom of heaven, which Christ gave His apostles before His ascension, are not recorded. And from the Epistles of St. Paul (1 Cor. 5-9 and Col. 4,16) we learn that part of the Scriptures have even been lost. Although Contardo Ferrini entertained great love for the Scriptures, he did not regard them as the only authority in matters of faith, but paid equal respect to the teachings of Holy Church.

— Scripture and the appointment to teach go hand in hand.

2. Holy Writ must not be our only source of faith. Christ did not say, "Distribute Bibles!" But He did say: "Teach all nations!" (Mt. 28,19). Holy Writ itself ought to assure us that it is the only source of our faith if that were the case; but nowhere can we find a statement to that effect. Neither is the meaning of Holy Writ plain to all who read it. Nowhere do we find it stated just what belongs to Holy Writ; our separated brethren have learned that from the teachers of the Catholic Church. — Let nothing and nobody keep you from heeding the teachings of the Catholic Church.

3. At no time was Holy Scripture used as the only source of faith. Certainly not in the beginning of Christianity; for then the Gospels and Epistles had not yet been written and distributed. Nor at any later time; for even Protestantism has not held the Bible to be the only rule, since the observance of Sunday, the baptism of infants, and many other practices are not mentioned in the Bible. Should non-Catholics reproach you for neglecting the Bible, let your answer be: Holy Scripture tells us nowhere that we should read the word of God, but it does tell us to hear the word of God. From Sunday to Sunday, the Catholic Church gives us the explanation of the Scriptures. Intelligent and leading Protestants themselves complain of the mischief done by the so-called free interpretation of the Bible. As far as reading the Bible is concerned, good Catholics read and pray it often in the prayers of the liturgy, especially the missal and the divine office. And the Church has granted an indulgence of three hundred days to the faithful who spend at least a quarter of an hour in reading Holy Scripture with the great reverence due to the word of God and after the manner of spiritual reading.

PRAYER OF THE CHURCH

May the faithful, O Lord, be strengthened by Thy graces, that having received them, they may yearn for still more and through this yearning receive them anew in greater measure. Through Christ our Lord. Amen.

OCTOBER 28
BLESSED THOMAS OF FLORENCE
Confessor, First Order

THOMAS was the son of a butcher of Florence, named Bellaci. His parents raised him in the fear of God; but when he had grown to young manhood, he strayed from the path of virtue by associating with bad companions. Matters came to a point where parents warned their sons to have nothing to do with Thomas Bellaci, and it was a disgrace to be found in his company. Then a rich man in town, who was also very wicked, made Thomas his friend and used the daring young man for many a villainous act. There came a day when a grievous crime was committed in Florence, and Thomas was accused of it. Although this time he was really guiltless, his reputation put him in danger of being condemned to severe punishment.

In his extremity he appealed to his patron, only to learn the worthlessness of such friendship. Thomas was not even received at the home of his patron. Calling again, he was told in plain words that so disreputable a person as he should never again venture to approach.

Crushed at the turn of events, Thomas paced the streets until he met a pious priest who had succeeded in bringing more than one such young man to his senses. Thomas at first rebuffed the priest. But when the priest continued to show him much sympathy, Thomas opened up his heart and told his story. The priest consoled him, and invited him to his home, saying that he would do everything in bis power for him. Actually he had Thomas declared innocent of the crime imputed to him.

Thomas now resolved to make amends for his disorderly life under the direction of his rescuer. He broke off his former associations and joined a pious society of which the priest was director. Instead of wandering about the streets and taverns, he was now seen busy at his work and visiting churches; instead of indulging in games and riotous pleasures, he now devoted himself to prayer and works of penance. The more he was filled with the grace of God, the more he longed to leave the world and to give himself to a life of penance.

Near Fiesole, the Friars Minor had recently built a convent that was renowned for the saintly lives of its members. There Thomas asked to be admitted as a lay brother. His request was considered carefully and then granted. The penance Thomas did in the convent proved the sincerity of his conversion. By fasting, keeping vigils, and scourging himself, he became a model friar. His clothing consisted of the cast-off clothes of his brethren. He performed the humblest tasks with the most perfect obedience.

The sincere conversion of Brother Thomas was rewarded by God with extraordinary graces. At prayer he was frequently rapt in ecstasy, so that his body was often seen raised on high. He was favored with remarkable spiritual gifts so that, although he was a lay brother, he was appointed master of novices. He trained many holy men who in time became glories of the order.

In the course of time Pope Martin V entrusted Thomas with the task of preaching against the heretical Fraticelli, whose complete extinction is attributed to him and his fellow Friars Minor. Thomas also founded many convents in southern Italy and elsewhere. Pope Eugene IV finally sent him with other Franciscans to the Orient to promote the reunion of the Eastern with the Western Church. There he encountered great hardships, hunger, and cruel imprisonment; and he had hopes of winning the martyr's crown. However, he was released when the pope sent a large sum of money for his ransom.

Returning to Italy, Thomas intended to make the request to be sent back to the Orient. But he died on the journey to Rome, in the convent of Rieti, on October 31, 1447. Because of the many miracles which were wrought through his intercession, his veneration increased steadily; and Pope Clement XIV beatified him. His feast is observed by the Franciscans on October twenty-fifth, and by the Capuchins on the thirty-first.

ON SINCERE CONVERSION

1. In Blessed Thomas we see verified the words of God: "I desire not the death of the wicked, but that the wicked turn away from his way and live" (Ezech. 33,11). We must never despair of the conversion of a sinner. But we should pray for his conversion rather than expect to achieve it by human efforts, for true conversion must come from God and the impulse of His grace. God usually permits temporal evil to befall the sinner, as in the case of Thomas, and then makes use of some human being, like the pious priest who met Thomas, to prepare the way of grace in the wayward soul. That is the decisive moment for the soul of the sinner; then we must pray much for him, especially to the Immaculate Heart of Mary, the refuge of sinners, that he may not refuse the rescuing hand offered him. — Have you always used the right approach in attempting the conversion of sinners?

2. Consider that true conversion shows itself in resolutely breaking with sin. When Blessed Thomas suddenly became a changed man, he gave up all sinful pleasures and avoided the occasions of sin. "If you turn to the

Lord with all your heart," said Samuel to the Israelites, "put away strange gods from among you" (1 Kings 7,3). Unless that is done, there is no true conversion. The objects of sin must be put away: bad books, tempting gifts, sinful finery; unjustly acquired goods must be restored; and we must forgive our enemy from our heart. Like Blessed Thomas, we should substitute good and pious associations in place of those that led us into sin. Would that every conversion were so sincere that the soul would count as harmful and destructive whatever it once welcomed on the path of sin. "The things that were gain to me, the same I have counted loss for Christ" (Phil. 3,7). — Have you acquired such insight into the value of things?

3. Consider that true conversion requires that corresponding satisfaction be made. Note the zeal for penance that characterized Blessed Thomas and how he persevered in it until the end of his life. It is the marvelous way of God's wisdom and longsuffering that it turns so many notorious sinners into brilliant lights of sanctity, who are urged by the remembrance of their past sins to so much greater penance. Thus the sinner Mary Magdalen was forgiven much because she manifested such great love for Christ by her tears and good works. In like manner, our Lord called the penitent Margaret of Cortona his daughter, because she was so eager to atone for the evil she had committed. Similar zeal for penance took possession of St. Paul, St. Augustine, and our holy Father St. Francis. May it also urge us to eliminate sin and its inclinations in us, so that we may live as true children of God.

PRAYER OF THE CHURCH

O God, who in Thy marvelous kindness dost make just men out of sinners, and vessels of election out of vessels of wrath, mercifully grant that, at the intercession of Blessed Thomas, Thy confessor, we may be redeemed from the slavery of sin and ever enjoy the freedom of Thy children. Through Christ our Lord. Amen.

OCTOBER 29
THE SERVANT OF GOD CATHARINE OF BOSNIA
Widow, Third Order

BOSNIA, in the Balkan peninsula, was a separate kingdom at one time. It suffered much from invasions of the Turks about the middle of the fifteenth century, especially after the glorious victory of St. John Capistran at Belgrade had checked their further advance. Anxious to strengthen the Christian religion in her land against impending dangers, pious Queen Catharine of Bosnia supported the blessed activities of the Friars Minor in every possible way.

About the year 1468, however, the Turks seized the kingdom. They took the king captive and demanded that he abjure the Catholic Faith; but he remained firm and preferred to suffer a cruel death. His son, however, allowed himself to be influenced by threats and promises to accept Islam. Catharine, who was much more grieved over the apostasy of her son than over the death of her husband and the loss of the kingdom, was forced to flee from the land. She took refuge in Rome, where Pope Sixtus IV received her with great honor.

Having experienced in such a frightful manner how perishable all earthly things are, the queen concerned herself only with eternal and imperishable things. She wore the habit of the Tertiaries, with which she is said to have been clothed by the pope himself, for he was also a member of the Franciscan Order. Rome was edified at her humility, piety, and patience. She was a thoughtful mother to the poor, and gave the last of what she had rescued from her possessions to alleviate their needs. She never complained of her lot, but prayed without ceasing for her unfortunate son and for her beloved country which was so sorely oppressed. It was a great consolation for Catharine to know that the Friars Minor secretly remained there in order to encourage the Christians who were living under the Turkish government.

The sorely tried queen died blessedly on October 25, 1487. In accordance with her request she was entombed in the Franciscan church of Aracoeli, Rome.

ON THE PERISHABILITY OF MATERIAL THINGS

1. Learn from the life of the servant of God Catharine how perishable are material things. Wealth and royal glory are sometimes suddenly lost through misfortune, and in every case there is soon an end to the happiness of riches, honors, and earthly delights. "Where are the princes

of the nations?" asks the Prophet; and he answers: "They are cut off and are gone down to hell" (Bar. 3,16-19). Yes, so perishable and undependable are earthly goods that many a one, even while possessing them, is troubled by the fear of losing them. "I saw in all things vanity, and vexation of mind, and that nothing was lasting under the sun" (Eccl. 2,11). Why should anyone wish to give up peace of heart or even the joys of heaven for their sake? — And yet, how many there are that actually do that!

2. Not only are material goods undependable, but human beings are likewise undependable, and we should not stake our happiness on any of them. Catharine was certainly justified in believing she could depend on her son, whom she had devoutly raised, to take his father's place after the latter had gone to eternity. And what was her experience with him? For the sake of earthly happiness he fell away from the Faith and caused greater grief to his mother's heart than any other misfortune could have done. Man is like a reed; if you count on him as your support and staff, the staff will easily break and the splinters will cause additional pain to your hand. A curse has been uttered against the man who forsakes God and trusts in man: "Cursed be the man who trusts in man, and whose heart departs from the Lord" (Jer. 17,5).

3. Consider what should claim our hearts, since material goods are so perishable and we can count so little on human beings. We should desire eternal goods and place our whole trust in God who alone is imperishable and unchangeable. Then, if those who are near and dear to you should be taken away from you, you can say with David: "My father and my mother have left me, but the Lord has taken me up" (Ps. 26,10). And if your earthly goods, honors and pleasures are lost, or if they have never been your portion, you will not grieve too much. For higher goods, heavenly treasures, eternal joys, and imperishable honors will be your portion if you patiently bear temporal wants. — Endeavor to merit those goods by a Christian life and the practice of good works.

PRAYER OF THE CHURCH

O God, who makest the faithful to be of one mind and will, grant that Thy people may love what Thou dost command and desire what Thou dost promise; that amid the changing things of this world, our hearts may be fixed where true joy is found. Through Christ our Lord. Amen.

OCTOBER 30
BLESSED ANGELO OF ACRI
Confessor, First Order

 HILE St. Leonard of Port Maurice was bringing about a remarkable change of morals in northern and central Italy, Blessed Angelo was equally successful in southern Italy among the peasant population of the province of Calabria. Born in the little town of Acri, and having spent his youthful years in perfect innocence, he entered the Capuchin convent.

But he did not persevere. The rigorous life frightened him and he returned home. He asked to be re-admitted and his request was granted, but again he weakened and left the convent. Unable to find peace, he made a third attempt, and was again permitted to enter. When the enemy of souls tried anew to shake his resolution, he cast himself upon his knees before a crucifix and cried out: "O Lord, I cannot trust myself. You know my weakness. Assist me with Your grace!"

God gave him special graces and he came forth victorious from the struggle. He now resolved to consecrate each hour of the day to some special mystery of the Passion of Christ. This furnished him with such strength and joy in his vocation that henceforth everything seemed easy.

As a priest his fervor at holy Mass was sometimes so great that he was rapt in ecstasy and would spend a long time in thanksgiving, crying out with our holy Father St. Francis: "O Love that is not loved! O Love, O Love!"

Ordered to prepare himself to preach missions, Angelo did so with the greatest care. He was to begin his mission career with the Lenten sermons at Carigliano in 1702. He began by addressing the large congregation with much zeal, but he had not advanced far when his memory failed him. He stopped short and had to leave the pulpit in confusion.

Returning to his cell, he cast himself on his knees, acknowledged his shortcomings, and pleaded with God to make His will known to him. Then he heard a voice saying: "Fear nothing, I will grant you the gift of preaching." Angelus asked: "Who are you?" At that moment his cell shook and he heard the words: "I am who am. In future you will preach in a familiar and simple style, so that all may understand your words."

Now Angelo understood what God wanted of him. He resolved at once to drop that artificial style of preaching which depends for its success on personal effort, and to prepare more by prayer and meditation, trusting in the help of God. The results were proof that God was working through him. In future he spoke with such clarity, power, and heavenly unction that his hearers were deeply moved.

Father Angelo did untold good as he traveled from parish to parish. But once again a great humiliation awaited him. It was in Naples, where the cardinal-archbishop had urged him to preach. There were some who jeered and laughed at him because of his simple language. But when Angelo called upon the congregation at the next sermon to pray for an unfortunate soul that was going to meet with a sudden death, and the principal scoffer presently dropped dead while leaving the church, the people recognized that they had mocked a saint. Now they listened to his lessons as to one sent by God, and God Himself confirmed his words by many miracles. Blessed Angelo also received the grace to read the hearts of men, so that he disclosed to them the sins they concealed or forgot in confession.

After laboring untiringly in the vineyard of the Lord for more than thirty-six years, Angelo died, worn out by work but rich in heavenly merits, on October 30, 1739. The many miracles that occurred even after his death induced Pope Leo XII to beatify him in the year 1825. The Franciscans and the Capuchins celebrate the feast of Blessed Angelo on October thirtieth.

ON THE SIGNS THAT IDENTIFY THE WORKS OF GOD

1. The works of God are frequently begun amid much criticism and difficulty. It was, without doubt, the devil who twice succeeded in diverting Angelo from his vocation, for in it the latter was finally to wrest many souls from hell. Many of the saints, especially St. Theresa, looked upon it as a sign that an undertaking was inspired by God and would save many souls, if the devil went to much trouble to hinder it. That is why we should not let ourselves be intimidated if hell seems to be loosed against any of our undertakings, but rather regard it as a sign that the work is of God and will be blessed by Him. With firm hope in God we must steadfastly overcome all hardships, according to the words of the Prince of the Apostles: "Resist him, strong in faith" (1 Pet. 5,9). — To what extent have you permitted yourself to be stopped by the devil in the performance of good works? Has he perhaps crushed most of your resolutions right from the start?

2. Consider that God Himself often lets the good works He inspires us to perform meet with ill success in the beginning, as He did in the case of Blessed Angelo. Usually we trust too much in our own efforts. We must, of course, do our part also in the work assigned to us by God. Although almighty God granted the gift of preaching to Blessed Angelo, so that his

personal efforts were no longer needed in the ordinary manner, it would, generally speaking, be presumptuous to expect such intervention. Still, we must depend for the success of our undertakings on the grace and blessing of God, so that in all our labors, we cheerfully acknowledge with the Apostle: "Not I, but the grace of God with me" (1 Cor. 15,10). — Do you make this acknowledgment?

3. Consider that failure may attend us even at the end of our work, as Blessed Angelo experienced in Naples. Almighty God permits that to happen, so that the praise of men may not be the motive which prompts us to do our work. False motives can easily spoil the work of even God's chosen souls. Humiliations are the best remedy against this dangerous poison. They preserve the soul from pride, and strengthen it to act only from the purest motives, so that we can say with the Prophet: "Not to us, O Lord, not to us, but to Thy name give glory" (Ps. 113,1). When the soul is dead to itself and to the world, then will it be a fitting tool for the works of God. Then will we prove to be a source of blessing to many souls here upon earth, and merit for ourselves a crown of glory in heaven.

PRAYER OF THE CHURCH

O God, wonderful in Thy saints, who didst attract to Thyself the soul of Blessed Angelo, let us through his merits and intercession ever despise the things of earth and, through the continual contemplation of heavenly things, be set aright in the love for our heavenly home. Through Christ our Lord. Amen.

<hr/>

OCTOBER 31
THE SERVANT OF GOD PAMPHILUS OF MAGLIANO
Confessor, First Order

HIS learned and saintly friar was born on August 22, 1824, in Magliano dei Marsi. His family name was Pierbattista, and in baptism he received the name of John Paul. He was given the name of Pamphilus when he entered the Franciscan Order at the age of sixteen.

On July 5, 1839, he pronounced his solemn vows as a member of the Abruzzi province, and on December 18, 1846, he was ordained to the holy priesthood. Soon after his ordination he was placed at the head of the departments of philosophy and theology in his province. The general of the order recognized his exceptional talent and ability, and called him to Rome in 1852, appointing him to the chair of theology at the College of St. Isidore.

It was during this stay at St. Isidore's that Bishop Timon of Buffalo was negotiating to secure a community of Franciscans for educational and missionary work in his diocese. Father Pamphilus had long felt a call to sacrifice his life in the "American foreign missions." Two other Italian fathers were as anxious as he to exercise the sacred ministry in neglected regions of the United States. Bishop Timon gladly accepted their offer. Fortified with the blessing of the vicar of Christ and commissioned by the minister general to start a new province when circumstances permitted it, the little group of Franciscan pioneers, with Father Pamphilus as superior, set out on May 10, 1855. They reached New York on June twentieth.

Twelve years make up the span of Father Pamphilus' activities on American soil. What he accomplished in this period seems almost incredible. When one reflects that at his coming there was no Franciscan community of any kind in the eastern states, and few Catholic churches in western New York, these accomplishments seem prodigious. A custody of six formed friaries; two new communities of sisters, one at Allegany, New York, the other, the Sisters of St. Francis of Mary Immaculate, at Joliet, Illinois; five well-organized Franciscan parishes, twenty-two mission churches, a college and seminary (St. Bonaventure's College and Seminary) and two academies for young women — these institutions point to a ministry crowded with activity and crowned with success, but accomplished at the price of great hardship amid humanly insurmountable obstacles. It was a mystery even to his brethren how he could do so much work.

It is difficult at times for human nature to realize it, yet afflictions of body or soul are an unmistakable sign of divine favor. So it seems that almighty God meant to give posterity the surest proof of the sterling character of this saintly Franciscan when He sent him trials and sorrows after a span of years spent solely in His service and for His honor and glory. This must have been a heavy cross, but Father Pamphilus bore it with truly Christian fortitude and patience — a true soldier of the misunderstood Christ.

At the summons of the minister general, Father Pamphilus hastened to Rome, where he gave a detailed account of his activities in America. He then humbly begged to be relieved of his burden, that he might retire to one of the friaries of his native Italy.

In the solitude of the cloister of San Francesco on the banks of the muddy Tiber, he took up his abode. Shortly after his arrival this friary was confiscated by the Italian government, and he repaired to that of San Pietro in Montorio. Here he welcomed the opportunity to take up his pen in defense of his faith and to record the glories of his order. Among his extensive literary contributions, his History of the Franciscan Order is the greatest. He had the happiness of seeing two volumes published and receive great praise in and out of the order. As he began to formulate plans for the third volume, he was seized with a serious illness from which he never recovered. He died on November 15, 1876.

Father Pamphilus will be remembered and loved as a builder, author, preacher, and professor of rare ability, who was filled with the seraphic spirit, Catholic in word and deed, and loyal to the Chair of Peter; with a heart going out in tender sympathy to every race; an ardent imitator of the sweet Poverello of Assisi; profoundly learned, thirsting for souls, affable, kind, and childlike. He has been referred to as the embodiment of the Franciscan educational ideal.

ON TRUE HEROISM

1. What greater joy does a soldier experience than that of victory? No matter how battered and bruised his body, if victory in a noble cause was his, it remains a pleasant memory for the rest of his life. Witness the proud figure and firm gait of the veterans of the various wars who take their places in a parade. Hear the tales of gallant deeds they relate. But if they are proud of their feats, what shall we say of the heroes in the spiritual combat? Can any battlefield compare with that to which the soldier of Christ must go, or any enemy, with the cohorts of Satan? How glorious is the victory of the soldier of Christ if he has won the battle against so mighty a foe! With firm step he may cross the threshold of eternity to join the ranks of God's heroes when his General greets him: "Well done, good and faithful servant, enter into the joy of your Lord" (Mt. 25,23).

2. But there are degrees of heroism. Of all the battles we must wage, few require greater virtue than to keep silent in the time of suffering. We long to defend ourselves when unjustly accused; nature prompts us to seek consolation from our friends; our evil inclinations urge us to retaliate. And so, Thomas a Kempis (3,28) says, "It is no small prudence to be silent in the evil time and not to be disturbed by the judgment of men." The saintly Franciscan Father Pamphilus was misunderstood and misinterpreted by those who were nearest to him, those on whose support he should have been able to depend. This test of his virtue was a difficult one, yet he bore

it with a patience that was admirable and truly heroic. No word of resentment ever passed his lips. He was a true soldier of the misunderstood Christ! — What an example for us! May it impel us to make greater efforts to fight our battles more courageously.

3. "Jesus held his peace" (Mt. 26,63). By a single word Christ could have confounded His accusers and become the object of praise and admiration. But the great General chose otherwise. He knew that His followers would expect to learn from Him how to proceed in their struggles with the enemy, and so He taught them the surest lesson — silence. How frequently we aggravate a situation by speaking when our heart is disturbed. We fail against charity, justice, and patience; and instead of victory, we carry away with us only the consciousness of defeat. — Let us take heart from the example of saintly Father Pamphilus, who, in imitation of his divine leader, preserved the majesty of calmness in the face of trial and thus gave us a lasting lesson of true heroism.

PRAYER OF THE CHURCH
(No. 28 under "Various Prayers")

O God, who by the patience of Thine only-begotten Son hast crushed the pride of the enemy of old, grant us, we beseech Thee, devoutly to keep in mind all that He endured in His love for us, and thus by the help of His example to bear our troubles with equanimity. Through the same Christ our Lord. Amen.

NOVEMBER

NOVEMBER 1
THE SERVANT OF GOD MARY OF THE PASSION CHAPPOTIN
Virgin, Third Order

ANTES in France is the native city of this religious foundress, who did so much for the foreign missions. She was born there in 1839, and was a descendant of the old French family of the Chappotins de Neuville. The Franciscan spirit of poverty and humility was evident in her at a very early age. In 1860 she was admitted to the Poor Clare convent at Nantes, but the following year she was sent home because her health failed.

Three years later, Mary joined the Sisters of St. Mary Reparatrix, and the next year she was sent to India. Having labored with great success among the heathens there, Providence directed her to Rome. There at the bidding of Pope Pius IX, she founded the congregation of the Missionaries of Mary. As a result of arrangements with the minister general of the Franciscan Order, her foundation was affiliated with the Third Order of St. Francis and took the name of the Franciscan Missionaries of Mary.

Truly Franciscan in spirit, the foundress urged her sisters to offer themselves as victims for the Church and for souls, to honor the Blessed Sacrament and the Immaculate Mother of God in a very special way, and in the heathen missions to employ all their resources for the salvation of souls. With real Franciscan charity she devoted herself to the care of the lepers.

At her death in 1904, the congregation numbered eighty-six houses in all parts of the world. She was extremely happy when the news was conveyed to her in 1900 that seven sisters had been martyred for the Faith in China. She considered this the baptism of blood for her congregation. On one occasion she made this statement: "I wish I had two lives: one with which I could always pray, the other, with which to perform all the duties God imposes on me." A cardinal once said: "Her very presence is somehow a power and an inspiration. Her example, her gifts and virtues are a continual lesson. Her maternal heart is a safe refuge for her daughters."

In 1904, the jubilee year of the Immaculate Conception, Mary passed on to the eternal vision of God. God glorified her by many signs and wonders shortly after her death, and so urgent were the petitions of her clients that the cause of her beatification was soon introduced. This cause is still pending in Rome.

ON IMITATING MARY

1. The Blessed Virgin Mary may well serve as our leader. The servant of God Mother Mary learned this by experience. She rose to virtue and saintliness by following in the footsteps of Our Lady. The Blessed Virgin has given us an example of all the virtues we need to get to heaven. She proved her humble faith in the stable of Bethlehem and on the journey to Egypt. She showed thoughtful charity on her visit to Elizabeth and at the wedding feast at Cana. We behold her unwavering patience amid suffering as she stands underneath the Cross of Jesus. And sin had no part in her. With good reason Holy Church places on her lips the words: "Blessed is the man who hears me" (Prov. 8,34). — Cling to Mary, and you will not go astray.

2. We should be filled with confidence when we imitate Mary. Let us take pleasure in honoring her in our hearts by frequent little acts of piety. In our external conduct, let us imitate her faith, her charity, her patience and her purity. Let us not only sing hymns of devotion to her, but let us live so that we may never cause her sorrow or make her ashamed of us. By our words and actions we should strive to fulfill the prophecy: "Behold, from henceforth all generations shall call me blessed" (Lk. 1,48). — How practical is your veneration of the Mother of God?

3. Fear may well form part of our veneration of Mary. We should fear to love her too little, especially since everything we do for the love of the Mother of God reflects on her Divine Son. We should fear to be separated from Mary, which happens when we commit sin. May the words which Holy Mother Church places on the lips of the Blessed Virgin ever resound in our hearts: "He who shall find me shall find life, and shall have salvation from the Lord. But he who shall sin against me, shall hurt his own soul" (Prov. 8,35-36). — Let us be mindful of the words: "We follow you with all our heart, and we fear you" (Dan. 3,41).

PRAYER OF THE CHURCH

Grant, we beseech Thee, O Lord God, that we Thy servants may evermore enjoy health of mind and body, and through the glorious intercession of blessed Mary ever virgin be delivered from present sorrows and enjoy everlasting gladness. Through Christ our Lord. Amen.

NOVEMBER 2
THE SERVANT OF GOD MARY CATHARINE SEGER
Virgin, Second Order

MARY CATHARINE SEGER entered the Order of Poor Clares at Munich, Bavaria, at a very early age. Moved by her piety, her superiors chose her to found the new convent at Graz in Styria, and as the first abbess there, she labored with marked success.

In the spirit of charity, she cherished a most tender compassion for the holy souls in purgatory, and she did all in her power to shorten their pains by means of prayer and acts of sacrifice. For that reason God permitted them on occasion to appear to her in great numbers to plead for her help. When Mary Catharine effected their release, they would appear again to express their gratitude. Our Lord called her to her heavenly home in the year 1637.

ON COMPASSION FOR THE HOLY SOULS

1. Consider that the poor souls, who came from purgatory to ask Mary Catharine for help, also call on us for compassion. "Miseremini mei, miseremini mei — have mercy on me, have mercy on me," thus the Church represents them as appealing to us on this day when we commemorate the departed souls. "Have pity on me," the suffering soul calls out, "at least you, my friends; for the hand of the Lord has touched me" (Job 19,21). They suffer great woe under the chastening hand of the all-holy and all-just God. A departed fellow sister once appeared to St. Margaret Mary Alacoque and related that because of unkind words of which she was guilty at times, she was now suffering pain as of glowing needles constantly piercing her tongue. Some religious writers are of the opinion that the souls in purgatory are cleansed by the same pains which affect the damned eternally. Many of the souls who are suffering so dreadfully this very day were near and dear to us on earth; they are expecting special help from us today. — Are you giving them this help?

2. Consider that the souls in purgatory are so much the more deserving of our compassion as they cannot help themselves nor hasten their release. As long as man is on earth, he can acquire merit for heaven by every good work he does and every act of penance he performs; and at the same time he can render satisfaction for the punishments for which he would otherwise have to atone in purgatory. The extent of this satisfaction is gauged by the devotion and contrition with which he performs the penances. According to St. Bernard, such voluntary atonement on earth may often atone a hundred times as much as similar suffering in purgatory. And so the admonition is addressed to us: "Work the works (of penance) while it is day; the night comes when no man can work" (Jn. 9,4). Night has come for the poor souls, their hands are tied so that they can no longer do anything, but must suffer until the last farthing is paid, unless someone else comes to their assistance. Does not such helplessness deserve our compassion? — Have you entertained such compassion in the past, especially towards the most forsaken souls?

3. Consider how we can make our compassion for the poor souls effective. We can call upon the divine mercy in their behalf and offer up for them the sufferings of Jesus Christ. We can assist them by our prayers, by holy Communion, and most effectively by the holy sacrifice of the Mass and by indulgences. We can offer to God on their behalf the hardships of life and special works of penance. God's goodness will accept such charity from us, and His justice will be appeased by it. And as for the souls for whom we apply these good works, we may confidently hope that they will be released or at least have their sufferings made easier. — How have you manifested your compassion for the poor souls in the past? What are you resolved to do for them each day from now on?

PRAYER OF THE CHURCH (All Souls' Day)

O God, the Creator and Redeemer of all the faithful, grant to the souls of Thy servants and handmaids departed the remission of all their sins, that through pious supplications they may obtain the pardon which they have always desired. Through Christ our Lord. Amen.

NOVEMBER 3
THE SERVANT OF GOD MARY RUIZ
Virgin, Third Order

ARY was born of a distinguished family about the year 1420 at Alcarez, Spain. Her devout parents reared her in the fear of God from her youth. Averse to all worldly ado and aspirations, she took no pleasure in the idle and frivolous fiction, which was so widely circulated in those days. She read the lives of the saints instead, drawing lessons of heavenly wisdom from the virtuous examples found in them.

Like the holy hermits and penitents, Mary sought retirement and had a room arranged in an out-of-the-way part of her home, in the seclusion of which she devoted herself to fervent prayer and austere penance. Nevertheless the fame of her virtue and beauty led many prominent young men to ask her hand in marriage. But all such proposals and all the persuasion of her father could not separate her from the Divine Bridegroom she had chosen.

Mary was invested with the habit of the Third Order, and her example encouraged several of her young friends to do the same thing. Later she invited them all to come and live in her home, where, united in sisterly charity, they served God with holy zeal. In 1468 Pope Innocent VIII raised this pious group of young women to the rank of a religious congregation, placed them under the obedience of the Franciscan provincial of Carthagena, and appointed Mary Ruiz their first superior.

In this capacity she built, in addition to a new convent, a church which she placed under the patronage of St. Mary Magdalen. Up to a ripe old age, she labored unceasingly and zealously at her own perfection and that of her sisters.

By special grace from on high, the day of her death was revealed to her. She prepared herself with the greatest care, and the Lord received her into His kingdom on the appointed day in the year 1500.

ON READING

1. Consider how wisely the servant of God Mary acted by not spending her time in reading useless worldly stories and romances. How dangerous such reading can be, even if the books contain nothing that is in itself bad, St. Theresa tells us from her own experience: "My mother," she says, "was very virtuous; but I acquired none of her good qualities, and one of her weaknesses became quite detrimental to me. She delighted in reading tales

of chivalry, and permitted her children to do the sanie thing. She never neglected her duties on that account, but I neglected many a necessary and better occupation while I read by the hour, although this greatly displeased my father, and I was obliged to keep the books hidden from his sight. As a result, I became negligent in my religious practices, indulged in all kinds of frivolities, and would surely have come to a tragic end, had God's special grace not opened my eyes." — Have you perhaps had a similar sad experience? May the grace of God help you today to see the danger to which you are exposing yourself.

2. Consider how our servant of God Mary made her choice of reading matter like a truly wise virgin. While she carefully avoided all useless and dangerous books, she derived from the good and pious books she read the desire to progress in virtue. There were few books at that time, and it was not easy to get them. Printing had not yet been invented, and the books were all written by hand. Now, with books printed by the thousands, they can be bought cheaply and circulated easily. Of course, bad books have increased in greater number than good ones, and it is necessary to be on our guard in the choice of our reading material. There is plenty of good material which has been printed, and we should gladly spend a moderate sum in order to secure good books and periodicals supplying instruction and inspiration for leading a Christian life as well as reasonable diversion. — Have you made good use of this means for yourself and your family?

3. Consider that even in the use of good books and publications, one must carefully guard against abuse. First of all, not every book is fit reading matter for every person. Many a book that is useful and good for adults, would be dangerous and harmful for children; they should not be permitted to read such books. Secondly, in books and especially in daily papers that are otherwise good in themselves there are at times articles that are more harmful to virtue than useful; such articles should not be read. Thirdly, reading is always harmful when it is prompted by mere curiosity and a passion for reading; many a duty will be neglected and little good will come of it. Thomas a Kempis (1,3) says: "Because many take more pains to be learned than to lead good lives, therefore they often go astray and bear no fruit at all, or but little. But when the day of judgment comes, it will not be asked of us what we have read, but what we have done." — Take care now that you may not be put to shame on that day.

PRAYER OF THE CHURCH
(Over the People, Thursday in Passion Week)

Be gracious to Thy people, we beseech Thee, O Lord, that, rejecting what is displeasing to Thee, they may rather be filled with delight in Thy commandments. Through Christ our Lord. Amen.

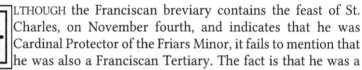

NOVEMBER 4
ST. CHARLES BORROMEO
Bishop and Cardinal, Third Order

LTHOUGH the Franciscan breviary contains the feast of St. Charles, on November fourth, and indicates that he was Cardinal Protector of the Friars Minor, it fails to mention that he was also a Franciscan Tertiary. The fact is that he was a close follower of the Poverello, a prelate according to the heart of St. Francis; and he deserves to be recognized, honored, and imitated as one of the greatest saints of the Third Order. In his life of St. Charles Borromeo, Orsenigo says that "enrolled in the Third Order of St. Francis, he not only faithfully wore the habit ... but above all ... took the poverty of St. Francis of Assisi as the model for his life."

Charles was born in the castle of Arona in 1538. His father was Count Gilbert Borromeo; his mother belonged to the Medici family; and his uncle was Pope Pius IV. It may seem strange to hear that he received the tonsure and was appointed a titular abbot, which entitled him to a big income, when he was only twelve years old; and that ten years later, before he was ordained a priest, his uncle called him to Rome and made him administrator of the Papal States as well as the archdiocese of Milan, and also a cardinal. However, Cardinal Borromeo, who was then only twenty-two years old, was an exceptional young man, endowed with extraordinary gifts of mind and heart, deeply spiritual, and devoted wholeheartedly to the welfare of the Church. It was due to the young cardinal's vigorous efforts and leadership that the Council of Trent was re-opened and carried to a successful conclusion three years later, in 1563. In that same year he was ordained a priest and consecrated a bishop.

The archdiocese of Milan was in a deplorable condition; and in 1565 Pope Pius IV yielded to Cardinal Borromeo's request and permitted him to go to his see and personally to set things in order and to carry out the decrees of the Council of Trent. Charles remained there for the rest of his life; and the reform of the Milan archdiocese was his great life's work. It is amazing how indefatigably he devoted himself to his work and how much he accomplished. In 1569 an attempt was made on his life. A bullet struck him as he was kneeling in prayer, but he was miraculously preserved from harm. Far from stopping him, the difficulties he encountered only made him so much more dogged in carrying out his program. He never tired visiting the parishes; he established the Confraternity of Christian Doctrine for the proper instruction of the children; he saw to it that the sacred liturgy was carried out in a worthy manner; he founded the Oblates of St. Ambrose in order to lead the priests to personal holiness; and he conducted five provincial and eleven diocesan synods.

But it was the example of his own saintly life that made the deepest impression on his flock and produced the best results. He was indeed an exemplary Tertiary, a true son of St. Francis. He avoided all personal finery, and his clothes were so shabby that even beggars thought they were unfit to be worn. He was ingeniously humble, and was careful to hide his merits, his penances, and his private devotions so that no praise might come to him. He did not hesitate to wash dishes, to enter the dirtiest hovels of the poor, and to instruct a poor man by sitting down with him on the roadside. When a pestilence broke out in 1576, he remained at his post in Milan, and personally ministered to the sick and dying. He succored the poor until his funds were depleted; and then he sold his possessions, including his bed, to procure means to help them. After that he no longer encountered any opposition.

Rich in merits, esteemed by all, he died in 1584, only forty-six years old. He was beatified in 1601 and canonized in 1610. His tomb occupies a place of honor on the altar of the chapel in the crypt of the great cathedral of Milan. St. Charles is venerated in a special manner as a patron against pestilences. (Cf. Biersack, p. 21-22; *Forum,* 1938, p. 548-549, and 1943, pp. 328-329, 349.)

ON THE VALUE OF THE THIRD ORDER

1. Consider how Divine Providence made use of St. Francis to renew the world. Sensuality and avarice had shaken the very foundations of Christian life. To counteract them, St. Francis founded his order on poverty and renunciation. The First Order of the Friars Minor and the Second Order of the Poor Clares were to practice these virtues by taking vows and living in religious communities. Those called to the religious life in either of these two orders were to be outstanding examples and

incentives to the world. The Third Order was intended for Christians living in the world who were desirous of assuring their salvation, and supplied ways and means by which they, too, could counteract the dangers of sensuality and avarice. It was for this reason that St. Charles, though a prince of the Church, faithfully observed the rule of the Third Order and imitated the poverty of St. Francis. For this reason, too, the late Popes from Pius IX to Pius XII have declared that nothing could be more pleasing to them than that the Third Order be spread far and wide. — What does this mean for you?

2. Consider how the Third Order protects its members from the dangers of the world. Pope Leo XIII revised the rule to fit the present age, so that its practices of piety and mortification can be more easily observed by every Christian, also by those who belong to the working class. Twelve Our Fathers are said daily, holy Mass is attended daily if possible, the sacraments are received frequently, once a month being the minimum, and two extra fastdays are observed during the year. Wise precepts are laid down for the practice of virtues which will counteract sensuality and avarice, as well as promote submission to temporal and spiritual authority. Modern Christians who are really interested in their salvation do well to unite in Christian brotherhood to achieve these purposes. — If you are a member of the Third Order, ask yourself whether you are really living according to the rule.

3. Consider the powerful aids which are provided in the Third Order. In it people associate with others who have the same purpose in mind and publicly pledge themselves to that purpose. Their example encourages them mutually, their common association is a constant stimulus. The members say a common prayer, and God looks upon that common prayer of millions with favor. At the monthly meetings they receive useful instruction. They are joined in one spiritual family and in a certain communion of graces with all the children of St. Francis, even with their Seraphic Father and the numerous saints of his three orders who have already been glorified. With what confidence may the Tertiaries call upon their sainted forebears to assist them! — As a Tertiary, do not forget to recommend to their intercession also the souls of the departed members of the order.

PRAYER OF THE CHURCH

Keep Thy Church, O Lord, under the unfailing protection of Thy holy confessor and bishop, Charles; and as his shepherdlike vigilance has exalted him in glory, so may his intercession make us always fervent in Thy love. Through Christ our Lord. Amen.

❧❧❧❧❧❧❧❧❧❧❧

NOVEMBER 5
BLESSED JANE MARY OF MAILLE
Widow, Third Order

ANE, the daughter of the wealthy baron of Maillé, was born at the chateau of her father near St. Quentin in France. Because she possessed from her earliest youth a tender devotion and love for the Blessed Virgin Mary, she was given the additional name of Mary at confirmation, and from then on she always used it with her baptismal name. Under the direction of a Franciscan, who conducted the divine services at the chateau, she strove earnestly to attain perfection. Self-denial, mortification, prayer, and works of charity towards her neighbor were the special means she employed.

She was scarcely fifteen years old when her father died. Jane Mary was placed under the guardianship of her grandfather, who was already quite advanced in years, and who therefore believed it his duty to see his grandchild settled in life as soon as possible. He chose as her husband Baron Robert of Silly, a man who was noble both by birth and by virtue. On the evening of their wedding day the grandfather died suddenly. This made such an impression on the pious husband that he readily yielded to the wish of his young wife to live in virginity.

The young couple's first concern was to order their household in a Christian fashion. Only virtuous and God-fearing persons were admitted as their servants; all had to observe the commandments of God and of the Church faithfully; frivolous conversations, cursing and swearing, as well as games of chance, were not tolerated. In everything their master and mistress set the best example. Jane Mary interested herself also in all the needs of her people, and never sent a needy person away from her door without giving him assistance.

But the cross is the real test of all true fidelity towards God; and it was not to be wanting in this house either. A terrible war broke out between England and France. The Baron of Silly and his vassals took the field in defense of their country. But the war was disastrous for France. Mortally wounded, the baron was brought to his chateau; but hardly had he arrived there, when the English took possession of it and led him away as a prisoner. Through the efforts of his faithful wife, he obtained his freedom;

but he died not long afterwards.

Now Jane withdrew entirely from the world. She left her vast possessions in the hands of relatives, while she moved to a little house near the Franciscan church in Tours. Dressed in the ash-gray habit of the Third Order, she went out to nurse the sick and the poor; the remaining time she spent in prayer. She prayed especially that God might bless the labors of priests, particularly those who preached the divine word. She prayed most of all for the universal Church, which at that time had to endure one of its severest trials. Christendom was divided into two groups — one pope resided in Italy, another in France, and even saintly people did not know which one was the rightful head of the Church. Confusion and many scandals were the inevitable results. Had the Church been the work of human hands, it must certainly have gone to ruin. In answer to the prayers of many pious souls, God came to the assistance of the Church, and Jane Mary had the consolation before her death of seeing the Church again united under one head.

She died in the year 1414, at the age of eighty-two years. When her remains, clothed in the habit of the Third Order, were brought into the church, the body appeared to have the freshness of youth. The veneration paid to her since her death was approved by Pope Pius IX. The feast of Blessed Jane Mary is observed by the Franciscans on November sixth, by the Conventuals on April eleventh, and by the Third Order Regular on March twenty-ninth.

PRAYING FOR PRIESTS AND FOR HOLY CHURCH

1. Like Jane Mary, all believing and devout Christians have ever held in high esteem the blessed labors of good priests. Our holy Father St. Francis says in his Testament: "We should honor all theologians and those who interpret the word of God, as persons who impart to us spirit and life." But to enable them to do that, much grace and blessing from heaven are necessary, and this the faithful should draw down on the priests by their prayers. Therefore the Apostle Paul writes to the Romans: "I beseech you, therefore, brethren, through our Lord Jesus Christ, and by the charity of the Holy Ghost that you help me in your prayers for me to God" (Rom. 15,30). — Do you also pray for your priests?

2. Consider that every Catholic ought to pray for Holy Church. True, the Church is the work of God and shall not be confounded as long as the world lasts. But she is made up of human beings and is placed among them. That is why she encounters oppositions from people who are outside the pale of the Church; and, what is still worse, there can arise

within the Church aberrations, schisms, and scandals. While all this mischief will not cause the Church to go to ruin, yet many a soul can be lost in consequence. That is why so many prayers of the liturgy call upon God to spare His Church from all schism and error. If the welfare of the Church is truly a matter of personal concern to us, then we, too, will often raise our hearts in silent prayer for the Church.

3. Consider that we ourselves must do something if our prayer for the Church and her priests is to be effective and to please God. We ourselves must be good and true children of the Church, observe her precepts faithfully, use her means of grace diligently. We must revere and love the priests, but especially the directors of our souls, listen attentively to their teachings, follow their directions, and not pay attention to what is purely human in them, according to the example of St. Francis, who says in his Testament: "I will not consider any sin in them because I behold in them the Son of God, and they are my lords." We must, finally, as good lambs and sheep of the flock of Christ, aim to please our Lord by the Christian virtues of humility, love of God and neighbor, contempt of what is temporal, and appreciation of what is eternal. Then will our prayer also be pleasing to God and find a hearing.

PRAYER OF THE CHURCH

O Lord, Jesus Christ, friend of humility and charity, who didst inflame Blessed Jane Mary with Thy love, and didst lavish upon her Thy heavenly gifts, teaching her to despise the fortunes of this world, grant that we, who venerate her in celebrating her feast, may also follow her by humility and contempt of things temporal. Who livest and reignest forever and ever. Amen.

NOVEMBER 6
BLESSED MARGARET OF LORRAINE
Widow, Second Order

ARGARET was born of the ancient noble family of the dukes of Lorraine. Her earnest efforts to lead a virtuous life attracted attention very early in her life.

After the death of her husband, Duke René of Alengçon, she assumed the government of the duchy. In this she was guided solely by Catholic principles; and by means of prudent economy, she managed to save a neat amount which she used to render aid to the poor and the needy. She took particular pleasure in nursing the sick and the lepers. She built churches, convents, and hospitals everywhere.

The subject matter taught in the schools and the instruction of the people were objects of particular solicitude to her. Hardhearted landlords and selfish officials were dealt with by her with the greatest severity. Still, she remained very humble, and spent a great part of her day in meditating on the sufferings of Christ and in performing works of penance.

In later years, after she had turned the government over to her son, she was invested with the habit of the Third Order. And when that no longer satisfied her desire for perfection, she entered the convent of the Poor Clares at Argenton, which she herself had founded. There she died a saintly death in the year 1527. Pope Benedict XV approved her veneration. The feast of Blessed Margaret is observed on November sixth by the Franciscans and the Capuchins.

ON ASPIRING TO PERFECTION

1. Every Christian is obliged to strive for perfection. It is not without reason that our Lord says: "Be you therefore perfect as your heavenly Father is perfect" (Mt. 5,48). This obligation does not require the impossible of us. Everyone can love his neighbor, do good, and overcome himself. Blessed Margaret aspired to perfection as a child, a woman, a ruler, a widow, a religious, and she succeeded in achieving her goal. — Imitate her in this endeavor.

2. Sometimes striving for perfection may become a difficult task. This may be due to our associates, or to external circumstances. Blessed Margaret did not permit herself to be restrained in her efforts to reach perfection, neither by human beings, nor by the high station in which she found herself. But we must above all bear in mind that perfection does not consist in external practices, but rather in the disposition of our heart. The motive must be the love of God. All for the love of God! — Let this sentiment grow in you, and you will grow in perfection.

3. Obstacles are really a help in our efforts to attain to perfection. The Apostle writes: "Patience has a perfect work" (Jas. 1,4). Let us, therefore, preserve patience in all the vicissitudes of life, meet all opposition with patience, evince patience in sickness and trials, and we can then be sure that we are on the road of perfection and will advance on it. — Rejoice if you are put to the test.

PRAYER OF THE CHURCH

O God, the Author of every virtue, who didst illumine with extraordinary merits Thy blessed servant Margaret in every station in life, grant us through her intercession, that we may live holily in the state to which Thou hast called us, and may ever give a good example. Through Christ our Lord. Amen.

❦❦❦❦❦❦❦❦❦❦

NOVEMBER 7
BLESSED HELEN ENSELMINI
Virgin, Second Order

ELEN, a member of the ancient noble family of the Enselmini, was born in Padua in 1208. Early in life she entertained an ardent desire to become a bride of Christ; and so, when St. Francis established a convent of Poor Clares in her native city in 1220, she received the habit of St. Clare from the hands of St. Francis himself. St. Anthony of Padua was her director, and under his guidance the young novice advanced rapidly in religious perfection.

In order to purify His spouse thoroughly, our Lord began to send her grievous and painful maladies when she was but eighteen years of age; she became lame, blind, and dumb, and remained thus until her death. She bore this trial with heroic constancy and perfect surrender to her suffering and crucified Saviour.

But as a recompense, she was also strengthened and enlightened by abundant heavenly consolation. In spirit she saw the glory of the blessed in heaven, especially that of our holy Father St. Francis and all the religious who were faithful to their vocation. God permitted her also to behold the sufferings of the souls in purgatory, in order to encourage her to pray the more zealously for them and to bear her own sufferings with still greater patience.

Finally, on November 4, 1242, God called her to her eternal home. She was thirty-four years old, and had spent twenty-two years in the convent. Her body has remained incorrupt to the present day, and numerous miracles have been wrought at her intercession. In 1695 Pope Innocent XII approved the public veneration given to her since her death. The Franciscans and the Capuchins observe her feast on November seventh, and the Conventuals on the sixth.

ON PATIENCE IN TIME OF SICKNESS

1. If you are afflicted with illness, reflect that it has been sent to you by God, for, without the will of our heavenly Father, not a hair falls from our head. Our Lord Himself assures us of this. Perhaps you have been the cause of your illness: through want of precaution, immoderate exertion, intemperance, or other sins. But even then it is God's hand that sends you the sickness as a penance, and you can do nothing better than accept the penance for the amendment of your life, and bear it patiently. — Examine yourself and see whether you have borne bodily sufferings in this spirit in the past. Offer them up also for the poor souls, who must suffer more than you in purgatory.

2. But sickness is not always a punishment for sins committed. When the disciples saw the man born blind, they asked our Lord: "Master, who has sinned, this man or his parents, that he should be born blind?" Our Lord replied by saying that neither the blind man nor his parents had caused the blindness by their sins, but that it was permitted "that the works of God should be made manifest in him" (Jn. 9,2-3). So it was with the innocent soul of Blessed Helen: she was afflicted with sickness that the power and grace of God might be made manifest in her, and her virtue might be proved in patience. — If our Lord permits you to be afflicted with illness, perhaps it is because He wants to try you to see whether your piety is genuine, whether your love of God will continue also in the time of suffering. If, with the grace of God, you stand the test in patience, you promote the glory of God and insure your salvation. — Have you stood the test in the past?

3. Consider that even if sickness comes from God, it is not contrary to God's will that we apply the proper remedies to restore our health. We may, and we should call in a physician when the sickness is serious. Holy Scripture says: "The most High has created medicines out of the earth, and a wise man will not abhor them" (Eccli. 38,4). It is part of patience in illness willingly to take the prescribed medicines, to follow the directions of the physician, and not to become impatient even if there is no improvement. Moreover, it is not contrary to patience if we pray and ask others to pray for the restoration of our health. Nor is it wrong to speak of our sufferings and pains. If that is done in a simple and truthful manner, it is better than if the patient remains silent in the hope of being admired and pitied all the more; such silence is rather disguised love of praise and vanity. Be unassuming and forthright in days of sickness as well as in days of good health. Accept whatever God sends you; apply the proper remedies and then leave everything in His hands. In this way you

will merit His good pleasure and work out your salvation.

PRAYER OF THE CHURCH

O God, Thou strength of those who are in health and remedy of the sick, who didst adorn Thy virgin, Blessed Helen, with marvelous strength in illness and with innocence of life, grant us at her intercession patiently to endure sickness and vicissitudes, to amend our lives and attain to everlasting happiness in heaven. Through Christ our Lord. Amen.

NOVEMBER 8
BLESSED JOHN DUNS SCOTUS
Confessor, First Order

DURING the first decade of the fourteenth century, the most famous teacher at the universities of Cambridge, Oxford, and Paris was Father John Duns of Scotland— the Blessed John Duns Scotus. Not only did he possess one of the keenest and most penetrating minds the world has ever seen, but he was also a humble Friar Minor and close follower of St. Francis of Assisi.

Born in 1266 at Littledean in Scotland of an Irish family which had settled in Scotland, he received his early education from his Franciscan uncle, Father Elias Duns, in the friary at Dumfries. He was clothed with the Franciscan habit in 1279 or 1280; and even before his ordination he taught theology to his brethren (1289-1290). Bishop Oliver Sutton of Lincoln, England, ordained him a priest on St. Patrick's Day, March 17, 1291. After he had continued his studies at Paris and Oxford for some eight years, he began to lecture at Cambridge in 1301 and the following year taught at the Sorbonne, Paris. At that time Philip the Fair was engaged in a disgraceful quarrel with Pope Boniface VIII, and Father John fearlessly defended the spiritual supremacy of the Vicar of Christ. Thus he incurred the anger of the French king, and together with his thirty confreres of the Paris friary he was forced to flee from the country.

Returning to England, Father John then taught at Oxford for some three years (1303-1306), and there obtained the doctor's degree in 1304. Soon the fame of his genius and learning spread abroad, and students came in great numbers to sit at the feet of the new teacher. "From almost every corner of the globe," wrote Rodulphus, "large numbers came to see and hear him whom they reverenced as an oracle from heaven." The title of the Subtle Doctor was conferred on Father John; for, as Rodulphus wrote, "there was nothing so recondite, nothing so abstruse that his keen mind could not fathom and clarify; nothing so knotty that he, like another Oedipus, could not unravel; nothing so fraught with difficulty or enveloped in darkness that his genius could not expound." Another writer declared: "He described the Divine Nature as if he had seen God; the attributes of the celestial spirits as if he had been an angel; the felicities of a future state as if he had enjoyed them; and the ways of Providence as if he had penetrated into all Its secrets."

In 1306 Father John returned to Paris; and there came to be known as the Doctor of Mary, after he had championed her Immaculate Conception and refuted all the objections of the learned men of the time against this prerogative of Our Lady. "The perfect Mediator," Father John pointed out, "must, in some one case, have done the work of mediation most perfectly, which would not be, unless there is some one person, at least, in whose regard the wrath of God was anticipated and not merely appeased." In 1854, Pope Pius IX solemnly declared the doctrine of Father John, which had always been accepted by the ordinary faithful, to be an article of faith: at the first moment of her conception, Mary was preserved free from the stain of original sin, in view of the merits of Christ.

The seal of the Church's approval was also placed on Father John's Christocentric doctrine, when the feast of Christ the King was instituted in 1925. "Duns Scotus," writes Father Gemelli, "conceived the universe in the form of a gigantic pyramid, built up of every kind of genera and species, rising upward by degrees, the lower stages united in their most noble part to the higher ... 'Jesus Christ is the culminating logical point of creation.' " Thus, the Second Person of the Blessed Trinity would have assumed a human nature even if Adam had not sinned. Because Adam sinned Christ came as Redeemer of the human race, but He is at the same time the King of creation.

In 1307 Father John was sent to Cologne, and there he died and was buried in the Minoritenkirche or Friars' Church. The date usually given as that of his death is November 8, 1308; but documents recently discovered seem to indicate that he lived for some time longer. Father John was honored as a saint, and his tomb has been visited through the centuries by large numbers of the faithful. During the Second World War the Friars' Church, which was formerly in the care of the Conventuals, was demolished; and while it was being rebuilt, the relics of Blessed John Duns Scotus were kept in a secret place in the famous cathedral, except for an arm which is now kept in an ancient sarcophagus in the crypt of the Franciscans' new church in another part of the city.

Since 1710, at least, the diocese of Nola in Italy, has observed the feast of Blessed John with an Office and Mass on November eighth. The confirmation by the Holy See of his cult as Blessed is now being sought in Rome. A new critical edition of the writings of Blessed John Duns Scotus was begun in 1927, and the first volumes have been published. It is hoped that this work will speed the day of his beatification and canonization. (Cf. *Forum*, 1942, pp. 399-401; *The Provincial Chronicle of St. John Baptist Province*, Cincinnati, Ohio, Special Marian Issue, 1954, pp. 59-68; Beraude de Saint-Maurice, *John Duns Scotus*, a book published by the Franciscan Institute, and a pamphlet condensation published by Franciscan Herald Press.)

ON THE IMMACULATE CONCEPTION

1. Consider that, like a true son of St. Francis, Blessed John Duns Scotus was eager to honor the Mother of God, whom St. Francis made the mother and patroness of his order. Scotus defended this exceptional privilege, which from the first moment of her conception kept Mary free from original sin, whereas it has tainted the soul of all other human beings. Because of this privilege the serpent, whose head she was destined to crush, never had any power over Mary. It was a consolation to the faithful, and to the Franciscan Order in particular, when this truth was declared a dogma on December 8, 1854. The Supreme Pontiff extended a great kindness to the Franciscan Order on that occasion. In all Franciscan churches the faithful can gain a plenary indulgence on this feast, and all Franciscan priests have the privilege of saying the Mass of the Immaculate Conception every Saturday throughout the year except on certain specified days. — Let us celebrate this glorious privilege of Mary with great joy throughout the year!
2. Consider how we should honor the Immaculate Conception. We should render her homage and give thanks to God, who in view of the merits of Christ preserved her from every stain of sin. But we should also look up to her on account of the great care with which she kept her soul free from every personal sin, even though she was never assailed by any evil inclination. Since we are so filled with evil inclinations, should it not be a matter of particular concern to us to guard against sin? — What care have we taken in the past?
3. Consider that the Immaculate Conception should be our special refuge in danger of sin. She who was always free from stain has no greater desire than that her children may preserve their purity of heart. And the prince of darkness, whose power was helpless against her at her very conception,

fears her more than the opposition of all men and saints together. Fly to her in the first moments of temptation. Say devoutly the little indulgenced prayers: O Mary, conceived without sin, pray for us who have recourse to you! Sweet Heart of Mary, be my salvation! O my Queen, O my Mother, remember that I am your own; keep me, guard me, as your property and possession! — Whenever you have called on her with a sincere heart, you may be sure that you have not lost the grace of God. If you faithfully take refuge with her, she will watch over you until you have reached a place near her in heaven.

PRAYER OF THE CHURCH

O God, who by the Immaculate Conception of the Virgin Mary didst prepare a worthy dwelling place for Thy Divine Son, we beseech Thee that, as Thou, foreseeing the death of this Thy Son, didst preserve her from all stain, so Thou wouldst also permit us, purified through her intercession, to come to Thee. Through the same Christ our Lord. Amen.

NOVEMBER 9
BLESSED MARGARET COLONNA
Virgin, Second Order

MEMBER of the princely Roman family of the Colonna, Margaret was born in Rome, the capital of Christendom, in 1210. Very early in life she lost both her parents. She was then placed under the guardianship of her two brothers, John and James. When she had grown to young womanhood, her older brother insisted that she enter a brilliant marriage. But Margaret, whose name signifies pearl, held her virginity in such high regard that she was willing to sacrifice all the glamor of the world in order to retain it. She firmly refused to yield to her brother's plan, declaring that she would be espoused to none other than the immortal Spouse of souls. Her younger brother championed her resolution.

With two maids, Margaret withdrew to a quiet country house belonging to her family and situated in the mountains near Palestrina. There the group devoted themselves to practices of piety and penance, as well as to works of charity. They wore coarse garments, similar to those of the Poor Clares, and mapped out their daily routine as far as possible according to the strict rule of that order.

In her new life, Margaret's relatives caused her many trials and annoyances. But she considered them as marks of the love of her Divine Bridegroom seeking in this way to disengage her heart from the world, so that she might belong to Him alone. And Christ our Lord actually appeared to her at this time and placed a crown of lilies on her head and a ring upon her finger.

In order to secure the merit of obedience, she and her companions meant to join the Poor Clares of Assisi, who had already offered to receive them. But a grievous illness attacked Margaret and prevented her plan. Somewhat restored to health, she consulted her younger brother James in Rome, who had meanwhile become a priest and cardinal. At his suggestion, and with the approval of Pope Urban IV, Margaret turned the country house on the quiet mountain near Palestrina into a Poor Clare convent where she and several like-minded young women observed the rule of St. Clare as well as her continued infirmity permitted it. Almighty God rewarded her pious zeal with many consolations.

Also favors of another kind were not wanting. Our Lord gave her an opportunity to taste a little of the sufferings He had endured. A wound opened in her right side and kept growing wider and deeper, causing her untold suffering during the last seven years of her life. She thanked God for this favor up to the last day of her life. When that day came, she said before receiving Holy Viaticum: "I thank Thee, dear Lord, for having permitted my body to become weak and infirm, so that I could the more freely return my soul to Thee." Assisted in her last moments by her brother James, and the prayers of her sisters, she surrendered her soul into the hands of God on December 30, 1284.

Later, when the convent of Palestrina was transferred to Rome, the sisters took with them the precious remains of their mother and foundress and had them entombed in their new convent of St. Sylvester. Innumerable miracles occurred at the grave of this holy virgin. In 1847 Pope Pius IX gave renewed approval to the veneration paid to her for centuries. The feast of Blessed Margaret is celebrated by the Franciscans on November seventh, and by the Capuchins on December thirtieth.

ON SUFFERING AS A SIGN OF GOD'S LOVE

1. Consider how the love of God manifested itself in the many sufferings that were sent to Blessed Margaret. At a very early age she was deprived of her parents; and who would not feel compassion for the little orphan? But God used this means to disengage her heart from the world, so that

it seemed to pass into eternity with her departed parents, for she now determined to devote herself entirely to the service of God. Her relatives turned against her, they mocked and derided her, and so her heart was no longer attached to anyone in the world, and she could belong to God whole and undivided. God may permit us to suffer a painful loss which we regard perhaps as a great misfortune. Often it is only a manifestation of His love, a grace which detaches our hearts from the perishable things of earth and turns them towards the imperishable and eternal things of heaven. He permits certain people to whom we have been much attached to become unfaithful and turn against us, so that we may turn our hearts to Him, the eternally faithful One. — In the past you have perhaps complained where you should have rejoiced with the Prophet: "The snare is broken and we are delivered" (Ps. 123,7).

2. Consider how God sent Margaret additional sufferings in order to lead her to still greater perfection. Serious illness and continued infirmity tended to disengage her even from herself, for she had to give up her intentions of entering a strict convent and commit herself entirely to God's plans. She did not resent this in any way but was filled with the sweetest consolation in making this sacrifice to the Beloved of her soul. "When you shall arrive thus far," says Thomas a Kempis (2,12), "that tribulation shall be sweet to you, then think that it is well with you, for you have found a paradise on earth." — Are self-love and imperfect love of God the reason why you have not yet found this paradise on earth?

3. Consider that God's love manifested itself in the sufferings He sent Blessed Margaret, in as much as He led her to eternal glory on this secure and meritorious way. According to all theologians, it is a sign of predestination if God leads a soul along the pathway of suffering. The pain of these sufferings, however, does not compare with the glory that will be the soul's portion in eternity. That is why Thomas a Kempis says again (2,12): "If there had been anything better and more beneficial to man's salvation than suffering, Christ certainly would have showed it. But now He manifestly exhorts us all: if any man will come after Me, let him deny himself, and take up his cross and follow Me." — May we be encouraged by the example and strengthened by the intercession of Blessed Margaret.

PRAYER OF THE CHURCH

O God, who didst inflame the virgin Blessed Margaret with Thy love and glorify her through her contempt for the world, grant us at her intercession ever faithfully to carry the cross and to cling only to Thee. Through Christ our Lord. Amen.

NOVEMBER 10
BLESSED MATTHIA NAZZAREI
Virgin, Second Order

THE family of the Nazzarei was one of the wealthiest and most distinguished of Matelica in the Italian province of the March. Matthia, however, esteemed virtue and nobility of soul more than all worldly nobility, and resolved, for love of Christ, to consecrate herself to His service in the state of virginity.

When, therefore, her father planned to marry her to a young nobleman, Matthia firmly refused, declaring she was already espoused to the heavenly Bridegroom. Her father endeavored to force her into the marriage, but she fled from home to a convent of the Poor Clares where her aunt was the abbess. When her aunt hesitated to receive the fugitive, Matthia cut off her hair, and, laying aside her expensive garments, put on the first old habit she found.

Thus attired, she met her father in the reception room of the convent, when the enraged man appeared with the determination of bringing her back by force. Matthia dealt so gently and yet so convincingly with her father that he willingly gave his consent to her entrance into the convent.

After receiving the habit, Matthia showed such zeal and such perfection in virtue, not only during the year of probation, but afterwards as well, that when the abbess died a few years later, the sisters unanimously chose Matthia as her successor, despite her youthful years. The bishop of Camerino gladly gave his approval to their choice.

The youthful abbess looked upon herself not as the first in rank but rather as the lowliest among her sisters. She always picked out the lowliest tasks for herself. She was a shining example of all the religious virtues. She so loved to obey others that she made obedience pleasant to her subjects and never experienced any opposition from her sisters. A true daughter of St. Clare, she loved poverty and observed it faithfully. She turned over the rich inheritance she received from her father to the poor and to pious projects, not retaining even the smallest part of it for herself. To preserve her virtue from every shadow of impurity, she was very austere with herself throughout life, observing fasts and practicing rigorous corporal penance. She gained strength to persevere on the way of perfection by her habit of uninterrupted prayer.

Almighty God granted her the gifts of prophecy and of miracles, and the sick and the oppressed came from far and near to seek counsel and assistance from her.

Matthia lived thus for more than forty years until the day of her death, which she had foretold. On that day she gathered the sisters about her, fervently admonished them to persevere in chastity, poverty, and obedience, and in holy charity. On the feast of the Holy Innocents in the year 1300, she gave her pure soul back to God. At her grave many crippled people received the health of their limbs again, the blind received their sight and the deaf their hearing. Pope Clement XIII and Pope Pius VI approved the annual celebration of her feast. It is observed by the Franciscans on November seventh, and by the Capuchins on December thirtieth.

ON RELIGIOUS SUPERIORS

1. Consider that God permitted Matthia to be elected abbess of her convent, although she was still very young. "The lots are in the hands of the Lord" (Ps. 30,16). Human beings can do no more at an election than choose the person they believe to be the fittest for the position. But they cannot know whether he really is the best person for the office. For that reason all who are concerned in the results should imitate the first Christians (Acts 1,24) and pray that God may guide the electors to select him whom He finds best for the position.

2. Consider that those who have been elected superiors as well as all who have been placed over us according to God's plans, must be looked upon as representatives of God. For that reason, we owe them obedience and respect, though in our judgment they may be lacking in the required qualifications. Jesus Christ taught that lesson in the house of Nazareth. Joseph was the least of the three inmates of that home, but he had been appointed by God as head of the family. So Mary and Jesus, the Eternal Wisdom, were both subject to him. What merit would you derive from your obedience if you rendered it merely because you found your superiors wise, kind, and congenial. Your obedience would no longer be virtue and would win no merit for eternity. — What merit has your obedience won in the past?

3. Consider that even superiors who are full of faults must be honored as representatives of God. A crucifix that has been damaged is nevertheless a representation of our crucified Saviour. Your superior is the representative of God in what concerns you, no matter how bad he may

be personally. Hence St. Peter writes: "Servants, be subject to your masters with all fear, not only to the good and gentle, but also to the froward" (1 Pet. 2,18). Did not Mary and Joseph honor the pagan emperor and go to Bethlehem when he issued the edict of enrollment? The Divine Child will also come to you some day and be a merciful judge, if you honor the authority of those whom He has placed over you.

PRAYER OF THE CHURCH

Graciously hear us, O God, our salvation: and grant that we who are gladdened by the festival of blessed Matthia, Thy virgin, may learn from it loving devotion to Thee. Through Christ our Lord. Amen.

NOVEMBER 11
THE SERVANT OF GOD BONAVITA
Confessor, Third Order

WE have already made the acquaintance of many saints and saintly persons of the Franciscan family who were descendants of noble and prominent families. Some may draw the conclusion that even among the saints those are preferred who were once people of rank.

That, however, is not the case; only virtue counts in the life of the saints. But since it is in itself a great virtue if anyone who is wealthy and prominent sacrifices the conveniences of the world to serve God in humility and mortification, and because God rewards such a sacrifice with extraordinary graces, it so happens that, among those who devote themselves to a life of piety, there are many persons of rank who have attained heroic sanctity.

Then, too, the virtues of prominent persons are more liable to be recorded and handed down to posterity, whereas the hidden virtue and sanctity of many a person among the lowly will be brought to light only at the last judgment. And yet, there are records also of many from the humbler ranks of life who have given the most remarkable examples of virtue and proofs of holiness. Such a servant of God was Bonavita.

Born of lowly parents in the little Italian town of Lugo, he earned his livelihood as a smith. Although his hands were black and sooty, he preserved his soul immaculately white and clean even from his youth. His life agreed with his name; "bona vita" means "good life."

After joining the Third Order of St. Francis, he advanced rapidly in true holiness. Among the members of the order in his parish, none was more temperate in his manner of living, none more humble of heart, none kinder towards the poor than Bonavita. One day in winter he saw a poor person approach half naked and shivering from cold; promptly he took off his coat and gave it to the needy person. As he went on his way home without a coat, the children ran after him and made fun of him. But Bonavita walked on quietly as though he saw and heard nothing.

His thoughts were continually occupied with God. When he was in his smithy, fanning the flame of his forge with the bellows, he would ask God to set his heart aflame with the fire of His love. God blessed his charity towards his neighbor with miracles. Often the bread which he was distributing to the poor was multiplied in his hands. By merely making the Sign of the Cross he healed many sick persons. By the Sign of the Cross, he once extinguished a fire in Lugo, which had already burned many houses to the ground and was continuing to spread. On another occasion when he was about to drive some oxen through a stream, he made the Sign of the Cross in order to be preserved from misfortune; the waters at once divided, and he passed through with the oxen on dry ground.

However, he too had his crosses and trials. For a long time he was sorely tempted by the devil; but with the help of God he was successful in overcoming all temptations. He was only thirty-seven years old when God called him to eternal bliss in the year 1375. His body was laid to rest in the Franciscan church at Lugo, and on special feastdays his head, which is enclosed in a precious shrine, is exposed for veneration.

ON PRACTICAL CHRISTIANITY

1. In order to be holy it is sufficient to be imbued with the spirit of active Christianity as was the servant of God Bonavita. It was not the miracles he performed that constituted his sanctity; it consisted rather in humility and purity, in his love of God and neighbor. Even if he had wrought no miracles, he would have been as great a saint. Christianity was compared by Christ Himself with a seed. A dead germ has no value; a living germ draws to itself the virtues of the soil and produces a plant according to the nature of the seed. Thus does living Christianity absorb all the thoughts and actions of a person and produce a life such as that of Bonavita. Such a person can say with the Apostle: "I live, now not I, but Christ lives in me" (Gal. 2,20).

2. Consider that a Christian life consists first of all in having a living faith,

for which reason Christians are also called the faithful. Without a firm and unshaken faith in all that God has revealed and the Catholic Church proposes for our belief, we cannot be numbered among the faithful. But this faith must be a lively one, it must manifest itself in our words and actions. "Shall faith (without works) be able to save him?" (Jas. 2,14). Do you wish to know whether Christ lives in you, then examine the thoughts and sentiments of your heart, to see whether you adhere firmly to all the truths of the Faith. Consider the language that proceeds from your lips, whether it conforms with the teachings and the precepts of the Catholic Faith and of Christian charity; examine your deeds, whether they reveal an active Christian spirit. There are some Christians to whom the words apply: "You have the name of being alive, but you are dead" (Apoc. 3,1). — You are called a Christian, but in reality are you one?

3. Consider that as Christians we must shape our lives according to the example of Christ. "Put me as a seal upon your heart, as a seal upon your arm" (Cant. 8,6), says Christ to His beloved. The seal which is impressed on lacquer or wax leaves an exact image of itself. True, the impression is of a different composition, not so valuable and not so stable as the seal itself, nevertheless it is entirely similar in appearance and design. Aim, therefore, to make the thoughts that take root in your heart, the words that proceed from your lips, the deeds of your arms and hands conformable to those which Christ thought, spoke, and did. Ask yourself at times: Would Christ have acted in this way? He from whom we have received the name of Christians, must be the model we should aim to reproduce in our lives.

PRAYER OF THE CHURCH (Third Sunday after Easter)

O God, who dost show the light of Thy truth unto those who go astray, that they may return to the path of righteousness, grant, that we who are of the Christian Faith may abhor whatever is contrary to that name and strive after that which is in agreement with it. Through Christ our Lord. Amen.

NOVEMBER 12
BLESSED RAYNIER OF AREZZO
Confessor, First Order

AYNIER was born at Arezzo, Tuscany, of the noble family of the Mariani. From his earliest years he was noted for his piety and humility, and when he asked to be admitted into the Franciscan Order, he desired to be only a lay brother. His thought was that he might thus be unobserved by the world and in a better position to lead a life entirely hidden in God.

In his efforts to attain to sanctity he took our Saviour as his model, and his eminently virtuous life soon made him a model to all the brethren. He distinguished himself in a very pronounced way by fraternal charity, profound humility, perfect obedience, and truly evangelical poverty. That is why the servant of God Benedict of Arezzo, a missionary in the East, who had received the holy habit from the hands of St. Francis himself and had been named provincial of Syria, chose Brother Raynier as his constant companion on his apostolic travels.

Brother Raynier also formed a close friendship with Brother Masseo, who had been a beloved companion of St. Francis. He listened eagerly to whatever Masseo could tell him of the remarkable life and holy conduct of St. Francis, and he strove to imitate the things he heard.

Blessed Raynier died a holy death in the year 1304 at Borgo San Sepolcro near Arezzo. His mortal remains rest there in the church of the Friars Minor Conventual, and are highly venerated by the people even to this day. In 1802 Pope Pius VII approved the veneration accorded to him for the previous five centuries and entered his name among the blessed. The Franciscans celebrate his feast on November twelfth, and the Conventuals and Capuchins on the third.

ON THE IMITATION OF CHRIST

1. Consider what a wise choice Blessed Raynier made when he chose Christ as his model, for Christ came into this world not only to redeem us, but also to enlighten us and to show us the way to heaven. That is why He speaks of Himself as the light of the world, and says: "I am the way, and the truth, and the life" (Jn. 14,6). He is the true and only certain way to eternal life. His teachings and His conduct on earth direct us how to act properly in every circumstance of life. Could we do better than to follow the lessons of our Divine Master? — Have the life and teachings of Christ been the rule of your conduct in the past?

2. Consider that the imitation of Christ differs widely from the life and the principles of the world. The world says: Make life comfortable for yourself, acquire fame and honor, amass money and worldly goods, then you will acquire prestige and be in a position to enjoy life. Christ, on the other hand, practiced and taught humility, poverty, self-denial, and the carrying of the cross. And so He tells the world: "I am not of this world" (Jn. 17,16), and He says that His disciples, too, are not of this world. — When you reflect on your past life and its ambitions, what have you to say for yourself? Are you of this world, or do you belong to the disciples of Christ?

3. "To many this seems a hard saying," says Thomas a Kempis (2,12): "Deny yourself, take up your cross, and follow Jesus." "But it will be much harder," he continues, "to hear that last word: 'Depart from me, you cursed, into everlasting fire.' " And yet, he who will not listen to the words of Christ and imitate Him by self-denial and the carrying of the cross will hear those other words of condemnation when eternity comes. For there is no other way that leads to salvation than that of the imitation of Christ. "He who is not with Me, is against me," our Lord Himself has said (Mt. 12,30). And, "he who will not take up his cross and follow Me is not worthy of Me" (Mt. 10,38). But whoever seeks to follow Him will not be denied the necessary grace to do so, provided he will beseech God for the needed assistance.

PRAYER OF THE CHURCH

O Lord Jesus Christ, who didst make Thy confessor Blessed Raynier admirable in imitating Thee and walking the hard road of humility, poverty, obedience, and patience, grant that we, through his intercession and by the imitation of his example, may live in a manner pleasing to Thee. Who livest and reignest forever and ever. Amen.

NOVEMBER 13
ST. DIDACUS OF ALCALA
Confessor, First Order

IDACUS was born about 1400 at San Nicolas in Andalusia, of poor and God-fearing parents. He entered the Third Order of St. Francis when he had scarcely reached young manhood, and under the direction of a devout Tertiary priest, he served

God for a long time as a hermit. Consumed with the desire for still greater perfection, he later entered the Franciscan convent at Arizafa in Castile and was there admitted to solemn vows as a lay brother.

His rapid progress in virtue made him a model to all his companions. His soul was continually occupied with God in prayer and meditation. From this source he gathered such supernatural insight concerning God and the mysteries of Faith that learned theologians listened with astonishment to the inspiring conversations of this uneducated lay brother.

Since Brother Didacus manifested great zeal for souls and willingness for sacrifice, his superiors sent him with other brethren to the Canary Islands, which at that time were still inhabited by wild infidels. Didacus was eager for martyrdom, and in this spirit bore with dauntless patience the many hardships that came his way. Both by word and example he helped in converting many infidels. In 1445 he was appointed guardian of the chief friary on the islands at Fortaventura.

Recalled to Spain, he went to Rome in 1450 at the command of the Observant Vicar general, St. John Capistran, to attend the great jubilee and the canonization ceremonies of St. Bernardin of Siena. On this occasion an epidemic broke out among the many friars assembled in the large convent of Aracoeli. Didacus attended the sick with great charity and trust in God. And God did not fail him. Despite the lack of supplies in the city at the time, Didacus always had ample provisions for his patients. He miraculously restored many of them to health by merely making the Sign of the Cross over them. Leaving Rome, he returned to Spain, where, as in the former days, he was a source of great edification to the friars in every convent in which he lived.

When he felt that the end of his life was drawing near, he asked for an old and worn-out habit, so that he might die in it as a true son of the poor St. Francis. With his eyes fixed on the crucifix, he breathed forth his soul on November 12, 1463, saying the words: "O faithful wood, O precious nails! You have borne an exceedingly sweet burden, for you have been deemed worthy to bear the Lord and King of heaven."

Months passed before it was possible to bury Didacus, so great was the concourse of people who came to venerate his remains. Not only did his body remain incorrupt, but it diffused a pleasant odor. After it was laid to rest in the Franciscan church at Alcalá de Henares astounding miracles continued to occur at his tomb. Pope Sixtus V, himself a Franciscan, canonized Brother Didacus in 1588. The three branches of the First Order celebrate the feast of St. Didacus on November thirteenth. He is the special patron of those friars who are brothers. The Spanish for Didacus is Diego, and Mission San Diego in California was named for the Franciscan St. Didacus.

GOD CHOOSES THE LOWLY

1. In the office for the feast of St. Didacus, we find the following words: "See your vocation, brethren, that there are not many wise according to the flesh, not many mighty, not many noble; but the foolish things of the world has God chosen that He may confound the wise" (1 Cor. 1,26). The life of St. Didacus proves the truth of these words. Born of poor parents in a lowly station, and having no schooling of any kind, he was able to discuss the loftiest matters to the great astonishment of learned men. How ashamed of themselves will learned men be in the presence of this plain brother at the judgment-seat of God, unless they serve God, like him, in genuine humility. What the world accounts as foolishness is wisdom in the sight of God; but the wisdom of the world will be put to shame at the final reckoning. — To which principle do you hold?

2. Consider why God chooses the lowly to lavish His grace on them and make them really great. The Apostle tells us, "that no flesh shall glory in His sight" (1 Cor. 1,29). Almighty God bestows His grace on human beings so that they can do great things, but they should not ascribe what is accomplished to themselves; they should rather give the glory to God. Because the wise ones of this world and the wealthy and the prominent so readily give to themselves the credit for what they do, they receive less grace to accomplish that which is supernatural, and so they devote themselves to what is material and perishable. But when the learned, the wealthy, and the prominent of this earth are at the same time humble, God chooses them also, as He once chose St. Paul, St. Augustine, and the saintly King Louis. The latter thought more of the crown of thorns which had been placed on the head of our Lord than he thought of his own royal crown. — Have you made yourself undeserving of God's graces because you sought your own honor?

3. Consider that God admits only those souls to eternal bliss and heavenly glory who remain humble in their own eyes though they have accomplished great things. Endowed with the most brilliant gifts of nature and of grace, Lucifer contemplated himself and became puffed up — and immediately he was deprived of his throne among the angels and was thrust into hell. Didacus, who was greatly esteemed by the world and by his brethren because of the marvelous things God accomplished through him, nevertheless thought little of himself and wished to leave this world clothed in a poor and worn-out habit. In heaven he received a place once

occupied by the proud angels. "Everyone who exalts himself shall be humbled; and he who humbles himself shall be exalted" (Lk. 14,11).

PRAYER OF THE CHURCH

Almighty and eternal God, who in Thy wonderful condescension hast chosen the weak of this world to confound the strong, mercifully grant to our lowliness, that through the pious intercession of Thy holy confessor St. Didacus, we may deserve to be raised to eternal glory in heaven. Through Christ our Lord. Amen.

NOVEMBER 14
BLESSED GABRIEL FERRETTI
Confessor, First Order

GABRIEL was born in 1385 and belonged to the ancient ducal family of the Ferretti. His devout parents raised him in the fear of God, and in his eighteenth year he entered the Franciscan Order. His efforts at acquiring virtue won for him so great a degree of the respect and confidence of his brethren that, shortly after his ordination to the priesthood, when he was only twenty-five years old, he was appointed to preach missions in the March of Ancona. For fifteen years he devoted himself to this important task with blessed success.

He was then assigned to the office of guardian of the convent of Ancona, and later he was elected provincial of the province of the March. In both offices he was careful to guide his subjects well. He shirked no labor, and he could be very severe if it was necessary to correct an evil. He achieved the greatest results, however, by his own bright example of virtue, which induced weak and lax characters to exert themselves manfully in observing the rule.

The following incident is proof of his great humility and piety. Once while he was journeying to Assisi, he went into the Franciscan church at Foligno to pray. The sacristan, who took him for a brother, bade him serve the Mass of a priest who had just gone to the altar. The humble provincial obeyed. But when the guardian of the convent recognized the venerable superior of the province of the March in the server, he severely reproached the sacristan. But Father Gabriel defended the sacristan, saying: "To serve Mass is a great privilege. The angels would consider themselves honored. So do not blame the brother for conferring that honor on me!"

Gabriel's zeal to promote the interests of the order was as great as his humility. At San Severino he restored a convent that had fallen into ruin. At Osimo he built a new convent. The convent at Ancona he enlarged, in order to accommodate the great number of novices attracted to it by the fame of his sanctity.

He possessed an ardent love of God and the Blessed Virgin Mary, and he unwittingly gave expression to it in all his sermons. Frequently he was favored with visions of our Lord and of the Blessed Virgin.

Rich in virtue and merits, he died on November 12, 1456, in the convent at Ancona, assisted in his last hour by the servant of God Gregory of Alba, and St. James of the March. The latter delivered his funeral oration. To this day his body is incorrupt, and the many miracles wrought through his intercession have increased the devotion of the faithful to him. Pope Benedict XIV and Pope Clement XIII solemnly confirmed his veneration. The feast of Blessed Gabriel is observed by the Franciscans and Capuchins on November twelfth.

ON THE VIGILANCE EXERCISED BY SUPERIORS

1. Blessed Gabriel Ferretti distinguished himself as provincial by the vigilance he kept over his subjects. This is a most important duty of those in authority, whether they are parents, employers, teachers, spiritual or temporal superiors. They must make a careful check of the conduct of their subjects and of the dangers that threaten them, in order to warn them in time and forestall the danger of their being lost. As the Apostle says, they must "render an account of your souls" (Heb. 13,17). How many young and inexperienced souls are lost here and hereafter, because their superiors do not watch over them. What a terrible accounting the superiors thus store up for themselves! "I will require the blood of this victim," says the Lord, "at the hand of the watchman" (Ezech. 33,6). — Will such blood perhaps be required of you?

2. Consider that the vigilance of Blessed Gabriel extended also to the temporal needs of his brethren. Thus he restored convents that had fallen into ruin, enlarged such as were not spacious enough, and built new ones. Parents, employers, and others in authority must watch over the temporal needs of their subjects, and keep them provided with clothing, shelter, food, and whatever else is necessary for their corporal well-being. If that is done, the subjects will be indebted to their superiors and more readily heed their admonitions and warnings. Such watchfulness is the sacred

duty of every Christian, for the Apostle says: "If any man have not care of his own, and especially of those of his house, he has denied the faith, and is worse than an infidel" (1 Tim. 5,8). — Have you always been faithful to this duty?

3. Consider that there is a third kind of vigilance that superiors must exercise, and that is vigilance over themselves, so that they may not cause harm to their subjects. Parents, for example, must refrain from saying many a thing, must avoid doing many a thing which is otherwise permissible, when their children are about to hear and see. Masters and mistresses cannot expect their servants to be attached to the house and economical and contented, if they themselves are lavish in their expenditures, live in luxury, and indulge in all sorts of dissipation till late at night. No superior will find willing subjects if he always conducts himself in a proud and domineering way. Such a spirit also drives away the grace of God, which is doubly necessary for superiors. The Holy Ghost gives them the following admonition: "The greater you are, the more humble yourself in all things, and you shall find grace before God" (Eccli. 3,20).

PRAYER OF THE CHURCH

O God, who dost graciously look down from the throne of Thy majesty upon the lowly, but dost look upon the proud with disfavor, grant us Thy servants, that through the merits and the example of Blessed Gabriel, Thy confessor, we may renounce worldly vanity and pleasure, and may deserve to receive the reward which Thou hast promised to the humble. Through Christ our Lord. Amen.

NOVEMBER 15
BLESSED JOHN OF PEACE
Confessor, Third Order

JOHN CINI was the son of distinguished parents, and was born at Pisa in the year 1353. He was a soldier by profession, and at one time joined other citizens of his native town in a war against the Florentine republic. The company to which he was attached fell into an ambush laid by the enemy. Nearly all of his companions were slain, and it was only by a special dispensation of Providence that he escaped unharmed. Filled with gratitude for this favor, he vowed to spend the remainder of his life in the service of God. But since the ties of matrimony prevented him from entering a convent, he joined the Third Order of St. Francis.

From that time he lived a strict penitential life, wore a heavy iron chain as a belt next to his body, and practiced many other forms of mortification. The greatest part of his time was spent in works of piety and charity.

He founded a pious society at Pisa, the members of which contributed regularly to a common fund which was secretly distributed to poor people who were ashamed to beg. He succeeded in implanting so solid a spirit of charity in this confraternity, that as long as the organization existed, which was up to the disturbances of the French Revolution at the end of the eighteenth century, this noble work was continued.

John died a blessed death on November 12, 1433, and was buried in the cemetery at Pisa. His fellow citizens erected a magnificent memorial over his grave, and the faithful went there in great numbers to invoke his intercession with God. In 1856 his remains were transferred to the church of the Friars Minor Conventual at Pisa, and Pope Pius IX confirmed his veneration. The feast of Blessed John Cini or Blessed John of Peace, as he is more often called, is celebrated on November twelfth by the Franciscans, the Conventuals, and the Third Order Regular. (Cf. *Forum,* 1947, pp. 333-334; *These Made Peace,* pp. 161-163.)

ON CARE FOR THE TIMID POOR

1. Consider how God Himself wished to care for the timid poor through His servant Blessed John. It was providential that when Blessed John wished to devote himself to the service of God, he could not enter a convent because of the ties of matrimony. So he resolved to serve God in the world by serving God's poor, searching out bashful poor people, and secretly bringing them alms, all of which he could not have done in a convent. Thus, also, a charitable confraternity was founded, which continued to exist for four hundred years after his death. God still provides for such timid poor by means of similar societies which the spirit of God has called into existence, such as the St. Vincent de Paul Society. — If you possess anything of the spirit of Blessed John, you will be glad to join such charitable organizations and help spread them.
2. Consider the several ways in which we can aid the timid poor. We can see to it that alms are sent to them, and the less openly this is done, the more meritorious it will be for us. Better still it would be to take a poor person into one's employ, even if his work is not so perfect or necessary

as that of another. We can encourage other employers to do the same for the love of God. We can see to it that they are promptly paid for their work. If there are children in such families, we can take it upon ourselves to make provision for them. As landlords, we can give them cheaper rent. In all these ways we are helping the needy and at the same time preserving their sense of self-respect. — In cases such as these, have you done to others what you would wish to have done to yourself?

3. Consider why this kind of charity is particularly pleasing to God. Generally there is a greater need in such families than in those whom everybody knows to be poor, and therefore Christian charity requires that we come to their assistance first. By helping them secretly, we shield their honor, on which so much depends. We also preserve their children and perhaps an entire generation from beggardom, a condition which readily passes on to children and the children's children, to the great detriment of their souls. These bashful poor are for the most part people of a more virtuous kind, who accept their poverty in the spirit and in imitation of Christ. The words of Christ are particularly applicable to the good deeds we render such people: "As long as you did it to one of these My least brethren, you did it to Me" (Mt. 25,40).

PRAYER OF THE CHURCH

O God, who didst make Blessed John illustrious by his spirit of penance and unusual charity, grant us, Thy servants, that following in his footsteps, we may check the desires of our bodies and souls, show mercy to the poor here on earth, and thereby merit to receive the imperishable crown of mercy in heaven. Through Christ our Lord. Amen.

<hr />

NOVEMBER 16
ST. AGNES OF ASSISI
Virgin, Second Order

WHEN St. Clare received the veil in 1212, she left behind her at home a young sister of fourteen named Agnes. In answer to Clare's prayers and inspired by God, Agnes betook herself to the same convent where Clare was then staying only sixteen days after her sister's departure from home.

Their father, much enraged, hastened to the convent in company with several relatives. He used force to remove her and was in the act of dragging her along by the hair, when Agnes suddenly became fixed to the spot. The united efforts of the entire company were powerless to move her. In a burst of fury her uncle, Monaldo, drew his sword to strike her. But he was seized with a violent pain in his arm and the weapon dropped from his hand. Overcome with fear, he and the rest of the band fled from the scene.

Agnes was overjoyed and returned to her sister Clare. St. Francis then led the two maidens to the convent of St. Damian, where he gave the holy habit also to Agnes. She now endeavored to imitate her saintly sister in everything, and devoted all her spare time to prayer and contemplation. She lived a very austere life, partaking only of bread and water, and wearing a coarse garb all her life.

St. Francis soon recognized the rich treasure of virtue hidden in this privileged soul. When a new convent of Poor Clares was to be founded at Florence in 1221, St. Francis sent Agnes, despite her youth, to act as superior there. Later he sent her also to Mantua and to several other cities in northern Italy to establish additional houses of the order. Wherever she went, she edified everybody by her holy life. Many devout young women renounced the world in order to consecrate themselves to God in monastic seclusion under her direction. She had the gift of infusing the Franciscan spirit into them, both by word and example.

She was favored with many extraordinary graces by God. In the great fervor of her devotion she was often raised above the earth, and once our Lord appeared to her in the form of an infant. From Holy Thursday until Holy Saturday she was once so rapt in the contemplation of the sufferings of Christ that she was under the impression she had spent but an hour in this mystical state.

When St. Clare was about to die, she sent for Agnes to assist her in her final days. In her last moments Clare addressed her sister in these words: "My beloved sister, it is the will of God that I go, but be comforted, you will soon come and rejoin me with our Lord." Three months later Agnes followed her sister to eternity. It was on November 16, 1253. Her body rests in Assisi in a side chapel of the church of St. Clare. Numerous miracles occurred at her tomb, and Pope Benedict XIV canonized her. The feast of St. Agnes is celebrated by the three branches of the First Order as well as the Third Order Regular on November sixteenth.

ON THE FRANCISCAN SPIRIT

1. On the feast of St. Agnes, Holy Church has us pray for the seraphic or Franciscan spirit. In what does that spirit consist? The seraphic spirit

consists in ardent holy love, in a heart which seeks and sees God in all things and is bent on spending itself for His honor and using all things to glorify Him. The seraphic spirit takes its name from the Seraphim, who are ever aflame with love for God. Our seraphic Father St. Francis was all aglow with this love of God and, like the three young men in the fiery furnace, wished all creatures to join in praising God. St. Agnes was at times so inflamed with this love that she was bodily raised above the earth. This love of God is conspicuous in all the saints of the Franciscan Order, for which reason the order itself is often spoken of as the Seraphic Order. As in the material world everything is attracted to the sun and revolves around it, so should all rational creatures be drawn to God and all the desires of their hearts should tend towards Him. — Do you possess this seraphic spirit?

2. Consider the obstacles that oppose this seraphic spirit in the heart of man. There is, above all, worldliness which makes us attached to material goods, sensual pleasures, and earthly honors, and thus hinders us from rising to God. Christ spoke thus to the Jews: "You are from beneath — that is, earthly-minded — I am from above" (Jn. 8,23). That is the reason, said He, why they could not come to Him, and would die in their sins. Sins for which atonement has not yet been made also stand in the way and prevent the flame of love from rising upwards. Finally, conceit and pride hold many people captive. Such pride cast Lucifer out of heaven, and it permits no human heart to rise to God. Therefore, detachment from material things, penance for sins committed, and sentiments of humility must prepare our hearts, otherwise they will not be in a condition to receive so much as a spark of true divine love. — What is it that prevents you from truly loving God?

3. Consider that this fire of love, which fills the heart with the seraphic spirit, must come from the Father of Light. What we can do, is make ourselves receptive for this grace. But, if we do our part, God will give it to us, for He said: "I am come to cast fire on the earth, and what will I but that it be kindled?" (Lk. 12,49). Let us, therefore, pray for the seraphic spirit and do what lies in us that it may not be weakened or stifled in us. Then, too, let us be mindful, especially during this month which is devoted to the souls in purgatory, of these souls who are filled with the seraphic spirit but suffer great anguish in their desire for God. Let us pray that God may satisfy their ardent longing.

PRAYER OF THE CHURCH

O Lord Jesus Christ, who didst set up Blessed Agnes before many virgins as a model and guide to evangelical perfection, grant, we beseech Thee, that the seraphic spirit, which she so wisely taught and confirmed by her holy example, may be preserved in us from all taint. Who livest and reignest forever and ever. Amen.

NOVEMBER 17
BLESSED SALOME
Virgin, Second Order

ALOME was a daughter of the royal family of Prince Lescon V, and a sister of Boleslas the Chaste, the virginal spouse of Blessed Kinga. She was born at Cracow, the capital of Poland, in 1201. At the age of three, according to the custom of the time, she was betrothed to Prince Colman of Hungary, a brother of St. Elizabeth of Thuringia, and was sent to the court of King Andrew II in order to be raised according to the customs of the country.

The little girl proved to be a child of grace and a model to all with whom she associated. When the day of her marriage arrived, both spouses resolved to preserve their virginity. They preserved their vow intact to the end of their lives.

The pious couple vied with each other in their practices of piety and penance. With the consent of her husband, Salome received the habit of the Third Order at the hands of her confessor, a Franciscan friar. Following her example, many of the ladies at the court renounced worldly pomp and vanity, and the palace took on the appearance of a convent. Even when her husband became king of Galicia, and Salome, in addition to the crown that was hers by birth, received a royal crown, she remained the simple daughter of St. Francis in the Order of Penance.

King Colman fell in battle against the Tatars in 1225. Salome then resolved to consecrate herself to God, and used her wealth in supporting the poor and in building churches. In 1240 she entered the convent of the Poor Clares at Zawichost. The convent was later removed to the vicinity of Cracow, to protect it against the inroads of the Tatars, and it was known as St. Mary of the Stairs. Here Salome continued to live for twenty-eight years, highly respected by her fellow sisters because of her virtue. On several occasions she was elected to the office of abbess.

When she was sixty-seven years old, she was seized with an illness one day during holy Mass, and she predicted that her death would follow shortly. Admonishing those about her deathbed to practice charity and harmony, and faithfully observe the rule, she died November 17, 1268, favored and fortified in her last hour with a vision of our Lady and the Child Jesus. A heavenly sign that she was receiving a third crown, the best of them all, was the fact that her sisters in religion, at the moment of her death, saw a brilliant star rise from her lips and mount to heaven.

When her body was exhumed seven months after burial, it was found incorrupt and giving forth a sweet odor. She was then entombed in the Franciscan church at Cracow beside her husband, King Colman. Many miracles occurred in testimony of her sanctity, whereupon Pope Clement X beatified her. The feast of Blessed Salome is observed by the three branches of the First Order on November seventeenth.

ON PURITY OF HEART

1. Consider how precious is the virtue of purity of heart, which shone so brightly in Blessed Salome. Christ pronounced Salome blessed in advance when He said: "Blessed are the clean of heart, for they shall see God" (Mt. 5,18). Blessed are such souls even here on earth, for they possess that interior bliss which results from a good conscience and from the right order of things preserved despite the warring emotions of the heart. The pure of heart also win the affections of their fellowmen, just as little children are beloved by everyone. The greatest blessing of purity, however, is the assurance of eternal happiness; for, says Eternal Truth, "they shall see God." — Should we not be eager to acquire this precious virtue?

2. Consider what constitutes purity of heart. It consists, not only in rejecting all indecent, impure desires and affections, but also in conquering all the other passions which stain the soul, especially injustice and avarice, pride and vanity, lying and deceit. In answer to the question as to who will be admitted to the vision of God, the Psalmist says: "The innocent in hands, and clean of heart, who has not taken his soul in vain, nor sworn deceitfully to his neighbor" (Ps. 23,4). — How do matters stand with you?

3. Consider how we can preserve purity of heart. Be ever mindful of the high origin of your soul. A person of high birth needs only to remember his distinguished extraction in order to refrain from doing anything unbecoming. Your soul is of a most distinguished origin. It has been created by God Himself according to His image and likeness; it has come forth from baptism a child of God and an heir of heaven. If sensuality, pride, or avarice attack your soul and threaten to stain it, say with Blessed

Salome: "I am of too noble an extraction, I am too distinguished in birth to yield to anything of that sort," and then banish the tempter with contempt. — Mindful, however, of your weakness, do not fail to plead with the prophet: "Create a clean heart in me, O God!" (Ps. 50,12).

PRAYER OF THE CHURCH

O God, who didst combine in Blessed Salome contempt of an earthly kingdom with the luster of virginity in the married state, grant, we beseech Thee, that imitating her example, we may serve Thee with a pure and humble heart and deserve to attain to the imperishable crown of glory in heaven. Through Christ our Lord. Amen.

NOVEMBER 18
BLESSED JANE OF SIGNA
Virgin, Third Order

ANE was born in 1244 near Signa, not far from Florence. Her parents were poor and devout peasants, and from her earliest years Jane tended her father's sheep. Prayer and meditation were her favorite pastime during the long solitary hours in meadow and wood. If she sought the company of other shepherds, it was not from boredom, but rather to pray with her associates or to show them how to serve God, avoid sin, and practice virtue. How pleasing this conduct was in the eyes of God was shown in the following incident.

A terrible storm broke out. Jane fled with her flock to the tree where she was accustomed to hold her pious gatherings, and lo, while a hailstorm and cloudburst raged all about, not a drop of water fell on Jane and her flock. Noticing this, the other shepherds sought out Jane with their flocks when a storm arose, and always they experienced the same wonderful protection. "Jane's tree," a giant oak measuring over fourteen feet in circumference, is alive to this day, and is religiously preserved by the people of the country in memory of the miracle.

At other times, the waters of the Arno were swollen by rain or melting snow and made an impassable barrier between Jane and her home. Full of confidence in God, Jane would then spread her cloak on the waters, and kneeling on it, she would reach the opposite shore in safety.

Led by curiosity and devotion, the people began to seek out the virgin and her flock. This wounded her humility as well as her love of recollection. So she laid aside her shepherd's staff, and sought her dearly loved solitude in another state of life.

About an hour's distance from her native town was the Franciscan convent of Carmignano. There Jane received the habit of the Third Order at the age of twenty-three, and then had herself shut up in a cell which she had constructed on the bank of the Arno. There she lived in great austerity and intimate union with God for forty years. At the same time she never wearied of comforting and assisting the poor, the sick, and the sorrowful who came to her. God bestowed on her extraordinary graces, and at her intercession granted miraculous assistance to many. A blind man received his sight again; a dear child was restored to life.

Her earthly sojourn ended on November 9, 1307, when she was sixty-three years old. A miraculous ringing of bells at the time attracted the townsfolk to her hermitage. As there was no door to the cell, the wall was broken down, and Jane was found lying dead on the floor, with a bundle of fagots under her head as a pillow, like a person asleep.

Her virginal remains repose in the parish church of St. John the Baptist, in a side chapel built for the purpose; and to this day her body is incorrupt. Her cell, too, has been preserved, although it has since been converted into a chapel. Because of the many miracles wrought at her tomb, especially during epidemics and floods, Pope Pius VI, on September 7, 1798, approved the continued veneration given to Blessed Jane, and permitted the celebration of her feast. The Franciscans observe the feast of Blessed Jane on November seventeenth, and the Conventuals on the ninth. (Cf. *These Made Peace*, pp. 34-37.)

ON CHILDLIKE CONFIDENCE IN GOD

1. The childlike confidence by which Blessed Jane obtained miraculous help for herself and others is a gift which God usually gives to simple and devout souls. They are conscious of their own helplessness, but they see in God a powerful and loving Father, to whom they hasten to make their needs known just as a child hastens to its mother. Other people think first of themselves, and count on their own wisdom and resources. When these means are exhausted, they next appeal to other people, and only when all means have failed and they begin to lose heart, do they turn to God. — Is it surprising that little help is forthcoming?

2. Consider the basis on which we should build up simple and childlike trust in God. This confidence must rest on our relations with God. We are His children. By creation we became God's children: "He gave us breath and life" (2 Mac. 7,32). By redemption and baptism we are His children in

a higher, supernatural way, so that by the love of our heavenly Father "we are called and should be the sons of God" (1 Jn. 3,1). No one in the world is so close to us as is God, our heavenly Father. Then why not at all times have our recourse to Him first of all? And He is a Father full of love. He has even assured us that if a mother should forget her children, He will not forget us (Is. 49,15). Moreover, His power is unlimited, so that He can help us in all our needs and put to flight all our foes. Then why not approach Him with unlimited confidence?

3. Consider that the man who persists in living in sins has no right to expect help from God, nor he who expects help in sinful, or vain and worldly designs; that would be presumption and blasphemy. But the penitent sinner may return to God with childlike confidence — that is why the Son of God related the parable of the prodigal son. Even in material things he may confidently hope that God will give him whatever promotes his temporal and eternal well-being. How contented and how fortunate we shall be, if in childlike simplicity, we confidently leave ourselves and our affairs in God's fatherly hands.

PRAYER OF THE CHURCH

O God, the friend of simple souls, who didst first of all reveal to shepherds the birth of Thy Divine Son, and who hast given us in Blessed Jane fresh examples of simplicity and innocence, grant that through her intercession Thy servants may follow her steps in the ways of simplicity of heart and innocence. Through the same Christ our Lord. Amen.

NOVEMBER 19
ST. ELIZABETH OF HUNGARY
Widow, Third Order

IN 1207 a daughter was born to pious King Andrew II of Hungary. She received the name of Elizabeth in baptism. The child was so lovable that the wealthy landgrave of Thuringia and Hesse sought her as the bride of his eldest son Louis. His request was granted, and a solemn embassy went to get Elizabeth, then only three years old, so that she could be raised at her future husband's castle.

The two children loved each other like brother and sister, and vied with each other in acts of piety and charity. Those who beheld Elizabeth at prayer might well have believed they saw an angel. Her greatest joy was to give things to the poor. When she grew a little older, she visited the poor and the sick, and waited on them with as much reverence as if she were serving Christ Himself.

The proud dowager Landgravine Sophia was displeased with Elizabeth's conduct and endeavored to talk her son into sending Elizabeth back to Hungary and choosing a bride of more princely ways. But Louis was aware of the treasure he possessed in Elizabeth. Succeeding his father at the age of eighteen he took over the government and married Elizabeth. Their marriage was unusually happy, and Louis gave his wife full liberty to do all the good her heart desired.

At Eisenach Elizabeth built a large hospital. During a famine she daily fed nine hundred needy people. The story is told that once when she was on her way with her cloak full of good things for her dear poor and sick, she met her husband, who teasingly blocked her path until she would show him what she was carrying away this time. How astonished was he to behold fresh, fragrant roses in midwinter. Reverently he permitted his spouse to go on her charitable way.

When Louis was away, it was Elizabeth's duty to take over the regency, and this she did with great prudence and care. Whatever spare time she had, she spent on the poor, the sick, and especially the lepers. It is related that once she took in a little leper boy whom no one cared to have about, and after caring for him as if he were her own child, placed him in the royal bed. But Louis returned unexpectedly at this time, and the angry dowager ran to tell him what Elizabeth had done and how she would surely cause him to be infected. Quite stirred, Louis went to the bed and tore aside the covers. But he was amazed and moved to tears when he beheld there the form of the Crucified. Turning to his wife, he said: "Dear Elizabeth, you may always receive guests like that. I shall even thank you for it."

But Elizabeth, too, was to be tried by the crucible of suffering. Emperor Frederick II set out on a crusade to the Holy Land in 1227, and pious Landgrave Louis joined the expedition. But he died on the way, in southern Italy. When the news reached Thuringia, Louis' brothers rose up against Elizabeth. She was driven out of the palace; only two faithful maids went with her. In Eisenach the people dared not give her shelter fearing the resentment of the new masters. It was midwinter and night was at hand. The daughter of a king, a widowed princess, with four little children, the youngest scarcely two months old, was completely destitute and homeless.

A man finally offered her shelter in a stable. Grateful for the kindness,

Elizabeth thought of how the Son of God on coming down from heaven, was refused admittance at all the doors of Bethlehem and found refuge in a stable. The thought filled her with greater joy than she had ever experienced in her palace. At midnight, when the bells of the nearby Franciscan convent, which she had built, announced the chanting of the Divine Office, she begged the friars to sing the Te Deum in thanksgiving for the favor that she and her children were made so like Jesus.

With her faithful servants, Elizabeth now arranged things as best she could. She spun flax for a livelihood, saving something from the meager income to give to the poor.

Later Elizabeth was reinstated in the Wartburg, and Emperor Frederick II, whose wife had died, asked her hand in marriage. But Elizabeth had so learned to love poverty and seclusion that she had no desire for worldly greatness. Her children were given the education due to princes, but she and her two maids repaired to a small house near the Franciscan church in Marburg. Elizabeth had joined the Third Order of St. Francis during the lifetime of her husband. Indeed, she was the first member in Germany, and received a message from St. Francis himself. Now, vested with the habit and the cord, she led a quiet religious life, meanwhile nursing the sick in the hospitals, and submitting her whole life to the direction of the learned and devout Friar Conrad.

Our Lord announced to her that He would soon call her to heaven. She told her Father Confessor, who had fallen seriously ill, that he would recover, but that she would die soon. Within four days she became ill, and was prepared for her final hour by her confessor, who had recovered.

Elizabeth was admitted into heaven on November 19, 1231, when she was only twenty-four years old. The miracles that took place at her tomb were so numerous that Pope Gregory IX canonized her already in 1235. She is the special patroness of the sisters of the Third Order Secular of St. Francis, and also of some religious sisterhoods of the Third Order Regular. Pope Leo XIII placed all charitable organizations of women under her patronage. The feast of St. Elizabeth is celebrated on November nineteenth by the three branches of the First Order as well as the Third Order Regular. (Cf. Nesta de Robeck, *Saint Elizabeth of Hungary*.)

ON NOBILITY OF SOUL

1. Consider how noble Elizabeth was by birth: the daughter of a king, the wife of a prince who governed a beautiful and wealthy country. But nobility of soul meant more to her who was God's child, destined to serve the Most High here on earth, and to be an heir of the heavenly kingdom.

Filled with the spirit of God, Elizabeth appreciated her dignity from childhood on. She found her sweetest delight in being united with God by prayer and pious practices, and her favorite occupation was to serve God in His poor and sick members. She did this with such holy sentiments that our Lord deigned to take the place of the leper she was nursing. She was always aware of the nobility of her own soul and acted accordingly. — Is your soul not equally noble? Are your sentiments and conduct in keeping with your nobility?

2. Many people believe that the way to maintain their dignity is by proud and domineering manners and by exterior pomp and finery. Elizabeth thought otherwise. She looked upon vain pomp as a form of slavery in which the soul basely serves the detestable vice of pride, the sin through which our first parents lost their nobility in Paradise. The Son of God gave His own blood to atone for that sin; and only by means of that royal purple have we been restored to the position of children of God. That is why Elizabeth loathed everything that savored of pride, always remaining as humble and submissive as a child. — Do you permit the nobility of your soul to be sullied by pride and vanity?

3. Consider how almighty God prepares the soul, which He has endowed with such nobility, for its destiny in eternity. In company with all the angels and saints the soul is to enjoy the most intimate union with God. That is why God permits many trials and hardships to come upon human beings, so that their fidelity may be proved and everything unworthy may first be removed. But he who tries to escape the test of the cross and seeks sensual pleasures makes himself unworthy of nobility of soul and exposes himself to the danger of losing it. He who wants to be faithful to God but submits only imperfectly to His ordinances must pass through a severe purification in purgatory before he can enter heaven. Only the soul that has been thoroughly purified here on earth can be admitted to heaven immediately after death. When Elizabeth departed from this life, her soul was radiant in the full brilliance of its nobility. In trials she had thanked God in the words of the Te Deum; and then she submitted to the strict guidance of a confessor who completed the preparation of her soul for heaven. — While there is time, prepare your soul so that, when you die, it may be ready for heaven.

PRAYER OF THE CHURCH

Enlighten, O God of mercy, the hearts of Thy faithful, and through the prayers of Blessed Elizabeth, do Thou cause us to think little of worldly prosperity and ever to be gladdened by that consolation which is of heaven. Through Christ our Lord. Amen.

❧❧❧❧❧❧❧❧❧❧❧❧

NOVEMBER 20
BLESSED ELIZABETH THE GOOD
Virgin, Third Order

LIZABETH was born November 25, 1386, at Waldsee, Württemberg. Her father, John Achler, and his pious mother reared her from youth in the fear and love of God. As a child she was quite generally called Die Gute Beth — "Good Beth," because of her great charity and meekness. She joined the Third Order Secular when she was fourteen.

At the age of seventeen, following her spiritual director's advice, Elizabeth entered the convent of the Third Order Regular at Reute, near her native town. She bent all her efforts to do everything, even the smallest things, as perfectly as possible, so that her confessor declares in her biography, he could often find no matter for absolution. Although the rules of her community did not prescribe strict enclosure, nevertheless Elizabeth so loved solitude and retirement that she never crossed the threshold of her convent; she was, therefore, often called the anchoress.

In order to purify her, our Lord sent her severe spiritual sufferings. He even permitted her associates to look upon her as a hypocrite and to treat her as such. But she persevered with an even frame of mind in charity, patience, and humility, and she was finally vindicated in a very striking way.

God also sent her acute and severe maladies. Meditation on the sufferings of our Saviour was her sweetest comfort during these sieges, and she was frequently heard to cry out: "O Lord, why dost Thou not punish me still more? Oh, let me understand Thy holy sufferings, and experience the pains Thou didst endure!" Her one regret was that in younger days she had not reflected enough on the sufferings of our Saviour.

Almighty God rewarded her steadfastness with supernatural graces, and permitted her to discern the secrets of the human heart and of the future. While the Council of Constance was in session, she foretold the settlement of the schism which existed in the Church at the time, and the election of Pope Martin V. Toward the close of her life, our Lord favored her with the marks of His five wounds.

He called her to Himself on the thirty-fourth anniversary of her birth,

November 25, 1420. In her agony she asked that the story of our Lord's suffering be read to her, and at the words, "And He gave up the ghost," she, too, surrendered her pure soul into the hands of God. Immediately after her death the people began venerating her as a saint, and Pope Clement VIII approved her veneration. Her remains repose in a precious shrine in the convent church at Reute, and to this day numerous devout pilgrims travel there in order to invoke her intercession. Her feast is observed on November seventeenth by the Franciscans, and on the twenty-fifth by the Conventuals. (Cf. *These Made Peace,* pp. 122-125.)

ON THE SUFFERINGS OF CHRIST

1. Blessed Elizabeth drew sweet consolation from the sufferings of Christ. The only regret she had was that she had not made them the object of her meditation sooner. In the sufferings of Christ she appreciated the love which the Son of God bears humankind, and the more she reflected on the severity and anguish of this suffering, the more clearly she perceived the great love of Christ. That was sweet comfort to her. — Do we not find consolation in recalling the sacrifices that another has endured for our sake? With the Apostle each of us must say of the sacrifice of Christ: "He loved me and delivered Himself for me" (Gal. 2,20).

2. Consider how dear the sufferings of Christ must be to us when we reflect on what they accomplished. They redeemed us from our sins and saved us from eternal damnation. They are the price of our soul. That was the thought Elizabeth had, and that is why she consecrated her whole life to her Redeemer, and kept aloof from human beings as much as possible. The Apostle says also to us: "You are bought with a price, be not made the bond slaves of men" (1 Cor. 7,23); and again: "For you are bought with a great price. Glorify and bear God in your body" (1 Cor. 6,20). — Do you glorify and serve God, who bought you at so great a price, or must you admit that you are a slave of human respect or perhaps of your lower passions?

3. Consider that Blessed Elizabeth regarded the sufferings of Christ as precious balm to comfort and strengthen her in the spiritual afflictions heaven sent her. If your soul grows weary in the struggle against temptation; if it is almost ready to collapse under the burden of material trouble and worry, then think of your Saviour and how He was tempted by the devil, persecuted by the Jews, and tormented by weariness and hunger. If you have to endure bodily sufferings and various maladies, look devoutly on your suffering Saviour in the Garden of Gethsemane, at the pillar of the scourging, crowned with thorns, and hanging on the cross.

You will then bear your sufferings more patiently for the sake of Him who suffered much more for love of you.

PRAYER OF THE CHURCH

May the devotion to the sufferings of Thine only-begotten Son increase in us, O Lord, and may the remembrance of them be steadily enlivened in our hearts after the example of Thy virgin Blessed Elizabeth. Through Christ our Lord. Amen.

NOVEMBER 21
THE SERVANT OF GOD RUFINUS OF ASSISI
Confessor, First Order

UFINUS, born in Assisi, descended from a noble family, and was a cousin of St. Clare. In 1210 he became a follower of St. Francis as a brother, and thus he was one of the Poverello's early companions. Possessing great purity of soul, he had the gift of prayer and of contemplation in an unusual degree. He waited on St. Francis with special affection in times of illness, and thus had occasion to be one of the first to see the five wounds which St. Francis received and so carefully concealed. Later he often gave testimony concerning the stigmata.

In spite of his childlike simplicity, he experienced some of the severest temptations and struggles. One day he was filled with great sadness, for it seemed to him that he was rejected by God and destined for eternal damnation. To add to the confusion, Satan appeared to him in the form of the crucifix and said to him: "O Brother Rufinus, foolish man! Since you are not one of those who are predestined to eternal life, enjoy the pleasures of this world as long as you can. Do not afflict yourself with such severe penances. Above all, have nothing to do with this madcap son of Pietro Bernardone, who is a greater son of iniquity than you are."

Filled with fear, Rufinus was seized with even greater sadness, but spoke to nobody about it, not even to St. Francis, since mistrust of Francis had entered into his heart. Enlightened by God, St. Francis knew what was bothering the soul of his disciple. He showed Rufinus how he had been deceived, and told him that, if the devil ever appeared to him again, he was to turn away from him in disgust and remember that he was an angel of darkness.

When Satan again appeared to Rufinus in the form of the crucifix and addressed reproaches to him because he had revealed everything to the "son of Bernardone," Rufinus promptly and with holy indignation told him that he was the father of lies and should depart. The evil spirit left, and with him went the temptation and the dryness of spirit with which Rufinus had been afflicted.

Rufinus now served God again with joy and with greater confidence in St. Francis than he had hitherto known. He lived about a half century after the death of St. Francis, and was able to speak of his virtues and miracles as an eyewitness. His bones rest in the Basilica of St. Francis at Assisi, where the remains of other early disciples of the Poverello have likewise been placed.

ON THE TEMPTATION OF DIFFIDENCE

1. Consider how dangerous is the temptation to lose confidence. It is the temptation that came over Brother Rufinus and that still tortures many souls who are trying to serve God. If souls who are given to sadness and melancholy do not receive an early answer to prayers, they give way to the feeling that God does not hear their prayers, and they believe it is useless for them to pray. And for that very reason their further prayers are fruitless, because they are lacking in confidence. "Let not that man think that he shall receive anything of the Lord" (Jas. 1,7). Then the enemy often comes along and increases this distrust to the point of despair. How many a soul has fallen a prey to these snares, and given itself over to a life of worldly pleasure resulting in eternal ruin! Cast from you the first inclination to distrust of God as soon as it assails you; say with the Apostle: "I know whom I have believed" (2 Tim. 1,12), and with holy Job, "Although he should kill me, I will trust in him" (Job 13,15). — The temptation will surely vanish if you act thus.

2. Consider that the temptation to lose trust in God is usually bound up, as in the case of Brother Rufinus, with distrust in those who have been appointed by God to guide us: our parents, religious superiors, and especially our Father Confessor. The tempter knows only too well how important it is for us to have confidence in these persons, if their guidance is to help us and promote our advancement in virtue. Christ Himself has said of them: "He who hears you, hears me" (Lk. 10,16). That is why the enemy of our salvation seeks to prejudice us against them under all sorts of pretexts. There is no salvation in such cases but to make the snare known, disclosing the difficulties to one's confessor in a childlike way and trusting him rather than the serpent. — Have you always done that?

3. Consider that there is a kind of distrust that is really beneficial. It is distrust of self: of our own insight, our own strength, our own constancy. One reason why many a soul begins to distrust God and His representatives is because it believes it knows better than anyone else what is good and beneficial for it. But woe to the person who relies upon himself! Commit yourself with childlike confidence to the guidance of God and those whom He has placed over you. Then you may trustfully say: "In thee, O Lord, have I hoped, let me never be confounded" (Ps. 30,2).

PRAYER OF THE CHURCH
(Over the People, Wednesday in Passion Week)

Give ear to our prayers, almighty God, and on those to whom Thou grantest confidence in Thy loving kindness, bestow also the effects of Thy wonted mercies. Through Christ our Lord. Amen.

NOVEMBER 22
THE SERVANT OF GOD MAGÍN CATALA
Confessor, First Order

F the one hundred and thirty Franciscans who labored as missionaries in the famous "old missions" of the state of California during the three-quarters of a century from 1769 to 1845, the one who, more than any other, gained the reputation of being a saint was Father Magín Catalá, the Holy Man of Santa Clara.

He and a twin brother were born in January, 1761, at Montblanch in Catalonia, Spain. Their father was a doctor and notary, and their mother was the daughter of a prominent merchant. Both gave their children an example of genuine piety. Magín joined the Franciscans in Barcelona when he was sixteen, and eight years later he was ordained a priest. The following year, 1786, he was permitted to join the Mission College of San Fernando in Mexico City; and there he remained until 1792, when he was sent to the California missions.

Arriving at Monterey in July, 1793, he was appointed chaplain of the Saavedra expedition to Nootka, on the west coast of Vancouver Island. A year later he returned, and was sent to Santa Clara Mission. Here he remained for the rest of his life, a period of thirty-six years. After three years he was made senior missionary and henceforth devoted himself exclusively to the spiritual care of the Indians, while his companion, Father Viader, had charge of material affairs. Besides the Indians who lived at Santa Clara, there were ten other Indian settlements which belonged to the mission; and these were regularly visited by the missionaries.

During the thirty-six years that Father Magín was at Santa Clara Mission, no less than five thousand persons were baptized, nearly all of them Indians. Father Magín was soon afflicted with a very painful sickness, inflammatory rheumatism; and though this malady caused him constant suffering, he continued to minister to the Indians faithfully and perseveringly. Twice, in 1800 and 1804, he received permission to go back to Mexico; but each time his love for the Indians kept him at his post.

That in itself was heroism of a high degree, but Father Magín added other penances; and he spent long nights in prayer before the Blessed Sacrament in the mission church, and before a life-size crucifix, which still occupies a place of honor in the restored mission church. Eyewitnesses declared that the figure of the Crucified Saviour was seen to bend down to embrace Father Magín and to lift him above the ground. When Father Magín died at daybreak on November 22, 1830, the Indians cried: "The saint has left us!" He was buried on the Gospel side of the sanctuary in the church; and in 1907, after the restoration of the church, the Jesuits of Santa Clara University transferred his remains to a newly prepared vault in the same place, to the left of the Altar of the Crucifix. There the devout faithful may still be seen visiting Father Magín's grave and asking his intercession at the throne of God, as did the early Californians who used to pray: "Soul of Padre Magín, assist me!"

About a half century after the death of Father Magín, in 1882, a movement was set on foot for his beatification. Two years later, at the canonical process held in California, sixty-two witnesses of Padre Magín's personal virtues and holiness of life were examined; and the acts of the ecclesiastical court were sent to Rome. Interest in the cause of Father Magín was revived in 1907; and after a second process was conducted in California in 1908 and 1909, the documents were taken to Rome the following year. The cause of Father Magín's beatification is still pending in Rome. A prayer for the successful completion of the cause was authorized by Archbishop Hanna of San Francisco in 1916, and approved once more by Archbishop Mitty in 1937. In recent years new interest in the cause has been aroused by Father Aloysius Stern, S.J., who as a missionary to the Indians at Nootka, Vancouver Island, experienced the power of Father Magín's intercession in 1909, when his efforts were suddenly crowned with success after five disheartening years. (Cf.

Engelhardt, *The Holy Man of Santa Clara*; and a pamphlet compiled by Father Stern and distributed by the University of San Francisco.)

ON GRATITUDE FOR THE TRUE FAITH

1. We give so little thought to the gift of the Faith. The servant of God Father Magín was well aware of the great grace of faith, and the knowledge impelled him to do all in his power to bring this gift to the Indians. And how grateful they were to him for leading them into the fold of the Faith. It is to be feared that our dear Lord has reason to find fault with the most of us: "If you knew the gift of God!" (Jn. 4,10). — Repeat with heart and lips: "O God, accept my thanks for the gift of the true Faith."

2. We give so little thought to the blessings associated with the Faith. Everything depends on the words of Christ: "He who believes and is baptized shall be saved" (Mk. 16,16). The end toward which the Faith leads us is the vision of God in a blessed eternity. That bliss no eye has seen, nor ear heard, neither has it entered into the heart of man. — May this thought awaken in us sentiments of sincere gratitude for the Faith.

3. How shall we manifest our gratitude for the gift and the blessings of faith? Offer up holy Mass and Communion frequently in thanksgiving. Gratitude is pleasing to God; and yet it is a rare thing. Live according to the teachings of your Faith and guard yourself and those entrusted to your care from the enemies of the Faith. Remove from your homes all godless papers and magazines! Cease to procure from the libraries books that undermine the Faith! Be zealous to promote the Faith! — Have you acted in this manner?

PRAYER OF THE CHURCH

Almighty and eternal God, who didst grant Thy servants by professing the true Faith, to acknowledge the glory of the Eternal Trinity and also to worship the Unity in the power of Thy majesty; we beseech Thee, that by steadfastness in this Faith we may at all times be defended from all adversity. Through Christ our Lord. Amen.

NOVEMBER 23
BLESSED JOHN BAPTIST BULLAKER
Martyr, First Order

HIS MARTYR of the Franciscan Order was born at Chichester, England, in 1604. He was the only son of a devout physician, and received the name of Thomas in baptism. When he was eighteen years old, he resolved to become a priest and a missionary. At first he thought of going to the missions in the West Indies; but when it was pointed out to him later on that England was a preferable field for his labors, he gladly returned to his native land and there won the martyr's crown.

Because all the Catholic institutions had been suppressed in England, he first went to France, where with the consent of his zealous parents he studied at the Jesuit College at St. Omer.

About this time God filled him with a strong desire to enter the Franciscan Order. And so, when he was nineteen years old, he was invested with the habit of St. Francis in the convent of Our Lady of the Ladder of Heaven in Valladolid, Spain, receiving the name of John Baptist.

He was ordained to the priesthood in 1628, and soon afterwards he was sent by his superiors as a missionary to England. On foot and without money, he set out on his journey. At Bordeaux he met the captain of a ship who volunteered to take him to England. The captain proved to be a traitor. As soon as they arrived in England, he turned Father John over to a magistrate. But Providence spared Father John for still greater things; for, unaccountably he gained his freedom. For fourteen years he then worked in secret, amid many hardships, persecutions, and dangers of all sorts. He undertook the task of comforting Catholics who had been imprisoned, strengthening them through the holy sacraments.

In 1640 it was revealed to him that he would die a martyr's death. On Sunday, September 11, 1642, a maid in one of the houses in London where he was accustomed to say holy Mass in secret, betrayed him to an apostate for five pieces of gold. This man arrested him during the celebration of holy Mass and dragged him before a magistrate in London.

Father John professed and defended his religion with great candor and invincible firmness, and so he was condemned to death. He was placed on a hurdle and dragged through the muddy streets to Tyburn, the place of execution. Unafraid, and filled with holy joy, the martyr mounted the ladder to the gallows. The sheriff then hanged him, and while he yet breathed, the usual barbarous practice of quartering was inflicted on him, his heart, still palpitating, being shown to the crowd. Finally, his head was struck off and placed on a pole on London bridge, and the four pieces of his body on the four gates of the city.

All this took place before a great crowd of people on October 12, 1642. In 1929 Pope Pius XI beatified him together with one hundred and thirty-five other martyrs. Strangely enough, the feast of Blessed John Baptist Bullaker has not been added to any of the Franciscan calendars. (Cf. *Forum*, 1942, pp. 338-340; Steck, *Franciscans and the Protestant Revolution*, pp. 251-271.)

ON THE VALUE OF THE HOLY SACRAMENTS

1. How highly Blessed John Baptist Bullaker must have regarded the holy sacraments. He exposed himself to the risk of losing his life amid painful torture in order to bring the consolation of the sacraments to his countrymen. He was right, for the holy sacraments are the precious channels of grace by means of which our Saviour dispenses His grace to mankind for their purification and salvation. It was not too much for our Divine Saviour to undertake a life of hardship and death on the Cross in order to make the stream of divine grace, which had been stopped by sin, once more accessible to mankind. So Father John thought it should not be too much for His servants to risk their lives in order to direct the stream of grace to men through the channels of the holy sacraments. — Do you regard the sacraments and the dispensers of them in this light?

2. Reflect on the wisdom of Christ our Lord in providing for all human needs by means of the seven sacraments. In baptism original sin is effaced and man is born again to the life of sanctifying grace. In confirmation the life of grace is strengthened against the storms of the world, and by means of the Sacrament of the Altar it is nourished. Penance restores life if it was lost after baptism. Extreme unction remits the remains of sin and strengthens the soul for its last struggle and its passage to eternity. By means of holy orders, the ministers of the sacraments and the teachers of Christendom continue to function, and matrimony provides for the continuation and education of the Christian people. — Admire the wisdom of Christ and thank Him fervently for having made you a child of the Catholic Church in which alone the sacraments are duly and validly dispensed.

3. Consider that we must do our part if the sacraments are to produce their proper effects. Since grace is extended to us each time the sacraments are validly administered, it is for us to see to it that no obstacle be in the way of our receiving the grace. A mortal sin on our soul would be a fatal hindrance, making it impossible for us to receive the fruits of

Christ's bloody sacrifice on the Cross — it would be a sacrilege. Venial sin and inordinate attachment to material things tend to prevent us from receiving the fullness of the graces which would otherwise be ours. — Woe to the person who approaches the sacraments sacrilegiously! Should we not exercise the greatest care that the sacraments may have their fullest effect in us?

PRAYER OF THE CHURCH
(Postcommunion on Saturday in September Ember Week)

May Thy sacraments, we beseech Thee, O Lord, perfect in us what they contain, that we may receive in truth what we now celebrate under outward signs. Through Christ our Lord. Amen.

NOVEMBER 24
THE SERVANT OF GOD MARGARET SINCLAIR
Virgin, Second Order

 CHARMING mystery of divine grace is presented to us in the life of Margaret Sinclair. The cradle of this servant of God, who was born in 1900, was in the house of a simple and devout workingman's family in Edinburgh. Her whole life bears the impress of simple ways and childlike sentiment. In her solicitude for the salvation of the soul of a wayward boy, Margaret kept company with him for nearly three years, always declining his proposals of marriage with the remark that she had no desire to marry.

Life in a large city is always attended with special dangers for youth, but Margaret armed herself against them by intimate friendship with our Saviour in the tabernacle and in holy Communion. Her associates in the furniture factory where she worked for several years kept a careful guard over their language when Margaret was about, for, they said, "she is a saintly girl."

But this does not mean that she was long-faced and forbidding in manner. The contrary is the case. She possessed the real Franciscan disposition, which is always cheerful and spreads sunshine everywhere. She enjoyed games, she danced, she loved music and attractive clothes, and took the greatest delight in making other people happy. But her conversation, her letters and her diary manifested a depth of thought and knowledge surpassing that of educated girls of her age. To a friend whom she was trying to attract to the practice of daily holy Communion she said: "You should not go to holy Communion because you are good, but because you are trying and want to be good."

At last this working girl yielded to the attraction she had always felt for convent life and joined the Poor Clares. "Oh, yes," she said to her confessor, who was sounding her out, "matrimony is a great sacrament, but I wish to be alone with my Saviour." On July 21, 1923, she was received as a postulant at the Poor Clare convent in London, and the following year she was clothed with the holy habit. A year later she made her profession as an extern sister. She had now entered upon her life's career, but little did she dream that it would be short-lived.

Margaret had contracted tuberculosis of the throat, and shortly after profession she was obliged to go to a sanitarium. This was a great trial for the young Poor Clare. She said in her own simple way: "The life of a Poor Clare is made up of prayer and penance. That is exactly what I have here: prayer and penance." And so, despite her sufferings, Sister Mary Frances of the Five Wounds, as she was known in religion, was always cheerful, happy, and contented. Those about her drew inspiration from her fortitude. A visiting priest remarked: "If she belongs to the slums, she is only another example of the miracles of God's grace, which we priests are privileged to witness in the souls of those who, though materially poor, are rich in the things of the spirit."

She suffered untold agony for more than six months, but she retained a clear mind to the very end. Her one desire was to be with God. Her confessor reports that she suffered a veritable purgatory in a certain thirst of the soul which baffled description, and which sometimes poured itself out in the whisper: "I want to see Him!"

Margaret's beautiful death was the echo of the holy life of a beautiful soul. She was filled with joy at being permitted to go to God. She died on November 24, 1925. Although she had spent but twenty-five years on earth, she was rich in merits and ripe for heaven. Her body, at first buried at Kensall Green Cemetery, Notting Hill, was later brought back to her home town and now rests in Mt. Vernon Cemetery at Liberton. The process of her beatification is now being carried on in Rome. (Cf. *Forum*, 1942, p. 280.)

THE DUTIES OF OUR VOCATION

1. The duties of our state of life and the Christian religion harmonize well with each other. Those who read the life story of Margaret Sinclair will probably ask: "What did she do that is so extraordinary?" But neither sainthood nor religion require anything extraordinary; they are found rather in the simple, ordinary fulfillment of the duties of our state of life.

The Apostle writes: "Endeavor to be quiet, and do your business, and work with your own hands as we command you" (1 Thess. 4,11). — Simple, ordinary, and faithful, let that also be your motto.

2. Cheerfulness is also compatible with religion and holiness. This, too, is evident in the life of Sister Mary Frances. She was always cheerful. She spread sunshine everywhere by her straightforward and unaffected cheerfulness and good humor. And why not? It is written: "Serve the Lord with gladness" (Ps. 99,2). And Christ commanded His disciples: "May My joy be in you and your joy be filled" (Jn. 15,11). How foolish are they, then, who believe that religion and cheerfulness are opposed to each other. — Let us also manifest to the world by a truly genuine spirit of cheerfulness that we are good Christians.

3. Recreation is likewise compatible with religion and piety. Let us again look at the life of Margaret Sinclair. She took pleasure in attractive clothes, in dancing, in music, in games, and yet she became a saint. All that is necessary is that we strive to sanctify our recreation as well as our work by the right intention. "Wine and music rejoice the heart; but the love of wisdom is above them both" (Eccli. 40,20). We should not be too absorbed in these things and make them an end in themselves, but rather use them in moderation in order to serve God better and more cheerfully. — Let us, then, be sensible in our attitude toward recreation.

PRAYER OF THE CHURCH

O God, the protector of those who hope in Thee, without whom nothing is strong, nothing holy, pour forth Thy mercies in us, so that under Thy guidance and direction we may so pass through the things of time, that we may not lose those of eternity. Through Christ our Lord. Amen.

𝕺𝕽𝕯𝕺𝕽𝕯𝕺𝕽𝕯𝕺𝕽𝕯𝕺𝕽𝕯

NOVEMBER 25
THE SERVANT OF GOD PAUL PIUS PERAZZO
Confessor, Third Order

ERAZZO was not a hermit, nor a friar, but an everyday train dispatcher, proof again that no station in life is a hindrance to holiness. Moreover, he did not live several hundred years ago; but he belongs to our own times, having died as recently as 1911, and he is already far along the way to be declared blessed.

Turin, the city that has gained fame because of the saintly Tertiary priests it produced — Don Bosco, Cottolengo, and Cafasso — is also associated with the name of Paul Pius Perazzo. He was born on July 5, 1846, at Nizza, Monferrato; and his excellent parents raised their boy to be one of God's little soldiers. He regarded everything with an astounding awareness of God's providence. One day, as a little boy, he was fanning the coals in the open fireplace, and stumbled right into the coals. His clothes caught fire and he got some very bad burns. But he never uttered a whimper, nor shed a tear. Ruefully regarding his crippled thumb, he said merely: "Mamma, I guess I shall never be able to write again; that thumb will not behave any more."

He once lost first place in class, and the professor felt called upon to sympathize with him. "Never mind, Paul, you'll beat him again next time." "Oh, professor," said Paul with genuine astonishment in his tone, "I have never thought of studying to beat others. Only for the fun of it, and because that is what I am here for."

But he devoted himself to studies in such a way that it began taking a toll on his health. So his priestly uncle, who supervised his studies, advised that he get a job before it was too late. And that is how Paul got to be a railroader.

He found it difficult to give up formal application to study, and continued privately to keep himself informed on certain subjects that would be serviceable to him in railroad work. He worked for five years without a salary, sometimes for ten, twelve, or more hours a day. He got to be a small-town freight clerk then, and in 1867 he was promoted to Turin itself.

Meanwhile a nice young lady fell in love with the dignified and yet charming young railroad clerk. Her mother consulted Mother Perazzo. Since it was really a desirable match, for the girl was a good girl and well-to-do, Paul's mother put the case before him. "Just as you say, mother," was the reply. But his mother had no intention of deciding the matter for him: "It is for you to say, not for me," she told him. "Very well then, mother," he replied, "if I am to make the choice, shall we say the affair is off once and for all?" And that is how it happened that Paul lived and died a bachelor.

But he took another bride, and that was the Church. He became more and more interested and posted in the doctrines of the Church, the better to meet the anti-Catholic and anti-religious attacks that were so bitter at that time, especially among men of his class. He joined the Third Order of St. Francis on St. Joseph's day in 1875, and became a real apostle of the truth by word and example. That gained for him the respect of his associates, but it also brought upon him the hardest trial an ambitious young man can meet. Young Perazzo was making good when the crudest and most unjust discrimination was launched against him on account of his religious convictions and his refusal to drop the practice of his religion.

It showed itself first in little annoyances. His pay was not raised, while that of others around him, who owed everything to him, rose constantly. In 1886, after twenty-five years of service, he was indeed made assistant freight agent at Porta Nuova in Turin, and two years later chief agent. But then, unreasonable duties had also been added to his work and every pretext was found to rob him of his holidays.

When the time came that he was eligible for promotion, he was totally ignored and younger men got the coveted positions. He remained freight agent at Porta Nuova for twenty years without a promotion or an increase in salary. An influential friend made an appeal in his behalf, only to be repulsed with the contemptuous remark that "the government has no money for prayer-patterers like Perazzo or to give favors to priests and monks." In Italy, as in other European countries, it must be remembered, the railroads are operated by the government.

In 1911 he would have completed fifty years of service and been eligible for a pension; but, instead, they found reason to dismiss him with two days' notice in the year 1908. He died November 22, 1911, in the year that he should have been pensioned, and went to his true home where services like his receive a just reward. People began speaking of him and honoring him as a saint; and his cause of beatification is now pending in Rome. (Cf. *Forum,* 1938, pp. 475-476; and 1953, pp. 287-288.)

ADVERSITIES ARE STEPPING-STONES TO SANCTITY

1. When we reflect on the heroic manner in which Paul Perazzo bore the annoyances and injustices inflicted on him in his work, we are not surprised that his process for beatification was set on foot immediately after his death. God had tried His servant and had found him faithful. "Gold and silver are tried in the fire, but acceptable men in the furnace of humiliation" (Eccli. 2,5). And St. James says: "Blessed is the man who endures temptation; for, when he has been proved, he shall receive the crown of life." — Can you expect to receive a crown if you are not willing to bear a trial in patience?

2. The trials of Paul Perazzo extended over nearly half a century. A less saintly man would soon have given up the Faith or at least have ceased to love and practice it; or he would have grown embittered with everything and everybody. Not so, Paul Perazzo. He stuck to his job, was faithful to

his religious practices, and sociable with his fellow workers. He used these trials as stepping-stones to sanctity, and though the road was long and weary at times, he was rewarded in the end when the God of sanctity welcomed him to the land of eternal rest. — If in our trials and sufferings we imitate the conduct of Paul Perazzo, we, too, shall attain to a degree of sanctity that will be our passport to heavenly bliss.

3. The extent of our love of God is manifested by the manner in which we bear the trials He sends us. "Brave as death itself is love." That has been demonstrated by the holy martyrs. But those who have shed their blood for the Faith are not the only martyrs. Fidelity to duty can be a slow martyrdom, requiring sacrifice and sufferings that are equal to bodily martyrdom and sometimes demanding greater fortitude because of the length of time involved. Here again we can look up to the servant of God Paul Perazzo as a shining example of this twentieth century. Love of God alone could have induced him to hold fast to the Faith, when he found himself persecuted because of his religious convictions and afflicted with trials that were indeed a test of heroic sanctity. But he persevered, and as St. Matthew tells us (24,13), "He who shall persevere to the end, shall be saved." — Profit by the trials of life so that you will gain the strength and courage of Paul Perazzo, and they will become stepping-stones from earth to heaven.

PRAYER OF THE CHURCH
(Secret, Eleventh Sunday after Pentecost)

Look with mercy, we beseech Thee, O Lord, upon our homage, that the Gift we offer may be accepted by Thee and be the support of our frailty. Through Christ our Lord. Amen.

✸✸✸✸✸✸✸✸✸

NOVEMBER 26
ST. LEONARD OF PORT MAURICE
Confessor, First Order

LEONARD was born in 1676 at Port Maurice, a seaport near Genoa, the son of Dominic Casanova, a ship captain. Dominic raised his children with so much care that three of his sons entered the Franciscan Order, and his only daughter took the veil.

When Leonard was thirteen years old, he went to Rome to enter the renowned Roman college where St. Aloysius once pursued his studies. There he so distinguished himself by piety, diligence, and good works that he was called another Aloysius. After completing his college studies he thought of entering the medical profession. But he soon perceived that God was calling him to another state of life. He happened to visit the church connected with the Franciscan convent of St. Bonaventure in Rome when the choir intoned the verse at Compline, "Converte nos Deus, salutaris noster! — Convert us, O God, our salvation!" The young man was strangely impressed by these words and took them as a call from heaven to enter the order and devote himself to God's service.

On October 2, 1697, his request for the holy habit was granted, and eventually he became the glory of the friary of St. Bonaventure. His exact observance of the rule was admirable; likewise his fervor at prayer, his burning love of Jesus and Mary, his rigorous penance, his humility, and his tireless charity toward bis neighbor. It was his ardent desire to preach the Gospel to the pagans in China and to shed his blood for the Faith. But his delicate constitution for a while even prevented him from preaching. Consumption seemed to have claimed him as a victim; but, at the intercession of the Blessed Virgin, he was miraculously restored to health.

He now devoted himself with renewed zeal to parish missions. Amid great hardships and dangers, he spent twenty-four years as a missionary, covering every section of Italy and the island of Corsica, which was then notorious for lawless inhabitants. The power of his words made a deep impression because of his strict life; and he converted innumerable sinners. Meanwhile he did not forget himself. For his benefit and that of his brethren engaged in preaching missions, he built a retreat house at Incontro near Florence, where the missionaries could withdraw for a time in order to prepare themselves for future activities by a life of seclusion and penance. During his sojourns there, he scourged his body without compassion in order to obtain mercy for himself and for poor sinners. Then he wrote down his well-known resolutions, which he kept until his death.

In Rome he founded several pious confraternities, especially that of the Sacred Heart. He taught the people frequently to say the little ejaculation: "My Jesus, mercy!" Wherever he went, he spread the devotion of the Way of the Cross and perpetual adoration of the Blessed Sacrament. In a special manner he also fostered devotion to the Immaculate Conception of the Blessed Virgin; and to the intercession of the Immaculate Virgin he attributed all the good he had ever received or done in his life.

Pope Benedict XIV held Father Leonard in high esteem. The pope secured the promise from him not to die in any other city but Rome, and Father Leonard kept his promise. Returning to Rome from a mission in Bologna, he died in the convent of St. Bonaventure, November 26, 1751. God glorified him in life but still more after his death by numerous miracles. Pope Pius VI, who had known him personally, beatified him in 1796; and Pope Pius IX canonized him June 29, 1867. Pope Pius XI appointed him patron of all parish missionaries. His feast is celebrated by the Franciscans and the Conventuals on November twenty-sixth, and by the Third Order Regular on the twenty-seventh. (Cf. *Forum*, 1949, pp. 355-358.)

ON PARISH MISSIONS

1. Filled with zeal for souls, St. Leonard desired to go to the foreign missions, but God had destined him to give missions to the Christian people of his own country. Urgent though it may be to spread the Faith among the heathens, it is sometimes more necessary to make believers in Christ live according to their faith. "If you be the children of Abraham," Christ said to the Jews, "do the works of Abraham" (Jn. 8,39). There is at times great need to revive that spirit. Evil conditions creep in. Young people become dissolute, older people grow careless and lukewarm, so that it is necessary from time to time to employ extraordinary means to correct these conditions. Zealous priests then arrange to have a mission given in their parishes. — Have you always recognized their importance?
2. Consider what a blessing a mission is for a parish. The missionaries, sent by their spiritual superiors, can say with the Apostle: "We are ambassadors of Christ, God, as it were, exhorting by us. For Christ, we beseech you, be reconciled to God" (2 Cor. 5,20). Moreover, they bring with them, so to say, the special grace of God, so that mission days are days of greater salvation than other days. All are admonished: "Today when you hear his voice, harden not your hearts!" (Ps. 94,8). The most hardened sinners are converted, enmities are reconciled, injustices are rectified, the hearts of all are drawn to God, and the happy priest can say with the prophet: "O Lord, remember no longer our iniquities. Behold, see, we are all thy people" (Is. 64,9). — Do what you can to make missions as effective as possible.
3. Consider that the salvation of those for whom a mission is conducted depends on whether or not they derive fruit from the mission. Your heart should not be like a sand pile, which grows very warm when the sun beats down on it, but remains as barren as before. It is necessary to put into practice what you learn at the mission: faithful observance of the laws of

God, perseverance in complying with the duties of your state of life, of justice, patience, fraternal charity, piety. In order to persevere, do as St. Leonard so urgently advised: receive the sacraments frequently and regularly, join pious confraternities and faithfully observe their regulations, recommend yourself often to the Blessed Mother of God, and keep a careful guard on yourself, so that, should you ever stray from the path of duty, you may at once repent and return to your first fervor. — Have you kept the resolutions you made at the last mission?

PRAYER OF THE CHURCH

O God, who didst clothe Thy confessor, St. Leonard, with admirable sanctity and invincible power of speech that he might move the hardened hearts of sinners to penance by his preaching of the Gospel, grant us, we beseech Thee, that through his merits and intercession we may be able to draw forth from our hearts tears of contrition. Through Christ our Lord. Amen.

NOVEMBER 27
BLESSED BERNARDIN OF FOSSA
Confessor, First Order

BERNARDIN was a descendant of the distinguished family of the Amici, and saw the light of the world at Fossa near Aquila in the province of Naples. His parents sent him to Aquila to pursue his higher studies, and later to Perugia, where he applied himself to the study of civil and canon law. There he was moved by the sermons of St. James of the March to become a Franciscan.

In 1445 St. James himself gave him the holy habit of St. Francis and the name of Bernardin, in honor of the great preacher of penance St. Bernardin of Siena, who had died the previous year at Aquila. Taking this great saint as his model, Bernardin of Fossa made giant strides on the path of virtue and in the study of sacred theology. He was named to the post of apostolic missionary, and in this capacity he traveled through Italy, Dalmatia, and Croatia with marvelous results.

After he was elected provincial of the province of St. James, this province became a pattern of religious discipline and order. Later he was made general procurator of the entire order in Rome. Despite the many duties attached to these offices, he never discontinued preaching and laboring for the salvation of souls. Twice the episcopal dignity was offered him in the city of Aquila, and the Holy Father expressed his earnest desire that he accept it. But by his earnest pleadings he managed to divert attention to someone else, for it was his most fervent wish to live and die as a humble son of St. Francis.

After a life rich in labor and merit, God called him to Himself on November 29, 1503, when he was eighty-three years old. Blessed Vincent of Aquila was privileged to see his soul, radiant in glory and accompanied by a host of angels, ascending to heaven. The fame of his sanctity spread far and wide, and in 1828 Pope Leo XII confirmed the veneration which had been given to him for more than three centuries. The feast of Blessed Bernardin is observed by the Franciscans and the Capuchins on November twenty-seventh.

ON CHRISTIAN COMPASSION

1. Compassion for the many souls who were on the road that leads to eternal ruin urged Blessed Bernardin to labor zealously and up to an advanced age for their salvation. St. Teresa was filled with similar compassion when, in a vision, she once saw souls falling into hell like snowflakes, and she offered up her many sufferings and prayers for the conversion of sinners. Should not the heart of every Christian be touched with compassion when he sees how many people are living day after day with no thought of God, and how many of the eighty thousand people who die daily are eternally lost? — Pray often for the conversion of sinners, especially for those who are soon to die.

2. Consider that Christian compassion, which is the fruit of Christian charity, must also extend to the natural life and needs of our fellowmen. We should have compassion for the poor, the sick, the sorrowful, and the oppressed. This sincere and heartfelt sympathy is sometimes a greater comfort to the suffering than temporal aid, and it is, as a rule, the mark of the true children of God to sympathize with each of their fellowmen as if he were their own brother, since God is the Father of all. "The just," says Holy Writ, "regards the lives of his beasts, but the hearts of the wicked are cruel" (Prov. 12,10). — Does your heart experience compassion, or is it cold and callous?

3. But there is also a false sympathy, which is not Christian. If a mother, for example, does not want to punish a child for its faults because she does not want to hurt the child; if we are unwilling to refuse a person what is forbidden for fear of offending him; if we refrain from acquainting a person who is seriously ill with his condition for fear of disturbing him — we love the body more than the soul. That would be as unchristian as

having more compassion for an animal than for a human being. — Have you permitted yourself to be led astray by such false compassion? If so, change your attitude and pray God to give you the sincere disposition of Christian charity and Christian mercy.

PRAYER OF THE CHURCH

O God, who didst inflame Blessed Bernardin with the ardor of the seraphic spirit, and didst make him an admirable preacher of the divine word in order to achieve the salvation of souls, grant us the grace to practice the works of charity as he practiced them and thus to obtain Thy mercy. Through Christ our Lord. Amen.

☙❧☙❧☙❧☙❧☙❧☙

NOVEMBER 28
ST. JAMES OF THE MARCH
Confessor, First Order

JAMES was born in the March of Ancona. His parents raised him in the fear and love of God, and in due time he was sent to the University of Perugia, where he studied civil and canon law with such remarkable success that he received a doctor's degree in both subjects. Despite the fact that brilliant positions were already open to him, he soon recognized the vanity of the world and felt a singular attraction for the religious life. At first he thought of joining the contemplative Carthusians, but almighty God, who had destined him to labor for the salvation of thousands of souls in the active life, led him to the Order of St. Francis.

During his novitiate James distinguished himself by the practice of all the virtues, so that he became a model of religious perfection. In order to preserve angelic purity, which he had kept unsullied from his youth, he led a most austere life. He never slept more than three hours, and that on the bare floor; the remainder of the night he spent in meditating on the sufferings of Christ. He constantly wore a coat of mail having sharp points, and scourged himself daily. Like our holy Father St. Francis, he observed a forty-day fast seven times a year. Bread and water were his regular fare, although he sometimes added uncooked beans or vegetables. Some years later, St. Bernardin of Siena prevailed upon him to mitigate these austerities somewhat in order to conserve his strength.

Soon after his ordination, when he was thirty years old, he was sent out as a missionary. He undertook this high calling with untiring zeal. For more than fifty years he traveled through Italy, Dalmatia, Croatia, Albania, Bosnia, Austria, Bohemia, Saxony, Prussia, Poland, Denmark, Norway, Sweden, and Russia. During the years 1427 and 1428 he preached in Vienna, Augsburg, Ratisbon, Ulm, Limburg, Brandenburg, and Leipzig. Inspired by his apostolic example, more than two hundred of the noblest young men of Germany were impelled to enter the Franciscan Order. The crowds who came to hear him were so great that the churches were not large enough to accommodate them, and it became imperative for him to preach in the public squares.

At Milan he was instrumental in converting thirty-six women of bad repute by a single sermon on St. Mary Magdalen. It is said that he brought fifty thousand heretics into the bosom of the Church, and led two hundred thousand unbelievers to baptism. In addition, God granted St. James such wisdom, that popes and princes availed themselves of his services, seeking counsel from him. He possessed the gifts of miracles and of prophecy in great measure, yet his humility surpassed all these distinctions. He was offered the archiepiscopal dignity of the see of Milan, but he declined it with the words: "I have no other desire upon earth than to do penance and to preach penance as a poor Franciscan."

Worn out by his many labors as well as advanced age, he died at Naples November 28, 1476, in the eighty-fifth year of his life, sixty years of which were consecrated to God in the religious state. He was entombed in the Franciscan church at Naples, where his body can still be seen in a crystal coffin, incorrupt, flexible, and emitting a fragrant perfume. Pope Benedict XIII canonized St. James in 1726. His feast is celebrated by the three branches of the First Order as well as the Third Order Regular on November twenty-eighth.

ON THE POWER OF THE WORD OF GOD

1. Consider the marvelous effects of the word of God as preached by St. James. Great numbers of unbelievers were baptized, obstinate heretics abandoned their erroneous beliefs, public sinners were sincerely converted, and a great number of young men generously consecrated their lives to the service of God. Without doubt, the sanctity of the preacher helped. But the real reasons for these remarkable conversions lay in what he preached and in the grace of God. He had to say as all the preachers of the word of God must say: "I am the voice of one calling, but the word I announce to you is not the word of a man, 'it is indeed the word of God, who works in you'" (1 Thess. 2,13). — Do you always have the proper

respect for the word of God when you hear it announced from the pulpit or when you read it in the Scriptures?

2. Consider how the power of the divine word is described for us in the Scriptures themselves. The prophets call it a hammer that crushes hearts that seem to be made of rock; a fire that brings light to the darkness of hearts and warms them (Jer. 23,29). They compare it with a rain that falls from heaven and soaks the earth, waters it, and makes it fruitful (Is. 55,10). Not without reason does the Apostle call it a two-edged sword that pierces the soul and the spirit, the joints and the marrow, and is a discerner of the thoughts and the intents of hearts (Heb. 4,12). But it is also a soothing oil (Ps. 54,22), a healing balsam for the sick soul, and in sorrow it is a sweet consolation, sweeter than honey in the mouth (Ps. 118,103). — Have you never experienced these effects of the divine word in yourself? Love it, then, and say with the servant of God Thomas a Kempis (4,11): "Thanks be to Thee, O Lord Jesus, Light of eternal Light, for the table of holy doctrine which Thou hast ministered to us by Thy servants, the Prophets and Apostles, and other teachers."

3. Consider that the divine word will truly manifest its power if our hearts are well prepared to receive it. Jesus Christ compares the word of God with a seed (Lk. 8) that produces manifold fruits, but only when the soil in which it is sown has been well cultivated. Your heart must not be constantly occupied with distracting thoughts like an open road; it must not be as hard as a rock because of conceit and self-will; moreover, it must not be overrun with the thorns of avarice, sensuality and pride. It must rather be a pure, a recollected, a willing heart; then it will taste the sweetness of the divine word, which will produce fruit thirty, sixty, a hundredfold. — Let us begin thoroughly to cleanse our hearts from sin.

PRAYER OF THE CHURCH

O God, who in order to save souls and to call back sinners from the abyss of vice to the path of virtue, didst make Thy confessor St. James a distinguished preacher of the Gospel, mercifully grant that through his intercession we may repent of all our sins and attain to eternal life. Through Christ our Lord. Amen.

NOVEMBER 29
BLESSED HUMILIS OF BISIGNANO
Confessor, First Order

ALABRIA was the birthplace of Blessed Humilis; the year was 1582. In baptism he received the name of Luke Anthony, and at a very early age he gave evidence of great love of God and holy things. His parents spared no efforts to give their boy a good training. He obeyed not only their commands but even their least wishes. The noisy games of his associates held no attraction for him; he found his delight in prayer and in going to church. His confessor was aware of the special gifts God was granting to the boy, and permitted him, at a very early age, to receive holy Communion frequently.

As a young man, he spent the time he could spare from his heavy duties in the fields and with the flocks by meditating on the sufferings of our Saviour before a crucifix. At eighteen, when it was necessary to choose a vocation, Luke Anthony began to pray fervently for light. He joyfully came to the conclusion that he was called to be a lay brother in the Franciscan Order.

But a cross awaited him at the start. Obstacles presented themselves, and the fulfillment of his cherished desire had to be postponed for quite a time. He did not, however, lose courage, but began to lead a life like that of a strict and zealous religious. Nine years passed by before the hindrances were removed. He was now admitted as a lay brother at Bisignano, and received the name that fitted him so well, Brother Humilis, that is, the humble one.

He was a model to his brethren. A devoted client of the Immaculate Virgin, he obtained from her through much prayer and mortification the virtue of purity to such a degree that he seemed to be an angel in the flesh. But his love of poverty and humility were just as great. He dreaded all honor or distinction accorded to him, and publicly acknowledged himself to be the greatest sinner. But our Lord, who exalts the humble and gives wisdom to the simple, gave supernatural light to Humilis, so that learned men came to him for advice and instruction in their problems. Pope Gregory XV had him come to Rome, and always received him with special kindness. Urban VIII also appreciated him highly and often discussed matters with him.

Illness finally forced Humilis to return to his convent at Bisignano for medical attention. But his life was drawing to a close. He suffered severe pains with dauntless patience until the moment of his death. Crucifix in hand, he fixed his eyes intently on it and entered into celestial joy on

November 16, 1637. The remarkable favors which God granted him in life
and after his death were carefully examined by Pope Pius IX and approved
as miraculous. Pope Leo XIII enrolled his name among the blessed. The
feast of Blessed Humilis is celebrated by the Franciscans on November
twenty-seventh.

ON THE IMAGE OF THE SACRED HEART OF JESUS

1. Devotion to the Sacred Heart of Jesus is a sign that we are filled with
love of Christ. We find that love in the thoughts and sentiments of Blessed
Humilis. From the days of his youth his heart was imbued with love for
Jesus Crucified, as he reflected on the great love of Christ for us poor
mortals. The love of Jesus Christ, of which the heart is the symbol, is the
real spiritual object of devotion to the Sacred Heart. "Behold the heart
which has loved men so much," our Lord said to St. Margaret Mary
Alacoque, and then He showed her His Heart, from which flames of fire
proceeded. — Do you often reflect on the great love of the Heart of Jesus,
and do you respond to it with love? Often repeat the ejaculation: "Heart
of Jesus, burning with love for us, inflame our hearts with love for Thee!"
2. Consider that, when our Lord showed St. Margaret Mary His Sacred
Heart with the flames of fire proceeding from it, a cross stood out amid
the flames, and the Heart itself was surrounded by a crown of thorns. He
meant to indicate that His love, for which He gave the last drop of His
Blood on the Cross, has received only a meager response from so many
Christians, whose coldness, lack of fidelity, and continual offenses are like
a renewed crowning with thorns. The heathen soldiery wound a crown
for the head of our Lord; unfaithful Christians wind a crown about His
Heart. — Have you been guilty of this offense? Imitating the zeal with
which Blessed Humilis practiced mortification, do what you can to make
amends for your past infidelities.
3. Consider that there is no true devotion to the Sacred Heart unless we
strive to imitate His virtues. Among these, our Lord Himself points out
two in particular: "Learn of Me, because I am meek and humble of heart"
(Mt. 11,29). Recall the marvelous proofs of humility and meekness which
our Lord gave us during His life and in the hour of death. These were the
mirror of virtues upon which Blessed Humilis centered his attention.
Plead with our Lord, that at the intercession of His servant Humilis, you
may, like him, imitate these virtues of our Lord.

PRAYER OF THE CHURCH

O Lord, Jesus Christ, who art meek and humble of heart, grant us the grace so to imitate Thy blessed confessor Humilis, who gave us so unusual an example of humility and meekness, that we may renounce the vanities of this life and ever serve Thee, who livest and reignest forever and ever. Amen.

NOVEMBER 30
THE SERVANT OF GOD JOHN OF MONTECORVINO
Confessor, First Order

NE of the most heroic figures in the history of foreign missions is Father John of Montecorvino, a successful pioneer missionary in various countries of the Orient for about half a century, of which he spent some nine years in Armenia and Persia, one in India, and thirty-four in China. He was the first Catholic missionary in India since apostolic times, and the founder of the first Catholic missions in China. During the last two decades of his life he was Patriarch of the Entire Orient and Archbishop of Khanbaliq (later on called Peking and Peiping).

In 1247, the same year in which Father John of Piano di Carpine returned from his pioneer journey across Asia to Mongolia, John was born in a town of southern Italy, called Montecorvino. As a young man he was a soldier, a judge, and a doctor; but, like St. Francis, he turned his back on a brilliant career in the world and joined the ranks of the Friars Minor. After he had been ordained a priest, he soon distinguished himself as a learned teacher and preacher. At the same time he practiced austere penance and strove to imitate the poor and humble St. Francis as closely as possible.

He was thirty-two years old in 1279 when he went as a missionary to Lesser Armenia and Persia, where he and other Franciscans labored with great success and established what was called the Vicarate of East Tartary. This was an organized mission territory, extending from the Caucasus Mountains to the Indus River, and comprising no less than twenty-three friaries or central missions by the end of the thirteenth century. Father John, in particular, became well versed in the languages of this region, and by his preaching gained numerous converts. Frequently, within the space of a week or a month, many thousands were baptized.

In 1289 the two rulers of Armenia and Persia sent Father John as their envoy to the Supreme Pontiff, Nicholas IV. This pope had been the Franciscan Father Jerome Massi of Ascoli, and he had served as minister general and then papal legate to the Greeks. A great missionary pope, he wrote no less than two thousand letters to promote the missions in Asia. He appointed Father John as his legate and sent him back to the Orient with twenty-six letters and a large number of missionary friars.

One of the pope's letters was addressed to the Great Khan in China, and so it happened that Father John traveled to that country, by way of India, about the same time that Marco Polo was returning to Europe from the court of Kublai Khan. In India Father John tarried for thirteen months, visiting various parts of the country and baptizing about a hundred persons. He arrived in southeastern China in 1293, and proceeded to the capital, where he was well received, and where he remained for the rest of his life except for about one year which he spent in Tenduk. In the latter kingdom, which comprised the provinces of Shensi, Shansi, and Kansu, he succeeded in converting the Nestorian ruler and many of the people to the Catholic Faith.

In Khanbaliq, the capital of China, however, he had to contend with the opposition of the Nestorians for five years. During this period, he nevertheless succeeded in winning over many of the schismatic Alans; and these became the nucleus of the Christian community in the capital. In 1299 he was able to build his first church; and choir boys whom he had trained there chanted the divine office. He also learned the Tatar language, and translated into it the Psalter and the New Testament. Another Franciscan, Father Arnold of Cologne, came to his aid in 1303; and by the end of the next year, they had baptized six thousand persons. From All Saints Day, 1305, to February, 1306, four hundred more received baptism; and at this time Father John built his second church.

This we learn from two letters Father John wrote in 1305 and 1306. These reports were taken from Persia to Rome by Blessed Thomas of Tolentino; and in 1307 Pope Clement V appointed Fr. John Patriarch of the Entire Orient and Archbishop of Khanbaliq. Seven Franciscan bishops and numerous friars were sent to his aid; and though many of these died on the way, the work in China now made extraordinary progress. Missions were established also in other parts of the country, and additional bishops and friars arrived.

As archbishop, Father John continued his apostolic labors with great success, converted the schismatic Armenians who built a third church in the capital, and extended his missionary efforts also to the pagan Mongols and Chinese. We are told that in 1311 he baptized the Great Khan, called

Khai Khan or U-tsun, shortly before he died, as well as his mother. The archbishop was eighty-one years old when he died in 1328, honored as a saint by the pagans as well as the Christians. Contemporary documents speak of him as leading "a good and very austere life," and being "a capable and holy man," "a man of a very good life, pleasing to God and the world." In more recent times, various prelates of China have repeatedly requested the Holy See to beatify him. The First Plenary Council of China, held at Shanghai in 1924, likewise asked that Archbishop John of Montecorvino be enrolled among the blessed, because of "his heroic missionary virtues and very active zeal in preaching the Catholic Faith." His cause of beatification is now pending in Rome. (Cf. *In Journeyings Often*, pp. 56-79.)

ON MISSIONARY ZEAL

1. God wishes us to manifest zeal for the missions. He gave the command: "Go, therefore, teach all nations and baptize them" (Mt. 28,19). Missionaries, like John of Montecorvino, certainly carried out this command. But what can the missionaries do if their fellow Catholics at home do not supply the means to build churches, schools, and asylums and provide catechists? — Remember that you, too, have an obligation to render help to the work of the missions.

2. The heathens need our assistance. They are many in number. More than a billion. But their misery is still greater. They have no idea of the meaning of life, of eternity, of Christ, and of His Blessed Mother, of those wells of grace, the sacraments, of consolation in sorrow, of the dignity of women, of the value of the soul. Are we going to say to the heathens: "What is that to us? Look you to it!" (Mt. 27,4). They are all our brothers in Christ. — Reflect on this frequently, and do for them whatever you are able to do.

3. The missionaries themselves need our co-operation. They make the sacrifice of their home, their health, and their life. How great were the sacrifices which John of Montecorvino made in order to win the heathens for Christ! Shall they be forced to say that their fellow Catholics at home have left them in the lurch? — Do not wait till you are approached, but regard co-operation in mission activity the sacred duty of a Christian.

PRAYER OF THE CHURCH

Behold, O God, our protector, and look upon the face of Thy Christ, who gave Himself as a ransom for us all, and grant that from the rising of the sun even to the going down, Thy name may be great among the Gentiles, and that in every place there may be sacrifice, and a clean oblation offered to Thy name. Through Christ our Lord. Amen.

DECEMBER

DECEMBER 1
BLESSED ANTHONY BONFADINI
Confessor, First Order

NTHONY was born in Ferrara in the year 1400. He did not become a Franciscan until he was about thirty-eight years old. As a friar, he devoted himself without ceasing to the practice of virtue, distinguishing himself by his poverty and humility. He took special delight in spending his time in contemplation before a crucifix, seeking to atone for his sins by acts of penance and prayer.

After he was ordained a priest he applied himself with fervor to the care of souls. His great desire was to go to the foreign missions, and he thanked God when he was assigned to the missions of the Orient.

Forced to return home after what was too brief a stay for his zeal, he stopped in Palestine on the way and visited the holy places with tender love and devotion.

Back in his native land, he again applied himself to the apostolic ministry, until broken by hardship and infirmity he had to desist from these labors. He died a saintly death on December 1, 1482, in the convent at Cotignola. Pope Leo XIII approved the veneration given to him through four centuries; and his feast is observed by the three branches of the First Order on December first.

ON THE VALUE OF OBEDIENCE

1. Obedience is not an easy sacrifice, for we offer up to God the most valuable thing we have, our free will. St. Gregory the Great says: "In all the other virtues we offer God what we possess, but in obedience we offer ourselves." But because God Himself requires obedience of us, no prayers, communions, fasts, and the like can be pleasing to Him without obedience. When Blessed Anthony was called home from the missions in the Orient, he found it very difficult to comply with the order given him. Still because obedience required it, he adapted himself to the new

arrangement. — Let us esteem obedience as highly as he did.

Obedience is very meritorious. There are really two virtues included in obedience: there is the act of self-renunciation, and, inasmuch as we see God's representatives in our superiors, there is an act of faith in the words of our Lord: "He who hears you, hears Me" (Lk. 10,16). In this way obedience becomes a divine service. — Has your obedience to date always been in accordance with this Christian view of it?

2. Failure to obey is attended with great responsibility. Our first parents failed against obedience and it brought great misfortune to them and to mankind. Thousands of young people who have not permitted their parents or superiors to give them any orders, have, as a result, shed many bitter tears, but too late. — Remember the words of Scripture: "It is like the sin of witchcraft to rebel, and like the sin of idolatry to refuse to obey" (1 Kings 15,23).

PRAYER OF THE CHURCH

O God, who didst make Thy blessed confessor Anthony distinguished by sanctity of life and zeal for souls, grant that by his intercession we may ever advance in virtue. Through Christ our Lord. Amen.

࿇࿇࿇࿇࿇࿇

DECEMBER 2
BLESSED BENTIVOLIO BUONI
Confessor, First Order

ENTIVOLIO was born at San Severino in the March of Ancona toward the close of the twelfth century, and belonged to the distinguished family of the Buoni. About the time that he grew into young manhood, reports of St. Francis and his newly founded order reached his native town, and shortly after a Franciscan preached at San Severino. Bentivolio was so impressed by his words and his whole appearance, that he became eager to join the new order.

Triumphing over the first objections of his father, he went to Assisi and received the holy habit from the hands of St. Francis himself. Soon he distinguished himself among the brethren by exceptional virtue. Especially noteworthy were his humility, his patience, his obedience, and his childlike simplicity.

He possessed the rare gift of affording both pleasure and edification by his pious conversation about heavenly things. Although he seemed to say it all in an offhand manner, nevertheless, everybody felt that it came from a holy heart, and some invisible power seemed to move them to strive for perfection. Once a bright star was seen shining on his forehead, a sign that he was filled with the fire of the Holy Ghost.

After he had become a priest and confessor, Bentivolio labored with blessed success in the holy tribunal of the confessional. At prayer, to which he was most devoted, he was often seen in ecstasy; sometimes he was even raised high above the earth.

God glorified him by many other miracles before and after his death, so that the veneration that was paid to him at his grave in the Franciscan church at San Severino constantly increased. Pope Pius IX gave the Church's approval to this veneration, thus declaring him blessed. His feast is observed by the Franciscans on December first, by the Conventuals on the fourteenth, and by the Capuchins on January second.

ON PIOUS CONVERSATION

Consider how the piety and holiness of Blessed Bentivolio was evident in his devout conversation. Just as one can tell by the ticking of a clock whether everything is in proper working order within, so, as a rule, one can detect in a person's conversation how matters stand interiorly with him. He who thinks only of profits and gain speaks continually of trade and business. He who is filled with self-love speaks continually of himself and considers others unimportant. He who is vain speaks of clothes and beauty. He whose heart is not clean takes pleasure in indecent speech. He who has God in his heart converses with pleasure about God and religious matters. — What does your speech betray? If Christ were to appear to you as He once did to the disciples on the way to Emmaus, and were to ask: "What are these discourses which you hold with one another?" (Lk. 14,17) what would you have to answer?

In the Gospel account about these same disciples, consider how useful pious conversation is. The disciples spoke about Jesus, full of sorrow over His bitter Passion, and immediately Jesus was with them to console them. Jesus in turn conversed with them about the things which Holy Scripture relates of Him, and they acknowledged that their hearts were aflame while He spoke. Pious conversation draws God, His light, His consolation, and His assistance down on us. It enkindles in the hearts of the persons speaking and in those with whom they speak the love of God and zeal for His service, as everybody experienced when Blessed Bentivolio spoke. — Have you not had this same experience yourself?

Consider that pious conversation edifies only when it comes in simplicity from a devout heart. If it consists only of affected remarks made on any and every occasion in order to impress others with one's piety, then it produces boredom and disgust. A devout heart and not vanity should guide you in regard to the time when it is fitting to direct the conversation to pious subjects. Thus, if a person speaks of fortunate or unfortunate circumstances: recall that God directs all things to the best advantage of those who love Him, and no misfortune is so great as falling into sin. Or, someone speaks about beautiful things: ask yourself what is all the beauty on earth compared with that of heaven? Thus visible things remind us of those that are invisible, and pious conversation about them directs our hearts and our steps to the way that leads to heaven.

PRAYER OF THE CHURCH

O God, who didst reveal Thy glory through the words and miracles of Thy blessed confessor Bentivolio, mercifully grant that through his intercession and merits we may be directed to behold Thy sublime Majesty. Through Christ our Lord. Amen.

DECEMBER 3
BLESSED GERARD CAGNOLI
Confessor, First Order

 ERARD was born in Valenza near the River Po, and belonged to the noble family of the Cagnoli. For fourteen years his mother lay ill, and during all this time Gerard waited on her with the tender devotion of a loving son. After her death he distributed his inheritance among the poor, and, impelled by motives of piety, he set out to visit the more notable shrines of Italy. Then going on to Sicily, he chose for himself a cell at the foot of Mt. Etna, where he planned to live in perfect seclusion and to devote himself entirely to God and to the salvation of his soul.

Moved, however, by the fame of the virtue and miracles of St. Louis the bishop, who was a Franciscan, he hastened to obtain admission into the Franciscan Order. From Randazzo, where he had been invested, he was transferred to Palermo. Here he took great delight in performing the humblest duties. As a cook, and later on as porter, he gained the esteem of his confreres, as well as of the people, by his conscientiousness, his spirit of prayer, and his charity towards others, especially towards the poor and needy.

God almighty favored him with the gift of prophecy and other graces. After the Blessed Virgin acquainted him with the time of his death, he peacefully surrendered his soul to Him to whom he had dedicated all his thoughts and affections. Gerard died in the year 1342 at age of seventy-five. His body rests in the church of St. Francis at Palermo.

Pope Pius X ratified the veneration paid to him from time immemorial, placing his name among the Blessed of the Church. His feast is observed on December first by the Franciscans, on January third by the Conventuals, and on January second by the Capuchins.

ON THE LOVE OF RETIREMENT

1. A good Christian should welcome retirement at least on occasion. For, this bustling and seductive world "is seated in wickedness" (1 Jn. 5,19). And, continues St. John (1, 2,15), "if any man love the world, the charity of the Father is not in him." Hence, it was Christian prudence on the part of Blessed Gerard to renounce all his possessions, all honors and pleasures, to live apart from the world and devote himself to those matters which pertain to heaven and to eternity. — Should this not inspire you with a desire to seek out the blessed quiet and the quiet blessedness of a retreat house?

2. Contact with the world often has harmful effects on us. Often we take with us nothing less than "a weight upon our conscience and a dissipated heart" (Imit. 1,20). We occupy ourselves with things that do not concern us. We pass judgments which we cannot fully substantiate. We see and hear many things that give rise to grave temptations for us and which have a detrimental influence on our life of prayer. "It is easier," says Thomas a Kempis (1,20), "to keep retired at home than to be enough upon one's guard abroad." — Think often and well of the wise saying: Love to be alone and you will preserve your heart unsullied.

3. The blessed results of a retired life are many. "Whoever withdraws himself from acquaintances and friends, to him will God with His holy angels draw near" (a Kempis 1,20). God is with us in the quiet round of our household duties because we are with Him. There we shall always be at peace with ourselves and with men. Hence the wise saying: "Do you wish to be great in the estimation of men, then shun being seen by men."

PRAYER OF THE CHURCH

Grant, we beseech Thee, O almighty God, that spurred on to a better life
by the example of Blessed Gerard, Thy confessor, we may be led to imitate
the life of him whose festival we commemorate. Through Christ our Lord.
Amen.

DECEMBER 4
THE SERVANT OF GOD LUCY SANCIA
Widow, Second Order

UCY was born at Carmona in Spain towards the close of the
fifteenth century. From youth she devoted herself with filial
piety to the service of the Blessed Virgin and devoutly
venerated the mystery of the Immaculate Conception.

When she grew up into a young woman, her parents gave her in
marriage to a physician who was very worldly-minded. This gave her
occasion for much grief, which she could confide to no one but to her
crucified Lord and His holy Mother. Whenever occasion offered itself, she
would repair to a remote and secluded church where she could pour out
her heart to God without being disturbed.

It so happened on a certain Sunday that she was deeply absorbed in
prayer when a heavy storm arose, followed by such a downpour of rain
that the entire neighborhood was flooded. This delayed her return home,
and she was forced to spend the entire night in the church. Next morning
she returned home with a heavy heart, filled with dread of the reproaches
that her husband would make, but at the same time recommending herself
to the care of the Queen of heaven.

To her astonishment, she found her husband in the best of humor; her
absence had remained unnoticed. Lucy recognized in this the protection
of Mary, and, amid tears of gratitude, she gave her husband a complete
account of what had happened. He was so affected that he promised to
reform his life, and from then on granted her perfect freedom in the
exercise of works of charity and of piety.

A few years later, when Lucy had become a widow, she obtained
permission from Pope Leo X to convert a house she had bought into a
convent, and there she founded a congregation of Sisters of the Third
Order in the year 1513. The result was that her dissatisfied relatives
caused her much annoyance and sorrow. But her humility, patience, and

holy prudence helped her to triumph over these difficulties. Later she obtained the privilege of enclosure for this congregation and incorporation with the Conceptionist Poor Clares, who had been founded by Blessed Beatrice da Silva and were subject to the minister general of the Franciscans. Then she and her companions were invested with the habit of these Poor Clares and pronounced their vows in accordance with their rule.

After a long life filled with good works, she died a blessed death. Her spiritual daughters revered her as a saint.

ON DOMESTIC PEACE

1. Consider how important it is in the eyes of God that peace reign in the home. Christ, our Lord, commanded His disciples: "In whatsoever house you enter, first say: 'Peace be to this house' (Lk. 10,5). Holy Church prescribes that when her priests enter a house on a spiritual errand, they should use this same salutation, and our holy Father St. Francis writes in his testament: "This greeting the Lord revealed to me, that we should say: 'The Lord give you His peace.' " The fact is, that when there is peace in a house, there will also be joy, and life will be a pleasure. In such a home everyone is intent on discharging his duty well, and God's blessing assures the temporal and spiritual well-being of its inmates. But where peace does not abide, every other effort to attain happiness will be ineffectual. How great the merit of the servant of God Lucy who succeeded in keeping peace in her home in spite of the difficulties caused by her erring husband! She could say with the Psalmist: "With them who hated peace I was peaceable" (Ps. 119,6). So it was that the Blessed Mother of God came to her assistance in a marvelous way to preserve peace. To this favor God added the complete conversion of Lucy's husband and, finally, permitted her to enjoy true peace in a spiritual dwelling, from which she was to enter into the eternal peace of the house of God. — If you follow her example, you will share her happiness in eternity.

2. Consider that all the inmates of a house must cooperate so that peace and harmony may reign there, just as every member of the body must function properly and in harmony with the other members to keep the body in a healthy condition. The person that can succeed best in promoting domestic peace is the mother, the housewife, or the one taking her place. She is like the heart in the body of a family. If the heart beats evenly, a person may rest content, even if his head sometimes aches or one of the other members begins to rebel. Hence, the great ecclesiastic John of Avila writes that, to accomplish peace, a housewife must have the

heart of a child, of a mother, and of a stepmother, that is, she must be submissive and yielding like a child, full of love and solicitude like a mother, and prudent and insistent like a good stepmother. — Happiness and blessing will come to the house which has such a mother.

3. Consider how sinful and despicable it would be for anyone to disturb this domestic peace, whether he is a resident of the house or not, whether he is a neighbor or a relative. There is little comfort for such people in the old jingle, which says:

> He who deludes a simple soul,
> Or belies an honest one,
> Or causes strife 'twixt man and wife,
> The devil's laugh has won.

Keep a careful guard against such mischievous allies of Satan, and with the aid of fervent prayer, despite the difficulties involved, strive to preserve peace and harmony.

PRAYER OF THE CHURCH
(For the Preservation of Harmony)

O God, the giver of peace and lover of charity, give unto Thy servants true harmony in accordance with Thy will, that we may be delivered from all the temptations which beset us. Through Christ our Lord. Amen.

DECEMBER 5
BLESSED NICHOLAS TAVELICH
Martyr, First Order

ICHOLAS was the son of a noble and wealthy family of Dalmatia. His illustrious parents gave him a good education, and his progress in learning was marvelous. But no less marvelous was his progress in virtue.

When Nicholas finished his studies, a bright future smiled upon him. Everything the world could give was at his command and awaited his pleasure. However, he resolved to quit the world and enter the Order of St. Francis. In spite of the great obstacles and the stubborn opposition he met, he received the humble habit of St. Francis and made his novitiate with the simplicity and docility of a child.

Manual labor, study, prayer, and mortification were his delight and chief employment. After he was ordained a priest, his fervor in saying holy Mass caused general edification and all were impressed by his sermons.

Due to his great learning and piety, he was sent as a missionary to Bosnia, a most difficult field of labor. Undaunted, Nicholas labored with ardent zeal among the heretics, refuting their false doctrines, repaying insult with blessing, visiting the sick, comforting the afflicted. He gained innumerable souls for Christ by his extreme kindness and charity.

Many esteemed him as another Christ, while others persecuted him with relentless hatred. At heart he loved the latter more, for he desired martyrdom and thought they might procure for him the coveted crown. This thought gave him tremendous supernatural strength. It increased his charity and zeal, his spirit of prayer, meditation and penance. But, after twelve years of tireless labor in Bosnia, all opposition died down, and Nicholas was convinced he must seek martyrdom elsewhere.

He now asked for permission to go to the Holy Land, where so many of his brethren had already attained the martyr's crown. The permission was granted to him, and he was sent to Jerusalem. Once more he led a hidden life of prayer, penance, and study, but more than ever he yearned to die the death of a martyr, desiring, like Christ, to be an oblation of love for the salvation of others.

On November 11, 1391, he entered the Turkish mosque and with the zeal of a Saint Paul preached to a vast assembly there. He pleaded with tact and eloquence that Christ and His religion be accepted by the Turks in their hearts and homes. Before he had finished, he was apprehended and taken to the magistrates.

Questioned as to his faith, Nicholas joyfully professed his belief in the one true Church of Christ, defending it against every objection. This incensed the court to such an extent that he was knocked to the ground and attacked with great fury. Beaten almost to death, he was dragged into a dungeon, chained hand and foot, and kept there for three days without food or drink.

On the fourth day he was taken out into the street, where he died the glorious death of a martyr, slashed to pieces with scimitars. God glorified His martyr by miracles, and Pope Leo XIII solemnly confirmed the veneration paid to him from time immemorial; and requests for his canonization have recently been sent to the Holy See. The feast of Blessed Nicholas is celebrated by the Franciscans and the Capuchins on December fifth, and by the Conventuals on the first.

ON ETERNAL GOODS

1. Eternal goods should be treasured above all things. Reflecting on the permanence of heavenly goods, Blessed Nicholas left everything the world offered him and became a poor Franciscan. He followed the admonition of our Lord: "Lay not up to yourselves treasures on earth, where the rust and the moth consume, and where thieves break through and steal. But lay up to yourselves treasures in heaven, where neither the rust nor the moth consume, and where thieves do not break through nor steal" (Mt. 6,19-20). — Which treasures do you seek to acquire?

2. Eternal goods are not properly evaluated. Most people are bent on acquiring temporal goods, money, possessions, distinctions, honor, and pleasure. They put themselves to much trouble by day and by night to acquire them. How many there are who ignore the goods of eternity for the sake of some temporal benefit, a momentary pleasure! The words of our Lord are directed to them: "I have sworn in My wrath! They shall not enter into My rest" (Heb. 3,11). — Which goods are you trying to acquire? Temporal goods are quite worthless. They are transient and cannot satisfy the heart of man. Solomon reveled in worldly luxury, and in the end he was forced to admit: "I was weary of my life when I saw that all things under the sun are evil, and all vanity and vexation of spirit" (Eccl. 2,17). — Do not permit yourself to be dazzled by the things of this world.

PRAYER OF THE CHURCH

O God, who didst glorify Thy confessor Blessed Nicholas by zeal in spreading the Gospel and by the palm of martyrdom, grant in answer to our prayer, that we may merit to walk in his footsteps and through his intercession deserve to receive the victor's reward of eternal life. Through Christ our Lord. Amen.

♦♦♦♦♦♦♦♦♦♦

DECEMBER 6
THE SERVANT OF GOD ANGELO OF MONTELEONE
Confessor, First Order

NGELO was invested with the holy habit of St. Francis very early in life. In due time he filled the position of professor of theology in his convent with considerable success and credit. But when he heard of the convent established by the servant of God Paul Trinci, in which the rule of St. Francis was observed with particular exactness, he joined him and became one of his most zealous disciples.

He was a devotee of prayer and meditation, and his favorite subject was the sufferings of Christ. He celebrated holy Mass and recited the Divine Office with the greatest fervor. In gratitude for the blessings of creation and redemption, he genuflected devoutly a thousand times in the course of a day and night. God blessed him for this with many graces and great success in the accomplishment of his sacerdotal duties.

As a preacher he succeeded in converting a great number of sinners in Florence and other cities. The people venerated him as a saint, and he was commissioned to establish several convents in which the friars strictly observed the rule of the Franciscan Order.

When Angelo was dying, he was required by his superior to reveal, for the honor of God and the edification of his brethren, what special graces he had received from God. Then he admitted, though reluctantly, that he considered it a special grace from God that he had not spoken an idle or useless word for the space of thirty years.

He died in the convent at Florence in the year 1399. His cord, which is reverently preserved at Fiesole, has restored health to many persons to whom it has been applied.

CONCERNING EVENING PRAYERS

1. The devout heart of the servant of God Angelo impelled him, so to say, continuously to thank God for His great benefits both by day and by night. The least we can do is give daily thanks by a devout night prayer. Each day is a new gift of God; as human beings we should thank Him for our creation, and as Christians for our redemption. Many other benefits are added to these each day: health, food and drink, happiness, and God's blessing on our work; sometimes, misfortune that is intended to save us from arrogance and remind us of God; and many special graces on particular days. You ought to thank God for all these gifts each evening. Kneel devoutly with the servant of God Angelo and say with the Psalmist: "Let my prayer be directed as incense in Thy sight, the lifting up of my hands as an evening sacrifice" (Ps. 140,2). — How has your night prayer been said in the past?

2. At our night prayer we should also review the day that has passed. Recalling the benefits God has granted us, let us examine ourselves in regard to the manner in which we have used them, and ask ourselves whether we have repaid Him with faithful service. Frequently we shall

find that we have been guilty of much neglect of duty, and have perhaps used God's benefits to offend Him. Such acknowledgment should impel every honest heart to make a sincere act of contrition and a firm purpose to do better on the following day. Would that by this practice we might arrive at a state of vigilance over ourselves similar to that which the servant of God Angelo achieved, who for thirty years avoided every useless word. —What have you done each evening to correct your faults? 3. Consider that at our night prayer we should also recommend ourselves to the divine protection for the night. The hours of the night form a large part of our life. We should consecrate even the night to God by taking our rest for the purpose of complying with our duties on the following day. Often the enemy of our salvation prepares temptations for soul and body during the darkness of the night. Recommend yourself, therefore, to the protection of God and of His holy angels, as Holy Church teaches us to do in the canonical hours.

PRAYER OF THE CHURCH
(At Compline)

Visit, we beseech Thee, O Lord, this habitation, and drive far from it all the snares of the enemy; let Thy holy angels dwell in it always and preserve us in peace, and may Thy blessing be upon us forever. Through Jesus Christ our Lord. Amen.

DECEMBER 7
ST. MARY JOSEPH ROSSELLO
Virgin, Third Order

IT was in the little seaport of Albissola that Mary Joseph came into this world on May 27, 1811, in a truly Christian family and one richly blessed with children. When she was but sixteen years of age, she entered the Third Order.

She had spent seven years in the service of a wealthy but childless couple, when she earnestly desired to enter a convent. But she was refused admission because she had no dowry. The couple for whom she worked hesitated to furnish the dowry, because they were unwilling to give up the girl whom they loved and intended to make their heir. Divine Providence came to her assistance.

The bishop of Savona knew of the special talent Mary Joseph

possessed, of gathering young girls about her and instructing them in their religion. So he purchased a house, furnished two rooms as classrooms, and entrusted the work of teaching to Mary Joseph and a few other young women who were similarly qualified. And so, in the year 1837, there was organized the Institute of the Daughters of Mercy. A few years later the little band of teachers pronounced their vows.

Mary Joseph administered the office of superior during the space of forty years. She placed her community under the protecting care of Our Lady of Mercy and of St. Joseph. A favorite motto of hers, which she was often heard to repeat, was "The hands should be at work, the heart with God."

Her own experience taught her a lesson, and so she received good girls into her community without a dowry. Her love for the sick sisters was expressed in the statement: "We must look upon our sick sisters as our most reliable support. They, by their patience, their suffering, and their prayers, maintain the house and, in fact, the whole institute, since they seek and obtain for us from the Father of Mercy the blessing of heaven."

The community has grown in a remarkable manner. There are more than three thousand sisters in two hundred houses spread over Italy, Argentina, and the United States. Mother Mary Joseph departed from this life on December seventh in the year 1880. She was beatified in 1938, and canonized in 1949. However, her feast is not observed in any of the Franciscan calendars.

ON IDLENESS

1. We should flee idleness. Holy Scripture says: "Idleness has taught much evil" (Eccli. 33,29). St. Francis calls it a cesspool of bad thoughts, and experience shows that idleness is the devil's workshop. Hence St. Mary Joseph acted according to the principle: "Hands at work." Work is a duty for everybody. "In the sweat of your face shall you eat bread" (Gen. 3,19). — Let yourself be guided by these principles and flee idleness as you would the plague.
2. We should avoid busy idleness. Those who neglect their own duties while they concern themselves so much the more about the business of others are guilty of a form of idleness. Also those who occupy themselves with all kinds of hobbies, but do not want to perform the duties of their state of life. They are everywhere and nowhere, and are a burden to everyone. St. Francis compared this kind of people to flies, which seem to exist for no other purpose than to molest others. — Do you belong to these

annoying flies?

3. We should never just "kill time" or waste it in idleness. This can be done chiefly by following the admonition of the Apostle: "Let all things be done according to order" (1 Cor. 14,40). Hence, we should divide our day between work, prayer, and recreation. Besides this, we should reflect on the account we shall have to render of the time and the talents loaned to us. — Reflect that, according to the words of our Saviour, only faithful servants can enter into the kingdom of heaven.

PRAYER OF THE CHURCH

Be merciful, O Lord, to our prayers and heal our indolence, so that we may obtain the remission of our sins and at all times rejoice in Thy blessing. Through Christ our Lord. Amen.

DECEMBER 8
THE SERVANT OF GOD BEATRICE RAINERI
Virgin, Second Order

AFTER the Venetian government gained possession of the large island of Euboea in the Aegean Sea, a number of Venetian families settled there. The distinguished family of the Raineri also acquired a considerable estate in Euboea and lived in the city of Negropont. In 1471, however, the island was invaded by the Turks, who at once occupied Negropont and plundered the homes of the prominent Venetians.

Beatrice, a devout daughter of the house of Raineri, made a successful escape to a neighboring mountain. But she was overcome with great fear when she realized that she was alone and helpless in a country occupied by the enemy. She knelt down and pleaded for help from heaven.

The Queen of heaven appeared to her, consoled her, and promised to take her devout client under her special protection. She told her that she would arrive safely in Venice and there she would serve God among the Poor Clares. When the Blessed Virgin disappeared, Beatrice saw a venerable old man standing near her. He led Beatrice to the sea, where a boat was ready to sail for Venice. On the boat she met a distinguished lady, Polyxena by name, who had lost her husband and her wealth as a result of the invasion of the Turks, and was likewise fleeing from the place. They resolved to remain together as companions.

Upon their arrival in Venice, they found hospitality with a devout young woman who had used her great wealth in building a hospice for pilgrims to the Holy Land. In time this hospice was converted into a convent of Poor Clares called Holy Sepulcher convent because it possessed a beautiful painting of the Holy Sepulcher.

Beatrice distinguished herself among the members of the convent by penance, obedience, humility, patience, charity towards her neighbor, and fervor at prayer. She was favored with extraordinary graces by God. Many sick persons were miraculously cured by her, and she was often rapt in ecstasy while at prayer.

In another vision our Blessed Lady again assured Beatrice of her maternal protection; and then she died a blessed death, in the year 1509, venerated as a saint by those who knew her.

ON THE DOCTRINE OF THE IMMACULATE CONCEPTION

1. This doctrine agrees with the most elementary ideas of the divine goodness. Who can imagine that the eternal Father, having the power to save His daughter from the tyranny of Satan, though that tyranny were to last but an instant, would not have saved her from it even for that instant? Who can suppose that the infinite love of God the Son would have endured even for a moment to behold His mother tainted by the defilement and degradation, which Adam's disobedience left as a heritage to his children? Would the spouse of the Holy Ghost have been anything but immaculate? Surely, even by us, who in so faint a measure perceive the hatefulness of sin, the very thought must be rejected. – Let us renew our faith in this mystery. Let us thank and bless the Most Holy Trinity, who at Mary's conception poured out upon her soul the riches of her great privilege.

2. This doctrine has its basis in the divine maternity. In taking human form, Christ wished to provide for a mother who had never been in the power of Satan. He owed that to Himself as the God-man. The dogma that all men are redeemed by Christ is in no way contrary to this doctrine. The plan of the redemption was conceived from all eternity and from all eternity God could provide properly for Mary's exemption from original sin. Mary was then preserved from original sin for the sake of the merits of the Redemption as foreseen and ordained by God. – Reflect devoutly on this mystery of the grace of God.

3. This doctrine teaches us that only one person was preserved from original sin. The rest of humankind remained subject to the law of original sin and its consequences: suffering, hardship, death. Contrary to the tenets

of atheistic communism and materialism, heaven will never be found anywhere on the face of the earth. And while the authors of the new paganism endeavor to unleash the animal in man, the picture of the Immaculate Mother of God, with the serpent under her feet, tells us: "You shall reign over the beasts of the earth and over all that is bestial within you!" — Always remember this, and do all you can to rejoice and honor Mary Immaculate.

PRAYER OF THE CHURCH

O God, who by the Immaculate Conception of the Virgin didst prepare a worthy dwelling-place for Thy Son, we ask, that, as by the foreseen death of this Thy Son Thou didst keep her from all stain, so too Thou wouldst permit us, purified through her intercession, to come to Thee. Through the same Christ our Lord. Amen.

༄ঔৡঔৡঔৡঔৡঔৡঔ

DECEMBER 9
BLESSED FRANCIS ANTHONY FASANI
Confessor, First Order

ORN in 1681 at Lucera, southeastern Italy, Francis Anthony was the son of very poor peasants; but he was a bright lad, and received a good education from the Conventual Franciscans in his native town. When he was fourteen he received the habit of St. Francis among the Conventuals, and in 1705 he was ordained to the priesthood. He was then sent to the Sacro Convento, adjoining the basilica in Assisi where St. Francis is buried, for the purpose of continuing his studies. Two years later he received the doctorate in theology, and he was then appointed lector of philosophy in the college conducted by the Conventuals in his home town. He was promoted successively to regent of studies, guardian, and provincial, which latter office he held from 1721 to 1723. After that he served as master of novices, and then as pastor of the church of St. Francis in Lucera. A bishopric was offered to him, but he declined it.

From the process of beatification we learn that Francis Anthony was diligent in study, fervent in piety, prompt in his obedience to his superiors, devout in meditation, and most exact in the fulfillment of all his duties. He was also mortified and given to the exercises of penance even to bloodshed. From his youth he was an "angel in the flesh, more an angel than a man."

Among the devotions that he cherished there were especially a tender love for the Immaculate Mother of God, a childlike affection for the Infant Jesus, and fervent adoration, also night adoration, of the Holy Eucharist. Once, while he was absorbed in prayer, someone who happened to be in the church heard a voice saying: "This priest prays much for his people."

As a priest, he also became an eloquent preacher, a lover of the poor, a friend of the unfortunate. He was a missionary, a retreat-master, and a Lenten preacher. For hours he would sit in the confessional, hearing and absolving the sins of his penitents, consoling the afflicted, warning the hardened of heart. He spent much time in visiting the sick, the orphans, and the imprisoned. As a pastor he was a real father to his people.

After thirty-five years in the priesthood and a life of penance, union with God, and intense labor for the salvation of souls, God called Father Francis Anthony to Himself on November 29, 1742. On that day the people of Lucera came hurrying to the church of St. Francis, exclaiming, as did the children at the death of St. Anthony of Padua: "The saint is dead! The saint is dead!" And for two hundred years since then, they have continued to kneel and pray at his tomb. The cause of his beatification was introduced in Rome in 1832; and in 1951 Pope Pius XII solemnly enrolled him among the blessed. The Conventuals celebrate the feast of Blessed Francis Anthony on December ninth.

ON THE VENERATION OF THE SAINTS

1. The important feature in venerating the saints is imitating their virtues; but it is not the only feature. The saints deserve personal honor too, such as we give them by observing their feastdays, adorning their images, extolling their virtues in sermons, singing hymns and reciting prayers in their honor. In honoring them we honor God Himself, as the Psalmist admonishes us: "Praise the Lord in his saints" (Ps. 150,1). For, after all, we honor them because of the graces God granted to them and because of the fidelity they showed towards God. — Can you also say with the Psalmist: "To me Thy saints, O God, have been made exceedingly honorable"? (Ps. 138,17).

2. Consider that the veneration of the saints will be particularly helpful to us if we confidently ask them to intercede for us. They are with God, they behold Him face to face, and as beloved children of God they can do much for us poor sinners by their intercession. From personal experience they know our needs and the many dangers to which we are exposed here below. Hence they take pleasure in carrying our prayers to the throne of

God, and holy Mother Church induces us to call upon them: "Pray for us, all ye saints of God!" — Do you call upon the saints with confidence?

3. Consider the powerful protection the saints procure for us. Their merits and sufferings, not seldom endured in a cruel martyrdom, plead to God for mercy and grace as do the open wounds of Christ. Moreover, their loving solicitude for our salvation urges them to pray for us at the throne of God. Thus Onias, the high-priest, once beheld the prophet Jeremias in a vision, and said: "This is the lover of his brethren who prays much for the people" (2 Mac.15,14). If the saints were so zealous for the salvation of souls while they were still on earth, as we perceive in Blessed Francis Anthony, what, then, may we not expect of them now that they have arrived at their eternal home with God!

PRAYER OF THE CHURCH

Grant, we pray, O Lord, that Thy faithful people may ever rejoice in venerating Thy blessed servant Francis Anthony and all Thy saints and may be aided by their unceasing prayers. Through Christ our Lord. Amen.

DECEMBER 10
BLESSED HUGOLINUS MAGALOTTI
Confessor, Third Order

HUGOLINUS was a scion of the famous and noble family of the Magalotti. He was born toward the close of the fourteenth century on an estate near the city of Camerino, Italy. His mother died while he was still quite young, but his excellent father was deeply concerned about the education of the boy, so that nothing was left wanting. By his obedience, affection, and other virtues Hugolinus gave much joy to his father. His lively temperament caused him many a struggle, but the guidance of his father and the grace of God helped him overcome his evil inclinations.

As he grew older, Hugolinus applied himself to the study of the sciences. Spiritual books, however, held the greatest attraction for him. He read them constantly, impressed their lessons on his mind and heart, and regulated his life accordingly. He did not speak much, but his example edified everybody.

After his father died, the youth thought he heard addressed to him the words of our Lord to the rich young man: "If you wish to be perfect, go, sell what you have, and give to the poor" (Mt. 19,21). Hugolinus did not hesitate a moment. He sold all his possessions and divided the proceeds among the poor, particularly the widows and orphans. Stripped of all material things, he withdrew to a hermitage, where he led a truly celestial life. Prayer and meditation were the nourishment of his soul; and on his body he imposed the severest fasts and mortifications.

The enemy of virtue did not neglect to attack him severely. One time he would tempt him by stirring up sensual desires and reminding him of the pleasures he could enjoy out in the world. At other times he would frighten him by appearing to him in horrible forms. But Hugolinus proved to be a good soldier of Jesus Christ; prayer, penance, and especially trustful appeal to the Immaculate Mother of God, made him victorious in every struggle.

God rewarded the fidelity of His servant with extraordinary favors. Enlightened by God, he gave advice and consolation to the faithful, who appealed to him in great numbers. He miraculously restored health to many sick persons.

When he perceived that his end was drawing near, he became even more intimately united with God. Having received the last sacraments several times, he died peacefully in the Lord in 1373. His body was laid to rest in the church of St. John the Baptist at Figni, Camerino, and immediately the people began to venerate him. This veneration was approved by Pope Pius IX, and Pope Leo XIII permitted his feast to be celebrated. The Franciscans, the Conventuals, and the Third Order Regular observe the feast of Blessed Hugolinus on December eleventh. (Cf. Biersack, p. 64; *These Made Peace,* pp. 126-127.)

ON VOLUNTARY POVERTY

1. Consider how many wealthy young men and young women, like Blessed Hugolinus, divested themselves of their material goods in order to walk the way of perfection. They considered material goods a hindrance to perfection, and renounced them, just as a person entering a race rids himself of everything that can be in his way. They were taught this lesson by Jesus Christ Himself: "If you wish to be perfect, go, sell what you have and give to the poor" (Mt. 19,21). If the renunciation of material goods leads to perfection and sanctity, surely the inordinate accumulation of such goods must lead to imperfection and sin. — How do you regard material goods?

2. Consider that not only the words of our Lord, but still more His

example, impelled devout souls to embrace voluntary poverty with all its consequences. Jesus Christ had all the good things in the world at His disposal, but He preferred to be born in poverty, to live in poverty and privation, and to die in poverty. For love of Jesus and to be like Him, St. Francis, and many thousands before and after him, left a life of comfort and wealth in order to share the poverty and want of Christ. St. Francis called poverty his queen and bride, because the King of heaven espoused her in the Crib and remained true to her up to the Cross. It is the Holy Spirit that inspires men with the love of poverty and privation. He is called, in the sequence of Pentecost, the Father of the Poor. Whoever longs for a life of social eminence, and is not willing to put up with privation, is being led by the spirit of the world. — By which spirit are you guided? 3. Consider the reward which Christ promises to those who embrace a life of poverty. He rewards them a hundredfold already here on earth. Even in temporal matters they enjoy a security which the children of the world often strive for in vain. None of the thousands who followed St. Francis in voluntary poverty in the past seven hundred and fifty years, were ever in want, whereas many who once were rich have died in hunger and misery. But our Lord gives the hundredfold reward especially in spiritual things, which are worth a hundred times more: peace of heart, joy of spirit, interior peace that surpasses all that is sensual. The complete reward will be given to the poor followers of Christ in eternity, where a great treasure awaits them in heaven. According to the measure of their poverty will their riches be in heaven; for, as St. Thomas says, "the poorer we are here for love of God, the richer we will be there," where God will reward us.

PRAYER OF THE CHURCH

Most kind and merciful God, who didst deign to give to Blessed Hugolinus, Thy confessor, a love of seclusion and the grace of evangelical poverty, grant us, Thy servants, to follow his example and to receive a like reward. Through Christ our Lord. Amen.

DECEMBER 11
BLESSED PETER OF SIENA
Confessor, Third Order

ETER was a simple combmaker of Siena, and was faithfully devoted to his work. He sanctified it by prayer and united his hardships with the fatigue of our Saviour in His work at Nazareth. In his love for penance he joined the Third Order of St. Francis, and not only observed its rule exactly, but added still more rigorous works of penance. If work piled up, so that he was kept from spending more time in prayer, he would offer up his work instead.

He managed always to find time for certain special devotions which he performed each evening with his devout wife.

When his wife died at an early age leaving no children, Peter found he was free to lead a life wholly in accord with his pious wishes. He saw in the poor and the sick, children whom God entrusted to his care. He shared his goods with them, visited them, comforted and nursed them in need. He continued to work at his trade, but devoted more time to prayer, even many hours of the night. He had the grace of intimate union with God and fostered special devotion to our Blessed Lady. She frequently appeared to him and treated him as a mother does a beloved son.

The more intimately Peter was permitted to enjoy this heavenly intercourse, the less he conversed with men. He spoke only when necessity or charity required it. In selling his combs, he would state the price and then place his finger on his lips so as to keep from speaking unnecessarily. His price always suited his customers, because they knew that his wares were good and that he never overcharged anyone.

In his great love for our holy Father St. Francis, Peter asked the friars of the Franciscan convent of Siena for permission to live there. The friars, aware of his extraordinary virtue, arranged a cell for him. This cell became for him an abode of delight. He would spend entire nights in prayer, enjoying the company of the holy angels and their queen, of the holy apostles, and of St. Francis himself, who would instruct him and fill his soul with heavenly consolation.

For a long time Peter also had to endure apparitions and temptations from the evil spirits. Peter overcame them by his humility; and the higher he was raised by God, the more deeply did he descend in the opinion he had of himself. He confessed his smallest failings amid torrents of tears. One day he wrote out the sins and failings of his whole life, and then for his own humiliation, he read the whole list. God gave him the assurance that all his sins were forgiven, and all that he had written and read was miraculously erased.

His humble reserve never permitted him to speak when older people, priests, or religious were present, unless he was invited to do so. But, as everyone knew that he was favored with heavenly enlightenment, he was frequently called on to give advice. A religious once asked him what he should do regarding weariness at prayer. He answered: "Do not on that account curtail the time allotted to it. Sometimes we gain more by patient waiting than by receiving."

God wrought many miracles through His humble servant. He died December 4, 1289. His tomb in the Franciscan church in Siena was adorned with a beautiful marble memorial. So many miraculous cures occurred at his grave that pilgrims came there from all parts of Italy. The veneration paid to him from the time of his death was approved by Pope Pius VII. His feast is celebrated by the Franciscans on December eleventh, by the Conventuals on the fourth, and by the Third Order Regular on the fifth. (Cf. Biersack, pp. 151-152; *These Made Peace,* pp. 22-26.)

ON SILENCE

1. Consider how Blessed Peter acquired the virtue of silence through constant conversation with God. Familiar conversation with God dreads useless converse with men, and no sincere Christian soul loves idle talk. Moses, the friend of God, said to the Lord: "Since Thou hast spoken to thy servant, I have more impediment and slowness of tongue" (Ex. 4,10). Silence also helps us speak with God and pray with devotion. Just as the warmth of a room gradually diminishes if the doors are left open, so will devotion leave the heart of a man whose mouth is constantly open in useless conversation. "If you desire to withdraw from superfluous talking," says Thomas a Kempis (1,20), "you will find time sufficient and proper to spend in good meditations." — Is your lack of devotion at prayer due to talkativeness?

2. Consider that it is advisable to acquire the habit of silence in order to avoid offending God and man. "In the multitude of words," says the Holy Spirit, "there shall not want sin" (Prov. 10,19). How often are charity, truth, and justice violated, while envy, vanity, and conceit are greatly nourished by it! On the other hand, he who speaks little has little responsibility. Often people believe they are making a favorable impression on their fellowmen by their conversation, whereas the opposite is the case. They become a nuisance to others. Hearing them always speaking about a third party, their hearers may justly fear that they too will be the subject of their gossip. Remember that one day you

will have to give an account of every word you have uttered.

3. Consider the merit and the virtue that can be gained by means of silence. Sacred Scripture admonishes us: "Be not full of words in a multitude of ancients" (Eccli. 7,15). "Interrupt not others in the midst of their discourse." "Answer not a word before you hear" (Eccli. 11,8). Short and simple as these maxims are, it is only by real self-control that you will be able to carry them out. But if you do overcome yourself for the love of God, it will add to your store of merits in eternity. You will learn to be modest and humble, and perceive how foolish and out of place was much of your past conversation. "The heart of fools is in their mouth: and the mouth of wise men is in their hearts" (Eccli. 21,29). — Reflect on the beautiful example of Blessed Peter and strive to acquire reserve similar to his in your speech.

PRAYER OF THE CHURCH

We beseech Thee, O Lord, subdue the conceit of our soul by the spirit of holy humility, Thou who didst so admirably reward the humility of Thy confessor Blessed Peter with heavenly graces. Through Christ our Lord. Amen.

❧❧❧❧❧❧❧❧❧❧❧

DECEMBER 12
VENERABLE INNOCENT OF CHIUSA
Confessor, First Order

INNOCENT CALDERERO, a Sicilian by birth, showed signs of his future sanctity when he was still a boy. He loved seclusion, and while other boys were busy at play, he would withdraw to some quiet place and pray. As a young man, he entered the Franciscan Order as a lay brother, and soon proved to be a model of virtue. His love of solitude was so great, that he not only avoided all contact with the world, but endeavored as much as possible to remain unobserved even in the convent. Still, his virtues could not long remain a secret to his brethren.

He sought at all times to sacrifice his will by preferring to do the will of another. He regarded obedience to his superiors as the guide of his least action. If the choice was left to him, he always picked what was the more lowly and uninviting.

By fasts, scourgings, and other rigorous penances, he vanquished the

evil spirit, who tempted him often and severely. As a reward for his
fidelity and diligence in striving for perfection, he was frequently favored
with apparitions of our Blessed Lady, and with intimate association with
the holy angels. He fostered special devotion to the great St. Anne, and
often sought help from her in his trials and tribulations. His life was a
continual preparation for death, the place and the time of which were
revealed to him many years in advance.

After serving God in the religious state for fifty-two years, he
departed from this life at Rome in 1631, when he was seventy-four years
old. Immediately upon his death all Rome hastened to view his remains
and to pay him respect. At first he was laid to rest in the choir of St.
Peter's in Montorio, but in 1653, at the request of the pious Empress
Eleonore of Austria and with the approbation of Pope Innocent X, his
body was transferred to the Franciscan church of St. Francis across the
Tiber.

At the process of his beatification, which was introduced by Pope
Innocent XII in 1692, two hundred and ninety reliable witnesses testified
under oath to the sanctity of his life, and many, to miracles wrought at his
intercession. However his cause is still pending in Rome.

ON PRAYER FOR THE LIVING

1. Like Venerable Brother Innocent we should pray much and often. We
should pray for ourselves; we should pray for the faithful departed who
can no longer help themselves; and we should also pray for our fellowmen
who are still living among us, especially for the sick, the afflicted, and the
oppressed. St. James admonishes all: "Pray for one another that you may
be saved" (Jas. 5,16). The closer our association is with anybody, or the
more we are indebted to him in gratitude, the greater is our obligation to
pray for him. Parents, brothers and sisters, and benefactors have therefore
a special claim on our prayers. But we may not exclude any fellowman
from a share in our prayers, not even our worst enemy. — Have you been
faithful to this obligation of prayer?
2. We should also recommend ourselves to the prayers of others,
especially of devout and God-fearing souls. In his epistles St. Paul often
recommends himself to the prayers of the faithful, and God Himself told
the friends of Job, when they had sinned in speech, to recommend
themselves to the prayers of this just sufferer. Prayers said for us by
someone else more readily incline God to help us, for they are prayers
prompted by charity. Above all the intercession of a just soul is helpful for
"the prayer of a just man avails much" (Jas. 5,16). On the other hand,

nobody may hold himself excused from the common duty of prayer because he has recommended himself to the prayers of others. Remember that God's promise to hear our prayers is attached first and foremost to our own individual prayers. "For everyone who asks, receives" (Mt. 7,8). "All things whatsoever you ask when you pray, believe that you shall receive and they shall come unto you" (Mk. 11,24). — Recommend yourself, therefore, to the prayers of others, but do not neglect to pray for yourself.

3. Consider that we should pray especially for those on whom the general welfare of mankind depends. The general welfare is each one's particular welfare as well. Therefore the Apostle writes, "I desire therefore first of all that supplications, prayers, intercessions, and thanksgivings be made for all men: for kings, and for all who are in high station, that we may lead a quiet and peaceful life in all piety and chastity" (1 Tim. 2,1). He who prays for the temporal and spiritual authorities, prays for himself and all those who are entrusted to their care. The time you spend in such prayer is not lost to you.

PRAYER OF THE CHURCH
(For Prelates and Those under Their Care)

Almighty and everlasting God, who alone workest great marvels, send down upon Thy servants and the flocks entrusted to them, the spirit of Thy saving grace; and that they may please Thee in truth, pour forth upon them the continual dew of Thy blessing. Through Christ our Lord. Amen.

DECEMBER 13
THE SERVANT OF GOD JANE OF LUXEMBOURG
Virgin, Third Order

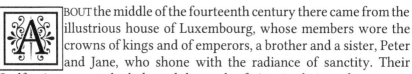

ABOUT the middle of the fourteenth century there came from the illustrious house of Luxembourg, whose members wore the crowns of kings and of emperors, a brother and a sister, Peter and Jane, who shone with the radiance of sanctity. Their Godfearing parents had planted the seeds of piety in their souls at a very early age.

In true fraternal affection the Countess Jane attached herself to her brother, and he became her teacher and guide on the way of perfection. In the prime of life both made the vow of perpetual chastity. Peter turned his attention to the priestly state, and Jane resolved to serve her heavenly Bridegroom in the convent. Nothing could make her waver in her resolve, neither the many flattering offers for her hand nor the persuasion of her parents.

On one occasion she attended a sermon in the company of her parents. The preacher used as his text the words of our Lord; "Go sell what you have and give to the poor, and you shall have treasure in heaven" (Mt. 19,21). Jane was so seized with holy longing that right there in public she fell down at the feet of her father, begging him not to withhold his consent any longer, but to permit her to follow her earnest desire.

Her father now gave in. Complying with her wish, he himself took Jane to the convent of the sisters of the Third Order of St. Francis at Monzel, France. There in the presence of her parents and her pious brother she received the holy habit. From that day forward she served God with great fervor in the quiet of seclusion, in prayer, vigils, fasting, and work. She became a model to her fellow sisters and a glory to her convent.

Meanwhile her brother had become a priest and archdeacon of Dreux and Chartres. Later he was appointed bishop of Metz, and in the year 1386 he was made a cardinal of Holy Church. Nevertheless he always remained the most trusted friend and spiritual guide of his sister. He died shortly after being elevated to the cardinalate, on July 2, 1387. Jane had now but one desire, to leave this earth and to be with Christ. Finally, our Lord heard her fervent prayer and took her to Himself in 1404.

Her body was laid to rest in the convent church at Monzel, and the heart of her brother (who was canonized in 1572 and is known as St. Peter of Luxembourg) was buried with her, so that the hearts that were so intimately united during life might not be separated in death.

LOVE AMONG BROTHERS AND SISTERS

1. Consider that divine grace does not destroy the bonds of nature, but rather ennobles them. It was thus that Jane and Peter loved each other. Our Saviour Himself was pleased to honor such noble love, for He often visited the home of His three friends of Bethania, Lazarus, Mary, and Martha, who despite their differences in disposition, lived together in peace and harmony. Peaceful community life of that kind is praised by the Holy Spirit in the words: "Behold how good and how pleasant it is for brethren to dwell together in unity" (Ps. 132,1). — Have you always endeavored to live in harmony with your brothers and sisters, or do quarreling, dissention, and jealousy reign among you? Cain nursed the

latter sentiments until he rose to murder his brother Abel.

2. Consider that fraternal love does not require that the family must always remain together. Often that would be mere natural love and attachment; it might at times even interfere with higher duties. Rather, holy love does not interfere with the individual's duty to follow the vocation to which God has called him, as we see in the life of the holy brother and sister Peter and Jane. Even though such persons do not live together, their hearts are always united. They are sincerely devoted to each other, each aims to do for the other what can be done to promote his vocation, and in time of need each comes to the other's assistance as far as it is possible for him to do so. — Do you possess this supernatural love, or is yours only the natural kind?

3. Consider that fraternal love can never mean cooperation in that which is sinful. We may never defend what is wrong because those we love have done it. We may not do anything that will offend God because those we love require it of us. Were we to do that, almighty God could say to us: "He who loves brother and sister more than Me is not worthy of Me."

PRAYER OF THE CHURCH
(No. 9 under "Various Prayers")

O God, the giver of peace and the lover of charity, give to Thy servants true concord in accordance with Thy will, that we may be delivered from all the temptations which beset us. Through Christ our Lord. Amen.

DECEMBER 14
BLESSED NICHOLAS FACTOR
Confessor, First Order

 HE FEAST of SS. Peter and Paul in 1520 was the birthday of Nicholas. His parents were devout Christians of Valencia, Spain. As a child of five he already manifested signs of his future sanctity. He fasted three times a week and gave the food he did not touch to the poor. With cheerful words he comforted the sick, and on visiting the leper hospital, he would at times kiss the wounds of the afflicted persons. A Moorish maid in his home was so affected at the conduct of the holy child that she was attracted to the Catholic Faith, took instructions, and was baptized. As a young man he continued his labors of love and encouraged his companions and fellow students to do likewise.

Meanwhile, his father was busy making plans for this son of his, who was so distinguished because of his brilliant talents and handsome appearance. Nicholas, however, saw in his father's projects great danger of being turned away from the path of God's commandments. Upon due consideration and advice, he resolved to enter the Order of St. Francis and donned the holy habit in the convent in Valencia. After he had finished his novitiate and his studies, and had been ordained a priest, Nicholas asked to be sent to the foreign missions. The request was not granted by his superiors, but they did send him to preach and convert the Mohammedans, who were very numerous in Spain at that time.

With the blessing of obedience he cheerfully took up the task assigned him, and he was rewarded with remarkable success. The means he employed were uninterrupted prayer and rigorous interior and exterior mortification. He never went into the pulpit without first having taken the discipline three times. It is said that for two years he kept vigil every night at the foot of the cross, meditating on the sufferings of our Saviour. Despite these austerities his complexion always remained ruddy, and he was affable and cheerful in his association with others. His comeliness caused him many a temptation; but his modesty, humility, and piety turned all the snares of the evil spirits to naught, so that he preserved his purity of body and soul unsullied.

God permitted him to read the hearts of men, and on several occasions he suddenly presented himself to unfortunate persons who were about to commit suicide, showed them the seriousness of their sins, and dissuaded them from carrying out their godless design. He also had great success in various positions in the order itself, as novice master, guardian, definitor, and confessor to the Poor Clares of Madrid and Valencia.

Rich in merits, he was finally called home to receive his heavenly reward on December 23, 1583, in the convent of Mary and Jesus near Valencia. Because of the great crowds who gathered to view the body, it lay in state for ten days in the church. A pleasant odor emanated from it, and it remained as flexible as the body of a living person. Three years after his death, King Philip II of Spain wished to see it again, and it was found to be still incorrupt.

Because of the many miracles wrought at his tomb, Pope Pius VI beatified him on August 18, 1786. His feast is celebrated by the Franciscans on December fourteenth.

ON THE TEN COMMANDMENTS

1. Consider the zeal which Blessed Nicholas displayed in observing the commandments of God. To avoid failing against them, he scorned a brilliant career in the world, and for further protection he built a wall about the commandments with the evangelical virtues. All through his priestly life he made it a point to help others know and observe the commandments. There is no other way to salvation for Christians than the observance of the commandments of God. On the day God gave them to the Israelites, He spoke as follows: "These words which I command you this day, shall be in your heart; and you shall tell them to your children, and you shall meditate upon them sitting in your house and walking on your journey, sleeping and rising" (Deut. 6,6-7). — Have you thus esteemed the commandments of God?

2. Consider how the Ten Commandments comprise all the duties of a Christian towards God and his neighbor. The first three refer to his duties towards God: adoration, which refuses to consider anything on a higher or an equal level with Him; respect for His holy name and for everything that pertains to God; and worship of God, for which a definite day is set aside. The remaining seven commandments teach us our duties towards our fellowmen: first of all, towards those to whom we owe special respect, then towards every fellowman, in the things that pertain to his life, to his family, to his possessions, and to his honor, not only exteriorly but also in our thoughts and desires. The Lord said to Moses: "Who shall give them to have such a mind, to fear Me and keep all My commandments at all times, that it may be well with them and with their children forever" (Deut. 5,29). — Have you merited this blessing by your faithful observance of the commandments?

3. Consider that there are various motives for observing the commandments. We must observe them at least because we fear God; if we observe them only because we fear men, we merit nothing for eternity. But the love of God is a far nobler motive than the fear of God, and it is far more meritorious to observe the commandments from motives of the love of God. That is why at the profession ceremonies in the Third Order we promise in a special way that as true children of St. Francis we will observe the commandments of God. — Let us endeavor to observe them from motives of love.

PRAYER OF THE CHURCH

O God, who didst grant Blessed Nicholas, who was inflamed with such extraordinary love, the grace to imitate Thee with a pure heart, grant us, Thy servants, that, filled with the same spirit and aglow with love, we may run the way of Thy commandments without impediment. Through Christ our Lord. Amen.

DECEMBER 15
BLESSED CONRAD OF OFFIDA
Confessor, First Order

BORN at Offida, a little town in the diocese of Ascoli, in 1237, Conrad grew up under the watchful care of his devout parents in innocence and a seriousness unusual in a child of his age. He entered the Franciscan Order as a youth of fourteen. As a friar he devoted himself to prayer, meditation, and the faithful observance of the rule, as well as to thorough study of the sacred sciences. Though he was destined for the priesthood, it pleased his humility to do some of the most disagreeable and wearying duties performed by the brothers.

In Blessed Peter of Treja (or Montecchio) he found a companion of similar disposition, animated with burning zeal, love of God, and unwearying desire for sanctity. The two formed a holy friendship and joined in constant imitation of their Saviour and of their holy Father St. Francis. In this way Conrad made such progress in perfection that some of the first disciples of St. Francis who were still alive at that time, used to call him the "second St. Francis."

Like the holy Founder, he was often favored with apparitions of our Lady and of the saints. Once on the feast of the Purification, when he was meditating on the significance of the feast, our Lady deigned, in the presence of his friend Peter of Treja, to place the Divine Child in his arms. He was given the grace to touch and convert the hearts of sinners by his sermons. He was also the spiritual director of the holy Tertiary, Blessed Benvenuta.

But the farther his reputation spread, the more did he seek the seclusion of solitary convents, endeavoring as much as possible to keep aloof from the world. Sometimes he went to Mt. La Verna, at other times to Pirolo. But he felt most at home in the convent in Forano, where he again met Peter of Treja and, together with him, led a truly celestial life. It was here that God granted him the gift of miracles and of prophecy.

After nearly half a century of such a life, he died on December 12, 1306, while preaching the Advent sermons at Bastia near Assisi. In the year 1320 his body was transferred from Bastia to the church of the Friars Minor in Perugia, and from there in 1872 to the cathedral where it is greatly venerated by the people. In view of the many miracles wrought at his intercession during the centuries following his death, Pope Pius VII, on April 21, 1817, confirmed the veneration paid to him. The three branches of the First Order celebrate the feast of Blessed Conrad on December fourteenth.

MARY AND HER DIVINE CHILD

1. Consider that God has often permitted His saints to take the Divine Child in their arms from the hands of Mary, His Mother. That happened also in the life of Blessed Conrad. God permitted this as a token of His tender love for the saints. At the same time it shows through whom we should expect to receive Christ. Just as Mary was chosen by the Most Holy Trinity to bring the Redeemer to mankind in general, so is each individual to receive Jesus through her. For that reason, St. Bernard admonishes us: "Seek for grace, but seek it through Mary!" — If you wish to receive the Divine Child into your heart on the feast of Christmas, then diligently venerate Mary, the Mother of Divine Grace, during Advent.
2. Consider that in offering the Divine Child to the saints, Mary gave us to understand that her most ardent wish is to fill our hearts with love for her Divine Son. If you wish to please our Lady, strive to increase the love of God in your heart. Do not let your devotion consist in mere pious sentiments, but aim for her sake to make yourself and others, as far as you can, daily more pleasing to her Divine Son. When you look at her picture with the Divine Child in her arms, beg her for her blessing in the words: "Nos cum prole pia, benedicat Virgo Maria" — "May the Virgin Mary mild bless us with her holy Child."
3. Consider what particular virtues made Blessed Conrad deserving to be so highly favored by Christ and His Mother. These virtues were his profound humility, for he thought nothing of himself and wished to remain hidden from the world; his tender piety, for it kept his heart constantly directed towards God, no matter where he was or what he was doing; and his holy zeal to fulfill the duties of his state of life. Examine yourself and see how far you resemble him in these virtues.

PRAYER OF THE CHURCH

Increase in our hearts, O Lord, sentiments of true piety, and grant us through the intercession of Thy blessed confessor Conrad, the grace to imitate the shining example of his remarkable humility and devotion. Through Christ our Lord. Amen.

◇◆◇◆◇◆◇◆◇◆◇◆

DECEMBER 16
VENERABLE MARY CRUCIFIXA
Virgin, Third Order

EFORE the birth of this child, a saintly Franciscan brother prophesied her future sanctity to her mother. He also said that as the child grew older, it would be crippled, and would later receive the habit of the Third Order of St. Francis. All these events were fulfilled.

Born in the city of Naples on February 19, 1782, she received the name of Mary Josephine in baptism. She was educated in a convent, and at a very early age showed an unusual love of prayer. She was even favored with divine revelations, and she entertained no desire but to serve God all her life in the convent.

At the age of thirteen, however, she was called home by her parents in order to help them in the work of the household and the raising of the younger children. Mary cheerfully obeyed their call and assisted her parents to the best of her ability. Some time later, however, when she realized that her parents were making plans for her marriage, she begged God amid many tears to send her an illness that would make her unfit. She was then afflicted with arthritis, which so contracted her body that she became a cripple and could move about only with the help of crutches.

Despite her affliction, she continued in her pious practices and even in the performance of many heavy household duties. She did it all in so cheerful a manner that the rest of the family were in admiration at it and esteemed her more and more highly. They even joined in her devout exercises so that their home soon resembled a convent rather than a family residence.

In 1802 Mary was received into the Third Order of St. Francis, and henceforth wore the Tertiary habit publicly. At her reception she received the name of Mary Crucifixa of the Wounds of Our Lord, and there was never a lack of proof that she was really crucified with Jesus. Her corporal sufferings increased steadily as she grew older; to this were added unbelievable torments of soul and the most horrible molestations of the evil spirit. But the sufferings of Christ and the sorrows of our Lady were a consolation to her, and the tender devotion she cherished to the Infant

Jesus helped her persevere in her sweet disposition.

As Mary was unable to leave the house, she was permitted to have a private oratory at home in which holy Mass could be said. She found the sweetest delight in decorating this little sanctuary for the Infant Jesus. One must, says her biographer, go to this oratory personally to get an idea of the care she took in adorning this room. The altar and the walls are covered with artistic tapestries and laces which she herself made despite her great affliction. Only God knows how many hours of the night she sacrificed in this work.

Finally the day arrived when she was taken to the sanctuary of heaven. She died on the first day of her accustomed novena to the Infant Jesus before the feast of Christmas, December 16, 1826. Her body reposes in the church of St. Lucy in Naples; and the steady stream of answers to prayer and the miracles that have been wrought caused the process of her beatification to be introduced in 1842. She has been declared Venerable, and her cause is still pending in Rome.

ON LOVE FOR THE INFANT JESUS

1. Consider with what fervor and perseverance Mary Crucifixa proved her love of the Infant Jesus. She is truly a model for us all. "If anyone love Me," says the Lord, "he will keep My word" (Jn. 14,23). Mary gave evidence of such love already in her childhood. When her parents called her home from the convent to assist in the household work, much as she wished to remain at the convent, she obeyed at once. She had no definite assurance of her vocation to the religious state, and therefore felt bound to sacrifice her pious plans to the certain dictates of the Fourth Commandment. — Have you been willing to sacrifice your inclinations, even your pious ones, to the observance of the commandments? Without that willingness, the true love of God does not dwell in your heart. "He who loves Me not, keeps not My words" (Jn. 14,24).

2. Consider how Mary Crucifixa stood the test of her love of Jesus. In order to belong to Christ alone as His virginal spouse, she asked to be afflicted with illness. The prayer was granted. Not only her body, but also her soul was tortured with the most painful sufferings for many years. All these waters of tribulation could not quench her love for the Divine Bridegroom; rather, like a holy oil, they inflamed it more and more, so that those about her were kindled with it. "Many," says Thomas a Kempis (2,11), "praise and bless Jesus as long as they receive consolations from Him. But if Jesus hide Himself and leave them for a little while, they either murmur or fall into excessive dejection." — How have you stood the test

of your love for Jesus in the past?

3. Consider how the tenderness of Mary's love of Jesus manifested itself. All the sufferings she had to endure did not keep her from carefully adorning the altar of her little chapel where He was to come to her at holy Mass. Souls who truly love God can also say with the Psalmist: "I have loved, O Lord, the beauty of Thy house, and the place where Thy glory dwelleth" (Ps. 25,8). — Can you say as much? But remember that also your heart is a place where God wishes to dwell. If you love Him, adorn it with virtues that are pleasing to Him. Endeavor during the novena before Christmas which begins today, to make it a pleasing abode for His arrival.

PRAYER OF THE CHURCH
(Second Sunday in Advent)

Arouse our hearts, O Lord, to prepare the way for Thine only-begotten Son, that we may be found worthy upon His arrival to serve Thee with a clean heart. Through the same Christ our Lord. Amen.

ᎧᏋᏋᏋᎧᏋᏋᎧᏋᏋᎧᏋᏋ

DECEMBER 17
BLESSED BARTOLO OF SAN GIMIGNANO
Confessor, Third Order

ARTOLO BUONPEDONI, the last descendant of the ancient and illustrious house of the counts of Mucchio, was born at San Gimignano in northern Italy in 1228. For twenty years his pious mother, who had been childless, begged God to give her a son. St. Peter, whose intercession she had invoked, appeared to her in a dream and assured her that her petition would soon be granted. She bore a son, who was given the name Bartholomew, or Bartolo, in baptism. The child grew up in innocence and piety.

When he reached young manhood, he felt that he was called by God to the priesthood. But his father, the count, a proud and worldly-minded man, preferred his son to be a stately knight and famous soldier. He became very angry at his son and used every means to break his resolve.

Matters went so far that the boy fled from the anger of his father to the convent of the Benedictines at Pisa. There he did duty as an infirmarian although still in secular clothes. As his eminent virtues became manifest, the fathers offered him the religious habit. Then one night he was granted a vision. Our Saviour, covered with wounds and holding a scourge in His hand, addressed the young man: "Bartolo, not in this habit are you to attain the celestial crown; it is to be through suffering and wounds, and in the garb of penance."

Bartolo then resolved to request the habit of the Third Order of St. Francis and to embrace the life of a secular priest. After several years of preparation he was ordained by the bishop of Volaterra and appointed assistant priest at Picciola, and twelve years later, pastor of Pichena. In this capacity he labored with extraordinary zeal. All the income of his parish was used for good purposes, especially for works of mercy in behalf of the sick and needy. One night he met a poor traveler, whom he invited to spend the night with him. At midnight he heard a voice say: "Bartolo, you have given hospitality to Jesus Christ." Going to the room where his guest had been lodged, he found that the guest had disappeared.

When Bartolo was fifty-two years old, he was attacked by the dread disease of leprosy, which was so rampant at that time. He resigned his parochial duties, and withdrew to the leper hospital near San Gimignano. He lived there nearly twenty years, gradually wasting away from suffering and leprosy, but always manifesting the most heroic patience. It was a marvelous circumstance that no one ever showed any disgust for his wounds, but rather perceived a sweet odor emanating from them.

A week before his death our Lord appeared to him, to tell him that the end of his terrible suffering was at hand. He died December 12, 1300. His body was laid to rest in the church of St. Augustine at San Gimignano and numerous miracles occurred at his tomb. He was beatified in 1910 by Pope Pius X. His feast is observed on December fourteenth by the Franciscans, on the twelfth by the Conventuals, and on May eleventh by the Third Order Regular. (Cf. Biersack, pp. 10-11; *These Made Peace*, pp. 31-34.)

ON BEHOLDING CHRIST IN THE NEEDY

1. In the lives of the saints there are frequent instances like the one Blessed Bartolo experienced, when Christ in the form of a poor man accepted charity at their hands. Our Lord does that as a reward to the saints and a lesson to us. They trained themselves ever to see Christ in the person of the poor and the destitute. To reward their charity, our Lord sometimes showed them that He accepts such charity as rendered to Himself. But for us it should be a good lesson. The works of mercy can prove meritorious only if they are rendered to the needy for love of God. That is why the Apostle writes: "If I should distribute all my goods to feed the poor and have not charity, it profits me nothing" (1 Cor. 13,3). — Have you always practiced the works of mercy with such sentiments?

2. Consider that Christ makes it our duty to practice the works of mercy with such Christian sentiments. We have received from His hands invaluable benefits for body and soul. We owe Him thanks and return gifts for these blessings as far as lies in our power. But Christ is not in need of our gifts. So He leaves us the poor and the needy, and we are to share with them, in God's stead, the good things we have received from Him. Whoever refuses to do this is in danger of the judgment of God: "As long as you did it not to one of these least, neither did you do it to Me. Depart from Me into everlasting fire" (Mt. 25,41).

3. Consider that Blessed Bartolo was deemed worthy at the last to become like Christ by his sufferings and dread illness. Just as unmistakably as the marks of the wounds present St. Francis to us as an image of the Crucified, so do sickness, poverty, contempt, and persecution make us like Christ if we bear them cheerfully for love of Christ and after His example. — God grant that in such circumstances we may recognize our likeness with Christ and our filial relationship with God Himself!

PRAYER OF THE CHURCH
Preserve, O Lord, Thy family in Thy continued goodness; that we, who rely solely on the hope of Thy heavenly grace, may also be defended by Thy heavenly protection. Through Christ our Lord. Amen.

DECEMBER 18
THE SERVANT OF GOD FRANCES SCHERVIER
Virgin, Third Order

"ONE is as it were rich, when he has nothing; and another is as it were poor, when he has great riches" (Prov. 13,7). This passage of Scripture fits the servant of God, Frances, who with all her heart espoused holy poverty and thus came into the possession of the grace of God.

Born in 1819, Frances Schervier was a descendant of a distinguished family in the old imperial city of Aachen or Aix-la-Chapelle. While she was perhaps not prominent in the eyes of the world, she enjoyed the distinction of extraordinary supernatural privileges from the very days of her youth. Her desire to enter a religious order was thwarted by the early death of her mother in 1832, when Frances was only thirteen years old. She was obliged to remain at home and attend to the household. But she did not let these circumstances prevent her from caring in a very special way for the poor and the sick. So lavish was her liberality that one of the old servants once remarked: "One of these days the child will have dragged everything out of the house." Later she was an active member of several benevolent societies of women and also of what was known as St. John's soup kitchen, a charitable enterprise organized to feed the needy.

Frances joined the Third Order of St. Francis in 1844. Henceforth she and four other young women resolved to lead a community life. They found a dwelling at the old city gate of St. James, and took possession of their first religious abode on the eve of the feast of St. Francis in 1845. Prayer and works of mercy were their principal occupation. Mother Frances and her first companions — the number soon increased to twenty-three — received the religious habit on August 12, 1851, and a new religious family was formed. Very appropriately she called the new congregation the Sisters of the Poor of St. Francis. The poverty of St. Francis and his love for the poor of Christ superseded everything else in the eyes of the foundress. On one occasion she wrote to her sisters: "The impress of poverty and penance should mark even our chapels and churches and be their distinctive feature."

The first foundation of the Sisters of the Poor of St. Francis in the United States was made in 1858. Twice Mother Frances came to the United States, the first time in 1863, and the second time in 1868. During her first sojourn in this country, she joined her sisters in ministering to wounded soldiers of the Civil War, and to the sick, the homeless, and the orphaned. The second time, while visiting the various institutions conducted by her sisters, she also lent a helping hand in caring for the sick, the aged, and the poor.

Mother Frances sacrificed everything for the poor out of love for God, and she was amply repaid by Him who cannot be outdone in generosity. Her foundation increased visibly, and to this day it enjoys the special blessing of Divine Providence. At her holy death on December 14, 1876, Mother Frances was mourned by thousands of daughters in religion as well as by the poor, and was venerated as a saint. Unusual conversions and other remarkable events occurred even during her lifetime in answer to her trustful prayer, and since her departure from this world, such things have happened even more frequently. Her cause of beatification is now being carried on in Rome. (Cf. *Forum*, 1945, pp. 166-168, 189.)

ON ALMSGIVING

1. Almsgiving is a source of blessings. The servant of God Mother Frances experienced this truth. It is of course not granted to all of us to do for the

poor what she did. Still, we should all keep in mind the words of Scripture, "He who gives to the poor, shall not want" (Prov. 28,27). Those who are in need are the wards of God. He who helps them will undoubtedly obtain blessings from God for himself and those entrusted to his care. — Is it not worth your while to merit those blessings for yourself?

2. The blessings attached to almsgiving depend on the measure of our charity. St. Paul writes: "He who sows sparingly, shall also reap sparingly; and he who sows in blessings, shall also reap of blessings" (2 Cor. 9,6). In places where people give generously, everything usually prospers; while, where the poor are despised, people are not happy in their possessions. — Be mindful of the words of our Lord: "Give, and it shall be given to you" (Lk. 6,38).

3. Almsgiving exercises us in virtues that promote our temporal welfare, so that whoever gives to the poor will experience the truth of the text: "Some distribute their own goods, and grow rich" (Prov. 11,24). Keeping in mind the need of the poor, the charitable readily limit their personal outlay to that which is necessary, they take good care of their own property, they practice economy, permitting no waste, no luxury. In this way their good deeds react blessedly on themselves as well as on the poor. — Take this to heart and act accordingly.

PRAYER OF THE CHURCH

We beseech Thee, O Lord, that Thy grace may ever precede and accompany our deeds; let it tend to make us ever mindful of good works. Through Christ our Lord. Amen.

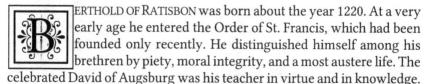

DECEMBER 19
THE SERVANT OF GOD BERTHOLD OF RATISBON
Confessor, First Order

ERTHOLD OF RATISBON was born about the year 1220. At a very early age he entered the Order of St. Francis, which had been founded only recently. He distinguished himself among his brethren by piety, moral integrity, and a most austere life. The celebrated David of Augsburg was his teacher in virtue and in knowledge.

The master soon recognized the great gifts with which God favored Berthold, and provided for their complete development. And so Berthold became an outstanding spiritual leader and the greatest and most powerful preacher of his time in the entire German empire. Like a two-edged sword the word of God proceeding from his lips pierced the hearts of his hearers and moved the most hardened sinners to repentance. Often the concourse of people who came to hear him was so great that no church could accommodate them — sometimes the number rose to a hundred thousand — and he was forced to address the people in the open air, speaking to them from a pulpit built in a tree. To this day there is a vast open area in Bohemia called Berthold's field, because on several occasions Berthold addressed such crowds there.

One day at Ratisbon, Berthold was preaching in forceful terms against the vice of impurity. A woman of evil repute in the audience was so overcome with sorrow over her past sinful life that she dropped dead. Berthold's fervent prayer restored her to life, and she confessed her sins with sincere contrition. Other sinners converted through Berthold sought to atone for their sins by a life of strict seclusion and rigorous penitential practices. The people of Ratisbon were so edified at their spirit of penance that they built a convent and a chapel for them, which they dedicated to St. Mary Magdalen. The convent exists to this day and is occupied by the daughters of St. Clare.

Berthold was favored with the gift of prophecy, and foretold certain catastrophes and other future events, all of which were fulfilled in every detail.

Rich in heavenly merits, Berthold died in his native town of Ratisbon on December 13, 1272, and was laid to rest by the pious people of the town, but the faithful from Bohemia and Hungary made pilgrimages to it as to the tomb of a saint. Following the suppression of the convents in 1811, the mortal remains of this great servant of God were withdrawn from public veneration. But he still speaks to the modern world in some of his sermons which have been preserved. The following consideration is taken from them:

ON THE THREE SNARES

1. The evil spirits lay numberless snares for us poor mortals, to keep us from reaching eternal salvation. But there are three snares that are more dangerous than the rest. The first of them they lay for us when we come into the world, and the second, as we pass through the world, and the third, when we pass out of the world. Once a child in the womb of its mother has a soul, that soul will live forever. But to keep that soul from seeing the face of God and enjoying eternal salvation, the devils lay snares to keep it from being baptized; for without baptism it cannot enter eternal

bliss. They do what they can to keep the child from being born alive. If it is born alive, they use various tricks to have its baptism put off. Once it has been baptized, they try to involve it in bad habits, for they know that such habits will stick to the child for life. That is why husband and wife should take good care of the life of the child, should by all means not put off baptism, and should keep their little ones from getting into bad habits, while they start them in good habits as early as possible. — Have you always acted like a Christian in this matter or have you perhaps helped the devil lay his snares?

2. As we pass through life, the evil spirits lay snares for us by means of sinful love and sinful fears. They stir up men's senses to seek satisfaction in intemperance, impurity, vanity, and pride, and they ensnare thousands of souls with false love. Other souls, and sometimes the very same ones, they fill with false fears that they will not be able to make their way through life, and so they incite them to greed, avarice, and injustice. The evil spirits entrap practically all men with one or the other of these snares. Which snare do you need to fear the most?

3. It is when we pass out of this world that the evil spirits lay the last snare for us, and that snare is doubt. Sometimes they attack the dying person with doubts against faith; that is why we should try to strengthen our faith during life and to renew the acts of faith each morning and evening. But the evil spirits more often tempt men in their last hour with doubt of the mercy of God. That is why we should atone for our sins while there is time, and do much good, so that it may outweigh the evil we have done. But even if his wicked deeds outnumbered his good deeds, let the dying person still not despair, but look up to God and to Mary, and trust in the Blood of Christ, one drop of which is more than enough to outbalance all our sins. — May God grant all Christians the grace to pass to the eternal shores with such happiness that they can say with the Psalmist: "Our soul has been delivered as a sparrow out of the snare of the fowlers" (Ps. 123,7).

PRAYER OF THE CHURCH (Seventeenth Sunday after Pentecost)
Grant, we beseech Thee, O Lord, that Thy people may avoid all contacts with the devil, and with pure mind follow Thee, the only God. Through Christ our Lord. Amen.

DECEMBER 20
THE SERVANT OF GOD ELIZABETH OF AUSTRIA
Widow, Third Order

N 1554 there was born to the German Emperor Maximilian II a daughter who was named Elizabeth. Like her holy patron Elizabeth of Hungary, she was destined to be an honor to her house and to the Third Order. At an early age Elizabeth manifested tender sympathy for the needy, and such piety that she would sometimes arise at night and spend several hours on her knees in prayer.

When she was only fifteen years old, she was married to King Charles IX of France. But her husband died within four years after their marriage. The nineteen-year-old widow now returned to Vienna. She resolved not to marry again, but to devote her life solely to the service of God and to godly deeds. She publicly entered the Third Order of St. Francis and gave the Tertiaries of Vienna a most edifying example. Dressed in the plainest garment, so as to escape all notice, she visited churches and took part in processions and other devotions. At home she always spent much time in prayer, observed rigorous fasts, and avoided all public amusements.

She took much pleasure in serving the sick in the hospitals. She also visited the homes of the city in search of the poor sick and provided them with medicine and other supplies. To many of these people her kindness and cordial service gave even greater comfort than the corporal aid she rendered them. Occasionally she invited poor people to dine at her home, where she herself sat down at table with them, especially on Thursdays, when she would prepare a plentiful table for poor people in honor of the Last Supper.

In the spirit of humility she often performed the lowliest duties in a convent of Poor Clares which she had founded, often cooking the meals for the poor there. She was also much interested in the upkeep of churches, but she was even more concerned about having worthy priests to conduct the services and attend to the care of souls. She loved to help talented young men pursue their studies and get a good education in preparation for the sacred ministry.

After accomplishing a great amount of good in the twenty years of her widowhood, she died in Vienna in 1592, to the great sorrow of the entire imperial city. The humble queen had chosen the following text from the office of the dead for her epitaph: "Since I sin daily and yet do not do penance, the fear of death disturbs me. As in hell there is no redemption, have mercy on me, O God, and save me!" Several miracles have occurred at her tomb.

ON SOLICITUDE FOR GOOD PRIESTS

1. Among the many good works undertaken by the servant of God Elizabeth, surely the noblest and the best was her solicitude for good priests. What a blessing a good priest is for a Christian community! "When a priest celebrates," says Thomas a Kempis (4,5), "he honors God, he rejoices the angels, he edifies the Church, he helps the living, he obtains rest for the dead." And what an amount of good the priest does in his sacerdotal activities! He is the educator of youth, the counsellor of adults, the savior of sinners, the comfort of the sick and the dying. Those who provide the Church with a good priest have a share in all these blessings. — Have you ever paused to consider what opportunities you have to help young men to reach the goal of the priesthood?

2. Consider how we can provide for good priests. Parents can provide their sons with the education needed for the clerical state, and brothers and sisters can co-operate in this great charity. Of course, no parents may compel a son to embrace the priesthood, or persuade him by the promise of worldly advantages. Such a boy might easily prove to be a hireling or even a wolf to the flock of Christ, and then, woe to the one who misled him. But to consent that a son may follow his vocation, and to make sacrifices that he may achieve his goal, is a highly meritorious work. Perhaps we can contribute to the education of young men who wish to become priests. All of us can at least pray for good priests. The Ember Days have been especially instituted to obtain worthy priests from God by means of penance, fasting, and prayer. What Holy Scripture says about the need of priests is applicable to our times as well: "The harvest indeed is great, but the laborers are few" (Mt. 9,37). — Have you done your duty in the past in regard to this matter?

3. Consider that our solicitude for good priests should manifest itself in a special way by supporting them in their activities. We should gladly follow their advice, cheerfully contribute to the good works they promote, and help establish their influence. It is only when good Catholics give them this co-operation that priests can hope to labor with success. Do not criticize what they say, even if it does not always suit you. They are ambassadors of Christ, and through them God exhorts the faithful (2 Cor. 5,20). Beware of undermining their influence and of giving them a bad name. That would burden you with a dreadful responsibility. Often pray that God may keep the priests of His Church free from scandal and that He may bless their activities.

PRAYER OF THE CHURCH (Fifteenth Sunday after Pentecost)

Let Thy constant pity, O Lord, cleanse and defend Thy Church, and since without Thee we cannot abide in safety, may we ever be governed by Thy grace. Through Christ our Lord. Amen.

DECEMBER 21
THE SERVANT OF GOD HERMAN OF GERSTHAGEN
Confessor, First Order

 T MUEHLHAUSEN in Thuringia, Germany, in the year 1224, the saintly Father Herman of Gersthagen entered the Franciscan Order. Humility was his favorite virtue. Out of love for God he always sought the least and most abject in everything, believing that this was in conformity with the vocation of a Friar Minor. He was particularly careful in the observance of poverty, so that, as far as material things were concerned, he contented himself strictly with what was indispensable. Yet he sacrificed himself completely, with indefatigable zeal, for the salvation of souls. He journeyed to the most inhospitable regions of northern Germany, which were but sparsely settled at that time, to preach the Gospel to the poor and to administer to them the Church's means of salvation. He instructed the ignorant, led back the erring, comforted the disconsolate, and assisted the dying with truly paternal solicitude.

He administered the sacrament of penance with special charity and blessed success. In all things he was like a bright star in the newly established Franciscan Order in the north of his country. Almighty God also glorified him in life and after death by many signs and wonders. Herman raised several dead persons to life, nine blind persons received their sight, three regained their speech, and numerous sick persons had their health restored to them.

After his death Herman was also invoked to restore lost objects, and to the peasants he was a special patron for recovering lost cattle.

His tomb is in the convent church at Muehlhausen, where he died in 1287. Three centuries later, when the church was taken over by the Lutherans, the people declared that they still saw a brilliant light over his grave on special feastdays.

ON THE VIRTUE OF HUMILITY

1. The Apostle St. Paul writes: "For if any man think himself to be something whereas he is nothing, he deceives himself" (Gal. 6,3). These words point to the surest foundation for humility, namely, the knowledge that we are nothing. Pride is only empty conceit and self-deception. "Reflect," says St. Bernard, "what you were, what you are, and what you will be." You were nothing, for you were created out of nothing. Of yourself you are nothing, for what you are comes from God's bounty and grace. And you will return to dust and ashes, as Holy Church reminds you on every Ash Wednesday. Think frequently of these truths, and your pride is bound to vanish.

2. Consider that holy humility is also the foundation of all the other virtues. In his sincere efforts to reach perfection, Father Herman practiced this virtue above all the rest. Just as the root of a tree furnishes it with life and growth, so must humility sustain the soul, for God gives His grace to the humble, and from grace proceeds all that is good. He who wishes to accumulate virtue without humility is like a person who carries dust about in the wind: the wind of his pride immediately scatters everything about. Yes, his imaginary virtue makes the proud man still more arrogant, and thus he displeases God, as did the Pharisees in the Temple. — Have you properly evaluated the virtue of humility? How valuable in the sight of God are your other virtues?

3. Learn from the example of Father Herman that true humility is no hindrance to the accomplishment of great good. On the contrary, it is a great aid and makes a person better qualified for great things, since almighty God chooses for the most important undertakings "the weak things, the base things of the world and the things that are not, that no flesh shall glory in His sight" (1 Cor. 1,29). The proud man turns away in fear when difficulty presents itself, because he fears there will be no particular honor in it for him. The humble man does not consider his honor but the honor of God, and in everything that is done for that purpose, he depends upon the Almighty for assistance and says with the Apostle: "I can do all things in him who strengthens me" (Phil. 4,3). The Lord never permits those to be confounded who trust in Him. — In difficult circumstances have you always placed your trust in the grace of God? Or have you allowed pride to make you ashamed of defeat, and so deter you from noble enterprises?

PRAYER OF THE CHURCH
(Third Sunday in Lent)

We beseech Thee, almighty God, look upon the desires of Thy lowly servants and stretch forth the right hand of Thy majesty to be our defense. Through Christ our Lord. Amen.

DECEMBER 22
ST. FRANCES XAVIER CABRINI
Virgin, Third Order

ORN in 1850 at Sant'Angelo di Lodi in Lombardy, Mary Frances Cabrini was the youngest in a peasant family of thirteen children. Even as a child she was known for her piety and love of prayer; and she dreamed of being a missionary in China. At eighteen she received her teacher's certificate; and when her parents died the following year, she sought admission in two different sisterhoods but was rejected because of her poor health. During the next ten years, she devoted herself to teaching and directing a school for orphans, and satisfied her zeal by giving catechism instructions and visiting the poor during free time. During a smallpox epidemic in 1872 she did heroic work as a nurse.

But Mary Frances still wanted to be a missionary; and in 1880, with the encouragement of the bishop of Lodi, she and a few companions took up their residence in a former Franciscan friary and thus founded a new religious community, namely the Missionary Sisters of the Sacred Heart. Previously Mother Frances Xavier, as Mary Frances was now called, had been an exemplary Tertiary of St. Francis of Assisi. In the decree of the Sacred Congregation of Rites on the heroic quality of her virtues we find the following statement: "She imitated to a high degree the virtue of three saints who bear the name of Francis, and modeled her life according to their example. Thus she imitated the virtues and example of St. Francis of Assisi, whose Third Order rule she professed and holily observed." And even after founding a new sisterhood, Mother Cabrini continued to derive inspiration from the example of the Poverello for her mission of apostolic charity.

In 1888 Mother Cabrini's institute received the approval of the Holy See; and the next year Pope Leo XIII directed her to go, not to China, but to the United States, and to make the Italian emigrants in that country the object of her charitable and apostolic work. With six companions, Mother Cabrini arrived in the United States, March 31, 1889; and, though she also visited Central and South America, she spent the greater part of her remaining life in the United States. She became a United States citizen at Seattle in 1909. At first she encountered many difficulties, but soon she accomplished the apparently impossible. And amidst feverish activity, she always maintained great tranquility of soul and prayerful union with God, entrusting all her undertakings to God with unbounded trust in Divine Providence.

When the cause of her beatification was commenced in 1928, her sisters, two thousand in number, were caring for sixty-seven institutions in eight countries of America and Europe. Mother Cabrini suffered from fevers for months at a time, but she kept up her amazing activities for God and for souls until she died at Columbus Hospital in Chicago on December 22, 1917, at the age of sixty-seven. She was beatified in 1938, and canonized in 1946, the first United States citizen to be thus raised to the full honors of the altar.

The feast of St. Frances Xavier Cabrini, "Mother of the Emigrants," is observed on December twenty-second. Her body rests beneath the high altar in the chapel of Mother Cabrini High School, in the northernmost part of Manhattan, New York City. (Cf. Ciognani, *Sanctity in America*, pp. 107-114; *Forum*, 1944, pp. 361-363, and 1946, pp. 217-218.)

SERVING GOD IN OUR NEIGHBOR

1. Consider how St. Frances Xavier understood how one must serve God. Much of the time that she would have liked to spend in prayer, she used in the service of others because they needed her help and direction and advice. That is what is called by St. Francis de Sales, leaving God for God's sake. Apparently one neglects something in the service of God, but in reality one serves Him the better by the practice of charity towards one's neighbor. Thomas a Kempis (1,15) also says: "For the benefit of one that is in need, a good work is sometimes freely to be left undone, or rather to be changed for what is better." — Have you acted accordingly in the past?
2. Consider that Christ our Lord Himself teaches us that certain laws permit of exceptions in special cases. He healed a sick person on the Sabbath day, and permitted His hungry disciples to pluck ears of corn although the Pharisees accused Him on that account of violating the Sabbath. Thus our holy Father St. Francis also urged a weak brother to eat out of time on a fastday, and himself ate with him to encourage him. So

there may arise instances where the commandment to refrain from servile work, to attend holy Mass, to fast, and so forth, does not obligate us, yes, where the need of the neighbor or our own may demand that we refrain from observing the commandment, especially if our superiors or our confessor so direct us. In such cases it would be pharisaical justice, and often perverse self-will, to persist in carrying it out. — Have you ever done this?

3. Consider that it is indeed not permitted for any person's sake to do evil or omit an obligatory good act from which we are not excused. But the good deeds and pious exercises which we perform of our own accord, we can at times with merit neglect or put off for the sake of others, especially if complying with them would be burdensome or annoying to others. Thus the Apostle says: "To the weak I became weak that I might gain the weak. I became all things to all men that I might save all" (1 Cor. 9,22).

PRAYER OF THE CHURCH (Eighth Sunday after Pentecost)

Of Thy mercy, O Lord, we beseech Thee, grant us the mind ever to think and to do what is right, that we who have no being apart from Thee, may live according to Thy will. Through Christ our Lord. Amen.

DECEMBER 23
THE SERVANT OF GOD BERNARDIN OF BUSTI
Confessor, First Order

LTHOUGH St. Francis was not a learned man and many of his first associates were simple and unlearned like the fishermen of Galilee, still the holy founder did not in any way despise learning. Rather he esteemed it and desired that it be fostered in his order hand in hand with piety.

Bernardin, of the prominent patrician family of the Busti of Milan, excelled equally in both. After his preparatory studies, the young man devoted himself to the study of law at the famous University of Pavia, where he acquired eminent knowledge. But knowledge did not satisfy his heart; rather he feared the reputation and the pride which so readily accompany it. For that reason he preferred the Order of Friars Minor to his profession as a lawyer. He received the holy habit in the province of Milan.

After his novitiate and profession, he devoted himself, at the command of his superiors, to the study of sacred theology, distinguishing himself among his fellow students. In particular he prepared himself for the office of preaching under the renowned preacher of the order, Father Michael of Carcano, and then labored with great blessing as one of the most distinguished orators of Italy. Especially by preaching on the sufferings of Christ and devotion to the Blessed Virgin, did he convert numerous sinners and lead many good Christians to perfection.

Upon general request, he committed his sermons to writing. Through the recent invention of printing they were then published far and wide as a blessing to many, appearing in editions even outside of Italy. In addition, Bernardin wrote several learned works of canonical and moral content. But he also bequeathed to our day proofs of his piety, for his piety never grew cold amid all his labors as a preacher and missionary. He composed an Office of the Immaculate Conception of the Blessed Virgin, and the touchingly devout Office of the Holy Name of Jesus, which, with minor changes, was introduced in the Franciscan Order for the feast of the Holy Name, and was later prescribed for the entire Church by Pope Innocent XIII.

Rich in merits and universally reputed as a saint because of his outstanding virtues, he died at Melignano in 1500.

LEARNING AND PIETY

1. By divine inspiration Bernardin recognized, even as a young man, how dangerous learning is by itself. He understood the words of St. Paul: "Knowledge puffs up" (1 Cor. 8,1). For that reason he entered the humble order of St. Francis. There he devoted himself to the practices of piety, and his piety taught him to use his knowledge for the glory of God and the salvation of souls. Thus he fulfilled those other words of the Apostle in the same text, "but charity edifies." — Would that learning were universally employed in this manner!

2. Consider that in itself learning is good, since it ennobles the intellect, a faculty which places man on a higher plane than the other earthly creatures. Learning also serves the temporal and eternal interests of men. For many it is a necessity because of their vocation; for instance, in the case of the priest. Through the mouth of the Prophet, the Lord says: "Because you have rejected knowledge, I will reject you" (Os. 4,6). But in order to avoid being puffed up because of learning, man should remember what Thomas a Kempis (1,2) says: "If it seem to you that you know many things, know, for all that, that the things you are ignorant of are still more," and "The more you know and the better, so much heavier will your

judgment be, unless your life be also more holy." Christ Himself says: "And the servant who knew the will of his Lord, and did not according to his will, shall be beaten with many stripes" (Lk. 12,47).

3. Consider that a moderate amount of learning, required in one's avocation and acquired with humility and a sense of duty, is much better for a Christian than much knowledge with vain conceit. All knowledge has, after all, only the purpose to perceive the right road to eternal happiness. But that is perceived more surely by a humble heart that loves God than by the conceited learning of many others put together. Holy Scripture says: "The soul of a holy man discovers sometimes true things more than seven watchmen that sit in a high place to watch" (Eccli. 37,18).

PRAYER OF THE CHURCH
(Sixth Sunday after Pentecost)

O God of Hosts, the giver of all good things, implant in our hearts the love of Thy name; make us to grow in fervor; foster in us that which is good; and in Thy loving kindness, of that which Thou fosterest, be Thou Thyself the safeguard. Through Christ our Lord. Amen.

DECEMBER 24
THE SERVANT OF GOD CONSTANCE, QUEEN OF ARAGON
Widow, Second Order

OMETIMES wicked fathers have good children, and not seldom does it devolve upon saintly daughters to atone for the sins of their fathers. Constance fulfilled this mission. Her father was Manfred, son of the wicked Emperor Frederick II. Stepping into the footsteps of his father, he heeded neither the precepts nor the rights of the Church. He usurped the kingdom of Sicily against the will of the pope, to whom, at that time, the disposition of it belonged. In consequence, he was excommunicated by the pope.

His pious daughter Constance prayed much and performed severe penances and mortifications in order to obtain from God the conversion of her father. Gladly would she have made the sacrifice of her entire life in a strict order in atonement for his crime, but she was obliged to yield to the will of her father and give her hand in marriage to the king of Aragon.

In the married state she endeavored to sanctify herself and her

THE SERAPHIC ORDER

children, a task in which she succeeded so admirably that her daughter Elizabeth, Queen of Portugal, is numbered among the saints of the Catholic Church.

After the death of her husband, Constance was obliged to hold the reins of government in Aragon for eight years. During this period she edified all by her Christian love of enemies. Charles of Anjou had robbed her father of his throne and of his life; he had also driven her cousin Conradin from his throne in Naples and had caused him to be executed in the market place of that city. Now the son of Charles was made prisoner by the fleet of Constance, and taken to her residence in Barcelona. But far from taking revenge on the son of the enemy of her family, she visited him in prison and made his condition as easy as possible. Yes, when the royal court pronounced the sentence of death upon him, she refused steadfastly to have the sentence executed. "How could I," said she, "justify myself before my Judge, who on the Cross pleaded forgiveness for His enemies?"

After Constance abdicated, she entered the Order of St. Clare, in which she lived sixteen years, devoting herself to prayer and the practices of penance until her saintly death in the year 1301.

ON LOVE FOR ONE'S ENEMIES

1. Christ our Lord says: "You have heard that it has been said: An eye for an eye and a tooth for a tooth. You shall love your neighbor, and hate your enemy. But I say to you, love your enemies" (Mt. 5,38.43-44). In the Old Testament it was said that he who had done evil to another, should be sentenced to suffer a like evil, and therefore it was said: Eye for eye, tooth for tooth. The Scribes and the Pharisees, who interpreted Holy Scripture according to their own ideas, deduced from this text that personal revenge was justified, and that anyone could inflict on his enemy the same injury that he had suffered. Such revenge, says our Lord, is not in conformity with His doctrine: "But I say to you: Love your enemies." Let us marvel at the clear and sublime doctrine of Christ, and let us strive, like Queen Constance, to carry it out when the occasion arises.

2. Consider that the world still adheres to the pharisaical principles of repaying like with like, because it is in accord with the inclinations of tainted human nature. Yes, it seems at times as if it were regarded as a disgrace to act otherwise. We do good and are friendly to those who act in the same manner towards us, but show hatred and enmity towards those who hate us. But our Divine Saviour asks: "Do not also the heathens this?" (Mt. 5,47). To us, however, He says: "Do good to those who hate

you, and pray for those who persecute and calumniate you, that you may be the children of your Father who is in heaven" (Mt. 5,44). To which group do you want to belong, to the heathens or to the children of God? 3. Consider what should induce us to love our enemies. Our enemy himself may not deserve it, that is true; but our enemy is a child of God, even though he be an ill-bred one, and God wishes that we love him as His child, just as we still love our own ill-bred child. God will, without doubt, punish our enemy, as He in His wisdom sees proper; but we should, out of love for God, forgive him and do him good, so that God may forgive us the wrong we have done against Him. "But if you will not forgive men; neither will your Father forgive you your offenses" (Mt. 6,15). Did not the Son of God give us the most beautiful example, when on the Cross He prayed for His deadly enemies? And our heavenly Father lets His sun shine on the good and on the bad. Do we not go to the same Table of the Lord with those against whom we have an aversion?

PRAYER OF THE CHURCH
(Ninth Postcommunion under "Various Prayers")

Pour forth upon us, O Lord, the spirit of Thy charity, that those whom Thou hast sated with the one Bread from heaven, Thou mayest in Thy goodness make of one mind. Through Christ our Lord. Amen.

DECEMBER 25
BLESSED JACOPONE DA TODI
Confessor, First Order

ABOUT the year 1230 a son was born to the noble family of the Benedetti at Todi in northern Italy. He received the name of Giacomo (Jacomo) or James in baptism. As a young man he devoted himself to the study of law and soon became a very capable and celebrated lawyer. At the same time he was very proud, vain, and worldly-minded. His young wife Vanna, on the other hand, was humble, devout, and generous. She regretted the worldly disposition of her husband, and endeavored to make amends before God for many of his failings.

One day in 1268, yielding to the wish of her husband, she attended a public tournament which was being held at Todi. Suddenly and unexpectedly, the stand in which she and many other noble women were seated, collapsed, and she was fatally injured. When her clothes were removed, it was seen that she wore about her waist a penitential girdle. James was deeply shaken at the sight. It was surely for me, he thought to himself, that she was doing such penance.

On the spot he resolved to abandon the vanities of the world, to live in extreme poverty, and for Christ's sake to become a fool.

He divided his possessions among the poor and entered the Third Order. Clothed in rags, he went about the streets of the city, an object of derision to the children and of horror to the adults, mocked at as a fool and despised as a penitent by many who had once admired him as a learned and prominent man. In derision he was given the name of Jacopone, that is, "Crazy Jim." He rejoiced in the name so much that he never wanted to be called otherwise.

After ten years of such humiliation he asked to be admitted into the Order of Friars Minor. The repute of his folly, however, had gone ahead of him to the convent, and so he met with difficulties. He then composed a beautiful poem, which is still extant, on the vanity of the world, and its merit opened the way for his admission into the order in 1278. From that time forward he lived an unusually rigorous life, striving hard to achieve perfection in every virtue. Out of humility he declined to be ordained a priest, yet he accomplished much good by his thoughtful and tender hymns, which he wrote in the vernacular.

Is it possible for a good and holy man to find himself suddenly on the wrong side in a conflict? That is what happened to Brother Jacopone in his old age. Having become a leader of the Spirituals, those friars who sought to imitate the poverty of St. Francis in a very strict manner, Jacopone also became associated with the two Colonna cardinals, Jacopo and Pietro, who were regarded as protectors of the Spirituals. These cardinals were also friends of Pope St. Celestine V, who ruled the Church during the latter half of 1294 and then resigned. Unfortunately, the Colonna cardinals rebelled against Celestine's successor, Boniface VIII, and questioned the validity of his election. Jacopone, who was undoubtedly in good faith, was with the Colonna cardinals when their fortress at Palestrina fell in September, 1298; and so, at the age of sixty-eight he was excommunicated and thrown into prison. Although Jacopone now realized he had made a mistake and begged Boniface VIII for absolution, it was only five years later, in October, 1303, that Boniface's successor, Benedict XI, absolved him and released him from his dungeon.

Jacopone had borne the hardships of his imprisonment in the spirit of penance; and he now spent the last three years of his life among his brethren, a more spiritual man than before. It was probably at this time that he wrote that masterpiece of Latin hymnology, the *Stabat Mater*. During those last years he did not cease to weep. "I weep," he said, "because Love is not loved." On Christmas eve, 1306, while he and some of his brethren were in the Poor Clare convent at Collazzone, Jacopone knew that his last hour had come; and, like St. Francis, he welcomed Sister Death with song. His friend, Blessed John of La Verna, miraculously appeared on the scene and administered the last sacraments to him. Then Jacopone sang one of his favorite poems: "Jesus, in Thee is all our trust, high hope of every heart." When he had finished his song, he closed his eyes; and, it is claimed, he died from excess of love for the Infant Jesus, just as the priest who was celebrating the midnight Mass intoned the Gloria in excelsis Deo; "Glory to God in the highest, and on earth peace to men of good will!"

From the time of his death, Brother Jacopone was venerated as a saint; and in popular devotion he has been called Blessed Jacopone through the centuries. In 1596 his remains were enclosed in a magnificent tomb and placed in the Church of San Fortunato at Todi. At different times, for instance in 1868-1869, attempts were made to have his cause of beatification introduced in Rome; but thus far his veneration as Blessed has not been officially approved. (Cf. Underhill, *Jacopone da Todi, A Spiritual Biography*, pp. 1-211.)

ON THE NATIVITY OF CHRIST

1. On Christmas Day our hearts should be enkindled with holy love. In Bethlehem we find the Son of God lying like any poor child on coarse straw and wrapped in swaddling clothes. And why? In order to bring salvation to us sinners. The sacrifices of the Old Law were not enough. So the Son of God said to His Father: "A body Thou hast given Me; behold I come" (Heb. 10,5). It is with this body that He begins today to atone for us. — Beholding this marvelous spectacle, turn away as our holy Father St. Francis and Blessed Jacopone did from the love of the world, and exclaim: "Dear Babe of Bethlehem, we offer Thee our love!"

2. On Christmas Day our hearts should be aglow with joy and gratitude. Let us acknowledge that, if this Babe had not been born, we should all have been lost for all time. But there is the comforting message: "This day is born to you a Saviour, who is Christ the Lord" (Lk. 2,11). With Francis and Blessed Jacopone we will rejoice over the birth of our Saviour, and give joyful expression to our sincere gratitude. — Say with gratitude and joy: "Dear Child, I love Thee with all my heart, in joy and in sorrow too."

3. On Christmas Day our hearts should expand with readiness to make

sacrifices. We should pledge ourselves to carry out to the full the Christmas message, "Glory to God in the highest, and peace on earth to men of good will" (Lk. 2,14). In other words, we should say to the Divine Child: "I will do all I can for Thee and Thy honor." We should make Him the offering of our will. All that is implied in the term good will. — Pray that your good will may manifest itself in action. Say with our holy Father St. Francis: "Let us love the Babe of Bethlehem."

PRAYER OF THE CHURCH

O God, who dost rejoice us annually with the festival of our redemption, grant that we may confidently look upon Thine only-begotten Son, whom we now cheerfully embrace as our Redeemer, when He shall come as our Judge, Jesus Christ, our Lord, who liveth and reigneth forever and ever. Amen.

DECEMBER 26
BLESSED JEREMY LAMBERTENGHI
Confessor, Third Order

ORN at Como, Italy, Jeremy or Jeremias Lambertenghi was the son of a family which belonged to the nobility. After a youth spent in innocence and the practices of piety, he joined the Third Order Regular (T.O.R.) and made such rapid progress in virtue that he soon reached a high degree of sanctity.

After his ordination to the priesthood, he devoted most of his time to the preaching of the word of God. In this capacity he reaped a rich harvest of souls, one reason being the fact that God gave special efficacy to his apostolic work by miracles.

Also after his death in 1513, God testified to the holiness of his life by many miracles; and he has been honored as a saint ever since his demise. Because of the suppression of convents in Italy his remains have been transferred several times from one place to another; and they now rest in the cathedral at Forli in the Romagna, where they are held in great veneration.

Toward the end of the nineteenth century, petitions were sent to the Holy See requesting official approval of the cult of Blessed Jeremy, which had been kept up for some four centuries; and according to Holzapfel (1908) this approval has been granted. However, the feast of Blessed

Jeremy, for some reason or other, does not appear in any of the Franciscan calendars, not even in that of the Third Order Regular.

ON THE CHRISTMAS TREE

1. The Christmas tree is a Christian custom. Recent investigations prove that there is no vestige of anything pagan or Protestant about it; rather, it originated in Catholic Alsace. In fact, when it was first introduced, which was in the middle of the seventeenth century, it was strongly opposed by the Protestants. Nevertheless, it has been introduced everywhere, and cannot be separated from the feast of Christmas. One is tempted to apply to it the words of Scripture: "The tree was great and strong, the sight of it was even to the ends of all the earth" (Dan. 4,8). — Let us then keep up the beautiful custom of the Christmas tree.
2. The Christmas tree is a custom full of meaning. Being a tree of the kind that does not wither, it is a figure of the tree of life in the midst of Paradise (Gen. 2,9). Its fruits were to give us eternal life, but sin prevented that. Through the Babe lying in the crib we can once more partake of its fruits, for He is the Life, who has come that we may have life. The lights on the Christmas tree remind us of Him whom St. John calls the "true light which enlightens every man who comes into this world" (Jn. 1,9). This Light is, for the time being, hidden in the stable in the form of a little child. — How well crib and Christmas tree fit together!
3. The Christmas tree is a consoling custom. Many beautiful as well as tasty things are hung on its branches and Christmas gifts lie at its base. Why all this? In order to direct our thoughts to the many graces we receive through our redemption, from the Child lying in the crib, God's gift to us, without whom we should have been lost. — As you stand before the Christmas tree, thank God for His great love of mankind, and vow to love Him sincerely in return.

PRAYER OF THE CHURCH

Grant, we beseech Thee, almighty God, that we, who are filled with the new light of Thy Incarnate Word, may show forth in our works that which by faith shineth in our minds. Through the same Christ our Lord. Amen.

DECEMBER 27
BLESSED THEODORIC COELDE
Confessor, First Order

CERTAIN picture of Theodoric bears the following true description of him: "An extraordinary preacher, author of the first German catechism, angel of peace, hero of charity, illustrious both in life and after his death for his virtues and miracles." The official acts of the order give him the title of Blessed, for the confirmation of which a petition has been sent to the Holy See.

Theodoric Coelde was born in 1435. He studied philosophy and theology in Cologne, and then joined the Canons Regular of St. Augustine. But the sermons of an eloquent Franciscan made so deep an impression on the young Augustinian, that, like St. Anthony of Padua, he resolved to become a Franciscan. He became a member of the province of Lower Germany, where religious observance was held in high esteem.

In 1489 an epidemic broke out in Brussels. During the two years that the disease raged, Father Theodoric ministered to the sick in a truly heroic manner. Neither lack of food, drink, and sleep, nor distance nor difficult roads could keep him from searching out the places where the plague had struck, in order to hear the confessions of the dying, give them holy Communion, and administer extreme unction. Old records speak of thirty-two thousand dying persons to whom Theodoric was an apostle of charity during the two years of the plague.

He labored also with unusual success as an author. His works include meditations on the sufferings of Christ, a little work called Daily Interior Practice, and his Little Book of Devotions in the Love of Jesus and Mary. His Mirror for Christians was the first German catechism and achieved unusual fame. It appeared for the first time in 1470 in Brabant, and a thirty-fourth edition appeared in Cologne in 1708.

As a priest Theodoric possessed the special gift of settling dissensions and reconciling people who were at odds with each other. As a religious he did much to establish regular observance, and as superior of the convent of Brussels, he converted it, as Venerable Father General Francis Quiñones declared, into a dwelling of saints.

On December 11, 1515, while preaching to the people, he mentioned that his death was near at hand. At noon he failed to appear at the community meal, remaining in his cell. One of the brethren was sent to see what was the matter, and found him there kneeling, with hands folded, but lifeless.

He was immediately venerated by the people as a saint, especially as a patron against contagious disease.

'

THE RULE OF LIFE OF BLESSED THEODORIC

1. In the evening always call to mind how you have spent the day, and to what extent you may have sinned by word and thought, by thoughtlessness and intentionally, and by the neglect of the good you could and should have done.

2. If you must give an order, do it in gentle terms and a kind manner. You will thus gain the love and affection of all men.

3. If you wish to enjoy peace, do not be ambitious. Do not aspire to an office, and do not envy others for the offices they hold. It is no small thing to govern human beings. Whoever entertains such desires does not possess the spirit of God.

4. Love to be alone, converse with God, shun the company of men, do not become intimate with anybody. You will then preserve a good conscience and have God as your Friend.

5. Just as people strive daily to increase their wealth and temporal goods, so aim to become wealthier in the goods of the soul.

PRAYER OF THE CHURCH
Grant us, we beseech Thee, O Lord our God, that we who rejoice in the celebration of the nativity of our Lord Jesus Christ, may live so worthily that we may deserve to be admitted into His company. Amen.

❦❧❦❧❦❧❦❧❦❧❦❧❦

DECEMBER 28
THE SERVANT OF GOD MARGARET STADLER
Virgin, Second Order

IT is well known that our holy Father St. Francis had great devotion to the holy Childhood of Jesus. He was the first who built a crib, such as we have it at Christmas, and with the approval of the pope he had the holy sacrifice of the Mass offered up before it. The childlike purity and simplicity of his soul as well as his ardent love for the Word made flesh drew him to this devotion, and many of his children followed his example.

Of his followers, the members of the Second Order, the Poor Clares, whose spirit finds expression particularly in the virtues of the holy Childhood, are known for their tender devotion to the Divine Child.

Among them the servant of God Margaret distinguished herself in a special way. She lived in the convent at Sefflingen, not far from Ulm in Suabia. One day while she was absorbed in contemplating the lovableness of God who came into this world as a child, hours passed without Margaret being aware of it. At the time she should have been at her duties in the kitchen.

But while our Divine Saviour fed His spouse with heavenly sweetness, He wished also to provide for the bodily nourishment of her fellow sisters. For a singularly beautiful little boy was seen in the kitchen preparing the food, and when it was set before the sisters at mealtime, they declared that they had never tasted anything so delicious. But the wonderful little cook had vanished.

From that time on, Margaret practiced even more faithfully the devotion to the Child Jesus. Rich in heavenly merits, her life came to a close in the year 1521.

ON DEVOTION TO THE HOLY INFANCY

1. Consider how Mother Church herself encourages us to honor the holy Childhood of Jesus by the observance of Christmas and the ensuing season which extends to the feast of the Purification of the Blessed Virgin Mary. We make the best of this observance if we frequently reflect upon the great love of our Saviour in coming into this world as a little child, and living so many years in humble seclusion in order to win quiet and humble hearts for Himself. How pleasing to our Lord the devotion to His holy Childhood is, we learn from the fact that He has appeared to so many holy souls in the form of a child, as, for example, to St. Anthony, to St. Felix, to St. Veronica Giuliani, and others. In the form of a child, too, He performed Margaret's place in the convent kitchen.

2. Consider how the sentiments of love, innocence, and simplicity from which this devotion proceeded in the case of our holy Father St. Francis will also increase in our hearts by means of this same devotion. What can a soul that has nothing in common with the world desire more earnestly than to be imbued with this innocent, childlike spirit so pleasing to God? Therefore, practice this devotion to the Child Jesus not only during the Christmas season but throughout the year. — For the sake of the dear Child Jesus, take a cheerful interest in children, especially those who are poor and neglected.

3. All true veneration calls for imitation as well. In the matter of devotion to the holy Infancy, the point which parents and superiors should imitate consists in this, that, like Joseph and Mary, they exercise continual

solicitude for those entrusted to their care; while children and subordinates should practice obedience and submission like the Child Jesus, and all of whatever station should learn to be humble and modest. And if they have not remained children by their innocence, let them make amends for all their transgressions by sincere penance, and thus return to the innocence of childhood. For our Lord says: "Unless you be converted and become as little children, you shall not enter into the kingdom of heaven" (Mt. 18,3).

PRAYER OF THE CHURCH

O God, whose only-begotten Son has appeared in the substance of our flesh, grant, we beseech Thee, that by Him in whom outwardly we recognize our likeness, we may deserve to be inwardly created anew. Who with Thee liveth and reigneth forever and ever. Amen.

DECEMBER 29
THE SERVANT OF GOD DIDACUS OF SINAGRA
Confessor, Third Order

 IDACUS was born in Sicily. As a young man he was one day making a journey when he was attacked by robbers. They kidnapped him, and when no one could be found to pay a ransom for him, they forced him under threats of death to be their servant. But he kept God before his mind even in this terrible predicament and never took part in the crimes committed by the bandits. When Sixtus V ascended the papal throne in 1585, he made it his first task to root out banditry in the Papal States. The band to which Didacus was attached, was also seized, brought to justice, and condemned to atone for its crimes by the death penalty. Didacus had been caught with the robbers, but instead of being condemned to death, he was condemned to the galleys. His quiet resignation and unchanging piety soon convinced the authorities of his innocence, and so, after an imprisonment of eighteen months, they set him free.

But the sad experience he had undergone made a deep impression on his soul. He resolved to quit the world and to devote the remaining days of his life only to the service of God and to the task of his salvation. He, therefore, entered the Third Order of St. Francis, and then withdrew to a high mountain known as Mount St. Philip. There he spent twenty-five

888

THE SERAPHIC ORDER

years in a secluded cave, leading a very rigorous and God-pleasing life. Enriched by many virtues and glorified by many miracles, he died peacefully in the Lord in 1612.

ON THE DISPENSATIONS OF PROVIDENCE

1. Consider how admirable are the ways of God. He permitted Didacus to become a servant of robbers and a galley slave in order to make a saint of him. Who would have believed that Joseph, sold by his brothers and carried into Egypt, was on the way to be the first in rank after the king himself? Who could have told Job in advance, when he was robbed of his cattle, when his children were buried under the wreckage of his home, and he himself was covered all over with sores and sitting on a dunghill, that this way was leading him to greater wealth than he had previously? Truly, "how incomprehensible are the judgments of God. For who has known the mind of the Lord? Or who has been His counsellor?" (Rom. 11,34). In humility let us adore the ways of God and say with the Apostle: "Of him, and by Him, and in Him are all things. To Him be glory forever" (Rom. 11,36).

2. Consider that sometimes the ways of God are rough and difficult, but they are ways of salvation nevertheless. There is much that is inordinate in all of us. If we are to become citizens of heaven, there is still much sawing, planing, and filing to be done. There is still much that must be atoned for before we can enter into the kingdom of heaven. That is why the mercy of God often leads us along rough ways, so that at the end of our life He can lead us into everlasting glory. When blind Tobias sat at home, derided even by his wife, he sighed and said to the Lord. "Thou art just, O Lord, and all Thy judgments are just, and all Thy ways are mercy" (Tob. 3,2). — Do you pray in such a way?

3. Consider that with all our wisdom, we could never find better ways to true happiness than those by which God's providence leads us. We often think that something else would be better for us. But the Lord declares to us through the Prophet: "My thoughts are not your thoughts, nor your ways My ways" (Is. 55,8,9). Hence, Thomas a Kempis admonishes us in the name of the Lord: "Son, commit your cause to Me always; I will dispose of it well in due season. Await My appointment and then you shall experience greater success than if you had vehemently pursued a thing" (3,39). — May the grace of God give us this holy resignation and childlike confidence.

PRAYER OF THE CHURCH
(Saturday of Whitsun Week)

In Thy bounty, O Lord, we beseech Thee, pour forth into our hearts the Holy Ghost, by whose wisdom we were created, and by whose providence we are guided. Through Christ our Lord. Amen.

⊗⊗⊗⊗⊗⊗⊗⊗

DECEMBER 30
THE SERVANT OF GOD JACOBA OF SETTESOLI
Widow, Third Order

JACOBA or Giacoma was a young noblewoman of Rome. After her husband died she remained a widow and raised her two sons in virtue and in the fear of the Lord. When she learned of the holy and penitential life of St. Francis, she desired to make his acquaintance and to seek his advice in the spiritual difficulties she encountered.

The desire was gratified when St. Francis came to Rome to obtain from the pope the sanction of his rule. The sermons and admonitions of St. Francis so affected her, and Jacoba was so filled with enthusiasm for the love of God and the renunciation of the world, that she transferred all her possessions to her two sons, the better to devote herself to the salvation of her soul and the practice of good works.

For this reason, too, she entered the Third Order and submitted entirely to the direction of the friars. She arranged that a hospice in the Trastevere or Trans-Tiber section of Rome be furnished for them, and provided like a loving mother for their needs, especially for those of the sick brethren.

When St. Francis felt that his end was approaching, he sent her notice, as he had promised, by means of the following letter, which is still preserved: "Know, beloved sister in Christ, that God in His goodness has revealed to me the end of my life. It is very near at hand. If you wish to find me still alive, make haste so that you will be at St. Mary of the Angels by next Sunday. Bring with you some ash-gray cloth to be used as a shroud for my body, and wax candles for my burial."

But before the letter was sent to Rome, Jacoba with her two sons and a great retinue arrived at the Portiuncula. She was led to the bed of the dying saint and fell at his feet as if in ecstasy, until St. Francis bade her arise. Then she related: "In prayer last evening I heard a voice, which said: "If you wish to see Brother Francis alive, go at once to St. Mary of the Angels; take with you whatever will be necessary for his burial as well as the refreshments that you used to provide for him when he was ill at Rome. So I came hither and brought everything with me."

Francis thanked God and partook of a little nourishment which she had brought him. During the last four days of his life, Jacoba remained at St. Mary of the Angels in order to give the dying man whatever comfort and assistance she could.

After his death, the body of the saint was wrapped in the cloth Jacoba had provided. She also assisted the brethren in arranging the funeral, which she attended amid many tears.

Then Jacoba went back to Rome to put her affairs in order, after which she renounced the world completely, and returned to Assisi, where she spent the remaining days of her life watching and praying at the tomb of her spiritual father. On February 8, 1239, she, too, died a blessed death and was laid to rest in the same church where St. Francis had been buried.

CONCERNING CHRISTIAN BURIAL

1. What Jacoba did for the burial of St. Francis was the corporal work of mercy called burying the dead. This act of mercy includes everything that is associated with the Christian burial of a deceased person. We may judge for ourselves how pleasing this was to God from the fact that God announced to Jacoba the approaching death of St. Francis by means of a special revelation. And the archangel Raphael pointed out to Tobias how God rewards this pious act: "When you prayed with tears and buried the dead, I offered your prayer to the Lord" (Tob. 12,12). How pleasing to God it must be when we honor with a Christian burial the bodies which were temples of God here on earth and which will be endowed with eternal glory in heaven! — Have you practiced this corporal work of mercy?

2. Consider that the honors of a Christian burial do not consist of worldly pomp and a grand funeral procession. Such things attract attention, but awaken very little devotion; and oftentimes the honor of the living rather than that of the dead is the real motive behind it all. It is much better to be mindful of the poor at a funeral, and come to the assistance of the departed by means of holy Masses. Think of how you yourself would wish your funeral to be conducted.

3. Consider that it is especially meritorious if from pious motives you accompany the remains of poor people to the grave — people who have few friends and relatives and would otherwise have little honorable escort.

It is like the funeral procession which Joseph of Arimathea, Nicodemus, and the pious women formed to take our Lord from Mount Calvary to His grave. The rule of the Third Order prescribes that Tertiaries attend the funeral of a departed member and devoutly pray the rosary. A quiet and devout funeral procession is certainly the truest honor and the dearest tribute one can offer the deceased.

PRAYER OF THE CHURCH

O God, of whose mercy it is that the souls of Thy faithful people do rest in peace, graciously grant unto Thy servants and handmaids and unto all that here and everywhere rest in Christ, the forgiveness of their sins; that, absolved from every offense, they may rejoice forever with Thee. Through Christ our Lord. Amen.

DECEMBER 31
BLESSED ANTHONY OF HUNGARY
Confessor, Third Order

 LMIGHTY God Himself instituted a jubilee in the Old Testament (Lev. 25). It was celebrated every fifty years, and a certain remission of debt was associated with it. So a jubilee year was also celebrated in the Christian Church of old every fifty years, and later on every twenty-five years, to which a plenary indulgence, or the remission of the temporal punishment due to sin, was attached. Sometimes, too, an extraordinary jubilee indulgence is granted because of some special occasion.

In former times, however, the jubilee indulgence could not be gained in all parts of the Catholic world, as nowadays, but only in Rome. The Jubilee indulgence of the year 1350 was a solemn one and was attended by a large number of persons. Millions of pilgrims came from every country of Europe. In Italy the highways were crowded with people going to Rome to visit the tombs of the Apostles.

The holy man Anthony had also come that year from Hungary, in order to share in the graces of the indulgence at Rome. After he had performed his devotions there, he went to Assisi to gain the Portiuncula indulgence, and there he also joined the Third Order of St. Francis. Continuing his journey, he became ill at Foligno, and that is how he came to the hospital of the Holy Spirit.

At the hospital he received very loving care, and to it, next to God, he ascribed the recovery of his health. In gratitude, Anthony, who was free to do as he wished, resolved to remain in the hospital, and to consecrate his life to the service of the sick. He did that until his death, with so much love and humility that he became a model to all the nurses in the institution. In addition, he led a very strict life, and obtained from God the grace of contemplation at prayer. He died in 1398, honored by all as a saint.

Almighty God showed how pleased He was with Anthony's extraordinary sense of gratitude and the holiness of his life by numerous miracles which occurred at his grave. As a consequence his body was exhumed in the year 1608; and, clad in the garb of the Third Order, it was laid out in a precious gold-plated shrine over the high altar of the hospital church at Foligno.

ON GRATITUDE

1. We should give thanks at the end of each day. The saints are outstanding examples of gratitude, some of them devoting their days and even their nights to this holy task. Should we not at least give thanks at the close of each day, manifesting our gratitude for all the benefits God has bestowed on us? Gratitude is a rare virtue, and it is very pleasing to God. Kneel down before the Most High every evening and say with the Psalmist: "Let my prayer be directed as incense in Thy sight, the lifting up of my hands as an evening sacrifice" (Ps. 140,2). — What kind of night prayers do you say?

2. We should give thanks to God when He sends us crosses. We do not know what is profitable to us toward a happy death and everlasting life. We seem to think that everything must always go well with us here on earth. Then, when the night comes, that is, when our good fortune begins to decline, we become dejected and give up. Yet, the Apostle says: "Count it all joy when you fall into diverse temptations" (Jas. 1,2). Why rejoice? Because in every temptation and trial we must see the kind hand of God, seeking to make us ripe for heaven by means of suffering. — In the time of suffering, be courageous to make a sincere act of thanksgiving to God.

3. We should also give thanks at the end of the year. Another year has gone by. Let us thank God that we are still alive. Let us thank God that we have been the beneficiaries of so many blessings for body and soul. Let us thank God that we have been saved from a bad death. "Give thanks always for all things in the name of our Lord Jesus Christ, to God, and the Father" (Eph. 5,20). Today, above all, let us give special thanks to God,

since there are so many people who are spending this day offending God by boisterous amusements, intemperance, and other sins, instead of rendering thanks to Him. — A grateful heart deserves and always receives new graces and blessings.

PRAYER OF THE CHURCH

O God, whose mercy is boundless, and whose bounty is an inexhaustible treasury, we thank Thy gracious majesty for all the benefits Thou hast bestowed upon us, and we implore Thy mercy at all times that Thou mayest not forsake those whose prayers Thou hast heeded, but wouldst rather prepare them for the eternal reward. Through our Lord Jesus Christ Thy Son, who liveth and reigneth with Thee and the Holy Ghost, God forever and ever. Amen.

Appendix I

FRANCISCAN SAINTS AND BLESSED
(Chronological List)[3]

1220 S Accursius, Friar Minor, brother, martyr
1220 S Adjutus, Friar Minor, brother, martyr
1220 S Berard, Friar Minor, priest, martyr
1220 S Otto (Otho), Friar Minor, priest, martyr
1220 S Peter, Friar Minor, priest, martyr
1226 S Francis of Assisi, founder of three orders, deacon
1227 S Angelo, Friar Minor, priest, martyr
1227 S Daniel, Friar Minor, priest, martyr
1227 S Domnus, Friar Minor, brother, martyr
1227 S Hugolinus, Friar Minor, priest, martyr
1227 S Leo, Friar Minor, priest, martyr
1227 S Nicholas, Friar Minor, priest, martyr
1227 S Samuel, Friar Minor, priest, martyr
1231 S Anthony of Padua, Friar Minor, priest, doctor
1231 S Elizabeth of Hungary, Tertiary, widow
1231 B John of Perugia, Friar Minor, priest, martyr
1231 B Peter of Sassoferrato, Friar Minor, brother, martyr
1232 B Bentivolio Buoni, Friar Minor, priest
1232 B Benvenute of Gubbio, Friar Minor, brother
1233 B Peregrin of Falerone, Friar Minor, brother
1236 B Agnellus of Pisa, Friar Minor, priest
1236 B Philippa Mareria, Poor Clare, virgin
1236 B Rizzerio of Muccia, Friar Minor, priest
1237 B Roger of Todi, Friar Minor, priest
1242 B Helen Enselmina of Padua, Poor Clare, widow
1242 B Raymond Carboneri of Narbonne, Friar Minor, priest, martyr
1242 B Stephen of Narbonne, Friar Minor, priest, martyr
1242 B Veridiana of Attavanti, Tertiary, virgin
1245 B Gerard Mecatti of Villamagna, Tertiary
1246 B Humiliana Cerchi, Tertiary, widow
1250 B Giles (Guy) de Vinotelli of Cortona, Friar Minor, priest
1252 S Ferdinand III, King of Castile and Leon, Tertiary
1252 S Rose of Viterbo, Tertiary, virgin

---

[3] The date given is the year of death.

1253 S Agnes of Assisi, Poor Clare, virgin
1253 S Clare of Assisi, foundress of Poor Clares, virgin
1254 B Andrew Caccioli of Spello, Friar Minor, priest
1258 B Liberatus of Lauro, Friar Minor, priest
1260 B Gandolph of Binasco, Friar Minor, priest
1260 B Luchesio (Lucius) of Poggibonsi, first Tertiary
1262 B Giles of Assisi, Friar Minor, cleric
1268 B Salome of Cracow, Poor Clare, widow
1270 B Isabelle of France, Poor Clare, virgin
1270 S Louis IX, King of France, Tertiary
1271 B John Penna, Friar Minor, priest
1272 B Christopher of Romagnola, Friar Minor, priest
1274 S Bonaventure, Friar Minor, bishop, cardinal, doctor
1276 S Benvenute Scotivoli of Osimo (Ancona), Friar Minor, bishop
1276 B Gregory X, Tertiary, pope
1278 S Zita of Lucca, Tertiary, virgin
1280 B Novellon of Faenza, Tertiary, hermit
1282 B Agnes of Prague (Bohemia), Poor Clare, virgin
1282 B Torello of Poppi, Tertiary, hermit
1285 B Luke Belludi, Friar Minor, priest
1289 B Conrad Miliani of Ascoli, Friar Minor, priest
1289 B John Buralli of Parma, Friar Minor, priest
1289 B Peter of Siena, Tertiary
1292 B Kinga (Cunegunda) of Poland, Poor Clare, virgin
1297 S Margaret of Cortona, Tertiary, penitent
1298 B Yolande (Jolenta), Tertiary, widow
1299 B Gerard of Lunel, Tertiary, hermit
1299 S Louis of Toulouse, Friar Minor, bishop
1300 B Bartolo of San Gimignano, Tertiary, priest
1302 B Andrew Segni of Conti, Friar Minor, priest
1303 S Yves (Ivo) of Brittany, Tertiary, priest
1304 B Amatus Ronconi, Tertiary, hermit
1304 B James of Pieve (Castelpieve), Tertiary, martyr
1304 B John Pelingotto, Tertiary, hermit
1304 B Peter of Treja, Friar Minor, priest
1304 B Raynier of Arezzo, Friar Minor, brother
1307 B Jane of Signa, Tertiary, virgin
1308 S Clare of Montefalco, Tertiary, virgin
1309 B Angela of Foligno, Tertiary, widow
1310 B Christina Macabai (Menabuoi) of Valdarno, Tertiary, virgin
1316 B Raymond Lull, Tertiary, martyr
1320 B Matthia Nazzarei, Poor Clare, virgin

1320 B Waldo (Vivald) of San Gimignano, Tertiary, hermit
1321 B Thomas of Tolentino, Friar Minor, martyr
1322 B Francis Venimbene of Fabriano, Friar Minor, priest
1323 B John of La Verna, Friar Minor, priest
1323 B Elzear of Sabran, Tertiary
1323 B Peter Cresci of Foligno, Tertiary
1326 B Clare of Rimini, Poor Clare, widow
1327 S Roch of Montpellier, Tertiary
1330 B Bartholomew Pucci, Friar Minor, priest
1331 B Odoric Matiussi of Pordenone, Friar Minor, priest
1336 S Elizabeth (Isabella), Queen of Portugal, Tertiary, widow
1340 B Benvenute Mareri of Recanati, Friar Minor, brother
1340 B Gentle Finiguerra of Matelica, Friar Minor, priest, martyr
1345 B Gerard Cagnoli of Valencia, Friar Minor, brother
1350 B Francis Zanferdini of Pesaro, Tertiary, hermit
1350 B Julian Cesarello of Valle, Friar Minor, priest
1351 S Conrad Confalonieri of Piacenza, Tertiary
1355 B Petronilla of Troyes, Poor Clare, virgin
1356 B Michelina of Pesaro, Tertiary, widow
1358 B Delphina of Glandeves, Tertiary, widow
1364 B Charles of Blois, Duke of Brittany, Tertiary
1373 S Bridget of Sweden, Tertiary, widow
1373 B Hugolinus Magalotti of Camerino, Tertiary, hermit
1380 B Margaret Colonna, Poor Clare, widow
1390 B Sanctes Brancosini of Montefabro, Friar Minor, brother
1391 B Nicholas Tavelich of Illyria (Dalmatia), Friar Minor, priest, martyr
1396 B Conrad of Offida, Friar Minor, priest
1397 B John of Cetina, Friar Minor, priest, martyr
1397 B Peter of Duenas, Friar Minor, brother, martyr
1400 B Lucy Caltagirone, Third Order Regular, virgin
1400 B Oddino Barotti of Fossano, Tertiary, priest
1404 B William Cufitella of Scicli, Tertiary, hermit
1409 B James of Strepar, Friar Minor, bishop
1414 B Jane Mary Maillé, Tertiary, widow
1420 B Elizabeth the Good Achlerin, Third Order Regular, widow
1431 S Joan of Arc, Tertiary, virgin
1433 B John of Peace Cini of Pisa, Tertiary
1435 B Angelina of Marsciano, Third Order Regular, widow
1435 B Peter Gambacorta of Pisa, Tertiary, hermit
1440 S Frances of Rome, Tertiary, widow
1444 S Bernardin of Siena, Franciscan, priest
1444 B Felicia Meda of Milan, Poor Clare, virgin

1447 S Coleta (Colette) of Corbie, Poor Clare, virgin
1447 B Thomas of Florence, Franciscan, brother
1449 B Nicholas of Forcapalena, Tertiary, priest, hermit
1451 B Herculan of Piagale, Franciscan, priest
1451 B Matthew of Girgenti, Franciscan, bishop
1456 B Gabriel Ferretti, Franciscan, priest
1456 S John Capistran, Franciscan, priest
1456 S Peter Regalado, Franciscan, priest
1458 B Bernard of Baden, Tertiary
1460 B Archangelo Piacenza of Calatafimi, Franciscan, priest
1461 B Anthony of Stroncone, Franciscan, brother
1463 S Catharine Vigri of Bologna, Poor Clare, virgin
1463 S Didacus of Alcalá de Henares, Franciscan, brother
1472 B Antonia of Florence, Poor Clare, widow
1476 S James of the March, Franciscan, priest
1478 B Seraphina Sforza, Poor Clare, widow
1479 B Mark Fantuzzi of Bologna, Franciscan, priest
1482 B Anthony Bonfadini of Ferrara, Franciscan, priest
1482 B Pacificus of Cerano (Ceredano), Franciscan, priest
1482 B Simon of Lypnica, Franciscan, priest
1485 B John Dukla, Franciscan, priest
1490 B Christopher of Milan, Franciscan, priest
1490 B Beatrice of Silva, foundress Conceptionist Poor Clares, virgin
1490 B James of Bitecto (Jadera), Illyria (Dalmatia), Franciscan, brother
1490 B Peter of Mogliano, Franciscan, priest
1491 B Eustochium of Messina, Poor Clare, virgin
1491 B Vitalis of Bastia, Tertiary, hermit
1492 B Balthasar Ravaschieri of Chiavari, Franciscan, priest
1494 B Bernardin of Feltre, Franciscan, priest
1495 B Angelo Carletti of Chiavasso, Franciscan, priest
1496 B Mark of Montegallo, Franciscan, priest
1498 B Elizabeth Amodei, Tertiary, virgin
1503 B Bernardin Amici of Fossa, Franciscan, priest
1503 B Louise Albertoni, Tertiary, widow
1503 B Louise of Savoy, Poor Clare, widow
1504 B Timothy of Montecchio, Franciscan, priest
1504 B Vincent of Aquila, Franciscan, brother
1505 S Jane of Valois, Tertiary, widow
1505 B Ladislas of Gielniow, Franciscan, priest
1507 B Francis of Calderola, Franciscan, priest
1510 S Catharine of Genoa, Tertiary, housewife
1510 B Mark Marconi, Tertiary, hermit

1510 B Jeremy Lambertenghi, Third Order Regular, priest
1513 B Paula Montaldi of Volta, Poor Clare, virgin
1514 B Paula Gambara-Costa, Tertiary, widow
1518 B Giles of Lorenzana, Franciscan, brother
1521 B Margaret of Lorraine, Poor Clare, widow
1524 B Baptista Varani, Poor Clare, virgin
1535 B Lawrence Masculi of Villamagna, Franciscan, priest
1535 S Thomas More, Tertiary, martyr
1538 B John Forest, Franciscan, priest, martyr
1539 B John Baptist Righi of Fabriano, Franciscan, priest
1540 S Angela Merici, Tertiary, foundress of Ursulines, virgin
1562 S Peter of Alcantara, Franciscan, priest
1567 S Salvator of Horta, Franciscan, brother
1572 S Anthony Hornaer, Franciscan, priest, martyr
1572 S Anthony of Weert, Franciscan, priest, martyr
1572 S Cornelius Wikan of Dorstat, Franciscan, brother, martyr
1572 S Francis Rod, Franciscan, priest, martyr
1572 S Godfrey Mervelan, Franciscan, priest, martyr
1572 S Jerome van Weert, Franciscan, priest, martyr
1572 S Nicasius (Nicaise) Hes or Jonson, Franciscan, priest, martyr
1572 S Nicholas Pieck, Franciscan, priest, martyr
1572 S Peter van Asche (Askan), Franciscan, brother, martyr
1572 S Theodoric of Emden, Franciscan, priest, martyr
1572 S Willehad (Wilhad) Dan, Franciscan, priest, martyr
1583 B Nicholas Factor of Valencia, Franciscan, priest
1584 S Charles Borromeo, Tertiary, cardinal, bishop
1589 S Felix of Cantalice, Capuchin, brother
1589 S Benedict the Moor, Franciscan, brother
1592 S Paschal Baylon, Franciscan, brother
1597 S Anthony of Nagasaki, Tertiary, martyr
1597 S Bonaventure of Miyako, Tertiary, martyr
1597 S Cosmas Zakeya, Tertiary, martyr
1597 S Francis Blanco, Franciscan, priest, martyr
1597 S Francis Falegname of Miyako, Tertiary, martyr
1597 S Francis the Doctor of Miyako, Tertiary, martyr
1597 S Francis of S Michael de la Parilla, Franciscan, brother, martyr
1597 S Gabriel Ise, Tertiary, martyr
1597 S Gonsalvo Garcia of India, Franciscan, brother, martyr
1597 S Joachim Sakakibara, Tertiary, martyr
1597 S Leo Ibaraki Karasumaru, Tertiary, martyr
1597 S Leo Kinuya, Tertiary, martyr
1597 S Louis Ibaraki, Tertiary, martyr

1597 S Martin of the Ascension de Aguirre, Franciscan, priest, martyr
1597 S Matthias of Miyako, Tertiary, martyr
1597 S Michael Kozaki, Tertiary, martyr
1597 S Paul Ibaraki, Tertiary, martyr
1597 S Paul Suzuki, Tertiary, martyr
1597 S Peter Baptist Blasquez, Franciscan, priest, martyr
1597 S Peter Sukejiro, Tertiary, martyr
1597 S Philip of Jesus de las Casas of Mexico, Franciscan, cleric, martyr
1597 S Thomas Danki, Tertiary, martyr
1597 S Thomas Kozaki, Tertiary, martyr
1598 B Godfrey Maurice Jones, Franciscan, priest, martyr
1600 B Sepastian of Aparicio, Franciscan, brother
1602 B Andrew Hibernon, Franciscan, brother
1604 B Seraphin of Montegranaro, Capuchin, priest
1606 B Julian of S Augustine, Franciscan, brother
1610 S Francis Solano, Franciscan, priest
1612 S Joseph of Leonissa, Capuchin, priest
1617 B Peter of the Assumption, Franciscan, priest, martyr
1618 B John of S Martha, Franciscan, priest, martyr
1619 B Hippolyte Galantini, Tertiary
1619 S Lawrence of Brindisi, Capuchin, priest, doctor
1622 B Apollinaris Franco, Franciscan, priest, martyr
1622 S Fidelis of Sigmaringen, Capuchin, priest, martyr
1622 B Francis of S Bonaventure of Japan, Franciscan, cleric, martyr
1622 B Leo of Satsuma, Tertiary, cleric, martyr
1622 B Lucy Freites, Tertiary, widow, martyr
1622 B Paul of S Clare of Japan, Franciscan, brother, martyr
1622 B Peter of Avila, Franciscan, priest, martyr
1622 B Richard of S Ann, Franciscan, priest, martyr
1622 B Vincent of S Joseph Ramirez, Franciscan, brother, martyr
1623 B Francis Galvez, Franciscan, priest, martyr
1624 B Louis Baba, Tertiary, martyr
1624 B Louis Sasada, Franciscan, priest, martyr
1624 B Louis Sotelo, Franciscan, bishop-elect, martyr
1625 B Benedict of Urbino, Capuchin, priest
1627 B Aloysius Maki, Tertiary, martyr
1627 B Anthony of S Francis of Japan, Franciscan, brother, martyr
1627 B Bartholomew Laurel of Mexico, Franciscan, brother, martyr
1627 B Francis Kuhioye, Tertiary, martyr
1627 B Francis of S Mary, Franciscan, priest, martyr
1627 B Gaspar Vaz, Tertiary, martyr
1627 B John Maki, Tertiary, martyr

1627 B Louis Matsuo Soemon, Tertiary, martyr
1627 B Luke Kiemon, Tertiary, martyr
1627 B Martin Gomez of Japan, Tertiary, martyr
1627 B Mary Vaz, Tertiary, martyr
1627 B Michael Kizaemon, Tertiary, martyr
1627 B Thomas O Jinemon, Tertiary, martyr
1627 B Thomas Tzuji, Tertiary, priest, martyr
1628 B Anthony of S Bonaventure, Franciscan, priest, martyr
1628 B Dominic of S Francis of Japan, Franciscan, brother, martyr
1628 B Dominic Nihachi, Tertiary, martyr
1628 B Dominic Tomachi, Tertiary, martyr
1628 B Francis Nihachi, Tertiary, martyr
1628 B John Romano Chikugo, Tertiary, martyr
1628 B John Tomachi, Tertiary, martyr
1628 B Lawrence Yamada, Tertiary, martyr
1628 B Louise Chikugo, Tertiary, martyr
1628 B Louis Nihachi, Tertiary, martyr
1628 B Matthew Alvarez of Japan, Tertiary, martyr
1628 B Michael Tomachi, Tertiary, martyr
1628 B Michael Yamada, Tertiary, martyr
1628 B Paul Tomachi, Tertiary, martyr
1628 B Thomas Tomachi, Tertiary, martyr
1631 B John of Prado, Franciscan, priest, martyr
1632 B Gabriel of S Magdalen, Franciscan, brother, martyr
1632 B Jerome Torres of Japan, Third Order Regular, priest, martyr
1637 B Humilis of Bisignano, Franciscan, brother
1638 B Agathangelo of Vendome, Capuchin, priest, martyr
1638 B Cassian of Nantes, Capuchin, priest, martyr
1640 B Hyacintha Mariscotti, Third Order Regular, virgin
1642 B John Baptist (Thomas) Bullaker, Franciscan, priest, martyr
1645 S Mariana of Jesus de Paredes, Tertiary, virgin
1663 S Joseph of Copertino, Conventual, brother
1667 B Bernard of Corleone, Capuchin, brother
1670 S Charles of Sezze, Franciscan, brother
1679 B Joachim of S Ann Wall, Franciscan, priest, martyr
1684 B Bonaventure of Barcelona, Franciscan, brother
1694 B Bernard of Offida, Capuchin, brother
1711 B Bonaventure of Potenza, Conventual, priest
1721 S Pacificus of San Severino (Septempeda), Franciscan, priest
1727 S Veronica of Giuliani, Poor Clare, virgin
1729 B Thomas of Cori, Franciscan, priest
1734 S John Joseph of the Cross, Franciscan, priest

1737 B Mary Magdalen Martinengo of Brescia, Poor Clare, virgin
1739 B Angelo of Acri, Capuchin, priest
1740 S Theophilus of Corte, Franciscan, priest
1742 B Francis Anthony Fasani, Conventual, priest
1744 B Mary Crescentia Hoess of Kaufbeuren, Third Order Regular, virgin
1750 B Crispin of Viterbo, Capuchin, brother
1751 S Leonard of Port Maurice, Franciscan, priest
1781 S Ignatius Laconi, Capuchin, brother
1787 BFelix of Nicosia, Capuchin, brother
1791 SMary Frances of the Five Wounds, Tertiary, virgin
1794 B Apollinaris Morel, Capuchin, priest, martyr
1794 B John Baptist Triquerie, Conventual, priest, martyr
1794 B John Francis Burté, Conventual, priest, martyr
1794 B Josephine Leroux, Poor Clare, virgin, martyr
1794 B Severin George Girault, Third Order Regular, priest, martyr
1801 B Didacus Joseph of Cadiz, Capuchin, priest
1812 B Giles Mary of S Joseph, Franciscan, brother
1815 B Leopold Gaich, Franciscan, priest
1816 B John of Triora, Franciscan, priest, martyr
1833 S Mary Bartholomea Capitanio, Tertiary, virgin, foundress
1842 S Joseph Benedict Cottolengo, Tertiary, priest
1846 S Mary Magdalen Postel, Tertiary, virgin, foundress
1847 S Vincenta Gerosa, Tertiary, virgin, foundress
1850 B Vincent Pallotti, Tertiary, priest, founder
1854 S Joachima de Mas y de Vedruna, Tertiary, virgin, foundress*
1859 S John Mary Vianney, Tertiary, priest
1860 B Carmel Volta, Franciscan, priest, martyr
1860 B Emmanuel Ruiz, Franciscan, priest, martyr
1860 B Engelbert Kolland of Tyrol, Franciscan, priest, martyr
1860 B Francis Pinazzo D'Aspuentes, Franciscan, brother, martyr
1860 B John James Fernandez, Franciscan, brother, martyr
1860 S Joseph Cafasso, Tertiary, priest
1860 B Nicholas Mary Alberca de Torres, Franciscan, priest, martyr
1860 B Nicanor Ascasius, Franciscan, priest, martyr
1860 B Peter Soler, Franciscan, priest, martyr
1863 S Michael Garicoits, Tertiary, priest, founder
1866 B Francis Mary of Camporubeo, Capuchin, brother
1880 S Mary Josepha Rosello, Tertiary, virgin, foundress
1888 S John Bosco, Tertiary, priest, founder
1894 S Conrad of Parzham, Capuchin, brother
1900 B Andrew Bauer, Franciscan, brother martyr
1900 B Anthony Fantosati, Franciscan, bishop, martyr

1900 B Cesidio Giacomantonio, Franciscan, priest, martyr
1900 B Elias Facchini, Franciscan, priest, martyr
1900 B Francis Fogolla, Franciscan, bishop, martyr
1900 B Gregory Grassi, Franciscan, bishop, martyr
1900 B John Chiang of Nan-tzu, Tertiary, cleric, martyr
1900 B John Chiang of Tae-kuo, Tertiary, cleric, martyr
1900 B John Wan of Hsin-li-t'sun, Tertiary, cleric, martyr
1900 B Joseph Mary Gambaro, Franciscan, priest, martyr
1900 B Mary Adolphine Dierkx, Third Order Regular (F.M.M.), virgin, martyr
1900 B Mary Amandine Jeuris, Third Order Regular (F.M.M.), virgin, martyr
1900 B Mary Clare Nanetti, Third Order Regular (F.M.M.), virgin, martyr
1900 B Mary Hermine Grivot, Third Order Regular (F.M.M.), virgin, martyr
1900 B Mary of Peace Giuliani, Third Order Regular (F.M.M.), virgin, martyr
1900 B Mary of S. Just Moreau, Third Order Regular (F.M.M.), virgin, martyr
1900 B Mary of Ste. Natalie Kerguin, Third Order Regular (F.M.M.), virgin, martyr
1900 B Francis Chiang-jun of Chi-tzu-san, Tertiary, martyr
1900 B Matthias Fu-en-tei of Sho-chow, Tertiary, martyr
1900 B Patrick Chun, Tertiary, cleric, martyr
1900 B Peter Chiang-pan-niu of Tu-lin-sa, Tertiary, martyr
1900 B Peter Wu-an-pan of Liu-lin-t'sun, Tertiary, martyr
1900 B Philip Chiang, Tertiary, cleric, martyr
1900 B Simon Cheng, Tertiary, martyr
1900 B Theodoric Balat, Franciscan, priest, martyr
1900 B Thomas Shen, Tertiary, martyr
1902 B Contardo Ferrini, Tertiary
1905 B Mary Assunta Pallotta, Third Order Regular (F.M.M.), virgin
1914 S Pius X, Tertiary, pope
1917 S Frances Xavier Cabrini, Tertiary, virgin, foundress

APPENDIX II

FRANCISCAN MISSIONARY SAINTS

T is of interest to note that of the 355 Franciscan saints and blessed whose names appear in Appendix I, 62 died in the 13th century, 45 in the 14th, 43 in the 15th, 64 in the 16th, 67 in the 17th, 20 in the 18th, 51 in the 19th, and 3 in the 20th. A large percentage of these saints and blessed died as martyrs, namely 151 or 43 per cent. Many of these martyrs were missionaries in foreign lands and native Christians of these countries; 5 died in England during the Protestant Reformation; 11 were put to death by Calvinists in Holland; 5 were victims of the French Revolution.

At least 85 of the Franciscan saints and blessed were missionaries who left their native lands to establish the Church and propagate the Faith in other parts of the world:

(1) *Africa*: S Francis himself preached to the sultan in Egypt. The five protomartyrs, SS Berard and his companions (1220), and seven more of the first friars, SS Daniel and his companions, (1227) died in Morocco. B Conrad of Ascoli (1289) was a missionary in Libya. Others in northern Africa were B Giles of Assisi, B Raymond Lull, and S Anthony of Padua. B John of Prado died a martyr in Morocco in 1631. And the two Capuchins, BB Agathangelo and Cassian, won the martyr's crown in Abyssinia seven years later.

(2) *Canary Islands*: These islands were still mission country when S Didacus of Alcala (1463) served here as a catechist.

(3) *China*: B Odoric of Pordenone (1331), a world missionary, assisted Archbishop John of Montecorvino during the last three years of his life. B John of Triora (1816) was a missionary in central China during difficult times. And the Boxer Persecution of 1900 gave the martyr's crown to no less than 15 Franciscan missionaries from Europe: BB Bishop Gregory Grassi and 7 fellow Franciscans, and BB Mother Mary Ermeline Grivot and 6 other Franciscan Missionaries of Mary. B Mary Assunta Pallotta of the same sisterhood died in China in 1905.

(4) *Holy Land*: B Nicholas Tavelich (1391) was one of many Franciscan missionaries and martyrs in the Holy Land.

(5) *India:* B Thomas of Tolentino (1321) and his companions were on their way to China when they died as martyrs in India.

(6) *Japan:* No less than 18 Franciscan missionaries, now saints or blessed, came to Japan from Europe, India, and Mexico, and died there as martyrs in the 16th and 17th centuries: SS Peter Baptist (1597) and his five confreres, and BB Apollinaris Franco (1622) and 11 others.

(7) *Orient:* B Raynier of Arezzo (1304) and B Anthony Bonfadini (1482) labored as missionaries in the Near East; and the Capuchin S Joseph of Leonissa (1612) suffered at the hands of the Turks in Constantinople.

(8) *Persia:* B Gentle of Matelica (1304) was one of many medieval Franciscan missionaries in Persia when it was still a Mongol khanate.

(9) *Russia:* B James of Strepar (1409) and B John of Dukla preached the Gospel to the Russians in the 14fh and 15th centuries. B Ladislas of Gielniow (1505) was a missionary in Lithuania.

(10) *South America:* S Francis Solano (1610) is called the Apostle of Argentina and Peru; he was a pioneer missionary in Tucuman (Argentina), Bolivia, Paraguay.

(11) *Syria:* BB Emmanuel Ruiz (1860) and seven other Franciscans were missionaries in Damascus, when they died there for the Faith at the hands of the Druses.

(12) *Moslems of Spain:* The Moors were still in control of a large part of Spain when two pairs of Franciscan missionaries were put to death for preaching the Catholic Faith among them: BB John of Perugia and Peter of Sassoferrato (1231) and BB John of Cetina and Peter of Dueñas (1397).

(13) *Schismatic Greeks:* Many attempts were made in the Middle Ages to bring the Orthodox Greek Church back into the Catholic fold, and some were successful for a time. Among those who devoted themselves to this work were B John of Parma (1289) and B Thomas of Florence (1447).

(14) *Albigensians of France:* These heretics made the southern part of France a mission field for a long time. BB Raymond and Stephen of Narbonne (1242) were missionary martyrs in this area; and B Christopher of Romagnola (1272) labored here as a missionary.

(15) *Calvinists of Switzerland:* The Capuchin S Fidelis of Sigmaringen (1622) was sent as missionary to these Protestants by the newly established Sacred Congregation of the Propagation of the Faith, and he became its protomartyr.

Not included among the 85 Franciscan saints and blessed who went to other lands as missionaries are the great preachers and parish missionaries: S Bernardin of Siena (1444), "the people's preacher" who began the devotion to the Holy Name; S John Capistran (1456), who gained numerous converts in Italy, Austria, Germany, Poland, and helped to win a great victory over the Turks at Belgrade; S James of the March, who is said to have converted 50,000 heretics and to have led 200,000 unbelievers to baptism, especially in the German states; S Lawrence of Brindisi (1619), Capuchin, linguist, and preacher in several countries of central Europe, who likewise contributed to a victory over the Turks at Stuhlweissenburg; S Leonard of Port Maurice (1756), who has been declared special patron of parish missions and missionaries.

S Lawrence of Brindisi has been declared a Doctor of the Church by Pope John XXIII (December, 1958), thus raising the number of Franciscans who hold this title to three. S Bonaventure, the Seraphic Doctor, and St. Anthony of Padua, the Evangelical Doctor, are the other two. S Bernardin of Siena is likewise being proposed for the same honor by the Franciscan postulator general. Recently S Bernardin was named special patron of those who are engaged in public relations work, and S Clare of Assisi was chosen as patron of television.

Noteworthy is the fact that 50 of the Franciscan saints and blessed were natives of Japan, and 11 of China. In different books one finds their surnames spelled in different ways. For the correct spelling of the Japanese names we are indebted to Father Bernardin Schneider, O.F.M., and Father Thomas Uyttenbroeck, O.F.M., of Japan, and for the Chinese names, according to the Wade system of transcription, to Father Boniface Pfeilschifter, O.F.M., formerly a missionary in China.

APPENDIX III

FRANCISCAN SAINTS AND BLESSED (355)
(Alphabetical List)

A. SAINTS (114)[4]

I. First Order (57)

1. *Before* 1440 (17)

S Accursius, bro., mart., 1220
S Adjutus, bro., mart., 1220
S Angelo, priest, mart., 1227
S Anthony of Padua, priest, 1231
S Benvenute of Osimo, bishop, 1282
S Berard, priest, mart., 1220
S Bonaventure, cardinal, 1274
S Daniel, priest, mart., 1227
S Domnus, bro., mart., 1227

2. *Franciscans* (32)

S Anthony Hornaer, priest, mart., 1572
S Anthony of Weert, priest, mart., 1572
S Benedict the Moor, bro,, 1589
S Bernardin of Siena, priest, 1444
S Charles of Sezze, bro., 1670
S Cornelius Wikan, bro., mart., 1572
S Didacus of Alcalá, bro., 1463
S Francis Blanco, priest, mart., 1597
S Francis of S Michael, bro., mart., 1597
S Francis Rod, priest, mart., 1572
S Francis Solano, priest, 1610
S Godfrey Mervelan, priest, mart., 1572
S Gonzalo Garcia, bro., mart., 1597

---

[4] In the Introduction, S Joachima de Mas y de Vedruna, canonized April 12, 1959, is counted among the Blessed. Hence, mention is made of 113 Saints and 242 Blessed, instead of 114 Saints and 241 Blessed.

.

S James of the March, priest, 1476
S Jerome of Weert, priest, mart., 1572
S John Capistran, priest, 1456
S John Joseph of the Cross, priest, 1734
S Francis of Assisi, deacon, 1226
S Hugolinus, priest, mart., 1227
S Leo, priest, mart., 1227
S Louis of Toulouse, bishop, 1297
S Nicholas, priest, mart., 1227
S Otto, priest, mart., 1220
S Peter, priest, mart., 1220
S Samuel, priest, mart., 1227
S Leonard of Port Maurice, priest, 1756
S Martin of the Ascension, priest, mart., 1597
S Nicasius Hes, priest, mart., 1572
S Nicholas Pieck, priest, mart., 1572
S Pacificus of San Severino, priest, 1721
S Paschal Baylon, bro., 1592
S Peter Askan, bro., mart., 1572
S Peter Baptist Blasquez, priest, mart., 1597
S Peter of Alcantara, priest, 1562
S Peter Regalado, priest, 1456
S Philip of Jesus, cleric, mart., 1597
S Salvator of Horta, bro., 1567
S Theodoric of Emden, priest, mart., 1572
S Theophilus of Corte, priest, 1740
S Willehad Dan, priest, mart., 1572

3. *Conventuals* (1)

S Joseph of Copertino, priest, 1663

4. *Capuchins* (7)

S Conrad of Parzham, bro., 1894
S Felix of Cantalice, bro., 1585
S Fidelis of Sigmaringen, priest, mart., 1622
S Ignatius Laconi, bro., 1781

II. Second Order (5)

S Agnes of Assisi, virg., 1253
S Catharine of Bologna, virg., 1463
S Clare of Assisi, virg., 1253

III. Third Order (52)

1. Regular (1)
S Hyacintha Mariscotti, virg., 1640

2. Secular (51)
S Angela Merici, virg., 1540
S Anthony of Nagasaki, mart., 1597
S Bartholomea Capitanio, virg., 1833
S Bonaventure of Miyako, mart., 1597
S Bridget of Sweden, widow, 1373
S Catharine of Genoa, widow, 1510
S Charles Borromeo, cardinal, 1584
S Clare of Montefalco, virg., 1308
S Conrad of Piacenza, conf., 1351
S Cosmas Zakeya, mart., 1597
S Elizabeth of Hungary, widow, 1231
S Elizabeth of Portugal, queen, 1336
S Elzear of Sabrano, conf., 1323
S Ferdinand III, king, 1252
S Frances of Rome, widow, 1440
S Frances Xavier Cabrini, virg., 1917
S Francis the Doctor of Miyako, mart., 1597
S Francis Falegname of Miyako, mart., 1597
S Gabriel of Ise, mart., 1597
S Jane of Valois, widow, 1505
S Joachim Sakakibara, mart., 1597
S Joachima de Mas-Vedruna, virg., 1854
S Joseph of Leonissa, priest, 1612
S Lawrence of Brindisi, priest, 1619
S Seraphin of Montegranaro, bro., 1604
S Coleta of Corbie, virg., 1447
S Veronica Giuliani, virg., 1727
S Joan of Arc, virg., 1431
S John Bosco, priest, 1888
S John Mary Vianney, priest, 1859
S Joseph Benedict Cottolcngo, priest, 1842

S Joseph Cafasso, priest, 1860
S Leo Ibaraki Karasumaru, mart., 1597
S Leo Kinuya, mart., 1597
S Louis Ibaraki, mart., 1597
S Louis IX of France, king, 1270
S Margaret of Cortona, penitent, 1297
S Mariana of Jesus Paredes, virg., 1645
S Mary Frances of the Five Wounds, virg., 1791
S Mary Joseph Rosello, virg., 1880
S Mary Magdalen Postel, virg., 1846
S Matthias of Miyako, mart., 1597
S Michael Garicoits, priest, 1863
S Michael Kozaki, mart., 1597
S Paul Ibaraki, mart., 1597
S Paul Suzuki, mart., 1597
S Peter Sukejiro, mart., 1597
S Pius X, pope, 1914

B. BLESSED (241)

I. First Order (127)

1. *Before* 1440 (38)

B Agnellus of Pisa, priest, 1236
B Andrew of Spello, priest, 1254
B Andrew of Segni, priest, 1302
B Bartholomew Pucci, priest, 1330
B Bentivolio Buoni, priest, 1232
B Benvenute of Recanati, bro., 1340
B Benvenute of Gubbio, bro., 1232
B Conrad of Ascoli, priest, 1289
B Conrad of Offida, priest, 1396
B Christopher of Romagnola, priest, 1272
B Francis of Fabriano, priest, 1322
B Gandolph of Binasco, priest, 1260
B Gentle of Matelica, priest, mart., 1340
B Gerard Cagnoli, bro., 1345
B Giles of Assisi, cleric, 1262
B Guy of Cortona, priest, 1250
B James of Strepar, bishop, 1409

B John of Parma, priest, 1289
B John of La Verna, priest, 1322
B John of Cetina, priest, mart., 1397
B John of Perugia, priest, mart., 1231

2. *Franciscans* (74)

B Andrew Bauer, bro., mart., 1900
B Andrew Hibernon, bro., 1602
B Angelo of Chiavasso, priest, 1495
B Anthony Bonfadini, priest, 1482
B Anthony Fantosati, bishop, mart., 1900
B Anthony of S Bonaventure, priest, mart., 1628
B Anthony of S Francis, bro., mart., 1627
B Anthony of Stroncone, bro., 1461
B Julian of Valle, priest, 1350
B Liberatus of Lauro, priest, 1258
B Luke Belludi, priest, 1285
B Nicholas Tavelich, priest, mart., 1391
B Odoric of Pordenone, priest, 1331
B Peregrin of Falerone, bro., 1233
B Peter of Dueñas, bro., mart., 1397
B Peter of Sassoferrato, bro., mart., 1231
B Peter of Treja, priest, 1304
B Raymond Carboneri, priest, mart., 1242
B Raynier of Arezzo, bro., 1304
B Rizzerio of Muccia, priest, 1236
B Roger of Todi, priest, 1237
B Sanctes of Montefabro, bro., 1390
B Stephen of Narbonne, priest, mart., 1242
B Thomas of Tolentino, priest, mart., 1321
B John of Penna, priest, 1271
B Apollinaris Franco, priest, mart., 1622
B Archangelo of Calatafimi, priest, 1460
B Balthasar Ravaschieri, priest, 1492
B Bartholomew Laurel, bro., mart., 1627
B Bernardin of Feltre, priest, 1494
B Bernardin of Fossa, priest, 1503
B Bonaventure of Barcelona, bro., 1684
B Cesidio Giacomantonio, priest, mart., 1900
B Carmel Volta, priest, mart., 1860

B Christopher of Milan, priest, 1485
B Dominic of S Francis, bro., mart., 1628
B Elias Facchini, priest, mart., 1900
B Emmanuel Ruiz, priest, mart., 1860
B Engelbert Kolland, priest, mart., 1860
B Francis of Calderola, priest, 1507
B Francis Fogolla, bishop, mart., 1900
B Francis Galvez, priest, mart., 1623
B Francis of S Bonaventure, cler., mart., 1622
B Francis of S Mary, priest, mart., 1627
B Francis Pinazzo, bro., mart., 1860
B Gabriel Ferretti, priest, 1456
B Gabriel of Magdalena, bro., mart., 1632
B Giles Mary of S Joseph, bro., 1812
B Giles of Lorenzana, bro., 1518
B Godfrey Maurice Jones, priest, mart., 1598
B Gregory Grassi, bishop, mart., 1900
B Herculan of Piagale, priest, 1451
B Humilis of Bisignano, bro., 1637
B James of Bitecto, bro., 1490
B Joachim (John) Wall, priest, mart., 1679
B John Baptist Bullaker, priest, mart., 1642
B John Baptist of Fabriano, priest, 1539
B John Dukla, priest, 1484
B John Forest, priest, mart., 1538
B John James Fernandez, bro., mart., 1860
Conventuals (4)
B Bonaventure of Potenza, priest, 1711
B Francis Anthony Fasani, priest, 1742
Capuchins (11)
B Agathangelo of Vendome, priest, mart., 1638
B John of Prado, priest, mart., 1631
B John of S Martha, priest, mart., 1618
B John of Triora, priest, mart., 1816
B Joseph Mary Gambaro, priest, mart., 1900
B Julian of S Augustine, bro., 1606
B Ladislas of Gielniow, priest, 1505
B Lawrence of Villamagna, priest, 1535
B Leopold Gaich, priest, 1815
B Louis Sasada, priest, mart., 1624
B Louis Sotelo, bishop-elect, mart., 1624

B Mark of Bologna, priest, 1479
B Mark of Montegallo, priest, 1496
B Matthew of Girgenti, bishop, 1451
B Nicanor Ascan, priest, mart., 1860
B Nicholas Factor, priest, 1583
B Nicholas Mary Alberca, priest, mart., 1860
B Pacificus of Cerano, priest, 1482
B Peter of Avila, priest, mart., 1622
B Peter of Mogliano, priest, 1490
B Paul of S Clare, bro., mart., 1622
B Peter of the Assumption, priest, mart., 1617
B Peter Soler, priest, mart., 1860
B Richard of S Ann, priest, mart., 1622
B Sebastian of Aparicio, bro., 1600
B Simon of Lypnica, priest, 1482
B Theodoric Balat, priest, mart., 1900
B Thomas of Cori, priest, 1729
B Thomas of Florence, bro., 1447
B Timothy of Montecchio, priest, 1504
B Vincent of Aquila, bro., 1504
B Vincent Ramirez, bro., mart., 1622
B John Baptist Triquerie, priest, mart., 1794
B John Francis Burté, priest, mart., 1794
B Angelo of Acri, priest, 1739
B Apollinaris Morel, priest, mart., 1794
B Benedict of Urbino, priest, 1625
B Bernard of Corleone, bro., 1667
B Bernard of Offida, bro., 1694
B Cassian of Nantes, priest, mart., 1638
B Crispin of Viterbo, bro., 1750

II. Second Order (22)

B Agnes of Prague, virg., 1282
B Antonia of Florence, widow, 1472
B Baptista Varani, virg., 1524
B Beatrice of Silva, virg., 1490
B Clare of Rimini, widow, 1326
B Eustochium of Messina, virg., 1491
B Felicia Meda of Milan, virg., 1444
B Helen Enselmine of Padua, virg., 1242

B Isabella of France, virg., 1270
B Josephine Leroux, virg., mart., 1794
B Kinga (Cunegunda) of Poland, virg., 1292

III. Third Order (92)

1. Regular (15)

B Angelina of Marsciano, widow, 1435
B Elizabeth the Good, virg., 1420
B Jeremy Lambertenghi, priest, 1513
B Jerome Torres, priest, mart., 1632
B Lucy of Caltagirone, virg., c. 1400
B Mary Adolphine Dierkx, virg., 1900
B Mary Amandine Jeuris, virg., 1900
B Mary Assunta Pallotta, virg., 1905

2. Secular (77)

B Aloysius Maki, mart., 1627
B Amatus Ronconi, hermit, 1304
B Angela of Foligno, widow, 1309
B Bartolo of San Gimignano, priest, 1300
B Bernard of Baden, conf., 1458
B Charles of Blois, duke, 1364
B Christina of Tuscany, virg., 1310
B Contardo Ferrini, conf., 1902
B Delphina of Glandeves, virg., 1358
B Didacus Joseph of Cadiz, priest, 1801
B Francis Mary of Camporubeo, bro., 1866
B Felix of Nicosia, bro., 1787
B Louise of Savoy, widow, 1503
B Margaret Colonna, virg., 1380
B Margaret of Lorraine, widow, 1521
B Mary Magdalen Martinengo, virg., 1737
B Matthia of Nazarei, virg., 1320
B Paula Montaldi, virg., 1514
B Petronilla of Troyes, virg., 1355
B Philippa Mareri, virg., 1236
B Salome of Cracow, virg., 1268
B Seraphina Sforza, widow, 1478

B Yolande (Jolenta), widow, 1298
B Mary Clare Nanetti, virg., 1900
B Mary Crescentia Hoess, virg., 1744
B Mary Hermine Grivot, virg., 1900
B Mary of Peace Giuliani, virg., 1900
B Mary of St. Just Moreau, virg., 1900
B Mary of Ste. Natalie Kerguin, virg., 1900
B Severin George Girault, priest, mart., 1794
B Dominic Nihachi, mart., 1628
B Dominic Tomachi, mart., 1628
B Elizabeth Amodei, virg., 1498
B Francis Chiang-jun, mart., 1900
B Francis Kuhioye, mart., 1627
B Francis Nihachi, mart., 1628
B Francis of Pesaro, hermit, 1350
B Gaspar Vaz, mart., 1627
B Gerard Lunel, hermit, 1299
B Gerard of Villamagna, hermit, 1245
B Gregory X, pope, 1276
B Hippolyte Galantini, conf., 1619
B Hugolinus Magalotti, hermit, 1373
B Humiliani of Cerchi, widow, 1246
B James of Pieve, priest, mart., 1304
B Jane Mary of Maillé, widow, 1414
B Jane of Signa, virg., 1307
B John Chiang of Nan-tzu, cleric, mart., 1900
B John Chiang of Tae-kuo, cleric, mart., 1900
B John of Peace Cini, conf., 1433
B John Maki, mart., 1627
B John Pelingotto, hermit, 1304
B John Tomachi, mart., 1628
B John Romano Chikugo, mart., 1628
B John Wan, cleric, mart., 1900
B Lawrence Yamada, mart., 1628
B Leo of Satsuma, mart., 1622
B Louis Baba, mart., 1624
B Louise Albertoni, widow, 1503
B Louise Chikugo of Nagasaki, mart., 1628
B Louis Matsuo Soemon, mart., 1627
B Louis Nihachi, mart., 1628
B Luchesio of Poggibonsi, conf., 1260

B Lucy Freites, mart., 1622
B Luke Kiemon, mart., 1627
B Mark Marconi, hermit, 1510
B Martin Gomez, mart., 1627
B Mary Vaz, mart., 1627
B Matthew Alvarez, mart., 1628
B Matthias Fu-en-tei, mart., 1900
B Michael Kizaemon, mart., 1627
B Michael Tomachi, mart., 1628
B Michael Yamada, mart., 1628
B Michelina of Pesaro, widow, 1356
B Nicholas of Forcapalena, priest, hermit, 1449
B Novellon of Faenza, hermit, 1280
B Oddino Barotti, priest, 1400
B Patrick Chun, cleric, mart., 1900
B Paula Gambara-Costa, widow, 1515
B Paul Tomachi, mart., 1628
B Peter Chiang-pan-niu, mart., 1900
B Peter Cresci, conf., 1323
B Peter of Pisa, hermit, 1435
B Peter of Siena, conf., 1289
B Peter Wu-an-pan, mart., 1900
B Philip Chiang, cleric, mart., 1900
B Raymond Lull, mart., 1316
B Simon Cheng, mart., 1900
B Thomas O Jinemon, mart., 1627
B Thomas Tomachi, mart., 1628
B Thomas Tsuji, priest, mart., 1627
B Thomas Shen, mart., 1900
B Torello of Poppi, hermit, 1282
B Veridiana of Attavanti, virg., 1242
B Vincent Pallotti, priest, 1850
B Vitalis of Bastia, hermit, 1491
B Waldo of San Gimignano, hermit, 1320
B William Cufitella of Scicli, hermit, 1404

The total number of Franciscan canonized saints and formally or equivalently declared blessed is 355. Of this number, 184 belong to the First Order (55 before 1440; 106 Franciscans; 18 Capuchins; 5 Conventuals); 27 to the Second Order; and 144 to the Third Order (16 Regular; 128 Secular).

Not included in this total are the following 17 founders of religious orders and congregations who are said to have been members of the Third Order:

S Alphonse Mary Liguori, 1787 (Redemptorists)
S Anthony Mary Claret, 1870 (Claretians)
S Cajetan, 1547 (Theatines)
S Camillus of Lellis, 1614 (Camillians)
S Caspar del Bufalo, 1837 (Precious Blood Fathers)
S Francis de Paul, 1507 (Minims)
S Ignatius of Loyola, 1556 (Jesuits)
S Jane Frances de Chantal, 1641 (Visitation Nuns)
S John Baptist de la Salle, 1719 (Christian Brothers)
B John Colombini, 1367 (Jesuats)
S John of God, 1550 (Hospital Brothers of Mercy)
S John Eudes, 1680 (Eudists)
S Louise de Marillac, 1660 (Sisters of Charity)
S Paul of the Cross, 1775 (Passionists)
B Peter Julian Eymard, 1868 (Blessed Sacrament Fathers)
S Philip Neri, 1595 (Oratorians)
S Vincent de Paul 1660 (Vicentians)
Neither does the total of Franciscan saints and blessed include the following four canonized Cordbearers of S Francis:
S Benedict Joseph Labre, pilgrim, 1783 (see April 16)
S Bernadette (Mary Bernarda) Soubirous, virgin, 1879 (see April 16)
S Francis de Sales, bishop, 1622 (see January 29)
S Joseph Calasanza, founder of the Piarists, 1648

Excluded from the total of Franciscan saints and blessed are the following 38 members of one of the orders of S Francis who have received and still retain the title of Blessed in popular devotion. Confirmation of their cult as Blessed, that is, formal or equivalent beatification, is now being sought in Rome by the Franciscan postulator general for those who are marked with an asterisk (cf. Acta Ordinis Fratrum Minorum, 1950, pp. 19-34).

*B Agnes of Bavaria, Poor Clare, 1352
*B Agnes Peranda, Poor Clare, 1281
*B Albert de Albertis, Friar Minor, priest, minister general, 1239
B Albert of Sarziano, Franciscan, priest, 1450 (see August 5)
*B Amadeus Menez of Portugal, Franciscan, priest, 1487 (see August 10)
B Anthony of Hungary, Tertiary, 1398 (see December 31)
*B Anthony Tigrini, Friar Minor, brother, 1313

*B Balthasar of Castronuovo, Franciscan, priest, 1525
*B Barbara of Bavaria, Poor Clare, 1474
B Benvenuta of Ancona, Tertiary, 13th century
*B Bernardin Caimi, Franciscan, priest, 1450
B Blanche, queen, mother of St. Louis IX, Tertiary, 1253 (see August 23)
*B Bona of Armagnac, Poor Clare, 1462
*B Bonincontri of Rome, Tertiary, priest, 13th century
*B Clara of Barcelona, Poor Clare, end of 13th century
*B Davanzato, Tertiary, priest, 13th century (see August 30)
*B Elias of Bourdeille, Franciscan, archbishop of Tours, cardinal, 1484
B Jacopone of Todi, Friar Minor, brother, 1306 (see December 25)
*B James of Todi, Friar Minor, brother, 1310
*B James Oldo of Lodi, Tertiary, priest, 1404 (see April 10)
*B John Duns Scotus, Friar Minor, priest, 1308 (see November 8)
B John of Lobedau, Friar Minor, 1264 (see October 9)
*B John the Discalced, Friar Minor, priest, 1349
B John Velita, Tertiary, friend of S Francis (see Forum, 1949, pp. 336-338)
B Julian of Germany, Franciscan, 1486 (see September 21)
B Jutta of Thuringia, Tertiary, widow, 1264 (see June 26)
B Luitgard of Wittichen, Poor Clare, 1348
*B Michael Carcano, Franciscan, priest, 1485
B Paschaline of Foligno, Tertiary, companion of B Angela of Foligno, 1313
*B Peter of Guarda, Franciscan, brother, 1505
B Pica, Tertiary, mother of S Francis (see April 14)
B Robert Malatesta, Tertiary, 1412 (see October 13)
*B Sixtus Brioschi of Milan, Franciscan, priest, 1482
B Theodoric Coelde of Munester, Franciscan, priest, 1515 (see December 27)
B Thomas of Foligno, Tertiary, 1377 (see September 16)

Appendix IV

FRANCISCAN COMPOSITE CALENDAR

JANUARY

Day	Roman	Franciscan	Conventual	Capuchin	Third Order Regular
2				B Bentivolio Buoni B Gerard Cagnoli	
3			B Gerard Cagnoli		
4			B Angela of Foligno		B Angela of Foligno
5			B Roger of Todi		
7			B Matthew of Girgenti		
14		B Odoric of Pordenone B Roger of Todi B Giles of Lorenzana	B Odoric of Pordenone		
16		SS Berard and Companions	SS Berard and Companions	SS Berard and Companions	SS Berard and Companions
19		B Thomas of Cori B Charles of Sezze B Bernard of Corleone		B Bernard of Corleone	B James of Pieve
22			B John B. Triquerie		
23	Sup.	Espousals of the B.V.M.			
28				B Odoric of Pordenone B Roger of Todi B Giles of Lorenzana	B Paula Gambara-Costa
29	Roman	S Francis de Sales	S Francis de Sales	S Francis de Sales	S Francis de Sales
30		S Hyacintha Mariscotti	S Hyacintha Mariscotti	S Hyacintha Mariscotti	
31	Roman	S John Bosco	S John Bosco	S John Bosco	B Louis Albertoni

Note: "Roman" after the date indicates that the feast is also in the Roman Missal;
"Sup.", that it is in the Supplement of the Roman Missal for some places;
"U.S.", that it is in the Supplement of the Roman Missal for the United States.

FEBRUARY

1				B Veridiana
3		B Andrew of Segni	B Matthew of Girgenti	
4	S Joseph of Leonissa	S Joseph of Leonissa	S Joseph of Leonissa	S Joseph of Leonissa
5 U.S.*	SS Peter B. and Companions	SS Peter B. and Companions	SS Peter B. and Companions	SS Peter B. and Companions
7	B Rizzerio of Muccia B Giles Mary of S Joseph B Anthony of Stroncone	B Rizzerio of Muccia		
8		SS Peter B. and Companions	B Eustochium	
13	B John of Triora		B Rizzerio of Muccia B Anthony of Stroncone B Andrew of Segni	
14	S Jane of Valois			
15	Transfer, S Anthony	Transfer, S Anthony		
16	B Philippa Mareri (Simple) B Eustochium B Veridiana	B Philippa Mareri	B Philippa Mareri	
17	B Luke Belludi (Simple) B Andrew of Segni B Peter of Treja	B Luke Belludi	B Luke Belludi	
19	S Conrad of Piacenza	S Conrad of Piacenza	S Conrad of Piacenza	S Conrad of Piacenza
20		B Peter of Treja	B Peter of Treja	
22 Sup. (on 26)	S Margaret of Cortona	S Margaret of Cortona	S Margaret of Cortona	S Margaret of Cortona
25	B Sebastian of Aparicio		B Isabella of France (or 26)	
26	B Antonia of Florence B Angela of Foligno B Louise Albertoni (Simple)		B Antonia of Florence (or 29)	
	Mysteries, Way of Cross			

Fri. after Ash-Wednesday
* In the U.S., S Philip of Jesus only.

MARCH

First Fri.	Mysteries, Way of Cross			
2		B Isabella of France B Agnes of Prague	B Agnes of Prague	
5	S John Jos. of the Cross	S John Jos. of the Cross	S John Jos. of the Cross	S John Jos. of the Cross
6	S Coleta	S Coleta	S Coleta	S Coleta
9°	S Catharine of Bologna	S Catharine of Bologna	S Catharine of Bologna	S Catharine of Bologna
11	B Agnellus of Pisa B John B. of Fabriano B Christopher of Milan		B Agnellus of Pisa	
13		Transfer, S Bonaventure		
14	Transfer, S Bonaventure			B Torello of Poppi
16				S Salvator of Horta
18	S Salvator of Horta		S Salvator of Horta	
20	B John of Parma B Mark of Montegallo B Hippolyte Galantini	B Agnellus of Pisa B John of Parma	B John of Parma B Mark of Montegallo	B Hippolyte Galantini
22	S Benvenute of Osimo	S Benvenute of Osimo	S Benvenute of Osimo	S Catharine of Genoa
22 U.S.				S Benvenute of Osimo
23			S Catharine of Genoa	
26	B Didacus Jos. of Cadiz		B Didacus Jos. of Cadiz	
28 Roman	S John Capistran	S John Capistran	S John Capistran	
29				B Jane Mary of Maillé
30	S Peter Regalado	S Peter Regalado	S Peter Regalado	

° Roman Missal has S Frances of Rome on this day (March 9).

APRIL

First Fri.	Mysteries, Way of Cross			
3	B Gandolph of Binasco B John of Penna B William of Scicli (Simple)	B Gandolph of Binasco B John of Penna	B Gandolph of Binasco B John of Penna	

4	S Benedict the Moor	S Salvator of Horta S Benedict the Moor	S Benedict the Moor	S Benedict the Moor
5				
6	B Mary Crescentia Hoess			B Mary Crescentia Hoess
7		B William of Scicli		B William of Scicli
8	B Julian of S Augustine			
9		B Thomas of Tolentino B Gentle of Matelica	B Thomas of Tolentino B Gentle of Matelica	
10			B Mark of Bologna	
11		B Jane Mary of Maillé		
12			B Angelo of Chiavasso	
16 Sup.*	Sol. Com. of S Francis S Benedict Jos. Labre S Bernadette Soubirous	Sol. Com. of S Francis	Sol. Com. of S Francis S Benedict Jos. Labre	S Benedict Jos. Labre
17		S Benedict Jos. Labre		
18	B Andrew Hibernon			
19	B Conrad of Ascoli (Simple) B Mark of Bologna B Angelo of Chiavasso	B Conrad of Ascoli	B Conrad of Ascoli	
21	S Conrad of Parzham	S Conrad of Parzham	S Conrad of Parzham	S Conrad of Parzham
22	B Francis of Fabriano (Simple)	B Francis of Fabriano	B Francis of Fabriano	
23	B Giles of Assisi (Simple)	B Giles of Assisi	B Giles of Assisi	
24 Roman	S Fidelis of Sigmaringen	S Fidelis of Sigmaringen	S Fidelis of Sigmaringen	
28	B Luchesio	B Luchesio		B Luchesio
29		S Joseph Benedict Cottolengo S Joseph Cafasso		
30	S Joseph Benedict Cottolengo		B Benedict of Urbino	
Second Saturday after Easter			Mother of the Divine Shepherd (Roman Sup., on Sept. 3)	

* In the Roman Missal Supplement, S Benedict Joseph Labre only.

MAY

Day				
1		B Petronilla of Troyes		
2		B Julian of Valle		
5		B Benvenute of Recanati		
6		B Bartholomew Pucci		
11			B Julian of Valle B James of Bitecto B Ladislas of Gielniow	B Bartolo of San Gimignano B Waldo of San Gimignano
12	S Ignatius of Laconi		S Ignatius of Laconi	S Ignatius of Laconi
13		B Gerard of Villamagna	B Petronilla of Troyes	S Peter Regalado
14	B Benedict of Urbino B Julian of Valle B James of Bitecto		B Bartholomew Pucci B Benvenute of Recanati	B Gerard of Villamagna
17	S Paschal Baylon	S Paschal Baylon	S Paschal Baylon	
18	S Felix of Cantalice	S Felix of Cantalice	S Felix of Cantalice	S Felix of Cantalice
19	S Theophilus of Corte	S Theophilus of Corte S Yves of Britanny	S Theophilus of Corte S Yves of Britanny	S Yves of Britanny
20	Roman — S Bernardin of Siena	S Bernardin of Siena	S Bernardin of Siena	
21	B Ladislas of Gielniow B Crispin of Viterbo B Waldo of San Gimignano	B John of Cetina B Peter of Dueñas	B Humiliana Cerchi	B Humiliana of Cerchi
22	B John Forest B Godfrey Maurice Jones B Joachim of S Ann Wall	B Humiliana Cerchi	B John of Cetina B Peter of Dueñas	
23	B Bartholomew Pucci B Benvenute of Recanati B Gerard of Villamagna			
24	B John of Prado B John of Cetina B Peter of Dueñas			B Gerard of Lunel

Date	Rank				
25		Dedication, Basilica, Assisi Transfer, S Francis	Dedication, Basilica, Assisi Transfer, S Francis	Dedication, Basilica, Assisi Transfer, S Francis	Dedication, Basilica, Assisi Transfer, S Francis
26		S Mariana de Paredes			S Mariana de Paredes
27	Sup.	Mary Mediatrix of Graces			
29		B Stephen of Narbonne B Raymond of Narbonne (Simple)	B Stephen of Narbonne B Raymond of Narbonne	B Stephen of Narbonne B Raymond of Narbonne	
30	Sup.	S Ferdinand III, King	S Ferdinand III, King	S Ferdinand III, King	S Ferdinand III, King
JUNE					
1	Roman (on May 31)	S Angela Merici	S Angela Merici	S Angela Merici	B John Pelingotto
2		B Herculan of Piagale B Felix of Nicosia B John Pelingotto		B Herculan of Piagale	
3	Sup. (on May 30)				S Joan of Arc
3			B John Pelingotto B Andrew of Spello	B Andrew of Spello B Felix of Nicosia	
7			Both Churches, Rivotorto	B Baptista Varani	
8		B Isabella of France (Simple) B Agnes of Prague B Baptista Varani			
9		B Andrew of Spello (Simple) B Pacific of Cerano B Lawrence of Villamagna			
13	Roman	S Anthony of Padua	S Anthony of Padua	S Anthony of Padua	S Anthony of Padua
15		B Yolande of Poland B Humiliana Cerchi B Paula Gambara-Costa (Simple)	B Yolande of Poland	B Yolande of Poland	

JULY

16			B Guy of Cortona	B Guy of Cortona	B Michelina of Pesaro
20		S Joseph Cafasso			
23		B Guy of Cortona (Simple)			
27		B Benvenute of Gubbio	B Benvenute of Gubbio	B Benvenute of Gubbio	
3		BB Gregory Grassi & Comps.	B Raymond Lull		B Raymond Lull
4	Roman				
8		S Elizabeth of Portugal	S Elizabeth of Portugal	S Elizabeth of Portugal	
9		SS Nicholas and Companions	SS Nicholas and Companions	S Veronica Giuliani	SS Nicholas and Companions
10		BB Emmanuel Ruiz & Comps.			
11	Sup. (on Jul. 9)	S Veronica Giuliani	S Veronica Giuliani	SS Nicholas and Companions	S Veronica Giuliani
12			B Godfrey Maurice Jones		
13	U.S. (on Jul. 24)	S Francis Solano	S Francis Solano		
14	Roman	S Bonaventure	S Bonaventure	S Bonaventure	S Bonaventure
15		Most Holy Sepulchre	B Angelina of Marsciano		
16		Canonization, S Francis	Canonization, S Francis	Canonization, S Francis	
21		B Angelina of Marsciano		S Francis Solano	B Angelina Marsciano
23		S Lawrence of Brindisi		S Lawrence of Brindisi	S Lawrence of Brindisi
24		B Kinga of Poland (Simple) B Petronilla of Troyes B Felicia Meda	S Lawrence of Brindisi	B Kinga of Poland	S Francis Solano
27		B M Magdalen Martinengo	B Kinga of Poland	B M Magdalen Martinengo	B Novellon of Faenza
28			B Louise of Savoy		
30		B Simon of Lypnica (Simple) B Peter of Mogliano B Archangelo Calatafimi		B Simon of Lypnica B Peter of Mogliano B Archangelo Calatafimi	S Thomas More

AUGUST

	Portiuncula (O.L. of Angels)	Portiuncula (O.L. of Angels)	Portiuncula (O.L. of Angels)	Portiuncula (O.L. of Angels)
2	S Dominic	S Dominic	S Dominic	S Dominic
4 Roman				
5		B Francis of Pesaro		
7	B Agathangelo B Cassian		B Agathangelo B Cassian	
9 Roman	S John Mary Vianney	S John Mary Vianney	S John Mary Vianney	B Francis of Pesaro
11		B John of La Verna	B Louise of Savoy	
12 Roman	S Clare of Assisi	S Clare of Assisi	S Clare of Assisi	S Clare of Assisi
13	B John of La Verna (Simple) B Vincent of Aquila B Novellon of Faenza		B John of La Verna B Vincent of Aquila	
14			B Sanctes of Montefabro	
17 Sup.	S Roch of Montpellier	S Roch of Montpellier		S Roch of Montpellier
18	B Beatrice of Silva B Paula Montaldi		B Paula Montaldi	S Clare of Montefalco
19	S Louis of Toulouse	S Louis of Toulouse	S Louis of Toulouse	S Louis of Toulouse
25 Roman	S Louis IX of France	S Louis IX of France	S Louis IX of France	S Louis IX of France
26	B Timothy of Montecchio B Bernard of Offida	Seven Joys of Our Lady	S Roch of Montpellier	
27	Seven Joys of Our Lady (Roman Missal on this day: S Joseph Calasanza)	Seven Joys of Our Lady (Roman Missal on this day: S Joseph Calasanza)		

SEPTEMBER

1	B John of Perugia (Simple) B Peter of Sassoferrato	B John of Perugia B Peter of Sassoferrato	B Bernard of Offida	
2	B John Francis Burté B Apollinaris Morel B Severin Girault	B John Francis Burté	B Apollinaris Morel B John of Perugia B Peter of Sassoferrato	

		S Pius X	S Pius X	S Pius X	
3	Roman				B Severin Girault
4		S Rose of Viterbo	S Rose of Viterbo	S Rose of Viterbo	S Rose of Viterbo
5		B Thomas of Tolentino B Gentle of Matelica B Raymond Lull (Simple)		B Gentle of Matelica	
6		B Liberatus of Lauro B Peregrin of Falerone B Sanctes of Montefabro (Simple)	B Liberatus of Lauro	B Timothy of Montecchio B Liberatus of Lauro B Peregrin of Falerone	
7			B Peregrin of Falerone		
9		B Seraphina Sforza (Simple) B Louise of Savoy B Michelina of Pesaro		B Seraphina Sforza	
10		BB Apollinaris and Comps.			B Apollinaris and Comps.
11		B Bonaventure of Barcelona			
13				B Francis of Calderola	
16				B Francis of Camporosso	
17	Roman	Stigmata of S Francis	Stigmata of S Francis	Stigmata of S Francis	Stigmata of S Francis
18	Roman	S Joseph of Copertino	S Joseph of Copertino	S Joseph of Copertino	
23		Finding, S Clare	Finding, S Clare		
24		S Pacificus of San Severino	S Pacificus of San Severino	S Pacificus of San Severino	S Pacificus of San Severino
25		B Francis M of Camporosso			
26		B Delphina B Lucy of Caltagirone	B Lucy of Caltagirone		B Lucy of Caltagirone
27		S Elzear of Sabran	S Elzear of Sabran	S Elzear of Sabran	S Elzear of Sabran
28		B John of Dukla (Simple) B Bernardin of Feltre B Francis of Calderola		B Bernardin of Feltre	
30			B Felicia Meda		

OCTOBER

	Roman				
1		B Francis of Pesaro / B Nicholas of Forcapalena	B John of Dukla	B John of Dukla	B Nicholas of Forcapalena
3		Transfer, S Clare	Transfer, S Clare		
4	Roman	S Francis of Assisi	S Francis of Assisi	S Francis of Assisi	S Francis of Assisi
5				B Felicia Meda / Franciscan All Souls	
6		S M Frances of Five Wounds	S M Frances of Five Wounds	S M Frances of Five Wounds	S M Frances of Five Wounds
8	Roman	S Bridget of Sweden	S Bridget of Sweden	S Bridget of Sweden	
10		SS Daniel and Companions	SS Daniel and Companions	SS Daniel and Companions	SS Daniel and Companions
12		S Seraphin of Montegranaro	S Seraphin of Montegranaro	S Seraphin of Montegranaro	S Seraphin of Montegranaro
19	Roman	S Peter of Alcantara	S Peter of Alcantara	S Peter of Alcantara	
21		B James of Strepar (Simple) / B Matthew of Girgenti	B James of Strepar	B James of Strepar	
23		B Josephine Leroux			
25		B Christopher of Romagnola / B Balthasser of Chiavari / B Thomas of Florence (Simple)			
26		B Bonaventure of Potenza	B Bonaventure of Potenza		
27		B Contardo Ferrini (Simple)			
30		B Angelo of Acri		B Angelo of Acri	
31				B Christopher of Romagnola / B Thomas of Florence	

NOVEMBER

3			B Christopher of Romagnola / B Raynier of Arezzo / Franciscan All Souls	B Raynier of Arezzo	

4 Roman	S Charles Borromeo	S Charles Borromeo	S Charles Borromeo	
5	Relics in Fran. Churches	Relics in Fran. Churches	Relics in Fran. Churches	Relics in Fran. Churches
6	B Margaret of Lorraine B Jane Mary of Maillé (Simple)	B Helen Enselmina	B Margaret of Lorraine	
7	B Helen Enselmina (Simple) B Margaret Colonna B Matthia Nazzarei		B Helen Enselmina	
9		B Jane of Signa		
12	B Raynier of Arezzo (Simple) B Gabriel Ferretti B John of Peace	B John of Peace	B Gabriel Ferretti	B John of Peace
13 Roman	S Didacus of Alcalá	S Didacus of Alcalá	S Didacus of Alcalá	
16	S Agnes of Assisi	S Agnes of Assisi	S Agnes of Assisi	S Agnes of Assisi
17	B Salome (Simple) B Jane of Signa B Elizabeth the Good	B Salome	B Salome	
19 Roman	S Elizabeth of Hungary	S Elizabeth of Hungary	S Elizabeth of Hungary	S Elizabeth of Hungary
25		B Elizabeth the Good		
26 Sup.	S Leonard of Port Maurice	S Leonard of Port Maurice		
27	B Bernardin of Fossa B Humilis of Bisignano	Manifestation of Our Lady of the Miraculous Medal	B Bernardin of Fossa	S Leonard of Port Maurice
28	S James of the March	S James of the March	S James of the March	S James of the March
29	Franciscan All Saints	Franciscan All Saints	Franciscan All Saints	Franciscan All Saints

DECEMBER

1	B Anthony Bonfadini B Bentivolio Buoni B Gerard Cagnoli (Simple) Franciscan All Souls	B Anthony Bonfadini B Nicholas Tavelich	B Anthony Bonfadini	B Delphina and Comps.
2				Franciscan All Souls
4		B Peter of Siena		
5	B Nicholas Tavelich		B Nicholas Tavelich	B Peter of Siena
8 Roman	Immaculate Conception Patroness of Fran. Order	Immaculate Conception	Immaculate Conception	Immaculate Conception
9		B Francis Anthony Fasani		
11	B Peter of Siena B Hugolinus Magalotti	B Hugolinus Magalotti		B Hugolinus Magalotti
12 U.S.	Our Lady of Guadalupe (in U.S.)			
12	Finding, S Francis	Finding, S Francis B Waldo B Bartolo of San Gimignano	Finding, S Francis	Finding, S Francis
13	Finding, S Francis (in U.S.)			
14	B Nicholas Factor B Conrad of Offida B Bartolo of San Gimignano	B Bentivolio Buoni B Conrad of Offida	B Conrad of Offida	
15	Mary, Queen of Fran. Order	Mary, Queen of Fran. Order	Mary, Queen of Fran. Order	Mary, Queen of Fran. Order
30				B Margaret Colonna B Matthia Nazzarei

APPENDIX V

SPECIAL FRANCISCAN FEASTDAYS

SINCE this is a book of saints, a biographical sketch of a Franciscan saint, blessed, or saintly person is presented also for those days on which a feast of our Lord or our Lady or some other special feast is observed. In the Franciscan calendar there are 25 special feasts which are not in the universal Roman missal and breviary, at least not in the same form; and it will be well to add a brief explanation of these feasts, except those of Portiuncula (August 2) and the Stigmata of S Francis (September 17). In regard to the latter, an exception has been made, and an account is offered on the days indicated. Incidentally, S Francis of Assisi is the only saint since the time of the apostles who has two feasts in the Roman calendar, September 17 and October 4. The special feasts in the Franciscan calendar are the following:

(1) *January 23: Espousals of the Blessed Virgin Mary with S Joseph.* In 1537 Pope Paul III permitted the Franciscans to celebrate this feast, and in the course of time it was extended also to several other groups. It was removed from the Church's calendar in 1913; but in 1928, the Franciscans were again permitted to observe the feast. According to the Jewish law, marriage included the erusim and the nissuim, which have been translated as the betrothal and the marriage. But these English terms are an incorrect translation. The erusim, or espousals, meant a real marriage contract; however, between the erusim and the nissuim, or taking home, there was, in the case of a virgin, usually an interval of a year, during which she lived in seclusion at the home of her parents. Although the feast is celebrated on January 23, Mary was espoused to Joseph probably on November 25, 7 B.C., when she was about thirteen years and two months old (Cf. Columbia, May, 1954, pp. 4, 18). It is quite certain that the Annunciation took place about four months later, March 25, 6 B.C.

(2) *February 15: Transfer of the Body of S Anthony of Padua.* When S Anthony died on June 13, 1231, his body was buried in the little Franciscan Church of S Mary in Padua. By 1263, the building of the present great basilica was advanced far enough so that his remains could be placed beneath the high altar. When the coffin was opened on this occasion, it was found that the saint's body had been reduced to ashes except for a few bones, but his tongue was intact and life-like. S Bonaventure, who was present as minister general of the Friars Minor,

took the tongue reverently into his hands and exclaimed: "O blessed tongue, which has always blessed God and caused others to bless Him, now it appears evident how great were your merits before God!" The tongue of S Anthony was then placed in a special reliquary, and can still be seen today in a separate chapel on the epistle side of the basilica. In 1310 the basilica was almost finished, and the remains of S Anthony were transferred to a tomb in the middle of the nave. The final transfer of the relics of S Anthony to their present chapel on the Gospel side of the basilica took place in 1350. It is the latter transfer that is commemorated on February 15. (Cf. Everyman's Saint, pp. 17-18, 89-90.)

(3) *First Friday of March (Fran.) or Friday after Ash-Wednesday (Conv.): Mysteries of the Way of the Cross.* The Stations of the Cross which one sees on the walls of almost every Catholic church belong to a devotion which was introduced and promoted by the sons of S Francis. As guardians of the holy places in Palestine, the Franciscans began to walk along the Via Dolorosa or Sorrowful Way from the Praetorium to Golgatha, prayerfully recalling the events in the Passion of our Lord which occurred en route. They still do this every day at 3:15 in the afternoon, rain or shine. This devotion was introduced by them also in Europe; and in 1686 Pope Innocent XI granted to the faithful who made the Way of the Cross the same indulgences which were gained by visiting the holy places in Jerusalem. S Leonard of Port Maurice (1751) is especially known for his great zeal in promoting the devotion of the Way of the Cross. It was Pope S Pius X who in 1906 granted the Franciscans permission to celebrate a special feast of the Mysteries of the Way of the Cross. — At the present time, the faithful can gain a plenary indulgence as often as they go the Way of the Cross; and an additional plenary indulgence is granted to them, if they receive holy Communion on the same day. A remarkable feature of the plenary indulgence attached to the Way of the Cross is the fact that the usual conditions for such an indulgence are not required, namely confession, Communion, and vocal prayers, not even for the intentions of the Holy Father. All that need be done, besides being in the state of grace, is to walk from station to station and to meditate briefly at each one on some phase of the Passion, not necessarily the one depicted at the station. Those who can not visit the Stations where they are erected in church or outdoors, can gain the same indulgences by holding in their hands a specially blessed Stations Crucifix and reciting twenty Paters, Aves, and Glorias. The sick who can not say these Paters etc. need only kiss such a crucifix or look upon it and at least mentally say a short ejaculation in honor of the Passion, for instance "My Jesus, mercy!", the favorite prayer of S Leonard.

(4) *March 14: Transfer of the Body of S Bonaventure.* The Franciscans and Conventuals, on this day, commemorate the transfer of the relics of S Bonaventure to the new Franciscan church in Lyons, France, which took place in 1434. At this time, one arm of the saint was taken to his birthplace, Bagnorea, near Viterbo, Italy.

(5) *April 16: Solemn Commemoration of Our Holy Father S Francis.* The three branches of the First Order observe this feast to recall the first oral approval of the First Order which S Francis obtained from Pope Innocent III. On this occasion S Francis and the first friars also received the tonsure and the permission to preach penance. The traditional date of this event is April 16, 1209, although Joergensen and others think it should be the summer of 1210. On April 16 the Franciscans also renew their vows annually. (Cf. *As the Morning Star*, pp. 160-161.)

(6) *Second Saturday after Easter: Our Lady, Mother of the Divine Shepherd.* This feast is observed by the Capuchins on this day, because the Gospel of the Mass on the following day (Second Sunday after Easter) consists of the words of our Lord (from John 10,11-16) in which He describes Himself as the Good Shepherd, who laid down His life for His sheep.

(7&8) *May 25: Dedication of the Patriarchal Basilica of Our Holy Father S Francis at Assisi, and Commemoration of the Transfer of the Body of S Francis.* This feast and commemoration are observed by all the branches of the Franciscan Order. When S Francis died in 1226, he was buried in the Church of S George in Assisi (now a chapel in Santa Chiara, and the shrine of the original San Damiano Crucifix.) Two years later S Francis was solemnly canonized, and the building of San Francesco at the other end of the town was begun. In May, 1230, the body of the saint was transferred to the new church; and in 1253, on the anniversary of the transfer, Pope Innocent IV consecrated the Church of San Francesco. Pope Benedict XIV (1740-1758) raised it to the rank of a patriarchal basilica and papal chapel. (Cf. *As the Morning Star*, pp. 167-168.)

(9) *May 27: Our Lady, Mediatrix of Graces.* The Franciscans celebrate this feast to honor Mary as the one through whose hands her Divine Son deigns to bestow all graces on men. It was instituted by the Tertiary Pope Benedict XV (1914-1922), but its celebration is limited to the Franciscans and certain other groups and places.

(10) *July 15: The Most Holy Sepulchre of our Lord Jesus Christ.* It was on

July 15, 1099, that the First Crusade freed Jerusalem from the Saracens. Since 1917, the Franciscans, inasmuch as they are the custodians of the holy places, are privileged to celebrate this special feast of the Holy Sepulchre on July 15.

(11) *July 16: Commemoration of the Canonization of Our Holy Father S Francis.* While celebrating the feast of Our Lady of Mount Carmel on July 16, the three branches of the First Order of S Francis also commemorate, on this day, the canonization of their holy founder, which took place on July 16, 1228, less than two years after his death. The pope who enrolled S Francis among the Church's canonized saints was Gregory IX (1227-1241), who as Cardinal Ugolino had been the personal friend and adviser of the Poverello. (Cf. *As the Morning Star*, pp. 153-156, 166.)

(12) *August 2: Dedication of the Patriarchal Basilica of S Mary of the Angels (Portiuncula).* See August 2 in this volume. Noteworthy is the fact that, although the anniversary of the consecration of the great basilica which was built over the Portiuncula chapel is observed on this day, the office and the Mass are not taken from the common of such feasts but are really the proper office and Mass of a feast of Our Lady, namely Our Lady of the Angels. (Cf. *As the Morning Star*, p. 170.)

(13) *August 4: Our Holy Father S Dominic.* The founder of the Order of Friars Preacher, who died in 1221 and was canonized in 1234, was a personal friend and admirer of S Francis; and for this reason the entire Franciscan Order celebrates his feast with special solemnity. S Francis gave S Dominic the cord he was wearing as a remembrance and token of friendship, and for this reason S Dominic is regarded as the first Cordbearer of S Francis. In places where there are convents of the Friars Preacher and the Friars Minor, it is customary for a Dominican to celebrate the solemn Mass on October 4 in the Franciscan church and for a Franciscan to sing the Mass on August 4 in the Dominican church.

(14) *August 26 or 27: The Seven Joys of Our Lady.* The Franciscans celebrate this feast on August 27 and the Conventuals on August 26. Pope S Pius X authorized them to celebrate this feast in 1906. The original day was the Sunday after the octave of the Assumption, but in 1914 it was transferred to the octave day itself; and in 1942, when the feast of the Immaculate Heart of Mary was assigned to that day, that of the Seven Joys was moved to August 26 or 27. The Franciscans wear the Rosary of the Seven Joys on their cord. (Cf. October 16 in this volume.)

September 17: The Imprinting of the Stigmata of Our Holy Father S Francis.
See September 17 in this volume. This feast was instituted for the
Franciscan Order by B Benedict XI (1303-1304), and extended to the whole
Church by Pope Paul V (1605-1621). The latter was persuaded to do this
by the Jesuit cardinal and doctor of the Church, S Robert Bellarmine. (Cf.
As the Morning Star, pp. 161-162.)

September 23: The Finding of the Body of S Clare. For some six centuries the
body of S Clare lay buried deep under the high altar of Santa Chiara, the
church in Assisi which had been built in her honor. In 1850 Pope Pius IX
granted permission that excavations be made, and after seven days the
stone coffin containing the body of the saint was found. When it was
opened, it was discovered that the body of S Clare, though blackened with
age, was still incorrupt. It was put into a crystal coffin, and this was placed
in the crypt of the church after it was completed in 1872. The feast of the
Finding of the Body of S Clare, which was instituted by Pope Pius IX, is
celebrated by the Franciscans and Conventuals as well as the Poor Clares.
October 3: Commemoration of the Transfer of the Body of S Clare. With
the Poor Clares, the Franciscans and Conventuals also commemorate the
transfer of the body of S Clare from the Church of S George in Assisi,
where it was buried after her death in 1253, to the new Church of Santa
Chiara which was built beside it. The latter was commenced in 1255, the
year in which S Clare was canonized; and it was completed five years
later, in 1260. The transfer took place on October 3 of that year.

*October 5, November 3, December 1: The Commemoration of All the Dead of
the Franciscan Order.* Besides All Souls Day on November 2, the Franciscan
Order observes a Franciscan All Souls Day — the Capuchins on October
5, the Conventuals on November 3, and the Franciscans and Third Order
Regular on December 1. On this day the Office for the Dead and a holy
Mass are said, not only for all the deceased members of the Franciscan
Order, but also for their departed relatives and benefactors, and for all
those who are buried in Franciscan cemeteries.
November 5: The Holy Relics Preserved in Franciscan Churches. The
Second Ecumenical Council of Nicaea (787) and the Council of Trent
(1545-1563) defended and approved the veneration of the relics of the
saints. It is the saints themselves whom we honor when we venerate their
relics. By such veneration, we also give expression to our faith in the
resurrection of the body; for, at the Last Judgment, the relics of the saints
will be reunited as glorified bodies with their souls and share their eternal
happiness in heaven. Through the relics of the saints, God has wrought

countless wonders.

November 27: Manifestation of Our Lady of the Miraculous Medal. In 1830-1831 Our Lady appeared four times to S Catharine Laboure in Paris and instructed her to have the Miraculous Medal struck. On these occasions Our Lady showed herself to S Catharine as the Immaculate Conception; and, the Miraculous Medal is really the Medal of the Immaculate Conception. On the medal are the words of the little prayer which Our Lady herself wishes us to say: "O Mary, conceived without sin, pray for us who have recourse to you!" This feast is observed by the Conventuals.

November 29: All Saints of the Franciscan Order. In addition to All Saints Day on November 1, the entire Franciscan Order celebrates a Franciscan All Saints Day. All the saints and blessed mentioned in this book, in fact, all the members of the three orders of S Francis who have attained their goal in heaven, whether known or unknown, are honored in a special manner on this day. November 29 was selected for this feastday, because on that day in 1223 Pope Honorius III gave his approval to the final rule which S Francis gave to the Friars Minor, a rule which pointed out a new way to sanctity. By observing it faithfully many have become saints; and by celebrating the feast of all Franciscan saints, we are inspired and encouraged to follow in their footsteps. (Cf. As the Morning Star, pp. 171-172.)

December 8: The Immaculate Conception of the Blessed Virgin Mary, Patroness of the Franciscan Order. Although the feast of the Immaculate Conception is also in the Roman calendar since 1854, it is celebrated with special solemnity by the Franciscan Order, because under this title Our Lady is the patroness of the order. Long before 1854, ever since 1477, the Franciscan Order has been privileged to celebrate the feast of the Immaculate Conception. The Franciscan feast was extended to Spain and its possessions in 1761; and after the American hierarchy had chosen the Immaculate Conception as the patroness of the United States in 1846, the feast of the Immaculate Conception was likewise celebrated in this country. (Cf. November 8 in this volume, and Second Franciscan National Marian Congress, San Francisco, California, 1954.)

December 12: Our Lady of Guadalupe. On December 9, 10, 11, and 12, 1531, Our Lady appeared as an Indian maiden to the Indian Juan Diego on Tepeyac Hill, just north of Mexico City, and once, on December 12, to his sick uncle, Juan Bernardino, who was cured. On the last day, she arranged miraculous roses in Juan Diego's rough mantle and told him to carry them to the Franciscan Bishop Zumárraga. When the Indian unfolded his mantle before the bishop, the miraculous painting of Our Lady of Guadalupe was seen for the first time. That image is venerated today in the large and beautiful basilica which was built at the foot of Tepeyac Hill. Guadalupe, as this place is called, is a Marian shrine comparable in many respects to Lourdes and Fatima. Together with all of Latin America and some dioceses in the United States, the Franciscans of the United States and Canada, by a special grant, celebrate the feast of Our Lady of Guadalupe, Patroness of the Americas, on December 12.

December 12 or 13: Finding of the Body of Our Holy Father S Francis. The church which was built at Assisi in honor of S Francis soon after his death (1228-1230) was a double church, and the body of the saint was buried deep under the lower church. In the course of time the exact location of the tomb was forgotten; and with the permission of the Holy See, excavations were made in 1818 for the purpose of finding the relics. After 52 nights of hard work, the stone coffin containing the bones and ashes of S Francis was found. A third underground church was then hewn out of the solid rock upon which the church had been built; and there the relics of S Francis are venerated today. Pope Leo XII instituted a special feast to commemorate the finding of the body of S Francis. It is observed by the Franciscan Order on December 12, except in the Americas where it is kept on the following day. (Cf. As the Morning Star, pp. 168-169.)

December 15: The Blessed Virgin Mary, Queen of the Franciscan Order. As Thomas of Celano tells us in his Second Life of S Francis, "what is a very special source of joy is the fact that he chose her (Mary) as the Patroness of his order; and he entrusted to her shielding mantle his children whom he was to leave that she might guard and protect them unto the end." In 1910 Pope S Pius X permitted the members of the three orders of S Francis to add to the Litany of Loreto the invocation: "Queen of the Franciscan Order, pray for us!" And in 1950 Pope Pius XII granted them a special feast, with a proper office and Mass, honoring Our Lady as Queen of the Franciscan Order. The day chosen for this feast is December 15, formerly the octave day of the Immaculate Conception. The children of S Francis through the centuries have always distinguished themselves by their devotion to Mary and by their efforts to promote this devotion among the faithful. The latest feast of Our Lady to be introduced into the Roman calendar, that of Mary, Queen of the Universe, which is celebrated on the last day of May, owes its institution in great measure to the late Canadian Franciscan missionary bishop, the Most Reverend Ange-Marie Hiral, who already in January, 1946, had dedicated his cathedral in Port

Said at the entrance to the Suez Canal, "the crossroad of the world," to Maria, Regina Mundi — Mary, Queen of the World. (Cf. Forum, 1957, p. 149.)

APPENDIX VI

SAINTLY FRANCISCANS
(Three Orders of St. Francis)

HE list of saintly Franciscans of the three orders of S Francis which follows is only a partial one. Emphasis is placed on those whose cause of beatification has been introduced and those who have died in the 19th and 20th centuries. Those servants of God of whom sketches appeared in The Poverello's Round Table (abbreviated PRT) but who had to cede their places to canonized saints, formally or equivalently declared blessed, American martyrs, and others of special interest, are included in the following list with a reference to the day to which they were originally assigned. Special pains were taken to include all known modern Tertiaries who distinguished themselves by the holiness of their lives. The names of those servants of God who are mentioned in this volume on one of the days of the year are not repeated in the list given here. *Heroes* is an abbreviation of the compiler's Heroes of the Cross, and Heralds of his Heralds of the King.

I. First Order

A. Friars Minor (before 1440)

Ademar of Fignac, priest, d. 1320 (cf. PRT, July 18)
Aldobrand of Florence, priest, martyr in Persia, c. 1282 (cf. In Journeyings Often, pp. 177, 179)
Angelus of Spoleto, priest, martyr in Kipchak (Russia), c. 1323 (ibid., pp. 178, 179)
Anthony of Armenia, priest, martyr in Persia, c. 1282 (ibid., pp. 177, 179)
Conrad of Saxony, priest, martyr in Georgia (Russia), 1288 (ibid., pp. 179)
De Rosatis of Milan, Anthony, priest, martyr in Armenia, 1314 (ibid., pp. 177, 179)
Dominic, Friar, priest, martyr in Kipchak (Russia), c. 1333 (ibid., pp. 180)
Francis of Borgo San Sepolcro, brother, martyr in Persia, 1314 (ibid., pp. 177, 179)
Francis of Fermo or Petriolo, priest, martyr in Armenia, 1314 (ibid., pp. 177, 179)
James of Florence, bishop, and 4 companions, martyrs in Turkestan, 1362 (ibid., pp. 122, 139, 180)

Kador, John, priest, martyr in Armenia, 1383 {ibid,., pp. 168, 177, 180)
Matthew of Escandel of Hungary, priest, martyr in China, c. 1400 (ibid., pp. 127, 143, 180)
Monald of Ancona, priest, martyr in Armenia, 1314 {ibid., pp. 177, 179)
Pepoli, Nicholas, brother, companion of S Francis, d. 1229 (cf. PRT, May 1)
Peter the Small, priest, martyr in Kipchak (Russia), c. 1340 (cf. In Journeyings Often, pp. 178, 180)
Richard of Burgundy, bishop, and 5 companions (3 priests and 2 brothers), martyrs in Almaligh or Sinkiang, China, 1339 (ibid., pp. 123, 133, 135, 180)
Stephen of Gross-Wardein, Hungary, priest, martyr, d. 1334 (ibid., pp. 178, 180; PRT, April 27)
Stephen of Hungary, priest, martyr in Georgia (Russia), 1288 (cf. In Journeyings Often, pp. 177, 179)
William of England, priest, martyr in Georgia (Russia), 1288 (ibid., pp. 177, 179)

B. Franciscans

Alberti of Calenzana, Bernardin, priest, 1591-1653; cause pending
Aloysius of Bergamo, brother, d. 1806; cause pending
Anthony of S Ann, brother, martyr in Oceania, d. 1610; cause pending
Atonna, Berard, priest, 1842-1917; cause pending
Ballardini of Breno, Louis, priest, 1616-1679; cause pending
Balthasar of Castronuovo, priest, 1460-1525; cause pending
Bardesi, Peter, brother, 1649-1700; cause pending
Bartolomei of Orvieto, Peter Dominic, priest, 1682-1738; cause pending
Beineke, Chrysostom, priest, d. 1879 cf. Heralds, pp. 158-161)
Benedict of Poggibonsi, priest, 1591-1659, cause pending
Boehle, Apollinaris, brother, d. 1936 (cf. Heralds, p. 723)
Cherubin of S Lucia, Ven., priest, 1545-1587; cause in progress
Cichetti of Acre Casale, Marianus, brother, 1778-1866; cause pending
Classen, Ignatius, priest, d. 1945 (cf. Heralds, p. 741)
Conley, Leander, priest, d. 1954 (cf. Heralds, p. 747)
Dal Vago of Portugruaro, Bernardin, priest, min. gen., archb., 1822-1895; cause pending
Dalmazzo of Cuneo, Benign, priest, 1673-1744; cause pending
Dangelosanto of Picciano, Francis, brother, 1773-1851; cause pending
Daniel and 5 companions, martyrs of Alkmaar, Holland, d. 1572; cause pending
Davino of Collodi, Francis, priest, 1793-1863; cause pending
De Palacios, Peter, brother, in Brazil, d. 1570 (cf. Forum, 1943, p. 139)
Drengler, Canute, brother, d. 1936 (cf. Heralds, p. 719)

Echevarria Gorostiaga, Felix, priest, and 6 companions, martyrs in Spain, d. 1936; cause pending

Esquiu, Mamerto, bishop, in Argentina, 1826-1883; cause pending

Faulhaber, Bonaventure, priest, d. 1907 (cf. Heralds, p. 693)

Fontana of Premosello, Generosus, priest, 1729-1804; cause pending

Francis of S Anthony, brother, 1680-1764; cause pending

Galvao, Anthony of S Ann, priest, in Brazil, 1739-1822 (cf. Forum, 1942, pp. 93-96, 120)

Garcia Acosta, Andrew Philemon, brother, 1800-1853; cause pending

Giovanelli, Aloysius, priest, 1727-1803; cause pending

Giraldi, Joseph, brother, 1853-1889; cause pending

Gomez, Ven. John, brother, d. 1530; cause in progress

Grass, Juniper, brother, d. 1918 (cf. Heralds, p. 697)

Habig, Boniface, cleric, d. 1918 (cf. Heralds, p. 701)

Helm of Fulda, Leonard, priest, d. 1664 (cf. PRT, July 20)

Hesse, Erasmus, brother, d. 1878 (cf. Heralds, p. 154-155)

Hou, Gabriel, priest, martyr in China, d. 1931 (cf. PRT, September 20)

John Baptist of Burgundy, priest, 1700-1726; cause pending

Kummer, Wendelin, brother, d. 1878 (cf. Heralds, pp. 155-157)

Kuo, Thomas, priest, martyr in China, d. 1931 (cf. PRT, September 20)

Lawrence of Revello, brother, 1582-1623; cause pending

Lilli of Cappadocia, Salvator, priest, and 10 companions, martyrs in Armenia, d. 1895; cause pending

Lombardi of Monsano, Lawrence, priest, 1716-1797; cause pending

Longo of Manliano, Michaelangelo, priest, 1812-1886; cause pending

Lopez, Peter, priest, 1816-1898; cause pending

Madrigal, John Baptist, priest, d. 1608 (cf. PRT, June 24)

Mallmann, Maternus, priest, d. 1878 (cf. Heralds, pp. 155-158)

Mangano of Naples, Francis, priest, 1763-1841; cause pending

Marini of Recanati, Paul, priest, 1771-1842; cause pending

Marianus of Orszelar, priest, d. 1632 (cf. PRT, July 16)

Martyrs in China, 1 bishop, 24 priests and 4 brothers in addition to those here mentioned by name (cf. In Journeyings Often, pp. 303-304)

Martyrs of the French Revolution, 8 Franciscans, with John Poulin and 145 others, 1793-1796; cause pending

Martyrs of the United States, 41 fathers and brothers, in addition to the 34 mentioned in this volume (cf. Heroes of the Cross; The Martyrs of the United States of America)

Maupas of Parma, Linus, priest, jail chaplain, 1866-1924; cause pending (cf. Forum, 1947, pp. 18-19, and 1954, pp. 329-331)

Mazzarello, Modestin of Jesus and Mary, priest, 1802-1854; cause pending

Michaelangelo of S Francis, brother, 1740-1800; cause pending

Mucchielli of Ghisone, Francis, cleric, 1777-1832; cause pending

Musso, Leopold M., brother, 1855-1922; cause pending

Oddi, Didacus, brother, 1839-1919; cause pending
Oliveri of Sommariva, Hugolinus, brother, 1725-1772; cause pending
Pagani, Ven. Anthony, priest, 1526-1589; cause in progress
Paschal Mary, brother, d. 1936 (cf. Forum, 1937, p. 155)
Pelletier, Didacus, brother, in Canada, 1657-1699
Philip of Velletri, priest, 1704-1754; causing pending
Philippovich, Simon, priest, 1732-1802; cause pending
Prosperi of Bagnaia, Peter, priest, 1660-1742; cause pending
Ricci, Hermigild, bishop, martyr, in China, d. 1931 (cf. PRT, September 20)
Rinklake, Leo, priest, d. 1873 (cf. Heralds, pp. 154-155)
Sacconi, Anthony M., bishop, martyr, in China, 1741-1785; cause pending
Sarobe, Pius, priest, 1830-1912; cause pending
Scalmato, Ven. Anthony, priest, 1476-1559; cause in progress
Schrempp, Vincent, priest, d. 1941 (cf. Heralds, p. 735)
Sebastian of S Joseph, priest, martyr, in Oceania, 1566-1610; cause pending
Sillero, Sebastian of Jesus, brother, 1665-1734; cause pending
Strauch y Vidal, Raymond, bishop, martyr, 1760-1823; cause pending
Thaddeus of Tocco, brother, 1533-1639; cause pending
Thyssen, Henry, priest, 1755-1844; cause pending
Tolksdorf, Paulinus, priest, d. 1931 (cf. Heralds, p. 713)
Valadier of Bussieres, Simon, priest, 1842-1881; cause pending
Verhaeghen, Theotim, bishop, martyr, in China, 1840-1904, with 2,388 companions of the First and Third orders; cause pending
Viale, James, priest, 1834-1916; cause pending
Wadding, Luke, priest, 1588-1657 (cf. Forum, 1946, pp. 359-362, and 1957, p. 41).
Wiewer, Aloysius, priest, d. 1901 (cf. Heralds, pp. 154-164)
Witte, Everard, brother, in Holland, 1868-1950 (cf. Forum, 1951, p. 287, and 1952, pp. 47-48)
Yerovi, Joseph Mary, bishop, 1819-1867; cause pending
Yung, Amandus, brother, d. 1878 (cf. Heralds, pp. 154-155)
Zeng, Bonaventure, priest, martyr, d. 1931 (cf. PRT, September 20)
C. Conventuals

Agricola of Amberg, Bavaria, Bartholomew, priest, d. 1627; cause in progress
Bambozzi, Benvenute, priest, 1809-1875; cause pending
Cervini, Francis, priest, d. 1519; cause pending
Cesa of Avellino, Ven. Joseph M., priest, d. 1749; cause in progress
Chylinski, Ven. Raphael, priest, 1694-1741; cause in progress (cf. Forum, 1950, p. 191)
De Philippis of Itri, Ven. Innocent, brother, d. 1761; cause in progress

Gessi, Francis, priest, d. 1673; cause pending
Giannecchini, Mark Dominic, priest, d. 1767; cause pending
Girardelli of Muro Lucano, Ven, Dominic, priest, d. 1683; cause in progress
Katarzyniec, Venantius, priest, 1889-1921; cause pending (cf. Forum, 1950, p. 381)
Kolbe, Maximilian, priest, d. 1941 in prison camp, as martyr of charity; cause pending (cf. Forum, 1949, p. 127, and 1950, January to December)
Loverne of Canicactineo, Dominic, brother, d. 1713; cause pending
Lucci, Ven. Anthony, bishop, d. 1752; cause in progress
Palentieri, Jerome, bishop, d. 1619; cause pending
Sandreau, Angelo Anthony, priest, d. 1752; cause pending

D. Capuchins

Amigo Ferrer, Aloysius, bishop, 1854-1934; cause pending
Anthony Mary of Vauro, priest, 1825-1907; cause pending
Barberini, Bonaventure, archbishop, 1674-1743; cause pending
Bassost, Francis, priest, martyr, in San Francisco, California, d. 1872 (cf. Heroes of the Cross, pp. 208-209; Martyrs of the United States of America, p. 121)
Benedict of Beaucaire and 4 companions, martyrs, d. 1790; cause pending
Belvisolti, Ignatius of S Agatha, priest, 1686-1770; cause pending
Bonaventure of Occimiano, priest, 1700-1772; cause pending
Champigne of Paris, Honoratus, priest, 1567-1624; cause pending
Charles of Abbiategrasso, priest, 1825-1829; cause pending
Charles of Montrone, priest, 1690-1763, cause pending
Diliberto of Palermo, Joseph Mary, cleric, 1864-1886; cause pending
Felix of Marola, brother, d. 1707; cause pending
Francis of Licodia, brother, 1600-1682; cause pending
Francis of Bergamo, priest, 1536-1626; cause pending
Francis "a Praecepto", priest, 1564-1645; cause pending
Galli of Rome, Dominic Anthony, priest, 1746-1813; cause pending
Giles Mary of Lugliano, priest, 1681-1763; cause pending
Hartmann, Anastasius, bishop, in Switzerland, 1803-1866 (cf. Forum, 1942, p. 213)
Ignatius of Monsonio, priest, 1537-1613; cause pending
Innocent of Calatagirone, priest, 1589-1655; cause pending
Jeremy of Wallachia, brother, 1556-1625; cause pending
Jerome of Camerata, priest, 1549-1627; cause pending
Joachim of Canicactineo, priest, 1831-1905; cause pending
John Francis of Lucca, priest, d. 1655; cause pending
Joseph of Carabantes, priest, 1628-1694; cause pending
Lawrence of Zibello, priest, 1695-1781; cause pending

Leonard of Chartres, priest, martyr, at Annapolis, N. S., d. 1655 (cf. Heroes of the Cross, pp. 240-243)

Leopold of Castelnuovo, priest, 1864-1942; cause pending (cf. Forum, 1954, pp. 269-272)

Louis of Mazareno, priest, 1708-1763; cause pending

Malacrino of Rhegio, Jesuald, priest 1725-1803; cause pending

Mandic of Castelnuovo, Leopold, priest, 1866-1942; cause pending

Maolini, Marcellin, brother, d. 1909 (cf. Forum, 1941, pp. 9-10)

Marcuello of Adoain, Stephen, priest, 1808-1880; cause pending Mark of Aviano, priest, 1631-1699; cause pending (cf. Forum, 1954, p. 191)

Massaja, William, cardinal, 1809-1889

Molinari, Nicholas, bishop, 1707-1792; cause pending

Plunkett, Christopher, priest, martyr in Virginia, d. 1697 (cf. Heroes of the Cross, pp. 228-230; Martyrs of the United States of America, pp. 75-76)

Raynier of Borgo San Sepolcro, brother, 1511-1589; cause pending

Scalderone of Laculibero, Francis, priest, 1717-1804; cause pending

Scalvinoni of Bertio, Innocent, priest, 1844-1890; cause pending

Simón y Ródenas, Francis, bishop, 1849-1914; cause pending

Thomas of Olera, Ven., brother, 1563-1631 (cf. Forum, 1943, pp. 9-14)

Thomas of S Donato, brother, d. 1648; cause pending

II. Second Order

Alphonsa of Trivandrum, India, 1910-1946 (cf. *Forum*, 1951, pp. 318- 319, and 1956, pp. 129-140)

Antigo, Ann Mary, 1602-1676; cause pending

Belloni, Ven. Antonia M., 1625-1719; cause in progress

Berengaria of Portugal, d. c. 1565 (cf. PRT, December 27)

Biagini, Mary Aloisia, 1770-1811; cause pending

Clara Ortolana, d. 1689 (cf. PRT, October 28)

Do Lado of Portugal, Mary, d. 1633; cause pending

Elizabeth of Torre, d. 1510 (cf. PRT, May 6)

Fornari, Ven. Clara Isabella, 1697-1744; cause in progress

Gherzi, Ven. Clara Isabella, 1742-1800; cause in progress

Jacques, Louise Marie, 1901-1942 (cf. Forum, 1954, pp. 206-208, 212, 219)

Jane of Jesus, foundress of Recollect Poor Clare Penitents, 1576-1648; cause pending

Jeronima of the Assumption, Ven., in the Philippines, d. 1630; cause in progress

Martyrs of Ptolemais, 74 Poor Clares, slain by Mohammedans in 1289

Martyrs of Tripoli, 69 Poor Clares, slain by Mohammedans in 1289

Martyrs of Zawichost, Poland, 59 Poor Clares, slain by Tatars c. 1260

Mary of Jesus, Ven., Conceptionist Poor Clare, 1576-1637; cause pending

Mary of Sorrows and Protection, Conceptionist Poor Clare, 1831-1891; cause pending

Nobili, Cecilia, 1630-1655; cause pending

Romero Balmaseda, Teresa of Jesus, Conceptionist Poor Clare, 1861-1910; cause pending

Steiner, Mary Agnes Clara, 1813-1862; cause pending

Von Kuefstein Odescalchi, Mary Clare of S Francis, Capuchin Poor Clare, 1834-1933 (cf. Forum, 1941, pp. 262, 293, 335)

III. Third Order

A. Regular

Basil, Mary Francis, foundress of the Franciscan Sisters of Mill Hill

Bertarelli, Anna Felicia, foundress of 5 convents of Franciscan Tertiaries, 1688-1773; cause pending (cf. Forum, 1952, p. 255)

Buettler, Mary Bernard, foundress of the Franciscan Sisters of Our Lady Help of Christians in Colombia, 1848-1924; cause pending (cf. Forum, 1956, p. 160)

Bugni, Clare, d. 1511 (cf. PRT, September 19)

Caiani, Margaret, foundress of the Franciscan Minim Sisters of the Sacred Heart, 1863-1921; cause pending

Chevrier, Ven. Anthony, founder of the Franciscan Societies of Priests and Sisters "del Prado", 1826-1879; cause in progress

Cony, Maria Antonia, Brazilian member of the Sisters of S Francis of Penance and Christian Charity, 1900-1939 (cf. Forum, 1954, pp. 93, 159)

Farolfi, Mary Clare Seraphina of Jesus, foundress of the Franciscan Missionary Poor Clare Sisters of the Blessed Sacrament, 1853-1917; cause pending

Fietz, Mary Clare, member of the School Sisters of the Third Order of S Francis of Graz, Austria; cause pending (cf. Forum, 1954, p. 63)

Frances of Hagenau, d. 1675 (cf. PRT, July 1)

Gonzalez, Bridget, d. 1551 (cf. PRT, October 15)

Hagenauer, Barbara, d. 1570 (cf. PRT, June 26)

Hueber, Marie, foundress of the Third Order Convent Sisters of Tyrol, 1643-1705 (cf. Forum, 1952, pp. 359-362)

Hummel, Berta, artist, Franciscan sister, 1909-1946 (cf. Forum, 1955, p. 96, and 1957, p. 302)

Jansens, Lawrence, Tertiary brother, d. 1692 (cf. PRT, July 25)

Lapini, Anna Maria, foundress of the Franciscan Sisters of the Holy Stigmata, 1809-1860; cause pending

Lega, Mary Theresa, foundress of the Sisters of the Holy Family of the Third Order of S Francis, 1812-1890; cause pending

Lilia Maria of the Most Holy Crucified One, Ven., foundress of the Sisters of the Third Order of S Francis of Viterbo, 1690-1773; cause pending

Mary Aloisia of the Most Blessed Sacrament, foundress of the Franciscan Sisters Adorers of the Cross, 1826-1886; cause pending

Micarelli, Mary Josepha of the Infant Jesus, foundress of the Franciscan Sisters of the Infant Jesus, 1845-1909; cause pending

Mussart, Vincent, founder of Third Order community, d. 1637 (cf. PRT, October 3)

Nisch, Ulrica, member of the Franciscan Sisters of Mercy of the Holy Cross, 1882-1913

Peter de Betancourt, Ven., founder of Bethlehemite Brothers in Spanish America, a Franciscan teaching and nursing brotherhood which adopted the rule of S Augustine in 1687, 1619-1667 (cf. Forum, 1941, pp. 199-202)

Ranixe, Mary Leonarda, foundress of the Sisters of S Clare of the Annunciation, 1796-1875; cause pending

Sailer, Mary Catharine, d. 1684 (cf. PRT, October 14)

Scherer, Mary Theresa, foundress of the Franciscan Sisters of Mercy of the Holy Cross, 1825-1888: cause pending (cf. Forum, 1950, p. 352)

Siedliska, Mary Frances, foundress of the Franciscan Sisters of the Holy Family of Nazareth, 1842-1902; cause pending

Streitel, Frances, foundress of the Franciscan Sisters of the Sorrowful Mother, 1844-1911; cause pending

Tombrock, Immaculata, foundress of the Missionary Sisters of the Immaculate Conception of the Mother of God, 1887-1938 (cf. Forum, 1942, pp. 177-178, 120)

Troiani, Mary Catharine of S Rose, foundress of the Franciscan Missionary Sisters of Egypt, 1813-1887; cause pending

Truszkowska, Mary Angela, foundress of the Felician Sisters, d. 1899; cause pending (cf. Forum, 1951, p. 159)

Vendramini, Elizabeth, foundress of the Elizabethan Franciscan Tertiary Sisters of Padua, 1790-1860; cause pending

Wattson, Paul James Francis, founder of the Society of the Atonement, 1863-1940 (cf. Forum, 1940, p. 418; Gannon, Father Paul of Graymoor)

White, M. Lurana Frances, foundress of the Franciscan Sisters of the Atonement

B. Secular

Aalberse, P. J. M., professor of Technical High School of Delft, Holland, 1871-1948

Adriana of Cortona, virgin, sister of S Margaret of Cortona, 13th century (cf. PRT, July 17)

Allard, Joseph, industrialist in southern France, 1853-1941

Anna of Medina, virgin, d. 1602 (cf. PRT, September 3)

Ariens, Alphonse, secular priest, 1860-1928; cause pending

Barban, Eurosia, mother of two priests, 1866-1932 (cf. Pemffo, Stelle)

Barelli, Armida, speaker, writer, helped found Catholic University of Milan, 1882-1952 (cf. Forum, 1953, pp. 199-205)

Baretta, Louis, of Brussels, artist, 1866-1918

Batthyany-Strattmann, Ladislas, prince, physician, 1876-1931 (cf. Forum, 1931, pp. 119-120, and 1948, pp. 134-138)

Battistini, Matthias, opera singer of Europe, d. 1928

Bays, Margaret, seamstress, in Switzerland, 1815-1879; cause pending (cf. Forum, 1955, pp. 223-224)

Beaufaux, Charles, attorney, 1886-1941 (cf. Forum, 1952, pp. 133, 160)

Belpaire, Maria Elisa, of Antwerp, 1853-1948

Benavente, Hyacinth, of Madrid, author, Nobel Prize winner, d. 1955

Benedict XV, pope, d. 1922

Bermejo, Ven. Anthony Alonso, founder of Hospital of S Michael Archangel, in Spain, 1678-1758; cause in progress

Bernardi, Margaret, virgin, 1683-1743; cause introduced in 1770

Berube, Thomas, of Canada, motorman of street-car, 1884-1938

Beskow, Nils, Scandinavian author, 1863-1946

Bettazzi, Rudolfo, college professor, 1861-1941 (cf. Forum, 1942, p. 62, and 1955, pp. 46-48, 52)

Borsi, Giosue, 1888-1915 (cf. Forum, pp. 332-336, 347)

Bosco, Margaret, mother of S John Bosco, 1788-1856 (cf. Peruffo, Stelle)

Branly, Edouard, pioneer of wireless, 1846-1940 (cf. Forum, 1940, p. 527)

Bullesi, Giles, Italian seaman, 1905-1929

Calabria, John, secular priest, 1873-1954 (cf. Forum, 1955, pp. 176, 180)

Camacho, Maria de la Luz, Mexican martyr, 1907-1934 (cf. Heroes, pp. 252-254)

Castagna, Francis, doctor and professor of economics and political science, 1898-1941 (cf. Forum, 1942, pp. 61-62)

Ceolato, Rosina,1894-1930 (cf. Peruffo, Terziari d'Oggi)

Chen, Francis, martyr in China, d. 1931 (cf. PRT, September 20)

Chiron, Joseph Mary, French secular priest, 1797-1852; cause begun in 1937

Chmielowski, Adam, of Poland, 1846-1916 (cf. Peruffo, Cavalieri)

Christopher of S Catharine, Spanish secular priest, founder of Hospital of Jesus of Nazareth, 1638-1690; cause pending

Cifuentes, Abdon, of Chile, 1836-1928 (cf. Peruffo, Cavalieri)

Cimabue, John, painter, c. 1240-c. 1302

Clement, Andree, actress, d. 1954 (cf. Forum, 1955, pp. 77-80)

Coccapani, Louis, teacher, social worker, 1849-1931; cause pending (cf. Forum, 1955, pp. 11-13)

Columbus, Christopher, discoverer of the New World, 1451-1506; cause pending

Comoglio, Josephine, virgin, 1847-1899; cause pending

Comoglio, Teresa, virgin, 1843-1891, sister of Josephine; cause pending
Cortes, Donoso, 1809-1853
Costantino, Antonio Cuoghi, professor, 1850-1930 (cf. Forum, 1958, pp. 114-115)
Cuervo, Rufino José, scholar, 1844-1910
Cultrera, Sebastiana, mother of four religious, 1850-1935 (cf. Peruffo, Stelle)
Debaerdemaecker, Jules Jozef, of Holland, 1877-1944
De Béthune, Baron Jan, architect, 1821-1894
De Châtillon, Baroness, 1819-1885
De Foulques, Maria, 1861-1929 (cf. Peruffo, Terziari d'Oggi)
De Gailhard-Bancel, Hyacinth, French deputy, 1850-c. 1935 (cf. Forum, 1952, p. 105)
De Groeve, Alfons, of Holland, 1885-1945
Dehon, Leo John, priest, founder of Sacred Heart Fathers (Hales Corners, Wisconsin), 1843-1925; cause pending
De Lamarre, Victor, of Canada, "the strongest man that ever lived," 1888-c.1944 (cf. Forum, 1956, pp. 149-156)
De la Vallée-Poussin, Louis, scholar, 1869-1939
Dempsey, Timothy, of St. Louis, secular priest, "the American Cottolengo," d. 1936
De Mun, Albert, writer, orator, organizer, statesman, member of the French chamber of deputies, 1841-1914 (cf. Forum, 1940, p. 419, 1949, pp. 67-70, 91, and 1957, p. 158)
De Nicolai, Pauline, benefactor of the Holy Land missions, 1811-1868
De Pardo Bazan, Emilia, Spanish author, 1851-1921
Deprez, Firmin, founder with Tertiaries Prosper Thuysbaert and Hilaire Gravez of the Flemish student association "Amicitia", 1890-1916
De Reynold, Alfred, French colonel, d. 1929 (cf. Forum, 1931, p. 118)
De Segur, Hertogin, mother of Msgr. de Segur, 1799-1874
De Segur, Monsignor, 1820-1881
De Vialar, Emilia, in Portugal, foundress of Sisters of S Joseph, 1797-1856
De Urquijo, José Maria, in Spain, d. 1936 (cf. Pemffo, Terziari d'Oggi)
Diersen, Henry, man of all work for Sisters of Notre Dame in Cleveland, 1858-1938 (cf. Forum, 1939, pp. 187-188)
Dietrich, Johann, artist, 1846-1936 (cf. Forum, 1938, pp. 499-501)
Diotallevi, Rosa, virgin, 1908-1930; cause begun in 1946
Domingo y Sol, Emmanuel, secular priest, founder of Congregation of Priest-Workers, 1836-1909; cause pending
Dupanloup, Felix, bishop, 1802-1878 (cf. Forum., 1949, pp. 39-42)
Dumerin, Teresa, of Paris, foundress of Society of Friends of the Poor (cf. Peruffo, Cavalieri)
Dutton, Joseph, helper of Father Damian at Molokai, 1843-1931 (cf. Forum, 1948, pp. 327-331)

Fati, Argene, virgin, 1890-1926; cause pending (cf. Peruffo, Terziari d'Oggi)

Ferron, Marie Rose, stigmatic, 1902-1936 (cf. Forum, 1947, pp. 383-384, and 1951, p. 96)

Fey, Clara, in Holland, foundress of the Sisters of the Poor Child Jesus, 1815-1894

Flanagan, Edward, priest, monsignor, founder of Boys Town, Nebraska, d. 1948

Flores, Gonsalvo, martyr in Mexico, d. 1927

Flynn, Elinor, of New York, actress, 1910-1938 (cf. Forum, 1938, pp. 573-575, and 1957, p. 194)

Folger, Frieda, foundress of the Seraphic Mass Association of the Capuchins, 1868-1954 (cf. Forum, 1955, p. 95)

Fowler, Anna, English convert, nurse of lepers at Molokai

Francis of China, died from effects of imprisonment at the age of eighty, d. 1875 (cf. PRT, August 8)

Fuchs, Alfred, convert from Judaism, journalist, "martyr" of Dachau, d. 1942

Fullerton, Lady Georgiana Charlotte, convert, author, translator, poet, 1812-1885 (cf. Musser, Franciscan Poets, p. 199)

Gabriel of Trejo, cardinal, d. 1630 (cf. PRT, December 19)

Galici, Leonard, d. 1634 (cf. PRT, June 17)

Galvani, Louis, scientist, 1737-1798 (cf. Forum, 1938, pp. 333-334)

Garcia Farian, José, martyr in Mexico under Calles

Gardi, Teresa, virgin, 1769-1837; cause pending

Gattorno, Anna Rosa, widow, foundress of the Institute of the Daughters of S Ann, 1831-1900; cause pending

Gendre, Frederick, introduced S Vincent de Paul Society into Switzerland, 1819-1900

Giehrl, Emmy, widow, writer, bed-ridden for 53 years, 1837-1915 (cf. Forum, 1939, pp. 139-140)

Giotto di Bondone, artist, architect, c.1276-c.1337 (cf. Forum, 1956, p. 42)

Giovannetti, Rosina, violincellist, 1896-1929 (cf. Peruffo, Terziari d'Oggi)

Gonin, Marius, of France, 1873-1937; cause pending (cf. Forum, 1938, pp. 330-332; 1952, pp. 103-105; 1953, p. 351)

Goretti, Assunta, mother of S Mary Goretti, 1866-1954 Gounod, Charles, musician, 1818-1893

Goyau, Georges, of France, author, 1869-1939 (cf. Forum, 1940, pp. 419-421)

Grosoli-Pironi, John, senator, 1859-1937 (cf. Peruffo, Cavalieri)

Guasti, Angiolina, 1854-1937 (cf. Peruffo, Terziari d'Oggi)

Guasti, Caesar, 1822-1889; cause pending

Guillena, Jane, widow, d. 1646 (cf. PRT, July 2)

Hallack, Cecily Rosemary, author, d. 1939 (cf. Forum, 1957, pp. 224-227)

Hallenbarter, Leo, historian, artist, journalist, d. 1952 (cf. Forum, 1955, pp. 303-304)

Harmel, Leon, of France, 1829-1915 (cf. Forum, 1942, pp. 340-341; 1949, pp. 3-8; 1951, p. 287; 1957, p. 158)

Hauptmann, Gerhard, convert from Socialism, Nobel Prize winner in 1912, d. 1946

Hauser, Conrad, school teacher, 1857-1936 (cf. Forum, 1938, pp. 377-378)

Heim, George, priest, 1885-1938 (cf. Forum, 1939, pp. 43-44) Helleputte, Joris, minister of state, 1852-1925

Hubrich, Mary, first Catholic lay woman to go to a foreign mission from the United States as a medical missionary (left Joliet, Illinois, for Wuchang, China, in 1924)

Jackson, Arthur, 1900-1953 (cf. Forum, 1953, pp. 298-299)

Jaegen, Jerome, bank director, 1841-1919 (cf. Forum, 1938, pp. 402-404)

Jammes, Francis, French poet, 1868-1938

Jane of Silva, virgin, d. c.1617 (cf. PRT, December 26)

Jodice, Anthony, jurist, 1866-1952 (cf. Forum, 1953, pp. 151-16)

Joergensen, Johannes, Danish author, d. 1956 (cf. Forum, 1956, pp. 287-288; 1957, p. 12)

John of India, martyr, d. 1339 (cf. In Journeyings Often, 122-130)

Kenway, Bernard Charles, of Canada, d. 1951 (cf. Forum, 1952, pp. 105-106)

Killing, William, mathematician, professor, 1847-1923 (cf. Forum, 1947, pp. 329-333; 1955, pp. 109-112)

Klorer, Rosa Lang, of Alsace, died at Canton, Ohio, at 89, 1849-1938 (cf. Forum, 1939, p. 164)

Kolping, Adolph, apostle of young workingmen and founder of the Kolping Society, 1815-1865 (cf. Forum, 1949, pp. 99-102 and 163-165; 1956, p. 91)

Kuhn, Antoinette Marie, 1907-1939 (cf. Forum, 1949, pp. 259-262, 283-284)

Lamot, Margaret, English convert, founded association of Tertiary women doctors for the missions in India

Lamour, Louise Mary Elizabeth, doctor of literature, 1903-1937 (cf. Forum, 1938, pp. 451-452)

Laporta, August, doctor, in Holland, 1864-1919

Laroudie, John Baptist, Parisian workingman, 1825-1889 (cf. Forum, 1949, pp. 227-230)

Latour, Lolosa, doctor, d. 1920

Lavalliere, Eve, actress, 1866-1929 (cf. Forum, 1943, p. 331; 1948, pp. 291-294, 323-326, 350-351, 358-361; 1950, p. 159; 1957, p. 192)

Lavigerie, cardinal, founder of the White Fathers of Africa, 1825-1892

Le Cardonnel, Louis, priest, poet, 1862-1936

Ledochowska, Mary Theresa, foundress of the Sodality of S Peter Claver,

1863-1922 (cf. Forum, 1932, p. 120)

Legendre, Lucien, of France, founded or revived 24 different societies and projects of a religious nature, 1886-1932 (cf. Forum, 1940, pp. 386-387, 391)

Leo XIII, pope, d. 1903

Leonori, Aristide, architect, 1856-1928; cause pending (cf. Forum, 1938, pp. 354-356)

Lestra, Madame Jean, of France, died at 88, 1863-1951 (cf. Forum 1954, pp. 77-78, 91)

Letonnelier, Augustina, mother of 12 children, 1853-1917 (cf. Forum, 1958, pp. 49-52)

Lévesque, James Claude, agricultural engineer, 1922-1947 (cf. Forum, 1952, pp. 231-233)

Lippens, Polydor, father of Belgian telegraphy, d. 1899

Lo Pa Hong, Joseph, rich man of Shanghai, noted for charities, martyr (cf. Forum, 1931, p. 118; 1940, pp. 329-331)

Loyson, Mary Angela, former Carmagnole of the French Revolution, penitent, d. 1840 (cf. Forum, 1936, p. 71)

Lozinski, Zygmunt, bishop of Pinsk, Poland, 1870-1932 (cf. Forum, 1939, pp. 91-92)

Lueger, Karl, of Vienna, 1844-1910 (cf. Forum, 1942, pp. 169-174)

MacNutt, Francis Augustus, convert, 1863-1927 (cf. his autobiography A Papal Chamberlain and Forum, 1955, pp. 377-378)

Maffei, Giacomo, university student, d. 1935 (cf. Forum, 1938, pp. 523-525)

Manning, cardinal, archbishop of Westminster, 1807-1892

Manzoni, Alexander, author, 1785-1873 (cf. Forum, 1949, pp. 323-326, 352)

Marchisio, Clement, priest, 1833-1903

Marcotte, Hormisdas, blacksmith, father of 15 children, New Bedford, Mass., 1863-1937 (cf. Forum, 1939, pp. 163-164)

Marianna of Jesus, Ven., virgin, in Spain, d. 1620; cause introduced in 1692

Marie Joseph B. of Trie sur Baise, mother, widow, d. after 1938 (cf. Forum, 1952, pp. 259-262)

Marucchi, Orasio, great scholar of the Catacombs, d. 1931 (cf. Forum, 1931, p. 119)

Marson, Louis, doctor, 1901 P-1952 (cf. Forum, 1953, pp. 331-332)

Martin, Louis, father of S Teresa, the Little Flower (cf. Forum, 1939, pp. 20-22; 1957, p. 77)

Martin, Zelia, mother of S Teresa, the Little Flower, 1831-1877 (cf. Forum, 1939, pp. 20-22; 1945, pp. 267-269, 288; 1957, p. 77)

Martyrs of the French Revolution, 3 Tertiaries, with John Poulin and 145 others, 1793-1796; cause pending

Mary Angela of the Crucified One, virgin, 1846-1932; cause pending

Max of Saxony, Prince, priest, professor, 1870-1951 (cf. Forum, 1952, p. 131)

Mazzola-Zelger, Sophie, d. 1941 (cf. Forum, 1942, p. 62)

McGuinness, John, 1901-1945 (cf. Forum, 1947, pp. 262-265; 1957, p. 123)

Michael of the Angels, hermit, d. 1628 (cf. PRT, June 18)

Moreno, Garcia, president of Ecuador, martyr, 1821-1895 (cf. Forum, 1948, pp. 163-165, 191, 195-198)

Murillo, Bartholomew Stephen, Spanish painter, 1617-1632 (cf. Forum, 1931, p. 118)

Nascimbene, Joseph, priest, pastor, protonotary apostolic, founder of the Institute of the Little Sisters of the Holy Family, 1851-1922; cause pending.

Nobels, Jan, leader of the Christian workers' movement in Holland, d. 1923

Nosek, Francis, of Czechoslovakia, 1886-1935 (cf. Peruffo, Terziari d'Oggi)

Nuncia of Naples, widow, d. 1596 (cf. PRT, November 1)

O'Connell, Daniel, Irish patriot, 1775-1847

Pacchioni, Nino, 1912-1936 (cf. Peruffo, Terziari d'Oggi)

Pacelli, Philip, consistorial advocate at the Vatican, father of Pope Pius XII, 1836-1916

Pacelli, Virginia Graziozi, mother of Pope Pius XII, 1844-1920

Papini, Giovanni, author (cf. Forum, 1956, p. 319; 1957, p. 13)

Patmore, Coventry, English convert, poet, 1823-1896 (cf. Musser, Franciscan Poets, pp. 157-172)

Pecci, Countess, mother of the poor, mother of Pope Leo XIII, 1773- 1824

Pellico Silvio, Italian author, 1789-1854

Petit, Bertha, mystic, promoter of the devotion to the Immaculate and Sorrowful Heart of Mary, 1870-1943

Pius IX, pope, 1792-1878; cause introduced in 1922 Pius XI, pope, d. 1939

Pius XII, pope, d. 1958 (cf. Forum, pp. 400-407, 409)

Poppe, Edward, priest, 1890-1924; episcopal cause opened in 1946 and closed in 1951 (cf. Forum, 1952, pp. 255 and 323-326)

Pottier, Antonine, of Belgium, priest, 1849-1923

Queiser, Bertha, 1877-1951 (cf. Forum, 1952, pp. 45-47)

Ranken, George Elliott, editor of the London Tablet, 1828-1889

Rasponi del Sale, Augusta, countess, 1864-1942 (cf. Peruffo, Cavalieri)

Reichensperger, August, founder in 1852 of the German Catholic Party, later the Centre Party, 1808-1895

Reinhard, Paula, German author, 1851-1908

Ricci de Grimaldi, Innocentia, virgin, 1599-1624; cause pending

Richard, Francis Benjamin, cardinal, archbishop of Paris, d. 1908: cause pending

Ripon, Earl of (George F. S. Robinson), English convert in 1874, governor

general of India in 1880-1884, friend of the natives of India, 1827-1909
Roggen, Anna, medical missionary
Rohringer, Rosa, martyr, 1906-1950 (cf. Forum, 1951, pp. 191-192)
Ronca, Vincent, 1740-1824; cause pending
Rosaz, Edward Joseph, bishop of Susa, Piedmont, and founder of Franciscan Sisters at a retreat for girls, 1830-1903; cause pending (cf. Forum, 1954, p. 95)
Rossi, Justine, mother of 11 children, 1843-1940 (Peruffo, Stelle)
Rothe, Tancred, doctor of law, jurist, 1851-1935 (cf. Forum, 1938, 426-428)
Rubbens, Edmond, Fleming of Belgium, lawyer, minister of labor and social welfare, minister of colonies, 1894-1938
Rusconi, Beatrice, widow, d. 1490 (cf. PRT, July 22)
Ruys de Beerenbrouk, Charles Joseph Mary, of Holland, lawyer, deputy to lower chamber, prime minister three times, cabinet member till his death, 1873-1936 (cf. Forum, 1939, pp. 115-116; 1957, p. 271)
Ryan, Abram J., "the poet priest of the South," c. 1839-1886 (cf. Musser, Franciscan Poets, pp. 204-214).
Salonne, Marie Paula, author, 1902-1947 (cf. Forum, 1952, pp. 167-170)
Salvadore, Julius, 1862-1928; cause pending (cf. Forum, 1958, pp. 276-278)
Sanna, Ven. Elizabeth, widow, 1788-1857; cause introduced in 1880
Sarto, Margaret Sanson, mother of Pope S Pius X
Savelberg, P. J., priest, founder of Tertiary congregations of sisters and brothers in Holland, 1824-1907
Schollaert, Frans, stateman, 1851-1917
Sengmueller, Sebastian and Catherine, husband and wife (cf. Forum, 1939, p. 296)
Seipel, Monsignor, chancellor of Austria, 1876-1932
Servois, Marie Aimee, wife, on staff of Catholic newspaper La Croix of Limoges, France, d. 1939 (cf. Forum, 1939, pp. 237-238)
Simoni, Agnes, university student, 1929-1953 (cf. Forum, 1953, pp. 362-363)
Sorge, Reinhard Johann, German author, 1892-1916 (cf. Forum, 1957, p. 124)
Sotelo, Calvo, 1893-1936
Soubirous, Pierre, brother of S Bernadette, d. 1931 (cf. Forum, 1931, p. 117)
Souchon, Jean, father of ten children, 1900-1944 (cf. Forum, 1953, pp. 299-300, 318)
Spieler-Meyer, Hilda, of Switzerland, 1896-1953
Spoetl, Maria, of Switzerland, artist, d. 1953 (cf. Forum, 1955, p. 96)
Starace, Carmine, author, scholar, senator, d. 1955 (cf. Forum, 1958, pp. 190-191)

Starr, Eliza Allen, convert, author, artist, 1824-1901 (cf. Catholic Encyclopedia, vol. XIV, p. 250)

Suarez, Marco Fidel, president of Ecuador, 1855-1927 (cf. Peruffo, Cavalieri)

Tang, Peter, priest, martyr in Shensi, China, d. 1912

Teichmann, Constance, of Antwerp, 1824-1896

Telghuis, Wilhelmina, of Antwerp, 1824-1907

Termier, Pierre, geologist, 1859-1930 (cf. Forum, 1931, p. 119)

Thompson, Francis Joseph, poet, 1859-1907 (cf. Musser, Franciscan Poets, pp. 12-25)

Thuysbaert, Prosper, of Holland, lawyer, 1853-1908

Tinel, Edgar, musician of Brussels, 1854-1912

Tolli, Philip, founder of Societá Antischiavistica d'ltalia, 1843-1924 (cf. Peruffo, Cavalieri)

Tonnet, Ferdinand, died in concentration camp, 1894-1945

Tovini, Joseph, father of 12 children, lawyer, social worker, d. 1897 (cf. Forum, 1931, p. 119)

Tremblay, Jules, Canadian author of prose and poetry, honored by French Academy, 1883-1928

Trinci de Serrone, Frances, 1557-1607; cause pending

Van Cauwelaert, August, of Antwerp, 1885-1945

Van den Abeele, Hendrik, organist, 1869-1931

Vaughan, Herbert, cardinal, archbishop of Westminister, founder of Franciscan Sisters of Mill Hill (cf. Forum, 1951, p. 331; Musser, Franciscan Poets, p. 200)

Verdaguer, Jacinto, priest and poet of Catalonia

Verhaegen, Arthur, baron, leader of Christian workers' movement, 1847-1917

Vincent of Nicosia, d. 1601 (cf. PRT, June 29)

Vliebergh, Emiel, "the Flemish Ferrini," 1872-1925

Volpicelli, Ven. Catharine, virgin, foundress of the Institute of the Handmaids of the Sacred Heart of Jesus, 1839-1894; cause in progress

Von Hofmannsthal, Hugo, German author, 1874-1929

Von Ketteler, Emmanuel, bishop, 1811-1877 (cf. Forum, 1948, pp. 13-15, and 43-46)

Von Krane, Anna, German author

Von Ringseis, John Nepomuk, physician of Munich, 1785-1879 (cf. Forum, 1936, p. 334)

Von Sturmfelder-Homek, Baron Karl Friedrich, Bavarian statesman, d. 1936 (cf. Forum, 1936, p. 120)

Vrau, Camille Ferron, French manufacturer; cause begun

Vrau, Philip, brother of Camille Ferron, French manufacturer; cause begun (cf. Forum, 1931, p. 96)

Vyncke, Amaat, of Holland, priest, 1850-1888

Wang, Matthias, martyr in China, d. 1955

Weale, James, convert, father of 10 children, archeologist, historian, liturgist, 1832-1917

Weerts, Jan, of Holland, d. 1889

Westermaier, Maximilian, scientist, professor, 1852-1903; cause begun in 1948 (cf. Forum, 1950, pp. 128, 160; 1952, pp. 195-198, 224)

Windthorst, Ludwig, lawyer, judge, member of German Reichstag, leader of Catholic Center Party in Germany, opponent of Bismarck, 1812- 1891 (cf. Forum, 1941, pp. 235-237; 1948, pp. 227-230; 1957, p. 272)

Wolf, Nicholas, of Switzerland, 1756-1832 (cf. Forum, 1954, pp. 109-112)

Yamamoto, Sinziro Stephen, admiral of Japan, 1877-1942 (cf. Peruffo, Cavalieri)

Zerman, Henry, general, 1867-1938 (cf. Peruffo, Terziari d'Oggi)

Zolli, Eugenio, convert, Biblical scholar, 1881-1956 (cf. Forum, 1956, pp. 338-339, 342)

"The Saints and Blessed of the Third Order are to us a luminous cloud of witnesses; showing by their words and lives that though humility and charity are the highest reaches of perfection, nevertheless the way is easy and open to all in every state of life."

—Cardinal Manning

BIBLIOGRAPHY

The following is a select list of hooks and pamphlets in the English language about Franciscan saints, blessed, and saintly persons. Most of the lives of Franciscan saints and blessed which have been printed are in other languages (cf. for instance, the bibliography in These Made Peace). Of a few Franciscan saints, such as S Francis and S Anthony, numerous English lives have been published; and of these only a few are mentioned here.

A. Reference Works

Anon., *Franciscan Supplement to the Daily Missal*, 350 pp. St. Anthony Guild Press, Paterson, N.J., 1942.
Attwater, Donald, *A Dictionary of Saints*, 320 pp. Burns, Oates, and Washbourne, London, 1938. New edition, 1958, has 2,500 entries.
Benedictine Monks of S Augustine Abbey, Ramsgate, *The Book of Saints*, 3rd edn., 328 pp. Macmillan, London, 1942.
Foy, Felician A., O.F.M., *The 1958 National Catholic Almanac*, 704 pp. St. Anthony Guild Press, Paterson, N.J., 1957.
Herscher, Irenaeus, O.F.M., *Franciscan Literature, A Preliminary Check List*, 151 pp. St. Bonaventure University, St. Bonaventure, N.Y., 1952.
Holweck, F. G., *A Biographical Dictionary of the Saints*, 1053 pp. Herder, St. Louis, 1924.
Nelson, Joseph A., ed., *Roman Breviary in English*, 4 vols. Benziger Brothers, N.Y., 1950.
Webster's Biographical Dictionary, 1697 pp. G. and C Merriam, Springfield, Mass., 1943.

B. Collections of Lives

Attwater, Donald, *Butler's Lives of the Saints*, Supplementary Volume, 200 pp. Burns, Oates, and Washbourne, London, 1949.
Butler, Alban, *The Lives of the Saints*, Now Edited, Revised, and Copiously Supplemented by Herbert Thurston, S.J., and Donald Attwater, 12 volumes, one for each month. Burns, Oates, and Washbourne, London, 1933-1938. Revised four volume edition, 1956.
Biersack, Louis, O.F.M.Cap., *The Saints and Blessed of the Third Order of St. Francis*, 186 pp. St. Anthony Guild Press, Paterson, N.J., 1943.

Barth, Sister M. Aquinas, *The Poverello's Round Table*, 811 pp. Joliet, 111., 1939.

Bauer, Benedict, O.S.B., *Saints of the Missal*, 2 vols., tr. by Raymond Meyerpeter, O.S.B. Herder, St. Louis, 1957 and 1958.

Catholic Encyclopedia, 15 vols. Robert Appleton, N.Y., 1907-1912. Index and Supplement, The Encyclopedia Press, N.Y., 1914 and 1922.

Cicognani, Amleto Giovanni, Sanctity in America, revised edn., 228 pp. St. Anthony Guild Press, Paterson, N.J., 1941.

De Robeck, Nesta, *Among the Franciscan Tertiaries*. London, 1929.

Devas, Dominic, O.F.M., *Franciscan Essays*. Herder, St. Louis, 1924.

Erbacher, Sebastian, O.F.M., ed., *Seraphic Days, Franciscan Thoughts and Affections on the Principal Feasts of Our Lord and Our Lady and All the Saints of the Three Orders of the Seraph of Assisi* (written by Angelico Chavez, O.F.M.), 327 pp. Duns Scotus College, Detroit, 1940.

Engelbert, Omer, Lives of the Saints, tr. by Christopher and Anne Fremantle, 500 pp. McKay, N.Y., 1951.

Franciscan Herald, monthly. Franciscan Herald Press, Chicago, 1913-1940.

Franciscan Herald and Forum, monthly. Franciscan Herald Press, Chicago, 1940-1958.

Goodier, Alban, S.J., *Saints for Sinners*. Sheed and Ward, N.Y., 1930.

Habig, Marion A., *Heralds of the King, The Franciscans of the St. Louis-Chicago Province*, 1858-1958, 895 pp. Franciscan Herald Press, Chicago, 1958.

—, *Heroes of the Cross, An American Martyrology*, 3rd edn., 271 pp. St. Anthony Guild Press, Paterson, N.J., 1947.

—, *In Journeyings Often, Franciscan Pioneers in the Orient*, 338 pp. Franciscan Institute, St. Bonaventure, N.Y., 1953.

Hallack, Cecily, and Peter F. Anson, *These Made Peace, Studies in the Lives of the Beatified and Canonized Members of the Third Order of St. Francis of Assisi*, 287 pp. Burns and Oates, London, and St. Anthony Guild Press, Paterson, N.J., 1957

Leon (de Clary), Pére, O.F.M., *Lives of the Saints and Blessed of the Three Orders of Saint Francis*, 4 vols., tr. from Auréole Séraphique. Franciscan Convent, Taunton, England, 1885-1887.

Little Flowers of St. Francis, A Modern English Translation from the Latin and the Italian with Introduction, Notes, and Biographical Sketches by Raphael Brown. Hanover House, Garden City, New York, 1958.

Malloy, Mary, *Legends of St. Francis* (two booklets on S Francis, S Anthony, and the early companions of S Francis). Franciscan Herald Press, Chicago.

Martindale, Cecil C., S.J., *What Are the Saints?* Sheed and Ward, N.Y.,

1934.

Musser, Benjamin Francis, *Franciscan Poets*, 274 pp. Macmillan, N.Y., 1933.

Nesbitt, Marian, *Little Lives of Great Tertiaries*. Benziger, N.Y., 1928.

Ozanam, Anthony Frederick, *The Franciscan Poets in Italy of The Thirteenth Century*, tr. by A. E. Nellen and N. C. Craig. David Nutt, London, and Scribner's, N.Y., 1914.

Powers, James M., ed., *The Martyrs of the United States of America and Related Essays* by His Excellency Most Reverend John Mark Gannon, Archbishop-Bishop of Erie, 196 pp. Erie, Pa., 1957.

Royer, Fanchon, *The Franciscans Came First*, 200 pp. St. Anthony Guild Press, Paterson, N.J., 1951.

Steck, Francis Borgia, O.F.M., *Franciscans and the Protestant Revolution in England*, 344 pp. Franciscan Herald Press, Chicago, 1920.

Third Order Forum, quarterly from 1922, bimonthly from 1931, monthly from 1938. Chicago.

Biographies

Anon., *Franciscan Martyrs of Damascus*. Dublin, 1927.

—, *Giosue Borsi* (pamphlet). Kenedy, N.Y., 1940.

—, *Missionary Martyrs* (Franciscan martyrs of the Boxer Persecution in China), pamphlet, Franciscan Missionaries of Mary, North Providence, R.I.

—, *Mother Immaculata of Jesus*. Missionary Sisters of the Immaculate Conception, West Paterson, N.J.

—, *St. Louis, King of France*. Herder, S Louis, 1913.

Allibert, *St. Benedict the Moor*. Kenedy, N.Y.

Anson, Peter F., *Hermit of Cat Island, the Life of Fra Jerome Hawes*, 286 pp. Kenedy, N.Y., 1957.

Antony (Woodcock), Catherine Mary, *St. Anthony of Padua* (Lives of the Friar Saints series). London, 1911.

Bayer, Robert, *Piety in Overalls* (Matt Talbot), pamphlet. Franciscan Herald Press, Chicago.

—, *White Violet of Edinburgh* (Margaret Sinclair), pamphlet. Franciscan Herald Press, Chicago.

Bazzocchini, Benvenute, O.F.M., *A Seraphic Flower* (B Mary Assunta Pallotta), 68 pp. Franciscan Missionaries of Mary, N. Providence, R.I.

Beahn, John E., *A Man Born Again* (S Thomas More), 208 pp. Bruce, Milwaukee, 1954.

—, *A Rich Young Man* (novelized life of S Anthony of Padua), 250 pp. Bruce, Milwaukee, 1953.

Beebe, Catherine, *St. John Bosco and the Children's Saint, Dominic*

Savio (Vision Book). Farrar, Straus, and Cudahy, N.Y., and Burns and Oates, London, 1956.

Belloc, Hillaire, *Joan of Arc,* 85 pp. McMullen, now Farrar Straus, and Cudahy, N.Y., 1949.

Beraude de Saint Maurice, *John Duns Scotus, A Teacher for Modern Times,* tr. by Columban Duffy, O.F.M. Franciscan Institute, St. Bonaventure, N. Y., 1955. Also a condensation of this book in pamphlet form, by Benedict Leutenegger, O.F.M. Franciscan Herald Press, Chicago, 1958.

Bielak, Valeria, *The Servant of God Mary Theresa Countess Ledochowska,* new edn., 226 pp. Sodality of S Peter Claver, St. Paul, Minn., 1945.

Bittle, Celestine, O.F.M.Cap., *A Herald of the Great King, Stephen Eckert, O.F.M.Cap.* Bruce, Milwaukee, 1933.

Block, Irvin, *Christopher Columbus* (Real Book). Garden City Books, Garden City, N.Y., 1953.

Borden, Lucille Papin, *Without Staff or Scrip* (S Frances X. Cabrini), 400 pp. Macmillan, N.Y., 1945.

Brady, Charles A., *Stage of Fools* (novelized life of S Thomas More), 381 pp. Dutton, N.Y., 1953.

Brady, Ignatius, O.F.M., *The Life and Writings of St. Clare of Assisi,* 190 pp. Franciscan Institute, St. Bonaventure, N.Y., 1953.

Brophy, Liam, *St. Raymond Lull* (Herald Book), in preparation. Franciscan Herald Press, Chicago, 1959.

Brown, Raphael, *St. Charles of Sezze* (Herald Book), in preparation. Franciscan Herald Press, Chicago, 1959.

Burks, Arthur J., *Bells Over the Amazon* (the story of Fr. Hugo Mense, O.F.M., modern pioneer missionary among the Mundurucu Indians in the Brazilian jungles), 241 pp. David McKay, N.Y., 1952.

Caron, G., *Good Father Frederick Janssoone, O.F.M.* Three Rivers, Canada, 1932.

Carroll, Malachy, *The Story of Matt Talbot,* 110 pp. Mercier Press, Cork, 1949.

Case, Howard D., ed., *Joseph Dutton (Memoirs), the Story of 44 Years Service Among the Lepers of Molokai,* Hawaii. Honolulu Star-Bulletin, 1927.

Catharine of Genoa, St., *Treatise on Purgatory and The Dialogue,* tr. by Helen Douglas Irvine, 150 pp. Sheed and Ward, N.Y., 1947.

Clergue, Helen, *The Saint of Toulouse,* A Study of a Great Religious Personality. The Mitre Press, London, 1932.

Costelloe, Laurence, O.F.M., *St. Bonaventure, The Seraphic Doctor* (*Lives of the Friar Saints series*). London, 1911.

Cotter, Marie, *Westward by Command* (S Frances X. Cabrini), 160 pp.

Mercier Press, Cork.

Craven, Mrs. Augustus, *Life of Lady Georgiana Fullerton*, tr. by Henry James Coleridge, S. J. Richard Bentley and Son, London, 1888.

Cullen, Thomas F., *Mother Mary of the Passion*. Franciscan Missionaries of Mary, N. Providence, R.I.

Curtayne, Alice, *St. Anthony of Padua*. Franciscan Herald Press, Chicago, 1932.

Cuthbert (Hess), Father, O.S.F.C., *A Tuscan Penitent, The Life and Legend of St. Margaret of Cortona*. Burns, Oates, and Washbourne, London.

—, *Life of St. Francis of Assisi*. Longmans Green and Co., London and N.Y., 1910, 1912, 1921, 1927, 1935.

Da Masserano, Giuseppe Maria, O.F.M., *The Life of St. Leonard of Port Maurice*, tr. by Antonio Isoleri, 370 pp. Kilner, Philadelphia, 1909.

David of Augsburg, *Spiritual Life and Progress*, tr. by Dominic Devas, O.F.M., 2 vols. Burns, Oates, and Washbourne, London, 1937.

De Chérancé, Leopold, O.F.M.Cap., *St. Margaret of Cortona, The Magdalen of the Seraphic Order*, tr. by R. F. O'Connor. Sealy, Bryers, and Walker, Dublin, and Benziger Brothers, N.Y., 1903.

De la Gorce, Agnes, *St. Benedict Joseph Labre*, tr. by Rosemary Sheed, 213 pp. Sheed and Ward, N.Y., 1952.

De Montreuil, Baron, *The Life of Saint Zita, A Servant Girl of Lucca*, tr. from the French, 165 pp. P. O'Shea, N.Y., 1859.

De Porrentruy, Louis Antoine, *Saint of the Eucharist, St. Paschal Baylon*, tr. by Oswald Staniforth, O.S.F.C. 1905.

Derleth, August, *Columbus and the New World* (Vision Book). Farrar, Straus, and Cudahy, N.Y. and Burns and Oates, London, 1957.

De Robeck, *Nesta, St. Clare of Assisi*, 250 pp. Bruce, Milwaukee, 1951

—, *Saint Elizabeth of Hungary*, 200 pp. Bruce, Milwaukee, 1954.

—, *Vico Necchi* (Herald Book), in preparation. Franciscan Herald Press, Chicago, 1959.

Devas, Dominic, O.F.M., *A Modern Franciscan* (Father Arsenius Mary de Servieres, of France, Canada, and England, d. 1898), translated from the French, 146 pp. Benziger, N.Y., 1914.

—, *Life of St. Leonard of Port Maurice, O.F.M.*, 1676-1751. Burns, Oates, and Washbourne, London, 1920.

—, *Mother Mary of the Passion, Foundress of the Franciscan Missionaries of Mary*, 1839-1904. Longmans, Green, and Co., N.Y., 1924.

—, *St. Peter of Alcantara's Treatise on Prayer and Meditation*, tr. with an introduction and sketch of the saint's life (also John of Bonilla's Pax Animae), 211 pp. Newman, Westminster, Md., 1949.

De Wohl, Louis, *St. Joan the Girl Soldier* (Vision Book). Farrar, Straus, and Cudahy, N.Y., 1957.

Diethelm, Walter, O.S.B., *St. Pius X the Farm Boy Who Became Pope* (Vision Book). Farrar, Straus, and Cudahy, N.Y., 1956.

Dobbins, Dunstan, O.S.F.C., *St. Conrad of Parzham. The Friary, Crawley*, England, 1934.

Doherty, Eddie, *Matt Talbot*, 200 pp. Bruce, Milwaukee, 1953.

Driscol, Annette, *Tertiaries of Our Day* (Lady Georgiana Fullerton and Lady Herbert Lea), pamphlet. Franciscan Herald Press, Chicago.

Duerk, Hilarion, O.F.M., *Two Royal Saints* (St. Louis IX and St. Elizabeth), pamphlet. Franciscan Herald Press, Chicago, 1926.

Dunigan, Louis, O.F.M., *Broadway to Heaven* (Elinor Flynn), pamphlet. Franciscan Herald Press, Chicago.

Elmer, Victor, *St. Bernardine of Siena, Orator of Reform*, pamphlet. St. Anthony Guild Press, Paterson, N.J.

Engelhardt, Zephyrin, O.F.M., *Holy Man of Santa Clara*, or *Life, Virtues, and Miracles of Father Magín Catalá, O.F.M.* J. H. Barry, San Francisco, Calif., 1909.

Farrow, John, *Story of Thomas More*. Sheed and Ward, N.Y., 1954.

Fitzgerald, Vincent, O.F.M., *Saint John Capistran* (Lives of the Friar Saints series), Longmans, Green, and Co., London and N.Y., 1911.

Forbes, F. A., *Margaret Sinclair, in Religion Sister Mary Francis of the Five Wounds, Extern Sister of the Poor Clare Collettines*, 1900-1925. Herder, St. Louis, 1931.

Fullerton, Lady Georgiana, *The Life of St. Frances of Rome*, 136 pp. D. and J. Sadlier, N.Y.

Franciscan Fathers, Father Luke Wadding. Clonmore and Reynolds, Dublin, and Burns, Oates, and Washbourne, London, 1957.

Franciscan Institute, *The Legend and Writings of Saint Clare of Assisi*, Introduction, Translation, Studies. Franciscan Institute, St. Bonaventure, N.Y., 1953.

Geiger, Maynard, O.F.M., tr., Palou's *Life of Fray Junipero Serra*. Academy of American Franciscan History, Washington, D.C., 1954.

Ghéon, Henri, *Secrets of the Saints* (S John M. Vianney and S John Bosco included). Sheed and Ward, N.Y., 1944.

Gilbert, Father, O.S.F.C., *Blessed Agnellus and the English Grey Friars*. Burns, Oates, and Washbourne, London, 1937.

Giordani, Igino, *Pius X, A Country Priest* tr. by Thomas J. Tobin, 205 pp. Bruce, Milwaukee, 1954.

Gossens, Bruno, O.F.M.Cap., *The Venerable Mother Frances Schervier*, tr. from the German, by Ferdinand Gruen, 64 pp. Kenedy, N.Y., 1935.

Goyau, Georges, *Valiant Women, Mother Mary of the Passion and the Franciscan Missionaries of Mary*, tr. by George Telford, 310 pp. Sheed and Ward, London and N.Y., 1947.

Habig, Marion A., O.F.M., *As the Morning Star, The Passing of St.*

Francis, 218 pp. McMullen, N.Y., 1947. (A list of English works on S Francis on pp. 209-218.)

—, Contardo Ferrini, *A Modern Hero of the Faith*, pamphlet, 22 pp. St. Anthony Guild Press, N.J., 1942.

—, Everyman's Saint, *The Life, Cult, and Virtues of St. Anthony of Padua*, 200 pp. St. Anthony Guild Press, Paterson, N.J., 1954. (A list of English works on S Anthony on pp. 189-191.)

—, *Maggie, The Life-Story of Margaret Lekeux*, adapted from a biography by her brother Father Martial, O.F.M., 215 pp. Franciscan Herald Press, Chicago, 1931, 1932.

—, *Man of Peace, St. Francis of Assisi*, pamphlet, 35 pp. St. Anthony Guild Press, Paterson, N.J., 1941.

—, *Pioneering in China, Father Francis Xavier Engbring, O.F.M.*, the First Native American Priest in China (1857-1895), with Sketches of His Missionary Comrades, 155 pp. Franciscan Herald Press, Chicago, 1930.

—, Race and Grace; *St. Benedict the Negro*, 1526-1589, pamphlet, 56 pp. Franciscan Herald Press, Chicago, 1944.

—, Saint Francis Solano, *Apostle of Argentine and Peru*, pamphlet, 24 pp. S Anthony Guild Press, Paterson, N.J., 1942.

—, *The Franciscan Père Marquette*, A Critical Biography of Father Zénobe Membré, O.F.M., *La Salle's Chaplain and Missionary Companion*, 1645-1689 (Franciscan Studies, no. 13), 314 pp. Wagner, N.Y., 1934.

—, Vico Necchi, *Leader of Catholic Action*, pamphlet, 26 pp. St. Anthony Guild Press, Paterson, N.J., 1945.

Heath, Ven. Paul, O.F.M., *Self-Communings of a Martyr*, tr. by James Meyer, O.F.M., 156 pp. Franciscan Herald Press, Chicago, 1947.

Hegener, Mark, O.F.M., *The Poverello, St. Francis of Assisi*, 92 pp. Franciscan Herald Press, Chicago, 1956.

Herbert, Mary E., *Venerable* (now Blessed) *Vincent Pallotti*, 1795-1850, new edn. by Father Wilwers. Pallottine Fathers, Milwaukee, 1945.

Hiral, Ange-Marie, O.F.M., *The Revelations of Margaret of Cortona*, tr. by Raphael Brown, 90 pp. Franciscan Institute, St. Bonaventure, N.Y., 1952.

Hofer, Johannes, *St. John Capistran*, Reformer, tr. by Patrick Cummins, O.S.B. Herder, St. Louis, 1943.[5]

Hollis, Christopher, *Thomas More*. Bruce. Milwaukee, 1935.

Homan, Helen Walker, *Francis and Clare, Saints of Assisi* (Vision Book). Farrar, Straus, and Cudahy, N.Y., 1956.

---

[5] This work is now back in print from Mediatrix Press.

—, *St. Anthony and the Christ Child* (Vision Book). Farrar, Straus, and Cudahy, N.Y., 1958.

Hubbard, Margaret Ann, *St. Louis and the Last Crusade* (Vision Book). Farrar, Straus, and Cudahy, N.Y., 1958.

Huennermann, Wilhelm, *Flame of White, St. Pope Pius X*, tr. by an Ursuline nun (a novelized biography), in preparation. Franciscan Herald Press, Chicago, 1959.

Hughes, Henry Louis, *Frederick Ozanam.* Herder, St. Louis, 1933.

—, *St. John Bosco*, 1815-1888, Founder of the Salesian Congregation, Herder, St. Louis, 1934.

Ince, Elizabeth M., *St. Thomas More of London* (Vision Book). Farrar, Straus, and Cudahy, N.Y., 1957.

Jarrett, Bede, O.P., *Contardo Ferrini.* Herder, St, Louis, 1933.

Jeiler, Ignatius, O.F.M., *A Life of Venerable* (now Blessed) *Mary Crescentia Hoess*, tr. by Clementin Deymann, O.F.M. N.Y., 1886.

—, *The Venerable Mother Frances Schervier*, tr. by Bonaventure Hammer, O.F.M., 3rd edn., 492 pp. Herder, St. Louis, 1913.

Joergensen, Johannes, *An Autobiography*, tr. from the Danish by Ingeborg Lund, 2 vols. Longmans, Green, and Co., N.Y., 1929.

—, *Don Bosco.* Burns, Oates, and Washbourne, London, 1934.

—, *Saint Francis of Assisi*, A Biography, tr. from the Danish by T. O'Connor Sloane. Longmans, Green, and Co., N.Y., 1912, 1913, 1928, 1938, 1944. Image Books edn., Garden City, N.Y., 1955.

Johnston, S.M., *Cameo of Angela* (S. Angela Merici), 181 pp. Franciscan Herald Press, Chicago, 1958.

Joselma, Sister, O.S.F., *The Littlest Brother* (Achatius, a child Franciscan; cf. PRT, June 11). Franciscan Herald Press, Chicago.

King, Kenneth M., *Mission to Paradise, The Story of Junípero Serra and the Missions of California.* Franciscan Herald Press, Chicago, 1956.

Kerr, Lady Amabel, *A Son of St. Francis, St. Felix of Cantalice.* Herder, St. Louis, 1900.

Kerr, Cecil, Teresa Higginson, *School Teacher and Mystic*, 1844-1905, Herder, St. Louis, 1929.

Legaré, Romain, O.F.M., *Good Father Frederick Janssoone, O.F.M.*, tr. by Raphael Brown, in preparation. Franciscan Herald Press, Chicago, 1959.

Leutenegger, Benedict, O.F.M., *Apostle of America, Fray Antonio Margil*, 64 pp. Franciscan Herald Press, Chicago, 1956.

Lomask, Milton, *The Curé of Ars, The Priest Who Outtalked the Devil* (Vision Book). Farrar, Straus, and Cudahy, N.Y., 1958.

Lovasik, Father, *The Singing Heart* (Antoinette Marie Kuhn), 144 pp. Radio Replies Press, St. Paul, Minn., 1948.

Lummis, Charles F., *Flowers of Our Lost Romance* (pp. 50-87 on B

Sebastian of Aparicio). Houghton, Mifflin, Boston and N.Y., 1929.

Malloy, Louise, *Paschal Baylon, the Saint of the Eucharist*, pamphlet. Franciscan Herald Press, Chicago, 1926.

Manning, Anne, *The Household of Sir Thomas More*, 158 pp. Herder, St. Louis, 1905.

Marquardt, Philip, P.F.M., *On Crutches to Heaven, Being a Life of Brother Simon*, O.F.M., new edn. Franciscan Herald Press, Chicago, 1958.

Mason, Sister M. Liguori, O.S.F., *Mother Magdalen Daemen and Her Congregation*, 1835-1935, 440 pp. Stella Niagara, N.Y., 1935.

Mauriac, Francois, Margaret of Cortona, tr. by Barbara Wall. Clonmore and Reynolds, Dublin, 1949.

May, Julian, *The Friar Brand, St. John Capistran* (Herald Book), in preparation. Franciscan Herald Press, Chicago, 1959.

Maynard, Theodore, *Richest of the Poor* (St. Francis of Assisi). Garden City Books, Garden City, N.Y., 1948, 1949.

—, *The Long Road of Father Serra*, 300 pp. Appleton, Century, Crofts, N.Y., 1954.

—, *Through My Gift* (Mother Frances Schervier), 320 pp. Kenedy, N.Y., 1952.

—, *Too Small a World* (S Frances X. Cabrini), 350 pp. Bruce, Milwaukee, 1945.

McAuliffe, Harold J., S.J., *Father Tim* (Father Timothy Dempsey of St. Louis, d. 1936), 162 pp. Bruce, Milwaukee, 1944.

McNabb, Vincent, O.P., *St. Elizabeth of Portugal.* Sheed and Ward, N.Y.

McReavy, L. I., *Eve Lavalliére, A Modern Magdalen*, 1866-1929, 191 pp. Herder, S Louis, 1934.

Meersman, Achilles, O.F.M., *Climbing down to Glory* (Brother Everard Witte, O.F.M.) 68 pp. Everybody's St. Anthony, Bangalore, India, 1958.

Meyer, James, O.F.M., *Blessed by a Curse* (B Luchesio), pamphlet. Franciscan Herald Press, Chicago.

Meynell, Everard, *The Life of Francis Thompson*, 5th revised edn. Scribner's, N.Y., 1926.

Mindorff, Elgar, O.F.M., *Man of the Eucharist, Saint Paschal Baylon, O.F.M.* pamphlet. St. Francis Book Shop, Cincinnati, 1949.

Monchamp, Georges, *Father Victoria Delbrouck, A Franciscan Martyr of Our Days*, tr. from the German by Father Leo Heinrichs, O.F.M. St. Bonaventure Monastery, Paterson, N.J., 1910.

Monnin, Alfred, *The Life of the Curé of Ars*, tr. by Bertram Wolferstan, S.J., new edn. Herder, St. Louis, 1927.

Moonen, Remaclus, O.F.M., *Life of Valentine Paquay, O.F.M.* Malines, 1926.

Morgan, Thomas B., *A Reporter at the Papal Court, A Narrative of the*

Reign of Pope Pius XI. Longmans, Green, and Co., N.Y., 1938.

Murphy, Edward F., Eve Lavalliere (a novelized life), 375 pp. Doubleday, N.Y., 1949.

Nesbitt, Marian, *St. Anthony of Padua*, pamphlet. Franciscan Herald Press, Chicago, 1926.

O'Brien, Isidore, O.F.M., *Enter St. Anthony.* St. Anthony Guild Press, Paterson, N.J., 1932.

—, *St. Anthony of Padua*, pamphlet. St. Anthony Guild Press, Paterson, NJ.

O'Connor, Armel, *The Life of St. Peter of Alcantara.* Herald, Birmingham, England, 1915.

Oré, Luis Jerónimo, O.F.M., *The Martyrs of Florida,* tr. by Maynard Geiger, O.F.M. Wagner, N.Y., 1937.

Orsenigo, Cesare, *Life of St. Charles Borromeo,* tr. by Rudolp Kraus, 390 pp. Herder, St. Louis, 1943.

O'Shea, Joseph A., O.F.M., *The Life of Father Luke Wadding.* Dublin, 1885.

O'Sullivan, D. J., *Life of Mother Mary Lawrence,* F.M.M. Propagation of the Faith Society, 1919.

Oursler, Fulton and Will, *Father Flanagan of Boys Town.* Doubleday, N.Y., 1949.

Partridge, F. J., *The Life of St. Bridget of Sweden.* London, 1888.

Parsons, Mrs., *The Life of Saint Collette.* Burns, Oates, and Washbourne, London, 1879.

Pastrovicchi, Angelo, O.F.M.Conv., *St. Joseph of Copertino,* tr. by Francis S. Laing, O.F.M.Cap. Herder, St. Louis, 1918

Pauline, Sister, *Frances Schervier, Mother of the Poor,* 88 pp. St. Clare Convent, Cincinnati, 1946.

Peers, Edgar Allison, *Ramon Lull.* Macmillan, N.Y., 1929.

Perotti, Leonard D., St. Salvator of Horta, pamphlet. St. Anthony Guild Press, Paterson, N.J., 1941.

Perrin, Elixabeth Sainte-Marie, *St. Collette and Her Reform,* tr. by Mrs. Conor Maguire. Herder, St. Louis, 1924.

Perry, Frederick, *St. Louis, the Most Christian King.* Putnam, N.Y., 1901.

Poor Clare, A, *A Lily of the Cloister, Sister M. Celine of the Presentation,* tr. from the French by Mary Caroline Watt, 236 pp. Burns, Oates, and Washbourne, London, 1923.

Powers, Gabriel Francis, *Woman of the Bentivoglios.* Ave Maria, Notre Dame, Ind., 1921.

Redpath, Sister Helen, *God's Ambassadress* (S Bridget of Sweden), 216 pp. Bruce, Milwaukee, 1947.

Reichert, Aquilin, O.F.M.Conv., *Mother Frances Streitel, Her Life and Work,* 277 pp. Convent of the Sorrowful Mother, Milwaukee, 1949.

Reus, John B., S.J., Under Angel Wings (Franciscan Sister M. Antonia Cony), tr. by Conall O'Leary, O.F.M., 215 pp. St. Anthony Guild Press, Paterson, N.J., 1954.

Romb, Anselm M. O.F.M.Conv., Mission to Cathay (B Odoric of Pordenone), 153 pp. St. Anthony Guild Press, Paterson, N.J., 1956.

Royer, Franchon, St. Francis Solanus, Apostle to America, 207 pp. St. Anthony Guild Press, Paterson, N.J., 1955.

Sargent, Daniel, Thomas More, Sheed and Ward, N.Y., 1933, 1934, 1935.

Salotti, Cardinal, Life of Sister Assunta (B Mary Assunta Pallotta). Franciscan Missionaries of Mary, N. Providence, R.I.

Schimberg, A. P., The Great Friend, Frederick Ozanam, 345 pp. Bruce, Milwaukee, 1946.

—, Tall in Paradise, St. Colette of Corbie. Marshall Jones Co., Francestown, N.H., 1948.

Schoppe, Eric, O.F.M., Saint of the Eucharist (S Paschal Baylon), pamphlet. St. Anthony Guild Press, Paterson, N.J.

Seton, Walter W., Blessed Giles of Assisi (British Society of Franciscan Studies, vol. VIII). Manchester, 1918.

—, Some New Sources for the Life of Blessed Agnes of Bohemia (British Society of Franciscan Studies, vol. VII), 176 pp. University Press, Aberdeen, 1915.

Smith, Jeremiah, O.F.M.Conv., Knight of the Immaculate (Father Maximilian Kolbe), 70 pages. Franciscan Herald Press, Chicago, 1952.

Stacpoole-Kenny, Louise M., Francis de Sales, A Study of the Gentle Saint. Burns, Oates, and Washbourne, London, 1924.

Stang, Joseph, Margaret Sinclair, pamphlet. St. Anthony Guild Press, Paterson, N.J., 1941.

—, Matt Talbot, pamphlet. Our Sunday Visitor, Huntington, Ind., 1940.

Stano, Gaetano M., O.F.M.Conv., Blessed Francis Anthony Fasani, tr. by Raphael Huber, O.F.M.Conv., 62 pages. Basilica SS XII Apostoli, Rome, Italy, 1951.

Steck, Francis Borgia, ed., tr., Motolinia's History of the Indians of New Spain (with a life of Motolinia), 378 pp. Academy of American Franciscan History, Washington, D.C., 1953.

Stern, Aloysius S., S.J., Magín Catalá, O.F.M., The Holy Man of Santa Clara, pamphlet, 20 pp. University of San Francisco, San Francisco, Calif. 1955.

Strub, Celestine, O.F.M., Little Violet of Jesus (Poor Clare nun of Coyoacán, Mexico), pamphlet. Franciscan Herald Press, Chicago, 111.

Taylor, Emmett, No Royal Road, Father Luca Pacioli, O.F.M.Conv., and His Times, 1445-1514, 450 pp. University of North Carolina Press, 1943.

Thaddeus, Father, O.F.M., Life of Blessed Father John Forest. N.Y., 1886.

Thompson, Blanche Jennings, *St. Elizabeth's Three Crowns* (Vision Book). Farrar, Straus, and Cudahy, N.Y., 1958.

Thureau-Dangin, Paul, *Life of St. Bernardino of Siena*, tr. by Baroness G. von Huegel. Macmillan, London, 1902, 1906, 1911.

Tibesar, Antonine, O.F.M., ed., *Writings of Junípero Serra*, 4 vols. Academy of American Franciscan History, Washington, D.C., 1956-1957.

Toynbee, Margaret R., *S. Louis of Toulouse and the Process of Canonisation in the Fourteenth Century* (British Society of Franciscan Studies, vol. XV). Manchester University Press, 1929.

Trindade, Enrique Golland, O.F.M., *Matt Talbot, Worker and Penitent*, tr. by Conall O'Leary, O.F.M., 130 pp. St. Anthony Guild Press, Paterson, N.J., 1954.

Trochu, Francis, *St. Bernadette Soubirous*, 400 pp. Pantheon, N.Y., 1958.

Underhill, Evelyn, *Jacopone da Todi, Poet and Mystic, 1228-1306, A Spiritual Biography with a Selection from the Spiritual Songs* Translated by Mrs. Theodore Beck, 521 pp. J. M. Dent and Sons, London, 1919.

Van den Broek, Silvére, O.F.M., *The Spiritual Legacy of Sister Mary of the Holy Trinity, Louisa Jacques, 1901-1942* (a Poor Clare), 364 pp. Newman, Westminster, Md., 1950.

Ward, Maisie, *St. Bernardino of Siena*. London, 1944.

Wedge, Florence, *My Brother Benedict* (S Benedict the Moor), pamphlet. Franciscan Printery, Pulaski, Wis., 1957.

White, Helen C., Dust on the King's Highway (novelized life of Father Francisco Garcés), 470 pp. Macmillan, N.Y., 1947.

—, *Watch in the Night* (novelized life of Jacopone da Todi). Macmillan, N.Y., 1933.

Wiegand, Sister M. Gonsalva, *Sketch Me, Berta Hummel* (life of Sister M. Innocentia of the Franciscan Sisters of Siessen), 94 pp. Grail Publications, St. Meinrad, Ind., 1951.

Williams, Alfred, *Frederick Ozanam, pamphlet*. St. Anthony Guild Press, Paterson, N.J., 1940

Windeatt, Mary Fabyan, *Song in the South* (S Francis Solano), 191 pp. Sheed and Ward, N.Y., and Grail Publications, St. Meinrad, Inc., 1946.

Winowska, Maria, *Our Lady's Fool, Father Maximilian Kolbe, Friar Minor Conventual*, tr. by Therese Plumereau. Newman, Westminster, Md., 1952.

Yeo, Margaret, *Reformer, St. Charles Borromeo*, 317 pp. Bruce, Milwaukee, 1938.

INDEX OF SAINTS

---

[6] Names without any designation are those of Servants of God; S means Saint; B means Blessed; and V means Venerable.

Archangel of Calatafimi, B, Jul 28
Balthassar of Chiavari, B, Oct 24
Baptista of Piacenza, Oct 17
Baptista Varani, B, June 11
Bartholomew Pucci, B, May 23
Bartolo of San Gimignano, B, Dec 17
Beatrice of Silva, B, Aug 18
Beatrice Raineri, Dec 8 Berard and Companions, S, Jan 16
Bernard of Baden, B, Jul 15
Bernard of Corleone, B, Jan 20
Bernard of Offida, B, Aug 27
Bernard of Quintavalle, Jul 2
Bernardin of Busti, Dec 23
Bernardin of Feltre, B, Sept 29
Bernardin of Fossa, B, Nov 27
Bernardin of Siena, S, May 20
Benedict Joseph Labre, S, Apr 16
Benedict of Urbino, B, May 14
Benedict the Moor, S, Apr 4
Bentivolio Buoni, B, Dec 2
Benvenute of Gubbio, B, June 29
Benvenute of Osimo, S, Mar 22
Benvenute of Recanati, B, May 27
Berthold of Ratisbon, Dec 19
Blanche, Queen of France, B, Aug 23
Bonaventure, S, Jul 14
Bonaventure of Barcelona, B, Sept 11
Bonaventure of Potenza, B, Oct 26
Bonavita of Lugo, Nov 11
Bridget of Sweden, S, Oct 8
Caesar of Speyer, Apr 1
Cassian of Nantes, B, Aug 7
Catharine of Bologna, S, Mar 9
Catharine of Bosnia, Oct 29
Catharine of Genoa, S, Mar 23
Catharine, Queen of England, Jan 6
Cecilia Joanelli-Castelli, Jul 18
Charles Borromeo, S, Nov 4
Charles of Blois, B, Sept 20
Charles of Sezze, S, Jan 18
Christina of Tuscany, B, Jan 4
Christopher of Milan, B, Mar 13
Christopher of Romagnola, Oct 25
Clare of Assisi, S, Aug 12
Clare of Montefalco, S, Aug 16
Clare of Rimini, B, Feb 10
Coleta of Corbie, S, Mar 6
Conrad of Ascoli, B, Apr 19

Gabriel Ferretti, B, Nov 14
Gabriel Mary, B, Aug 29
Gandolph of Binasco, B, Apr 3
Gentle (Gentil) of Matelica, B, Sept 7
George of Augsburg, V, Oct 7
Gerard Cagnoli, B, Dec 3
Gerard Lunel, B, May 6
Gerard of Villamagna, B, May 28
Giles Mary of S Joseph, B, Feb 8
Giles of Assisi, B, Apr 23
Giles of Lorenzana, B, Jan 15
Godfrey Maurice Jones, B, May 9
Gregory Grassi and Companions, B, Jul 4
Gregory X, B, Jan 10
Guy of Cortona, B, June 27
Helen Enselmini, B, Nov 7
Herman of Gersthagen, Dec 21
Herculan of Piagale, B, June 2
Hippolyte Galantini, B, Mar 19
Hugh of Digne, Mar 10
Hugolinus Magalotti, B, Dec 10
Humiliana Cerchi, B, June 16
Humilis Martinez, Feb 1
Humilis of Bisignano, B, Nov 29
Hyacintha Mariscotti, S, Jan 30
Ignatius Laconi, S, May 12
Illuminatus of Rieti, June 24
Innocent of Berzo, V, Apr 13
Innocent of Chiusa, V, Dec 12
Isabella of France, B, June 8
Ivo of Britanny, S, May 16
Jacoba of Settesoli, Dec 30
Jacopone da Todi, B, Dec 25
James Oldo, B, Apr 10
James of Bitecto, B, May 11
James of Pieve, B, Jan 26
James of the March, S, Nov 28
James of the Rosary, Oct 16
James of Strepar, B, Oct 21
Jane Mary of Maillé, B, Nov 5
Jane Mary of the Cross, V, Mar 25
Jane of Luxembourg, Dec 13
Jane of S Erasmus, Jan 7
Jane of Signa, B, Nov 18
Jane of the Cross, V, May 3
Jane of Valois, S, Feb 14
Jeremy Lambertenghi, B, Dec 26
Joan of Arc, S, June 3

Jutta of Thuringia, B, June 26
Kinga of Poland, B, Jul 24
Ladislas of Gielniow, B, May 21
Lawrence of Brindisi, S, Jul 23
Lawrence of Villamagna, B, June 14
Leo Heinrichs, Mar 29
Leonard of Port Maurice, S, Nov 26
Leonore Gusman, June 21
Leopold of Gaiche, B, Apr 2
Liberatus of Lauro, B, Sept 6
Liberatus Weiss and Companions, Mar 3
Louise Albertoni, B, Feb 27
Louise of Savoy, B, Sept 14
Louis, King of France, S, Aug 25
Louis of Arazilo, Jan 27
Louis of Casoria, Mar 31
Louis of Toulouse, S, Aug 19
Luchesio (Lucius) of Poggibonzi, B, Apr 28
Lucy of Caltagirone, B, Sept 22
Lucy Sancia, Dec 4 Luke Belludi, B, Feb 17
Magdalen Dahmen (Daemen), Aug 3
Magdalen of Rottenburg, Jul 22
Magín Catalá, Nov 22
Michael Garicoits, S, May 15
Michelina of Pesaro, B, Sept 15
Margaret of Colonna, B, Nov 9
Margaret Lekeux, Mar 7
Margaret of Cortona, S, Feb 22
Margaret of Lorraine, B, Nov 6
Margaret of Luxembourg, Aug 24
Margaret Sinclair, Nov 24
Margaret Stadler, Dec 28
Marie Celine, May 2
Mark Marconi, B, Feb 24
Mark of Bologna, B, Apr 17
Mark of Montegallo, B, Mar 21
Martin of Valencia, Aug 31
Mary Ann of Jesus de Paredes, S, May 26
Mary Assunta Pallotta, B, Apr 7
Mary Bartholomea Capitanio, S, June 4
Mary Bernadette Soubirous, S, Apr 16
Mary Catharine Seger, Nov 2
Mary Cresentia Hoess, B, Apr 6
Mary Crucifixa, V, Dec 16
Mary Emmanuela, Sept 23
Mary Fidelis Weiss, Feb 2
Mary Frances of the Five Wounds, S, Oct 6
Mary Joseph Rosello, S, Dec 7

Philippa Mareri, B, Feb 16
Philippa of Lorraine, Mar 2
Philomena Jane Genovese, Jul 1
Pica of Assisi, B, Apr 14
Pius X, S, Sept 3
Portiuncula, Aug 2
Raymond Lull, B, Sept 8
Raymond of Narbonne, B, May 29
Raynier of Arezzo, B, Nov 12
Rizziero of Muccia, B, Feb 7
Robert Malatesta, B, Oct 13
Robert, King of Naples, Jan 17
Roch of Montpellier, S, Aug 17
Roger of Todi, B, Jan 13
Roland of Chiusi, June 30
Rose of Viterbo, S, Sept 4
Rufinus of Assisi, Nov 21
Salome of Cracow, B, Nov 17
Salvator of Horta, S, Mar 18
Sancia, Queen of Naples, Jul 6
Sanctes of Montefabro, B, Sept 13
Sebastian of Aparicio, B, Feb 25
Seraphina Sforza, B, Sept 9
Seraphin of Montegranaro, S, Oct 12
Severin Girault, B, Sept 2
Simon of Lypnica, B, Jul 30
Simon Van Ackeren, May 1
Stephen Eckert, Feb 11
Stephen of Narbonne, B, May 29
Stigmata of S Francis, Sept 17
Sylvester of Assisi, Mar 4
Thomas Bullaker, B, Nov 23
Thomas More, S, Jul 31
Thomas of Cori, B, Jan 19
Thomas of Florence, B, Oct 28
Thomas of Foligno, B, Sept 16
Thomas of Tolentino and Companions, B, Sept 5
Theodoric Coelde, B, Dec 27
Theodoric Loet, Apr 12
Theophilus of Corte, S, May 19
Timothy of Montecchio, B, Aug 26
Torello of Poppi, B, Mar 16
Valentine Paquay, Jan 11
Veridiana Attavanti, B, Feb 15
Veronica Giuliani, S, Jul 11
Vico (Ludovico) Necchi, Jan 9
Victricius Weiss, Oct 11
Vincenta Gerosa, S, June 4

Vincent of Aquila, B, Aug 14
Vincent Pallotti, B, Jan 21
Vitalis of Bastia, B, May 31
Waldo (Vivaldo) of San Gimignano, B, May 8
Walter Lopez, Jul 7
Walter of Treviso, Oct 15
William Cufitella of Scicli, B, Apr 9
Yolande of Poland, B, June 15
Yves of Brittany, S, May 16

INDEX OF SAINTS

Corringenda: To the list of those called Blessed in popular devotion (see Appendix III, at the end) should be added: B Francis of Pavia, Franciscan, 15th century La Franceschina, vol. I, pp. 140-170). — The surname of the Servant of God Magdalen Dahmen (Aug 3), spelled thus in Dehey, Religious Orders of Women in the United States (p. 453), should be Daemen. — Poggibonzi (Apr 28 and Aug 28) should be spelled Poggibonsi; and Chiavasso (Apr 20) should be Chivasso.

INDEX OF MEDITATIONS

Printed in the USA
CPSIA information can be obtained
at www.ICGtesting.com
LVHW051202181223
766713LV00029B/362/J